Key Notation Used in the Text

α	Certainty equivalent factor
A	Assets
AFC	Annual financing cost
APR	Annual percentage rate
ATCF	After-tax cash flow
B	(1) Debt in a firm's capital structure
	(2) Market value of a firm's debt
β_j	Beta (systematic risk) for security *j*
β_l	Leveraged beta
β_u	Unleveraged beta
c	Unit production cost
C	Value of a call option
CAPM	Capital Asset Pricing Model
CF	Cash flow
CL	Current liabilities
D	Common stock dividends
Dep	Depreciation
DCL	Degree of combined leverage
DFL	Degree of financial leverage
DOL	Degree of operating leverage
D_p	Preferred stock dividends
E	(1) Common equity in a firm's capital structure
	(2) Market value of a firm's equity
	(3) Exercise price of an option
e	Exponential *e*; value $\approx$ 2.71828
EAT	Earnings after taxes
EBIT	Earnings before interest and taxes
EBT	Earnings before taxes
EPS	Earnings per share
EVA	Economic value added
F	(1) Forward rate in foreign exchange
	(2) Fixed costs
FCF	Free cash flow
FIFO	First-in, first-out inventory valuation
FV	Future value
FVAN	Future value of an annuity
FVAND	Future value of an annuity due
FVIF	Future value interest factor
FVIFA	Future value interest factor of an annuity
g	Expected annual growth rate in earnings, dividends, and/or stock price
i	Interest rate per time period
I	Interest payments before taxes
i_{eff}	Annual effective interest rate
i_f	Interest rate in the foreign currency country
IFE	International Fisher effect
i_h	Interest rate in the home currency country
i_{nom}	Annual nominal interest rate
i_R	Real rate of return
IRR	Internal rate of return
k	A percentage required return or cost of capital; discount rate
k_a	Weighted (marginal) cost of capital
k_a^*	Risk-adjusted weighted cost of capital (required return) on an investment
k_d	Required return on a bond; pretax cost of debt; yield to maturity on a bond
k_e	Required return on common stock; cost of internal equity
k'_e	Cost of external equity
k_i	After-tax cost of debt
k_j	Required return from security *j*
k_p	Required return on preferred stock; Cost of preferred stock financing
LBO	Leveraged buyout
LIBOR	London interbank offer rate
LIFO	Last-in, first-out inventory valuation
m	Frequency of compounding per time period
M	Maturity value of a bond
M_e	Market price of stock ex-rights
M_o	Market price of stock rights-on
MACRS	Modified accelerated cost recovery system of depreciation
MC	Marginal cost

Key Notation Used in the Text

MR	Marginal revenue
MVA	Market value added
n	Number of time periods
N	Number of rights required to purchase one share of stock
N(d)	Value of a cumulative normal density function in option value models
NAL	Net advantage to leasing
NCF	Net cash flow
NINV	Net investment
NPV	Net present value
NWC	Net working capital
O	Operating costs
p	(1) Probability of occurrence of a specific rate of return
	(2) Price per unit
P_{net}	Net proceeds to firm from the sale of a security
P_s	Current stock price in option value calculations
P_t	Price of a security at time period t
PB	Payback period
P/BV	Market price per share ÷ book value per share
P/E	Market price per share ÷ current earnings per share
P_f	(1) Preferred stock in a firm's capital structure
	(2) Market value of a firm's preferred stock
PI	Profitability index
PMT	Annuity payment
PPP	Purchasing power parity
PV	Present value
PVAN	Present value of an annuity
PVAND	Present value of an annuity due
PVIF	Present value interest factor
PVIFA	Present value interest factor of an annuity
PVNCF	Present value of net (operating) cash flows
PVPER	Present value of a perpetuity
PVPERD	Present value of a perpetuity due
π_f	Expected foreign country inflation rate
π_h	Expected home country inflation rate
Q	Quantity
q	Number of units sold
Q_b	Breakeven quantity
ρ	Correlation coefficient
r	(1) Internal rate of return of a project
	(2) Single rate of return of a security
$\hat{r}$	Expected return
R	(1) Revenues
	(2) Theoretical value of a right
RADR	Risk-adjusted discount rate
r_f	Risk-free rate of return
r_j	The jth possible return from a security or project
r_m	Rate of return on the market portfolio
r_p	Rate of return on a portfolio of securities
ROE	Return on equity
ROI	Return on investment (assets)
σ	Standard deviation
S_0	Spot rate in a foreign currency at time 0
S	(1) Sales
	(2) Subscription price of a right
s	Unit selling cost
SML	Security Market Line
θ	Risk premium
T	Marginal tax rate
t	Time period indicator
TC	Total cost
TR	Total revenue
v	Coefficient of variation
V	Variable cost per unit
w	Portion (weight) of funds invested in a particular security in a portfolio
Y	Investment in property, plant and equipment
z	Number of standard deviations

Contemporary Financial Management

FOURTEENTH EDITION

R. CHARLES MOYER
College of Business, University of Louisville

JAMES R. McGUIGAN
JRM Investments

RAMESH P. RAO
Spears School of Business, Oklahoma State University

Cengage

Australia • Brazil • India • Mexico • Singapore • United Kingdom • United States

Cengage

Contemporary Financial Management, 14e

R. Charles Moyer,
James R. McGuigan,
and Ramesh P. Rao

For product information and technology assistance, contact us at **asia.infoindia@cengage.com**

For permission to use material from this text or product, submit all requests online at **www.cengage.com/permissions**

ISBN-13: 978-93-5573-455-6
ISBN-10: 93-5573-455-7

Cengage Learning India Pvt. Ltd.
T-303, 3rd Floor
DAV Complex, Plot 3
Mayur Vihar Phase 1
Delhi-110091

Cengage is a leading provider of customized learning solutions with employees residing in nearly 40 different countries and sales in more than 125 countries around the world. Find your local representative at **www.cengage.com**

Cengage is committed to creating inclusive and diverse products, including perspectives that represent the diversity of people across all backgrounds, identities, opinions, and experiences. If you have any feedback related to this, please contact us at **support.cengage.com**

To learn more about Cengage products, platforms and services, visit at **www.cengage.co.in**

Disclaimer:
This book contains link to resources which are a part of the imported edition. The same may not be available with the Indian edition. The buyer needs to purchase a copy of the imported edition to have full access to those resources. In no event the publisher shall be liable for any limitation or performance due to unavailability of these resources.

Printed by:
Saurabh Printers Pvt Ltd
67A-68 Ecotech Ext-I Greater Noida, Tel-0120-2341180

Printed in India
Print Number: 03 Print Year: 2024

To Sally, Craig, and Laura
RCM

To Claire
JRM

To Uma, Anil, and Nikhil
RPR

About the Authors

R. CHARLES MOYER

is a Professor of Finance and Entrepreneurship and Dean Emeritus of the College of Business at the University of Louisville. Prior to this position, Dr. Moyer held the GMAC Insurance Chair in Finance and was Dean of the Babcock Graduate School of Management, Wake Forest University, was a Professor of Finance and Chairman of the Department of Finance at Texas Tech University, and previously taught at the University of Houston, Lehigh University, and the University of New Mexico. He earned his B.A. in economics (*cum laude*) from Howard University, where he was elected to Phi Beta Kappa, and received his M.B.A. and Ph.D. in Business from the University of Pittsburgh. Dr. Moyer spent a year at the Federal Reserve Bank of Cleveland and a year as a Sears-AACSB Federal Faculty Fellow at the Maritime Administration, U.S. Department of Commerce. Professor Moyer has taught in executive education programs and is frequently called upon to provide expert testimony in public utility rate cases across the nation. Dr. Moyer is a director of Capitala Finance Corp. and Summit Biosciences Inc.

In addition to coauthoring *Contemporary Financial Management*, 14th Edition, Dr. Moyer also coauthored *Managerial Economics*, 14th Edition (Cengage, 2017), and *Fundamentals of Contemporary Financial Management*, 2nd Edition (South-Western, 2007). He has published extensively in leading finance and economic journals, including *Financial Management*, *Journal of Financial and Quantitative Analysis*, *Journal of Finance*, *Financial Review*, *Journal of Financial Research*, *International Journal of Forecasting*, *Journal of Economics and Business*, and *Journal of Industrial Organization*, publishing over 90 articles and books. Dr. Moyer has served as a vice president of the Financial Management Association, as a director of the Financial Management Association, the Eastern Finance Association, and the Southern Finance Association, as a Secretary/Treasurer of the Financial Management Association, and as President of the Southern Finance Association.

JAMES R. McGUIGAN

currently owns and operates his own numismatic investment firm. Prior to this endeavor, he was Associate Professor of Finance and Business Economics in the School of Business Administration at Wayne State University, where he taught in the undergraduate and masters programs for 10 years. He also taught at the University of Pittsburgh and Point Park College. Dr. McGuigan received his undergraduate degree from Carnegie-Mellon University. His graduate degrees are from the Graduate Schools of Business at the University of Chicago (M.B.A.) and the University of Pittsburgh (Ph.D.). He has published articles dealing with his research on options in the *Journal of Financial and Quantitative Analysis*. In addition to his interests in financial management, Dr. McGuigan has coauthored books in managerial economics, including *Managerial Economics*, 14th Edition (Cengage, 2017), which he coauthored with R. Charles Moyer and Frederick Harris, and *Fundamentals of Contemporary Financial Management*, 2nd Edition (South-Western, 2007), coauthored with R. Charles Moyer and Ramesh P. Rao.

RAMESH P. RAO

is a professor and holds the Paul C. Wise Chair of Finance in the Spears School of Business, Oklahoma State University. Previously he was on the faculty at Texas Tech

University, Wayne State University, and the University of Toledo. He earned a B.S. at the University of the Philippines, an M.B.A. from the Asian Institute of Management, and a Ph.D. from Texas Tech University. He has coauthored over 80 journal articles in publications such as *Journal of Business, Journal of Finance, Journal of Banking and Finance, Financial Management, Journal of Business Finance and Accounting, Journal of Empirical Finance, Journal of Financial Research, Financial Review*, and *Journal of Applied Corporate Finance*. In addition to coauthoring *Contemporary Financial Management*, 14th Edition, Dr. Rao also coauthored *Fundamentals of Contemporary Financial Management*, 2nd Edition (South-Western, 2007). He is an associate editor of *Journal of Financial Research* and *Financial Review*. He was a former coeditor of the *Journal of Applied Finance* (2007–2013). He is former program chair and president of the Southwestern Finance Association and a director of the Asian Finance Association. He has been recognized for his teaching and research excellence including the following awards: 2007 Southwestern Finance Association Outstanding Educator of the Year Award, Richard W. Poole Research Excellence Award (2015–2016, 2012–2013, 2009–2010, and 2008–2009), Chandler-Frates & Reitz Teaching Excellence Award-MBA Program (OSU-Tulsa campus, 2008), Regents Distinguished Research Award (2007), Merrick Foundation Teaching Award (2003), and MBA Outstanding Faculty Award (2003).

Brief Contents

PART 5 Working Capital Management

PART 6 Additional Topics in Contemporary Financial Management

Contents

PART 2 Determinants of Valuation

PART 3 The Capital Investment Decision

PART 5 Working Capital Management

Preface

The financial management field continues to experience exciting change and growth. Financial practitioners are increasingly employing new financial management techniques, sophisticated computer resources, and mega databases to aid in their decision making. "Financial engineers" continue to create new derivative financial instruments and transactions, including options, financial futures contracts, options on futures contracts, foreign currency swaps, and interest rate swaps, to help managers deal with risk and enhance shareholder wealth. Many industries have been restructured because of the pressures of global competition. Leveraged buyout transactions from sophisticated investors have forced managers to make more careful use of their firms' resources. The growing private equity market has added another dimension to the focus on sound management of a firm's resources. Corporate reformers have focused attention on the structure of corporate governance relationships and the impact of alternative managerial compensation packages on firm performance. The Internet has transformed the way securities are bought and sold and the way companies access new capital. At the same time, financial researchers have made important advances in the areas of valuation, cost of capital, capital structure theory and practice, option valuation (including "real" options associated with capital investments), risk management, and dividend policy. Access to and content of the Internet have greatly expanded, making timely financial information increasingly available to customers, investors, and financial managers.

The financial crisis and recession that began in late 2007 and continued into 2010 had a major impact on the financial marketplace and the practice of financial management. This crisis in the financial markets identified structural weaknesses in many financial institutions, including commercial banks, quasi-governmental financial entities, regulatory practices, and various aspects of risk management. The lessons from this experience will have long-lasting impacts on financial markets and the strategies employed by financial managers and investors. This 14th Edition of *Contemporary Financial Management* addresses the cause of this crisis and its impacts on the practice of finance.

The future promises to be a more exciting time for finance professionals. Financial managers have refocused their attention on the core objective of maximizing shareholder wealth. Managers who act contrary to the interests of shareholders face the prospect of an unfriendly takeover, a corporate restructuring, pressure from domestic and foreign competitors, pressure from private equity investors, or pressures from shareholder groups and institutional investors. Firms increasingly must find operating savings necessary to remain competitive, as managers continue to struggle to find the optimal capital structure for their firm. The central importance of cash flows in the financial management of a firm has never been more apparent. The European economic and monetary unification and the near collapse of that union in the wake of the financial crisis of 2008–2010, and the growing importance of countries such as China and India, all require contemporary financial managers to possess greater knowledge of doing business in an international marketplace. Recent turmoil in the commodity, currency, and interest rate markets highlight the importance of financial risk management tools. In addition, the standards of ethical behavior adopted by managers of business enterprises become even more important.

Contemporary Financial Management, 14th Edition, incorporates these changes—the increased focus on shareholder wealth maximization and cash flow management, an emphasis on the international aspects of financial management, a concern for the ethical behavior of managers, the role of private equity investors, and the lessons learned in the financial crisis that impacted all aspects of risk management—into a text designed primarily for an introductory course in financial management. The book is also suitable for management development programs and as a reference aid to practicing finance professionals.

The 13th Edition of *CFM* was well received by our many adopters. In the 14th Edition we retain the core features of that edition. We appreciate the many users and adopters who continue to offer suggestions for content additions and enhancements. As in the past, we have incorporated many of these suggestions into this edition. This edition has been extensively updated throughout, including the addition of numerous contemporary examples and references.

We recognize that students enter this course with a wide variety of backgrounds in mathematics, economics, accounting, and statistics. The only presumption we make regarding prior preparation is that all student users have had one course in financial accounting.

Organization of the Text

This text provides an introduction to both analytical tools and descriptive materials that are useful in financial management. Because this is an introductory-level text, however, it does *not* attempt to make the reader an expert in every aspect of financial decision making. Instead, it is intended to do the following:

- Acquaint the reader with the types of decisions faced by financial managers
- Develop a framework for analyzing these decisions in a systematic manner
- Provide the reader with the background necessary to pursue more advanced readings and courses in financial management

Although the subject matter in this text is divided into distinct parts, in reality and practice, the various types of financial decisions are interrelated and should not be considered in isolation from one another.

Each chapter begins with a summary preview of the key concepts from the chapter. This is followed by a financial challenge faced by a real firm(s) and related to the material in the chapter. Next, Learning Objectives are identified for each chapter. At the end of each chapter is a point-by-point summary of the chapter and extensive sets of discussion questions and problems, including "Self-Test Problems" with detailed solutions that you can use to test your understanding of the text material. A glossary of key terms is provided at the end of the book. Some chapters also have more complex, integrative case problems. Where appropriate, special international financial management issues and entrepreneurial finance issues are discussed. The book also has "Ethical Issues" sections integrated throughout. "Check" answers to selected problems appear at the end of the book. You will find an overview of the CFM Excel templates that are available for solving many of the complex chapter problems and cases at the book's Web site (www.cengagebrain.com).

Parts of the Text

Part One, Introduction. Chapter 1 discusses the role and objectives of financial management, introduces the various forms of business organization, discusses the importance of ethical business practices, and reviews the structure of the financial management function. Chapter 2 reviews the major elements of the U.S. and international financial marketplace. It includes a discussion of the structure of the U.S. financial system and the role of stock exchanges. Also included are introductions to various types of derivative securities and international financial management. Chapter 2 also contains an extensive discussion of the causes and impacts of the financial crisis beginning in late 2007. Chapter 3 considers the financial statements and ratios that can be used to evaluate the financial performance of a firm. Chapter 4 presents various techniques for analyzing cash flows and forecasting future financial performance.

Part Two, Determinants of Valuation. Valuation is a central theme of the book. Chapter 5 develops the concept of the time value of money. This concept is used in the valuation of securities and the evaluation of investment projects expected to provide benefits over a number of years. The present value rule is also introduced. Chapter 6 applies the basic valuation model to fixed income securities, such as bonds and preferred stock. Chapter 7 deals with the valuation of common stock and the role of investment bankers. Chapter 8 provides a comprehensive introduction to the concept of risk in finance and the relationship between risk, required return, and the shareholder wealth maximization goal of the firm.

Part Three, The Capital Investment Decision. This portion of the text focuses on capital expenditures—that is, investments in long-term assets. Chapters 9 and 10 present the fundamentals of capital budgeting, namely, the process of investing in long-term assets. Chapter 9 deals with the measurement of the cash flows (benefits and costs) associated with long-term investment projects. Chapter 10 considers various decision-making criteria that can be used when choosing projects that will maximize the value of the firm. Chapter 11 extends the concepts developed in Chapter 10 by considering some of the decision-making techniques that attempt to deal with the problem of the risk associated with a specific project's cash flows.

Part Four, The Cost of Capital, Capital Structure, and Dividend Policy. Chapter 12 illustrates the principles of measuring a firm's cost of capital. The cost of funds to a firm is an important input in the capital budgeting process. Chapters 13 and 14 address the relationship of the cost of capital to the firm's capital structure. Chapter 15 discusses the factors that influence the choice of a dividend policy and the impact of various dividend policies on the value of a firm.

Part Five, Working Capital Management. Chapters 16 through 18 examine the management of a firm's current asset and liability accounts—that is, net working capital. Chapter 16 provides an overview of working capital management, with emphasis on the risk-return trade-offs involved in working capital decision making. Chapter 16 also covers the management of secured and unsecured short-term credit. Chapter 17 deals with the management of cash and marketable securities, and Chapter 18 focuses on the management of accounts receivable and inventories.

Part Six, Additional Topics in Contemporary Financial Management. Chapter 19 deals with lease financing and intermediate-term credit. Chapter 20 focuses on option-related funding alternatives, i.e., derivative securities, including convertible securities, and warrants. Chapter 21 examines various techniques for managing risk, including the use of derivative securities. Chapter 22 discusses the factors that affect exchange rates and foreign exchange risk. Chapter 23 examines corporate restructuring decisions, including mergers and acquisitions, the role of private equity investors, bankruptcy, and reorganization.

Distinctive Features

In this 14th Edition, we continue our commitment to provide a comprehensive, correct, and well-written introduction to the field of financial management. The current edition reflects the many refinements that have been made over the years in previous editions. In addition, we have created a text package that fully reflects contemporary financial management developments in the book's pedagogical aids, organizational design, and ancillary materials.

Pedagogical Features

CFM has been carefully designed to assist the student in learning and to stimulate student interest.

Distinctive pedagogical features include:

1. **Financial Challenges.** Each chapter begins with an illustration of a financial management problem faced by a firm or individual. These exciting lead-ins come from real-firm situations, including Medtronic, Lexus, Hertz, Apple Inc., Ford Motor, Twitter, Facebook, Boeing, Novo Nordisk, Source Gas Distribution, ExxonMobil, Sears, Procter & Gamble, Berkshire Hathaway, Verizon, and JPMorgan Chase. These examples focus on financial problems in the topic area of the chapter and highlight the importance of learning sound financial management principles. The "Financial Challenges" have been extensively revised and updated from the 13th Edition, including numerous totally new examples.
2. **Foundation Concepts.** These concepts are introduced early in the text. Their central importance in the study of finance is highlighted by specially designated icons indicating that these are "Foundation Concepts" and hence worthy of extra attention by the student. Important foundation concepts are identified throughout the book, including the determinants of the return on equity, the valuation of assets, the valuation of common stock, cash flow estimation principles, capital budgeting decision models, business risk, financial risk, and the weighted cost of capital.
3. **International Issues.** To emphasize and reinforce the global nature of financial decision making, we have included "International Issues" sections throughout the book to illustrate the global issues associated with making financial decisions. By covering international finance in two chapters—and throughout, with the "International Issues" features—we ensure that all students will be exposed to important international dimensions of financial management decisions, and we provide an opportunity for in-depth coverage of some of the more important international finance topics.
4. **Ethical Issues.** "Ethical Issues" sections are integrated throughout to present some of the ethical dilemmas facing financial managers. These sections raise sensitivities to ethical issues and usually conclude with questions and issues for further classroom discussion.
5. **Entrepreneurial Issues.** In recognition of the important and growing role of small and medium-sized firms in the American business environment, we have included "Entrepreneurial Issues" sections that appear in appropriate places throughout the book and emphasize unique finance-related problems and concerns of entrepreneurs.
6. **Extensive and Fully Integrated Examples of the Financial Policies and Problems That Face Real Firms.** Throughout the book, we have illustrated financial management concepts by using problems facing real firms. By minimizing the number of hypothetical firm situations and using data and situations facing actual firms that students will recognize and relate to, CFM has further enhanced the realism and excitement of the field of finance.
7. **Calculator Application Illustrations.** Many chapters have easy-to-follow, step-by-step calculator keystrokes to solve many of the time value of money examples developed in the text. These "Calculator Applications" sections are set up in a generic calculator format and can be used with virtually any financial calculator.

8. **Spreadsheet Strategies.** Many chapters have illustrative examples of how spreadsheet software (Microsoft Excel) can be used to solve finance problems, including time value of money problems, stock and bond valuation, and capital budgeting.
9. **Intuitive Use of Notation.** Notation in the text is simplified and intuitive to aid student learning. Inside the front cover, we have provided a handy summary of the key notation used throughout the book.
10. **Internet Applications.** This edition provides numerous references to interesting Internet applications. The applications provide students with handy references that can be used to explore the Internet for additional information and data dealing with chapter topics.
11. **Extensive Problem Sets.** Many of the end-of-chapter problems contain a surfeit of information, forcing students to identify the relevant material needed to solve the problem. The problem sets provide students and instructors with a greater breadth of problem coverage than in many other texts. In addition, the problems have been identified with a difficulty rating ranging from basic to intermediate to challenging. In several finance textbooks, problems are labeled to indicate the type of problem to be solved. We have specifically chosen not to include this information because we believe that recognition of the problem type is an important part of the learning process. However, we understand the differing needs and goals of instructors, and thus have provided these categories in Appendix A of the Instructors' Resource Manual, so that it can be easily shared with students if desired. Selected check answers to some of the end-of-chapter problems appear at the end of the text.
12. **Self-Test Problems.** Each chapter includes end-of-chapter "Self-Test Problems," with detailed solutions at the end of the text that students can use for further practice and enhanced understanding of the concepts developed in the chapter.
13. **Integrative Cases.** At the end of appropriate chapters, an expanded set of comprehensive "Integrative Cases" are provided. Many of these cases can be used in conjunction with the Excel models, available on the Moyer Student Companion Web site, to demonstrate the power of computers in performing sensitivity analysis.
14. **Excel™ Problems.** Throughout the text, problems that can be solved using Excel are highlighted with an Excel icon. To help solve these problems, more than 20 user-friendly, flexible, downloadable Excel models are available at www.cengagebrain.com and require no prior knowledge of Excel.

Organizational Design

Contemporary Financial Management is organized around the objective of maximizing the value of the firm for its shareholders. This objective is introduced early in the book, and each major financial decision is linked to the impact it has on the value of the firm. The distinctive content features are designed to complement this objective:

1. **Emphasis on the fundamental concepts of cash flow, net present value, risk-return relationships, and market efficiency.** There are four concepts that are central to a complete understanding of most financial management decisions:
   a. The importance of cash flows as the relevant source of value to a firm
   b. The significance of the net present value rule for valuing cash flows
   c. The relationship between risk and return in the valuation process
   d. The efficiency of the capital markets
2. **Unique treatment of problems of international financial management.** In a business world that is increasingly global, it is important that finance students be aware

of the most important dimensions of international finance. Some texts provide a single chapter dealing with a potpourri of international issues, but due to time constraints, many instructors have difficulty in covering this material. Other texts use a series of short international topic sections scattered throughout the book, but this approach does not provide the in-depth coverage needed for some international finance topics, such as hedging exchange rate risk. In the 14th Edition of *CFM*, important international finance relationships, including the operation of foreign currency markets, exchange rate determination, and the role of multinational firms in the global economy, are covered in Chapter 2 ("The Domestic and International Financial Marketplace"). More advanced international topics, such as international parity relationships and the management of foreign exchange risk, are introduced in Chapter 22, "International Financial Management." In addition, international viewpoints are covered in other chapters where appropriate.

3. **Comprehensive and integrated coverage of ethical issues facing financial managers.** Financial managers seeking to maximize shareholder wealth must also confront difficult ethical dilemmas. "Ethical Issues" sections are integrated throughout and present some of the ethical dilemmas facing financial managers. This treatment of the ethical dimensions of financial management is consistent with the AACSB's recommendations for coverage of these issues.
4. **Early coverage of institutional characteristics and valuation models for financial instruments.** We have provided separate chapters (Chapters 6 and 7) dealing with the valuation of fixed income securities and common stock. These chapters also define all of the important characteristics of each of these security types and cover the institutional aspects of the markets for these securities, including the reading and understanding of security transaction information from sources such as *The Wall Street Journal*. This structure provides students with both an institutional understanding of bonds, preferred stock, and common stock and an understanding of the valuation process for securities in the financial marketplace.
5. **Early coverage of time value of money concepts.** Time value of money concepts are covered in depth in Chapter 5. This treatment provides students with the exposure needed to fully understand the valuation process that is central to the goal of shareholder wealth maximization. In addition, this coverage of the time value of money involves students in useful practical applications early on in the course, setting an early tone of relevance for the course.
6. **The importance of cash flow analysis is introduced early and reemphasized throughout the text.** Chapter 1 introduces students to the importance of the cash flow concept. This concept is then applied extensively in the context of financial planning and forecasting (Chapter 4), valuation (Chapters 6 and 7), capital budgeting (Chapters 9, 10, and 11), dividend policy (Chapter 15), working capital management (Chapter 16), and corporate restructuring (Chapter 23).
7. **Attention to unique problems of financial management in entrepreneurial finance.** In recognition of the important and growing role of small and medium-sized firms in the American business environment, we have included "Entrepreneurial Issues" sections, which appear in appropriate places throughout the book and emphasize unique finance-related problems and concerns of entrepreneurs (small businesses).
8. **Extensive development of the cash flow estimation process in capital budgeting.** Perhaps the most important step in the capital budgeting process is the estimation of cash flows for potential projects. *CFM* devotes an entire chapter (Chapter 9) to

this topic, with a chapter appendix detailing alternative depreciation methods and their tax consequences.

9. **A detailed discussion of real options that are embedded in many capital investment projects.** Finance scholars and practitioners have increasingly focused attention on "embedded options" in capital investment projects, such as the option to abandon, the option to expand, and the option to defer investments. These options add value to an investment project above that normally identified in a net present value calculation. Chapter 10 includes an extensive intuitive discussion of real options in capital budgeting.
10. **Coverage of modern financial analysis and performance appraisal concepts.** The increased attention given to the objective of shareholder wealth maximization has brought about the development of new performance appraisal models that can be used to judge a firm's performance and motivate managers to create value. The "Market Value Added" and "Economic Value Added" concepts, developed by Stern-Stewart, are covered in Chapter 3 ("Evaluation of Financial Performance").
11. **Broad, integrated treatment of working capital management.** For many small and medium-sized companies, the management of working capital can present more challenges than any other area of financial management. A thorough and up-to-date three-chapter section on working capital management is included.
12. **Introduction to new financial instruments and strategies.** Financial futures contracts, options, interest rate swaps, corporate restructuring, and leveraged buyouts (LBOs), to name but a few, have become increasingly important to contemporary financial managers. These topics are introduced to the student in an applied context that illustrates their value to financial managers.
13. **Frequent coverage of the impact of agency relationships in financial management.** The impact of principal-agent relationships on decisions in the areas of goal setting, valuation, capital structure, dividend policy, and corporate restructuring are presented throughout the book.
14. **Extensive coverage of the impact of the financial crisis that began in late 2007.** The 14th Edition of *CFM* provides extensive coverage of the impact of the financial crisis (that began in 2007–2008 and continued into 2010) on the practice of financial management. In addition to an in-depth and intuitive presentation in Chapter 2, it is also referenced many times in the following chapters.

Materials for the Student

- Excel™ Models. These models are designed to solve a wide variety of financial management problems. Problems in the text that can be solved using these models are indicated with an Excel logo next to the problem. The models require absolutely no prior knowledge of Excel. All of the models are designed so they can be used to solve actual business financial analysis problems, not just simplified textbook examples.
- e-Lectures. Difficult concepts from each chapter are explained and illustrated via streaming video and animated tutorials. These video clips and tutorials can be extremely helpful review and clarification tools if a student has trouble understanding an in-class lecture or is a visual learner who has difficulty grasping concepts as presented in the text.
- Ask-the-Author Video. In the ask-the-author video segments, the text author, R. Charles Moyer, discusses the most difficult concept for the students to grasp from the chapter. Because the author is the best person to explain his book, these video clips are invaluable to students who need just a little extra help without extra class time.

Materials for the Instructor

- An Instructor's Resource Manual (IRM), revised by the text authors, is available to instructors. It contains detailed solutions to the end-of-chapter questions and problems, and documentation for the Excel templates included in the back of the manual. The solutions to text questions and problems have been thoroughly checked to assure their accuracy. In addition, topical categories of the end-of-chapter questions and problems are listed in an appendix. The IRM is available to instructors in electronic format only, on the text Web site.
- An extensive Test Bank, revised by Mary Fox Luquette of the University of Louisiana, offers over 1,800 multiple-choice questions and problems. This unique test bank is designed with the instructor in mind, and includes AACSB designations for each question and problem. Approximately 60 percent of the questions are "fact" questions, taken directly from the discussion in the text. Approximately 20 percent of the questions are "elementary problem" questions that closely parallel problem examples developed in the chapter and easier problems at the end of the chapter. Approximately 20 percent of the questions are "challenging problems" that require the student to apply concepts developed in the chapter to new problem situations.
- A set of PowerPoint Presentation Slides, revised by William T. Chittenden of Texas State University, provide the text's graphs and tables along with lecture notes and is available at the text Web site. These can be printed for use as transparency masters or acetates.
- Aplia™ for Finance! The best-selling homework solution in education today, Aplia is trusted by more than 500,000 students at more than 650 institutions worldwide. Aplia for Finance offers an online homework system that improves learning by increasing student effort and engagement—without requiring more work from the instructor. Aplia's original, autograded finance assignments ensure that students grasp the skills and concepts presented in the text through interactive problem sets, news analyses, tutorials in math, accounting, statistics, economics, and financial calculators. Visit www.aplia.com for a full Aplia for Finance demonstration online.

Acknowledgments

The authors wish to acknowledge the helpful comments provided by many of our adopters and reviewers, from our first edition through this 14th Edition. We are also grateful for the invaluable comments from our survey respondents, who are included here:

Jean Abbott
Jean Abbott
Hez A. Aubey
Peter W. Bacon
Dean Baim
Richard Bauer
Carl Beidleman
Thomas Berry
Gordon R. Bonner
Jerry D. Boswell
Denis Boudreux
Don Bowlin
Jay T. Brandi
Peter Brucato
William Brunsen
Anthony K. Byrd
W. Thomas Carls
Kenneth Carow
P. R. Chandy
Robert Chatfield
Tylor Claggett
Brandon Cline
Maclyn L. Clouse
C. Mitchell Conover
David B. Cox
John Crockett
Orkunt Dalgic
Lynn E. Dellenbarger, Jr.
Shreesh Deshpande
J. David Diltz
Vernon Dixon
Shannon Donovan
Rudolph D'Souza
William Dukes
John Dunkelberg
Fred Ebeid
John W. Ellis
Holger Engberg
Marilyn Ettinger
Keith W. Fairchild
Edward Farragher
Donald Fehrs
Mike Ferri
Jane Finley
Shifra Fraifeld
John Gawryk
Richard Gendreau
James Gentry
Michael Gombola
James Greenleaf
Kamal Haddad
Thomas Hamilton
Thomas Hardy
Charles Harper
Rick Harris
Mahboubul Hassan
Delbert Hastings
Eric Haye
Patrick Hays
Shantaram P. Hedge
Robert Hehre
George Hettenhouse
L. Dean Hiebert
K. P. Hill
Shalom Hochman
Barbara Howard
Thomas Howe
Jim Hsieh
Pearson Hunt
Aditya Mohan Jadhav
Nemiraja Jadiyappa
Ravi Kumar Jain
Keith B. Johnson
R. Larry Johnson
Charles P. Jones
Raymond G. Jones, Jr.
Peppy M. Kenny
Kee Kim
Thomas Klaasen
Daniel P. Klein
Timothy Koch
Robert S. Kravchuk
Thomas M. Kreuger
Harry R. Kuniansky
Robert Lamy
Keith Laycock
Thomas D. Legg
Joseph J. Levitzky
Thomas J. Liesz
David Lindsley
Charles Linke
Danny S. Litt
Mike Lockett
Robert Lutz
Inayat U. Mangla
Wayne M. Marr
Rand Martin
Robert McElreath
Z. Lew Melnyk
Richard Meyer
Stuart Michelson
Edward M. Miller
Billy C. Moore
Scott Moore
Allen D. Morton
Tammie Simmons Mosley
Robert Nash
Eddie O'Neal
Robert A. Olsen
Coleen G. Pantalone
Ajay Patel
Walter W. Perlick
Susan M. Phillips
Mario Picconi
Pegaret Pichler
Anthony Plath
Alwyn du Plessis
Barbara Poole
Ralph Pope
Dwight Porter

Robert Porter
Rose M. Prasad
Dianna Preece
Kelly Price
Dennis Proffitt
Russ Ray
Charles Rayhorn
Bruce Resnick
Jesse Reyes
William B. Riley
Charles T. Rini
John T. Rose
Jack H. Rubens
Carolyn J. Ryan
Gary C. Sanger
Richard Sapp
Robert G. Schwebach
Robert Schweitzer
Bernard A. Shinkel
Mark Shrader
Phillip Sisneros
Donald Simonson
Frank Smith
John Speltz
Richard F. Sperring
Uma Sridharan
Vic Stanton
Gordon M. Stringer
Paul Swanson
Rolf K. Tedefalk
Richard J. Teweles
Chan Kok Thim
Niranjan Tripathy
K. C. Tseng
Anthony M. Tuberose
George Ulseth
David Upton
Howard E. Van Auken
Sue Visscher
Charles Wade
Richard A. Wall
Alan Weatherford
Samuel C. Weaver
Marsha Weber
Herbert Weinraub
Jill Wetmore
J. Daniel Williams
E. Walter Wilson
Lawrence Wolken
Dr. Kenneth Yung
Richard Zock
J. Kenton Zumwalt

and the following business professionals:

Gordon B. Bonfield
Richard H. Brock
Roy V. Campbell
Gary Costley
Norman Dmuchowski
David Dupree
Stephen H. Grace
Samuel C. Hadaway
R. Lee Haney
Raymond A. Hay
Lawrence Ingrassia
Ira G. Kawaller
Carl J. Lange
Martin H. Lange
Chris Layton
Lewis Lehr
C. Londa
Paul MacAvoy
Frank Mastrapasqua
John H. Maxheim
John McKinnon
Thomas R. Mongan
Robert B. Morris III
T. Boone Pickens
Jack S. Rader
M. W. Ramsey
William J. Regan
Albert J. Robison
Julie Salamon
Kenneth Schwartz
Terry J. Winders
Greg Young

We are also indebted to Lehigh University, Texas Tech University, the University of Houston, the University of New Mexico, Wayne State University, Wake Forest University, Oklahoma State University and the University of Louisville for the considerable support they provided in this or earlier editions.

We owe thanks, as well, to our deans and fellow faculty members at our universities for the encouragement and assistance they provided on a continuing basis during the preparation of the manuscript. Special thanks are due to Mohsen Mollagholamali for his diligent help in updating real data and examples used in Chapters 13–15, 21, and 23; to Subbu Iyer for authoring the Ethical Issues feature in Chapter 21; and to Anil P. Rao for authoring the Financial Challenge lead-in for Chapters 3 and 23.

Finally, we wish to express our thanks to the Finance team members at Cengage Learning. We are particularly appreciative of the support provided by our editors and marketing staff: Joe Sabatino as senior product manager, Brad Sullender as content developer, Nate Anderson as marketing manager, Sharon Smith as production manager, and Mark Hopkinson as media developer.

R. Charles Moyer
James R. McGuigan
Ramesh P. Rao

PART 1

Introduction

CHAPTER 1
The Role and Objective of Financial Management

CHAPTER 2
The Domestic and International Financial Marketplace

CHAPTER 3
Evaluation of Financial Performance

CHAPTER 4
Financial Planning and Forecasting

Part One provides an overview of the field of financial management. Chapter 1 considers the goal of the firm, discusses the role of financial management in the firm, and describes the alternative forms of business organizations. The determinants of value are also introduced. The chapter also considers the organization of the financial management function, the relationship between finance and other business disciplines, and various careers that are available in finance. Chapter 2 presents key elements of the U.S. financial marketplace, including the structure of the U.S. financial system and the role of stock exchanges. Also included is an introduction to the various types of financial derivative securities. The causes and consequences of the financial market and economic crisis of 2008–2009 are discussed. The last part of the chapter contains an introduction to international financial management, including multinational enterprises and the foreign currency markets and exchange rates. Chapter 3 deals with the use of financial ratios to evaluate a firm's financial performance. Chapter 4 examines various financial planning and forecasting techniques, including percentage of sales forecasting methods and cash budgets.

CHAPTER 1

The Role and Objective of Financial Management

KEY CHAPTER CONCEPTS

1. *Shareholder wealth* is defined as the present value of the expected future returns to the owners of the firm. It is measured by the market value of the shareholders' common stock holdings.
2. The primary normative goal of the firm is to make the most efficient use of the firm's resources and thereby to maximize shareholder wealth.
3. Achievement of the shareholder wealth maximization goal is constrained by social responsibility concerns and problems arising out of agency relationships.
4. The market value of a firm's stock is determined by the magnitude, timing, and risk of the cash flows the firm is expected to generate. Managers can take a variety of actions to influence the magnitude, timing, and risk of the firm's cash flows. These actions are often classified as investment, financing, and dividend decisions.
5. Ethical standards of performance frame the bounds of decision making by leaders, managers, and other employees.
6. The most important forms of business organization are the:
    a. Sole proprietorship
    b. Partnership—both limited and general
    c. Corporation
7. Corporations have the advantages of limited liability for owners, potentially perpetual life, and the ability to raise large amounts of capital. Even though they account for less than 18 percent of U.S. firms, corporations account for 81 percent of U.S. business revenues.
8. The finance function is usually headed by a chief financial officer.
    a. Financial management responsibilities are often divided between the controller and treasurer.
    b. The controller normally has responsibility for all activities related to accounting.
    c. The treasurer is normally concerned with the acquisition, custody, and expenditure of funds.

FINANCIAL CHALLENGE

Issues Confronting Financial Managers

- In September 2015, the U.S. Environmental Protection Agency disclosed that it had discovered that Volkswagen (VW) was using software designed to deceive regulators about the true amount of emissions being expelled by its diesel-powered cars sold in the United States. Subsequently it was learned that the scope of this deception also included cars sold in Europe and other parts of the world. Between September and late November 2015, the market value of VW declined by a whopping 37 percent. VW set aside $10 billion to pay for the consequences of this deception. The CEO of VW and other top managers of the company resigned. Now VW's management team is faced with the challenge of determining how this fraud was allowed to occur for so many years, how to reassure customers that the company can be trusted in the future, how to reassure regulators that this type of fraud will never happen again, and how to pay for the fines and costs associated with correcting the emissions problems. In late November 2015, the management team began a series of meetings to determine how they can cut their budgets going forward to pay the multibillion-dollar costs. Undoubtedly the company will have to cancel or limit many desirable capital projects in the coming years, further reducing the long-term value of the firm.[1] Ethical breaches such as this one can have short-term positive impacts on revenues and profits, but disastrous long-term impacts on firm value. The importance of ethical behavior by a company's managers is a key element in achieving the goal of shareholder wealth maximization.
- The global financial collapse of 2008–2009 had wide-ranging impacts in the United States and internationally. Iceland, a beautiful island nation of just over 300,000 inhabitants, had long been known for its rich fishing industry. Icelanders pride themselves for their reputation as confident, risk-taking adventurists. Because of its extensive geothermal and hydroelectric power sources, the country has been able to attract a growing aluminum industry. In the 1990s a new generation of Icelandic bankers set the goal of transforming Iceland into a global financial powerhouse. Commercial banks expanded their business to include hedge fund investments, investment banking, and private equity. Soon the financial sector was worth more than the country's entire gross domestic product. This growth could be supported only by debt provided by the international wholesale credit markets. As its economy grew, retail investors were attracted to the high rates of return offered by Icelandic banks and hedge funds, and by the appreciation in the country's currency, the krona. In October 2008, just after the collapse of Lehman Brothers, a major U.S. investment bank, the Icelandic financial system collapsed. Each of the major banks went into receivership, local companies declared bankruptcy, and the country's currency dropped in value from 63 krona to the dollar to 130 krona to the dollar.[2] The story of Iceland is another tale of uncontrolled risk, overoptimistic return expectations, and hubris. In this course you will learn about important elements of the international financial system and ways to manage financial risk.

© Darren Brode/Shutterstock.com

- In July 2015 Apple announced that the cash on its balance sheet totaled $203 billion, making it the first company in history to have more than $200 billion in cash. In July 2014 Apple's cash balances stood at $164.5 billion. Strong operating cash flows over the previous year account for

---

[1]For more detail on the VW fraud case and its implications, see, for example, W. Boston and M. Spector, "VW Draws Regulators' Ire," *The Wall Street Journal*, November 19, 2015, pp. B1–B2.

[2]For a detailed account of the Iceland dilemma, see Asgeir Jonsson, *Why Iceland?* (New York: McGraw-Hill, 2009).

FINANCIAL CHALLENGE — CONTINUED

the rapid growth in its cash position. This growing cash balance was achieved even though the company paid out $3.1 billion in dividends and repurchased $4 billion in stock during the previous quarter. What do managers plan to do with this huge cash hoard? Nearly 90 percent of the cash is held offshore in its overseas subsidiaries. If the cash were brought back to the United States, Apple would face a monstrous tax bill. That is why Apple also borrowed $10 billion during the last quarter to help meet dividend and share buyback commitments, and to fund operations. Like many other large firms, Apple is waiting for an improvement in the tax treatment of offshore cash balances. In the meantime, its board and management need to plan for capital investments, new product development costs, and make decisions regarding how to compensate shareholders through dividends and share buybacks.

The situations described here provide a small taste of the important questions regularly facing financial managers. The financial concepts and tools needed to deal with these types of problems are the subject matter of this book.

CHAPTER OBJECTIVES

Upon completion of this chapter, you should have a clear understanding of the following topics:

1. The primary goal of the firm
2. The determinants of the value of a firm
3. The meaning and implications of agency problems in a corporation
4. The importance of ethics in running a business organization
5. The major types of business organizations and their distinguishing features
6. The role and function of the financial manager
7. The relationship between finance and other business disciplines

1-1 Introduction

HTTP:
Yahoo! maintains a finance portal site for access to an extensive range of data, tools, and financial analysis and commentary.
finance.yahoo.com

Financial managers have the primary responsibility for acquiring funds (cash) needed by a firm and for directing those funds into projects that will maximize the value of the firm. The field of financial management[3] is an exciting and a challenging one, with a wide range of rewarding career opportunities in the fields of corporate financial management, investment banking, investment analysis and management, portfolio management, commercial banking, real estate, insurance, risk management, wealth management, and the public sector.

Articles appear regularly in the major business periodicals, such as *The Wall Street Journal*, *Bloomberg BusinessWeek*, *Fortune*, *Forbes*, and *The Financial Times*, describing

[3]The terms *financial management*, *managerial finance*, *corporate finance*, and *business finance* are virtually synonymous and are used interchangeably. Most financial managers, however, seem to prefer either *financial management* or *managerial finance*.

financial managers' involvement in important and challenging tasks. Consider, for example, the options facing Ford Motor's management in 2009 when it was deciding whether to accept U.S. government loan assistance. Imagine the challenges faced by U.S.–based capital goods manufacturers like Boeing, Caterpillar, Cummins, and Lockheed as they face competition in 2015 and beyond from European firms. Between 2011 and late 2015, the value of the euro had declined from \$1.48/euro to \$1.06/euro. A decrease in the value of the euro (which is the same as an increase in the value of the dollar) makes imports from European companies much cheaper for U.S. companies and consumers, while exports from the U.S. become much more expensive for European firms and consumers.

Imagine being a portfolio manager who invested \$10 million, on behalf of her clients, in Apple, Inc. in July 2014. At that time Apple's stock was trading at \$95 per share. By November 2015 the stock had risen to over \$117 per share, an increase of approximately 23 percent. Was this the time to take profits for her client, or should she continue to hold the Apple stock? In November some analysts, such as those from Goldman Sachs, predicted an additional 43 percent increase in value over the coming year, while others believed that the stock was fully valued, or even overvalued, at the current price.

Any business has important financial concerns, and its success or failure depends in a large part on the quality of its financial decisions. Every key decision made by a firm's managers has important financial implications. Managers daily face questions like the following:

- Will a particular investment be successful?
- Where will the funds come from to finance the investment?
- Does the firm have adequate cash or access to cash—through bank borrowing agreements, for example—to meet its daily operating needs?
- Which customers should be offered credit, and how much should they be offered?
- How much inventory should be held?
- Is a merger or an acquisition advisable?
- How should cash flows be used or distributed? That is, what is the optimal dividend policy? Or should shares be repurchased?
- In trying to arrive at the best financial management decisions, how should risk and return be balanced?
- Are there "intangible" benefits (for example, real option aspects) from an investment project that the firm is considering that will affect the accept/reject decision emerging from traditional quantitative analysis procedures?

This text presents an introduction to the theory, institutional background, and analytical tools essential for proper decision making in these and related areas. As a prospective manager, you will be introduced to the financial management process of typical firms. By learning how the financial management process works, you will establish a key building block for a successful management career.

1-2 The Goal of Shareholder Wealth Maximization

III Foundation Concept

Shareholder wealth

Effective financial decision making requires an understanding of the goal(s) of the firm. What objective(s) *should* guide business decision making—that is, what should management try to achieve for the owners of the firm? The most widely accepted objective of the firm is to make the most efficient use of the firm's resources and thereby maximize the value of the firm for its owners; that is, to *maximize shareholder wealth*. **Shareholder wealth** is represented by the market price of a firm's common stock.

Warren Buffett, CEO of Berkshire Hathaway, an outspoken advocate of the shareholder wealth maximization objective, and a premier "value investor," says it this way:

> Our long-term economic goal ... is to maximize the average annual rate of gain in intrinsic business value on a per-share basis. We do not measure the economic significance or performance of Berkshire by its size; we measure by per-share progress.[4]

The shareholder wealth maximization goal states that management should seek to maximize the present value of the expected future returns to the owners (that is, shareholders) of the firm. These returns can take the form of periodic dividend payments or proceeds from the sale of the common stock. **Present value** is defined as the value today of some future payment or stream of payments, evaluated at an appropriate discount rate. The **discount rate** takes into account the returns that are available from alternative investment opportunities during a specific (future) time period. As we shall see in Chapter 5, the longer it takes to receive a benefit, such as a cash dividend or price appreciation of the firm's stock, the lower the value investors place on that benefit. In addition, the greater the **risk** associated with receiving a future benefit, the lower the value investors place on that benefit. Stock prices, the measure of shareholder wealth, reflect the *magnitude*, *timing*, and *risk* associated with future benefits expected to be received by stockholders.

Present value

discount rate

risk

Shareholder wealth is measured by the market value of the shareholders' common stock holdings. **Market value** is defined as the price at which the stock trades in the marketplace, such as on the New York Stock Exchange. Thus, total shareholder wealth equals the number of shares outstanding times the market price per share.

Market value

$$\text{Shareholder wealth} = \text{Number of shares outstanding} \times \text{Market price per share} \tag{1.1}$$

The objective of shareholder wealth maximization has a number of distinct advantages. First, this objective explicitly considers the timing and the risk of the benefits expected to be received from stock ownership. Similarly, managers must consider the elements of timing and risk as they make important financial decisions, such as capital expenditures. In this way, managers can make decisions that will contribute to increasing shareholder wealth.

Second, it is conceptually possible to determine whether a particular financial decision is consistent with this objective. Stock prices provide a direct measure of the success of decisions made by a firm's managers.

Third, shareholder wealth maximization is an impersonal objective. Stockholders who object to a firm's policies are free to sell their shares *under more favorable terms* (that is, at a higher price) *than are available under any other strategy* and invest their funds elsewhere. If an investor has a consumption pattern or risk preference that is not accommodated by the investment, financing, and dividend decisions of that firm, the investor will be able to sell his or her shares in that firm at the best price, and purchase shares in companies that more closely meet the investor's needs.

For these reasons, the shareholder wealth maximization is the key performance metric in financial management. However, concerns for the social responsibilities of business, the existence of other objectives pursued by some managers, and problems that arise from agency relationships may cause some departures from pure wealth-maximizing behavior by owners and managers. (These problems are discussed later.) Nevertheless, the shareholder wealth maximization goal provides the standard against which actual decisions can be judged and, as such, is the objective assumed in financial management analysis.

1-2a Stakeholder Concerns

Most firms recognize the importance of the interests of all their constituent groups, or **stakeholders**—customers, employees, suppliers, and the communities in which they

stakeholders

[4]Berkshire Hathaway, Inc., *Annual Report* (2001). More recently (*Annual Report*, 2010), Buffett adds that their goal is to increase the intrinsic value at a rate of growth in excess of the *Standard & Poor's 500* Stock Price Index (S&P 500), thus providing an objective standard against which success can be measured. (See Chapter 2 for more information on the S&P stock index.)

operate—and not just the interests of stockholders. For example, firms normally recognize responsibilities to various constituencies, such as:

- To sustain an optimum return on investment for *stockholders*
- To be perceived by *customers* as a provider of quality service
- To demonstrate that *employees* are the firm's most valuable resource
- To provide corporate leadership in the *communities* it serves
- To operate compatibly with environmental standards and initiate programs that are sensitive to environmental issues [*community*]

A diversity of opinion exists regarding what stakeholder concerns should be addressed by private companies. The concept is somewhat subjective and is neither perceived nor applied uniformly by all firms. In most instances, a manager who takes an appropriate long-term perspective in decision making, rather than focusing only on short-term accounting profits, will recognize responsibility to all of a firm's constituencies and will help lead the company to the maximization of value for shareholders, while balancing concerns of other stakeholders. In essence, concern for the interests of stakeholders can be viewed as the *means* to the *end* of maximizing long-term shareholder wealth.

1-2b Divergent Objectives

The goal of shareholder wealth maximization specifies how financial decisions should be made. In practice, however, not all management decisions are consistent with this objective. For example, Joel Stern and Bennett Stewart have developed an index of managerial performance that measures the success of managers in achieving a goal of shareholder wealth maximization.[5] Their performance measure, called *Economic Value Added*, is the difference between a firm's annual after-tax operating profit and its total annual cost of capital. Many highly regarded major corporations, including Coca-Cola, AT&T, Quaker Oats, Briggs & Stratton, and CSX, have used the concept. The poor performances of other firms may be due, in part, to a lack of attention to stockholder interests and the pursuit of goals more in the interests of managers.

In other words, there often may be a divergence between the shareholder wealth maximization goal and the *actual* goals pursued by management. The primary reason for this divergence has been attributed to *separation of ownership and control* (management) in corporations.

Separation of ownership and control has permitted managers to pursue goals more consistent with their own self-interests as long as they satisfy shareholders sufficiently to maintain control of the corporation. Instead of seeking to maximize some objective (such as shareholder wealth), managers may "satisfice," or seek acceptable levels of performance, while maximizing their own welfare.

Maximization of their own personal welfare (or utility) may lead managers to be concerned with long-run survival (job security). The concern for long-run survival may lead managers to minimize (or limit) the amount of risk incurred by the firm, since unfavorable outcomes can lead to their dismissal or possible bankruptcy for the firm. Likewise, the desire for job security is cited as one reason why management often opposes takeover offers (mergers) by other companies. Giving senior managers "golden parachute" contracts to compensate them if they lose their positions as the result of a merger is one approach designed to ensure that they will act in the interests of shareholders in merger decisions, rather than in their own interests.

Other firms expect top managers and directors to have a significant ownership stake in the firm. When they do, it is more likely that they will be thinking about ways to increase that stock price every day they go to work.

---

[5] J. M. Stern, J. S. Shiely, and I. Ross, *The EVA Challenge* (New York: Wiley, 2001). This performance measure is discussed more fully in Chapter 3.

1-2c Agency Problems

Agency relationships
principals
agent

The existence of divergent objectives between owners and managers is one example of a class of problems arising from agency relationships. **Agency relationships** occur when one or more individuals (the **principals**) hire another individual (the **agent**) to perform a service on behalf of the principals.[6] In an agency relationship, principals often delegate decision-making authority to the agent. In the context of finance, two of the most important agency relationships are the relationship between stockholders and creditors and the relationship between stockholders (owners) and managers.

Stockholders and Creditors A potential agency conflict arises from the relationship between a company's owners and its creditors. Creditors have a fixed financial claim on the company's resources in the form of long-term debt, bank loans, commercial paper, leases, accounts payable, wages payable, taxes payable, and so on. Because the returns offered to creditors are fixed whereas the returns to stockholders are variable, conflicts may arise between creditors and owners. For example, owners may attempt to increase the riskiness of the company's investments in hopes of receiving greater returns. When this occurs, bondholders suffer because they do not have an opportunity to share in these higher returns. For example, when RJR Nabisco (RJR) was acquired by KKR, the debt of RJR increased from 38 percent of total capital to nearly 90 percent of total capital. This unexpected increase in financial risk caused the value of RJR's bonds to decline by nearly 20 percent. In response to this loss of value, Metropolitan Life Insurance Company and other large bondholders sued RJR for violating the bondholders' rights and protections under the bond covenants. RJR and Metropolitan ultimately settled the suit to the benefit of Metropolitan. Similar concerns arose in several large financial firms, including Wachovia, AIG, Merrill Lynch, and Lehman Brothers, during the economic crisis of 2008–2009. The issue of bondholder rights remains controversial, however.

In order to protect their interests, creditors often insist on certain protective covenants in a company's bond indentures.[7] These covenants take many forms, such as limitations on dividend payments, limitations on the type of investments (and divestitures) the company can undertake, poison puts,[8] and limitations on the issuance of new debt. The constraints on the owner-managers may reduce the potential market value of the firm. In addition to these constraints, bondholders may also demand a higher fixed return to compensate for risks not adequately covered by bond indenture restrictions.

Stockholders and Managers Inefficiencies that arise because of agency relationships have been called *agency problems*. These problems occur because each party to a transaction is assumed to act in a manner consistent with maximizing his or her own utility (welfare). The example cited earlier—the concern by management for long-run survival (job security) rather than shareholder wealth maximization—is an agency problem. Another example is the consumption of on-the-job perquisites (such as the use of company airplanes, limousines, and luxurious offices) by managers who have no (or only a partial) ownership interest in the firm. Shirking by managers is also an agency-related problem.

In May 2012, JPMorgan Chase called a surprise news conference call to announce a loss of at least $2 billion because of trading in risky credit default swaps that were made in the office of the chief investment officer, Ina Drew. The trades that led to the massive losses

---

[6]See Amir Barnea, R. Haugen, and L. Senbet, *Agency Problems and Financial Contracting* (Englewood Cliffs, NJ: Prentice Hall, 1985) for an overview of the agency problem issue. See also Jean-Jacques Laffont and David Martimort, *The Theory of Incentives: The Principal-Agent Model* (Princeton, NJ: Princeton University Press, 2001).

[7]Protective covenants are discussed in greater detail in Chapters 6 and 19.

[8]A "poison put" is an option contained in a bond indenture that permits the bondholder to sell the bond back to the issuing company at face value under certain circumstances, such as a leveraged buyout that raises the risk for existing debt holders.

were managed by a trader in the firm's London offices. These trades occurred because of a conflict of incentives between the traders and the risk-management profile desired by JPMorgan's CEO, Jamie Dimon. Seven employees lost their jobs, the market value of JPMorgan's stock declined by nearly $39 billion in the two months following the announcement of the trading losses, and the reputations of JPMorgan and its CEO were severely damaged.

agency costs

These agency problems give rise to a number of **agency costs**, which are incurred by shareholders to minimize agency problems. Examples of agency costs include:

1. Expenditures to structure the organization in such a way as to minimize the incentives for management to take actions contrary to shareholder interests
2. Expenditures to monitor management's actions, such as paying for audits of managerial performance and internal audits of the firm's expenditures
3. Bonding expenditures to protect the owners from managerial dishonesty
4. The opportunity cost of lost profits arising from complex organizational structures that prevent management from making timely responses to opportunities

A number of different mechanisms are available to reduce the agency conflicts between shareholders and managers. These include corporate governance, managerial compensation, and the threat of takeovers.

Corporate Governance As a result of accounting scandals and the increased perception of excessive executive compensation (relative to company performance), the Securities and Exchange Commission (SEC), the securities exchanges (NYSE, AMEX, NASDAQ), The Conference Board (a business research organization), and other experts have made various proposals concerning how best to deal with the issues of corporate governance.

First, the board of directors of a corporation should have a majority of independent directors. Independent directors are individuals who are not current or former employees of the company and who have no significant business ties to the company. Additionally, the committee responsible for nominating members of the board of directors must be composed only of independent directors. Furthermore, the post of chairman of the board of directors should be split from the CEO position; or, alternatively, an independent lead, or presiding, director should chair board meetings. Also, all members of the audit and compensation committees must be independent directors. Finally, the company must disclose whether it has adopted a code of ethics for the CEO and senior financial officers and, if not, explain why it has not done so.

Many of these proposals have been implemented by public companies. In addition to these proposed changes in how corporations govern themselves, the Sarbanes-Oxley Act, passed by Congress in 2002, mandated various changes in the processes used by corporations to report their financial results.

Managerial Compensation Properly designed compensation contracts can help to align shareholder-management conflicts. For example, providing part of the compensation in the form of stock or options to purchase stock can reduce agency conflicts. Stock options granted to managers entitle them to buy shares of the company at a particular price (**exercise price**). Typically, the options are set at an exercise price greater than the price of the stock at the time options are granted and can be exercised only after a certain period of time has elapsed. These conditions are imposed so that managers won't be tempted to cash in their options immediately and leave the company. More important to stock value, this is an attempt to align their interests more closely with those of the shareholders. Many firms, including Disney and Home Depot, provide key executives with significant stock options that increase in value with improvements in the firm's stock price. Two of the largest payoffs from the exercise of options were the $706 million

exercise price

received in 2001 by Lawrence Ellison, chairman and CEO of Oracle, and the $570 million paid in 1998 to Michael Eisner, chairman and CEO of Disney. In 2012 Apple's new CEO, Tim Cook, received a compensation package totaling $378 million.

Some critics have argued that stock options tend to distort executive decisions by emphasizing short-term performance and giving them incentives to engage in accounting tricks to inflate the company's stock price. As a result, some firms have adopted alternative incentive compensation policies. One plan is to offer "restricted stock" to company executives. Such stock cannot be sold unless the manager remains with the company for a stated period of time. Microsoft, for example, stopped issuing stock options in 2003 and instead began offering restricted stock to its executives (and all other employees). For Microsoft managers, the restricted shares vest, or can be sold, over a five-year period. Another approach is to offer executives "performance shares," which are stock grants based on the company meeting specific performance targets. For example, in 2003 General Electric (GE) stopped issuing stock options to its CEO and instead offered 250,000 performance share units. Each performance share unit was equal to one share of common stock. Half of the performance share units will vest in five years if GE's cash flow increases at an average rate of 10 percent or more per year. The other half of the performance share units will vest in five years if GE's shareholder return meets or exceeds the cumulative five-year return of companies in the *Standard & Poor's 500* Stock Price Index (S&P 500).[9] The potential value of these performance share units at the time of issue was approximately $7.5 million, which was more than half of the CEO's total compensation package.

Threat of Takeovers Takeovers also can serve as an important deterrent to shareholder-management conflicts. The argument goes as follows: If managers act in their self-interest, then share values will be depressed, providing an incentive for someone to take over the company at a depressed level. The acquirer can then benefit from instituting policies that are consistent with shareholder wealth maximization, such as eliminating underperforming units and cutting overhead.

In addition to these mechanisms, we will learn in later chapters that certain corporate financial policies, such as dividends and capital structure, can also serve to control agency conflicts. Remaining agency problems give rise to costs that show up as a reduction in the value of the firm's shares in the marketplace.

1-3 Maximization of Shareholder Wealth: Managerial Strategies

If the managers of a firm accept the goal of maximizing shareholder wealth, how should they achieve this objective? One might be tempted to argue that managers will maximize shareholder wealth if they maximize the profits of the firm. After all, profit maximization is the predominant objective that emerges from static microeconomic models of the firm. Unfortunately, the profit maximization objective has too many shortcomings to provide consistent guidance to the practicing manager.

Before discussing some of these shortcomings, it is useful to highlight one important managerial decision rule that emerges from the microeconomic profit maximization model. To maximize profits, we learned in microeconomics that a firm should expand output to the point where the marginal (additional) cost (MC) of the last unit produced and sold just equals the marginal revenue (MR) received. To move beyond that output level will result in greater additional costs than additional revenues and hence lower profits. To fail to produce up to the point where $MC = MR$ results in a lower level of

[9]See Chapter 2 for more information on this index.

total profits than is possible by following the rule. This fundamental rule, that an economic action should be continued up to the point where the marginal revenue (benefit) just equals the marginal cost, offers excellent guidance for financial managers dealing with a wide range of problems. For example, we shall see that the basic capital expenditure analysis model is simply an adaptation of the $MC = MR$ rule. Other applications appear in the working capital management and capital structure areas.

Despite the insights it offers financial managers, the profit maximization model is not useful as the central decision-making model for the firm for several reasons. First, the standard microeconomic model of profit maximization is *static*; that is, it lacks a time dimension. Profit maximization as a goal offers no explicit basis for comparing long-term and short-term profits. Major decisions made by financial managers *must* reflect the time dimension. For example, capital expenditure decisions, which are central to the finance function, have a long-term impact on the performance of the firm. Financial managers must make trade-offs between short-run and long-run returns in conjunction with capital investment decisions.

profit (or earnings or income)

The second limitation of the profit maximization objective has to do with the definition of **profit (or earnings or income)**. Generally accepted accounting principles (as discussed in Chapter 3) result in literally hundreds of definitions of profit for a firm because of the latitude permitted in recognizing and accounting for costs and revenues. For example, Carolina Power & Light Company (CPL) was forced to reduce its earnings by \$81.6 million because of an unfavorable regulatory treatment of its Harris nuclear plant. To offset this impact on the firm's earnings, CPL "changed its method of accounting for revenues to accrue unbilled revenues as of the date service is rendered, rather than when billed. The net effect of this accounting change was an increase in net income of \$77 million, or \$0.92 per share."[10] This arbitrary accounting change had *no* impact on the cash flows or economic well-being of CPL and hence had no impact on its value.

Even if we could agree on the appropriate accounting definition of profit, it is not clear whether a firm should attempt to maximize total profit, the rate of profit, or earnings per share (EPS).

Consider Columbia Beverages Inc., a firm with 10 million shares outstanding that currently earns a profit of \$10 million after tax. If the firm sells an additional 1 million shares of stock and invests the proceeds to earn \$100,000 per year, the total profit of the firm will increase from \$10 million to \$10.1 million. However, are shareholders better off? Prior to the stock sale, earnings per share are \$1 (\$10 million profit divided by 10 million shares of stock). After the stock sale, EPS decline to \$0.92 (\$10.1 million in earnings divided by 11 million shares). Although total profit has increased, EPS have declined. Stockholders are not better off as a result of this action.

This example might lead one to conclude that managers should seek to maximize EPS (for a given number of shares outstanding). This, too, can result in misleading actions. For example, consider a firm with total assets at the start of the year of \$10 million. The firm is financed entirely with stock (1 million shares outstanding) and has no debt. After-tax earnings are \$1 million, resulting in a return on stockholders' equity of 10 percent (\$1 million in earnings divided by \$10 million in stockholders' equity), and EPS are \$1. The company decides to retain one-half of this year's earnings (increasing assets and equity to \$10.5 million) and pay out the balance in stockholders' dividends. Next year the company's earnings total \$1.029 million, resulting in EPS of \$1.029. Are shareholders better off because of the decision by managers to reinvest \$500,000 in the firm? In this example, a strong argument can be made that the position of shareholders has deteriorated. Although EPS increased from \$1 per share to \$1.029 per share, the realized return on stockholders' equity actually declined, from 10 percent to 9.8 percent (\$1.029 million

[10]Carolina Power & Light Company, "Letter to Members of the Financial Community," January 25, 1991.

divided by $10.5 million of stockholders' equity). In essence, the company's managers reinvested $500,000 of stockholders' money to earn a return of only 5.8 percent ($0.029 million of additional earnings divided by $0.5 million of additional investment). This type of investment is not likely to result in maximum shareholder wealth. Shareholders could do better by investing in bonds yielding more than 5.8 percent.

The third major problem associated with the profit maximization objective is that it provides no direct way for financial managers to consider the risk associated with alternative decisions. For example, two projects generating identical future expected cash flows and requiring identical outlays may be vastly different with respect to the risk of the expected cash flows. Similarly, a firm can often increase its EPS by increasing the proportion of debt financing used in the firm's capital structure. However, leverage-induced increases in EPS come at the cost of increased financial risk. The financial marketplace will recognize the increased risk of financial distress that accompanies increases in debt financing and will value the resulting EPS accordingly.

1-3a Determinants of Value

If the profit maximization objective does not provide the proper guidance to managers seeking to maximize shareholder wealth, what rules should these managers follow? First, it is important to recognize that the maximization of shareholder wealth is a market concept, not an accounting concept. Managers should attempt to maximize the market value of the company's shares, not the accounting or **book value** per share. The book value reflects the historic cost of assets, not the earning capacity of those assets. Also, the book value does not consider the risk associated with the assets.

book value

Three major factors determine the market value of a company's shares of stock: the *amount of the cash flows expected to be generated for the benefit of stockholders*; *the timing of these cash flows*; and *the risk of the cash flows.*

Cash Flow

Throughout the book, we stress the importance of cash flows in the practice of financial management. **Cash flow** relates to the actual cash generated or paid by the firm. Only cash can be used to acquire assets, and only cash can be used to make valuable distributions to investors. In contrast, the accounting system focuses primarily on a matching over time of the historic, cost-based revenues and expenses of a company, resulting in a bottom-line earnings figure. But accounting earnings are often misleading because they do not reflect the actual cash inflows and outflows of the firm. For example, an accountant records depreciation expense on an asset each period over the depreciable life of that asset. Depreciation is designed to reflect the decline in value of that asset over time. However, depreciation itself results in no cash outflow.[11] The entire cash outflow occurred when the asset was originally purchased.

Cash flow

Timing of Cash Flows

The market value of a share of stock is influenced not only by the amount of the cash flows it is expected to produce, but also by the timing of those cash flows. If faced with the alternatives of receiving $100 today or $100 three years from today, you would surely choose the $100 today because you could invest that $100 for three years and accumulate the interest. Thus, financial managers must consider both the magnitude of the cash flows they expect to generate and the timing of these cash flows, because investors will reflect these dimensions of return in their valuation of the enterprise.

Risk

Finally, the market value of a share of stock is influenced by the perceived risk of the cash flows it is expected to generate. The relationship between risk and required return is an important concept in financial management and is discussed in detail in Chapter 8. In general, *the greater the perceived risk associated with an expected cash*

[11]Because depreciation is used in computing a firm's tax liability, it can affect *after-tax* cash flows. This concept is discussed further in Chapters 4 and 9.

flow, the greater the rate of return required by investors and managers. Thus, financial managers must also consider the risk of the cash flows expected to be generated by the firm because investors will reflect this risk in their valuation of the enterprise.

1-3b Managerial Actions to Influence Value

How can managers influence the magnitude, timing, and risk of the cash flows expected to be generated by the firm in order to maximize shareholder wealth? Many factors ultimately influence the magnitude, timing, and risk of a firm's cash flows and thus the price of the firm's stock. Some of these factors are related to the external economic environment and are largely outside the direct control of managers. Other factors can be directly manipulated by the managers. Figure 1.1 illustrates the factors affecting stock prices.

FIGURE 1.1

Factors Affecting Stock Prices

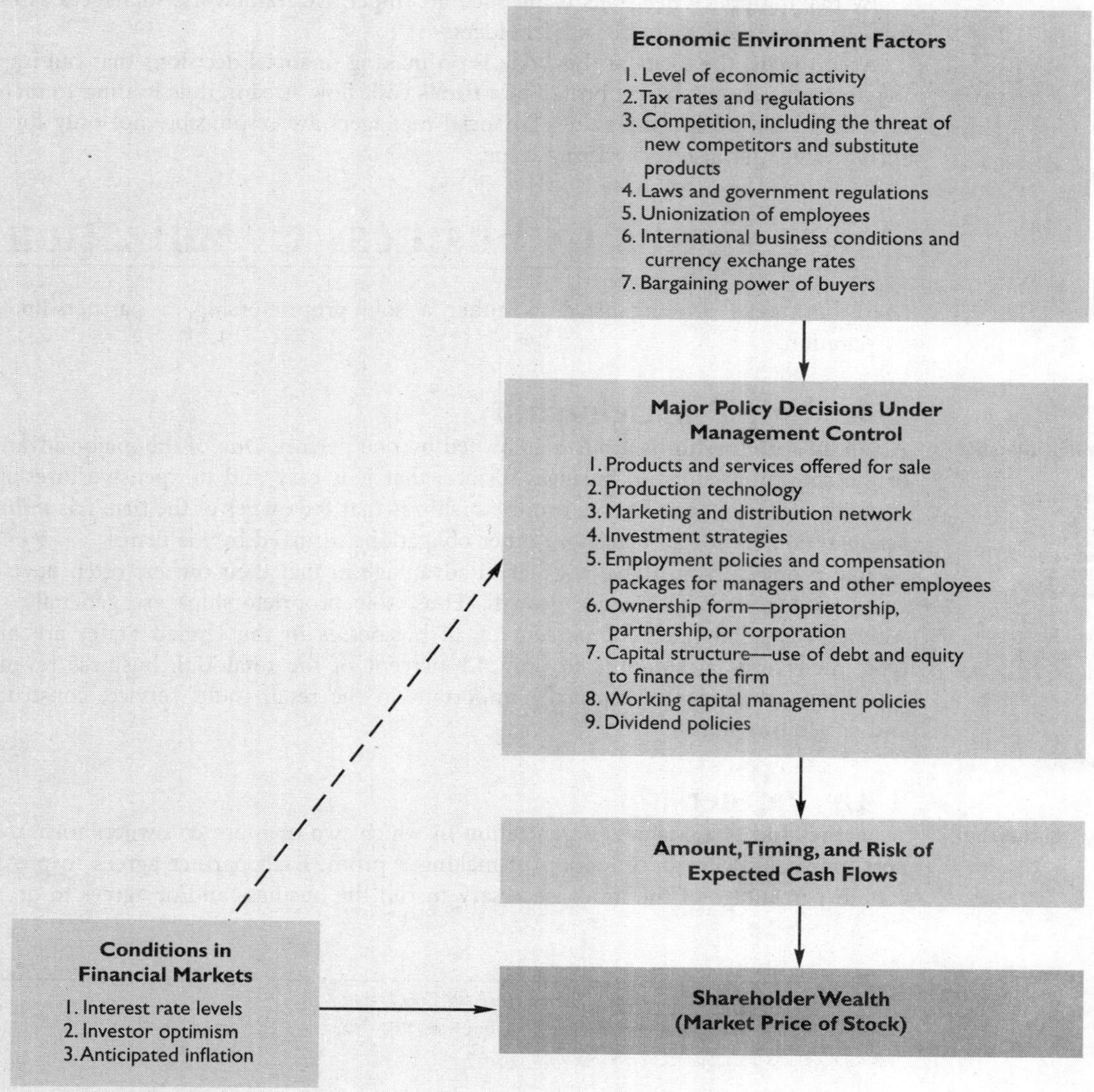

The top panel enumerates some of the factors in the economic environment that have an impact on the strategic decisions managers can make. Even though economic environment factors are largely outside the direct control of managers, managers must be aware of how these factors affect the policy decisions under the control of management.

In this context, it is useful to consider a competitive strategy framework developed initially by Michael E. Porter and developed further by Alfred Rappaport.[12,13] Porter and Rappaport recommend that managers formulate an overall competitive strategy analyzing five competitive forces that can influence an industry's structure and can thereby ultimately affect the market prices of stocks of individual companies in a particular industry. The five competitive forces are:

1. The threat of new entrants
2. The threat of substitute products
3. The bargaining power of buyers
4. The bargaining power of suppliers
5. The rivalry among current competitors

By making policy decisions using such a competitive framework, managers can be in a position to create value for shareholders.

Accordingly, the focus of this book is on making financial decisions that can improve the amount, timing, or risk profile of a firm's cash flow stream, thus leading to increases in shareholder wealth and value. Financial managers are responsible not only for *measuring* value, but also for *creating* value.

1-4 Forms of Business Organization

Most businesses are organized as either a sole proprietorship, a partnership, or a corporation.

1-4a Sole Proprietorship

sole proprietorship

A **sole proprietorship** is a business owned by one person. One of the major advantages of the sole proprietorship business form is that it is easy and inexpensive to establish. A major disadvantage of a sole proprietorship is that the owner of the firm has *unlimited personal liability* for all debts and other obligations incurred by the firm.

HTTP:
The Small Business Administration offers some very helpful tips and information on running a small business, including financial guidance, local resources, and disaster assistance.
www.sba.gov

Sole proprietorships have another disadvantage in that their owners often have difficulty raising funds to finance growth. Thus, sole proprietorships are generally small. Although approximately 72 percent of all businesses in the United States are of this type, their revenue amounts to only 4.1 percent of the total U.S. business revenue.[14] Sole proprietorships are especially important in the retail trade, service, construction, and agriculture industries.

1-4b Partnership

partnership

A **partnership** is a business organization in which two or more co-owners form a business, normally with the intention of making a profit. Each partner agrees to provide a certain percentage of the funds necessary to run the business and/or agrees to do some

[12]Michael E. Porter, *Competitive Advantage* (New York: Free Press, 1985), Chapter 1.

[13]Alfred Rappaport, *Creating Shareholder Value* (New York: Free Press, 1986), Chapter 4.

[14]Internal Revenue Service, *Statistics of Income*, www.irs.gov.

portion of the necessary work. In return, the partners share in the profits (or losses) of the business.

general partnership

Partnerships may be either general or limited. In a **general partnership**, each partner has unlimited liability for all of the obligations of the business. Thus, general partnerships have the same major disadvantage as sole proprietorships. Approximately 17 percent of all partnerships in the United States are of this type.

limited partnership

A **limited partnership** usually involves one or more general partners and one or more limited partners. Although the limited partners may limit their liability, the extent of this liability can vary and is set forth in the partnership agreement. Limited partnerships are common in real estate ventures.

Partnerships have been relatively important in the agriculture, mining, oil and gas, finance, insurance, real estate, and services industries. Overall, partnerships account for about 10 percent of all U.S. business firms and less than 15 percent of total business revenues.[15]

Partnerships are relatively easy to form, but they must be re-formed when there is a change in the makeup of the general partners. Partnerships have a greater capacity to raise capital than sole proprietorships, but they lack the tremendous capital attraction ability of corporations.

1-4c Corporation

corporation

A **corporation** is a "legal person" composed of one or more actual individuals or legal entities. It is considered separate and distinct from those individuals or entities. Money contributed to start a corporation is called *capital stock* and is divided into shares; the owners of the corporation are called *stockholders* or *shareholders*.

Corporations account for less than 18 percent of all U.S. business firms but about 81 percent of U.S. business revenues and approximately 61 percent of U.S. business profits.[16]

HTTP:
Do you know who the 400 richest people in America are? Which are the 200 best-run small companies? The 500 largest private firms? *Forbes* magazine can tell you.
www.forbes.com

The corporate form of business organization has four major advantages over both sole proprietorships and partnerships.

- **Limited liability**. Once stockholders have paid for their shares, they are not liable for any obligations or debts the corporation may incur. They are liable only to the extent of their investment in the shares.
- **Permanency**. The legal existence of a corporation is not affected by whether stockholders sell their shares, which makes it a more permanent form of business organization.
- **Flexibility**. A change of ownership within a corporation is easily accomplished when one individual merely sells shares to another. Even when shares of stock are sold, the corporation continues to exist in its original form.
- **Ability to raise capital**. Due to the limited liability of its owners and the easy marketability of its shares of ownership, a corporation is able to raise large amounts of capital, which makes large-scale growth possible.

However, the ability to raise capital comes with a cost. In the typical large corporation, ownership is separated from management. This gives rise to potential conflicts of goals and certain costs, called *agency costs*, which were discussed earlier. However, the ability to raise large amounts of capital at relatively low cost is such a large advantage of the corporate form over sole proprietorships and partnerships that a certain level of agency costs is tolerated.

As a "legal person," a corporation can purchase and own assets, borrow money, sue, and be sued. Its officers are considered to be *agents* of the corporation and are authorized to act on the corporation's behalf. For example, only an officer, such as the treasurer, can sign an agreement to repay a bank loan for the corporation.

---

15 Internal Revenue Service, *Statistics of Income*, www.irs.gov.

16 Internal Revenue Service, *Statistics of Income*, www.irs.gov.

ETHICAL ISSUES

The Practice of Financial Management

In recent years, interest in the ethical dimensions of business practice has exploded. Front-page stories of the stock trading scandals involving the use of insider information that led to the downfall of Dennis Levine, Ivan Boesky, Raj Rajaratnam (Galleon Group), the Treasury bond trading scandal at Salomon Brothers that severely damaged Salomon's reputation and resulted in its top managers being forced to resign, the billions of dollars of questionable loans made by savings and loan executives that caused the collapse of much of the savings and loan industry, and the collateralized mortgage obligation (CMO) debacle that played a crucial role in the 2008–2009 financial collapse have focused attention on the ethical practices followed by business and financial managers.

Webster's defines ethics as "the discipline dealing with what is good or bad, right or wrong, or with moral duty and obligation."[a] John J. Casey defines business ethics as follows: "At its best, business ethics is excellence in management applied with fairness and dispatch. It involves hard-headed thought, not a sentimental reaction. It also involves articulate, effective communication to all parties...."[b] Casey identifies a number of techniques that managers can keep in mind when addressing the ethical dimensions of a business problem:

- Clarify the parameters of the problem
- Involve the right team of participants at the outset
- Collect all the facts bearing on the problem
- Articulate the harm and benefit that may result from proposed actions
- Weigh the consequences of alternatives
- Seek equity for those who may be affected

Other action guidelines that have been suggested for managers include to:

- Ensure that personal interests do not conflict with business decisions being made
- Respect the confidentiality of information entrusted to you
- Make decisions based on rational, objective business analysis rather than on inappropriate factors, such as race, sex, or religion
- Act fairly in dealing with customers while protecting the legitimate interests of the business.[c]

Ethical considerations impact all kinds of business and financial management decisions. Some financial decisions with important ethical dimensions, such as the collateralized mortgage obligations issued by large banks which led to the global financial collapse in 2008–2009, command national attention.

However, financial managers encounter day-to-day decisions that have important ethical dimensions. For example, as a new bank loan officer, should you recommend approval of a loan to a longtime friend, even though she does not quite meet the normal loan standards of the bank? As an account executive for a brokerage firm, should you recommend to your clients the securities of firms that have poor environmental management records or that deal in such products as alcohol and tobacco? Should you tell your father-in-law that your firm is likely to become a candidate for a takeover before this is publicly announced? As a division manager being evaluated in part on a return-on-assets calculation, should you lease assets to keep them out of the asset base for evaluation purposes and thereby enhance your apparent performance? When discussing the earnings performance of your company in quarterly and annual reports, should the discussion be limited to only GAAP (Generally Accepted Accounting Principles) definitions of earnings, like Apple and Netflix do, or should you urge investors to focus on alternative definitions of earnings that make the company's performance appear to be better (as many other rapidly growing tech firms do)?

This brief sampling of the areas of business and financial-management decision making that possess important ethical dimensions provides a feel for the breadth of ethical issues facing financial managers. In most cases, the answers to these questions are not clear-cut. Actual decision making is very complex and involves many trade-offs among parties with competing interests. However, explicitly recognizing the costs and benefits associated with each of these decisions and making the decision in an atmosphere of balanced objectivity and fairness can help financial managers avoid apparent or real breaches of their ethical trust.

An important concern for financial managers, who are entrusted with the resources of stockholders and are expected to maximize the value of these

ETHICAL ISSUES — CONTINUED

resources, is: How does a concern for ethics in the practice of financial management impact the goal of shareholder wealth maximization? Firms that expect employees to act according to a code of ethics in their business dealings can expect to have reduced litigation and damages expenses. A recent survey concluded that some 90 percent of the *Fortune* 500 companies have adopted a published code of conduct for their managers and other employees. High ethical standards are respected by customers and valued by investors. One could argue that ethical business dealings build long-term value for investors, whereas breaches of standards of business ethics may provide short-term gains at the expense of future returns and long-term value.

Throughout the text, we will highlight ethical issues that confront financial managers as they make important financial decisions. Our objective is to raise your consciousness of these issues, rather than to make moral judgments about what is right or wrong in each case. Those judgments are best left to you as topics of lively discussions with your classmates.

[a] *Webster's Third New International Dictionary* (Chicago: Merriam Webster, 1981).
[b] John J. Casey, "The New Urgency for Ethics in Banking," *The Banker* (March/April 1991): 44–50.
[c] Ibid., 48–49.

Corporate Organization and Governance In most corporations, the stockholders elect a *board of directors*, which, in theory, is responsible for overseeing the management of the corporation. In practice, however, the board of directors usually deals with broad policy matters, leaving the day-to-day operations of the business to the *officers*, who are selected by the board. Corporate officers normally include a *chairman of the board*, *chief executive officer* (CEO), *chief operating officer* (COO), *chief financial officer* (CFO), *president*, *vice president(s)*, *treasurer*, and *secretary*. In some corporations, one person holds more than one office; for instance, many small corporations have a person who serves as secretary-treasurer. In most corporations, the president and various other officers are also members of the board of directors. These officers are called "inside" board members, whereas other board members are called "outside" or independent board members. A corporation's board of directors usually contains at least three members.

Corporate Securities In return for the use of their funds, investors in a corporation are issued certificates, or *securities*. Corporate securities represent claims against the assets and future earnings of the firm.

HTTP:
Most major corporations today maintain extensive Web sites, displaying their histories, products, services, financial statements, and much more. Check out the Web sites of Ford, GM, and Boeing, and explore a few of their many links.

www.ford.com
www.gm.com
www.boeing.com

There are two types of corporate securities. Investors who lend money to the corporation are issued *debt securities*; these investors expect periodic interest payments, as well as the eventual return of their principal. Owners of the corporation are issued *equity securities*. Equity securities take the form of either *common stock* or *preferred stock*. Common stock is a residual form of ownership; that is, the claims of common stockholders on the firm's earnings and assets are considered only after all other claims—such as those of the government, debt holders, and preferred stockholders—have been met. Common stockholders are considered to be true owners of the corporation. Common stockholders possess certain rights or claims, including dividend rights, asset rights, voting rights, and preemptive rights.[17] In Chapters 6 and 7, we illustrate how to obtain information about a company's common stock and debt securities from such sources as *The Wall Street Journal* and *finance.yahoo.com*.

Preferred stockholders have priority over common stockholders with regard to the firm's earnings and assets. They are paid cash dividends before common stockholders. In

[17] Stockholder rights are discussed in greater detail in Chapter 7.

addition, if a corporation enters bankruptcy, is reorganized, or is dissolved, preferred stockholders have priority over common stockholders in the distribution of the corporation's assets. However, preferred stockholders are second in line behind the firm's creditors.

Because of the advantages of limited liability, permanency, and flexibility and because ownership shares in corporations tend to be more liquid (and hence relatively more valuable) than ownership interests in proprietorships and partnerships, it is easy to see why the majority of business conducted in the United States is done under the corporate form of organization.

1-4d Other Types of Business Organizations

Though sole proprietorships, partnerships, and corporations are the three basic forms of business organization, there are other types or organizations sometimes referred to as *hybrid organizations*, which have features of each of these basic forms.

The *subchapter S corporation* is one such example. The Internal Revenue Code permits companies with 100 or fewer domestic stockholders, and that meet certain other requirements, to register as an S corporation. With the S corporation, stockholders avoid the double taxation of earnings and pay taxes similar to partnerships. The S corporation, however, preserves the other benefits of the corporate setup, including limited liability. In recent years, there has been an increase in the number of firms registering as S corporations for tax purposes.

An increasingly popular form of hybrid organization is the *limited liability company (LLC)*. Like the S corporation, the earnings of the LLC flow through to the owners (called *members*) and are taxed at the individual level. Also, like the corporation, the LLC members have the benefit of limited liability. The LLC has fewer restrictions than the S corporation in terms of who can qualify as owners and greater flexibility in terms of accounting requirements. For example, the members need not be domestic, and from an accounting perspective no annual reports need to be filed. Examples of an LLC include Domino's Pizza LLC as well as SourceGas LLC, a natural gas company headquartered in Denver. The LLC legal form of business organization is frequently used by early-stage start-up companies.

The *limited liability partnership (LLP)* is another type of business organization where all partners have limited liability. LLPs are taxed like any other partnership; thus, they share the tax advantage of regular partnerships and sole proprietorships. A form of LLP is the professional limited liability partnership (PLLP), which is a partnership formed to render specific professional services such as legal, accounting, or medical services. Examples of LLPs include Baker Botts LLP (legal practice) and PwC LLP (accounting and other management services). Goldman Sachs, a well-known investment banking firm, was a limited partnership until May 1999, when it converted to the corporate form in order to have better access to capital to finance growth, enable broad employee ownership of the firm, and enable the firm to engage in strategic acquisitions.

1-5 Organization of the Financial Management Function

Many firms divide the decision-making responsibilities of management among several different officers, which often include those in manufacturing, marketing, finance, personnel, and engineering. A sample organization chart emphasizing the finance function is shown in Figure 1.2. The finance function is usually headed by a vice president of

FIGURE 1.2
Sample Organization Chart

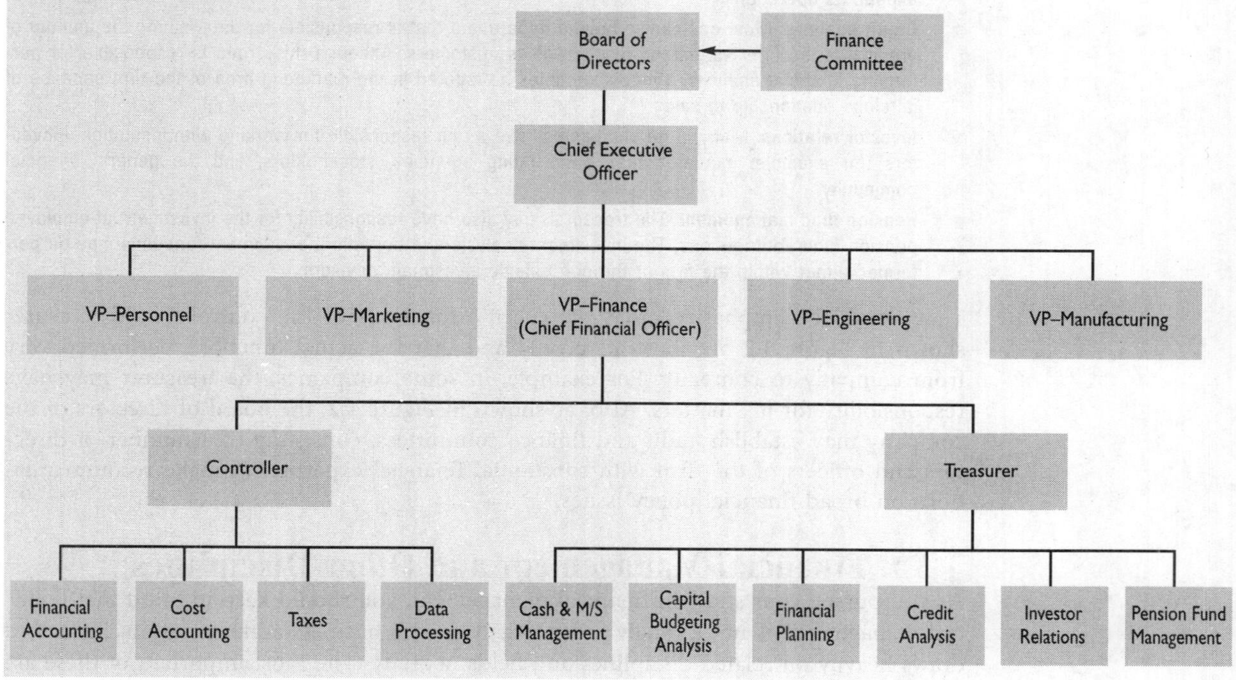

finance, or *chief financial officer (CFO)*, who reports to the president or the CEO. In some corporations the CFO may also be a member of the board of directors. In addition to overseeing the accounting, treasury, tax, and audit functions, today's CFO often has responsibility for strategic planning, monitoring and trading foreign currencies, managing the risk from volatile interest rates, and monitoring production and inventory levels. CFOs also must be able to communicate effectively with the investment community concerning the financial performance of the company.

The chief financial officer often distributes the financial management responsibilities between the *controller* and the *treasurer*. The controller normally has responsibility for all accounting-related activities. These include such functions as the following:

- **Financial accounting.** This function involves the preparation of the financial statements for the firm, such as the balance sheet, income statement, and the statement of cash flows.
- **Cost accounting.** This department often has responsibility for preparing the firm's operating budgets and monitoring the performance of the departments and divisions within the firm.
- **Taxes.** This unit prepares the reports that the company must file with the various government (local, state, and federal) agencies.
- **Data processing.** Given its responsibilities involving corporate accounting and payroll activities, the controller may also have management responsibility for the company's data-processing operations.

The treasurer is normally concerned with the acquisition, custody, and expenditure of funds. These duties often include the following:

- **Cash and marketable securities management.** This group monitors the firm's short-term finances—forecasting its cash needs, obtaining funds from bankers and other sources when needed, and investing any excess funds in short-term interest-earning securities.

- **Capital budgeting analysis.** This department is responsible for analyzing capital expenditures—that is, the purchase of long-term assets, such as new facilities and equipment.
- **Financial planning.** This department is responsible for analyzing the alternative sources of long-term funds, such as the issuance of bonds or common stock, that the firm will need to maintain and expand its operations.
- **Credit analysis.** Most companies have a department that is responsible for determining the amount of credit that the firm will extend to each of its customers. Although this group is responsible for performing financial analysis, it may sometimes be located in the marketing area of the firm because of its close relationship to sales.
- **Investor relations.** Many large companies have a unit responsible for working with institutional investors (for example, mutual funds), bond rating agencies, stockholders, and the general financial community.
- **Pension fund management.** The treasurer may also have responsibility for the investment of employee pension fund contributions. The investment analysis and portfolio management functions may be performed either within the firm or through outside investment advisors.

It should be emphasized that the specific functions of the controller and treasurer shown in Figure 1.2 are illustrative only and that the actual functions performed vary from company to company. For example, in some companies, the treasurer may have responsibility for tax matters. Also, as shown in Figure 1.2, the board of directors of the company may establish audit and finance committees, consisting of a number of directors and officers of the firm with substantial financial expertise, to make recommendations on broad financial policy issues.

1-5a Financial Management and Other Disciplines

As you pursue your study of financial management, you should keep in mind that financial management is not a totally independent area in business administration. Instead, it draws heavily on related disciplines and fields of study. The most important of these are *accounting* and *economics*; in the latter discipline, both *macroeconomics* and *microeconomics* are significant. *Marketing*, *production*, *human resources management*, and the study of *quantitative methods* also have an impact on the financial management field. Each of these is discussed here.

Accounting Financial managers manage a firm's financial and physical assets and secure the funding needed to support these assets. Accountants keep score of the firm's performance. Financial managers often turn to accounting data to assist them in making decisions. Generally a company's accountants are responsible for developing financial reports and measures that assist its managers in assessing the past performance and future direction of the firm and in meeting certain legal obligations, such as the payment of taxes. The accountant's role includes the development of financial statements, such as the *balance sheet*, the *income statement*, and the *statement of cash flows*.

Financial managers are primarily concerned with a firm's cash flows, because they often determine the feasibility of certain investment and financing decisions. The financial manager refers to accounting data when making future resource allocation decisions concerning long-term investments, when managing current investments in working capital, and when making a number of other financial decisions (for example, determining the most appropriate capital structure and identifying the best and most timely sources of funds needed to support the firm's investment programs).

In many small and medium-sized firms, the accounting function and the financial management function may be handled by the same person or group of persons. In such cases, the distinctions just identified may become blurred.

HTTP:
The Web site maintained by *The Economist* magazine provides extensive background reading on many financial issues you will encounter in this course.

www.economist.com

Similarly, *The Wall Street Journal's* Web site is a rich source of information and examples of issues central to this course.

online.wsj.com/home-page

Economics There are two areas of economics with which the financial manager must be familiar: *microeconomics* and *macroeconomics*. Microeconomics deals with he economic decisions of individuals, households, and firms, whereas macroeconomics looks at the economy as a whole.

The typical firm is heavily influenced by the overall performance of the economy and is dependent on the money and capital markets for investment funds. Thus, financial managers should recognize and understand how monetary policies affect the cost of funds and the availability of credit. Financial managers should also be versed in fiscal policy and how it affects the economy. What the economy can be expected to do in the future is a crucial factor in generating sales forecasts as well as other types of forecasts.

ENTREPRENEURIAL ISSUES

Shareholder Wealth Maximization

Entrepreneurial finance deals with the financial issues facing small businesses—an important sector of the U.S. economy. Small business firms may be organized as sole proprietorships, partnerships, or corporations. According to criteria used by the Small Business Administration, over 95 percent of all business firms are considered small. These firms account for the majority of private sector employment and a large majority of the net growth in new jobs.

It is difficult to arrive at a precise definition of a small, or entrepreneurial, business; however, the characteristics of small business firms can be identified. In general, small businesses are not the dominant firm in the industries in which they compete, and they tend to grow more rapidly than larger firms. Small firms have limited access to the financial markets, and they often do not have the depth of specialized managerial resources available to larger firms. Small firms also have a high failure rate.

In our discussion of the goals of the firm, we concluded that the predominant goal of financial managers is to maximize shareholder wealth, as measured by the price of the firm's stock. Many entrepreneurial corporations are closely held, and their stock trades infrequently, if ever. Other entrepreneurial firms are organized as sole proprietorships, partnerships, or LLCs. In these cases, there is no readily accessible external measure of performance. Consequently, these firms often rely more heavily on accounting-based measures of performance to track their progress. Accounting-based measures of performance are discussed in Chapter 3. In spite of the lack of an objective, readily available measure of performance, the fundamental decisions made by entrepreneurs are unaltered. That is, the firm should invest resources in projects expected to earn a rate of return *at least* equal to the required return on those projects, considering the project's risk. However, because many entrepreneurs are poorly diversified with respect to their personal wealth (that is, they have a large proportion of their own wealth tied up in the firm), many of these owners are more concerned about avoiding risks that could lead to financial ruin than are managers of public corporations.

As discussed earlier, in the large modern corporation, there is a concern that a firm's managers may not always act in the interests of the owners (the agency problem). This problem is less severe in many entrepreneurial businesses because managers and owners are often one and the same. An entrepreneur who consumes "excessive" perks is merely reducing his or her ability to withdraw profits from the firm. To the extent that the manager is the owner, there is no owner-manager agency problem. Of course, the potential for agency-related conflicts between entrepreneurs and lenders still exists and may be greater in the closely held firm. As a consequence, many small firms find it difficult to acquire capital from lenders without also giving the lender an option on a part of the ownership in the firm or having the entrepreneur personally guarantee the loan.

Throughout this book, we identify situations where the entrepreneurial financial management of small businesses poses special challenges. In general, we find that small firms often lack the depth of managerial talent needed to apply sophisticated financial planning techniques. Also, because significant economies of scale are often associated with using sophisticated financial management techniques, these techniques may not be justified on a cost-benefit analysis basis in small companies.

FIGURE 1.3
Impact of Other Disciplines on Financial Management

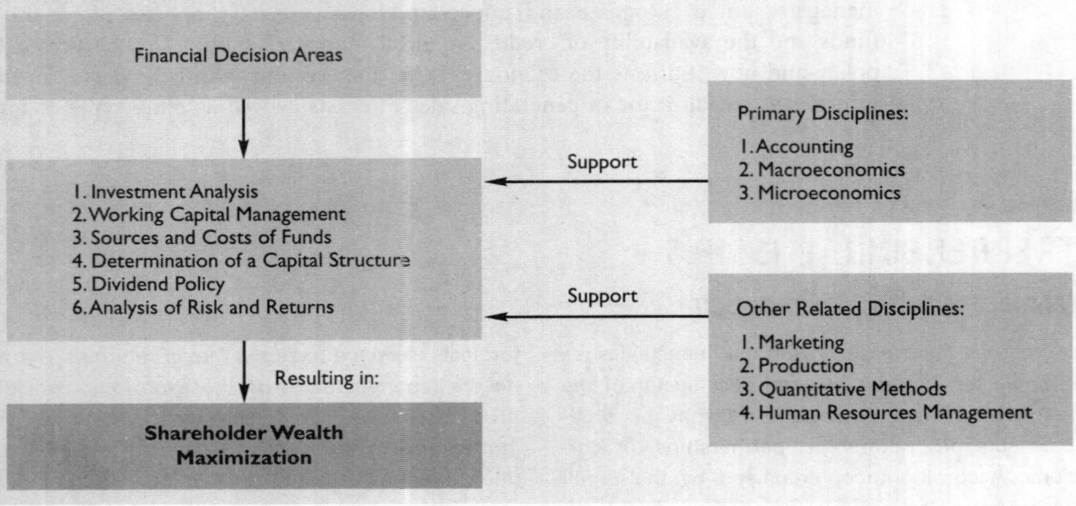

The financial manager uses microeconomics when developing decision models that are likely to lead to the most efficient and successful modes of operation within the firm. Specifically, financial managers use the microeconomic concept of setting marginal cost equal to marginal revenue when making long-term investment decisions (*capital budgeting*) and when managing cash, inventories, and accounts receivable (*working capital management*).

1-5b Marketing, Production, Quantitative Methods, and Human Resources Management

Figure 1.3 depicts the relationship between financial management and its primary supportive disciplines. Marketing, production, quantitative methods, and human resources management are indirectly related to the key day-to-day decisions made by financial managers.

For example, financial managers should consider the impact of new product development and promotion plans made in the marketing area because these plans will require capital outlays and have an impact on the firm's projected cash flows. Similarly, changes in the production process may necessitate capital expenditures, which the firm's financial managers must evaluate and then finance. The tools of analysis developed in the quantitative methods area are frequently helpful in analyzing complex financial management problems. Compensation policies may impact the extent of agency problems in a firm.

HTTP:
Looking for a job? Yahoo provides a Web portal for hundreds of career opportunities and job search Web sites.

careers.yahoo.com

1-6 Career Opportunities in Finance

The finance profession offers a number of exciting career opportunities. As illustrated in the organization chart in Figure 1.2, the corporate finance function encompasses a wide range of activities involved with acquisition and expenditure of the firm's resources. In addition to careers in corporate finance, opportunities are available in the financial services sector. The financial services sector includes such businesses as commercial banks, securities brokers, investment banks, mutual funds, pension funds, real estate companies, and insurance companies.

1-7 Professional Finance Affiliations and Certifications

There are several professional organizations for practicing financial managers. These organizations include the Financial Executives Institute, the Institute of Chartered Financial Analysts, and the Financial Management Association. These organizations provide an opportunity for professional interaction and lifelong learning.

The Financial Management Association (FMA) serves as a bridge between the academic study of finance and the application of financial principles by financial managers. This is achieved through the sponsorship of several annual conferences and publication of a number of journals including *Financial Management* and *Journal of Applied Finance*. The FMA sponsors student chapters at many universities and sponsors the National Honor Society, the only national honorary organization for students of finance. The FMA also holds an annual meeting featuring the presentation of financial research, panel discussions led by leading academic and financial practitioners, and tutorials on new developments in finance. Additional membership information can be obtained from the Financial Management Association Web site (see www.fma.org for more information). Several professional certifications are available. These certifications may enhance your career prospects and are even required for certain positions. Brief descriptions of some of the certifications follow.

- **Certified Financial Manager (CFM).** The Institute of Management Accounting sponsors the CFM designation. It is designed to recognize the qualifications and expertise of professionals engaged in financial management.
- **Certified Financial Planner (CFP).** The CFP designation identifies the holder as being qualified to provide financial planning services for individuals.
- **Chartered Financial Analyst (CFA).** The CFA qualification is granted by the CFA Institute. The CFA designation is a globally recognized qualification in the area of investment and portfolio management.
- **Certified Treasury Professional (CTP).** Sponsored by the Association for Financial Professionals, the CTP designation is a desirable qualification for those pursuing careers in cash/treasury management.

In general these certifications require that you sit for and pass one or more exams and may also require relevant work experience.

1-8 Summary

- The primary normative goal of financial management decision making is the *maximization of shareholder wealth* as measured by the price of the firm's stock.
- *Agency relationships*, such as the relationship between stockholders and managers and the relationship between owners and lenders, give rise to certain agency problems and costs that can have an important impact on firm performance.
- The amount, timing, and risk of the cash flows generated by a firm are, in large part, determined by key financial management decisions, including investment decisions, dividend decisions, financing decisions, and ownership structure decisions. These decisions must be made in the context of factors in the broader economic environment.

- The three primary forms of business organization are the *sole proprietorship*, the *partnership*, and the *corporation*. Corporations have certain advantages over the other two forms of business organization, especially for large businesses.
- A corporation is defined as a "legal person" composed of one or more actual individuals or legal entities. The owners of a corporation are called *stockholders* or *shareholders*. The stockholders elect a *board of directors* that usually deals with broad policy matters, whereas the day-to-day operations are supervised by the corporate *officers*.
- Corporations issue *debt securities* to investors who lend money to the corporation and *equity securities* to investors who become owners.
- The optimal form of organization for a business enterprise is influenced by such factors as cost, complexity, owner liability, business continuity, need for raising capital, the owners' desire to maintain decision-making authority, and tax considerations.
- The finance function is usually headed by a vice president or *chief financial officer*. The financial management responsibilities are often divided between the *controller* and the *treasurer*. The controller normally has responsibility for all accounting-related activities. The treasurer is normally concerned with the acquisition, custody, and expenditure of funds.
- Financial management is closely related to other areas of business decision making, particularly accounting and economics.
- The finance profession offers a number of exciting career opportunities both within the corporate finance function and in the financial services sector.

Important Equation

Shareholder wealth = Number of shares outstanding × Market price per share

1-9 Questions and Topics for Discussion

1. Define *shareholder wealth*. Explain how it is measured.
2. What are the differences between shareholder wealth maximization and profit maximization? If a firm chooses to pursue the objective of shareholder wealth maximization, does this preclude the use of profit maximization decision-making rules? Explain.
3. Which type of corporation is more likely to be a shareholder wealth maximizer—one with wide ownership and no owners directly involved in the firm's management, or one that is closely held?
4. Is the shareholder wealth maximization goal a short- or long-term goal? Explain your answer.
5. It has been argued that shareholder wealth maximization is not a realistic normative goal for the firm, given the social responsibility activities that the firm is "expected" to engage in (such as contributing to the arts, education, etc.). Explain why these social responsibility activities are not inconsistent with shareholder wealth maximization.
6. Explain why management may tend to pursue goals other than shareholder wealth maximization.
7. Explain what is meant by *agency relationships* and *agency costs*.
8. Give some examples of agency costs incurred by shareholders in the agency relationship between the shareholders (owners) and management of a firm.

9. What is the source of potential agency conflicts between owners and bondholders? Who is the agent and who is the principal in this relationship?
10. Explain the differences in the responsibilities of the treasurer and the controller in a large corporation.
11. Explain the relationship between financial management and (a) microeconomics and (b) macroeconomics.
12. Why is EPS not a consistently good measure of a firm's performance?
13. Metropolitan Life Insurance Company, Swiss Bank Corporation, and several other holders of RJR Nabisco bonds filed suit against the company to prevent it from completing the leveraged buyout acquisition from Kohlberg Kravis Roberts. Why do you think the bondholders wanted to block this transaction? What arguments can you make for and against the bondholders' case?
14. What are the major factors that determine the value of a firm's stock?
15. Under pressure from outside investors including corporate raider Carl Icahn, USX Corporation, the parent corporation for U.S. Steel and Marathon Oil, announced a plan to split its stock into separate steel and energy issues. The market response to this action was immediately positive, with the stock price of USX increasing $2.37 to close at $31.25 on the day of the announcement. Why do you think this action by USX was so well received by the stock market?
16. In 2012 Kodak declared bankruptcy. How can you reconcile a bankruptcy declaration with a management pledged to maximize shareholder wealth?
17. How can the adherence to high standards of ethical business practice contribute to the goal of shareholder wealth maximization?
18. Compare the potential for agency problems in sole proprietorships, partnerships, and corporations. In light of your analysis, why is the corporate form of organization so popular?

CHAPTER
2

The Domestic and International Financial Marketplace

KEY CHAPTER CONCEPTS

1. In the U.S. financial system, funds flow from net savers (such as households) to net investors (such as businesses) through financial middlemen and financial intermediaries.
    a. Financial middlemen include securities brokers and investment bankers.
    b. Financial intermediaries include commercial banks, thrift institutions, investment companies, and finance companies.
2. Financial markets are classified as money or capital markets and primary or secondary markets.
    a. Short-term securities with maturities of one year or less are traded in money markets. Long-term securities have maturities of more than one year and are traded in capital markets.
    b. New securities are traded in the primary markets. Existing securities are traded in the secondary markets, such as the New York Stock Exchange and NASDAQ.
3. Companies engaged in international financial transactions face such problems as political and exchange rate risk in addition to those risks encountered in domestic transactions.
4. The exchange rate is the rate at which a currency can be converted into another currency.
    a. The spot rate is the present exchange rate for immediate delivery.
    b. The forward rate is the present exchange rate for deliveries of currencies in the future.
5. The Eurocurrency market is an important alternative to domestic sources of financing for multinational firms. LIBOR, the London InterBank Offer Rate, is the basic interest rate against which Eurocurrency loans are priced.
6. In efficient capital markets, security prices represent an unbiased estimate of the true economic value of the cash flows expected to be generated for the benefit of that security holder.
7. Holding period returns measure the actual or expected return from holding a security, including price changes and distributions, such as dividends or interest.

FINANCIAL CHALLENGE

Burger King's "Whopper" of a Tax-Motivated Merger

On December 12, 2014, Burger King Worldwide, Inc., a U.S. company, and Tim Hortons, Inc., announced the completion of an $11 billion merger to establish a new Canadian-headquartered company named Restaurant Brands International. One of the primary motivations for this merger was the potential that the merger would save between $400 million and $1.2 billion in U.S. taxes between 2015 and 2018. As a result of the merger, Burger King can avoid $117 million in U.S. taxes on profits that it held offshore in 2014. In addition, it will not have to pay U.S. taxes on any profits earned in the United States between 2015 and 2018. Burger King's largest shareholders will also save up to $820 million in capital gains taxes due to the tax inversion.

Tax inversion mergers have been increasing in popularity among U.S.-headquartered companies since the mid-1990s, but the pace of these transactions has rapidly accelerated. In 2014, over 55 percent of all inversion deals since 1990 were completed and, in spite of efforts by the U.S. Treasury to make these transactions more difficult to complete, they have continued. The tax losses to the U.S. Treasury from these transactions is estimated to be more than $41 billion over the next decade.

Some examples of large, international tax inversion mergers include:

- Alkermes (U.S.) with Elan Drug Technologies (Ireland)—tax rate reduced from 26 percent before the merger to 18 percent after the merger
- Eaton (U.S.) with Cooper Industries (Ireland)—tax rate reduced from 9 percent before the merger to 1 percent after the merger
- Actavis (U.S.) with Warner Chilcott (Ireland)—tax rate reduced from 39 percent before the merger to 17 percent after the merger
- Endo Health Solutions (U.S.) with Palatin Labs (Ireland)—tax rate reduced from 29 percent before the merger to 20 percent after the merger
- Medtronic (U.S.) with Covidien (Ireland)—tax rate reduced from 20 percent before the merger to 16 percent after the merger
- AbbVie (U.S.) with Shire (U.K.)—tax rate reduced from 22 percent before the merger to 13 percent after the merger

© Tupungato/Shutterstock.com

Some other large U.S. companies that have reincorporated in countries with lower corporate tax rates than those in the United States include Accenture, Ingersoll Rand, Tyco International, and Seagate Technology. In late 2015, Pfizer announced an agreement to merge Ireland-based Allergan in a $150 billion transaction that would save Pfizer around $2 billion per year in taxes and reduce its average tax rate from 25 percent to 17 percent. Coca-Cola Enterprises, a U.S. bottler and distributor, was also progressing with a merger with two European Coke bottlers to create a new UK-based company.

As these examples of tax inversion mergers illustrate, managers that seek to maximize returns for a company's shareholders need to be aware of the tax strategies and corporate structure strategies that are available both domestically and internationally. In a highly interconnected global economy, it is very difficult for one country to maintain noncompetitive tax rates for very long. In this chapter we introduce the structure and operation of domestic and international financial markets and provide an overview of the elements of U.S. tax policies that impact both investors and companies.

Sources: M. Clark, "Burger King Could Dodge $1.2 Billion in U.S. Taxes," *International Business Times* (November 20, 2015); and J. Novack, "The Tax Inversion Rush—in One Handy Graphic," *Forbes/Personal Finance* (September 10, 2014).

CHAPTER OBJECTIVES

Upon completion of the chapter, you should have a clear understanding of the following:

1. The role and significant aspects of financial markets
2. The structure and operation of U.S. securities markets
3. Currency markets and their importance to companies and the global economy
4. The meaning of market efficiency
5. The calculation of holding period returns
6. An overview of the financial crisis of 2007–2010
7. An overview of the U.S. corporate income tax structure

2-1 Introduction

This chapter provides a look at the domestic and international marketplaces within which firms operate. These financial marketplaces serve the role of allocating scarce resources from saving units (such as individuals) to investing units (such as firms). We provide an overview of the operation of the U.S. and international financial systems, distinguishing between the money and capital markets. The major financial intermediaries are discussed, and the operation and structure of secondary security markets are presented. The concept of an efficient market is developed. This is followed by an illustration of how to calculate holding period returns for any investment. The chapter also provides an overview of the financial crisis that started in 2007 and its implications for financial markets and business in general. The chapter concludes with an overview of the U.S. tax system. The existence of corporate and personal income taxes has important implications for financial managers. Because so many financial decisions are based on after-tax cash flows, finance and business professionals must have a basic understanding of tax matters. (Appendix 2A at the end of this chapter contains an overview of the U.S. corporate income tax structure.)

2-2 An Overview of the U.S. Financial System

The U.S. financial system serves an important function in the efficient operation of the economy. The financial system is the vehicle that channels funds from saving units (savers) to investing units. The rates of return that investing units must pay for the capital supplied by savers are determined competitively in financial markets. As we shall see later in the book, investment activity undertaken by firms is influenced by the rate of return (cost of capital) the firms must pay to attract resources from savers. Accordingly, it is important for financial managers to understand the elements and functioning of the financial marketplace so that capital costs can be minimized for any set of investments a firm undertakes.

In considering any economy as a whole, the actual savings for a given period of time must equal the actual investments. This phenomenon is called the *saving-investment cycle*. The saving-investment cycle depends on net savers, or *surplus spending units*, and net investors, or *deficit spending units*. The cycle is completed when the surplus spending units transfer funds to the deficit spending units. The main purpose of the U.S. financial system—including the financial markets and all financial institutions—is to facilitate this transfer of funds. Figure 2.1 graphically depicts this continual flow.

The deficit or surplus spending units consist of households, businesses, or government entities. Generally, households, as a group, are net savers, whereas businesses and government entities, as a group, tend to be net borrowers. However, the terms *surplus* or *deficit spending units* do not necessarily connote anything about a particular entity's financial health. Businesses as a group tend to be comprised of deficit spending units because they often invest in growth opportunities that cannot be financed by internally generated funds alone. They have to obtain funds through the sale of stock or debt issues to finance new projects. The federal government, more often than not, is a deficit spending unit because the tax revenues it generates are less than its cash outflows, resulting in a net deficit. Households overall are classified as surplus spending units because, as a group, they earn more than they spend on current consumption.

We have been talking about surplus and spending units at the aggregate level. On an individual basis, a particular unit may be a surplus or a deficit spending unit. So not all households are surplus spending units; a young family may be a deficit spending unit, while an older, retired couple may be classified as a surplus spending unit. Likewise, a start-up company in a growth industry, such as biotechnology, may be a deficit spending unit; but a large firm in a mature industry, such as oil exploration and refining, is likely to be a surplus spending unit. Furthermore, even if a firm or an entity is a surplus (deficit) spending unit, it may still borrow (invest) funds. A firm with an excess of cash flow over its spending may still borrow over the course of a year to finance seasonal needs such as the buildup in inventory in anticipation of the year-end holiday selling season.

Figure 2.1 shows that funds flow from surplus spending units, such as households, to deficit spending units, such as businesses, through *financial middlemen* and *financial intermediaries*. Financial middlemen include *brokers*, who bring together buyers and sellers of securities; *dealers*, who sell securities to investors out of an inventory they carry; and *investment bankers*,[1] who assist corporations in selling their securities. These securities are called *primary claims*, because they are sold directly by the borrower and bought directly by the saver (lender).

Financial intermediaries include commercial banks, thrift institutions, investment companies, pension funds, insurance companies, and finance companies. They differ from financial middlemen in that they issue *secondary claims* to the ultimate lender instead of primary claims. (A bank savings account is an example of a secondary claim.) A financial intermediary may lend money to a corporation, even though there is a small chance that the corporation will default on its loan. In general, individuals or households are unwilling to lend funds to a corporation under these circumstances, but they will allow a commercial bank to use their funds, because the bank can guarantee them both liquidity and safety.

Thus, financial intermediaries facilitate the transfer of funds. They are compensated for their services by an *interest rate spread*. For example, a bank might loan money to a business at an average of 5 percent interest, pay depositors an average of 1.5 percent interest, and use the 3.5 percent difference to pay employee salaries and other expenses,

[1]The role of investment bankers in corporate finance is discussed in greater detail in Chapter 7.

FIGURE 2.1
Flow-of-Funds Diagram

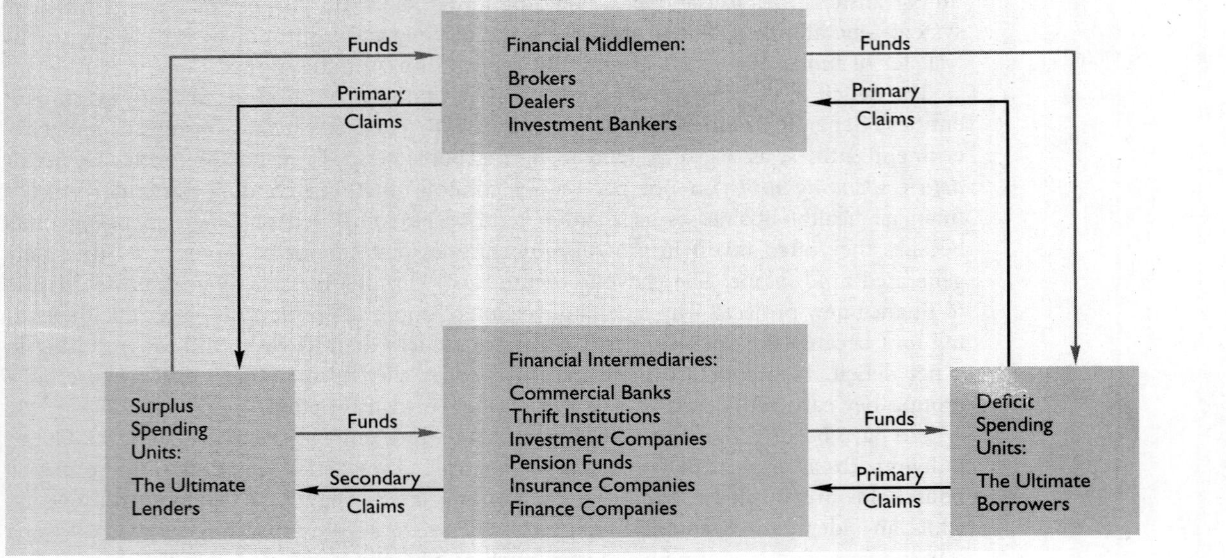

as well as to provide a return to their stockholders. The various financial intermediaries are examined in greater detail later in this section.

2-2a Financial Assets

Although *money* is the most obvious financial asset, there are others as well, including *debt securities* and *equity securities.* Both debt and equity securities represent claims against the assets and future earnings of the corporation. Debt and equity securities are financial *assets* of the investors who own them, and, at the same time, these securities appear on the *liabilities and stockholders' equity* side of the issuing company's balance sheet.

2-2b Financial Markets

Financial markets are the vehicles through which financial assets are bought, sold, and traded. Financial markets are generally classified as money or capital markets and primary or secondary markets.

money markets
capital markets

Money and Capital Markets

Money markets deal in short-term securities having maturities of one year or less. **Capital markets** deal in long-term securities having maturities greater than one year. (In both cases, the one-year break point is somewhat arbitrary.)

Most large corporations participate in the money markets, especially when they have more cash on hand than needed to run their businesses. For example, Facebook Inc. had over $11 billion in cash and short-term investments at the end of (fiscal year) 2014—approximately 82 percent of its current assets and 28 percent of its total assets. By investing in money market securities, the company earned interest rather than leaving its funds in non-interest-bearing commercial bank checking accounts.

Corporations enter the capital markets to obtain long-term funds, either debt or equity. Many corporations are unable to generate enough funds *internally* to satisfy their needs, so they raise additional funds *externally* in the capital markets. This is especially true for rapidly growing early stage companies.

primary financial market

Primary and Secondary Markets An investor who purchases *new* securities is participating in a **primary financial market**. Net proceeds from the sale of new securities go directly to the issuing company. On virtually any given business day, *The Wall Street Journal* contains announcements about the issuance of new debt and equity securities. (These are called *tombstones* because of their resemblance to epitaphs.) Figure 2.2 shows a tombstone announcement for the sale of new shares of common stock by ARIBA Corporation. The company issued 5.75 million shares of common stock through an underwriting syndicate of investment bankers for $23 per share. Note that part of the offering was sold via the Internet. There is a trend toward more Internet-based distributions of new offerings, including a large offering in 2004 by Google.

secondary financial market

An investor who resells existing securities is participating in a **secondary financial market**. Secondary markets are well established in the United States, where stocks can be traded on the "floor" of a security exchange, such as the New York Stock Exchange (NYSE), or in the over-the-counter (OTC) market, most notably NASDAQ. The structure and operation of the secondary markets is discussed in greater detail in the following sections. The operation of the primary markets is examined in Chapter 7.

2-2c Financial Intermediaries

A variety of different financial intermediaries exists to facilitate the flow of funds between surplus spending units and deficit spending units. These different financial intermediaries specialize in the types of deposits they accept (sources of funds) and the types of investments they make (uses of funds).

Commercial Banks Commercial banks accept both demand deposits (in the form of checking accounts) and time deposits (in the form of savings accounts and certificates of deposit). These funds are loaned to individuals, businesses, and governments. Commercial banks are an important source of short-term loans. Seasonal businesses, such as retailers, certain manufacturers (for example, those who deal in leisure products), some food processors, and builders often require short-term financing to help them through peak periods. Many other types of businesses have a more or less continuing need for short-term financing and make prior arrangements with their banks to borrow on short notice. For example, in 2015, Ford Motor arranged a $13.4 billion revolving credit agreement with its banks. This established revolving credit agreement gives Ford quick access to substantial funds as they are needed in the operation of the firm. As this example illustrates, banks provide significant amounts of both temporary and more "permanent" short-term financing for businesses.[2]

term loans

Banks are also a major source of **term loans**, which have initial maturities between 1 and 10 years and are usually repaid in installments over the life of the loan.[3] The proceeds from term loans can be used to finance current assets, such as inventory or accounts receivable, and to finance the purchase of fixed plant facilities and equipment, as well as to repay other debts.

Thrift Institutions Thrift institutions include savings and loan associations, mutual savings banks, and credit unions. These institutions accept both demand and time deposits. Savings and loan associations and mutual savings banks invest most of

[2]Short-term bank credit is discussed further in Chapter 16.

[3]Term loans are examined in Chapter 19.

FIGURE 2.2

Tombstone Announcement for ARIBA Common Stock Sale

Morgan Stanley Dean Witter is a service mark of Morgan Stanley Dean Witter & Co.

This announcement is neither an offer to sell nor a solicitation of an offer to buy any of these Securities. The offer is made only by the Prospectus.

5,750,000 Shares

ARIBA®

Common Stock

Price $23 a Share

Copies of the Prospectus may be obtained in any State from only such of the undersigned as may legally offer these Securities in compliance with the securities laws of such State.

MORGAN STANLEY DEAN WITTER

DAIN RAUSCHER WESSELS
a division of Dain Rauscher Incorporated

DEUTSCHE BANC ALEX. BROWN

MERRILL LYNCH & CO.

Internet Distribution Offered By

DISCOVER BROKERAGE DIRECT — E*TRADE SECURITIES

ING BARING FURM SELZ LLC — EDWARD D. JONES & CO., L.P.

SG COWEN — SOUNDVIEW TECHNOLOGY GROUP

ADAMS, HARKNESS & HILL, INC. — FIRST UNION CAPITAL MARKETS CORP.

NEEDHAM & COMPANY, INC. — C.E. UNTERBERG, TOWBIN

Morgan Stanley Dean Witter is a service mark of Morgan Stanley Dean Witter & Co.

their funds in home mortgages, whereas credit unions are engaged primarily in consumer loans. Many thrift institutions have been acquired by commercial banks in recent years. The role of thrifts in financing has declined greatly.

Investment Companies Investment companies, such as mutual funds, real estate investment trusts (REITs), and business development companies (BDCs), pool the funds of many investors and invest these funds in various types of assets. Mutual funds invest in specific financial assets—such as debt and equity securities of corporations or money market instruments—according to the objectives of the fund. Mutual funds attempt to achieve superior performance through diversification[4] and professional investment management. REITs, as the name suggests, invest their pool of funds in real estate. BDCs generally provide financing, both debt and equity, to early stage companies that do not have access to bank financing. Some of the big mutual fund families are Vanguard, Fidelity, and T. Rowe Price.

Pension Funds Pension funds pool the contributions of employees (and/or employers) and invest these funds in various types of financial assets, such as corporate securities, or real assets, such as real estate. One of the largest pension funds is the California Public Employees Retirement System (CalPERS), with over $293 billion in assets as of November 2015.

Insurance Companies Insurance companies receive periodic or lump-sum premium payments from individuals or organizations in exchange for agreeing to make certain future contractual payments. Life insurance companies make payments to a beneficiary based on certain events, such as the death or disability of the insured party. Property and casualty insurance companies make payments when a financial loss occurs due to such events as fire, theft, accident, and illness. The premiums received are used to build reserves to pay future claims. These reserves are invested in various types of assets, such as corporate securities.

Finance Companies Finance companies obtain funds by issuing their own debt securities and through loans from commercial banks. These funds are used to make loans to individuals and businesses. Some finance companies are formed to finance the sale of the parent company's products. Well-known examples are GE Capital, CIT Group, and IBM Global Financing.

2-3 The Structure and Operation of U.S. Security Markets

As discussed earlier, capital markets are usually classified as either *primary* or *secondary* markets. New securities are issued in the primary markets, and the firms issuing these securities receive the proceeds from their sale, thus raising new capital. Outstanding securities are traded in the secondary markets, where owners of these securities may sell them to other investors. The corporations whose securities are traded in the secondary markets do not share in the proceeds from these sales.

Although primary and secondary markets are separate, they are closely related. Smoothly functioning secondary markets aid the primary markets, because investors tend to be more willing to purchase new securities when they know they can sell them

[4] *Diversification* is the act of investing in a set of securities having different risk-return characteristics. The topic is covered in Chapter 8.

in the secondary market. In fact, the potential liquidity available in the secondary markets may make investors more willing to accept slightly lower returns on their investments, thereby lowering the cost companies have to pay for their funds.

2-3a Security Exchanges and Stock Market Indexes

Listed security exchanges
OTC security markets

Secondary markets can be classified as either listed security exchanges or over-the-counter (OTC) markets. **Listed security exchanges** operate at designated places of business and have requirements governing the types of securities they can list and trade. The **OTC security markets** do not have centralized places of business but rather exist as networks of security dealers connected by a communications system of telephones and computer terminals that allow the dealers to post the prices at which they are willing to buy and sell various securities.

Listed Security Exchanges

The New York Stock Exchange (NYSE), sometimes called the *Big Board*, was founded in 1792 and is the largest stock exchange in the United States. Over 2,800 firms are listed on the NYSE. Trading on individual common and preferred stocks and bonds takes place on the exchange. For a company's stock to be listed and traded on the NYSE, the company must meet certain minimum requirements with regard to the number of shares of stock outstanding, the number of shareholders, the geographical distribution of shareholders, the value of assets, the market value of shares, and the net income level. As a result, the NYSE tends to list the stock of larger firms.

Trading on the NYSE is conducted by members of the exchange. Basically there are two types of members: floor brokers and designated market makers. Floor brokers execute orders, acting as agents, on the "floor" of the exchange for clients. When you as an investor want to buy or sell a security (for example, common stock of IBM), the order is channeled through a floor broker. Designated market makers play a special role as members of the exchange. They are entrusted with maintaining a fair and an orderly market in the stocks assigned to them. Among other things, designated market makers ensure sufficient liquidity and minimal volatility in the stocks assigned to them. The NYSE is owned by the Intercontinental Exchange, which owns several stock, bond, futures, and options exchanges, and also owns a large electronic trading entity.

In addition to the national exchanges, there are a number of smaller regional exchanges located around the country. Trading activities on the NYSE and the major regional exchanges are listed together and reported in the financial press as the *NYSE Composite Transactions*.

HTTP:
The United States' national and OTC exchanges support extensive Web sites where they describe themselves, the stocks they trade, how to become listed on their exchanges, and so on.

www.nyse.com
www.amex.com
www.nasdaq.com

Over-the-Counter (OTC) Markets

Securities not listed on exchanges are said to be traded "over the counter." In general, these include stocks of small and relatively unknown companies, although a growing number of large companies, such as Microsoft, many bank and insurance company stocks, a majority of corporate bonds and preferred stocks, and most U.S. Treasury and municipal bonds are traded in OTC markets. The OTC market consists of numerous security dealers linked by an electronic network of computer terminals and telephones, through which they make offers to buy and sell securities for their clients and for their own accounts. The OTC dealers who are willing to buy and sell a security for their own account are said to *make a market* in that security. These dealers maintain an inventory of certain securities from which they sell to interested buyers and to which they add by buying from interested sellers. The dealers post bid and ask prices on the securities in which they make a market. The *bid price* is the price at which the dealer is willing to buy a given security; the *ask price* is the price the dealer is willing to sell a given security. For any given dealer, the ask price is going to

spread

be greater than the bid price. This difference is known as the **spread**, which is how the dealer makes a profit.

A specific example of an OTC market is the NASDAQ. NASDAQ is a network of dealers and brokers scattered all over the world that conduct business through a sophisticated electronic marketplace. As in the case of organized stock exchanges, only securities meeting certain requirements are eligible to be listed in the NASDAQ. There are currently approximately 3,100 actively traded issues in the NASDAQ. NASDAQ is owned by NASDAQ OMX, which owns several securities exchanges in the United States and internationally.

Stock Market Indexes Stock market indexes give a broad indication of how the stock market or a segment of it performed during a particular day. The most frequently quoted stock market index is the Dow Jones Industrial Average (DJIA), which is based on the stock prices of 30 large, well-established industrial corporations.[5] The DJIA is calculated by adding the prices of the 30 stocks and dividing by a number that reflects prior stock dividends and splits. When a radio announcer says "The market was up five points today," the announcer means the DJIA was up five points.

The Dow Jones Transportation Average is based on 20 major railroad, airline, and trucking stocks, and the Dow Jones Utility Average is derived from 15 major utility stocks. The DJIA is combined with the transportation and the utility averages to form the Dow Jones Composite Average.

The Standard & Poor's 500 Stock Price Index (S&P 500), another frequently quoted stock market index, is significantly broader than the DJIA. It is compiled from the stock prices of 400 leading industrial firms, 20 transportation firms, 40 utilities, and 40 financial institutions. The S&P 500 is a *market value–weighted index*. This means, for example, that a stock whose total market value is $2 billion influences the index twice as much as a stock whose total market value is $1 billion.

Figure 2.3 provides a listing and data on major stock market indexes.

2-3b Regulation of the Security Markets

HTTP:
The government is an important player in our financial markets— from policies, rules, and regulations, to injecting and withdrawing money. Visit this site for scores of government-related links (SEC, Treasury, etc.).

www.yahoo.com/government

Both the individual states and the federal government regulate the securities business. Beginning with Kansas in 1911, each of the 50 states (with the exception of Delaware) has passed so-called blue sky laws. The term *blue sky* came about when some risky securities were called nothing more than "pieces of blue sky." In spite of these state laws, many investors received incomplete and even fraudulent security information during the 1920s. This fact, combined with the 1929 stock market crash and the general reform spirit of the 1930s, led to the enactment of two principal pieces of security legislation—the Securities Act of 1933 and the Securities Exchange Act of 1934—and the establishment of the **Securities and Exchange Commission (SEC)**.

Securities and Exchange Commission (SEC)

The primary purpose of the SEC is to ensure full disclosure of security information so that investors, individuals, and institutions alike have credible and timely information on which to base their investment decisions. This disclosure is accomplished by requiring firms to file comprehensive reports (called *forms*), either periodically or as needed. For example, firms with publicly held securities are required to file annual reports (known as the *10-K Form*) and quarterly reports (known as the *10-Q Form*) with the SEC within a specified time after the end of the fiscal period. Firms are also required to file **proxy statements** (also called *14-A Filing*) prior to annual shareholder meetings, detailing, among other things, matters to be discussed and voted upon. Firms also have to file special

proxy statements

[5]Dow Jones and Company is a financial company that publishes *The Wall Street Journal*. Every day, the values of all the major stock market indexes are listed in *The Wall Street Journal* and in the financial section of most major newspapers.

FIGURE 2.3

Major U.S. Stock-Market Indexes

	LATEST High	LATEST Low	LATEST Close	LATEST Net chg	LATEST % chg	52-WEEK RANGE High	52-WEEK RANGE Low	52-WEEK RANGE % chg	% CHG YTD	% CHG 3-yr. ann.
Dow Jones										
Industrial Average	17752.16	17485.49	**17737.16**	247.66	1.42	18312.39	15666.44	**0.3**	−0.48	**12.1**
Transportation Avg	8196.96	8063.05	**8 91.33**	133.03	1.65	9217.44	7466.97	**−9.1**	−10.4	**18.8**
Utility Average	563.52	554.13	**562.80**	3.77	0.67	652.11	541.97	**−5.4**	−8.9	**8.3**
Total Stock Market	21562.66	21229.73	**21547.29**	341.61	1.61	22287.78	19528.72	**1.4**	0.6	**15.3**
Barron's 400	534.46	526.31	**534.14**	8.59	1.63	586.75	497.51	**−0.5**	−1.3	**16.1**
Nasdaq Stock Market										
Nasdaq Composite	5078.80	5001.67	**5075.20**	89.19	1.79	5218.86	4506.49	**8.5**	7.2	**21.2**
Nasdaq 100	4657.63	4580.72	**4653.44**	87.63	1.92	4719.05	4016.32	**10.2**	9.8	**22.5**
Standard & Poor's										
500 Index	2085.31	2051.99	**2083.58**	33.14	1.62	2130.82	1867.61	**1.7**	1.2	**15.3**
MidCap 400	1442.82	1421.43	**1442.44**	23.90	1.68	1549.44	1351.29	**0.8**	−0.7	**14.8**
SmallCap 600	692.97	682.71	**692.62**	10.16	1.49	742.13	641.76	**3.5**	−0.4	**16.6**
Other Indexes										
Russell 2000	1172.02	1153.39	**1171.75**	18.54	1.61	1295.80	1083.91	**1.2**	−2.7	**14.7**
NYSE Composite	10436.00	10285.37	**10429.60**	143.84	1.40	11239.66	9601.42	**−4.6**	−3.8	**9.6**
Value Line	462.19	454.53	**461.95**	7.42	1.63	522.42	431.31	**−6.7**	−8.0	**10.8**
NYSE Arca Biotech	3793.47	3705.04	**3791.51**	83.68	2.26	4431.87	3280.93	**14.4**	10.2	**38.0**
NYSE Arca Pharma	541.98	534.73	**541.30**	8.78	1.65	605.94	509.74	**−0.6**	1.6	**15.1**
KBW Bank	76.03	74.60	**76.00**	1.55	2.08	80.41	66.40	**4.8**	2.3	**17.2**
PHLX§ Gold/Silver	45.58	43.35	**45.48**	1.85	4.24	82.07	43.63	**−36.1**	−33.9	**−35.0**
PHLX§ Oil Service	179.23	174.65	**179.00**	4.21	2.41	249.27	155.39	**−25.6**	−15.1	**−5.2**
PHLX§ Semiconductor	662.57	651.65	**662.14**	6.32	0.96	746.08	559.59	**1.8**	−3.6	**23.0**
CBOE Volatility	19.45	16.80	**16.85**	−1.99	−10.56	40.74	11.82	**20.7**	−12.2	**0.9**

§Philadelphia Stock Exchange

Source: SIX Financial information WSJ Market Data Group and *Wall Street Journal* (November 19, 2015).

forms prior to the issuance of new securities (for example, new stock or bond issues) to the public and report other unusual events of material importance (for example, a potential merger or divestiture) in a timely manner. The SEC is also responsible for enforcing insider trading regulations and laws that are designed to prevent insiders from taking advantage of their "inside" knowledge at the expense of all other outside shareholders. For example, under insider trading regulations, executives of a firm are barred from trading on the firm's stock in anticipation of news that they are aware of but that has not been released to the public. Finally, the SEC is involved in governing the activities of investment bankers and certain other financial intermediaries including mutual funds, investment management companies, and purveyors of financial advice and research.

One of the most significant changes in financial markets regulation occurred with the passage of the Sarbanes-Oxley Act of 2002. The act was legislated in the aftermath of the scandals of Enron, Tyco, WorldCom, and the Internet stock market bubble in the early 2000s. The act resulted in major changes to disclosure and financial reporting by public corporations and how key financial institutions conduct business, including auditors, law offices, and investment banks. Some of the significant changes are as follows:

- Top management is directly responsible for the accuracy of the firm's financial statements. The SEC now requires that the CEO and chief financial officer (CFO) certify the accuracy of the financial statements and the adequacy of the firm's internal control system.

- The act strengthened the independence and accountability of the audit committee of the firm's board of directors.
- The act created a new Public Company Accounting Standards Board to oversee the auditing industry, instituting new rules to improve the independence and credibility of auditors and the auditing function. The act requires that auditors now certify a firm's financial control system and report any material weaknesses.
- The act institutes new rules to ensure independence of financial analysts and create structural separation between financial analysts and investment bankers working for the same firm.

2-4 The Global Economy and Multinational Enterprises

The importance of understanding the global economy can be seen in the volume of exports and imports in the United States. In 2014, U.S. goods and services exports totaled over $2.35 trillion and merchandise imports totaled over $2.85 trillion. The difference between merchandise exports and imports is the *goods and services trade balance.* In 2014, the United States had a *goods and services trade deficit* of approximately $500 billion, representing a substantial increase from the deficit in 1991 of $65 billion (U.S. Dept. of Commerce: National Trade Data).

Business enterprises participate in the global marketplace in a wide variety of ways. Some firms simply *export* finished goods for sale in another country and/or *import* raw materials or products from another country for use in their domestic operations. At the other end of the spectrum are *multinational enterprises.* A **multinational corporation** has direct investments in manufacturing and/or distribution facilities in more than one country. Often, these foreign operations are structured as more or less freestanding subsidiaries. Among the largest multinational firms are such U.S. firms as General Motors, Ford, IBM, ExxonMobil, General Electric, and Procter & Gamble. Large multinational Japanese firms include Toyota, Hitachi, Matsushita, Nissan, and Toshiba. Major European multinationals include Royal Dutch Shell, BMW, British Petroleum, Siemens, Volkswagen, Unilever, and Nestlé.

multinational corporation

The rise of the multinational firm has drastically changed the way business is done around the world. The multinational organization makes it relatively easy for firms to transfer the key factors of production—land, labor, and capital—to the location where they can be most productive, which represents a dramatic change from the time when the factors of production were thought to be immobile and only goods and services could be moved easily across borders. As a result, the process of resource allocation and business decision making has become more complex. At the same time, multinational firms have the opportunity to benefit from imperfections that arise in various national markets for capital and other factors of production. Furthermore, whether a firm is engaged in international transactions, the decline of trade barriers and the increasing ease of moving assets to those countries where they will be the most productive adds a new element of competition for all firms. It is no longer possible for a U.S. manufacturer, such as Ford Motor Company, to worry just about its domestic competitors. Over the past two decades, Japanese, South Korean, and German auto companies have built plants in the United States that directly compete with U.S.-based companies, and Toyota has become one of the three largest sellers of cars in the United States.

All firms engaged in international business transactions face unique problems and risks not encountered by firms that operate in only one country. First, there are difficulties associated with doing business in different currencies. Financial transactions between

U.S. firms and firms (or individuals) in foreign countries normally involve foreign currency that ultimately has to be converted into U.S. dollars. Therefore, firms that do business internationally are concerned with the *exchange rate* between U.S. dollars and foreign currencies. Second, problems arise because of different government regulations, tax laws, business practices, and political environments in foreign countries.

2-5 Foreign Currency Markets and Exchange Rates

Whenever a U.S. firm purchases goods or services from a firm in another country, two currencies normally are involved. For example, when a U.S. company purchases materials from a United Kingdom (U.K.) supplier, the U.K. firm usually prefers payment in U.K. pounds, whereas the U.S. company prefers to make payment in U.S. dollars. If the sales agreement requires that payment be made in pounds, the U.S. company will have to exchange (that is, *sell*) dollars to obtain the required number of pounds. The exact amount of dollars the U.S. company will have to sell depends on the **exchange rate** between the two currencies.

exchange rate

Suppose, for example, that the exchange rate at the time of the transaction is $1.50 per pound, £. Furthermore, assume that the U.K. supplier and the U.S. firm have agreed on a price of £2 million for the materials. Therefore, the U.S. firm will have to exchange $3.0 million (that is, £2,000,000 × $1.50/pound) to obtain the U.K. currency to pay for the purchase.

Foreign currency needed for international financial transactions can be exchanged for domestic currency in most countries either at large commercial banks or at a central bank operated by the government. The volume of foreign currency transactions is very large. For example, the Bank for International Settlements estimates that daily, worldwide foreign currency trading exceeded $5.5 trillion in 2014. By 2019, this volume is expected to reach nearly $8.0 trillion. The most important foreign currency trading centers are in New York, Tokyo, Hong Kong, Singapore, Bahrain, Frankfurt, Zurich, London, San Francisco, and Los Angeles.

2-5a The Eurocurrency Market

Eurocurrency

A **Eurocurrency** is a currency that is deposited in a bank located outside the country of origin. Eurocurrencies are created when, for example, a U.S. firm transfers dollars from a bank in the United States to a bank outside the United States. Also, someone outside the United States may receive dollars in connection with a business transaction or because of a purchase in the foreign exchange market. When these dollars are deposited in a bank outside the United States, they become **Eurodollars.** The bank may either be a foreign bank, such as Deutsche Bank, or a foreign branch of a U.S. bank, such as JPMorgan Chase, located in Frankfurt. Other important Eurocurrencies include Euroyen and Eurosterling (Japanese yen and U.K. pounds), deposited outside their country of origin. The majority of the Eurocurrencies outstanding are U.S. dollar–denominated.

Eurodollars

HTTP:
LIBOR is a very important interest rate in the world of finance, but so are the SIBOR, TIBOR, and a lot of other IBORs. Can you guess what the S and T in the above terms mean? Using a search engine, see whether you're correct.

As an illustration, consider the following example. BMW sells a car to an American dealer for $60,000. The American dealer pays BMW with a check for $60,000 drawn on JPMorgan Chase. BMW must then decide what to do with this check. BMW could immediately sell the dollars (buy euros). However, BMW wants to retain the dollars for use later on (perhaps to pay for goods purchased from U.S. firms), so it buys a Eurodollar deposit by depositing the check in Deutsche Bank in Germany. The typical Eurocurrency deposit is a nonnegotiable time deposit with a fixed term to maturity. Maturities range from overnight to as long as five years.

The Eurocurrency market provides an important alternative to domestic sources of funds for multinational firms. For example, in the United States, large, well-established multinational corporations can borrow funds either in the domestic financial market or in the international financial marketplace, such as the Eurocurrency market. If General Motors chooses to borrow in the Eurodollar market, it would receive a Eurodollar loan from a foreign bank, such as Barclays Bank in London or Deutsche Bank in Frankfurt. The interest rate in the Eurodollar market is usually related to the *London InterBank Offered Rate*, or *LIBOR*. **LIBOR** is the interest rate at which banks in the Eurocurrency market lend to each other. The cost to borrow in the Eurocurrency market is usually stated as a margin above LIBOR. Typically, Eurodollar borrowing rates are between 0.5 percent and 3 percent over LIBOR, with a median of about 1.5 percent. Eurocurrency loans range in maturity up to 10 years for the best quality borrowers.

LIBOR

2-5b The Euro: A Common European Currency

On January 4, 1999, 11 countries of the European Union (EU) turned over control of their monetary policies to a new European Central Bank, and the single European currency, the **euro**, was born. During a transition period, the euro was being used only for paperless transactions. But on January 1, 2002, euro bills and coins began circulation, and six months later, the national currencies of these 11 countries ceased to exist. This move toward a single European currency is the logical outgrowth of the development of a single European market, where goods, services, and people flow freely across national borders. The use of a common currency eliminates exchange costs associated with converting from one currency to another and also the uncertainty of exchange rate fluctuations among these countries. The euro initially traded in the foreign currency marketplace at a rate of about \$1.17 per euro. By late 2001, however, the value of the euro declined to about \$0.88 because of a number of factors, including the relative strength of the U.S. and European economies. In early 2013, the euro rose in value to approximately \$1.30, and by late 2015 it was valued at about \$1.06 per euro. The euro is a major international currency, rivaling the dollar in importance. However, recent financial difficulties and budget deficits by several euro-area countries have raised serious questions about the long-term viability of the euro as a common European currency.

euro

2-5c Direct and Indirect Quotes

Exchange rates can be expressed as either *direct quotes* or *indirect quotes*. A **direct quote** is the home currency price of one unit of foreign currency. For example, from the perspective of a U.S. firm, a quote of \$1.30 per euro would be a direct quote. An **indirect quote** is the foreign currency price of one unit of the home currency. A quote of 0.7692 euro/\$ would be an indirect quote from the perspective of a U.S. firm. Direct quotes and indirect quotes have a reciprocal relationship. Accordingly, the indirect quote was derived by taking the reciprocal (1 ÷ \$1.30/euro) of the direct quote.

direct quote

indirect quote

2-5d Spot Rates

Exchange rates between U.S. dollars and the currencies of most countries are reported daily in *The Wall Street Journal*. Table 2.1 lists the (direct quote) exchange rates between U.S. dollars and various currencies as of February 25, 2013, and November 18, 2015. These quotes are for trades made among banks in amounts of \$1 million or more. Smaller, retail transactions usually result in fewer units of a foreign currency per dollar. The quotes in Table 2.1 are known as spot rates. **Spot rates** represent the rate of exchange for currencies being bought and sold for immediate delivery.[6]

spot rates

---

[6]The date at which money must be exchanged among the parties in a spot foreign currency transaction is known as the *value date*. It is customarily set as the second working day after the date on which the transaction is concluded. For example, a spot transaction entered into in Frankfurt on Monday will not normally be settled until the following Wednesday.

TABLE 2.1

Spot Foreign Exchange Rates (Direct Quotes)

		Exchange Rate (U.S. Dollars)	
Country	**Currency**	**February 25, 2013**	**November 18, 2015**
Australia	Dollar	$1.0258	$0.7111
U.K.	Pound	$1.5165	$1.5236
Canada	Dollar	$0.9745	$0.7517
India	Rupee	$0.01845	$0.01514
Japan	Yen	$0.010891	$0.008088
South Africa	Rand	$0.1129	$0.0706
Switzerland	Franc	$1.0728	$0.9805
Euro area	Euro	$1.3062	$1.0660

Source: *The Wall Street Journal* (February 26, 2013 and November 19, 2015).

Banks profit from their foreign currency transactions by buying currencies at one rate (bid) and selling them at another, higher rate (ask or offer). For example, a bank may quote the euro at $1.0658 bid, and $1.0662 offer.

2-5e Forward Rates

forward rates

In addition to spot transactions, currencies can also be bought and sold today for delivery at some future time, usually 30, 90, or 180 days from today. In these cases, **forward rates** are used, rather than spot rates. Table 2.2 lists some forward exchange rates as of February 25, 2013.

A comparison of the spot and forward rates in Tables 2.1 and 2.2 shows that the 30-, 90-, and 180-day forward rates for the Japanese yen (U.K. pound) is above (below) its spot rate, indicating a market expectation that it will gain (lose) value relative to the dollar over these time horizons.

The premium or discount between the spot rate, S_0, and a forward rate, F, for a currency (relative to the dollar, for example) can be expressed on an *annualized* percentage basis (using direct quotes) as follows:

$$\text{Annualized forward premium or discount} = \left(\frac{F - S_0}{S_0}\right)\left(\frac{12}{n}\right)(100\%) \tag{2.1}$$

where n is the number of months in the forward contract. A positive value calculated using Equation 2.1 indicates that a currency is trading at a forward premium relative to the dollar, whereas a negative value indicates a forward discount.

TABLE 2.2

Forward Foreign Exchange Rates

	Exchange Rate (U.S. Dollars) February 25, 2013		
Currency	**1-Month Forward**	**3-Month Forward**	**6-Month Forward**
U.K. pound	$1.5162	$1.5158	$1.5152
Japanese yen	0.010893	0.010898	0.010908
Swiss franc	1.0731	1.0739	1.0752

Source: *The Wall Street Journal* (February 26, 2013).

Calculator Solutions[a]

Key	Enter
n	*0.5*
i	
PV	*−1.5165*
PMT	
FV	*1.5152*
	Solution
i	*−0.17145*

Using the exchange rates from Tables 2.1 and 2.2, the following annualized discount for the six-month forward quote on the U.K. pound can be calculated:

$$\text{Annualized discount} = \left(\frac{1.5152 - 1.5165}{1.5165}\right)\left(\frac{12}{6}\right)(100\%)$$
$$= -0.17145\%$$

Thus we can say that the U.K. pound was trading at a forward discount relative to the U.S. dollar (that is, the U.S. dollar is expected to gain slightly relative to the U.K. pound).

As shown later in the book (Chapter 22), firms engaged in international transactions can use the forward foreign exchange market to hedge against the risk of adverse fluctuations in exchange rates.

2-5f Foreign Currency Futures

A foreign currency *futures* contract is similar to a forward contract. Both call for the delivery of a specified amount of some item, such as a foreign currency, at a future point in time at a price set at the present time. A **forward contract** is normally a contract between two individuals who are known to each other, such as an importer and a commercial bank. Performance on the contract by the seller and the buyer depends on the character and capacity of the two parties. Because these contracts are negotiated between two individuals, forward contracts can be established for any future time period and for any quantity of any item that is agreeable to the parties. Forward contracts are not liquid; that is, it is difficult or impossible for either party to transfer their interest in the contract to another party once the contract has been agreed upon. The seller of the contract must deliver the promised item at the time agreed to in the contract, and the buyer must pay for it and accept delivery.

forward contract

futures contract

In contrast to a forward contract, a **futures contract** is an *exchange traded agreement* that calls for the delivery of a *standardized amount* of an item (such as 125,000 euros) at a *standardized maturity date*. The most important foreign currency futures market in the United States is the Chicago Mercantile Exchange (CME). Contracts traded on the CME mature on the third Wednesday of the contract month, with the last trading day being two days prior to that. Unlike forward contracts, there is virtually no performance risk in a futures contract. Rather than the buyer and seller of the contract dealing directly with each other, the exchange clearinghouse acts as the buyer and seller of all contracts. Buyers and sellers of futures contracts must post collateral (as their performance bond). Each day the value of the contract is "marked to market," with all gains and losses being paid between the parties in cash. If payment is not made, the contract is sold by the clearinghouse and the performance bond of the defaulting party is charged for any losses. In essence, one can think of a futures contract as a series of forward contracts that are settled each day. Only about 5 percent of foreign currency futures contracts are settled by means of delivery of the underlying currency from the seller to the buyer. More commonly, the parties will offset their position prior to expiration by making a transaction opposite to the original one. For example, a buyer of a contract for 125,000 euros with delivery in March usually sells an identical contract prior to expiration. The sale of an identical contract by an initial buyer of the same contract fully offsets the position from the perspective of the clearinghouse.

HTTP:
Futures magazine will tell you why coffee prices are surging to record highs while cattle prices are plummeting.
www.futuresmag.com

Table 2.3 shows foreign currency futures contract quotations for the euro as of November 18, 2015. The first line under the headings indicates that the contract is for euros, that the contract is traded on the CME, that the contract is for 125,000 euros, and that the prices are direct quotes ("$ per euro"). The next two lines provide quotes

[a]The determination of a forward discount or premium on a currency can also be done with the aid of a financial calculator. Consider the calculation of the forward discount on the Canadian dollar. This may differ slightly from the value computed using Equation 2.1 due to the compounding impacts that are more correctly reflected in the calculator solution.

TABLE 2.3

Futures Contract Quotation

Contract Date	Open	High	Low	Settle	Change	Open Interest
Euro FX (CME)—Euro 125,000; $ per Euro						
Dec	1.0648	1.0698	1.0620	1.0650	−.0002	421,697
March '16	1.0678	1.0723	1.0650	1.0678	−.0001	13,269

Source: *The Wall Street Journal* (November 19, 2015).

for the contracts maturing on the third Wednesday of December 2015 and March 2016. The column numbers indicate that the opening price of the December 2015 contract was $1.0648 per euro, the high price for the day was $1.0698, the low price for the day was $1.0620, and the closing price (settle) was $1.0650. This was a decrease of $0.0002 from the previous day. There were 421,697 contracts (open interest) in existence. As the last trading date approaches, the open interest declines dramatically and only a small minority of the contracts will actually be in existence (and therefore require delivery of euros from the seller to the buyer) at expiration. Also, this table indicates much more trading interest in the near-term contract (December) than in the longer-term contract (March 2016).

2-5g Foreign Currency Options

options

call option

put option

Whereas forward and future currency contracts reflect an *obligation* to either buy or sell a currency at a future date, **options** are contracts that give the option buyer the *right, but not the obligation,* to either buy or sell a fixed amount of a foreign currency at a fixed price at a time up to, or at, the expiration date of the option. There are two fundamental types of options. A **call option** is an option to buy something, such as foreign currency, and a **put option** is an option to sell (foreign currency). An *American option* gives the holder the right to buy (call options) or sell (put options) the underlying currency at any time prior to expiration. In contrast, a *European option* gives the holder the right to buy or sell the underlying currency only at expiration. Large commercial banks offer customized options for all major currencies with exercise periods of up to a year. In addition, foreign currency options are traded on the Philadelphia Stock Exchange and the Chicago Mercantile Exchange. Foreign currency options provide an alternative to forward and futures contracts for firms seeking to control their foreign exchange risk. Chapter 20 develops the principles of option valuation, and Chapters 21 and 22 illustrate the use of options to hedge foreign currency risk.

2-6 Market Efficiency

III

Foundation Concept

A central theme of much of the academic finance and financial economics research since the 1960s has been the *efficiency* of the capital markets. The more efficient capital markets are, the more likely it is that resources will find their highest (risk-adjusted) return uses. Capital market efficiency is an implicit assumption in many decision models widely used in finance. Consequently, this concept is important to a full understanding of these decision models.

efficient capital market

In an **efficient capital market**, *stock prices provide an unbiased estimate of the true, or intrinsic, value of an enterprise.* Stock prices reflect a *present value* estimate of the firm's *expected cash flows*, evaluated at an appropriate *required rate of return*. The required rate of return is determined by conditions in the financial markets, including the supply of funds from savers, the investment demand for funds, and expectations regarding future inflation rates. The required rate of return on a security also depends on the seniority of the security, the maturity of that security, the business and financial risk of the firm issuing the security, the risk of default, and the marketability of the security. The *efficiency of the capital markets* is the important "glue" that bonds the present value of a firm's net cash flows—discounted at the appropriate risk-adjusted required rate of return—to shareholder wealth as measured by the market value of a company's common stock. Hence, in this section of the chapter, the concept of market efficiency is defined, the evidence regarding the extent of capital market efficiency is reviewed briefly, and some important implications of market efficiency are identified.

2-6a Information and Capital Market Efficiency

Capital markets are efficient if security prices instantaneously reflect in an unbiased manner all economically relevant information about a security's prospective returns and the risk of those returns. What is meant by "all economically relevant information"? Information is a message about future events that may occur. Relevant information can be used by an individual to take actions that will change the welfare of that individual. Messages that an individual cannot act upon to change his or her welfare have little value. For example, a cotton farmer who grows cotton on irrigated land might be willing to pay for accurate weekly rainfall forecasts, because these forecasts can be used to establish the most efficient irrigation schedule. In contrast, once a dry-land cotton farmer has planted his fields, weekly rainfall forecasts are of little use, because there are no actions the farmer can take on a day-to-day basis using this information.

In addition to being able to act upon the information in a manner that will affect one's welfare, one must be able to correlate the information with the future events when they occur. For example, if your broker always told you that a stock you had identified looked like a "good buy," this message would have little value to you, because you know that some of these stocks will perform well and others will not. In contrast, if your broker recommends stocks to buy and stocks to sell based upon his or her estimate of each security's return prospects and is right more often than he or she is wrong, then this message constitutes economically relevant information.

In security markets, some messages are economically relevant to investors and others are not. If a message has no impact on the future return or risk prospects of a security, it is not relevant to investors and should not be correlated with security performance; that is, it does not constitute information. For example, the news that a company has changed the format of the presentation of its financial reports is not information because this cosmetic change has no impact on the return or risk of that company's securities. In contrast, if the company announces that it has adopted a new accounting convention that will result in significant tax savings, this news is information because it affects the return stream from that company's securities.

To illustrate the market efficiency concept, consider the case of HP, Inc., the computer and printer company (ticker symbol HPQ). On November 24, 2015, HP, Inc. reported disappointing fourth-quarter earnings relative to analyst expectations. In addition, fourth-quarter revenues declined by 9 percent year over year to $25.7 billion. Personal computer sales declined by 14 percent, and printer and supplies revenues were also down 14 percent. In the face of this surprising decline in revenues and earnings, and the expectation of additional disappointments in coming quarters, the stock price declined substantially. As can be seen in Figure 2.4, between November 19 and the close of trading on November 24, there had been a modest increase in the price of HPQ, rising from about $13.75 to as high as $14.75 on November 24. After the close of trading on the 24th, when the company released its fourth-quarter results, the market was swift to react. The stock price opened on November 25 at $13.25 and quickly fell to less than $12.50 per share, a decline of over 15 percent. The stock continued to trade in this new lower price range for the next several weeks. In an efficient market, one would expect that the announcement of a significant change in a company's future earning prospects would result in a very rapid decline in the stock price. As Figure 2.4 shows, the price adjustment occurred almost instantaneously, as expected.

If markets are inefficient, or slow to react to new information, one could easily attain abnormal profits by trading on the stock after the release of information. Specifically, if the information is positive, you would buy the stock when the information is released and then sell it a few days later after the stock has risen to its new equilibrium level. You can also profit from negative news releases by selling the stock first and then buying it back a few days later when the stock has settled to a new lower level. The latter type of transaction is called **short-selling**. In a short sale you essentially sell a stock that you do not own by "borrowing" it from another investor (this is done by the stockbroker on your behalf) and then replacing it later by purchasing it, presumably, at a lower price.

short-selling

2-6b Degrees of Market Efficiency

The HP example illustrates the concept of market efficiency with respect to publicly available information, such as company news releases. The finance discipline recognizes several degrees of market efficiency based on the type of information under consideration: *weak-form efficiency*, *semistrong-form efficiency*, and *strong-form efficiency*.

FIGURE 2.4

Daily Stock Price for HPQ Around Disappointing Earnings Announcement

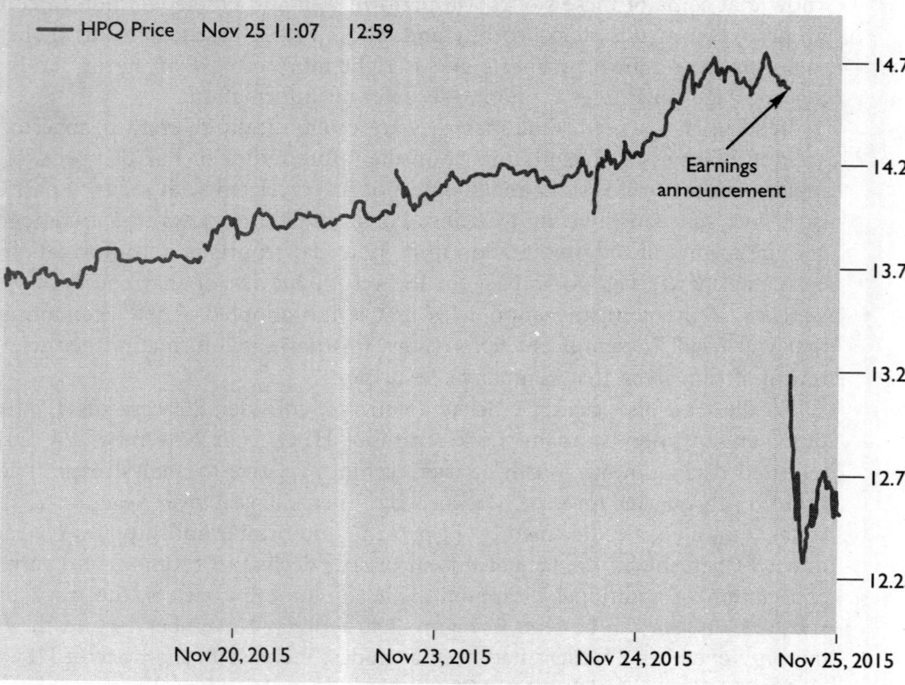

Source: YCharts.com

Weak-Form Efficiency With weak-form market efficiency, no investor can expect to earn excess returns[7] based on an investment strategy using such information as historical price or return information. All stock market information, including the record of past stock price changes and stock trading volume, is fully reflected in the current price of a stock.

Tests of the weak-form market efficiency hypothesis have included statistical tests of independence of stock price changes from various day-to-day periods.[8] These studies have concluded that stock price changes over time essentially are statistically independent and that a knowledge of past price changes cannot be used to predict future changes. Other tests have concluded that stock price changes over time essentially are statistically independent and that a knowledge of past price changes cannot be used to predict future changes. Other tests have looked for the existence of longer-term cycles in stock prices, such as monthly or seasonal cycles.[9] In addition, numerous trading rules based solely on past market price and volume information have been tested. Pinches, in a review of much of this research, has concluded that "with some exceptions, the studies of mechanical trading rules do not indicate that profits can be generated by these rules."[10] In conclusion, the evidence indicates that U.S. capital markets are efficient in a weak-form context.

Semistrong-Form Efficiency With semistrong-form market efficiency, no investor can expect to earn excess returns based on an investment strategy using any publicly available information. Announcements of earnings changes, stock splits, dividend changes, interest rate changes, money supply levels, changes in accounting practices that affect a firm's cash flows, takeover announcements, and so on are quickly and unbiasedly incorporated in the price of a security. A finding of semistrong-form market efficiency implies that the market is also weakly efficient because the information set considered in the weak-form case is also publicly available. Once information is made public in a semistrong-form efficient capital market, it is impossible for investors to earn excess returns (after considering trading costs) from transactions based upon this information because the security price will already reflect the value of this information. Studies of stock splits, new issues, stock listing announcements, earnings and dividend announcements, stock acquisition announcements, and announcements of analyst recommendations support the notion of semistrong-form market efficiency, at least after the cost of commissions on transactions is considered.[11] There have been a few apparent observed violations of semistrong-form market efficiency, but in many cases, alternative explanations for these exceptions have been found. Overall, the evidence on semistrong-form market efficiency tends to support this level of market efficiency.

---

[7]Excess returns are returns that exceed those that can be expected considering the risk assumed by the investor. In Chapter 8, we formally develop models of the relationship between returns and appropriate measures of risk.

[8]See, for example, Sidney S. Alexander, "Price Movements in Speculative Markets: Trends or Random Walks?" *Industrial Management Review* (May 1961): 7–26; Eugene F. Fama, "The Behavior of Stock Market Prices," *Journal of Business* (January 1965): 34–105; and Eugene F. Fama and James MacBeth, "Risk, Return and Equilibrium: Empirical Tests," *Journal of Political Economy* (May/June 1973): 607–636.

[9]C. W. Granger and O. Morgenstern, *Predictability of Stock Market Prices* (Boston, MA: D. C. Heath, 1970).

[10]George Pinches, "The Random Walk Hypothesis and Technical Analysis," *Financial Analysts Journal* (March/April 1970): 104–110.

[11]See, for example, Eugene Fama, L. Fisher, M. Jensen, and R. Roll, "The Adjustment of Stock Prices to New Information," *International Economic Review* (February 1969): 1–21; Frank K. Reilly, "Further Evidence on Short-Run Results for New Issue Investors," *Journal of Financial and Quantitative Analysis* (March 1974): 165–177; Stanley Block and Marjorie Stanley, "The Financial Characteristics and Price Movement Patterns of Companies Approaching the Unseasoned Securities Market in the Late 1970s," *Financial Management* (Winter 1980): 30–36; Richard W. Furst, "Does Listing Increase the Market Price of Common Stocks?" *Journal of Business* (April 1970): 174–180; R. Richardson Pettit, "Dividend Announcements, Security Performance and Capital Market Efficiency," *Journal of Finance* (December 1972): 993–1007; Michael Firth, "The Information Content of Large Investment Holdings," *Journal of Finance* (December 1975): 1265–1281; and Peter L. Davies and Michael Canes, "Stock Prices and the Publication of Second-Hand Information," *Journal of Business* (January 1978): 43–56.

Strong-Form Efficiency With strong-form market efficiency, security prices fully reflect *all* information, both public and private. Thus, in a strong-form efficient capital market, no individual or group of individuals should be able to consistently earn above-normal profits, including insiders possessing information about the economic prospects of a firm. The existence of individuals, such as investment banker Dennis Levine (see the "Ethical Issues" section), who have traded illegally on the basis of inside information and have earned phenomenal profits until they were caught and prosecuted by the Securities and Exchange Commission, provides graphic evidence that strong-form efficiency does not hold.

2-6c Implications of Market Efficiency for Financial Managers

In general, we can conclude that capital markets are quite efficient, both in an informational and an operational sense. The observed efficiency of capital markets has some very important implications for financial managers.

Timing or Gambling In a weak-form efficient capital market, we know there are no detectable patterns in the movement of stock and bond prices. Companies often indicate that they have delayed a stock or bond offering in anticipation of more favorable capital market conditions; that is, a higher stock price or lower interest rates. Since there are no predictable patterns of stock price and interest rate movements over time, financing decisions based upon improved market timing are not likely to be productive, on average. If a stock has traded as high as $30 per share recently but is now trading only at $28, management may delay a proposed new stock issue in anticipation of a higher future price. If this delay is based upon a market timing argument—such as "the market is now temporarily depressed"—rather than on some inside information known only to management that suggests that the stock is currently undervalued, then the strategy is not likely to be successful. In some instances, the stock price will increase in the direction of the target, while in others, it will decline even further. In weak-form efficient capital markets, financial decisions based on timing market cycles are not able to consistently lead to higher returns than are available to managers who do not attempt to time their financial decisions to take advantage of market cycles.

An Expected NPV of Zero In an efficient capital market, all securities are perfect substitutes for one another, in the sense that each security is priced such that its purchase represents a zero net present value investment. (In general, the net present value of any investment is the present value of benefits minus the present value of costs of **outlays**. This concept is covered in more detail in later chapters.) This is another way of saying that required returns equal expected returns in efficient capital markets. For example, if you buy one share of Apple Inc. stock for $116, the present value of the market expectation of its cash flows is equal to $116. Hence, this purchase has a net present value of zero. If you buy for $65 one share of stock in Duke Energy, a diversified energy firm with considerably less risk and lower earnings growth prospects than Apple, the present value of the market expectation of its cash flows is equal to $65. The difference between the risk and expected returns of the two companies' stocks is reflected in their market prices and the discount rate used by the market to evaluate the expected future cash flows. Only if an investor possesses information that is not known to the marketplace—for example, insider knowledge of a major new oil strike by an oil firm or of a pending takeover attempt—will the investment in a stock or bond have a positive net present value.

outlays

Expensive and Unnecessary Corporate Diversification If capital markets are efficient and all securities are fairly priced, on average, investors can accomplish much on their own without the help of a firm's financial managers. For example, consider Eastman Kodak's acquisition of Sterling Drug. In 1988, Eastman Kodak paid $89.50 per share to acquire Sterling Drug. During the previous year, Sterling traded for as little as $35.25 per share. As a stockholder of Eastman Kodak, you could have achieved the same diversification in your portfolio simply by buying shares of Sterling Drug in the open market.[12] McDonalds had a similar failed diversification experience when it attempted to move into the lodging business in 2001. The corporate landscape is littered with numerous failed diversification examples. In spite of this poor performance record, financial managers of many firms continue to make acquisitions of other companies in order to achieve "the benefits of diversification." In efficient capital markets, this type of activity is better left to individual investors.

Security Price Adjustments In efficient capital markets, security prices reflect expected cash flows and the risk of those cash flows. If a transaction, such as an accounting change, does not impact the firm's expected *cash flows* or the risk of those cash flows, then the transaction should have no impact on security prices. Investors are not fooled by cosmetic accounting or other nonmaterial transactions.

Efficient capital markets research has shown that accounting format changes having no impact on a firm's cash flows do not result in changes in the firm's value. Actions such as including the capitalized value of financial leases on a firm's balance sheet, providing an inflation-adjusted income statement and balance sheet, company name changes, stock splits, and stock dividends unaccompanied by a rise in earnings and/or dividends have no significant impact on stock prices. In contrast, any event impacting actual cash flows—such as a change in inventory valuation designed to reduce tax obligations—or the risk of these cash flows—such as an announcement by a public utility company that it will sell all of its nuclear power plants—will be reflected quickly in the stock price.

Prices in efficient capital markets have a story to tell. For example, the response of the market to the proposed acquisition of King Pharmaceuticals by Mylan Laboratories in 2004 suggests that this combination was not perceived to be value enhancing. On the date of the merger announcement, the price of Mylan stock fell by 16 percent to $15.51. The merger was ultimately called off and Mylan's stock regained its loss in value.

2-6d Behavioral Finance Perspectives on the Financial Marketplace

HTTP:

Visit www.investorhome.com/psych.htm and www.aobf.org for more on behavioral finance issues.

In spite of an extensive body of literature indicating that the capital markets in the United States and other financially sophisticated economies are highly efficient, these markets are not perfectly efficient. We continue to find anomalous events that are inconsistent with fully efficient markets. For example, the speculative "bubble" of the late 1990s that saw the run-up in prices of Internet stocks and their subsequent decline indicates trading behavior that may not be consistent with fully rational investment decision making. Similar anomalies have impacted real estate markets, most recently in the run-up to the economic downturn of 2008–2009.

[12]Eastman Kodak ultimately divested itself of its ownership of Sterling Drug, taking a considerable loss, when it failed to realize the expected benefits from the acquisition. As a result of several other strategic miscues, Eastman Kodak was forced to file for bankruptcy in January 2012.

These anomalies have led to the development of new financial models suggesting that investors sometimes behave irrationally. Behavioral finance seeks to understand how departures from totally rational decision making by investors and other market participants can help to explain otherwise curious market occurrences.[13]

Various psychological considerations may lead to market inefficiencies. One example is the refusal by some investors to sell a losing stock, since it means giving up hope and admitting that the investor made a mistake in purchasing the security. Another example is fixating on a price target for a stock (or the market) and filtering out evidence that the investor (or analyst) may be wrong. A final example is the tendency for some investors to focus too heavily on up or down price trends. As a consequence, the investor tends to extrapolate past performance too far into the future. Coupled with a consideration of circumstances where arbitrage may not work quickly to eliminate valuation anomalies, behavioral finance research seeks to provide a richer understanding of the way financial markets work. There is evidence that behavioral approaches to understanding market price patterns may have some merit. However, most researchers believe that, *over the long run*, securities markets are efficient; that is, the market price of a company's stock represents an unbiased estimate of the intrinsic value of the company.

2-7 Holding Period Returns

holding period return

The return from holding an investment is called the *holding period return, holding period yield*, or *realized rate of return*. The **holding period return** can be defined by the following equation.

$$\text{Holding period return (\%)} = \frac{\text{Ending price} - \text{Beginning price} + \text{Distributions received}}{\text{Beginning price}} \times (100\%) \tag{2.2}$$

Distributions include the interest on debt or the dividends on stock. To illustrate, suppose you purchased one share of Boeing common stock for $120 a year ago. During the year, you received $3.64 in dividends, and you now sell the share for $147.00. Your holding period return would be calculated as:

$$\text{Holding period return (\%)} = \frac{\$147.00 - \$120.00 + \$3.64}{\$120.00} \times 100\% = 25.53\%$$

Foundation Concept

Returns are expressed as a percentage or fraction and are frequently quoted on an annual basis. However, holding period returns can be calculated for any time period. But, in order for a calculated holding period return to be a meaningful number, it must be compared to other returns computed using equal time periods.

The return just computed is called a *realized*, or *ex post* (after the fact), return. Realized returns differ from *expected*, or *ex ante* (before the fact), returns. Although ex ante returns are calculated in the same manner as ex post returns, ending prices and distributions for expected returns are *estimated* values, whereas ending prices and distributions for realized returns are *actual* values.

[13]An excellent collection of behavioral finance research can be found in Richard H. Thaler, ed., *Advances in Behavioral Finance* (New York: Russell Sage Foundation, 1993). See also Andrei Shleifer, *Inefficient Markets: An Introduction to Behavioral Finance* (New York: Oxford University Press, 2000), and E. Burton and S. Shah, *Behavioral Finance: Understanding the Social, Cognitive, and Economic Debates* (Hoboken, NJ: Wiley, 2013).

ETHICAL ISSUES

Insider Trading

In 1942, a young lawyer at the Securities and Exchange Commission, reacting to a complaint that a company president had purchased stock after telling shareholders that earnings had declined when he knew earnings were strong, wrote an initially obscure rule, Rule 10b-5. Rule 10b-5 and subsequent SEC rules have since been broadly interpreted and used as the justification for prosecuting insider trading.[a] Insider trading is defined as an individual (the insider) buying or selling securities on the basis of material, nonpublic information.

The story of Dennis Levine, the Drexel Burnham investment banker who spent over two years in federal prison after his conviction on insider trading charges, provides insights into the ethical dilemmas facing young managers. In 1978, the 25-year-old Levine began trading on insider information while working as a trainee at Citibank and earning a salary of $19,000. He began with seemingly innocent trades based on "hot stock tips" from another Citibank employee about pending mergers. His first insider trade earned him no return at all because the rumored merger did not materialize. But in seven years, Levine built his personal wealth from $39,750 to $11.5 million based on insider trades.

As his profits grew, his greed grew as well. He stated, "I was confident that the elaborate veils of secrecy I had created ... would protect me. And Wall Street was crazy in those days. These were the 1980s, remember, the decade of excess, greed, and materialism.... In this unbelievable world of billions and billions of dollars, the millions I made trading on nonpublic information seemed almost insignificant."[b]

Levine rationalized his actions with the belief (which is true, at least in part) that insider trading is a victimless crime. Henry Manne, one of the leading legal experts on insider trading, states, "The insiders' gain is not made at the expense of anyone. The occasionally voiced objection to insider trading—that someone must be losing the specific money the insiders make— is not true in any relevant sense."[c] Furthermore, the first criminal prosecution of insider trading did not occur until 1978, the year when Levine first began to use inside information for his private gain.

There is considerable controversy about the criminal status of insider trading. Criminal prosecutions under Rule 10b-5 have been rare. However, in a high-profile prosecution, Martha Stewart, CEO of Martha Stewart Living Omnimedia, was convicted of lying to government investigators about her sale of securities based on inside information. More general agreement exists regarding the ethics of insider trading for personal gain by individuals who have been entrusted with confidential information. The Levine story illustrates how easy it is for aggressive young managers to step over the bounds of ethical behavior early in their careers.

Do you agree with Manne that insider trading is a victimless crime? Who should be considered an insider for purposes of enforcing the rule? Can you think of any reasons why insider trading should be permitted?

[a]There is considerable controversy whether Rule 10b-5 was ever intended for the purpose of criminally prosecuting insider trading. Indeed, in passing the 1934 Securities Act, Congress considered making insider trading illegal but rejected the idea. It was not until 1961 that the SEC claimed it could use Rule 10b-5 to bring a civil case. Only in 1978 did SEC and federal prosecutors use this rule to bring a criminal case. Only eight insider trading cases had gone to trial by the end of 1990. For a more complete discussion of the evolution and application of Rule 10b-5, see Gordon Crovitz, "The SEC Overstepped When It Made Insider Trading a Crime," *The Wall Street Journal* (December 19, 1990): A17.

[b]Dennis B. Levine, "The Inside Story of an Inside Trader," *Fortune* (May 21, 1990): 80–89.

[c]Henry G. Manne, "In Defense of Insider Trading," *Harvard Business Review* (November/December 1966): 113–122.

2-8 Overview of the Financial Crisis beginning in 2007

In this section we present an overview of the financial crisis that started in 2007 and continued into 2010. Though our focus is from the U.S. perspective, where the crisis largely originated, in many ways the crisis was a global one that has affected many

INTERNATIONAL ISSUES

Market Efficiency Outside the United States[a]

As previously mentioned, extensive testing of the efficiency of security markets in the United States has led researchers to conclude that the major capital markets in this country are quite efficient in their operation and in the way in which investors process new, economically relevant information. An important question facing the manager of a multinational firm that desires to raise capital outside the United States is: Are foreign capital markets also efficient with respect to security pricing and the processing of new information?

Extensive tests of the efficiency of capital markets outside the United States have also been conducted. These studies concluded that the capital markets in the major industrialized countries, such as Japan, Canada, the United Kingdom, and most of Western Europe, are reasonably efficient.

Outside the major industrialized countries, capital markets function without the frequency of trading and liquidity that are necessary for efficient markets. For example, one day in Cairo, the total number of trades on the Cairo Stock Exchange was eight! Transferring shares in Egypt is a complicated, bureaucratized process that requires many signatures, the payment of transfer taxes, and the reissue of stock certificates by the issuing company (a signature is required by two members of the company's board of directors). Overall, it can take between two and three months before the purchaser receives the shares. Brokers in Cairo have an unspoken agreement that prices will not be allowed to move more than 10 percent a day. When someone wants to buy shares from a broker in Egypt, the first question that is usually asked is "Why?" The broker always suspects that the buyer is privy to some inside information. Insider trading is not illegal in Egypt.[b] The inefficiency of the Cairo Exchange holds for the capital markets in many developing countries. Hence, most of the capital that is raised by multinational firms is acquired in countries with well-developed, efficiently functioning capital markets.

Even if the capital markets of the major industrialized countries are relatively efficient, it may still be true that international capital markets, in general, are not efficient. For example, to the extent that there are barriers to the free flow of capital among the major world capital markets, it is possible that a multinational firm can use these barriers to reduce the overall cost of raising capital. Some of the barriers that have been identified include the following:

1. *Legal restrictions* limit the amount of foreign investment by some institutional investors. Some countries limit the amount of foreign ownership of domestic industries in an attempt to prevent a loss of local control.
2. *High transactions costs* may also make the free flow of capital across country borders difficult. These high costs include the cost of gathering information, trading costs, fees for managing international investments, and security custodial service fees.
3. *Taxation policies* between nations sometimes discourage the flow of capital across borders.
4. International investments are subject to greater *political risks* than are domestic investments. These risks range from expropriation to limits on the repatriation of profits and assets.
5. *Foreign exchange risks*, that is, the risks of unfavorable movements in the value of foreign currencies, also act as a deterrent to the flow of capital across national borders.

These factors may lead to somewhat segmented international capital markets. To the extent that international capital markets are not fully integrated, opportunities may exist for multinational firms that are willing to aggressively manage their investment and capital-raising functions to gain some advantage over less internationally integrated firms.

[a]This section is based, in part, on Bruno Solnick, *International Investments*, 2nd ed. (Reading, MA: Addison-Wesley, 1991).
[b]G. Brooks, "To Play the Market in Egypt Requires a Lot of Patience," *The Wall Street Journal* (March 23, 1989): A1.

regions, including Europe, Asia, and Latin America. The financial crisis provides a first-hand look at many of the aspects of financial markets covered in this chapter and their importance to the economy as a whole and to corporations in particular. The crisis also is instructive in teaching us how firms could have protected themselves or at least minimized the effects of the crisis. Many of these lessons are related to topics covered in this textbook.

2-8a Causes of the Financial Crisis

Economists generally agree on a confluence of factors that ultimately led to the start of the financial crisis in 2007: a real estate housing bubble, low interest rates, the creation of complex mortgage-backed securities, and the use of high leverage by individuals and corporations.

Most economists agree that the financial crisis was closely associated with the real estate bubble in the United States that peaked in 2006. An asset bubble occurs when an asset (for example, real estate, gold) sells for very inflated values that are not justified by its fundamentals. Figure 2.5 shows the U.S. home price index from 1991 to 2010. Note how the index value rises exponentially in the early 2000s and peaks in the first half of 2007, followed by a dramatic drop that continued through 2009.

The natural question to ask is, why did real estate prices increase so much? From basic economics we know that the price of any asset is a function of the demand and supply for it. In this case we experienced significant increases in demand for housing in the early 2000s. This increase can be attributed to a number of factors. Chief among them is the extraordinarily low mortgage interest rates that were available to potential homeowners. Figure 2.6 shows a graph of U.S. mortgage interests rates since 1985. Note the very low interest rates beginning in the early 2000s. These low rates have been traced to the easy money supply and low interest rate policies followed by the U.S. Federal Reserve in the aftermath of the 2001 Internet bubble. The Fed followed an easy money policy to prevent the 2001 stock market bubble from spreading to the wider

FIGURE 2.5

Index of U.S. Home Prices (Purchase-Only, Seasonally Adjusted Index, January 1991–January 2010)

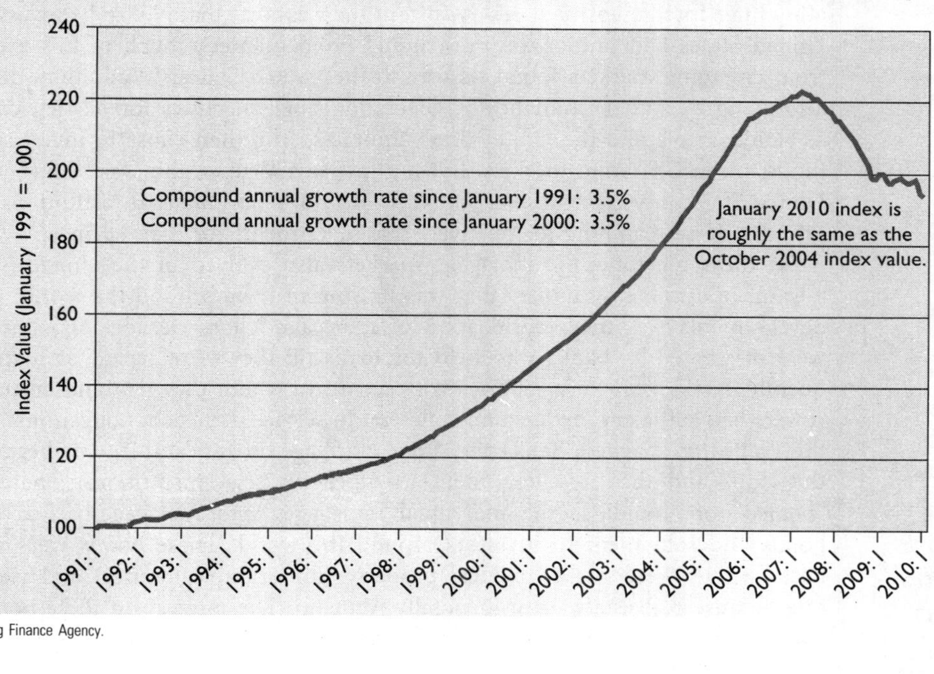

Source: Federal Housing Finance Agency.

FIGURE 2.6

U.S. Mortgage Interest Rates

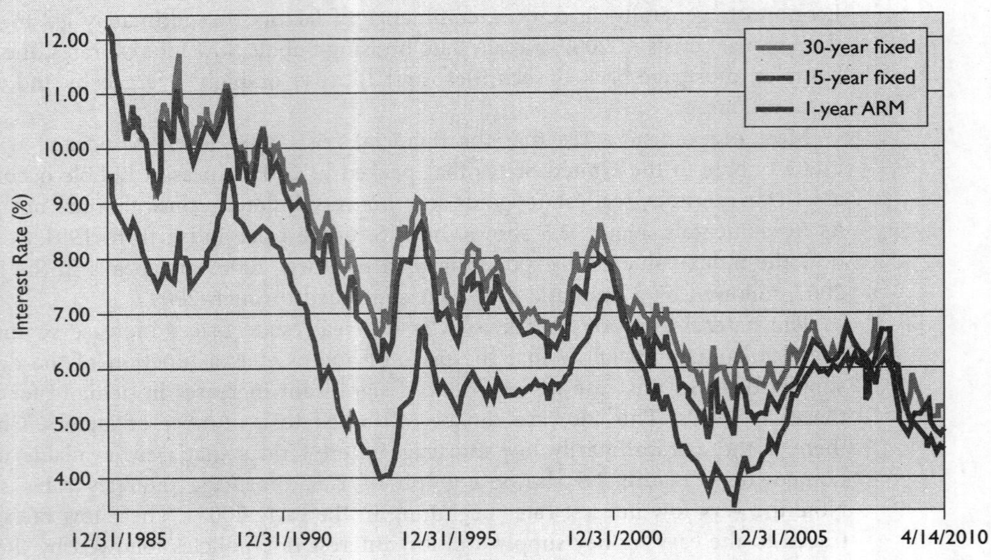

Source: Bankrate.com.

economy. The low interest rates meant that banks, which (as you learned in this chapter) are major financial intermediaries, could borrow money at extremely low interest rates, and could lend money to home buyers (and others) at very low rates.

The cheap money also came from foreign sources, especially the emerging markets. Emerging market economies, such as China, South Korea, India, and others, were generating huge foreign currency reserves from their exports that had to be invested. Since the United States had one of the most liquid bond markets, much of this excess liquidity from emerging markets found its way to the United States. In addition, oil prices were also going up rather dramatically, generating huge surpluses for oil-rich countries such as Saudi Arabia and the United Arab Emirates, who then chose to invest some of these funds in the U.S. bond markets. But not just sovereign wealth was being invested in the United States. Investments also poured in from foreign financial institutions and companies that were searching for relatively safe investments for their savings.

At the same time, the mortgage markets also evolved in the United States to take advantage of the easy money that was flowing in from around the world. One of these developments was the securitization of mortgage loans. Decades ago, mortgage loans were originated by banks who held the loans till they were repaid or matured. Consequently, banks were very cautious with regard to whom they lent and ensured that borrowers had sufficient income and collateral to service their debt obligations. Beginning in the 1980s this changed. Banks and other mortgage brokers and lenders began originating the loans and then reselling them to other financial institutions. These institutions "pooled" or "bundled" the individual mortgages into mortgage-backed securities or bonds and sold them to investors around the world. These bonds were very popular because they were backed by real property (for example, houses) and viewed as very safe because real estate prices generally went up. The interest on these bonds was paid from interest collected from the underlying mortgages. Institutions found these bonds attractive compared to investing in Treasury bonds because they provided a higher yield but were seemingly not that much riskier.

This securitization reached a new and dangerous level in the early 2000s. To exploit the demand for these mortgage-backed securities, investment banks figured a way to expand the supply of the bonds by reaching down into more and more risky mortgages, known as subprime mortgages. Subprime mortgages are mortgages made to borrowers who are of questionable credit risk. These borrowers have a high probability of defaulting on their loans but were willing to pay a higher interest rate because of their high risk of default. The innovation that was made was to bundle these risky subprime mortgages and then to offer derivative securities on the pools with different risk profiles from very safe to very risky. In other words, the underlying pool of risky loans was "sliced and diced" into several layers of securities of varying risk-and-return profiles. The very safe securities carried a low rate of interest and low default risk rating; the riskiest layer of securities carried high interest rates but would also assume the greatest default risk. (Default risk and ratings are covered in Chapter 6.) Since interest rates were very low overall, these higher-yielding securities became very popular. As long as real estate prices were going up and the economy and employment levels were high, these derivative securities enjoyed a great deal of popularity as actual default risk on these bonds was very low.

Many of the big banks were actively engaged in creating these complex securities and also trading in them through their specialized trading subsidiaries. Some of them had significant exposure to the riskiest classes of these complex mortgage-backed securities. Banks also used significant amounts of leverage in their trading activities. It was not uncommon to use leverage multiples of 50 or 60 times; that is, for every dollar invested, $50 was borrowed.

Increasing leverage throughout the economy was also a contributor to the financial crisis. Home borrowers increasingly went for zero-down-payment loans. Often, home borrowers were young couples and families that had not built up any sizable savings to use as down payments for the homes, preferring instead to borrow 100 percent of the home's value. Bankers, of course, were willing to do this because of the cheap and easy availability of funds. The growth in housing values also promoted the popularity of home equity lines of credit. The increase in housing prices meant that the equity that owners had in their houses had gone up. Homeowners could use this equity as collateral to borrow from banks (that is, a home equity line of credit). These loans were used to finance purchases of new cars, appliances, and even vacations. Additionally, many homeowners found it attractive to refinance their homes at new lower interest rates to a higher loan amount, because their house values had gone up, and to use the excess loan amount to purchase items such as cars and appliances.

Firms were not immune from this loan binge. Many firms, attracted by the low interest rates, increased the leverage in their balance sheets and used the proceeds to engage in new investments and acquisitions that did not necessarily add value to the firm (that is, negative net present value investments; see Chapter 10 for the discussion on net present value).

The increase in home prices was unsustainable, and the markets realized this in late 2006. Also, holders of the complex securities began to question the true quality of the securities they held. As house prices started spiraling downward, the construction industry came to a screeching halt, resulting in mass layoffs in the industry. This had a domino effect that eventually spread to other industries and to higher economy-wide unemployment. The unemployment in turn resulted in an increasing trend in defaults of mortgage loans and other loans (home equity loans, credit card debt, installment loans for auto purchases, etc). Many homeowners simply walked away from their homes and let financial institutions take possession of their homes, which were worth much less than the loan balances on the property.

Recall that many of these mortgage loans were packaged into complex derivative securities. The owners of these securities suffered huge losses as well because the underlying assets of these "toxic" assets were comprised of subprime mortgages that were now in default or near default. Banks and financial institutions were some of the biggest investors in these securities. As the values of these securities fell, regulation required that they write down the values of these assets against their capital. This created a liquidity pressure for financial institutions, leading to an almost complete credit freeze, wherein banks were even distrustful of loaning money to other banks for fear of not being able to collect on their obligations. This fear, however, was not an imagined one. It was real. Many banks and financial institutions were caught in this liquidity trap, leading to their eventual liquidation or takeover by a stronger financial institution. The failed firms included many large financial institutions, including Washington Mutual, Countrywide, Merrill Lynch, Bear Stearns, and Lehman Brothers. It also included many banks (for example, Citicorp and Bank of America) that were severely crippled and were saved only because of the capital infusions by the U.S. Treasury. In all, the U.S. government invested over $700 billion in the so-called bailout of financial institutions.

2-8b How Firms Were Affected by the Financial Crisis

In as much as this book is about corporate financial management, it is important to discuss how the financial crisis affected businesses in general. As the financial crisis ultimately affected the wider economy, it led to significant unemployment and the severest recession since the Great Depression of the 1930s. This meant that businesses experienced significant losses in revenue and profits. These losses were reflected in lower stock prices, as evidenced by the dramatic drop in various stock market indexes. Figure 2.7 shows the Dow Jones 30 Index level for 2003–2013. Note the significant drop in the index from about the end of 2007 to the beginning of 2009, when it hit a low of 7,062. This was followed by a sustained market recovery into 2015. In late 2015 the Dow Jones Average was over 17,000. Many businesses had to scale back, while many others went bankrupt. Virtually all aspects of the real estate industry were devastated—from builders to brokers to

FIGURE 2.7

Dow Jones Industrial Average Index (2003–2013)

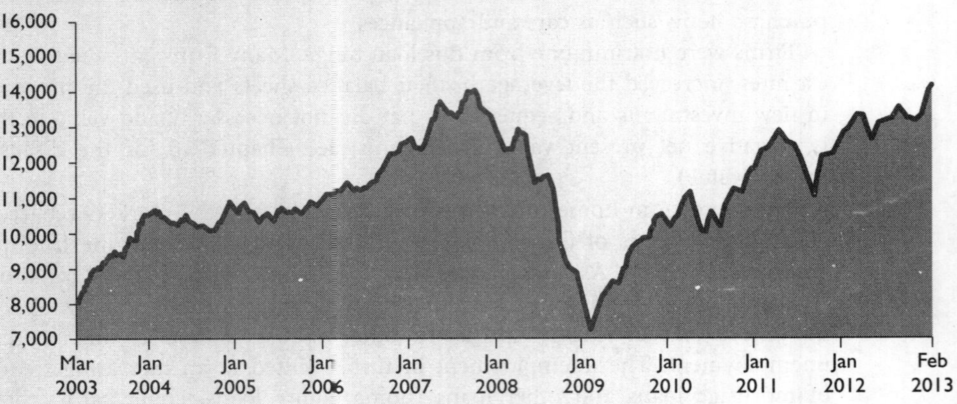

Source: money.msn.com (February 26, 2013).

financial institutions. Firms that survived did so because they had the foresight to prepare for the severe recession or were able to react quickly enough to limit the damage. Ford Motor Company, for example, had the foresight to prepare for the recession by improving its liquidity position. They did this by tapping into their substantial revolving lines of credit. (See Chapter 16 for a discussion of lines of credit.) This gave them a significant cash balance to weather the recession and, more importantly, to develop new, highly efficient cars that would appeal to cost-conscious consumers during the recession and also be prepared with an exciting line of cars when the economy picked up. Their chief U.S. competitors, General Motors and Chrysler, on the other hand, were caught flatfooted and ultimately had to be bailed out by the U.S. Treasury to prevent their possible liquidation.

The recession also showed that firms that were nimble, that had low business risk, and that exerted tight controls on their fixed costs and variable costs were able to weather the economic storm much better. For example, WalMart, one of the largest department/grocery store chains in the world, not only did not suffer much during the financial crisis, but it actually thrived during the crisis by catering to the cost-conscious consumer and redoubled its focus on offering products for the lowest price possible. They were able to do this because of their business model, which minimizes business risk, and their practice of managing their fixed and variable costs very tightly. (Business risk, variable cost, and fixed cost concepts are covered in detail in Chapters 13 and 14, especially the appendix). Southwest Airlines is another example of a company that managed to limit the negative effects of the financial crisis and the recession through cost control and various risk-management practices such as hedging its fuel cost purchases. (Risk management is covered in Chapter 21.) Leverage was also an important determinant of how a firm fared during this recession. Firms that got carried away by the low interest rates and ended up with too much debt in their capital structure struggled to meet their payments during the recession. Examples of firms that struggled because of excessive leverage include General Motors and Chrysler. (Capital structure is covered in Chapter 14.)

2-9 Income Taxes and Financial Management

A knowledge of tax laws and regulations is essential in making a wide variety of business decisions that affect shareholder wealth, such as what form of business organization to select, what types of securities to issue, and what investment projects to undertake.

Specific provisions of the federal tax laws applicable to corporations are discussed in Appendix 2A.

2-9a Implications of Income Taxes for Financial Managers

HTTP:
Additional tax information is available at
www.irs.gov
and
www.taxhelponline.com

Although the effect of income taxes on financial decisions is discussed in detail where appropriate throughout the book, a brief review of some of the critical areas of concern is provided in this section.

Capital Structure Policy Taxes have important implications for capital structure policy because the interest payments associated with debt financing are deductible from earnings when computing a company's income tax liability, whereas common stock dividends and preferred stock dividends are not deductible. In other words, for a company with positive pretax earnings and a 40 percent income tax rate, a new debt issue that increases interest expenses by $1,000,000 per year would cost the company (that is, reduce after-tax income) only $600,000—$1,000,000 interest expense less $400,000 tax savings (= 0.40 × $1,000,000). This tax advantage of debt is a prime reason for leveraged buyouts and financial restructurings.

Dividend Policy A firm's dividend policy may be influenced by personal income taxes. When dividends are paid to common stockholders, these dividends are taxed immediately as income to the shareholder. If, instead of paying dividends, a firm retains and reinvests its earnings, the price of the stock can be expected to increase. Personal taxes owed on common stock appreciation are deferred until the stock is sold. The ability to defer personal taxes on retained earnings causes some investors (for example, those in high marginal tax brackets) to prefer retention and reinvestment and ultimately capital gains rather than immediate dividend payments. This investor preference can have an impact on corporate dividend policy, particularly in small, closely held companies.

Capital Budgeting Capital expenditure decisions are also influenced by corporate income taxes. Capital expenditures require an outlay of *after-tax* dollars in order to acquire the needed assets. The assets are expected to generate a stream of operating income that is subject to tax. A tax-deductible expense associated with many capital expenditures is depreciation. Depreciation provides a **tax deduction** equal to a part of the original cost of a depreciable asset, such as machinery or buildings. The tax code details the methods that may be used to depreciate assets. Because depreciation is a non-cash expense (the cash outlay was made when the asset was purchased), it simply reduces taxable income and hence reduces the amount of taxes that must be paid. Changes in the tax code that speed up (slow down) the depreciation rate increase (decrease) the present value of the cash flows from the investment project and make the project a more (less) desirable investment. Therefore, financial managers must pay close attention to expected tax law changes.

tax deduction

Leasing The decision to lease or buy an asset is often motivated by its tax effects. If the lessee (asset user) is losing money or not subject to taxation (for example, a non-profit enterprise), leasing may be advantageous because the lessor (asset owner) can reflect the tax benefits of ownership in the lease rate charged to the lessee.

These and other tax effects of financial decisions will be encountered throughout the text and in the practice of financial management.

2-9b Tax Rate Used in the Text

U.S. tax laws impose progressive tax rates on corporate income—the larger the income, the higher the tax rate. As discussed in Appendix 2A, during 2015, the largest corporations paid a federal marginal tax rate (that is, tax rate on the next dollar of income) of 35 percent. Throughout the text, however, we use an *assumed* marginal tax rate of 40 percent rather than the *actual* corporate marginal tax rate of 35 percent. There are two reasons for following this convention. First, it simplifies many of the calculations. Second, most firms are also subject to state-imposed income taxes. A 40 percent rate is an excellent approximation of the *combined* federal and state income tax rates facing most firms.

2-10 Summary

- The main purpose of an economy's financial system is to facilitate the transfer of funds from *surplus spending units* to *deficit spending units. Financial middlemen,* such as investment bankers, bring together the surplus and deficit spending units in the capital markets so that funds can be transferred.

Financial intermediaries, such as commercial banks, receive *primary claims* from their borrowers and issue *secondary claims* to their lenders. Secondary claims have different risk and liquidity characteristics than primary claims.

- *Financial assets* consist of *money, debt securities*, and *equity securities*.
- Financial markets are the vehicles through which financial assets are bought and sold. They include *money* or *capital markets* and *primary* or *secondary markets*. Money markets deal in securities with maturities of approximately one year or less, while capital markets deal in securities with maturities greater than one year. Primary markets are those in which *new* securities are issued; secondary markets are those in which *existing* securities are traded.
- *Capital markets* are considered to be *efficient* if security prices instantaneously and fully reflect, in an unbiased way, all economically relevant information about a security's prospective returns and the risk of those returns.
- A *Eurocurrency* is a currency deposited in a bank located outside the country of origin. The Eurocurrency market is an important alternative to domestic sources of financing for multinational firms. The interest rate charged for Eurocurrency loans is tied to LIBOR, the London InterBank Offered Rate.
- The *exchange rate* is the rate at which one currency can be converted into another. The *spot rate* is the rate of exchange for currencies being bought and sold for *immediate delivery today*. The *forward rate* is the rate of exchange between currencies to be delivered at a future point in time—usually 30, 90, and 180 days from today. The *futures rate* is also a rate of exchange between currencies to be delivered at a future point in time. In contrast to forward contracts, futures contracts are standardized with respect to size and delivery date and are traded on organized exchanges, such as the International Monetary Market. Foreign currency *options* give the option holder the *right* to buy or sell a foreign currency at a fixed price over some time horizon.
- Investment returns are normally measured using the holding period return concept.

Important Equations

$$\text{Annualized forward premium or discount} = \left(\frac{F - S_0}{S_0}\right)\left(\frac{12}{n}\right)(100\%)$$

$$\text{Holding period return (\%)} = \frac{\text{Ending price} - \text{Beginning price} + \text{Distributions received}}{\text{Beginning price}} \times (100\%)$$

2-11 Questions and Topics for Discussion

1. Describe and discuss the saving-investment cycle.
2. What roles do financial middlemen and financial intermediaries play in the operation of the U.S. financial system? How do the two differ?
3. How do money and capital markets differ?
4. Describe the various types of financial intermediaries, including the sources of their funds and the types of investments they make.
5. What factors need to be considered when determining the optimal form of organization for a business enterprise?
6. How do primary and secondary financial markets differ?
7. What is the primary distinction between the trading process on the New York Stock Exchange and the OTC markets?
8. Describe the concept of market efficiency. In what sense is this concept an important part of the shareholder wealth maximization objective?

9. If a capital market is not efficient, what is the impact on a firm seeking to raise capital in that market? Why?
10. Define the following terms:
    a. Multinational corporation
    b. Spot exchange rate
    c. Forward exchange rate
    d. Direct quote versus indirect quote
    e. Option
    f. LIBOR
    g. Euro

2-12 Self-Test Problems

ST1. Three months ago, you purchased 100 shares of TCBY Enterprises for $11 per share. The stock has just paid a 10-cent-per-share dividend, and the current price per share is $8.75. What has been your holding period return on this stock?

ST2. What is the premium or discount between the spot rate and the three-month forward rate for the Swiss franc on February 25, 2013? What does this imply about the future spot rate for Swiss francs? (See Tables 2.1 and 2.2.)

ST3. What does the evidence in Table 2.3 indicate about the expected future value of the euro relative to the dollar?

ST4. Compute the indirect quote for the rand, rupee, and yen as of February 25, 2013. (Refer to Table 2.1.)

2-13 Problems*

BASIC

1. Using the data contained in Figure 2.3, what 52-week rate of return, excluding dividend yields, would an investor have received by purchasing the following portfolios of stocks?
    a. The stocks in the Dow Jones Industrial Average
    b. The stocks in the New York Stock Exchange Composite Average
    c. The stocks in the NASDAQ 100 Average
    d. The stocks in the Russell 2000 Index

    Assume that you purchased the stocks in the various averages in the same proportions that they are in the averages.

BASIC

2. An investor bought 100 shares of Venus Corporation common stock one year ago for $40 per share. She just sold the shares for $44 each, and during the year, she received four quarterly dividend checks for $40 each. She expects the price of the Venus shares to fall to about $38 over the next year. Calculate the investor's realized percentage holding period return.

BASIC

3. An investor bought 10 Ellis Industries, Inc. long-term bonds one year ago, when they were first issued by the company. In addition, he bought 200 shares of the company's common stock at the same time for $30 per share. He paid $1,000 each for the bonds, and today, the bonds are selling at $950 each (long-term interest rates have increased slightly over the past year). The bonds have a stated interest rate of 12 percent per year. The investor received an interest payment equaling $60 per bond six months ago and has just received another $60 per bond interest payment.

*Color blocks behind the numbers denote problems that have check answers provided at the end of the book.

Calculate the investor's percentage holding period return for the one year he has held the bonds.

BASIC **4.** Suppose a U.S. Treasury bill, maturing in 30 days, can be purchased today for $99,500. Assuming that the security is held until maturity, the investor will receive $100,000 (face amount). Determine the percentage holding period return on this investment.

BASIC **5.** Suppose a Midwest Telephone and Telegraph (MTT) Company bond, maturing in one year, can be purchased today for $975. Assuming that the bond is held until maturity, the investor will receive $1,000 (principal) plus 6 percent interest (that is, $0.06 \times \$1000 = \$60$). Determine the percentage holding period return on this investment.

INTERMEDIATE **6.** a. National Telephone and Telegraph (NTT) Company common stock currently sells for $60 per share. NTT is expected to pay a $4 dividend during the coming year, and the price of the stock is expected to increase to $65 a year from now. Determine the *expected* (ex ante) percentage holding period return on NTT common stock.

b. Suppose that one year later, NTT's common stock is selling for $75 per share. During the one-year period, NTT paid a $4 common stock dividend. Determine the *realized* (ex post) percentage holding period return on NTT common stock.

c. Repeat Part b given that NTT's common stock is selling for $58 one year later.

d. Repeat Part b given that NTT's common stock is selling for $50 one year later.

INTERMEDIATE **7.** One year ago, you purchased a rare Indian-head penny for $14,000. Because of the recession and the need to generate current income, you plan to sell the coin and invest in Treasury bills. The Treasury bill yield now stands at 8 percent, although it was 7 percent one year ago. A coin dealer has offered to pay you $12,800 for the coin. Compute the holding period return on this investment.

INTERMEDIATE **8.** Six months ago, you purchased a tract of land in an area where a new industrial park was rumored to be planned. This land cost you $110,000, and the seller offered you an interest-free loan for 70 percent of the land cost. Today, the industrial park project was formally announced, and an attorney for the developer has just offered you $190,000 for your land. If you accept this offer, what will be your holding period return on this investment?

CHALLENGE **9.** The stock of Tips, Inc., a new firm operating a chain of sports betting parlors, has just been sold in an initial public offering at a price of $25 per share. One week after this offering, the stock has risen in value to $35. You believe the stock will rise to $45 over the coming year. You do not expect Tips to pay any dividends over the year. If you require a rate of return on this stock of 18 percent, do you believe this is a good investment at the current price of $35?

INTERMEDIATE **10.** Japanese Motors exports cars and trucks to the U.S. market. On February 25, 2013, its most popular model was selling (wholesale) to U.S. dealers for $20,000. What price must Japanese Motors charge for the same model on November 18, 2015, to realize the same amount (of Japanese yen) as it did in 2013? (Refer to Table 2.1.)

CHALLENGE **11.** Valley Stores, a U.S. department store chain, annually negotiates a contract with Alpine Watch Company, located in Switzerland, to purchase a large shipment of watches. On February 25, 2013, Valley purchased 10,000 watches for a total of 1.26 million Swiss francs. Refer to Table 2.1 and determine the following:

a. The total cost and cost per watch in U.S. dollars

b. The total cost and cost per watch in U.S. dollars of 12,000 watches purchased on November 18, 2015, assuming that Alpine's price per watch (in Swiss francs) remains unchanged

INTERMEDIATE **12.** Determine the percentage change in the value of the following currencies relative to the U.S. dollar between February 25, 2013 and November 18, 2015. (Refer to Table 2.1.)

a. Rupee
b. Pound
c. Yen
d. Euro
e. Canadian dollar

CHALLENGE **13.** Over the past 10 years, your $15,000 in gold coins has increased in value by 200 percent. You plan to sell these coins today. You have paid annual storage and insurance costs of $500 per year. Assay expenses at the time of sale are expected to total $400. What is your 10-year (not annualized) holding period return on this investment?

● APPENDIX 2A

TAXES

Introduction

Both individuals and businesses must pay taxes on their incomes. The type and rates of taxation that businesses must pay depend on how they are organized. Generally, when organized as a corporation, business income is taxed at corporate rates, whereas business income of sole proprietorships and partnerships is taxed at the rates of the individual owners or partners.[1] Since corporations are the dominant form of business organization (in terms of sales), this appendix focuses on corporate income taxes.

Federal income tax laws were first enacted by the government in 1913 and have been changed numerous times since then. This appendix contains a brief introduction to some tax law concepts and provides the background needed for understanding tax issues discussed in the book.

Corporate Income Taxes

In general, the taxable income of a corporation is calculated by subtracting business expenses from revenues. Tax-deductible[2] business expenses normally include the cost of goods sold, selling and administrative expenses, depreciation allowances,[3] and interest expenses. Federal income taxes are computed on the resulting taxable income. The current (2015) tax rates imposed on corporations are shown in Table 2A.1.

The benefits of the 15 percent and 25 percent rates are phased out (or "recaptured") by imposing an additional 5 percent tax (that is, 39 percent instead of 34 percent) on taxable income between $100,001 and $335,000. The benefit of the 34 percent rate on taxable income between $335,000 and $10,000,000 is phased out by imposing an additional 3 percent tax (that is, 38 percent instead of 35 percent) on taxable income between $15,000,001 and $18,333,333. The effect of these provisions is that corporations with taxable incomes in excess of $18,333,333 pay a flat rate of 35 percent on all taxable income.

The calculation of the total tax for various levels of taxable income is shown in Table 2A.2. The *average tax rate* of a corporation is calculated by dividing the total tax by taxable income. The **marginal tax rate** of a corporation is defined as the tax rate on the next dollar of taxable income. For large corporations with taxable incomes exceeding $18,333,333, the effective marginal and average tax rates will be equal to 35 percent.

marginal tax rate

In addition to paying taxes on *operating* or *ordinary income*, corporations must also pay taxes on *capital gains income* and *dividend income*.

Capital Gains Income

Capital gains
capital losses

Capital gains income received by corporations is currently (2015) taxed at the same marginal tax rate as ordinary income. Corporate **capital losses** are deductible only against capital gains. Net capital losses may be carried back and applied against net

[1]One exception is the S corporation, which is discussed later in this appendix.

[2]A *tax deduction* differs from a *tax credit*. A tax deduction is subtracted from a firm's revenues in calculating taxable income, whereas a tax credit is a direct deduction from the firm's tax liability.

[3]A detailed discussion of depreciation methods is contained in Appendix 9A.

TABLE 2A.1

2015 Corporate Tax Rates

Taxable Income	Marginal Tax Rate	Tax Calculation Base Tax + (Marginal Tax Rate × Amount over Base Income)
Up to $50,000	15%	$ 0 + (15% × Amount over $0)
$50,001–$75,000	25%	$ 7,500 + (25% × Amount over $50,000)
$75,001–$100,000	34%	$ 13,750 + (34% × Amount over $75,000)
$100,001–$335,000	39%*	$ 22,250 + (39% × Amount over $100,000)
$335,001–$10,000,000	34%	$ 113,900 + (34% × Amount over $335,000)
$10,000,001–$15,000,000	35%	$ 3,400,000 + (35% × Amount over $10,000,000)
$15,000,001–$18,333,333	38%**	$ 5,150,000 + (38% × Amount over $15,000,000)
Over $18,333,333	35%	35% × Taxable Income

*Includes additional 5% "recapture" tax under the Tax Reform Act of 1986.

**Includes additional 3% "recapture" tax under the Revenue Reconciliation Act of 1993.

TABLE 2A.2

Computation of Corporate Income Taxes

Taxable Income ($)	Marginal Tax Rate (%)	Tax Calculation	Average Tax Rate (%)
25,000	15%	$0 + (.15 × $25,000) = $3,750	15.0
75,000	25	$7,500 + (.25 × $25,000) = $13,750	18.33
100,000	34	$13,750 + (.34 × $25,000) = $22,250	22.25
250,000	39	$22,250 + (.39 × $150,000) = $80,750	32.3
1,250,000	34	$113,900 + (.34 × $915,000) = $425,000	34.0
2,500,000	34	$113,900 + (.34 × $2,165,000) = $850,000	34.0
12,500,000	35	$3,400,000 + (.35 × $2,500,000) = $4,275,000	34.2
17,500,000	38	$5,150,000 + (.38 × $2,500,000) = $6,100,000	34.86
25,000,000	35	.35 × $25,000,000 = $8,750,000	35.0
125,000,000	35	.35 × $125,000,000 = $43,750,000	35.0

gains in the prior three years. Any remaining net capital loss may be carried forward for five years and applied against capital gains in those years.

Dividend Income

Dividends received by a corporation are normally entitled to a 70 percent exclusion from federal income taxes. To illustrate, suppose that the Hastings Corporation owns stock in the Fremont Corporation and that Fremont pays $100,000 in dividends to Hastings during 2015. Hastings has to pay taxes on only 30 percent of the $100,000, or $30,000. (The other 70 percent, or $70,000, is excluded; that is, received tax-free. However, Fremont had to pay taxes on its income before paying the $100,000 to Hastings, because *dividends paid by a firm are not considered tax-deductible expenses.*) The $30,000 of taxable dividend income is taxed at ordinary income tax rates.[4] Assuming that Hastings is large

[4]For corporate shareholders that own between 20 percent and 80 percent of the voting power and value of the stock of a dividend-paying corporation, there is an 80 percent dividends-received exclusion. There is a 100 percent dividends-received exclusion if a corporation owns more than 80 percent of the stock of a dividend-paying corporation.

ENTREPRENEURIAL ISSUES

S Corporations

The Internal Revenue Code allows certain small businesses to take advantage of the corporate form of organization while having their business income taxed directly to their shareholders at individual income tax rates. To qualify for S corporation status, a firm may not have more than 100 shareholders.

The primary benefit of **S corporations** is the avoidance of the *double taxation of dividends.* With a regular corporation, earnings are taxed twice—once at the corporate level and a second time as dividends at the individual level. With an S corporation, the company's earnings are passed (tax-free) to the shareholders and taxed only once as personal income. Despite the fact that the top personal tax rate is higher than the top corporate rate for companies with less than $10 million in income, the combination of the corporate and personal taxes is usually greater than the single personal tax paid by S corporation shareholders on an equivalent amount of income.

A further advantage of the S corporation form of organization is that the company can often pass losses to shareholders who can then use these losses to offset other income and thus reduce their tax liability.

S Corporations

enough to have a marginal tax rate of 35 percent, the tax on the dividends is $30,000 × 0.35 = $10,500. For corporations having a marginal tax rate of 35 percent, intercompany dividends are taxed at an effective rate of 10.5 percent; that is, (1 − 0.7) × 35 percent.

Loss Carrybacks and Carryforwards

Corporations that sustain net operating losses during a particular year are permitted by tax laws to apply the losses against any taxable income in other years, thereby lowering the taxes owed in those years. If such a loss is applied against a previous year, it is called a *loss carryback*; if it is applied against a succeeding year, it is called a *loss carryforward.*

The tax laws specify that a corporation's net operating loss may be carried back 2 years and forward 20 years to offset taxable income in those years. For example, suppose the NOL Corporation incurs a net operating loss totaling $200,000 in 2015. This loss may be carried back two years to 2013. If the NOL Corporation had 2013 taxable income of $125,000, for example, it could receive a tax refund equal to the taxes it paid for that year. The remaining $75,000 portion of the 2015 net operating loss could be carried back to 2014.

Questions and Topics for Discussion

1. What are the differences between the operating income, capital gains income, and dividend income of a corporation: At approximately what rates are these different types of income taxed?
2. What is an *S corporation*?
3. What do you think is the reason for the 70 percent corporate-dividend exclusion?

Self-Test Problems

ST1. During the past year, Alcore Enterprises, Inc., had sales of $3 million, cost of goods sold of $1.8 million, operating expenses of $800,000, and interest expenses of $200,000. Alcore paid preferred stock dividends of $100,000 and common stock dividends of $200,000 during the year. Alcore also retired maturing debt totaling $1.5 million during the year. Using the U.S. federal corporate tax rates shown in Table 2A.1, what was Alcore's taxable income and its total tax liability for the year? What are Alcore's average and marginal tax rates?

ST2. Jenkins Product, Inc., had sales of $5 million, cost of goods sold of $3 million, other operating expenses of $1 million, and interest expenses of $200,000 last year. During the year, Jenkins sold a plant and its associated equipment for $1.2 million. The book value of the plant and equipment was $500,000. What is Jenkins's taxable income and what taxes are due?

Problems*

BASIC

1. Last year, Idaho Steel Corporation had taxable ordinary income of $2 million and capital gains income of $500,000. The company also had $50,000 in dividend income and paid its stockholders $150,000 in dividends. Calculate the Idaho Steel Corporation's tax bill.

INTERMEDIATE

2. Last year the Selling Corporation had earnings before interest and taxes (operating income) equal to $1 million. It paid $200,000 in dividends to its stockholders and $100,000 in interest to its creditors. During the year, the company also repaid a bank loan of $150,000. Assuming a corporate income tax rate of 40 percent on all taxable income, calculate the Selling Corporation's tax bill.

INTERMEDIATE

3. Clapper Industries reported taxable income of $290,000.

a. What is Clapper's marginal tax rate based on the corporate tax rate table in this appendix?

b. What is Clapper's average tax rate?

c. If Clapper's taxable income increases to $410,000, what will be Clapper's marginal and average tax rates?

CHALLENGE

4. Using the tax rates shown in Table 2A.1, determine the expected annual tax liability of Kaiser Enterprises (a new firm formed in 2015), if the firm anticipates the following stream of taxable income:

Year	Taxable Income
2015	$30,000
2016	80,000
2017	(150,000)
2018	125,000
2019	150,000
2020	(75,000)

INTERMEDIATE

5. The CIG Power Corporation expects to report earnings before interest and taxes of $25 million this year. Management has determined that the firm needs $10 million of new capital this year to fund its anticipated capital investments. One alternative is to borrow the funds from a syndicate of banks at a 15 percent rate of interest. Alternatively, CIG could sell $10 million of a new preferred stock that pays annual dividends of $1.4 million. The marginal tax rate for CIG is 40 percent.

*Color blocks behind the numbers denote problems that have check answers provided at the end of the book.

a. What will be the "earnings after tax and available for common stockholders" if the money is borrowed?
b. What will be the "earnings after tax and available for common stockholders" if preferred stock is sold?

INTERMEDIATE **6.** Canon Corporation expects to receive $3 million of dividend income from the shares of stock it holds in Fuji Enterprises. Canon currently owns 15 percent of Fuji's outstanding stock. Canon's marginal tax rate is 40 percent and its average tax rate is 37 percent. What after-tax amount of cash will Canon receive from Fuji?

CHALLENGE **7.** Patriot Industries recently sold its fin fabrication machine for $150,000. The machine originally cost $500,000 and has a current book value of $100,000. Patriot's marginal tax rate is 35 percent for ordinary income and 35 percent for capital gains income.
a. What amount of gain has Patriot received from this transaction?
b. Is this a capital or ordinary gain?
c. How much tax must Patriot pay on this transaction?

CHALLENGE **8.** Amexicorp, Inc., a producer of security systems, had sales of $400 million, cost of goods sold of $150 million, operating expenses of $100 million, and interest expense of $100 million. Amexicorp also received $10 million in dividends from other corporations in which it had less than a 20 percent ownership stake. During the year, Amexicorp also sold for $20 million assets that are carried on its books at a book value of $17 million. Amexicorp paid preferred stock dividends totaling $10 million during the year. Common stock dividends paid were $5 million. Use the tax rates shown in Table 2A.1.
a. What is Amexicorp's after-tax net income available to common stockholders?
b. What would have been Amexicorp's after-tax net income available to common stockholders if the assets that were sold had a book value of $25 million?

CHAPTER 3

Evaluation of Financial Performance

KEY CHAPTER CONCEPTS

1. The evaluation of financial performance involves a series of techniques that can be used to help identify the strengths and weaknesses of a firm.
2. Financial ratios, which use data from a firm's balance sheet, income statement, statement of cash flows, and certain market data, are often used when evaluating the financial performance of a firm.
   a. *Liquidity* ratios indicate a firm's ability to meet its short-term financial obligations.
   b. *Asset management* ratios indicate how efficiently a firm is using its assets to generate sales.
   c. *Financial leverage management* ratios indicate a firm's capacity to meet short- and long-term debt obligations.
   d. *Profitability ratios* measure how effectively a firm's management generates profits.
   e. *Market-based ratios* reflect the financial market's assessment of a company's performance.
   f. *Dividend policy ratios* indicate the dividend practices of a firm.
3. Common-size financial statements express financial items as percentages (rather than dollar amounts) and are useful in evaluating financial performance.
4. Trend analysis evaluates a firm's performance over time, whereas comparative analysis evaluates a firm's performance relative to other firms.
5. When evaluating a firm's performance based on its balance sheet, income statement, and a series of financial ratios, a good financial analyst must be aware of the accounting techniques used by the firm and mindful of the quality of the firm's earnings and its balance sheet.

FINANCIAL CHALLENGE

It "Hertz" to Restate Earnings[1]

© aureliefrance/Shutterstock.com

Between 2011 and 2013, Hertz, one of the largest car rental companies, displayed impressive financial and accounting performance. Over that time frame, Hertz stock generated a 94.8 percent three-year cumulative return, and Hertz increased their net income from $176 million in 2011, to $243 million in 2012, and $346 million in 2013. When the market opened on June 5, 2014, Hertz was trading at an all-time high of $30.25. By the end of trading on November 14, 2014, Hertz was trading at $21.69, for a return of −28.3 percent. What caused this large decline in share price? On June 6, 2014, Hertz issued a Form 8-K acknowledging that they would need to restate their financial statements for 2011. Likewise, on November 14, 2014, Hertz issued a Form 8-K stating they would have to restate their financial statements for 2012 and 2013 as well, and also disclosed that they were under investigation from the SEC. Hertz had made errors involving depreciation, the allowance for doubtful accounts, and allowances for uncollectible amounts, amongst other errors. Additionally, Hertz disclosed the presence of four categories of material weaknesses in their internal control over financial reporting.

Hertz's earnings numbers led investors to believe the company was more profitable than it actually was. This, in turn, led to an inflated share price. Once news came out that the previously disclosed earnings numbers were of poor quality, the share price fell back down, as investors realized that the earnings numbers were likely inflated. As it turns out, the net effect of the aforementioned errors was to overstate net income by a total of $144 million from 2011 to 2013.

This example demonstrates the importance of balance sheet and earnings quality. Users of financial statements rely heavily on the numbers included in the financial statements, earnings chief among them, in order to make decisions regarding the firm. For example, shareholders and potential shareholders may use the numbers included in financial statements to determine the value of the company and therefore whether to buy or sell the stock. Banks may use financial statement numbers to determine whether a firm is creditworthy. This reliance on financial statements is what necessitates proper internal controls (e.g. internal audits) and external auditing, to ensure that financial statements are accurate and reliable.

Hertz Net Income and Restatements (in millions)

	2011	2012	2013
Hertz net income (as originally filed)	176	243	346
Cumulative misstatements	−31	−62	−51
Cumulative misstatement as a % of net income	−18	−26	−15

Sources: "1. Hertz Completes Financial Restatement; Provides 2015 Business Outlook," 07/16/2015. *PR Newswire*, July 16, 2015, http://www.prnewswire.com/news-releases/hertz-completes-financial-restatement-provides-2015-business-outlook-300114669.html; Hertz Form 8-K, June 6, 2014, http://www.sec.gov/Archives/edgar/data/47129/000110465914044345/a14-14905_18k.htm; Hertz Form 8-K, November 14, 2014, http://www.sec.gov/Archives/edgar/data/47129/000110465914080651/a14-24382_18k.htm; and Hertz 2014 Form 10-K, July 16, 2014, http://www.sec.gov/Archives/edgar/data/47129/000004712915000009/thc2014form10-k.htm.

[1]The authors thank Anil P. Rao for writing this opening vignette.

CHAPTER OBJECTIVES

Upon completion of this chapter, you should have a clear understanding of the following:

1. The major financial statements
2. How to calculate and interpret financial ratios
3. The limitations of financial statements and financial ratio analysis

3-1 Introduction

This chapter reviews the basic accounting statements and concepts and deals with the evaluation of financial performance, using financial statement analysis. A carefully executed financial statement analysis can assist financial managers in assessing the current financial condition of a firm. Trend analysis and common-size financial statements can assist financial managers in detecting changes in a firm's financial performance over time.

3-1a Uses of Financial Analysis

financial analysis

A **financial analysis** assists in identifying the major strengths and weaknesses of a business enterprise. It indicates whether a firm has enough cash to meet obligations; a reasonable accounts receivable collection period; an efficient inventory management policy; sufficient property, plant, and equipment; an efficient cost structure; sufficient profits; and an adequate capital structure—all of which are necessary if a firm is to achieve the goal of maximizing shareholder wealth. Financial analysis can also be used to assess a firm's viability as an ongoing enterprise and to determine whether a satisfactory return is being earned for the risks taken. Financial analysis helps a firm's management to discover specific problem areas in time for remedial action. For example, the analysis may show that a firm is carrying an excessive accounts receivable balance, which if not looked into may lead to liquidity problems in the future. The results of a financial analysis may indicate facts and trends that can aid the financial manager in planning and implementing a course of action consistent with the goal of maximizing shareholder wealth.

HTTP:
Many search engines maintain a finance area with extensive financial information and links to hundreds of different financial sites. Begin by looking at Yahoo's Web site, then follow the links to their financial information/data.
finance.yahoo.com

Financial analyses are also used by persons other than financial managers. For example, credit managers may examine basic financial ratios of a prospective customer when deciding whether to extend credit. Security analysts use financial analysis to help assess the investment worth of different securities. Bankers use the tools of financial analysis when deciding whether to grant loans. Financial ratios have been used successfully to forecast such financial events as impending bankruptcy. Unions refer to financial ratios when evaluating the bargaining positions of certain employers. Finally, students and other job hunters may perform financial analyses of potential employers to determine career opportunities.

3-1b Interpreting Financial Ratios

financial ratio

A **financial ratio** is a relationship that indicates something about a company's activities, such as the ratio between current assets and current liabilities or between its accounts receivable and its annual sales. Financial ratios enable an analyst to make a comparison of a company's financial condition over time or in relation to other firms. Ratios essentially standardize various elements of financial data for differences in the size of a series of financial data when making comparisons over time or between firms. For example, the total profits of Exxon Mobil normally are many times those of Noble Energy, because Exxon Mobil is a much larger firm than Noble Energy. For the fiscal year ending December 31, 2014, Exxon Mobil had net income of $32.5 billion compared to $1.2 billion for Noble Energy. By computing a ratio such as net profits divided by total assets, the relative performance of the two firms can be assessed more accurately.

Successful financial ratio analysis requires that an analyst keep in mind the following points:

- Any discussion of financial ratios is likely to include only a representative sample of possible ratios. Many other ratios can be developed to provide additional insights. In some industries, such as banking, analysts use special ratios unique to the activities of the firms in those industries.
- Financial ratios are only "flags" indicating potential areas of strength or weakness. A thorough analysis requires the examination of other data as well.
- Frequently a financial ratio must be dissected to discover its true meaning. For example, a low ratio may be caused by either a low numerator or a high denominator. Good financial analysts examine both the numerator and the denominator before drawing any conclusions.
- A financial ratio is meaningful only when it is compared with some standard, such as an industry ratio trend, a ratio trend for the specific firm being analyzed, or a stated management objective.
- When financial ratios are used to compare one firm with another, it is important to remember that differences in accounting techniques may result in substantial differences in financial ratios. Failure to consider this may lead to incorrect conclusions.

3-2 Basic Classifications of Financial Ratios

THOMSON ONE Business School Edition

Because different groups inside and outside a company have varying objectives and expectations, they approach financial analysis from different perspectives. For example, suppliers and short-term creditors are likely to be most concerned with a firm's current liquidity and near-term cash-generating capacity. Bondholders and holders of preferred stock, who have long-term claims on a company's earnings and assets, focus on the firm's cash-generating ability over the long run and on the claims other investors have on the firm's **cash flows**. Common stockholders and potential investors are especially interested in measures of profitability and risk, because common stock prices are dependent on the amount and stability of a firm's future earnings and dividends. Management is concerned with all aspects of financial analysis on both a short- and a long-term basis, because it is responsible for conducting the firm's day-to-day operations and earning a competitive rate of return for risks taken, and thereby maximizing shareholder wealth.

cash flows

No single financial ratio can begin to answer all these analytical needs. In fact, six different groups of ratios have been developed:

- *Liquidity ratios* indicate a firm's ability to meet short-term financial obligations.
- *Asset management ratios* indicate how efficiently a firm is using its assets to generate sales.
- *Financial leverage management ratios* indicate a firm's capacity to meet short- and long-term debt obligations.
- *Profitability ratios* measure how effectively a firm's management generates profits on sales, assets, and stockholders' investments.

- *Market-based ratios* measure the financial market's evaluation of a company's performance.
- *Dividend policy ratios* indicate the dividend practices of a firm.

Each type is discussed in detail in this chapter.

3-2a Key Financial Statements

The financial statements of the Drake Manufacturing Company, a medium-sized firm that produces various replacement components for the lawn equipment industry, will be examined to illustrate how ratios are used in financial analysis. Data will be used from Drake's *balance sheet* for the years ending December 31, 2015 and 2016, and from its *income statement* for the year 2016.

balance sheet

The Balance Sheet The **balance sheet** shown in Table 3.1 contains information on Drake's *assets, liabilities,* and *stockholders' equity.* The figures provide a "snapshot" view of the firm's financial health on December 31, 2016, and December 31, 2015. Drake's assets are recorded on the balance sheet at the price the company paid for them (that is, at historic cost). The liabilities are amounts the firm owes its creditors, and the **stockholders' equity** (also termed *net worth* or *owners' equity*) is the difference between total assets and total liabilities. The stockholders' equity accounts in Table 3.1 are (1) common stock ($10 par value), (2) contributed capital in excess of par, and (3) retained earnings.

stockholders' equity

TABLE 3.1

Drake Manufacturing Company Balance Sheet (in Thousands of Dollars)

	December 31, 2016		December 31, 2015	
ASSETS				
Cash		$ 2,540		$ 2,081
Marketable securities		1,800		1,625
Accounts receivable, net		18,320		16,850
Inventories		27,530		26,470
Total current assets		$50,190		$47,026
Plant and equipment	$43,100		$39,500	
Less: Accumulated depreciation	11,400		9,500	
Net plant and equipment		$31,700		$30,000
Total assets		$81,890		$77,026
LIABILITIES AND STOCKHOLDERS' EQUITY				
Accounts payable		$ 9,721		$ 8,340
Notes payable—bank (10%)		8,500		5,635
Accrued taxes payable		3,200		3,150
Other current liabilities		2,102		1,750
Current portion of long-term debt		2,000		2,000
Total current liabilities		$25,523		$20,875
Long-term debt ($9\frac{5}{8}$ % mortgage bonds)*		$22,000		$24,000
Total liabilities		$47,523		$44,875
Common stock ($10 par value)	$13,000		$13,000	
Contributed capital in excess of par	10,000		10,000	
Retained earnings	11,367		9,151	
Total stockholders' equity		$34,367		$32,151
Total liabilities and stockholders' equity		$81,890		$77,026

*Mortgage bonds require a $2,000(000) annual payment to a sinking fund.

income statement

EAT

The Income Statement The **income statement** in Table 3.2 indicates Drake's performance during the year ended December 31, 2016. The *cost of sales*, *operating expenses*, *interest expenses*, and *taxes* are deducted from the revenues generated, or *net sales*, to arrive at the firm's *earnings after taxes* (**EAT**, also known as net income, net earnings, or net profit). The statement in Table 3.2 also shows how the firm's earnings are distributed between dividend payments to stockholders and earnings reinvested in the firm.

common-size balance sheet

common-size income statement

Common-Size Financial Statements Common-size financial statements are also helpful in financial analysis. A **common-size balance sheet** shows the firm's assets and liabilities and stockholders' equity as a percentage of total assets, rather than in dollar amounts. Table 3.3 shows the Drake Company's common-size balance sheet on December 31, 2016, and December 31, 2015. A **common-size income statement** lists the firm's income and expense items as a percentage of net sales, rather than in dollar amounts. Table 3.4 contains Drake's common-size income statement for the year ended December 31, 2016. Common-size financial statements allow trends in financial performance to be detected and monitored more easily than with financial statements showing only dollar amounts.

statement of cash flows

The Statement of Cash Flows The **statement of cash flows** is useful in financial analysis, too. It indicates how a firm generated cash flows from its operations, how it

TABLE 3.2

Drake Manufacturing Company Income Statement (in Thousands of Dollars)

For the Year Ended December 31, 2016		
Net sales		$112,760
Cost of sales		85,300
Gross margin		$ 27,460
Operating expenses:		
Selling	$ 6,540	
General and administrative*	9,400	
Total operating expenses		15,940
Earnings before interest and taxes (EBIT)		$ 11,520
Interest charges:		
Interest on bank notes	$ 850	
Interest on mortgage bonds	2,310	
Total interest charges		3,160
Earnings before taxes (EBT)		$ 8,360
Federal and state income taxes at a combined 40% rate		3,344
Earnings after taxes (EAT) and available for common stockholders		$ 5,016
OTHER INFORMATION:		
Dividends paid on common stock		$ 2,800
Earnings retained in the firm		$ 2,216
Shares outstanding (000)		1,300
Market price per share		$ 24
Book value per share		$ 26.44
Earnings per share		$ 3.86
Dividends per share		$ 2.15

*Includes $150(000) in annual lease payments and $1,900(000) in depreciation expense.

TABLE 3.3

Drake Manufacturing Company Common-Size Balance Sheet

	December 31, 2016	December 31, 2015
ASSETS		
Cash	3.1%	2.7%
Marketable securities	2.2	2.1
Accounts receivable, net	22.4	21.9
Inventories	33.6	34.4
Total current assets	61.3%	61.1%
Net plant and equipment	38.7	38.9
Total assets	100.0%	100.0%
LIABILITIES AND STOCKHOLDERS' EQUITY		
Current liabilities	31.2%	27.1%
Long-term debt (9⅝ % mortgage bonds)	26.8	31.2
Total liabilities	58.0%	58.3%
Stockholders' equity	42.0	41.7
Total liabilities and stockholders' equity	100.0%	100.0%

TABLE 3.4

Drake Manufacturing Company Common-Size Income Statement

For the Year Ended December 31, 2016	
Net sales	100.0%
Cost of sales	75.7
Gross margin	24.3%
Operating expenses	14.1
Earnings before interest and taxes (EBIT)	10.2%
Interest charges	2.8
Earnings before taxes (EBT)	7.4%
Federal and state income taxes at a combined 40% rate	3.0
Earnings after taxes (EAT) and available for common stockholders	4.4%

used cash in investing activities, and how it obtained cash from financing activities. The statement of cash flows is analyzed in the next chapter.

3-2b Liquidity Ratios

Liquidity ratios

A firm that intends to remain a viable business entity must have enough cash on hand to pay its bills as they come due. In other words, the firm must remain *liquid*. One way to determine whether this is the case is to examine the relationship between a firm's current assets and approaching obligations, which are captured in the current liabilities. **Liquidity ratios** are quick measures of a firm's ability to provide sufficient cash to conduct business over the next few months. *Cash budgets* provide the best assessment of a firm's liquidity position. They are discussed in the next chapter.

This section discusses two different liquidity ratios—the *current ratio* and the *quick ratio*.

Current Ratio

The current ratio is defined as follows:

(3.1)
$$\text{Current ratio} = \frac{\text{Current assets}}{\text{Current liabilities}}$$

Current assets include the cash a firm already has on hand and in the bank plus any assets that can be converted into cash within a "normal" operating period of 12 months, such as marketable securities (also known as cash equivalents) held as short-term investments, accounts receivable, inventories, and prepayments. Current liabilities include any financial obligations expected to fall due within the next year, such as accounts payable, notes payable, the current portion of long-term debt due, other payables, and various accruals such as taxes and wages due.

Using data from Table 3.1, Drake's current ratio at year-end 2016 can be calculated as $50,190/$25,523 = 1.97, or about 2:1. Or, it can be said that Drake's current assets *cover* its current liabilities about two times.

The ratio is interpreted to mean that to satisfy the claims of short-term creditors exclusively from existing current assets, Drake must be able to convert each dollar of current assets into at least $0.51 of cash ($1.00/1.97 = $0.507, or $0.51). The *industry average* for the current ratio is 2.40 times,[2] meaning that the average firm in the industry must convert only $0.42 ($1.00/2.40 = $0.416, or $0.42) of each dollar of current assets into cash to meet short-term obligations.

The fact that Drake's current ratio is below the industry average does *not* necessarily mean that the firm is not well-managed. Nor does it mean that Drake's creditors are any less well protected than the creditors of competing firms, because no two firms—even those in the same industry—are identical. In fact, ratios that suggest the presence of a problem in one firm may be quite satisfactory for another firm.[3] By the same token, a higher current ratio for Drake than that for the industry is not necessarily indicative of better liquidity. For example, a higher current ratio may be due to greater inventory levels compared to the industry, which, in turn, could be indicative of the firm's having trouble moving things "off the shelf." Drake's current ratio provides only *one* standard for measuring liquidity. The financial analyst must dissect, or go behind, the ratio to discover why it differs from the industry average and determine whether a serious problem exists.

Quick Ratio

The quick ratio is defined as follows:

(3.2)
$$\text{Quick ratio} = \frac{\text{Current assets} - \text{Inventories}}{\text{Current liabilities}}$$

This ratio, sometimes called the "acid test," is a more stringent measure of liquidity than the current ratio. By subtracting inventories from current assets, this ratio recognizes that a firm's inventories are often one of its least-liquid current assets.[4] This is, of course, more applicable to some industries than to others. For example, if you are an apparel manufacturer, the ability to liquidate your inventory at fair value is highly doubtful. On the other hand, if you manufacture a commodity product such as newsprint, you may have greater confidence in the value of the inventory, especially if the prices are stable.

---

[2]Industry averages are obtained from various sources. The "Sources of Comparative Financial Data" section later in this chapter discusses a number of such sources.

[3]Many practitioners view a current ratio of 1.5 times (1.5) as satisfactory for industrial firms. Public utilities, on the other hand, typically function with considerably lower ratios. However, a financial analyst must be very cautious when using any of these rules of thumb. The safe level of a current ratio is a function of how fast the firm's current assets and liabilities turn over. In the case of a public utility, the accounts receivable turn over on a monthly basis—much faster than in the typical industrial firm. Thus, public utilities are able to safely sustain lower current ratios than industrial firms.

[4]Some analysts also subtract prepaid expenses from current assets in the calculation of the quick ratio because prepayments are difficult to convert back to cash.

Referring to the figures on Drake's balance sheet (Table 3.1), the firm's quick ratio at year-end 2016 is calculated as follows:

$$\frac{\$50{,}190 - \$27{,}530}{\$25{,}523} = \frac{\$22{,}660}{\$25{,}523} = 0.89 \text{ times}$$

The industry average is 0.92 times; Drake's quick ratio is nearly equal to that.

The quick ratio is interpreted to mean that Drake's cash and other current assets one step removed from cash—that is, marketable securities and accounts receivable—are equal to 89 percent of the current liabilities. The crucial assumption behind the quick ratio is that a firm's accounts receivable may be converted into cash within the "normal" collection period (and with little "shrinkage") or within the period of time for which credit was initially granted.

An analyst who doubts the liquidity of a firm's receivables may wish to prepare an *aging schedule.* The following one lists Drake's accounts receivable as of December 31, 2016:

Days Outstanding	Amount Outstanding (in Thousands of Dollars)	Percentage of Total
Less than 30	$ 9,450	51.6%
30–59	5,161	28.2
60–89	2,750	15.0
Over 90	959	5.2
Total accounts receivable	$18,320	100.0%

Unfortunately, the data required to prepare an aging schedule are not normally available to outside analysts. Hence, the aging schedule is useful primarily for internal analysis.

To evaluate the figures contained in an aging schedule, an analyst would need to consider Drake's selling terms. If, for example, Drake's customers are expected to pay within 40 days (which, in fact, they are), then the aging schedule indicates that many accounts are past due. However, because only 5.2 percent of the firm's receivables have been outstanding over 90 days, the major problem appears to be with slow-paying rather than uncollectible accounts. Some analysts adjust the quick ratio *downward* if a significant percentage of a firm's receivables are long past due and have not been written off as losses. Adjusting Drake's quick ratio downward involves the following calculation:

$$\frac{(\text{Current assets} - \text{Inventories}) - \text{Accounts outstanding over 90 days}}{\text{Current liabilites}} = \frac{\$22{,}660 - \$959}{\$25{,}523} = 0.35 \text{ times}$$

The 0.04 difference between the quick ratio, 0.89 times, and the adjusted ratio, 0.85 times, is probably insignificant. Therefore, even if Drake's accounts over 90 days old were considered uncollectible, this alone would not indicate any real problem for the firm.

3-2c Asset Management Ratios

One objective of financial management is to determine how a firm's resources can be best distributed among the various asset accounts. If a proper mix of cash, receivables, inventories, property, plant, and equipment can be achieved, the firm's asset structure will be more effective in generating sales revenue.

asset management ratios

Asset management ratios indicate how much a firm has invested in a particular type of asset (or group of assets) relative to the revenue the asset is producing. By comparing asset management ratios for the various asset accounts of a firm with established industry norms, the analyst can determine how efficiently the firm is allocating its resources.

This section discusses several types of asset management ratios, including the *average collection period*, the *inventory turnover ratio*, the *fixed-asset turnover ratio*, and the *total asset turnover ratio*.

Average Collection Period The average collection period is the average number of days an account receivable remains outstanding. It is usually determined by dividing a company's year-end receivables balance by the average daily credit sales (based on a 365-day year).[5]

(3.3)
$$\text{Average collection period} = \frac{\text{Accounts receivable}}{\text{Annual credit sales} \div 365}$$

Using figures from both Drake's balance sheet (Table 3.1) and the income statement (Table 3.2), the average collection period at year-end 2016 can be calculated as \$18,320/(\$112,760/365) = \$18,320/\$308.93 = 59.3 days. Because the industry average for this ratio is 47 days, Drake's ratio is substantially above the average.

Drake's credit terms call for payment within 40 days. The ratio calculations show that 59.3 days of sales are tied up in receivables, meaning that a significant portion of Drake's customers are not paying bills on time. (This is also indicated by the aging schedule of the firm's accounts receivable.) The analyst interprets this ratio to mean that Drake has allocated a greater proportion of total resources to receivables than the average firm in the industry. If the company implemented a more vigorous collection program and reduced the collection period to the industry norm of 47 days, some of these funds would be released for investment elsewhere or for debt reduction. The released funds of (59.3 days − 47 days) × \$308.93 per day = \$3,800 could be invested in other assets that might contribute more significantly to profitability.[6]

An average collection period substantially above the industry norm is usually not desirable and may indicate too liberal a credit policy. Ultimately, a firm's managers must determine if the liberal credit policy generates enough incremental sales and profits to justify the incremental cost.[7] In contrast, an average collection period far *below* the industry norm may indicate that the firm's credit terms are too stringent and are hurting sales by restricting credit to the very best customers. Although moderate- to slow-paying customers may seem troublesome individually, they can be profitable as a group, and a credit policy that is too tight may drive them to competing firms.

Inventory Turnover Ratio The inventory turnover ratio is defined as follows:

(3.4)
$$\text{Inventory turnover} = \frac{\text{Cost of sales}}{\text{Average inventory}}$$

Whereas the cost of sales is usually listed on a firm's income statement, the average inventory has to be calculated. This can be done in a number of ways. For example, if a firm has been experiencing a significant and continuing rate of growth in sales, the average inventory may be computed by adding the figures for the beginning and ending inventories for the year and dividing by 2.[8] If sales are seasonal or otherwise subject to wide fluctuations, however, it would be better to add the month-end inventory balances for the entire year and divide by 12.

Some analysts calculate inventory turnover as simply the ratio of annual sales to ending inventory. Although the *sales-to-inventory ratio* is technically inferior to and gives

---

[5]When credit sales figures are not available (which is frequently the case), total sales figures are customarily used in calculating the ratio, resulting in an *overstatement* of the average daily credit sales and an *understatement* of the average collection period. When firms have seasonal sales, an analyst should calculate an average of the end-of-month receivables balances. When comparing average collection period ratios with industry norms, the analyst must make sure the industry ratios have been computed in the same manner as the particular firm's ratios.

[6]Recall that the analysis for Drake is being done in terms of thousands of dollars. Hence, the actual released funds total approximately \$3.8 million.

[7]Chapter 18 contains an example of this type of incremental analysis.

[8]Note that the beginning inventory is the same as the ending inventory for the preceding period (year).

different results from those of more commonly used ratios, it may be satisfactory if used consistently when making comparisons between one firm and the industry as a whole. However, the problem with this ratio is that it tends to differ from one firm to another, depending on policies regarding markups on the cost of sales.

Because Drake's sales are spread evenly over the year and its growth rate has been fairly moderate, the average inventory can be calculated by taking the average of the beginning and ending inventory balances, ($27,530 + $26,470)/2 = $27,000. Dividing the cost of sales by this figure, $85,300/$27,000, gives an inventory turnover ratio of 3.16 times. This is considerably below the industry norm of 3.9 times, indicating that Drake has a larger investment in inventory relative to the sales being generated than the average firm. If the company could increase its inventory turns up to the industry average of 3.9 times, its average inventory investment in 2016 would be $21,872 ($85,300/3.9). The released funds, $27,000 − $21,872 = $5,128, could be used either for investment in other potentially more profitable assets or possibly for debt reduction.[9]

Two factors may be responsible for Drake's apparently excessive amount of inventory:

- The firm may be attempting to carry all possible types of replacement parts so that every order can be filled immediately. Drake should carefully examine this policy to determine whether the incremental cost of carrying large stocks of inventory is justified by the incremental profits earned on additional sales.[10]
- Some of Drake's inventory may be damaged, obsolete, or slow moving. Stock falling into these categories has questionable liquidity and should be recorded at a value more reflective of the realizable market value.

If a firm's inventory turnover ratio is too high, it may mean that the firm is frequently running out of certain items in stock and losing sales to competitors. For inventory to contribute fully to profitability, the firm has to maintain a reasonable balance of inventory levels. In general, inventory turnover ratios have gone up over the last three decades because of improvements in supply chain management and operations management. The popularity of "just-in-time" inventory management has meant that firms can operate with very low levels of inventory and yet meet customer demand for their products.

Fixed-Asset Turnover Ratio The fixed-asset turnover ratio is defined as follows:

$$\text{Fixed-asset turnover} = \frac{\text{Sales}}{\text{Net fixed assets}} \quad \textbf{(3.5)}$$

This ratio indicates the extent to which a firm is using existing property, plant, and equipment to generate sales.

The balance sheet figures that indicate how much a firm has invested in property, plant, and equipment are affected by several factors, including the following:

- The cost of the assets when acquired
- The length of time since acquisition
- The depreciation policies adopted by the firm
- The extent to which fixed assets are leased rather than owned

Because of these factors, it is possible for firms with virtually identical plants to have significantly different fixed-asset turnover ratios. Thus, the ratio should be used primarily for year-to-year comparisons within the same company, rather than for intercompany comparisons.

---

[9]Recall that the analysis for Drake is being done in terms of thousands of dollars. Hence, the actual released funds total approximately $5.128 million.

[10]The management of inventory is discussed in Chapter 18.

Drake's fixed-asset turnover ratio is \$112,760/\$31,700 = 3.56 times, considerably below the industry average of 4.6 times. However, a financial analyst should acknowledge the shortcomings of the ratio and perform further analyses before concluding that the company makes inefficient use of its property, plant, and equipment.

Total Asset Turnover Ratio The total asset turnover ratio is defined as follows:

(3.6)
$$\text{Total asset turnover} = \frac{\text{Sales}}{\text{Total assets}}$$

It indicates how effectively a firm uses its total resources to generate sales and is a summary measure influenced by each of the asset management ratios previously discussed.

Drake's total asset turnover ratio is \$112,760/\$81,890 = 1.38 times, whereas the industry average is 1.82 times. In view of Drake's other asset turnover ratios, the firm's relatively poor showing with regard to this ratio is not surprising. Each of Drake's major asset investment programs—accounts receivable, inventory, and property, plant, and equipment—has been found apparently lacking. The analyst could look at these various ratios and conclude that Drake is not generating the same level of sales from its assets as other firms in the industry.

3-2d Financial Leverage Management Ratios

financial leverage management ratios

Whenever a company finances a portion of assets with any type of fixed-charge financing—such as debt, preferred stock, or leases—the firm is said to be using *financial leverage.* **Financial leverage management ratios** measure the degree to which a company is employing financial leverage and, as such, are of interest to creditors and owners alike.

Both long- and short-term creditors are concerned with the amount of leverage a company employs because it indicates the company's risk exposure in meeting debt service charges (that is, interest and principal repayment). A company that is heavily financed by debt offers creditors less protection in the event of bankruptcy. For example, if a company's assets are financed with 85 percent debt, the value of the assets can decline by only 15 percent before creditors' funds are endangered. In contrast, if only 15 percent of a company's assets are debt financed, asset values can drop by 85 percent before jeopardizing the creditors.

Owners are interested in financial leverage because it influences the rate of return they can expect to realize on their investment and the degree of risk involved. For example, if a firm is able to borrow funds at 6 percent and employ them at 10 percent, the owners earn the 4 percent difference and are likely to view financial leverage favorably. On the other hand, if the firm can earn only 3 percent on the borrowed funds, the −3 percent difference (3%−6%) will result in a lower rate of return to the owners.[11]

Either balance sheet or income statement data can be used to measure a firm's use of financial leverage. The balance sheet approach gives a *static* measure of financial leverage at a specific point in time and emphasizes *total* amounts of debt, whereas the income statement approach provides a more *dynamic* measure and relates required interest payments on debt and other fixed liability charges to the firm's ability to pay. Both approaches are employed widely in practice.

There are several types of financial leverage management ratios, including the *debt ratio*, the *debt-to-equity ratio*, the *times interest earned ratio*, and the *fixed-charge coverage ratio.*

[11]The trade-off between risk and return resulting from the use of financial leverage is discussed in Chapters 13 and 14.

Debt Ratio The debt ratio is defined as follows:

(3.7) $$\text{Debt ratio} = \frac{\text{Total debt}}{\text{Total assets}}$$

It measures the proportion of a firm's total assets that is financed with creditors' funds. As used here, the term *debt* encompasses all short- and long-term liabilities.

Bondholders and other long-term creditors are among those likely to be interested in a firm's debt ratio. They tend to prefer a low debt ratio because it provides greater protection in the event of liquidation or some other major financial problem. As the debt ratio increases, so do a firm's fixed-interest charges. If the debt ratio becomes too high, the cash flows a firm generates during economic recessions may not be sufficient to meet interest payments. Thus, a firm's ability to market new debt obligations when it needs to raise new funds is crucially affected by the size of the debt ratio and by investors' perceptions about the risk implied by the level of the ratio.

Debt ratios are stated in terms of percentages. Drake's debt ratio as of year-end 2016 is ($25,523 + $22,000)/$81,890 = $47,523/$81,890 = 0.58, or 58 percent. The ratio is interpreted to mean that Drake's creditors are financing 58 percent of the firm's total assets. This figure is considerably higher than the 47 percent industry average, indicating that Drake has less unused borrowing capacity than the average firm in the industry.

A high debt ratio implies a low *proportionate equity base*, that is, the percentage of assets financed with equity funds. As the proportionate equity base declines, investors are more hesitant to acquire a firm's debt obligations. Whether Drake can continue to finance its assets with 58 percent of "outsider" money largely depends on the growth and stability of future earnings and cash flows.

Because most interest costs are incurred on long-term borrowed funds (greater than one year to maturity) and because long-term borrowing places multiyear, fixed financial obligations on a firm, some analysts also consider the ratio of *long-term debt-to-total assets*, or *long-term debt-to-equity* (discussed in the following section). Another modification that is sometimes made in these ratios is to include the capitalized value of noncancellable financial leases (discussed in Chapter 19) in the numerator. Some analysts also include a firm's preferred stock with its debt when computing these ratios because preferred stock dividends, like interest requirements, are usually viewed as contractual obligations of the firm.

Debt-to-Equity Ratio The debt-to-equity ratio is defined as follows:

(3.8) $$\text{Debt-to-equity ratio} = \frac{\text{Total debt}}{\text{Total equity}}$$

It is similar to the debt ratio and relates the amount of a firm's debt financing to the amount of equity financing. The debt-to-equity ratio, in actuality, is not really a new ratio. It is simply the debt ratio in a different format.

The debt-to-equity ratio is also stated as a percentage. Drake's debt-to-equity ratio at year-end 2016 is $47,523/$34,367 = 1.383, or 138.3 percent. Because the industry average is 88.7 percent, Drake's ratio indicates that the firm uses more than the usual amount of borrowed funds to finance its activities. Specifically, it raises nearly $1.38 from creditors for each dollar invested by stockholders, which is interpreted to mean that the firm's debt suppliers have a lower margin of safety than is common in the industry. In addition, Drake has a greater potential for financial distress if earnings do not exceed the cost of borrowed funds.

Times Interest Earned Ratio The times interest earned ratio is defined as follows:

(3.9) $$\text{Times interest earned} = \frac{\text{Earnings before interest and taxes (EBIT)}}{\text{Interest charges}}$$

Often referred to as simply *interest coverage*, this ratio tells an analyst the extent to which the firm's current earnings are able to meet current interest payments. The **EBIT** figures are used because the firm makes interest payments out of operating income, or EBIT. When the times interest earned ratio falls below 1.0, the continued viability of the enterprise is threatened because the failure to make interest payments when due can lead to bankruptcy.

EBIT

You may have noticed that unlike the two previous leverage ratios (debt ratio and debt-to-equity ratio), which are based on the balance sheet, this ratio employs income statement data. Some analysts think this is a better measure of long-term solvency (ability to service long-term obligations) than a balance sheet–based measure of leverage as it tells you how much earnings (EBIT) a firm has per dollar of interest expense. To the extent that interest expense is paid from earnings, a firm that has no earnings will be unable to pay its interest obligations.[12] It is possible that a firm may have a low debt ratio *and* a low interest coverage ratio (and vice versa), which is why many analysts consider the interest coverage ratio to be a stronger measure of long-term solvency.

Drake's times interest earned ratio for 2016 is \$11,520/\$3,160 = 3.65 times. In other words, it covers annual interest payments 3.65 times; this figure is considerably below the industry norm of 6.7 times. This ratio is further evidence that the company makes extensive use of creditors' funds to finance its operations.

Fixed-Charge Coverage Ratio The fixed-charge coverage ratio is defined as follows:

(3.10)

$$\text{Fixed-charge coverage} = \frac{\text{EBIT} + \text{Lease payments}}{\text{Interest} + \text{Lease payments} + \text{Preferred dividends before tax} + \text{Before-tax sinking fund}}$$

It measures the number of times a firm is able to cover total *fixed charges*, which include (in addition to interest payments) preferred dividends and payments required under long-term lease contracts. Many companies are also required to make *sinking fund* payments on bond issues, which are annual payments aimed at either retiring a portion of the bond obligation each year or providing for the ultimate redemption of bonds at maturity.[13]

In calculating the fixed-charge coverage ratio, an analyst must consider each of the firm's obligations on a *before-tax* basis. However, because sinking fund payments and preferred stock dividends are not tax deductible and therefore must be paid out of after-tax earnings, a mathematical adjustment has to be made. After-tax payments must be divided by $(1 - T)$, where T is the marginal tax rate. This effectively converts such payments to a before-tax basis, or one that is comparable to the EBIT.[14] And, since lease payments are deducted in arriving at the EBIT, they must be added back into the numerator of the ratio because the fixed charges (in the denominator) also include lease payments.

---

[12]Strictly speaking, this is only true of earnings that equate to cash flows. The next chapter distinguishes between earnings and cash flows.

[13]Sinking fund provisions are covered in greater detail in Chapter 6.

[14]The rationale for this computation is as follows:

$$\begin{aligned}\text{Earnings after taxes} &= \text{Earnings before taxes} - \text{Taxes}\\ &= \text{Earnings before taxes} - \text{Earnings before taxes} \times T\\ &= \text{Earnings before taxes } (1 - T)\\ \frac{\text{Earnings after taxes}}{1-T} &= \text{Earnings before taxes}\end{aligned}$$

The fixed-charge coverage ratio is a more severe measure of a company's ability to meet fixed financial obligations. With figures from Drake's income statement for 2016,[15] the fixed-charge coverage ratio can be calculated as follows:

$$\frac{\$11{,}520 + \$150}{\$3{,}160 + \$150 + \$2{,}000/(1 - 0.4)} = \frac{\$11{,}670}{\$6{,}643} = 1.76 \text{ times}$$

Because the industry average is 4.5 times, once again it is apparent that Drake provides creditors with a smaller margin of safety—that is, a higher level of risk—than the average firm in the industry. As a result, Drake is probably straining its relations with creditors. If a tight money situation developed in the economy, Drake's high debt and low coverage ratios would most likely limit the firm's access to new credit sources, and Drake might be forced to curtail operations or borrow on prohibitively expensive and restrictive terms.

3-2e Profitability Ratios

More than any other accounting measure, a firm's *profits*[16] demonstrate how well its management is making investment and financing decisions. If a firm is unable to provide adequate returns in the form of dividends and share price appreciation to investors, it may be unable to maintain, let alone increase, its asset base. **Profitability ratios** measure how effectively a firm's management is generating profits on sales, total assets, and, most importantly, stockholders' investment. Therefore, anyone whose economic interests are tied to the long-run survival of a firm will be interested in profitability ratios.

profitability ratios

There are several types of profitability ratios, including the *gross profit margin ratio*, the *net profit margin ratio*, the *return on investment ratio*, and the *return on stockholders' equity ratio*.

Gross Profit Margin Ratio

The gross profit margin ratio is defined as follows:

(3.11)
$$\text{Gross profit margin} = \frac{\text{Sales} - \text{Cost of sales}}{\text{Sales}}$$

It measures the relative profitability of a firm's sales after the cost of sales has been deducted, thus revealing how effectively the firm's management is making decisions regarding pricing and the control of production costs.

Drake's gross profit margin ratio for 2016 is \$27,460/\$112,760 = 24.4 percent, just slightly below the industry average of 25.6 percent. This percentage indicates that either Drake's pricing policies or its production methods are not quite as effective as those of the average firm in the industry. Differences in inventory accounting methods (and, to a lesser extent, depreciation methods) used by Drake and the firms included in the industry average also influence the cost of sales and, by extension, the gross profit margin.

Net Profit Margin Ratio

The net profit margin ratio is defined as follows:

(3.12)
$$\text{Net profit margin} = \frac{\text{Earnings after taxes (EAT)}}{\text{Sales}}$$

It measures how profitable a company's sales are after all expenses, including taxes and interest, have been deducted.

Some analysts also compute an *operating profit margin ratio*, defined as EBIT/sales. It measures the profitability of a firm's operations before considering the effects of

[15]Some analysts exclude preferred dividend payments when computing the fixed-charge coverage ratio. In the calculation that follows, the \$150 represents annual long-term lease payments and the \$2,000 represents sinking fund obligations.

[16]The terms *profits*, *earnings*, and *net income* are used interchangeably in this discussion.

financing decisions. Because the operating profit margin is computed before considering interest charges, this ratio is often more suitable for comparing the profit performance of different firms.

A variant of the operating profit margin is the EBITDA margin, defined as (earnings before interest, taxes, depreciation, and amortization)/sales. The advantage of this ratio is that it is not influenced by noncash expenses such as depreciation and amortization, which vary with firm age and the particular depreciation policy followed by the firm. Also, EBITDA is highly correlated with the cash flow of the firm, which is a better measure of the soundness of a firm than its accounting earnings.

Drake's net profit margin ratio for 2016 is \$5,016/\$112,760 = 4.45 percent, which is below the industry average of 5.1 percent and is interpreted to mean that the company is earning 0.65 percent less on each dollar of sales than the average firm in the industry. This percentage indicates that Drake may be having difficulty controlling either total expenses (including interest, operating expenses, and the cost of sales) or the prices of its products. In this case, the former is probably more accurate, because Drake's financial structure contains a greater proportion of debt, resulting in more interest charges.

Return on Investment (Total Assets) Ratio The return on investment ratio is defined as follows:

(3.13)
$$\text{Return on investment} = \frac{\text{Earnings after taxes (EAT)}}{\text{Total assets}}$$

It measures a firm's net income in relation to the total asset investment.

Drake's 2016 return on investment ratio, \$5,016/\$81,890, is 6.13 percent, which is considerably below the industry average of 9.28 percent and is a direct result of the firm's low asset management ratios and low profit margins.

Some analysts also like to compute the ratio of EBIT to total assets. This measures the operating profit rate of return for a firm. An after-tax version of this ratio is earnings before interest and after tax (EBIAT) divided by total assets. These ratios are computed before interest charges and may be more suitable when comparing the operating performance of two or more firms that are financed differently.

Return on Stockholders' Equity Ratio The return on stockholders' equity ratio is defined as follows:

(3.14)
$$\text{Return on stockholders' equity} = \frac{\text{Earnings after taxes (EAT)}}{\text{Stockholders' equity}}$$

It measures the rate of return that the firm earns on stockholders' equity. Because only the stockholders' equity appears in the denominator, the ratio is influenced directly by the amount of debt a firm is using to finance assets.

Drake's 2016 return on stockholders' equity ratio is \$5,016/\$34,367 = 14.60 percent. Again, Drake's ratio is below the industry average of 17.54 percent. The firm's low asset management ratios and low profit margins result in profitability ratios inferior to the industry norms, even after the effects of debt financing (financial leverage) are considered.

3-2f Market-Based Ratios

The financial ratios discussed in the previous four groups are all derived from accounting income statement and balance sheet information provided by the firm. Analysts and investors are also interested in the financial market's assessment of the performance of

market-based ratios

a firm. The **market-based ratios** for a firm should parallel the accounting ratios of that firm. For example, if the accounting ratios of a firm suggest that the firm has more risk than the average firm in the industry and has lower profit prospects, this information should be reflected in a lower market price of that firm's stock.

Price-to-Earnings (P/E) Ratio

The price-to-earnings ratio is defined as follows:

$$\text{P/E} = \frac{\text{Market price per share}}{\text{Current earnings per share}} \tag{3.15}$$

(Some security analysts use the next year's projected earnings per share in the denominator. This makes sense since when buying a stock, investors are buying the *future* earnings stream of the company.)

The P/E ratio tells us how much the market (investors) is willing to pay per dollar of earnings of the firm. In general, *the lower the firm's risk, the higher its P/E ratio* should be. In addition, *the better the growth prospects of its earnings, the greater is the P/E multiple.* For example, Arm Holdings, which makes microprocessors and is prominent in the high-growth mobile device sector and a major supplier to Apple's iPhones, had a P/E ratio of 46.3 in late 2015. On the other hand, Intel, a much larger rival but one that had been unable to break into the high-growth mobile device sector and therefore had lower future growth expectations, had only a P/E ratio of 15.2 in late 2015.

Drake's current 2016 earnings per share are $3.86 (earnings of $5,016 ÷ 1,300 shares).[17] If Drake's current market price is $24 per share, its P/E ratio is 6.22 times. This is below the industry average of eight times, and indicates that Drake has either higher risk than the average firm, lower growth prospects, or both.

As a supplement to the price-to-earnings ratio, financial analysts sometimes also examine a firm's *stock price to cash flow* and *stock price to free cash flow ratio.* In these alternative ratios, rather than dividing the stock price by earnings per share, we divide it by cash flow per share and free cash flow per share, respectively. Cash flow per share is calculated as (EAT + Depreciation − Preferred dividends, if any) ÷ Common shares outstanding. Some financial experts prefer to use price to cash flow ratio over price to earnings ratio because depreciation is a noncash expense. Price to free cash flow is a stricter measure that reduces the cash flow by the amount of capital expenditures. Cash flow and free cash flow are often viewed as a better measure than earnings of the financial soundness of a firm. Earnings data can sometimes be misleading because accounting rules give companies discretion in such areas as the recognition of revenues that have not been received and the allocation of costs over different time periods.[18] For example, Integrated Resources and Todd Shipyards had good earnings but had negative cash flow and were ultimately forced to file for bankruptcy.

Market Price-to-Book Value (P/BV) Ratio

The market-to-book ratio is defined as follows:

$$\text{P/BV} = \frac{\text{Market price per share}}{\text{Book value per share}} \tag{3.16}$$

Generally, the higher the rate of return a firm is earning on its common equity relative to the return required by investors (the cost of common equity), the higher will be the P/BV ratio.

---

[17]If Drake had preferred shares outstanding, we would have to subtract preferred dividends from net earnings (EAT) before dividing by common shares outstanding. Also note that we calculated our own earnings per share. Accounting rules require that firms report both basic and diluted earnings per common share in their financial statements. The *basic earnings per share* is calculated as net income after payment of preferred dividends divided by the *average* number of common shares outstanding during the course of the year. The *diluted earnings per share* calculation takes into account the potential dilutive effect of convertible securities and/or stock options outstanding. For example, in 2014 Netflix reported basic and diluted earnings per share of $4.44 and $4.32, respectively.

[18]The issue of earnings quality is discussed in greater detail later in the chapter.

The book value per share of common stock is determined by dividing the total common stockholders' equity for a firm by the number of shares outstanding. In the case of Drake at year-end 2016, the book value per share is equal to $26.44 (stockholders' equity of $34,367 divided by 1,300 shares outstanding).[19] With a market price per share of $24, the market-to-book ratio for Drake is 0.91. This compares unfavorably with the industry average of 1.13.

It should be noted that, because the market-to-book ratio contains the book value of the common stockholders' equity in the denominator (remember that common stockholders' equity is equal to total assets minus total liabilities),[20] it is affected by the accounting treatments used by a firm in such crucial areas as inventory valuation and depreciation. For this reason, comparisons between firms can often be misleading.

EV-EBITDA (EV/EBITDA) Multiple Sometimes simply known as the *EBITDA multiple*, it is the enterprise value of the firm divided by earnings before interest, taxes, depreciation, and amortization.[21] It is calculated as follows:

(3.17)
$$\frac{\text{EV}}{\text{EBITDA}} = \frac{\text{Enterprise value}}{\text{Earnings before interest, taxes, depreciation, and amortization}}$$

Unlike the P/B and P/E ratios, the EBITDA multiple takes into account the entire capital structure of the firm, that is, the values of debt and equity, and earnings (cash flow), available to all capital holders. Thus, it is an aggregate measure of value that tells us the overall worth of the company per dollar of earnings (cash flow) available to all capital holders. Enterprise value is calculated as the sum of the market value of common stock plus the market value of debt.[22] Because the market value of debt is hard to obtain, we usually substitute the book value of debt in its place. The EBITDA multiple is especially useful when a firm is considering buying another firm and is trying to determine how much to pay for it.

For Drake, the market value of equity is calculated as the price per share multiplied by common shares outstanding: $24 × 1,300 = $31,200. The book value of debt is $47,523. Adding the two values yields an enterprise value for Drake of $78,723. Drake's EBITDA is obtained by taking the EBIT and adding back depreciation (Drake did not report any amortization): $11,520 + $1,900 = $13,420. Taking the ratio of EV to EBITDA gives Drake's EBITDA multiple: $78,723/$13,420 = 5.87. This compares with an industry EBITDA multiple of 7.0. Thus, Drake, taking the firm as a whole, is valued at a discount compared to the rest of the industry. This is consistent with the lower P/E ratio for Drake compared to the industry average.

3-2g Dividend Policy Ratios

The two primary dividend policy ratios, the payout ratio and the dividend yield, give insights regarding a firm's dividend strategies and its future growth prospects.

Payout Ratio The payout ratio indicates the percentage of a firm's earnings that are paid out as dividends to its common shareholders. It is defined as:

(3.18)
$$\text{Payout ratio} = \frac{\text{Dividends per share}}{\text{Earnings per share}}$$

---

[19] If Drake had preferred stock outstanding, then the preferred stock amount would have to be subtracted from stockholders' equity to arrive at common stockholders' equity.

[20] This assumes the firm does not have any preferred stock.

[21] Some analysts prefer to subtract cash from enterprise value in the numerator.

[22] If the firm utilizes preferred stock in its capital structure, then the market value of preferred stock is also included as part of enterprise value. If the market value of preferred stock is unavailable, the book value may be substituted.

In the case of Drake, the payout ratio is equal to 55.7 percent ($2.15 annual 2016 dividends ÷ $3.86 annual 2016 earnings per share). As discussed in Chapter 15, companies are extremely reluctant to cut their dividends because of the negative signal such an action transmits to the financial marketplace. Accordingly, companies with stable earnings are more likely to pay out a greater proportion of their earnings as dividends than are companies with more volatile earnings. Also, companies with a large, continuing number of high-return investment projects are less likely to pay out a high proportion of earnings as dividends because of their need for the capital to finance these projects.

dividend yield

Dividend Yield A stock's **dividend yield** is the expected yearly dividend divided by the current stock price, or:

$$\text{Dividend yield} = \frac{\text{Expected dividend per share}}{\text{Stock price}} \tag{3.19}$$

The current dividend yield for Drake is 8.96 percent ($2.15 dividend divided by the $24 stock price). As discussed in Chapter 7, the returns received by an investor in common stock are the sum of the dividend yield and expected growth in the company's earnings, dividends, and ultimately its stock price. Stocks with a low dividend yield often indicate high expected future growth. High dividend yields, such as are common for utility companies, are frequently indicators of low future growth prospects. *Very* high dividend yields often signal a company facing financial difficulty that the market expects to be accompanied by future cuts in the dividend amount.

3-3 Summary of Financial Ratio Analysis

Table 3.5 lists all the financial ratios calculated for the Drake Manufacturing Company, summarizing the comparative financial ratio analysis undertaken for the firm.

The assessment column to the right of the table contains an evaluation of each of Drake's ratios in comparison with the industry averages. For example, the firm's liquidity position is rated fair to satisfactory. Although its current ratio is somewhat below the industry norm, its quick ratio is satisfactory, indicating that Drake probably has sufficient liquidity to meet maturing obligations. The firm's asset structure is not generating sufficient sales revenues, however. Drake's asset management ratios indicate that the firm is investing too much in receivables and inventories, as well as property, plant, and equipment, relative to the sales volume being generated. Thus, Drake should consider implementing more stringent credit and collection policies as well as better inventory controls. The firm should also evaluate its investment in property, plant, and equipment to determine whether reductions could be made without impairing operations.

Drake's financial leverage ratios indicate that the firm is using significantly more debt to finance operations than the average firm in the industry. Because of its poor coverage ratios, the company may have difficulty obtaining debt financing for further asset additions. In the event of an economic slowdown, Drake's creditors would probably reevaluate the firm's borrowing capacity and make fewer funds available to it. If Drake wants to restore its borrowing capacity, it should take steps to increase its equity base. The market-based ratios confirm the analysis performed using Drake's financial statements, and the dividend policy ratios indicate that the firm may have low growth prospects.

It should be emphasized that the ratios discussed in this analysis are interrelated. For example, Drake is using more debt and investing more in receivables and inventories than the average firm in the industry. If the company could reduce its investment in receivables and inventories and use the released funds to lower debt, *both* the asset management ratios and the financial leverage ratios would be closer to the industry averages.

3-4 Trend Analysis

trend analysis

Thus far, the analysis of the Drake Manufacturing Company has focused solely on the year 2016. This has provided a fairly complete, if rather static, picture of the company's situation at that particular point in time in comparison with industry standards. To gain insight into the direction the company is moving, however, a trend analysis should be performed. A **trend analysis** indicates a firm's performance *over time* and reveals whether its position is improving or deteriorating relative to other companies in the industry.

A trend analysis requires that a number of different ratios be calculated over several years and plotted to yield a graphic representation of the company's performance. Figure 3.1 depicts a trend analysis for the Drake Company for the years 2010–2016 and indicates the direction the firm has been taking for the past several years. Each of the four different categories of financial ratios is represented in the figure. For example, it is evident that the firm's liquidity position—as measured by the quick ratio—has declined gradually over the seven-year period, falling to slightly below the industry average in 2016. Unless this downward trend continues, however, liquidity should not be a major problem for the firm.

The trend analysis tells another story about the firm's leverage and profitability. Drake's use of debt has exceeded the industry average since 2012. The asset management ratios—the total asset turnover ratio and the average collection period ratio—indicate that the company has used much of this new debt to finance additional assets, including a buildup in receivables. Unfortunately, the new assets have not produced offsetting increases in profits. As a result, returns on investment have dropped below the industry standards by increasing amounts over the past seven years.

In summary, the comparative financial ratio analysis and the trend analysis combined provide a fairly clear picture of Drake's performance. As is evident from the analysis, Drake has employed excessive debt to finance asset additions that have not been sufficiently productive in generating sales revenues. The result is returns on investment and stockholders' equity that are significantly lower than the industry average. If the firm intends to reverse these trends, it will have to make more effective use of assets and reduce the use of creditors' funds. These steps will enable the firm to improve relations with creditors and potentially increase profitability and reduce risk for its owners.

3-5 Analysis of Profitability: Return on Investment

THOMSON ONE Business School Edition

The preceding discussion of ratios indicates that a firm's return on investment (ROI) is defined as the ratio of earnings after taxes (EAT) to total assets. The ROI ratio can be examined more closely to provide additional insights into its significance.

TABLE 3.5

Ratio Analysis Summary for the Drake Manufacturing Company

Ratio	Definition
LIQUIDITY	
1. Current ratio	$\frac{\text{Current assets}}{\text{Current liabilities}}$
2. Quick ratio (acid test)	$\frac{\text{Current assets} - \text{Inventories}}{\text{Current liabilities}}$
ASSET MANAGEMENT	
3. Average collection period	$\frac{\text{Accounts receivable}}{\text{Credit sales}/365}$
4. Inventory turnover	$\frac{\text{Cost of sales}}{\text{Average inventory}}$
5. Fixed-asset turnover	$\frac{\text{Sales}}{\text{Fixed assets}}$
6. Total asset turnover	$\frac{\text{Sales}}{\text{Total assets}}$
FINANCIAL LEVERAGE MANAGEMENT	
7. Debt ratio	$\frac{\text{Total debt}}{\text{Total assets}}$
8. Debt-to-equity ratio	$\frac{\text{Total debt}}{\text{Total equity}}$
9. Times interest earned	$\frac{\text{Earnings before interest and taxes (EBIT}}{\text{Interest charges}}$
10. Fixed-charge coverage	$\frac{\text{EBIT} + \text{Lease payments}}{\text{Interest} + \text{Lease payments} + \text{Preferred stock dividends before tax} + \text{Before-tax sinking fund}}$
PROFITABILITY	
11. Gross profit margin	$\frac{\text{Sales} - \text{Cost of sales}}{\text{Sales}}$
12. Net profit margin	$\frac{\text{Earnings after taxes (EAT)}}{\text{Sales}}$
13. Return on investment	$\frac{\text{Earnings after taxes (EAT)}}{\text{Total assets}}$
14. Return on stockholders' equity	$\frac{\text{Earnings after taxes(EAT)}}{\text{Stockholders' equity}}$
MARKET-BASED	
15. Price-to-earnings ratio	$\frac{\text{Market price per share}}{\text{Current earnings per share}}$
16. Market-to-book ratio	$\frac{\text{Market price per share}}{\text{Book value per share}}$
17. EV-EBITDA Multiple	$\frac{\text{Enterprise value}}{\text{Earnings before interest, taxes, depreciation, and amortization}}$
DIVIDEND POLICY	
18. Payout ratio	$\frac{\text{Dividends per share}}{\text{Earnings per share}}$
19. Dividend yield	$\frac{\text{Expected dividends per share}}{\text{Stock price}}$

(Continued)

TABLE 3.5

Ratio Analysis Summary for the Drake Manufacturing Company *(Continued)*

Calculation	Industry Average	Assessment
$\frac{\$50{,}190}{\$25{,}523} = 1.97$ times	2.40 times	Fair
$\frac{\$22{,}660}{\$25{,}523} = 0.89$ times	0.92 times	Satisfactory
$\frac{\$18{,}320}{\$112{,}760/365} = 59.3$ days	47 days	Unsatisfactory
$\frac{\$85{,}300}{(\$27{,}530 + \$26{,}470)/2} = 3.16$ times	3.9 times	Unsatisfactory
$\frac{\$112{,}760}{\$31{,}700} = 3.56$ times	4.6 times	Poor
$\frac{\$112{,}760}{\$81{,}890} = 1.38$ times	1.82 times	Poor
$\frac{\$47{,}523}{\$81{,}890} = 58$ percent	47 percent	Poor
$\frac{\$47{,}523}{\$34{,}367} = 138.3$ percent	88.7 percent	Poor
$\frac{\$11{,}520}{\$3{,}160} = 3.65$ times	6.7 times	Poor
$\frac{\$11{,}520 + \$150}{\$3{,}160 + \$150 + \$2{,}000/(1 - 0.4)} = 1.76$ times	4.5 times	Poor
$\frac{\$27{,}460}{\$112{,}760} = 24.4$ percent	25.6 percent	Fair
$\frac{\$5{,}016}{\$112{,}760} = 4.45$ percent	5.10 percent	Unsatisfactory
$\frac{\$5{,}016}{\$81{,}890} = 6.13$ percent	9.28 percent	Poor
$\frac{\$5{,}016}{\$34{,}367} = 14.60$ percent	17.54 percent	Poor
$\frac{\$24}{\$3.86} = 6.22$ times	8.0 times	Poor
$\frac{\$24}{\$26.44} = 0.91$ times	1.13 times	Poor
$\frac{\$78{,}723}{\$13{,}420} = 5.87$ times	7.0 times	Poor
$\frac{\$2.15}{\$3.86} = 55.7$ percent	28 percent	High, implying low growth prospects or lower earnings risk
$\frac{\$2.15}{\$24} = 8.96$ percent	4.2 percent	High, implying low growth prospects

FIGURE 3.1

Trend Analysis of the Financial Ratios for the Drake Manufacturing Company from 2010 to 2016

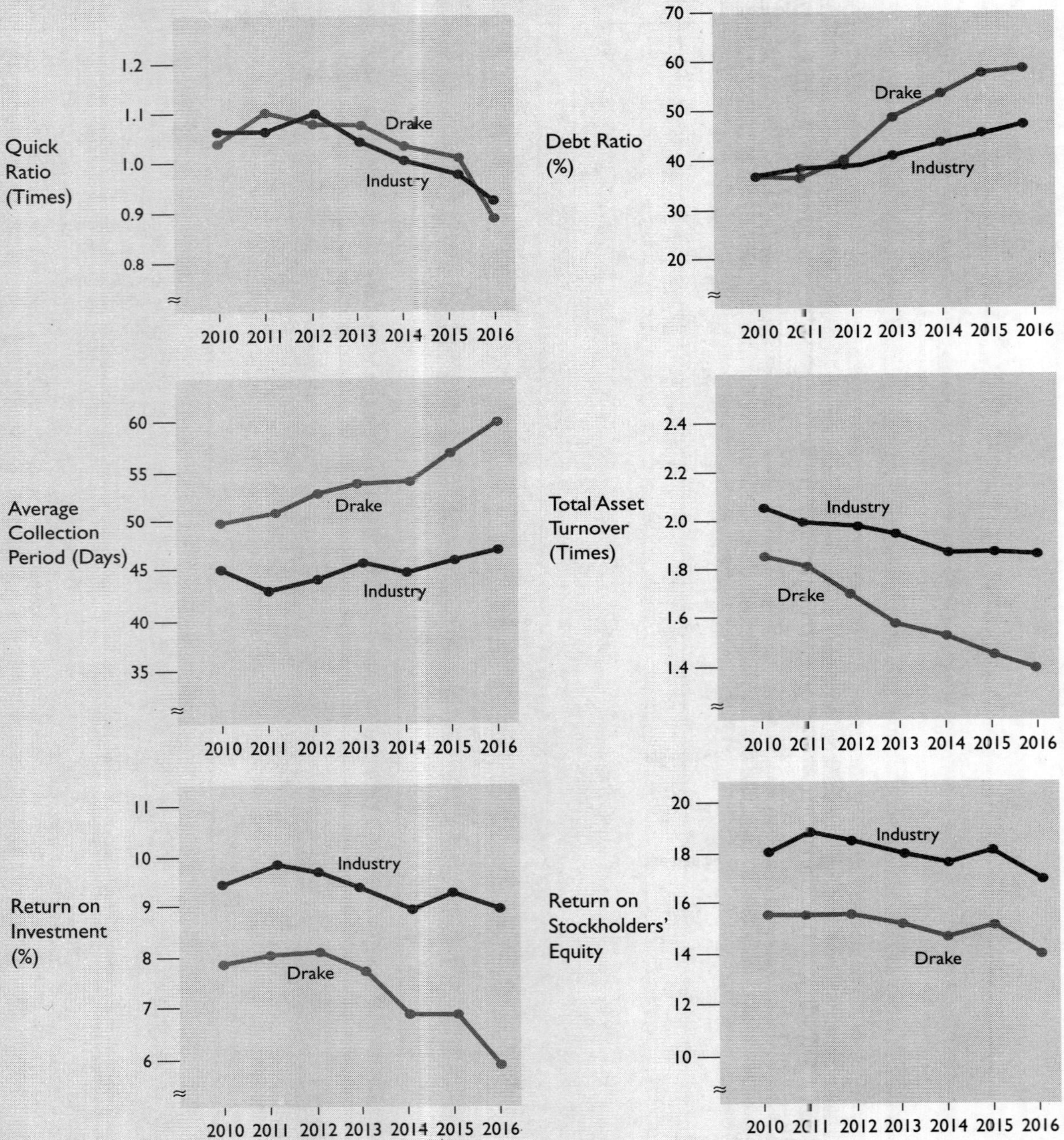

The ROI can also be viewed as a function of the net profit margin times the total asset turnover because the net profit margin ratio = EAT/sales and the total asset turnover ratio = sales/total assets:

(3.20)
$$\text{ROI} = \frac{\text{EAT}}{\text{Total assets}} = \frac{\text{EAT}}{\text{Sales}} \times \frac{\text{Sales}}{\text{Total assets}}$$

It is important to examine a firm's ROI in terms of "margin" and "turnover," because each plays a major role in contributing to profitability. "Margin" measures the profit earned per dollar of sales but ignores the amount of assets used to generate sales. The ROI relationship brings these two components together and shows that a deficiency in either one will lower a firm's return on investment.

Using the figures from the net profit margin ratio and total asset turnover ratio calculated previously for the Drake Company, the firm's ROI for 2016 can be computed as 4.45% × 1.377 = 6.13 percent. Note that this figure is equal to the one obtained by calculating the ROI directly: EAT/Total assets = \$5,016/\$81,890 = 6.13 percent. Figure 3.2, called a *modified DuPont chart* because it was developed and first used by the DuPont Corporation, illustrates this relationship. For purposes of comparison, the industry average ROI = 5.10% × 1.82 = 9.28 percent. The ROI relationship shows Drake to be deficient in both margin and turnover relative to the industry average. Improvement in either area would increase the firm's ROI.

FIGURE 3.2

Modified DuPont Analysis for the Drake Manufacturing Company, 2016

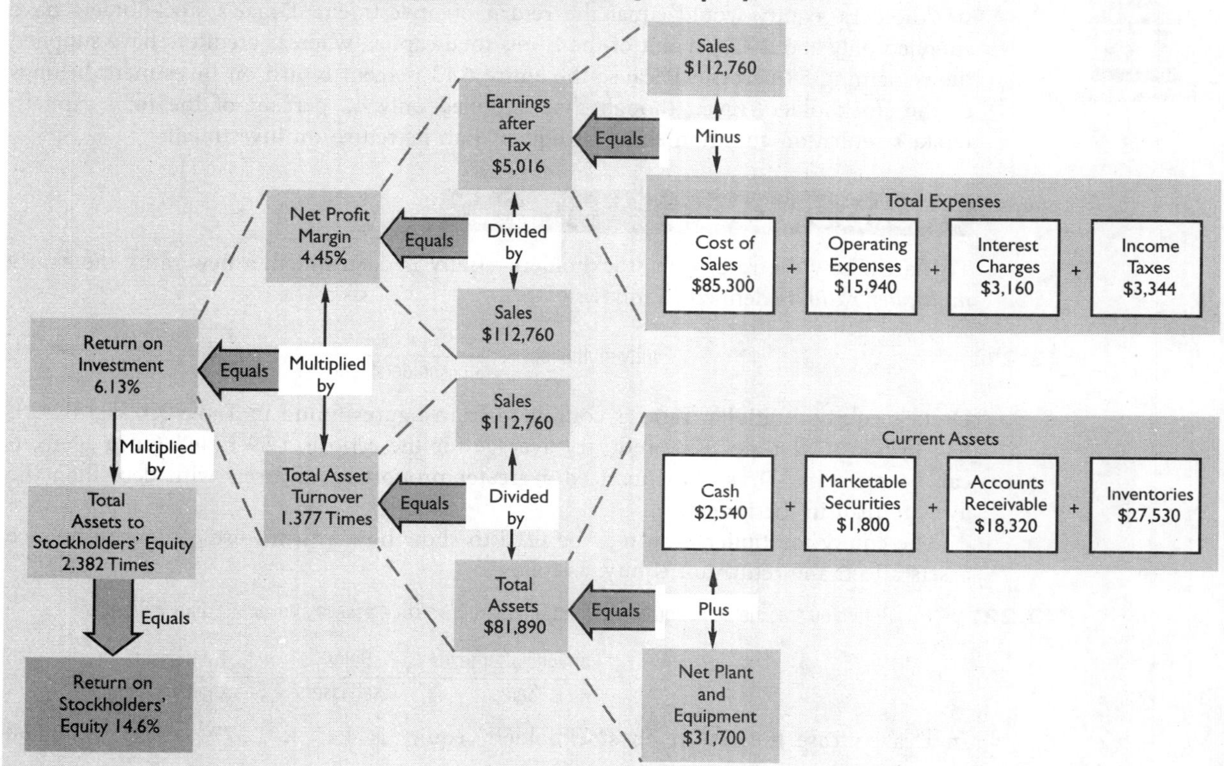

To improve its *margin*, for example, Drake must either increase sales revenues more than costs or decrease costs more than sales revenues. To improve its *turnover*, the firm must either increase sales revenue or reduce the asset level required to support the current sales volume. The DuPont chart illustrates the relationship between a firm's ROI and the factors that determine it. By working back through the DuPont chart, an analyst can begin to pinpoint potential areas for improvement that will enhance the firm's ROI.

The relative contributions of the net profit margin and the asset turnover ratio in the ROI relationship differ from industry to industry. Specifically, the turnover ratio is dependent largely on a firm's investment in property, plant, and equipment. Firms with large investments in fixed assets tend to have low turnover ratios; public utilities, railroads, and large industrial firms fall into this category. If these companies are to succeed, their relatively low turnover ratios must be offset by correspondingly high margins to produce competitive ROIs. For example, electric and gas utilities typically have net profit margins of 10–15 percent. In contrast, other industries require much lower investments in fixed assets, resulting in higher turnover ratios. A typical example is the retail grocery chain industry, which has margins of only 1 or 2 percent. Firms in this industry often achieve turnovers of 10 times or more. If a grocery chain had a lower turnover, its ROI probably would not be sufficient to attract investors.

3-6 Analyzing Profitability Through Return on Stockholders' Equity

Foundation Concept

Figure 3.2 also shows Drake's return on stockholders' equity, which is computed as 14.60 percent. If the firm were financed solely with common equity (stock), the return on stockholders' equity would equal the return on investment. Drake's stockholders have supplied only about 42 percent of the firm's total capital, whereas creditors have supplied the remaining 58 percent. Because the entire 6.13 percent return on investment belongs to the stockholders (even though they supplied only 42 percent of the total capital), Drake's return on common equity is higher than its return on investment.

THOMSON ONE Business School Edition

To clarify how the return on stockholders' equity is determined, a new ratio, the *equity multiplier ratio*, is defined as follows:

(3.21)
$$\text{Equity multiplier} = \frac{\text{Total assets}}{\text{Stockholders' equity}}$$

Drake's equity multiplier ratio is computed from figures found in Table 3.1 as $81,890/$34,367 = 2.382 times. The industry average for the ratio is 1.89 times. Once again, it can be seen that Drake has financed a greater proportion of assets with debt than the average firm in the industry.

The equity multiplier ratio may be used to show how a firm's use of debt to finance assets affects the return on equity, as follows:

(3.22)
$$\text{Return on stockholders' equity} = \text{Net profit margin} \times \text{Total asset turnover} \times \text{Equity multiplier}$$
$$= \frac{\text{Earnings after taxes}}{\text{Sales}} \times \frac{\text{Sales}}{\text{Total assets}} \times \frac{\text{Total assets}}{\text{Stockholders' equity}}$$

In Drake's case the return on stockholders' equity is 4.45 × 1.377 × 2.382 = 14.60 percent.

Although this figure is the same as the return on equity computed directly by dividing earnings after tax by stockholders' equity, the calculations shown illustrate more clearly how Drake managed to magnify a 6.13 percent return on total investment into a 14.60 percent return on stockholders' equity by making more extensive use of debt financing than did the average firm in the industry. This increased use of debt has improved Drake's return on equity but has also increased its risk—more likely resulting in a decline in Drake's stock price relative to other, similar firms.

3-7 Sources of Comparative Financial Data

THOMSON ONE Business School Edition

An analyst may refer to a number of sources of financial data when preparing a comparative financial analysis, including the following:

HTTP: www.dnb.com

- **Dun & Bradstreet**. Dun & Bradstreet (D&B) prepares a series of 14 key business ratios for 800 different lines of business. These ratios are based on the financial statements of some hundreds of thousands of companies. Because of the extensive coverage, D&B reports are useful for assessing the performance of small and medium-sized companies. D&B reports three values for each ratio—the *median*, the *upper quartile*, and the *lower quartile*. The median is the figure that falls in the middle when individual ratios of sampled firms are arranged by size. The figure halfway between the median and the ratio with the highest value is the upper quartile, and the figure halfway between the median and the ratio with the lowest value is the lower quartile. By reporting three values for each ratio, D&B enables the analyst to compare a particular firm with the "average" (median) firm, as well as with the "typical" firms in the top and bottom halves of the sample. The D&B publication containing the data is titled *Industry Norms and Key Business Ratios*.

HTTP: www.rmahq.org/RMA

- **Risk Management Association**. This national association of bank loan and credit officers uses information provided by loan applications to compile 19 ratios for over 800 industries. Like D&B, Risk Management Association reports the median, upper quartile, and lower quartile for each ratio. Data are presented for six categories of firm size. This source is especially useful to the analyst gathering information about smaller firms. The Risk Management Association publication containing the data is titled *Annual Statement Studies*.

HTTP: www.census.gov/econ/qfr

- **Quarterly Financial Report for Manufacturing, Mining, Trade, and Selected Trade Industries**. Produced quarterly by the U.S. Census Bureau, the report includes analyses of the firms by industry and asset size, along with presentations of financial statements in ratio form.
- **Moody's (now called Mergent) or Standard & Poor's Industrial, Financial, Transportation, and Over-the-Counter Manuals**. These contain a large amount of balance sheet and income statement data, as well as other relevant background information about a firm.

HTTP: www.moodys.com www.standardandpoors.com

- **Annual reports**. Most corporations publish an annual report containing income statement and balance sheet data, along with other information of interest. Annual reports can be easily obtained from the company's Web site or by contacting the company.
- **10K reports**. Every widely held firm is required annually to file a 10K report with the SEC. These reports contain income statement and balance sheet data, plus a wide range of other relevant information dealing with the firm's past and current performance and expected future prospects. The 10K reports can be accessed online from the SEC's Web site (www.sec.gov).
- **Trade journals**. These are published by trade associations and contain a great deal of financial and other types of information on member firms.
- **Commercial banks**. Banks frequently compile financial reports on selected industries.
- **Internet/electronically accessible data sources**. A number of Internet/electronically accessible databases are also available to assist in financial analysis. These tend to be expensive but are used extensively by the finance profession and available at many universities. Standard and Poor's Capital IQ Platform has data on thousands of public and private companies including data on financial statement variables, market prices (for public companies), ownership, governance, and management, among many

HTTP:
Financial data on firms (financial statements, ratio analyses, histories, products, profit projections, etc.) are available at many Web sites. Some are free, and others charge a monthly fee. Here are a few:

www.hoovers.com
www.sec.gov
www.bloomberg.com
www.corpfinet.com
www.valueline.com
finance.yahoo.com
money.msn.com

others. Both current and historical data are available. The Thomson Reuters *Worldscope* database contains financial data on over 50,000 companies from around the world. The University of Chicago *CRSP* database contains stock price information for thousands of U.S. companies going back to 1926. Thomson Reuters *Datastream* contains security price information for stocks and bonds for thousands of firms across the globe. *Value Line* provides summary financial data and forecasts of future performance for over 1,700 widely followed firms and more limited information on an additional 1,800 small and medium-sized firms. The *Value Line* database is available both in hard copy and via Internet. Most of these data sources can be accessed via the Internet, but most require subscription. However, in a number of Internet sources, financial information on companies and the markets in general is available for free. Search engines such as Yahoo! and Google are an excellent source of financial data. Several of these Internet sources are noted in the margin.

3-8 A Word of Caution About Financial Ratio Analysis

Throughout the analysis of the Drake Manufacturing Company, we emphasized that an analyst must exercise caution when evaluating a firm's financial ratios. Although ratios can provide valuable information, they can also be misleading for a number of reasons.

generally accepted accounting principles (GAAP)

First, ratios are only as reliable as the accounting data on which they are based. The financial statements of most U.S. companies are prepared in accordance with **generally accepted accounting principles (GAAP).**[23] In the United States, the Financial Accounting Standards Board issues *Statements of Financial Accounting Standards* (SFAS), which describe accounting rules that companies must follow in preparing their financial statements. Even though careful financial analysis can provide excellent insights into the direction and relative strength of the firm, the financial analyst must keep in mind that GAAP gives firms considerable latitude in reporting their financial positions. Different firms follow different accounting procedures for inventory valuation, depreciation, reporting long-term leases, pension fund contributions, and mergers and acquisitions, to name just a few. These, in turn, affect reported earnings, assets, and owners' investments. Unless the analyst makes adjustments for accounting reporting differences, ratio comparisons between individual companies and with various industry norms cannot be viewed as definitive.

Second, with the exception of disclosing upper and lower quartile values, firms that compile industry norms often do not report information about the dispersion, or distribution, of the individual values around the mean ratio. If the reported ratios are dispersed widely, the industry average will be of questionable value because it may not reflect the so-called typical firm in the industry. Furthermore, the standard of comparison probably should not be the "typical" firm, but rather the better-performing firms in the industry. Without some measure of dispersion, however, ratios for these better-performing firms cannot be determined.

comparative analysis

Third, valid **comparative analysis** depends on the availability of data for appropriately defined industries. Some industry classifications are either too broad or too narrow to be reliable sources of comparative data when an analyst is evaluating a particular firm. Most firms operate in more than one industry, which makes analysis more difficult.

Fourth, it is important to remember that financial ratios provide a *historic* record of the performance and financial condition of a firm. Further analysis is required before this historic record can be used as a basis for future projections.

[23]Most of the countries outside of the United States follow the International Financial Reporting Standards (IFRS). Although U.S. GAAP and IFRS standards have a lot in common, there are also differences. Many believe that in the future there will be convergence between U.S. GAAP and IFRS.

Finally, comparisons of a firm's ratios with industry norms may not always be what they seem. Ratios comparing unfavorably with industry norms should be construed as red flags indicating the need for further investigation—not signals of impending doom. On the other hand, even if a firm's ratios compare favorably with those of the better-performing firms in the industry, it does not necessarily mean the firm is performing adequately. If, for example, the industry itself is experiencing a declining demand for its goods and services, favorable ratio comparisons may simply indicate that a firm is not decaying as rapidly as the typical firm in the industry. Thus, comparisons of selected ratios—particularly those relating to profitability—must be made with *national* industry averages in order to determine whether a particular firm in a particular industry is justified in making further investments.

In summary, ratios should not be viewed as substitutes for sound business judgment. Instead, they are simply tools that can help management make better decisions.

3-9 Earnings and Balance Sheet Quality and Financial Analysis

When performing a financial analysis of a firm, an analyst must be mindful of the *quality of the earnings* reported by a firm, as well as the *quality of the firm's balance sheet.* These two dimensions of financial analysis can have a critical impact on the final assessment of the firm's financial condition.

3-9a Earnings Quality

When one is considering the quality of a firm's earnings, two key factors should be kept in mind. First, high-quality earnings tend to be cash earnings. The proportion of a firm's earnings that can be viewed as cash earnings is greatly influenced by the firm's procedures with respect to sales revenue recognition. For example, a firm may recognize a sale at the time a contract is signed, a down payment is made, or when the full proceeds from the sale are actually collected as cash. Generally, the closer the recognition of a sale is to the time the full proceeds from that sale are collected, the higher is the quality of the firm's reported earnings.

Although there is frequently a close correlation between a firm's earnings and its cash flows over time, generally accepted accounting principles give companies substantial latitude in the reporting of earnings. Distortions in earnings can arise from such issues as the time of revenue recognition, the establishment of reserves for such items as loan loss provisions in banking, the amortization of intangible assets, and the like.

The earnings management tricks used by some companies include:[24]

1. *Timing store openings and asset sales in a way that keeps earnings growing at a smooth rate.* General Electric has been a master at using this strategy over the years.

---

[24]N. Byrnes, R. Melcher, and D. Sparks, "Earnings Hocus-Pocus," *Business Week* (October 5, 1998): 134–142; J. Fox, "Learn to Play the Earnings Game (and Wall Street Will *Love* You)," *Fortune* (March 31, 1997): 77–80; R. Smith and S. Lipin, "Are Companies Using Restructuring Costs to Fudge the Figures?" *The Wall Street Journal* (January 30, 1996): A11; David Dreman, "Fantasy Earnings," *Forbes* (October 1, 2001): 134; and J. Revell, "Forget About Earnings," *Fortune* (June 11, 2001): 224; James Bandler and Mark Maremont, "Xerox to Pay $10 Million in SEC Case," *The Wall Street Journal* (April 2, 2002): A3; Jonathon Weil, "Another AOL Time Warner Writeoff?" *The Wall Street Journal* (August 23, 2002): C1; Jessie Drucker, "Motorola's Profit: Special Again?" *The Wall Street Journal* (October 15, 2002): C1; Gardiner Harris, "At Bristol-Myers, Ex Executives Tell of Numbers Games," *The Wall Street Journal* (December 12, 2002): A1; Gardiner Harris, "Bristol-Myers Says Accounting Was 'Inappropriate,' Inflated Sales," *The Wall Street Journal* (March 11, 2003): A2; Scott Thurm, "Buyers Beware: The Goodwill Games," *The Wall Street Journal* (August 14, 2012), http://www.wsj.com/articles/SB100008723963904440427045775873026255354444 (accessed January 1, 2016); Jack Adamo, "Even GAAP Is Better Than These Adjustments," *Barron's* (November 4, 2013): 45.

2. *Acceleration (or delay) of shipments at the end of a quarterly reporting period to either increase sales in a weak quarter or defer sales into the next quarter when the current quarter's numbers are especially strong.* For example, Bristol-Myers Squibb in early 2003 stated that its reported sales had been inflated by as much as $2.75 billion between 1999 and 2002 because of what is known as "channel stuffing." This involved offering financial incentives to wholesalers to purchase enough of the company's products at the end of each quarter in order to meet the sales targets established by senior management. Zoomlion, a large Chinese construction equipment manufacturer, reported a 65 percent increase in excavator sales for 2012 even though the rest of the industry reported declining shipments. It turns out that Zoomlion "stretched the credit terms" to its customers, encouraging them to increase their purchases from the firm.[25] Several other prominent and not so prominent companies, including Coca-Cola, McAfee (Network Associates), and Nortel, have admitted to misleading revenue recognition practices. Rather than shifting sales, some firms attempt to shift costs to an earlier or later period. Diamond Foods, which manufactures snack items (Emerald nuts, Pop Secret popcorn, and Kettle chips), is alleged to have shifted some of the costs associated with payments to growers for nuts it purchased to the following year, thereby inflating its earnings for the 2010 fiscal year. The inflated earnings initially led to a spike in the stock price, only to lead to a sudden drop a few weeks later when the potential fraud was exposed.
3. *Capitalizing normal operating expenses.* America Online capitalized and wrote off over two years the cost of the free disks and ads it used to lure new customers. Without this accounting treatment, the company would have reported losses instead of the profits it actually recorded. Under criticism, the company finally abandoned this practice in 1997.
4. *Extending depreciable life of assets.* A common ploy to inflate earnings during difficult times is to increase the useful life of an asset, thereby reducing the depreciation expense and increasing earnings. Between 1988 and 1996, Waste Management made several changes to the useful life of various fixed assets, resulting in inflated earnings to the tune of $1.7 billion, which had to be restated subsequently.
5. *Taking "big bath" write-offs and using "spin" control for bad earnings.* Many companies have found that if they take large so-called one-time write-offs, it will be easier to meet earnings objectives in future years. AOL set the record for the largest write-down ever—a *$54.2 billion* pretax charge to cover the decline in goodwill assets it booked from its acquisition of Time Warner. More recently, in 2015 Microsoft wrote off $7.6 billion related to its acquisition of the Nokia phone business made just a year prior for $7.2 billion. While such "big bath" write-offs tend to be one-off events, many companies can be classified as repeat offenders. Boston Scientific, a manufacturer of medical care devices (e.g., pacemakers, stents, defibrillators) wrote off nearly $10 billion in asset value between 2007 and 2010 for a variety of reasons, including lower growth in Europe, lower projections due to the financial crisis, and overpayment for its purchase of Guidant (pacemaker manufacturer). Other repeat offenders include AT&T, Tyco International, and International Paper.

   In other instances, firms have resorted to "spinning," where they opportunistically blame their poor earnings on coincidental external events that may not really be the true cause of their underperformance. For example, Namico, the Dutch maker of vitamins and food supplements, blamed their poor performance on plunging sales in the United States due to the effects of terrorism. At the same time, sales

---

[25]Credit terms are discussed in Chapter 18.

by most of Namico's U.S. competitors steadily grew. In this case, "competition" seems to be cleverly disguised as terrorism.

6. *Increasing reserves in good times and drawing down on them in bad times.* Many companies create reserves for product returns, bad loans, retirement benefits, layoffs, and insurance losses. In good years, these reserve allocations can be overfunded so that, in bad years, they can be drawn against while protecting reported earnings. For example, in a settlement with the Securities and Exchange Commission (SEC), which included a $10 million fine, Xerox was required to make $400 million in adjustments to its 1997–2000 financial statements as the result of the improper establishment and release of reserves. The SEC was attempting to crack down on the use of such "cookie-jar" reserves. Commercial banks, with their loan-loss reserves, are especially able to use these practices to manage earnings.

   In a similar vein, Cisco, the largest manufacturer of networking equipment, took a $2.2 billion charge in the spring of 2001 for "obsolete" inventories. This charge was not shown as a normal expense of doing business, as is the usual way for recording inventory losses, but rather as a special, nonoperating income write-off. Then in the quarter ending in July 2001 Cisco reported that it had sold off $187 million of this "worthless" inventory and booked the proceeds as a reduction in operating expenses, thereby improving reported profits. Other serial abusers of accounting practices include Amazon.com, Yahoo!, and Qualcomm.
7. *Focusing on adjusted (non-GAAP) earnings rather than traditional or GAAP earnings.* Increasingly firms have (mis)led analysts to focus on "adjusted" or "core" or non-GAAP earnings rather than traditional or GAAP earnings, arguing that the latter often include one-time charges or temporary effects that do not reflect future earnings. While in theory, it may be a good idea to call attention to non-GAAP earnings, the motives are often to inflate earnings and increase stock price in the short run. Groupon (a daily couponing Web site), for example, in their public offering filing (IPO filing) tried to promote their earnings definition that excluded marketing costs, ostensibly to obtain a higher stock price. The Securities Exchange Commission, however, disallowed it before the firm went public.

The above examples illustrate the different ways in which firms try to manage "earnings." While most of these methods are not illegal, some rise to a level that are considered fraudulent and that require the firm to restate its earnings, similar to the example illustrated in the Financial Challenge feature at the beginning of the chapter. According to the research firm Audit Analytics, 275 large public companies had to restate their earnings in 2012, compared to 153 in 2009.

3-9b Balance Sheet Quality

The quality of a firm's balance sheet should also be of concern to a financial analyst. If the assets on a firm's balance sheet have a market value equal to or greater than the book value at which they are being carried, this enhances the quality of the firm's balance sheet. In contrast, if a significant portion of the assets of a firm has a market value substantially below book value, the quality of the firm's balance sheet is reduced. For example, Hewlett-Packard in 2012 had to write down $8.8 billion of the value of an enterprise technology firm, Autonomy, that it purchased for $11 billion just a year prior. It turned out that the purchase price was based on grossly overstated profitability of Autonomy. Commercial banks regularly write off a portion of their loan portfolios when it becomes clear that particular loans will not be repaid. In the aftermath of the recent global financial crisis, many banks had to significantly write down the value of their risky subprime loans and other assets. The International Monetary Fund (IMF) estimated the total write-down globally to exceed $1.3 trillion between 2008 and 2009. Citigroup alone accounted for over $100 billion of that. These actions greatly reduce a firm's equity ratios. Similarly, if a firm has significant amounts of inventory that cannot be moved, the quality of the balance sheet is reduced until the firm charges off this low-quality inventory.

In addition to asset quality issues, an analyst should also be aware of hidden liabilities. These liabilities may take the form of such things as long-term lease obligations not appearing on the company's balance sheet or uninsured losses arising from pending lawsuits. When large potential liabilities exist, an analyst must be quite careful before drawing conclusions about the adequacy of a firm's capital structure, based upon an analysis of its reported balance sheet.

ETHICAL ISSUES

The Sarbanes-Oxley Act and the Financial Reporting Process[a]

The accounting scandals involving such well-known companies as Enron, WorldCom, HealthSouth, Adelphia Communications, and Tyco International led to a crisis in investor confidence and a loss of faith in the reporting of financial results by corporations. Various proposals have been put forth to deal with these issues, some of which were codified into law with the passage of the Sarbanes-Oxley Act of 2002.

The primary values of good corporate governance and financial reporting should include *transparency*, *accountability*, and *integrity*.

Transparency. Companies should be willing to provide information needed by their various stakeholders (for example, shareholders, bondholders, customers) to make informed decisions. Information is transparent when it provides the user with a clear understanding of the results of the company's operations—namely, its income and cash flows, assets and liabilities, and other aspects of its business.

Accountability. There must be a strong commitment to a culture of accountability among all the participants, including the board of directors, officers of the corporation, and its external auditors. Each individual must take responsibility for carrying out his or her role in the financial reporting process.

Integrity. Transparency and accountability depend on individuals trying to "do the right thing." Doing what is expedient or even permissible is not acceptable. Integrity is the foundation for the various stakeholders being able to trust the information generated by companies.

The Sarbanes-Oxley law contains various provisions that seek to restore the public's faith in the financial reports issued by companies. The act places responsibilities on the various parties involved in the corporate reporting process.

Audit committee. The audit committee of the board of directors must consist of independent directors. At least one member of the audit committee must meet specified criteria as a "financial expert" and, if not, the reason for the absence of such a member must be specified.

Company executives. The CEO and CFO must affirm the completeness and accuracy of the company's quarterly and annual reports. Certifying a report that does not conform to the law subjects the officer to a fine of up to $1 million and a jail sentence of up to 10 years.

External auditors. The external auditor is prohibited from providing major nonaudit services to the company while engaged in an audit capacity.

The Sarbanes-Oxley Act established the Public Company Accounting Oversight Board, under the direction of the SEC, to monitor compliance with the law. Whether this law will restore investor trust and confidence depends on many factors. These include the qualifications and character of company directors, whether the directors remain vigilant, and the amount of information management shares with the board. As Nell Minow, editor of the *Corporate Library*, a governance research service, noted, "There is no structure that can't be subverted."[b]

[a]Michael Schroeder, "Cleaner Living but Fewer Riches," *The Wall Street Journal* (July 22, 2003): C1.
[b]Amy Borrus et al., "Reform: Business Gets Religion," *Business Week* (February 3, 2003): 40.

Enron Corporation, the high-flying energy-producing and trading concern that failed in 2001, hid more than a billion dollars in liabilities in a web of partnerships and subsidiaries that were not reflected in the consolidated balance sheet of the parent corporation. In another example, FedEx reported \$1.93 billion of debt, which represented 7 percent of its firm value. This compared very favorably with the 15 percent estimated for its competitor, UPS. When operating leases, which are reported in the footnotes but not in the balance sheet, are included, the ratio for FedEx is 56 percent and only 22 percent for UPS. These differences lead to very different conclusions about the relative leverage of the two companies.[26]

In contrast, some firms have significant hidden assets. These assets may be physical assets, such as real property that has appreciated in value but is carried on the firm's books at cost, or securities that are carried on the books at cost even though the market value of these securities has increased above the original cost. These hidden assets may also consist of intangibles, such as valuable patents or brand names. For example, Amazon paid \$1.1 billion for online shoe seller Zappos.com in 2009. Two-thirds of the price reflected goodwill—that is, the brand value of Zappos.

This list of balance sheet and earnings quality issues is not all-inclusive, but it does give an indication of the extent to which a surface analysis of a firm's financial statements can lead to misleading conclusions about the financial condition of that firm. As Professor Shyam Sunder of Yale has said, "Off-balance sheet financing is a nice, gentlemanly label given to misrepresentation." Good financial analysts develop an eye for this type of deception.

3-10 Market Value Added/Economic Value Added:[27] An Alternative Measure of Performance

As already discussed, traditional financial analysis focuses on a set of financial ratios derived primarily from accounting information. Using an approach such as DuPont analysis, a firm's financial performance can be dissected into its component elements. The ultimate measure of firm performance is the return on stockholders' equity. Although insights can be gained from this type of analysis, traditional financial analysis suffers from weaknesses inherent in reported accounting information, and it does not directly consider risk in the measure of performance. The greatest shortcoming of traditional financial analysis is the lack of a direct tie between performance, as measured using financial ratios, and shareholder wealth, as measured by the market price of a firm's stock.

3-10a The Market Value Added Concept

market value added (MVA)

One measure of performance that does not have such shortcomings is **Market Value Added (MVA)**. MVA and the related Economic Value Added (EVA) measures were developed by Stern Stewart & Company. MVA is defined as the market value of debt, preferred equity, and common equity capitalization, less capital. Capital is a measure of

[26] Jacqueline Doherty, "Out of the Footnotes, Into the Spotlight," *Barron's* (June 6, 2011): 29.

[27] Irwin Ross, "The Stern Stewart Performance 1000," *Bank of America Journal of Applied Corporate Finance* (Winter 1999): 122–134.

all the cash raised from investors or retained from earnings to fund new investments in the business, since the company's inception.

(3.23) $$\text{MVA} = \text{Market value} - \text{Capital}$$

MVA is the capital market's assessment of the accumulated net present value (NPV) of all of the firm's past and projected investment projects. (Net present value is discussed in Chapter 10.) It measures the amount of wealth generated by the firm since its inception.

3-10b Economic Value Added

economic value added (EVA®)

Economic Value Added (EVA®) is a measure of operating performance that indicates how successful a firm has been at increasing the MVA of the enterprise in any given year. Analysts and investors often focus on EVA rather than MVA because they are more interested in the year-to-year performance of a company than its cumulative performance since inception. EVA is defined as:

(3.24) $$\text{EVA} = [\text{Return on total capital } (r) - \text{Cost of capital } (k)] \times \text{Capital}$$

where r = net operating profits after tax divided by beginning of year capital and k = weighted after-tax cost of capital. (Weighted after-tax cost of capital is discussed in Chapter 12.) Using this relationship, it can be seen that a firm's managers can increase EVA by (1) increasing operating efficiency and thereby increasing r; (2) committing new resources to the enterprise that promise a return in excess of the firm's weighted (and risk-adjusted) cost of capital; (3) redirecting resources from projects that do not earn adequate returns (relative to the cost of capital) and show little promise of doing so in the future, to more productive uses, including the payment of dividends and reduction of debt levels if no adequate-return projects are present; and (4) optimizing the capital structure to yield a lower cost of capital k.

HTTP:
evadimensions.com/

EVA can be thought of as the incremental contribution of a firm's operations to the creation of MVA. MVA is the present value of all expected future EVA. Firms that consistently earn returns in excess of their cost of capital will have positive EVA, thereby enhancing the MVA of the enterprise. Table 3.6 shows the EVA for some of the best and worst performing firms ranked by that measure in early 2012 from a list of approximately 1,500 firms. The table shows that Apple was the top performer, generating \$27.5 billion in EVA over the preceding year. This is not surprising in view of the extraordinary success Apple has had in bringing out new products in its iPhone, iPad, and other related product lines. In addition, Apple is known for premium pricing of its products and very efficient management. At the other extreme are companies such as Sears, which lost \$1.9 billion in EVA as it struggles to compete with more ably managed competitors like Walmart, which ranked among the top EVA generators.

One important implication of the MVA and EVA concepts is that growth in earnings does not necessarily add to the value of an enterprise (MVA) unless it is achieved by making (and managing) investments such that they earn a return in excess of the cost of capital (positive EVA).

The EVA and MVA concepts provide a useful alternative way to focus on the performance of an enterprise in the context of the objective of maximizing the value of the enterprise. This way of looking at financial analysis is appealing because it explicitly ties together the investment decisions with measures of firm performance. As such, financial managers and analysts may find this approach to firm performance analysis a useful complement to more traditional approaches.

TABLE 3.6

EVA Values for Select Firms

Rank	Company	Industry	EVA ($ million)
1	APPLE INC	Computers & Peripherals	27,524
2	MICROSOFT CORP	Software	17,470
3	WAL-MART STORES INC	Food & Staples Retailing	9,980
4	GOOGLE INC	Internet Software & Services	7,750
5	INTEL CORP	Semiconductors & Semiconductor Equipment	7,497
6	JOHNSON & JOHNSON	Pharmaceuticals	7,429
7	INTL BUSINESS MACHINES CORP	IT Services	6,841
8	ORACLE CORP	Software	6,696
9	GENERAL ELECTRIC CO	Conglomerates & Machinery	6,561
10	COCA-COLA CO	Food & Beverage	5,747
1493	CENTURYLINK INC	Diversified Telecommunication Services	−1,413
1494	MICRON TECHNOLOGY INC	Semiconductors & Semiconductor Equipment	−1,511
1495	VERISIGN INC	Internet Software & Services	−1,586
1496	VERIZON COMMUNICATIONS INC	S Diversified Telecommunication Services	−1,705
1497	DISNEY (WALT) CO	Media	−1,816
1498	SEARS HOLDINGS CORP	Specialty Retail	−1,933
1499	CBS CORP	Media	−2,083
1500	MOTOROLA SOLUTIONS INC	Communications Equipment	−2,276
1501	TIME WARNER INC	Media	−3,914
1502	JDS UNIPHASE CORP	Communications Equipment	−6,731

Source: EVA Dimensions (www.evadimensions.com).

INTERNATIONAL ISSUES

Financial Analysis of Multinational Corporations

The tools of financial analysis developed in this chapter are useful in evaluating the financial performance of purely domestic U.S. firms as well as firms with small international operations. However, assessing the financial performance and condition of a firm with sizable international operations is generally more complicated than analyzing a firm whose operations are largely domestic.

Part of the complication involves the translation of foreign operating results from the host country's currency to U.S. dollars. To illustrate, suppose Sara Lee's European Union operations show net earnings of 200 million euros. Sara Lee reports its results to stockholders denominated in U.S. dollars. Therefore, the euro income must be translated into U.S. dollars. The *dollar* amount of Sara Lee's euro earnings depends on the exchange rate between dollars and euros. If this exchange rate is 1.2 euros per dollar, the dollar earnings from 200 million euros are reported as $166.67 million (200 million euros/1.2 euros per dollar). But if the exchange rate changes to 1.5 euros/dollar, the dollar value of 200 million euros drops to $133.33 million. Conversely, strengthening of the euro to 0.8 euros per dollar increases the dollar value of 200 million euros to $250 million. Thus the earnings reported by a U.S.-based company with sizable foreign operations depend not only on the local currency earnings, but also on the exchange rate between the dollar and the local currency. When the U.S. dollar is relatively strong against a foreign currency—that is, when the dollar will buy more euros, for example—foreign earnings translate into fewer dollars than when the dollar is relatively weak.

An additional complication in financial analysis of multinational firms arises because of fluctuating exchange rates. What happens to the dollar value on the parent (Sara Lee) balance sheet of Sara Lee's European assets and liabilities as the exchange rate between euros and dollars changes? According to Statement of Accounting Standards No. 52, which deals with international accounting, assets and liabilities are normally translated at the exchange rate in effect on the balance sheet date. However, any gains or losses resulting from the translation of asset and liability accounts are not reflected on the income statement and therefore also are not included in the retained earnings figure on the balance sheet. Instead, gains and losses from foreign translation are reported separately on the balance sheet as a part of stockholders' equity, usually under a heading such as "Cumulative foreign exchange translation adjustment," or "Translation adjustments." For example, during 2005, GE reported more than a negative $4 billion in its translation adjustments account. This decrease did not affect GE's 2005 earnings, but it did change stockholders' equity on its balance sheet.

Financial managers and analysts will have to be knowledgeable about the complex international aspects of financial statement analysis.

3-11 Inflation and Financial Statement Analysis

Inflation can cause a number of problems for a financial analyst who is trying to assess the performance of a firm over time and in comparison with other firms in the industry. In particular, *inventory profits*—short-lived increased profits that occur as a result of the timing of price increases—can make a significant difference in a firm's reported earnings from year to year.

For example, consider a supply company that buys equipment parts wholesale from the manufacturer for $4.00 each and sells them at a retail price of $5.00 each, realizing a profit of $1.00 per unit. Suppose the manufacturer announces a price increase of $0.50 per unit to $4.50, effective on the first of next month. If the supply company passes the increase on to customers and announces a price increase of its own to $5.50, also effective on the first of next month, it will realize a gross profit of $1.50 on every unit sold that originally cost $4.00. In other words, the company will make additional profit on the units already in inventory *prior to the price increase*. Once it begins purchasing parts from the manufacturer at the new price of $4.50 per unit, it will revert to its original $1.00 profit. In the meantime, however, the timing of the price increase will allow the company to enjoy short-lived increased profits, or inventory profits.

Most companies do not want to pay income taxes on inventory profits, preferring to use these funds to replenish inventories—especially in inflationary times. Fortunately, there is a way of avoiding or deferring the necessity of reporting these higher profits. The

LIFO *last-in, first-out* (**LIFO**) inventory valuation method assumes that the items a firm uses from inventory are those that were acquired most recently. Thus, they can be *priced out* of the inventory based on the most recent inventory acquisition costs. In contrast, the

FIFO *first-in, first-out* (**FIFO**) method of inventory valuation, which assumes that the items a firm uses from inventory are the oldest items in inventory, results in the firm's having to show a higher profit and therefore pay higher income taxes.

The accounting method used for inventory will affect a firm's profits and its balance sheet. Hence, any financial ratio that contains balance sheet inventory figures (for example, the total asset turnover ratio) or net income will vary from one firm to another, depending on the firm's accounting treatment of inventory. Another effect of inflation on financial statements is the tendency for the value of fixed assets to be understated. Also, to the extent that inflation causes a rise in interest rates, the value of long-term debt outstanding will decline. Thus, a firm will appear to be more financially leveraged in an inflationary period than is actually the case.

Inventory profits and inflation are only two factors that can affect a firm's reported earnings. Differences in the reporting of earnings, the recognition of sales, and other factors can also make comparisons between firms somewhat misleading. Again, a good financial analyst will always "go behind" the figures stated on a firm's income statement or balance sheet to find out what is actually occurring within a company.

3-12 Summary

- Financial ratios fall into six categories:
    1. *Liquidity ratios*, which measure a firm's ability to meet its maturing obligations
    2. *Asset management ratios*, which measure how efficiently a firm is using resources to generate sales
    3. *Financial leverage management ratios*, which indicate a firm's capacity to meet short- and long-term debt obligations
    4. *Profitability ratios*, which measure the firm's ability to generate profits on sales, assets, and owners' investment
    5. *Market-based ratios*, which measure the market's (investors') perceptions of a firm's performance and risk
    6. *Dividend policy ratios*, which indicate the dividend practices of a firm
- *Common-size financial statements*, which express financial items in percentages, are helpful in detecting and monitoring financial trends.
- *Trend analysis* introduces the element of time into financial ratio analysis. It gives the analyst a more dynamic view of a company's situation than does a pure comparative financial ratio analysis alone.
- The relationship of the return on investment (ROI) to "margin" and "turnover" can be used to determine whether one or both are deficient in contributing to the profitability of a firm.
- To gain further insight into the relative financial position of a firm, the analyst must compare the financial ratios with *industry averages*. The more diversified the firm, the more difficult it will be to make such a comparison. Two major sources of industry ratios are Dun & Bradstreet and Risk Management Association.
- The quality of a firm's balance sheet is enhanced as the ratio of the market value of the firm's assets to the book value of those assets increases and as the amount of hidden liabilities that appears on the firm's balance sheet decreases.
- The *Market Value Added* concept is the market's assessment of the accumulated value created from a firm's past and projected investment projects.
- *Economic Value Added* is a *yearly* measure of the operating performance of a firm, considering investor return requirements.
- Financial statements of multinational firms are influenced by fluctuating foreign exchange rates.

Important Equations

$$\text{Current ratio} = \frac{\text{Current assets}}{\text{Current liabilities}}$$

$$\text{Quick ratio} = \frac{\text{Current assets} - \text{Inventories}}{\text{Current liabilities}}$$

(Continued)

Important Equations (*Continued*)

$$\text{Average collection period} = \frac{\text{Accounts receivable}}{\text{Annual credit sales}/365}$$

$$\text{Inventory turnover} = \frac{\text{Cost of sales}}{\text{Average inventory}}$$

$$\text{Fixed-asset turnover} = \frac{\text{Sales}}{\text{Net fixed assets}}$$

$$\text{Total asset turnover} = \frac{\text{Sales}}{\text{Total assets}}$$

$$\text{Debt ratio} = \frac{\text{Total debt}}{\text{Total assets}}$$

$$\text{Debt-to-equity ratio} = \frac{\text{Total debt}}{\text{Total equity}}$$

$$\text{Times interest earned} = \frac{\text{Earnings before interest and taxes (EBIT)}}{\text{Interest charges}}$$

$$\text{Fixed-charge coverage} = \frac{\text{EBIT} + \text{Lease payments}}{\text{Interest} + \text{Lease payments} + \text{Preferred dividends before tax} + \text{Before-tax sinking fund}}$$

$$\text{Gross profit margin} = \frac{\text{Sales} - \text{Cost of sales}}{\text{Sales}}$$

$$\text{Net profit margin} = \frac{\text{Earnings after taxes (EAT)}}{\text{Sales}}$$

$$\text{Return on investment} = \frac{\text{Earnings after taxes (EAT)}}{\text{Total assets}}$$

$$\text{Return on stockholders' equity} = \frac{\text{Earnings after taxes (EAT)}}{\text{Stockholders' equity}}$$

$$\text{P/E} = \frac{\text{Market price per share}}{\text{Current earnings per share}}$$

$$\text{P/BV} = \frac{\text{Market price per share}}{\text{Book value per share}}$$

$$\text{EV-EBITDA Multiple} = \frac{\text{Enterprise value}}{\text{Earnings before interest, taxes, depreciation, and amortization}}$$

$$\text{Payout ratio} = \frac{\text{Dividends per share}}{\text{Earnings per share}}$$

(Continued)

Important Equations (*Continued*)

$$\text{Dividend yield} = \frac{\text{Expected dividend per share}}{\text{Stock price}}$$

$$\text{ROI} = \frac{\text{EAT}}{\text{Total assets}} = \frac{\text{EAT}}{\text{Sales}} \times \frac{\text{Sales}}{\text{Total assets}}$$

$$\text{Equity multiplier} = \frac{\text{Total assets}}{\text{Stockholders' equity}}$$

$$\text{Return on stockholders' equity} = \text{Net profit margin} \times \text{Total asset turnover} \times \text{Equity multiplier}$$
$$= \frac{\text{Earnings after taxes}}{\text{Sales}} \times \frac{\text{Sales}}{\text{Total assets}} \times \frac{\text{Total assets}}{\text{Stockholders' equity}}$$

$$\text{MVA} = \text{Market value} - \text{Capital}$$

$$\text{EVA} = [\text{Return on total capital } (r) - \text{Cost of capital } (k)] \times \text{Capital}$$

3-13 Questions and Topics for Discussion

1. What are the primary limitations of ratio analysis as a technique of financial statement analysis?
2. What is the major limitation of the current ratio as a measure of a firm's liquidity? How may this limitation be overcome?
3. What problems may be indicated by an average collection period that is substantially above or below the industry average?
4. What problems may be indicated by an inventory turnover ratio that is substantially above or below the industry average?
5. What factors limit the use of the fixed-asset turnover ratio in comparative analyses?
6. What are the three most important determinants of a firm's return on stockholders' equity?
7. What specific effects can the use of alternative accounting procedures have on the validity of comparative financial analyses?
8. How can inflation affect the comparability of financial ratios between firms?
9. What is the relationship between a firm's P/E multiple and that firm's risk and growth potential?
10. Discuss the general factors that influence the quality of a company's reported earnings and its balance sheet.
11. Why would you anticipate a lower P/E ratio for a typical natural gas utility than for a computer technology firm, such as Apple?
12. Many large corporations, such as General Motors, have written off large amounts of their nonperforming (or poorly performing) assets as they have shrunk their operations. What is the impact of these asset write-offs on the future return on assets, future return on common equity, and future financial leverage ratios? What impact would you expect these write-offs to have on the market value of the firm's equity securities? Why?

13. The Farmers State Bank recently has been earning an "above average" (compared to the overall banking industry) return on total assets of 1.50 percent. The bank's return on common equity is only 12 percent, compared with an industry average of 15 percent.
a. What reasons can you give for the bank's low return on common equity?
b. What impact do you think this performance by the bank is having on the value of its debt and equity securities?

14. What is the relationship between EVA and MVA?

3-14 Self-Test Problems

The following financial data for the Freemont Corporation are to be used in answering self-test problems 1–6.

Balance Sheet ($000)

Assets		Liabilities & Stockholders' Equity	
Cash	$ 1,500	Accounts payable	$12,500
Marketable securities	2,500	Notes payable	12,500
Accounts receivable	15,000	Total current liabilities	$25,000
Inventory	33,000	Long-term debt	22,000
Total current assets	$52,000	Total liabilities	$47,000
Fixed assets (net)	35,000	Common stock (par value)	5,000
Total assets	$87,000	Contributed capital in excess of par	18,000
		Retained earnings	17,000
		Total stockholders' equity	$40,000
		Total liabilities and stockholders' equity	$87,000

Income Statement ($000)

Sales (all on credit)	$130,000
Cost of sales	103,000
Gross margin	$ 27,000
Operating expenses*	16,000
Earnings before interest and taxes	$ 11,000
Interest expense	3,000
Earnings before taxes	$ 8,000
Income tax	3,000
Earnings after taxes	$ 5,000

**Includes $200(000) in lease payments*

Other Information

Stock price	$9.50
Book value/share	$8.00
Number of shares	5,000 (000)

ST1. Calculate the following liquidity ratios:
a. Current ratio
b. Quick ratio

ST2. Calculate the following asset management ratios:
a. Average collection period
b. Inventory turnover
c. Fixed-asset turnover
d. Total asset turnover

ST3. Calculate the following financial leverage management ratios:
a. Debt ratio
b. Debt-to-equity ratio
c. Times interest earned ratio
d. Fixed-charge coverage ratio

ST4. Calculate the following profitability ratios:
a. Gross profit margin
b. Net profit margin
c. Return on investment
d. Return on stockholders' equity

ST5. Calculate the following market-based ratios:
a. Price-to-earnings ratio
b. Market price-to-book value ratio

ST6. Express the return on stockholders' equity ratio as a function of the net profit margin, total asset turnover, and equity multiplier ratios.

ST7. Thompson Electronics, Inc., is presently 100 percent equity financed and has assets of $100 million. Thompson's present net income is $9 million, and the company's marginal and average tax rates are 40 percent. In addition, Thompson has 4 million common shares outstanding, and its current annual dividend is $0.75 a share. Currently, the company is able to borrow 10 percent *perpetual* debt, that is, debt that has no maturity date. What amount of 10 percent perpetual debt would Thompson have to borrow in order to increase its return on stockholders' equity to 15 percent, assuming that the debt proceeds are used to retire equity?

3-15 Problems*

BASIC

1. Vanity Press, Inc., has annual credit sales of $1.6 million and a gross profit margin of 35 percent.
a. If the firm wishes to maintain an average collection period of 50 days, what level of accounts receivable should it carry? (Assume a 365-day year.)
b. The inventory turnover for this industry averages six times. If all of Vanity's sales are on credit, what average level of inventory should the firm maintain to achieve the same inventory turnover figure as the industry?

BASIC

2. Pacific Fixtures lists the following accounts as part of its balance sheet.

Total assets	$10,000,000
Accounts payable	$ 2,000,000
Notes payable (8%)	1,000,000
Bonds (10%)	3,000,000
Common stock at par	1,000,000
Contributed capital in excess of par	500,000
Retained earnings	2,500,000
Total liabilities and stockholders' equity	$10,000,000

*Color blocks behind the numbers denote problems that have check answers provided at the end of the book.

Compute the return on stockholders' equity if the company has sales of $20 million and the following net profit margin:

a. 3 percent
b. 5 percent

BASIC **3.** Clovis Industries had sales in 2016 of $40 million, 20 percent of which were cash. If Clovis normally carries 45 days of credit sales in accounts receivable, what are its average accounts receivable balances? (Assume a 365-day year.)

BASIC **4.** Williams Oil Company had a return on stockholders' equity of 18 percent during 2016. Its total asset turnover was 1.0 times, and its equity multiplier was 2.0 times. Calculate the company's net profit margin.

CHALLENGE **5.** Using the data in the following table for a number of firms in the same industry, do the following:

a. Compute the total asset turnover, the net profit margin, the equity multiplier, and the return on equity for each firm.
b. Evaluate each firm's performance by comparing the firms with one another. Which firm or firms appear to be having problems? What corrective action would you suggest the poorer performing firms take? Finally, what additional data would you want to have on hand when conducting your analyses?

	Firm			
(in Millions of Dollars)	**A**	**B**	**C**	**D**
Sales	$20	$10	$15	$25
Net income after tax	3	0.5	2.25	3
Total assets	15	7.5	15	24
Stockholders' equity	10	5.0	14	10

BASIC **6.** Tarheel Furniture Company is planning to establish a wholly owned subsidiary to manufacture upholstery fabrics. Tarheel expects to earn $1 million after taxes on the venture during the first year. The president of Tarheel wants to know what the subsidiary's balance sheet would look like. The president believes that it would be advisable to begin the new venture with ratios that are similar to the industry average.

Tarheel plans to make all sales on credit. All calculations assume a 365-day year. In your computations, you should round all numbers to the nearest $1,000.

Based upon the industry average financial ratios presented here, complete the projected balance sheet for Tarheel's upholstery subsidiary.

	Industry Averages
Current ratio	2:1
Quick ratio	1:1
Net profit margin ratio	5%
Average collection period	20 days
Debt ratio	40%
Total asset turnover ratio	2 times
Current liabilities/stockholders' equity	20%

Forecasted Upholstery Subsidiary Balance Sheet

Cash	____	Total current liabilities	____
Accounts receivable	____	Long-term debt	____
Inventory	____	Total debt	____
Total current assets	____	Stockholders' equity	____
Net fixed assets	____	Total liabilities and stockholders' equity	____
Total assets	____		

INTERMEDIATE

7. The Sooner Equipment Company has total assets of $100 million. Of this total, $40 million was financed with common equity and $60 million with debt (both long term and short term). Its average accounts receivable balance is $20 million, and this represents an 80-day average collection period. Sooner believes it can reduce its average collection period from 80 to 60 days without affecting sales or the dollar amount of net income after taxes (currently $5 million). What will be the effect of this action on Sooner's return on investment and its return on stockholders' equity if the funds received by reducing the average collection period are used to buy back its common stock at book value? What impact will this action have on Sooner's debt ratio?

INTERMEDIATE

8. The Jamesway Printing Corporation has current assets of $3.0 million. Of this total, $1.0 million is inventory, $0.5 million is cash, $1.0 million is accounts receivable, and the balance is marketable securities. Jamesway has $1.5 million in current liabilities.

a. What are the current and the quick ratios for Jamesway?
b. If Jamesway takes $0.25 million in cash and pays off $0.25 million of current liabilities, what happens to its current and quick ratios? What happens to its real liquidity?
c. If Jamesway sells $0.5 million of its accounts receivable to a bank and uses the proceeds to pay off short-term debt obligations, what happens to its current and quick ratios?
d. If Jamesway sells $1.0 million in new stock and places the proceeds in marketable securities, what happens to its current and quick ratios?
e. What do these examples illustrate about the current and quick ratios?

INTERMEDIATE

9. Gulf Controls, Inc., has a net profit margin of 10 percent and earnings after taxes of $600,000. Its current balance sheet follows:

Current assets	$1,800,000	Current liabilities	$ 600,000
Fixed assets	2,200,000	Long-term debt	1,000,000
Total assets	$4,000,000	Common stock	500,000
		Retained earnings	1,900,000
		Total liabilities and stockholders' equity	$4,000,000

a. Calculate Gulf's return on stockholders' equity.
b. The industry average ratios are as follows:

Net profit margin	6%
Total asset turnover	2.5 times
Equity multiplier	1.4 times

Compare Gulf Controls with the average firm in the industry. What is the source of the major differences between the Gulf and the industry average ratios?

CHALLENGE **10.** Using the following data for Jackson Products Company, answer Parts a through g:

Jackson Products Company's Balance Sheet December 31, 2016

Cash	$ 240,000	Accounts payable	$ 380,000
Accounts receivable	320,000	Notes payable (9%)	420,000
Inventory	1,040,000	Other current liabilities	50,000
Total current assets	$1,600,000	Total current liabilities	$ 850,000
Net plant and equipment	800,000	Long-term debt (10%)	800,000
Total assets	$2,400,000	Stockholders' equity	750,000
		Total liabilities and stockholders' equity	$2,400,000

Income Statement for the Year Ended December 31, 2016

Net sales (all on credit)		$3,000,000
Cost of sales		1,800,000
Gross profit		$1,200,000
Selling, general, and administrative expenses		860,000
Earnings before interest and taxes Interest:		$340,000
Notes	$37,800	
Long-term debt	80,000	
Total interest charges		117,800
Earnings before taxes		$ 222,200
Federal income tax (40%)		88,880
Earnings after taxes		$ 133,320

Industry Averages

Current ratio	2.5:1
Quick ratio	1.1:1
Average collection period (365-day year)	35 days
Inventory turnover ratio	2.4 times
Total asset turnover ratio	1.4 times
Times interest earned ratio	3.5 times
Net profit margin ratio	4.0%
Return on investment ratio	5.6%
Total assets/stockholders' equity (equity multiplier) ratio	3.0 times
Return on stockholders' equity ratio	16.8%
P/E ratio	9.0 times

a. Evaluate the liquidity position of Jackson relative to that of the average firm in the industry. Consider the current ratio, the quick ratio, and the net working capital (current assets minus current liabilities) for Jackson. What problems, if any, are suggested by this analysis?

b. Evaluate Jackson's performance by looking at key asset management ratios. Are any problems apparent from this analysis?

c. Evaluate the financial risk of Jackson by examining its times interest earned ratio and its equity multiplier ratio relative to the same industry average ratios.

d. Evaluate the profitability of Jackson relative to that of the average firm in its industry.
e. Give an overall evaluation of the performance of Jackson relative to other firms in its industry.
f. Perform a DuPont analysis for Jackson. What areas appear to have the greatest need for improvement?
g. Jackson's current P/E ratio is seven times. What factor(s) are most likely to account for this ratio relative to the higher industry average ratio?

INTERMEDIATE **11.** Given the following data for Profiteers, Inc., and the corresponding industry averages, perform a trend analysis of the return on investment and the return on stockholders' equity. Plot the data and discuss any trends that are apparent. Also, discuss the underlying causes of these trends.

	Years				
	2012	**2013**	**2014**	**2015**	**2016**
Profiteers, Inc.					
Net profit margin	14%	12%	11%	9%	10%
Asset turnover	1.26 ×	1.22 ×	1.20 ×	1.19 ×	1.21 ×
Equity multiplier	1.34 ×	1.40 ×	1.61 ×	1.65 ×	1.63 ×

	Years				
	2012	**2013**	**2014**	**2015**	**2016**
Industry Averages					
Net profit margin	12%	11%	11%	10%	10%
Asset turnover	1.25 ×	1.27 ×	1.30 ×	1.31 ×	1.34 ×
Equity multiplier	1.42 ×	1.45 ×	1.47 ×	1.51 ×	1.53 ×

INTERMEDIATE **12.** If a company sells additional common stock and uses the proceeds to increase its inventory level and to increase its cash balances, what is the near-term (immediate) impact (increase, decrease, no change) of this transaction on the following ratios?
a. Current ratio
b. Return on stockholders' equity
c. Quick ratio
d. Debt to total assets
e. Total asset turnover

INTERMEDIATE **13.** Keystone Resources has a net profit margin of 8 percent and earnings after taxes of $2 million. Its current balance sheet is as follows:

Current assets	$ 6,000,000	Current liabilities	$ 3,500,000
Fixed assets	10,000,000	Long-term debt	5,500,000
Total assets	$16,000,000	Common stock	2,000,000
		Retained earnings	5,000,000
		Total liabilities and stockholders' equity	$16,000,000

a. Calculate Keystone's return on stockholders' equity.
b. Industry average ratios are

Net profit margin	10%
Total asset turnover	2.0 times
Equity multiplier	1.5 times

What does a comparison of Keystone to these averages indicate about the firm's strengths and weaknesses?

c. Keystone has inventories of $3.2 million. Compute the firm's quick ratio.

INTERMEDIATE **14.** Palmer Chocolates, a maker of chocolates that specializes in Easter candy, had the following inventories over the past year:

Month	Inventory Amount
January	$25,000,000
February	60,000,000
March	90,000,000
April	30,000,000
May	20,000,000
June	22,000,000
July	25,000,000
August	38,000,000
September	50,000,000
October	60,000,000
November	70,000,000
December	30,000,000

Palmer had sales of $290 million over the past year. Cost of sales constituted 50 percent of sales. Calculate Palmer's inventory turnover using beginning of year inventory, end of year inventory, and a monthly average inventory. Which method do you feel is most appropriate? Why?

BASIC **15.** The stock of Jenkins Corporation, a major steel producer, is currently selling for $50 per share. The book value per share is $125. In contrast, the price per share of Dataquest's stock is $40, compared to a book value per share of $10. Dataquest, a leading software developer, has a copyright on the best-selling database management program. Why do these two firms have such dramatically different market-to-book ratios?

CHALLENGE **16.** Hoffman Paper Company, a profitable distributor of stationery and office supplies, has an agreement with its banks that allows Hoffman to borrow money on a short-term basis to finance its inventories and accounts receivable. The agreement states that Hoffman must maintain a current ratio of 1.5 or higher *and* a debt ratio of 50 percent or lower. Given the following balance sheet, determine how much additional money Hoffman could borrow at this time to invest in inventory and accounts receivable without violating the terms of its borrowing agreement.

Cash	$ 50,000	Current liabilities	$ 200,000
Accounts receivable	150,000	Long-term debt	300,000
Inventory	250,000	Stockholders' equity	630,000
Fixed assets (net)	680,000		
Total assets	$1,130,000	Total liabilities and stockholders' equity	$1,130,000

CHALLENGE

17. Sun Minerals, Inc., is considering issuing additional long-term debt to finance an expansion. Currently, the company has $50 million in 10 percent debt outstanding. Its after-tax net income is $12 million, and the company is in the 40 percent tax bracket. The company is required by the debt holders to maintain its times interest earned ratio at 3.5 or greater.

a. What is the present coverage (times interest earned) ratio?
b. How much additional 10 percent debt can the company issue now and maintain its times interest earned ratio at 3.5? (Assume for this calculation that earnings before interest and taxes remain at their present level.)
c. If the interest rate on additional debt is 12 percent, how much unused "debt capacity" does the company have?

INTERMEDIATE

18. The balance sheet and income statement of Eastland Products, Inc., are as follows:

Balance Sheet, December 31, 2016 (in Millions of Dollars)

Current assets	$ 40	Current liabilities	$ 30
Fixed assets, net	110	Long-term debt	40
		Common stock ($1 par)	5
		Contributed capital in excess of par value	20
		Retained earnings	55
Total assets	$150	Total liabilities and equity	$150

Income Statement for Year Ended December 31, 2016 (in Millions of Dollars)

Sales	$120
Cost of sales	80
EBIT	$ 40
Interest	5
EBT	$ 35
Taxes (40%)	14
Net income (EAT)	$ 21

Additional Information

Total dividends	$10 million
Market price of common stock	$32 a share
Number of common shares issued	5 million

Using these data, determine the following:

a. Earnings per share
b. Price-to-earnings ratio
c. Book value per share
d. Market-to-book ratio
e. EV-EBITDA multiple. Assume the cost of sales includes $10 million in depreciation expenses. Assume there are no amortization expenses.
f. How much of the retained earnings total was added during 2016?
g. Show Eastland's new balance sheet after the company sells 1 million new common shares in early 2017 to net $30 a share. Part of the proceeds, $10 million, is used to reduce current liabilities, and the remainder is temporarily deposited in the company's bank account. Later, this remaining amount (along with additional long-term debt financing) will be invested in new manufacturing facilities.

INTERMEDIATE **19.** Fill in the balance sheet for the Jamestown Company based on the following data (assume a 365-day year):

- **Sales = $3,650,000**
- **Total asset turnover = 4×**
- **Current ratio = 3:1**
- **Quick ratio = 2:1**
- **Current liabilities to net worth = 30%**
- **Average collection period = 20 days**
- **Total debt to total assets = 0.4**

Balance Sheet

Cash	____	Accounts payable	____
Accounts receivable	____	Total current liabilities	____
Inventory	____	Long-term debt	____
Total current assets	____	Stockholders' equity	____
Fixed assets			
Total assets	____	Total liabilities and equity	____

INTERMEDIATE **20.** The Southwick Company has the following balance sheet ($000):

Assets		**Liabilities and Stockholders' Equity**	
Cash	$ 500	Accounts payable	$ 1,750
Marketable securities	750	Notes payable	1,250
Accounts receivable	2,000	Total current liabilities	$ 3,000
Inventory	2,500	Long-term debt	1,750
Total current assets	$ 5,750	Total liabilities	$ 4,750
Plant and equipment (net)	5,000	Common stock ($1 par)	1,000
Total assets	$10,750	Contributed capital in excess of par	2,000
		Retained earnings	3,000
		Total stockholders' equity	$ 6,000
		Total liabilities and stockholders' equity	$10,750

Financial Ratios

Current ratio	1.92
Quick ratio	1.08
Debt-to-equity ratio	0.79

Evaluate the impact of each of the following (independent) financial decisions on Southwick's current, quick, and debt-to-equity ratios:

a. The firm reduces its inventories by $500,000 through more efficient inventory management procedures and invests the proceeds in marketable securities.

b. The firm decides to purchase 20 new delivery trucks for a total of $500,000 and pays for them by selling marketable securities.

c. The firm borrows $500,000 from its bank through a short-term loan (seasonal financing) and invests the proceeds in inventory.

d. Southwick borrows $2 million from its bank through a five-year loan (interest due annually, principal due at maturity) and uses the proceeds to expand its plant.

e. The firm sells $2 million (net) in common stock and uses the proceeds to expand its plant.

INTERMEDIATE **21.** Armbrust Corporation is the maker of fine fitness equipment. Armbrust's bank has been pressuring the firm to improve its liquidity. Which of the following actions proposed by the CFO do you believe will actually achieve this objective? Why or why not?

a. Sell new equity and use the proceeds to purchase a new plant site.

b. Use cash and marketable securities to pay off short-term bank borrowings and accounts payable.

c. Borrow long-term and use the proceeds to pay off short-term debt.

d. Sell surplus fixed assets and invest the proceeds in marketable securities.

BASIC **22.** Use Yahoo's finance site, finance.yahoo.com, to access the data needed to perform a comparative financial analysis of Delta Airlines and Southwest Airlines (Hint: Enter the ticker symbol for the firm and get the stock quote for the firm).

CHAPTER 4

Financial Planning and Forecasting

KEY CHAPTER CONCEPTS

1. Firms need to conduct two types of planning: strategic planning, and a subset, operational planning.
   a. Strategic planning is long range in nature and deals with the overall direction of the firm.
   b. Operational planning serves as a blueprint detailing where the firm wants to be at some future point in time and what resources are needed to get there.
2. Financial forecasting involves the estimation of the firm's future needs for funds. Pro forma financial statements, that is, balance sheets, income statements, and cash budgets, are an integral part of financial forecasting. They show the results of assumed events rather than actual events.
3. Cash flows are the ultimate source of financial value. Therefore, cash flow analysis and forecasting are important parts of a firm's financial plans.
4. After-tax cash flow is equal to earnings after tax plus noncash charges.
5. The statement of cash flows shows the effects of a firm's operating, investing, and financing activities on its cash balance.
6. The percentage of sales forecasting method is used in estimating the amount of additional financing that a firm will need for a given increase in sales, based on certain assumptions about the relationship between sales and the various asset and liability accounts.
7. A cash budget is the projection of a firm's cash receipts and disbursements over a future time period and is useful in determining the amount of short-term funds the firm will need to borrow.

FINANCIAL CHALLENGE

How Planning Saved Ford Motor Company from Bankruptcy

Friedrich Stark/Alamy Stock Photo

In 2006, the U.S. auto industry was enjoying near peak auto sales at slightly over 17 million units (trucks and cars). However, dark clouds loomed on the horizon. The U.S. consumer was overleveraged with unsustainable levels of credit card, mortgage, and other consumer debt. Additionally, a real estate bubble was in the making, and gasoline prices were trending upward. This and other factors conspired to create the financial crisis of 2007–2010. (For more on this, see the section titled "Overview of the Financial Crisis Beginning in 2007" in Chapter 2.) Not surprisingly, the financial crisis had disastrous consequences for the auto industry, particularly on the Big Three U.S. auto manufacturers (General Motors, Ford Motor, and Chrysler), who were overinvested in fuel-inefficient trucks and sport utility vehicles. The Big Three also had several other challenges including an inflated cost structure owing to expensive unionized wage contracts and a bloated management structure.

One firm, however, fared better than the others during the ensuing financial crisis. Both General Motors and Chrysler had to resort to government bailout money to sustain their operations. Both of these firms also declared bankruptcy in 2009. Ford Motor was the only Big Three U.S. auto firm that did not seek government bailout money and that did not declare bankruptcy. What set Ford Motor apart from the other two U.S. auto companies? In a word, it was planning. In 2006, the board and top management of Ford realized that they were on a collision course with financial distress, if something was not done soon. With the help of their new CEO, Alan Mulally, formerly head of Boeing, and the board of directors, Ford's top management put together a strategic plan called "The Way Forward." The plan's aim was to restructure the company to meet the challenges it was facing and was going to face in the coming years.

The plan contained many elements discussed in this chapter, including strategic, operational, and financial aspects. The plan included shuttering many plants, investing in new fuel-efficient models, changing the way decisions are made, and so on. All of this, however, takes money. Despite record losses in 2006 (over \$14 billion), Ford raised \$18 billion in new debt. Because of the losses, Ford could raise these funds only because it offered up virtually all of its assets as collateral. Even so, the debt cost was quite high, prompting the major rating agencies to push Ford's bond rating further into the junk category. Rather than a large offering of debt in 2006, Ford could have chosen the alternative of raising the debt as it needed, thus avoiding having to pay interest on idle funds. In fact, several analysts had criticized Ford for taking on this massive amount of debt, even though it did not need it right away. However, Ford's management viewed the debt as an insurance policy against the uncertainty that was just around the corner and was thus willing to pay a little extra for this safety. This turned out to be prescient on the part of management in as much as the credit markets froze in 2008 during the height of the financial crisis. As a result, Ford did not have to resort to government bailout funds, while the other two U.S. auto firms had no choice.

Because of its planning, Ford suffered a smaller loss in its market share during the downturn and was able get back to its pre-crisis market share by 2010, while GM and Chrysler suffered significant declines in their market shares. In 2010 Ford had a market share of 16.4 percent, which exceeded the 16 percent market share it held prior to the crisis in 2007. On the other hand, GM had an 18.8 percent market share in 2010, considerably less than the 23.9 percent share held in 2007; while Chrysler's market share in 2010 was 9.2 percent, down from 12.5 percent in 2007. The planning paid off in profitability when Ford announced a net income of \$2.7 billion in 2009, the first profitable year in four years. GM has since emerged from bankruptcy and so has Chrysler, though it is now owned by the Italian auto giant Fiat. Ford continues to lead in profitability with an operating profit

FINANCIAL CHALLENGE — CONTINUED

margin of 2.6 percent in 2014, which compares very favorably with an operating profit margin of approximately 1 percent each for GM and Fiat Chrysler. Additionally, Ford has worked down its debt. At the end of 2014, its long-term debt was 38 percent of total assets, down from a peak of 59 percent in 2009. Ford regained its investment grade rating on its debt in 2012 after having lost it for seven years.

Sources: Bryce G. Hoffman, "Ford Bets the House," *The Detroit News* (November 28, 2006), taken from www.detnews.com; Bill Koenig, "Ford Borrows $18B for Restructuring," *The Denver Post* (November 27, 2010), taken from denverpost.com; Ian Armitage, "Ford CEO Alan Mulally: The Turnaround Specialist," (August 10, 2010), www.manufacturingdigital.com.

CHAPTER OBJECTIVES

Upon completion of this chapter, you should have a clear understanding of the following:

1. The importance of financial planning
2. Interpreting the statement of cash flows
3. Forecasting the funds needed using the percentage of sales method and pro forma financial statements
4. Developing a cash budget

4-1 Introduction

To grow and prosper, firms have to conduct two types of planning exercises: *strategic planning* and—a subset of strategic planning—*operational planning*. Financial planning is a critical component of the operational planning process.

4-2 Financial Planning

Strategic planning is long range in nature and deals with the overall direction of the firm. It is largely concerned with anticipating significant new developments and changes that will have a major impact on the industry and the firm. For example, few firms anticipated 20 years ago that e-commerce would become as big as it has. Companies that did not anticipate this major development lost market share to small, agile start-up firms that immediately capitalized on this new marketing opportunity. Take, for instance, Barnes & Noble, the largest bookstore chain in the world. A few years ago, when the Internet was still in its nascent stages, Barnes & Noble did not think trading via this medium was going to be a significant factor. For one thing, they felt the experience of going to a bookstore and browsing through the aisles could not be duplicated. As Barnes & Noble found out, this idea couldn't be further from the truth. Amazon.com, a firm that began operations only in July 1995, caught the Internet wave and now commands a majority share of all books purchased over the Internet (Today, Amazon sells just about everything, not just books). Barnes & Noble did ultimately start selling its books through the Internet but remains a distant second to Amazon.com. With a proper strategic planning process, Barnes & Noble probably could have positioned itself to better take advantage of the opportunities presented by the Internet medium.

While strategic planning focuses more on the overall direction of the business and the industry, *operational planning, as the phrase denotes, is designed to be a blueprint detailing where the firm wants to be at some future point in time and what resources are needed to get it there.* Operational plans are generally conducted at two levels—long term and short term. Long-term plans are typically done over a five-year planning horizon, while short-term plans are conducted over a 12- to 18-month window. This chapter focuses on the operational rather than strategic plan of the firm (and especially on its financial aspect). The operational plan begins with a series of *operational objectives* that define *where the firm wants to be at the end of the planning period.* These objectives are very specific. Some examples are:

- Raise market share from 12.5 percent to 17 percent in 12 months.
- Reduce debt to total assets ratio from 65 percent to 40 percent in two years.
- Raise operating profit margin from 8 percent to 9.5 percent in one year.
- Roll out a new line of electric vehicles in three years.
- Decrease dependence on sales to the defense industry from 60 percent to under 40 percent in two years.

To address these objectives, the firm must develop an operational plan, which consists of a *marketing plan*, a *production plan*, a *human resource plan*, and a *financial plan*. The marketing plan lays out the marketing resources needed to meet the operational objectives and includes such things as advertising strategy, marketing promotions, channels of distribution and distribution incentives, and assignment of sales territory. The production plan consists of facilities needed to achieve the operational objectives including the number of shifts, plant refurbishment and expansions, vendor and supplier arrangements, inventory control, etc. The human resource plan is concerned with the personnel aspect of the objectives. It looks at the managerial and labor pool that is needed to attain the objectives. The financial plan *lays out the financial resources that are needed to achieve the operational (including the financial) objectives of the firm.* Operational planning is crucial to a firm's survival in the short and long run. The lack of adequate operational planning has doomed many a firm, both small and large.

Figure 4.1 presents an overview of the corporate planning process as described here. The strategic plan is determined by the long-term goals of the firm, but it also affects the operational objectives of the firm. The operational objectives in turn are implemented via the operational plan, which consists of marketing, production, human resource, and financial plans. The dashed line from the operational plan to operational objectives and back to the operational plan indicates that the operational plan should be continually monitored to see if the objectives are being met or not. If the objectives are not met, then the operational plan needs to be adjusted so that it is in alignment with the objectives. Thus, the operational plan is not only a *planning* device, but it is also a *monitoring* device.

FIGURE 4.1

An Overview of the Corporate Planning Process

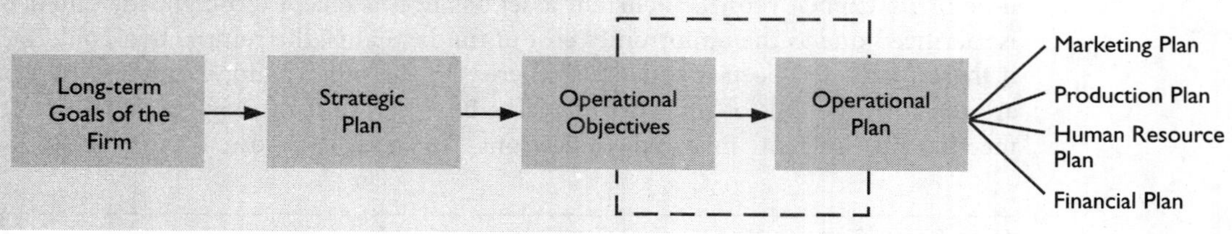

An integral part of the operational plan and the financial plan are the financial forecasts. However, before discussing various financial forecasting techniques, the next section focuses on cash flow analysis, which is an important element of financial planning.

4-3 Cash Flow Analysis

Foundation Concept

Traditional financial ratio analysis can be a useful tool to an analyst trying to evaluate a firm's performance. However, many of the key performance measures, such as return on sales, assets, and equity, rely on accounting income concepts. Accounting income is not the relevant source of value in a firm—cash flow is. Only cash can be spent. Accounting income, in contrast, does not reflect the actual cash inflows and outflows in a firm. Consequently, in this section we illustrate and define further the cash flow concept.

THOMSON ONE | Business School Edition

The concept of *cash flow* is one of the central elements of financial analysis, planning, and resource allocation decisions. Cash flows are important because the financial health of a firm depends on its ability to generate sufficient amounts of cash to pay its creditors, employees, suppliers, and owners.

4-3a The Cash Flow Generation Process

Financial managers are concerned primarily with raising funds (cash) for use by the firm and investing those funds in assets that can be converted into a stream of cash flows accruing to the firm and its owners. If the value today of the stream of cash flows generated by the assets of a firm exceeds the cost of those assets, the investments undertaken by the firm add value to the firm. When financial managers perform this primary function of acquiring funds and directing the investment of those funds into value-maximizing projects, they must balance the risk (variability) and timing of the expected cash flow stream against the magnitude of the expected returns. The cash flow generation process for a firm is illustrated in Figure 4.2.

A firm can raise funds by issuing different types of financial securities, including both debt and equity types.[1] Financing decisions such as these are summarized on the liabilities and owners' equity side of the balance sheet. In addition to selling securities, a firm can raise cash by borrowing from a lender such as a commercial bank. Funds can also be raised by generating cash flow internally. Internal cash flows include cash generated from operations and cash generated by the sale of assets.

Once cash is available, a decision must be made to invest it in one or more assets. The acquisition of the best long-term assets is crucial, because once acquired, long-term assets impact the firm for a long time. Long-term assets can be sold if necessary but sometimes only at a significant loss. Current assets, or working capital, such as cash, accounts receivable, and inventory, are held for operating purposes and generally offer little or no explicit return. If current asset balances are kept too high, shareholder wealth is sacrificed due to the opportunity cost of funds; that is, the returns that could be earned if these funds had been invested elsewhere. On the other hand, if current asset balances are too low, the risk of the firm increases because the firm may encounter difficulty in meeting its current financial obligations. In addition, low current asset balances

[1]Chapter 6 discusses various types of debt securities, and Chapter 7 discusses various types of equity securities.

FIGURE 4.2

A Firm's Cash Flow Generation Process

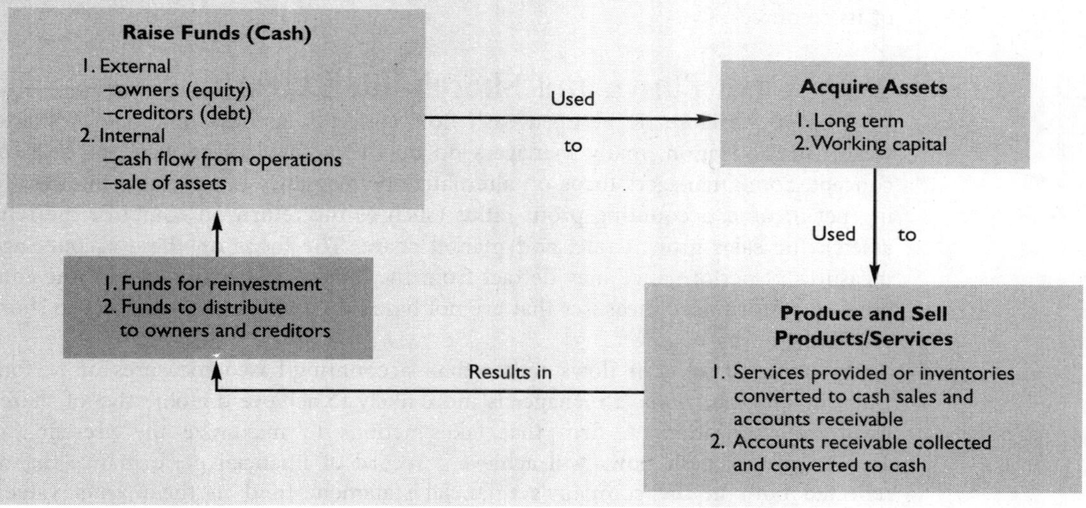

(particularly inventories and accounts receivable) may prevent a firm from responding to the needs of prospective customers in a timely and profitable way.

Eventually, all assets are transformed into a cash flow. Plant and equipment generate a product or service. Inventory is gradually sold and generates cash sales or accounts receivable. Cash flow is generated as accounts receivable are collected. Then, the firm must decide how much of its cash flow to use to acquire additional assets, pay off creditors, and distribute to its owners.

4-3b Importance of Cash Flows

The valuation of debt and equity securities is based upon the present value of the cash flows that these securities are expected to provide to investors.[2] Similarly, the value of a capital expenditure is equal to the present value of the cash flows that the asset is expected to produce for the firm. In addition, cash flows are central to the prosperity and survival of a firm. For example, rapidly expanding firms often grow faster than their ability to generate internally the cash flows needed to meet operating and financial commitments. As a result, these firms may be faced with difficult financial decisions regarding the external sources of funds needed to sustain rapid growth. On the one hand, increases in debt to support expansion result in an increase in the firm's financial risk. On the other hand, if new shares of stock are sold, ownership in the firm may be diluted more than is desired by the firm's controlling group of owners. Therefore, managers need to pay close attention to the projected cash flows associated with investment and firm expansion strategies.

As you learned in your accounting courses and as is discussed in Chapter 3, generally accepted accounting principles (GAAP) provide considerable latitude in the determination of the net income. As a consequence, GAAP concepts of net income do not provide a clear indication of the economic performance of a firm. Cash flow

[2]The present value concept is discussed in detail in Chapter 5.

concepts are unambiguous and provide the necessary insight for managers making a wide range of financial resource allocation decisions. Investors also find that cash flow concepts provide a clear measure of performance. Accordingly, the concept of cash flow assumes great importance in the analysis of a firm's performance and the management of its resources.

4-3c Cash Flows and Shareholder Wealth

In spite of the close tie between cash flow concepts and the objective of shareholder wealth maximization, many managers do not seem to place enough emphasis on this concept. Some managers focus on alternative performance measures, including accounting net income, accounting profit ratios (such as the return on equity or the return on assets), the sales growth rate, and market share. The focus on these accounting-based measures of performance may detract from the long-term performance of the company, because performance measures that are not based on cash flows are subject to short-term manipulation by managers.

By emphasizing cash flows rather than accounting-based measures of performance when making decisions, a manager is more likely to achieve the objective of shareholder wealth maximization. A firm that takes actions to maximize the present value of expected future cash flows will achieve a record of financial performance that will be reflected both in the company's financial statements and in the market value of its stock.

4-3d The Cash Flow Concept

after-tax cash flow (ATCF)

The income statement can be modified to provide a quick measure of the **after-tax cash flow (ATCF)** that is available from current operations to make capital expenditures, pay dividends, and repay debt. Accordingly, the ATCF is generally a more important number than the net income or earnings after taxes (EAT) figure. One shortcoming of the ATCF is that it does not consider additional cash tied up in (or released from) net working capital.

ATCF is found by adding back noncash charges to EAT:

$$\text{ATCF} = \text{EAT} + \text{Noncash charges} \tag{4.1}$$

Noncash charges consist of such items as depreciation and deferred taxes. Hence:

$$\text{ATCF} = \text{EAT} + \text{Depreciation} + \text{Deferred taxes} \tag{4.2}$$

Depreciation *Depreciation* is defined as the systematic allocation of the cost of an asset over more than one year. The annual depreciation expense recorded for a particular asset is an allocation of its original cost and does not represent a cash outlay. As a result, a company's annual depreciation expense is added to earnings after taxes in calculating after-tax cash flow. For example, in 2014, Panera Bread Company had earnings after taxes of $179 million. Its depreciation expense of $124 million must be added to the earnings after taxes amount in calculating Panera Bread's ATCF.[3]

Deferred Taxes After-tax cash flow also differs from earnings after taxes by the amount of a company's *deferred taxes*. In accordance with generally accepted accounting principles and specifically in accordance with Statement of Financial Accounting Standards No. 96, a company usually reports a different income tax expense amount to its stockholders than it actually pays in cash during that year. Frequently, the income tax amount shown on the company's income statement is larger than the income tax

[3] Panera Bread Company 2014 10-K Annual Report.

amount actually paid. The difference between the tax amount reported to stockholders and the cash amount actually paid is referred to as a *deferred tax* because it is due to be paid by the company sometime in the future. For example, during 2014, Panera Bread reported the following earnings amounts to its stockholders:

Earnings before taxes	\$277 million
Less income taxes	98 million
Earnings after taxes	\$179 million
Income taxes:	
Current portion	\$87.5 million
Deferred	10.5 million

In calculating Panera Bread's 2014 after-tax cash flow, the deferred tax amount, \$10.5 million, is added to the earnings after tax, because the deferred taxes were subtracted as an expense in determining earnings but did not constitute a cash payment by Panera Bread in 2014.

Deferred taxes generally occur because of temporary differences in the stated amounts of assets and liabilities *for financial reporting purposes* and for tax purposes. Even though deferred taxes can occur for a variety of reasons, some of the more common reasons include differences between financial reporting and tax methods regarding accounting for depreciation, inventories, and pensions. Many companies use the straight-line depreciation method to calculate the income they report to their stockholders and an accelerated depreciation method to calculate taxable income. This practice usually results in the taxes currently owed being less than they would be if the company used straight-line depreciation methods for tax purposes, thus resulting in deferred taxes. A company effectively can continue to defer payment of these taxes as long as it continues to purchase a sufficient amount of new fixed assets. When it ceases purchasing such assets or purchases fewer of them, it will have to pay the deferred taxes.

The effect of depreciation and deferred income taxes on the after-tax cash flows of the Ellwood Appliance Company is illustrated in Table 4.1. Using straight-line depreciation for financial reporting purposes results in reported income taxes of \$8.0 million and EAT of \$12.0 million. Using accelerated depreciation (MACRS)[4] for tax purposes results in a current income tax payment of \$7.2 million, with the balance of \$0.8 million (that is, \$8.0 million − \$7.2 million) being deferred. If the tax records for Ellwood are available, the ATCF of \$22.8 million can be calculated by adding the depreciation amount of \$12.0 million to the earnings after taxes amount of \$10.8 million. If the tax records are not available, the ATCF can be calculated using Equation 4.2, as follows:

$$\text{ATCF} = \$12.0 + \$10.0 + \$0.8 = \$22.8 \text{ (million)}$$

4-3e The Statement of Cash Flows

THOMSON ONE Business School Edition

The statement of cash flows, together with the balance sheet and the income statement, constitute a major portion of a company's financial statements. The *statement of cash flows* shows the effects of a company's *operating*, *investing*, and *financing* activities on its cash balance. The principal purpose of the statement of cash flows is to provide

[4]MACRS, or Modified Accelerated Cost Recovery System, is explained in Appendix 9A.

TABLE 4.1

Ellwood Appliance Company: After-Tax Cash Flow (ATCF) Calculation

(A) Calculation of Taxes for Financial Reporting and Tax Purposes ($ Million)

	Financial Reporting Purposes	Tax Purposes
Sales	$100.0	$100.0
Expenses, excluding depreciation	70.0	70.0
Depreciation:		
Straight-line	10.0	
MACRS*		12.0
Earnings before taxes	$ 20.0	$ 18.0
Taxes (40%)	8.0	7.2
Earnings after taxes (EAT)	$ 12.0	$ 10.8

(B) Partial Income Statement Reported to Stockholders ($ Million)

	Financial Reporting Purposes
Earnings before taxes	$20.0
Federal income taxes (40%)	
Current	7.2
Deferred	0.8
Total federal income tax	$ 8.0
Earnings after tax	$12.0
Plus: Noncash charges	
Depreciation	10.0
Deferred taxes	0.8
After-tax cash flow (ATCF)	$22.8

*MACRS stands for Modified Accelerated Cost Recovery System and is explained in Appendix 9A.

relevant information about a company's cash receipts and cash payments during a particular accounting period. The statement of cash flows provides a more complete indication of the sources (and the uses) of a firm's cash resources over time.

The procedures for preparing the statement of cash flows are presented in Statement of Financial Accounting Standards No. 95, issued by the Financial Accounting Standards Board (FASB) in November 1987. It requires companies to include a statement of cash flows when issuing a complete set of financial statements for annual periods ending after July 15, 1988. The FASB encourages companies to prepare their statement of cash flows using the *direct* method of presenting cash flows from operating activities.

Statement of Cash Flows: Direct Method Table 4.2 shows an example of a statement of cash flows using the direct method for the Summit Furniture Company, a retail chain of furniture stores. During 2016, Summit's "cash flows from operating activities" totaled $14,600,000 ($142,000,000 cash received from customers, plus $600,000 of interest received, less $120,000,000 paid to suppliers and employees, less $2,000,000 interest paid, less $6,000,000 of income taxes paid). Summit's investing activities used net cash of $18,000,000. The company spent $19,000,000 on capital expenditures and received $1,000,000 in proceeds from the sale of an asset. During the year the net cash provided by financing activities equaled $3,600,000. The $3,600,000 is calculated as the difference between financing activities that require cash outflows and those that result in cash inflows. Summit had financing cash outflows totaling $3,100,000 ($2,600,000 repayment of long-term debt and $500,000 of dividends paid out) and financing cash

TABLE 4.2

Summit Furniture Company Statement of Cash Flows for the Year Ended December 31, 2016

Increase (Decrease) in Cash and Cash Equivalents* (000)		
Cash Flows from Operating Activities:		
Cash received from customers	$ 142,000	
Cash paid to suppliers and employees	(120,000)	
Interest received	600	
Interest paid (net of amount capitalized)	(2,000)	
Income taxes paid	(6,000)	
Net cash provided (used) by operating activities		$ 14,600
Cash Flows from Investing Activities:		
Proceeds from sale of asset	1,000	
Capital expenditures	(19,000)	
Net cash provided (used) by investing activities		(18,000)
Cash Flows from Financing Activities:		
Net borrowings under bank line-of-credit agreement	1,000	
Repayments of long-term debt	(2,600)	
Proceeds from issuance of long-term debt	4,000	
Proceeds from issuance of common stock	1,700	
Dividends paid	(500)	
Net cash provided (used) by financing activities		3,600
Net increase (decrease) in cash and cash equivalents		200
Cash and cash equivalents at beginning of year		5,000
Cash and cash equivalents at end of year		$ 5,200

*Cash and cash equivalents include currency on hand, bank deposits and similar accounts, and short term (maturities less than three months), highly liquid investments.

inflows totaling $6,700,000 (bank borrowing of $1,000,000 plus proceeds from the issuance of long-term debt of $4,000,000 plus proceeds from the issuance of common stock of $1,700,000). The overall change in cash is calculated as follows:

$$\begin{aligned}\text{Net cash increase (decrease)} &= \text{Net cash provided (used) by operating activities}\\ &\quad + \text{Net cash provided (used) by investing activities}\\ &\quad + \text{Net cash provided (used) by financing activities} \qquad (4.3)\\ \text{Net cash increase (decrease)} &= \$14{,}600{,}000 - \$18{,}000{,}000 + \$3{,}600{,}000\\ &= \$200{,}000\end{aligned}$$

The statement of cash flows presented in Table 4.2 provides Summit's management, investors, and creditors with a summary of its cash flows for the year. In particular, Summit's operations provided net cash of $14,600,000; however, the company used a total of $18,000,000 in its investing activities. As a result, if Summit wanted to keep its cash balance at about $5,000,000, the company's financing activities would have to provide $3,400,000 of net cash ($18,000,000 − $14,600,000). In fact, Summit's financing activities actually did provide $3,600,000, causing the ending cash balance to be $5,200,000, or $200,000 above the beginning $5,000,000.

Statement of Cash Flows: Indirect Method A sampling of recent annual reports shows that very few companies present their statement of cash flows using the direct method. Instead, most companies use the indirect, or reconciliation, method to report the net cash flow from operating activities. The *indirect method* involves adjusting net income to reconcile it to net cash flow from operating activities. Table 4.3 shows the

TABLE 4.3

Panera Bread Company Consolidated Statements of Cash Flows (in thousands)

	For the fiscal year ended		
	December 30, 2014	December 31, 2013	December 25, 2012
Cash flows from operations:			
Net income	$ 179,293	$ 196,169	$ 173,448
Adjustments to reconcile net income to net cash provided by operating activities:			
Depreciation and amortization	124,109	106,523	90,939
Stock-based compensation expense	10,077	10,703	9,094
Tax benefit from exercise of stock options	(3,089)	(8,100)	(8,587)
Deferred income taxes	10,459	10,356	20,334
Loss on disposals of property and equipment	1,547	5,764	3,995
Other	3,070	589	475
Changes in operating assets and liabilities, excluding the effect of acquisitions and dispositions:			
Trade and other accounts receivable, net	(22,139)	3,021	(31,414)
Inventories	(895)	(2,186)	(2,440)
Prepaid expenses and other	(8,524)	(841)	(10,995)
Deposits and other	239	1,449	161
Accounts payable	1,978	8,162	(6,513)
Accrued expenses	35,288	13,372	49,246
Deferred rent	1,067	5,868	5,718
Other long-term liabilities	2,599	(2,432)	(4,005)
Net cash provided by operating activities	335,079	348,417	289,456
Cash flows from investing activities:			
Additions to property and equipment	(224,217)	(192,010)	(152,328)
Acquisitions, net of cash acquired	—	(2,446)	(47,951)
Purchase of investments	—	(97,919)	—
Proceeds from sale of investments	—	97,936	—
Proceeds from sale-leaseback transactions	12,900	6,132	4,538
Net cash used in investing activities	(211,317)	(188,307)	(195,741)
Cash flows from financing activities:			
Proceeds from issuance of long-term debt	100,000	—	—
Debt issuance costs	(193)	—	(1,097)
Repurchase of common stock	(159,503)	(339,409)	(31,566)
Exercise of employee stock options	1,116	573	4,455
Tax benefit from exercise of stock options	3,089	8,100	8,587
Proceeds from issuance of common stock under employee benefit plans	3,247	2,842	2,462
Payment of deferred acquisition holdback	(270)	(4,112)	(2,055)
Net cash used in financing activities	(52,514)	(332,006)	(19,214)
Net increase (decrease) in cash and cash equivalents	71,248	(171,896)	74,501
Cash and cash equivalents at beginning of period	125,245	297,141	222,640
Cash and cash equivalents at end of period	$ 196,493	$ 125,245	$ 297,141

Source: Panera Bread Company Annual Report (2014).

statements of cash flows using the indirect method for Panera Bread Company for the fiscal year ending December 30, 2014.

Panera Bread had net income (EAT) of $179 million for the 2014 fiscal year. Converting this net income to cash flow requires adding back noncash expenses, including depreciation, amortization, and deferred taxes. Next, the firm adjusted net income from the accrual method (required by GAAP) to the cash amount by showing increases and decreases in its various current asset and liability accounts. After these adjustments, Panera Bread had net cash from operations of $335 million for the year. The firm used $211 million in investing activities, primarily for purchases of property, plant, and equipment. Financing activities used up $52.5 million, consisting mainly of a $100 million debt issue (source of funds) and a $159.5 million use of funds for buying back stock in the company. The net effect of Panera Bread's activities for the year ended December 30, 2014, was an increase in cash and cash equivalents of approximately $71 million. The statement of cash flows gives a good feel for the effect Panera Bread's operating, investing, and financing activities had on its cash position.

4-4 Financial Forecasting

Financial forecasting consists of various techniques that can be used to determine the amount of additional financing a firm will require in the future. If internal sources of funds (cash) are not sufficient to achieve its goals, then the firm must seek to obtain external funding from the capital markets.

pro forma financial statements

This section presents an overview of the financial forecasting process, with emphasis on the important role of pro forma financial statements. **Pro forma financial statements**, showing the results of some *assumed* event, rather than an *actual* event, are usually an integral part of a financial forecast. For example, an operating budget that shows the level of net income that can be expected if sales and expenses are at a given assumed level next year is a pro forma income statement. Short-term forecasts, those that deal with one year or less, tend to be rather detailed, whereas long-term forecasts are more general. This section discusses the percentage of sales forecasting method, cash budgets, the pro forma statement of cash flows, computerized financial forecasting and planning models, and using financial ratios to forecast future financial performance.

4-4a Percentage of Sales Forecasting Method

percentage of sales forecasting method

The **percentage of sales forecasting method** permits a company to forecast the amount of financing it will need for a given increase in sales. This method is simple and can provide information useful in preparing pro forma financial statements and in estimating future funds needs. The method assumes that (1) present asset levels are optimal with respect to present sales and (2) most items on the balance sheet increase in proportion to sales increases. The use of this method is illustrated with the following example of the Industrial Supply Company (ISC).

The present (2016) ISC balance sheet and income statement are shown in Table 4.4. Management forecasts that sales will increase by 25 percent, or $3,750,000, next year to $18,750,000 and that expenses, including interest and taxes, will increase to $17,750,000.

One of management's primary concerns is the amount of funds (cash) needed to finance this sales growth. Until now, the company has financed its growth by using both internally and externally generated funds. The company has reinvested most of its past earnings, primarily into additional inventory. The company has also used external financing in the form of short-term borrowings from its bank.

TABLE 4.4

Industrial Supply Financial Statements

Balance Sheet	(Actual) December 31, 2016	(Pro Forma) December 31, 2017	Comments
Assets			
Cash	$ 500,000	$ 625,000	25% increase (*assumption*)
Accounts receivable	2,000,000	2,500,000	25% increase (*assumption*)
Inventories	4,000,000	5,000,000	25% increase (*assumption*)
Total current assets	$ 6,500,000	$ 8,125,000	
Fixed assets, net	$ 1,000,000	$ 1,250,000	25% increase (*assumption*)
Total assets (A)	$ 7,500,000	$ 9,375,000	
Liabilities and Equity			
Accounts payable (CL)	$ 1,500,000	$ 1,875,000	25% increase (*assumption*)
Notes payable	1,000,000	1,750,000	{$1,000,000 + AFN = $1,000,000 + $750,000
Total current liabilities	$ 2,500,000	$ 3,625,000	
Long-term debt	500,000	500,000	No change (*assumption*)
Stockholders' equity	4,500,000	5,250,000	{$4,500,000 + R/E = $4,500,000 + $750,000
Total liabilities and equity	$ 7,500,000	$ 9,375,000	
Income Statement	**2016**	**2017**	
Sales (S)	$15,000,000	$18,750,000	25% increase (*forecasted*)
Expenses, including interest & taxes	14,250,000	17,750,000	*Forecasted*
Earnings after taxes (EAT)	$ 750,000	$ 1,000,000	
Dividends paid (D)	250,000	250,000	No change (*assumption*)
Retained earnings	$ 500,000	$ 750,000	
Selected Financial Ratios			
Current ratio	2.60 times	2.24 times	Decreased
Debt ratio	40%	44%	Increased
Return on stockholders' equity	16.7%	19.0%	Increased
Net profit margin on sales	5.0%	5.33%	Increased

To determine the amount of additional financing necessary to reach the expected $18,750,000 annual sales level, the ISC management has made the following observations about the company's various assets and liabilities:

1. **Cash**. Management feels that the company's cash balances are generally adequate for the present sales level and would have to increase proportionately as sales increase.
2. **Accounts receivable**. The company's present average collection period is approximately 49 days. Management feels that the company's present credit policies are appropriate for its type of business. As a result, they feel that the average collection period will remain approximately constant and that accounts receivable will increase proportionately as sales increase.
3. **Inventory**. Management feels that the company's inventory is properly managed at present. Therefore, they feel inventory would have to increase proportionately for sales to increase.

4. **Fixed assets.** The company is a distributor with relatively few fixed assets (delivery trucks, forklifts, office equipment, storage racks, and so forth). Because the company's fixed assets *are being used at nearly full capacity,* management feels that fixed assets will have to increase as sales grow. For financial planning purposes, management is willing to assume that the *net* fixed asset figure on the balance sheet will increase proportionately as sales increase.
5. **Accounts payable.** The company now maintains good relations with its suppliers. As the company purchases more inventory, its accounts payable balance will increase proportionately as sales increase.
6. **Notes payable and long-term debt.** Notes payable and long-term debt do not necessarily have a direct relationship to the sales level. For example, a portion of the company's future cash flows may be used to pay off the present debt.

In summary, as the company's sales increase, its assets will increase proportionately to support the new sales. In addition, the current liabilities that vary directly with sales, namely accounts payable, will also increase. The difference between the forecasted asset increase and the forecasted current liability increase is equal to the total financing the company will need. This relationship can be expressed in equation form as follows:

$$\begin{aligned}\text{Total financing needed} &= \text{Forecasted asset increase} - \text{Forecasted current liability increase}\\ &= \frac{A}{S}(\Delta S) - \frac{CL}{S}(\Delta S)\end{aligned} \qquad \textbf{(4.4)}$$

where A is the company's present level of assets *that vary proportionately with sales,* S is the company's present sales, CL is the company's present level of current liabilities *that vary proportionately with sales* (that is, accounts payable), and ΔS is the forecasted sales increase.[5]

A portion of the total financing needed can be generated internally from increased retained earnings. Specifically, the increased retained earnings generated during the time period when sales increase from S to $S + \Delta S$ can be expressed in equation form as follows:

$$\begin{aligned}\text{Increased retained earnings} &= \text{Forecasted earnings after taxes} - \text{Dividends}\\ &= \text{EAT} - D\end{aligned} \qquad \textbf{(4.5)}$$

The additional financing needed can be calculated by subtracting the increased retained earnings from the total financing needed:

$$\begin{aligned}\text{Additional financing needed} &= \text{Total financing needed} - \text{Increased retained earnings}\\ &= \left[\frac{A}{S}(\Delta S) - \frac{CL}{S}(\Delta S)\right] - [EAT - D]\end{aligned} \qquad \textbf{(4.6)}$$

With reference to the ISC example, the additional financing needed to support a sales increase of \$3,750,000 up to the \$18,750,000 level can now be calculated. Assume that management forecasts expenses to be \$17,750,000 and EAT to be \$1,000,000 during the coming year. Assume further that the company plans to maintain its dividend payments at the same level in 2017 as in 2016. Inserting these data into Equation 4.6 yields:

$$\begin{aligned}\text{Additional financing needed} &= \left[\frac{\$7{,}500{,}000}{\$15{,}000{,}000}(\$3{,}750{,}000) - \frac{\$1{,}500{,}000}{\$15{,}000{,}000}(\$3{,}750{,}000)\right]\\ &\quad -(\$1{,}000{,}000 - \$250{,}000)\\ &= \$750{,}000\end{aligned}$$

[5]Current liabilities, such as accounts payable, that automatically expand (contract) as the volume of business increases (decreases) are often referred to as "spontaneous" sources of financing. Chapter 16 contains a more detailed discussion of short-term sources of funds.

The approximate amount of additional financing that will be needed to finance ISC's forecasted growth in sales from \$15,000,000 to \$18,750,000 is \$750,000.[6] Even though the financing will be needed gradually as sales increase, the ISC management has to decide whether to (1) borrow on a short-term basis, (2) borrow on a long-term basis, (3) sell additional common stock, or (4) cut dividends. The factors that influence the debt versus equity decision are discussed in Chapters 13 and 14, the factors that influence the short-term versus long-term debt decision are discussed in Chapter 16, and the factors that influence the dividend decision are discussed in Chapter 15. As this example illustrates, *the investment, financing, and dividend decisions of the firm are interdependent.*

Table 4.4 shows ISC's pro forma financial statements for 2017, *assuming* that all of the additional financing needed is in the form of short-term notes payable. Examination of the selected financial ratios shows that this financing plan will increase the net profit margin on sales from 5.0 percent to 5.33 percent and increase the return on stockholders' equity from 16.7 percent in 2016 to 19.0 percent in 2017. However, it also reduces the firm's current ratio (measure of liquidity) from 2.60 to 2.24 times and increases its debt ratio (measure of leverage) from 40 percent to 44 percent. ISC management would have to weigh these factors in determining how to obtain the \$750,000 of additional financing needed.

The percentage of sales forecasting method for calculating financing needs is a useful and convenient cash flow forecasting technique. However, as with all analytical techniques, the application of this method should be supplemented by any additional factors that are unique to the particular situation.

One such factor is *economies of scale*. Economies of scale may result in nonlinear relationships between sales and certain types of assets. In other words, the relationships may not be strictly proportional, as assumed in the model. For example, a 10 percent increase in sales may only require a 5 percent increase in fixed assets or inventories. Another factor in some industries is that capacity can be added only in *discrete* or *"lumpy" increments*. Once output reaches the capacity of an existing production facility, expansion requires building another facility. This causes fixed assets to increase in a stepwise manner as sales are increased, rather than increasing proportionately.

4-4b Cash Budgeting

Even though the percentage of sales forecasting method is a useful tool that can provide insights regarding financing needs associated with projected sales increases, *cash budgets* can estimate more precisely *both* the *amount* of financing needed by a firm and the *timing* of those financing needs. Cash budgeting plays an important role in the firm's financial forecasting process. Effective cash budgeting can help management identify potential cash flow problems. Usually, cash flow problems are easier to solve when they are anticipated. In addition to a detailed discussion of cash budgets, this section contains a brief overview of budgeting.

An Overview of Budgeting *Budgets* are simply pro forma financial statements that detail a firm's financial forecasts. They show how the company's cash will be spent on labor, materials, and capital goods and indicate how cash will be obtained.

Budgets are used to *plan*, *coordinate*, and *control* a firm's operations. They are essential to *planning* because they represent the company's objectives in numerical terms, such as dollars of sales, units of production, pounds of raw materials, and dollars of financing required from the capital markets. Once a firm has made financial plans, it refers to the budgets when *coordinating* its overall activities. For example, the purchasing department

[6]The \$750,000 figure assumes that none of the present notes payable or long-term debt will have to be repaid during the year.

examines the budgets when deciding how best to integrate purchasing activities with monthly production requirements to ensure the availability of sufficient raw materials. The production and marketing departments then work together to guarantee that sufficient finished goods inventories are on hand. Finally, the finance department coordinates the company's need for funds with the requirements of the purchasing, production, and marketing departments.

The projected figures in a firm's budgets are also used as a *control* device against which actual figures are compared. This ensures that the various departments and divisions are functioning properly and working together toward the objectives developed in the planning phase.

A firm's budgets are based on the *assumption* of certain future sales and production levels. As pro forma financial statements, budgets predict *what* a company's financial statements will look like if specific plans are realized.

cash budget

Cash Budgets

A **cash budget** is the projection of a company's cash receipts and disbursements over some future period of time. Typically, a cash budget is prepared on an annual basis and subdivided into months. However, more detailed and refined cash budgeting is done on a weekly or even daily basis by some companies that employ good ongoing cash management procedures.

Cash budgets are useful in determining the amount of short-term funds the firm may need to borrow to cover any projected cash shortages. Short-term borrowed funds are almost always easier to obtain when the need for them is anticipated. In addition to planning for any cash shortages, the cash budget also indicates the periods when the firm may have cash surpluses. This information is helpful in managing the firm's marketable securities investments. Thus, the cash budget is one of the most important short-range financial forecasting tools. In addition, cash budgets can be useful for control and coordination purposes.

To explore actual cash budgeting procedures, the Midwestern Manufacturing Company Central Division will be examined. Table 4.5 illustrates a cash budget worksheet

TABLE 4.5

Cash Budget Worksheet—Midwestern Manufacturing Company

Midwestern Manufacturing Company—Central Division Cash Budget Worksheet First Quarter, 2017

	December	January	February	March
Budget of Receipts from Sales				
Estimated sales	$540,000	$500,000	$550,000	$620,000
Estimated credit sales	486,000	450,000	495,000	558,000
Estimated receipts:				
Cash sales		$ 50,000	$ 55,000	$ 62,000
Collections of accounts receivable:				
70% of last month's credit sales		$340,200	$315,000	$346,500
30% of current month's credit sales		135,000	148,500	167,400
Total accounts receivable collections		$475,200	$463,500	$513,900
Budget of Payments for Purchases				
Estimated purchases*	$275,000	$302,500	$341,000	
Estimated payments of accounts payable**		$275,000	$302,500	$341,000

*Purchases are estimated at 55 percent of next month's sales.

**Payments are estimated to lag purchases by one month.

TABLE 4.6

Cash Budget—Midwestern Manufacturing Company

Midwestern Manufacturing Company—Central Division Cash Budget*
First Quarter, 2017

	December	January	February	March
Sales	$ 540,000	$ 500,000	$ 550,000	$ 620,000
Projected cash balance, beginning of month		$ 61,000	$ 50,700	$ 50,000
Receipts:				
Cash sales		50,000	55,000	62,000
Collection of accounts receivable		475,200	463,500	513,900
Total cash available		$ 586,200	$ 569,200	$ 625,900
Disbursements:				
Payment of accounts payable		$ 275,000	$ 302,500	$ 341,000
Wages and salaries		158,000	154,500	145,500
Rent		17,000	17,000	17,000
Other expenses		4,500	7,000	8,000
Taxes		81,000	—	—
Dividends on common stock		—	—	30,000
Purchase of new equipment (capital budget)		—	70,000	—
Total disbursements		$ 535,500	$ 551,000	$ 541,500
Excess of available cash over disbursements		$ 50,700	$ 18,200	$ 84,400
Cash loans needed to maintain balance of $50,000		—	31,800	—
Loan repayment		—	—	(31,800)
Projected cash balance, end of month		$ 50,700	$ 50,000	$ 52,600

*Prepared December 15, 2016.

for that division for the first quarter of 2017, prepared as of the middle of December 2016. Table 4.6 is an actual cash budget for the time period.

The first step in cash budget preparation is the estimation of cash receipts, which results directly from the sales forecast. Midwestern has found that, on the average, about 10 percent of total sales in any given month are cash sales. The remaining 90 percent are credit sales.[7]

About 30 percent of the company's credit sales are collected during the month in which the sale is made, and all of the remaining 70 percent are collected during the following month. Thus, the total accounts receivable the company can expect to collect during January are equal to 70 percent of the forecasted December credit sales plus 30 percent of the forecasted January credit sales.

$$(0.70 \times \$486{,}000) + (0.30 \times \$450{,}000) = \$340{,}200 + \$135{,}000$$
$$= \$475{,}200$$

The forecasted cash receipts for February and March are calculated the same way.

The next step in cash budgeting is the scheduling of *disbursements*, or payments the firm must make to others. Many of these items remain relatively constant from month to month and thus are relatively easy to budget. Others, however, such as the payment of accounts payable for purchases of merchandise, raw materials, and supplies, are more complicated. The key determinants of a firm's schedule of payables are the level of purchases per period and the terms given by suppliers.

[7]Estimated December credit sales are 90 percent of estimated December sales; that is, 0.90 × $540,000 = $486,000.

Frequently, accounts payable become due before goods are sold and cash is received; this can lead to temporary cash shortages. In fact, many companies experience cash difficulties immediately after a good sales period. Inventories are depleted and must be replenished, but cash is low because collections from the good sales period have not yet been received. Midwestern's purchases generally are estimated to be 55 percent of next month's sales. This percentage is based on the company's past experience and can vary considerably among industries and companies. (Note that depreciation does not appear as a disbursement in the cash budget, because it is a noncash charge.)

After cash receipts and disbursements have been estimated, the next step in the cash budgeting process is the determination of a desired cash balance at the beginning of each month. This minimum cash balance figure is usually a function of several factors, including the nature of the business, tax laws, and bank requirements. Table 4.6 lists Midwestern's projected cash balance for the beginning of January, February, and March. Note that the projected cash balance at the *beginning* of each month is equal to the projected cash balance at the *end* of the previous month. In this example, $50,000 is assumed to be the most appropriate minimum cash balance for the first quarter, 2017.[8]

Table 4.6 shows that Midwestern expects to need a short-term loan of $31,800 in February to maintain a minimum cash balance of $50,000 because the company expects a decrease in the collection of accounts receivable in February, brought about by slightly lower than normal sales expected in January. In addition, the company plans to purchase new equipment in February, which will cost $70,000; this also contributes to the expected need for a short-term loan.

If the company planned to spend much more money than this on new equipment, it might decide to secure longer term financing at this time, instead of the short-term loan. The proceeds from longer term financing could be budgeted as a separate cash receipt in February, permitting the company to separate short-term and long-term cash needs.

With a projected need for a short-term loan in February, the cash budget in Table 4.6 shows that the loan can probably be paid at the end of March because the available cash balance of $84,400 will still be above $50,000 after repayment of $31,800. The company has indicated the repayment on the cash budget by adding another side caption: Loan repayment.[9]

Most companies follow this same general format for cash budgeting, yet few companies use *exactly* the same format. A company's actual cash budgeting system will depend on its business and its accounting procedures. Computerized financial spreadsheet models are useful in constructing and analyzing cash budgets.

4-4c Pro Forma Statement of Cash Flows

The statement of cash flows can also be used to determine how much additional financing a company will need in some future period. Suppose the Summit Furniture Company, whose statement of cash flows for 2016 was shown earlier in Table 4.2, is preparing a cash flow forecast for 2017 in the fall of 2016.

Operating Activities Based on sales and cost projections for the coming year, management forecasts that net cash provided by operations will be $21,000,000, as shown in Table 4.7.

---

[8]Cash management is discussed further in Chapter 17.

[9]Note that the cash budget does not include any interest payments on this loan (or interest earned on investments of excess cash). These items generally have a relatively small impact on cash flows. However, they can be added to the cash budget if necessary.

TABLE 4.7

Pro Forma Statement of Cash Flows for the Year Ending December 31, 2017—Summit Furniture Company

Increase (Decrease) in Cash and Cash Equivalents* (000)			Comments
Cash Flows Expected from Operating Activities:			
Cash received from customers	$ 170,000		Forecasted cash receipts and disbursements
Cash paid to suppliers and employees	(140,000)		
Interest received	500		
Interest paid (net of amount capitalized)	(2,500)		
Income taxes paid	(7,000)		
Expected net cash provided (used) by operating activities		$ 21,000	
Cash Flows Expected from Investing Activities:			
Proceeds from sale of assets	—		
Capital expenditures	(25,000)		Planned capital expenditures
Expected net cash provided (used) by investing activities		(25,000)	
Cash Flows Expected from Financing Activities:			
Net borrowings under bank line-of-credit agreement	2,000		
Repayment of long-term debt	(3,000)		
Proceeds from issuance of long-term debt	7,000		
Proceeds from issuance of common stock	—		
Dividends paid	(500)		
Expected net cash provided (used) by financing activities		**5,500**	= 25,000 + 1,500 − 21,000
Expected Net Increase (Decrease) in Cash and Cash Equivalents		1,500	Required increase in cash
Cash and Cash Equivalents at Beginning of Year		5,200	From Table 4.2
Expected Cash and Cash Equivalents at End of Year		$ 6,700	Desired cash balance

*Cash and cash equivalents include currency on hand, bank deposits and similar accounts, and short-term (maturities less than three months), highly liquid investments.

Investing Activities Expansion of its warehouse and the opening of two new stores will require a capital expenditure of $25,000,000 during the coming year. Unlike the previous year, no asset sales are expected during 2017.

Financing Activities In order to support the higher level of sales in 2017, the company estimates that it will have to increase its cash and cash equivalents by $1,500,000, that is, from $5,200,000 at the beginning of 2017 to $6,700,000 at the end of the year. Substituting the relevant data into Equation 4.3 yields the amount of additional financing required by financing activities during the year:

$$\$1{,}500{,}000 = \$21{,}000{,}000 + (-\$25{,}000{,}000) + \text{Net cash provided (used) by financing activities}$$

$$\text{Net cash provided (used) by financing activities} = \$5{,}500{,}000$$

The pro forma statement of cash flows in Table 4.7 details how Summit expects to achieve $5,500,000 of net cash provided by financing activities. The company must repay $3,000,000 in long-term debt that comes due during 2017. Furthermore, the company has decided to maintain dividend payments at the current (2016) $500,000 level and not to issue any new common stock. Needed cash will be raised using a combination of short-term and long-term sources—namely, by borrowing $2,000,000 under a bank line-of-credit agreement and by issuing $7,000,000 in long-term debt.

4-4d Computerized Financial Forecasting and Planning Models

financial planning models

In recent years, many companies have spent considerable amounts of time and money developing models to represent various aspects of their financial planning process, as well as cash flow forecasting. These are generally called **financial planning models** and are usually implemented using computerized software. A detailed discussion of these models is beyond the scope of this text because it requires a familiarity with a number of quantitative techniques, such as regression analysis and linear programming—topics not covered here. A brief general introduction to the topic is provided for informational purposes, however.

Financial planning models are often classified according to whether they are *deterministic* or *probabilistic* and whether they attempt to *optimize* (that is, achieve the most desirable level of) the value of some objective function, such as net income or stock price.

deterministic model

A **deterministic model** gives a single-number forecast of a financial variable or variables without stating anything about its probability of occurrence. An example of a deterministic model is a computerized representation of a firm's operating budget, or a *budget simulator*. Companies that employ budget simulators enter estimated future revenues and expenses into the computer and receive as output an estimate of various financial variables, such as net income and earnings per share. The model tells the company nothing about the chances of achieving these estimates, nor does it indicate whether the company will be able to manage its resources in such a way as to attain higher levels of these variables.

sensitivity analysis

The main advantage of deterministic models is that they allow the user to perform *sensitivity analyses* quickly and easily. A **sensitivity analysis** essentially consists of rerunning the model to determine the effect on the output variables of changes in the input variables. For example, a company may want to know *what* its net income will be *if* it discontinues some product line. Thus, sensitivity analysis is also called *what-if* analysis.

Some companies prepare different budgets to reflect different assumptions about the type of year they expect to have. For instance, a company may compile three separate budgets to reflect *pessimistic*, *realistic*, and *optimistic* assumptions about the coming year. Such scenario analysis is especially helpful in preparing for unexpected events such as the U.S./global financial crisis of 2008–2009. One company that owes its success to such planning is JDS Uniphase, a high-tech communications equipment manufacturer. Each year, JDS prepares three sales scenarios for the coming year with supporting plans for each. This exercise turned out to be especially astute during the recent financial storm when sales fell by 15 percent in the 2009 fiscal year for the firm. Because of their scenario planning, the company was prepared to put into motion a series of actions before it was too late. As a result, despite the sales crunch, the firm did not experience any cash shortfalls.[10] Whereas these scenario analysis models are essentially deterministic, they represent a first step toward the use of probabilistic models.

probabilistic models

Probabilistic models are becoming increasingly popular because they often provide financial decision makers with more useful information than other models. Whereas deterministic models yield single-point estimates, probabilistic models yield more general probability distributions. To illustrate, suppose a company is planning to build a new plant. Instead of estimating a single sales figure, the company's planners might estimate a 25 percent chance that the firm's sales will be \$2 million, a 50 percent chance that they will be \$3 million, and a 25 percent chance that they will be \$4 million. The use of a probabilistic planning model yields output in the form of a probability distribution,

[10] Cari Tuna, "Theory and Practice: Pendulum Is Swinging Back on 'Scenario Planning,'" *The Wall Street Journal* (July 6, 2009): B6.

which gives the company's planners more useful information than a deterministic model would. In the case of complex probabilistic models, more input is necessary.[11]

optimization models

Optimization models determine the values of financial decision variables that optimize (that is, maximize or minimize) some objective function such as profits or costs. For example, consider an oil refinery whose capacity and production costs are known. By combining these known figures with estimates of the sales prices for gasoline and heating fuel, it is possible, with the use of an optimization model, to specify what output product mix will achieve an optimal level of operating income. Optimization models are not used widely in finance, even though various applications have been proposed in the financial literature.

4-4e Using Financial Ratios to Forecast Future Financial Performance

A type of forecasting that analysts and managers are interested in involves predicting a firm's financial events. Such events include bankruptcy, being acquired by another company, going public, dividend changes, and the like. An exhaustive coverage of forecasting financial events is beyond the scope of this text; instead, we present a brief overview of how one such event—bankruptcy—can be forecasted using financial data.

Whereas traditional financial ratio analysis may be useful in predicting bankruptcy, one of its primary limitations is that it looks at only one ratio at a time and then relies on the analyst to form a judgment about the overall financial profile of the firm. Recently, more powerful statistical techniques have been applied to assist analysts in making judgments about the financial condition of the firm.

discriminant analysis

Discriminant analysis is a statistical technique that helps the analyst classify observations (firms) into two or more predetermined groups based on certain characteristics of the observation. In the context of financial statement analysis, the characteristics typically are financial ratios.

One early application of discriminant analysis in finance was a model developed by Edward Altman to predict bankruptcy of firms.[12] Altman identified five financial ratios that contributed significantly to the predictive accuracy of his model:

1. Net working capital/Total assets
2. Retained earnings/Total assets
3. EBIT/Total assets
4. Market value of total equity (common and preferred)/Book value of total debt
5. Sales/Total assets

Altman's basic model was developed from a sample of 66 manufacturing firms—half of which went bankrupt. On the basis of the analysis, he established a guideline score, which could be used to classify firms as either financially sound or headed toward bankruptcy. The lower the score, the greater the probability of bankruptcy; the higher the score, the lower the probability of bankruptcy. In other words, the lower the values of the five ratios just listed, in general, the greater the probability of bankruptcy.

Since Altman's original model, there have been more refined models using better statistical techniques (logit, neural networks, etc.) and additional ratios that have achieved bankruptcy prediction accuracy of 100 percent one year preceding bankruptcy and as much as 93 percent three years preceding bankruptcy.[13]

---

[11]Additional examples of probabilistic models are discussed in Chapter 11.

[12]Edward I. Altman, "Financial Ratios, Discriminant Analysis, and the Prediction of Corporate Bankruptcy," *Journal of Finance* (September 1968): 589–609.

[13]Jodi Bellovary, Don Giacomino, and Michael Akers, "A Review of Bankruptcy Prediction Studies: 1930 to Present," *Journal of Financial Education* (Winter 2007): 1–42.

4-5 Summary

- For growth and survival, firms have to conduct two types of planning exercises:

  1. The strategic plan is long range in nature and deals with the overall direction of the firm.
  2. The operational plan addresses the operational objectives of the firm. It serves as a blueprint detailing where the firm wants to be at some future point in time and what resources are needed to get it there. Operational plans are generally conducted at two levels—long term and short term.

- The operational plan consists of a marketing plan, a production plan, a human resource plan, and a financial plan. The marketing plan lays out the marketing resources needed to meet the operational objectives and includes such things as advertising strategy, marketing promotions, channels of distribution and distribution incentives, and assignment of sales territory. The production plan consists of facilities needed to meet the operational objectives, including the number of shifts, plant refurbishment and expansions, vendor and supplier arrangements, inventory control, etc. The human resource plan is concerned with the personnel aspect of the objectives. The financial plan lays out the financial resources that are needed to achieve the operational objectives of the firm including the financial objectives of the firm.
- The cash flow concept is a fundamental concept in finance. Financial managers focus on raising cash to invest in assets that will, in turn, generate future cash flows for the firm and its owners.
- After-tax cash flow is equal to earnings after taxes plus noncash charges. Depreciation and deferred taxes are examples of noncash charges.
- The statement of cash flows is a major financial statement showing the effects of a firm's operating, investing, and financing activities on its cash balance.
- Financial forecasting involves the projection and estimation of a firm's future cash needs. The percentage of sales method, cash budgeting, the pro forma statement of cash flows, and computerized financial planning models are used in financial forecasting. Pro forma financial statements are usually an integral part of any financial plan. *Pro forma financial statements* show the results of some *assumed* rather than *actual* events.
- The *percentage of sales* method is used to estimate the amount of additional financing that will be needed to support a given future sales level.
- *Cash budgets* are projections of cash receipts and disbursements over some future time period. The steps involved in preparing a cash budget include the following:

  1. Estimating cash receipts based on historical information about the collection of receivables
  2. Scheduling disbursements
  3. Determining a minimum cash balance
  4. Calculating the amount of loans required to cover any cash shortages

- A *financial planning model* is a computerized representation of some aspect of a firm's financial planning process. Financial planning models are usually classified according to whether they are *deterministic* or *probabilistic* and whether they seek to *optimize* the value of some objective function.

Important Equations

$$\text{ATCF} = \text{EAT} + \text{Noncash charges}$$

$$\text{ATCF} = \text{EAT} + \text{Depreciation} + \text{Deferred taxes}$$

$$\begin{aligned}\text{Total financing needed} &= \text{Forecasted asset increase} - \text{Forecasted current liability increase}\\ &= \frac{A}{S}(\Delta S) - \frac{CL}{S}(\Delta S)\end{aligned}$$

$$\begin{aligned}\text{Additional financing needed} &= \text{Total financing needed} - \text{Increased retained earnings}\\ &= \left[\frac{A}{S}(\Delta S) - \frac{CL}{S}(\Delta S)\right] - [\text{EAT} - D]\end{aligned}$$

4-6 Questions and Topics for Discussion

1. What are *deferred taxes,* and how do they come into being?
2. What are *pro forma financial statements*?
3. What is the *percentage of sales forecasting method*? What are some of the limitations financial analysts should be aware of in applying this method?
4. What is a *cash budget*? What are the usual steps involved in preparing a cash budget?
5. Illustrate how the statement of cash flows can be used as a financial planning technique.
6. Explain the difference between deterministic and probabilistic financial planning models.

4-7 Self-Test Problems

ST1. Jenkins Properties had gross fixed assets of $1,000 at the end of 2015. By the end of 2016, these had grown to $1,100. Accumulated depreciation at the end of 2015 was $500, and it was $575 at the end of 2016. Jenkins has no interest expenses. Jenkins expected sales during 2016 to total $500. Operating expenses (exclusive of depreciation) were forecasted to be $125. Jenkins's marginal tax rate is 40 percent.

a. What was Jenkins's 2016 depreciation expense?

b. What was Jenkins's 2016 earnings after taxes (EAT)?

c. What was Jenkins's 2016 after-tax cash flow using Equation 4.1?

d. Show that EAT less the increase in *net* fixed assets is equivalent to after-tax cash flow less the increase in *gross* fixed assets.

ST2. Piedmont Products Inc. (PPI) has current sales of $60 million. Sales are expected to grow to $80 million next year. PPI currently has accounts receivable of $9 million, inventories of $15 million, and net fixed assets of $21 million. These assets are expected to grow at the same rate as sales over the next year. Accounts payable are expected to increase from their current level of $15 million to a new level of $19 million next year. PPI wants to increase its cash balance at the end of next year by $3 million over its current cash balance. Earnings after taxes next year are forecasted to be $12 million. PPI plans to pay a $2 million dividend. PPI's marginal tax rate is 40 percent.

How much external financing is required by PPI next year?

ST3. Use the percentage of sales forecasting method to compute the additional financing needed by Lambrechts Specialty Shops, Inc. (LSS), if sales are expected to increase from a current level of $20 million to a new level of $25 million over the coming year. LSS expects earnings after taxes to equal $1 million over the next year (2017). LSS intends to pay a $300,000 dividend next year. The current year balance sheet for LSS is as follows:

Lambrechts Specialty Shops, Inc. Balance Sheet as of December 31, 2016

Cash	$ 1,000,000	Accounts payable	$ 3,000,000
Accounts receivable	1,500,000	Notes payable	3,000,000
Inventories	6,000,000	Long-term debt	2,000,000
Net fixed assets	3,000,000	Stockholders' equity	3,500,000
Total assets	$11,500,000	Total liabilities and equity	$11,500,000

All assets, except "cash," are expected to vary proportionately with sales. Of total liabilities and equity, only "accounts payable" is expected to vary proportionately with sales.

ST4. Refer to the Summit Furniture Company example (Table 4.2). Recalculate the cash and cash equivalents at the end of 2016 assuming that (1) the company had 2016 capital expenditures of $22,000; (2) it paid dividends of $800; and (3) it did not issue any common stock. Assume that Summit's other cash flows are the same as those shown in Table 4.2.

4-8 Problems*

BASIC

1. Last year, Blue Lake Mines, Inc., had earnings after tax of $650,000. Included in its expenses were depreciation of $400,000 and deferred taxes of $100,000. The company also purchased new capital equipment for $300,000 last year. Calculate Blue Lake's after-tax cash flow for last year.

BASIC

2. Prepare a statement of cash flows (using the indirect method) for the Midland Manufacturing Corporation for the year ending December 2016, based on the following comparative balance sheets.

Midland Manufacturing Corporation
Comparative Balance Sheets (in Millions of Dollars)*

	December 31, 2015	December 31, 2016
Assets		
Current assets:		
Cash	$ 4.9	$ 0.8
Accounts receivable, net	7.2	7.5
Inventories	13.8	14.5
Total current assets	$ 25.9	$ 22.8
Property and equipment	$ 80.7	$115.0
Less: Accumulated depreciation	16.3	25.8
Net property and equipment	$ 64.4	$ 89.2
Total assets	$ 90.3	$112.0
Liabilities and Stockholders' Equity		
Current liabilities:		
Accounts payable	$ 8.0	$ 9.5
Other current liabilities	6.0	8.2
Total current liabilities	$ 14.0	$ 17.7
Long-term debt	18.8	31.8
Deferred federal income taxes	1.2	1.4
Stockholders' equity:		
Common stock	$ 3.0	$ 3.0
Additional paid-in capital	29.0	29.0
Retained earnings	24.3	29.1
Total stockholders' equity	$ 56.3	$ 61.1
Total liabilities and stockholders' equity	$ 90.3	$112.0

*Net income for the year ended December 31, 2016, totaled $8.3 million; dividends paid during the same period totaled $3.5 million; $2.0 million of long-term debt was retired in 2016; and fixed assets were sold during 2016 for $1.0 million.

*Color blocks behind the numbers denote problems that have check answers provided at the end of the book.

CHALLENGE

3. Consider the Industrial Supply Company example (Table 4.4) again. Assume that the company plans to maintain its dividend payments at the same level in 2017 as in 2016. Also assume that all of the additional financing needed is in the form of short-term notes payable. Determine the amount of additional financing needed and pro forma financial statements (that is, balance sheet, income statement, and selected financial ratios) for 2017 under each of the following conditions:

	Increase in Sales	Increase in Expenses
a.	$3,750,000	$3,750,000
b.	$3,000,000	$2,800,000
c.	$4,500,000	$4,000,000

CHALLENGE

4. Prepare a cash budget for Atlas Products, Inc., for the first quarter of 2017, based on the following information:

The budgeting section of the corporate finance department of Atlas Products has received the following sales estimates from the marketing department:

	Total Sales	Credit Sales
December 2016	$825,000	$770,000
January 2017	730,000	690,000
February 2017	840,000	780,000
March 2017	920,000	855,000

The company has found that, on average, about 25 percent of its credit sales are collected during the month when the sale is made, and the remaining 75 percent of credit sales are collected during the month following the sale. As a result, the company uses these figures for budgeting.

The company estimates its purchases at 60 percent of next month's sales, and payments for those purchases are budgeted to lag the purchases by one month. Various disbursements have been estimated as follows:

	January	February	March
Wages and salaries	$250,000	$290,000	$290,000
Rent	27,000	27,000	27,000
Other expenses	10,000	12,000	14,000

In addition, a tax payment of $105,000 is due on January 15, and $40,000 in dividends will be declared in January and paid in March. Also, the company has ordered a $75,000 piece of equipment. Delivery is scheduled for early January, and payment will be due in February.

The company's projected cash balance at the beginning of January is $100,000, and the company desires to maintain a balance of $100,000 at the end of each month.

CHALLENGE

5. Prepare a cash budget for Elmwood Manufacturing Company for the first three months of 2017 based on the following information:

Month	Estimated Sales	Estimated Factory Overhead	Estimated Selling and Administrative Expenses
December 2016	$ 4,600,000	$640,000	$1,250,000
January 2017	6,400,000	650,000	1,275,000
February 2017	11,200,000	670,000	1,285,000
March 2017	8,400,000	670,000	1,310,000
April 2017	7,000,000	680,000	1,300,000

The company has found that approximately 40 percent of sales are collected during the month the sale is made and the remaining 60 percent are collected during the month following the sale. Material purchases are 30 percent of next month's estimated sales, and payments lag these purchases by one month. Labor costs are 35 percent of next month's sales and are paid during the month incurred. Factory overhead and selling and administrative expenses are paid during the month incurred. In addition, a payment for new equipment of $1.5 million is due in February. Also, a tax payment of $1.6 million and a dividend payment of $650,000 are due in March.

The company's projected cash balance at the beginning of January is $1.5 million. Furthermore, Elmwood desires to maintain a $750,000 cash balance at the end of each month.

CHALLENGE

6. The Podrasky Corporation is considering a $200 million expansion (capital expenditure) program next year. The company wants to know approximately how much additional financing (if any) will be required if it decides to go through with the expansion program. The company currently has $400 million in net fixed assets on its books. Next year, the company expects to earn $80 million after interest and taxes. The company also expects to maintain its present level of dividends, which is $15 million. If the expansion program is accepted, the company expects its inventory and accounts receivable each to increase by approximately $20 million next year. Long-term debt retirement obligations total $10 million for next year, and depreciation is expected to be $80 million. The company does not expect to sell any fixed assets next year. The company maintains a cash balance of $5 million, which is sufficient for its present operations. If the expansion is accepted, the company feels it should increase its year-end cash balance to $8 million because of the increased level of activities. For planning purposes, assume no other cash flow changes for next year.

CHALLENGE

7. Baldwin Products Company anticipates reaching a sales level of $6 million in one year. The company expects earnings after taxes during the next year to equal $400,000. During the past several years, the company has been paying $50,000 in dividends to its stockholders. The company expects to continue this policy for at least the next year. The actual balance sheet and income statement for Baldwin during 2016 follow.

Baldwin Products Company Balance Sheet as of December 31, 2016

Cash	$ 200,000	Accounts payable	$ 600,000
Accounts receivable	400,000	Notes payable	500,000
Inventories	1,200,000	Long-term debt	200,000
Fixed assets, net	500,000	Stockholders' equity	1,000,000
Total assets	$2,300,000	Total liabilities and equity	$2,300,000

Income Statement for the Year Ending December 31, 2016	
Sales	$4,000,000
Expenses, including interest and taxes	$3,700,000
Earnings after taxes	$ 300,000

a. Using the percentage of sales method, calculate the additional financing Baldwin Products will need over the next year at the $6 million sales level. Show the pro forma balance sheet for the company as of December 31, 2017, assuming that a sales level of $6 million is reached. Assume that the additional financing needed is obtained in the form of additional notes payable.

b. Suppose that the Baldwin Products' management feels that the average collection period on its additional sales—that is, sales over $4 million—will be 60 days, instead of the current level. By what amount will this increase in the average collection period increase the financing needed by the company over the next year?

c. If the Baldwin Products' banker requires the company to maintain a current ratio equal to 1.6 or greater, what is the maximum amount of additional financing that can be in the form of bank borrowings (notes payable)? What other potential sources of financing are available to the company?

INTERMEDIATE

8. In the Industrial Supply Company example (Table 4.4), it was assumed that the company's fixed assets were being used at nearly full capacity and that net fixed assets would have to increase proportionately as sales increased. Alternatively, suppose that the company has excess fixed assets and that *no increase* in net fixed assets is required as sales are increased. Assume that the company plans to maintain its dividend payments at the same level in 2017 as in 2016. Determine the amount of additional financing needed for 2017 under each of the following conditions:

	Increase in Sales	Increase in Expenses
a.	$3,750,000	$3,750,000
b.	$3,000,000	$2,800,000
c.	$4,500,000	$4,000,000

INTERMEDIATE

9. Berea Resources is planning a $75 million capital expenditure program for the coming year. Next year, Berea expects to report to the IRS earnings of $40 million after interest and taxes. The company presently has 20 million shares of common stock issued and outstanding. Dividend payments are expected to increase from the present level of $10 million to $12 million. The company expects its current asset needs to increase from a current level of $25 million to $30 million. Current liabilities, excluding short-term bank borrowings, are expected to increase from $15 million to $17 million. Interest payments are $5 million next year, and long-term debt retirement obligations are $8 million next year. Depreciation next year is expected to be $15 million on the company's financial statements, but the company will report depreciation of $18 million for tax purposes.

How much external financing is required by Berea for the coming year?

INTERMEDIATE

10. Appalachian Registers, Inc. (ARI) has current sales of $50 million. Sales are expected to grow to $75 million next year. ARI currently has accounts receivable of $10 million, inventories of $15 million, and net fixed assets of $20 million. These assets are expected to grow at the same rate as sales over the next year. Accounts payable are expected to increase from their current level of $10 million to a new level of $13 million next year. ARI wants to increase its cash balance at the end of next year by

$2 million over its current cash balances, which average $4 million. Earnings after taxes next year are forecasted to be $10 million. Next year, ARI plans to pay dividends of $1 million, up from $500,000 this year. ARI's marginal tax rate is 34 percent.

How much external financing is required by ARI next year?

BASIC **11.** Do a Google search for "Preparing a Cash Flow Forecast." Choose a site that provides cash flow forecasting tools and templates. Prepare a one-page memo to your instructor summarizing what you found and compare it to the cash flow forecasting discussion in this chapter.

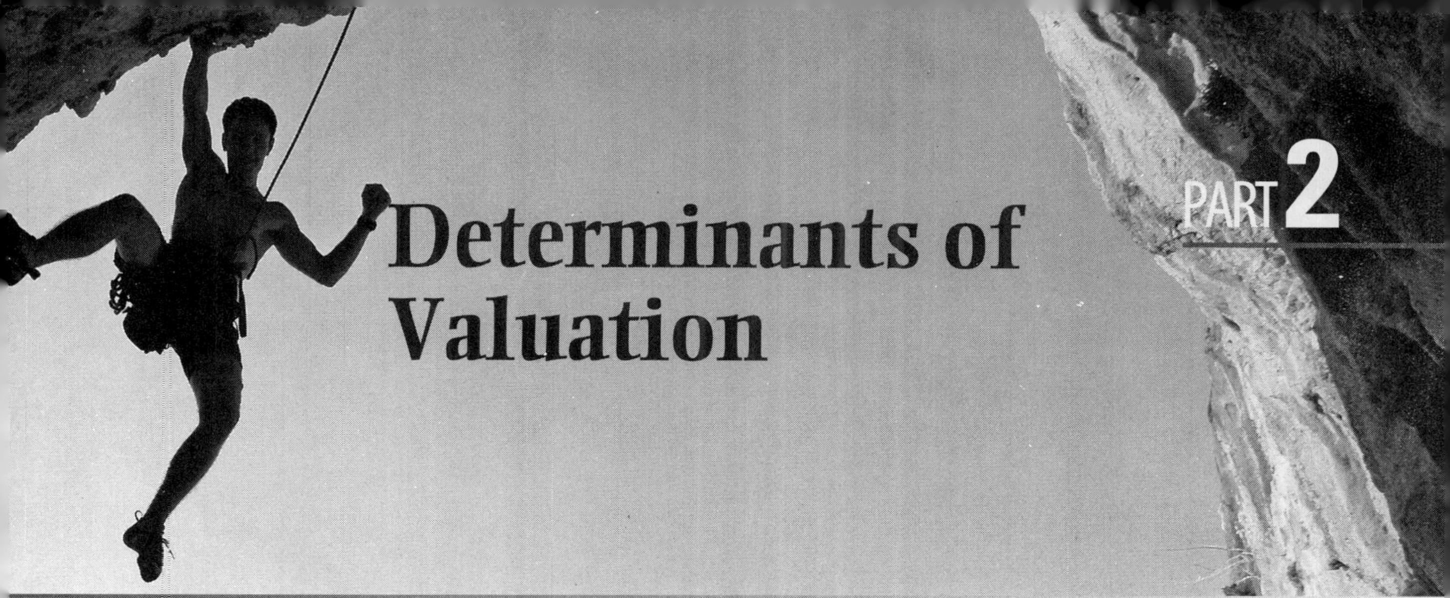

PART 2

Determinants of Valuation

CHAPTER 5
The Time Value of Money

CHAPTER 6
Fixed-Income Securities: Characteristics and Valuation

CHAPTER 7
Common Stock: Characteristics, Valuation, and Issuance

CHAPTER 8
Analysis of Risk and Return

The primary objective of financial management is to maximize the value of the stock of the firm's shareholders. This part discusses the valuation process in detail. Chapter 5 deals with the time value of money, which is essential for any serious analysis of important financial decisions that impact an enterprise over a number of years. Chapters 6 and 7 build valuation models for a firm's securities. Chapter 6 focuses on the valuation of fixed-income securities—namely, bonds and preferred stock. Chapter 7 deals with the valuation of common stock. Chapter 7 also discusses the offering process for securities. Chapter 8 explores the determinants of risk and relates risk to the valuation process. These chapters are important because valuation is the dominant theme carried throughout the text and it is related to all financial decisions.

CHAPTER 5

The Time Value of Money

KEY CHAPTER CONCEPTS

1. The concept of interest:
   a. Simple interest is paid on the principal sum only.
   b. Compound interest is paid both on the initial principal amount and on any interest earned but not withdrawn during earlier periods.
2. Future (compound) value calculations determine the value at some point in time in the future of a given amount invested today, earning some compound rate of interest, *i*, per period.
3. Present value calculations determine the value today (present value) of some amount to be received in the future.
4. An annuity is a series of equal periodic payments.
   a. Ordinary annuity payments are made at the end of each period.
   b. Annuity due payments are made at the beginning of each period.
5. The future value of an annuity calculation determines the future value of an annuity stream of payments.
6. The present value of an annuity calculation determines the present value of an annuity stream of payments.
7. The net present value rule is the primary decision-making rule used throughout the practice of financial management.
   a. The net present value of an investment is equal to the present value of the future cash flows minus the initial outlay.
   b. The net present value of an investment made by a firm represents the contribution of that investment to the value of the firm and, accordingly, to the wealth of shareholders.
8. Other important topics include:
   a. Compounding frequency
   b. Determining the present value of perpetuities
   c. Determining the present value of uneven cash flow streams
   d. Determining the present value of deferred annuities

FINANCIAL CHALLENGE

Pension Obligations and the Discount Rate

Most larger companies, as well as federal, state, and local governments and not-for-profit organizations, offer their employees pension benefits. Two basic types of plans are offered—defined contribution plans, for example 401(k)s, and defined benefit plans. With a defined contribution plan, through contributions from the employer and/or employee, the plan is fully funded on the day the employee retires, and the employer has no further financial liability to the pension plan. With a defined benefit plan, the employer is obligated to provide a given amount of retirement benefits to the employee, usually based on the number of years worked and the salary or other forms of compensation received. The employer (and possibly also the employee) is supposed to deposit a sufficient amount of assets, such as money or securities, into a fund to cover these future obligations. Many companies are switching to defined contribution plans in order to limit their future pension liabilities. The number of defined benefit plans fell from 103,346 in 1975 to 46,543 in 2010. Among larger companies, 584 of the *Fortune* 1000 companies had defined benefit plans in 2011 compared with 633 companies in 2004.

The amount that the employer needs to set aside today in a defined benefit plan to meet future pension obligations depends on the discount rate, that is, the interest rate or rate of return, the pension plan expects to earn between when the funds are invested and when the required pension payments are due. The lower the discount rate, the larger will be the required contributions to the plan. For example, if the pension plan can generate an 8 percent rate of return, a $1,000 pension payment due in 20 years generates a $215 payment obligation today. However, if the plan can earn only a 4 percent return over the next 20 years, then the present pension liability increases to $456.

With interest rates at or near historic lows, employers were faced with the need to increase contributions to their pension plans. For example, despite contributing $3.4 billion to its pension plans, which was $2 billion more than legally required, Ford's unfunded pension liability increased to $18.7 billion in 2012. This was due in part because the company had to lower the discount rate used in calculating its future pension liabilities from 4.6 percent to 3.84 percent. Similarly, because of lackluster investment returns, as well as increased benefit payments and failure in the past to adequately fund its pension obligations, many state and local governments were faced with serious pension fund deficits. For example, according to Standard and Poor's, Illinois had a $94.6 billion deficit in its pension funds in 2012. It was estimated that the state's pension fund covered only 40.4 percent of its future obligations—the lowest of any state. For planning purposes, Illinois' various pension plans used projected discount rates between 7 percent and 8.5 percent, whereas actual 10-year average rates of return were much lower—ranging from 2.4 percent to 3.6 percent.

© Monkey Business Images/Shutterstock.com

Many decisions that companies and individual investors make involve streams of returns that are spread out over future time periods. To make informed choices, decision makers must have a working knowledge of the time value of money—the topic of this chapter.

Sources: David Reilly, "Illinois Pension Plans Should Go Dutch," *The Wall Street Journal* (February 19–20, 2011): B18; John A. Sugden, "U.S. State Pension Funding: Strong Investment Returns Could Lift Funded Returns, but Longer Term Challenges Remain," www.standardandpoors.com/ratingsdirect (June 24, 2014): 1–22; Mike Ramsey and Vipal Monga, "Low Rates Force Companies to Pour Cash into Pensions," *The Wall Street Journal* (February 4, 2013): A1.

CHAPTER OBJECTIVES

Upon completion of this chapter, you should have a clear understanding of the following:

1. The meaning of interest and discount rates
2. The concept of future and present values and how to calculate these values
3. The meaning and implication of compounding and compounding frequency
4. How to calculate the future and present values of an annuity and the present value of a perpetuity
5. The meaning and calculation of effective interest rates
6. The application of present and future value concepts to special situations such as growth rates and loan amortization

5-1 Introduction

HTTP:
Click on the Investment Analysis Calculator button at
www.cengage.com/finance/moyer
for an interactive financial calculator for future and present value calculations.

Understanding the time value of money is crucial to effective financial management. In fact, anyone who is involved with money should have some comprehension of the time value of money. Consider the following:

- A banker who makes loans and other investments
- A financial officer whose job includes consideration of various alternative sources of funds in terms of their cost
- A company manager who must choose among various alternative investment projects
- A securities analyst who evaluates the securities that a firm sells to investors
- An individual who is confronted with a host of daily financial problems ranging from personal credit account management to deciding how to finance a new home purchase

Each of these individuals makes frequent use of the time value of money. Many people fear that a working knowledge of the time value of money concept might be too difficult to master. However, the availability of interest tables, financial calculators, and spreadsheet programs such as Excel makes the subject readily accessible.

Although an understanding of the time value of money is useful in and of itself, it is also a necessary prelude to the following topics:

- Valuation of securities and other assets
- Capital budgeting (the analysis of investment projects)
- The cost of capital
- Working capital (short-term asset and liability) management
- Lease analysis

This chapter introduces the concepts and skills necessary to understand the time value of money and its applications. The analysis in this chapter assumes that you will use either a financial calculator, an Excel spreadsheet, or the interest tables (Tables I through IV) at the end of the book to solve problems. Calculator and spreadsheet solutions are presented for many of the examples in this chapter. However, we are primarily interested in having you learn the principles of the time value of money.

5-1a A Word About Notation

A brief discussion of financial notation is in order before we begin our discussion of the time value of money. In finance, as a general rule, lowercase letters are used to denote percentage rates and lengths of time, whereas capital letters are used to denote money or dollar amounts. For example, we use i to denote the interest rate, n to denote the number of periods, *PMT* to denote cash payments, PV to denote the **present value** dollar amount, and FV to denote the **future value** dollar amount. One important exception in this text is that we use T to denote the tax rate instead of t. Lowercase t denotes time. Our use of i to denote the interest rate is similar to the notation used on most financial calculators. However, later in the text, for example in Chapter 6, when the interest rate becomes a specific required rate of return, we use k to denote required return, as is the custom used by many financial analysts.

present value
future value

5-1b CFM Excel Templates

Another feature of *Contemporary Financial Management*, 14th edition, is the availability of Excel templates to solve a wide range of complex financial management problems, including the loan amortization problems encountered in this chapter. These templates are designed to be used in conjunction with the Excel electronic spreadsheet program. The CFM Excel templates require *no prior knowledge of Excel* and are menu driven. The templates are available at the book's Web site (www.cengage.com/finance/moyer). As part of the problem section of selected chapters, we have included problems that can be solved using these templates. These problems are identified by an Excel icon printed next to the problem number.

5-2 The Use of Financial Calculators and Spreadsheets

The concepts in this chapter are illustrated using four methods. Time value of money problems may be solved using *mathematical formulas*, *special interest factor tables* provided at the end of the textbook, *financial calculators*, and *spreadsheet software*. The serious business student should plan on becoming adept at the use of financial calculators and spreadsheet software, such as Microsoft Excel, to solve time value of money problems efficiently. Spreadsheet software also has many applications across all business disciplines. In addition to applications in this chapter, spreadsheets are useful in solving *security valuation*, *capital budgeting*, and *financial forecasting problems*. Most employers consider it an asset if a potential employee is already familiar with the use of spreadsheets.

While the use of financial calculators and spreadsheets is encouraged, we urge students to familiarize themselves as well with the formulas and the use of the tables in solving the basic time value of money problems. Solving problems initially by using formulas and the tables provides a better appreciation of what is happening on a conceptual level. We have found that going straight to the calculators or to spreadsheets often results in students thinking in mechanical terms—inputting numbers into a calculator or a spreadsheet with little appreciation for what it is they are really trying to do in the problem.

HTTP:
If you need to calculate present value and future value but don't have access to a handheld calculator or a spreadsheet, try one of many Web sites that have built-in time-value calculators, such as the one at Salem Five.

www.salemfive.com

5-2a Calculator Solution

The calculator solutions are illustrated in the margins throughout the chapter. The same basic steps are involved regardless of which financial calculator you use. There are five basic keys that are utilized for solving time value of money problems. You can think of each key as a specific variable. While the location and specific notation may vary between calculators, usually the five keys are grouped together. An example of a margin calculator solution is shown in the margin on this page.

The five basic keys are:

n i PV PMT FV

n = Number of periods
i = Interest rate per period
PV = Present value amount
PMT = Payment
FV = Future value amount

Calculator Solutions

Key	Enter
n	1.0
i	14.0
PV	
PMT	
FV	−28.50
	Solution
PV	25.00

As a general guideline, you should do the following before using a financial calculator to solve a time value of money problem:

1. Set number of payments per year to 1.
2. Clear the time value of money registers so that values held over from a previous problem do not affect your current calculations.
3. Set payments to end-of-period mode.
4. Some calculators are preset to display only two decimal places; while this may be sufficient in most instances, we suggest removing this feature, to use floating-decimal.

5-2b Spreadsheet Solution

Spreadsheet solutions are presented for selected problems in special boxes throughout the chapter. Although a variety of spreadsheets exist, we will be illustrating problems in this chapter using Microsoft Excel. Spreadsheets are simply a series of the rows and columns making up a matrix of cells. The rows are identified by numbers while the columns are referenced by letters. A sample spreadsheet is shown here:

Spreadsheet Strategies

	A	B	C	D	E	F	G	H
2								
3								
4								
5								
6								
7								
8								
9								
10								
11								
12								
13								
14								
15								
16								
17								
18								
19								

Individual cells are identified by the row and column in which they are located. For example, the highlighted cell in the sample spreadsheet above is B4—column B, row 4. The cells may contain text material, numbers, or formulas. In solving time value of money problems, we will be using several time value of money *functions* built into the spreadsheet software. Functions are formulas built into the spreadsheet, sparing us the need to actually enter the formulas. The functions we will be using are:

PV—to calculate present value

FV—to calculate future value

PMT—to calculate payments

NPER—to calculate the number of periods

RATE—to calculate the interest rate or discount rate

These functions are used to calculate the corresponding variable, given other known values for the problem.

5-3 Interest

Money can be thought of as having a time value. In other words, an amount of money received today is worth more than the same dollar amount would be if it were received a year from now.[1] The primary reason that a dollar today is worth more than a dollar to be received sometime in the future is that the current dollar can be invested to earn a rate of return. (This holds true even if risk and inflation are not considerations.) Suppose, for example, that you had $100 and decided to put it into a savings account for a year. By doing this, you would temporarily give up, or forgo, spending the $100 however you wished, or you might forgo the return that the $100 might earn from some alternative investment, such as U.S. Treasury bonds. Or you might forgo paying an additional $100 on your mortgage. Similarly, a bank that loans money to a firm forgoes the opportunity to earn a return on some alternative investment.

interest

principal

rate of interest

Interest is the return earned by or the amount paid to someone who has forgone current consumption or alternative investment opportunities and "rented" money in a creditor relationship.[2] The **principal** is the amount of money borrowed or invested. The term of a loan is the length of time or number of time periods during which the borrower can use the principal. The **rate of interest** is the percentage on the principal that the borrower pays the lender per time period as compensation for forgoing other investment or consumption opportunities.

5-4 Simple Interest

simple interest

Simple interest is the interest paid (in the case of borrowed money) or earned (in the case of invested money) on the principal only. The amount of simple interest is equal to the product of the principal times the rate per time period times the number of time periods:

(5.1)
$$I = PV_0 \times i \times n$$

[1]The terms *amount of money, cash flow,* and *payment* are used interchangeably throughout the chapter.

[2]Although other forms of returns are dealt with throughout the text, this discussion is limited to borrowing–lending situations.

where I = the simple interest in dollars; PV_0 = the principal amount at time 0, or the present value; i = the interest rate per time period; and n = the number of time periods. The following problems illustrate the use of Equation 5.1.

1. *What is the simple interest on \$100 at 10 percent per annum for six months?* Substituting \$100 for PV_0, 10 percent (0.10) for i, and $^6/_{12}$ (0.5) for n yields the following:

$$\begin{aligned} I &= \$100 \times 0.10 \times 0.5 \\ &= \$5 \end{aligned}$$

2. *If Isaiah Williams bought a house and borrowed \$30,000 at a 10 percent annual interest rate, what would be his first month's interest payment?* Substituting \$30,000 for PV_0, 10 percent (0.10) for i, and $^1/_{12}$ for n yields the following:

$$\begin{aligned} I &= \$30{,}000 \times 0.10 \times \frac{1}{12} \\ &= \$250 \end{aligned}$$

3. *Mary Schiller receives \$30 every three months from a bank account that pays a 6 percent annual interest rate. How much is invested in the account?* Because PV_0 is the unknown in this example, Equation 5.1 is rearranged:

$$PV_0 = \frac{I}{i \times n} \tag{5.2}$$

Substituting \$30 for I, 0.06 for i, and ¼ (0.25) for n yields the following:

$$\begin{aligned} PV_0 &= \frac{\$30}{0.06 \times 0.25} \\ &= \$2{,}000 \end{aligned}$$

It also is useful to be able to calculate the amount of funds a person can expect to receive at some point in the future. In financial mathematics, the terminal, or future, value of an investment is called FV_n and denotes the principal plus interest accumulated at the end of n years. It is written as follows:

$$FV_n = PV_0 + I \tag{5.3}$$

4. *Raymond Gomez borrows \$1,000 for 9 months at a rate of 8 percent per annum. How much will he have to repay at the end of the 9-month period?* Combining Equations 5.1 and 5.3 to solve for FV_n results in the following new equation:

$$FV_n = PV_0 + (PV_0 \times i \times n) \tag{5.4}$$

Substituting \$1,000 for PV_0, 0.08 for i, and ¾ (9 months = ¾ of 1 year) for n yields the following:

$$\begin{aligned} FV_{3/4} &= \$1{,}000 + (1{,}000 \times 0.08 \times 3/4) \\ &= \$1{,}060 \end{aligned}$$

This problem can be illustrated using the following timeline:

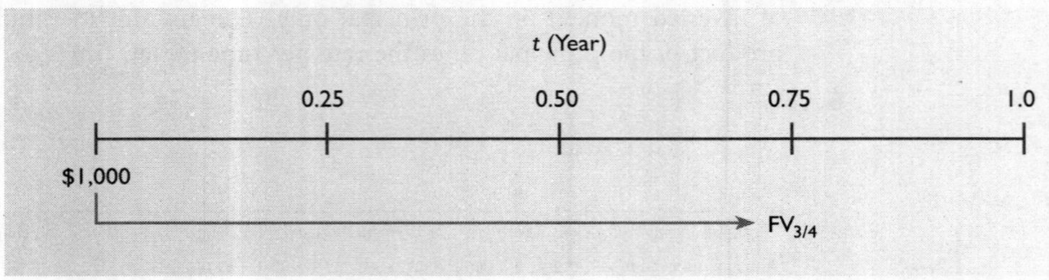

5. *Marie Como agrees to invest \$1,000 in a venture that promises to pay 10 percent simple interest each year for two years. How much money will she have at the end of the second year?* Using Equation 5.4 and assuming two 10 percent simple interest payments, the future value of Marie's investment at the end of two years is computed as follows:

$$
\begin{aligned}
FV_2 &= PV_0 + (PV_0 \times i \times 2)\\
&= \$1{,}000 + (\$1{,}000 \times 0.10 \times 2)\\
&= \$1{,}200
\end{aligned}
$$

This problem can be illustrated using the following timeline:

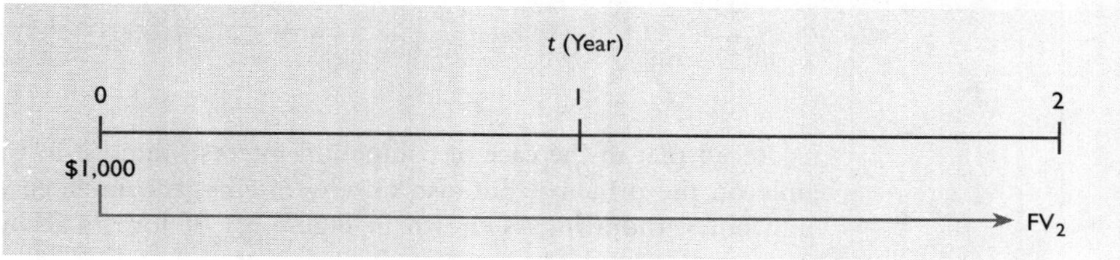

HTTP:
Is the time value of money an important concept in the world of business? Try typing "present value" (a generic term) into a major search engine, such as Google, and watch how many millions of hits you obtain. Then take a look at the different kinds of hits (calculators, tutorials, graphs, advisers/consultants, etc.).

www.google.com

In general, in the case of *simple interest*, the future, or terminal, value (FV_n) at the end of n years is given by Equation 5.4.

5-5 Compound Interest and Future Value

compound interest

Compound interest is interest that is paid not only on the principal but also on any interest earned but not withdrawn during earlier periods. For example, if Jerry Jones deposits \$1,000 in a savings account paying 6 percent interest compounded annually, the future (compound) value of his account at the end of one year (FV_1) is calculated as follows:

(5.5)

$$
\begin{aligned}
FV_1 &= PV_0\,(1 + i)\\
&= \$1{,}000\,(1 + 0.06)\\
&= \$1{,}060
\end{aligned}
$$

This problem can be illustrated using the following timeline:

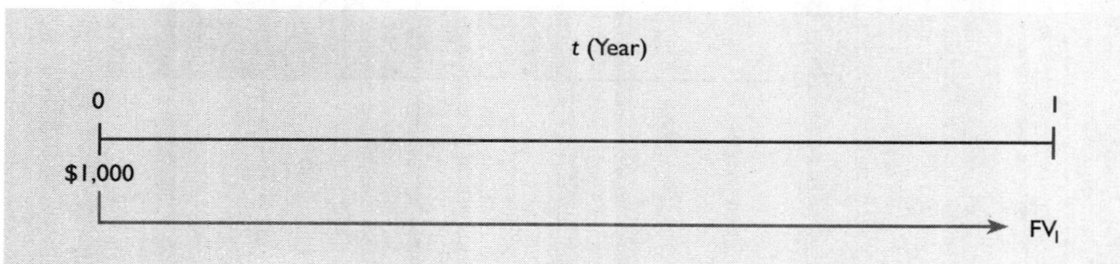

If Jones leaves the \$1,000 *plus* the accumulated interest in the account for another year, its worth at the end of the second year is calculated as follows:

$$\begin{aligned} FV_2 &= FV_1(1+i) \\ &= \$1{,}060(1+0.06) \\ &= \$1{,}123.60 \end{aligned} \tag{5.6}$$

This problem can be illustrated using the following timeline:

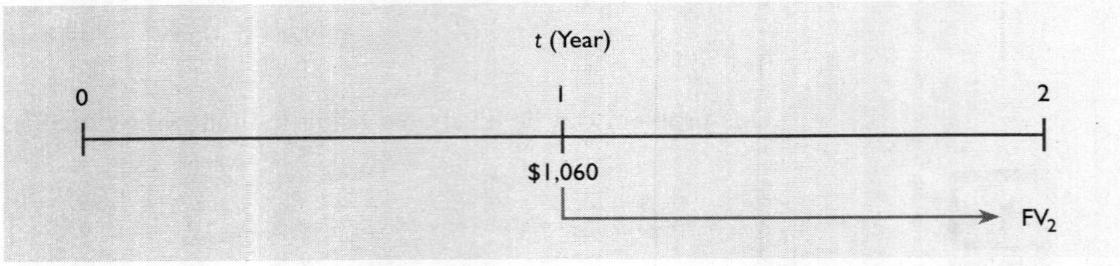

Recall that in the case of compound interest, interest in each period is earned not only on the principal but also on any interest accumulated during previous periods and not withdrawn. As shown in Figure 5.1, if Jones's account paid simple interest instead of compound interest, its value at the end of two years would be $1,120 instead of $1,123.60. The $3.60 difference is the interest on the first year's interest, 0.06 × $60.

FIGURE 5.1

Simple Versus Compound Interest

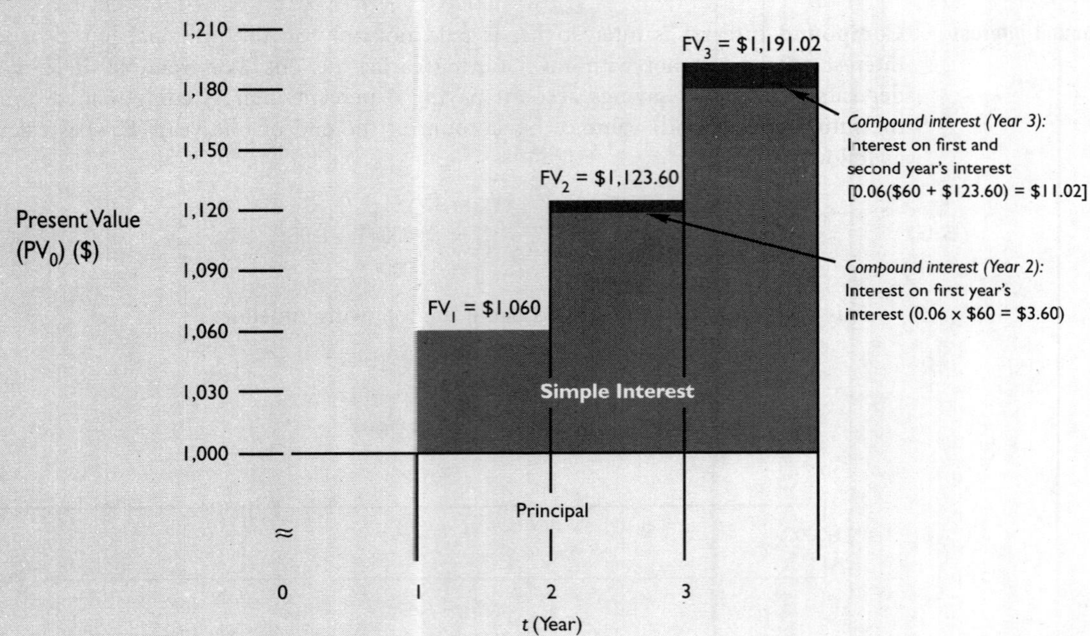

If Jones makes no withdrawals from the account for another year, it will total the following at the end of the third year:

(5.7)
$$\begin{aligned} FV_3 &= FV_2(1+i) \\ &= \$1{,}123.60(1+0.06) \\ &= \$1{,}191.02 \end{aligned}$$

This problem can be illustrated using the following timeline:

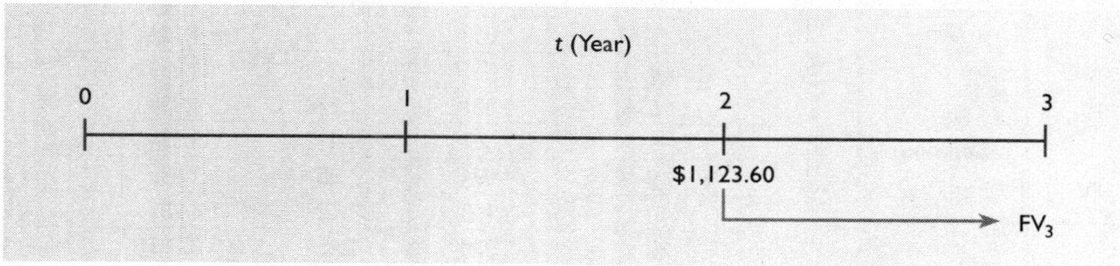

Figure 5.1 illustrates that if the account paid only simple interest, it would be worth only $1,180 at the end of three years. The $11.02 difference (that is, $1,191.02 – $1,180) is the interest on the first and second years' interest, 0.06 × ($60 + $123.60).

A general formula for computing future values can be developed by combining Equations 5.5 and 5.6. Substituting Equation 5.5 into Equation 5.6 yields the following equation:

$$FV_2 = PV_0(1+i)(1+i)$$

or

(5.8)
$$FV_2 = PV_0(1+i)^2$$

This equation can be further generalized to calculate the future value at the end of period *n* for any payment compounded at interest rate *i*:

(5.9)
$$FV_n = PV_0(1+i)^n$$

Although Equation 5.9 is useful for solving future value problems involving one, two, three, or even four years into the future, it is rather tedious to use this equation for problems involving longer time periods. For example, solving for 20 years into the future would require calculating $(1 + i)^{20}$. *Future value interest factors* (FVIFs) are commonly used to simplify such computations. Table I at the end of the book provides a listing of future value interest factors for various interest rates covering up to 60 periods (years or other time periods). Because each future value interest factor is defined as:

(5.10)
$$FVIF_{i,n} = (1+i)^n$$

the FVIF may be thought of as the value that $1 today grows to in *n* periods at a periodic interest rate of *i*.

Equation 5.9 may be rewritten as follows:

(5.11)
$$FV_n = PV_0(FVIF_{i,n})$$

where i = the nominal interest rate per period and n = the number of periods.

To better understand Table I, it is helpful to think of each factor as the result of investing or lending $1 for a given number of periods, *n*, at interest rate *i*. The solution for any amount other than $1 is the product of that principal amount times the factor for a $1 principal amount.

Calculator Solutions[a]

Key	Enter
n	20
i	6
PV	−1,000
PMT	
FV	
	Solution
FV	3,207

TABLE 5.1

Future Value Interest Factors (FVIFs) for $1 at Interest Rate *i* for *n* Periods*

End of Period (*n*)	Interest Rate (*i*) 1%	5%	6%	8%	10%
1	1.010	1.050	1.060	1.080	1.100
2	1.020	1.102	1.124	1.166	1.210
3	1.030	1.158	1.191	1.260	1.331
4	1.041	1.216	1.262	1.360	1.464
5	1.051	**1.276**	1.338	1.469	1.611
8	1.083	1.477	1.594	1.851	2.144
9	1.094	1.551	1.689	**1.999**	2.358
10	1.105	**1.629**	1.791	2.159	2.594
20	1.220	2.653	**3.207**	4.661	6.728
25	1.282	3.386	4.292	6.848	10.835

*The values in this and similar tables in this text have been rounded off to three places. When large sums of money are involved, more accurate tables or financial calculators should be used.

A portion of Table I is reproduced as Table 5.1. Table 5.1 can be used to determine the value of $1,000 compounded at 6 percent for 20 years:

$$\begin{aligned} FV_{20} &= PV_0(FVIF_{0.06,20}) \\ &= \$1{,}000(3.207) \\ &= \$3{,}207 \end{aligned}$$

The 3.207 figure is arrived at by reading down the 6 percent, or 0.06, column and across the 20 row under the "End of Period (*n*)" heading to where the row and column meet.

5-5a Solving for the Interest Rate

Calculator Solutions[b]

Key	Enter
n	10
i	
PV	−1,000
PMT	
FV	1,629
	Solution
i	5.0

In some compound value problems, the present value (PV_0) and future value (FV_n) are given and the objective is to determine the interest rate (i) that solves Equation 5.11. For example, the future value interest factor for an investment requiring an initial outlay of $1,000 and promising a $1,629 return after 10 years is as follows:

$$\begin{aligned} FVIF_{i,10} &= \frac{FV_{10}}{PV_0} \\ &= \frac{\$1{,}629}{\$1{,}000} \\ &= 1.629 \end{aligned}$$

When one reads across the 10-year row in Table 5.1, 1.629 is found in the 5 percent column. Thus, the investment yields a 5 percent compound rate of return.

5-5b Solving for the Number of Compounding Periods

The future value interest factor tables can also be used to determine the number of annual compounding periods (n). For example, to determine how long it would take

[a]The future value amount can also be computed using a financial calculator. When no value appears above a "key box," such as *PMT* in this example, it is not necessary to enter any value to solve the problem.

Students who are planning to use a financial calculator should become familiar with the keystrokes needed to solve time value of money problems. The manual accompanying your financial calculator and the insert card in this text explain the basic operations required to solve the examples and problems.

[b]The interest rate can also be computed using a financial calculator.

Calculator Solutions[c]

Key	Enter
n	
i	8
PV	–1,000
PMT	
FV	2,000
	Solution
n	9.0

for \$1,000 invested at 8 percent to double, search the 8 percent column in Table 5.1 to locate a future value interest factor of 2.000. The closest value to this figure is 1.999. Reading to the left of this figure, it can be seen that the original \$1,000 would be worth nearly \$2,000 in nine years.[3] This problem can also be solved algebraically:

$$FV_n = PV_0(FVIF_{0.08,n})$$

$$FVIF_{0.08,n} = \frac{FV_n}{PV_0}$$

$$= \frac{\$2,000}{\$1,000}$$

$$= 2.000$$

Compounding can also be illustrated graphically. Figure 5.2 shows the effects of time, n, and interest rate, i, on the growth of a \$100 investment. As the figure shows, the higher the compound interest rate, the faster the growth rate of the value of the initial principal. The notion that an interest rate may be thought of as a *growth rate* will be useful during later discussions of valuation and cost of capital.

5-6 Present Value

The compound, or future, value calculations answer the question: What will be the future value of a given amount invested today, compounded at some rate of interest, i? The financial decision maker, however, is often faced with another type of problem: Given some future value, FV_n, what is its equivalent value today? That is, what is its present value, PV_0? The solution requires *present value* calculations, which are used to determine the dollar amount today, PV_0, that is equivalent to some promised future dollar amount, FV_n. The equivalence depends upon the rate of interest (return) that can be earned on investments during the time period under consideration.

The relationship between compound value and present value can be shown by rewriting Equation 5.9 to solve for PV_0:

$$FV_n = PV_0(1+i)^n \tag{5.9}$$

or

$$PV_0 = FV_n\left[\frac{1}{(1+i)^n}\right] \tag{5.12}$$

where $1/(1 + i)_n$ is the reciprocal of the compound value factor. The process of finding present values is frequently called *discounting*. Equation 5.12 is the basic discounting formula.

To illustrate the use of Equation 5.12, suppose your banker offers to pay you \$255.20 in five years if you deposit X dollars today at an annual 5 percent interest rate. Whether the investment would be worthwhile depends on how much money you must deposit, or

[3]In a shortcut solution to this type of problem known as the "Rule of 72," the number 72 is divided by the interest rate to determine the number of years it would take for a sum of money to double. In this case, 72/8% = 9. The Rule of 72 can also be used to determine the interest rate required for a sum of money to double in a given number of years: 72/9 = 8%. The Rule of 72 does not yield exact figures, but it can be used to calculate good approximations.

[c]The number of compounding periods can also be computed using a financial calculator.

FIGURE 5.2

Growth of a $100 Investment at Various Compound Interest Rates

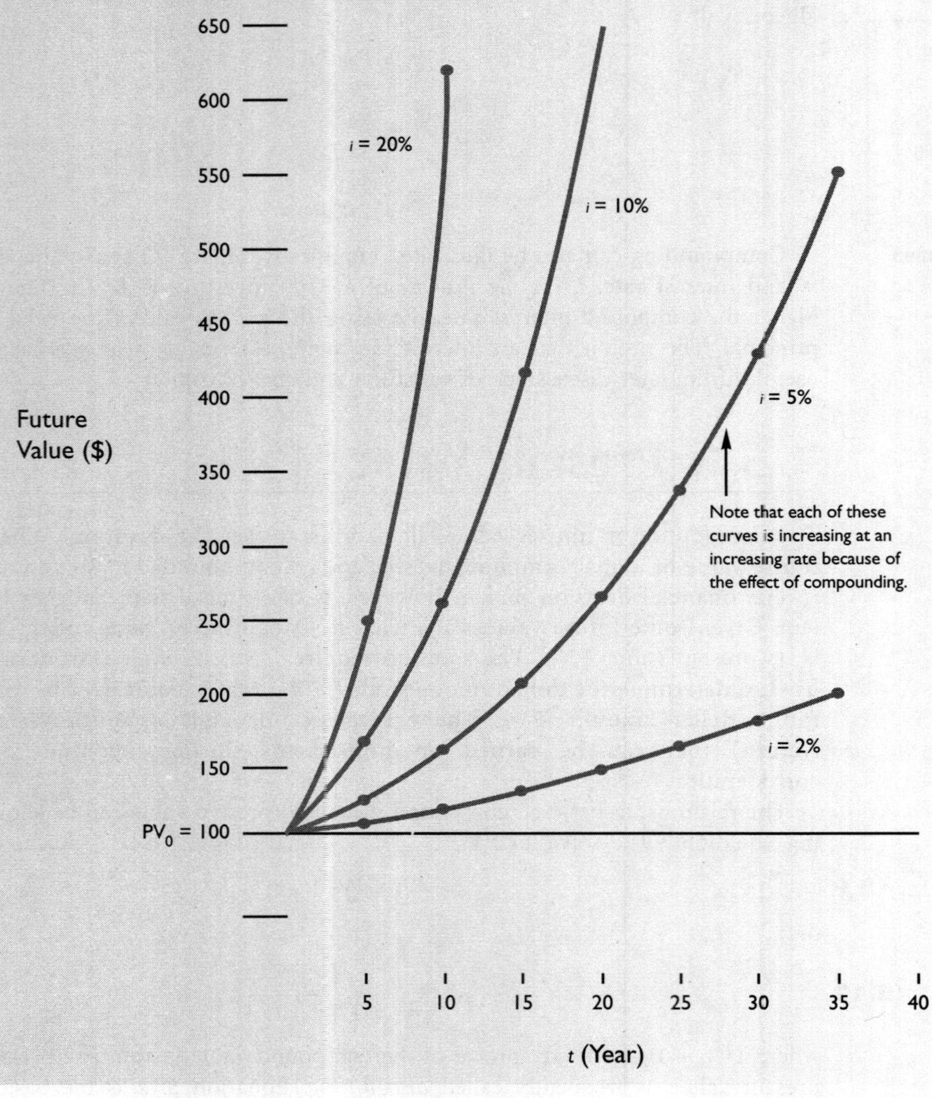

the *present value* of the *X* dollars. FVIF tables, such as Table 5.1 presented earlier, can be used to solve the problem as follows:

$$PV_0 = FV_5\left(\frac{1}{FVIF_{0.05,5}}\right)$$
$$= \$255.20\left(\frac{1}{1.276}\right)$$
$$= \$200$$

This problem can be illustrated with the following timeline:

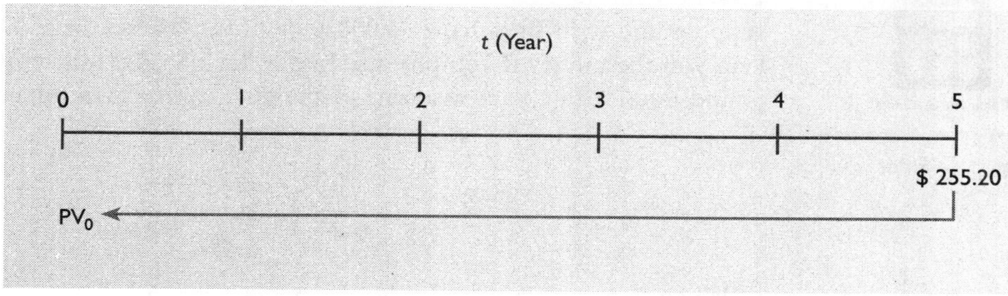

Thus, an investment of $200 today would yield a return of $55.20 in five years.

Because determining the reciprocals of the compound value interest factors, $1/(1+i)^n$, can be a tedious process, *present value interest factors* (PVIFs) commonly are used to simplify such computations. Defining each present value interest factor as:

(5.13) $$\text{PVIF}_{i,n} = \frac{1}{(1+i)^n}$$

Equation 5.12 can be written in the following form:

(5.14) $$\text{PV}_0 = \text{FV}_n(\text{PVIF}_{i,n})$$

Calculator Solutions

Key	Enter
n	20
i	10
PV	
PMT	
FV	−1,000
	Solution
PV	149

Table II at the end of the book provides a number of present value interest factors. A portion of Table II is reproduced here as Table 5.2.

For example, Table 5.2 can be used to determine the present value of $1,000 received 20 years in the future discounted at 10 percent:

$$\begin{aligned}\text{PV}_0 &= \text{FV}_{20}(\text{PVIF}_{0.10,20})\\ &= \$1{,}000(0.149)\\ &= \$149\end{aligned}$$

Thus, $149 invested today at 10 percent interest compounded annually for 20 years would be worth $1,000 at the end of the period. Conversely, the promise of $1,000 in 20 years is worth $149 today, given a 10 percent interest rate.

TABLE 5.2

Present Value Interest Factors (PVIFs) for $1 at Interest Rate *i* for *n* Periods

	Interest Rate (*i*)					
End of Period (*n*)	**1%**	**5%**	**6%**	**8%**	**10%**	**13%**
1	0.990	0.952	0.943	0.926	0.909	0.885
2	0.980	0.907	0.890	0.857	0.826	0.783
3	0.971	0.864	0.840	0.794	0.751	0.693
4	0.961	**0.823**	**0.792**	0.735	0.683	0.613
5	0.951	0.784	0.747	0.681	0.621	0.543
8	0.923	0.677	0.627	0.540	0.467	0.376
10	0.905	0.614	0.558	0.463	0.386	0.295
20	0.820	0.377	0.312	0.215	**0.149**	0.087
25	0.780	0.295	0.233	0.146	0.092	0.047

5-6a Solving for Interest and Growth Rates

Calculator Solutions

Key	Enter
n	4
i	
PV	5,000
PMT	
FV	−6,250
	Solution
i	5.74

Present value interest factors can also be used to solve for interest rates. For example, suppose you wish to borrow $5,000 today from an associate. The associate is willing to loan you the money if you promise to pay back $6,250 four years from today. The compound interest rate your associate is charging can be determined as follows:

$$PV_0 = FV_4(PVIF_{i,4})$$
$$\$5{,}000 = \$6{,}250(PVIF_{i,4})$$
$$(PVIF_{i,4}) = \frac{\$5{,}000}{\$6{,}250} = 0.800$$

When one reads across the 4-year row in Table 5.2, 0.800 is found between the 5 percent (0.823) and 6 percent (0.792) columns. Interpolating between these two values yields:

$$i = 5\% + \frac{0.823 - 0.800}{0.823 - 0.792}(1\%) = 5.74\%$$

Thus, the effective interest rate on the loan is 5.74 percent per year, compounded annually.

Calculator Solutions

Key	Enter
n	5
i	
PV	−4.01
PMT	
FV	5.63
	Solution
i	7.02

Another common present value application is the calculation of the compound rate of growth of an earnings or a dividend stream. For example, Procter & Gamble (P&G) had earnings of $4.01 per share in 2014. Suppose these earnings are expected to grow to $5.63 in 2019. Over this five-year period, what is the expected compounded annual rate of growth in P&G's earnings? The answer to this problem can be obtained by solving for the present value interest factor over the five-year period as follows:

$$\$4.01 = \$5.63(PVIF_{i,5})$$
$$PVIF_{i,5} = 0.712$$

From Table II, we find this approximate present value interest factor in the 5-year row under the 7 percent interest, or growth rate, column. Hence the compound annual rate of growth in P&G's earnings per share is forecasted to be 7 percent. A more precise calculation using a calculator yields 7.02 percent.

discount rate

The discounting process can also be illustrated graphically. Figure 5.3 shows the effects of time, n, and interest rate, i, on the present value of a $100 investment. As the figure shows, the higher the **discount rate**, the lower the present value of the $100.

5-7 Annuities

annuity
ordinary annuity
annuity due

An **annuity** is the payment or receipt of equal cash flows per period for a specified amount of time.[4] An **ordinary annuity** is one in which the payments or receipts occur at the *end* of each period, as shown in Figure 5.4. An **annuity due** is one in which payments or receipts occur at the *beginning* of each period, as shown in Figure 5.5. Most lease payments, such as apartment rentals and life insurance premiums, are annuities due.

In a four-year ordinary annuity, the last payment is made at the *end* of the fourth year. In a four-year annuity due, the last payment is made at the end of the third year (the *beginning* of the fourth year).

[4]This discussion focuses primarily on periods of one year.

FIGURE 5.3

Present Value of $100 at Various Discount Rates

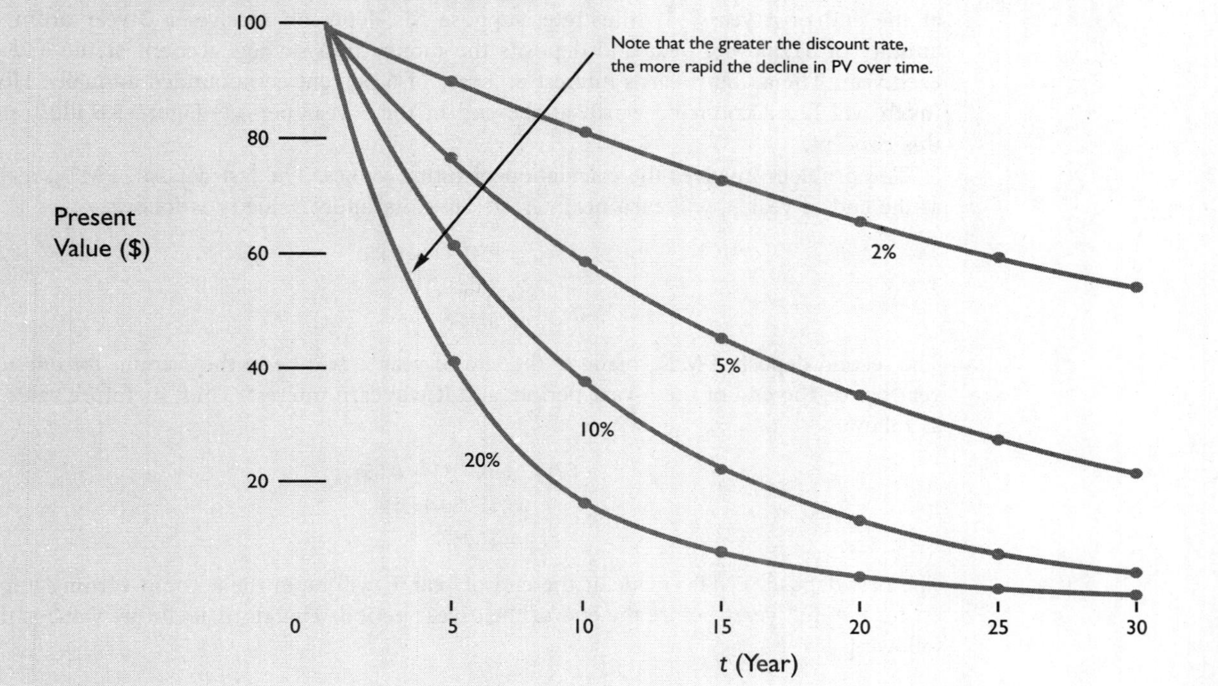

FIGURE 5.4

Timeline of an Ordinary Annuity of $100 per Period for Four Periods

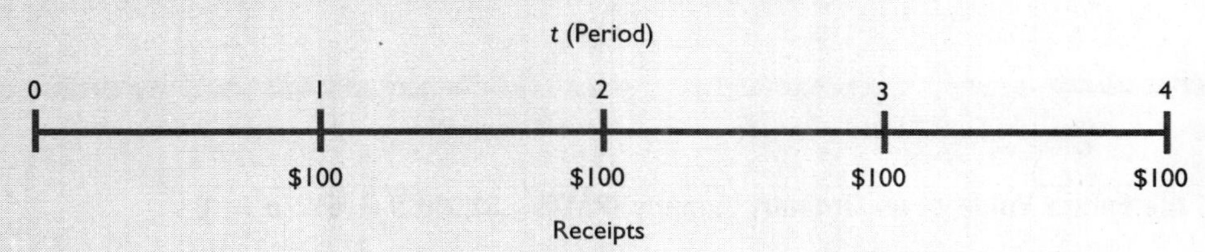

FIGURE 5.5

Timeline of an Annuity Due of $100 per Period for Four Periods

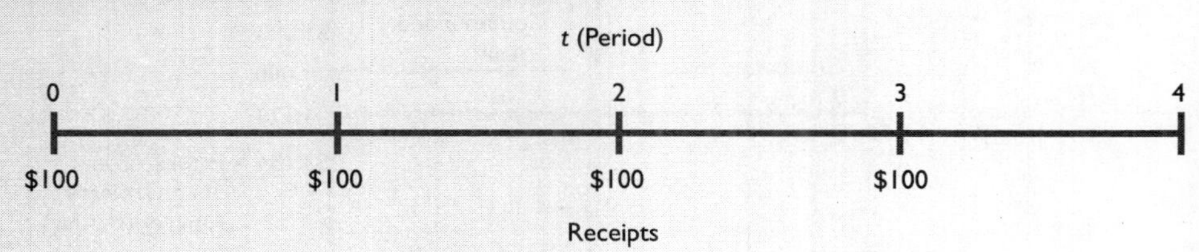

5-7a Future Value of an Ordinary Annuity

A future value of an ordinary annuity ($FVAN_n$) problem asks the question: If an amount PMT is deposited in an account at the end of each year for *n* years, and if the deposits earn interest rate *i* compounded annually, what will be the value of the account at the end of *n* years? To illustrate, suppose Ms. Jefferson receives a 3-year ordinary annuity of $1,000 per year and deposits the money in a savings account at the end of each year. The account earns interest at a rate of 6 percent compounded annually. How much will her account be worth at the end of the 3-year period? Figure 5.6 illustrates this concept.

The problem involves the calculation of future values. The last deposit, PMT_3, made at the end of year 3, will earn no interest. Thus, its future value is as follows:

$$\begin{aligned} FV_{3rd} &= PMT_3(1+0.06)^0 \\ &= \$1{,}000(1) \\ &= \$1{,}000 \end{aligned}$$

The second deposit, PMT_2, made at the end of year 2, will be in the account for one full year before the end of the 3-year period, and it will earn interest. Thus, its future value is as follows:

$$\begin{aligned} FV_{2nd} &= PMT_2(1+0.06)^1 \\ &= \$1{,}000(1.06) \\ &= \$1{,}060 \end{aligned}$$

The first deposit, PMT_1, made at the end of year 1, will be in the account earning interest for two full years before the end of the 3-year period. Therefore, its future value is the following:

$$\begin{aligned} FV_{1st} &= PMT_1(1+0.06)^2 \\ &= \$1{,}000(1.124) \\ &= \$1{,}124 \end{aligned}$$

FIGURE 5.6

Timeline of the Future Value of an Ordinary Annuity (PMT = \$1,000; i = 6%; n = 3)

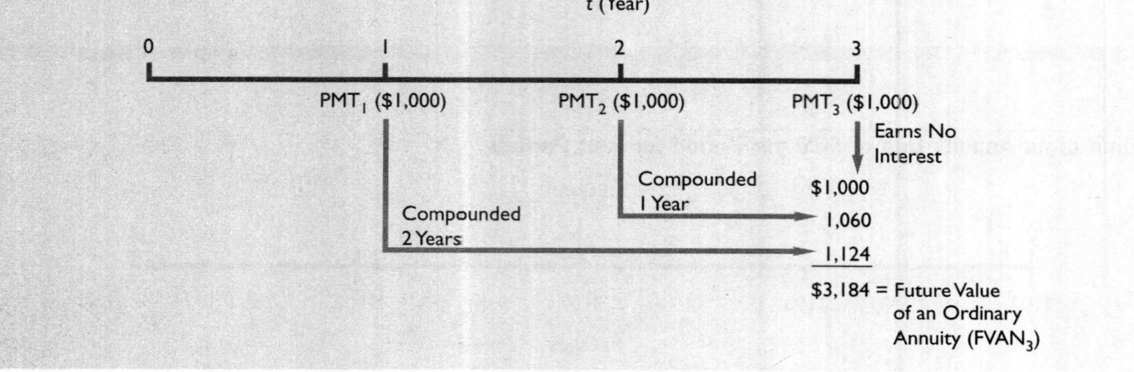

Calculator Solutions

Key	Enter
n	3
i	6
PV	
PMT	−1,000
FV	
	Solution
FV	3,184

The sum of the three figures is the future value of the annuity:

$$\begin{aligned} FVAN_3 &= FV_{3rd} + FV_{2nd} + FV_{1st} \\ &= \$1{,}000 + \$1{,}060 + \$1{,}124 \\ &= \$3{,}184 \end{aligned}$$

The future value of an annuity interest factor (FVIFA) is the sum of the future value interest factors presented in Table I. In this example, the future value of an annuity interest factor is calculated as:

$$\begin{aligned} FVIFA_{0.06,3} &= FVIF_{0.06,2} + FVIF_{0.06,1} + FVIF_{0.06,0} \\ &= 1.124 + 1.060 + 1.000 \\ &= 3.184 \end{aligned}$$

Tables of the future value of an ordinary annuity interest factors are available to simplify computations. Table III at the end of the book provides a number of future value of an annuity interest factors. A portion of Table III is reproduced here as Table 5.3. FVIFAs can also be computed as follows:

(5.15)
$$FVIFA_{i,n} = \frac{(1+i)^n - 1}{i}$$

This formula can be used when you do not have access to interest tables with the appropriate values of i and n or to a financial calculator.

The future value of an ordinary annuity ($FVAN_n$) may be calculated by multiplying the annuity payment, PMT, by the appropriate interest factor, $FVIFA_{i,n}$:

(5.16)
$$FVAN_n = PMT(FVIFA_{i,n})$$

Table 5.3 can be used to solve the problem involving Jefferson's annuity. Because PMT $= \$1{,}000$, the interest factor for $n = 3$ years, and $i = 6\%$ is 3.184, the future value of an ordinary annuity can be calculated as follows:

$$\begin{aligned} FVAN_3 &= PMT(FVIFA_{0.06,3}) \\ &= \$1{,}000(3.184) \\ &= \$3{,}184 \end{aligned}$$

TABLE **5.3**

Future Value of an Ordinary Annuity Interest Factors (FVIFA) for \$1 per Period at Interest Rate *i* for *n* Periods

	Interest Rate (i)			
End of Period (n)	**1%**	**5%**	**6%**	**10%**
1	1.000	1.000	1.000	1.000
2	2.010	2.050	2.060	2.100
3	3.030	3.152	**3.184**	3.310
4	4.060	4.310	4.375	4.641
5	5.101	5.526	5.637	6.105
10	10.462	12.578	13.181	15.937
20	22.019	33.066	36.786	57.275
25	28.243	47.727	54.865	98.347

The spreadsheet solution is shown here.

Spreadsheet Strategies

	A	B	C	D	E	F	G	H	I
2									
3		Using a Spreadsheet to Find Future Value of an Ordinary Annuity							
4									
5				Years					
6			0	1	2	3			
7				$1,000.00	$1,000.00	$1,000.00			
8									
9		Interest rate =	6.00%						
10									
11		Future value of an Ordinary Annuity=	$3,183.60						
12									
13									

Comment: Enter years and cash flows.

Future value of a regular annuity is calculated using the annuity formula, +FV(rate,nper,pmt,PV type) and then taking the absolute value of the resulting answer: "+ABS(FV($C$9,(F6−C6),D7,0,0))." FV, rate, nper, pmt, and PV stand for the future value, periodic interest rate, number of periods in an annuity, annuity value, and present value, respectively. And type is zero for regular annuity and one for annuity due.

Sinking Fund Problem Future value of an annuity interest factors can also be used to find the annuity amount that must be invested each year to produce a future value. This type of problem is sometimes called a **sinking fund problem**. Suppose the Omega Graphics Company wishes to set aside an equal, annual, end-of-year amount in a "sinking fund account" earning 9.5 percent per annum over the next five years. The firm wants to have $5 million in the account at the end of five years to retire (pay off) $5 million in outstanding bonds. How much must be deposited in the account at the end of each year?

sinking fund problem

This problem can be solved using either Equation 5.16 or a financial calculator. Substituting $n = 5$, $FVAN_5 = \$5{,}000{,}000$, and $i = 0.095$ into Equation 5.16 yields:

$$\$5{,}000{,}000 = PMT(FVIFA_{0.095,5})$$

Calculator Solutions

Key	Enter
n	5
i	9.5
PV	
PMT	
FV	−5,000,000
	Solution
PMT	827,182

Since the interest rate of 9.5 percent is not in Table III, one must use Equation 5.15 to determine $FVIFA_{0.095,5}$.

$$\$5{,}000{,}000 = PMT\left(\frac{(1+0.095)^5 - 1}{0.095}\right)$$

$$PMT = \$827{,}182$$

By depositing approximately $827,182 at the end of each of the next five years in the account earning 9.5 percent per annum, Omega will accumulate the $5 million needed to retire the bonds.

5-7b Future Value of an Annuity Due

Calculator Solutions[d]

Key	Enter
n	3
i	6
PV	
PMT	−1,000
FV	
	Solution
FV	3,375

Table III at the end of the book (future value of an annuity interest factors) assumes *ordinary* (end-of-period) annuities. For an *annuity due*, in which payments are made at the *beginning* of each period, the interest factors in Table III must be modified.

Consider the case of Jefferson cited earlier. If she deposits $1,000 in a savings account at the *beginning* of each year for the next three years and the account earns 6 percent interest, compounded annually, how much will be in the account at the end of three years? (Recall that when the deposits were made at the end of each year, the account totaled $3,184 at the *end* of three years.)

Figure 5.7 illustrates this problem as an *annuity due*. PMT_1 is compounded for three years, PMT_2 for two years, and PMT_3 for one year. The correct *annuity due* interest

[d]The problem must be solved with the calculator in the *beginning of period* payment mode. This amount is larger than the $3,184 obtained in the ordinary annuity example given previously by an amount equal to $1 + i$, or 1.06 in this particular example.

FIGURE **5.7**

Timeline of the Future Value of an Annuity Due (PMT = \$1,000; *i* = 6%, *n* = 3)

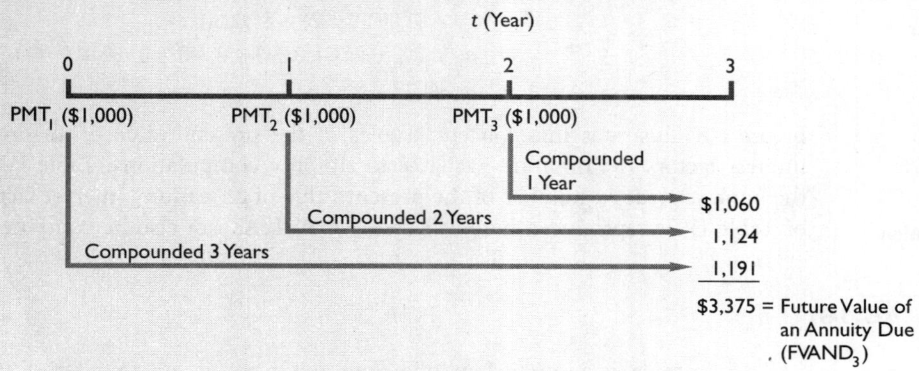

factor may be obtained from Table III by multiplying the FVIFA for three years and 6 percent (3.184) by 1 plus the interest rate (1 + 0.06). This yields a FVIFA for an annuity due of 3.375, and the future value of the annuity due ($FVAND_n$) is calculated as follows:

(5.17)

$$FVAND_n = PMT[FVIFA_{i,n}(1 + i)]$$
$$FVAND_3 = \$1{,}000(3.375)$$
$$= \$3{,}375$$

The spreadsheet solution is shown here.

Spreadsheet Strategies

	A	B	C	D	E	F	G	H	I
2									
3		Using a Spreadsheet to Find Future Value of an Annuity Due							
4									
5				Years					
6			0	1	2	3			
7				$1,000.00	$1,000.00	$1,000.00			
8									
9		Interest rate =	6.00%						
10									
11		Future value of an Annuity Due=	$3,374.62						
12									
13									

Comment: Enter years and cash flows.

Note: Future value of an annuity due is calculated using the annuity formula, +FV(rate,nper,pmt,PV,type) and then taking the absolute value of the resulting answer: "+ABS(FV($C$9,(F6−C6),D7,0,1))."

5-7c Present Value of an Ordinary Annuity

The present value of an ordinary annuity ($PVAN_0$) is the sum of the present value of a series of equal periodic payments.[5] For example, to find the present value of an ordinary \$1,000 annuity received at the end of each year for five years discounted at a 6 percent rate, the sum of the individual present values would be determined as follows:

HTTP:

The next time you win the lottery and can't wait to spend the money, a company named Stonestreet will buy your winning lottery ticket by giving you its present value, that is, cash in hand today.

www.stonestreet.com

[5]This discussion focuses primarily on annual payments.

Calculator Solutions

Key	Enter
n	5
i	6
PV	
PMT	−1,000
FV	
	Solution
PV	4,212

$$
\begin{aligned}
\text{PVAN}_0 &= \$1{,}000(\text{PVIF}_{0.06,1}) + \$1{,}000(\text{PVIF}_{0.06,2}) \\
&\quad + \$1{,}000(\text{PVIF}_{0.06,3}) + \$1{,}000(\text{PVIF}_{0.06,4}) \\
&\quad + \$1{,}000(\text{PVIF}_{0.06,5}) \\
&= \$1{,}000(0.943) + \$1{,}000(0.890) + \$1{,}000(0.840) \\
&\quad + \$1{,}000(0.792) + \$1{,}000(0.747) \\
&= \$1{,}000(0.943 + 0.890 + 0.840 + 0.792 + 0.747) \\
&= \$4{,}212
\end{aligned}
$$

Figure 5.8 illustrates this concept. Tables of the present value of an ordinary annuity interest factors (PVIFA) are available to simplify computations. Table IV at the end of the book provides a number of the present value of an annuity interest factors. A portion of Table IV is reproduced here as Table 5.4. PVIFAs can also be computed as follows:

(5.18)
$$\text{PVIFA}_{i,n} = \frac{1 - \dfrac{1}{(1+i)^n}}{i}$$

This formula is useful when one does not have access to interest tables with the appropriate values of i and n or a financial calculator.

FIGURE 5.8

Timeline of a Present Value of an Ordinary Annuity (*PMT* = \$1,000; *i* = 6%; *n* = 5)

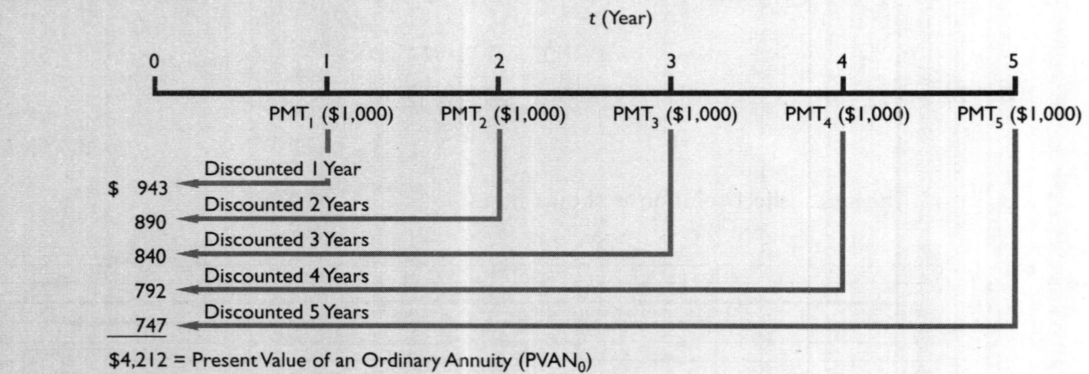

TABLE 5.4

Present Value of an Ordinary Annuity Interest Factors (PVIFA) for \$1 per Period at Interest Rate *i* for *n* Periods

	Interest Rate (*i*)			
End of Period (n)	**1%**	**5%**	**6%**	**10%**
1	0.990	0.952	0.943	0.909
2	1.970	1.859	1.833	1.736
3	2.941	2.723	2.673	2.487
4	3.902	3.546	3.465	3.170
5	4.853	4.329	**4.212**	**3.791**
10	9.471	7.722	7.360	6.145
20	18.046	12.462	11.470	8.514
25	22.023	14.094	12.783	9.077

The present value of an annuity can be determined by multiplying the annuity payment, PMT, by the appropriate interest factor, $PVIFA_{i,n}$:

$$\text{PVAN}_0 = \text{PMT}(\text{PVIFA}_{i,n}) \tag{5.19}$$

With reference to Table 5.4 to determine the interest factor for $i = 6\%$ and $n = 5$, the present value of an annuity in the previous problem can be calculated as follows:

$$\begin{aligned}\text{PVAN}_0 &= \text{PMT}(\text{PVIFA}_{0.06,5})\\ &= \$1{,}000(4.212)\\ &= \$4{,}212\end{aligned}$$

The present value of an ordinary annuity found by using a spreadsheet is shown here.

Spreadsheet Strategies

	A	B	C	D	E	F	G	H	I
2									
3		Using a Spreadsheet to Find Present Value of an Ordinary Annuity							
4									
5		Comment: Enter years and cash flows.		Years					
6			0	1	2	3	4	5	
7				$1,000.00	$1,000.00	$1,000.00	$1,000.00	$1,000.00	
8									
9		Interest rate =	6.00%						
10									
11		Present Value of an Ordinary Annuity=	$4,212.36						
12									
13									
14									
15									
16									

Present value of a regular annuity is calculated using the PV function +PV(rate,nper,pmt,FV,type) where PV, rate, nper, pmt, and FV stand for the present value, periodic interest rate, number of periods in an an annuity, annuity value, and future value, respectively. And, type is zero for regular annuity and one for annuity due. The final answer is obtained by taking the absolute value of the resulting answer: Excel formula: "+ABS(PV($C$9,(H6−C6),D7,0,0))"

Calculator Solutions

Key	Enter
n	5
i	
PV	−100,000
PMT	26,378
FV	
	Solution
i	10.0

Solving for the Interest Rate

Present value of an annuity interest factors can also be used to solve for the rate of return expected from an investment.[6] Suppose IBM purchases a machine for $100,000. This machine is expected to generate annual cash flows of $26,378 to the firm over the next five years. What is the expected rate of return from this investment?

Using Equation 5.19, we can determine the expected rate of return in this example as follows:

$$\begin{aligned}\text{PVAN}_0 &= \text{PMT}(\text{PVIFA}_{i,5})\\ \$100{,}000 &= \$26{,}378(\text{PVIFA}_{i,5})\\ \text{PVIFA}_{i,5} &= 3.791\end{aligned}$$

From the 5-year row in Table 5.4 or Table IV, we see that a PVIFA of 3.791 occurs in the 10 percent column.[7] Hence, this investment offers a 10 percent expected rate of return.

Calculator Solutions

Key	Enter
n	4
i	9.0
PV	−10,000
PMT	
FV	
	Solution
PMT	3,086.69

Loan Amortization and Capital Recovery Problems

Present value of an annuity interest factors can be used to solve a *loan amortization problem,* where the objective is to determine the payments necessary to pay off, or amortize, a loan, such as a home mortgage.

For example, suppose you borrowed $10,000 from Lexington State Bank. The loan is for a period of four years at an interest rate of 9.0 percent. It requires that you make four equal, annual, end-of-year payments that include both principal and interest on the outstanding balance.[8] This problem can be solved using either Equation 5.19 or a financial calculator. Substituting $n = 4$, $\text{PVAN}_0 = \$10{,}000$, and $i = 0.09$ into Equation 5.19 yields:

[6] This interest rate, or rate of return, is referred to by various names in finance, depending on the type of "investment" under consideration. When evaluating a bond (fixed-income security), this rate is referred to as the *yield-to-maturity* (YTM) (see Chapter 6). In the analysis of capital expenditure decisions, this rate is known as the *internal rate of return* (IRR) (see Chapter 10). Finally, when calculating the cost of bank loans and other types of credit, this rate is known as the *annual percentage rate* (APR) (see Chapter 16).

[7] Interpolation can be used to find the approximate interest rate when the PVIFA falls between two values in the table. See the examples discussed earlier involving PVIFs for an illustration of this technique.

[8] Loan repayment schedules other than equal periodic payments are discussed in Chapter 19.

$$\$10{,}000 = PMT(PVIFA_{0.09,4})$$
$$10{,}000 = PMT(3.240)$$
$$PMT = 3{,}086.42$$

loan amortization schedule

By making four annual, end-of-year payments to the bank of $3,086.69 (see the more accurate calculator solution in the margin), you will completely pay off your loan, plus provide the bank with its 9.0 percent interest return. This can be seen in the **loan amortization schedule** developed in Table 5.5. At the end of each year, you pay the bank $3,087. During the first year, $900 of this payment is interest (0.09 × $10,000 remaining balance), and the rest ($2,187) is applied against the principal balance owed at the beginning of the year. Hence, after the first payment, you owe $7,813 ($10,000 − $2,187). Similar calculations are done for years 2, 3, and 4. A spreadsheet solution to this problem is shown below.

Spreadsheet Strategies

	A	B	C	D	E	F	G	H
3								
4				Using a Spreadsheet to Amortize an Annual Loan				
5								
6		Loan amount=		$10,000				
7		Interest rate=		9%				
8		Loan term=		4				
9		Loan payment=		$3,086.69				
10								
11								
12								
13				Amortization Table				
14		Year	Beginning		Interest	Principal	Ending	
15			Balance	Payment	Paid	Paid	Balance	
16		1	$10,000.00	$3,086.69	$900.00	$2,186.69	$7,813.31	
17		2	7,813.31	$3,086.69	$703.20	$2,383.49	$5,429.82	
18		3	5,429.82	$3,086.69	$488.68	$2,598.00	$2,831.82	
19		4	2,831.82	$3,086.69	$254.86	$2,831.82	$0.00	
20		Totals		$12,346.75	$2,346.75	$10,000.00		
21								
22				Formulas Used in the Amortization Table:				
23		Year	Beginning		Interest	Principal	Ending	
24			Balance	Payment	Paid	Paid	Balance	
25		1	=+D6	=+$D$9	=+C16*$D$7	=+D16-E16	=+C16-F16	
26		2	=+G16	=+$D$9	=+C17*$D$7	=+D17-E17	=+C17-F17	
27		3	=+G17	=+$D$9	=+C18*$D$7	=+D18-E18	=+C18-F18	
28		4	=+G18	=+$D$9	=+C19*$D$7	=+D19-E19	=+C19-F19	
29		Totals		=+SUM(D16:D19)	=+SUM(E16:E19)	=+SUM(F16:F19)		
30								
31								
32								
33								
34								

Comment: Payment is calculated using the PMT function (PMT(rate,nper,PV)) and then taking the absolute value of the resulting answer: "+ABS(PMT(D7,D8,D6))."

Comment: Ending balance must be zero. Addition of interest paid and principal paid must be equal to total of payments.

TABLE 5.5

Loan Amortization Schedule: Lexington State Bank

End of Year	Payment	Interest (9.0%)	Principal Reduction	Remaining Balance
0	—	—	—	$10,000
1	$3,087	$900	$2,187	7,813
2	3,087	703	2,384	5,429
3	3,087	489	2,598	2,831
4	3,087	255	2,832	0

Present value of an annuity interest factors can also be used to find the annuity amount necessary to recover a capital investment, given a required rate of return on that investment. This type of problem is called a **capital recovery problem.**

capital recovery problem

5-7d Present Value of an Annuity Due

Annuity due calculations are also important when dealing with the present value of an annuity problem. In these cases, the interest factors in Table IV must be modified.

Calculator Solutions[e]

Key	Enter
n	5
i	6
PV	
PMT	−1,000
FV	
	Solution
PV	4,465

Consider the case of a 5-year annuity of $1,000 each year, discounted at 6 percent. What is the present value of this annuity if each payment is received at the *beginning* of each year? (Recall the example presented earlier, illustrating the concept of the present value of an ordinary annuity, in which each payment was received at the *end* of each year and the present value was $4,212.) Figure 5.9 illustrates this problem.

The first payment received at the beginning of year 1 (end of year 0) is already in its present value form and therefore requires no discounting. PMT_2 is discounted for one period, PMT_3 is discounted for two periods, PMT_4 is discounted for three periods, and PMT_5 is discounted for four periods.

The correct *annuity due* interest factor for this problem may be obtained from Table IV by multiplying the present value of an ordinary annuity interest factor for five years and 6 percent (4.212) by 1 plus the interest rate (1 + 0.06). This yields a PVIFA for an annuity due of 4.465, and the present value of this annuity due ($PVAND_0$) is calculated as follows:

$$PVAND_0 = PMT[PVIFA_{i,n}(1+i)] \tag{5.20}$$

$$PVAND_0 = \$1{,}000(4.465)$$

$$= \$4{,}465$$

FIGURE 5.9

Timeline of a Present Value of an Annuity Due (PMT = $1,000; *i* = 6%; *n* = 5)

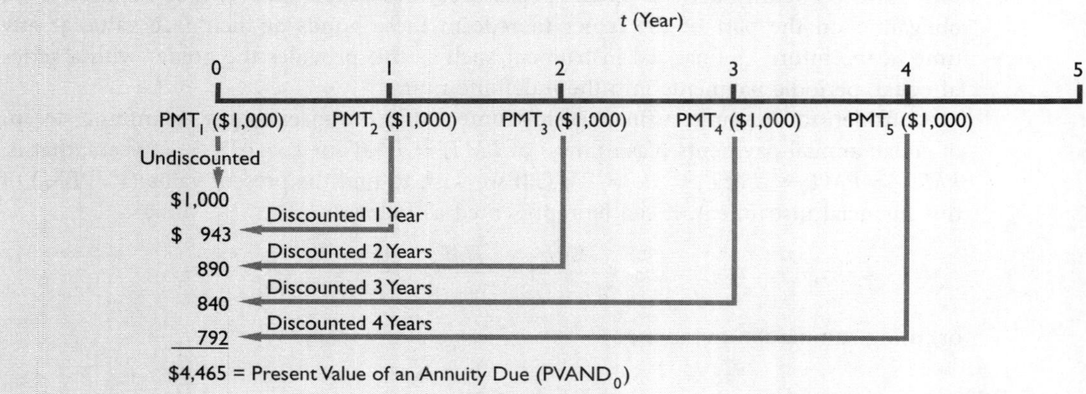

[e]The problem must be solved with the calculator in the beginning of period payment mode. This amount is larger than the $4,212 obtained in the ordinary annuity example presented previously by an amount equal to 1 + *i*, or 1.06.

A spreadsheet solution to this problem is shown here.

Spreadsheet Strategies

	A	B	C	D	E	F	G	H	I
2									
3		Using a Spreadsheet to Find Present Value of an Annuity Due							
4									
5					Years				
6			0	1	2	3	4	5	
7				$1,000.00	$1,000.00	$1,000.00	$1,000.00	$1,000.00	
8									
9		Interest rate =	6.00%						
10									
11		Present Value of an Annuity Due	$4,465.11						
12									
13									
14									
15									
16									

Comment:
Enter years and cash flows.

Present value of an annuity due is calculated using the PV function +PV(rate,nper,pmt,FV,type) where PV, rate, nper, pmt, and FV stand for the present value, periodic interest rate, number of periods in an annuity, annuity value, and future value, respectively. And type is zero for regular annuity and one for annuity due. The final answer is obtained by taking the absolute value of the resulting value.
Excel formula: "+ABS(PV($C$9,(H6–C6),D7,0,1))"

Annuity due calculations are especially important when dealing with rental or lease contracts because it is common for these contracts to require that payments be made at the beginning of each period.

5-8 Present Value: Some Additional Cash Flow Patterns

The discussion of present value thus far has focused on two cash flow patterns: single payments and annuities. The present value of three additional types of cash flow streams are examined in this section: namely, *perpetuities*, *uneven cash flows*, and *deferred annuities*. Examples of these types of cash flows are encountered in many different areas of financial decision making.

5-8a Perpetuities

perpetuity

A **perpetuity** is a financial instrument that promises to pay an equal cash flow per period forever: that is, an infinite series of payments. Therefore, a perpetuity may be thought of as an infinite annuity. Some bonds (and some preferred stocks) take the form of a perpetuity because these special securities never mature; that is, there is no obligation on the part of the issuer to redeem these bonds at their face value at any time in the future. A financial instrument such as this provides the holder with a series of equal, periodic payments into the indefinite future.

Consider, for example, a financial instrument that promises to pay an infinite stream of equal, annual payments (cash flows) of $PMT_t = PMT$ for $t = 1, 2, 3, \ldots$ years; that is, $PMT_1 = PMT_2 = PMT_3 = \ldots = PMT$. If we wish to find the present value (PVPER_0) of this financial instrument, it can be represented as follows:

$$\text{PVPER}_0 = \frac{PMT}{(1+i)^1} + \frac{PMT}{(1+i)^2} + \frac{PMT}{(1+i)^3} + \cdots$$

or, using summation notation, as:

(5.21)

$$\text{PVPER}_0 = \sum_{t=1}^{\infty} \frac{PMT}{(1+i)^t}$$

where i equals the rate of return required by an investor in this financial instrument. It should be apparent that Equation 5.21 represents a special type of annuity where the number of periods for the annuity equals infinity. This type of problem cannot be solved using Table IV.

An examination of the PVIFA interest factors for 10 percent (in Table IV) indicates that the value in the 10 percent column increases as the number of years increases, but at a decreasing rate. For example, the PVIFA factor for 10 percent and 10 years is 6.145, whereas the factor for 10 percent and 20 years is only 8.514 (much less than twice the 10-year factor). The limiting value in any column of Table IV is 1 divided by the interest rate of that column, i. In the case of a 10 percent perpetuity, the appropriate interest factor is 1/0.10, or 10. Thus Equation 5.21 can be rewritten as follows:

(5.22)
$$\text{PVPER}_0 = \frac{PMT}{i}$$

For example, assume that Great Plains Energy series E preferred stock promises payments of $4.50 per year forever and that an investor requires a 10 percent rate of return on this type of investment. How much would the investor be willing to pay for this security?

In this example, the value of a $4.50 perpetuity at a 10 percent required rate of return is:

$$\begin{aligned}\text{PVPER}_0 &= \frac{\$4.50}{0.10}\\ &= \$45\end{aligned}$$

In Chapter 6, the concept of a perpetuity is examined in greater detail in the valuation of preferred stocks and perpetual bonds.

5-8b Present Value of an Uneven Payment Stream

Many problems in finance—particularly in the area of capital budgeting—cannot be solved according to the simplified format of the present value of an annuity because the periodic cash flows are not equal. Consider an investment that is expected to produce a series of *unequal* payments (cash flows), PMT_1, PMT_2, PMT_3, ..., PMT_n, over the next n periods. The present value of this uneven payment stream is equal to the sum of the present values of the individual payments (cash flows). Algebraically, the present value can be represented as:

$$\text{PV}_0 = \frac{\text{PMT}_1}{(1+i)^1} + \frac{\text{PMT}_2}{(1+i)^2} + \frac{\text{PMT}_3}{(1+i)^3} + \cdots + \frac{\text{PMT}_n}{(1+i)^n}$$

or, using summation notation, as:

(5.23)
$$\text{PV}_0 = \sum_{t=1}^{n} \frac{\text{PMT}_t}{(1+i)^t}$$

(5.24)
$$= \sum_{t=1}^{n} \text{PMT}_t(\text{PVIF}_{i,t})$$

where i is the interest rate (that is, required rate of return) on this investment and $\text{PVIF}_{i,t}$ is the appropriate interest factor from Table II. It should be noted that the payments can be either positive (cash *in*flows) or negative (*out*flows).

Consider the following example. Suppose the Eaton Corporation is evaluating an investment in new equipment that will be used to manufacture a new product it has developed. The equipment is expected to have a useful life of five years and yield the following stream of cash flows (payments) over the five-year period:

End of Year t	Cash Flow PMT_t
1	+\$100,000
2	+150,000
3	−50,000
4	+200,000
5	+100,000

Note that in year 3, the cash flow is negative. (This is due to a new law that requires the company to purchase and install pollution abatement equipment.) The present value of these cash flows, assuming an interest rate (required rate of return) of 10 percent, is calculated using Equation 5.24 as follows:

$$\begin{aligned} PV_0 &= \$100{,}000(PVIF_{0.10,1}) + \$150{,}000(PVIF_{0.10,2}) \\ &\quad - \$50{,}000(PVIF_{0.10,3}) + \$200{,}000(PVIF_{0.10,4}) \\ &\quad + \$100{,}000(PVIF_{0.10,5}) \\ &= \$100{,}000(0.909) + \$150{,}000(0.826) \\ &\quad - \$50{,}000(0.751) + \$200{,}000(0.683) + \$100{,}000(0.621) \\ &= \$375{,}950 \end{aligned}$$

Figure 5.10 illustrates a timeline for this investment. The present value of the cash flows (\$375,950) would be compared with the initial cash outlay (that is, net investment in year 0) in deciding whether to purchase the equipment and manufacture the product.

As will be seen later in the text, during the discussion of capital budgeting, calculations of this type are extremely important when making decisions to accept or reject investment projects.

FIGURE 5.10

Timeline of a Present Value of an Unequal Payments (i = 10%; n = 5)

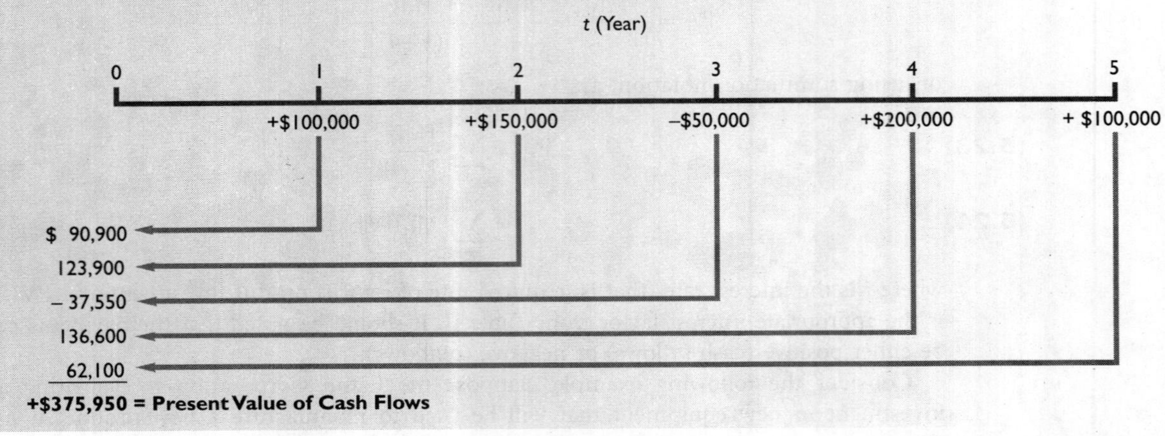

A spreadsheet solution for a simple series of uneven cash flows ($100, $200, and $300) is illustrated here.

Spreadsheet Strategies

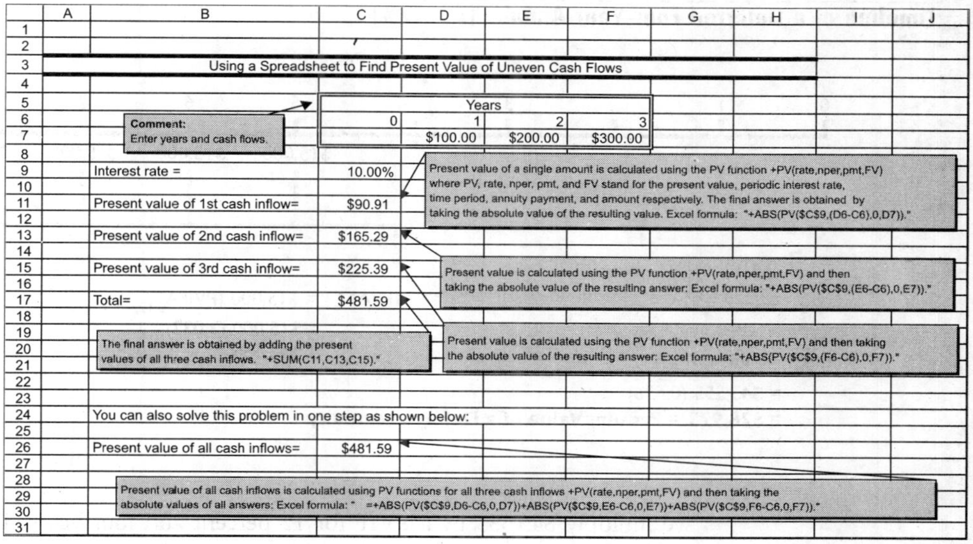

5-8c Present Value of Deferred Annuities

Frequently, in finance, one encounters problems where an annuity begins more than one year in the future. For example, suppose that you wish to provide for the college education of your daughter. She will begin college five years from now, and you wish to have $15,000 available for her at the beginning of each year in college. How much must be invested today at a 12 percent annual rate of return in order to provide the 4-year, $15,000 annuity for your daughter?

This problem can be illustrated in the timeline given in Figure 5.11. Four payments of $15,000 each are required at the end of years 5, 6, 7, and 8. Of course, this problem could be solved by finding the sum of the present values of each of the payments as follows:

Year t	**Payment PMT_t**	**$PVIF_{0.12,t}$**	**Present Value**
5	$15,000	0.567	$ 8,505
6	$15,000	0.507	$ 7,605
7	$15,000	0.452	$ 6,780
8	$15,000	0.404	$ 6,060
	Present Value of Deferred Annuity =		$28,950

It should be apparent that this would be an extremely tedious method of calculation in the case of a 10-year-deferred annuity, for example. Figure 5.11 illustrates one alternative means of solving this problem. First, you can calculate the present value of the 4-year annuity, evaluated at the end of year 4 (remember that this is the same as the beginning of year 5). This calculation is made by multiplying the annuity amount ($15,000) by the PVIFA for a 4-year, 12 percent annuity. This factor is 3.037 and can be obtained from Table IV. Next, the present value of the annuity ($45,555), evaluated at the end of year 4 ($PVAN_4$), must be discounted back to the present time (PV_0). Hence,

FIGURE 5.11

Timeline of a Deferred Four-Year Annuity ($i = 12\%$)

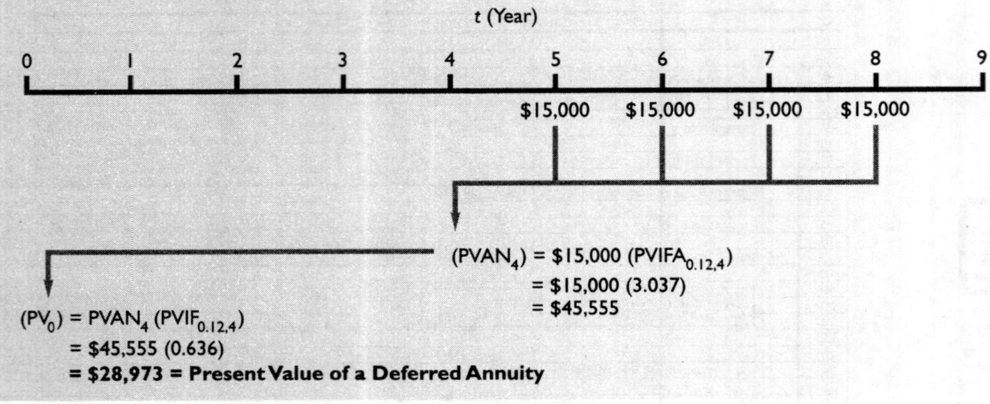

we multiply \$45,555 by a PVIF for 12 percent and four years. This factor, obtained from Table II, is equal to 0.636. The present value of the deferred annuity is \$28,973. (This differs from the amount calculated earlier due to rounding in the tables. No difference will exist if this problem is solved with a calculator or tables that are carried out to more decimal places.)[9]

If you have \$28,973 today and invest it in an account earning 12 percent per year, there will be exactly enough money in the account to permit your daughter to withdraw \$15,000 at the beginning of each year in college. After the last withdrawal, the account balance will be zero.

5-9 Compounding Periods and Effective Interest Rates

The frequency with which interest rates are compounded (for example, annually, semiannually, quarterly, and so on) affects both the present and future values of cash flows as well as the effective interest rates being earned or charged.

5-9a Effect of Compounding Periods on Present and Future Values

Thus far, it has been assumed that compounding (and discounting) occurs annually. Recall the general compound interest equation:

$$FV_n = PV_0(1 + i)^n \tag{5.9}$$

where PV_0 is the initial deposit, i is the annual interest rate, n is the number of years, and FV_n is the future value that will accumulate from the annual compounding of PV_0.

[9]An alternative way to solve this problem is to multiply the annuity payment (\$15,000) by the difference between ($PVIFA_{0.12,8}$) and ($PVIFA_{0.12,4}$). By subtracting ($PVIFA_{0.12,4}$) from ($PVIFA_{0.12,8}$) you are viewing this problem as an eight-year annuity that has no payments during the first four years. In this case, the calculation yields: $PV_0 = \$15,000(4.968 - 3.037) = \$28,965$. (The slight difference from the amount calculated earlier is due to rounding in Table IV.)

nominal interest rate
effective interest rate

An interest rate of i percent per year for n years is assumed. In the remainder of this section, this annual **nominal interest rate** will be designated i_{nom} to differentiate it from the annual **effective interest rate,** i_{eff}.

In some circumstances, interest on an account is compounded *semiannually* instead of annually; that is, half of the nominal annual interest rate, $i_{nom}/2$, is earned at the end of six months. The investor earns additional interest on the interest earned *before* the end of the year, or $(i_{nom}/2)PV_0$. In calculating interest compounded semiannually, Equation 5.9 is rewritten as follows:

$$FV_n = PV_0\left(1 + \frac{i_{nom}}{2}\right)^{2n}$$

The same logic applies to interest compounded *quarterly*:

$$FV_n = PV_0\left(1 + \frac{i_{nom}}{4}\right)^{4n}$$

In general, the compound interest for any number of periods during a year may be computed by means of the following equation:

(5.25)
$$FV_n = PV_0\left(1 + \frac{i_{nom}}{m}\right)^{mn}$$

where m is the number of times during the year the interest is compounded and n is the number of years. (The limiting case of continuous compounding and discounting is discussed in Appendix 5A.)

Table 5.6 contains the future value, FV_1, of $1,000 earning a nominal interest of 10 percent for several different compounding frequencies. For example, the future value (FV_1) of $1,000 compounded *semiannually* ($m = 2$) at a nominal interest rate (i_{nom}) of 10 percent per year by Equation 5.25 is:

Calculator Solutions

Key	Enter
N	2
i	5
PV	-1,000
PMT	
FV	
	Solution
FV	1,102.50

$$FV_1 = \$1{,}000\left(1 + \frac{0.10}{2}\right)^{2\times 1}$$
$$= \$1{,}102.50$$

As Table 5.6 shows, the more frequent the compounding, the greater the future value of the deposit and the greater the *effective* interest rate. Effective interest, in contrast to *nominal* interest, is the *actual* rate of interest earned by the lender and is generally the most economically relevant definition of interest rates.

The relationship between present values and compound values suggests that present values will also be affected by the frequency of compounding. In general, the present

TABLE **5.6**

Effects of Different Compounding Frequencies on Future Values of $1,000 at a 10 Percent Interest Rate

Initial Amount	Compounding Frequency	Future Value, FV_1 (End of Year 1)
$1,000	Yearly	$1,100.00
1,000	Semiannually	1,102.50
1,000	Quarterly	1,103.81
1,000	Monthly	1,104.71
1,000	Daily	1,105.16
1,000	Continuously*	1,105.17

*For advanced applications, it is useful to know that continuous compounding is obtained by letting m approach infinity in $FV_n = PV_0\,(1 + i/m)^{mn}$. In this case, $\lim_{m\to\infty}(1 + i/m)^m = e^i$, and the compound value expression becomes $FV_n = PV_0\,(e)^{in}$, where e is the exponential number having the approximate value of 2.71828. See Appendix 5A for a complete discussion of continuous compounding and discounting.

TABLE 5.7

Effects of Different Compounding Frequencies on Future Values of $1,000 at a 10 Percent Interest Rate

Amount	Compounding Frequency	Present Value, PV_0
$1,000	Yearly	$909.09
1,000	Semiannually	907.03
1,000	Quarterly	905.95
1,000	Monthly	905.21
1,000	Daily	904.85
1,000	Continuously	904.84

value of a sum to be received at the end of year n, discounted at the rate of i_{nom} percent and compounded m times per year, is as follows:

(5.26)
$$PV_0 = \frac{FV_n}{\left(1 + \frac{i_{nom}}{m}\right)^{mn}}$$

Calculator Solutions

Key	Enter
N	4
i	2.5
PV	
PMT	
FV	−1,000
	Solution
PV	905.95

Table 5.7 contains a number of present values, PV_0, for $1,000 received one year in the future discounted at a nominal interest rate of 10 percent with several different compounding frequencies. For example, the present value (PV_0) of $1,000 compounded *quarterly* ($m = 4$) at a nominal interest rate (i_{nom}) of 10 percent per year by Equation 5.26 is:

$$PV_0 = \frac{\$1{,}000}{\left(1 + \frac{0.10}{4}\right)^{4\times 1}} = \$905.95$$

As shown in Table 5.7, the more frequent the compounding, the smaller the present value of a future amount.

Throughout the text, much of the analysis assumes annual compounding instead of compounding for more frequent periods because it simplifies matters, and because the differences between the two are small. Similarly, unless otherwise stated, cash flows from a security or investment project are assumed to be received in a lump sum at the beginning or end of each period. More frequent compounding periods require more extensive tables or the use of a financial calculator.

Regardless of the frequency of compounding, it is important to recognize that *effective* rates of interest are the relevant rates to use for financial and economic analysis. The next section considers the calculation of effective interest rates in greater detail for those cases where compounding is done more than one time a year.

5-10 Effective Rate Calculations

The previous section illustrated the fact that the more frequently an annual *nominal* rate of interest is compounded, the greater is the *effective* rate of interest being earned or charged. Thus, if you were given the choice of receiving (1) interest on an investment, where the interest is compounded annually at a 10 percent rate, or (2) interest on an investment, where the interest is compounded semiannually at a 5 percent rate every six months, you would choose the second option, because it would yield a higher effective rate of interest.

Given the annual *nominal* rate of interest (i_{nom}), the *effective* annual rate of interest (i_{eff}) can be calculated as follows:

$$i_{eff} = \left(1 + \frac{i_{nom}}{m}\right)^m - 1 \tag{5.27}$$

where m is the number of compounding intervals per year.[10]

For example, suppose a bank offers you a loan at an annual nominal interest rate of 12 percent compounded quarterly. What effective annual interest rate is the bank charging you? Substituting $i_{nom} = 0.12$ and $m = 4$ into Equation 5.27 yields:

$$\begin{aligned} i_{eff} &= \left(1 + \frac{0.12}{4}\right)^4 - 1 \\ &= 0.1255 \end{aligned}$$

or 12.55 percent.

There are also situations in finance where one is interested in determining the interest rate during each compounding period that will provide a given annual effective rate of interest. For example, if the annual effective rate is 20 percent and compounding is done quarterly, you may wish to know what quarterly rate of interest will result in an *effective* annual rate of interest of 20 percent.

In general, the rate of interest per period (where there is more than one compounding period per year), i_m, which will result in an effective annual rate of interest, i_{eff}, if compounding occurs m times per year, can be computed as follows:

$$i_m = (1 + i_{eff})^{1/m} - 1 \tag{5.28}$$

In this example, the quarterly rate of interest that will yield an annual effective rate of interest of 20 percent is:[11]

$$\begin{aligned} i_m &= (1 + 0.20)^{0.25} - 1 \\ &= (1.04664) - 1 \\ &= 0.04664 \text{ or } 4.664\% \end{aligned}$$

HTTP:
For the current rates on mortgages, leases, car loans, home equity loans, savings, educational loans, etc., in your area of the country, visit the Money Cafe.

www.moneycafe.com

Thus, if you earn 4.664 percent per period and compounding occurs four times per year, the effective annual rate earned will be 20 percent. This concept is encountered in Chapter 6 in the discussion of the valuation of bonds that pay interest semiannually.

5-11 Net Present Value Rule

Foundation Concept

To achieve the objective of shareholder wealth maximization, a set of appropriate decision rules must be specified. In Chapter 1, we saw that the economic decision rule of setting *marginal cost equal to marginal revenue* (MC = MR) provides a framework for making many important resource allocation decisions. The MC = MR rule is best suited for situations in which the costs and benefits occur at approximately the same time.

---

[10]Note that annual effective interest rates are equivalent to annual nominal interest rates in the case where compounding occurs only one time per year, at year end. This can be shown by substituting $m = 1$ into Equation 5.27:

$$\begin{aligned} i_{eff} &= \left(1 + \frac{i_{nom}}{1}\right)^1 - 1 \\ &= 1 + i_{nom} - 1 \\ &= i_{nom} \end{aligned}$$

[11]Finding the ¼ or 0.25 root of (1 + 0.20) can be done easily with any financial or scientific calculator, using the root function on the calculator.

Many financial decisions, however, require that costs be incurred immediately but result in a stream of benefits over several future time periods. In these cases, the *net present value rule* provides appropriate guidance for decision makers.

net present value (NPV)

The **net present value (NPV)** of an investment is equal to the present value of the expected future cash flows generated by the investment minus the initial outlay of cash, or:

$$\text{NPV} = \text{Present value of future cash flows } \textit{minus} \text{ Initial outlay} \tag{5.29}$$

The future cash flows are discounted back to the present at a required rate of return that reflects the perceived risk of the investment.

The net present value of an investment made by a firm represents the contribution of that investment to the value of the firm and, accordingly, to the wealth of shareholders. For example, if Hewlett Packard (HP) expects a new line of servers to have a positive net present value of $750 million, the value of HP's common stock can be expected to increase by $750 million at the time the investment is made, all other things being equal. Thus, the net present value concept can be viewed as the bridge between cash flows and the goal of shareholder wealth maximization.

The net present value concept provides a framework for evaluating future *cash flows* from an investment or a firm. For example, in 2001, Airbus was considering whether to launch a new superjumbo jet (A-380) project in competition with Boeing's 747 family of jumbo jets. The development cost of the new plane was estimated to be $12 billion. The success of the project would hinge on the final costs of development, the cost of production, the price per plane, and the number of planes expected to be sold. Each of these factors is a key determinant of the annual net cash flows from the project. Airbus ultimately concluded that the expected cash flows were sufficient to justify the investment (that is, positive net present value). Boeing, in contrast, scrapped plans for a superjumbo model because they did not feel there would be sufficient demand for these giant planes.

Indeed, the NPV rule is central to the practice of financial management. You will find this rule constantly applied throughout your study of finance.

5-12 Summary

- An understanding of *interest* is crucial to sound financial management. *Simple interest* is interest earned or paid on the principal only. *Compound interest* is interest paid not only on the principal but also on any interest earned but not withdrawn during earlier periods.
- An *annuity* is the payment or receipt of a series of equal cash flows per period for a specified number of periods. In an *ordinary annuity,* the cash flows occur at the *end* of each period. In an *annuity due,* the cash flows occur at the *beginning* of each period.
- Table 5.8 below summarizes the equations used to compute the future and present values of the various cash flow streams.
- In solving financia mathematics problems, it is necessary to answer two questions:
  1. Do we need a future value or a present value?
  2. Are we dealing with a single payment or an annuity?

Once these questions have been successfully answered, the following table can be used to select the appropriate table of interest factors:

	Future Value	Present Value
Single Payment	Table I	Table II
Annuity	Table III	Table IV

- *Sinking fund problems* determine the annuity amount that must be invested each year to produce a future value.

● TABLE 5.8

Summary of Future and Present Value Equations

Type of Calculation	Equation	Interest Factor Table	Equation Number
Future value of a single payment	$FV_n = PV_0(FVIF_{i,n})$	Table I	5.11
Future value of an (ordinary) annuity	$FVAN_n = PMT(FVIFA_{i,n})$	Table III	5.16
Future value of an annuity due	$FVAND_n = PMT[FVIFA_{i,n}(1+i)]$	Table III	5.17
Present value of a single payment	$PV_0 = FV_n(PVIF_{i,n})$	Table II	5.14
Present value of an (ordinary) annuity	$PVAN_0 = PMT(PVIFA_{i,n})$	Table IV	5.19
Present value of an annuity due	$PVAND_0 = PMT[PVIFA_{i,n}(1+i)]$	Table IV	5.20
Present value of an uneven payment stream	$PV_0 = \sum_{t=1}^{n} PMT_t(PVIF_{i,t})$	Table II	5.24
Present value of a (ordinary) perpetuity	$PVPER_0 = \frac{PMT}{i}$	—	5.22

Definitions:
n = number of time periods of discounting or compounding (usually years).
i = annual rate of interest (that is, annual nominal interest rate).
PMT = annuity cash flow (that is, amount of cash flow paid or received for a specified number of years, or forever in the case of a perpetuity). In an ordinary annuity, the cash flows are received at the end of each year. In an annuity due, the cash flows are received at the beginning of each year.
PMT_t = payment (cash flow) in period t.

- *Capital recovery problems* determine the annuity amount necessary to recover some initial investment.
- The more frequently compounding occurs during a given period, the higher the *effective* interest rate on an investment. More frequent compounding results in higher future values and lower present values than less frequent compounding at the same interest rate.
- The appropriate compounding or discount rate to use in a particular decision-making situation depends upon the general level of interest rates in the economy, the time frame used for analysis, and the risk of the investment being considered.
- The net present value rule is central to financial analysis. The net present value (NPV) of an investment is equal to the present value of the future cash flows minus the initial outlay. Future outlays are discounted back to the present at a required rate of return that reflects the perceived risk of the investment.
- The net present value of an investment made by a firm represents the contribution of the investment to the firm and, accordingly, to the wealth of shareholders.

Important Equations

$$FV_n = PV_0(1+i)^n$$

$$FV_n = PV_0(FVIF_{i,n})$$

$$PV_0 = FV_n(PVIF_{i,n})$$

$$FVAN_n = PMT(FVIFA_{i,n})$$

$$FVAND_n = PMT[FVIFA_{i,n}(1+i)]$$

$$PVAN_0 = PMT(PVIFA_{i,n})$$

$$PVAND_0 = PMT[PVIFA_{i,n}(1+i)]$$

$$PVPER_0 = \frac{PMT}{i}$$

Important Equations (*Continued*)

$$PV_0 = \sum_{t=1}^{n} \frac{PMT_t}{(1+i)^t}$$

$$= \sum_{t=1}^{n} PMT_t(PVIF_{i,t})$$

$$FV_n = PV_0\left(1 + \frac{i_{nom}}{m}\right)^{mn}$$

$$PV_0 = \frac{FV_n}{\left(1 + \frac{i_{nom}}{m}\right)^{mn}}$$

$$i_{eff} = \left(1 + \frac{i_{nom}}{m}\right)^{m} - 1$$

$$i_m = (1 + i_{eff})^{1/m} - 1$$

NPV = Present value of future cash flows minus initial outlay

5-13 Questions and Topics for Discussion

1. Which would you rather receive: the proceeds from a 2-year investment paying 5 percent simple interest per year, or from one paying 5 percent compound interest? Why?
2. Which is greater: the future value interest factor (FVIF) for 10 percent and two years, or the present value interest factor (PVIF) for 10 percent and two years?
3. What happens to the present value of an annuity as the interest rate increases? What happens to the future value of an annuity as the interest rate increases?
4. Which would you prefer to invest in: a savings account paying 6 percent compounded annually, or a savings account paying 6 percent compounded daily? Why?
5. What type of contract might require the use of annuity due computations?
6. What effect does more frequent compounding have on present values?
7. Why should each of the following be familiar with compounding and present value concepts?
   a. A marketing manager
   b. A personnel manager
8. Explain the Rule of 72. How can it be used in finance applications? (See footnote 3.)
9. What is the relationship between present value and future value?
10. What is the difference between an ordinary annuity and an annuity due? Give examples of each.

11. If the required rate of return increases, what is the impact on the following?
a. A present value of an annuity
b. A future value of an annuity

12. Explain how future value of an annuity interest factors can be used to solve a sinking fund problem.

13. Describe how to set up a loan amortization schedule.

14. November 21, 1980, was the day of a tragic fire in the MGM Grand Hotel in Las Vegas. At the time of the fire, the hotel had only $30 million of liability insurance. One month after the fire, the hotel bought an extra $170 million of liability coverage for a premium of $37.5 million, retroactive to November 1, 1980 (before the fire). Based on your knowledge of present value concepts, why would insurers be willing to issue insurance to MGM under these conditions?

15. A savings account advertises that "interest is compounded continuously and paid quarterly." What does this mean?

16. Give an example of a perpetuity. How does a perpetuity differ from an annuity?

17. Explain how to determine the present value of an uneven cash flow stream.

18. Evaluate the following statement: "The development of powerful, inexpensive microcomputers has made the hand calculator as obsolete as the slide rule."

19. What is the relationship between the concepts of net present value and shareholder wealth maximization?

5-14 Self-Test Problems

ST1. Calculate the value in five years of $1,000 deposited in a savings account today if the account pays interest at a rate of:
a. 8 percent per year, compounded annually
b. 8 percent per year, compounded quarterly

ST2. A business is considering purchasing a machine that is projected to yield cash savings of $1,000 per year over a 10-year period. Using a 12 percent discount rate, calculate the present value of the savings. (Assume that the cash savings occur at the end of each year.)

ST3. Simpson Peripherals earned $0.90 per share in 2010 and $1.52 in 2015. Calculate the annual growth rate in earnings per share over this period.

ST4. You own a small business that is for sale. You have been offered $2,000 per year for five years, with the first receipt at the end of four years. Calculate the present value of this offer, using a 14 percent discount rate.

ST5. Yolanda Williams is 35 years old today and is beginning to plan for her retirement. She wants to set aside an equal amount at the end of each of the next 25 years so that she can retire at age 60. She expects to live to an age of 80 and wants to be able to withdraw $50,000 per year from the account on her 61st through 80th birthdays. The account is expected to earn 10 percent per year for the entire period of time. Determine the size of the annual deposits that she must make.

ST6. First State Bank offers a certificate of deposit that pays a 4.75 percent annual rate compounded monthly. Determine the effective annual percentage interest rate on this CD.

5-15 Problems*

BASIC **1.** How much will $1,000 deposited in a savings account earning a compound annual interest rate of 6 percent be worth at the end of the following number of years?
a. 3 years
b. 5 years
c. 10 years

BASIC **2.** If you require a 9 percent return on your investments, which would you prefer?
a. $5,000 today
b. $15,000 five years from today
c. $1,000 per year for 15 years

BASIC **3.** The Lancer Leasing Company has agreed to lease a hydraulic trencher to the Chavez Excavation Company for $20,000 a year over the next eight years. Lease payments are to be made at the beginning of each year. Assuming that Lancer invests these payments at an annual rate of 9 percent, how much will it have accumulated by the end of the eighth year?

BASIC **4.** The Mutual Assurance and Life Company is offering an insurance policy under either of the following two terms:
a. Make a series of twelve $1,200 payments at the beginning of each of the next 12 years (the first payment being made today).
b. Make a single lump-sum payment today of $10,000 and receive coverage for the next 12 years.

If you had investment opportunities offering an 8 percent annual return, which alternative would you prefer?

BASIC **5.** Determine the present value, discounted at 6 percent per year of $50,000 to be received five years from today if the interest rate is compounded:
a. Semiannually
b. Quarterly

BASIC **6.** A leading broker has advertised money multiplier certificates that will triple your money in nine years; that is, if you buy one for $333.33 today, it will pay you $1,000 at the end of nine years. What rate of return will you earn on these money multiplier certificates?

BASIC **7.** What is the present value of $800 to be received at the end of eight years, assuming the following annual interest rate?
a. 4 percent, discounted annually
b. 8 percent, discounted annually
c. 20 percent, discounted quarterly
d. 0 percent

BASIC **8.** Mr. Jones bought a building for $60,000, payable on the following terms: a $10,000 down payment and 25 equal annual installment payments to include principal and interest of 10 percent per annum. Calculate the amount of the installment payments. How much of the first year's payment goes toward reducing the principal amount?

BASIC **9.** A firm purchases 100 acres of land for $200,000 and agrees to remit 20 equal annual end-of-year installments of $41,067 each. What is the true annual interest rate on this loan?

*Color blocks behind the numbers denote problems that have check answers provided at the end of the book.

BASIC **10.** Susan Robinson is planning for her retirement. She is 30 years old today and would like to have $600,000 when she turns 55. She estimates that she will be able to earn a 9 percent rate of return on her retirement investments over time; she wants to set aside a constant amount of money every year (at the end of the year) to help achieve her objective. How much money must Robinson invest at the end of each of the next 25 years to realize her goal of $600,000 at the end of that time?

INTERMEDIATE **11.** What would you be willing to pay for a $1,000 bond paying $70 interest at the end of each year and maturing in 25 years if you wanted the bond to yield the following rates of return?

a. 5 percent
b. 7 percent
c. 12 percent

(*Note:* At maturity, the bond will be retired and the holder will receive $1,000 in cash. Bonds are typically issued with $1,000 face, or par, values. The actual market value at any point in time will tend to rise as interest rates fall and fall as interest rates rise.)

BASIC **12.** A life insurance company offers loans to its policyholders against the cash value of their policies at a (nominal) annual interest rate of 8 percent, compounded quarterly. Determine the effective annual percentage interest rate on these loans.

BASIC **13.** Two investment opportunities are open to you: Investment 1 and Investment 2. Each has an initial cost of $10,000. Assuming that you desire a 10 percent return on your initial investment, compute the net present value of the two alternatives options and evaluate their relative attractiveness:

Investment 1		Investment 2	
Cash Flows	**Year**	**Cash Flows**	**Year**
$5,000	1	$8,000	1
6,000	2	7,000	2
7,000	3	6,000	3
8,000	4	5,000	4

BASIC **14.** Your great-uncle Claude is 82 years old. Over the years, he has accumulated savings of $80,000. He estimates that he will live another 10 years at the most and wants to spend his savings by then. (If he lives longer than that, he figures you will be happy to take care of him.)

Uncle Claude places his $80,000 into an account earning 10 percent annually and sets it up in such a way that he will be making 10 equal annual withdrawals—the first one occurring one year from now—such that his account balance will be zero at the end of 10 years. How much will he be able to withdraw each year?

INTERMEDIATE **15.** You decide to purchase a building for $30,000 by paying $5,000 down and assuming a mortgage of $25,000. The bank offers you a 15-year mortgage requiring annual end-of-year payments of $3,188 each. The bank also requires you to pay a 3 percent loan origination fee, which will reduce the effective amount the bank lends to you. Compute the annual percentage rate of interest on this loan.

INTERMEDIATE **16.** An investment promises to pay $6,000 at the end of each year for the next five years and $4,000 at the end of each year for years 6 through 10.

a. If you require a 12 percent rate of return on an investment of this sort, what is the maximum amount you would pay for this investment?

b. Assuming that the payments are received at the *beginning* of each year, what is the maximum amount you would pay for this investment, given a 12 percent required rate of return?

CHALLENGE **17.** You are considering investing in a bond that matures 20 years from now. It pays an annual end-of-year coupon rate of interest of 8.75 percent, or $87.50 per year. The bond currently sells for $919. Your marginal income tax rate (applied to interest payments) is 28 percent. Capital gains are taxed at the same rate as ordinary income. What is your *after-tax* rate of return if you buy this bond today and hold it until maturity?

INTERMEDIATE **18.** Your parents have discovered a $1,000 bond at the bottom of their safe-deposit box. The bond was given to you by your late great-aunt Hilda on your second birthday. The bond pays interest at a rate of 5 percent per annum, compounded annually. Interest accumulates and is paid at the time the bond is redeemed. You are now 27 years old. What is the current worth of the bond (principal plus interest)?

INTERMEDIATE **19.** Your mother is planning to retire this year. Her firm has offered her a lump-sum retirement payment of $50,000 or a $6,000 lifetime annuity—whichever she chooses. Your mother is in reasonably good health and expects to live for at least 15 more years. Which option should she choose, assuming that an 8 percent interest rate is appropriate to evaluate the annuity?

BASIC **20.** Strikler, Inc., has issued a $10 million, 10-year bond issue. The bonds require Strikler to establish a sinking fund and make 10 equal, end-of-year deposits into the fund. These deposits will earn 8 percent annually, and the sinking fund should have enough accumulated in it at the end of 10 years to retire the bonds. What are the annual sinking fund payments?

BASIC **21.** Construct a loan amortization schedule for a 3-year, 11 percent loan of $30,000. The loan requires three equal, end-of-year payments.

INTERMEDIATE **22.** Mitchell Investments has offered you the following investment opportunity:

- $6,000 at the end of each year for the first 5 years, plus
- $3,000 at the end of each year from years 6 through 10, plus
- $2,000 at the end of each year from years 11 through 20.

a. How much would you be willing to pay for this investment if you required a 12 percent rate of return?

b. If the payments were received at the beginning of each year, what would you be willing to pay for this investment?

BASIC **23.** Upon retirement, your goal is to spend five years traveling around the world. To travel in the style to which you are accustomed will require $250,000 per year at the beginning of each year. If you plan to retire in 30 years, what are the equal, annual, end-of-year payments necessary to achieve this goal? The funds in the retirement account will compound at 10 percent annually.

INTERMEDIATE **24.** You deposit $4,500 per year at the end of each of the next 25 years into an account that pays 10 percent compounded annually. How much could you withdraw at the end of each of the 20 years following your last deposit? (The 25th and last deposit is made at the beginning of the 20-year period. The first withdrawal is made at the end of the first year in the 20-year period.)

INTERMEDIATE **25.** You deposit $10,000 at the end of each of the next four years into an account that pays 12 percent annually. What is the account balance at the end of 10 years?

BASIC **26.** Determine the value at the end of three years of a $10,000 investment (today) in a bank certificate of deposit (CD) that pays a nominal annual interest rate of 8 percent, compounded:

a. Semiannually
b. Quarterly
c. Monthly

BASIC **27.** An investment requires an outlay of $100,000 today. Cash inflows from the investment are expected to be $40,000 per year at the end of years 4, 5, 6, 7, and 8. If you require a 20 percent rate of return on this type of investment, should the investment be undertaken?

BASIC **28.** An investment of $100,000 is expected to generate cash inflows of $60,000 in one year and $79,350 in two years. Calculate the expected rate of return on this investment to the nearest whole percent.

INTERMEDIATE **29.** An investment offers the following year-end cash flows:

End of Year	Cash Flow
1	$20,000
2	$30,000
3	$15,000

Using a 15 percent interest rate, convert this series of irregular cash flows to an equivalent (in present value terms) 3-year annuity.

CHALLENGE **30.** James Street's son, Harold, is 10 years old today. Harold, a studious young fellow, is already making plans to go to college on his 18th birthday, and his father wants to start putting money away now for that purpose. Street estimates that Harold will need $18,000, $19,000, $20,000, and $21,000 for his freshman, sophomore, junior, and senior years, respectively. He plans on making these amounts available to Harold at the beginning of each of these years.

Street would like to make eight annual deposits (the first of which would be made on Harold's 11th birthday, one year from now, and the last on his 18th birthday, the day he leaves for college) in an account earning 10 percent annually. He wants the account to eventually be worth enough to *just* pay for Harold's college expenses. Any balances remaining in the account will continue to earn the 10 percent.

How much will Street have to deposit in this "planning" account each year to provide for Harold's education?

INTERMEDIATE **31.** How much must you deposit at the end of each quarter in an account that pays a nominal interest rate of 20 percent, compounded quarterly, if at the end of five years you want $10,000 in the account? (*Hint*: In working with the compound interest tables when solving this problem, you need to adjust the interest rate and the number of compounding periods to reflect quarterly, rather than annual, compounding.)

CHALLENGE **32.** IRA Investments develops retirement programs for individuals. You are 30 years old and plan to retire on your 60th birthday. You want to establish a plan with IRA that will require a series of equal, annual, end-of-year deposits into the retirement account. The first deposit will be made one year from today on your 31st birthday. The final payment on the account will be made on your 60th birthday. The retirement plan will allow you to withdraw $120,000 per year for 15 years, with the first withdrawal on your 61st birthday. Also, at the end of the 15th year, you wish to withdraw an additional $250,000. The retirement account promises to earn 12 percent annually.

What periodic payment must be made into the account to achieve your retirement objective?

CHALLENGE **33.** You have just had your 30th birthday. You have two children. One will go to college 10 years from now and require four beginning-of-year payments for college expenses of $10,000, $11,000, $12,000, and $13,000. The second child will go to college 15 years from now and require four beginning-of-year payments for college expenses of $15,000, $16,000, $17,000, and $18,000. In addition, you plan to retire in 30 years. You want to be able to withdraw $50,000 per year (at the end of each year) from an account throughout your retirement. You expect to live 20 years beyond retirement. The first withdrawal will occur on your 61st birthday.

What equal, annual, end-of-year amount must you save for each of the next 30 years to meet these goals, if all savings earn a 13 percent annual rate of return?

CHALLENGE **34.** You are currently 30 years of age. You intend to retire at age 60 and you want to be able to receive a 20-year, $100,000 beginning-of-year annuity with the first payment to be received on your 60th birthday. You would like to save enough money over the next 15 years to achieve your objective; that is, you want to accumulate the necessary funds by your 45th birthday.

a. If you expect your investments to earn 12 percent per year over the next 15 years and 10 percent per year thereafter, how much must you accumulate by the time you reach age 45?

b. What equal, annual amount must you save at the end of each of the next 15 years to achieve your objective, assuming that you currently have $10,000 available to meet your goal? Assume the conditions stated in Part a.

INTERMEDIATE **35.** Steven White is considering taking early retirement, having saved $400,000. White desires to determine how many years the savings will last if $40,000 per year is withdrawn at the end of each year. White feels the savings can earn 10 percent per year. How many years will White's savings last, given these parameters?

CHALLENGE **36.** Suppose today is July 1, 2014, and you deposit $2,000 into an account today. Then you deposit $1,000 into the same account on *each* July 1, beginning in 2015 and continuing until the last $1,000 deposit is made on July 1, 2020. Also, assume that you withdraw $3,000 on July 1, 2022. Assuming a 7 percent annual compound interest rate, what will be the balance in the account at the close of business on July 1, 2024?

CHALLENGE **37.** Your son, Charlie, has just turned 15. Charlie plans to go to college to study electronics on his 18th birthday. College is expected to cost Charlie $15,000, $16,000, $17,000, and $18,000 for each of his four years in school. You want these funds to be available to him at the beginning of each year in college. In addition, you want to give Charlie a $25,000 graduation gift on his 22nd birthday so that he can get a start on his career or on graduate school.

You currently have $8,000 to meet these obligations. You want to save an equal amount at the end of each of the next six years to meet the remaining obligations. If your investments earn 10 percent pretax and your marginal tax rate is 30 percent, how much must you save at the end of each of the next six years?

CHALLENGE **38.** Frank Chang is planning for the day when his child, Laura, will go to college. Laura has just turned eight and plans to enter college on her 18th birthday. She will need $25,000 at the beginning of each year in school. Frank plans to give Laura a Mercedes-Benz as a combination graduation and 22nd birthday present. The Mercedes is expected to cost $55,000. Frank currently has $10,000 saved for Laura. Also, Frank expects to inherit $25,000 nine years from now that will be used for Laura's education. Frank expects to be able to earn 7 percent after tax on any investments. How much must Frank save at the end of each of the next 10 years in order to provide for Laura's education and the Mercedes?

CHALLENGE **39.** Ted Gardiner has just turned 30 years old. He has currently accumulated $35,000 toward his planned retirement at age 60. He wants to accumulate enough money over the next 30 years to provide for a 20-year retirement annuity of $100,000 at the beginning of each year, starting with his 60th birthday. He plans to save $5,000 at the end of each of the next 10 years. What equal amount must he save at the end of years 11 through 30 to meet this objective? The interest rate for the first 10 years will be 5 percent. After that time, the interest rate is expected to be 7 percent.

CHALLENGE **40.** Torbet Fish Packing Company wants to accumulate enough money over the next 10 years to pay for the expected replacement of its digitalized, automated scaling machine. The new machine is expected to cost $200,000 in 10 years. Torbet currently has $10,000 that it plans to invest over the next 10 years to help pay for the new machine. Torbet wants to put away an equal, end-of-year amount into a sinking fund investment account at the end of each of the next 10 years. Earnings on all of the investments are expected to be 7 percent for the first five years and 9 percent thereafter. What equal, end-of-year amount must Torbet save each year over the next 10 years to meet these needs?

INTERMEDIATE **41.** Crab State Bank has offered you a $1,000,000 five-year loan at an interest rate of 11.25 percent, requiring equal annual end-of-year payments that include both principal and interest on the unpaid balance. Develop an amortization schedule for this loan.

CHALLENGE **42.** Garrett Erdle has just turned 26 years of age. Although Garrett currently has a negative net worth, he expects to pay off all of his financial obligations within four years and then to embark on an aggressive plan to save for retirement. He wishes to be able to withdraw $100,000 per year during the first 10 years of retirement (the first withdrawal coming on his 61st birthday) and $150,000 during the next 10 years of retirement. As a precaution against unexpected longevity, he would like to have a net worth of $500,000 after the withdrawal on his 80th birthday. Garrett expects the after-tax return on his investments to be 6 percent until he turns age 50, and 7 percent thereafter. What equal annual amount must Garrett save at the end of each year (the first deposit will occur on his 31st birthday and the last deposit will occur on his 60th birthday) to meet these retirement goals?

CHALLENGE **43.** Bobbi Proctor does not want to "gamble" on Social Security taking care of her in retirement. Hence she wants to begin to plan now for retirement. She has enlisted the services of Hackney Financial Planning to assist her in meeting her goals. Proctor has determined that she would like to have a retirement annuity of $200,000 per year, with the first payment to be received 36 years from now at the end of her first year of retirement. She plans a long, enjoyable retirement of about 25 years. Proctor wishes to save $5,000 at the end of each of the next 15 years, and an unknown, equal end-of-period amount for the remaining 20 years before she begins her retirement. Hackney has advised Proctor that she can safely assume that all savings will earn 12 percent per annum until she retires, but only 8 percent thereafter. How much must Proctor save per year during the 20 years preceding retirement?

CHALLENGE **44.** You have decided to start planning for your retirement by analyzing different retirement plans. The plan offered by IRA Managers requires you to deposit $5,000 at the beginning of each of the next 30 years. The retirement plan guarantees a 10 percent annual compounding rate over the 30-year time period. When you retire at the end of the 30th year, the interest earned on the money in the account is guaranteed to increase to a 12 percent annual rate. If you plan on making 20 equal withdrawals at the beginning of each year from the account (with the first withdrawal made at the end of the 30th year—the first year of retirement), how much can you withdraw?

45. Determine the monthly rate of interest that will yield an effective annual rate of interest of 12 percent.

46. Try using one of the many Internet calculators, such as the one at Salem Five, to calculate your time-value problems.

a. Suppose you wanted to borrow \$100,000 for 25 years at 8 percent. Using Salem Five's calculator, find your monthly payment.

b. Using Salem Five's "Savings and Investment Planner," find how much \$2,000 saved at the end of each of the next 30 years will grow to be, assuming it earns a constant 10 percent per year.

HTTP:
www.salemfive.com

INTEGRATIVE CASE PROBLEM

Time Value of Money

Assume that you are 30 years old today and expect to retire when you reach age 65. If you were to retire *today*, you would like a fixed (pretax) income of $60,000 per year (in addition to Social Security) for a period of 15 years (your approximate life expectancy at age 65). However, you realize that price inflation will erode the purchasing power of the dollar over the next 35 years and you want to adjust your desired retirement income at age 65 to reflect the decline in the purchasing power of the dollar. In addition to the fixed annual income, payable at the *beginning* of each year starting at age 65, you want to have assets (that is, securities investments) of $1,000,000, either for your own needs or to donate to heirs, when you reach 80 years old.

Empirical studies have estimated the average compound rate of price inflation and returns on stocks and bonds over the past 70 years to be approximately:

	Compound Rate
Inflation	3%
Common stocks	11
Corporate bonds	6
Equally weighted portfolio	8.5
(50% common stocks, 50% bonds)	

Assume that these rates will remain the same over the next 50 years and that you can earn these rates of return, after transactions costs, by investing in stock and/or bond index mutual funds. Also assume that contributions to your retirement fund are made at the *end* of each year. Finally, assume that income taxes on the returns from any retirement investments (for example, IRAs or 401(k) plans) can be deferred until you withdraw the funds beginning at age 65.

1. Determine your required inflation-adjusted annual (pretax) income at age 65. Assume that this annual amount remains constant from age 65 to age 80.
2. Determine the amount you must accumulate by age 65 to meet your retirement goal, assuming that you invest in:
   a. Common stocks
   b. Corporate bonds
   c. Equally weighted portfolio (50 percent common stocks, 50 percent bonds)
3. Determine the annual investment in *common stocks* required to accumulate the funds determined in question 2, assuming that the first payment is made at age:
   a. 30
   b. 40
   c. 50
4. Determine the annual investment in *corporate bonds* required to accumulate the funds determined in question 2, assuming that the first payment is made at age:
   a. 30
   b. 40
   c. 50

5. Determine the annual investment in an *equally weighted portfolio* (50 percent common stocks, 50 percent bonds) required to accumulate the funds determined in question 2, assuming that the first payment is made at age
   a. 30
   b. 40
   c. 50
6. What conclusions can be drawn from the answers to questions 3, 4, and 5?

APPENDIX **5A**

CONTINUOUS COMPOUNDING AND DISCOUNTING

Continuous Compounding

In Chapter 5 we assumed that interest was received (or growth in a stream of payments occurred) at discrete points in time, such as at the end of each year, semiannually, quarterly, and so forth. It was shown that a nominal rate of i_{nom} percent per year results in a greater than i_{nom} percent effective rate per year if compounding occurs more frequently than one time at the end of the year. Specifically, the future value (FV_n) of some initial amount (PV_0) is given by Equation 5.25:

$$FV_n = PV_0\left(1 + \frac{i_{nom}}{m}\right)^{mn}$$

where i_{nom} is the nominal annual rate of interest or growth, m is the number of times per year that compounding occurs, and n is the number of years compounding occurs. (Recall from footnote 10 in Chapter 5 that an annual nominal interest rate is equivalent to an effective annual rate in the case where compounding occurs once a year at the end of the year.)

As shown earlier in Table 5.6, the more often the compounding takes place each year, the greater will be the future value of some present amount. Another way of looking at this is to indicate that the more often compounding takes place each year, the greater is the *effective* rate of interest (or growth) compared to the stated annual *nominal* rate.

At the limit, we could accrue, or compound, interest *continuously*. In this limiting case, the future value equation for continuous compounding becomes:

(5A.1)
$$FV_n = PV_0(e)^{i_{nom}n}$$

where e is approximately equal to the value 2.71828. (This value is the base number in natural logarithms.) If you have a financial or scientific calculator, the value of $e^{i_{nom}n}$ normally can be found by multiplying the nominal rate i by the number of years n and then punching the e^x key.

For example, if $1,000 is invested for one year at a nominal rate of 10 percent compounded continuously, the future value at the end of that year is given as follows:

$$FV_1 = \$1{,}000(e)^{0.10(1)} = \$1{,}000(2.71828)^{0.10}$$
$$= \$1{,}105.17$$

In the case where the $1,000 is invested at a nominal rate of 10 percent for three years, the future value, assuming continuous compounding, is equal to:

$$FV_3 = \$1000(e)^{0.10(3)} = \$1{,}000(2.71828)^{0.30}$$
$$= \$1{,}349.86$$

Continuous Discounting

Equation 5A.1 can also be modified to reflect continuous discounting. At the limit where compounding takes place continuously, present values can be computed as follows:

(5A.2)
$$PV_0 = \frac{FV_n}{(e)^{i_{nom} n}}$$

or equivalently:

(5A.3)
$$PV_0 = FV_n(e)^{-i_{nom} n}$$

For example, if $1,349.86 is to be received three years from now at the continuously compounded rate of 10 percent, the present value can be computed as follows:

$$\begin{aligned} PV_0 &= \frac{\$1{,}349.86}{(2.71828)^{0.10(3)}} \\ &= \$1{,}000 \end{aligned}$$

Effective Rate Calculations

When a *nominal* annual rate, i_{nom}, of interest (or growth) is known and compounding occurs continuously, it is easy to compute the *effective* annual rate using the following expression:[1]

(5A.4)
$$i_{eff} = e^{i_{nom}} - 1$$

For example, if the nominal annual rate is 20 percent and compounding occurs continuously, the effective annual rate is computed as follows:

$$\begin{aligned} i_{eff} &= 2.71828^{(0.2)} - 1 \\ &= 1.2214 - 1 \\ &= 0.2214 \text{ or } 22.14\% \end{aligned}$$

The effective rate is higher than the nominal rate because, with continuous compounding, the money is working harder; that is, interest is being accumulated more frequently (continuously), and this accumulated interest is available to earn its own interest on an ongoing (continuous) basis.

Self-Test Problems

ST1. What is the future value of $1,000 invested for seven years at a nominal interest rate of 10 percent compounded continuously?

ST2. What is the present value of receiving $5,000 eight years from now if the nominal discount rate is 9 percent, discounted continuously?

ST3. Calculate the effective annual rate if the nominal annual rate is 12 percent, compounded continuously.

---

[1] Equation 5A.4 is obtained from Equation 5.27 by letting m approach infinity:

$$i_{eff} = \lim_{m \to \infty} \left(1 + \frac{i_{nom}}{m}\right)^m - 1 = e^{i_{nom}} - 1$$

Problems*

BASIC

1. What is the future value of $10,000 invested for two years at a nominal interest rate of 12 percent, compounded continuously?

BASIC

2. You expect to receive $5,000 in five years. What is the present value of this future receipt at the continuously discounted rate of 12 percent?

INTERMEDIATE

3. The nominal rate of interest on a bank CD is 8 percent. If compounding occurs continuously, what is the effective annual rate?

INTERMEDIATE

4. Given a nominal annual interest rate of 20 percent, determine the effective annual rate with
   a. Annual compounding
   b. Quarterly compounding
   c. Monthly compounding
   d. Continuous compounding

INTERMEDIATE

5. What is the future value of $1,000 invested for 10 years at a nominal interest rate of 10 percent compounded continuously? How much higher is this value than the value obtained with annual compounding for 10 years at 10 percent?

INTERMEDIATE

6. What is the present value of receiving $1,500 twenty-five years from now if the nominal interest rate is 10 percent, discounted continuously?

*Color blocks behind the numbers denote problems that have check answers provided at the end of the book.

CHAPTER 6

Fixed-Income Securities: Characteristics and Valuation

KEY CHAPTER CONCEPTS

1. The characteristics of fixed-income (debt and preferred stock) securities are examined, including
    a. Types of each form of security
    b. Features
    c. Users
    d. Advantages and disadvantages
2. Reading and interpreting financial market data, including stock and bond price quotations, is an essential skill for an effective financial manager.
3. In the capitalization of cash flow method, the value of an asset is equal to the present value of the expected future cash flows discounted at the appropriate required rate of return.
4. The required rate of return is a function of the risk or uncertainty associated with the cash flows from the asset, as well as the risk-free rate.
5. The value of a bond with a finite maturity date is equal to the present value of the interest payments and principal payment (at maturity) discounted at the investor's required rate of return.
6. The yield-to-maturity of a bond is equal to the rate of return that equates the price of the bond to the present value of the interest and principal payments.
7. The value of a perpetual bond, or perpetuity, is determined by dividing the fixed interest rate per period by the required rate of return, since no calculation for payback of principal is needed in the valuation.
8. Preferred stocks are often treated as *perpetuities* with a value equal to the annual dividend divided by the required rate of return.
9. The market value or market price of an asset is the value placed on the asset by the marginally satisfied buyer and seller, who exchange assets in the marketplace.
10. Market equilibrium occurs when the price of an asset is such that the expected rate of return is equal to the required rate of return.
11. Bond refunding involves the replacement of a called bond issue with a lower interest cost issue.

FINANCIAL CHALLENGE

Verizon's Record Bond Issue

Verizon Communications, owner of 55 percent of Verizon Wireless, agreed to purchase the other 45 percent stake owned by Vodafone, its wireless partner, for $130 billion in September 2013. Verizon planned to finance the transaction with approximately equal portions of common stock and cash. At the time of the acquisition, the $61 billion cash portion of the transaction was the largest amount of cash ever employed in an acquisition.

As part of the financing package, Verizon planned to issue $49 billion in bonds, with maturities ranging between 10 and 30 years. The company and its investment bankers (underwriters) expected that it would take as long as a year to raise the needed funds in the bond market. The plan was to raise the funds in stages over time and include bonds denominated in different (non-U.S.) currencies, with an initial offering of approximately $20 billion. However, interest in the bonds was so strong that Verizon and its investment bankers decided to raise the entire $49 billion in the initial offering. Verizon reportedly received orders for approximately $100 billion of the new bonds from investors.

The amount of this bond offering was far in excess of the largest corporate bond sale up to this point in time—namely, the $17 billion in bonds issued by Apple earlier in 2013. The transaction made Verizon Communications the largest nonfinancial issuer of bonds with over $100 billion of debt outstanding. By raising all of the funds in the initial offering, Verizon avoided the risk of having to issue more debt in the future, possibly at higher interest rates. Also, Verizon avoided the risk of having to pay a $10 billion breakup fee if, for some reason, it was unable to raise the funds needed for the buyout.

This chapter discusses the characteristics of long-term debt, reviews the bond quality ratings available from bond rating companies, and develops the techniques of bond valuation.

Sources: Spencer E. Ante, et al, "Vodafone, Verizon Agree on $130 Billion Deal," *The Wall Street Journal* (September 2, 2013); Mike Cherney et al., "Verizon Readies for a Bond Blowout," *The Wall Street Journal* (September 11, 2013): A1; Mike Cherney and Matt Wirz, "Big Bond Gets a Big Reception," *The Wall Street Journal* (September 12, 2013): C1; Michael Calia, "Verizon Completes Deal for All of Verizon Wireless," *The Wall Street Journal* (February 21, 2014).

CHAPTER OBJECTIVES

Upon completion of this chapter, you should have a clear understanding of the following:

1. Types, features, and characteristics of long-term debt instruments (bonds)
2. The valuation of bonds
3. Determining the yield-to-maturity of bonds
4. Types, features, and characteristics of preferred stocks
5. The valuation of preferred stocks

6-1 Introduction

Companies issue various types of long-term securities to help meet their needs for funds. These include long-term debt (bonds),[1] preferred stock, and common stock. Long-term debt and preferred stock are sometimes referred to as *fixed-income securities*. Holders of these types of securities receive relatively constant distributions of interest or dividend payments over time and have a fixed claim on the assets of the firm in the event of bankruptcy.[2] For example, Ford Motor Company sold $250 million of bonds in 1992, at which time it agreed to pay its lenders an interest rate of 8⅞ percent, or $88.75 per year, until 2022 for each $1,000 of debt outstanding. The company was required to pay this interest rate, even though market interest rates have fluctuated. Similarly, DuPont issued $70 million of preferred stock in 1947. Investors paid $102 per share, and the company agreed to pay an annual dividend of $3.50 per share. Since then DuPont has continued to pay this amount, even though common stock dividends have been increased numerous times.

common stock

Common stock, on the other hand, is a *variable-income security*. Common stockholders are said to participate in a firm's earnings because they may receive a larger dividend if earnings increase in the future, or their dividend may be cut if earnings drop. For example, during a number of years of disappointing earnings, Ford reduced its annual dividend rate several times. Beginning in 2000 it cut the rate to $1.50 per share (from $1.88), $1.05 in 2001, $0.40 in 2002, and $0.25 in 2006. Beginning in the fourth quarter of 2006, it stopped paying dividends on its common stock. With improvements in the economy and the company's financial condition, Ford resumed dividend payments ($0.20 per share) in 2012. Investors in common stock have a residual claim on the earnings (and assets) of the firm since they receive dividends only after the claims of bondholders and other creditors, as well as preferred stockholders, have been met.

Fixed-income securities—long-term debt and preferred stock—differ from each other in several ways. For example, the interest paid to bondholders is a tax-deductible expense for the borrowing company, whereas dividends paid to preferred stockholders are not. Legally, long-term debt holders are considered creditors, whereas preferred stockholders are considered owners. Thus, a firm is not legally required to pay dividends to its preferred stockholders, and the failure to do so has less serious consequences than the failure to meet interest payment and principal repayment obligations on long-term debt. In addition, long-term debt normally has a specific maturity, whereas preferred stock is often perpetual.

A knowledge of the characteristics of the various types of long-term securities is necessary in developing valuation models for these securities. The valuation of long-term securities is important to a firm's financial managers, as well as to current owners, prospective investors, and security analysts. For example, financial managers should understand how the price or value of the firm's securities (particularly common stock) is affected by its investment, financing, and dividend decisions. Similarly, both current owners and prospective investors should be able to compare their own valuations of the firm's securities with actual market prices to make rational security purchase and sale decisions. Likewise, security analysts use valuation techniques in evaluating long-term corporate securities when making investment recommendations.

---

[1]The terms *long-term debt securities, debt,* and *bonds* are used interchangeably throughout the chapter.

[2]While floating rate debt and adjustable rate preferred stock have interest and dividend distributions that can fluctuate over time (as described later in the chapter), they are still classified as fixed-income securities.

This chapter focuses on the characteristics and valuation of fixed-income securities, namely, long-term debt and preferred stock. The next chapter contains a similar discussion of variable-income securities, namely, common stock.

6-2 Characteristics of Long-Term Debt

When a company borrows money in the capital markets, it issues long-term debt securities to investors. These bonds are usually sold in denominations of \$1,000 and constitute a promise by the issuing company to repay a certain amount of money (the \$1,000 principal) on a particular date (the maturity date) and to pay a specified amount of interest at fixed intervals (usually twice a year). Most debt has a **par value** of \$1,000, and debt prices are often expressed as a percentage of that value. For example, a market price listing of "87" indicates that a \$1,000 par value bond may be purchased for \$870.

par value

There are many different types of long-term debt. The type or types a company chooses to use will depend on its own particular financial situation and the characteristics of the industry as a whole.

6-2a Types of Long-Term Debt

Long-term debt is generally classified according to whether it is secured by specific physical assets of the issuing company. Secured debt issues are usually called **mortgage bonds**, and issues not secured by specific assets are called **debentures** or, occasionally, *debenture bonds*. The term **bond** is often used to denote any type of long-term debt security.

mortgage bonds
debentures
bond

Utility companies have been the largest users of mortgage bonds. In recent years, the use of mortgage bonds relative to other forms of long-term debt has declined, whereas the use of debentures has increased. Because debentures are unsecured, their quality depends on the general creditworthiness of the issuing company. As a result, they are usually issued by large, financially strong firms.

The yield differential between the mortgage bond and debenture alternatives is another example of the risk-return trade-off that occurs throughout finance. For example, suppose Mid-states Oil Company could issue either mortgage bonds or debentures. If the mortgage bonds could be sold with a 7 percent interest rate, the debentures would have to be sold at a higher rate—for example, 7¼ percent—to attract investors. This is due to the fact that investors require a higher return on debentures, which are backed only by the unmortgaged assets of the company and the company's earning power, than they do on mortgage bonds, which are secured by specific physical assets as well as the company's earning power.

Debt issues are also classified according to whether they are senior or junior.[3] **Senior debt** has a higher priority claim to a firm's earnings and/or assets than junior debt. Occasionally, the actual name of the debt issue will contain a "junior" or "senior" qualifier. In most instances, however, identification of how a particular company's debt issues are ranked requires an analysis of the restrictions placed on the company by the purchasers of the issue.

senior debt

Unsecured debt may also be classified according to whether it is *subordinated* to other types of debt. In the event of a liquidation or reorganization, the claims of *subordinated debenture holders* are considered only *after* the claims of *unsubordinated debenture holders*. In general, **subordinated debentures** are junior to other types of debt, including bank loans, and may even be junior to *all* of a firm's other debt.

subordinated debentures

[3]The senior–junior classification scheme is also used in connection with preferred and common stock. Preferred stock is junior to long-term debt and senior to common stock.

Equipment trust certificates are used largely by railroad and trucking companies. The proceeds from these certificates are used to purchase specific assets, such as railroad rolling stock. The certificate holders own the equipment and lease it to the company. Technically, equipment trust certificates are not true bonds, even though they are guaranteed by the issuing company, because the interest and principal are paid by the **trustee** (the financial institution responsible for looking after the investors' interests). Even so, they are classified as debt because they have all of the characteristics of debt.

trustee

Collateral trust bonds are backed by stocks or bonds of other corporations. This type of financing is principally of historic interest; it is used today primarily by holding companies. A holding company, for example, may raise needed funds by pledging the stocks and/or bonds of its subsidiaries as collateral. In this arrangement, the holding company serves as the *parent* company. The *subsidiary* borrows from the parent, and the parent borrows from the capital markets. This makes good sense because the parent company can generally get more favorable terms for its debt in the capital markets than the subsidiary.

Income bonds are also largely of historic interest, although they are still used occasionally today. **Income bonds** promise to pay interest only if the issuing firm earns sufficient income; if it does not, no interest obligation exists. These securities are rarely issued directly. Instead, they are often created in reorganizations following bankruptcy and are normally issued in exchange for junior or subordinated issues. Thus, unsecured income bonds are generally considered to be "weak" securities.

income bonds

Payment-in-kind (PIK) bonds are another type of "weak" security. PIK bonds permit cash-strapped companies to issue more debt to bondholders in lieu of cash interest payments. PIK bonds allow companies to conserve cash during lean times at the expense of adding to their debt obligations. These bonds helped fuel the private equity buyout boom prior to the financial crisis in 2008. For example, in 2007, KKR and TPG, two large private equity companies, issued $4.25 billion of PIK bonds to help finance the $43 billion purchase of TXU, a Dallas-based electric utility provider (now known as Energy Future Holdings). As a result of giving these bondholders more debt in lieu of cash interest payments, Energy Future Holdings PIK debt increased by $500 million to $4.75 billion in 2010. Energy Future Holdings was forced to file for bankruptcy protection in 2014 as a result of the company's massive debt load and falling natural gas prices.

Banks and finance companies often issue bonds backed by a stream of payments from consumer and commercial obligations, known as receivables. Credit card and automobile loan payments are the two primary types of receivables used in the market for *asset-backed securities*.

Pollution control bonds and *industrial revenue bonds* are issued by local governments rather than corporations. The interest paid to purchasers of municipal bonds is tax-exempt, and the interest rate is typically less than what a corporation would have to pay. The interest payments are guaranteed by the corporation for whose benefit the bonds are issued.

6-2b Features of Long-Term Debt

Long-term debt has a number of unique features. Several of these are discussed in the following paragraphs.[4]

[4]See Douglas R. Emery and John D. Finnerty, "A Review of Recent Research Concerning Corporate Debt Provisions," *Financial Markets, Institutions and Instruments* 1, No. 5 (December 1992): 23–39.

indenture

Indenture An **indenture** is a contract between a firm that issues long-term debt securities and the lenders. In general, an indenture does the following:

- It thoroughly details the nature of the debt issue.
- It carefully specifies the manner in which the principal must be repaid.
- It lists any restrictions placed on the firm by the lenders. These restrictions are called *covenants,* and the firm must satisfy them to keep from defaulting on its obligations.[5]

Typical restrictive covenants include the following:

1. A minimum coverage, or times interest earned, ratio the firm must maintain
2. A minimum level of working capital[6] the firm must maintain
3. A maximum amount of dividends the firm can pay on its preferred and common stock
4. Other restrictions that effectively limit how much leasing and issuing of additional debt the firm may do

Debt covenants are used to resolve agency problems among debtholders, stockholders, and managers.[7] Restrictive covenants, such as those listed, can be used to protect debtholders by prohibiting certain actions by shareholders or managers that might be detrimental to the market value of the debt securities and the ability of the firm to repay the debt at maturity. Debt covenants can also be used to alter the terms of a debt issue if a future significant corporate event should lower the market value of the debt issue. One such example of "event risk language" is a "poison put" covenant,[8] which allows bondholders to sell their debt back to the company at par value in the event of a leveraged buyout (LBO) transaction[9] and a downgrade in the credit rating of the debt issue to below investment grade.[10] International Paper's 1992 issue of 7⅝ percent notes, which matured in 2007, contained an option allowing holders to redeem the bonds at par (plus accrued interest) in the event of a ratings decline to less than investment grade.

Strong debt covenants can reduce managerial flexibility and thus impose opportunity costs on the firm. At the same time, strong covenants can result in higher credit ratings and lower borrowing costs to the firm by limiting transfers of wealth from bondholders to stockholders and placing limits on the bargaining power of management in any future debt renegotiations. The optimal package of covenants minimizes the sum of these costs.

Trustee Because the holders of a large firm's long-term debt issue are likely to be widely scattered geographically, the Trust Indenture Act of 1939 requires that a trustee represent the debtholders in dealings with the issuing company. A trustee is usually a commercial bank or trust company that is responsible for ensuring that all the terms and covenants set forth in the indenture agreement are adhered to by the issuing company. The issuing company must pay the trustee's expenses.

call feature

call price

Call Feature and Bond Refunding A **call feature** is an optional retirement provision that permits the issuing company to redeem, or *call,* a debt issue prior to its maturity date at a specified price termed the *redemption,* or **call price**. Many firms use

[5]A company defaults on its debt when it does not pay interest or required principal on time or when it violates one or more of the bond's restrictive covenants. When default occurs, the debt is often said to be "triggered," meaning that the entire principal amount comes due immediately. This could result in bankruptcy.

[6]*Working capital,* defined as the firm's investment in current assets less its current liabilities, is discussed in Chapter 16.

[7]Agency problems are discussed in Chapter 1.

[8]A *put option* is an option to sell an asset at a set price. Put options are discussed in Chapter 20.

[9]In a leveraged buyout (LBO), the buyer of a company borrows a large portion of the purchase price, using the purchased assets as collateral for the loan. LBOs are discussed in Chapter 23.

[10]Credit ratings are discussed later in this section.

the call feature because it provides them with the potential flexibility to retire debt prior to maturity if, for example, interest rates decline.

call premium

The call price is greater than the par value of the debt, and the difference between the two is the **call premium**. During the early years of an issue, the call premium is usually equal to about one year's interest. Some debt issues specify fixed call premiums, whereas others specify *declining* call premiums. For example, consider the Ford Motor Company $250 million of 8⅞ percent, 30-year debentures issued in 1992. Beginning on November 15, 2002, the company could retire all or part of this issue at 104.153 percent of par value, and the following year the redemption price was scheduled to drop to 103.737 percent of par. Similar reductions in the redemption price are scheduled for each year up to the year 2012. Thereafter, the bonds can be redeemed by the company at 100 percent of par value. Many bonds are not callable at all for several years after the initial date. For example, the Ford debentures were not callable until 2002—10 years after the issue date. This situation is referred to as a *deferred call.* Ford exercised its option to call the bond issue on November 15, 2003, at the stated call price of 103.737 percent of par value.

Details of the call feature are worked out in the negotiations between the underwriters and the issuing company before the debt is sold. Because a call feature gives the company significant flexibility in its financing plans, while at the same time potentially depriving the lenders of the advantages they would gain from holding the debt until maturity, the issuing company has to offer the investors compensation in the form of the call premium in exchange for the call privilege. In addition, the interest rate on a callable debt issue is usually slightly higher than the interest rate on a similar noncallable issue.

bond refunding

Because of the interest savings that can be achieved, a firm is most likely to call a debt issue when prevailing interest rates are appreciably lower than those that existed at the time of the original issue. When a company calls a relatively high interest rate issue and replaces it with a lower interest rate issue, the procedure is called **bond refunding**. This topic is discussed in Appendix B of Chapter 20.

Sinking Fund

Lenders often require that a borrowing company gradually reduce the outstanding balance of a debt issue over its life instead of having the entire principal amount come due on a particular date 20 or 30 years into the future. The usual method of providing for a gradual retirement is a sinking fund, so called because a certain amount of money is put aside annually, or "sunk," into a *sinking fund account.* For example, with the Ingersoll-Rand 7.20 percent 30-year debentures issued in 1995, the company is required to redeem $7.5 million of the bonds annually between 2006 and 2025, thus retiring 95 percent of the debt issue prior to maturity. In practice, however, a company can satisfy its sinking fund requirements either by purchasing a portion of the debt each year in the open market or, if the debt is callable, by using a lottery technique to determine which actual numbered certificates will be called and retired within a given year. The alternative chosen depends on the current market price of the debt issue. In general, if current interest rates are above the issue's coupon rate, the current market price of the debt will be less than $1,000, and the company should meet its sinking fund obligation by purchasing the debt in the open market. If, on the other hand, market interest rates are lower than the issue's coupon rate, and if the market price of the debt is above the call price, the company should use the call procedure.

Equity-Linked Debt

Some debt issues (and some preferred stock issues) are linked to the equity (common stock) of the firm through a conversion feature that allows the holder to exchange the security for the company's common stock at the option of the holder. Interest costs of a **convertible debt** issue are usually less than a similar debt

convertible debt

issue without the conversion option, because investors are willing to accept the value of the conversion privilege as part of their overall return. Another form of equity-linked debt is the issuance of warrants with debt securities. A **warrant** is an option to purchase shares of a company's common stock at a specified price during a given time period. Convertible securities and warrants are discussed in Chapter 20.

warrant

Typical Sizes of Debt Issues

Debt issues sold to the public through underwriters are usually in the range of $25 million to several hundred million dollars. In the past, some very large companies, such as Ford and AT&T, have sold multibillion-dollar bond issues to investors. Because the use of an underwriting group in a public offering involves considerable expense, it is usually uneconomical for a company to make a public offering of this nature for debt issues less than about $25 million. *Private placements*, however, frequently involve lesser amounts of money—for example, $5–10 million—because the entire debt issue is purchased by a single investor, such as an insurance company.

Coupon Rates

The coupon rates on new bonds are normally fixed and set equal to market interest rates on bonds of comparable quality and maturity so that the bonds sell at or near par value. However, during the inflationary period of the early 1980s, when interest rates reached record high levels and bond prices were quite volatile, highly rated companies began issuing bonds with *floating* coupon rates.

In 1998, Chase Manhattan (now JPMorgan Chase) issued $250 million in floating-rate notes that mature in 2028. The interest rate on this debt issue is equal to the London Interbank Offered Rate (LIBOR) plus 0.625 percent. Such floating rate debt protects investors against a rise in interest rates because the market price of the debt does not fluctuate as much as for fixed interest rate debt.

Original issue deep discount (OID) bonds have coupon rates below prevailing market interest rates at the time of issue and hence sell at a discount from par value. Some OID bond issues pay no interest and are known as *zero coupon* bonds. The Time Warner zero coupon discounted debenture issue of November 30, 1995, maturing on January 15, 2036, is one such example. One of the advantages to the issuing firm of these types of bonds is the reduction in (or elimination of) interest payments (a cash outflow) during the life of the bonds. Another advantage is the slightly lower cost (yield-to-maturity) of these issues compared with bonds that are issued at or near par value. The primary disadvantage of these types of bonds is the large cash outflow required by the firm at maturity. OID bonds have decreased in popularity due to changes in the tax laws, which eliminated the tax advantages to companies of these issues over debt issued at par, and the issuance by several brokerage firms of lower-risk substitutes. One such substitute is Merrill Lynch's TIGRs—Treasury Investment Growth Receipts—which are backed by U.S. Treasury bonds. The U.S. Treasury has also issued its own zero coupon bonds. These securities, which pay no interest, are purchased at a discount from face value and can then be redeemed for the full face value at maturity.

Maturity

The typical maturity on long-term debt ranges from 20 to 30 years. Occasionally, companies borrow money for 40 years or longer. This is particularly true during periods when inflation and interest rates are relatively low, such as the late 1990s and early 2000s and, more recently, following the financial crisis. Although relatively rare, a few companies have issued "century" bonds, which mature in *100 years*. In 1993, Walt Disney and Coca-Cola issued the first century bonds since 1954. Norfolk Southern, a large transportation company, has issued century bonds on several occasions since

1997. On the other end of the scale, companies in need of financing often are willing to borrow for as few as 10 years, especially if they feel that interest rates are temporarily high, as was true in the environment of the early 1980s—an environment characterized by high rates of inflation and historically high interest rates.

Like the floating rate bonds described earlier, which protect investors against interest rate risk, firms have also been issuing bonds that are redeemable at par *at the option of the holder*. These are known as *extendable notes* or *put bonds*. If interest rates rise and the market price of the bond falls, the holder can redeem them at par and reinvest the proceeds in higher-yielding securities. An example of a put bond is Ingersoll-Rand's 6.443 percent debenture issue of 1997 that matures in 2027. The debentures are redeemable for the full principal amount plus interest at the option of the holder on November 15, 2007, and each November 15 thereafter.

When performing bond valuation and yield-to-maturity calculations (described later in the chapter), bond investors should keep in mind that the realized maturity of a debt issue may differ from its stated maturity. This can occur for a variety of reasons. The bond indenture may include early repayment provisions through the exercise of a call option, required sinking fund payments, open market purchases, or tender offers. Also, maturity extensions or contractions may occur as the result of reorganization, merger, leveraged buyout (LBO), default, or liquidation.

6-2c Information on Debt Financing Activities

HTTP:
The Internet has made current information on bond prices widely available. For example, Morningstar provides timely price quotes for U.S. Treasury securities, municipal bonds, corporate bonds, and zero coupon bonds.

www.morningstar.com

See also

bondsonline.com

Every business day, financial newspapers contain information on debt financing activities. For example, *The Wall Street Journal* and *Barron's* contain articles on financing activities in the bond market. They also report announcements by underwriters concerning the characteristics of the new issues presently being offered.

The Wall Street Journal and *Barron's* also contain information on the secondary debt markets, including price quotations for the widely traded corporate debt issues listed on the New York Stock Exchange and U.S. government debt securities. In this section, we illustrate the information that can be obtained from corporate and government bond quotations.

Corporate Bonds The majority of existing debt issues (bonds) of U.S. corporations are traded in the over-the-counter (OTC) market. The OTC market is a network of security dealers who buy and sell bonds and stock from each other, either for their own account or for their retail clients.

Barron's publishes trading information on the 40 most actively traded bonds. Figure 6.1 shows this trading information for the week ending Friday, November 20, 2015. The first bond listed in that table was issued by Lockheed Martin, Inc. Note that, unlike common stocks, a firm may have several bonds outstanding. Figure 6.1 shows four other bonds issued by Lockheed Martin.

coupon rate

The first Lockheed Martin bond has a **coupon rate** of 3.55 percent and matures on January 15, 2026. The coupon rate is the interest rate paid on the bond. The interest is typically paid semiannually, but the rate is quoted as an annual rate. The dollar amount of interest to be received by the bondholder is equal to the coupon rate times the **principal** (or face) amount of the bond. Unless otherwise stated, the face amount of corporate bonds is $1,000. The 3.55 percent coupon rate on the Lockheed Martin bond means that an investor will receive $35.50 in interest every year (0.0355 × $1,000). The **maturity** date shows the length of life of the debt obligation. In this case, the bond matures on January 15, 2026. On the maturity date, Lockheed Martin will have to payback the principal or face amount in addition to the final interest payment due.

principal

maturity

FIGURE **6.1**

Corporate Bond Quotations

For the week ending Friday, November 20, 2015
Forty most active fixed-coupon corporate bonds

Company (Ticker)	Coupon	Maturity	Last Price	Last Yield	**EST Spread	UST†	EST $ Vol (000's)
Lockheed Martin (LMT)	3.550	Jan 15, 2026	100.262	3.519	128	10	659,190
Lockheed Martin (LMT)	4.700	May 15, 2046	101.292	4.620	159	30	524,160
Microsoft (MSFT)	3.125	Nov 03, 2025	99.931	3.133	87	10	400,239
Novartis Capital Corp (NOVX)	3.000	Nov 20, 2025	99.189	3.095	83	10	318,408
Societe Generate Sa (SOCGEN)	4.750	Nov 24, 2025	99.075	4.868	263	10	284,517
Societe Generate Sa (SOCGEN)	5.625	Nov 24, 2045	99.598	5.653	263	30	281,723
Lockheed Martin (LMT)	2.500	Nov 23, 2020	99.879	2.526	84	5	279,763
Microsoft (MSFT)	4.450	Nov 03, 2045	101.732	4.345	132	30	268,918
Citigroup (C)	6.125	Nov 15, 2049	102.000	5.657	263	30	264,729
Ge Capital International Funding Co (GE)	2.342	Nov 15, 2020	99.695	2.407	75	5	260,422
JPMorgan Chase (JPM)	7.900	Apr 30, 2049	103.250	6.431	341	30	246,777
Lockheed Martin (LMT)	4.500	May 15, 2036	100.526	4.460	143	30	226,083
Santander Issuances Sau (SANTAN)	5.179	Nov 19, 2025	100.557	5.107	287	10	224,983
Intercontinental Exchange (ICE)	3.750	Dec 01, 2025	100.637	3.673	141	10	224,138
Westpac Banking (WSTP)	2.600	Nov 23, 2020	100.126	2.573	89	5	211,736
Citigroup (C)	2.650	Oct 26, 2020	99.555	2.747	106	5	211,454
Kincer Morgan Energy Partners Lp (KMI)	5.950	Feb 15, 2018	102.864	4.576	335	3	208,459
Ace Ina Holdings (ACE)	4.350	Nov 03, 2045	99.900	4.356	133	30	207,996
Cvs Health (CVS)	3.875	Jul 20, 2025	102.241	3.592	133	10	202,015
Intercontinental Exchange (ICE)	2.750	Dec 01, 2020	100.249	2.697	101	5	200,072
Novartis Capital Corp (NOVX)	4.000	Nov 20, 2045	98.300	4.099	107	30	199,712
Lockheed Martin* (LMT)	1.850	Nov 23, 2018	100.073	1.825	62	3	197,326
AT&T (T)	3.400	May 15, 2025	96.664	3.823	157	10	196,053
Time Warner (TWX)	3.875	Jan 15, 2026	100.434	3.821	158	10	189,425
Halliburton Co (HAL)	5.000	Nov 15, 2045	100.382	4.975	195	30	189,299
Actavis Funding Scs (AGN)	3.800	Mar 15, 2025	99.546	3.858	162	10	188,607
Westpac Banking (WSTP)	1.950	Nov 23, 2018	100.061	1.929	70	3	184,302
JPMorgan Chase (JPM)	2.550	Oct 29, 2020	99.960	2.558	87	5	182,771
Hewlett Packard Enterprise Co (HPE)	4.900	Oct 15, 2025	98.333	5.116	287	10	179,371
Astrazeneca (AZN)	4.375	Nov 16, 2045	100.041	4.372	136	30	174,613
Kinder Morgan (KMI)	4.300	Jun 01, 2025	85.113	6.414	416	10	174,185
Auslralia and New Zealand Banking Group Ltd. (New York Branch) (ANZ)	2.700	Nov 16, 2020	100.645	2.561	88	5	171,468
Ally Financial (ALLY)	5.750	Nov 20, 2025	100.180	5.726	346	10	169,800
Microsoft (MSFT)	2.000	Nov 03, 2020	99.812	2.040	36	5	167,181
General Motors Financial Inc. (GM)	3.700	Nov 24, 2020	99.882	3.726	204	5	166,385
JPMorgan Chase (JPM)	3.900	Jul 15, 2025	103.089	3.511	125	10	165,469
Verizon Communications* (VZ)	6.550	Sep 15, 2043	120.362	5.162	215	30	165,253
Bank of America (BAC)	3.875	Aug 01, 2025	101.973	3.631	137	10	164,078
Microsoft (MSFT)	1.300	Nov 03, 2018	99.848	1.353	14	3	162,608
Qualcomm (QCOM)	3.450	May 20, 2025	94.170	4.201	195	10	161,247

Volume represents total volume for each issue; price/yield data are for trades of $1 million and greater. *Denotes a security whose last round lot trade did not take place on the last business day prior to publication. **Estimated spreads, in basis points (100 basis points is one percentage point), over the 2, 5, 10 or 30-year hot run Treasury note/bond. 2-year: 0.750 10/17; 5-year: 1.375 10/20; 10-year: 2.250 11/25; 30-year: 2.875 08/45. †Comparable U.S. Treasury issue.

Source: MarketAxess Corporate BondTicker-www.bondticker.com; Barron's (November 23, 2015): M48.

Following the maturity date is the last price at which the bond traded on the trading date in question. The last price is reported as a percent of the face value, following the convention used by brokers to quote bond prices. The closing price on the Lockheed Martin bond is 100.262. If you had actually bought a bond at this price, you would have paid $1002.62 (100.262 × $10). The next column (Last yield) shows the **yield-to-maturity** (YTM) of the bond. The YTM tells investors what rate of return (annual) they can expect to receive if the bond is purchased at the last price indicated and is held to maturity. The calculation of the YTM is illustrated later in the chapter. In this case, investors buying the Lockheed Martin bond at the quoted last price of 100.262 can expect to earn a rate of return of 3.519 percent if the bond is held to maturity.

yield-to-maturity

The next column shows the *estimated spread* between the YTM of the bond in question and a U.S. Treasury bond with a similar time remaining to maturity. In other words, the spread is calculated as the YTM of the corporate bond minus the YTM of the Treasury bond. This difference, or spread, is also known as the default risk spread. The default risk spread tells investors how much additional yield can be expected because of the assumption of default risk. Default risk is the risk that the issuer will be unable to pay its debt obligations (principal and interest) on this bond. All corporate bonds are subject to some default risk, while Treasury bonds, because they are issued by the U.S. government, are assumed to have no risk of default. Thus, default risk spreads increase as the risk of default of an issue increases. Default risk spreads may change over time, with spreads increasing when the economy is more uncertain. For the Lockheed Martin bond we are examining, the spread is 128 basis points, or 1.28 percentage points (100 basis points equal 1 percentage point). The next column shows the length of maturity of the U.S. Treasury bond used to compute the default risk spread. In this case, the 10-year Treasury bond was used. The final column shows the *estimated volume of trading* (in thousands of dollars of face amount of debt). A total of $659.19 million face amount of Lockheed Martin bonds were traded during the week ending on November 20, 2015. In general, the trading volume for bonds is considerably less than the volume of trading in the common shares of the same company.

Government Debt Securities The U.S. government raises funds by selling debt securities. These securities take the form of short-term Treasury bills, intermediate-term Treasury notes, and long-term Treasury bonds. U.S. Treasury bills have an initial maturity of 13, 26, or 52 weeks and pay $10,000 per bill to the holder at maturity. Treasury bills pay no explicit interest; rather, they are sold at a discount from maturity value. An investor who buys a bill at a discount and holds it to maturity will receive as interest the difference between the price paid and $10,000. The quote for a typical Treasury bill on November 20, 2015, follows:

Maturity	Bid	Asked	Wkly. Chg.	Ask Yld.
May 19, '16	0.30	0.29	-	0.26

The bill shown here matures on May 19, 2016, or in 181 days. The bid and asked prices indicate the *annualized* percentage discount from maturity value.[11] An *asked discount* of 0.29 percent translates into a cash discount from $10,000 of approximately $14.38 [(0.29 ÷ 100) ÷ (365 ÷ 181) × $10,000], or an asked price of $10,000 − $14.38 = $9,985.62. The *ask yld.* is the annualized yield an investor will receive by purchasing this bill and holding it to maturity.

Longer term government debt is issued in the form of Treasury notes and bonds. Treasury notes typically have an initial maturity ranging from 1 to 10 years. Treasury bonds typically have initial maturities ranging from 10 to 30 years. Like corporate

[11] A *bid price* is the price at which buyers are willing to purchase, and the *asked price* is the price at which sellers wish to sell. For Treasury bills, the "bid" and "asked" quotes represent discounts from face value

bonds, Treasury notes and bonds pay a stated coupon rate of interest semiannually. They are issued in denominations of multiples of $1,000. Treasury note and bond prices vary in units of $\frac{1}{32}$ of 1 percent of par value. Thus, a price quote of 94:17 means that the bond will sell for $94\ \frac{17}{32}$ percent of par, or $945.31.

6-2d Bond Ratings

HTTP:
For more detail on bond rating methodologies see
www.moodys.com
www.standardandpoors.com

Debt issues are rated according to their relative degree of risk by various financial companies, including Moody's Investors Services and Standard & Poor's (S&P) Corporation. These agencies consider a variety of factors when rating a firm's securities, including earnings stability, coverage ratios, the relative amount of debt in the firm's capital structure, and the degree of subordination, as well as past experience. According to Moody's rating scale, the highest-quality, lowest-risk issues are rated Aaa, and the scale continues down through Aa, A, Baa, Ba, B, Caa, Ca, and C. On the Standard & Poor's ratings scale, AAA denotes the highest-quality issues, and this rating is followed by AA, A, BBB, BB, B, and so on. S&P also has various C and D classifications for high-risk issues; the majority of debt issues, however, fall into one of the A or B categories. Figure 6.2 summarizes Moody's and S&P's **bond-rating** definitions. Debt issues rated Baa or higher by Moody's (or BBB or higher by Standard and Poor's are classified as *investment grade* debt.

bond-rating

Table 6.1 shows the relationship between S&P's bond ratings and bond yields. For comparison, U.S. Treasury bond yields are also shown. Note that for any maturity, the lower a bond's credit rating, the higher the yield—reflecting an increasing risk of default. Also note that the maturity risk premium is larger for industrial bonds (for example, as measured by the difference between the yield on a 5-year bond and a 20-year bond) than it is for Treasury bonds. As a risky bond's maturity increases, the chance for default also increases because there is more time for something to go wrong at a firm.

Companies with weak financial positions (for example, highly leveraged balance sheets or low earnings) often issue high-yield debt securities to obtain capital needed for internal expansion or for corporate acquisitions and buyouts. Such debt, also known as **junk bonds**, or *speculative grade* debt, is rated Ba or lower by Moody's (or BB or lower by Standard & Poor's) and typically yields 2–3 percentage points or more over the highest-quality corporate debt. Junk bonds constitute an important segment of all corporate debt outstanding. High yield (junk) bonds totaled $312 billion, or approximately 22 percent of the total value of all new U.S. corporate bond issues in 2014.[12]

junk bonds

6-2e Users of Long-Term Debt

Most large- and medium-size companies finance some portion of their fixed assets with long-term debt. This debt may be in the form of either secured bonds or unsecured debentures. Utilities rely on debt capital to a large degree and, as a group, are the largest users of secured bonds; the *first mortgage bonds* of a utility are typically a safe, low-risk investment. Manufacturing companies, in contrast, rely on debt capital to varying degrees and generally use unsecured debt more often than secured debt.

Many large companies have virtually continuous capital expenditure programs. Usually, a company will plan to finance any new assets at least partially with long-term debt. Because it is generally uneconomical to borrow small amounts of long-term capital, however, companies that have ongoing construction programs often gradually "draw down" on their short-term revolving credit agreements. Then, once every couple of years or so, a firm of this type will enter the capital markets and sell long-term debt. At that time, a portion of the proceeds is used to repay the short-term borrowings, and the cycle begins

[12]"U.S. Corporate Bond Issuance: Investment Grade and High Yield" (December 2, 2015), www.sifma.org/research/statistics.aspx.

FIGURE 6.2

Summary of Moody's and Standard & Poor's Long-Term Corporate Bond Rating Definitions[a]

Moody's Bond Ratings

Ratings represent the relative credit risk of a fixed income obligation (bond), indicating the possibility of default and the financial loss suffered in the event of default.

Investment Grade	
Aaa	Highest quality with minimal credit risk
Aa	High quality with very low credit risk
A	Upper-medium grade with low credit risk
Baa	Medium-grade with moderate credit risk
Speculative Grade	
Ba	Speculative elements with substantial credit risk
B	Speculative with high credit risk
Caa	Poor quality with very high credit risk
Ca	Highly speculative and either in or near default with some prospect of recovery of obligation
C	Lowest quality with little prospect of recovery of obligation

Note: A numerical modifier (1, 2, or 3) is added to each rating classification from Aa to Caa. The modifiers 1, 2, or 3 indicate that the obligation (bond) ranks in the upper end, middle range, or lower end, respectively, of the rating classification.

Standard & Poor's Bond Ratings

Credit ratings indicate the risk of default and are based on such considerations as likelihood of repayment of the obligation (bond), provisions (covenants) of the obligation, and the protection offered the holder of the obligation in the event of bankruptcy or reorganization.

Investment Grade	
AAA	Highest rating with extremely strong capacity to meet obligation
AA	Very strong capacity to meet obligation
A	Strong capacity to meet obligation
BBB	Adequate capacity to meet obligation
Speculative Grade	
BB	Less vulnerable to nonpayment but faces ongoing uncertainties that could affect the ability to meet obligation
B	More vulnerable to nonpayments but faces ongoing uncertainties that will likely affect the ability to meet obligation
CCC	Currently vulnerable to nonpayment and dependent on favorable conditions to meet obligation
CC	Highly vulnerable to nonpayment
C	Subordinated debt obligation, highly vulnerable to nonpayment, such as a bankruptcy situation where payments continue to be made
D	Payments are in default due to bankruptcy

Note: A plus (+) or minus (–) sign may be added to ratings between AA and CCC to show relative standing within the rating classification.

[a]For a more detailed discussion of bond ratings, see "Rating Symbols and Definitions" (August 2015) at www.moodys.com and "Standard & Poor's Ratings Definitions" (November 20, 2014) at www.standardandpoors.com.

Source: Based on www.standardandpoors.com; and www.moodys.com.

again. This procedure is called *funding* short-term debt; as a result, long-term debt is sometimes referred to as *funded debt*.

Most established companies attempt to maintain reasonably constant proportions of long-term debt and common equity in their capital structures. During the course of a company's normal profitable operations, though, long-term debt is gradually retired as it matures, and the retained earnings portion of common equity is increased. This in turn decreases the debt-to-equity ratio. Thus, to maintain their desired capital structures, companies have to raise long-term debt capital periodically. This gradual refunding of debt, along with the tax deductibility of interest, accounts for the fact that about 85 to 90 percent of the external long-term capital raised in the United States is in the form of debt.

TABLE 6.1

Treasury and U.S. Industrials Bond Yields*

Maturity	Treasurys	AAA	AA	A	BBB	BB+
		—U.S. Industrials—				
5	1.67	2.22	2.45	2.74	3.64	5.11
10	2.24	3.15	3.37	3.63	4.67	6.22
15	2.43	3.54	3.77	4.01	5.14	6.72
20	2.62	3.87	4.10	4.33	5.52	7.13
25	2.81	4.18	4.40	4.62	5.86	7.49

Data as of Nov. 24, 2015.
Source: Standard & Poor's Global Fixed Income Research.

6-2f Advantages and Disadvantages of Long-Term Debt Financing

From the issuing firm's perspective, the major advantages of long-term debt include the following:

- Its relatively low after-tax cost due to the tax deductibility of interest
- The increased earnings per share possible through financial leverage
- The ability of the firm's owners to maintain greater control over the firm

foreign bonds

INTERNATIONAL ISSUES

The International Bond Market[a]

In addition to raising capital in the U.S. financial markets, many U.S. firms go to other countries to raise capital. International bonds are sold initially to investors outside the home country of the borrower. There are two major types of long-term instruments in the international bond market—Eurobonds and foreign bonds.

Eurobonds are bonds issued by a U.S. corporation, for example, denominated in U.S. dollars but sold to investors outside the United States, such as in Europe and Japan. The bond offering is often underwritten by an international syndicate of investment bankers. For example, IBM could sell dollar-denominated bonds to investors in Europe or Japan. The Eurobond market has been used because there is less regulatory interference than in the issuing country and, in some cases, less stringent disclosure requirements. Eurobonds are also bearer bonds (the name and country of the bond owner is not on the bond), providing the bondholder with tax anonymity and an opportunity, perhaps, to avoid the payment of taxes. For these reasons, the cost of Eurobond financing may be below that of domestic financing.

Foreign bonds, in contrast, are underwritten by an investment banking syndicate from a single country. Foreign bonds are normally denominated in the currency of the country of sale. The bond issuer, however, is from a country other than the country in which the bonds are being issued. For example, Crown Holdings (formerly Crown Cork & Seal Company, Inc.), with 149 plants in 40 countries, might enter the foreign bond market to raise capital for a new plant to be built in France. These bonds could be sold in France and be denominated in euros, or they could be sold in another country and denominated in that country's currency.

The international bond market has grown rapidly, and it continues to provide firms with additional alternative sources of funds that are, in some cases, lower in cost than purely domestic financing.

[a]For more detail, see James C. Van Horne, *Financial Market Rates and Flows*, 6th ed. (Upper Saddle River, NJ: Prentice Hall, 2001): Chapter 14.

The following are the major disadvantages of long-term debt financing, from the firm's perspective:

- The increased financial risk of the firm resulting from the use of debt
- The restrictions placed on the firm by the lenders

From the investors' viewpoint, in general, debt securities offer stable returns and therefore are considered relatively low-risk investments compared with common stock investments. Because debtholders are creditors, however, they do not participate in any increased earnings the firm may experience. In fact, during periods of relatively high inflation, holders of existing debt find that their *real* interest payments decrease because the nominal interest payments remain constant.

6-3 Valuation of Assets

Foundation Concept

The value of any asset is based on the *expected future benefits*, or *cash flows*, the owner will receive over the life of the asset. For example, the value of a *physical asset*, such as a new piece of equipment or production plant, is based on the expected cash flows the asset will generate for the firm over its useful life. These cash flows are derived from increased revenues and/or reduced costs plus any salvage value received from the sale of the asset.[13]

Similarly, the value of a *financial asset*, such as a stock or bond, is based on the expected cash flows the asset will generate for the owner during the *holding period*. These cash flows take the form of interest or dividend payments over the holding period plus the amount the owner receives when the security is sold.

It is assumed throughout this and the following chapter that the firms under discussion are *going concerns*; that is, that their organization and assets will remain intact and be used to generate future cash flows. Techniques other than the ones described here must be used to value long-term securities of firms faced with the possibility of bankruptcy. In such cases, the **liquidation value** of the firm's assets is the primary determinant of the value of the various types of long-term securities.[14]

liquidation value

6-3a Capitalization of Cash Flow Method

One way of determining the value of an asset is to calculate the present value of the stream of expected future cash flows discounted at an appropriate *required rate of return*. This is known as the **capitalization of cash flow** method of valuation and is represented algebraically as follows:

capitalization of cash flow

(6.1)
$$V_0 = \sum_{t=1}^{n} \frac{CF_t}{(1+i)^t}$$

where V_0 is the value of the asset at time zero, CF_t the expected cash flow in period t, i the required rate of return or discount rate, and n the length of the holding period.

For example, assume that the cash flows, CF_t, of an investment are expected to be an annuity of $1,000 per year for $n = 6$ years, and the required rate of return, i, is 8 percent. Using the capitalization of cash flow method, the value of this investment is:

$$V_0 = \sum_{t=1}^{6} \frac{\$1{,}000}{(1+0.08)^t}$$

Recognizing this expression as the present value of an annuity ($PVAN_0$), the value of the investment is computed using Equation 5.19 of Chapter 5:

[13] Chapters 9 through 11 contain a detailed discussion of capital budgeting.

[14] This topic is discussed in Chapter 23.

$$V_0 = \$1{,}000\,(\text{PVIFA}_{0.08,6}) = \$1{,}000(4.623) = \$4{,}623 \quad (6.2)$$

Calculator Solutions[a]

Key	Enter
n	6
i	8.00
PV	
PMT	−1,000
FV	
	Solution
PV	4622.88

The *required rate of return, i*, on an asset is a function of the uncertainty, or risk, associated with the returns from the asset as well as the risk-free interest rate.[15] As indicated in Chapter 1, this function is upward sloping, indicating that the higher the risk, the greater the investor's required rate of return.

6-3b Market Value of Assets and Market Equilibrium

From Equation 6.1, it can be seen that the value of an asset depends on both the expected cash flows, CF_t, and the owner's (or prospective buyer's) required rate of return, *i*. However, potential buyers and sellers can have different opinions of an asset's value based on their individual assessments of the potential cash flows from the asset and individual required rates of return.

The *market price*, or *market value*, of an asset (such as shares of common stock) is determined in much the same way as the price of most goods and services in a market-oriented economy, namely, by the interaction of supply and demand. This interaction is shown in Figure 6.3. Potential buyers are represented by a *demand* schedule showing the maximum prices they are willing to pay for given quantities of an asset, and potential

FIGURE **6.3**

Market Price of an Asset

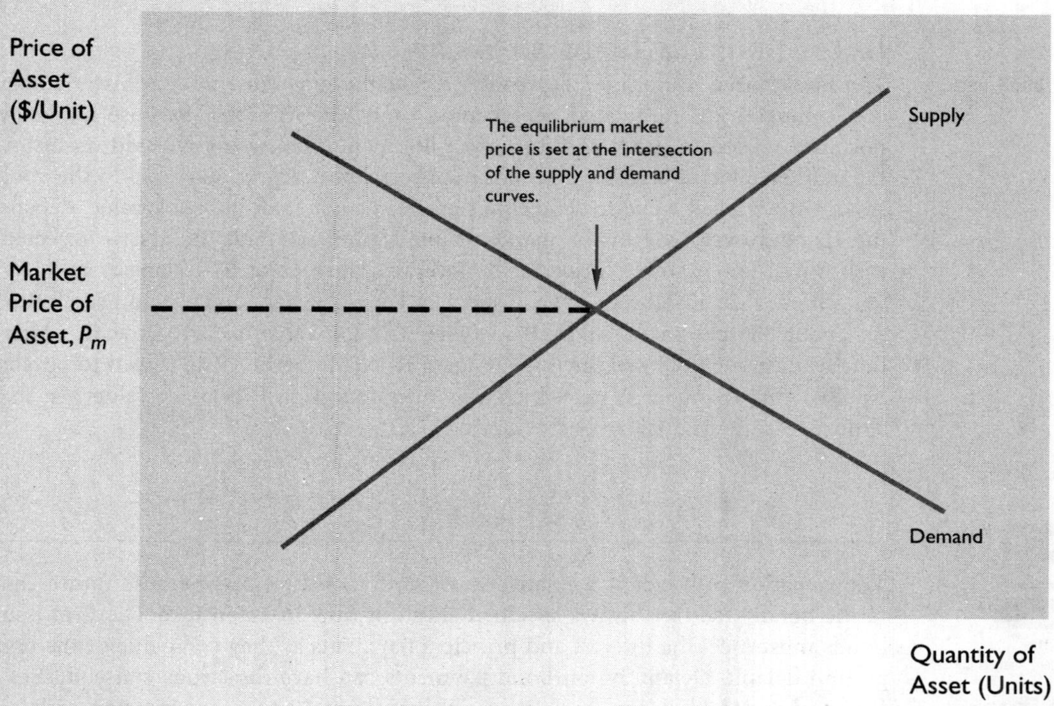

[15]A more detailed discussion of risk-return relationships is contained in Chapter 8.

[a]This solution is identical (rounded to the nearest dollar, $4,623, to that calculated earlier.

HTTP:
Finding the value of things is a huge industry. Using the Yahoo! search engine, type in "financial valuation" and look at some of the valuation companies (and their Web sites) that estimate market prices of real estate, corporations, partnerships, sole proprietorships, art, antiques, and other assets.

www.yahoo.com

sellers are represented by a *supply* schedule showing the minimum prices at which they are willing to sell given quantities of the asset. The transaction price, the price at which an asset is sold, occurs at the intersection of the demand and supply schedules. The intersection represents the *market value*, or *market price*, of the asset, P_m, in Figure 6.3.

The market price of an asset is the value placed on the asset by the *marginally satisfied buyer and seller* who exchange assets in the marketplace. A marginally satisfied buyer is one who paid his or her maximum acceptable price for the asset, and a marginally satisfied seller is one who received his or her minimum acceptable price for the asset. Clearly, many owners (potential sellers) will place a higher value on the asset than the current market price; likewise, many investors (potential buyers) will place a lower value on the asset than the current market price.

Market equilibrium exists whenever there is no tendency for the price of the asset to move higher or lower. At this point, the *expected* rate of return on the asset is equal to the marginal investor's *required* rate of return. *Market disequilibrium* occurs when investors' required rates of return, i, and/or the expected cash flows, CF_t, from the asset change. The market price adjusts over time—that is, it moves upward or downward—to reflect changing conditions, and a new market equilibrium is established.

Most financial assets are bought and sold in organized markets. The bonds, preferred stock, and common stock of many small, as well as most medium and large, firms are traded in one or more national or regional exchanges or in the OTC market. Because large numbers of competing buyers and sellers operate in the markets, the market price of a security represents a *consensus* judgment as to the security's value or worth. Although no such market-determined measure of value exists for securities of firms that are not publicly traded, their market values can be approximated using the market price of publicly traded securities of firms having similar operating and financial characteristics.

6-3c Book Value of an Asset

book value

The **book value** of an asset represents the *accounting* value, or the historic acquisition cost minus any accumulated depreciation or other write-offs. Because market value is normally related to expected future cash flows and book value is based on historic cost, the market value of an asset does not necessarily bear any relationship to the book value. In fact, the market value may be either greater or less than the book value, depending on the changes over time in the market capitalization rate and the asset's expected future cash flows. For example, prior to the leveraged buyout of RJR Nabisco in 1988 by the investment firm Kohlberg Kravis Roberts & Co., RJR Nabisco common stock was selling for about \$56 per share—more than twice its book value of \$24 per share. After a bidding war among potential buyers, Kohlberg Kravis Roberts & Co. agreed to purchase RJR Nabisco for \$109 per share, which was over four times its book value per share and almost twice its pre-takeover stock price.

6-4 Bond Valuation

HTTP:
Select the Investment Analysis Calculator button at

www.investopedia.com/calculator/bondprice.aspx

for an interactive financial calculator for bond valuation.

The valuation of bonds is a relatively straightforward process because future cash flows to the bondholder are always specified ahead of time in a contract. The firm issuing the bonds must meet the interest and principal payments as they come due or the bonds will go into default. Defaulting on bond payments can have disastrous consequences for the firm and its stockholders, such as possible bankruptcy and reorganization or liquidation.

Due to default risk, investors normally require a higher rate of return than the risk-free rate before agreeing to hold a firm's bonds. The required rate of return varies among bond issues of different firms, depending on their relative risks of default. All other things being equal, the greater the default risk on a given bond issue, the higher the required rate of return.

6-4a Bonds Having Finite Maturity Dates

Bonds that mature within finite periods of time pay the investor two types of returns: interest payments ($I_1, I_2, \ldots, I_n$) during each of the next n periods, and a principal payment (M) in period n. Period n is defined as the bond's *maturity date*, or the time at which the principal must be repaid and the bond issue retired.

The value of a bond can be computed by applying the capitalization of cash flow method to the series of cash flows:

(6.3) $$P_0 = \frac{I_1}{(1+k_d)^1} + \frac{I_2}{(1+k_d)^2} + \cdots + \frac{I_{n-1}}{(1+k_d)^{n-1}} + \frac{I_n + M}{(1+k_d)^n}$$

where P_0 is the present value of the bond at time zero, or its purchase date, and k_d is the investor's required rate of return on this particular bond issue.

Because all of the interest payments on a bond are normally equal (that is $I_1 = I_2 = \ldots = I_{n-1} = I_n = I$), Equation 6.3 can be simplified as follows:

(6.4) $$P_0 = \sum_{t=1}^{n} \frac{I}{(1+k_d)^t} + \frac{M}{(1+k_d)^n}$$

The first term in Equation 6.4 represents the present value of an *annuity* of I per period for n periods; the second term represents the present value of a *single payment* of M in period n. Equation 6.4 can be further simplified as follows:

(6.5) $$P_0 = I(\text{PVIFA}_{k_d,n}) + M(\text{PVIF}_{k_d,n})$$

To illustrate the use of Equation 6.5, consider the following example. Suppose Bell Communications Corporation (BCC) issued \$3 billion of 6 percent bonds maturing on March 15, 2023. The bonds were issued in \$1,000 denominations (par value). For purposes of simplifying this example, assume that the bonds pay interest on March 15 each year.[16]

An investor who was considering the purchase of one of these BCC bonds on March 15, 2016, and requires an 8 percent rate of return on this particular bond issue would compute the value of the bond as follows. These calculations assume that the investor will hold the bond until maturity and receive seven annual ($n = 7$) interest payments of \$60 each ($I = \$1{,}000 \times 0.06$) plus a principal payment, M, of \$1,000 at the end of the seventh year, March 15, 2023. The expected cash flows from this bond are shown in Figure 6.4. Inserting these

FIGURE 6.4

Cash Flows from a BCC Bond

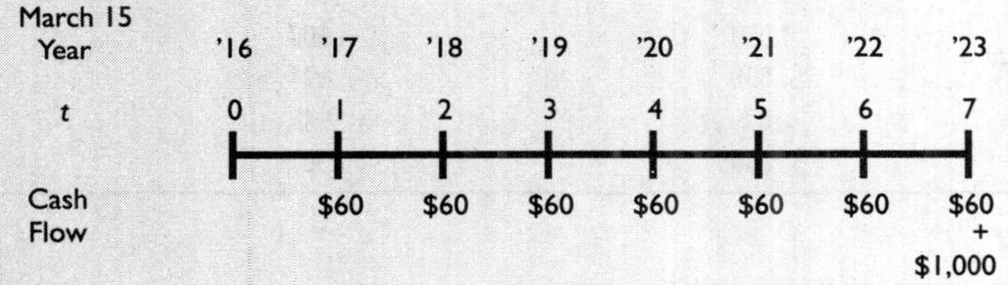

[16]In actuality, this bond issue pays interest *semiannually* on March 15 and September 15 each year.

Calculator Solutions[b]

Key	Enter
n	7
i	8.0
PV	
PMT	60
FV	1,000
	Solution
PV	−895.87

values along with $k_d = 8$ percent (0.08) into Equation 6.5 gives the following value for the bond:

$$P_0 = \$60(\text{PVIFA}_{0.08,7}) + \$1{,}000(\text{PVIF}_{0.08,7})$$
$$= \$60(5.206) + \$1{,}000(0.583)$$
$$= \$895.36 (\text{or } \$895)$$

In other words, an investor requiring an 8 percent return on this BCC bond would be willing to pay approximately $896 (calculator solution) for it on March 15, 2016.

The question often arises as to why investors would require an 8 percent rate of return on bonds that pay only 6 percent interest. The answer is that the required rate of return has increased since the bonds were originally issued. At the time of issue, the prevailing rate of interest (that is, the required rate of return) on bonds of this maturity and quality was approximately 6 percent. Hence, the coupon rate was set at 6 percent. Because of such factors as tight credit market conditions, higher inflation, increased firm risk, and so on, investors now require a higher rate of return to induce them to purchase these bonds.

An investor who desires more than an 8 percent rate of return on the BCC bond would value it at a price less than $896. Similarly, an investor who requires less than an 8 percent rate of return would value it at a price greater than $896. This *inverse relationship* between the required rate of return and the corresponding value of a bond to the investor is illustrated for bonds with 3-year and 15-year maturities in Table 6.2 and Figure 6.5. In other words, as the required rate of return increases, the value of the bond decreases, and vice versa.

The relationship between a bond's value and the investor's required rate of return depends on the time remaining before maturity. All other things being equal, the value of a longer term bond is affected more by changes in required rates of return than the value of a shorter term bond. As Table 6.2 and Figure 6.5 show, the variation in the value of the 15-year bond is considerably greater than the variation of the 3-year bond over the given range of required rates of return (2 to 10 percent).

Also, as can be seen in Table 6.2, when the required rate of return (prevailing market interest rate) is less than the coupon rate, the bond is valued at a *premium* over its par

TABLE 6.2

Value of 6 Percent Coupon Rate Bonds at Various Required Rates of Return

Required Rate of Return, k_d	Value of 15-Year Bond	Value of 3-Year Bond	Bond Value Relative to Par Value
2%	$1,514	$1,115	Premium
4	1,222	1,056	Premium
5	1,103	1,027	Premium
6	1,000	1,000	At Par
7	909	974	Discount
8	829	948	Discount
10	696	901	Discount

[b]The financial calculator solution and the solution obtained using Equation 6.5 and the interest tables differ slightly due to the use of interest tables with three decimal places of accuracy. Using more accurate interest tables gives an answer closer to $895.87, the true answer to this problem.

FIGURE 6.5

Relationships between the Value of a Bond and the Required Rate of Return

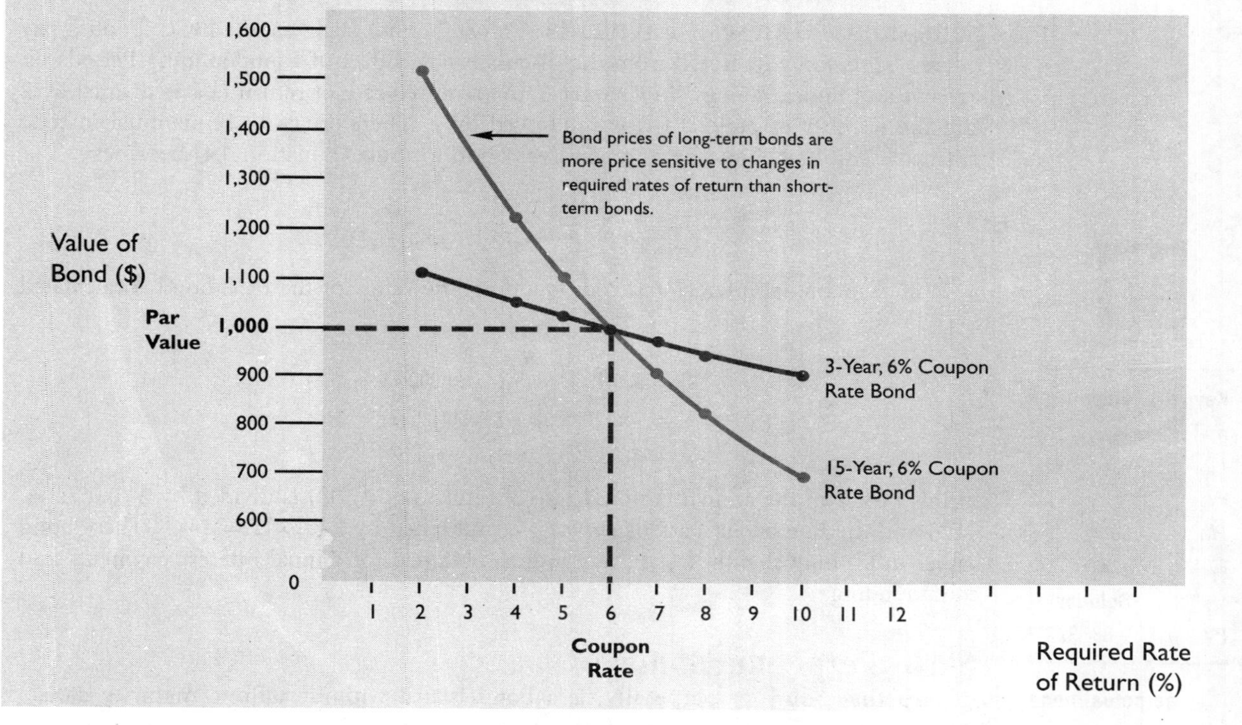

value of $1,000. Conversely, when the required rate of return is greater than the coupon rate, the bond is valued at a *discount* under its par value.

Investors who purchase a bond at the price determined by Equation 6.5 and *hold it until maturity* will realize their required rate of return, regardless of any changes in the market price of the bond.[17] However, if the market price of the bond declines due to a rise in prevailing interest rates and if the bond is sold *prior to maturity*, the investors will earn less than their required rate of return and may even incur a loss on the bond. This variation in the market price (and hence in the realized rate of return) of a bond (or any fixed income security) is known as **interest rate risk**.

interest rate risk

reinvestment rate risk

In addition to interest rate risk, bond investors are subject to reinvestment rate risk. **Reinvestment rate risk** occurs when a bond issue matures (or is called) and, because of a decline in interest rates, investors have to reinvest the principal at a lower coupon rate. For example, the owner of the Ford 30-year, 8⅞ percent debentures, purchased at the time of issue in 1992, is receiving $88.75 annual interest per bond. However, as noted earlier, this bond issue was callable beginning in 2002. If Ford decides to call the bonds, as it did in 2003, because of a decline in interest rates since the time of issue, the bondholder would probably be unable to reinvest the principal in another bond of comparable risk that yielded an 8⅞ percent (or higher) rate of return. Reinvestment rate risk also refers to the rate at which interest cash flows can be reinvested over

[17]This assumes that investors reinvest all interest received from the bond at a rate equal to the required rate of return on the bond. Otherwise, the realized return will differ slightly from the required return.

the life of the bond. When the reinvestment rate of interest cash flows is different from the yield-to-maturity on the bond, the return actually realized by a bond investor will be greater than (less than) the yield-to-maturity if the reinvestment rate is greater than (less than) the promised yield-to-maturity.

Semiannual Interest Payments Most bonds, such as the BCC bonds, pay interest *semiannually*. Recall from the discussion of "Effect of Compounding Periods on Present and Future Values" in Chapter 5, the required rate of return (k_d) is divided by 2 and the number of periods (n) is multiplied by 2. Therefore, with semiannual interest payments and compounding, the bond valuation formula (Equation 6.4) becomes:

(6.6)
$$P_0 = \sum_{t=1}^{2n} \frac{I/2}{(1 + k_d/2)^t} + \frac{M}{(1 + k_d/2)^{2n}}$$

With semiannual interest and compounding, the value for the BCC bond is calculated as follows:

Calculator Solutions

Key	Enter
n	14
i	4.0
PV	
PMT	30
FV	1,000
	Solution
PV	−894.37

$$\begin{aligned} P_0 &= \$30(\text{PVIFA}_{0.04,14}) + \$1{,}000(\text{PVIF}_{0.04,14}) \\ &= \$30(10.563) + \$1{,}000(0.577) \\ &= \$893.89(\text{or } \$894) \end{aligned}$$

In this problem, the annual required rate of return ($k_d = .08$) is divided by 2 ($0.08/2 = 0.04$) and the number of periods ($n = 7$) is multiplied by 2 ($7 \times 2 = 14$).[18] These bond values differ only slightly from the solutions obtained for annual interest payments and compounding.

6-4b Perpetual Bonds

perpetual bond

A **perpetual bond**, or perpetuity, is a bond issued without a finite maturity date.[19] Perpetual bonds promise to pay interest indefinitely, and there is no contractual obligation to repay the principal, that is, $M = 0$.

The valuation of a perpetual bond is simpler than the valuation of a bond having a finite maturity date. Assuming that the bond pays a fixed amount of interest, I, per period forever, the value is as follows:

(6.7)
$$P_0 = \sum_{t=1}^{\infty} \frac{I}{(1 + k_d)^t}$$

where k_d is the required rate of return. Equation 6.7 can be simplified to obtain the following expression:

(6.8)
$$P_0 = \frac{I}{k_d}$$

Consider, for example, the Canadian Pacific Limited Railroad's perpetual 4 percent debentures. What is the value of a $1,000 bond to an investor who requires an 8 percent

---

[18] It should also be noted that the use of a semiannual discount rate of 4 percent will result in a slightly greater than 8 percent effective annual discount rate. Based on the discussion of "Effective Rate Calculations" in Chapter 5, a semiannual discount rate of (see Equation 5.28):

$$\begin{aligned} i_2 &= (1 + 0.08)^{1/2} - 1 \\ &= 0.03923 \end{aligned}$$

or 3.923 percent should be used in the bond valuation calculation if the required annual return is 8 percent. However, we will ignore this complication in the remainder of this chapter.

[19] Perpetual bonds, also referred to as *consols*, are rare. Some countries, such as the United Kingdom, and some railroads, such as the Canadian Pacific and the Canadian National, have issued perpetual bonds.

ETHICAL ISSUES

Leveraged Buyouts and Bond Values

During the 1980s and early 1990s, many firms were acquired or financially restructured in a transaction called a *leveraged buyout* (LBO). In a typical LBO, the buyer of the firm borrows a large amount of the purchase price, using the purchased assets as collateral for a large portion of the borrowings. Debt ratios (debt to total capital) of 90 percent or more have not been uncommon in early LBOs.

LBOs have led to enormous wealth increases for the common stockholders of the acquired firm. For example, RJR Nabisco (RJR) shareholders saw the value of their common stock increase from the mid-50s price range to over $100 when the firm was acquired by Kohlberg Kravis Roberts in an LBO. Bondholders generally have not fared quite so well. The impact of most LBOs has been a decline in the bond ratings of the acquired or restructured firm because of the substantial increase in perceived risk. Declines in the market value of bonds for firms acquired in LBO transactions have averaged about 7 percent. In the case of the RJR transaction, these bondholder losses initially exceeded 20 percent.

In the RJR case, several large bondholders, notably Metropolitan Life Insurance and Hartford Insurance, sued RJR, claiming among other things that RJR management had the duty to disclose that it was considering the possibility of an LBO at the time it issued bonds six months prior to the announcement of the LBO. Metropolitan Life sought compensation for its bond losses not just on the recent bond issue, but also on earlier bond issues of RJR that it held.

Do you think that RJR bondholders and the bondholders in many other firms that were restructured with LBOs have a right to compensation from the firm's owners to offset bondholder losses in these transactions? What role do you think bond covenants should play in an analysis of the rights of bondholders and the obligations of management? How can bondholders protect themselves from losses arising out of LBOs?

rate of return on these Canadian Pacific bonds? Because $I = 0.04 \times \$1{,}000$, or $40, and $k_d = 8$ percent, Equation 6.8 can be used to compute the answer as follows:

$$P_0 = \frac{\$40}{0.08} = \$500$$

Thus, the investor would be willing to pay up to $500 for this bond.

6-4c Yield-to-Maturity of a Bond

The yield-to-maturity of a bond is the discount rate that equates the present value of all expected interest payments and the repayment of principal from a bond with the present bond price.[20] (In contrast, the **current yield**, which is equal to the annual interest payment divided by the current price, ignores the repayment of the principal.) If the current price of a bond, P_0, the uniform annual interest payments, I, and the maturity value, or principal, M, are known, the yield-to-maturity of a bond having a finite maturity date can be calculated by solving Equation 6.4 presented earlier for k_d:

current yield

$$P_0 = \sum_{t=1}^{n} \frac{I}{(1 + k_d)^t} + \frac{M}{(1 + k_d)^n}$$

Given values for any three of the four variables in this equation, one can solve for the value of the fourth variable. In the bond valuation calculation illustrated earlier in this

[20]The yield-to-maturity calculation assumes that cash flows from the bond occurring prior to maturity are reinvested at a rate equal to the yield-to-maturity.

Calculator Solutions

Key	Enter
n	7
i	
PV	−987.50
PMT	60
FV	1,000
	Solution
i	6.23

section, this equation was used to determine the value of a bond (P_0) when the value of k_d is known (along with the values of I and M). In the yield-to-maturity calculation that follows, the equation is used to determine k_d when the value of P_0 is known (along with the values of I and M).

For bonds with a call feature, the expected *yield to call* can also be computed. This is done by replacing the maturity value (M) by the call price and the number of years until maturity (n) by the number of years until the company can call the bond. If present interest rates are significantly below the coupon rate on the (callable) bond, then it is likely that the bond will be called in the future. In such a case, the relevant expected rate of return on the bond is the yield to call rather than the yield-to-maturity.

There are a number of ways to compute the yield-to-maturity of a bond. Most financial calculators are programmed to compute the yield-to-maturity, given P_0, I, n, and M. Also, special bond tables can be used to identify the yield-to-maturity for any particular bond.

Consider again the BCC 6 percent bonds maturing on March 15, 2023, discussed earlier. Again, assume that interest is paid annually on March 15 each year. Suppose that the bonds are selling for $987.50 on March 15, 2016 (seven years prior to maturity). Determine the bond's exact yield-to-maturity. Given $n = 7$, $I = \$60$, $P_0 = \$987.50$, and $M = \$1{,}000$, we can compute k_d. Therefore, the yield-to-maturity is 6.23 percent. (See Calculator Solution.)

The yield-to-maturity (or yield to call) can be used to compare the risk of two or more bonds that are similar *in all other respects*, including time to maturity. The bond with the higher yield-to-maturity is the one perceived to be the riskier by investors. Also, the yield-to-maturity on existing bonds can be used as an estimate of the required returns of investors on any new (and similar) bonds the firm may issue.

Zero Coupon Bonds For zero coupon bonds that pay no interest over their life, the only payment to holders is the principal payment at maturity. To illustrate the calculation of the yield-to-maturity for such a bond, consider the International Cellular zero coupon money multiplier notes that mature on April 21, 2024. Suppose these bonds (having a par value of $1,000) were purchased for $600 on April 21, 2016 (eight years prior to maturity). Determine the yield-to-maturity on these bonds.

Figure 6.6 shows cash flows from the purchase of an International Cellular zero coupon bond. Because there are no interest payments, the yield-to-maturity equation (Equation 6.5) can be simplified to:

$$P_0 = M(\text{PVIF}_{k_d,n}) \tag{6.9}$$

FIGURE 6.6

Cash Flows from the Purchase of an International Cellular Zero Coupon Bond

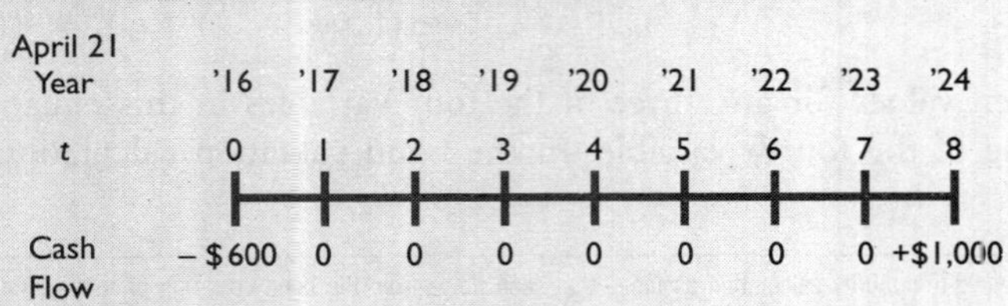

Substituting $n = 8$, $P_0 = \$600$, and $M = \$1{,}000$ into this expression yields:

$$\$600 = \$1{,}000(\text{PVIF}_{k_d,8})$$
$$(\text{PVIF}_{k_d,8}) = 0.600$$

Calculator Solutions

Key	Enter
n	8
i	
PV	−600
PMT	0
FV	1,000
	Solution
i	6.59

From Table II at the back of the book, we find this present value interest factor in the 8-year row between the 6 percent (0.627) and 7 percent (0.582) interest rate columns. Hence, by interpolation, the yield-to-maturity (k_d) on this zero coupon bond is approximately:

$$k_d = 6\% + \frac{0.627 - 0.600}{0.627 - 0.582}(1\%)$$
$$= 6.60\%$$

The exact yield-to-maturity is 6.59 percent. (See Calculator Solution.)

Perpetual Bonds The rate of return, or yield-to-maturity, on a *perpetual* bond can be found by solving the perpetual bond valuation equation presented earlier (Equation 6.8) for k_d:

$$P_0 = \frac{I}{k_d}$$

which gives:

(6.10) $$k_d = \frac{I}{P_0}$$

For example, recall the 4 percent Canadian Pacific Limited Railroad debentures described earlier. If the current price of a bond is \$640, what is the yield-to-maturity on the bond? Substituting $P_0 = \$640$ and $I = \$40$ (or 4 percent of \$1,000) into Equation 6.10 gives the following:

$$k_d = \frac{\$40}{\$640}$$
$$= 0.0625 \text{ (or 6.25 percent)}$$

6-5 Characteristics of Preferred Stock

preferred stock

As a source of capital for a firm, **preferred stock** occupies an intermediate position between long-term debt and common stock. Like common stock, preferred stock is part of the stockholders' equity. Like long-term debt, it is considered a fixed-income security, although preferred stockholders receive dividends instead of interest payments. Because the issuing firm often does not promise repayment at a specific date, preferred stock tends to be a more permanent form of financing than long-term debt. Dividends on preferred stock, like interest payments on long-term debt, normally remain constant over time.

The popularity of preferred stock financing has declined in recent decades. Dividends cannot be deducted from income for corporate income tax purposes, whereas interest payments are tax deductible. This means that for a company paying more than one-third of its income in taxes, the after-tax cost of preferred stock is greater than that of long-term debt, assuming that the pretax preferred stock and long-term debt rates are about the same and that the company makes no change in its capital structure.[21]

[21]For a given company at a particular time, preferred stock will often cost slightly more than long-term debt, even on a pretax basis, because investors require a higher return to compensate them for the greater risk involved with preferred stock. (See Chapter 12 for further discussion of this topic.) In contrast, preferred dividends received by corporate investors qualify for a 70 percent intercompany dividend exclusion, whereas interest income does not. Thus, a preferred stock offering that is largely purchased by other corporations may have a lower yield than similar debt offerings.

Preferred stock bears its name because it usually has preference, or priority, over common stock with regard to the company's dividends and assets. For example, if a company's earnings in a given year are insufficient to pay dividends on preferred stock, the company is not permitted to pay dividends on its common stock. In the event of a liquidation following bankruptcy, the claims on the firm's assets by preferred stockholders are subordinate to those of creditors but have priority over those of common stockholders.

6-5a Features of Preferred Stock

Like long-term debt, preferred stock has its own unique distinguishing characteristics. A number are discussed here.

Selling Price and Par Value The selling price, or issue price, is the per-share price at which preferred stock shares are sold to the public. Preferred stocks are typically issued at prices of $25, $50, or $100 per share.

par value

The **par value** is the value assigned to the stock by the issuing company and is frequently the same as the initial selling price. No relationship necessarily exists between the two, however. A preferred stock sold at $25 per share may have a $25 par value, $1 par value, or no par value at all. Regardless of what a preferred stock's actual par value is, however, in the event of liquidation, preferred stockholders are entitled to the issue price plus dividends, after the claims of creditors have been paid in full.

Preferred stock is usually designated by its dividend amount rather than its dividend percentage. For example, suppose Intermountain Power Company has a series of preferred stock that pays an annual dividend of $2.20, has a $1 par value, and was initially sold to the public at $25 per share. An investor would most likely refer to the stock as "Intermountain Power's $2.20 preferred."

Adjustable Rate Preferred Stock This type of preferred stock became popular in the early 1980s. With these issues, dividends are reset periodically and offer returns that vary with interest rates. For example, Chase Manhattan (now JPMorgan Chase) issued 9.1 million (series N) shares of adjustable rate preferred stock on April 29, 1994. The annual dividend rate was to be set quarterly at 85 percent of the highest of (1) the three-month U.S. Treasury Bill Rate, (2) the U.S. Treasury 10-year Constant Maturity Rate, and (3) the U.S. Treasury 30-year Constant Maturity Rate prior to each quarterly dividend period, with upper and lower limits of 10.50 percent and 4.50 percent, respectively.

cumulative

Cumulative Feature Most preferred stock is **cumulative.** This means that if, for some reason, a firm fails to pay its preferred dividend, it cannot pay dividends on its common stock until it has satisfied all or a prespecified amount of preferred dividends in arrears. The principal reason for this feature is that investors are generally unwilling to purchase preferred stock that is not cumulative.

Participation Stock is said to be *participating* if the holders share in any increased earnings the company might experience. Virtually all preferred stock, however, is *non-participating*; that is, the preferred dividend remains constant, even if the company's earnings increase. Any dividend increases resulting from higher earnings accrue directly to the common stockholders.

Maturity Preferred stock is technically part of a firm's equity capital. As such, some firms issue preferred stock that is intended to be *perpetual*, that is, a permanent portion of the stockholders' equity having no specific maturity date. Many preferred stock investors, however, desire sinking fund provisions, which guarantee that the issue will be retired over a specified time period.

Call Feature Like long-term debt, preferred stock can sometimes be redeemed, or *called*, at the issuing firm's option at some specified price. For example, Citigroup's 1997 (series R) adjustable rate preferred stock issue was callable (deferred call) on or after May 31, 1999, at a redemption price of $250 per share plus dividends accrued and unpaid to the redemption date.

Whereas the call feature allows the issuing company a measure of flexibility in its financing plans, the call feature is generally not attractive to investors. Thus, a firm usually must also provide investors with a *call premium*, or the difference between the call price and the original selling price, should it decide to attach a call feature to its preferred stock.

The probability that a firm will exercise the call privilege is likely to increase during times when market interest rates have decreased below those that existed at the time of issue. After calling the original issue, the firm can replace it with a lower cost issue.

Voting Rights As a general rule, preferred stockholders are not entitled to vote for the company's board of directors. However, special voting procedures frequently take effect if the company omits its preferred dividends or incurs losses for a period of time. In such a case, the preferred stockholders often vote as a separate group to elect one or more members of the company's board of directors. This ensures that the preferred holders will have direct representation on the board.

6-5b Trading of Preferred Shares

Following the initial sale of preferred stock by a firm, investors who purchase the shares may decide to sell them in the secondary markets. Large issues of actively traded preferred stock are listed on the major stock exchanges, such as the New York Stock Exchange. However, a majority of preferred stock issues are traded rather thinly, and these are traded OTC.

6-5c Users of Preferred Stock

In the past, utility companies have been the most frequent users of preferred stock financing, largely because of the regulatory treatment of preferred stock dividend payments. Utilities are permitted by their regulatory agencies to consider preferred dividends as an expense for rate-making purposes, thus reducing the after-tax cost disadvantage of preferred stock that deters nonutility firms from making extensive use of this form of financing. With deregulation, utility company use of preferred stock financing has been greatly reduced.

Large commercial banks are another group of preferred stock users. These banks, including Bank of America, Citigroup, and JPMorgan Chase, have issued preferred stock, partly to get additional equity into their capital structures.

Other occasional users of preferred stock financing are capital-intensive companies undertaking expansion programs. These companies may choose preferred stock as a means of securing long-term financing for the following reasons:

- Their capital structures and various other restrictions prevent the judicious use of additional long-term debt.
- Depressed common stock prices and the potential dilution of per-share earnings may cause them to decide against external common equity financing.

Often these same companies have relatively low marginal tax rates (because of losses and accelerated depreciation) that make the after-tax cost of preferred stock not appreciably different from that of long-term debt.

Also, the government used preferred stock to help stabilize the banking system in 2008. The U.S. Treasury, through the Troubled Asset Relief Program (TARP), received preferred stock in over 500 banks. The 16 largest banks to receive TARP funds issued over $200 billion in preferred stock to the government.

6-5d Advantages and Disadvantages of Preferred Stock Financing

From the issuing company's perspective, the principal advantage of preferred stock is that preferred dividend payments are potentially flexible. Omitting a preferred dividend in difficult times usually results in less severe consequences than omitting an interest payment on long-term debt.

In addition, preferred stock financing can increase a firm's degree of financial leverage. However, financial analysts may regard the issuance of preferred stock as equivalent to debt. In this case, the company is viewed as having used up a portion of its "debt capacity." In effect, the company has leveraged with preferred stock rather than long-term debt—at a greater after-tax cost.

From the investors' perspective, companies who purchase the preferred stock of other companies accrue certain tax advantages resulting from the 70 percent exclusion of intercompany dividends from federal income taxes. For example, an insurance company in the 35 percent tax bracket can invest in the preferred stock of another company and pay taxes equal to only about 10.5 percent of the preferred dividend income.[22] In contrast, the same insurance company would be required to include all the interest received in its taxable income.

The principal disadvantage of preferred stock financing is its high after-tax cost as compared with long-term debt because dividends cannot be deducted for income tax purposes. Thus the after-tax cost to the firm for preferred stock is generally greater than the after-tax cost of long-term debt, assuming that the firm's capital structure remains constant.[23] As a result, most companies considering long-term financing with fixed-income securities choose long-term debt over preferred stock. A complete discussion of the cost of debt and preferred stock is in Chapter 12.

6-5e Valuation of Preferred Stock

Most preferred stock pays regular, fixed dividends. Preferred dividends per share are normally not increased when the earnings of a firm increase, nor are they cut or suspended unless the firm faces serious financial problems. If preferred stock dividends are cut or suspended for a period of time for whatever reason, the firm is usually required to make up the past-due payments before paying any common stock dividends. Thus, the investor's expected cash return from holding most preferred stocks can be treated as a fixed, constant amount per period.

The investor's required rate of return on a preferred stock issue is a function of the risk that the firm will be unable to meet its dividend payments. The higher the risk, the higher the required rate of return. Because bondholders have a prior claim over preferred stockholders on the income and assets of a firm, it is riskier to hold a firm's preferred stock than to hold its bonds. As a result, investors normally require a higher rate of return on preferred stock than on bonds.

---

[22]The 10.5 percent figure is calculated by multiplying the portion of dividends that is subject to taxes, namely, 30 percent, by 35 percent.

[23]Tax code changes in 2013 increased the maximum tax rate on preferred stock dividends to 20 percent for individuals with taxable incomes greater than $400,000 ($450,000 for married couples). For taxpayers with incomes below these levels, the maximum rate remained at the 15 percent level set in 2003. A new Medicare tax of 3.8 percent on net investment returns for individuals with taxable incomes above $200,000 ($250,000 for married couples) also increased the maximum tax rate for many taxpayers. Despite these tax rate increases, preferred stock dividends remain somewhat more attractive to investors than interest on debt that is taxed at higher marginal tax rates.

Because many preferred stock issues do not have maturity dates, the cash flows from holding no-maturity preferred stock can be treated as a perpetual stream of payments, or a *perpetuity*. Capitalizing the perpetual stream of dividend payments gives the following valuation expression:

(6.11)
$$P_0 = \sum_{t=1}^{\infty} \frac{D_p}{(1 + k_p)^t}$$

where D_p is the dividend per period, and k_p is the investor's required rate of return.[24]

Equation 6.11 is similar to Equation 6.7 for a perpetual bond. Like the perpetual bond valuation model, this equation can be simplified into the following valuation model:

(6.12)
$$P_0 = \frac{D_p}{k_p}$$

To illustrate the use of Equation 6.12, assume that DuPont pays annual end-of-year dividends on its $4.50 series B cumulative preferred stock issue (issue price $100, par value of $0). What is the value of this stock to an investor who requires an 8 percent annual rate of return on the investment? Assume that the issue will not be called for the foreseeable future. Substituting $4.50 for D_p and 0.08 for k_p yields the following:

$$P_0 = \frac{\$4.50}{0.08}$$
$$= \$56.25$$

6-6 Summary

- The *capitalization of cash flow* method of valuation can be used to determine the value of a security to an investor. This involves calculating the present value of the stream of expected future cash flows discounted at the investor's required rate of return. The required rate of return is a function of the *risk* associated with the cash flows from the asset, as well as the risk-free rate.
- Long-term debt is generally classified according to whether it is *secured* by specific physical assets of the issuing company. Secured debt issues are *mortgage bonds*, whereas debt issues backed only by unmortgaged assets and the company's earning power are *debentures*.
- Long-term debt usually has the following features:

  1. The *indenture*, or the contract between the issuing company and the debtholders
  2. The *trustee*, who represents the debtholders in dealings with the company
  3. Some debt issues have a *call feature*, which gives the issuing company the option to retire the debt prior to maturity
  4. Some debt issues have a *sinking fund requirement*, which, in practice, means the company must gradually reduce the outstanding balance of the debt issue over its life

- Bond *refunding* occurs when a company redeems a callable issue and sells a lower-cost issue to take its place.
- The value of a *perpetual bond* is equal to the interest payment divided by the investor's required rate of return.
- The value of a *bond having a finite maturity date* is equal to the present value of the stream of interest and principal payments discounted at the investor's required rate of return.
- The *yield-to-maturity* on a bond is the rate of return the investor expects to earn if the bond is purchased at a given price and held until maturity.

[24]If an investor is considering purchasing a preferred stock issue that is expected to be called in the future, its value is calculated by capitalizing (that is, discounting) the call price plus the dividend payments to be received before the issue is called.

- Preferred stock usually has the following features:
  1. The *selling price*, or *issue price*, is the per-share price at which the shares are sold to the public.
  2. The *par value* is an arbitrary value assigned to the stock by the issuing company.
  3. Most preferred stock is *cumulative*; that is, dividends on common stock cannot be paid as long as any past or present preferred dividends remain unpaid.
  4. Virtually all preferred stock is *nonparticipating*; that is, preferred stock does not share in any increased earnings of the firm.
  5. Some preferred stock is *perpetual*, whereas other preferred stock is gradually retired by the firm.
  6. Preferred stock is often *callable*.
- From the issuing company's perspective, preferred stock financing is advantageous due to the potential flexibility of preferred dividend payments.
- The principal disadvantage of preferred stock financing is that dividends are not tax deductible, which causes the after-tax cost of preferred stock to the firm to be higher than the cost of long-term debt, all other things being equal.

Important Equations

$$P_0 = I(\text{PVIFA}_{k_d,n}) + M(\text{PVIF}_{k_d,n})$$

$$P_0 = \frac{I}{k_d}$$

$$k_d = \frac{I}{P_0}$$

$$P_0 = \frac{D_p}{k_p}$$

6-7 Questions and Topics for Discussion

1. Define the following terms associated with long-term debt:
   a. Indenture
   b. Trustee
   c. Call feature
   d. Sinking fund
   e. Conversion feature
   f. Coupon rate
2. Describe the basic features of each of the following types of bonds:
   a. Mortgage bonds
   b. Debentures
   c. Subordinated debentures
   d. Equipment trust certificates
   e. Collateral trust bonds
   f. Income bonds

3. Suppose a company simultaneously sold two long-term debt issues at par: $9\frac{1}{8}$ percent senior debentures and $9\frac{3}{8}$ percent subordinated debentures. What risk-return trade-off would be faced by an investor who was considering one of these issues?
4. What is the relationship between par value, market value, and book value for the following?
   a. Long-term debt
   b. Preferred stock
5. Define the following terms associated with preferred stock:
   a. Cumulative feature
   b. Participation
   c. Call feature
6. What variables must be known (or estimated) in applying the capitalization of cash flow method of valuation to a physical or financial asset?
7. Define the following:
   a. The market value of an asset
   b. Market equilibrium
8. What is the primary difference between the book value and the market value of an asset?
9. Describe the relationship between the coupon rate and the required rate of return that will result in a bond selling at
   a. A discount
   b. Par value
   c. A premium
10. How does the yield-to-maturity on a bond differ from the coupon yield or current yield?
11. Under what conditions will a bond's current yield be equal to its yield-to-maturity?
12. In what ways is preferred stock similar to long-term debt? In what ways is it similar to common stock?
13. Explain why bondholders often prefer a sinking fund provision in a bond issue.
14. Explain what is meant by *interest rate risk.*
15. Explain how a bond can be classified as a fixed-income security when the yield-to-maturity can fluctuate significantly over time, depending on the market price of the bond.
16. Describe the basic features of each of the following types of bonds:
    a. Floating rate bonds
    b. Original issue deep discount bonds
    c. Zero coupon bonds
    d. Extendable notes (put bonds)
17. Explain what is meant by *reinvestment rate risk.*
18. Compare the debt outstanding for Delta Airlines and Southwest Airlines. Use the *S&P Bond Guide* from your library to determine the bond rating of each of these firms. What reasons can you cite for the differences in bond ratings between the firms?

6-8 Self-Test Problems

ST1. What is the current value of a $1,000 par value perpetual bond to an investor who requires a 10 percent annual rate of return? The perpetual bond pays interest at the rate of 8 percent per year.

ST2. Cellular International zero coupon bonds (par value $1,000) mature on April 21, 2022. Calculate the yield-to-maturity if an investor purchased one of these bonds on April 21, 2016, at a price of $650.

ST3. Philips Industries has bonds outstanding ($1,000 par value) that mature 10 years from today and have a coupon interest rate of 9⅜ percent. Calculate the maximum price an investor should be willing to pay if the investor desires a 10 percent yield-to-maturity.

ST4. What is the value of a share of DuPont Series A $3.50 cumulative, perpetual preferred stock to an investor who requires a 6 percent annual rate of return on this security? This preferred stock was originally issued at $102 a share.

ST5. Use the data in Figure 6.1 to answer the following:
a. What is the coupon rate and year of maturity for the CVS Health bonds?
b. If you purchased one Halliburton bond, what price would you have to pay at the closing trade?
c. Why do you think the yield is greater for the Time Warner bond of 2026 than the Lockheed Martin bond of 2026?

ST6. A U.S. government bond was quoted as:

Rate	Maturity Mo/Yr	Bid	Asked	Chg*	Ask Yld
3	Sep 16	108:25	108:26	−10	0.57

*Chg is in 32nds of a percent.

a. How much would you have to pay for one of these $1,000 face value bonds?
b. What was the dollar amount of the price change on this bond?

6-9 Problems*

BASIC

1. Determine the value of a $1,000 Canadian Pacific Limited perpetual 4 percent debenture (bond) at the following required rates of return:
a. 4 percent
b. 5 percent
c. 6 percent

BASIC

2. Recently the high and low market prices of Canadian Pacific Limited's debentures (see problem 1) were $790 and $475, respectively. Determine the yield-to-maturity of one of these debentures if it was purchased under the following conditions:
a. At the high market price
b. At the low market price

INTERMEDIATE

Spreadsheet Strategies

3. Consider Fulton Manufacturing Company's 8¾ percent bonds that mature on April 15, 2028. Assume that the interest on these bonds is paid and compounded annually. Determine the value of a $1,000 denomination Fulton bond as of April 15, 2016, to an investor who holds the bond until maturity and whose required rate of return is:
a. 7 percent
b. 9 percent
c. 11 percent

What would be the value of the Fulton bonds at an 8 percent required rate of return if the interest were paid and compounded *semiannually*?

*Color blocks behind the numbers denote problems that have check answers provided at the end of the book.

CHALLENGE

4. Creative Financing, Inc., is planning to offer a $1,000 par value 15-year maturity bond with a coupon interest rate that changes every 5 years. The coupon rate for the first 5 years is 10 percent, 10.75 percent for the next 5 years, and 11.5 percent for the final 5 years. If you require an 11 percent rate of return on a bond of this quality and maturity, what is the maximum price you would pay for the bond? (Assume interest is paid annually at the end of each year.)

INTERMEDIATE

Spreadsheet Strategies

****5.** Adams Food Service has issued $7\frac{3}{8}$ percent bonds that mature on July 15, 2048. The bonds are callable at $1,037.08 on July 15, 2023. Assume that interest is paid and compounded annually. Determine the yield-to-maturity (to the nearest 10th of 1 percent) if an investor purchased a $1,000 denomination bond for $900 on July 15, 2016.

BASIC

Spreadsheet Strategies

****6.** BCC has issued $8\frac{1}{8}$ percent debentures that will mature on July 15, 2036. Assume that interest is paid and compounded annually. If an investor purchased a $1,000 denomination bond for $1,025 on July 15, 2016, determine the bond's yield-to-maturity. Explain why an investor would be willing to pay $1,025 for a bond that is going to be worth only $1,000 at maturity.

INTERMEDIATE

Spreadsheet Strategies

7. Consider the Leverage Unlimited, Inc., zero coupon bonds of 2020. The bonds were issued in 2002 for $100. Determine the yield-to-maturity (to the nearest $^1/_{10}$ of 1 percent) if the bonds are purchased at the:

a. Issue price in 2002. (*Note*: To avoid a fractional year holding period, assume that the issue and maturity dates are at the midpoint—July 1—of the respective years.)

b. Market price as of July 1, 2016, of $750.

c. Explain why the returns calculated in Parts a and b are different.

BASIC

Spreadsheet Strategies

8. If you purchase a zero coupon bond today for $225 and it matures at $1,000 in 11 years, what rate of return will you earn on that bond (to the nearest $^1/_{10}$ of 1 percent)?

INTERMEDIATE

Spreadsheet Strategies

9. In 2006, BCC issued $8\frac{5}{8}$ percent debentures that will mature on December 1, 2046.

a. If an investor purchased one of these bonds ($1,000 denomination) on December 1, 2016, for $1,050, determine the yield-to-maturity. Explain why investors would be willing to pay $1,050 on December 1, 2016, for one of these bonds when they are going to receive only $1,000 when the bond matures in 2046.

b. The BCC $8\frac{5}{8}$ percent debentures are callable by the company on December 1, 2021, at $1,044.50. Determine the *yield to call* as of December 1, 2016, assuming that BCC calls the bonds on that date.

BASIC

10. Determine the value of a share of DuPont Series A $3.50 cumulative preferred stock to an investor who requires the following rates of return:

a. 9 percent

b. 10 percent

c. 12 percent

INTERMEDIATE

11. Determine the value of a share of DuPont Series A $4.50 cumulative preferred stock, no par, to an investor who requires a 9 percent rate of return on this security. The issue is callable at $120 per share plus accrued dividends. However, the issue is not expected to be called at any time in the foreseeable future.

INTERMEDIATE

Spreadsheet Strategies

****12.** Consider again the BCC $8\frac{1}{8}$ percent debentures that mature on July 15, 2036 (see problem 6). Determine the yield to call if the bonds are called on July 15, 2022, at $1,016.55.

**Requires use of a financial calculator.

INTERMEDIATE **13. BCC has bonds that trade frequently, pay a 7.75 percent coupon rate, and mature in 2021. The bonds mature on March 1 in the maturity year. Suppose an investor bought this bond on March 1, 2016, and assume interest is paid annually on March 1. Calculate the yield-to-maturity assuming the investor bought the bond at the following price, as quoted in the financial press:

Spreadsheet Strategies

a. 100
b. 90
c. 105

CHALLENGE **14.** Hooks Athletics, Inc., has outstanding a preferred stock with a par value of $30 that pays a dividend of $2.50. The preferred stock is redeemable at the option of the stockholder in 10 years at a price equal to $30. The stock may be called for redemption by the company in 15 years at a price of $32.50. (Any stock that is not redeemed at the end of 10 years can be expected to be called by the company in 15 years.) If you know that investors require a 15 percent pretax rate of return on this preferred stock, what is the current market value of this preferred stock?

CHALLENGE **15.** Dooley, Inc., has outstanding $100 million (par value) bonds that pay an annual coupon rate of interest of 10.5 percent. Par value of each bond is $1,000. The bonds are scheduled to mature in 20 years. Because of Dooley's increased risk, investors now require a 14 percent rate of return on bonds of similar quality with 20 years remaining until maturity. The bonds are callable at 110 percent of par at the end of 10 years.

Spreadsheet Strategies

a. What price would the bonds sell for assuming investors *do not expect* them to be called?
b. What price would the bonds sell for assuming investors *expect* them to be called at the end of 10 years?

INTERMEDIATE **16.** Zabberer Corporation bonds pay a coupon rate of interest of 12 percent annually and have a maturity value of $1,000. The bonds are scheduled to mature at the end of 14 years. The company has the option to call the bonds in 8 years at a premium of 12 percent above the maturity value. You believe the company will exercise its option to call the bonds at that time. If you require a pretax return of 10 percent on bonds of this risk, how much would you pay for one of these bonds today?

Spreadsheet Strategies

CHALLENGE **17.** Waters, Inc., has outstanding a $100 million (face value) issue of bonds. The bonds pay a coupon rate of interest of 8 percent per annum. At the time the bonds were first issued, they sold at face value of $1,000 per bond. The bonds have 12 years remaining until maturity. They are "puttable" at the option of the bondholder at face value in five years. The bonds are not callable by the company. If you require a 9 percent return on bonds such as these with five years remaining until maturity and 8.2 percent on bonds such as these with 12 years remaining until maturity, how much would you pay for one of these bonds?

Spreadsheet Strategies

CHALLENGE **18.** World Tobacco has issued preferred stock ($10 par value) that pays an annual dividend of $0.84. The preferred stock matures in five years. At that time, holders of the stock will receive, at their option, either $10 or one share of common stock with a value up to $14. If the common stock is trading at a price above $14, the preferred stockholders will receive a fractional share of common stock worth $14. The current common stock price is $8.875. The common stock pays a 10 cent per share dividend. This dividend is expected to grow at a 10 percent rate per year for the next five years. If the market requires a 12 percent rate of return on a stock of this risk and maturity, what is the *maximum* value for which this share can be expected to trade?

Spreadsheet Strategies

INTERMEDIATE **19.** Zheng Enterprises, a multinational drug company specializing in Chinese medicines, issued $100 million of 15 percent coupon rate bonds in January 2011. The bonds had

**Requires use of a financial calculator.

an initial maturity of 30 years. The bonds were sold at par and were callable in five years at 110 (that is, 110 percent of par value). It is now January 2016, and interest rates have declined such that bonds of equivalent remaining maturity now sell to yield 11 percent. How much would you be willing to pay for one of these bonds today? Why?

BASIC **20.** Refer to the bonds appearing in Figure 6.1.

a. What is the coupon rate and year of maturity for the Qualcomm and Time Warner bonds?

b. How much would you have had to pay to buy one Bank of America bond at the closing trade?

c. Why is the yield-to-maturity on the Hewlett Packard Enterprise bonds of 2025 higher than the yield on the AT&T bonds of 2025?

BASIC **21.** The "asked" discount on a six-month Treasury bill was recently quoted as 3.02 percent. Approximately how much would you have to pay to buy one of these Treasury bills ($10,000 maturity value)?

BASIC **22.** How much would you have to pay for a U.S. government bond ($1,000 maturity value) scheduled to mature in November 2017 and quoted at 147:27 "asked"? The coupon rate on the bond is 9⅞ percent.

BASIC **23.** Zip Boys has outstanding zero coupon bonds maturing in 2018.

a. How would you compute the yield-to-maturity on bonds like these?

b. How do bondholders get a return when they buy these bonds?

INTERMEDIATE **24.** The bonds of Columbia Gas paid no interest in 1993 because the firm had declared bankruptcy. One issue of these bonds, the 8¼ percent coupon bonds due in 1996, was selling at 109 percent of par value, or for approximately $1,090. Why would someone pay $1,090 for the bonds of a bankrupt firm?

INTERMEDIATE **25.** Hexcel has a 7 percent coupon rate bond issue outstanding that matures in 2017. *The Wall Street Journal* reports a bond price of $582.50. These bonds are convertible into common stock. Why do you think a company would issue this type of bond?[9]

INTERMEDIATE ****26.** Disney Enterprises issued 7.55% senior debentures (bonds) on July 15, 1993, with a 100-year maturity (that is, due on July 15, 2093). Suppose an investor purchased one of these bonds on July 15, 2003 for $1,050.

a. Determine the yield-to-maturity (nearest $^1/_{100}$ of 1 percent) using the valuation formula for a bond with a finite maturity (Equation 6.5).

b. Determine the yield-to-maturity (nearest $^1/_{100}$ of 1 percent) using the valuation formula for a perpetual bond (Equation 6.8).

c. Explain why the answers to parts a and b are the same.

INTERMEDIATE **27.** Murphy's Brewhouse was a rapidly expanding chain of home-brew bars. The beer was not very good, but hopes were high when the company went public three years ago, because of founder/owner Kevin Murphy's promotional skills.

At the time the company went public, Murphy's also issued $50 million of 20-year maturity debentures at a coupon rate of 9 percent. These debentures were sold at par ($1,000 per bond). Shortly after this debenture issue, Murphy's received some very negative reviews, both in the gourmet beer magazines and on Wall Street. The company is currently struggling. Its stock has plummeted from $40 per share three years ago to less than $5. Earnings remain positive but disappointing at $0.03 per share, and the company is barely breaking even on a cash flow basis.

Murphy's debentures are currently selling at 40 cents on the dollar. The debentures are callable two years from now at $1,090. If you require a 20 percent rate of return on investments of this perceived risk level, should you buy these debentures?

**Requires use of a financial calculator.

CHAPTER 7

Common Stock: Characteristics, Valuation, and Issuance

KEY CHAPTER CONCEPTS

1. The characteristics of variable-income (common stock) securities include:

   a. Accounting aspects
   b. Stockholder rights
   c. Features
   d. Advantages and disadvantages

2. Investment bankers provide a number of important services within the operation of the capital markets.

3. Methods of selling securities in the primary capital markets include:

   a. Public cash offering
   b. Direct placement
   c. Rights offering to shareholders

4. In the general dividend valuation model, the value of a common stock is equal to the present value of all future dividend payments discounted at the investor's required rate of return.

5. In the constant growth dividend valuation model, the value of a common stock is equal to the next period's dividend divided by the difference between the investor's required rate of return and the dividend growth rate.

6. A zero growth dividend valuation model can be used when a firm's future dividend payments are expected to remain constant forever, as in a perpetuity.

7. A nonconstant growth dividend valuation model uses the present value of yearly dividends plus the present value of the expected stock price at the end of the period of nonconstant growth.

8. The valuation of small family held or privately held firm stock requires an explicit consideration of the marketability of that stock, whether the stock represents minority or majority ownership, and whether the stock is voting or nonvoting.

FINANCIAL CHALLENGE

Pricing Twitter's Initial Public Offering (IPO)

Twitter, founded in 2006, is an Internet service allowing users to send short (140-character) messages, called "tweets," to other users. Twitter's business model is to incorporate advertisements from its corporate clients in the tweets between users. Prior to its IPO in November 2013, Twitter had 230 million users and was unprofitable. In 2012 the company lost $79 million on total revenue of $317 million, and for the first three quarters of 2013, prior to its IPO, it lost $134 million on total revenue of $422 million. Despite its losses, investors were seeking to share in Twitter's potential for rapid growth. Some analysts were predicting that the company's revenue could increase by a factor of six or seven times over the next five years.

With strong demand for IPOs, Twitter and its investment advisors raised the issue price of Twitter's stock twice before the stock was going to begin trading on the New York Stock Exchange (NYSE). Three days prior to the planned trading date, they raised the price range from between $17 and $20 per share to between $23 and $25 per share. Then, on the day before trading opened, they increased the offering price to $26 per share. On the first day of trading on the NYSE, Twitter's shares opened at $45.10 and closed at $44.90, up 73 percent from the $26 IPO price. At this closing price, Twitter had a market capitalization of approximately $25 billion, which was greater than over half of the large capitalization companies that make up the Standard & Poor's 500 Stock Index.

© Friedrich Stark/Alamy

Given the high first-day closing price of the Twitter common stock, one could argue that Twitter "left money on the table" by not setting a higher issue price. For example, at an offering price of $45 per share, the company could have raised an additional $1.5 billion compared with the $26 issue price. However, Twitter and its investment advisors did not want to overprice the shares. By sacrificing some of the additional funds it could have raised from a higher offering price, they hoped to maintain goodwill with long-term investors who would tend to be more willing to buy shares in future Twitter stock issues.

In this chapter, the principle and tools used in the valuation of common stock are discussed, as are the institutional aspects of stock pricing and issuance.

Sources: Evelyn M. Rusli et al., "Twitter IPO Plan: Contrast Facebook," *The Wall Street Journal* (September 14–15, 2013): B1; Andy Kessler, "Why Twitter's IPO Is a Bigger Deal Than Facebook's," *The Wall Street Journal* (November 4, 2013): A19; Telis Demos et al., "Twitter Lifts Price Range in Heady WO Market," *The Wall Street Journal* (November 5, 2013): B1; Miriam Gottfried, "Revenue-Growth Hopes Feather Twitter's Nest," *The Wall Street Journal* (November 6, 2013): C18; Matt Jarzemsky, "Twitter Sets Its IPO Price @ $26," *The Wall Street Journal* (November 7, 2013): A1; Telis Demos et al., "Twitter Shares Take Wing with Smooth Trading Debut," *The Wall Street Journal* (November 8, 2013): A1.

CHAPTER OBJECTIVES

Upon completion of this chapter, you should have a clear understanding of the following:

1. The features and characteristics of common stocks
2. The securities offering process and the role of the investment banker
3. The valuation of common stocks

7-1 Introduction

Unlike long-term debt and preferred stock, which are normally fixed-income securities, common stock is a variable-income security. Common stockholders are said to participate in a firm's earnings because they may receive a larger dividend if earnings increase in the future or their dividends may be cut if earnings drop. For example, in 1974, Tucson Electric Power Company sold new common stock when annual dividends were $0.84 per share. By 1989, the annual rate was $3.90 per share, having been raised several times during the intervening years. However, during 1990, the company suffered substantial losses and cut its dividend to zero. Its common stock price dropped from about $65 a share in 1986 and 1987 to $3⅞ a share by early 1994. In 1996, the stock had a 1 for 5 reverse stock split and the company changed its name to UniSource Energy. At the end of 2000, its stock was trading at $19 per share. After a 10-year period of no dividend payments, the company resumed paying common stock dividends in 2000 ($0.32 per share). Since then, the company (now known as UNS Energy) has raised its dividend rate each year, paying $1.72 in 2013. Late in 2013, Fortis (Canada's largest gas and electric distributor) agreed to purchase UNS Energy for $60.25 per share, a 31 percent premium of UNS's closing share price.

Common stock also differs from long-term debt and preferred stock in that the market price tends to fluctuate more than the price of bonds and preferred stock, thus causing returns on common stock investments to vary more widely over time than returns on long-term debt or preferred stock.

This chapter describes the characteristics of common stock. The process by which securities are offered for sale and the role of the investment banker in this process are discussed. Finally, valuation models for common stock are developed.

7-1a Understanding Stock Quotations

Figure 7.1 shows selected stock quotations for common stocks traded on the New York Stock Exchange. Beginning at the left-hand side, the first column shows the stock's percentage price change for the calendar year to date. For example, the per-share price of DuPont common stock was down 4.48 percent from the beginning of 2015. The next two columns show the 52-week high (Hi) and low (Lo) for the stock. For DuPont, these were $76.61 and $47.11, respectively. The column immediately to the right of the stock name shows the ticker symbol used to identify this stock on the exchange's ticker tape, DD for DuPont. The next column shows the **dividend (percentage) yield**. For DuPont, the figure is 2.3 percent, calculated as the annual dividend divided by the closing price.

dividend (percentage) yield

The price-to-earnings or P/E ratio (the closing price divided by the sum of the latest four quarters of earnings per share) is shown next. The P/E ratio (21) indicates how much investors are willing to pay for $1 of current earnings from DuPont. Generally, the greater the risk of the firm, the lower will be its P/E multiple. Similarly, the P/E ratio will tend to be higher the more rapid the expected growth rate in future earnings. The next column lists the last or closing price for the day: $67.09 for DuPont. The final column shows the net change in price per share for the day, or the difference between this day's last price and the last price on the previous business day (or the last day on which a trade took place). For the day, the common stock of DuPont gained $0.17, or 17 cents per share.

FIGURE **7.1**
Selected Stock Quotations

Ytd % Chg	52-Week Hi	52-Week Lo	Stock	Sym	Yld %	PE	Last	Net Chg
−6.15	20.41	14.71	DDRCorp	DDR	4.0	dd	17.23	0.10
−7.18	92.27	73.23	DTEEnergy	DTE	3.6	15	80.17	0.29
13.00	97.62	81.25	Danaher	DHR	0.6	27	96.85	0.02
8.67	67.69	49.93	Darden	DRI	3.5	25	57.05	0.20
−1.87	85.17	70.12	DaVitaHlthcrPtrs	DVA	...	33	74.32	0.57
−10.60	98.23	71.85	Deere	DE	3.0	14	79.09	−0.91
37.75	25.14	17.15	DelhaizeGroupADR	DEG	1.8	49	24.96	0.09
20.45	90.57	66.10	DelphiAutomotive	DLPH	1.1	19	87.59	−0.13
−4.17	52	34.61	DeltaAir	DAL	1.1	13	47.14	0.27
−15.49	36.20	25.10	DeutscheBank	DB	3.3	dd	25.37	−0.01
−26.69	70.48	36.01	DevonEnergy	DVN	2.1	dd	44.87	−1.04
1.51	124.32	100.59	DiageoADR	DEO	3.7	19	115.81	−0.09
8.85	75.39	60.66	DigitalRealtyTrust	DLR	4.7	48	72.17	0.43
−13.19	66.72	50.20	DiscoverFinSvcs	DFS	2.0	12	56.85	−0.02
22.23	122.08	90	Disney	DIS	1.1	23	115.13	−3.54
−8.05	81.42	59.75	DollarGeneral	DG	1.4	17	65.01	−0.16
−12.39	80.89	66.52	DominionResources	D	3.8	22	67.37	0.15
15.38	119.73	91.90	Ddminos	DPZ	1.1	35	108.65	−0.50
9.65	32.32	26.66	DouglasEmmett	DEI	2.7	88	31.14	0.07
−9.24	79.50	55.50	Dover	DOV	2.6	17	65.09	−0.01
14.03	53.77	35.11	DowChemical	DOW	3.5	13	52.01	0.09
26.35	90.95	69.39	DrPepperSnap	DPS	2.1	24	90.57	0.78
−6.96	68	46.06	DrReddysLabADR	RDY	0.7	21	46.94	−2.80
−4.48	76.61	47.11	DuPont	DD	2.3	21	67.09	−0.17
−19.19	89.97	65.64	DukeEnergy	DUK	4.9	19	67.51	−0.21
0.84	22.70	17.60	DukeRealty	DRE	3.5	41	20.37	0.21

Source: *The Wall Street Journal* (November 28–29, 2015): B11.

When a company has preferred stock outstanding that is also traded on the New York Stock Exchange, the different classes of preferred stocks are listed in a separate table. DuPont has two preferred stock issues (pfA and pfB, which pay $3.50 and $4.50 per share, respectively). Unlike common stock dividends, the preferred stock dividend rate normally will not change over the time the issue is outstanding.

HTTP:
The American Association of Individual Investors will help you obtain all the information you need to make good investing decisions. It's a good lifetime resource for your investing needs.
www.aaii.com

7-2 Characteristics of Common Stock

A firm's common stockholders are its true owners. Common stock is a *residual form of ownership* in that the claims of common stockholders on the firm's earnings and assets are considered only *after* the claims of governments, debt holders, and preferred stockholders have been met. Common stock is considered a *permanent* form of long-term financing because, unlike debt and some preferred stock, common stock has no maturity date.

7-2a Common Stock and Accounting

Common stock appears on the right-hand side of a firm's balance sheet as part of the stockholders' equity. This is shown for the Lawrence Company in Table 7.1.

Stockholders' equity

Stockholders' equity includes both preferred stock (if any exists) and common stock. The total equity attributable to the common stock of the Lawrence Company is equal to the total stockholders' equity less the preferred stock:

$$\$117{,}820{,}000 - \$37{,}500{,}000 = \$80{,}320{,}000$$

In other words, the sum of the common stock account, contributed capital in excess of par value account, and retained earnings account equals the total common stockholders' equity.

book value per share

The **book value per share** of common stock is calculated as follows:

$$\text{Book value per share} = \frac{\text{Total common stockholders' equity}}{\text{Number of shares outstanding}} \tag{7.1}$$

In the case of the Lawrence Company,

$$\text{Book value per share} = \frac{\$80{,}320{,}000}{6{,}675{,}000} = \$12.03$$

A common stock's book value is calculated on the basis of balance sheet figures and does not necessarily have any relationship to the common stock's *market value*, which is based primarily on expectations concerning general economic conditions and the firm's future earnings.

par value

The amount shown in the common stock account is calculated by multiplying the number of shares actually outstanding by the **par value**, an arbitrary value assigned to shares of common stock.[1] To continue with this example, the Lawrence Company has 6.675 million shares outstanding and a $2 par value, resulting in a balance of $13.35 million.

To illustrate the nature of the contributed capital in excess of par value account, suppose Lawrence decides to raise an additional $12 million in external equity capital by selling 600,000 common shares at $20 each. The amount credited to the common

TABLE 7.1

Lawrence Company Stockholders' Equity, December 31, 2015 (in Thousands of Dollars)

Stockholders' Equity	
Preferred stock; $25 par value; authorized, 2,000,000 shares; issued and outstanding, 1,500,000 shares	$ 37,500
Common stock; $2 par value; authorized, 10,000,000 shares; issued and outstanding, 6,675,000 shares	13,350
Contributed capital in excess of par value*	28,713
Retained earnings	38,257
Total stockholders' equity	$117,820

*The *contributed capital in excess of par* account has several other frequently used names, including *capital surplus* and *additional paid-in capital*. Many accountants feel that the expression *capital surplus* is misleading, because it incorrectly implies that a firm has excess capital.

[1] At one time, par value was considered important for any possible liquidation proceedings, but today it has little, if any, real significance. Par value is normally a low figure and tends to be less than $5 per share. Occasionally, companies issue stock with no par value. In these instances, the balance in the common stock account is a "stated value."

stock account is \$1.2 million (600,000 shares times the \$2 par value). The remainder of the \$12 million is added to the contributed capital in excess of par value account. In other words, this account represents capital that is paid into the firm in excess of the par value when common stock is issued.

Additions to the retained earnings account occur as a result of earnings retained in the business, as opposed to earnings paid out to the stockholders as dividends. Retained earnings, which are internally generated funds, are one of the most important sources of capital for business.

7-2b Stockholder Rights

Common stockholders have a number of general rights, including the following:

- **Dividend rights**. Stockholders have the right to share equally on a per-share basis in any distribution of corporate earnings in the form of dividends.
- **Asset rights**. In the event of a liquidation, stockholders have the right to assets that remain after the obligations to the government (taxes), employees, and debt holders have been satisfied.
- **Preemptive rights**. Stockholders may have the right to share proportionately in any new stock sold. For example, a stockholder who owns 20 percent of a corporation's stock may be entitled to purchase 20 percent of any new issue.
- **Voting rights**. Stockholders have the right to vote on stockholder matters, such as the selection of the board of directors.

Whereas all stockholders have dividend and liquidation rights, in addition to voting rights (unless the stock is specifically nonvoting), preemptive rights exist in a relatively small minority of firms at the present time. (Preemptive rights are discussed in detail in Chapter 20.)

Stockholder Voting Rights A firm's stockholders elect its board of directors by means of either a *majority* or a *cumulative* voting procedure. Majority voting is similar to the voting that takes place in political elections; if two slates of people are running for the board, the one that receives more than 50 percent of the votes wins. With majority voting, it is possible that a group of stockholders with a minority viewpoint will have no representation on the board.

Cumulative voting, in contrast, makes it easier for stockholders with minority views to elect sympathetic board members. Because of this, cumulative voting is rare among major corporations and is frequently opposed by management. For example, in response to a shareholder proposal to adopt cumulative voting, General Mills' management recommended a vote against the proposal, arguing that it would result in dysfunctional partisanship on the board. In **cumulative voting**, each share of stock represents as many votes as there are directors to be elected. For example, if a firm is electing seven directors, a particular holder of 100 shares would have 700 votes and could cast all of them for *one* candidate, thereby increasing that candidate's chances for being elected to the board. The following formula can be used to determine the number of shares necessary to elect a certain number of directors:

cumulative voting

$$\text{Number of shares} = \frac{\begin{matrix}\text{Number of}\\ \text{directors}\\ \text{desired}\end{matrix} \times \begin{matrix}\text{Number of}\\ \text{shares}\\ \text{outstanding}\end{matrix}}{\begin{matrix}\text{Number of directors}\\ \text{being elected}\end{matrix} + 1} + 1 \tag{7.2}$$

Of course, it is possible that not all the shareholders will vote their shares. In this case, the calculation is based on the number of shares actually voting rather than the number of shares outstanding.

Consider the following example. The Markham Company has 11 members on its board and one million shares of common stock outstanding. If seven members were up for reelection in a given year and all the shares were voted, the number of shares necessary to elect one director would be as follows:

$$\frac{1 \times 1{,}000{,}000}{7+1} + 1 = 125{,}001$$

In addition to electing the board of directors, a firm's stockholders may vote from time to time on various other matters, such as whether to retain a particular auditing firm, or to increase the number of shares authorized.

The election of directors and other voting normally occur at the annual stockholders' meeting. Because it is usually not possible for all stockholders to attend, management—or anyone else—can solicit votes by *proxy*. Normally, a stockholder can expect to receive a single proxy statement from the firm's management requesting that stockholders follow management's recommendations. In the rather unlikely event that another group of stockholders sends out its own proxy statement, a *proxy fight* is said to occur. Proxy fights are most common when a company is performing poorly or is in the midst of a takeover attempt.

7-2c Other Features of Common Stock

This section covers other topics related to the ownership of common stock, including *common stock classes, stock splits, stock dividends,* and *stock repurchases.*

Common Stock Classes Occasionally, a firm may decide to create more than one class of common stock. The reason for this may be that the firm wishes to raise additional equity capital by selling a portion of the existing owners' stock while maintaining control of the firm. This can be accomplished by creating separate classes of stock with unequal voting rights. The Ford Motor Company is an example of a large, widely held company that has more than one class of common stock. Ford's 71 million shares of Class B stock are held entirely by Ford family interests and directors and officers of the company. This class has 40 percent of the total voting power. Ford's 3.938 billion shares of common stock are held by the public and have 60 percent of the total voting power. The two classes are otherwise equal.

stock split

Stock Splits If management feels that the firm's common stock should sell at a lower price to attract more purchasers, it can effect a **stock split**. There seems to be a feeling among some in the finance community that the optimum price range for a share of common stock should be roughly $15 to $60. Consequently, if a stock rises above this range, management may decide on a stock split to get the price back to a more desirable trading level.

For example, the per-share price of Nike common stock rose to $125 in 2015, at which time the board of directors declared a two-for-one stock split.

Frequently companies choose to raise their dividend levels at the time of a split. For example, when Nike split its stock two-for-one in 2015, it also increased its quarterly dividend by 14 percent, from $0.28 to $0.32 per share.

Many investors believe stock splits are an indication of good financial health. The mere splitting of a stock, however, should not be taken in and of itself as evidence that the stock will necessarily perform well in the future.

ETHICAL ISSUES

Unequal Voting Rights[a]

Many companies issue two (or more) classes of common stock with different voting rights. Insiders, such as the company founders, often receive common stock with more voting power than the shares held by other investors. It has been estimated that 10 percent or more of all listed companies have at least two classes of stock. The table below illustrates the voting power held by the founders of several public companies.

Company	Controlling Shareholders	Equity Stake (% of Shares)	Voting Power (%)
Dick's Sporting Goods	Edward Stack, others	37.7	85.8
Wm. Wrigley, Jr.[b]	William Wrigley, Jr., others	17.7	68.2
Ford Motor	Ford family & trusts	3.9	40
Comcast	Brian Roberts	0.4	33.3

Corporate governance experts claim that dual classes of stock with unequal voting power is undemocratic since this denies all shareholders voting power that is commensurate with the amount of capital they have at risk. Having shares with supervoting power allows these shareholders to elect directors who can choose policies that benefit this one class of shareholders rather than policies that are in the best interests of the corporation and the other class(es) of common stockholders.

Defenders of the dual class system claim that it protects companies from the stock market's obsession with short-term profits. When Dick's Sporting Goods was taken public by the founding Stack family in 2002, CEO Edward W. Stack received shares having 10 votes per share compared with outsiders' shares having only one vote. As Dick's CFO noted, this system ensures that "decisions are made for the long-term health of the business."

Also, some publishing companies, such as the New York Times Company and Dow Jones & Company (publisher of *The Wall Street Journal* and now part of News Corp.), claim that supervoting stock is needed to protect their editorial independence.

Furthermore, many investors are willing to invest in shares having unequal voting power as long as the company is successful in generating shareholder wealth. Presumably, investors are aware of the positive and negative aspects of dual-class companies. As a spokeswoman for Coors Brewing, a company that had a dual-class system before merging with Molson in 2005, explained, "If you approve of the way the company is managed and run, you buy the shares in the company, and if you don't, you sell them."

How would the existence of two classes of stock having unequal voting power affect your decision to invest in a company?

[a]Amy Borrus and Aaron Bernstein, "One Share, Many Votes," *BusinessWeek* (March 29, 2004): 94–95.
[b]Merged with Mars, Inc., in 2008.

From an accounting standpoint, when a stock is split, its par value is changed accordingly. For example, when the split is two-for-one, the par value is reduced by one-half and the number of shares is doubled. No changes occur in the firm's account balances or capital structure.

reverse stock splits

Reverse Stock Splits

Reverse stock splits are stock splits in which the number of shares is decreased. They are used to bring low-priced shares up to more desirable trading levels. One example was American International Group's (AIG) one-for-twenty reverse stock split in July 2009. After the government bailout of the company in September 2008 (by means of a combination of direct loans and preferred stock investments). AIG's stock price fell to under $2 per share, down from over $100 per share prior to the financial crisis. The reverse stock split raised the price to the $20-per-share range, which the company hoped would attract more institutional investors.

Many investors feel reverse stock splits indicate poor corporate health. For this reason, such splits are relatively uncommon.

stock dividend

Stock Dividends A **stock dividend** is a dividend to stockholders that consists of additional shares of stock instead of cash. Normally, stock dividends are in the 2 to 10 percent range—that is, the number of shares outstanding is increased by 2 to 10 percent. From an accounting (but not a cash flow) standpoint, stock dividends involve a transfer from the retained earnings account to the common stock and additional paid-in capital accounts.[2]

treasury stock

Stock Repurchases From time to time, companies repurchase some of their own shares (known as **treasury stock**). In addition to undertaking share repurchases as an alternative to the payment of cash dividends, which is discussed in Chapter 15, a company may have a number of other reasons for repurchasing its own stock. These include:

- **Disposition of excess cash**. The company may want to dispose of excess cash that it has accumulated from operations or the sale of assets. These funds are expendable because management may not feel that they can be invested profitably within the company in the foreseeable future.
- **Financial restructuring**. By issuing debt and using the proceeds to repurchase its common stock, the firm can alter its capital structure to gain the benefits of increased financial leverage.
- **Future corporate needs**. Stock can be repurchased for use in future acquisitions of other companies, stock option plans for executives, conversion of convertible securities, and the exercise of warrants.[3]
- **Reduction of takeover risk**. Share repurchases can be used to increase the price of a firm's stock and reduce a firm's cash balance (or increase its debt proportion in the capital structure) and thereby reduce returns to investors who might be considering an acquisition of the firm.

These reasons are not mutually exclusive—a firm may repurchase shares for a combination of reasons.

7-2d Advantages and Disadvantages of Common Stock Financing

One of the major advantages of common stock financing is that no fixed-dividend obligation exists, at least in principle. In practice, however, dividend cuts are relatively uncommon for companies paying a "regular" dividend, a fact that implies that corporate management generally views a firm's current level of dividends as a minimum for the future.[4] Nevertheless, common stock financing does allow firms a greater degree of flexibility in their financing plans than fixed-income securities. Thus, common stock is less risky to the firm than fixed-income securities. Limits on additional debt and the maintenance of working capital levels are only two of the constraints imposed on a firm when fixed-income security financing is employed.

In addition, common stock financing can be advantageous for a firm whose capital structure contains more than an optimal amount of debt. Under these circumstances, common stock financing can lower the firm's weighted cost of capital.[5]

From the investors' perspective, however, common stock is a riskier investment than debt securities or preferred stock. Because of this, investors in common stock require relatively high rates of return, and this means that the firm's cost for common stock financing is high compared with fixed-income securities.

---

[2] Chapter 15 contains a more detailed discussion of stock dividends.

[3] Warrants and convertible securities are examined in Chapter 20.

[4] See Chapter 15 for a discussion of dividend policy.

[5] See Chapters 12–14 for a discussion of the measurement of and the effect of capital structure on the firm's weighted cost of capital.

TABLE 7.2

Example of Diluted Per-Share Earnings as a Result of Common Stock Financing: Desert Electric Power Company

	Year Ended September 30	
	2015	2014
Net income available for common stock	$25,821,000	$20,673,000
Average number of common shares outstanding	15,600,000	12,122,007
Earnings per average share of common stock	$1.66	$1.71

From another perspective, external common stock financing frequently results in an initial dilution of per-share earnings, particularly if the assets acquired with the proceeds of the financing do not produce earnings immediately. Table 7.2, which contains figures for Desert Electric Power Company for 2014 and 2015, illustrates this point.

Notice that whereas the firm's net income increased in 2015 over 2014, its earnings per share declined because of the new shares issued. Thus, the additional issue of common shares can dilute the original owners' claims on the firm's earnings. If, on the other hand, the new assets earn a higher rate of return than the existing assets, the original owners will benefit from the increased earnings. Also, the problem of diluted earnings should be only temporary if the firm is investing wisely and should have no adverse consequences in a well-informed market.

A final disadvantage of external equity financing involves the relatively high issuance costs associated with common stock sold to the public.[6]

7-3 The Security Offering Process: Role of the Investment Banker

Investment bankers are financial middlemen who bring together suppliers and users of long-term funds in the capital markets and thereby play a key role in the security offering process. Whenever a large corporation is considering raising funds in the capital markets, it almost always enlists the services of an investment banker. In fact, most large industrial corporations have ongoing relationships with their investment bankers.

investment bankers

Investment bankers assist client corporations in the offering process in a variety of ways, including the following:

- Long-range financial planning
- The timing of security issues
- The purchase of securities
- The marketing of securities
- The arrangement of private loans and leases
- The negotiation of mergers

In summary, the investment banker is an important source of financial market expertise and an important part of the security offering process.

[6]Issuance costs for various sources of capital are discussed in the following sections of this chapter.

7-3a How Securities Are Sold

Firms can sell securities in the primary capital markets in one of three ways:

- By selling securities through investment bankers to the public in a *public cash offering*
- By placing a debt or stock issue with one or more large investors in a *private,* or *direct, placement*
- By selling common stock to existing stockholders through a *rights offering*

Investment bankers usually assist firms in all three methods of sale. Figure 7.2 is a flowchart that outlines the various methods and steps for the sale of corporate securities.

Public Cash Offerings Normally, when a corporation wishes to issue new securities and sell them to the public, it makes an arrangement with an investment banker whereby the investment banker agrees to purchase the entire issue at a set price. This is called a firm commitment **underwriting**. The investment banker then resells the issue to the public at a higher price.

underwriting

Underwriting can be accomplished either through *negotiations* between the underwriter and the issuing company, or by *competitive bidding*. A **negotiated underwriting** is simply an arrangement between the issuing firm and its investment bankers. Most large industrial corporations turn to investment bankers with whom they have had ongoing relationships. In **competitive bidding**, the firm sells the securities to the underwriter (usually a group) that bids the highest price. Many regulated companies, such as utilities and railroads, are required by their regulatory commissions (for example, the Federal Energy Regulatory Commission, the Interstate Commerce Commission, and state regulatory bodies) to sell new security issues in this way.

negotiated underwriting

competitive bidding

Security issues sold to the public through underwriters normally exceed $25 million in size; amounts in the billion-dollar or several hundred million–dollar range (particularly bond issues) are not uncommon. Due to the size of these issues, individual investment bankers usually do not want to underwrite an entire issue by themselves. Normally, a group of underwriters, called a **purchasing syndicate**, agrees to underwrite the issue in order to spread the risk.[7] Sometimes the purchasing syndicate can sell an entire issue to large institutional investors;[8] this is often true with high-quality debt issues. On other occasions—particularly with large debt issues or equity issues—the underwriters organize a *selling group* of security firms to market the issue to the public. It is not uncommon for a selling group responsible for marketing a large issue to number over 100 security firms. Figure 2.2 in Chapter 2 shows the underwriting syndicate for an ARIBA Corporation common stock offering.

purchasing syndicate

An important part of the negotiations between the issuing firm and the investment banker is the determination of the security's selling price. It is in the best interests of both the issuing firm and the underwriter to have the security "fairly priced." If the security is underpriced, the issuing firm will not raise the amount of capital it could have, and the underwriter may lose a customer. If the security is overpriced, the underwriter may have difficulty selling the issue, and investors who discover that they paid too much may choose not to purchase the next issue offered by either the corporation or the underwriter.

Occasionally, with smaller company issues, the investment banker agrees to help market the issue on a "best efforts" basis rather than underwriting it. Under this type of arrangement, the investment banker has no further obligation to the issuing company if

[7]In most cases, one to three underwriters agree to manage an issue, handling all legal matters, advertising, and so on. These firms are the *managing underwriters*.

[8]Institutional investors include life insurance companies, pension funds, mutual funds, and commercial banks.

FIGURE 7.2

How Securities Are Sold: A Flowchart

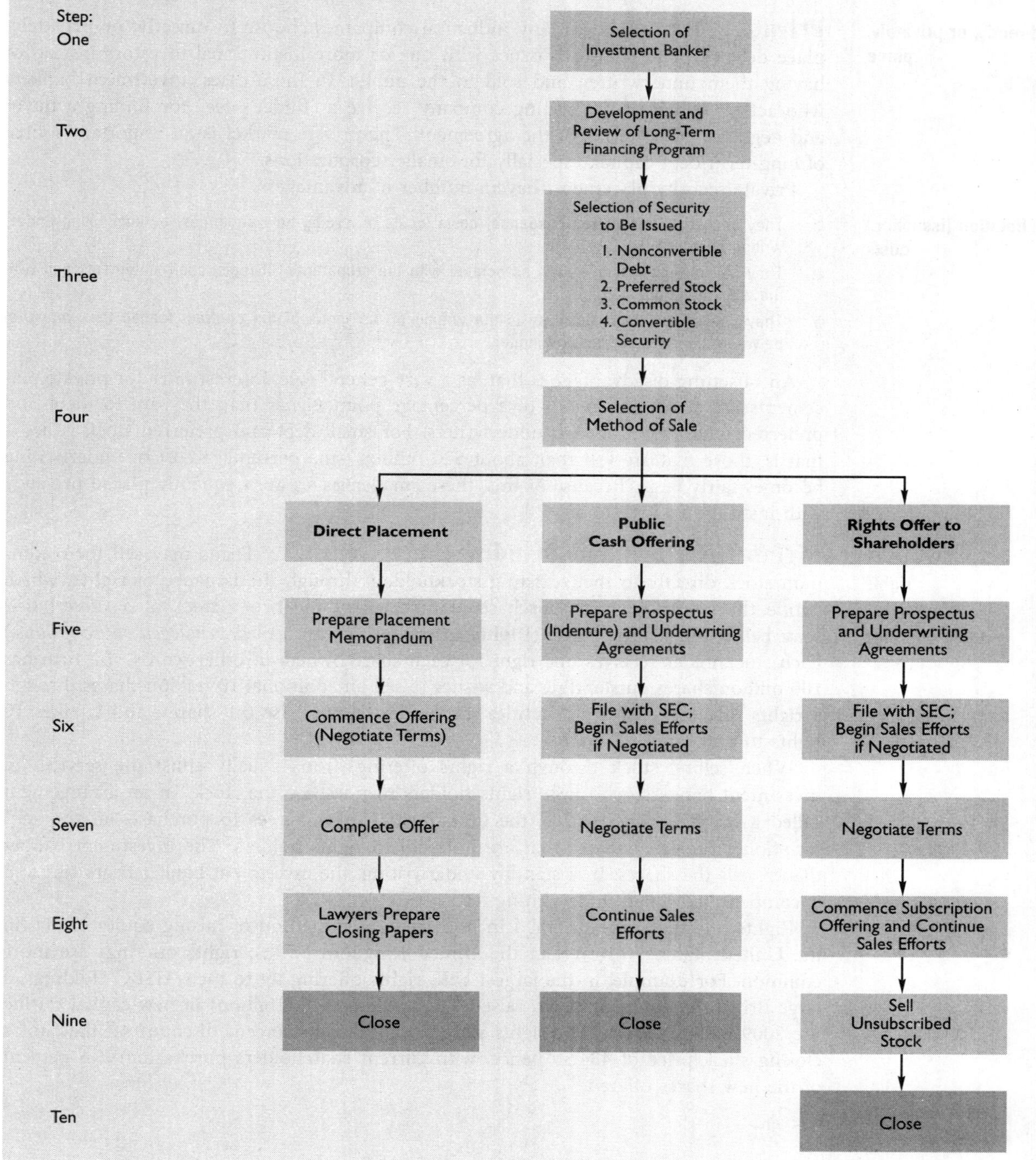

© Cengage Learning

some of the securities cannot be sold. The investment banker functions as a *dealer* in an underwriting situation and as a *broker* in a best-efforts situation. In a best-efforts offering, the investment banker does not assume the risk that the securities will not be sold at a favorable price.

directly, or privately, place

Private Placements

Many industrial companies choose to **directly, or privately, place** debt or preferred stock issues with one or more institutional investors instead of having them underwritten and sold to the public. In these cases, investment bankers who act on behalf of the issuing company receive a "finder's fee" for finding a buyer and negotiating the terms of the agreement. The private market is an important source of long-term debt capital, especially for smaller corporations.

Private security placements have a number of advantages:

flotation (issuance) costs

- They can save on **flotation (issuance) costs** (costs of issuing new securities) by eliminating underwriting costs.
- They can avoid the time delays associated with the preparation of registration statements and with the waiting period.
- They can offer greater flexibility in the writing of the terms of the contract (called the *indenture*) between the borrower and the lender.

An offsetting disadvantage is that, as a very general rule, interest rates for private placements are about one-eighth of a percentage point *higher* than they are for debt and preferred issues sold through underwriters. For small debt and preferred stock issues—that is, those that are less than about $20 million—the percentage cost of underwriting becomes fairly large. Because of this, these smaller issues are frequently placed privately with institutional investors.

rights

rights offerings

Rights Offerings and Standby Underwritings

Firms may sell their common stock directly to their existing stockholders through the issuance of **rights**, which entitle the stockholders to purchase new shares of the firm's stock at a *subscription price* below the market price. (**Rights offerings** also are called *privileged subscriptions.*) Each stockholder receives one right for each share owned; in other words, if a firm has 100 million shares outstanding and wishes to sell an additional 10 million shares through a rights offering, each right entitles the holder to purchase 0.1 shares, and it takes 10 rights to purchase one share.[9]

When selling stock through a rights offering, firms usually enlist the services of investment bankers, who urge rights holders to purchase the stock. In an arrangement called a *standby underwriting*, the investment banker agrees to purchase—at the subscription price—any shares that are not sold to rights holders. The investment banker then resells the shares. In a standby underwriting, the investment banker bears risk and is compensated by an underwriting fee.

Rights offerings have declined in popularity as a method of raising equity capital in the United States. However, in the United Kingdom (U.K.), rights offerings are more common. For example, in the largest U.K. rights offering up to then, HSBC Holdings, a large British banking company, raised £12.5 billion ($18.5 billion) in new capital during the 2009 banking crisis. The rights were priced at a 40 percent discount off the bank's closing stock price of 434.50 pence, with current shareholders purchasing 96.6 percent of the new shares offered.[10]

---

[9] Rights and rights offerings are discussed in greater detail in Chapter 20.

[10] "HSBC Raises $18.5 Billion in Massive Rights Issue," *The Wall Street Journal* (April 6, 2009): C1.

underwriting spread

Direct Issuance Costs

An investment banker who agrees to underwrite a security issue assumes a certain amount of risk and, in turn, requires compensation in the form of an *underwriting discount* or **underwriting spread**, computed as follows:

$$\text{Underwriting spread} = \text{Selling price to public} - \text{Proceeds to company} \tag{7.3}$$

Examples of underwriting spread amounts are shown in Table 7.3.

It is difficult to compare underwriting spreads for negotiated and competitive offerings because rarely are two offerings brought to market at the same time that differ only in the ways in which they are underwritten. Generally, underwriters receive lower spreads for competitively bid utility issues than for negotiated industrial offers. This is primarily because utilities tend to have a lower level of risk than industrial companies.

In addition to the underwriting spread, other direct costs of security offerings include legal and accounting fees, taxes, the cost of registration with the Securities and Exchange Commission, and printing costs. For small equity offerings of less than $10 million, these direct costs may exceed 10 percent of the gross proceeds from the offering, on average. For offerings with gross proceeds in the $20 million to $50 million range, direct costs averaged slightly less than 5 percent of gross proceeds. For large equity offerings (greater than $200 million), the direct issuance costs have averaged about 3.3 percent of gross proceeds.[11] An offering of 1.35 million shares of common equity by Service Corporation International had an underwriting spread of $2,160,000 and other direct issue expenses of $280,564. Direct costs of underwritten debt offerings are much lower than direct equity issuance costs, often ranging from 0.5 percent to 4.0 percent.

Generally, direct issuance costs are higher for common stock than for preferred stock issues, and direct issuance costs of preferred stock are higher than those of debt issues.

TABLE 7.3

Sample Underwriting Spreads for Selected Issues

Company	Issue Size (in Millions) of Dollars	Underwriting Spread (%)	S&P Rating*
Debt Issues			
First Interstate Bancorp.	$100	0.63	AA
CIGNA Corporation**	100	1.00	AA
Corning Glass Works**	100	1.00	A
U.S. Leasing International**	30	2.00	BBB
Jerrico, Inc.	40	1.88	BB
Petro-Lewis	85	3.35	B
Sunshine Mining Company	30	3.68	B
Common Stock Issues			
El Paso Electric Company	$ 57.5	3.26	
Ryder System, Inc.	83.4	3.88	
Southwest Airlines	34.7	3.89	
Service Corporation International	48.26	4.48	
Adage, Inc.	10.0	6.26	
Atlantic Southeast Airlines	5.2	8.00	

*Standard & Poor's (S&P) bond-rating scale is AAA (for the highest quality issues), AA, A, BBB, BB, B, CCC, CC, C.

**Convertible issues.

[11] Robert Hansen, "Evaluating the Costs of a New Equity Issue," *Midland Corporate Finance Journal* (Spring 1986): 42–55.

One reason for this is the amount of risk each type of issue involves. Common stocks usually involve more risk for underwriters than preferred stock, and preferred stock involves more risk than debt. Stock prices are subject to wider price movements than debt prices. Another reason for these differences in direct issuance costs is that investment bankers usually incur greater marketing expenses for common stock than for preferred stock or debt issues. Common stock is customarily sold to a large number of individual investors, whereas debt securities are frequently purchased by a much smaller number of institutional investors.

Direct issuance costs also depend on the quality of the issue. Low-quality debt issues, for example, tend to have higher percentage direct issuance costs than high-quality issues because underwriters bear more risk with low-quality issues and therefore require greater compensation. And finally, direct issuance costs are dependent on the size of the issue—costs tend to be a higher percentage of small issues, all other things being equal, because underwriters have various fixed expenses (such as advertising expenses, legal fees, registration statement costs, and so on) that are incurred regardless of the issue's size.

Other Issuance Costs In addition to direct costs, there are significant other costs associated with new security offerings, including:

1. The *cost of management time* in preparing the offering.
2. The *cost of underpricing* a new (initial) equity offering below the correct market value. Underpricing occurs because of the uncertainty associated with the value of initial public offerings and a desire to ensure that the offering is a success. For example, the initial public offering for LinkedIn, a business networking Web site, in May 2011 was priced at $45 per share. During the first day of trading, the share price reached a high of $122, before closing at $94—a gain of 109 percent. Examples such as this and many Internet company stocks in the late 1990s are extreme, although not uncommon, examples of the underpricing associated with many initial public offerings.
3. The *cost of stock price declines* for stock offerings by firms whose shares are already outstanding—so-called seasoned offerings. The announcement of new stock issues by a firm whose shares are already outstanding causes a price decline averaging about 3 percent for the outstanding shares.
4. The *cost of other incentives* provided to the investment banker, including the over-allotment or "Green Shoe" option. This option, often contained in underwriting contracts, gives the investment bankers the right to buy up to 15 percent more new shares than the initial offering amount at a price equal to the offering price. The option is designed to allow investment bankers to handle oversubscriptions. This option normally lasts for 30 days.

These indirect costs can, in aggregate, constitute a very significant expense associated with security offerings (especially for common equity). Ritter has estimated that the sum of direct issue costs and underpricing for new equity offerings averages over 31 percent for best-efforts offerings and over 21 percent for firm commitment underwritings.[12]

Registration Requirements The Securities Act of 1933 requires any firm offering *new* securities to the public to make a complete disclosure of all pertinent facts regarding these securities; the Securities Exchange Act of 1934 expanded the coverage to include trading in *existing* securities. The 1934 act also created the Securities and Exchange Commission (SEC), which is responsible for administering federal securities

[12]See J. R. Ritter, "The Costs of Going Public," *Journal of Financial Economics* (December 1987): 269–281.

legislation. These federal laws make no judgments regarding the quality of securities issues; they simply require full disclosure of the facts.[13]

Any company that plans to sell an interstate security issue totaling over $1.5 million and having a maturity greater than 270 days is required to register the issue with the SEC.[14] The procedure involves the preparation of a *registration statement* and a **prospectus**. The registration statement contains a vast amount of information about the company's legal, operational, and financial position; the prospectus summarizes the information contained in the registration statement and is intended for the use of potential investors.

prospectus

After a company has filed a registration statement and prospectus, there is normally a waiting period of 20 days before the SEC approves the issue and the company can begin selling the securities. During the waiting period, the company may use a preliminary prospectus in connection with the anticipated sale of securities. This preliminary prospectus is often called a "red herring" because it contains a statement, usually marked in red, saying that the prospectus is "not an offer to sell." When the registration statement is approved by the SEC, the new securities can be formally offered for sale. All buyers of the new securities must be provided with a final copy of the prospectus.

Shelf Registration In November 1983, the SEC permanently adopted a new registration option that it had allowed experimentally for the preceding one-and-a-half years. Rule 415 permits the *shelf registration* of debt and equity securities. The shelf registration option is available only to larger firms (the market value of outstanding equity must exceed $150 million) with a high (*investment grade*) rating. Under the shelf registration procedure, a firm files a *master registration* statement with the SEC. The company is then free to sell small increments of the offering over an extended time period (two years) merely by filing a brief *short-form statement* with the SEC only hours before the actual offering. By placing its new securities "on the shelf" awaiting an opportune time for issuance, the company has the capability to time their issuance with the specific financing needs of the firm and to take advantage of perceived favorable pricing windows in the market. There is some evidence that the shelf registration procedure is less costly than traditional underwriting for equity offerings.[15] In spite of this apparent cost advantage, shelf registrations of new equity offerings have not been popular.

7-4 Valuation of Common Stock

III

Foundation Concept

In principle, the valuation of common stock is no different from the valuation of other types of securities, such as bonds and preferred stock. The basic procedure involves capitalizing (that is, discounting) the expected stream of cash flows to be received from holding the common stock. This is complicated by several factors, however.

First, the expected cash flows from holding a common stock take two forms: the cash dividend payments made during the holding period, and/or changes in the price of the

[13] In recent years, some states have prohibited the sale of certain securities on the grounds of poor quality rather than because of any problems associated with the disclosure of information.

[14] Security issues of the federal government and nonprofit organizations do not have to be registered with the SEC. Bank and railroad issues are also exempt because these industries are regulated by other government agencies.

[15] S. Bhagat, M. W. Marr, and G. R. Thompson, "The Rule 415 Experiment: Equity Markets," *Journal of Finance* (December 1985): 1385–1401.

stock (capital gains or losses) over the holding period. All the cash flows received by the common stockholder are derived from the firm's earnings and can be either paid to shareholders in the current period as cash dividends or reinvested in the firm to (it is hoped) provide higher future dividends and a higher stock price.

Second, because common stock dividends are normally expected to grow rather than remain constant, the relatively simple annuity and perpetuity formulas used in the valuation of bonds and preferred stock are generally not applicable, and more complicated models must be used.

Finally, the expected cash flows from common stock are more uncertain than the cash flows from bonds and preferred stock. Common stock dividend payments are related to the firm's earnings in some manner, and it can be difficult to forecast future long-term earnings and dividend payments with a high degree of accuracy.

capitalization of cash flow valuation method

To better understand the application of the **capitalization of cash flow valuation method** to common stock, it is best to begin by considering a *one*-period dividend valuation model and then move on to consider multiple-period valuation models.

7-4a One-Period Dividend Valuation Model

Assume that an investor plans to purchase a common stock and hold it for *one* period. At the end of that period, the investor expects to receive a cash dividend, D_1, and to sell the stock for a price, P_1. What is the value of this stock to the investor today (time 0), given a required rate of return on the investment, k_e?

In the capitalization of cash flow valuation method, the discounted present value of the expected cash flows from the stock is calculated as follows:

$$P_0 = \frac{D_1}{1 + k_e} + \frac{P_1}{1 + k_e} \tag{7.4}$$

INTERNATIONAL ISSUES

Global Equity Markets

Large multinational corporations have increasingly been turning to international markets to raise both equity and debt capital. Large, non-U.S.-domiciled corporations may sell equity in the United States because of the size and liquidity of the market for new issues in this country. For example, Unilever NV, a Dutch company (marketer of such brands as Skippy, Lipton, Dove, and Q-tips), has its stock listed on both the New York and Amsterdam exchanges. By listing its stock in multiple country capital markets, Unilever NV hoped to reach more potential investors and perhaps realize some capital cost savings.

By dealing in global equity markets, multinational firms can take advantage of institutional differences from one country to another that may temporarily disadvantage a firm that is limited to selling its shares in a single capital market. Many multinational firms now have their shares trading in the United States, Japan, and Western European markets such as London and Paris. The existence of these markets permits nearly 24-hour-per-day trading in the stock of large multinational firms. Around-the-clock trading provides investors with opportunities to buy and sell shares at almost any time they wish. In addition, multinational firms can increase their name and product recognition abroad, to the benefit, it is hoped, of the firm's bottom-line performance.

As a truly global capital market emerges, it is clear that national borders will be less important in determining where, and in what form, capital will be acquired by a firm. Rather, firms can be expected to sell their shares in those markets with the greatest demand (and hence the lowest cost to the firm).

Calculator Solutions[a]

Key	Enter
n	1.0
i	14.0
PV	
PMT	
FV	–28.50
	Solution
PV	25.00

For example, if Ohio Engineering Company common stock is expected to pay a \$1.00 dividend and sell for \$27.50 at the end of one period, what is the value of this stock to an investor who requires a 14 percent rate of return? The answer is computed as follows:

$$\begin{aligned} P_0 &= \frac{\$1.00}{(1+0.14)} + \frac{\$27.50}{(1+0.14)} \\ &= \$1.00(\text{PVIF}_{0.14,1}) + \$27.50(\text{PVIF}_{0.14,1}) \\ &= \$1.00(0.877) + \$27.50(0.877) \\ &= \$24.99(\text{or } \$25) \end{aligned}$$

Thus, the investor who purchases the stock for \$25, collects the \$1 dividend, and sells the stock for \$27.50 at the end of one period will earn the 14 percent required rate of return.

7-4b Multiple-Period Dividend Valuation Model

The dividend valuation process just described can be generalized to a multiple-period case. The expected cash flows to the investor who purchases a share of common stock and holds it for n periods consist of dividend payments during each of the next n periods (D_1, D_2, …, D_n) plus an amount, P_n, from the sale of the stock at the end of the nth period. Capitalizing these expected cash flows at the investor's required rate of return, k_e, gives the following valuation equation:

$$P_0 = \frac{D_1}{(1+k_e)^1} + \frac{D_2}{(1+k_e)^2} + \cdots + \frac{D_n}{(1+k_e)^n} + \frac{P_n}{(1+k_e)^n} \tag{7.5}$$

Consider again the Ohio Engineering Company common stock. Suppose that the investor is considering purchasing a share of this stock and holding it for five years. Assume that the investor's required rate of return is still 14 percent. Dividends from the stock are expected to be \$1 in the first year, \$1 in the second year, \$1 in the third year, \$1.25 in the fourth year, and \$1.25 in the fifth year. The expected selling price of the stock at the end of 5 years is \$41.

Using Equation 7.5 and the appropriate present value interest factors (PVIFs), the value of the stock to the investor is computed as follows:

Calculator Solutions[b]

Key	Enter
i	14.0
CF_1	1.00
CF_2	1.00
CF_3	1.00
CF_4	1.25
CF_5	42.25
NPV	
	Solution
NPV	25.00

$$\begin{aligned} P_0 &= \$1.00(\text{PVIF}_{0.14,1}) + \$1.00(\text{PVIF}_{0.14,2}) \\ &\quad + \$1.00(\text{PVIF}_{0.14,3}) + \$1.25(\text{PVIF}_{0.14,4}) \\ &\quad + \$1.25(\text{PVIF}_{0.14,5}) + \$41.00(\text{PVIF}_{0.14,5}) \\ &= \$1.00(0.877) + \$1.00(0.769) + \$1.00(0.675) \\ &\quad + \$1.25(0.592) + \$1.25(0.519) + \$41.00(0.519) \\ &= \$24.99(\text{or } \$25) \end{aligned}$$

Note that the *current* value of a share of Ohio Engineering common stock is the same (that is, $P_0 = \$25.00$) regardless of whether the investor plans to hold it for one, five, or any other number of years.[16]

7-4c A General Dividend Valuation Model

In each of the valuation models described, the current value of the stock, P_0, is dependent upon the expected price of the stock at the end of the expected holding period.

[a]The FV amount of \$28.50 is equal to the sum of the dividend at the end of year 1 and the stock price at the end of year 1.

[b]To solve this problem with the aid of your calculator, it is necessary to use the cash flow function/keys (CF) on your calculator.

[16]The value of a stock at *any* point in time is simply the present value of all dividends expected to be paid from that time forward. Hence, the price P_5 of \$41 reflects the present value of dividends expected in years 6 through infinity.

Although this seems straightforward, providing accurate forecasts of stock prices when applying the models to specific stocks can be difficult. A final generalization permits the elimination of P_n from the model while showing that the dividend valuation models discussed are consistent with one another.

First, the value of the stock at the end of the nth period, P_n, must be redefined. Using the capitalization of cash flow approach, it can be shown that P_n is a function of all expected *future* dividends that the investor will receive in periods $n + 1$, $n + 2$, and so on. Discounting the stream of dividends at the required rate of return, k_e, gives the value of the stock at the end of the nth period:

(7.6)
$$P_n = \sum_{t=n+1}^{\infty} \frac{D_t}{(1 + k_e)^{t-n}}$$

Substituting Equation 7.6 into Equation 7.5 and simplifying yields the following *general dividend valuation model*:

(7.7)
$$P_0 = \sum_{t=1}^{\infty} \frac{D_t}{(1 + k_e)^{t}}$$

HTTP:
Click on the Investment Analysis Calculator at
www.cengage.com/finance/moyer
for an interactive financial calculator for common stock valuation.

Thus, *the value of a firm's common stock to the investor is equal to the discounted present value of the expected future dividend stream.* As was shown, the valuation of a firm's common stock given by the multiple-period model (Equation 7.5) is equivalent to the valuation given by the general model (Equation 7.7). The general dividend valuation model is applicable regardless of whether the stream of dividends over time is fluctuating or constant, increasing or decreasing.

Note that the general dividend valuation model treats the stream of dividends as a *perpetuity* having no finite termination date. Whereas this assumption is reasonable for firms that are going concerns, shorter time horizons must be used when considering firms that might be either acquired by other firms or liquidated in the foreseeable future.

Some rapidly growing firms (such as Salesforce.com and Amazon.com) reinvest all their earnings and do not pay current cash dividends. In fact, some profitable firms have *never* paid cash dividends for as long as they have been in existence and are not expected to do so in the near future. How can the general dividend valuation model be applied to the common stock of a firm such as this? It must be assumed that the firm will be able to start making regular, periodic cash dividend payments to its shareholders *at some time in the future.* Or, these returns could consist of the *proceeds from the sale of the firm's outstanding common stock,* should the firm be acquired by another company, or a final liquidating dividend (distribution), should the firm be liquidated.

As stated in Chapter 1, the primary goal of firms should be the *maximization of shareholder wealth* The general dividend valuation model (Equation 7.7) indicates that

shareholder wealth

shareholder wealth, as measured by the value of the firm's common stock, P_0, is a function of the expected stream of future dividend payments and the investor's required rate of return. Thus, when making financial decisions that are consistent with the goal of maximizing shareholder wealth, management should be concerned with how these decisions affect both the expected future dividend stream and the discount rate that investors apply to the dividend stream. The relationship between financial decision making and shareholder wealth is illustrated in Figure 7.3. A primary emphasis of the financial management function is attempting to define and measure this relationship.

FIGURE 7.3
Relationship Between Financial Decisions and Shareholder Wealth

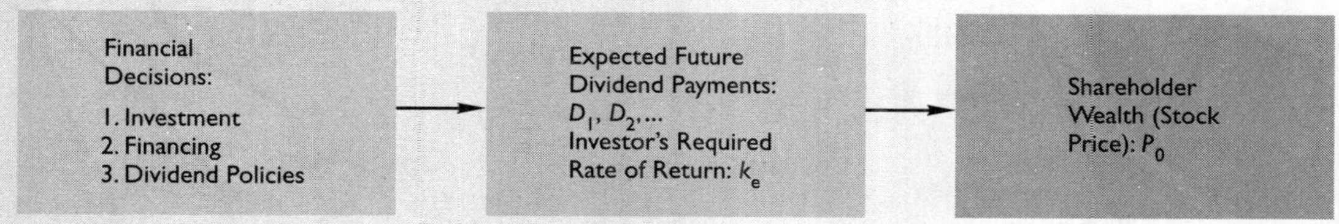

7-5 Applications of the General Dividend Valuation Model

The general dividend valuation model can be simplified if a firm's dividend payments over time are expected to follow one of several different patterns, including *zero growth*, *constant growth*, and *nonconstant growth*.

7-5a Zero Growth Dividend Valuation Model

If a firm's future dividend payments are expected to remain constant *forever*, then D_t in Equation 7.7, the general dividend valuation model, can be replaced by a constant value D to yield the following:

(7.8)
$$P_0 = \sum_{t=1}^{\infty} \frac{D}{(1 + k_e)^t}$$

This equation represents the value of a perpetuity and is analogous to those used for valuing a perpetual bond (Equation 6.7) and a preferred stock (Equation 6.11) developed in the previous chapter. It can be simplified to obtain:

(7.9)
$$P_0 = \frac{D}{k_e}$$

This model is valid only when a firm's dividend payments are expected to remain constant *forever*. Although few common stocks strictly satisfy these conditions, the model can still be used to approximate the value of a stock for which dividend payments are expected to remain constant for a relatively long period into the future. Figure 7.4 shows a zero growth dividend payment pattern.

To illustrate the zero growth dividend valuation model, assume that the Mountaineer Railroad common stock pays an annual dividend of \$1.50 per share, which is expected to remain constant for the foreseeable future. What is the value of the stock to an investor who requires a 12 percent rate of return? Substituting \$1.50 for D and 12 percent (0.12) for k_e in Equation 7.9 yields the following:

$$P_0 = \frac{\$1.50}{0.12} = \$12.50$$

FIGURE 7.4

Dividend Growth Patterns

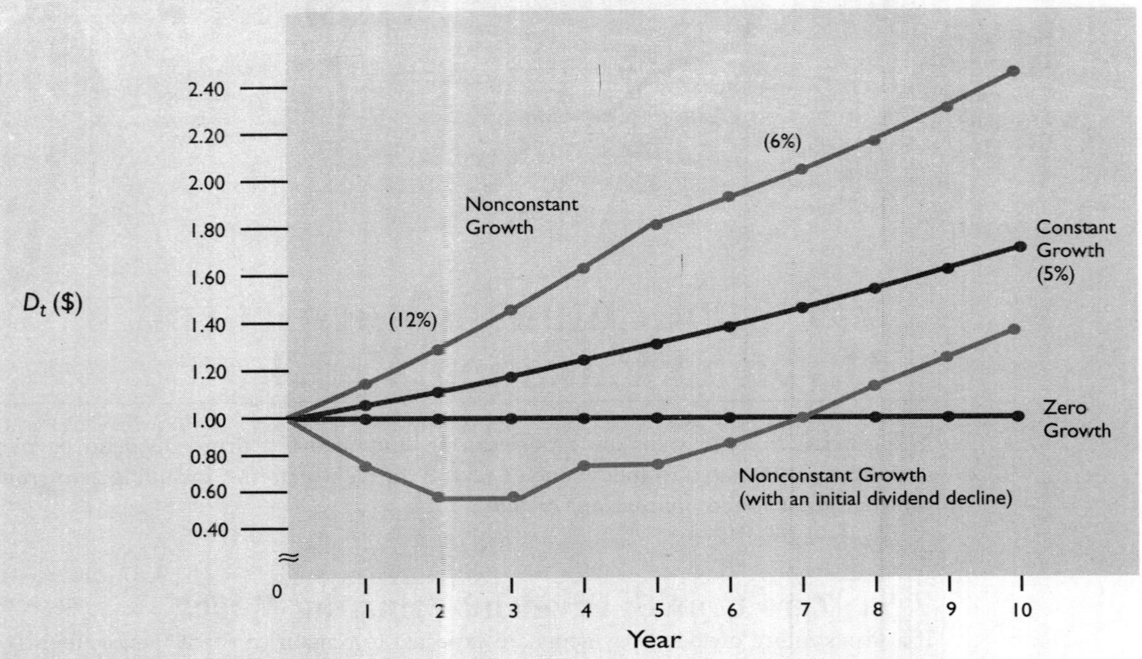

7-5b Constant Growth Dividend Valuation Model

If a firm's future dividend payments per share are expected to grow at a *constant rate*, *g*, per period forever, then the dividend at any future time period *t* can be forecast as follows:

(7.10)
$$D_t = D_0(1 + g)^t$$

where D_0 is the dividend in the current period ($t = 0$). The expected dividend in period 1 is $D_1 = D_0(1 + g)^1$, the expected dividend in period 2 is $D_2 = D_0(1 + g)^2$, and so on. The constant-growth curve in Figure 7.4 illustrates such a dividend pattern.

Substituting Equation 7.10 for D_t in the general dividend valuation model (Equation 7.7) yields the following:

(7.11)
$$P_0 = \sum_{t=1}^{\infty} \frac{D_0(1 + g)^t}{(1 + k_e)^t}$$

Assuming that the required rate of return, k_e, is greater than the dividend growth rate,[17] *g*, Equation 7.11 can be transformed algebraically to obtain the following simplified common stock valuation model:[18]

[17]If this assumption is not satisfied—that is, if the growth rate (g) is greater than or equal to the required rate of return (k_e)—then the market price (P_0) would be infinite.

[18]Equation 7.12 is often referred to in finance literature as the *Gordon model*, for Myron J. Gordon, who pioneered its use. See Myron J. Gordon, *The Investment, Financing, and Valuation of the Corporation* (Homewood, IL: Irwin, 1962).

(7.12)
$$P_0 = \frac{D_1}{k_e - g}$$

Note that in the constant growth valuation model (Equation 7.12), the dividend value in the numerator is D_1, that is, the dividend expected to be received one year from now. The model assumes that D_0, the current dividend, has just been paid and does not enter the (forward-looking) valuation process.

The constant growth valuation model (Equation 7.12) assumes that a firm's *earnings, dividends, and stock price are expected to grow at a constant rate, g, into the future.* Hence, to apply this model to a specific common stock, it is necessary to estimate the expected future growth rate, g. Considerable research evidence indicates that (1) the most accurate estimates of future growth are those provided by security analysts and (2) consensus analyst forecasts of growth are an excellent proxy for growth expectations of investors. Sources of analyst growth rate forecasts include:

1. *Value Line Investment Survey.* Value Line reports, even though they represent only one analyst's forecast for each company, are available online and at most public and university libraries and have been shown to be reasonably accurate and closely related to investor expectations.
2. *Zacks Earnings Estimates.* This provides summaries of long-term (five years) and short-term earnings growth expectations from more than 2,100 analysts covering more than 3,500 companies. Forecasts from Zacks are available online.
3. *Thomson Reuters.* This service is similar to that of Zacks and also can be accessed through the Internet.

HTTP:
Value Line can be accessed at
www.valueline.com
Zacks Investment Research can be accessed at
www.zacks.com
Thomson Reuters can be accessed at
www.thomsonreuters.com/products_services/financial

To illustrate the application of the constant growth valuation model, consider Eaton Corporation. Dividends for Eaton are expected to be \$2.20 per share *next year.* Suppose that earnings and dividends are expected to grow at about 7.5 percent annually. To determine the value of a share of this stock to an investor who requires a 10 percent rate of return, substitute \$2.20 for D_1, 7.5 percent (0.075) for g, and 10 percent (0.10) for k_e in Equation 7.12, which yields the following value for a share of Eaton's common stock:

$$P_0 = \frac{\$2.20}{0.10 - 0.075}$$
$$= \$88.00$$

The constant growth dividend valuation model can be used to illustrate the two forms of returns an investor can expect to receive from holding a common stock. Solving Equation 7.12 for k_e yields the following:

(7.13)
$$k_e = \frac{D_1}{P_0} + g$$

required rate of return

The investor's **required rate of return** is equal to the expected dividend yield, D_1/P_0, plus the price appreciation yield, g—the expected increase in dividends and, ultimately, in the price of the stock.

Thus, in the Eaton Corporation example, the investor's 10 percent required return, k_e, consists of a 2.5 percent dividend yield ($D_1/P_0 = \$2.20/\$88$) plus a growth return ($g$) of 7.5 percent annually.

The constant growth dividend valuation model will be encountered again in the discussion of the firm's cost of capital in Chapter 12.

7-5c Nonconstant Growth Dividend Valuation Model

Many firms experience growth rates in sales, earnings, and dividends that are *not* constant. Typically, many firms experience a period of above-normal growth as they exploit new technologies, new markets, or both; this generally occurs relatively early in a firm's life cycle. Following this period of rapid growth, earnings and dividends tend to stabilize or grow at a more normal rate comparable to the overall average rate of growth in the economy. The reduction in the growth rate occurs as the firm reaches maturity and has fewer sizable growth opportunities. The upper curve in Figure 7.4 illustrates a nonconstant growth pattern.[19]

Nonconstant growth models can also be applied to the valuation of firms that are experiencing temporary periods of poor performance, after which a normal pattern of growth is expected to emerge. (The lower nonconstant growth line in Figure 7.4 illustrates this type of pattern.) For example, during 1992 IBM paid a dividend of $1.21 per share. This dividend was cut to $0.40 in 1993 and to $0.25 in 1994. As IBM's restructuring efforts progressed, earnings and dividend growth resumed. Dividends in 1996 grew to $0.33 and continued growing each year, reaching $5.00 in 2015. An investor attempting to value IBM's stock at the beginning of 1993 should have reflected the declining-then-increasing pattern of dividend growth for the firm.

There is no single model or equation that can be applied when nonconstant growth is anticipated. In general the value of a stock that is expected to experience a nonconstant growth rate pattern of dividends is equal to the present value of expected yearly dividends during the period of nonconstant growth plus the present value of the expected stock price at the end of the nonconstant growth period, or:

(7.14)
$$P_0 = \begin{array}{c}\text{Present value of expected}\\ \text{dividends during period of}\\ \text{nonconstant growth}\end{array} + \begin{array}{c}\text{Present value of the expected}\\ \text{stock price at the end of the}\\ \text{nonconstant growth period}\end{array}$$

The stock price at the end of a nonconstant growth rate period can be estimated in a number of ways:

1. Security analysts such as *Value Line* provide an estimated (five-year) future price range for the stocks they follow.
2. *Value Line*, *Zacks*, and *Thomson Reuters* all provide earnings growth rate estimates for five years into the future. These growth rate estimates can be used to derive earnings per share (EPS) forecasts for five years in the future. The EPS forecasts can be multiplied by the expected price-to-earnings (P/E) multiple, estimated by looking at current P/E multiples for similar firms, to get an expected price in five years.
3. At the end of the period of nonconstant growth, an estimate of the value of the stock can be derived by applying the constant growth rate valuation model (Equation 7.12). For example, consider a firm expected to experience dividend growth at a nonconstant rate for m periods. Beginning in period $m + 1$, dividends are expected to grow at rate g_2 forever. The value of the stock, P_m, at the end of period m is equal to:

(7.15)
$$P_m = \frac{D_{m+1}}{k_e - g_2}$$

To demonstrate how this model works, suppose an investor expects the earnings and common stock dividends of HILO Electronics to grow at a rate of 12 percent per annum for the next five years. Following the period of above-normal growth, dividends are expected to grow at the slower rate of 6 percent for the foreseeable future. The firm

[19]The transition between the periods of above-normal and normal, or average, growth is usually not as pronounced as Figure 7.4 indicates. Typically, a firm's growth rate *declines gradually* over time from the above-normal rate to the normal rate. Growth models similar to Equation 7.14 can be developed to handle cases like this.

ENTREPRENEURIAL ISSUES

Valuation of Closely Held Firms

The ownership of many small firms is closely held. An active market for shares of closely held companies normally does not exist. As a result, entrepreneurs occasionally need to have the value of their enterprises estimated by independent appraisers. The reasons for these valuations include mergers and acquisitions, divestitures and liquidations, initial public offerings, estate and gift tax returns, leveraged buyouts, recapitalizations, employee stock ownership plans, divorce settlements, estate valuation, and various other litigation matters.

The principles of valuation developed in this chapter and applied to large publicly traded firms also apply to the valuation of small firms. Small firm valuation poses several unique challenges. When valuing the shares of a closely held corporation, many factors are considered, including the nature and history of the business, the general economic outlook and the condition and outlook of the firm's industry, earnings capacity, dividend paying capacity, the book value of the company, the company's financial condition, whether the shares represent a majority or minority (less than 50 percent) interest, and whether the stock is voting or nonvoting.

Specifically, however, in valuing a company that sells products and services, earnings capacity is usually the most important factor to be considered. Typically, the company as a whole is valued by determining a normal earnings level and multiplying that figure by an appropriate price/earnings multiple. This approach is known as the "capitalization of earnings" approach and results in a "going concern value." If the shares represent a minority interest in the corporation, a discount is taken for the lack of marketability of these shares.

Determination of Normal Earnings

The determination of an average, or "normal," earnings figure usually involves either a simple average or some type of weighted average of roughly the last five years of operations. For example, if the earnings of the company have been growing, some type of weighted average figure that places greater emphasis on more recent results is often used.

In some cases, the reported earnings of the company may not be an appropriate figure for valuation purposes. For example, suppose a portion of the salary paid to the president (and principal stockholder) really constitutes dividends paid as salary to avoid the payment of income taxes. In this situation, it is appropriate to adjust the reported earnings to account for these dividends.

Determination of an Appropriate Price–Earnings Multiple

The next step in the valuation process is to determine an appropriate rate at which to capitalize the normal earnings level. This is equivalent to multiplying the earnings by a price/earnings multiple. Had there been recent arms-length transactions in the stock, the price/earnings multiple would be known and observable in the financial marketplace. However, this situation rarely exists for closely held corporations. As a consequence, the analyst must examine the price/earnings multiple for widely held companies in the same industry as the firm being valued in an attempt to find firms that are similar to the firm of interest. The price/earnings multiple for these comparable firms is used to capitalize the normal earnings level.

Minority Interest Discount

The owner of a minority interest in a closely held corporation has an investment that lacks control and often marketability. There is usually either no market for the shares, or the only buyer is either the other owners or the corporation itself. In addition, the owner of minority interest shares generally receives little, if any, dividends. The minority interest shareholder lacks control and is not able to change his or her inferior position. As a result of these problems, it is a widely practiced and accepted principle of valuation that the value of minority interest shares should be discounted.

The usual procedure in valuing minority interest shares is to value the corporation as a whole. Next, this value is divided by the number of shares outstanding to obtain a per-share value. Finally, a discount is applied to this per-share value to obtain the minority interest share value. These discounts have ranged from a low of 6 percent to more than 50 percent.[a]

In conclusion, the basic valuation concepts are the same for small and large firms. However, the lack of marketability of shares for many small firms and the problem of minority interest positions pose special problems for the analyst.

[a]See George S. Arneson, "Minority Discounts Beyond Fifty Percent Can Be Supported," *Taxes: The Tax Magazine* (February 1981): 97–102; and Ruth R. Longenecker, "A Practical Guide to Valuation of Closely Held Stock," *Trusts and Estates* (January 1983): 32–41.

TABLE 7.4

Value of HILO Electronics Common Stock

Year, t	Dividend $D_t = \$2.00(1 + 0.12)^t$	Present Value Interest Factor, $PVIF_{0.15,\ t}$	Present Value, D_t
Present Value of First 5 Years' Dividends			
1	$\$2.00(1 + 0.12)^1 = \$2.24$	0.870	\$1.95
2	$2.00(1 + 0.12)^2 = 2.51$	0.756	\$1.90
3	$2.00(1 + 0.12)^3 = 2.81$	0.658	\$1.85
4	$2.00(1 + 0.12)^4 = 3.15$	0.572	\$1.80
5	$2.00(1 + 0.12)^5 = 3.53$	0.497	\$1.75
			\$9.25

Value of Stock at End of Year 5, $P_5 = \dfrac{D_6}{k_e - g_2}$

$$P_5 = \frac{D_6}{0.15 - 0.06}$$

$$D_6 = D_5(1 + g_2) = \$3.53(1 + 0.06) = \$3.74$$

$$P_5 = \frac{\$3.74}{0.15 - 0.06} = \$41.56$$

Present Value of P_5, $PV(P_5) = \dfrac{P_5}{(1 + k_e)^5} = \dfrac{\$41.56}{(1 + 0.15)^5} = \$41.56(PVIF_{0.15,\,5}) = \$41.56(0.497) = \$20.66$

Value of Common Stock, $P_0 = PV\text{(first 5 years' dividends)} + PV(P_5)$

$$P_0 = \$9.25 + \$20.66 = \$29.91$$

currently pays a dividend, D_0, of \$2 per share. What is the value of HILO common stock to an investor who requires a 15 percent rate of return?

Table 7.4 illustrates the step-by-step solution to this problem. First, compute the sum of the present values of the dividends received during the nonconstant growth period (years 1 through 5 in this problem). This equals \$9.25. Second, use the constant growth model to determine the value of HILO common stock at the end of year 5; P_5 equals \$41.56. Next, determine the present value of P_5, which is \$20.66. Finally, add the present value of the dividends received during the first five years (\$9.25) to the present value of P_5 (\$20.66) to obtain the total value of the common stock of \$29.91 per share. A timeline showing the expected cash flows from the purchase of HILO common stock is given in Figure 7.5.

FIGURE 7.5

Cash Flows from HILO Electronics Common Stock

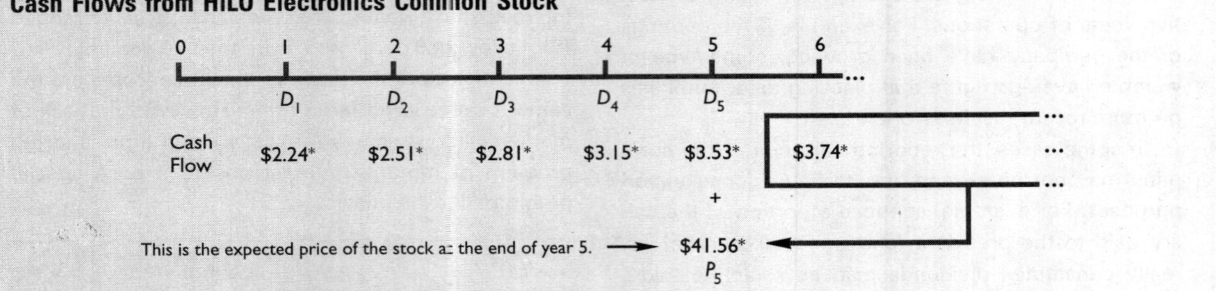

*Values as computed in Table 7.5.

7-6 Summary

- The common stockholders are the true owners of the firm; thus, common stock is a permanent form of financing. Common stockholders participate in the firm's earnings, potentially receiving larger dividends if earnings rise or smaller dividends if earnings drop.
- Stockholder rights include the following:

  1. The right to dividends
  2. The right to any assets remaining after senior claims are satisfied in a liquidation
  3. Voting rights
  4. The *preemptive right*, or the right to share proportionately in any new stock sold. This right is available in some firms but not in others.

- Common stock permits a firm greater flexibility in its financing plans than fixed-income securities because, in principle, no fixed-dividend obligation exists.
- Investment bankers assist firms in the security offering process by providing advice on a wide range of corporate financial transactions, including the timing and structure of new security offerings. New corporate securities are sold through *public cash offerings*, *private placements*, and *rights offerings*.
- Issuance costs for sales of common equity are normally significantly greater than those for corporate debt or preferred stock. There are significant economies of scale associated with security offerings.
- The valuation of *common stock* is considerably more complicated than the valuation of either bonds or preferred stock for the following reasons:

  1. The cash flows can take two forms, cash dividend payments and price appreciation.
  2. Common stock dividends are normally expected to grow and not remain constant.
  3. The cash flows from common stocks are generally more uncertain than the cash flows from other types of securities.

- In the *general dividend valuation model*, the value of a common stock is equal to the present value of all the expected future dividends discounted at the investor's required rate of return. Simpler common stock valuation models can be derived from assumptions concerning the expected growth of future dividend payments.
- One of the most commonly encountered simplified dividend valuation models is the *constant growth dividend valuation model*. In this model, the value of a common stock is equal to next year's dividend divided by the difference between the required rate of return and the expected growth rate.
- The valuation of stock in small corporations poses special challenges because of its limited marketability, lack of liquidity, and the difference between minority interest and controlling interest shares.

Important Equations

$$\text{Book value per share} = \frac{\text{Total common stockholders' equity}}{\text{Number of shares outstanding}}$$

$$\text{Number of shares} = \frac{\begin{array}{c}\text{Number of}\\ \text{directors}\\ \text{desired}\end{array} \times \begin{array}{c}\text{Number of}\\ \text{shares}\\ \text{outstanding}\end{array}}{\begin{array}{c}\text{Number of}\\ \text{directors}\\ \text{being elected}\end{array} + 1} + 1$$

$$\text{Underwriting spread} = \text{Selling price to public} - \text{Proceeds to company}$$

Important Equations (*Continued*)

$$P_0 = \sum_{t=1}^{\infty} \frac{D_t}{(1 + k_e)^t}$$

$$P_0 = \frac{D}{k_e}$$

$$D_t = D_0(1 + g)^t$$

$$P_0 = \frac{D_1}{k_e - g}$$

$$k_e = \frac{D_1}{P_0} + g$$

P_0 = Present value of expected dividends during period of nonconstant growth + Present value of the expected stock price at the end of the nonconstant growth period

7-7 Questions and Topics for Discussion

1. Define the following terms associated with common stock:
   a. Nonvoting stock
   b. Stock split
   c. Reverse stock split
   d. Stock dividend
   e. Book value
   f. Treasury stock
2. Does the retained earnings figure on a company's balance sheet indicate the amount of funds the company has available for current dividends or capital expenditures? Explain fully.
3. Discuss the reasons why a firm may repurchase its own common stock.
4. Explain the differences between par value, book value, and market value per share of common stock.
5. Discuss the various stockholder rights.
6. What factor or factors make the valuation of common stocks more complicated than the valuation of bonds and preferred stocks?
7. According to the general dividend valuation model, a firm that reinvests all its earnings and pays no cash dividends can still have a common stock value greater than zero. How is this possible?
8. Explain the relationship between financial decisions and shareholders' wealth.
9. Explain how *each* of the following factors would affect the valuation of a firm's common stock, assuming that all other factors remain constant:

a. The general level of interest rates shifts upward, causing investors to require a higher rate of return on securities in general.
b. Increased foreign competition reduces the future growth potential of the firm's earnings and dividends.
c. Investors reevaluate upward their assessment of the risk of the firm's common stock as the result of increased South American investments by the firm.

10. In the context of the constant growth dividend valuation model, explain what is meant by
a. Dividend yield
b. Price appreciation yield

11. Explain why the valuation models for a perpetual bond, preferred stock, and common stock with constant dividend payments (zero growth) are virtually identical.

12. Explain how the book value per share of common stock can change over time.

13. What is the difference between majority voting and cumulative voting?

14. What are the primary functions served by investment bankers?

15. What are the differences between a *direct placement*, a *public cash offering*, and a *rights offering* of securities?

16. Which do you think is more risky for a firm trying to raise capital—an *underwritten offering* or a *best-efforts offering?*

17. Identify the major issuance costs associated with a security offering by a corporation.

18. How does a *shelf registration* differ from other public security offerings?

7-8 Self-Test Problems

ST1. What is the current value of a share of Commonwealth Edison common stock to an investor who requires a 12 percent annual rate of return, if *next* year's dividend, D_1, is expected to be $3 per share and dividends are expected to grow at an annual rate of 4 percent for the foreseeable future?

ST2. The Edgar Corporation currently (D_0) pays a $2 per share dividend. This dividend is expected to grow at a 20 percent annual rate over the next three years and then to grow at 6 percent per year for the foreseeable future. What would you pay for a share of this stock if you demand a 20 percent rate of return?

ST3. Capitol Industries has 7 million shares of stock outstanding. In an election for the board of directors, 80 percent of the shares are voted. The company has seven directors on its board, all of whom are elected annually.
a. If the company uses a majority rule voting procedure, how many shares are required to elect
  i. One director
  ii. Two directors
  iii. A majority of the members of the board
b. If the company uses a cumulative voting procedure, how many shares are required to elect
  i. One director
  ii. Two directors
  iii. A majority of the members of the board

ST4. Referring to the following listing for Disney on November 27, 2015:

22.23 122.08 90 Disney DIS 1.1 23 115.13 −3.54

determine the
a. Closing price on November 27, 2015
b. Price change from the previous trading day

c. Dividend yield
d. Price/earnings ratio
e. Percentage change in price from January 1, 2015

ST5. Gibson Company Stockholders Equity, December 31, 2015 ($000)

Preferred Stock, $50 par value 1 million shares outstanding	$ 50,000
Common Stock, $1 par value 20 million shares authorized 15 million shares outstanding	15,000
Contributed capital in excess of par	210,000
Retained Earnings	235,000
Total Shareholders' Equity	$510,000

Determine the book value per share of Gibson common stock.

7-9 Problems*

BASIC

1. General Cereal common stock dividends have been growing at an annual rate of 7 percent per year over the past 10 years. Current dividends are $1.70 per share. What is the current value of a share of this stock to an investor who requires a 12 percent rate of return if the following conditions exist?

a. Dividends are expected to continue growing at the historic rate for the foreseeable future.
b. The dividend growth rate is expected to *increase* to 9 percent per year.
c. The dividend growth rate is expected to *decrease* to 6.5 percent per year.

INTERMEDIATE

Spreadsheet Strategies

2. The Foreman Company's earnings and common stock dividends have been growing at an annual rate of 6 percent over the past 10 years and are expected to continue growing at this rate for the foreseeable future. The firm currently (that is, as of year 0) pays an annual dividend of $5 per share. Determine the current value of a share of Foreman common stock to investors with each of the following required rates of return:

a. 12 percent
b. 14 percent
c. 16 percent
d. 6 percent
e. 4 percent

BASIC

3. The common stock of General Land Development Company (GLDC) is expected to pay a dividend of $1.25 next year and currently sells for $25. Assume that the firm's future dividend payments are expected to grow at a constant rate for the foreseeable future. Determine the implied growth rate of GLDC's dividends (and earnings), assuming that the required rate of return of investors is 12 percent.

INTERMEDIATE

Spreadsheet Strategies

4. Cascade Mining Company expects its earnings and dividends to increase by 7 percent per year over the next 6 years and then to remain relatively constant thereafter. The firm currently (that is, as of year 0) pays a dividend of $5 per share. Determine the value of a share of Cascade stock to an investor with a 12 percent required rate of return.

*Color blocks behind the numbers denote problems that have check answers provided at the end of the book.

INTERMEDIATE Spreadsheet Strategies

5. Over the past five years, the dividends of the Gamma Corporation have grown from \$ 0.70 per share to the current level of \$1.30 per share (D_0). This growth rate (computed to 1/10 of 1 percent accuracy) is expected to continue for the foreseeable future. What is the value of a share of Gamma Corporation common stock to an investor who requires a 20 percent return on her investment?

INTERMEDIATE Spreadsheet Strategies

6. Simtek currently pays a \$2.50 dividend (D_0) per share. Next year's dividend is expected to be \$3 per share. After next year, dividends are expected to increase at a 9 percent annual rate for three years and a 6 percent annual rate thereafter.

a. What is the current value of a share of Simtek stock to an investor who requires a 15 percent return on his or her investment?

b. If the dividend in year 1 is expected to be \$3 and the growth rate over the following three years is expected to be only 7 percent and then 6 percent thereafter, what will the new stock price be?

BASIC

7. What is the current per-share value of JRM Corporation to an investor who requires a 16 percent annual rate of return, if JRM's current per-share dividend is \$2 and is expected to remain at \$2 for the foreseeable future?

INTERMEDIATE Spreadsheet Strategies

8. The Seneca Maintenance Company currently (that is, as of year 0) pays a common stock dividend of \$1.50 per share. Dividends are expected to grow at a rate of 11 percent per year for the next four years and then to continue growing thereafter at a rate of 5 percent per year. What is the current value of a share of Seneca common stock to an investor who requires a 14 percent rate of return?

INTERMEDIATE Spreadsheet Strategies

9. Ten years ago, Video Toys began manufacturing and selling coin-operated arcade games. Dividends are currently \$1.50 per share, having grown at a 15 percent compound annual rate over the past five years. That growth rate is expected to be maintained for the next three years, after which dividends are expected to grow at half that rate for three years. Beyond that time, Video Toys's dividends are expected to grow at 5 percent per year. What is the current value of a share of Video Toys common stock if your required rate of return is 18 percent?

CHALLENGE

10. The chairman of Heller Industries told a meeting of financial analysts that he expects the firm's earnings and dividends to double over the next six years. The firm's current (that is, as of year 0) earnings and dividends per share are \$4 and \$2, respectively.

a. Estimate the compound annual dividend growth rate over the six-year period (to the nearest whole percent).

b. Forecast Heller's earnings and dividends per share for each of the next six years, assuming that they grow at the rate determined in Part a.

c. Based on the constant growth dividend valuation model, determine the current value of a share of Heller Industries common stock to an investor who requires an 18 percent rate of return.

d. Why might the stock price calculated in Part c not represent an accurate valuation to an investor with an 18 percent required rate of return?

e. Determine the current value of a share of Heller Industries common stock to an investor (with an 18 percent required rate of return) who plans to hold it for six years, assuming that earnings and dividends per share grow at the rate determined in Part a for the next six years and then at 6 percent thereafter.

CHALLENGE

11. Kruger Associates is considering a substantial investment in the stock of McIntyre Enterprises. McIntyre currently (time 0) pays a dividend of \$1.50 per share. This dividend is expected to grow at 15 percent per year for the next three years and 10 percent per year for the following three years. McIntyre's marginal tax rate is 40 percent. Kruger expects the value of the McIntyre stock to increase by 50 percent between now and the *beginning* of year 5. If Kruger requires a 12 percent rate of return on investments of this type, what value would Kruger place on the McIntyre stock?

INTERMEDIATE **12.** Piedmont Enterprises currently pays a dividend (D_0) of $1 per share. This dividend is expected to grow at a 20 percent per year rate for the next two years, after which it is expected to grow at 6 percent per year for the foreseeable future. If you require a 15 percent rate of return on an investment of this type, what price do you expect the stock to sell for *at the beginning of year 5*?

CHALLENGE **13.** Over the past 10 years, the dividends of Party Time Inc. have grown at an annual rate of 15 percent. The current (D_0) dividend is $3 per share. This dividend is expected to grow to $3.40 next year, then grow at an annual rate of 10 percent for the following two years and 6 percent per year thereafter. You require a 15 percent rate of return on this stock.

Spreadsheet Strategies

a. What would you be willing to pay for a share of Party Time stock today?
b. What price would you anticipate the stock selling for at the beginning of year 3?
c. If you anticipated selling the stock at the end of two years, how much would you pay for it today?

BASIC **14.** Canadian National Railway sold 10 million shares of stock to the public at $30 per share. The company received net proceeds from its underwriters of $287,506,114. What was the underwriting spread from this stock offering?

INTERMEDIATE **15.** Suppose you have accumulated a sizable investment (100,000 common shares) in Alpine Land and Development Company. You are dissatisfied with the performance of the current management and are considering running for the board of directors. The company has a nine-member board and a total of 1.5 million common shares outstanding. Assume that all shares will be voted in the upcoming election and that four of the nine board members are up for reelection.

a. If the voting procedure is cumulative, what number of shares is necessary to ensure your election to the board? Is it possible for you to be elected with fewer votes? Explain.
b. Suppose a close friend of yours also owns a good deal of Alpine and shares your feelings about the current management. If the voting procedure is cumulative, how many shares are necessary to elect both you and your friend to the board?
c. If the voting procedure is majority, how many votes are necessary for election in Parts a and b of this problem? Explain your answer.

INTERMEDIATE **16.** The stock of Carroll's Bowling Equipment currently pays a dividend (D_0) of $3. This dividend is expected to grow at an annual rate of 15 percent for the next three years. The dividend is expected to increase by $1 in year 4 and to grow at a constant annual rate of 6 percent thereafter. If you require a 24 percent rate of return on an investment such as this, how much would you be willing to pay per share?

INTERMEDIATE **17.** The stock of Dravo Corporation currently pays a dividend (D_0) at the rate of $2 per share. This dividend is expected to increase at a 9 percent annual rate for the next three years, at a 7 percent annual rate for the following two years, and then at 4 percent per year thereafter. What is the value of a share of stock of Dravo to an investor who demands a 24 percent rate of return on this stock?

Spreadsheet Strategies

INTERMEDIATE **18.** Excel Corporation has recently witnessed a period of depressed earnings performance. As a result, cash dividend payments have been suspended. Investors do not anticipate a resumption of dividends until two years from today, when a yearly dividend of $0.25 will be paid. That yearly dividend is expected to be increased to $0.75 in the following year and $1.50 in the year after that. Beyond the time when the $1.50 dividend is paid, investors expect Excel's dividends to grow at an annual rate of 5 percent into perpetuity. All dividends are assumed to be paid at the end of each year. If you require an 18 percent rate of return on Excel's stock, what is the value of one share of this stock to you today?

INTERMEDIATE

Spreadsheet Strategies

19. The Cremmins Coat Company has recently completed a period of extraordinary growth, due to the popularity of its yellow jackets. Earnings per share have grown at an average compound annual rate of 15 percent, while dividends have grown at a 20 percent annual rate over the past 10 years. The current dividend (D_0) rate is \$2 per share. Current earnings are \$3.25 per share. Earnings are expected to grow at an annual rate of 15 percent for the next three years and 6 percent per annum thereafter. Dividends are expected to grow by 25 percent during the coming year, by 15 percent per annum for the following two years, and by 6 percent per annum thereafter.

a. What price do you expect the stock to sell for today, if your required rate of return on equity for a firm of this risk level is 16 percent?

b. What price do you expect the stock to sell for at the beginning of year 2?

CHALLENGE

20. The VSE Corporation currently pays no dividend because of depressed earnings. A recent change in management promises a brighter future. Investors expect VSE to pay a dividend of \$1 next year (the end of year 1). This dividend is expected to increase to \$2 the following year and to grow at a rate of 10 percent per annum for the following two years (years 3 and 4). Chuck Brown, a new investor, expects the price of the stock to increase 50 percent in value between now (time zero) and the end of year 3. If Brown plans to hold the stock for two years and requires a rate of return of 20 percent on his investment, what value would he place on the stock today?

CHALLENGE

21. Sports Novelties, Inc., has experienced an explosion in demand for its feathered football novelties. The firm currently (time 0) pays a dividend of \$0.25 per share. This dividend is expected to increase to \$0.75 per share one year from now. It is expected to grow at a rate of 15 percent per year for the following seven years. Coley, a naive investor, seeks your advice regarding the current value of this stock. Coley plans to purchase this stock today, if the price is right, and to hold it for three years. He believes that the stock will increase in value to \$30 at the end of four years. What is the current value of this stock to Coley if he requires a 20 percent rate of return on stocks of this risk level?

CHALLENGE

22. The Blinkelman Corporation has just announced that it plans to introduce a new solar panel that will greatly reduce the cost of solar energy. As a result, analysts now expect the company's earnings, currently (year 0) \$1 per share to grow by 50 percent per year for the next three years, by 25 percent per year for the following three years, and by 8 percent per year thereafter. Blinkelman does not currently pay a dividend, but it expects to pay out 20 percent of its earnings beginning two years from now. The payout ratio is expected to become 50 percent in five years and to remain at that level. The company's marginal tax rate is 40 percent. If you require a 20 percent rate of return on a stock such as this, how much would you be willing to pay for it today?

CHALLENGE

23. Watkins, Inc., has experienced an explosion in demand for its ram football novelties. The firm currently (time 0) pays a dividend of \$0.50 per share. This dividend is expected to increase to \$1.00 per share one year from now. It is expected to grow at a rate of 20 percent per year for the next seven years. Susan seeks your advice regarding the current value of this stock. Susan plans to purchase this stock today, if the price is right, and to hold it for three years. She believes that the stock will increase in value to \$40 at the end of five years. What is the current value of this stock to Susan if she requires a 20 percent rate of return on stocks of this risk level?

CHALLENGE

24. Whitehurst Associates is considering a substantial investment in the stock of Ivanhoe Enterprises. Ivanhoe currently (time 0) pays a dividend of \$3 per share. This dividend is expected to grow at 15 percent per year for the next three years and 10 percent per year for the following three years. Ivanhoe's marginal tax rate is 40 percent. Whitehurst expects the value of the Ivanhoe stock to increase by 40 percent between now and the *beginning* of year 5. If Whitehurst requires a 12 percent rate of return on investments of this type, what value would Whitehurst place on the Ivanhoe stock?

CHALLENGE

25. The Alpha Tool Corporation has never paid a dividend, but the new company president has announced that the firm would pay its first dividend exactly two years from now. That dividend is expected to be $2 per share. It is anticipated that this dividend will grow by 15 percent for the following three years and by 10 percent for the two years after that. No explicit dividend forecast is available beyond that point in time, although the firm is expected to continue to pay some dividends every year. The stock's current price/earnings (P/E) multiple is 15 times. The company (and investigators) expect the P/E multiple to remain constant for the foreseeable future. Earnings per share at the end of year 6 are expected to be $7. The company's marginal tax rate is 40 percent and the firm has a capital structure consisting of 40 percent debt (at a pretax cost of 20 percent) and 60 percent common equity. If you require a 15 percent rate of return on this stock, how much would you pay for one share of stock today?

INTERMEDIATE

26. The following stock quotations were recently reported in *The Wall Street Journal*:

47.22	31.45	10.3	AT&T	T	3.6	21	39.43	0.26
97.15	72.53	0.1	Boeing	BA	1.6	31	88.91	−0.85
71.46	52.16	−8.7	JohnsJohns	JNJ	2.5	16	60.26	−0.08

a. What are the dividend yields on the common stock of AT&T, Boeing, and Johnson & Johnson?
b. What possible explanation can you give for the differences in the common stock dividend yields observed in Part a?
c. What is the current price–earnings ratio for Boeing and Johnson & Johnson?
d. What possible explanation can you give for the differences in the price–earnings ratios observed in Part c?
e. What was the previous day's closing price for AT&T's common stock?

INTERMEDIATE

27. Blue Moon Corporation has one million shares of common stock outstanding. In a typical annual election for the board of directors, shareholders representing 70 percent of the shares outstanding exercise their right to vote. The company has nine members on its board of directors, all of whom are elected annually.

a. If the company uses a majority voting procedure to elect its board, how many votes are required to elect:
   i. One director
   ii. Two directors
   iii. A majority of the members of the board of directors
b. If the company uses a cumulative voting procedure, how many votes are required to elect:
   i. One director
   ii. Two directors
   iii. A majority of the members of the board of directors

BASIC

28. The American Association of Individual Investors has put together a list of stock-picking techniques that "stand the test of time." Given what you learned in the last chapter about valuation, coupled with what you now know about stock, do you agree or disagree with their techniques? Why or why not?

HTTP:
www.aaii.com

29. Konawalski's Kustom Erdapfel Chips, Inc., is the maker of gourmet German-style potato chips. The company began business three years ago in rural North Carolina and grew quickly as the product became known. Konawalski is now poised for national growth. Some analysts call the firm the next Krispy Kreme. The company pays a dividend of $0.10 per share. Earnings per share are currently $0.50, and analysts expect both earnings and dividends to grow at 20 percent per year for the next five years. The stock price is expected to increase in value by 70 percent over the next three years. If you believe that investors require a 20 percent rate of return on a stock of this risk, what price would you recommend as the IPO price for Konawalski?

CHAPTER 8

Analysis of Risk and Return

KEY CHAPTER CONCEPTS

1. Risk represents the variability of possible future returns from an investment. Risk tends to increase as one looks farther into the future.
2. A *probability distribution* indicates the percentage chance of occurrence of each of the possible outcomes.
   a. The *expected value* is a measure of mean or average value of the possible outcomes, each having an associated probability of occurrence.
   b. The *standard deviation* is an important measure of the total risk or variability of possible outcomes, each having an associated probability of occurrence.
   c. The *coefficient of variation* is a useful total risk measure when comparing two investments with different expected returns.
3. The *required rate of return* on an investment—financial asset (security) or physical asset—is equal to the risk-free rate of return plus a risk premium.
   a. The *risk-free rate of return* refers to the return available on a short-term investment with no risk of default.
   b. The *risk premium* is a function of maturity risk, default risk, seniority risk, and marketability risk.
4. The required rate of return on an investment and the perceived risk of the return expected have a positive relationship: the greater the risk, the greater the expected return.
5. Portfolios are composed of two or more assets.
   a. The risk of a portfolio of assets depends on the risk of the individual assets in the portfolio and the correlation of returns between the pairs of assets in the portfolio.
   b. By combining assets that are less than perfectly positively correlated, portfolio risk can be *reduced* below the level of the weighted average risk of the individual assets.
6. *The Capital Asset Pricing Model (CAPM)* can be used to determine required rates of return on investments in financial or physical assets.
   a. The *systematic* risk of a security refers to that portion of the variability of an individual security's returns caused by factors affecting the security market as a whole.
   b. *Beta*, measured as the slope of a regression line between market returns and a security's returns, is a measure of systematic risk.
   c. The *unsystematic* risk of a security refers to the portion of the variability of a security's returns caused by factors unique to that security.
   d. The *security market line* expresses the relationship between the required returns from a security and the systematic risk of that security.

FINANCIAL CHALLENGE

Investment Diversification and Risk

"Don't put all of your eggs in one basket" constitutes one of the core investment principles. This strategy, known as *diversification*, refers to the practice of spreading your money among various investments, for example, stocks, bonds, and other assets, rather than putting all of your funds in one investment. The importance of this subject can be seen by typing the term "investment diversification" into Google—one obtains more than 22 million hits.

Data suggest that many investors do not adhere to this principle. Findings from the Federal Reserve's Survey of Consumer Finances indicate that, of households that own shares of stock directly (for example, not indirectly through financial institutions such as mutual funds), 36 percent have shares in only a single stock and 84 percent own shares in fewer than 10 stocks.

All companies face uncertain events that can have a significant impact on the market prices of their stocks and bonds. The investment strategy of buying securities (stocks or bonds) in individual companies, even large, industry-leading companies, and holding them for the long term does not guarantee investment success. Large (capitalization) companies have encountered financial difficulties from time to time throughout history. In the current decade, well-known companies, such as Kodak and American Airlines, sought reorganization under the bankruptcy laws. During the prior decade, General Motors, Chrysler, United Airlines, Delta Airlines, K-Mart, and Enron all filed for bankruptcy protection. Investments in small (capitalization) companies pose even greater risks. For every company, like Intel, Microsoft, or Google, that grows into a successful multibillion-dollar enterprise, there are hundreds of other small, start-up companies that go out of business, leaving investors with little or no return.

It is this type of risk that causes most investors to hold well-diversified portfolios (groups) of stocks. As will be seen in the chapter, studies have shown that a significant portion of the variability in the returns from common stocks can be reduced through diversification, that is, by moving from a portfolio containing a single stock to a portfolio containing as few as 20 stocks.

FINANCIAL CHALLENGE — CONTINUED

This chapter defines what is meant by risk and develops various techniques for measuring and managing risk that can be used by financial decision makers, such as corporate treasurers, money managers, and securities brokers. Individual investors can also use these techniques to assess the risks associated with their personal investments (for example, individual retirement accounts).

Source: Jason Zweig, "More Stocks May Not Make a Portfolio Safer," *The Wall Street Journal* (November 21–22, 2009): B1

CHAPTER OBJECTIVES

Upon completion of this chapter, you should have a clear understanding of the following:

1. The meaning of the concept of risk and measurement of risk
2. The difference between the risk of an individual asset and the risk of an asset viewed as part of a portfolio
3. The relationship between risk and required rate of return

8-1 Introduction

Chapter 1 provided a brief introduction to risk and the relationship between risk and return. Recall that the required rate of return on an investment—financial asset (security) or physical asset—was represented as an increasing function of that investment's perceived risk; that is, the greater the risk, the greater the required rate of return.[1]

This chapter develops the relationship between risk and return in greater detail and presents methods for measuring risk. Later sections of the chapter focus on investment diversification and portfolio risk analysis.

8-2 Meaning and Measurement of Risk

In Chapter 2, the return from holding an investment was defined in Equation 2.2 as:

$$\text{Holding period return}(\%) = \frac{\begin{matrix}\text{Ending}\\ \text{price}\end{matrix} - \begin{matrix}\text{Beginning}\\ \text{price}\end{matrix} + \begin{matrix}\text{Distributions}\\ \text{received}\end{matrix}}{\text{Beginning price}} \times 100\%$$

Distributions include interest on debt, dividends on common stock, rent on real property, and so on.

risk Recall that **risk** was defined in Chapter 1 as the possibility that actual future returns will deviate from expected returns. In other words, it represents the variability of returns. From the perspective of security analysis or the analysis of an investment in some project

[1]The terms *asset* and *security* are used interchangeably throughout the chapter to refer to investments in either financial assets (securities) or physical assets.

(such as the development of a new product line), risk is the *possibility that actual cash flows (returns) will be different from forecasted cash flows (returns).*

An investment is said to be *risk free* if the dollar returns from the initial investment are known with certainty. Some of the best examples of risk-free investments are U.S. Treasury securities. There is virtually no chance that the Treasury will fail to redeem these securities at maturity or that the Treasury will default on any interest payments owed. As a last resort, the Treasury can always print more money.[2]

In contrast, Ford Motor Company bonds constitute a *risky* investment because it is possible that the company will default on one or more interest payments and will lack sufficient funds to redeem the bonds at face value at maturity. In other words, the possible returns from this investment are *variable,* and each potential outcome can be assigned a *probability.*

If, for example, you were considering investing in Ford bonds, you might assign the probabilities shown in Table 8.1 to the three possible outcomes of this investment. These probabilities are interpreted to mean that an 80 percent chance exists that the bonds will not be in default over their life and will be redeemed at maturity, a 15 percent chance of interest default during the life of the bonds, and a 5 percent chance that the bonds will not be redeemed at maturity.

Hence, from an investment perspective, risk refers to the chance that returns from an investment will be different from those expected. We can define risk more precisely, however, by introducing some probability concepts.

HTTP:
Using the Google search engine, type in the search term "risk analysis" and look at the vast wealth of Internet information available for analyzing risk of any kind for any assets. Some of the hits may surprise you.

www.google.com

8-2a Probability Distributions

The *probability* that a particular outcome will occur is defined as the *percentage chance* (or likelihood) of its occurrence. A *probability distribution* indicates the percentage chance of occurrence of each of the possible outcomes. Probabilities may be determined either objectively or subjectively. An objective determination is based on past occurrences of similar outcomes, whereas a subjective one is merely an opinion expressed by an individual about the likelihood that a given outcome will occur. In the case of projects that are frequently repeated—such as the drilling of developmental oil wells in an established oil field—reasonably good objective estimates can be made about the success of a new project. Similarly, good objective estimates can often be made about the expected returns of Ford bonds. However, the expected returns from securities of new, small firms are often much more difficult to estimate objectively. Hence, highly subjective estimates regarding the likelihood of various returns are necessary. The fact that many probability estimates in business are at least partially subjective does not diminish their usefulness.

TABLE **8.1**

Probability of Default on Ford Bonds

Outcome	Probability
No default, bonds redeemed at maturity	0.80
Default on interest for one or more periods	0.15
No interest default, but bonds not redeemed at maturity	0.05
	1.00

[2]Note that this discussion of risk deals with *dollar returns* and ignores other considerations, such as potential losses in purchasing power. In addition, it assumes that securities are held until maturity, which is not always the case. Sometimes a security must be sold prior to maturity for less than face value because of changes in the level of interest rates.

8-2b Summary of Notation

Before examining specific measures of risk and return, it is useful to summarize the basic elements of notation used throughout the chapter.

r = single rate of return on a given security; a subscript denotes the rate of return on a particular security (or portfolio of securities), such as r_f, described next, and a hat (^) symbol denotes an *expected* rate of return

r_f = nominal riskless (risk-free) rate of return; the return offered on short-term U.S. Treasury securities

r_p = rate of return on a portfolio of securities

r_m = rate of return on the market portfolio, a portfolio consisting of all available securities, weighted by their respective market values; a broad-based security market index, such as the *Standard & Poor's 500* Stock Price Index (S&P 500) or the New York Stock Exchange Index, is normally used as a measure of total market returns

p = probability of occurrence of a specific rate of return

σ = standard deviation of the rate of return on a security (or portfolio of securities); the square root of the variance of returns

σ_p = standard deviation of the rate of return on a portfolio of securities

σ_m = standard deviation of the rate of return on the market portfolio

v = coefficient of variation

z = number of standard deviations that a particular value of a random variable (such as rate of return) is from its expected value

ρ = correlation coefficient between the returns on two securities

w = portion (weight) of funds invested in a given security within a portfolio

k_j = *required* rate of return on a given security

θ_j = risk premium required by investors on a given security

β_j = measure of the volatility (or risk) of a security's returns relative to the returns on the market portfolio

β_p = measure of risk of a portfolio of securities

8-2c Expected Value

Suppose an investor is considering an investment of $100,000 in the stock of either Duke Energy, a public utility firm, or Texas Instruments (TI), a maker of electronic equipment. By investing in the stock of either of these firms, an investor expects to receive dividend payments plus stock price appreciation. We will assume that the investor plans to hold the stock for one year and then sell it. Over the coming year, the investor feels there is a 20 percent chance for an economic *boom*, a 60 percent chance for a *normal* economic environment, and a 20 percent chance for a *recession.* Given this assessment of the economic environment *over the next year*, the investor estimates the probability distribution of returns from the investment in Duke and TI as shown in Table 8.2.

expected value

From this information, the *expected value* of returns (or expected return) from investing in the stock of Duke and TI can be calculated. The **expected value** is a statistical measure of the mean or average value of the possible outcomes. Operationally, it is defined as the weighted average of possible outcomes, with the weights being the probabilities of occurrence.

TABLE 8.2

Probability Distribution of Returns from Duke and TI

State of the Economy	Probability	Rate of Return Anticipated Under Each State of the Economy*	
		Duke	TI
Recession	0.2	10%	–4%
Normal year	0.6	18	18
Boom	0.2	26	40
	1.0		

*For example, a 10 percent rate of return for Duke means that the stock value plus dividends total $110,000 at the end of one year. Working with a *discrete* probability distribution, as this example does, indicates that there is no probability of a loss by investing in Duke. This, of course, is unrealistic. In the following discussion of continuous distributions, this assumption is relaxed.

TABLE 8.3

Expected Return Calculation for Investment in Duke and TI

Duke			TI		
r_j	p_j	$r_j \times p_j$	r_j	p_j	$r_j \times p_j$
10%	0.2	2.0%	–4%	0.2	–0.8%
18	0.6	10.8	18	0.6	10.8
26	0.2	5.2	40	0.2	8.0
	Expected return $= \hat{r} =$	18.0%		Expected return $= \hat{r} =$	18.0%

Algebraically, the expected value of the returns from a security or project may be defined as follows:

(8.1)
$$\hat{r} = \sum_{j=1}^{n} r_j p_j$$

expected return

where $\hat{r}$ is the **expected return**; r_j is the outcome for the jth case, where there are n possible outcomes; and p_j is the probability that the jth outcome will occur. The expected returns for Duke and TI are computed in Table 8.3. The expected return is 18 percent for both Duke and TI.

8-2d Standard Deviation: An Absolute Measure of Risk

standard deviation

The **standard deviation** is a statistical measure of the dispersion of possible outcomes about the expected value. It is defined as the *square root of the weighted average squared deviations of possible outcomes from the expected value* and is computed as follows:

(8.2)
$$\sigma = \sqrt{\sum_{j=1}^{n} (r_j - \hat{r})^2 p_j}$$

where σ is the standard deviation.

The standard deviation can be used to measure the variability of returns from an investment. As such, it gives an indication of the *risk* involved in the asset or security. The larger the standard deviation, the more variable are an investment's returns and the riskier is the investment. A standard deviation of zero indicates no variability and

TABLE 8.4

Computation of Standard Deviations of Return for Duke and TI

	j	r_j	$\hat{r}$	$r_j - \hat{r}$	$(r_j - \hat{r})^2$	p_j	$(r - \hat{r})^2 p_j$
Duke	1 (Recession)	10%	18%	−8%	64	0.2	12.8
	2 (Normal)	18	18	0	0	0.6	0
	3 (Boom)	26	18	+8	64	0.2	12.8
							$\sum_{j=1}^{n}(r_j - \hat{r})^2 p_j = 25.6$

$$\sigma = \sqrt{\sum_{j=1}^{n}(r_j - \hat{r})^2 p_j} = \sqrt{25.6} = 5.06\%$$

	j	r_j	$\hat{r}$	$r_j - \hat{r}$	$(r_j - \hat{r})^2$	p_j	$(r - \hat{r})^2 p_j$
TI	1 (Recession)	−4%	18%	−22%	484	0.2	96.8
	2 (Normal)	18	18	0	0	0.6	0
	3 (Boom)	40	18	+22	484	0.2	96.8
							$\sum_{j=1}^{n}(r_j - \hat{r})^2 p_j = 193.6$

$$\sigma = \sqrt{\sum_{j=1}^{n}(r_j - \hat{r})^2 p_j} = \sqrt{193.6} = 13.91\%$$

thus no risk. Table 8.4 shows the calculation of the standard deviations for the investments in Duke and TI.

As shown in the calculations in Table 8.4, TI appears riskier than Duke because possible returns from TI are more variable, measured by its standard deviation of 13.91 percent, than those from Duke, which have a standard deviation of only 5.06 percent.

This example deals with a *discrete* probability distribution of outcomes (returns) for each firm; that is, a *limited* number of possible outcomes are identified, and probabilities are assigned to them. In reality, however, many different outcomes are possible for the investment in the stock of each firm—ranging from losses during the year to returns in excess of TI's 40 percent return. To indicate the probability of *all* possible outcomes for these investments, it is necessary to construct a *continuous* probability distribution. This is done by developing a table similar to Table 8.2, except that it would have many more possible outcomes and their associated probabilities. The detailed table of outcomes and probabilities can be used to develop the expected value of returns from Duke and TI, and a continuous curve would be constructed to approximate the probabilities associated with each outcome. Figure 8.1 illustrates continuous probability distributions of returns for investments in the stock of Duke and TI.

As seen in this figure, the possible returns for Duke have a tighter probability distribution, indicating a lower variability of returns, whereas the TI possible returns have a flatter distribution, indicating higher variability and, by extension, more risk.

8-2e Normal Probability Distribution

The possible returns from many investments tend to follow a *normal* probability distribution. The normal probability distribution is characterized by a symmetrical, bell-like curve.

● FIGURE 8.1

Continuous Probability Distributions for the Expected Returns from Investments in the Duke and TI Stocks

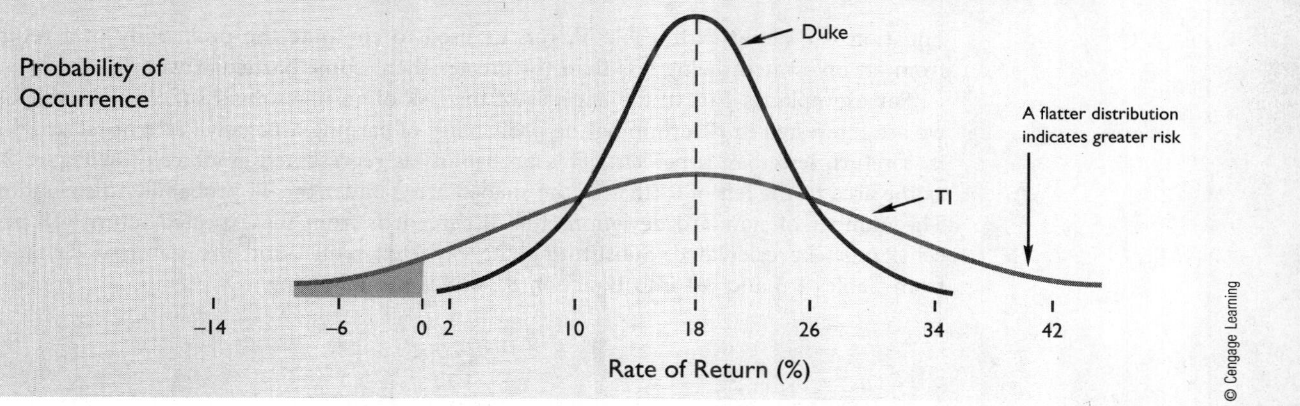

If the expected continuous probability distribution of returns is approximately normal, a table of the *standard normal probability distribution* (that is, a normal distribution with a mean equal to 0.0 and a standard deviation equal to 1.0, such as Table V at the end of the text) can be used to compute the probability of occurrence of any particular outcome. From this table, for example, it is apparent that the actual outcome should be between plus or minus 1 standard deviation from the expected value 68.26 percent of the time,[3] between plus or minus 2 standard deviations 95.44 percent of the time, and between plus or minus 3 standard deviations 99.74 percent of the time. This is illustrated in Figure 8.2.

● FIGURE 8.2

Areas Under the Normal Probability Distribution

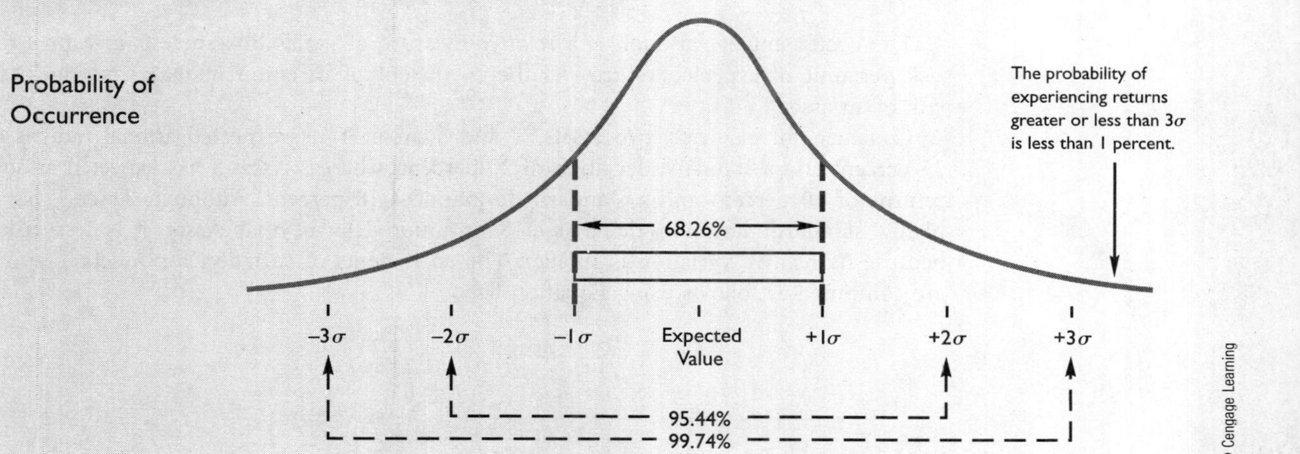

[3]For example, Table V indicates that there is a probability of 0.1587 of a value occurring that is greater than +1 from the mean *and* a probability of 0.1587 of a value occurring that is less than −1 from the mean. Hence, the probability of a value between $+1\sigma$ and -1σ is 68.26 percent, that is, $1.00-(2 \times 0.1587)$.

The number of standard deviations, z, that a particular value of r is from the expected value, $\hat{r}$, can be computed as follows:

(8.3)
$$z = \frac{r - \hat{r}}{\sigma}$$

Equation 8.3, along with Table V, can be used to compute the probability of a return from an investment being less than (or greater than) some particular value.

For example, as part of the analysis of the risk of an investment in TI stock, suppose we are interested in determining the probability of earning a negative rate of return, that is, a return less than 0 percent. This probability is represented graphically in Figure 8.1 as the area to the left of 0 (that is, the shaded area) under the TI probability distribution. The number of standard deviations that 0 percent is from the expected return (18 percent) must be calculated. Substituting the expected return and the standard deviation from Tables 8.3 and 8.4 into Equation 8.3 yields the following:

$$\begin{aligned} z &= \frac{0\% - 18\%}{13.91\%} \\ &= -1.29 \end{aligned}$$

In other words, the return of 0 percent is 1.29 standard deviations *below* the mean. From Table V, the probability associated with 1.29 standard deviations is 0.0985. Therefore, there is a 9.85 percent chance that TI will have returns below 0 percent. Conversely, there is a 90.15 percent (100 − 9.85) chance that the return will be greater than 0 percent.

8-2f Coefficient of Variation: A Relative Measure of Risk

The standard deviation is an appropriate measure of total risk when the investments being compared are approximately equal in expected returns and the returns are estimated to have symmetrical probability distributions. Because the standard deviation is an *absolute* measure of variability, it is generally *not* suitable for comparing investments with different expected returns. In these cases, the **coefficient of variation** provides a better measure of risk. It is defined as the ratio of the standard deviation, σ, to the expected return, $\hat{r}$:

coefficient of variation

(8.4)
$$v = \frac{\sigma}{\hat{r}}$$

The coefficient of variation is a *relative* measure of variability, since it measures the risk per unit of expected return. As the coefficient of variation increases, so does the risk of an asset.

Consider, for example, two assets, T and S. Asset T has expected annual returns of 25 percent and a standard deviation of 20 percent, whereas Asset S has expected annual returns of 10 percent and a standard deviation of 18 percent. Although Asset T has a higher standard deviation than Asset S, intuition tells us that Asset T is less risky, because its *relative* variation is smaller. The coefficients of variation for Assets T and S are computed as follows using Equation 8.4:

$$\begin{aligned} \text{Asset T}: \ v &= \frac{20\%}{25\%} \\ &= 0.8 \\ \text{Asset S}: \ v &= \frac{18\%}{10\%} \\ &= 1.8 \end{aligned}$$

Asset T's returns have a lower coefficient of variation than Asset S's; therefore, Asset T is the less risky of the two investments.

In general, when comparing two equal-sized investments, the standard deviation is an appropriate measure of total risk. When comparing two investments with different expected returns, the coefficient of variation is the more appropriate measure of total risk.[4]

8-2g Risk as an Increasing Function of Time

Most investment decisions require that returns be *forecasted* several years into the future. The riskiness of these forecasted returns may be thought of as an *increasing function of time*. Returns that are generated early can generally be predicted with more greater certainty than those that are anticipated farther out into the future.

Consider the risk facing Texas Instruments (TI) in its decision to market a new line of calculators. This project is expected to generate cash flows to TI of $2 million per year over the seven-year life of the project. Even though the expected annual cash flows are equal for each year, it is reasonable to assume that the riskiness of these flows increases over time as more and more presently unknown variables have a chance to affect the project's cash flows. Figure 8.3 illustrates this situation.

The distribution is relatively tight in year 1, because the factors affecting that year's cash flows (for example, demand and costs) are reasonably well known. By year 7, however, the distribution has become relatively flat, indicating a considerable increase in the standard deviation, which is caused by increased uncertainty about the factors that affect cash flows. For example, competitors may introduce similar (or improved) products, which would cause demand to decline for the TI calculators.

FIGURE 8.3

Risk of a Project over Time: Texas Instruments

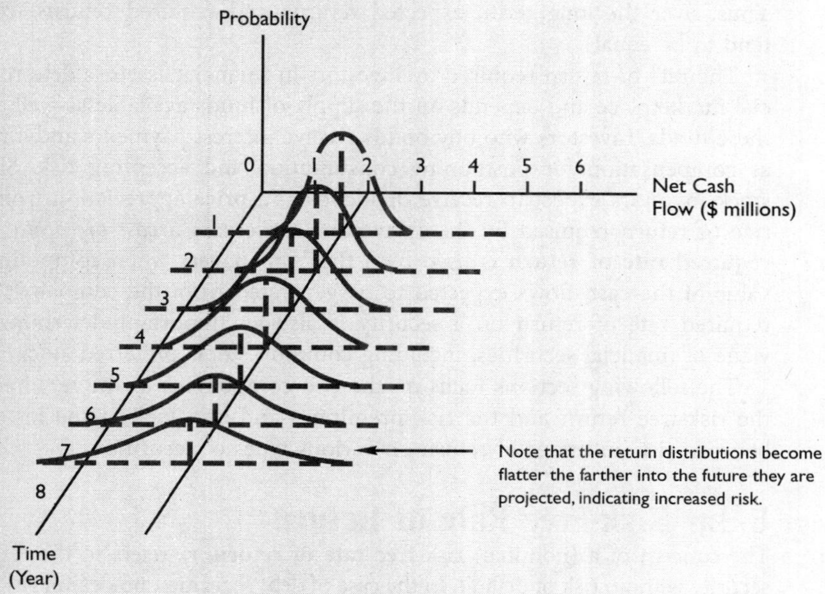

[4]The relationship between the coefficient of variation and several other measures of risk (including the standard deviation) is developed in John M. Wachowicz, Jr., and Ronald E. Shrieves, "An Argument for Generalized Mean-Coefficient of Variation Analysis," *Financial Management* (Winter 1980): 51–58.

Some types of cash flows are not subject to increasing variability. These include, for example, contractual arrangements, such as lease payments, in which the expected cash flows remain constant (or change at some predefined rate) over the life of the contract. In spite of the exceptions, it is reasonable to conclude that the riskiness of the cash flows from most investment projects gradually increases over time. Similarly, the riskiness of returns from most securities increases the farther into the future these returns are being considered. For instance, the interest return from the purchase of Ford bonds is nearly guaranteed for the next year. However, projecting the interest returns to be received 10 years in the future is much more difficult due to the potential impact of competition, new technology, and other factors that might cause Ford to have to default on the interest payment on its bonds.

8-3 Relationship Between Risk and Return

Foundation Concept

The trade-off between risk and return is a key element of effective financial decision making. This includes both decisions by individuals (and financial institutions) to invest in financial assets such as common stocks, bonds, and other securities and decisions by a firm's managers to invest in physical assets such as new plants and equipment.

In Chapter 1, the relationship between risk and required return was introduced. The relationship between risk and *required rate of return* can be expressed as follows:

$$\text{Required rate of return} = \text{Risk-free rate of return} + \text{Risk premium} \quad \textbf{(8.5)}$$

A *risk premium* is a potential "reward" that an investor expects to receive when making a risky investment. Investors are generally considered to be *risk averse*; that is, they expect, on average, to be compensated for the risk they assume when making an investment. Thus, over the long term, expected returns and required returns from securities will tend to be equal.

The rate of return required by investors in financial assets is determined in the financial marketplace and depends on the supply of funds available as well as the demand for these funds. Investors who buy bonds receive interest payments and a return of principal as compensation for postponing consumption and accepting risk. Similarly, common stock investors expect to receive dividends and price appreciation from their stock. The rate of return required by these investors represents a *cost of capital* to the firm. This

required rate of return

required rate of return is used by a firm's managers when computing the net present value of the cash flows expected to be generated from the company's investments. The required rate of return on a security is also an important determinant of the market value of financial securities, including common stock, preferred stock, and bonds.

The following sections focus on the two components of the required rate of return—the risk-free return and the risk premium—and also look at the historical relationship between risk and rates of return on various types of securities.

8-3a Risk-Free Rate of Return

risk-free rate of return

The concept of a (nominal) **risk-free rate of return**, r_f, refers to the return available on a security with no risk of default. In the case of debt securities, no default risk means that promised interest and principal payments are guaranteed to be made. Short-term U.S. government securities, such as Treasury bills, are generally considered to be risk-free investments.[5]

[5] Securities issued by the U.S. Treasury are used to finance the national debt and government operations.

The risk-free rate of return, r_f, is equal to the sum of a real rate of return and an expected inflation premium:

$$r_f = \text{Real rate of return} + \text{Expected inflation premium} \quad (8.6)$$

The *real rate of return* is the return that investors would require from a security having no risk of default in a period of no expected inflation. It is the return necessary to convince investors to postpone current, *real* consumption opportunities. The real rate of return is determined by the interaction of the supply of funds made available by savers and the demand for funds for investment. Historically, the real rate of return has been estimated to average in the range of 2 to 4 percent.

The second component of the risk-free rate of return is an *inflation premium* or *purchasing power loss premium*. Investors require compensation for expected losses in purchasing power when they postpone current consumption and lend funds. Consequently, a premium for expected inflation is included in the required return on any security. The inflation premium is normally equal to investors' expectations about future purchasing power changes. If, for example, inflation is expected to average 4 percent over some future period, the risk-free rate of return on U.S. Treasury bills (assuming a real rate of return of 3 percent) should be approximately equal to 3 percent + 4 percent = 7 percent by Equation 8.6. By extension, if inflation expectations suddenly increase from 4 to 6 percent, the risk-free rate should increase from 7 to 9 percent (3 percent real return plus 6 percent inflation premium).

At any point in time, the required risk-free rate of return on any security can be estimated from the yields on short-term U.S. government securities, such as 90-day Treasury bills.

When considering return requirements on all types of securities, it is important to remember that *increases in expected inflation rates normally lead to increases in the required rates of return on all securities.*

8-3b Risk Premium

risk premium

The **risk premium** assigned by an investor to a given security in determining the required rate of return (Equation 8.5) is a function of several different risk elements. These risk elements (and premiums) include:

- Maturity risk premium
- Default risk premium
- Seniority risk premium
- Marketability risk premium

Each of these risk elements is examined here.

term structure of interest rates

Maturity Risk Premium The return required on a security is influenced by the maturity of that security. The **term structure of interest rates** is the pattern of interest rate yields (required returns) for securities that differ only in the length of time to maturity. Plotting interest rate yields (%) on the vertical axis and the length of time to maturity (years) on the horizontal axis results in a yield curve. Two yield curves for U.S. government securities are shown in Figure 8.4.[6] Note the different shapes of the two yield curves. The yield curve for August 1981 is *downward sloping*, indicating that the

[6]The primary reason for examining U.S. government securities is that we are able to hold constant many of the factors affecting yields, such as default risk. Corporate debt security issues, even for the same company, often differ significantly with respect to their key provisions, including sinking fund, call, conversion, subordination, and mortgage features. Hence, these bond issues differ with respect to risk. Consequently, it is difficult to use corporate debt securities to make yield versus time-to-maturity comparisons. However, the same general conclusions concerning the term structure of interest rates apply to these securities.

FIGURE 8.4

Yield Curves Showing the Term Structure of Interest Rates for U.S. Treasury Securities

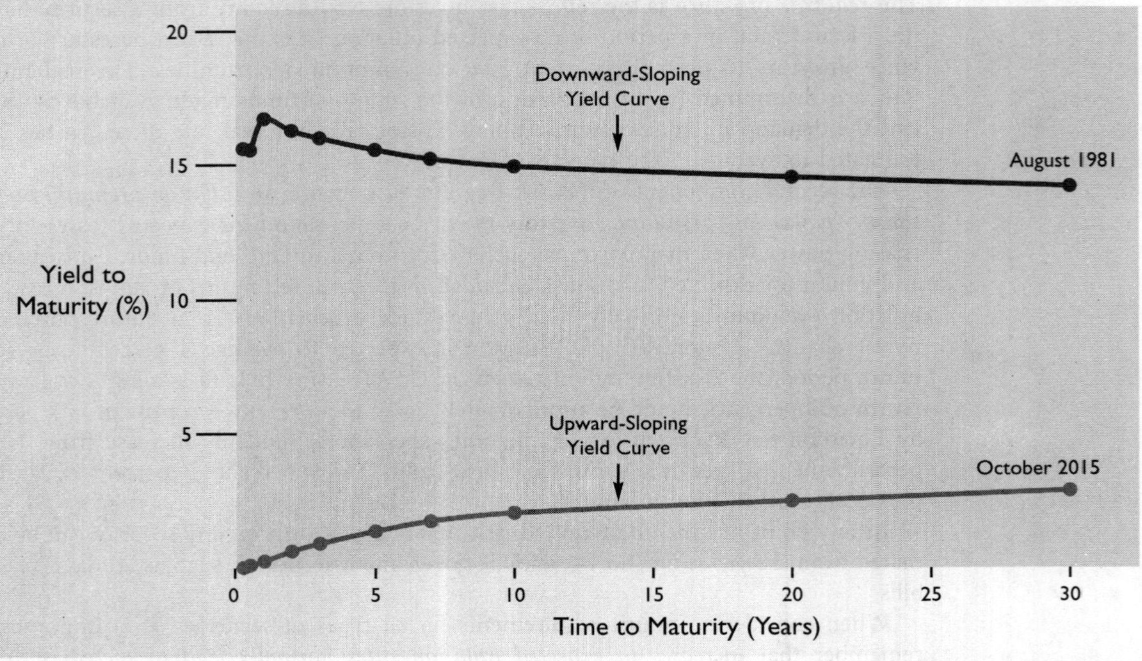

Sources: *Federal Reserve Bulletin* (October 1981): A27; *Selected Interest Rates* (weekly) (November 30, 2015): H. 15, www.federalreserve.gov.

longer the time to maturity, the lower the required return on the security. The yield curve for October 2015 is *upward sloping*, indicating that the longer the time to maturity, the higher the required return on the security.[7] In general, the yield curve has been upward sloping more often than it has been downward sloping.

A number of theories have been advanced to explain the shape of the yield curve, including the expectations theory, liquidity (or maturity) premium theory, and market segmentation theory.

According to the *expectations theory*, long-term interest rates are a function of expected future (that is, forward) short-term interest rates. If future short-term interest rates are expected to rise, the yield curve will tend to be upward sloping. In contrast, a downward-sloping yield curve reflects an expectation of declining future short-term interest rates. According to the expectations theory, current and expected future interest rates are dependent on expectations about future rates of inflation. Many economic and political conditions can cause expected future inflation and interest rates to rise or fall. These conditions include expected future government deficits (or surpluses), changes in Federal Reserve monetary policy (that is, the rate of growth of the money supply), and cyclical business conditions.

HTTP:
An excellent source of economic and financial data is the Federal Reserve Bank of St. Louis Web site.
www.stlouisfed.org

The *liquidity (or maturity) premium theory* of the yield curve holds that required returns on long-term securities tend to be greater the longer the time to maturity. The maturity premium reflects a preference by many lenders for shorter maturities because the **interest rate risk** associated with these securities is less than with longer-term

interest rate risk

[7] Upward- and downward-sloping yield curves are not the only possible shapes. At various times in the past, the yield curve has been relatively flat and also has been hump-shaped, that is, with high intermediate-term yields and low short-term and long-term yields.

securities. As discussed in Chapter 6, the value of a bond tends to vary more as interest rates change, the longer the term to maturity. Thus, if interest rates rise, the holder of a long-term bond will find that the value of the investment has declined substantially more than that of the holder of a short-term bond. In addition, the short-term bondholder has the option of holding the bond for the short time remaining to maturity and then reinvesting the proceeds from that bond at the new higher interest rate. The long-term bondholder must wait much longer before this opportunity is available. Accordingly, it is argued that whatever the shape of the yield curve, a liquidity (or maturity) premium is reflected in it. The liquidity premium is larger for long-term bonds than for short-term bonds.

Finally, according to the *market segmentation theory*, the securities markets are segmented by maturity. Furthermore, interest rates within each maturity segment are determined to a certain extent by the supply and demand interactions of the segment's borrowers and lenders. If strong borrower demand exists for long-term funds and these funds are in short supply, the yield curve will be upward sloping. Conversely, if strong borrower demand exists for short-term funds and these funds are in short supply, the yield curve will be downward sloping.

Several factors limit the choice of maturities by lenders. One such factor is the legal regulations that limit the types of investments commercial banks, savings and loan associations, insurance companies, and other financial institutions are permitted to make. Another limitation faced by lenders is the desire (or need) to match the maturity structure of their liabilities with assets of equivalent maturity. For example, insurance companies and pension funds, because of the long-term nature of their contractual obligations to clients, are interested primarily in making long-term investments. Commercial banks and money market funds, in contrast, are primarily short-term lenders because a large proportion of their liabilities is in the form of deposits that can be withdrawn on demand.

At any point in time, the term structure of interest rates is the result of the interaction of the factors just described. All three theories are useful in explaining the shape of the yield curve.

The Default Risk Premium U.S. government securities are generally considered to be free of default risk—that is, the risk that interest and principal will not be paid as promised in the bond indenture. In contrast, corporate bonds are subject to varying degrees of default risk. Investors require higher rates of return on securities subject to default risk. As seen in Table 8.5, the yields on bonds increase as the risk of default (indicated by the Moody's rating) increases, reflecting the positive relationship between

TABLE 8.5

Relationship Between Default Risk and Required Returns

	Yield	
Security	November 2008	October 2015
U.S. Treasury Bonds (20 years)	4.27	2.50
Aaa-rated Corporate Bonds (highest grade)	6.12	3.95
Baa-rated Corporate Bonds (medium grade)	9.21	5.34

Sources: *Selected Interest Rates, Historical Data*, H.15, www.federalreserve.gov; *Selected Interest Rates* (Weekly) (November 2015): H.15, www.federalreserve.gov.

risk and required return.[8] The spread between the required returns on bonds having various levels of default risk varies over time, reflecting the economic prospects and the resulting probability of default. For example, in November 2008, during the financial crisis, the spread between the required returns (yield) on Aaa-rated corporate bonds and Treasury bonds was 1.85 percentage points (6.12 versus 4.27). This compares with a spread of only 1.45 percentage points (3.95 versus 2.50) in October 2015, when the financial crisis had abated and the economy was headed in a positive direction. Likewise, the spread between Baa-rated and Aaa-rated corporate bonds narrowed significantly from 3.09 percentage points in November 2008 to 1.39 percentage points in October 2015.

Seniority Risk Premium Corporations issue many different types of securities. These securities differ with respect to their claim on the cash flows generated by the company and the claim on the company's assets in the case of default. A partial listing of these securities—from the least senior (that is, from the security having the lowest priority claim on cash flows and assets) to the most senior—includes the following: common stock, preferred stock, income bonds, subordinated debentures, debentures, second mortgage bonds, and first mortgage bonds.[9] Generally, the less senior the claims of the security holder, the greater the required rate of return demanded by investors in that security. For example, the holders of Aaa-rated (that is, the highest rating by Moody's) bonds issued by ExxonMobil are assured that they will receive interest and principal payments on these bonds except in the highly unlikely event that the company faces bankruptcy. In contrast, ExxonMobil common stockholders have no such assurance regarding dividend payments. Also, in the case of bankruptcy, all senior claim holders must be paid before common stockholders receive any proceeds from the liquidation of the firm. Accordingly, common stockholders require a higher rate of return on their investment in ExxonMobil stock than do the company's bondholders.

marketability risk

Marketability Risk Premium **Marketability risk** refers to the ability of an investor to buy and sell a company's securities quickly and without a significant loss of value. For example, there is very little marketability risk for the shares of stock of most companies that are traded on the New York Stock Exchange or listed on the NASDAQ system for over-the-counter stocks. For these securities, there is an active market. Trades can be executed almost instantaneously with low transaction costs at the current market price. In contrast, if you own shares in a rural Nebraska bank, you might find it difficult to locate a buyer for those shares (unless you owned a controlling interest in the bank). When a buyer is found, that buyer may not be willing to pay the price that you could get for similar shares of a larger bank listed on the New York Stock Exchange. The marketability risk premium can be significant for securities that are not regularly traded, such as the shares of many small and medium-size firms.

8-3c Business and Financial Risk[10]

Within individual security classes, one observes significant differences in required rates of return between firms. For example, the required rate of return on the common stock of AMR (parent of American Airlines), which filed for bankruptcy in 2011, was considerably higher than the required rate of return on the common stock of Southwest

[8]A more detailed discussion of bond ratings is contained in Chapter 6.

[9]The various forms of debt (that is, debentures and bonds) are described in Chapter 6.

[10]Business and financial risk are examined in greater detail in Chapter 13.

business risk

Airlines. The difference in the required rate of return on the securities of these two companies reflected differences in their business and financial risk. The **business risk** of a firm refers to the variability in the firm's operating earnings over time. Business risk is influenced by many factors, including the variability in sales and operating costs over a business cycle, the diversity of a firm's product line, the market power of the firm, and the choice of production technology. Over the period from 2001 to 2010, the operating profit margin ratio for Southwest Airlines was consistently higher and much less variable from year to year than for AMR. As a stronger, and more efficient firm, Southwest Airlines can be expected to have a lower perceived level of business risk and a resulting lower required return on its common stock (all other things held constant).

financial risk

Financial risk refers to the additional variability in a company's earnings per share that results from the use of fixed-cost sources of funds, such as debt and preferred stock. In addition, as debt financing increases, the risk of bankruptcy increases. For example, AMR had a much higher proportion of debt in its capital structure compared with Southwest Airlines. Unlike AMR, which incurred losses (more than $10 billion overall) in 8 of the 10 years prior to filing for bankruptcy, Southwest was profitable in each of these years. This difference in financial risk led to lower required returns on the common stock of Southwest Airlines compared to the common stock of AMR, all other things being equal.

Business and financial risk are reflected in the default risk premium applied by investors to a firm's securities. The higher these risks are, the higher the risk premium and required rate of return on the firm's securities.

8-3d Risk and Required Returns for Various Types of Securities

Figure 8.5 illustrates the relationship between required rates of return and risk, as represented by the various risk premiums just discussed. As shown in Figure 8.5, the lowest risk security is represented by short-term U.S. Treasury bills. All other securities have one or more elements of additional risk, resulting in increasing required returns by investors. The order illustrated in this figure is indicative of the general relationship between risk and required returns of various security types. There will be situations that result in differences in the ordering of risk and required returns. For example, it is possible that the risk of some junk (high-risk) bonds may be so great that investors require a higher rate of return on these bonds than they require on high-grade common stocks.

The relationship between risk and return can be observed by examining the returns actually earned by investors in various types of securities over long periods of time. Finance professionals believe that investor expectations of the relative returns anticipated from various types of securities are heavily influenced by the returns that have been earned on these securities over long periods in the past. Over the period from 1926 to 2014, investors in small-company common stocks earned average returns of 16.7 percent compared with 12.1 percent for investors in large-company stocks.[11] However, these higher returns on small-company stocks have come with substantially greater variability in annual returns. This variation, as measured by the standard deviation, has been approximately 32 percent for small-company stocks versus about 20 percent for large-company stocks. Returns on long-term corporate bonds have averaged about 6.4 percent, or slightly more than one-half the returns on large-company stocks, but the risk (standard deviation) of the returns on these bonds has also been much lower (8.4 percent). Short-term U.S. Treasury bills have offered the lowest average annual returns

[11] *Stocks, Bonds, Bills, and Inflation*: 2015 Classic Yearbook™ (Chicago: Morningstar, Inc., 2015): 40.

FIGURE 8.5

Conceptual Risk-Return Relationship

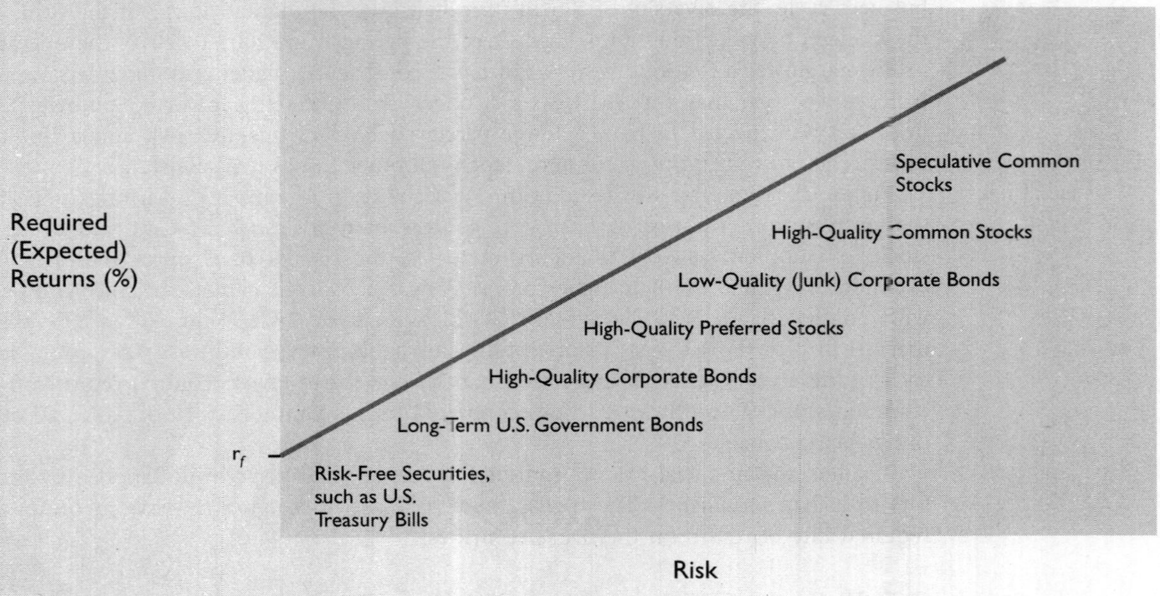

(3.5 percent) but have also had the lowest risk of all the securities examined (standard deviation of 3.1 percent). During the 89 years (1926–2014), inflation averaged 3.0 percent per year with a standard deviation of 4.1 percent.

8-4 Investment Diversification and Portfolio Risk Analysis[12]

The preceding sections examined the risk and returns associated with investments in single assets—either financial assets (securities) or physical assets. However, most individuals and institutions invest in a **portfolio** of assets, that is, a collection of two or more assets. Commercial banks invest in many different types of financial assets when they make loans to consumers and businesses; individuals invest in many different types of financial assets when they buy securities, such as bank certificates of deposit and corporate bonds and stocks; and corporations invest in many different kinds of physical assets when they acquire production and distribution facilities (that is, plant and equipment). Consequently, it is important to know how the returns from portfolios of investments behave over time—not just how the returns from individual assets in the portfolio behave. *Portfolio risk*, the risk associated with collections of financial and physical assets,

portfolio

[12]Two economists, Harry M. Markowitz and William F. Sharpe, were corecipients (along with Merton H. Miller) of the 1990 Nobel Prize for Economics for their pioneering work in portfolio theory (discussed in this section) and the Capital Asset Pricing Model (discussed in the following section). See Harry M. Markowitz, "Portfolio Selection," *Journal of Finance* 7 (March 1952): 77–91, and *Portfolio Selection: Efficient Diversification of Investments* (New York: John Wiley, 1959); William F. Sharpe, "A Simplified Model for Portfolio Analysis," *Management Science* (January 1963): 277–291, and "Capital Asset Prices: A Theory of Market Equilibrium Under Conditions of Risk," *Journal of Finance* (September 1964): 425–442.

is considered in this and the following two sections. The questions of importance are as follows:

- What return can be expected to be earned from the portfolio?
- What is the risk of the portfolio?

Consider the following example. Suppose that Alcoa (an aluminum producer) is considering diversifying into gold mining and refining. During economic boom periods, aluminum sales tend to be brisk; gold, on the other hand, tends to be most in demand during periods of economic uncertainty.[13] Therefore, let us assume that the returns from the aluminum business and the gold mining business are inversely, or *negatively*, related. If Alcoa expands into gold mining and refining, its overall return will tend to be less variable than individual returns from these businesses.

This effect is illustrated in Figure 8.6. Panel (a) shows the variation of rates of return in the aluminum industry over time; panel (b) shows the corresponding variation of returns from gold mining over the same time frame; and panel (c) shows the combined rate of return for both lines of business. As can be seen from this figure, when the return from aluminum operations is high, the return from gold mining tends to be low, and vice versa. The *combined* returns are more stable and therefore less risky.

This *portfolio effect* of reduced variability results because a *negative correlation* exists between the returns from aluminum operations and the returns from gold mining. The **correlation** between any two variables—such as rates of return or net cash flows—is a relative statistical measure of the degree to which these variables tend to move together. The correlation coefficient (ρ) measures the extent to which high (or low) values of one variable are associated with high (or low) values of another. Values of the correlation coefficient can range from $+1.0$ for *perfectly positively correlated* variables to -1.0 for *perfectly negatively correlated* variables. If two variables are unrelated (that is, uncorrelated), the correlation coefficient between these two variables will be 0.

correlation

FIGURE **8.6**

Illustration of Diversification and Risk Reduction: Alcoa

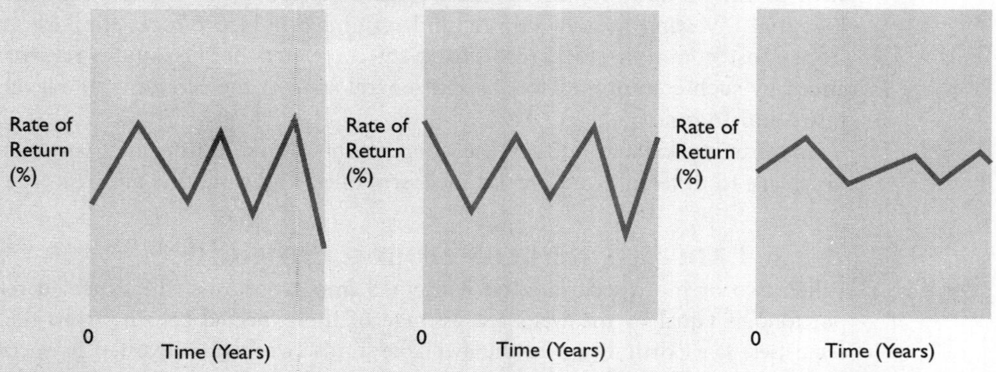

(a) Aluminum (b) Gold Mining (c) Aluminum and Gold Mining Combined

[13]As investors lose confidence in the economy's performance, many of them turn to gold as an investment. This drives the price of gold up and increases returns to gold mining firms, whose costs of operation are not directly related to the demand for gold.

FIGURE 8.7

Illustration of (a) Perfect Positive, (b) Perfect Negative, and (c) Zero Correlation for Two Investments

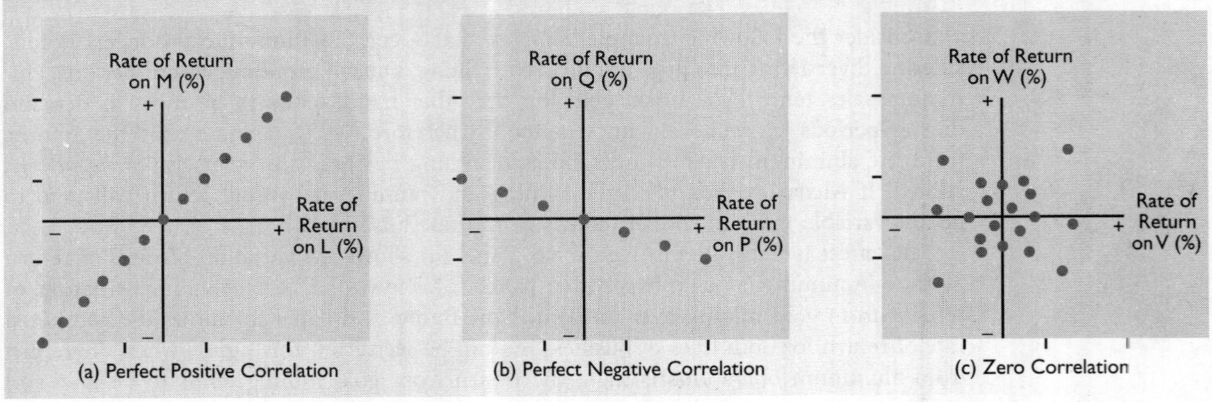

Figure 8.7 illustrates perfect positive correlation, perfect negative correlation, and zero correlation for different pairs of common stock investments. For perfect positive correlation, panel (a), high rates of return from Stock L are always associated with high rates of return from Stock M; conversely, low rates of return from L are always associated with low rates of return from M. For perfect negative correlation, panel (b), however, the opposite is true; high rates of return from Stock P are associated with low rates of return from Stock Q and vice versa. For zero correlation, panel (c), no perceptible pattern or relationship exists between the rates of return on Stocks V and W.

In practice, the returns from most investments a firm or an individual considers are positively correlated with other investments held by the firm or individual. For example, returns from projects that are closely related to the firm's primary line of business have a high positive correlation with returns from projects already being carried out and thus provide limited opportunities to reduce risk. In the Alcoa example, if Alcoa were to build a new aluminum smelter, it would not realize the risk reduction possibilities that investing in gold mining and refining would produce. Similarly, the returns from most common stocks are positively correlated because these returns are influenced by such common factors as the general state of the economy, the level of interest rates, and so on.

In order to explore further the concepts of diversification and portfolio risk, it is necessary to develop more precise measures of portfolio returns and risk.

8-4a Expected Returns from a Portfolio

When two or more securities are combined into a portfolio, the expected return of the portfolio is equal to the weighted average of the expected returns from the individual securities. If a portion, w_A, of the available funds (wealth) is invested in Security A, and the remaining portion, w_B, is invested in Security B, the expected return of the portfolio, r_p, is as follows:

(8.7)
$$\hat{r}_p = w_A\hat{r}_A + w_B\hat{r}_B$$

where $\hat{r}_A$ and $\hat{r}_B$ are the expected returns for Securities A and B, respectively. Furthermore, $w_A + w_B = 1$, indicating that all funds are invested in either Security A or Security B.

For example, consider a portfolio consisting of the common stock of American Electric Power (A), a public utility company, and Boeing (B), an aerospace producer. The expected returns on the two stocks are 12 percent ($\hat{r}_A$) and 16 percent ($\hat{r}_B$), respectively. A portfolio consisting of 75 percent (w_A) invested in American Electric Power and the remainder, or 25 percent (w_B), invested in Boeing would yield an expected return, by Equation 8.7, of:

$$\hat{r}_p = 0.75(12\%) + 0.25(16\%)$$
$$= 13.0\%$$

Table 8.6 (columns w_A and $\hat{r}_p$) and Figure 8.8 illustrate the relationship between the expected return for a portfolio containing Securities A and B and the proportion of the total portfolio invested in each security. For example, when $w_A = 1.0$ (100%) and $w_B = 0$ (because $w_A + w_B = 1.0$), the expected portfolio return is 12 percent, the same as the return for A. When $w_A = 0.5$ (50%) and $w_B = 0.5$ (50%), the expected portfolio return is 14 percent. As shown earlier, when $w_A = 0.75$ and $w_B = 0.25$, the expected portfolio return is 13 percent. Thus, it can be seen that the expected return from a portfolio of securities is simply equal to the weighted average of the individual security returns, where the weights represent the proportion of the total portfolio invested in each security. This results in the linear relationship shown in Figure 8.8.

In general, the expected return from any portfolio of n securities or assets is equal to the sum of the expected returns from each security times the proportion of the total portfolio invested in that security:

(8.8) $$\hat{r}_p = \sum_{i=1}^{n} w_i \hat{r}_i$$

8-4b Portfolio Risk

Although the expected returns from a portfolio of two or more securities can be computed as a weighted average of the expected returns from the individual securities, it is generally not sufficient merely to calculate a weighted average of the risk of each individual security to arrive at a measure of the portfolio's risk. Whenever the returns from the individual securities are not perfectly positively correlated, the risk of any portfolio of these securities may be reduced through the effects of diversification. Thus, **diversification** can be achieved by investing in a set of securities that have different risk-return

diversification

TABLE 8.6

Expected Returns and Portfolio Risk from a Portfolio of Stocks of American Electric Power (A) and Boeing (B)

Proportion Invested in Security A	Expected Return on Portfolio	Portfolio Risk σ_p (%)		
w_A (%)	r_p (%)	$\rho_{AB} = +1.0$	$\rho_{AB} = 0.0$	$\rho_{AB} = -1.0$
0.0%	16.0%	20.0%	20.0%	20.0%
25.0	15.0	17.5	15.0	12.5
33.333	14.67	16.67	13.74	10.0
50.0	14.0	15.0	11.2	5.0
66.667	13.33	13.33	9.43	0.0
75.0	13.0	12.5	9.01	2.5
100.0	12.0	10.0	10.0	10.0

Note: $\hat{r}_A = 12\%$; $\hat{r}_B = 16\%$; $\sigma_A = 10\%$; $\sigma_B = 20\%$.

FIGURE 8.8

Expected Return from a Portfolio of Stocks of American Electric Power (A) and Boeing (B)

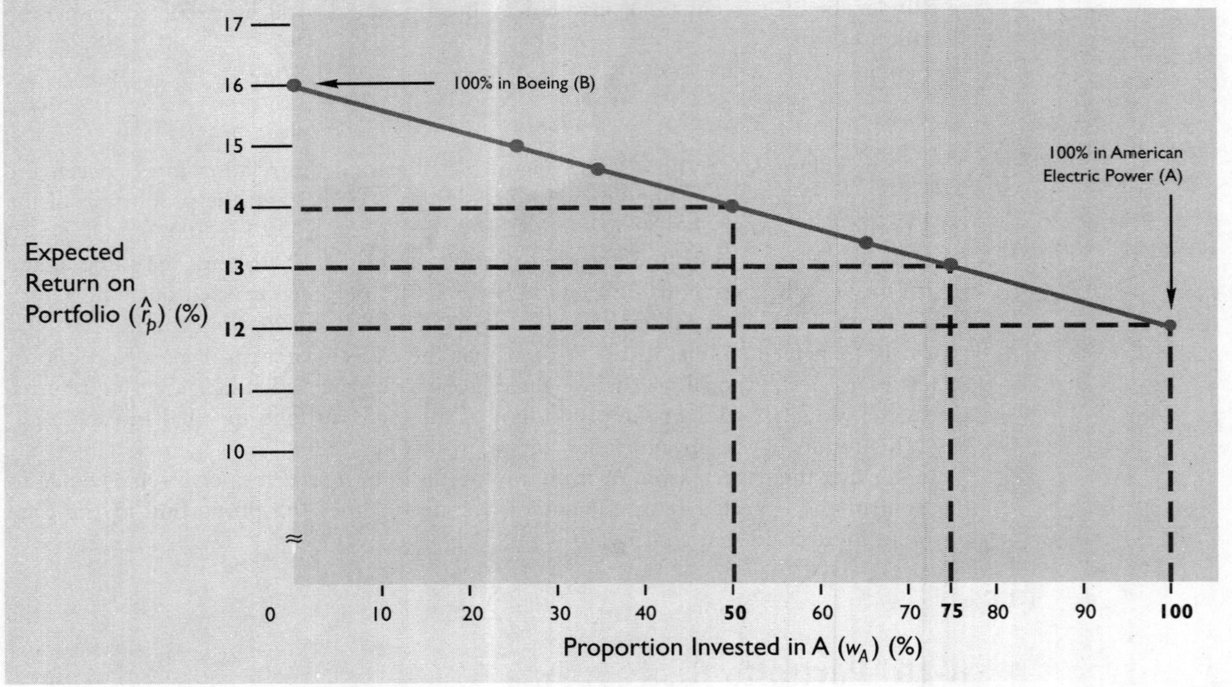

Note: $\hat{r}_A = 12\%$; $\hat{r}_B = 16\%$; $w_A + w_B = 1.0$ (100%). Data points in graph are from Table 8.6.

characteristics. The amount of risk reduction achieved through diversification depends on the degree of correlation between the returns of the individual securities in the portfolio. The lower the correlations among the individual securities, the greater the possibilities of risk reduction.

The risk for a two-security portfolio, measured by the standard deviation of portfolio returns, is computed as follows:

(8.9)
$$\sigma_p = \sqrt{w_A^2\sigma_A^2 + w_B^2\sigma_B^2 + 2w_A w_B \rho_{AB}\sigma_A\sigma_B}$$

where w_A is the proportion of funds invested in Security A; w_B is the proportion of funds invested in Security B; $w_A + w_B = 1$; σ^2_A is the variance of returns from Security A (or the square of the standard deviation for Security A, σ_A); σ^2_B is the variance of returns from Security B (or the square of the standard deviation for Security B, σ_B); and ρ_{AB} is the correlation coefficient of returns between Securities A and B.[14]

[14]In general, the risk of a portfolio containing *n* securities, as measured by the standard deviation of portfolio returns, is computed as follows:

$$\sigma_p = \sqrt{\sum_{i=1}^{n}\sum_{j=1}^{n} w_i w_j \rho_{ij}\sigma_i\sigma_j}$$

The double summation sign ($\sum\sum$) indicates that all possible combinations of *i* and *j* should be included in calculating the total value. Problem 16 at the end of the chapter examines the case of a three-security portfolio. Note that $\rho_{ij}\ \sigma_i\ \sigma_j$ is the covariance of returns between security *i* and security *j*.

Consider, for example, the portfolio discussed earlier consisting of the common stock of American Electric Power (A) and Boeing (B). The standard deviations of returns for these two securities are 10 percent (σ_A) and 20 percent (σ_B), respectively. Furthermore, suppose that the correlation coefficient (ρ_{AB}) between the returns on these securities is equal to +0.50. Using Equation 8.9, a portfolio consisting of 75 percent (w_A) invested in American Electric Power and 25 percent (w_B) in Boeing would yield a standard deviations of portfolio returns of:

$$\sigma_p = \sqrt{(.75)^2(10)^2 + (.25)^2(20)^2 + 2(.75)(.25)(+.50)(10)(20)}$$
$$= 10.90\%$$

With the techniques just described for calculating expected portfolio return and risk, we can now examine in greater detail the risk versus return trade-offs associated with investment diversification. The following three special cases illustrate how the correlation coefficient can affect portfolio risk.

Case I: Perfect Positive Correlation ($\rho = +1.0$) Table 8.6 (columns $\hat{r}_p$ and $\rho_{AB} = +1.0$) and panel (a) of Figure 8.9 illustrate the risk-return trade-offs associated with portfolios consisting of various combinations of American Electric Power (A) and Boeing (B) stock when $\rho_{AB} = +1.0$. *When the returns from the two securities are perfectly positively correlated, the risk of the portfolio is equal to the weighted average of the risk of the individual securities* (10 and 20 percent in this example). *Therefore, no risk reduction is achieved when perfectly positively correlated securities are combined in a portfolio.*

Case II: Zero Correlation ($\rho = 0.0$) Table 8.6 (columns $\hat{r}_p$ and $\rho_{AB} = 0.0$) and panel (b) of Figure 8.9 illustrate the possible trade-offs when $\rho_{AB} = 0.0$. In this case, we see that diversification can reduce portfolio risk below the risk of either of the securities that make up the portfolio. For example, an investment consisting of 75 percent in American Electric Power (A) stock and 25 percent in Boeing (B) stock has a portfolio standard deviation of only 9.01 percent, which is less than the standard deviations of either of the two securities (10 and 20 percent, respectively) in the portfolio. In general, *when the correlation coefficient between the returns on two securities is less than 1.0, diversification can reduce the risk of a portfolio below the weighted average of the total risk of the individual securities. The less positively correlated the returns from two securities, the greater the portfolio effects of risk reduction.* For example, the expected returns from an investment in two firms in different industries, such as ExxonMobil and Delta Airlines, should generally be less positively correlated than the expected returns between two firms in the same industry, such as ExxonMobil and Shell.

Case III: Perfect Negative Correlation ($\rho = -1.0$) Table 8.6 (columns $\hat{r}_p$ and $\rho_{AB} = -1.0$) and panel (c) of Figure 8.9 show the risk-return relationship when $\rho_{AB} = -1.0$. As illustrated, with perfectly negatively correlated returns, portfolio risk can be reduced to zero. In other words, *with a perfect negative correlation of returns between two securities, there will always be some proportion of the securities that will result in the complete elimination of portfolio risk.*

In summary, these three special cases serve to illustrate the effect that the correlation coefficient has on portfolio risk, as measured by the standard deviation. For any given pair of securities, the correlation coefficient is given (or can be estimated), and this number determines how much risk reduction can be achieved with various weighted combinations of the two securities.

FIGURE 8.9

Relationship Between Portfolio Expected Return and Risk for Stocks of American Electric Power (A) and Boeing (B)

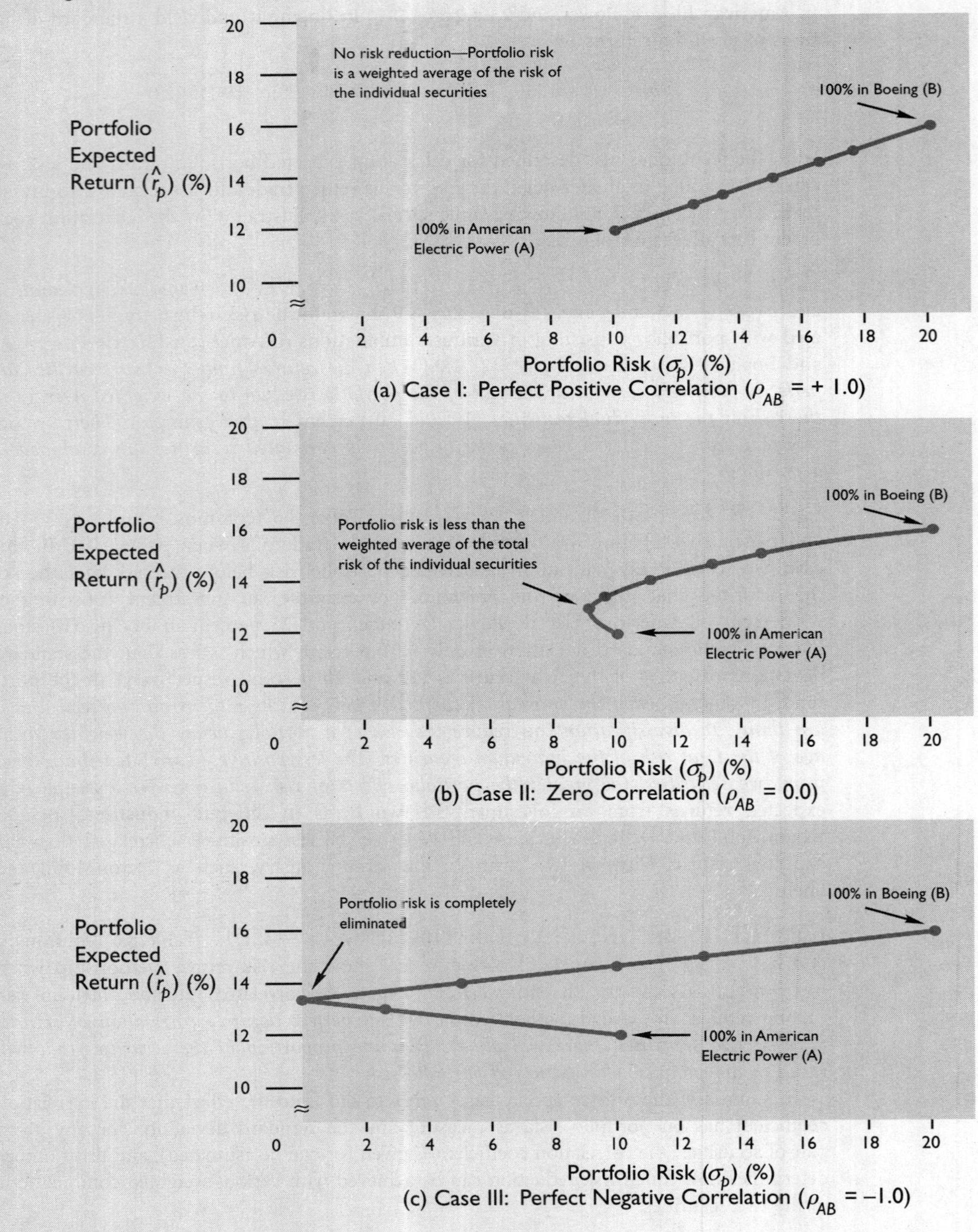

Note: $r_A = 12\%$; $r_B = 16\%$; $\sigma_A = 10\%$; $\sigma_B = 20\%$; $w_A + w_B = 1.0$ (100%). Data points in graphs are from Table 8.6.

8-4c Efficient Portfolios and the Capital Market Line

The risk-return relationships just discussed can be extended to analyze portfolios involving more than two securities. For example, consider the graph shown in Figure 8.10. Each dot within the shaded area represents the risk (standard deviation) and expected return for an individual security available for possible investment. The shaded area (or opportunity set) represents all the possible portfolios found by combining the given securities in different proportions. The curved segment from A to B on the boundary of the shaded area represents the set of **efficient portfolios**, or the **efficient frontier**. A portfolio is efficient if, for a given standard deviation, there is no other portfolio with a higher expected return, or for a given expected return, there is no other portfolio with a lower standard deviation.

efficient portfolios

efficient frontier

Risk-averse investors, in choosing their optimal portfolios, need only consider those portfolios on the efficient frontier. The choice of an optimal portfolio, whether portfolio A that minimizes risk or portfolio B that maximizes expected return or some other portfolio on the efficient frontier, depends on the investor's attitude toward risk (that is, risk aversion). More conservative investors will tend to choose lower-risk portfolios (closer to A); more aggressive investors will tend to select higher-risk portfolios (closer to B).

If investors are able to borrow and lend money at the risk-free rate (r_f), they can obtain any combination of risk and expected return on the straight line joining r_f and portfolio *m* as shown in Figure 8.11. When the market is in equilibrium, portfolio *m* represents the **Market Portfolio**, which consists of all available securities, weighted by

market portfolio

FIGURE 8.10
Portfolio Opportunity Set

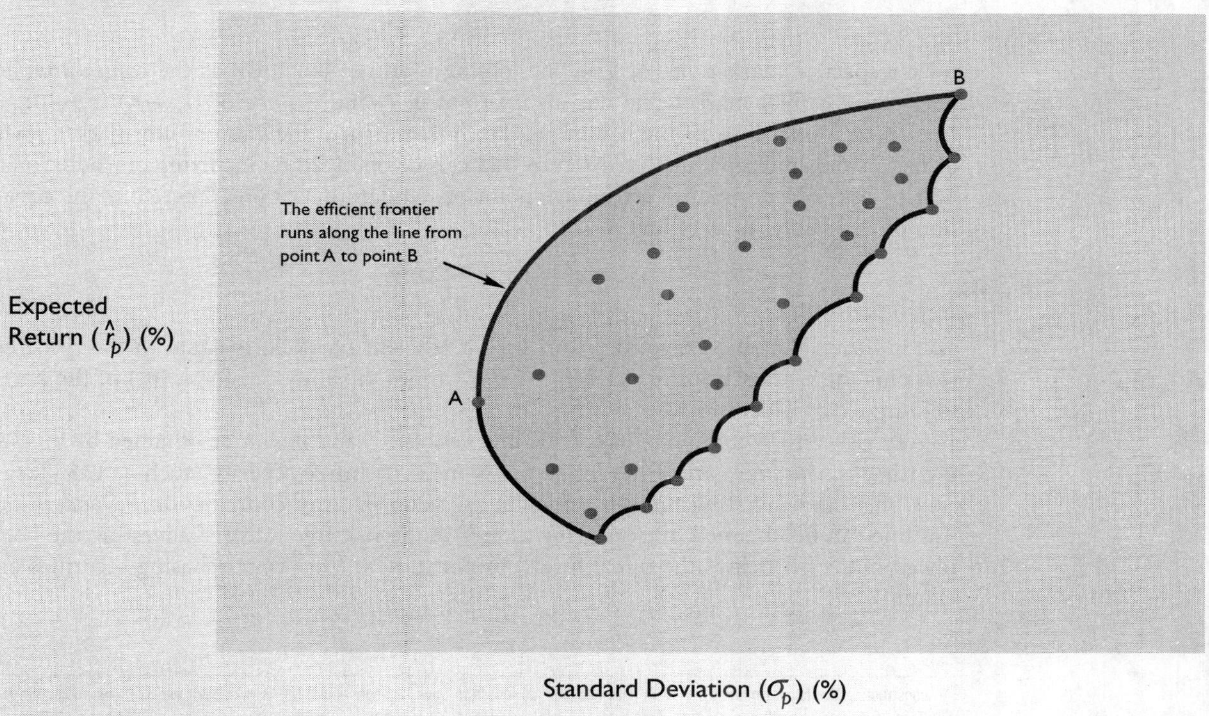

FIGURE 8.11
Capital Market Line

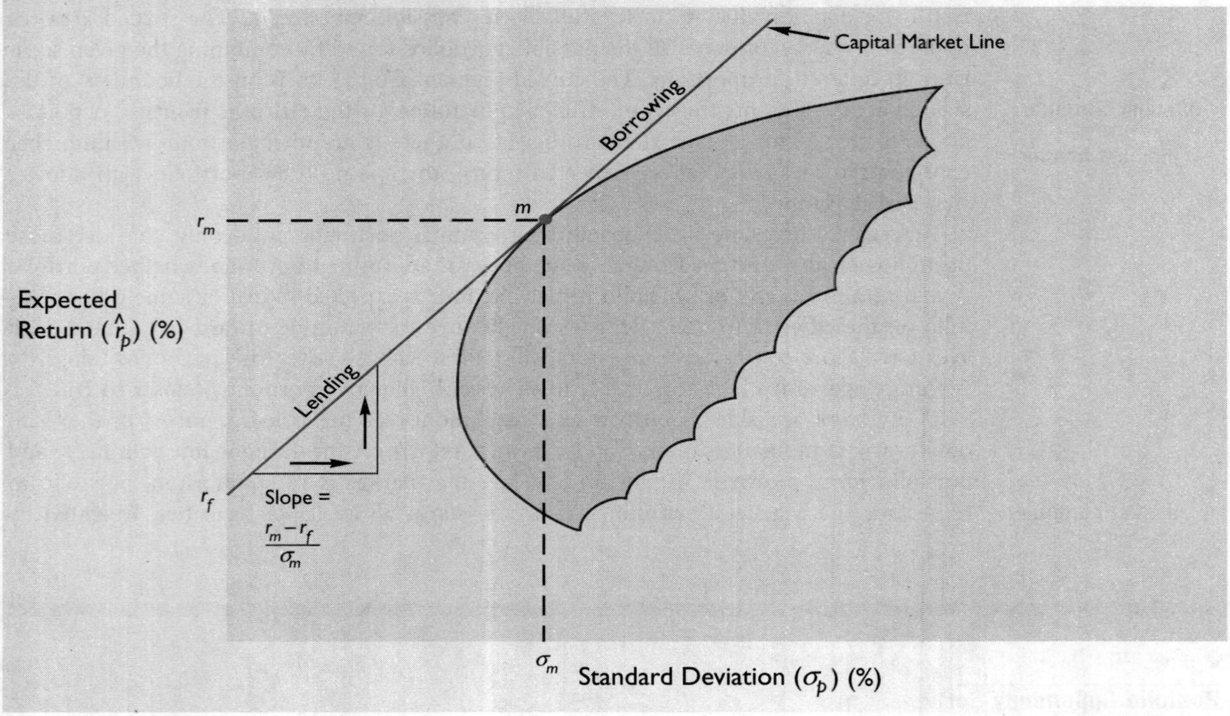

their respective market values. The line joining r_f and m is known as the *capital market* line.[15] The capital market line has an *intercept* of r_f and a *slope* of $(r_m - r_f)/(\sigma_m - 0) = (r_m - r_f)/\sigma_m$. The slope of the capital market line measures the equilibrium market price of risk or the additional expected return that can be obtained by incurring one additional unit of risk (one additional percentage point of standard deviation). Therefore, the equation of the capital market line is

$$\hat{r}_p = \hat{r}_f + \left(\frac{r_m - r_f}{\sigma_m}\right)\sigma_p \tag{8.10}$$

and indicates that the expected return for an efficient portfolio is equal to the risk-free rate plus the market price of risk $[(r_m - r_f)/\sigma_m]$ times the amount of risk (σ_p) of the portfolio under consideration.

Any risk-return combination on this line *between* r_f and m can be obtained by investing (that is, *lending*) part of the initial funds in the risk-free security (such as U.S. Treasury bills) and investing the remainder in portfolio m. Any combination *beyond* m on this line can be obtained by *borrowing* money at the risk-free rate and investing the borrowed funds (as well as the initial funds) in portfolio m (that is, purchasing securities on margin).

[15]In constructing the capital market line, it is assumed that all investors have homogeneous (that is, identical) expectations about the distributions of returns offered by securities. As a result of this assumption, all investors will perceive the same set of efficient portfolios.

With the ability to borrow and lend at the risk-free rate, the choice of an optimal portfolio for risk-averse investors involves determining the proportion of funds to invest in the Market Portfolio (m) with the remaining proportion being invested in the risk-free security. More conservative investors will tend to choose investments nearer to the r_f point on the capital market line. More aggressive investors will tend to select investments closer to, or possibly beyond, point m on the capital market line.

8-5 Portfolio Risk and the Capital Asset Pricing Model

The preceding analysis illustrates the possibilities for portfolio risk reduction when two or more securities are combined to form a portfolio. Unfortunately, when more than two securities are involved—as is usually the case—the number of calculations required to compute the portfolio risk increases geometrically. For example, whereas 45 correlation coefficients are needed for a portfolio containing 10 securities, 4,950 correlation coefficients must be computed for a portfolio containing 100 securities. In other words, a 10-fold increase in securities causes a greater than 100-fold increase in the required calculations.[16] In addition, a substantial computational undertaking is required to find the particular portfolio of securities that minimizes portfolio risk for a given level of return or maximizes return for a given level of risk, even for a portfolio that contains only a few securities. Obviously, a more workable method is needed to assess the effects of diversification on a portfolio of assets.

capital asset pricing model (CAPM)

One method that has gained widespread use in analyzing the relationship between portfolio risk and return is the **Capital Asset Pricing Model (CAPM)**. This model provides a strong analytical basis for evaluating risk-return relationships—both in the context of financial management and securities investment decisions. The remainder of this section discusses the development and application of the CAPM.

8-5a Systematic and Unsystematic Risk

As illustrated in the previous section, whenever the individual securities in a portfolio are less than perfectly positively correlated, diversification can reduce the portfolio's risk below the weighted average of the total risk (measured by the standard deviation) of the individual securities. Because most securities are positively correlated with returns in the securities market in general, it is usually not possible to eliminate all risk in a portfolio of securities. As the economic outlook improves, returns on most individual securities tend to increase; as the economic outlook deteriorates, individual security returns tend to decline. In spite of this positive "comovement" among the returns of individual securities, each security experiences some "unique" variation in its returns that is unrelated to the underlying economic factors that influence all securities. In other words, there are two types of risk inherent in each security:

- Systematic (market), or nondiversifiable, risk
- Unsystematic (unique), or diversifiable, risk

The sum of these two types of risk equals the total risk of the security:

(8.11)
$$\begin{matrix}\text{Total} \\ \text{risk}\end{matrix} = \begin{matrix}\text{Systematic risk} \\ \text{(nondiversifiable risk)}\end{matrix} + \begin{matrix}\text{Unsystematic risk} \\ \text{(diversifiable risk)}\end{matrix}$$

systematic risk

Systematic risk refers to that portion of the variability of an individual security's returns caused by factors affecting the market as a whole; as such, it can be thought of as being

[16]The number of correlation coefficients needed to evaluate an n-security portfolio is computed as $(n^2-n)/2$.

nondiversifiable. Systematic risk accounts for 25 to 50 percent of the total risk of any security. Some of the sources of systematic risk, which cause the returns from all securities to tend to move in the same direction over time, include the following:

- Interest rate changes
- Changes in purchasing power (inflation)
- Changes in investor expectations about the overall performance of the economy

Because diversification cannot eliminate systematic risk, this type of risk is the predominant determinant of individual security risk premiums.

unsystematic risk

Unsystematic risk is risk that is unique to the firm. It is the variability in a security's returns caused by such factors as the following:

- Management capabilities and decisions
- Strikes
- The availability of raw materials
- The unique effects of government regulation, such as pollution control
- The effects of foreign competition
- The particular levels of financial and operating leverage the firm employs

Since unsystematic risk is unique to each firm, an efficiently diversified portfolio of securities can successfully eliminate most of the unsystematic risk inherent in individual securities, as is shown in Figure 8.12. To effectively eliminate the unsystematic risk inherent in a portfolio's individual securities, it is not necessary for the portfolio to include a large number of securities. In fact, randomly constructed portfolios of as few as 20 to 25 securities on average can successfully diversify away a large portion of the unsystematic risk of the individual securities.[17] The risk remaining *after* diversification is market-related risk, or systematic risk, and it cannot be eliminated through diversification. Because unsystematic risk commonly accounts for 50 percent or more of the total risk of most individual securities, it should be obvious that the risk-reducing benefits of efficient diversification are well worth the effort.

Given the small number of securities required for efficient diversification by an individual investor, as well as the dominance of the securities markets by many large institutional investors who hold widely diversified portfolios, it is safe to conclude that the most relevant risk that must be considered for any widely traded individual security is its systematic risk. The unsystematic portion of total risk is relatively easy to diversify away.

8-5b Security Market Line (SML)

As discussed earlier in the chapter (see Equation 8.5), the return required of any risky asset is determined by the prevailing level of risk-free interest rates plus a risk premium. The greater the level of risk an investor perceives about a security's return, the greater the required risk premium will be. In other words, investors require returns that are commensurate with the risk level they perceive. In algebraic terms, the required return from any Security j, k_j, is equal to the following:

(8.12) $$k_j = r_f + \theta_j$$

where r_f is the risk-free rate and θ_j is the risk premium required by investors.

[17] A study by John Y. Campbell, Martin Lettau, Burton G. Malkiel, and Yexio Xu, "Have Individual Stocks Become More Volatile? An Empirical Exploration of Idiosyncratic Risk," *Journal of Finance* 56, no. 1 (February 2001): 1–43, of about 9,000 companies traded on the major U.S. stock exchanges suggests that the increased volatility (risk) of individual stocks over the period from 1962 to 1997 may have increased the number of stocks required to successfully diversify away a large portion of the unsystematic risk in security returns. Their results indicate that as many as 50 stocks may be required today to achieve the same amount of risk reduction as 20 stocks did in the past.

FIGURE 8.12

Unsystematic Risk and Portfolio Diversification

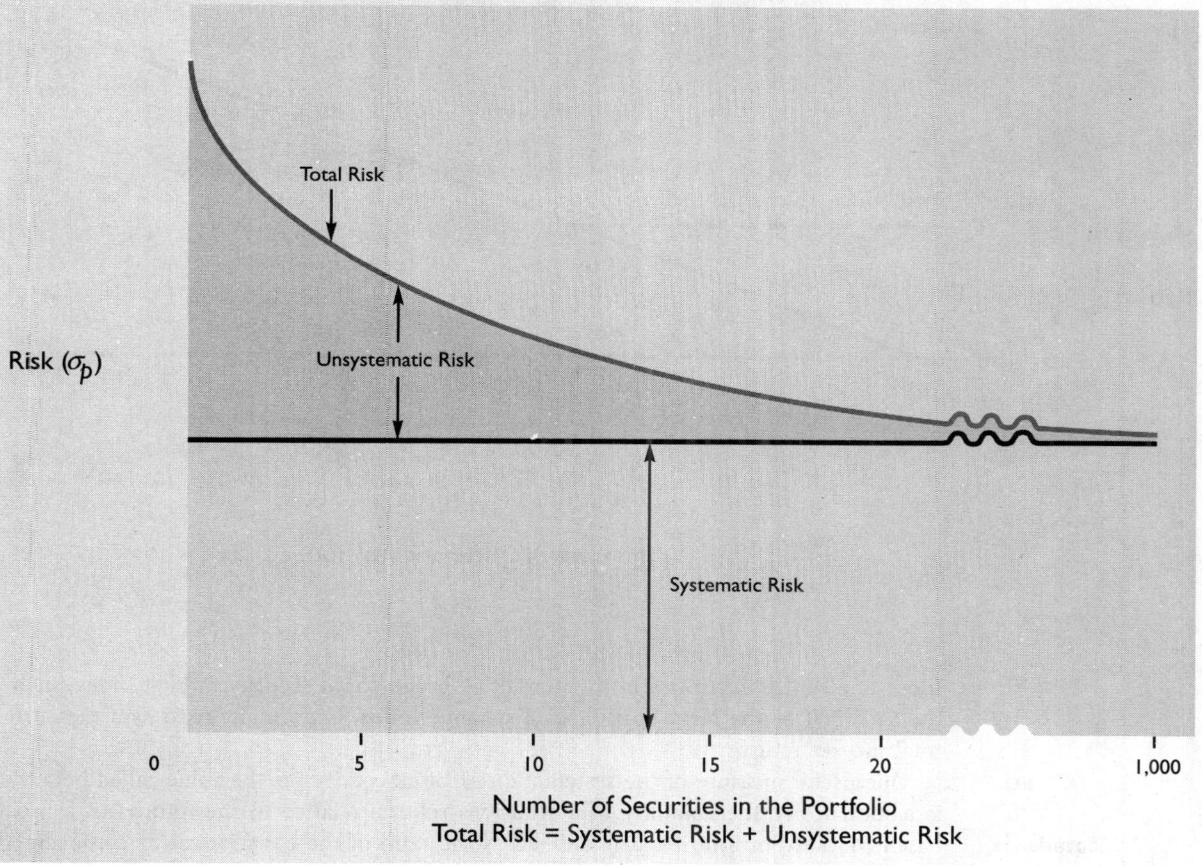

security market line (SML)

The **security market line (SML)** indicates the "going" required rate of return (k_j) on a security in the market for a given amount of *systematic risk* and is illustrated in Figure 8.13. The SML intersects the vertical axis at the risk-free rate, r_f, indicating that any security with an expected risk premium equal to zero should be required to earn a return equal to the risk-free rate. As systematic risk increases, so do the risk premium and the required rate of return. According to Figure 8.13, for example, a security having a risk level of *a* should be required to earn a 10 percent rate of return.

8-5c Beta: A Measure of Systematic Risk

Thus far, we have not addressed the question of the appropriate risk measure to use when considering the risk-return trade-offs illustrated by the SML. The previous discussion of risk in a portfolio context suggests that a measure of systematic risk is an appropriate starting point.

The systematic risk of a security is a function of the total risk of a security as measured by the standard deviation of the security's returns, the standard deviation of the returns from the Market Portfolio, and the correlation of the security's returns with

FIGURE 8.13

The Security Market Line (SML)

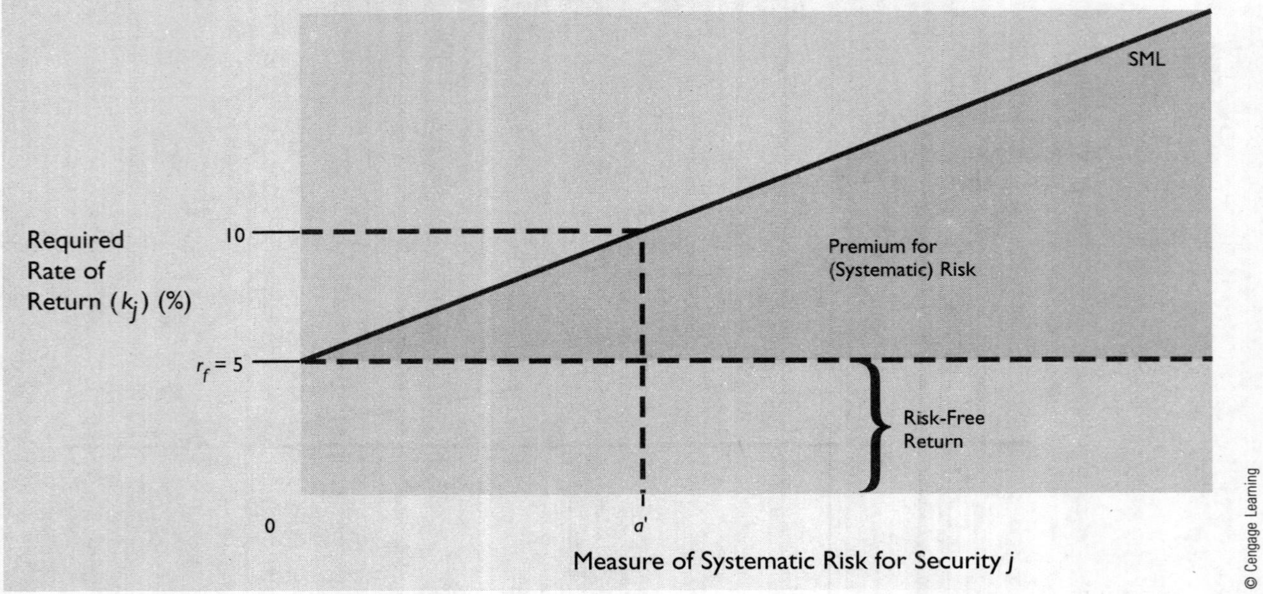

those of all other securities in the market. A broad-based security market index, such as the S&P 500 or the New York Stock Exchange Index, is normally used as a measure of total market returns.

beta One useful measure of the systematic risk of a Security j is the value called **beta**. Beta is a measure of the volatility of a security's returns relative to the returns of a broad-based Market Portfolio m. It is defined as the ratio of the **covariance** (or comovement) of returns on Security j and Market Portfolio m to the variance of returns on the Market Portfolio:

covariance

(8.13)

$$\beta_j = \frac{\text{Covariance}_{j,m}}{\text{Variance}_m}$$

$$\beta_j = \frac{\rho_{jm}\sigma_j\sigma_m}{\sigma_m^2}$$

where β_j is the measure of systematic risk for Security j; σ_j is the standard deviation of returns for Security j; σ_m is the standard deviation of returns for the Market Portfolio m; $\sigma^2{}_m$ is the variance of returns for the Market Portfolio m; and ρ_{jm} is the correlation coefficient between returns for Security j and Market Portfolio m.

In practice, beta may be computed as the slope of a regression line between periodic (usually yearly, quarterly, or monthly) rates of return on the Market Portfolio (as measured by a market index, such as the S&P 500) and the periodic rates of return for Security j, as follows:

(8.14)

$$k_j = a_j + \beta_j r_m + e_j$$

where k_j is the periodic percentage holding period rate of return for Security j; a_j is a constant term determined by the regression; *β_j is the computed historical beta for Security*

characteristic line

j; r_m is the periodic percentage holding period rate of return for the market index; and e_j is a random error term. This equation describes a line called Security *j*'s **characteristic line**.

Figure 8.14 shows the characteristic line for Alliance Motors. The slope (and intercept) of this line can be estimated using the least-squares technique of regression analysis. The slope of this line, or beta, is 0.97, indicating that the systematic returns from Alliance Motors common stock are slightly less variable than the returns for the market as a whole.

A beta of 1.0 for any security indicates that the security is of average systematic risk; that is, a security with a beta of 1.0 has the same risk characteristics as the market as a whole when only systematic risk is considered. When beta equals 1.0, a 1 percent increase (decline) in market returns indicates that the *systematic* returns for the individual security should increase (decline) by 1 percent.[18] A beta greater than 1.0—for example, 2.0—indicates that the security has greater-than-average systematic risk. In this case, when market returns increase (decline) by 1 percent, the security's systematic returns can

FIGURE 8.14

Characteristic Line for Alliance Motors

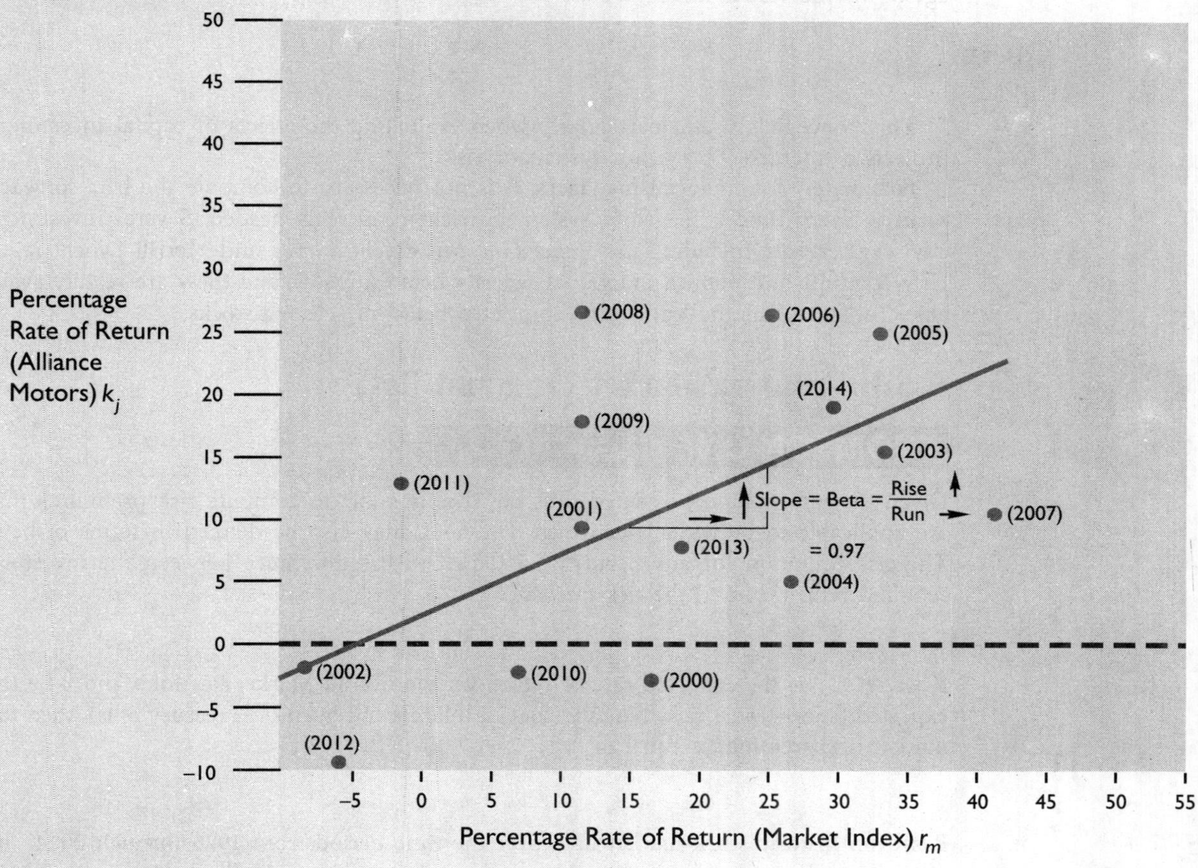

[18]Of course, there will also be *unsystematic* components to a security's returns at any point in time. We assume that these are diversified away in the portfolio.

TABLE 8.7

Interpretation of Selected Beta Coefficients

Beta Value	Direction of Movement in Returns	Interpretation
2.0	Same as market	Twice as risky (responsive) as market
1.0	Same as market	Risk equal to that of market
0.5	Same as market	Half as risky as market
0	Uncorrelated with market movements	No market-related risk
−0.5	Opposite of market	Half as responsive as market but in the opposite direction

be expected to increase (decline) by 2 percent. A beta of less than 1.0—for example, 0.5—is indicative of a security of less-than-average systematic risk. In this case, a 1 percent increase (decline) in market returns implies a 0.5 percent increase (decline) in the security's systematic returns. Table 8.7 summarizes the interpretation of selected betas.

The beta for the Market Portfolio as measured by a broad-based market index equals 1.0. This can be seen in Equation 8.13. Because the correlation of the market with itself is 1.0, the beta of the Market Portfolio must also be 1.0.

Finally, the beta of any portfolio of n securities or assets is simply the weighted average of the individual security betas:

(8.15)
$$\beta_p = \sum_{j=1}^{n} w_j \beta_j$$

This concept is useful particularly when evaluating the effects of capital investment projects or mergers on a firm's systematic risk.

Fortunately for financial managers, it is not necessary to compute the beta for each security every time a security's systematic risk measure is needed. Several investment advisory services, including the *Value Line Investment Survey* and Merrill Lynch, regularly compute and publish individual security beta estimates, and these are readily available. Table 8.8 lists the Value Line computed betas for selected stocks.

8-5d Security Market Line and Beta

THOMSON ONE Business School Edition

Given the information presented thus far, it is possible to compute risk premiums that are applicable to individual securities. The SML may also be defined in terms of beta. The risk premium for any Security j is equal to the difference between the investor's required return, k_j, and the risk-free rate, r_f:

(8.16)
$$\theta_j = k_j - r_f$$

If we let $\hat{r}_m$ be the expected rate of return on the overall Market Portfolio and $\hat{r}_f$ be the expected (short-term) risk-free rate (that is, the rate of return on Treasury bills), then the market risk premium is equal to:

$$\hat{\theta}_m = \hat{r}_m - \hat{r}_f$$

Based on historic stock market data over the time period from 1926 through 2014, the average market risk premium has been about 8.6 percent.[19] Other estimates based on

[19] *Stocks, Bonds, Bills and Inflation: 2012 Classic Yearbook*™ (Chicago: Morningstar, Inc., 2015): 40.

TABLE 8.8

Betas for Selected Stocks

Company	Value Line Beta	Company	Value Line Beta
Amazon.com	1.05	Hershey Foods	0.65
American Electric Power	0.70	Honeywell	1.10
American States Water	0.70	IBM	0.85
Apple	0.95	Intel	1.00
Avis Budget group	1.50	Johnson & Johnson	0.75
Bank of America	1.45	JPMorgan Chase	1.20
Berkshire Hathaway	0.80	Kellogg	0.65
Boeing	1.05	Krispy Kreme	1.15
Cheesecake Factory	0.85	Microsoft	1.00
Citigroup	1.45	Nike	0.80
Coca-Cola	0.70	Southwest Airlines	1.05
Coca-Cola Bottling	0.65	Target	0.70
Duke Energy	0.65	United Continental Holdings	1.05
DuPont	1.10	Wal-Mart Stores	0.65
ExxonMobil	0.95	Whirlpool	1.30
General Electric	1.15	WEC Energy Group	0.70
General Mills	0.70	Wynn Resorts	1.35
Harley-Davidson	1.15	Yahoo! Inc.	1.05

Source: *The Value Line Investment Survey* (New York: Value Line Publishing, Inc., November 27, 2015).

expected returns using security analyst data lead to somewhat lower equity risk premium estimates. The following discussion uses an average market risk premium of 8.2 percent.

For a security with average risk (β_j equal to 1.0), the risk premium should be equal to the market risk premium, or 8.2 percent. A security whose beta is 2.0, however, is twice as risky as the average security, so its risk premium should be twice the market risk premium:

$$\begin{aligned}\hat{\theta}_j &= \beta_j(\hat{r}_m - \hat{r}_f)\\ &= 2.0(8.2\%)\\ &= 16.4\%\end{aligned}$$

expected market return

The required return for any Security j may be defined in terms of its systematic risk, β_j, the **expected market return**, $\hat{r}_m$, and the expected risk-free rate, $\hat{r}_f$, as follows:

(8.17) $$k_j = \hat{r}_f + \beta_j(\hat{r}_m - \hat{r}_f)$$

For example, if the risk-free rate is 6 percent and $(\hat{r}_m - \hat{r}_f)$ is 8.2 percent, then the required rate of return for any security j is given by:

(8.18) $$k_j = 6 + 8.2\beta_j$$

The required return for DuPont, which has a beta of 1.10, can be computed using Equation 8.18:

$$\begin{aligned}k_j &= 6\% + 8.2\%(1.10)\\ &= 15.02\%\end{aligned}$$

Equation 8.17 provides an explicit definition of the SML in terms of the systematic risk of individual securities. The slope of the SML is constant throughout. When measured between a beta of 0 and a beta of 1.0, it is equal to $(\hat{r}_m - \hat{r}_f)/(1 - 0)$, or simply $\hat{r}_m - \hat{r}_f$. This slope represents the risk premium on an average risk security. Figure 8.15 illustrates the SML for Equation 8.18.[20] Given a risk-free rate of 6 percent and a market risk premium of 8.2 percent, the return required on a low-risk stock (for example, a security with a beta equal to 0.70, such as Coca-Cola) is 11.74 percent. The return required on a high-risk stock (for example, a security with a beta equal to 1.30, such as Whirlpool) is 16.66 percent, and the return required on a stock of average risk (such as Intel with a beta equal to 1.0) is 14.2 percent, the same as the market-required return.

Also, from Figure 8.15 we can determine what securities (assets) are attractive investments by comparing the *expected* return from a security with the return *required* for that security, given its beta. For example, Security A with a beta of 1.0 and an expected return of 16 percent would be an attractive investment because the expected return *exceeds* the 14.2 percent required return. In contrast, Security B with a beta of 1.50 is not an acceptable investment because its expected return (17 percent) is *less than* its required return (18.3 percent).

FIGURE 8.15

Security Market Line in Terms of Beta

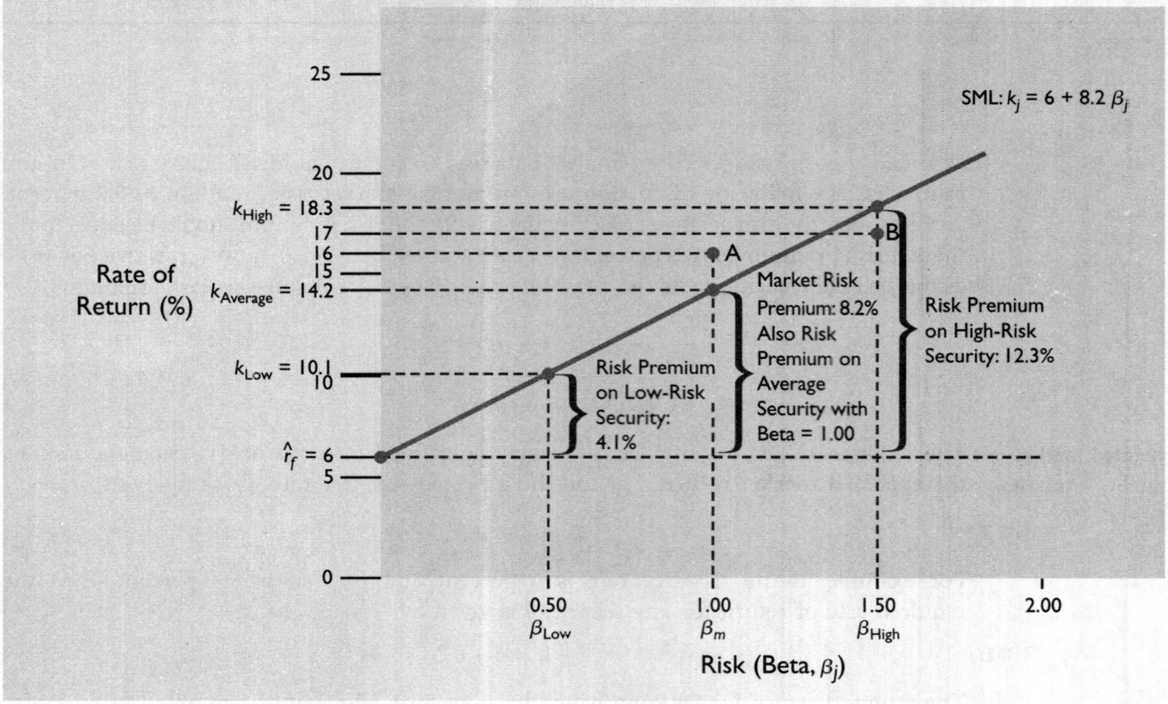

[20]Note that while the security market line (Figure 8.15 and Equation 8.18) and the capital market line discussed earlier (Figure 8.11 and Equation 8.10) have identical shapes (that is, straight lines) with the same intercept (r_f) on the vertical axis, they illustrate different relationships. The *security market line* defines the required (or expected) rate of return for an *individual security* (k_j) as a function of the *systematic risk* (measured by beta, β_j) of the security, whereas the *capital market line* measures the required (or expected) rate of return on a *portfolio* (r_p) in terms of the *total risk* (measured by the standard deviation, σ_p) of the portfolio.

8-5e Inflation and the Security Market Line

As discussed earlier in the chapter, the risk-free rate of return, r_f, consists of the real rate of return and the expected inflation premium. Because the required return on any risky security, k_j, is equal to the risk-free rate plus the risk premium, an increase in inflationary expectations effectively increases the required return on all securities. For example, if the risk-free rate of return increases by two percentage points, the required returns of all securities increase by two percentage points—the change in expected inflation. Thus, the required rate of return on a security of average risk (that is, beta equal to 1.0) would increase from 14.2 to 16.2 percent. When investors increase their required returns, they become unwilling to purchase securities at existing prices, causing prices to decline. It should come as no surprise, then, that security analysts and investors take a dim view of increased inflation.

8-5f Uses of the CAPM and Portfolio Risk Concepts

The concepts of portfolio risk, and the Capital Asset Pricing Model (CAPM), which relates required returns to systematic risk (beta), are powerful pedagogical tools to explain the nature of risk and its relationship to required returns on securities and physical assets. In Chapter 12, the CAPM is discussed as one technique that can be used to estimate the cost of equity capital. Chapter 12 also considers where the necessary data may be obtained to apply the model. Chapter 11 considers the use of CAPM-determined required rates of return as a technique to adjust for risk in the capital budgeting process.

INTERNATIONAL ISSUES

Diversification and Multinational Corporations

As we discussed earlier in the chapter, the degree to which diversification can reduce risk depends on the correlation among security returns. The returns from domestic companies (DMCs)—companies that are based and operate within a given country—tend to be positively related to the overall level of economic activity within the given country. Hence, these companies tend to have a relatively high degree of systematic risk. Since overall economic activity in different countries is not perfectly correlated, the returns from multinational companies (MNCs)—companies that operate in a number of different countries—may tend to have less systematic risk than those of DMCs. This suggests that further risk reduction benefits may be achieved by either:

1. Investing in MNCs, or
2. Investing directly in DMCs located in countries in which the MNC would otherwise operate.

If securities are traded in perfect financial markets, there should be no systematic advantage to holding shares in MNCs (Strategy 1) compared with owning shares directly in DMCs located in different countries (Strategy 2). However, if market imperfections exist, such as controls on capital flows, differential trading costs, and different tax structures, then MNCs may be able to provide diversification benefits to investors.

The empirical evidence is somewhat mixed.[a] Several studies have found that MNCs tend to have lower systematic risks (as measured by beta) as well as lower unsystematic risk than DMCs. Other studies have come to the opposite conclusion.

[a] See Israel Shaked, "Are Multinational Corporations Safer?" *Journal of International Business Studies* (Spring 1986): 83–101; Alfredo J. Mauri, "Influence of MNC Network Configuration Patterns on the Volatility of Firm Performance: An Empirical Investigation," *Management International Review* (November 2009).

8-5g Assumptions and Limitations of the CAPM

The theoretical CAPM and its applications are based upon a number of crucial assumptions about the securities markets and investors' attitudes, including the following:

- Investors hold well-diversified portfolios of securities. Hence, their return requirements are influenced primarily by the systematic (rather than total) risk of each security.
- Securities are traded actively in a competitive market, where information about a given firm and its future prospects is freely available.
- Investors can borrow and lend at the risk-free rate, which remains constant over time.
- There are no brokerage charges for buying and selling securities.
- There are no taxes.
- All investors prefer the security that provides the highest return for a given level of risk or the lowest amount of risk for a given level of return.
- All investors have common (homogeneous) expectations regarding the expected returns, variances, and correlations of returns among all securities.

While these assumptions may seem fairly limiting at first glance, extensions of the basic theory presented in this chapter, which relax the assumptions, have generally yielded results consistent with the fundamental theory.

Empirical studies of the CAPM have produced mixed results. Some researchers have found positive relationships between systematic (beta) risk and return. However, depending on the time period under examination, the results sometimes do not meet the standard tests of statistical significance.[21] Other investigators, using different stock price data, have found that variables other than systematic risk are better predictors of the performance of common stocks.[22] Their results suggest that differences in company size and the ratio of book-to-market values explain the differences in stock returns. Still other researchers have argued that the results of statistical tests of the relationship between systematic risk and return may be flawed because of the difficulty of obtaining accurate estimates of beta.[23] Their studies suggest that the use of market indexes, such as the S&P 500 Market Index, to measure returns on the true Market Portfolio can introduce significant errors into the process for estimating betas.

Despite the controversy concerning the validity of the CAPM, the model has been used extensively, both practically and conceptually, to consider the risk-return trade-off required by investors in the securities markets. For example, the CAPM (or a modification thereof) has been used in regulated public utility rate case testimony aimed at determining a reasonable allowed rate of return for the utility's investors.

However, users of this approach should also be aware of some of the major problems encountered in practical applications, which include the following:

- Estimating expected future market returns
- Determining the most appropriate estimate of the risk-free rate
- Determining the best estimate of an asset's *future* beta
- Reconciling the fact that some empirical tests have shown that investors do not totally ignore unsystematic risk, as the theory suggests

[21]Louis K. C. Chan and Josef Lakonishok, "Are the Reports of Beta's Death Premature?" *Journal of Portfolio Management* (Summer 1993): 51–62.

[22]Eugene F. Fama and Kenneth R. French, "The Cross-Section of Expected Returns," *Journal of Finance* 47 (June 1992): 427–465.

[23]Richard Roll, "A Critique of the Asset Pricing Theory's Tests. Part I: On Past and Present Testability of Theory," *Journal of Financial Economics* 4 (1977): 129–176.

ETHICAL ISSUES

High-Risk Securities

The decade of the 1980s experienced a dramatic growth in high-risk, so-called junk bonds. These are bonds with credit ratings below investment grade (BBB from Standard & Poor's and Baa3 from Moody's).[a] The lure of these securities was their high returns relative to the returns available from investment-grade corporate and U.S. government–issued debt securities. Junk bonds appeared to offer an easy way to quickly increase the yield on the portfolios of assets held by many financial institutions.

Although there are many complex reasons for the financial collapse of the savings and loan industry, at least in some cases the failure of large institutions can be traced to their overinvestment in high-risk debt securities. In the early 1990s, similar problems came to light in parts of the insurance industry. For example, in April 1991 insurance regulators in California seized control of Executive Life Insurance Company. The bond portfolio of Executive Life's parent company, First Executive Corporation, had a market value of $3 billion less than its $9.85 billion book value at the end of 1990. During the first quarter of 1991, the insurance company lost $465.9 million. The potential collapse of Executive Life placed in jeopardy the private pensions of thousands of workers whose employers had purchased retirement annuity contracts through the firm.

The problems caused by the savings and loan industry failure and the failure of large life insurance companies, such as First Executive, which had invested heavily in junk bonds, raise interesting issues of ethics and good business practice. Both savings and loan institutions and First Executive made a conscious decision to accept additional risk in the investment securities they purchased in exchange for additional expected return.

What standards of prudent business practice should be followed by firms when they attempt to improve their investment earnings performance? It is well known that, in the financial markets, higher returns can usually be achieved only by assuming greater risks. If this is true, should insurance companies completely avoid high-risk securities? How can these risks be managed effectively? What standards of voluntary disclosure of information to depositors and policyholders about the risk and return characteristics of the assets held by the institution do you believe are appropriate?

[a]See Chapter 6 for a discussion of bond credit ratings.

- Recognizing that measures of beta have been shown to be quite unstable over time, making it difficult to measure confidently the beta expected by investors
- Recognizing the growing body of evidence that suggests that required returns on most securities are determined by macroeconomic factors, such as interest rates and inflation, in addition to the risk-free rate of interest and the systematic risk of the security

8-6 Other Dimensions of Risk

This chapter has focused on various measures of variability in returns—either total variability, measured by the *standard deviation* and the *coefficient of variation*, or systematic variability, measured by *beta*. Although variability of returns is very important, it does not adequately consider another important risk dimension, that is, the risk of failure. In the case of an individual investment project, failure is a situation in which a project generates a *negative* rate of return. In the case of the entire firm, failure is the situation in which a firm loses money and is ultimately forced into bankruptcy.

For risk-averse investors, the risk of failure may play a large role in determining the types of investments undertaken. For example, the management of a firm is not likely to be eager to invest in a project that has a high risk of failure and that may ultimately cause the firm to fail if it proves to be unsuccessful. after all, the continued survival of the firm is tied closely to the economic well-being of management.

From a shareholder wealth maximization perspective, failure is a particularly undesirable occurrence. The direct and indirect costs of bankruptcy can be very high. Consequently, this failure risk is often an important determinant of investment risk. The risk and cost of failure can explain, in large part, the desire of many firms to diversify. In addition to reducing the overall risk of a firm, diversification can result in a lower probability of bankruptcy and thus lower *expected* costs incurred during bankruptcy. These costs include the following:

- The loss of funds that occur when assets are sold at distressed prices during liquidation
- The legal fees and selling costs incurred when a firm enters bankruptcy proceedings
- The opportunity costs of the funds that are unavailable to investors during the bankruptcy proceedings (for example, it took over eight years to settle the Penn Central bankruptcy)

Lower expected bankruptcy costs should increase shareholder wealth, all other things being equal.[24]

Diversification may also reduce a firm's cost of capital. By reducing the overall risk of the firm, diversification will lower the default risk of the firm's debt securities, and the firm's bonds will receive higher ratings and require lower interest payments. In addition, the firm may be able to increase the proportion of low-cost debt relative to equity in its optimal capital structure, further reducing the cost of capital and increasing shareholder wealth.[25]

Although we will focus primarily on return variability as our measure of risk in this book, the risk and cost of failure should also be kept in mind.

8-7 Summary

- The *risk* of a security or an investment project is generally defined in terms of the potential *variability* of its returns. When only one return is possible—for example, as with U.S. government securities held to maturity—there is no risk. When more than one return is possible for a particular project, it is risky.
- The *expected rate of return* from a security reflects the distributions an investor *anticipates* receiving from an investment. The *required rate of return* reflects the return an investor *demands* as compensation for postponing consumption and assuming risk. In efficient financial markets, required rates of return and expected rates of return should be approximately equal.
- The required rate of return on a security is a function of the general level of interest rates, as reflected in the risk-free rate of return, the maturity risk of the security, the default risk of the security, the business and financial risk of the firm that issues the security, the seniority risk of the security, and the marketability risk of the security.
- Risk is also influenced by the possibility of investment *diversification*. If a proposed project's returns are not *perfectly correlated* with the returns from the firm's other investments, the total risk of the firm may be reduced by accepting the proposed project. This is known as the *portfolio effect*.
- The *expected return from a portfolio* of two or more securities is equal to the weighted average of the expected returns from the individual securities.
- The *risk of a portfolio* is a function of both the risk of the individual securities in the portfolio and the correlation among the individual securities' returns.
- The *Capital Asset Pricing Model* (CAPM) is a theory that can be used to determine required rates of return on financial and physical assets.
- The *unsystematic* portion of the total risk in a security's return is that portion of return variability unique to the firm. Efficient diversification of a portfolio of securities can eliminate most unsystematic risk.

---

[24] The effects of bankruptcy costs on shareholder wealth (that is, market value of the firm) are examined in Chapter 13.

[25] The concept of optimal capital structure is discussed in Chapter 13.

- *Systematic risk* refers to the portion of total risk in a security's return caused by overall market forces. This risk cannot be diversified away in a portfolio. Systematic risk forms the basis for the risk premium required by investors in any risky security.
- The *security market line* (SML) provides an algebraic or a graphic representation of the risk-return trade-off required in the marketplace for risky securities. It measures risk in terms of systematic risk.
- An index of systematic risk for a security is the security's *beta*. Beta is determined from the slope of a regression line, the *characteristic line*, between the market return and the individual security's return. It is a measure of the volatility of a security's returns relative to the returns of the market as a whole.

Important Equations

$$\hat{r} = \sum_{j=1}^{n} r_j p_j$$

$$\sigma = \sqrt{\sum_{j=1}^{n} (r_j - \hat{r})^2 p_j}$$

$$z = \frac{r - \hat{r}}{\sigma}$$

$$v = \frac{\sigma}{\hat{r}}$$

Required rate of return = Risk-free rate of return + Risk premium

r_f = Real rate of return + Expected inflation premium

$$\hat{r}_p = w_A \hat{r}_A + w_B \hat{r}_B$$

$$\hat{r}_p = \sum_{i=1}^{n} w_i \hat{r}_i$$

$$\sigma_p = \sqrt{w_A^2 \sigma_A^2 + w_B^2 \sigma_B^2 + 2 w_A w_B \rho_{AB} \sigma_A \sigma_B}$$

$$\hat{r}_p = \hat{r}_f + \left(\frac{r_m - r_f}{\sigma_m}\right) \sigma_p$$

Total risk = Systematic risk (Nondiversifiable risk) + Unsystematic risk (Diversifiable risk)

$$\beta_j = \frac{\text{Covariance}_{j,m}}{\text{Variance}_m}$$

$$\beta_j = \frac{\rho_{jm} \sigma_j \sigma_m}{\sigma_m^2}$$

$$k_j = a_j + \beta_j r_m + e_j$$

Important Equations (*Continued*)

$$\beta_p = \sum_{j=1}^{n} w_j \beta_j$$

$$k_j = \hat{r}_f + \beta_j(\hat{r}_m - \hat{r}_f)$$

8-8 Questions and Topics for Discussion

1. Define the following terms:
   a. Risk
   b. Probability distribution
   c. Standard deviation
   d. Required rate of return
   e. Coefficient of variation
   f. Efficient portfolio
   g. Efficient frontier
   h. Capital market line
   i. Beta coefficient
   j. CAPM
   k. Correlation coefficient
   l. Portfolio
   m. Characteristic line
   n. Security market line
   o. Covariance
   p. Systematic risk
   q. Unsystematic risk
2. If the returns from a security were known with certainty, what shape would the probability distribution of returns graph have?
3. What is the nature of the risk associated with "risk-free" U.S. government bonds?
4. If inflation expectations increase, what would you expect to happen to the returns required by investors in bonds? What would happen to bond prices?
5. Under what circumstances will the coefficient of variation of a security's returns and the standard deviation of that security's returns give the same relative measure of risk when compared with the risk of another security?
6. Explain how diversification can reduce the risk of a portfolio of assets to below the weighted average of the risk of the individual assets.
7. What are the primary variables that influence the risk of a portfolio of assets?
8. Distinguish between unsystematic and systematic risk. Under what circumstances are investors likely to ignore the unsystematic risk characteristics of a security?
9. What effect do increasing inflation expectations have on the required returns of investors in common stock?
10. The stock of Amrep Corporation has a beta value estimated to be 1.4. How would you interpret this beta value? How would you evaluate the firm's systematic risk?
11. How is a security's beta value computed?
12. Under what circumstances can the beta concept be used to estimate the rate of return required by investors in a stock? What problems are encountered when using the CAPM?
13. The enclosed area in Figure 8.16 shows all the possible portfolios obtained by combining the given securities in different proportions (that is, the opportunity set).

FIGURE 8.16

Portfolio Opportunity Set

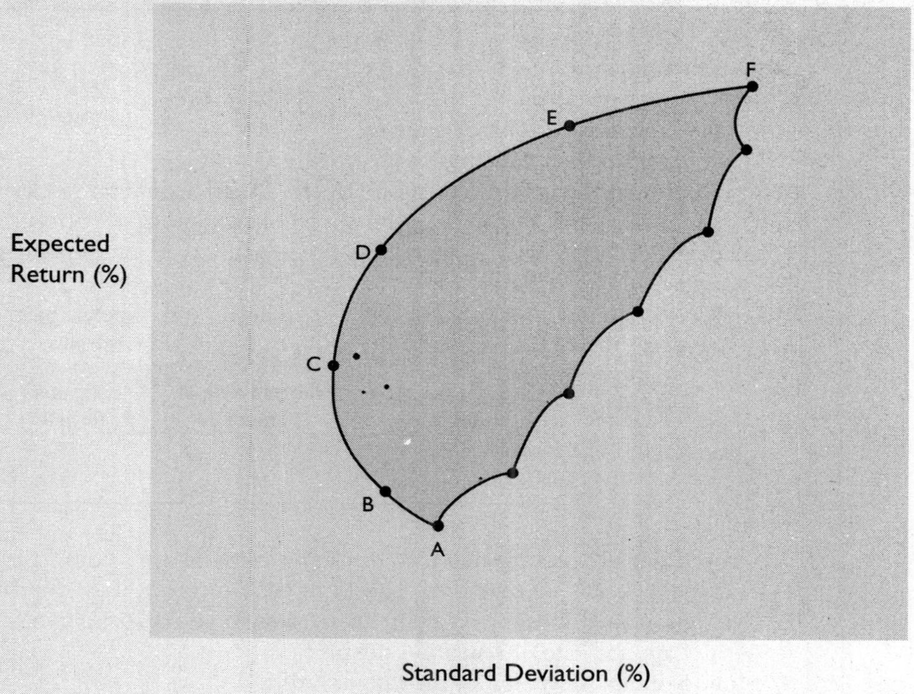

a. Which of the portfolios (A, B, C, D, E, or F) is (are) on the efficient frontier?
b. If an investor is interested in maximizing expected returns, which portfolio should be chosen?
c. If an investor is interested in minimizing risk (as measured by standard deviation), which portfolio should be chosen?

14. What is the *term structure* of interest rates?

15. What is the *risk structure* of interest rates?

16. How is *risk* defined in a financial sense?

17. Discuss the general relationship between risk and expected return.

18. What factors determine investors' required rates of return on corporate bonds? common stocks? U.S. government bonds?

19. Why do yield curves sometimes have a downward slope and at other times have an upward slope?

20. What is the primary difference between 20-year bonds issued by the U.S. government and 20-year bonds issued by IBM?

21. Is it possible for investors ever to require a lower rate of return on a company's equity than on its debt, assuming that the debt is in a junk-bond category of quality?

8-9 Self-Test Problems

ST1. Given the following possible returns (dividends plus capital gains) over the coming year from a $10,000 investment in Ford Motor Company common stock:

State of Economy	Probability	Return ($)
Recession	0.20	−1,000
Normal year	0.60	1,500
Boom	0.20	2,500

Determine the
a. Expected return
b. Standard deviation of returns
c. Coefficient of variation

ST2. Given that the rate of return on General Electric common stock over the coming year is normally distributed with an expected value of 15 percent and a standard deviation of 12 percent, determine the probability of earning a negative rate of return.

ST3. Two common stocks, Consolidated Edison and Apple, have the following expected return and standard deviation of return over the next year:

Common Stock	Expected Rate of Return	Standard Deviation
Consolidated Edison	12%	6%
Apple	20	15

Additionally, assume that the correlation coefficient of returns on the two securities is +0.50. For a portfolio consisting of 75 percent of the funds invested in Consolidated Edison and the remainder in Apple, determine the:
a. Expected rate of return on the portfolio
b. Standard deviation of the rate of return

ST4. Determine the beta of a portfolio consisting of equal investments in the following common stocks:

Security	Beta
Boeing	0.95
Daimler	1.25
Intel	1.15
Wal-Mart Stores	1.05

ST5. The risk-free rate of return is 6 percent, based on an expected inflation premium of 3 percent. The expected rate of return on the market portfolio is 15 percent.
a. Determine the required rate of return on Wisconsin Public Service (WPS) common stock, whose beta is 0.60.
b. Assume that the expected rate of return on the market portfolio remains constant but that the expected inflation premium increases from a current level of 3 percent to 4 percent. Determine the required rate of return on WPS common stock.
c. Assume that the expected inflation premium remains at 3 percent but that the expected return on the market portfolio increases to 16 percent. Determine the required rate of return on WPS common stock.

ST6. The yield to maturity on Xerox Corporation bonds maturing in 2026 is 8.40 percent. The yield to maturity on a similar maturity U.S. government Treasury bond is 7.55 percent. The yield to maturity on 90-day Treasury bills is 6.11 percent.

a. What is the maturity risk premium between the Treasury bill and the Xerox bond?
b. What is the default risk premium on the Xerox bond?

8-10 Problems*

BASIC

1. You have estimated the following probability distributions of expected future returns for Stocks X and Y:

Stock X		Stock Y	
Probability	Return	Probability	Return
0.1	−10%	0.2	2%
0.2	10	0.2	7
0.4	15	0.3	12
0.2	20	0.2	15
0.1	40	0.1	16

a. What is the expected rate of return for Stock X? For Stock Y?
b. What is the standard deviation of expected returns for Stock X? For Stock Y?
c. Which stock would you consider to be riskier? Why?

BASIC

2. The return expected from Project No. 542 is 22 percent. The standard deviation of these returns is 11 percent. If returns from the project are normally distributed, what is the chance that the project will result in a rate of return above 33 percent? What is the probability that the project will result in losses (negative rates of return)?

BASIC

3. The expected rate of return for the stock of Cornhusker Enterprises is 20 percent, with a standard deviation of 15 percent. The expected rate of return for the stock of Mustang Associates is 10 percent, with a standard deviation of 9 percent.
   a. Which stock would you consider to be riskier? Why?
   b. If you knew that the beta coefficient of Cornhusker stock is 1.5 and the beta of Mustang is 0.9, how would your answer to Part a change?

INTERMEDIATE

4. An investor currently has all of his wealth in Treasury bills. He is considering investing one-third of his funds in General Electric, whose beta is 1.30, with the remainder left in Treasury bills. The expected risk-free rate (Treasury bills) is 6 percent and the market risk premium is 8.8 percent. Determine the beta and the expected return on the proposed portfolio.

INTERMEDIATE

5. You are considering investing in two securities, X and Y. The following data are available for the two securities:

	Security X	Security Y
Expected return	0.10	0.07
Standard deviation of returns	0.08	0.04
Beta	1.10	0.75

a. If you invest 40 percent of your funds in Security X and 60 percent in Security Y and if the correlation of returns between X and Y is +0.5, compute the following:

   i. The expected return from the portfolio
   ii. The standard deviation of returns from the portfolio

*Color blocks behind the numbers denote problems that have check answers provided at the end of the book.

b. What happens to the expected return and standard deviation of returns of the portfolio in Part a if 70 percent of your funds are invested in Security X and 30 percent of your funds are invested in Security Y?

c. What happens to the expected return and standard deviation of returns of the portfolio in Part a if the following conditions exist?

   i. The correlation of returns between Securities X and Y is +1.0.
   ii. The correlation of returns between Securities X and Y is 0.
   iii. The correlation of returns between Securities X and Y is −0.7.

INTERMEDIATE **6.** You have the following information on two securities in which you have invested:

Security	Expected Return	Standard Deviation	Beta	Percent Invested (w)
Xerox	15%	4.5%	1.20	35%
Ford	12%	3.8%	0.98	65%

a. Which stock is riskier in a portfolio context? Which stock is riskier if you are considering them as individual assets (not part of a portfolio)?
b. Compute the expected return on the portfolio.
c. If the securities have a correlation of +0.60, compute the standard deviation of the portfolio.
d. Compute the beta of the portfolio.

BASIC **7.** Given a risk-free rate ($\hat{r}_f$) of 6 percent and a market risk premium ($\hat{r}_m - \hat{r}_f$) of 8.2 percent, calculate the required rate of return on each of the following stocks, based on the betas given in Table 8.8:

a. American Electric Power
b. Citigroup
c. General Mills
d. Wynn Resorts

BASIC **8.** The stock of Pizza Hot Inc., a Mexican pizza chain, has an estimated beta of 1.5. Calculate the required rate of return on Pizza Hot's stock if the SML is estimated as follows:

$$k_j = 0.06 + 0.094\beta_j$$

based on:

a. An initial inflation expectation of 4 percent
b. A new inflation expectation of 6 percent

INTERMEDIATE **9.** a. Suppose a U.S. Treasury bill, maturing in one year, can be purchased today for $92,500. Assuming that the security is held until maturity, the investor will receive $100,000 (face amount). Determine the rate of return on this investment.

b. Suppose a National Telephone and Telegraph (NTT) Company bond, maturing in one year, can be purchased today for $975. Assuming that the bond is held until maturity, the investor will receive $1,000 (principal) plus 7 percent interest (that is, 0.07 × $1,000 – $70). Determine the rate of return on this investment.

c. Determine the implied risk premium on NTT bonds.

INTERMEDIATE **10.** The real rate of interest has been estimated to be 3 percent, and the expected long-term annual inflation rate is 7 percent.

a. What is the current risk-free rate of return on one-year Treasury bonds?
b. If the yield on 10-year U.S. Treasury bonds is 12 percent, what is the maturity risk premium between a 10-year bond and a one-year bond?

c. If Delta bonds, scheduled to mature in 10 years, currently sell to yield 13 percent, what is the default risk premium on these bonds?
d. If investors in the common stock of Delta require a 16 percent rate of return, what is the seniority risk premium on Delta's common stock?

INTERMEDIATE **11.** Using Equation 8.17, suppose you have computed the required rate of return for the stock of Bulldog Trucking to be 16.6 percent. Given the current stock price, the current dividend rate, and analysts' projections for future dividend growth, you expect to earn a rate of return of 18 percent.
a. Would you recommend buying or selling this stock? Why?
b. If your expected rate of return from the stock of Bulldog is 15 percent, what would you expect to happen to Bulldog's stock price?

INTERMEDIATE **12.** The stock of Koch Brickyard Inc., is expected to return 14 percent with a standard deviation of 5 percent. Uptown Potbelly Stove Works' stock is expected to return 16 percent with a standard deviation of 9 percent.
a. If you invest 30 percent of your funds in Koch stock and 70 percent in Uptown stock, what is the expected return on your portfolio?
b. What is the expected risk of this portfolio if the returns for the two stocks have:

i. A perfect positive correlation (+1.0)?
ii. A slightly negative correlation (−0.2)?

INTERMEDIATE **13.** Security A offers an expected return of 15 percent with a standard deviation of 7 percent. Security B offers an expected return of 9 percent with a standard deviation of 4 percent. The correlation between the returns of A and B is +0.6. If an investor puts one-fourth of his wealth in A and three-fourths in B, what is the expected return and risk (standard deviation) of this portfolio?

INTERMEDIATE **14.** The return on the Tarheel Corporation stock is expected to be 14 percent with a standard deviation of 8 percent. The beta of Tarheel is 0.8. The risk-free rate is 7 percent, and the expected return on the market portfolio is 15 percent. What is the probability that an investor in Tarheel will earn a rate of return less than the required rate of return? Assume that returns are normally distributed.

CHALLENGE **15.** The stock of Jones Trucking is expected to return 13 percent annually with a standard deviation of 8 percent. The stock of Bush Steel Mills is expected to return 17 percent annually with a standard deviation of 14 percent. The correlation between the returns from the two securities has been estimated to be +0.3. The beta of the Jones stock is 0.9, and the beta of the Bush stock is 1.2. The risk-free rate of return is expected to be 8 percent, and the expected return on the market portfolio is 15 percent. The current dividend for Jones is $4. The current dividend for Bush is $6.
a. What is the expected return from a portfolio containing the two securities if 40 percent of your wealth is invested in Jones and 60 percent is invested in Bush?
b. What is the expected standard deviation of the portfolio of the two stocks?
c. Which stock is the better buy in the current market? Why?

INTERMEDIATE **16.** Equation 8.9 can be modified to compute the risk of a three-security portfolio as follows:

$$\sigma_p = \sqrt{w_A^2\sigma_A^2 + w_B^2\sigma_B^2 + w_C^2\sigma_C^2 + 2w_Aw_B\rho_{AB}\sigma_A\sigma_B + 2w_Aw_C\rho_{AC}\sigma_A\sigma_C + 2w_Bw_C\rho_{BC}\sigma_B\sigma_C}$$

You have decided to invest 40 percent of your wealth in Security A, 30 percent in Security B, and 30 percent in Security C. The following information is available about the possible returns from the three securities:

Security A		Security B		Security C	
Return	Probability	Return	Probability	Return	Probability
10%	0.25	13%	0.30	14%	0.40
12	0.50	16	0.35	18	0.30
14	0.25	19	0.35	22	0.30

Compute the expected return of the portfolio and the risk of the portfolio if the correlations between returns from the three securities are $\rho_{AB} = 0.70$; $\rho_{AC} = 0.60$; and $\rho_{BC} = 0.85$.

INTERMEDIATE **17.** The expected return and standard deviation of returns of General Mills common stock over the next year are estimated to be 20 percent and 12 percent, respectively. Assume that the returns are approximately normally distributed.

a. Determine the probability of incurring a loss (negative rate of return) from investing in this stock.

b. Determine the probability of earning a rate of return less than the risk-free rate of 6 percent.

INTERMEDIATE **18.** Three Rivers Investment Company desires to construct a portfolio with a 20 percent expected return. The portfolio is to consist of some combination of Security X and Security Y, which have the following expected returns, standard deviations of returns, and betas:

	Security X	Security Y
Expected return	15%	26%
Standard deviation	10%	20%
Beta	0.94	1.33

Determine the expected beta of the portfolio.

CHALLENGE **19.** The current (time zero) price of one share of Farrell Corporation's common stock is \$25. The price is expected to increase by \$5 over the coming year. The company is not expected to pay a dividend during the year. The standard deviation of the expected price change is \$3. The distribution of the end-of-year possible prices is approximately normal. Determine the probability of earning a return greater than 30 percent over the coming year from your investment in Farrell common stock.

INTERMEDIATE **20.** a. Estimate beta for each of the following securities assuming that the standard deviation of returns for the market portfolio (m) is 8.0 percent.

Security	Expected Return	Standard Deviation	Correlation Coefficient Between Returns for the Security and Market Portfolio
P	12%	10%	0.80
Q	18	20	0.60
R	15	15	0.40

b. Based on the Capital Asset Pricing Model, with a risk-free rate ($\hat{r}_f$) of 7 percent and a market risk premium ($\hat{r}_m - \hat{r}_f$) of 8.8 percent, which of the securities, P, Q, or R (if any) appear to be attractive investments?

INTERMEDIATE **21.** Two securities have the following characteristics:

	Security A	Security B
Expected return	15%	12%
Standard deviation	4%	6%
Beta	0.90	−0.25

Furthermore, the correlation of returns between the securities is −1.0. Determine the risk (standard deviation) of a portfolio consisting of equal proportions of Securities A and B.

CHALLENGE **22.** New Castle Company common stock has a beta of 1.50. The stock currently pays a dividend of $3 per share. The risk-free rate is 8 percent, and the market risk premium is expected to be 8.0 percent. The returns from New Castle stock are normally distributed with an expected value of 24 percent and a standard deviation of 12 percent.

a. Determine the required rate of return for New Castle's common stock.

b. Determine the probability that the stock of New Castle is undervalued at its current market price of $25 per share.

CHALLENGE **23.** The real rate of return has been estimated to be 2 percent given current economic conditions. The 30-day risk-free rate (annualized) is 5 percent. Twenty-year U.S. government bonds currently yield 8 percent. The yield on 20-year bonds issued by the Forester Hoop Company is 14 percent. Investors require an 18 percent return on Forester's common stock. The common stock of Brown's Forensic Products has a required return of 20 percent. Compute and identify all meaningful risk premiums. What might account for the difference in the required returns for Brown versus Forester?

CHALLENGE **24.** Bostonmarket.com stock has an estimated beta of 1.5. The stock pays no dividend and is not expected to pay one for the foreseeable future. The current price of the stock is $50. You expect this price to rise to $60 by the end of the coming year. You believe that the distribution of possible year-end prices is approximately normal with a standard deviation of $2.50. The risk-free rate of return is currently 4 percent and the market risk premium is 8.8 percent. What is the probability that bostonmarket.com's stock is currently overvalued?

CHALLENGE **25.** Suppose that a portfolio consists of the following stocks:

Stock	Amount	Beta
Chevron	$20,000	0.70
General Electric	40,000	1.30
Whirlpool	40,000	1.10

The risk-free rate ($\hat{r}_f$) is 5 percent and the market risk premium ($\hat{r}_m - \hat{r}_f$) is 8.8 percent.

a. Determine the beta for the portfolio.

b. Determine how much General Electric stock one must sell and reinvest in Chevron stock in order to reduce the beta of the portfolio to 1.00.

c. Determine the expected return on the portfolio in Parts a and b.

INTERMEDIATE **26.** Consider again the SML given by Equation 8.18 and shown in Figure 8.15. Assume that the risk-free rate ($\hat{r}_f$) of 6 percent is based on an expected inflation premium of 4 percent. Suppose expected inflation increases by two percentage points to 6 percent.

a. Write an equation for the SML given the increase in the expected inflation premium, assuming that all other factors remain constant.

b. Redraw the SML based on the new expected inflation premium.

c. Determine the required rate of return (k_j) on Amazon.com common stock before and after the expected increase in inflation. (See Table 8.8 for the appropriate beta.)

CHALLENGE **27.** International Many Foods, Inc.'s common stock has a beta of 0.9. The stock does not currently pay a dividend, but is expected to appreciate in value from a current price of $15 to $25 in the next five years. The risk-free rate is 6 percent and the market risk premium is 7.4 percent. If the standard deviation of the expected return from this stock is 2 percent, what is the probability that it is overvalued?

BASIC **28.** Visit the Bloomberg Web site (www.bloomberg.com) to assess the best performing mutual funds in recent periods. Is the ranking based on the last month somewhat consistent with the ranking of funds on the last year?

PART 3

The Capital Investment Decision

This part of the text looks at the financial management of the long-term asset portion of a firm's balance sheet. Investments in these assets (for example property, plant, and equipment) have a major impact on a firm's future stream of cash flows and the risk of those cash flows. As such, the long-term investment (capital budgeting) decision has a significant effect on the value of the firm. Chapter 9 deals with the measurement of cash flows from the long-term investments. Chapter 10 analyzes various investment decision criteria in light of the wealth maximization objective of the firm. Chapter 11 extends the analysis to consider techniques to account for differential levels of risk among projects.

CHAPTER 9

Capital Budgeting and Cash Flow Analysis

KEY CHAPTER CONCEPTS

1. *Capital budgeting* is the process of planning for purchases of assets whose cash flows are expected to continue beyond one year.
2. The *cost of capital* is defined as the cost of funds supplied to a firm. It represents the required rate of return a firm must earn on its investments and thus is an important input in the capital budgeting process.
3. There are four key steps in the capital budgeting process:
   a. Generating investment project proposals
   b. Estimating cash flows
   c. Evaluating alternatives and selecting projects to be implemented
   d. Reviewing a project's performance after it has been implemented and post-auditing its performance after termination
4. Investment projects can be generated by growth opportunities, by cost reduction opportunities, and to meet legal requirements and health and safety standards.
5. The initial outlay required to implement a project is called the *net investment* (NINV). It includes
   a. The installed cost of the assets
   b. Plus any initial net working capital requirements
   c. Less any cash inflows from the sale of replacement assets
   d. Plus or minus the tax consequences associated with the sale of existing assets and/or the purchase of new assets
6. The *net operating cash flow* from a project is equal to the change in net operating earnings after tax plus the change in depreciation minus the change in net working capital investment requirements associated with the adoption of a project. In the last year of a project's life, this net cash flow definition may have to be modified to reflect the recapture of the accumulated net working capital investment and any after-tax salvage value received.
7. The economic viability of a project can be affected by special tax considerations, such as the use of accelerated depreciation methods like the Modified Accelerated Cost Recovery System (MACRS) of depreciation.

FINANCIAL CHALLENGE

Ford Invests $1.3 Billion in Kentucky Truck Plant

Ford Motor Company has a long history of car and truck manufacturing in Louisville, Kentucky. In 1913 Ford opened a plant in Louisville to manufacture the Model T. Over the years Ford built new and expanded production facilities in Louisville as the firm grew and its needs changed. In 1955 Ford opened the Louisville Assembly Plant, a huge 3.1 million square foot facility on 180 acres. This plant has been home to the production of the Edsel, Ford Sunliners, Fairlanes, Galaxies, Ranger pickups, and the Ford Explorer. In 1969 Ford opened the Kentucky Truck Plant in Louisville, a plant that focuses on the production of heavier trucks.

Over the years, Ford has had to make a number of major capital investments in these plants to keep them competitive. For example, in 2012 Ford completed a $600 million revamp of the Louisville Assembly Plant, including the addition of new body, paint, and trim assembly lines. The plant reopened as the most flexible of Ford's domestic assembly plants. It is capable of producing up to six different models simultaneously. This renovation of a nearly 60-year-old plant was designed to make it the model for renovations at all of Ford's plants. With this new production model, the company expects to be able to operate the plant on three shifts, around the clock, to minimize the need for other stand-alone assembly plants, thus dramatically reducing costs. Employment at the plant is expected to grow from 1,100 prior to the makeover to 4,200.

In 2015 Ford announced plans for a $1.3 billion investment in the Kentucky Truck Plant to accommodate production of the next-generation 2017 Super Duty pickups. These plant modifications will permit Ford to switch all future generations of trucks from steel to aluminum bodies in order to reduce the truck's weight and thereby increase fuel economy. Ford also planned an additional $600 million investment to accommodate the next generation of the Ford Expedition and the Lincoln Navigator, both of which are expected to have aluminum bodies in their next models. These changes will add another 2,000 employees at the Kentucky Truck Plant.

When making these large multibillion-dollar investment decisions, Ford had to make an estimate of the impact of these investments on the future cash flows of the company. Only if the combination

© Markus Mainka/Shutterstock.com

FINANCIAL CHALLENGE — CONTINUED

of cost savings and revenue increases is large enough to offset the initial required expenditures, plus provide a competitive return to investors in the company, will a company make such investments. Capital investments such as these chart the course of a company's future for many years to come. Therefore, it is important that the related capital investment analysis be performed carefully and correctly.

This chapter develops the principles of capital investment analysis, with an emphasis on the estimation of the cash flows from a project. Chapter 10 considers appropriate decision criteria in the capital budgeting process that lead toward the maximization of shareholder wealth. Chapter 11 introduces techniques to account for differential levels of risk when making important investment decisions.

Sources: A. Priddle, "Ford Invests $1.3B, Adds 2,000 Jobs at Kentucky Plant," *Detroit Free Press*, December 1, 2015; G. Schneider, "Louisville Ford Plan Anticipates Aluminum Truck Jobs," *Louisville Courier-Journal*, January 30, 2015; B. Schreiner, "Ford Makes Big Investment in Louisville," *Associated Press*, June 13, 2012.

CHAPTER OBJECTIVES

Upon the completion of this chapter, you should have a clear understanding of the following:

1. The principles of estimating cash flows and their application
2. The identification and estimation of net investment and net cash flows
3. The effect of accelerated depreciation on net cash flow estimates

9-1 Introduction

This is the first of several chapters that explicitly deal with the financial management of the assets on a firm's balance sheet. In this and the following two chapters we consider the management of long-term assets. Later in the book (Chapters 16 to 18) the emphasis shifts to the management of short-term assets—that is, working capital decisions.

capital budgeting
capital expenditure

Capital budgeting is the process of planning for purchases of assets whose returns are expected to continue beyond one year. A **capital expenditure** is a cash outlay that is expected to generate a flow of future cash benefits lasting longer than one year. It is distinguished from a normal operating expenditure, which is expected to result in cash benefits during the coming one-year period. (The choice of a one-year period is arbitrary, but it does serve as a useful guideline.)

Several different types of outlays may be classified, for purposes of analysis, as capital expenditures and evaluated using the framework of capital budgeting models, including the following:

- The purchase of a new piece of equipment, real estate, or a building in order to expand an existing product or service line or enter a new line of business

- The replacement of an existing capital asset, such as a Boeing 767 airplane with a Boeing 787 Dreamliner
- Expenditures for an advertising campaign
- Expenditures for a research and development program
- Investments in permanent increases of target inventory levels or levels of accounts receivable
- Investments in employee education and training
- The refunding of an old bond issue with a new, lower interest issue
- Lease-versus-buy analysis
- Merger and acquisition evaluation

Total global business investments for all industries during 2014 exceeded $4 *trillion*. Capital expenditures are important to a firm both because they require sizable cash outlays and because they have a long-range impact on the firm's performance. For large companies, capital expenditures, including research and development outlays, as a percentage of sales typically range from 2 to 10 percent. For example, in 2014, Pepsi's capital expenditures and research and development totaled $2.86 billion and were about 4.3 percent of its sales for that year. Apple Inc.'s capital expenditures and research and development expenditures of $19.3 billion were 8.3 percent of its sales. In contrast, Pfizer (a large pharmaceutical company) spent over 19 percent of its sales on capital expenditures and research and development.

The following example illustrates the magnitude and long-term impact of capital expenditures for an individual company. In June 2002, Ford Motor Company announced plans to invest $5 billion to $6 billion in Volvo, its Swedish luxury-car subsidiary that it had purchased for $6.5 billion in 1999.[1] The bulk of the funds invested were to be used to build up to five new or redesigned midsize vehicle models. Also, part of the capital invested was to be used to expand its manufacturing facilities in Sweden and Belgium in order to be able to produce up to 600,000 units per year, compared with the 425,000 units it produced in 2001. These capital expenditures were being made despite a weak economy, a loss of $5.45 billion by Ford in the previous year, and a 15 percent drop in Volvo's U.S. sales during the first five months of 2002, compared with the previous year. Despite these concerns, Ford had confidence in Volvo's new products and the long-term health of the economy and the company. In 2010 Ford sold Volvo to a Chinese company for just $1.8 billion, a whopping $4.65 billion less than it had paid for the company in 1999, not to mention the investment of over $5 billion that had been made in Volvo over the period of its ownership. It took the new owners four years to return Volvo to profitability.

A firm's capital expenditures affect its future profitability and, when taken together, essentially plot the company's future direction by determining which products will be produced, which markets will be entered, where production facilities will be located, and what type of technology will be used. Capital expenditure decision making is important for another reason as well. Specifically, it is often difficult, if not impossible, to reverse a major capital expenditure without incurring considerable additional expense. For example, if a firm acquires highly specialized production facilities and equipment, it must recognize that there may be no ready used-equipment market in which to dispose of them if they do not generate the desired future cash flows. The losses incurred by Ford on its Volvo investments illustrate this point well. For these reasons, a firm's management should establish a number of definite procedures to follow when analyzing capital expenditure projects. Choosing from among such projects is the objective of capital budgeting models.

[1]Norihiko Shirouzu, "Ford to Invest up to $6 Billion in Volvo in Bid to Boost Sales," *The Wall Street Journal* (June 27, 2002): D8.

9-2 Key Terms and Concepts in Capital Budgeting

Before proceeding with the discussion of the capital budgeting process, it is necessary to introduce a number of terms and concepts encountered in subsequent chapters.

9-2a Cost of Capital

A firm's *cost of capital* is defined as the cost of the funds (debt, preferred and common equity) supplied to it and used to finance investments made by a company. It is also termed the *required rate of return* because it specifies the minimum necessary rate of return required by the firm's investors on new investments. If a firm earns returns on its new investments that exceed the cost of capital, shareholder wealth will increase. In this context, the cost of capital provides the firm with a basis for choosing among various capital investment projects. In this and the following two chapters, it is assumed that the cost of capital is a known value. Chapter 12 explores the methods used to determine the cost of capital.

9-2b How Projects Are Classified

A firm usually encounters several different types of projects when making capital expenditure decisions, including *independent projects, mutually exclusive projects*, and *contingent projects*. As is demonstrated in Chapter 10, project classification can influence the investment decision process.

independent project

Independent Projects

An **independent project** is one whose acceptance or rejection does not directly eliminate other projects from consideration. For example, a firm may want to install a new telephone communications system in its headquarters and replace a drill press during approximately the same time. In the absence of a constraint on the availability of funds, both projects could be adopted if they meet minimum investment criteria.

mutually exclusive project

Mutually Exclusive Projects

A **mutually exclusive project** is one whose acceptance precludes the acceptance of one or more alternative proposals. Because two mutually exclusive projects have the capacity to perform the same function for a firm, only one should be chosen. For example, BMW was faced with deciding whether it should expand its U.S. manufacturing complex in Spartanburg, South Carolina, or continue new model production in Germany. It ultimately chose the Spartanburg site; this precluded other alternatives.

contingent project

Contingent Projects

A **contingent project** is one whose acceptance is dependent on the adoption of one or more other projects. For example, a decision by Nucor to build a new steel plant in North Carolina is contingent upon Nucor investing in suitable air and water pollution control equipment. When a firm is considering contingent projects, it is best to consider together all projects that are dependent on one another and treat them as a single project for purposes of evaluation.

9-2c Availability of Funds

When a firm has adequate funds to invest in all projects that meet some capital budgeting selection criterion, such as has been true for Apple Inc., the firm is said to be operating without a *funds constraint*. Frequently, however, the total initial cost of the acceptable projects in the absence of a funds constraint is greater than the total funds the firm has available to invest in capital projects.[2] This is often true for small, rapidly growing firms. This fund shortage necessitates **capital rationing**, or setting limits on capital expenditures, and results in some special capital budgeting problems.[3]

capital rationing

9-3 Basic Framework for Capital Budgeting

According to economic theory, a firm should operate at the point where the marginal cost of an additional unit of output just equals the marginal revenue derived from the output. Following this rule leads to *profit maximization*. This principle may also be applied to capital budgeting decisions. In this context, a firm's marginal revenue is the rates of return earned on succeeding investments, and marginal cost may be defined as the firm's *marginal cost of capital* (MCC), that is, the cost of successive increments of capital acquired by the firm.

Figure 9.1 illustrates a simplified capital budgeting model. This model assumes that all projects have the same risk. The projects under consideration are indicated by lettered bars on the graph. Project A requires an investment of $2 million and is expected to generate a 24 percent rate of return. Project B will cost $1 million ($3 million minus $2 million on the horizontal axis) and is expected to generate a 22 percent rate of return,

FIGURE **9.1**

Simplified Capital Budgeting Model

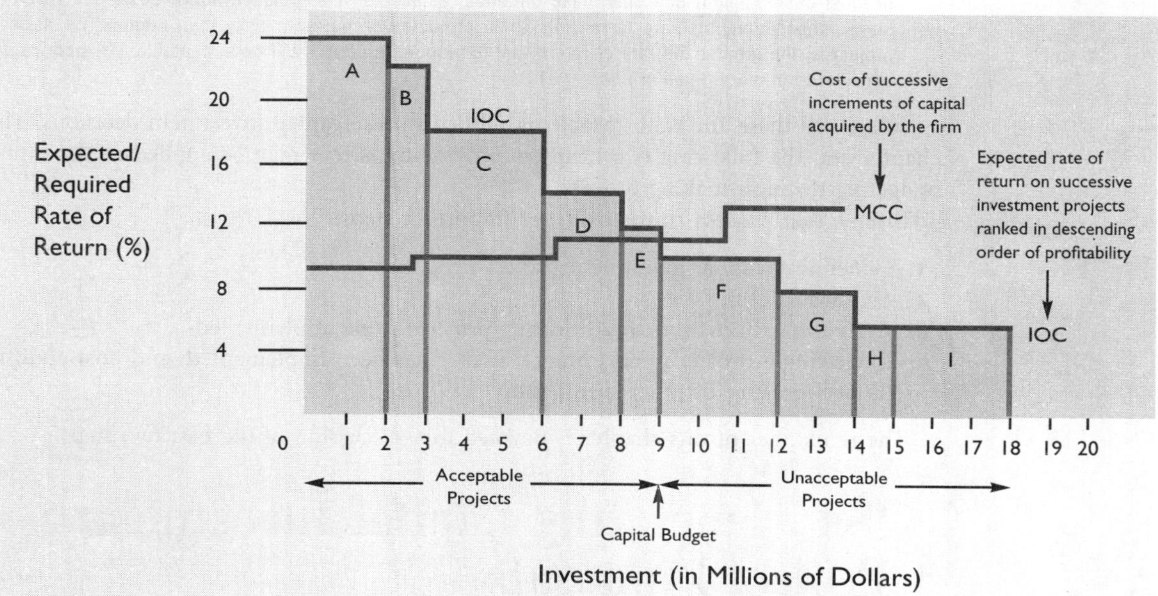

[2]Many times firms limit their capital expenditures, not because of a funds constraint but because of limited managerial resources needed to manage the project effectively.

[3]These are treated in Chapter 10.

and so on. The projects are arranged in descending order according to their expected rates of return, in recognition of the fact that no firm has an inexhaustible supply of projects offering high expected rates of return. This schedule of projects is often called the firm's *investment opportunity curve* (IOC). Typically, a firm will invest in its highest rate of return projects first—such as Project A—before moving on to less attractive alternatives.

The MCC schedule represents the marginal cost of capital to the firm. Note that the schedule increases as more funds are sought in the capital markets. The reasons for this include the following:

- Investors' expectations about the firm's ability to successfully undertake a large number of new projects
- The business risk to which the firm is exposed because of its particular line of business
- The firm's financial risk, which is due to its capital structure
- The supply and demand for investment capital in the capital market
- The cost of selling new stock, which is greater than the cost of retained earnings

The basic capital budgeting model indicates that, in principle, the firm should invest $9 million and undertake Projects A, B, C, D, and E, because the expected returns from each project exceed the firm's marginal cost of capital. Unfortunately, however, in practice, financial decision making is not this simple. Some practical problems are encountered in trying to apply this model, including the following:

- At any point in time, a firm probably will not know all of the capital projects available to it. In most firms, capital expenditures are proposed continually, based on results of research and development programs, changing market conditions, new technologies, corporate planning efforts, and so on. Thus, a schedule of projects similar to Figure 9.1 will probably be incomplete at the time the firm makes its capital expenditure decisions.
- The shape of the MCC schedule itself may be difficult to determine. (The problems and techniques involved in estimating a firm's cost of capital are discussed in Chapter 12.)
- In most cases, a firm can only make uncertain estimates of a project's future costs and revenues (and, consequently, its rate of return). Some projects will be more risky than others. The riskier a project is, the greater the rate of return that is required before it will be acceptable. (This concept is considered in more detail in Chapter 11.)

In spite of these and other problems, all firms make capital investment decisions. This chapter and the following two chapters provide tools that may be applied to the capital budgeting decision-making process.

Briefly, that process consists of four important steps:

1. Generating capital investment project proposals
2. Estimating cash flows
3. Evaluating alternatives and selecting projects to be implemented
4. Reviewing a project's performance after it has been implemented, and post-auditing its performance after its termination

The remainder of this chapter is devoted to a discussion of the first two steps.

9-4 Generating Capital Investment Project Proposals

Ideas for new capital investments can come from many sources, both inside and outside a firm. Proposals may originate at all levels of the organization—from factory workers up to the board of directors. Most large and medium-size firms allocate the responsibility for identifying and analyzing capital expenditures to specific staff groups. These groups can include cost accounting, industrial engineering, marketing research, research and development, and corporate planning. In most firms, systematic procedures are established to assist in the search and analysis steps. For example, many firms provide detailed forms that the originator of a capital expenditure proposal must complete. These forms normally request information on the project's initial cost, the revenues it is expected to generate, and how it will affect the firm's overall operating expenses. These data are then channeled to a reviewer or group of reviewers at a higher level in the firm for analysis and possible acceptance or rejection. Where a proposal goes for review often depends on how the particular project is *classified*.

9-4a Classifying Investment Projects

As noted earlier, there are several types of capital expenditures. These can be grouped into *projects generated by growth opportunities, projects generated by cost reduction opportunities*, and *projects generated to meet legal requirements and health and safety standards*.

Projects Generated by Growth Opportunities Assume that a firm produces a particular product that is expected to experience increased demand during the upcoming years. If the firm's existing facilities are inadequate to handle the demand, proposals should be developed for expanding the firm's capacity, such as Toyota's decision to expand Camry production by using part of a Subaru-owned plant in Indiana or Boeing's decision to open a major new airplane assembly plant in South Carolina. These proposals may come from the corporate planning staff group, from a divisional staff group, or from some other source.

Because most existing products eventually become obsolete, a firm's growth is also dependent on the development and marketing of new products. This involves the generation of research and development investment proposals, marketing research investments, test marketing investments, and perhaps even investments in new plants, property, and equipment. Firms in high-technology industries—such as electronics and pharmaceuticals—must undertake continuing programs of research and development to compete successfully. For example, Cisco spent over $6.2 billion on research and development in 2015. Johnson and Johnson spent $8.5 billion in 2014.

Projects Generated by Cost Reduction Opportunities Just as products become obsolete over time, so do plants, property, equipment, and production processes. Normal use makes older plants more expensive to operate because of the higher cost of maintenance and downtime (idle time). In addition, new technological developments may render existing equipment economically obsolete. These factors create opportunities for cost reduction investments, which include replacing old, obsolete capital equipment with newer, more efficient equipment.

Projects Generated to Meet Legal Requirements and Health and Safety Standards These projects include investment proposals for such things as pollution control, ventilation, and fire protection equipment. In terms of analysis, this group of projects is best considered as contingent upon other projects.

To illustrate, suppose USX wishes to build a new steel plant in Cleveland, Ohio. The decision will be contingent upon the investment in the amount of pollution abatement equipment required by state and local laws. Thus, the decision to invest in the new plant must be based upon the *total* cost of the plant, including the pollution abatement equipment, and not just the operating equipment alone. In the case of existing facilities, this type of decision making is sometimes more complex. For example, suppose a firm is told it must install new pollution abatement equipment in a plant that has been in operation for some time. The firm first needs to determine the lowest cost alternative that will meet these legal requirements. "Lowest cost" is normally measured by the smallest present value of net cash outflows from the project. Then management must decide whether the remaining stream of cash flows from the plant is sufficient to justify the expenditure. If it appears as though it will not be, the firm may consider building a new facility, or it may decide simply to close down the original plant.

9-4b Project Size and the Decision-Making Process

The classification of a proposed project influences the capital investment decision-making process. However, there are other factors to consider—in particular, the size of the expenditure required to carry out the project.

Most firms *decentralize* the decision-making function. For example, whereas the approval of the president and the board of directors may be needed for especially large outlays, such as Ford's $5 billion to $6 billion investment in Volvo discussed earlier in the chapter, a divisional vice president may be the final decision maker in the case of medium-size outlays. A plant manager may have responsibility for deciding on smaller outlays, and a department head in a particular plant may be authorized to approve small outlays. This decision chain of command varies with individual companies. In large firms, however, it is impossible for any one person to make every decision regarding proposed capital expenditures, and a decentralized system is usually employed.

III
Foundation Concept

9-5 Principles of Estimating Cash Flows

The capital budgeting process is concerned primarily with the estimation of the *cash flows* associated with a project, not just the project's contribution to accounting profits. Typically, a capital expenditure requires an initial *cash outflow*, termed the **net investment**. Thus it is important to measure a project's performance in terms of the *net (operating) cash flows* it is expected to generate over a number of future years.

net investment

Figure 9.2 shows the estimated cash flows for a particular project. After an initial net investment of $100,000, the project is expected to generate a stream of net cash inflows over its anticipated five-year life of $50,000 in year 1; $40,000 in year 2; $30,000 in year 3; $25,000 in year 4; and $5,000 in year 5. This type of project is called a conventional or **normal project**.

normal project

FIGURE 9.2

Illustration of Estimated Cash Flows for a Normal Capital Investment Project

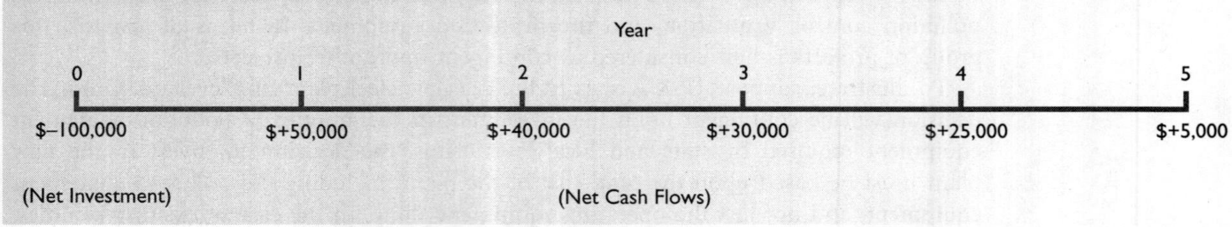

TABLE 9.1

Sample Cash Flow Patterns for Nonnormal Projects

	Year					
Project	**0**	**1**	**2**	**3**	**4**	**5**
X	−100,000	+80,000	+60,0000	−50,000	+75,000	+60,000
Y	−200,000	+150,000	+50,0000	+40,000	+30,000	−20,000
Z	−150,000	−20,000	−20,0000	−25,000	−25,000	−30,000

Nonnormal or nonconventional projects have cash flow patterns with either more than one or no sign change. Table 9.1 illustrates the cash flow patterns for three sample projects. Projects X and Y can cause some analytical problems, as we shall see in the discussion of the internal rate of return criterion in the following chapter. Project X might require that certain equipment be shut down and rebuilt in year 3, and Project Y could be an investment in a mining property, with the negative cash flow in year 5 representing abandonment costs associated with closing down the mine after its mineral wealth has been depleted. Finally, Project Z, which generates negative cash flows over the entire life of the investment, such as an investment in pollution control equipment, can be difficult to evaluate using the decision-making criteria developed in the next chapter.

Regardless of whether a project's cash flows are expected to be normal or nonnormal, certain basic principles should be applied during their estimation, including the following:

- **Cash flows should be measured on an incremental basis.** In other words, the cash flow stream for a particular project should be estimated from the perspective of how the entire cash flow stream of the firm will be affected if the project is adopted as compared with how the stream will be affected if the project is not adopted. Therefore, *all* changes in the firm's revenue stream, cost stream, and tax stream that would result from the acceptance of the project should be included in the analysis. In contrast, cash flows that would not be changed by the investment should be disregarded.
- **Cash flows should be measured on an after-tax basis.** Because the initial investment made on a project requires the outlay of after-tax cash dollars, the returns from the project should be measured in the same units, namely, after-tax cash flows.
- **All the indirect effects of a project should be included in the cash flow calculations.** For example, if a proposed plant expansion requires that working capital be increased for the firm as a whole—perhaps in the form of larger cash balances, inventories, or accounts receivable—the increase in working capital should be included in the *net investment* required for the project. A firm may also have to provide for further working capital increases as sales increase over the life of the project. These additional working capital requirements should be included in the yearly net cash flows as outflows. However, as the project winds down, net working capital balances decline; these should be included as inflows when determining yearly cash flows. Other indirect effects may occur when one division of a firm introduces a new product that competes directly with a product produced by another division. The first division may consider this product desirable, but when the impact on the second division's sales is considered, the project may be much less attractive. For example, in the Ford capital expenditure decision discussed earlier in the chapter, the company should have considered the impact of the increased output of Volvos on the demand for Ford's other luxury-car brands at the time—namely, Lincoln and Jaguar.
- **Sunk costs should not be considered when evaluating a project.** A *sunk cost* is an outlay that has already been made (or committed to be made). Because sunk costs cannot be recovered, they should not be considered in the decision to accept or reject a project. For example, in 2016, the Chemtron Corporation was considering constructing a new chemical disposal facility. Two years earlier, the firm had hired the R.O.E. Consulting Group to do an environmental impact analysis of the proposed site at a cost of $500,000. Because this $500,000 cost cannot be recovered whether the project is undertaken or not, it should not be considered in the accept-reject analysis taking place in 2016. The only relevant costs are the incremental outlays that will be made from this point forward if the project is undertaken.

- **The value of resources used in a project should be measured in terms of their opportunity costs.**

opportunity costs

Opportunity costs of resources (assets) are the cash flows those resources could generate if they are not used in the project under consideration. For example, suppose that the site Chemtron is considering to use for its disposal facility has been owned by the firm for some time. The property originally cost $500,000, but a recent appraisal indicates that the property could be sold for $2 million. Because Chemtron must forgo the receipt of $2 million from the sale of the site if the disposal facility is constructed, the appropriate opportunity cost of this piece of land is $2 million, not the original cost of $500,000.

These five principles of cash flow estimation may be applied to the specific problem of defining and calculating a project's *net investment* and *net cash flows.*

9-6 Net Investment (NINV)

The *net investment* (NINV) in a project is defined as the project's initial net cash outlay, that is, the outlay at time (period) 0. It is calculated using the following steps:

Step 1. The new project cost plus any installation and shipping costs associated with acquiring the asset and putting it into service[4]

PLUS

Step 2. Any increases in net working capital *initially* required as a result of the new investment

MINUS

Step 3. The net proceeds from the sale of existing assets when the investment is a replacement decision[5]

PLUS or MINUS

Step 4. The taxes associated with the sale of the existing assets and/or the purchase of the new assets[6]

EQUALS

The net investment (NINV).

The calculation of the net investment for two example projects is illustrated in later sections of the chapter dealing with asset expansion and asset replacement projects. Also discussed are some of the tax consequences that can influence the net investment of a project. These tax effects are the treatment of gains and losses from asset sales in the case of replacement decisions.

If a project generates additional revenues and the company extends credit to its customers, an additional initial investment in accounts receivable is required. Moreover, if additional inventories are necessary to generate the increased revenues, then an additional initial investment in inventory is required, too. This increase in initial working capital—that is, cash, accounts receivable, and inventories—should be calculated *net* of any automatic increases in current liabilities, such as accounts payable or wages and taxes payable, that occur because of the project. As a general rule, replacement projects require little or no net working capital increase. Expansion projects, on the other hand, normally require investments in additional net working capital.

[4]The asset cost plus installation and shipping costs form the basis upon which depreciation is computed.

[5]This is normally computed as the actual salvage value of the asset being replaced less any costs associated with physically removing or selling it.

[6]These taxes include any taxes associated with disposal of the old asset. The total tax effect may be either positive or negative; this is why it is either added to or subtracted from the new project cost.

FIGURE 9.3

Timeline of NINV for a Project with Multiple Period Outlays

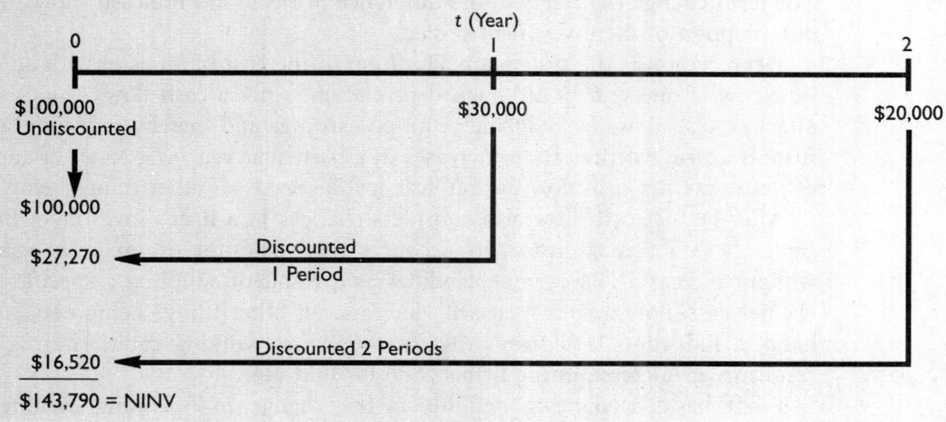

© Cengage Learning

Some projects require outlays over more than one year before positive cash inflows are generated. It may take several years to design and construct a new production facility, such as an automobile assembly plant. In these cases, the NINV for that project will be equal to the present value (at time 0) of this series of outlays, discounted at the firm's cost of capital. For example, consider a project requiring outlays of $100,000 in year 0, $30,000 in year 1, and $20,000 in year 2, with a cost of capital equal to 10 percent. The NINV or present value of the cash outlays is calculated as follows:[7]

Year t	Cash Outlay	$PVIF_{0.10,t}$	Present Value of Cash Outlay
0	$100,000	1.000	$100,000
1	30,000	0.909	27,270
2	20,000	0.826	16,520
			NINV = $143,790

Figure 9.3 illustrates this concept.

9-7 Net (Operating) Cash Flows

Capital investment projects are expected to generate after-tax cash flow streams after the initial net investment has been made. The process of estimating incremental cash flows associated with a specific project is an important part of the capital budgeting process.

net (operating) cash flows

Capital budgeting is concerned primarily with the after-tax **net (operating) cash flows** (NCF) of a particular project, or change in cash inflows minus change in cash outflows. For any year during the life of a project, these may be defined as the change in operating earnings after taxes, OEAT,[8] plus the change in depreciation, *Dep*, minus the

[7]For tax purposes, the installed cost of this asset would be $150,000—the actual cash outlays required to put the plant or equipment in service.

[8]Operating earnings after tax, OEAT, differs from earnings after tax, EAT, because OEAT *does not* consider interest expenses in its calculation. Net cash flows, NCF, as used for capital budgeting purposes, do not normally consider financing charges, such as interest, because these financing charges will be reflected in the cost of capital that is used to discount a project's cash flows. To include financing charges in NCF would result in double-counting these costs.

change in the net working capital investment required by the firm to support the project, NWC:[9]

(9.1)
$$NCF = \Delta OEAT + \Delta Dep - \Delta NWC$$

The term change (Δ) refers to the difference in cash (and noncash) flows *with* and *without* adoption of the investment project.

Depreciation is the systematic allocation of the cost of an asset with an economic life in excess of one year.[10] Although depreciation is not a cash flow, it does affect a firm's after-tax cash flows by reducing reported earnings and thereby reducing taxes paid by a firm. If a firm's depreciation increases in a particular year as a result of adopting a project, after-tax net cash flow in that year will increase, all other things being equal.

After-tax net cash flow also considers changes in a firm's investment in net working capital.[11] If a firm increases its accounts receivable, for example, in a particular year without increasing its current liabilities as a result of adopting a specific project, after-tax net cash flow in that year will decrease, all other things being equal. On the other hand, a reduction in a firm's investment in net working capital during a given year results in an increase in the firm's NCF for that year.

From basic accounting definitions, the change in operating earnings after taxes (ΔOEAT) in Equation 9.1 is equal to the change in operating earnings before taxes (ΔOEBT) times $(1 - T)$ where T is the marginal corporate income tax rate. Furthermore, ΔOEBT is equal to the change in revenues (ΔR) minus the change in operating costs (ΔO) minus the change in depreciation (ΔDep). Substituting these terms in Equation 9.1 yields the following definition of net cash flow:

(9.2)
$$NCF = (\Delta R - \Delta O - \Delta Dep)(1 - T) + \Delta Dep - \Delta NWC$$

Equation 9.2 can be further extended into an *operational* definition of NCF by defining ΔR as $R_w - R_{wo}$, ΔO as $O_w - O_{wo}$, and ΔDep as $Dep_w - Dep_{wo}$, where:

R_{wo} = Revenues of the firm *without* the project

R_w = Revenues of the firm *with* the project

O_{wo} = Operating costs exclusive of depreciation for the firm *without* the project

O_w = Operating costs exclusive of depreciation for the firm *with* the project

Dep_{wo} = Depreciation charges for the firm *without* the project

Dep_w = Depreciation charges for the firm *with* the project

The definition given in Equation 9.2 can be rewritten as follows:

(9.3)
$$\begin{aligned} NCF = {} & [(R_w - R_{wo}) - (O_w - O_{wo}) - (Dep_w - Dep_{wo})](1 - T) \\ & + (Dep_w - Dep_{wo}) - \Delta NWC \end{aligned}$$

These calculations and equations are summarized in Table 9.2. In the final year of a project's economic life, Equation 9.2 must be modified to reflect recovery of the incremental after-tax salvage value of the asset(s).

The following two sections illustrate the calculation of net cash flows using these equations.

[9] In years when a firm must increase its investment in net working capital (NWC) associated with a particular project, this increased investment in NWC *reduces* NCF. Normally, however, at the end of the life of a project, the NWC investment accumulated over the life of the project is recovered (for example, as inventories are sold and accounts receivable are collected). Thus, ΔNWC is negative (a reduction). Because of the minus sign before ΔNWC in Equation 9.1, the effect of a decline in the net working capital investments is an *increase* in NCF.

[10] Equation 9.1 provides an easy procedure for reflecting the cash flow impact of depreciation.

[11] Changes in net working capital can occur as part of the net investment at time 0 or at any time during the life of the project.

TABLE 9.2

Summary of Net Cash Flow Calculations and Equations

Calculation	Equation 9.1 and 9.2	Equation 9.3
Change in revenue	ΔR	$(R_W - R_{WO})$
Less: Change in operating costs	$-\Delta O$	$-(O_W - O_{WO})$
Less: Change in depreciation	$-\Delta Dep$	$-(Dep_W - Dep_{WO})$
Equals: Change in operating earnings before taxes	ΔOEBT	ΔOEAT
Less: Taxes	$-T(\Delta \text{OEBT})$	$-T(\Delta \text{OEBT})$
Equals: Change in operating earnings after taxes	ΔOEAT	ΔOEAT
Plus: Change in depreciation	$+\Delta Dep$	$+(Dep_W - Dep_{WO})$
Less: Change in net working capital	$-\Delta$NWC	$-\Delta$NWC
Equals: Net cash flow	NCF	NCF

9-7a Recovery of After-Tax Salvage Value

Whenever an asset that has been depreciated is sold, there are potential tax consequences that may affect the after-tax net proceeds received from the asset sale. These tax consequences are important when estimating the after-tax salvage value to be received at the end of the economic life of any project. As discussed earlier, the tax consequences of asset sales are also important when calculating the net investment required in a replacement investment project. There are four cases that need to be considered.

Case 1: Sale of an Asset for Its Book Value If a company disposes of an asset for an amount exactly equal to the asset's tax book value, there is neither a gain nor a loss on the sale and thus there are no tax consequences. For example, if Burlington Textile sells for $50,000 an asset with a book value for tax purposes of $50,000, no taxes are associated with this disposal. (In general, the tax book value of an asset equals the installed cost of the asset less accumulated tax depreciation.)

Case 2: Sale of an Asset for Less Than Its Book Value If Burlington Textile sells for $20,000 an asset having a tax book value of $50,000, Burlington Textile incurs a $30,000 pretax loss. Assuming that this asset is used in business or trade (an essential criterion for this tax treatment), this loss may be treated as an operating loss or an offset to operating income. This operating loss effectively reduces the company's taxes by an amount equal to the loss times the company's marginal tax rate.

Assume that the company's earnings before taxes is $100,000 (before consideration of the operating loss from the disposal of the asset). Taxes on these earnings are $100,000 times the company's marginal (40%) tax rate, or $40,000. (We use a 40% marginal tax rate throughout the book for ease of calculation. Actual current corporate marginal tax rates are discussed in Appendix 2A.) Because of the operating loss incurred by selling the asset for $20,000, the company's taxable income is reduced to $70,000 and the taxes decline to $28,000 (40% of $70,000). The $12,000 difference in taxes is equal to the tax loss on the sale of the old asset times the company's marginal tax rate ($30,000 × 40%).

Case 3: Sale of an Asset for More Than Its Book Value but Less Than Its Original Cost If Burlington Textile sells the asset for $60,000—$10,000 more than the current tax book value—$50,000 of this amount constitutes a tax-free cash inflow, and the remaining $10,000 is taxed as operating income. As a result, the firm's taxes increase by $4,000, or the amount of the gain times the firm's marginal tax rate ($10,000 × 40%). (The IRS treats this gain as a recapture of depreciation.)

Case 4: Sale of an Asset for More Than Its Original Cost If Burlington Textile sells the asset for $120,000 (assuming an original asset cost of $110,000), part of the gain from the sale is treated as ordinary income and part is treated as a long-term *capital gain*. The gain receiving ordinary income treatment is equal to the difference between the original asset cost and the current tax book value, or $60,000 ($110,000 − $50,000). The capital gain portion is the amount in excess of the original asset cost, or $10,000. Under the Revenue Reconciliation Act of 1993, both ordinary income and capital gains are taxed at the same corporate rate (35 percent).

9-7b Recovery of Net Working Capital

In the last year of a project that, over its economic life, has required incremental net working capital investments, this net working capital is assumed to be liquidated and returned to the firm as cash. At the end of a project's life, all net working capital additions required over the project's life are recovered—not just the initial net working capital outlay occurring at time 0. Hence, the total accumulated net working capital is normally recovered in the last year of the project. This *decrease* in net working capital in the last year of the project *increases* the net cash flow for that year, all other things being equal. Of course, no tax consequences are associated with the recovery of NWC.

9-7c Interest Charges and Net Cash Flows

Often the purchase of a particular asset is tied closely to the creation of some debt obligation, such as the sale of mortgage bonds or a bank loan. Nevertheless, it is generally considered *incorrect* to deduct the interest charges associated with a particular project from the estimated cash flows. This is true for two reasons.

First, the decision about how a firm should be financed can—and should—be made independently of the decision to accept or reject one or more projects. Instead, the firm should seek some combination of debt, equity (common stock), and preferred stock capital that is consistent with management's wishes concerning the trade-off between financial risk and the cost of capital. In many cases, this will result in a capital structure with the cost of capital at or near its minimum. Because investment and financing decisions should normally be made independently of one another, each new project can be viewed as being financed with the same proportions of the various sources of capital funds used to finance the firm as a whole.

Second, when a discounting framework is used for project evaluation, the discount rate, or cost of capital, already incorporates the cost of funds used to finance a project. Thus, including interest charges in cash flow calculations essentially would result in a double counting of costs.

9-7d Depreciation

depreciation

Depreciation was defined earlier as the systematic allocation of the cost of an asset over more than one year. It allows a firm to spread the costs of fixed assets over a period of years to better match costs and revenues in each accounting period. The annual depreciation expense recorded for a particular asset is simply an allocation of historic costs and does not necessarily indicate a declining market value. For example, a company that is depreciating an office building may find the building's market value *appreciating* each year.

There are a number of alternative methods of recording the depreciation of an asset for *financial reporting* purposes. These include straight-line depreciation and various accelerated depreciation methods. Under the straight-line depreciation method, the annual amount of an asset's depreciation is calculated as follows:

$$\text{Annual depreciation amount} = \frac{\text{Installed cost}}{\text{Number of years over which the asset is depreciated}} \tag{9.4}$$

The installed cost includes the purchase price of the asset plus shipping and installation charges, that is, Step 1 of the NINV calculation described earlier.

For *tax* purposes, the depreciation rate a firm uses has a significant impact on the cash flows of the firm. This is so because depreciation represents a *noncash* expense that is deductible for tax purposes. Hence, the greater the amount of depreciation charged in a period, the lower the firm's taxable income will be. With a lower reported taxable income, the firm's tax obligation (a cash outflow) is reduced and the cash inflows for the firm are increased.

For example, suppose that the Badger Company in a given year has revenues of $1,000,000, operating expenses exclusive of depreciation of $500,000, straight-line depreciation of $100,000, and a marginal tax rate of 40 percent.[12] Its operating cash flow is calculated in Part (a) of Table 9.3 to be $340,000. Now suppose Badger opts to use an accelerated depreciation method for tax purposes, rather than the straight-line method. As a result, its depreciation expense is recorded as $150,000 instead of $100,000. Its operating cash flow is now $360,000, as shown in Part (b) of Table 9.3.

A comparison of the two cash flow statements shows that the use of accelerated depreciation reduces operating earnings after taxes from $240,000 to $210,000 and reduces taxes from $160,000 to $140,000 but increases operating cash flow from $340,000 to $360,000. Hence, the use of accelerated depreciation for tax purposes is desirable for the firm because it reduces tax outlays and thereby increases cash flow. In general, a profitable firm will depreciate its assets as quickly as the tax law allows, and it should use whatever allowable method permits the highest percentage depreciation in the early years of an asset's life. The tax method currently used in the United States is

TABLE 9.3

Comparison of Straight-Line and Accelerated Depreciation Methods: Badger Company

	(a) Straight-Line Depreciation		(b) Accelerated Depreciation	
Revenues		$1,000,000		$1,000,000
Less: Operating expenses	$500,000		$500,000	
Depreciation	$100,000		$150,000	
Total		600,000		650,000
Operating earnings before taxes		$400,000		$350,000
Less: Taxes (40%)		160,000		140,000
Operating earnings after taxes		$240,000		$210,000
Plus: Depreciation		100,000		150,000
Operating cash flow (CF)		$340,000		$360,000

[12]This example assumes that net working capital remains constant.

Modified Accelerated Cost Recovery System (MACRS)

the **Modified Accelerated Cost Recovery System (MACRS)** method; it is explained in Appendix 9A.

The cash flow examples discussed in this chapter use straight-line depreciation to keep the calculations simple. In actual practice, companies today should use the MACRS method when computing the NCFs from a project. *The relevant depreciation number that should be used when computing the after-tax net cash flows expected from a capital expenditure project is the tax depreciation amount.*

9-8 Asset Expansion Projects

A project that requires a firm to invest funds in additional assets in order to increase sales (or reduce costs) is called an *asset expansion project*. For example, suppose the TLC Yogurt Company has decided to capitalize on the exercise fad and plans to open an exercise facility in conjunction with its main yogurt and health foods store. To get the project under way, the company will rent additional space adjacent to its current store. The equipment required for the facility will cost $50,000. Shipping and installation charges for the equipment are expected to total $5,000. This equipment will be depreciated on a straight-line basis over its five-year economic life to an estimated salvage value of $0. In order to open the exercise facility, TLC estimates that it will have to add about $7,000 initially to its net working capital in the form of additional inventories of exercise supplies, cash, and accounts receivable for its exercise customers (less accounts payable).

During the first year of operations, TLC expects its total revenues (from yogurt sales and exercise services) to increase by $50,000 above the level that would have prevailed without the exercise facility addition. These incremental revenues are expected to grow to $60,000 in year 2, $75,000 in year 3, decline to $60,000 in year 4, and decline again to $45,000 during the fifth and final year of the project's life. The company's incremental operating costs associated with the exercise facility, including the rental of the facility, are expected to total $25,000 during the first year and increase at a rate of 6 percent per year over the five-year project life. Depreciation will be $11,000 per year ($55,000 installed cost, assuming no salvage value, divided by the five-year economic life). TLC has a marginal tax rate of 40 percent. In addition, TLC expects that it will have to add about $5,000 per year to its net working capital in years 1, 2, and 3 and nothing in years 4 and 5. At the end of the project, the total accumulated net working capital required by the project will be recovered.

9-8a Calculating the Net Investment

First, we determine the net investment required for the exercise facility expansion. TLC must make a cash outlay of $50,000 to pay for the facility equipment. In addition, it must pay $5,000 in cash to cover the costs of shipping and installation of the equipment. Finally, TLC must invest $7,000 in initial net working capital to get the project under way. The four-step procedure discussed earlier for calculating the net investment yields the NINV required at time 0:

Purchase price of exercise equipment	$50,000
Plus: Shipping and installation	5,000
Plus: Initial net working capital required	7,000
Equals: Net investment (NINV)	$62,000

Note that steps 3 and 4 are not required in this problem since this is an asset expansion decision and no existing assets are being sold.

9-8b Calculating Annual Net Cash Flows

Next, we need to calculate the annual net cash flows associated with the project. The first-year net cash flows can be computed by substituting $\Delta R = \$50{,}000$, $\Delta O = \$25{,}000$, $\Delta Dep = \$11{,}000$, $T = 0.40$, and $\Delta \text{NWC} = \$5{,}000$ into Equation 9.2:

Year 1:

$$\begin{aligned} \text{NCF}_1 &= (\$50{,}000 - \$25{,}000 - \$11{,}000)(1 - 0.40) \\ &\quad + \$11{,}000 - \$5{,}000 \\ &= \$14{,}400 \end{aligned}$$

A similar calculation for the second year, where $\Delta R = \$60{,}000$, $\Delta O = \$25{,}000\,(1 + 0.06)^1 = \$26{,}500$, $\Delta Dep = \$11{,}000$, $T = 0.40$, and $\Delta \text{NWC} = \$5{,}000$, yields:

Year 2:

$$\begin{aligned} \text{NCF}_2 &= (\$60{,}000 - \$26{,}500 - \$11{,}000)(1 - 0.40) \\ &\quad + \$11{,}000 - \$5{,}000 \\ &= \$19{,}500 \end{aligned}$$

Finally, in the fifth year, TLC will recover its working capital investment of \$22,000, that is, \$7,000 (year 0) and \$5,000 (years 1, 2, and 3). Substituting $\Delta \text{NWC} = -\$22{,}000$, along with $\Delta R = \$45{,}000$ and $\Delta O = \$25{,}000\,(1 + 0.06)^4 = \$31{,}562$, $\Delta Dep = \$11{,}000$, and $T = 0.40$ into Equation 9.2 yields:

Year 5:

$$\begin{aligned} \text{NCF}_5 &= (\$45{,}000 - \$31{,}562 - \$11{,}000)(1 - 0.40) \\ &\quad + \$11{,}000 - \$22{,}000 \\ &= \$34{,}463 \end{aligned}$$

The calculations of annual cash flows for these years as well as for years 3 and 4 are summarized in Table 9.4. Note that since the equipment was fully depreciated and had no salvage value at the end of the fifth year, the after-tax salvage value was \$0.

The cash flows associated with the exercise facility project are illustrated with the time line in Figure 9.4.

In Chapter 10, several different capital budgeting decision models are applied to cash flows such as these to determine the desirability of capital investment projects.

TABLE 9.4

Calculation of Annual Net Cash Flows for TLC Exercise Facility

	Year 1	Year 2	Year 3	Year 4	Year 5
Change in revenues (ΔR)	\$50,000	\$60,000	\$75,000	\$60,000	\$45,000
Minus: Change in operating costs (ΔO)	25,000	26,500	28,090	29,775	31,562
Minus: Change in depreciation (ΔDep)	11,000	11,000	11,000	11,000	11,000
Equals: Change in operating earnings before tax (ΔOEBT)	\$14,000	\$22,500	\$35,910	\$19,225	\$2,438
Minus: Change in taxes (40%) (T)	5,600	9,000	14,364	7,690	975
Equals: Change in operating earnings after tax (ΔOEAT)	\$8,400	\$13,500	\$21,546	\$11,535	\$1,463
Plus: Change in depreciation (ΔDep)	11,000	11,000	11,000	11,000	11,000
Minus: Change in net working capital (ΔNWC)	5,000	5,000	5,000	0	−22,000
Plus: After-tax salvage	—	—	—	—	0
Equals: Net cash flow (NCF)	\$14,400	\$19,500	\$27,546	\$22,535	\$34,463

FIGURE 9.4

Estimated Cash Flows for TLC Investment Project

Year	0	1	2	3	4	5
	$-62,000	$14,400	$19,500	$27,546	$22,535	$34,463
	Net Investment	Net Cash Flows				

9-9 Asset Replacement Projects

The previous example of an asset expansion project illustrated the key elements of the calculation of a project's net investment and its annual net cash flows. In this section, we consider an *asset replacement* project. Asset replacements involve retiring one asset and replacing it with a more efficient asset.

Suppose Briggs & Stratton purchased an automated drill press 10 years ago that had an estimated economic life of 20 years. The drill press originally cost $150,000 and has been fully depreciated, leaving a current book value of $0. The actual market value of this drill press is $40,000. The company is considering replacing the drill press with a new one costing $190,000. Shipping and installation charges will add an additional $10,000 to the cost. The new machine would be depreciated to zero on a straight-line basis. The new machine is expected to have a 10-year economic life, and its actual salvage value at the end of the 10-year period is estimated to be $25,000. Briggs & Stratton's current marginal tax rate is 40 percent.

9-9a Calculating the Net Investment

Steps 1 and 2 of the net investment calculation are easy; the new project cost ($190,000) plus shipping and installation ($10,000) is $200,000. In this case, no initial incremental net working capital is required.

In steps 3 and 4, the net proceeds received from the sale of the old drill press have to be adjusted for taxes.

Because the old drill press is sold for $40,000, the gain from this sale is treated as a recapture of depreciation and thus taxed as ordinary income. Table 9.5 summarizes the

TABLE 9.5

Net Investment Calculation for Briggs & Stratton

Cost of new drill press	$190,000
Plus: Shipping and installation charges	10,000
Equals: Installed cost	$200,000
Plus: Increase in initial net working capital	0
Minus: Proceeds from sale of old drill press	40,000
Equals: Net investment before taxes	$160,000
Plus: Tax on gain from sale of old drill press (40% × $40,000)	16,000
Equals: Net investment (NINV)	$176,000

NINV calculation for Briggs & Stratton. As can be seen in this table, the NINV is equal to \$176,000.

9-9b Calculating Annual Net Cash Flows

Suppose Briggs & Stratton expects annual revenues during the project's first year to increase from \$70,000 to \$85,000 if the new drill press is purchased. (This might occur because the new press is faster than the old one and can meet the increasing demands for more work.) After the first year, revenues from the new project are expected to increase at a rate of \$2,000 a year for the remainder of the project life.[13]

Assume further that while the old drill press required two operators, the new drill press is more automated and needs only one, thereby reducing annual operating costs from \$40,000 to \$20,000 during the project's first year. After the first year, annual operating costs of the new drill press are expected to increase by \$1,000 a year over the remaining life of the project.[14] The old machine is fully depreciated, whereas the new machine will be depreciated on a straight-line basis. The marginal tax rate of 40 percent applies. Assume also that the company's net working capital does not change as a result of replacing the drill press.

The first-year net cash flow resulting from the purchase of the new drill press can be computed by substituting $R_w = \$85{,}000$, $R_{wo} = \$70{,}000$, $O_w = \$20{,}000$, $O_{wo} = \$40{,}000$, $Dep_w = \$20{,}000$ $(= \$200{,}000/10)$, $Dep_{wo} = \$0$, $T = 0.40$, and $\Delta\text{NWC} = \$0$ into Equation 9.3 as follows:

Year 1:

$$\begin{aligned}\text{NCF}_1 &= [(\$85{,}000 - \$70{,}000) - (\$20{,}000 - \$40{,}000)\\ &\quad -(\$20{,}000 - \$0)](1 - 0.4) + (\$20{,}000 - \$0) - \$0\\ &= \$29{,}000\end{aligned}$$

Using the different expected values for new revenues $R_w = \$87{,}000$ and new operating costs $O_w = \$21{,}000$ in the second year, the second-year net cash flows can be computed as follows:

Year 2:

$$\begin{aligned}\text{NCF}_2 &= [(\$87{,}000 - \$70{,}000) - (\$21{,}000 - \$40{,}000)\\ &\quad -(\$20{,}000 - \$0)](1 - 0.4) + (\$20{,}000 - \$0) - \$0\\ &= \$29{,}600\end{aligned}$$

Similar calculations are used to obtain the net cash flows in years 3 through 9.

Finally, in year 10, the \$25,000 estimated salvage from the new drill press must be added along with its associated tax effects. This \$25,000 salvage is treated as ordinary income because it represents a recapture of depreciation for tax purposes.

$$\begin{aligned}\text{NCF}_{10} &= [(\$103{,}000 - \$70{,}000) - (\$29{,}000 - \$40{,}000)\\ &\quad -(\$20{,}000 - \$0)](1 - 0.4) + (\$20{,}000 - \$0) - \$0\\ &\quad +\$25{,}000 \text{ salvage} - \text{tax on salvage}(0.4 \times \$25{,}000)\\ &= \$34{,}400 + \$25{,}000 - \$10{,}000\\ &= \$49{,}400\end{aligned}$$

Table 9.6 is a summary worksheet for computing the net cash flows for Briggs & Stratton during the 10-year estimated economic life of the new drill press.

---

[13]For simplicity, we have assumed that the revenue figure of \$70,000 without the project remains constant over the life of the project.

[14]For simplicity, we have assumed that the operating cost figure of \$40,000 without the project remains constant over the life of the project.

TABLE 9.6

Annual Net Cash Flow Worksheet for the Briggs & Stratton Drill Press Acquisition

	Year									
	1	2	3	4	5	6	7	8	9	10
Change in revenues ($R_W - R_{WO}$)*	$15,000	$17,000	$19,000	$21,000	$23,000	$25,000	$27,000	$29,000	$31,000	$33,000
Minus: Change in operating costs ($O_W - O_{WO}$)**	−20,000	−19,000	−18,000	−17,000	−16,000	−15,000	−14,000	−13,000	−12,000	−11,000
Minus: Change in depreciation ($Dep_W - Dep_{WO}$)***	20,000	20,000	20,000	20,000	20,000	20,000	20,000	20,000	20,000	20,000
Equals: Change in operating earnings before taxes (ΔOEBT)	$15,000	$16,000	$17,000	$18,000	$19,000	$20,000	$21,000	$22,000	$23,000	$24,000
Minus: Tax (40%)	6,000	6,400	6,800	7,200	7,600	8,000	8,400	8,800	9,200	9,600
Equals: Change in operating earnings after taxes (ΔOEAT)	$ 9,000	$ 9,600	$10,200	$10,800	$11,400	$12,000	$12,600	$13,200	$13,800	$14,400
Plus: Change in depreciation ($Dep_W - Dep_{WO}$)	20,000	20,000	20,000	20,000	20,000	20,000	20,000	20,000	20,000	20,000
Minus: Change in net working capital (ΔNWC)	0	0	0	0	0	0	0	0	0	0
Equals: Net cash flow before Salvage	$29,000	$29,600	$30,200	$30,800	$31,400	$32,000	$32,600	$33,200	$33,800	$34,400
Plus: Salvage	0	0	0	0	0	00	0	0	0	25,000
Minus: Tax on salvage (0.4 × salvage)	0	0	0	0	0	0	0	0	0	10,000
Equals: Net cash flow	$29,000	$29,600	$30,200	$30,800	$31,400	$32,000	$32,600	$33,200	$33,800	$49,400

*The change in revenues from undertaking a project may be either positive or negative.

**The change in operating costs may be either positive or negative. In this case, the firm's operating costs *decline* by $20,000 in year 1, for example; that is, the change in operating costs is *negative*, indicating a cost saving. This cost saving is *added* to the change in revenues (subtracting a negative number is the same as adding a positive number). If, in another situation, operating costs were to *increase* as a result of a project, the increased costs would be *subtracted* from the change in revenues.

**The change in depreciation may be either positive or negative. In this case, it is *positive* and has the effect of reducing the amount of taxable earnings, thus reducing the amount of taxes paid. Hence, this *increases* the cash flow from the project. If the change in depreciation were *negative*, it would have the effect of increasing the taxable earnings, increasing taxes paid, and *reducing* the cash flows from the project.

TABLE 9.7

Summary Project Cash Flows for Briggs & Stratton

Year	Net Investment and Net Cash Flows
0	−$176,000
1	29,000
2	29,600
3	30,200
4	30,800
5	31,400
6	32,000
7	32,600
8	33,200
9	33,800
10	49,400

Table 9.7 summarizes the net cash flows for the entire project. This schedule of net cash flows plus the NINV computed in the preceding section form the basis for further analysis. In Chapter 10, several different capital budgeting decision models are applied to similar cash flow streams from other projects to determine the investment desirability of these projects. The cash flows developed in this chapter are an essential input in the capital budgeting decision process.

9-10 Problems in Cash Flow Estimation

Because project cash flows occur in the future, there are varying degrees of *uncertainty* about the value of these flows. Therefore, it is difficult to predict the actual cash flows of a project. The capital budgeting process assumes that the decision maker is able to estimate cash flows accurately enough that these estimates can be used in project evaluation and selection. For this assumption to be realistic, a project proposal should be based on inputs from marketing managers regarding revenue estimates and inputs from the production and engineering staffs regarding costs and achievable levels of performance. Objective inputs from these sources can help reduce the uncertainty associated with cash flow estimation.

In addition, cash flow estimates for different projects may have varying degrees of uncertainty. For example, the returns from asset replacement projects are generally easier to forecast than the returns from new product introduction projects. Chapter 11 discusses some of the techniques used to incorporate risk analysis into capital budgeting decision models.

9-11 The Practice of Cash Flow Estimation for Capital Budgeting

The analysis presented in this chapter and throughout the book suggests that generating unbiased estimates of the cash flows from investment projects is extremely important to

ETHICAL ISSUES

Cash Flow Estimation Biases

The estimation of the cash flows associated with an investment project is the most important step in the capital expenditure evaluation process. If the cash flow estimates associated with a project are intentionally or unintentionally biased, a firm's resources are unlikely to be allocated to the set of investment projects that will maximize shareholder wealth.

There are several reasons why managers might produce biased cash flow estimates when preparing capital expenditure project proposals. First, a manager might be tempted to overestimate the revenues or underestimate the costs associated with a project if the manager is attempting to expand the resource base over which he or she has control. By biasing the estimates of a project's cash flows upward, a manager is likely to receive a larger share of the investment resources of the firm. Because managerial compensation is sometimes tied to the span of job responsibilities, managers may be tempted to expand this span of control at the expense of other areas in the firm.

Second, some firms tie employee compensation to performance relative to stated objectives—a compensation scheme often called *management by objective.* If a manager is confident that the best estimate of the cash flows from a proposed project is sufficiently large to guarantee project acceptance, the manager may be tempted to reduce these cash flow estimates to a level below the "most likely outcome" level, confident that the project will continue to be viewed as an acceptable investment and that it will be funded. However, once the project is under way, the project manager will feel less pressure to meet projected performance standards. The downward bias in the cash flow estimates provides a cushion that permits suboptimal management of the project while achieving the objectives enunciated when the project was first proposed.

What impact does intentionally biasing cash flow estimates for investment projects have on achieving the goal of shareholder wealth maximization?

the success of the firm. A survey supports this conclusion and provides considerable insight regarding the cash flow estimation procedures used by larger firms (*Fortune* 500).[15]

The majority of the firms responding to the survey had annual capital budgets of more than $100 million. Nearly 67 percent of the firms prepared formal cash flow estimates for over 60 percent of their annual capital outlays, and a majority produced detailed cash flow projections for capital investments requiring an initial outlay of $40,000 or more. Firms with high capital intensity and high leverage were more likely to have one or more persons, such as a financial analyst, treasurer, controller, or department manager, designated to oversee the process of cash flow estimation. This reflects the larger number of projects associated with capital-intensive firms and the need to effectively manage the risk associated with high leverage.

When asked about the type of cash flow estimates that were generated, 56 percent indicated that they used single-dollar estimates, 8 percent used a range of estimates, and 36 percent used both single-dollar estimates and a range of estimates. There was a significant positive correlation between firms that use both types of estimates and measures of operating and financial risk, suggesting that the use of a range of estimates is one procedure for managing high risk.

Forecasting methods employed by the respondent firms included subjective estimates from management, sensitivity analysis, consensus analysis of expert opinions, and computer simulation. Many firms used multiple cash flow forecasting techniques. The longer the forecasting horizon—that is, the longer the economic life of the project—the more likely a firm is to use multiple methods for forecasting future cash flows.

[15] Randolph A. Pohlman, E. S. Santiago, and F. L. Markel, "Cash Flow Estimation Practices of Large Firms," *Financial Management* (Summer 1988): 71–79.

Financial factors considered to be important in generating cash flow estimates include working capital requirements, project risk, tax considerations, the project's impact on the firm's liquidity, the anticipated rate of inflation, and expected salvage value. Important marketing factors considered include sales forecasts, the competitive advantages and disadvantages of the product, and product life. Important production factors include operating expenses, material and supply costs, overhead and expenses for manufacturing, capacity utilization, and start-up costs.

Three-fourths of the companies surveyed make comparisons between actual and projected cash flows, with nearly all the firms comparing actual versus projected initial outlays and operating cash flows over the project life; about two-thirds of these firms make comparisons of actual versus projected salvage values. The most accurate cash flow estimates are reported to be the initial outlay estimates, and the least accurate element of cash flow estimates is the annual operating cash flows. Cash flow forecasts were more accurate for equipment replacement investments than for expansion and modernization investments or for acquisitions of ongoing businesses. Firms with the information system in place to generate cash flow forecasts tend to produce more accurate forecasts than firms with less sophisticated capital project evaluation procedures.

9-12 Summary

- *Capital budgeting* is the process of planning for purchases of assets whose returns are expected to continue beyond one year.
- Projects may be classified as *independent, mutually exclusive*, or *contingent*. The acceptance of an independent project does not directly eliminate other projects from consideration; the acceptance of a mutually exclusive project precludes other alternatives; and the acceptance of a contingent project depends on the adoption of one or more other projects.
- There are four basic steps in the capital budgeting process: *the generation of proposals, the estimation of cash flows, the evaluation and selection of alternatives*, and *the post-audit or review*.
- Project cash flows should be measured on an *incremental after-tax* basis and should include all the indirect effects the project will have on the firm.
- Resources of a firm used in an investment project should be valued at their *opportunity cost* based upon the cash flows these resources could generate in their next-best alternative use.
- *Sunk costs* represent outlays that have already been made or committed and that cannot be recovered. Sunk costs should not be considered when evaluating an investment project.
- The *net investment* (NINV) in a project is the net cash outlay required to place the project in service. It includes the project cost *plus* any necessary increases in initial net working capital *minus* any proceeds from the sale of the old asset(s) (in the case of replacement decisions) *plus or minus* the taxes associated with the sale of the old asset(s) and/or the purchase of the new asset(s).
- The *net (operating) cash flows* (NCF) from a project are the incremental changes in a firm's operating cash flows that result from investing in the project. These flows include the changes in the firm's revenues, operating costs, depreciation, taxes, and net working capital with and without the project.
- An *asset expansion* project requires a firm to invest funds in additional assets to increase sales or reduce costs. *Asset replacements*, in contrast, involve retiring one asset and replacing it with a more efficient one.

Important Equations

$$\text{NCF} = \Delta\text{OEAT} + \Delta Dep - \Delta\text{NWC}$$

$$\text{NCF} = [(R_W - R_{WO}) - (O_W - O_{WO}) - (Dep_W - Dep_{WO})](1 - T) + (Dep_W - Dep_{WO}) - \Delta\text{NWC}$$

Important Equations (*Continued*)

$$\text{Annual depreciation amount} = \frac{\text{Installed cost}}{\text{Number of years over which the asset is depreciated}}$$

9-13 Questions and Topics for Discussion

1. Discuss how capital budgeting procedures might be used by each of the following:
   a. Personnel managers
   b. Research and development staffs
   c. Advertising executives
2. What is a mutually exclusive investment project? An independent project? A contingent project? Give an example of each.
3. What effect does capital rationing have on a firm's ability to maximize shareholder wealth?
4. What are the primary types of capital investment projects? Does a project's type influence how it is analyzed?
5. Cash flows for a particular project should be measured on an incremental basis and should consider all the indirect effects of the project. What does this involve?
6. What factors should be considered when estimating a project's NINV?
7. Depreciation is a noncash expense; why is it considered when estimating a project's net cash flows?
8. What are the potential tax consequences of selling an old asset in an asset replacement investment decision?
9. Why is it generally incorrect to consider interest charges when computing a project's net cash flows?
10. Distinguish between asset expansion and asset replacement projects. How does this distinction affect the capital expenditure analysis process?
11. How is the opportunity cost concept used in the capital budgeting process?

9-14 Self-Test Problems

ST1. The Fleming Company, a food distributor, is considering replacing a filling line at its Oklahoma City warehouse. The existing line was purchased several years ago for $600,000. The line's book value is $200,000, and Fleming management feels it could be sold at this time for $150,000. A new, increased capacity line can be purchased for $1,200,000. Delivery and installation of the new line are expected to cost an additional $100,000. Assuming Fleming's marginal tax rate is 40 percent, calculate the net investment for the new line.

ST2. International Foods Corporation (IFC) currently processes seafood with a unit it purchased several years ago. The unit, which originally cost $500,000, currently has a book value of $250,000. IFC is considering replacing the existing unit with a newer, more efficient one. The new unit will cost $700,000 and will require an additional $50,000 for delivery and installation. The new unit will also require IFC to increase its investment in initial net working capital by $40,000. The new unit will be depreciated on a straight-line basis over five years to a zero balance. IFC expects to sell the existing unit for $275,000. IFC's marginal tax rate is 40 percent.

If IFC purchases the new unit, annual revenues are expected to increase by $100,000 (due to increased processing capacity), and annual operating costs (exclusive of depreciation) are expected to decrease by $20,000. Annual revenues and operating costs are expected to remain constant at this new level over the five-year life of the project. IFC estimates that its net working capital investment will increase by $10,000 per year over the life of the project. At the end of the project's life (five years), all working capital investments will be recovered. After five years, the new unit will be completely depreciated and is expected to be sold for $70,000. (Assume that the existing unit is being depreciated at a rate of $50,000 per year.)

a. Calculate the project's net investment.
b. Calculate the annual net cash flows for the project.

ST3. Homecraft Stores (HSI), which operates a chain of retail warehouse-type stores, is considering opening a new store in the Tampa area. The store itself will cost $7 million to build. In addition, fixtures for the store are expected to cost $700,000, and installation of the fixtures is estimated to cost another $50,000. Initial net working capital (primarily due to inventory) is expected to be $600,000. HSI plans to build the Tampa store on land it purchased five years ago for $200,000. The land is presently worth $500,000 and is expected to remain at $500,000 while the store is being built. Calculate the net investment for the proposed Tampa store.

9-15 Problems*

INTERMEDIATE

1. The MacCauley Company has sales of $200 million and total expenses (excluding depreciation) of $130 million. Straight-line depreciation on the company's assets is $15 million, and the maximum accelerated depreciation allowed by law is $25 million. Assume that all taxable income is taxed at 40 percent. Assume also that net working capital remains constant.

a. Calculate the MacCauley Company's after-tax operating cash flow using both straight-line and accelerated depreciation.
b. Assuming that the company uses straight-line depreciation for book purposes and accelerated depreciation for tax purposes, show the income statement reported to the stockholders. What is the after-tax operating cash flow under these circumstances?

BASIC

2. Calculate the annual straight-line depreciation for a machine that costs $50,000 and has installation and shipping costs that total $1,000. The machine will be depreciated over a period of 10 years. The company's marginal tax rate is 40 percent.

BASIC

3. The Cooper Electronics Company has developed the following schedule of potential investment projects that may be undertaken during the next 6 months:

*Color blocks behind the numbers denote problems that have check answers provided at the end of the book.

Project	Cost (in Millions of Dollars)	Expected Rate of Return
A	$ 3.0	20%
B	1.5	22
C	7.0	7
D	14.0	10
E	50.0	12
F	12.0	9
G	1.0	44

a. If Cooper requires a minimum rate of return of 10 percent on all investments, which projects should be adopted?
b. In general, how would a capital budgeting constraint on the available amount of investment funds influence these decisions?
c. How would differing levels of project risk influence these decisions?

BASIC

4. Johnson Products is considering purchasing a new milling machine that costs $100,000. The machine's installation and shipping costs will total $2,500. If accepted, the milling machine project will require an initial net working capital investment of $20,000. Johnson plans to depreciate the machine on a straight-line basis over a period of eight years. About a year ago, Johnson paid $10,000 to a consulting firm to conduct a feasibility study of the new milling machine. Johnson's marginal tax rate is 40 percent.
   a. Calculate the project's net investment (NINV).
   b. Calculate the annual straight-line depreciation for the project.
   c. Calculate MACRS depreciation assuming this is a seven-year class asset (Appendix 9A).

BASIC

Spreadsheet Strategies

5. A new machine costing $100,000 is expected to save the McKaig Brick Company $15,000 per year for 12 years before depreciation and taxes. The machine will be depreciated on a straight-line basis for a 12-year period to an estimated salvage value of $0. The firm's marginal tax rate is 40 percent. What are the annual net cash flows associated with the purchase of this machine? Also compute the net investment (NINV) for this project.

BASIC

6. The Jacob Chemical Company is considering building a new potassium sulfate plant. The following cash outlays are required to complete the plant:

Year	Cash Outlay
0	$4,000,000
1	2,000,000
2	500,000

   Jacob's cost of capital is 12 percent, and its marginal tax rate is 40 percent.
   a. Calculate the plant's net investment (NINV).
   b. What is the installed cost of the plant for tax purposes?

BASIC

Spreadsheet Strategies

7. The Taylor Mountain Uranium Company currently has annual cash revenues of $1.2 million and annual cash expenses of $700,000. Depreciation amounts to $200,000 per year. These figures are expected to remain constant for the foreseeable future (at least 15 years). The firm's marginal tax rate is 40 percent.

   A new high-speed processing unit costing $1.2 million is being considered as a potential investment designed to increase the firm's output capacity. This new piece of equipment will have an estimated usable life of 10 years and a $0 estimated salvage value. If the processing unit is bought, Taylor's annual revenues are expected to increase to $1.6 million and annual expenses (exclusive of depreciation) will increase to $900,000. Annual depreciation will increase to $320,000. Assume that no increase in net working capital will be required as a result of this project. Compute the project's annual net cash flows for the next 10 years, assuming that the new processing unit is purchased. Also compute the net investment (NINV) for this project.

INTERMEDIATE

8. A firm has an opportunity to invest in a new device that will replace two of the firm's older machines. The new device costs $570,000 and requires an additional outlay of $30,000 to cover installation and shipping. The new device will cause the firm to increase its net working capital by $20,000. Both of the old machines can be sold—the first for $100,000 (book value equals $95,000) and the second for $150,000 (book value equals $75,000). The original cost of the first machine was $200,000, and the original cost of the second machine was $140,000. The firm's marginal tax bracket is 40 percent. Compute the net investment for this project.

INTERMEDIATE

Spreadsheet Strategies

9. Five years ago, the Mori Foods Company acquired a bean processing machine. The machine cost $30,000 and is being depreciated using the straight-line method over a 10-year period to an estimated salvage value of $0. A new, improved processor is now available, and the firm is considering making a switch. The firm's marginal tax rate is 40 percent. What are the after-tax cash flow effects of selling the old processing unit if it can be sold for the following prices?

a. $15,000
b. $5,000
c. $26,000
d. $32,000

INTERMEDIATE

Spreadsheet Strategies

10. Nguyen Inc. is considering the purchase of a new computer system (ICX) for $130,000. The system will require an additional $30,000 for installation. If the new computer is purchased, it will replace an old system that has been fully depreciated. The new system will be depreciated over a period of 10 years using straight-line depreciation. If the ICX is purchased, the old system will be sold for $20,000. The ICX system, which has a useful life of 10 years, is expected to increase revenues by $32,000 *per year* over its useful life. Operating costs are expected to decrease by $2,000 *per year* over the life of the system. The firm is taxed at a 40 percent marginal rate.

a. What net investment is required to acquire the ICX system and replace the old system?
b. Compute the annual net cash flows associated with the purchase of the ICX system.

INTERMEDIATE

Spreadsheet Strategies

11. Two years ago Agro Inc., purchased an ACE generator that cost $250,000. Agro had to pay an additional $50,000 for delivery and installation, and the investment in the generator required the firm to increase its net working capital position by $25,000. The generator, which is being depreciated over a period of five years using straight-line depreciation, has a current market value of $79,550. The firm's marginal tax rate is 40 percent. If the firm liquidates the asset for its current market value, compute the after-tax proceeds from the sale of the asset.

CHALLENGE

Spreadsheet Strategies

12. Benford Inc. is planning to open a new sporting goods store in a suburban mall. Benford will lease the needed space in the mall. Equipment and fixtures for the store will cost $200,000 and be depreciated over a five-year period on a straight-line basis to $0. The new store will require Benford to increase its net working capital by $200,000 at time 0. First-year sales are expected to be $1 million and to increase at an annual rate of 8 percent over the expected 10-year life of the store. Operating expenses (including lease payments and excluding depreciation) are projected to be

$700,000 during the first year and increase at a 7 percent annual rate. The salvage value of the store's equipment and fixtures is anticipated to be $10,000 at the end of 10 years. Benford's marginal tax rate is 40 percent.

a. Compute the net investment required for Benford.

b. Compute the annual net cash flows for the 10-year projected life of the store.

c. Compute the annual net cash flows assuming equipment and fixtures are depreciated using the seven-year asset class under MACRS (Appendix 9A).

CHALLENGE

Spreadsheet Strategies

13. A new machine costing $100,000 is expected to save the McKaig Brick Company $15,000 per year for 12 years before depreciation and taxes. The machine will be depreciated as a seven-year class MACRS asset. The firm's marginal tax rate is 40 percent. What are the annual net cash flows associated with the purchase of this machine? Also compute the net investment (NINV) for this project (*Hint*: See Appendix 9A for information on MACRS depreciation. This problem is the same as Problem 5 except for the depreciation method.)

CHALLENGE

Spreadsheet Strategies

14. Nguyen Inc. is considering the purchase of a new computer system (ICX) for $130,000. The system will require an additional $30,000 for installation. If the new computer is purchased, it will replace an old system that has been fully depreciated. The new system will be depreciated under the MACRS rules applicable to seven-year class assets. If the ICX is purchased, the old system will be sold for $20,000. The ICX system, which has a useful life of 10 years, is expected to increase revenues by $32,000 *per year* over its useful life. Operating costs are expected to decrease by $2,000 *per year* over the life of the system. The firm is taxed at a 40 percent marginal rate. (*Hint*: See Appendix 9A for information on MACRS depreciation. Except for the depreciation method, this problem is the same as Problem 10.)

a. What net investment is required to acquire the ICX system and replace the old system?

b. Compute the annual net cash flows associated with the purchase of the ICX system.

CHALLENGE

15. Argyl Manufacturing is evaluating the possibility of expanding its operations. This expansion will require the purchase of land at a cost of $100,000. A new building will cost $100,000 and will be depreciated on a straight-line basis over 20 years to a salvage value of $0. Actual land salvage at the end of 20 years is expected to be $200,000. Actual building salvage at the end of 20 years is expected to be $150,000. Equipment for the facility is expected to cost $250,000. Installation costs will be an additional $40,000 and shipping costs will be $10,000. This equipment will be depreciated as a seven-year MACRS asset. Actual estimated salvage at the end of 20 years is $0. The project will require net working capital of $70,000 initially (year 0), an additional $40,000 at the end of year 1, and an additional $40,000 at the end of year 2. The project is expected to generate increased EBIT (operating income) for the firm of $100,000 during year 1. Annual EBIT is expected to grow at a rate of 4 percent per year until the project terminates at the end of year 20. The marginal tax rate is 40 percent. (*Hint*: See Appendix 9A for information on MACRS depreciation.) Compute the initial net investment and the annual net cash flow from the project in year 20.

CHALLENGE

Spreadsheet Strategies

16. Ralph's Bow Works (RBW) is planning to add a new line of bow ties that will require the acquisition of a new knitting and tying machine. The machine will cost $1 million. It is classified as a seven-year MACRS asset and will be depreciated as such. Interest costs associated with financing the equipment purchase are estimated to be $50,000 per year. The expected salvage value of the machine at the end of 10 years is $50,000. The decision to add the new line of bow ties will require additional net working capital of $50,000 immediately, $25,000 at the end of year 1, and

$10,000 at the end of year 2. RBW expects to sell $300,000 worth of the bow ties during each of the 10 years of product life. RBW expects the sales of its other ties to decline by $25,000 (in year 1) as a result of adding this new line of ties. The lost sales level will remain constant at $25,000 over the 10-year life of the proposed project. The cost of producing and selling the ties is estimated to be $50,000 per year. RBW will realize savings of $5,000 each year because of lost sales on its other tie lines. The marginal tax rate is 40 percent. (*Hint*: See Appendix 9A for information on MACRS depreciation.) Compute the net investment (year 0) and the net cash flows for years 1 and 10 for this project.

CHALLENGE **17.** Bratton Stone Works is considering an expansion proposal that will require an outlay of $1 million for land and $5 million for equipment. The equipment will be depreciated under MACRS rules as a seven-year class asset. The salvage value of the equipment at the end of 10 years is expected to be $1 million. The actual life of the project is expected to be 10 years. At the end of 10 years, Bratton hopes to sell the land for S1.8 million. Revenues from the project are expected to be $700,000 per year. Operating costs are expected to be $200,000 per year. The ordinary and capital gains tax rate for Bratton is 40 percent. The project will require an additional investment in working capital of $250,000 in year 0 and $150,000 at the end of year 1. (*Hint*: See Appendix 9A for information on MACRS depreciation.) What net cash flow will this project produce in year 10?

CHALLENGE **18.** Locus Quintatus, Inc., a highly profitable maker of customized chariots, is planning to introduce a new model shortly. The firm must purchase equipment immediately at a cost of $900,000. Freight and installation costs for this equipment will be $100,000. The equipment will be depreciated as a seven-year class asset under MACRS. During the first year, Locus will have incremental operating expenses of $300,000 that are attributable to this project. Locus expects to be able to sell 1,000 chariots during year 2 at an average price of $800 each and to incur operating expenses of $300,000. Also, Locus expects its net working capital investment will increase by $50,000 during year 2. (Assume all operating costs and revenues are incurred at the end of each year.) The marginal tax rate for Locus is 40 percent. (*Hint*: See Appendix 9A for information on MACRS depreciation.) What is the required net investment, and what are the year 1 and year 2 net cash flows?

CHALLENGE **19.** Clyne Industries wants to market its new Slammin Jammin Basketball Goal Set. To bring this product to the market will require the purchase of equipment costing $650,000. Shipping and installation expenses associated with the equipment are estimated to be $50,000. In addition, Clyne will incur incremental employee training and recruiting expenses of $100,000, all of which will be incurred at time 0. Additional net working capital investments of $50,000 will be required at time 0, $25,000 in year 1, and $10,000 in year 2. Revenues are expected to be $250,000 in year 1 and grow at a rate of $25,000 per year through year 5, then decline by $25,000 per year until the project is terminated at the end of year 10. Annual operating expenses are expected to be $80,000 in year 1 and to grow at a rate of $10,000 per year until the end of the project life. Depreciation will be under MACRS for a seven-year class asset. The salvage value of the equipment at the end of 10 years is expected to be $50,000. The marginal, ordinary tax rate is 40 percent and the capital gains tax rate is 30 percent. (*Hint*: See Appendix 9A for information on MACRS depreciation.) Compute the expected net cash flow for year 10, the last year in the life of the project.

INTERMEDIATE **20.** Steber Packaging Inc. expects sales next year of $50 million. Of this total, 40 percent is expected to be for cash and the balance will be on credit, payable in 30 days. Operating expenses are expected to total $25 million. Accelerated depreciation is expected to total $10 million, although the company will only report $6 million of depreciation on its public financial reports. The marginal tax rate for Steber is 34 percent. Current assets now total $25 million and current liabilities total $15 million. Current assets are expected to increase to $30 million over the coming year. Current liabilities are expected to increase to $17 million. Compute the projected after-tax operating cash flow for Steber during the coming year.

CHALLENGE **21.** Hurley's Winery is planning to acquire a new grape masher. The masher will cost $100,000 including shipping and installation and will be depreciated as a seven-year MACRS asset. At the time the masher is purchased, Hurley will have to invest $5,000 in net working capital. Additional investments in net working capital are required at the end of year 1 ($3,000) and year 2 ($2,000). Net revenues attributable to the masher are expected to total $25,000 during year 1 and to grow by 5 percent per annum through the end of year 6. After that time, revenues are expected to decline by 10 percent per annum. Year 1 cash operating expenses are expected to total $10,000 and to grow at an annual rate of 10 percent per annum. Hurley expects to sell the masher at one second after midnight on the first day of year 8 for $10,000. The marginal tax rate for Hurley is 40 percent for ordinary income and 28 percent for capital gains. (*Hint*: See Appendix 9A for information on MACRS depreciation.) Compute the expected net cash flows for year 7. Include in your year 7 calculations the proceeds from the salvage value of the masher and recovery of net working capital at the beginning of year 8. For the purposes of present value calculations, you may assume that the end of year 7 is the same as the beginning of year 8.

INTERMEDIATE **22.** Hayward Enterprises, a successful imaging products firm, is considering expanding into the lucrative laser-engraved self-portrait business. It is expected that this new business will generate first-year revenues of $2 million. These revenues are expected to grow at 10 percent per year for the next 8 years. Year 1 incremental operating costs of this new business are expected to total $800,000 and to grow at 6 percent per year for the next eight years. The firm's marginal tax rate is 40 percent, but its average tax rate is only 35 percent. Depreciation expenses are expected to be $100,000 during year 1, $200,000 during year 2, and $150,000 during year 3. Capital outlays required at time 0 total $2 million, and another $500,000 will be required at the end of year 1. Net working capital investments of $50,000, $75,000, and $85,000 are expected at the end of years 1, 2, and 3 respectively. Calculate the expected net cash flows for year 3.

APPENDIX 9A

DEPRECIATION

Introduction to Depreciation

Prior to the establishment of the Modified Accelerated Cost Recovery System (MACRS) of depreciation, a number of alternative methods of depreciation were permitted by the IRS. These methods included straight-line depreciation and various accelerated methods.

Details are provided about the calculation of depreciation amounts under straight line and the Modified ACRS (MACRS) system of depreciation, which is used for assets placed in service after December 31, 1986.

Straight-Line Depreciation

Under the straight-line depreciation method, the annual amount of an asset's depreciation is calculated as follows:[1]

(9A. 1)
$$\text{Annual depreciation amount} = \frac{\text{Cost}}{\text{Estimated economic life (years)}}$$

For example, suppose Arrow Packaging Company purchases a machine that costs $12,000, and has a five-year economic life. The annual depreciation amount is 12,000/5 = $2,400. As shown in Table 9A.1, depreciation is constant each year, and the book value of the asset declines at a constant rate from $12,000 to $0 over the five-year period.

Straight-line depreciation is an appropriate method to employ when an asset is being used up fairly evenly over its lifetime. Many companies use straight-line depreciation for

TABLE 9A.1

Straight-Line Depreciation: Arrow Packaging Company

	Straight-Line Depreciation			
Year	Depreciation Base	Depreciation Rate	Depreciation Amount	End-of-Year Book Value
0	—	—	—	$12,000
1	$12,000	0.20	$2,400	9,600
2	12,000	0.20	2,400	7,200
3	12,000	0.20	2,400	4,800
4	12,000	0.20	2,400	2,400
5	12,000	0.20	2,400	0
Total			$12,000	

[1]Note that under pre-ACRS depreciation rules, the annual depreciation amount was determined as the cost of the asset less its estimated salvage value divided by the estimated economic life. In comparison, under the Accelerated Cost Recovery System provisions of the 1986 Tax Reform Act, no consideration is given to estimated salvage value in determining the annual depreciation amount. See Steven C. Dilley and James C. Young, *The Tax Reform Act of 1986: The New ACRS Rules* (Paramus, NJ: Prentice-Hall, 1986) for a discussion of the Accelerated Cost Recovery System and additional detail on MACRS.

TABLE 9A.2

MACRS Recovery Periods

Recovery Period and Asset Class*	Property Included in Class
3-Year	A small class of short-lived assets, including some special tools, some tractors, and racehorses (over two years old)
5-Year	Automobiles, light trucks, heavy general-purpose trucks, buses, oil-drilling equipment, information systems, certain semiconductor, textile, chemical, electronic, and manufacturing equipment, and dairy and breeder cattle
7-Year	Most manufacturing equipment, railroad track, office furniture and equipment, railroad cars and locomotives, airplanes, amusement parks, and mining equipment
10-Year	Vessels, barges, petroleum-refining equipment, railroad tank cars, and some manufacturing equipment
15-Year	Electric generation and distribution systems, cement-manufacturing equipment, nuclear power plants, natural gas pipelines, billboards, sewage treatment plants, and telephone distribution plants
20-Year	Most public utility property, sewer pipes, and railroad structures

*Most equipment is contained in the 7-year class.

financial reporting purposes—that is, in their reports to stockholders, because it usually results in a greater reported net income—and the MACRS accelerated depreciation method for federal income tax purposes, because accelerated depreciation can result in the deferment of tax payments.

Modified Accelerated Cost Recovery System (MACRS)

The Tax Reform Act of 1986 created the Modified Accelerated Cost Recovery System of depreciation.[2] Under this depreciation system, six classes of assets are established. All depreciable assets (new and used), except real estate, are assigned to one of these six classes. Regardless of the expected useful life of an asset, its annual depreciation is computed according to the rules for the class of assets to which it has been assigned.

Table 9A.2 summarizes the MACRS classes and depreciable lives that must be used under the 1986 Tax Act. The vast majority of business equipment, from office furnishings to machinery, is found in the seven-year class.

Depreciation Rate

Annual depreciation charges for each asset class are defined in Table 9A.3 for MACRS. The full installed cost of each asset forms the basis upon which depreciation is computed and charged. *Expected salvage value is not considered* in the depreciation calculations under MACRS.

Table 9A.3 provides the annual depreciation percentages. These percentages are multiplied by the installed cost of the asset when computing annual depreciation for any

[2]Under the Jobs and Growth Tax Relief Reconciliation Act of 2003, tangible property with a recovery period of 20 years or less that was placed in service between May 6, 2003, and January 1, 2005, was eligible for a 50 percent first-year depreciation bonus (in addition to the standard MARCS depreciation). Since the tax laws change from time to time, it is important for managers to have a working knowledge of the current provisions of these laws.

TABLE 9A.3

Depreciation Rates for MACRS Property Other Than Real Property*

Recovery Year	3-Year	5-Year	7-Year	10-Year	15-Year	20-Year
1	33.33%	20.00%	14.29%	10.00%	5.00%	3.750%
2	44.45	32.00	24.49	18.00	9.50	7.219
3	14.81	19.20	17.49	14.40	8.55	6.677
4	7.41	11.52	12.49	11.52	7.70	6.177
5		11.52	8.93	9.22	6.93	5.713
6		5.76	8.92	7.37	6.23	5.285
7			8.93	6.55	5.90	4.888
8			4.46	6.55	5.90	4.522
9				6.56	5.91	4.462
10				6.55	5.90	4.461
11				3.28	5.91	4.462
12					5.90	4.461
13					5.91	4.462
14					5.90	4.461
15					5.91	4.462
16					2.95	4.461
17						4.462
18						4.461
19						4.462
20						4.461
21						2.231

*Assumes that the half-year convention applies.

asset in the six classes. Note that the number of years of depreciation is always one greater than the number indicated in the asset class; for example, for a five-year class asset, depreciation is spread over a total of six years. The reason for this is that the 1986 Tax Reform Act requires that the half-year convention be followed. The half-year convention treats any asset placed in service during year 1 as being placed in service in the middle of the year. Consequently, the asset only receives one-half of the first year's depreciation. The half-year convention also applies to the last year of depreciation, thus making the number of years of depreciation one year longer than is indicated in the asset class name.

For example, assume General Electric acquires a $9.5 million piece of machinery, which requires $500,000 for shipping and installation. Under MACRS, this asset would be in the seven-year class. The depreciable basis for the asset is:

Asset cost	$9,500,000
Plus: Installation and shipping	500,000
Equals: Depreciable basis	$10,000,000

Table 9A.3 provides the depreciation rates applied to this seven-year asset that General Electric has acquired. The annual MACRS depreciation for this asset is computed as follows:

Year	MACRS Depreciation Rate	Amount of Depreciation (MACRS Rate × $10,000,000)
1	14.29%	$ 1,429,000
2	24.49	2,449,000
3	17.49	1,749,000
4	12.49	1,249,000
5	8.93	893,000
6	8.92	892,000
7	8.93	893,000
8	4.46	446,000
	100.00%	$10,000,000

MACRS Recovery Periods and Economic Life of an Asset

With the adoption of the MACRS recovery periods for all assets, there is no longer any direct relationship between the period over which tax depreciation is taken on an asset and that asset's economic life. Consequently, when estimating the cash flows from a project, there will normally be several years beyond the MACRS recovery period when no depreciation expense will be recorded. It is important to remember that cash flows for all projects (assets) should be projected over the full economic life of the project, not just the MACRS recovery period.

Real Property

The Tax Reform Act of 1986 established two classes of real property for depreciation purposes. The 27.5-Year Straight-Line Class includes residential rental property. The second class includes all nonresidential real property, such as office buildings. The recovery period for nonresidential real property was originally 31.5 years, but it was changed to 39 years in 1993 for property placed in service after May 12, 1993.

Depreciation for real property is computed on a straight-line basis. The amount of depreciation taken during the first year depends upon the month property is placed in service. Furthermore, a mid-month convention is used; that is, it is assumed that a building is placed in service in the middle of the first month and is therefore eligible for only one-half month's depreciation during month one.

For example, consider a $100,000 building placed in service during April 2013. The straight-line rate is 2.564 percent (1/39), and the depreciation on a $100,000 building for a full year is $2,564. Under the mid-month convention, April, the month the property is placed in service, is considered half a month. Thus, for 2013, the building owner gets 8.5 months of a full year's depreciation; this amounts to $1,819 using IRS-provided tables.

Questions and Topics for Discussion

1. What method of depreciation would you prefer, MACRS or straight-line, if your objective is to maximize the present value of your firm's cash flows?

Problems*

BASIC **1.** a. Calculate the annual MACRS depreciation for a machine in the seven-year MACRS asset class, assuming that the asset costs $20,000.

b. If you knew that the asset had an expected salvage value of $2,000 at the end of its 12-year economic life, would your answer to part a change?

BASIC **2.** Calculate the annual MACRS depreciation for a $20,000 truck that qualifies as a five-year MACRS asset. The truck is estimated to have a $7,000 salvage value six years from now.

BASIC **3.** Calculate the MACRS depreciation schedule for a drill press that costs $148,000 and has installation and shipping costs of $2,000. The drill press is classified as a seven-year MACRS asset.

INTERMEDIATE **4.** Calculate the depreciation schedule for a $100,000 office building placed in service in October 2013.

INTERMEDIATE **5.** Calculate the MACRS depreciation schedule for a milling machine that costs $47,500 and has installation and shipping costs of $2,500. The milling machine is classified as a seven-year MACRS asset. The milling machine is estimated to have a salvage value of $15,000 at the end of its 15-year economic life.

*Color blocks behind the numbers denote problems that have check answers provided at the end of the book.

CHAPTER 10

Capital Budgeting: Decision Criteria and Real Option Considerations

KEY CHAPTER CONCEPTS

1. The *net present value* of an investment project is defined as the present value of the stream of expected net cash flows from the project minus the project's net investment.
   a. A project is acceptable if its NPV is greater than or equal to zero.
   b. By maximizing the net present value of accepted projects, a firm will also maximize shareholder wealth.
2. The *profitability index* (PI) is the ratio of the preset value of expected net cash flows over the life of the project to the net investment.
   a. If the project has a PI equal to or greater than 1.0, it is acceptable.
   b. The PI can be used as a guide to resource allocation in a situation of capital rationing.
3. The *internal rate of return* (IRR) is defined as the discount rate that equates the present value of the expected net cash flows from a project with the present value of the net investment
   a. A project is acceptable if it has an IRR greater than or equal to the firm's cost of capital.
   b. The NPV and IRR approaches give the same accept-reject signals for independent projects, except in the case of mutually exclusive investment alternatives.
   c. The IRR approach can also lead to multiple internal rates of return in some cases.
4. The *payback period* of an investment is the period of time required for the cumulative cash inflows (net cash flows) from a project to equal the initial cash outlay.
   a. Weaknesses of the payback method include that it ignores the timing of cash flows and cash flows beyond the payback period.
   b. The payback technique can be used as a project liquidity measure and as a crude risk-screening technique.
5. Project post-audits and reviews can assist management in uncovering biases in the project analysis procedure of a firm, and can assist management in making abandonment decisions.
6. The use of conventional discounted cash flow techniques in capital budgeting without considering "real" options may result in a downward-biased estimate of the true value of a project's net present value.
7. For international projects, the present value of a project's net cash flows to the parent company is equal to the present value of the project's net cash flows from the foreign company converted into the home country currency.

FINANCIAL CHALLENGE

Boeing Stretches its Project Options for the 747-8

In 1969 Boeing introduced the Boeing 747, the largest commercial airliner ever built. It had the capacity to transport 500 passengers more than 6,000 miles in greater comfort and at a lower per-seat cost than other planes. Over the years more than 1,500 of these planes were sold in various model configurations. The latest version of the plane, the 747-8, was introduced in 2011. Thus far it has achieved orders for only 121 planes. The new model has a list price of $380 million, before the normal big discounts. At the end of 2015, Boeing reported a 747 order backlog of just 32 planes, 14 of which are configured as cargo planes and the balance as passenger planes. Competition for the 747 has come from Airbus, with its A380-800 double-deck plane. The A380 was introduced in 2005. Its sales have also been disappointing relative to expectations at launch. The current backlog is 141 planes and is shrinking quickly as new orders have been scarce. Indeed, much of the competition for the 747 has come from Boeing itself. It's new, more fuel efficient, longer-haul 777-9 model can accommodate up to 425 passengers and fly up to 8,700 nautical miles. This new model 777-9 will be the largest two-engine plane in the sky.

In spite of this new competition, Boeing continues to look at options to keep producing the 747-8. Boeing estimates that package haulers like UPS will need to replace nearly 250 aircraft over the next 5–10 years. Boeing hopes to get a share of that business because of some of the unique operating characteristics of the 747-8. In order to be successful in competing for this business, it is important for Boeing to retain the capability to continue building the plane. It is not practical to shut down and restart the 747 production line at Everett, Washington. Suppliers will move on to other projects, and skilled production workers would be lost during any period of a shut down. Hence, in order maintain the "real" option to produce and sell the 747-8 when new demand for the plane hopefully appears, Boeing has begun a strategy of slowing production rates to extend the production life of the 747-8. Up until April 2013, the monthly production rate for the 747-8 had been two planes per month. In April 2013 the build rate was reduced to 1.75 planes per month. Later in 2013 this rate was further reduced to 1.5 planes per month. In September 2015 the build rate was reduced to 1.3 per month, and in March 2016 to just 1 per month. Boeing may move even lower on this build rate. Over the past several years the company has greatly increased the efficiency of producing each plane. It now takes just 25 percent of the time to assemble one 747-8 as it did to assemble the first one. That, together with a streamlined parts operation and the aggressive implementation of many lean manufacturing processes, allows the 747-8 to remain profitable even at these lower production rates. Boeing is hoping to keep the plane in production until the 2020s.

Carlos Yudica/Shutterstock.com

In this chapter you will learn how to evaluate capital investments, and you will also learn about the importance of "real options," such as the option to continue manufacturing that is illustrated above, when making capital investment decisions.

Sources: G. Norris, "Boeing Signals Additional 747-8 Production Rate Cut," *Aviation Daily*, June 24, 2015; J. Johnsson and A. Rothman, "The Fate of America's Iconic 747 Jet is in Hands of Moscow Firm," *Bloomberg Business*, December 13, 2015; V. Bhaskara, "Boeing Cuts 747-8 Production Amidst VLA Weakness," *Airways News*, December 12, 2014; B. Zhang, "The Days of the Jumbo Jet Are Coming to an End," *Business Insider*, December 12, 2015, www.businessinsider.com.

CHAPTER OBJECTIVES

Upon completion of this chapter, you should have a clear understanding of the following:

1. Several widely used capital budgeting evaluation methods
2. The relative merits and limitations of the different capital budgeting evaluation methods

10-1 Introduction

This chapter looks at some widely used capital budgeting decision models, discussing and illustrating their relative strengths and weaknesses. When combined with the cash flow procedures developed in Chapter 9 and the time value of money procedures developed in Chapter 5, these models provide the basis for making capital expenditure decisions.

This chapter also examines project review and post-audit procedures and concludes by tracing a sample project through the capital budgeting analysis process.

10-2 Decision Models for Evaluating Alternatives

Four criteria are commonly used for evaluating and selecting investment projects:

- Net present value (NPV)
- Profitability index (PI)
- Internal rate of return (IRR)
- Payback (PB) period

10-2a Net Present Value

Foundation Concept

Recall from Chapter 5 that the net present value rule is the primary decision-making rule used throughout the practice of financial management. The net present value—that is, the present value of the expected future cash flows minus the initial outlay—of an investment made by a firm represents the contribution of that investment to the value of the firm and, accordingly, to the wealth of the firm's shareholders. In this chapter, we consider the net present value of capital expenditure projects.

net present value (NPV)

The **net present value (NPV)** of a capital expenditure project is defined as the present value of the stream of net (operating) cash flows from the project minus the project's net investment. The net present value method is also sometimes called the *discounted cash flow* (DCF) technique. The cash flows are discounted at the firm's required rate of return; that is, its *cost of capital.* A firm's cost of capital is defined as its minimum acceptable rate of return for projects of average risk.

The net present value of a project may be expressed as follows:

(10.1)
$$NPV = PVNCF - NINV$$

where NPV is the net present value; PVNCF, the present value of net (operating) cash flows; and NINV, the net investment.

For a series of uneven net (operating) cash flows, the net present value of a project may be calculated as follows:

(10.2)
$$NPV = \sum_{t=1}^{n} \frac{NCF_t}{(1+k)^t} - NINV$$

or

(10.3)
$$NPV = \sum_{t=1}^{n} NCF_t \times PVIF_{k,t} - NINV$$

where NCF_t is the net (operating) cash flow in year t, n is the expected project life (years), k is the cost of capital, and $PVIF_{k,t}$ is the present value interest factor (Table II). The net (operating) cash flow in the final year (n) of the project, NCF_n, includes any salvage value remaining at the end of the project's life. The summation sign (Σ) represents the arithmetic sum of the discounted cash flows for each year t over the life of the project (n years); that is, the present value of the net cash flows (PVNCF).

If all the net (operating) cash flows are equal over the life of the project, that is, an annuity $NCF = NCF_1 = NCF_2 = \ldots = NCF_n$, then Equation 10.3 can be expressed as follows:

(10.4)
$$NPV = NCF \times PVIFA_{k,n} - NINV$$

where $PVIFA_{k,n}$ is the present value of annuity interest factor (Table IV).

Spreadsheet Strategies

As mentioned in Chapter 9, the annual net cash flows for normal projects are usually positive after the initial net investment. Occasionally, however, one or more of the expected net cash flows over the life of a project may be negative. When this occurs, positive numbers are used for years having positive net cash flows (net inflows), and negative numbers are used for years having negative net cash flows (net outflows).

To illustrate net present value calculations, suppose Ace Lumber is considering two projects, A and B, having net investments and net cash flows as shown in Table 10.1. The net present value computations for the two projects are presented in Table 10.2. These calculations assume a 14 percent cost of capital. The calculations in these tables also assume that cash flows are received at the end of each year, rather than as a flow during the year. This assumption, although a normal one, tends to slightly understate a project's net present value or internal rate of return. Project A is shown in Table 10.2 to have a negative net present value of \$−1,387, and Project B has a positive net present value of \$7,735.

TABLE 10.1

Ace Lumber Company: Project Cash Flows

Year	Project A Net Cash Flow After Taxes NCF_t	Project B Net Cash Flow After Taxes NCF_t
1	$12,500	$5,000
2	12,500	10,000
3	12,500	15,000
4	12,500	15,000
5	12,500	25,000
6	12,500	30,000
	Net investment (NINV) = $50,000	Net investment (NINV) = $50,000

Decision Rule In general, a project should be accepted if its net present value is greater than or equal to zero and rejected if its net present value is less than zero. This is so because a positive net present value in principle translates directly into increases in stock prices and increases in shareholders' wealth. In the Ace Lumber example, Project A would be rejected because it has a negative net present value, and Project B would be accepted because it has a positive net present value.

TABLE 10.2

Ace Lumber Company: Net Present Value Calculations

Project A

Equation 10.4 (annuity)

Present value of an annuity of $12,500 for $n = 6$ years at $k = 14\%$:

PVNCF = $12,500 ($PVIFA_{0.14,6}$) = $12,500 (3.889)* = $ 48,613

Less: Net investment (NINV) $–50,000

Net present value (NPV) $ –1,387

Project B

Equation 10.3 (uneven cash flows)

Year	NCF_t	$PVIF_{0.14,t}$**	Present value $NCF_t \times PVIF_{0.14,t}$
1	$ 5,000	0.877	$ 4,385
2	10,000	0.769	7,690
3	15,000	0.675	10,125
4	15,000	0.592	8,880
5	25,000	0.519	12,975
6	30,000	0.456	13,680
PVNCF			$57,735
Less: Net investment (NINV)			–50,000
Net present value (NPV)			$ 7,735

*From the PVIFA table (Table IV)

**From the PVIF table (Table II)

Spreadsheet software may also be used to solve for NPV as illustrated here:

	A	B	C	D	E	F	G	H	I	J
1										
2										
3										
4		Using a Spreadsheet to Find Net Present Value of a Project								
5						Years				
6			0	1	2	3	4	5	6	
7		Project A	-$50,000	$12,500	$12,500	$12,500	$12,500	$12,500	$12,500	
8		Project B	-$50,000	$5,000	$10,000	$15,000	$15,000	$25,000	$30,000	
9										
10		Interest rate =	14.00%		Year 0 cash flow shown is the net investment, year 1-6 cash flows are net cash flows from project					
11										
12		You can solve the NPV in one step as shown below using the NPV function (+NPV(rate, values)+initial cash flow)								
13										
14		NPV (Project A)	-$1,391.66		Excel formula : "=+NPV($C$10,(D7:I7))+C7"					
15										
16		NPV (Project B)	$7,738.23							
17					Excel formula: "=+NPV($C$10,(D8:I8))+C8"					
18										
19										
20		Alternatively, you can solve for NPV by adding the present value of individual cash flows								
21		(Solution for Project B shown below)								
22										
23										
24										
25										
26		Net Investment (Year 0)=	-$50,000.00	Excel formula: "=+ABS(PV($C$10,(D6-C6),0,D8"						
27										
28		Present value of 1st NCF=	$4,385.96	Excel formula: "=+ABS(PV($C$10,(E6-C6),0,E8)"						
29										
30		Present value of 2nd NCF=	$7,694.68							
31				Excel formula: "=+ABS(PV($C$10,(F6-C6),0,F8))"						
32		Present value of 3rd NCF=	$10,124.57							
33				Excel formula: "=+ABS(PV($C$10,(G6-C6),0,G8))"						
34		Present value of 4th NCF=	$8,881.20							
35										
36		Present value of 5th NCF=	$12,984.22	Excel formula: "=+ABS(PV($C$10,(H6-C6),0,H8))"						
37										
38		Present value of 6th NCF=	$13,667.60							
39				Excel formula: "=+ABS(PV($C$10,(I6-C6),0,I8))"						
40		Total of all cash flows	$7,738.23	Excel formula: "=+SUM(C28:C38)+C26"						
41										
42										

If two or more *mutually exclusive* investments have positive net present values, the project having the largest net present value is the one selected. Assume, for example, that a firm has three mutually exclusive investment opportunities, G, H, and I, each requiring a net investment of $10,000 and each having a five-year expected economic life.[1] Project G has a net present value of $2,000; H has a net present value of $4,000; and I has a net present value of $3,500. Of the three, H would be preferred over the other two because it has the highest net present value and therefore is expected to make the largest contribution to the objective of shareholder wealth maximization.

Sources of Positive Net Present Value Projects What causes some projects to have a positive net present value and others to have a negative net present value? When product and factor markets are other than perfectly competitive, it is possible for a firm to earn above-normal profits (economic rents) that result in positive net present value projects. The reasons why these above-normal profits may be available arise from conditions that define each type of product and factor market and distinguish it from a perfectly competitive market. These reasons include the following barriers to entry and other factors:[2]

1. Buyer preferences for established brand names
2. Ownership or control of favored distribution systems (such as exclusive auto dealerships)

---

[1]Appendix 10A discusses procedures to use in evaluating mutually exclusive projects having unequal lives.

[2]D. Vickers, "Disequilibrium Structures and Financing Decisions in the Firm," *Journal of Business Finance and Accounting* (Autumn 1974): 375.

Calculator Solutions[a]

Project A

Key	Enter
CF_0	−50,000
$CF_{1–6}$	12,500
i	14
NPV	
	Solution
NPV	−1,392

Project B

Key	Enter
CF_0	−50,000
CF_1	5,000
CF_2	10,000
CF_3	15,000
CF_4	15,000
CF_5	25,000
CF_6	30,000
i	14
NPV	
	Solution
NPV	7,738

3. Patent control of superior product designs or production techniques
4. Exclusive ownership of superior natural resource deposits
5. Inability of new firms to acquire necessary factors of production (management, labor, equipment)
6. Superior access to financial resources at lower costs (economies of scale in attracting capital)
7. Economies of large-scale production and distribution arising from
    a. Capital-intensive production processes
    b. High initial start-up costs
8. Access to superior labor or managerial talents at costs that are not fully reflective of their value
9. Operating synergies when combining two companies in a merger.

These factors can permit a firm to identify positive net present value projects for internal investment. If the barriers to entry are sufficiently high (such as a patent on key technology) so as to prevent any new competition, or if the start-up period for competitive ventures is sufficiently long, then it is possible that a project may have a positive net present value. However, in assessing the viability of such a project, it is important that the manager or analyst consider the likely period of time when above-normal returns can be earned before new competitors emerge and force cash flows back to a more normal level. It is generally unrealistic to expect to be able to earn above-normal returns over the entire life of an investment project.

Thus, it may be possible for a firm to identify investment projects with positive net present values. However, if capital markets are efficient, the securities of the firm making these investments will reflect the value of these projects. Recall that the net present value of a project can be thought of as the *contribution to the value of a firm resulting from undertaking that particular project*. Therefore, even though a firm may be able to identify projects having expected positive net present values, efficient capital markets will quickly reflect these positive net present value projects in the market value of the firm's securities.

Suppose Project B in the preceding example was a new baby care product from Johnson & Johnson. Its positive net present value could be the result of buyer preferences due to Johnson & Johnson's established baby care business. Suppose Project A, on the other hand, involved a new soap product to compete with Procter & Gamble's Tide. Consumers' brand preferences for Tide, as well as Procter & Gamble's economies of scale for production and distribution, could easily cause Project A to have a negative net present value.

Advantages and Disadvantages of the Net Present Value Method The net present value of a project is the expected number of dollars by which the present value of the firm is increased as a result of adopting the project. Therefore, as we have pointed out, the net present value method is consistent with the goal of shareholder wealth maximization. The net present value approach considers both the magnitude and the timing of cash flows over a project's entire expected life.

A firm can be thought of as a series of projects, and the firm's total value is the sum of the net present values of all the independent projects that make it up. Therefore, when the firm undertakes a new project, the firm's value is increased by the net present value of the new project. The additivity of net present values of independent projects is referred to in finance as the *value additivity principle*.

[a]In order to solve this problem with the aid of your calculator, it is necessary to use the cash flow function/keys (CF) on your calculator. The calculator solutions and the solutions obtained using interest tables with three decimal places differ slightly. Using more accurate interest tables gives answers closer to the answers obtained using the calculator.

The net present value approach also indicates whether a proposed project will yield the rate of return required by the firm's investors. The cost of capital represents this rate of return; when a project's net present value is greater than or equal to zero, the firm's investors can expect to earn at least their required rate of return.

The net present value criterion has a weakness in that many people find it difficult to work with a present value dollar return rather than a percentage return. As a result, many firms use another present value–based method that is interpreted more easily: the internal rate of return method. It is discussed later in the chapter. Also, the traditional NPV approach does not consider the value of real options that are part of a proposed project. Real options are discussed later in the chapter.

10-2b Profitability Index

profitability index (PI)

The **profitability index (PI)**, or benefit-cost ratio, is the ratio of the present value of expected net cash flows over the life of a project (PVNCF) to the net investment NINV. It is expressed as follows:

(10.5)
$$\text{PI} = \frac{\text{PVNCF}}{\text{NINV}}$$

(10.6)
$$\text{PI} = \frac{\sum_{t=1}^{n} \text{NCF}_t/(1+k)^t}{\text{NINV}}$$

Assuming a 14 percent cost of capital, k, and using the Ace Lumber data from Table 10.2, the profitability index for Projects A and B can be calculated as follows:

$$\text{PI}_A = \frac{\$48{,}613}{\$50{,}000}$$
$$= 0.97$$
$$\text{PI}_B = \frac{\$57{,}735}{\$50{,}000}$$
$$= 1.15$$

The profitability index is interpreted as the present value return *for each dollar of initial investment.* In comparison, the net present value approach measures the total present value dollar return.

Decision Rule A project whose profitability index is greater than or equal to 1 is considered acceptable, whereas a project having a profitability index less than 1 is considered unacceptable.[3] In the case of Ace Lumber, Project B is acceptable, whereas Project A is not. When two or more *independent* projects with normal cash flows are considered, the profitability index, net present value, and internal rate of return approaches all will yield identical accept-reject signals; this is true, for example, with Projects A and B.

When dealing with mutually exclusive investments, conflicts may arise between the net present value and the profitability index criteria. This is most likely to occur if the alternative projects require significantly different net investments.

Consider, for example, the following information on Projects J and K. According to the net present value criterion, Project J would be preferred because of its larger net present value. According to the profitability index criterion, Project K would be preferred.

[3]When a project has a profitability index equal to 1, the present value of the net cash flows is exactly equal to the net investment. Thus, the project has a net present value of zero, meaning that it is expected to earn the investors' required rate of return and nothing more.

	Project J	Project K
Present value of net cash flows	\$25,000	\$14,000
Less: Net investment	20,000	10,000
Net present value (NPV)	\$5,000	\$4,000
$PI = \frac{\textbf{Present value of net cash flows}}{\textbf{Net investment}}$	**1.25**	**1.40**

When a conflict arises, the final decision must be made on the basis of other factors. For example, if a firm has no constraint on the funds available to it for capital investment—that is, no capital rationing—the net present value approach is preferred because it will select the projects that are expected to generate the largest *total dollar* increase in the firm's wealth and, by extension, maximize shareholder wealth. If, however, the firm is in a capital rationing situation, the profitability index approach may be preferred because it will indicate which projects will maximize the returns *per dollar of investment*—an appropriate objective when a funds constraint exists.

10-2c Internal Rate of Return

internal rate of return

The **internal rate of return** is defined as the discount rate that equates the present value of the net cash flows from a project with the present value of the net investment,[4] that is:

(10.7) $$\text{PVNCF} = \text{NINV}$$

Subtracting NINV from both sides of Equation 10.7 yields PVNCF $-$ NINV $= 0$, or NPV $= 0$, which shows that the internal rate of return is the discount rate that causes a project's net present value to equal zero. The internal rate of return for a capital expenditure project is identical to the yield-to-maturity for a bond investment.

A project's internal rate of return can be determined by means of the following equation:

(10.8) $$\sum_{t=1}^{n} \frac{\text{NCF}_t}{(1+r)^t} = \text{NINV}$$

or

(10.9) $$\sum_{t=1}^{n} \text{NCF}_t \times \text{PVIF}_{r,t} = \text{NINV}$$

where $\text{NCF}_t/(1+r)^t$ is the present value of net (operating) cash flows in period t discounted at the rate r, NINV is the net investment in the project, r is the internal rate of return, and $\text{PVIF}_{r,t}$ is the present value interest factor (Table II).

Subtracting the net investment, NINV, from both sides of Equation 10.8 yields the following:

$$\sum_{t=1}^{n} \frac{\text{NCF}_t}{(1+r)^t} - \text{NINV} = 0$$

This is essentially the same equation as that used in the net present value method (Equation 10.2).

The only difference is that in the net present value approach, a discount rate, k, is specified and the net present value is computed; whereas in the internal rate of return

[4]This also is called the *discounted cash flow (DCF)* rate of return.

method, the discount rate, r, which causes the project net present value to equal zero, is the unknown.

If all the net (operating) cash flows are equal over the life of the project, that is, an annuity $NCF = NCF_1 = NCF_2 = \ldots = NCF_n$, then Equation 10.9 can be expressed as follows:

$$NCF \times PVIFA_{r,n} = NINV \tag{10.10}$$

Calculator Solutions

Key	Enter
n	6
i	
PV	−50,000
PMT	12,500
FV	
	Solution
i	12.98

where $PVIFA_{r,n}$ is the present value of an annuity factor (Table IV).

The internal rate of return for Ace Lumber's Projects A and B can now be calculated. Because Project A is an annuity, its internal rate of return may be computed directly with the aid of a PVIFA table, such as Table IV.

Substituting NCF = \$12,500, NINV = \$50,000, $n = 6$ into Equation 10.10 yields:

$$\$12{,}500 \times PVIFA_{r,6} = \$50{,}000$$

$$PVIFA_{r,6} = \$50{,}000/\$12{,}500$$

$$= 4.000$$

Referring to Table IV and reading across the table for $n = 6$, it can be seen that the interest factor of 4.000 occurs near 13 percent, where it is 3.998. Thus, the internal rate of return for Project A is about 13 percent. The internal rate of return can also be calculated using a financial calculator or spreadsheet.

The internal rate of return for Project B is more difficult to calculate because the project is expected to yield uneven cash flows. In this case, the internal rate of return is computed with the help of a financial calculator or by using capital budgeting spreadsheet programs, such as the one available with this text. The internal rate of return for Project B is about 18.2 percent.

Calculator Solutions[b]

Key	Enter
CF_0	−50,000
CF_1	5,000
CF_2	10,000
CF_3	15,000
CF_4	15,000
CF_5	25,000
CF_6	30,000
IRR	
	Solution
IRR	18.19

The IRR may also be solved by using spreadsheet software, as illustrated here:

	A	B	C	D	E	F	G	H	I
1									
2									
3		Using a Spreadsheet to Find Internal Rate of Return of a Project							
4						Years			
5			0	1	2	3	4	5	6
6		Project A	-\$50,000	\$12,500	\$12,500	\$12,500	\$12,500	\$12,500	\$12,500
7		Project B	-\$50,000	\$5,000	\$10,000	\$15,000	\$15,000	\$25,000	\$30,000
8									
9		Interest rate =	14.00%						
10					Excel formula used (+IRR (Values, Guess)):				
11					"=+IRR(C6:I6,10)"				
12		IRR (Project A)	12.98%						
13									
14		IRR (Project B)	18.19%						
15									
16					Excel formula used (+IRR (Values, Guess)):				
17					"=+IRR(C7:I7,10)"				
18									

Figure 10.1 illustrates the relationship between net present value and internal rate of return. The figure plots the net present value of Project B (from Table 10.1) against the discount rate used to evaluate its cash flows. Note that at a 14 percent cost of capital, the net present value of B is \$7,735—the same figure that resulted from the computations performed in Table 10.2. The internal rate of return for Project B is approximately equal to 18.2 percent. Thus, the internal rate of return is a special case of the net present value computation.

Decision Rule

Generally, the internal rate of return method indicates that a project whose internal rate of return is greater than or equal to the firm's cost of capital should be accepted, whereas a project whose internal rate of return is less than the firm's cost of

[b] To solve this problem with the aid of your calculator, it is necessary to use the cash flow function/keys (CF) on your calculator.

FIGURE 10.1

NPV Profiles: Relationship between the Net Present Value and the Internal Rate of Return for Projects A and B: Ace Lumber Company

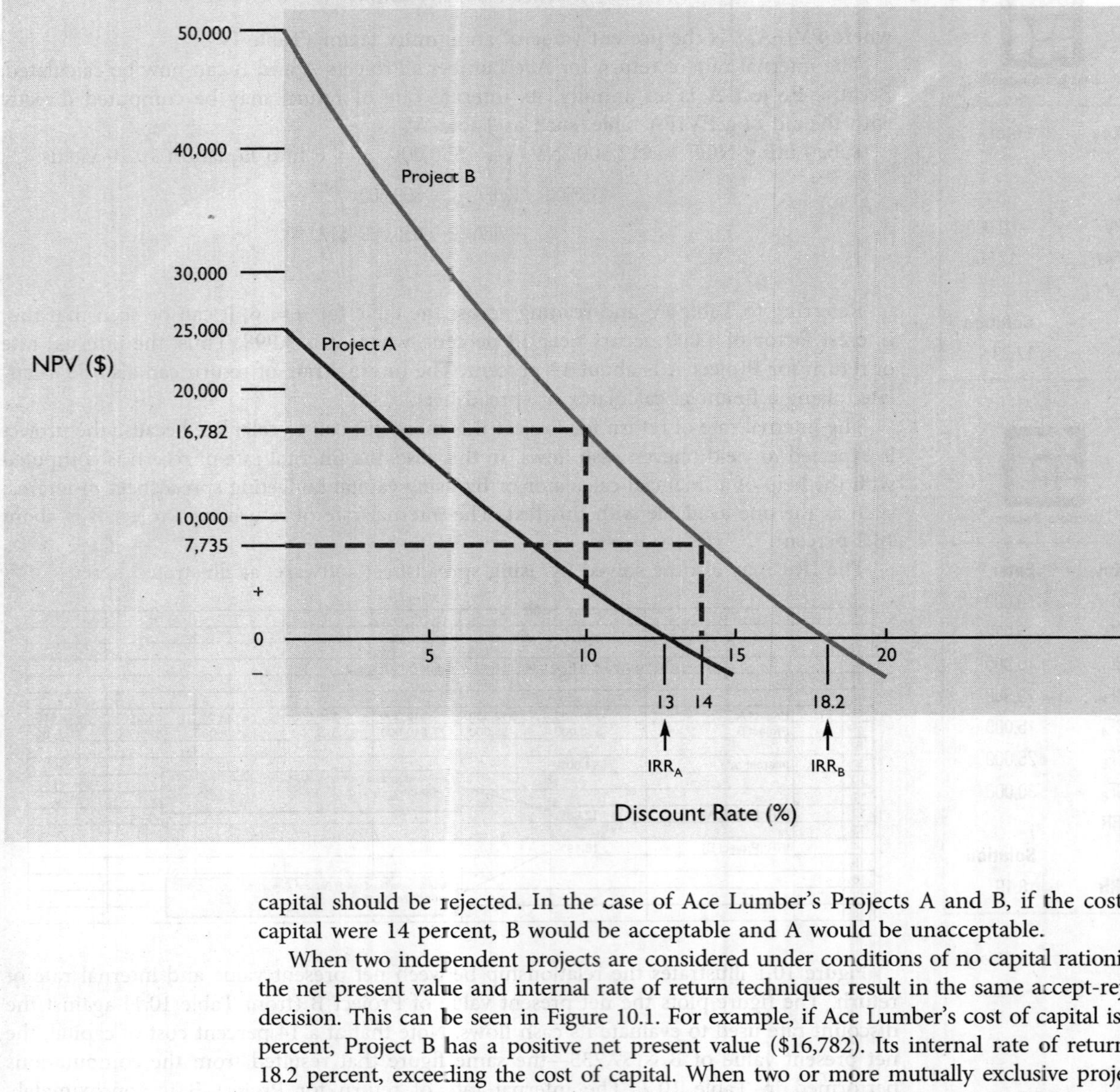

capital should be rejected. In the case of Ace Lumber's Projects A and B, if the cost of capital were 14 percent, B would be acceptable and A would be unacceptable.

When two independent projects are considered under conditions of no capital rationing, the net present value and internal rate of return techniques result in the same accept-reject decision. This can be seen in Figure 10.1. For example, if Ace Lumber's cost of capital is 10 percent, Project B has a positive net present value ($16,782). Its internal rate of return is 18.2 percent, exceeding the cost of capital. When two or more mutually exclusive projects are being considered, it is *generally* preferable to accept the project having the highest internal rate of return as long as it is greater than or equal to the cost of capital. In this case, if A and B were mutually exclusive, B would be chosen over A, as can be seen in Figure 10.1. Exceptions to this general rule are considered later in the chapter.

Advantages and Disadvantages of the Internal Rate of Return Method

The internal rate of return method is used widely in industry by firms that employ present value–based capital budgeting techniques. In a 1999 survey of 392 chief financial officers from a broad cross section of firms in the United States, it is documented that 74.9 percent of the respondents always or almost always use the NPV and that 75.7 percent always or almost always use the IRR to evaluate capital budgeting proposals.[5] The popularity of the internal rate of return method may be due to the fact that some people feel more comfortable dealing with the concept of a project's percentage rate of return than with its dollar amount of net present value. Like the net present value approach, the internal rate of return technique takes into account both the magnitude and the timing of cash flows over the entire life of a project in measuring the project's economic desirability.

multiple internal rates of return

However, some potential problems are involved in using the internal rate of return technique. The possible existence of **multiple internal rates of return** is one such problem. Whereas equating the net present value of a project to zero will yield only one internal rate of return, r, for *normal* investments, there are times when two or more rates may be obtained. Recall that a normal project has an initial cash outlay or outlays (net investment) followed by a stream of positive net cash flows. If for some reason—such as large abandonment costs at the end of a project's life or a major shutdown and rebuilding of a facility sometime during its life—the initial net investment is followed by one or more positive net cash flows (inflows) that then are followed by a negative cash flow,[6] it is possible to obtain more than one internal rate of return.

Whenever a project has multiple internal rates of return, the pattern of cash flows over the project's life contains more than one sign change, for example, $- \uparrow + + \uparrow -$. In this case, there are two sign changes (indicated by the arrows)—from minus to plus and again from plus to minus.

Consider the following investment, which has three internal rates of return—0, 100, and 200 percent:

Year	Net Cash Flows
0	$−1,000
1	+6,000
2	−11,000
3	+6,000

Unfortunately, none of these rates can be compared to the firm's cost of capital to determine the project's acceptability.

Although several techniques have been proposed for dealing with the multiple internal rate of return problem, none provide a simple, complete, and generally satisfactory solution. The best approach is to use the net present value criterion. If a project's net present value is positive, it is acceptable; if it is negative, it is not acceptable. Many financial calculators and software packages are available that compute internal rates of return, and they usually will warn the user when a potential multiple internal rate of return problem exists. Whenever this is a possibility, the use of the net present value method is preferred.

Finally, just as is the case with the NPV approach, the traditional IRR approach does not consider the value of a project's real option characteristics.

[5] Graham, John R., and Campbell R. Harvey, "The Theory and Practice of Corporate Finance: Evidence from the Field," *Journal of Financial Economics*, 60 (May/June 2001): 187–243.

[6] Table 9.1 in Chapter 9 illustrates two such projects, X and Y.

Net Present Value Versus Internal Rate of Return: The Reinvestment Rate Assumption As was indicated, both the net present value and the internal rate of return methods result in identical decisions to either accept or reject an *independent* project. This is true because the net present value is greater than (less than) zero if and only if the internal rate of return is greater than (less than) the required rate of return, *k*. In the case of *mutually exclusive* projects, however, the two methods may yield contradictory results; one project may have a *higher* internal rate of return than another and, at the same time, a *lower* net present value.

Consider, for example, *mutually exclusive* projects L and M described in the following table. Both require a net investment of $1,000. Using the internal rate of return approach, Project L is preferred, with an IRR of 21.5 percent compared with Project M's IRR of 18.3 percent. Using the net present value approach with a discount rate of 5 percent, Project M is preferred to Project L. Hence, it is necessary to determine which technique is the correct one to use in this situation.

	Project L	Project M
Net investment	$1,000	$1,000
Net cash flows		
Year 1	$ 667	$ 0
Year 2	$ 667	$1,400
Net present value at 5%	$ 240	$ 270
Internal rate of return	21.5%	18.3%

The outcome depends on what *assumptions* the decision maker chooses to make about the *implied reinvestment rate* for the net cash flows generated from each project. This can be seen in Figure 10.2. For discount (reinvestment) rates below 10 percent, Project M has a higher net present value than Project L and therefore is preferred. For discount rates greater than 10 percent, Project L is preferred using both the net present value and internal rate of return approaches. Hence, a conflict only occurs in this case for discount (cost-of-capital) rates below 10 percent. The net present value method assumes that cash flows are *reinvested at the firm's cost of capital*, whereas the internal rate of return method assumes that these cash flows are *reinvested at the computed internal rate of return*. Generally, the cost of capital is considered to be a more realistic **reinvestment rate** than the computed internal rate of return because the cost of capital is the rate the next (marginal) investment project can be assumed to earn. This can be seen in Figure 9.1 in Chapter 9, where the last acceptable project, Project E, offers a rate of return nearly equal to the firm's marginal cost of capital.

reinvestment rate

Consequently, in the absence of capital rationing, the net present value approach is normally superior to both the profitability index and the internal rate of return when choosing among mutually exclusive investments.

10-2d Payback (PB) Period

payback (PB) period

The **payback (PB) period** of an investment is the period of time required for the cumulative cash inflows (net cash flows) from a project to equal the initial cash outlay (net investment). If the expected net cash inflows are *equal* each year, then the payback

FIGURE 10.2

NPV Profiles: Net Present Value Versus Internal Rate of Return for Mutually Exclusive Alternatives

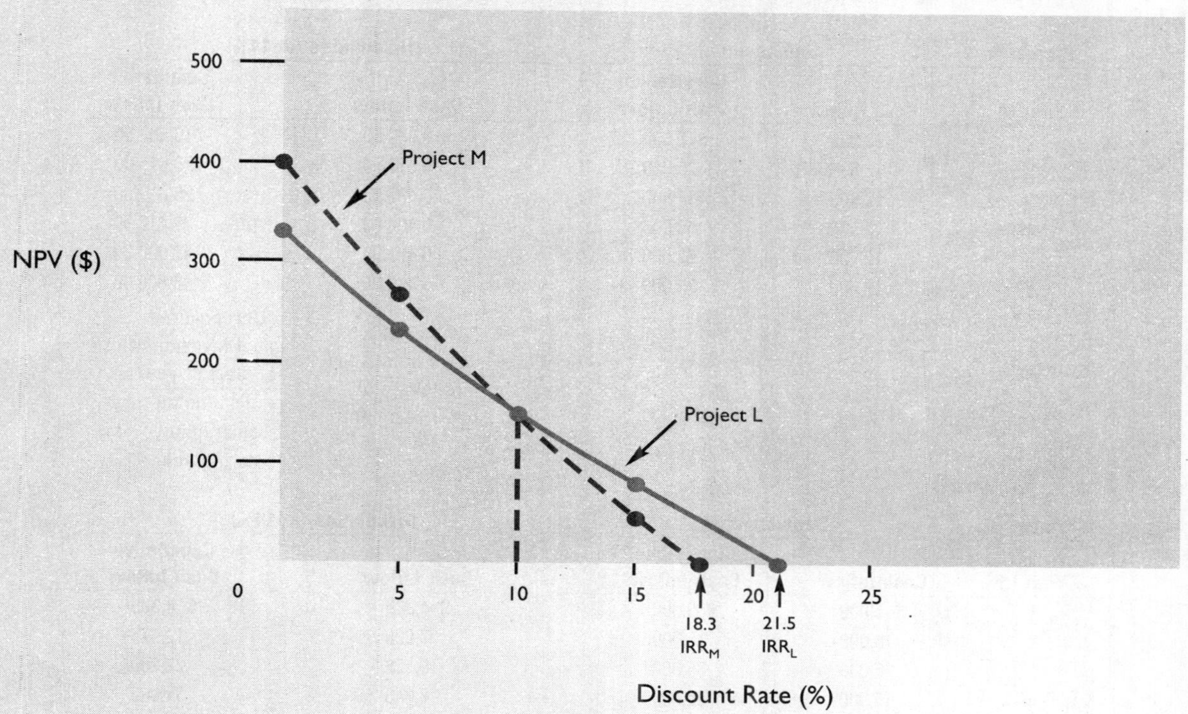

period is equal to the ratio of the net investment to the annual net cash inflows of the project:

(10.11)
$$PB = \frac{\text{Net investment}}{\text{Annual net cash inflows}}$$

When the annual cash inflows are not equal each year, slightly more complex calculations are required to compute the payback period. In this case, the analyst must add the yearly net cash flows until the cumulative total equals the net investment. The number of years it takes for this to occur is the project's payback period. One can also compute a *discounted* payback period, where the net cash inflows are discounted at the firm's cost of capital in determining the number of years required to recover the net investment in a project.

Table 10.3 illustrates the calculation of undiscounted and discounted (at a 14 percent required return) payback periods for Ace Lumber's Projects A and B, which were presented earlier in this section. In Panel (a) of the table we see that the *undiscounted* PB period is 4.0 years for Project A and 4.2 years for Project B. In Panel (b) we see that the discounted PB period for Project A is undefined. This occurs because the NPV of the project is negative, that is, the discounted cash inflows are less than the net investment. For Project B the discounted PB period is 5.43 years.

Decision Rule The decision criterion states that a project should be accepted if its payback period is less than or equal to a target maximum period. Otherwise, it

TABLE 10.3

Ace Lumber Company: Payback Period Calculations

Project A	(a) Undiscounted		(b) Discounted (at 14%)	
Year (t)	Cash Inflow	Cumulative Cash Inflow	Cash Inflow	Cumulative Cash Inflow
1	$12,500	$12,500	$10,962.50	$10,962.50
2	12,500	25,000	9,612.50	20,575.00
3	12,500	37,500	8,437.50	29,012.50
4	12,500	50,000	7,400.00	36,412.50
5	12,500	62,500	6,487.50	42,900.00
6	12,500	75,000	5,700.00	48,600.00

$$PB = \frac{\text{Net investment}}{\text{Annual cash inflow}} = \frac{50{,}000}{12{,}500} = 4.0 \text{ years}$$

$$PB = \begin{matrix}\text{Number of}\\ \text{years before full}\\ \text{recovery of}\\ \text{net investment}\end{matrix} + \frac{\begin{matrix}\text{Unrecovered}\\ \text{initial investment}\\ \text{at start of year}\end{matrix}}{\begin{matrix}\text{Discounted}\\ \text{cash inflow}\\ \text{during year}\end{matrix}} = \text{Undefined}$$

Project B	Undiscounted		Discounted (at 14%)	
Year (t)	Cash Inflow	Cumulative Cash Inflow	Cash Inflow	Cumulative Cash Inflow
1	$ 5,000	$ 5,000	$ 4,385	$ 4,385
2	10,000	15,000	7,690	12,075
3	15,000	30,000	10,125	22,200
4	15,000	45,000	8,880	31,080
5	25,000	70,000	12,975	44,055
6	30,000	100,000	13,680	57,735

$$PB = \begin{matrix}\text{Number of}\\ \text{years before full}\\ \text{recovery of}\\ \text{net investment}\end{matrix} + \frac{\begin{matrix}\text{Unrecovered}\\ \text{initial investment}\\ \text{at start of year}\end{matrix}}{\begin{matrix}\text{Cash inflow}\\ \text{during year}\end{matrix}} = 4 + \frac{(50{,}000 - 45{,}000)}{25{,}000} = 4.2 \text{ years}$$

$$PB = \begin{matrix}\text{Number of}\\ \text{years before full}\\ \text{recovery of}\\ \text{net investment}\end{matrix} + \frac{\begin{matrix}\text{Unrecovered}\\ \text{initial investment}\\ \text{at start of year}\end{matrix}}{\begin{matrix}\text{Discounted}\\ \text{cash inflow}\\ \text{during year}\end{matrix}} = 5 + \frac{(50{,}000 - 44{,}055)}{13{,}680} = 5.43 \text{ years}$$

should be rejected. However, the payback method has a number of serious shortcomings, and it should not be used in deciding whether to accept or reject an investment project.

Advantages and Disadvantages of the Payback Method The payback method suffers from the following serious disadvantages. First, the (undiscounted) payback method gives equal weight to all cash inflows within the payback period, regardless of when they occur during the period. In other words, the technique ignores the *time value of money.*

Assume, for example, that a firm is considering two projects, E and F, each costing $10,000. Project E is expected to yield cash flows over a three-year period of $6,000 during the first year, $4,000 during the second year, and $3,000 during the third year. Project F is expected to yield cash flows of $4,000 during the first year, $6,000 during the second year, and $3,000 during the third year. Viewed from the payback perspective, these projects are equally attractive, yet the net present value technique clearly indicates that Project E increases the value of the firm more than Project F.

Second, payback methods essentially ignore cash flows occurring after the payback period. Thus, payback figures are biased against long-term projects and can be misleading. For example, suppose a firm is considering two projects, C and D, each costing $10,000. It is expected that Project C will generate net cash inflows of $5,000 per year for 3 years and that Project D will generate net cash inflows of $4,500 per year forever. The PB period for Project C is 2 years ($10,000/$5,000), whereas the PB period for Project D is 2.2 years ($10,000/$4,500). If these projects were mutually exclusive, payback would favor C because it has the lower payback period. Yet Project D clearly has a higher net present value than Project C.

Third, payback provides no *objective* criterion for decision making that is consistent with shareholder wealth maximization. The payback method may reject projects with positive net present values. The choice of an acceptable payback period is largely a *subjective* one, and different people using essentially identical data may make different accept-reject decisions about a project.

The payback method is sometimes justified on the basis that it provides a measure of the *risk* associated with a project. Although it is true that less risk may be associated with a shorter payback period than with a longer one, risk is best thought of in terms of the *variability* of project returns. Because payback ignores this dimension, it is at best a crude tool for risk analysis.

A more valid justification for the use of the payback method is that it gives some indication of a project's desirability from a *liquidity* perspective because it measures the time required for a firm to recover its initial investment in a project. A company that is very concerned about the early recovery of investment funds—such as one investing overseas in a politically unstable area or one expecting a cash shortage in the future—might find this method useful.

In summary, payback is not a satisfactory criterion for investment decision making because it may lead to a selection of projects that do not make the largest possible contribution to a firm's value. It can be useful as a supplementary decision-making tool, however.

Table 10.4 presents a summary of the four capital budgeting methods discussed in the chapter.

10-3 Capital Rationing and the Capital Budgeting Decision

For each of the selection criteria previously discussed, the decision rule is to undertake *all* independent investment projects that meet the acceptance standard. This rule places no restrictions on the total amount of acceptable capital projects a company may undertake in any particular period.

However, many firms do not have unlimited funds available for investment. Rather than letting the size of their capital budget be determined by the number of profitable investment opportunities available, many companies choose to place an upper limit, or *constraint*, on the amount of funds allocated to capital investments. This constraint may be either *self-imposed* by the firm's management or *externally imposed* by conditions in the capital markets.

TABLE 10.4

Summary of the Capital Budgeting Methods

Model	Project Acceptance Criterion	Strengths	Weaknesses
Net present value (NPV)	Accept project if project has a positive or zero NPV; that is, if the present value of net cash flows, evaluated at the firm's cost of capital, equals or exceeds the net investment required.	Considers the timing of cash flows. Provides an objective, return-based criterion for acceptance or rejection. Most conceptually correct approach.	Difficulty in working with a dollar return value, rather than percentage returns.
Profitability index (PI)	Accept project if PI is greater than or equal to 1.0.	Same benefits as the NPV. Useful to guide decisions in capital rationing problems.	Sometimes gives decision that conflicts with NPV.
Internal rate of return (IRR)	Accept project if IRR equals or exceeds the firm's cost of capital.	Same benefits as the NPV. Easy to interpret the meaning of IRR.	Multiple rates of return problem. Sometimes gives decision that conflicts with NPV.
Payback (PB)	PB should not be used in deciding whether to accept or reject an investment project.	Easy and inexpensive to use. Provides a crude measure of project risk. Provides a measure of project liquidity.	No objective decision criterion. Fails to consider timing of cash flows.

For example, a very conservative firm may be reluctant to use debt or external equity to finance capital expenditures. Instead, it would limit capital expenditures to cash flows from continuing operations minus any dividends paid. Another firm may feel that it lacks the managerial resources to successfully undertake all acceptable projects in a given year and may choose to limit capital expenditures for this reason.

A number of externally imposed constraints might limit a firm's capital expenditures. For example, a firm's loan agreements may contain restrictive covenants that limit future borrowing. Similarly, a weak financial position, conditions in the securities markets, or both may make the flotation of a new bond or stock issue by the firm impossible or prohibitively expensive. Examples of such market-imposed constraints include depressed stock market prices, unusually high interest rates due to a "tight money" policy on the part of the Federal Reserve System, and a reluctance on the part of investors to purchase new securities if the firm has a large percentage of debt in its capital structure.

Several different methods can be used in making capital budgeting decisions under capital rationing. When the initial outlays occur in two (or more) periods, the methods are quite elaborate and require the use of linear, integer, or goal programming. However, when there is a single-period capital budgeting constraint, a relatively simple approach employing the profitability index can be used. Briefly, the approach consists of the following steps:

Step 1: Calculate the profitability index for each of a series of investment projects.

Step 2: Rank the projects according to their profitability indexes (from highest to lowest).

Step 3: Beginning with the project having the highest profitability index, proceed down through the list, and accept projects having profitability indexes greater than or equal to 1 until the entire capital budget has been utilized.

At times, a firm may not be able to use its entire capital budget because the next acceptable project on its list is too large, given the remaining available funds. In this case, the firm's management should choose among the following three alternatives:

Alternative 1: Search for another combination of projects, perhaps including some smaller, less profitable ones that will allow for a more complete utilization of available funds *and* increase the net present value of the combination of projects.

Alternative 2: Attempt to relax the funds constraint so that sufficient resources are available to accept the last project for which funds were not fully available.

Alternative 3: Accept as many projects as possible and either invest any excess funds in short-term securities until the next period,[7] pay out the excess funds to shareholders as dividends, use the funds to reduce outstanding debt, or do a combination of the above.

The following example illustrates how these alternatives can be applied to an actual capital budgeting decision. Suppose that management of the Old Mexico Tile Company has decided to limit next year's capital expenditures to $550,000. Eight capital expenditure projects have been proposed—P, R, S, U, T, V, Q, and W—and ranked according to their profitability indexes, as shown in Table 10.5. Given the $550,000 ceiling, the firm's management proceeds down the list of projects, selecting P, R, S, and U, in that order. Project T cannot be accepted because this would require a capital outlay of $25,000 in excess of the $550,000 limit. Projects P, R, S, and U together yield a net present value of $114,750 but require a total investment outlay of only $525,000, leaving $25,000 from the capital budget that is not invested in projects. Management is considering the following three alternatives:

Alternative 1: It could attempt to find another combination of projects, perhaps including some smaller ones, that would allow for a more complete utilization of available funds and increase the cumulative net present

TABLE 10.5

Old Mexico Tile Company: Ranking of Proposed Projects According to Their Profitability Indexes

Project (1)	Net Investment (2)	Net Present Value (3)	Present Value of Net Cash Flows (4)	PI = (4) ÷ (2)	Cumulative Net Investment	Cumulative Net Present Value
P	$100,000	$25,000	$125,000	1.25	$100,000	$25,000
R	150,000	33,000	183,000	1.22	250,000	58,000
S	175,000	36,750	211,750	1.21	425,000	94,750
U	100,000	20,000	120,000	1.20	525,000	114,750
T	50,000	9,000	59,000	1.18	575,000	123,750
V	75,000	12,500	87,500	1.17	650,000	136,250
Q	200,000	30,000	230,000	1.15	850,000	166,250
W	50,000	−10,000	40,000	0.80	900,000	156,250

[7] If a firm does not invest a portion of its available capital resources in projects earning a rate of return at least equal to the cost of capital, an implicit opportunity cost of lost earnings is incurred. However, as long as profitable investment alternatives exist, the firm should seek ways to fully use all available capital funds.

value. In this case, a likely combination would be Projects P, R, S, T, and V. This combination would fully use the $550,000 available and create a net present value of $116,250—an increase of $1,500 over the net present value of $114,750 from Projects P, R, S, and U.

Alternative 2: It could attempt to increase the capital budget by another $25,000 to allow Project T to be added to the list of adopted projects.

Alternative 3: It could merely accept the first four projects—P, R, S, and U—and invest the remaining $25,000 in a short-term security until the next period. This alternative would result in an NPV of $114,750, assuming that the risk-adjusted required return on the short-term security is equal to its yield.

In this case, *Alternative 1* seems to be the most desirable of the three. In rearranging the capital budget, however, Old Mexico Tile Company should never accept a project, such as W, that does not meet the minimum acceptance criterion of a positive or zero net present value (a profitability index greater than or equal to 1).

10-4 Reviewing and Post-Auditing an Accepted Project

A final important step in the capital budgeting process is the review of investment projects after they have been implemented. This can provide useful information on the effectiveness of the company's selection process. The **post-audit** procedure consists of comparing *actual* cash flows from an accepted project with *projected* cash flows that were estimated when the project was adopted. Because projected cash flows contain an element of uncertainty, actual values would not be expected to match estimated values exactly. Instead, a project review should be concerned with identifying systematic biases or errors in cash flow estimation on the part of individuals, departments, plants, or divisions and attempting to determine *why* these biases or errors exist. This type of analysis, when properly performed, can help a company's decision makers better evaluate investment proposals submitted in the future.

post-audit

The importance of the post-audit process has been highlighted in research by Brown and Miller.[8] They observed that in the common situation where bad projects outnumber good ones, the simple procedure of making unbiased cash flow estimates and choosing projects with positive net present values will result in an upwardly biased acceptance rate for proposed projects (and returns that are, on average, below those that are expected) if there is uncertainty regarding future cash flows. In a situation such as this, the firm needs to correct for this potential bias when projects are being reviewed. The information needed to make this necessary bias-eliminating correction can be gathered from careful project post-audits.

The importance of a good project review and tracking system is illustrated in the following example from Ameritech (merged with SBC Communications in 1999, which in turn merged with and adopted the AT&T name in 2005). Ameritech has a sophisticated tracking system that permits the company to identify the individual responsible for each

[8] Keith C. Brown, "A Note on the Apparent Bias of Net Revenue Estimates for Capital Investment Projects," *Journal of Finance* (September 1974): 1215–1216; K. C. Brown, "The Rate of Return on Selected Investment Projects," *Journal of Finance* (September 1978): 1250–1253; Edward M. Miller, "Uncertainty Induced Bias in Capital Budgeting," *Financial Management* (Autumn 1978): 12–18; and E. M. Miller, "The Competitive Market Assumption and Capital Budgeting Criteria," *Financial Management* (Winter 1987): 22–28.

estimate in a capital project proposal. When the tracking system was announced and initiated, budgets had already been submitted for the coming year. Divisions were permitted to take back their budgets and resubmit them in light of the new tracking system. Seven hundred projects disappeared from the new budgets, and many others had reduced estimates of benefits![9]

Another objective of the project review process involves determining whether a project that has not lived up to expectations should be continued or abandoned. The decision to abandon a project requires the company to compare the cost of abandonment with any future cash flows that are expected over the project's remaining life. These estimates of future cash flows will usually be more accurate after the project has been in service for a period of time.

10-5 A Comprehensive Example of Capital Budgeting: Opening a New Bank Branch

The First National Bank and Trust Company has a single banking office located in the downtown business district of a medium-size town. As the population moved to the suburbs, First National has seen its share of both local banking deposits and profits decline. Two of the bank's vice presidents have proposed that First National try to reverse this trend by building a branch in a new, affluent suburban community. They have presented the bank's executive committee with the following information.

The initial cost of the bank building and equipment is $1 million. This facility is expected to have a useful life of 20 years. Also, in 20 years at the end of the project, the branch building and its equipment are expected to be sold for a $200,000 salvage value. The branch building and its equipment will be depreciated over their 20-year life using straight-line depreciation to a zero balance. We have assumed straight-line depreciation for simplicity. As discussed in Appendix 9A, in actual practice the bank would use MACRS depreciation with a 39-year life on the building and a 7-year life on the equipment. The annual straight-line depreciation will be $1,000,000/20 = $50,000. The bank building is to be constructed on land leased for $20,000 per year. In addition to the $1 million investment for the building and equipment, the parent bank's net working capital must be increased by $100,000 to accommodate the new branch.

Based on customer surveys, population trends, the location of competitor banks, and the experience other area banks have had with their branches, it is estimated that the annual revenues from the new branch will be $400,000. Of this $400,000 in revenues, $50,000 will be drawn away from the bank's main office. (Assume that the main office will not attempt to cut its expenses because of this loss in revenues.)

In addition to the $20,000 annual expense for the land lease, the new branch will incur about $130,000 per year in other expenses, including personnel costs, utilities, and interest paid on accounts. Both expenses and revenues are expected to remain approximately constant over the branch's 20-year life.

The bank's marginal tax rate is 40 percent and its cost of capital (required rate of return) is 9 percent after taxes.

[9] "Capital Budgeting: A Panel Discussion," *Financial Management* (Spring 1989): 10–17.

Step 1: Computing the Net Investment

New project cost	$1,000,000
Plus: Increase in net working capital	100,000
Net investment (NINV)	$1,100,000

The net investment equals the new project cost ($1 million) plus the increase in net working capital ($100,000).

Step 2: Computing Net Cash Flows

Net increase in revenues ($400,000 − $50,000)	$350,000
Less: Operating costs of branch ($130,000 + $20,000)	150,000
Less: Depreciation	50,000
Operating earnings before taxes	$150,000
Less: Tax (40%)	60,000
Operating earnings after taxes	$90,000
Plus: Depreciation	50,000
Net cash flow (NCF_t)	$140,000

Net cash flows are calculated for years 1 through 19 by subtracting branch operating costs and depreciation from the incremental revenues of $350,000. This yields operating earnings before taxes from which taxes (at the 40 percent rate) are deducted to arrive at operating earnings after taxes. By adding back depreciation, the net cash flow equals $140,000 for each year from 1 through 19. Net cash flows in year 20 are computed by adding the $120,000 estimated after-tax salvage and the $100,000 return of working capital to the annual net cash flow of $140,000 to equal $360,000.[10]

The $100,000 working capital requirement is added back to the year 20 cash flows because at the end of 20 years, when the project is terminated, there will no longer be a need for this incremental working capital, and thus the working capital of $100,000 can be liquidated and made available to the bank for other uses.

Step 3: Arraying Project Cash Flows and Evaluating Alternatives

Net investment (NINV)	$1,100,000
Net cash flows (NCF_t):	
Years 1–19	140,000
Year 20	360,000

After the project cash flows have been computed and arrayed, the decision of whether to accept or reject the new branch project must be made. Next, the project is evaluated using three of the decision criteria discussed in this chapter, namely, net present value, internal rate of return, and profitability index.

[10]The $200,000 salvage value is taxable as ordinary income because the branch building and its equipment are fully depreciated at the end of the project. Therefore, the after-tax salvage cash flow is $200,000 minus 40 percent tax, or $120,000.

INTERNATIONAL ISSUES

A Framework for International Capital Expenditure Decisions[a]

The capital budgeting decision criteria discussed earlier in this chapter can also be used to evaluate international capital expenditure projects. To illustrate, suppose McCormick & Company, a U.S. spice company based in Maryland, is considering expanding its German spice operations.

The company plans to invest $5 million in additional German facilities. Based on this level of investment, McCormick estimates that its proposed German expansion project will generate annual net cash inflows of 1.5 million euros for a period of 10 years and nothing thereafter. Also, based upon its analysis of present German capital market conditions, McCormick has determined that the applicable German cost of capital, k, for the expansion project is 15 percent. The present value of the expected net cash flows from the project, denominated in the *foreign* currency, is calculated as follows:

$$PVNCF_f = \sum_{t=1}^{n} \frac{NCF_t}{(1+k)^t} \qquad \textbf{(10.12)}$$

Using Equation 10.12, a present value of approximately 7.53 million euros is obtained for the net cash flows of McCormick's proposed German expansion:

$$\begin{aligned} PVNCF_f &= \sum_{t=1}^{10} \frac{1.5 \text{ million}}{(1.15)^t} \\ &= 7.53 \text{ million euros} \end{aligned}$$

The present value of the project's net cash flows from the foreign viewpoint, $PVNCF_f$, is used to calculate the present value of the project's net cash flows to the parent company in the *home* country, $PVNCF_h$, as follows:

$$PVNCF_h = PVNCF_f \times S_0 \qquad \textbf{(10.13)}$$

where S_0 is the spot exchange rate expressed in units of home country currency per unit of foreign currency. Using a spot exchange rate of $0.80 per euro, the present value of the net cash flows to the parent company for McCormick's proposed expansion project is approximately $6.024 million.

$$\begin{aligned} PVNCF_h &= 7.53 \text{ million euros} \times \$0.80/\text{euro} \\ &= \$6.024 \text{ million} \end{aligned}$$

The project's net present value is calculated by subtracting the parent company's net investment in the project from $PVNCF_h$, the parent company's present value of the net cash flows:

$$NPV = PVNCF_h - NINV \qquad \textbf{(10.14)}$$

A net present value of approximately $1.024 million is obtained for the McCormick project.

$$\begin{aligned} NPV &= \$6.024 \text{ million} - \$5.0 \text{ million} \\ &= \$1.024 \text{ million} \end{aligned}$$

Based on this analysis, McCormick's proposed German expansion is an acceptable project.

The McCormick example assumes that an efficient capital market exists in the foreign country, as it does in Germany and other developed countries. Assets can be bought and sold and the required rates of return for projects can be determined from prices of other comparable assets in the foreign capital market.

The McCormick example also assumes that the amount and timing of the expected net cash flows to the foreign subsidiary are the same as for the parent company. If the amount and timing of the net cash inflows to the foreign subsidiary and the parent company are not the same, the evaluation of the capital expenditure project is more complex than the example presented in this section. Some of the reasons that the amount and timing of the net cash flows to the foreign subsidiary and parent may differ include the following:

- Differential tax rates for foreign and domestic companies in the country in which the project is planned
- Legal and political constraints on cash remittances from the foreign country to the home country
- Subsidized loans

The example presented in this section shows that the present value of a project's net cash flows to the parent company is simply the present value of the project's net cash flows from the foreign viewpoint converted into the home country currency at the current spot exchange rate.

[a]This section is based on James S. Ang and Tsong-Yue Lai, "A Simple Rule for Multinational Capital Budgeting," *The Global Finance Journal* 1, no. 1 (1989): 71–75. See also the special issue of *Managerial Finance*, "Capital Budgeting for the Multinational Enterprise," 22, no. 1 (1996).

- **Criterion 1: Net Present Value**

$$\begin{aligned}\text{NPV} &= \text{PVNCF} - \text{NINV}\\ &= \sum_{t=1}^{19}\frac{\$140{,}000}{(1+0.09)^t} + \frac{\$360{,}000}{(1+0.09)^{20}} - \$1{,}100{,}000\\ &= (\$140{,}000 \times \text{PVIFA}_{0.09,19})\\ &\quad + (\$360{,}000 \times \text{PVIF}_{0.09,20}) - \$1{,}100{,}000\end{aligned}$$

The first term in the net present value equation is the present value of an annuity of $140,000 for 19 years at 9 percent, the bank's cost of capital. Using the present value of an annuity table (Table IV), an interest factor of 8.950 may be found. The second term is the present value of $360,000 received in 20 years at 9 percent. From the present value table (Table II), an interest factor of 0.178 is found. Thus, the net present value of this project at a 9 percent cost of capital is as follows:

$$\begin{aligned}\text{NPV} &= \$140{,}000(8.950) + \$360{,}000(0.178) - \$1{,}100{,}000\\ &= \$1{,}253{,}000 + \$64{,}080 - \$1{,}100{,}000\\ &= \$217{,}080\end{aligned}$$

Using the net present value criterion and a cost of capital of 9 percent, this project would be acceptable because it has a positive net present value.

- **Criterion 2: Profitability Index**

The profitability index is the ratio of the present value of future net cash flows to the net investment. From the previous net present value calculation, we know that the present value of net cash flows at a 9 percent cost of capital is $1,317,080 ($1,253,000 + $64,080). Thus, the profitability index is computed as follows:

$$\begin{aligned}\text{PI} &= \frac{\text{PVNCF}}{\text{NINV}}\\ &= \frac{\$1{,}317{,}080}{\$1{,}100{,}000}\\ &= 1.20\end{aligned}$$

Because the profitability index is greater than 1, the new branch bank project is acceptable according to this criterion.

- **Criterion 3: Internal Rate of Return**

According to this method, a discount rate that makes the net present value of the project equal to zero must be found:

$$\text{PVNCF} - \text{NINV} = 0$$

or

$$\sum_{t=1}^{19}\frac{\$140{,}000}{(1+r)^t} + \frac{\$360{,}000}{(1+r)^{20}} - \$1{,}100{,}000 = 0$$

where r is the internal rate of return.

Since the calculated internal rate of return (r), equals 11.56 percent, which is greater than the cost of capital, the project is acceptable by this criterion.

Calculator Solutions[c]

Key	Enter
CF_0	−1,000,000
CF_{1-19}	140,000
CF_{20}	360,000
IRR	
	Solution
IRR	11.56

Based on these calculations, it appears that the new branch proposal will increase shareholder wealth and therefore should be undertaken. The only step remaining is to monitor the performance of the project to see if it meets, falls short of, or exceeds its projected cash flow estimates. Based on the actual results of this project, the bank's management will be able to evaluate other new branch bank proposals in a more knowledgeable manner.

[c] In order to solve this problem with the aid of your calculator, it is necessary to use the cash flow function/keys (CF) on your calculator.

10-6 Real Options in Capital Budgeting[11]

In our discussion of capital budgeting, we have used so-called conventional discounted cash flow techniques; that is, we determine a project's net present value by discounting the expected net cash flows at an applicable cost of capital, minus the net investment. This type of analysis does not consider the value of any operating (real) options that may be embedded in the project or the value of any options, or flexibilities, that the firm may choose to incorporate into the project's design. An option gives its holder the right, but not the obligation, to buy, sell, or otherwise transform an asset at a set price during a specified time period.

10-6a Classification of Real Options in Capital Budgeting

real options

Real options in capital budgeting can be classified in the following manner.

Investment Timing Options Delaying investment in a project, say for a year or so, may allow a firm to evaluate additional information regarding demand for outputs and costs of inputs, for example. Investing in a project today or waiting one year to invest in the same project is an example of two mutually exclusive projects. In this example, the firm should select the project with the higher net present value, assuming at least one project has a positive net present value. The "waiting-to-invest" option is a common real option.

Abandonment Option The option to discontinue a project is an important real option in capital budgeting. A project may be discontinued either by shutting it down completely and selling the equipment or by switching its use to an alternative product.

To illustrate how an abandonment option may influence the net present value of a project, consider a manufacturing firm that calculates a negative net present value on a proposed project to purchase a new lathe to make a series of industrial parts for a particular application. The project's negative net present value is based on a cash flow analysis that assumes that the lathe will produce the parts for the entire economic life of the project. This cash flow analysis does not take into consideration the option of the company to abandon the project and sell the lathe in the active secondary market that exists for lathes and other manufacturing equipment. Shutting down the project represents a put option to sell the project for the salvage value of equipment. Or the company could simply choose to switch from making the specific parts to another potentially more profitable product. The abandonment option is embedded in the project; its existence may limit the downside risk of the project. As demonstrated in the Financial Challenge at the beginning of the chapter, many times when a firm uses project-specific assets, such as those used to build the Boeing 747-8, abandonment options have a very small value. Indeed, delaying abandonment is often the best real option available to a firm.

Shutdown Options A firm may have the option of *temporarily* shutting down a project in order to avoid negative cash flows. Consider a mining or manufacturing operation characterized by relatively high variable costs. If output prices drop below variable

[11]This section is based on Nalin Kulatilaka and Alan J. Marcus, "Project Valuation Under Uncertainty: When Does DCF Fail?" *Journal of Applied Corporate Finance* (Fall 1992): 92–100. See also A. K. Dixit and R. S. Pindyck, "The Options Approach to Capital Investment," *Harvard Business Review* (May/June 1995): 105–119. An excellent set of articles dealing with the status of real option analysis in capital budgeting can be found in *Journal of Applied Corporate Finance* 14, no. 2 (Summer 2001). See also D. E. Stout, Y. A. Xie, and H. Qi, "Improving Capital Budgeting Decisions with Real Options," *Management Accounting Quarterly* 9, no. 4 (Summer 2008): 1–10.

ETHICAL ISSUES

The Use of Shareholder Resources

Managers are employed by the owners of a firm with the objective of maximizing wealth for the shareholders. As we have learned, this objective can be accomplished by investing in the set of projects possessing the maximum expected net present value. As discussed in Chapter 1, the managers of some firms, such as Berkshire Hathaway, have focused intently on this objective and have had good success in achieving their objective. Other managers, however, seem to have strayed frequently from this objective.

Investing in projects with negative net present values is most likely to occur in firms possessing large discretionary cash flows. Usually these are firms in mature industries with few true growth opportunities. Mature firms tend to generate substantial cash flows over which managers have considerable control. Marginal projects may be accepted, often with little analysis, because of their "strategic" importance to the firm. Managers may be reluctant to pay these "excess" cash flows out to shareholders as increased dividends because that will cause the firm to grow at a slower rate in the future.

As discussed in Chapter 3, Stern Stewart's Performance 1000 is a corporate performance measuring system designed to consider how effective managers have been in adding to their shareholders' investment.[a] Their "Market Value Added" (MVA) measure can be viewed as the "net present value of all of a company's past and projected capital investment projects." For example, Coca-Cola had an MVA of more than $103 billion; Exxon Mobil had about $153 billion in MVA; and Google had more than $150 billion of MVA. In contrast, AT&T had an MVA of less than −$37 billion and Bank of America had an MVA of less than −$111 billion.

What factors might cause managers to consistently adopt investment projects with negative net present values? What are the consequences of these decisions for shareholders? What are the consequences of these decisions for the U.S. economy?

[a]G. Bennett Stewart, III, "Announcing the Stern Stewart Performance 1000: A New Way of Viewing Corporate America," *Continental Bank: Journal of Applied Corporate Finance* (Summer 1990): 38–59.

costs, a business has the option to shut down until output prices recover and rise above variable costs. The shutdown option also reduces the downside risk of a project.

Growth Options A firm may have an opportunity to undertake a research program, build a small manufacturing facility to serve a new market, or make a small strategic acquisition in a new line of business. Each of these examples may be a negative net present value project, but each project can be viewed as having generated a growth option for the company, which, if exercised, may lead ultimately to a large positive net present value project.

To illustrate a growth option, suppose a company is considering a large Internet investment project that has the potential for either failure—that is, large losses with a high probability of occurrence—or success—that is, large profits with a low probability of occurrence. The investment consists of two stages. The first stage (today) is an investment in a Web site, and the second stage (one year from today) is an investment in an electronic commerce venture. The investment in the Web site has an NPV of $−10 million. Setting up the Web site (first stage) gives the company the option, but not the obligation, to invest in the electronic commerce business (second stage) one year from today.

HTTP:
Additional resources for classroom use in the discussion of real options can be found at
www.real-options.org

While the cash flows are highly uncertain, ranging from large losses to substantial profits, the best estimate today is that the electronic commerce business has an NPV of $−60 million. Based on the NPV decision rule, the Internet investment project would be unacceptable since it has an NPV of $−70 million ($−10 million + [$−60 million]).

However, one year from today, the company will have more information and be better able to estimate whether the electronic commerce business (second stage) is worth pursuing. At that time, suppose new information about the cash flows of the electronic commerce venture shows that it will be extremely profitable, yielding an overall NPV of $200 million for the Internet project. Clearly, the project would be worth undertaking at that time.

Investing in the Web site today, even though it has a negative NPV, preserves the company's option to invest in a positive NPV project in the future. By investing only in the Web site initially, the company is able to limit its downside risk ($–10 million NPV) while preserving the upside potential ($200 million NPV) for the Internet investment project.

Designed-In Options In addition to options that can occur naturally in projects, managers have the opportunity to include options in projects in order to increase net present value. These designed-in options are classified either as input flexibility options, output flexibility options, or expansion options.

Input flexibility options allow a firm to design into a project the capability of switching between alternative inputs because of input cost differences.

To illustrate a designed-in option, consider an electric power plant project that is evaluating whether to use a gas burner or an oil burner to power the turbines. The designed-in option in this instance would be a flexible dual-fuel boiler that can switch back and forth between gas and oil, depending on which energy source is cheaper to acquire and use. It may be, under certain conditions, that the flexible boiler project has a higher net present value than either of the projects using the gas-fired boiler or the oil-fired boiler, even though the initial cost of the flexible boiler is higher than the cost of either of the two single-fuel boilers. In other words, the value of the designed-in option may be greater than the additional cost of the flexible boiler.

Output flexibility options allow a firm to design into a project the capability of shifting the product mix of the project if demand or relative product prices dictate such a shift. Oil refineries normally have output flexibility options. Automobile manufacturers are increasing designing final assembly plants with the option to produce multiple, related vehicle models. For example, in 2012 Ford opened a redesigned car plant in Louisville, Kentucky. Ford spent $600 million to transform the plant into the most flexible one in the company, capable of producing up to six different vehicles at the same time.

Expansion options give project managers the ability to add future capacity to a project at a relatively low marginal cost. For example, consider a company that currently needs a manufacturing facility totaling 50,000 square feet. If instead, it builds a facility now with 70,000 square feet of space, the cost to the company to expand by 20,000 square feet in the future may be less than if it has to build a separate 20,000-square-foot facility later. Even if the need for the additional capacity never materializes, the value of the expansion option may justify the cost of the larger initial facility beforehand, particularly if significant uncertainty about future product demand exists.

While option valuation in actual capital budgeting projects is complicated, financial managers should recognize the presence of options in projects and should consider including designed-in options when possible in planning projects.

Using conventional discounted cash flow analyses in capital budgeting without considering real options often results in a downward-biased estimate of the true value of a project's net present value. Some operating options, such as an option to expand, may increase a project's upside potential, while other operating options, such as an option to abandon, may reduce a project's downside risk.

10-6b How Are Real Options Concepts Being Applied?[12]

Real options analysis is being used in different ways by leading companies. Some firms use real options concepts to frame a *way of thinking* about decision analysis problems involving capital investments. This may be viewed as the foundation level of use of real options concepts. When used as a way of thinking about corporate investment problems, real options analysis increases awareness of the value of the various options that may exist within a project. It also helps managers to recognize that valuable options can be created or destroyed because of the decision actions taken by managers. When used in this way, real options concepts help managers to think about risk and uncertainty as assets that can be exploited in a project, rather than negative factors that should be avoided. In addition, real options thinking helps to focus managers on the value of acquiring additional information before making irrevocable investment decisions.

Other firms use real options concepts as *an analytical tool.* These firms apply formal option pricing models, such as the Black-Scholes model and the binomial option pricing model, to formally value the option characteristics of investment projects.[13] More complex models are also being used by a growing number of firms to value the option characteristics of investment projects. Some firms that have used real options approaches when analyzing various investment project opportunities include:

- Genentech has used the real options approach to value drug development projects.
- Intel has used the real options approach to value investments in flexible manufacturing facilities.
- Chevron has used the real options approach to value oil and gas development projects.
- Ford and Toyota have used the real options concept when building new plants.
- Boeing has used the real options concept when scheduling the production rate for the 747-8 plane.

A large amount of advanced work on real options has been done and more is being done. Financial managers should attempt to incorporate options analyses in project evaluations whenever possible.

10-7 Summary

- The net present value of an investment made by a firm represents the contribution of the investment to the value of the firm and, accordingly, to the wealth of shareholders.
- The net present value is calculated by subtracting a project's net investment from the expected net cash flows discounted at the firm's cost of capital.
- The *profitability index* is the ratio of the present value of net cash flows to the net investment. It gives a measure of the relative present value return per dollar of initial investment. The profitability index is useful when choosing among projects in a capital rationing situation.
- The *internal rate of return* of a project is the discount rate that gives the project a net present value equal to zero.
- The net present value and internal rate of return approaches normally yield the same accept-reject decisions for a particular project. However, conflicts may arise when dealing with *mutually exclusive* projects. The reinvestment rate assumption embodied in the net present value approach—namely, that cash flows from a project are reinvested at the cost of capital—generally is more realistic than that underlying the internal rate of return method. For this reason, the net present value method is preferred to the internal rate of return method.
- Financial managers must be aware that using conventional discounted cash flow techniques in capital budgeting without considering real options results in a downward-biased estimate of the true value of a project's net present value.

---

[12]This discussion is based on A. Triantis and A. Borison, "Real Options: State of the Practice," *Journal of Applied Corporate Finance* (Summer 2001): 25–40.

[13]See Chapter 20 for a discussion of option pricing models, such as the Black-Scholes model.

Important Equations

$$\text{NPV} = \text{PVNCF} - \text{NINV}$$
$$= \sum_{t=1}^{n} \text{NCF}_t \times \text{PVIF}_{k,t} - \text{NINV}$$

$$\text{PI} = \frac{\sum_{t=1}^{n} \text{NCF}_t/(1+k)^t}{\text{NINV}}$$

$$\sum_{t=1}^{n} \frac{\text{NCF}_t}{(1+r)^t} = \text{NINV}$$

$$\sum_{t=1}^{n} \text{NCF}_t \times \text{PVIF}_{r,t} = \text{NINV}$$

$$\text{PB} = \frac{\text{Net Investment}}{\text{Annual net cash inflows}}$$

10-8 Questions and Topics for Discussion

1. How does the net present value model complement the objective of maximizing shareholder wealth?
2. When is it possible for the net present value and the internal rate of return approaches to give conflicting rankings of mutually exclusive investment projects?
3. When are multiple rates of return likely to occur in an internal rate of return computation? What should be done when a multiple rate of return problem arises?
4. Describe how the profitability index approach may be used by a firm faced with a capital rationing investment funds constraint.
5. What are the primary strengths and weaknesses of the payback approach in capital budgeting?
6. What are the primary objectives of the investment project post-audit review?
7. What major problems can you foresee in applying capital budgeting techniques to investments made by public sector and not-for-profit enterprises or organizations?
8. What effect would you expect the use of MACRS depreciation rules to have on the acceptability of a project having a 10-year economic life but a 7-year MACRS classification?
9. What are the primary types of real options in capital budgeting? Give examples of each type.

10-9 Self-Test Problems

ST1. Calculate the net present value of a project with a net investment of $20,000 for equipment and an additional net working capital investment of $5,000 at time 0. The project is expected to generate net cash flows of $7,000 per year over a 10-year estimated economic life. In addition, the net working capital will be recovered at the end of the project. The required return on the project is 11 percent and the company has a marginal tax rate of 40 percent. What is the meaning of the computed net present value figure?

ST2. Calculate the internal rate of return and profitability index for a project that is expected to generate eight years of annual net cash flows of $75,000. The project has a net investment of $360,000 and the required return on the project is 12 percent.

ST3. Two mutually exclusive projects (G and H) have the following expected cash flows:

Year	G	H
0	$−10,000	$−10,000
1	5,000	0
2	5,000	0
3	5,000	17,000

a. Calculate the internal rate of return for each project.
b. Calculate the net present value for each project, assuming the firm's weighted cost of capital is 12 percent.
c. Which project should be adopted? Why?

ST4. A junior executive is fed up with the operating policies of his boss. Before leaving the office of his angered superior, the young man suggests that a well-trained monkey could handle the trivia assigned to him. Pausing a moment to consider the import of this closing statement, the boss is seized by the thought that this must have been in the back of her own mind ever since she hired the junior executive. She decides to consider replacing the executive with a bright young baboon. She figures that she could argue strongly to the board that such "capital deepening" is necessary for the cost-conscious firm. Two days later, a feasibility study is completed, and the following data are presented to the president:

- It would cost $12,000 to purchase and train a reasonably alert baboon with a life expectancy of 20 years.
- Annual expenses of feeding and housing the baboon would be $4,000.
- The junior executive's annual salary is $7,000 (a potential saving if the baboon is hired).
- The baboon will be depreciated on a straight-line basis over 20 years to a zero balance.
- The firm's marginal tax rate is 40 percent.
- The firm's current cost of capital is estimated to be 11 percent.

On the basis of the net present value criterion, should the monkey be hired (and the junior executive fired)?

10-10 Problems*

BASIC

1. Calculate the net present value and profitability index of a project with a net investment of $20,000 and expected net cash inflows of $3,000 a year for 10 years if the project's required return is 12 percent. Is the project acceptable?

*Color blocks behind the numbers denote problems that have check answers provided at the end of the book.

BASIC

2. A firm wishes to bid on a contract that is expected to yield the following after-tax net cash flows at the end of each year:

Year	Net Cash Flow
1	$5,000
2	8,000
3	9,000
4	8,000
5	8,000
6	5,000
7	3,000
8	$−1,500

To secure the contract, the firm must spend $30,000 to retool its plant. This retooling will have no salvage value at the end of the 8 years. Comparable investment alternatives are available to the firm that earn 12 percent compounded annually. The depreciation tax benefit from the retooling is reflected in the net cash flows in the table.

a. Compute the project's net present value.
b. Should the project be adopted?
c. What is the meaning of the computed net present value figure?

Spreadsheet Strategies

3. A machine that costs $8,000 is expected to operate for 10 years. The estimated salvage value at the end of 10 years is $0. The machine is expected to save the company $1,554 per year before taxes and depreciation. The company depreciates its assets on a straight-line basis and has a marginal tax rate of 40 percent. What is the internal rate of return on this investment?

INTERMEDIATE

4. Jefferson Products Inc. is considering purchasing a new automatic press brake, which costs $300,000 including installation and shipping. The machine is expected to generate net cash inflows of $80,000 per year for 10 years. At the end of 10 years, the book value of the machine will be $0, and it is anticipated that the machine will be sold for $100,000. If the press brake project is undertaken, Jefferson will have to increase its net working capital by $75,000. When the project is terminated in 10 years, there will no longer be a need for this incremental working capital, and it can be liquidated and made available to Jefferson for other uses. Jefferson requires a 12 percent annual return on this type of project and its marginal tax rate is 40 percent.

a. Calculate the press brake's net present value.
b. Is the project acceptable?
c. What is the meaning of the computed net present value figure?
d. What is the project's internal rate of return?
e. For the press brake project, at what annual rates of return do the net present value and internal rate of return methods assume that the net cash inflows are being reinvested?

BASIC

5. An acre planted with walnut trees is estimated to be worth $12,000 in 25 years. If you want to realize a 15 percent rate of return on your investment, how much can you afford to invest per acre? (Ignore all taxes and assume that annual cash outlays to maintain your stand of walnut trees are nil.)

BASIC

6. A company is planning to invest $100,000 (before tax) in a personnel training program. The $100,000 outlay will be charged off as an expense by the firm this year (year 0). The returns from the program in the form of greater productivity and a reduction in employee turnover are estimated as follows (on an after-tax basis):

Years 1–10:	$10,000 per year
Years 11–20:	$22,000 per year

The company has estimated its cost of capital to be 12 percent. Assume that the entire $100,000 is paid at time 0 (the beginning of the project). The marginal tax rate for the firm is 40 percent. Should the firm undertake the training program? Why or why not?

INTERMEDIATE

7. Two mutually exclusive investment projects have the following forecasted cash flows:

Year	A	B
0	$–20,000	$–20,000
1	+10,000	0
2	+10,000	0
3	+10,000	0
4	+10,000	+60,000

a. Compute the internal rate of return for each project.
b. Compute the net present value for each project if the firm has a 10 percent cost of capital.
c. Which project should be adopted? Why?

INTERMEDIATE

8. Show that the internal rate of return of the following investment is 0, 100, and 200 percent:

Net investment	$ –1,000	Year 0
Net cash flows	+6,000	Year 1
	–11,000	Year 2
	+6,000	Year 3

INTERMEDIATE

Spreadsheet Strategies

9. Commercial Hydronics is considering replacing one of its larger control devices. A new unit sells for $29,000 (delivered). An additional $3,000 will be needed to install the device. The new device has an estimated 20-year service life. The estimated salvage value at the end of 20 years will be $2,000. The new control device will be depreciated over 20 years on a straight-line basis to $0. The existing control device (original cost = $15,000) has been in use for 12 years, and it has been fully depreciated (that is, its book value equals zero). Its scrap value is estimated to be $1,000. The existing device could be used indefinitely, assuming the firm is willing to pay for its very high maintenance costs. The firm's marginal tax rate is 40 percent. The new control device requires lower maintenance costs and frees up personnel who normally would have to monitor the system. Estimated annual cash savings from the new device will be $9,000. The firm's cost of capital is 12 percent.

Evaluate the relative merits of replacing the old control device using the net present value approach.

BASIC

10. A $1,230 investment has the following expected cash returns:

Year	Net Cash Flow
1	$800
2	200
3	400

Compute the internal rate of return for this project.

CHALLENGE

11. Imperial Systems has $1 million available for capital investments during the current year. A list of possible investment projects, together with their net investments and net present values, is provided in the following table:

Project	Net Investment	Net Present Value
1	$200,000	$20,000
2	500,000	41,000
3	275,000	60,000
4	150,000	5,000
5	250,000	20,000
6	100,000	4,000
7	275,000	22,000
8	200,000	−18,000

a. Rank the various investment projects in terms of their profitability indexes (computed to three decimal places).
b. In the order of decreasing profitability index values and considering the capital constraints, which projects should be adopted? Are all capital funds expended?
c. Is there another combination that produces a higher aggregate net present value than the one developed in Part b?
d. If less than the entire amount of available funds is invested, what is the opportunity cost of the unused funds?

CHALLENGE

12. The L-S Mining Company is planning to open a new strip mine in western Pennsylvania. The net investment required to open the mine is $10 million. Net cash flows are expected to be +$20 million at the end of year 1 and +$5 million at the end of year 2. At the end of year 3, L-S will have a net cash *outflow* of $17 million to cover the cost of closing the mine and reclaiming the land.

a. Calculate the net present value of the strip mine if the cost of capital is 5, 10, 15, 30, 71, and 80 percent.
b. What is unique about this project?
c. Should the project be accepted if L-S's cost of capital is 10 percent? 20 percent?

CHALLENGE

Spreadsheet Strategies

13. Fred and Frieda have always wanted to enter the blueberry business. They locate a 50-acre piece of hillside in Maine that is covered with blueberry bushes. They figure that the annual yield from the bushes will be 200 crates. Each crate is estimated to sell for $400 for the next 10 years. This price is expected to rise to $500 per crate for all sales from years 11 through 20.

In order to get started, Fred and Frieda must pay $150,000 for the land plus $20,000 for packing equipment. The packing equipment will be depreciated on a straight-line basis to a zero estimated salvage value at the end of 20 years. Fred and Frieda believe that at the end of 20 years, they will want to retire to Florida and sell their property.

Annual operating expenses, including salaries to Fred and Frieda and exclusive of depreciation, are estimated to be $50,000 per year for the first 10 years and $60,000 thereafter. The land is expected to appreciate in value at a rate of 5 percent per year. The couple's marginal tax rate is 30 percent for both ordinary income and capital gains and losses.

a. If the couple requires at least a 13 percent return on their investment, should they enter the blueberry business?

b. Assume that the land can be sold for only $50,000 at the end of 20 years (a capital loss of $100,000). Should the couple invest in the land and blueberry business? (Assume that the couple may claim the full amount of their capital loss in the year it occurs—year 20.)

CHALLENGE

Spreadsheet Strategies

14. The Sisneros Company is considering building a chili processing plant in Hatch, New Mexico. The plant is expected to produce 50,000 pounds of processed chili peppers each year for the next 10 years. During the first year, Sisneros expects to sell the processed peppers for $2 per pound. The price is expected to increase at a 7 percent rate per year over the 10-year economic life of the plant. The costs of operating the plant, exclusive of depreciation, including the cost of fresh peppers, are estimated to be $50,000 during the first year. These costs are expected to increase at an 8 percent rate per year over the next 10 years.

The plant will cost $80,000 to build. It will be depreciated as a 7-year MACRS asset. The estimated salvage at the end of 10 years is zero. The firm's marginal tax rate is 40 percent.

a. Calculate the net investment required to build the plant.

b. Calculate the annual net cash flows from the project.

c. If Sisneros uses a 20 percent cost of capital to evaluate projects of this type, should the plant be built?

d. Calculate the payback period for this project.

e. How many internal rates of return does this project have? Why?

INTERMEDIATE

15. Note the following information on two mutually exclusive projects under consideration by Wang Food Markets, Inc.

ANNUAL CASH FLOWS

Year	A	B
0	$−30,000	$−60,000
1	10,000	20,000
2	10,000	20,000
3	10,000	20,000
4	10,000	20,000
5	10,000	20,000

Wang requires a 14 percent rate of return on projects of this nature.

a. Compute the NPV of both projects.

b. Compute the internal rate of return on both projects.

c. Compute the profitability index of both projects.

d. Compute the payback period on both projects.

e. Which of the two projects, if either, should Wang accept? Why?

INTERMEDIATE

16. Channel Tunnel Inc. plans to build an additional 23-mile-long tunnel under the English Channel for added train service. The cost (NINV) of the tunnel is expected to be $3.3 billion. Net cash inflows are expected to equal $651 million per year. How many years must the firm generate this cash inflow stream for investors to earn their required 19 percent rate of return?

CHALLENGE

Spreadsheet Strategies

17. Commercial Hydronics is considering replacing one of its larger control devices. A new unit sells for $29,000 (delivered). An additional $3,000 will be needed to install the device. The new device has an estimated 20-year service life. The estimated salvage value at the end of 20 years will be $2,000. The new control device will be depreciated as a 7-year MACRS asset. The existing control device (original cost = $15,000) has been in use for 12 years, and it has been fully depreciated (that is, its book value equals zero). Its scrap value is estimated to be $1,000. The existing device could be used indefinitely, assuming the firm is willing to pay for its very high maintenance costs. The firm's marginal tax rate is 40 percent. The new control device requires lower maintenance costs and frees up personnel who normally would have to monitor the system. Estimated annual cash savings from the new device will be $9,000. The firm's cost of capital is 12 percent.

Evaluate the relative merits of replacing the old control device using the net present value approach. (This problem is the same as problem 9 except for depreciation method. Comparing the answers you get to problems 9 and 17, what effect does the use of MACRS depreciation have on the economic desirability of the project?)

INTERMEDIATE

Spreadsheet Strategies

18. The Taylor Mountain Uranium Company currently has annual revenues of $1.2 million and annual expenses exclusive of depreciation of $700,000. Depreciation amounts to $200,000 per year. These figures are expected to remain constant for the foreseeable future (at least 15 years). The firm's marginal tax rate is 40 percent.

A new high-speed processing unit costing $1.2 million is being considered as a potential investment designed to increase the firm's output capacity. This new piece of equipment will have an estimated usable life of 10 years and a $0 estimated salvage value. If the processing unit is bought, Taylor's annual revenues are expected to increase to $1.6 million, and annual expenses exclusive of depreciation will increase to $900,000. Annual depreciation will increase to $320,000. Assume that no increase in net working capital will be required as a result of this project. (*Note:* This problem is the same as problem 7 in Chapter 9, except for the following questions.)

a. Calculate the processing unit's net present value, using a 12 percent required return.

b. Should Taylor accept the project?

c. How many internal rates of return does the processing unit project have? Why?

d. Calculate the processing unit's internal rate of return.

CHALLENGE

Spreadsheet Strategies

19. Benford Inc. is planning to open a new sporting goods store in a suburban mall. Benford will lease the needed space in the mall. Equipment and fixtures for the store will cost $200,000 and be depreciated to $0 over a 5-year period on a straight-line basis. The new store will require Benford to increase its net working capital by $200,000 at time 0.

First-year sales are expected to be $1 million and to increase at an annual rate of 8 percent over the expected 10-year life of the store. Operating expenses (including lease payments but excluding depreciation) are projected to be $700,000 during the first year and to increase at a 7 percent annual rate. The salvage value of the store's equipment and fixtures is anticipated to be $10,000 at the end of 10 years.

Benford's marginal tax rate is 40 percent. (*Note:* This problem is the same as problem 12 in Chapter 9, except for the following questions.)

a. Calculate the store's net present value, using an 18 percent required return.
b. Should Benford accept the project?
c. Calculate the store's internal rate of return.
d. Calculate the store's profitability index.

CHALLENGE

Spreadsheet Strategies

20. Seco Dame Enterprises (SDE) acquired a robotic saw six years ago at a cost of $10 million. The saw was depreciated to its current book value of $0. Actual salvage value today is estimated to be $2 million. SDE's average tax rate is 30 percent, and its marginal tax rate is 40 percent. The weighted cost of capital for SDE is 15 percent.

A new robotic saw will cost $15 million. It will be depreciated under MACRS rules for a 7-year class asset. If SDE acquires the new saw, it estimates that its net working capital investment will decline, due to the reduced need to carry inventories of spare parts for this more reliable machine. Net working capital should decline from a current level of $1 million to a new level of $500,000 as a result of this purchase.

a. Calculate the net investment required to acquire the new saw.
b. The new saw is expected to reduce operating costs (exclusive of depreciation) for SDE by $800,000 per year over the asset's expected 10-year life. Also, the increased productivity of the new saw is expected to increase SDE's revenue by $2 million per year. Salvage value at the end of 10 years is expected to be $0. Calculate the annual net cash flows for this investment.
c. Compute the NPV for this project.

INTERMEDIATE

21. Project Alpha requires an outlay of $10,000 immediately. Project Alpha has a 1-year life and is expected to produce a net cash flow at the end of one year of $20,000. Project Beta, a mutually exclusive alternative to Alpha, requires an outlay of $20,000 immediately. It too is expected to have a 1-year life and to produce a net cash flow at the end of one year of $35,000.

a. Compute the internal rate of return for both projects. Compute the NPV for both projects, using a cost of capital of 10 percent.
b. Which project should be undertaken?

INTERMEDIATE

22. International Foods Corporation, a U.S.-based food company, is considering expanding its soup-processing operations in Switzerland. The company plans a net investment of $8 million in the project. The current spot exchange rate is SF6.25 per dollar (SF = Swiss francs). Net cash flows for the expansion project are estimated to be SF5 million for 10 years and nothing thereafter. Based on its analysis of current conditions in Swiss capital markets, International Foods has determined that the applicable cost of capital for the project is 16 percent. Calculate the net present value of the proposed expansion project.

INTERMEDIATE

23. You have just been named the chief financial officer of Fabco, a large metal fabricator located in Chama, New Mexico. The company has long been a user of the net present value method for evaluating its investment projects. The firm undertakes all projects offering a positive net present value, based upon data submitted by the project proposer. Fabco's weighted cost of capital has been estimated to be 15 percent. This capital cost has remained approximately constant over the past five years.

Over the past 5 years, Fabco has earned a return on assets averaging 8 percent. You are concerned about the apparent disagreement between Fabco's cost of capital and its earned returns. The CEO has asked you to prepare a report on the situation. What factors (both within and outside of the firm) might account for this *apparent* discrepancy in performance?

INTEGRATIVE CASE PROBLEM

Capital Budgeting

First Republic Bancorp is considering the acquisition of a new data processing and management information system. The system, including computer hardware and software, will cost $1 million. Delivery and installation of the system is expected to add $100,000 to this cost. To put this new system in place, the bank expects to have to make an investment of $50,000 in net working capital immediately and an additional net working capital investment of $25,000 at the end of year 1. The system has an expected economic life of 10 years. It will be depreciated as a 7-year asset under MACRS rules. Actual salvage value at the end of 10 years is expected to be $100,000, and the bank plans to sell the system for its salvage value at that time.

The new data processing system will save the bank the $190,000 fee per year that it currently pays to a computer time-sharing company. Operating, maintenance, and insurance costs for the system are estimated to total $50,000 during the first year. These costs are expected to increase at a rate of 7 percent per year over the 10-year period.

First Republic plans to sell excess computer time to a number of local firms. The demand function for this service during year 1 is estimated to be:

$$Q = 20{,}000 - 200P$$

where Q = number of units of computer time sold, and P = price per unit of computer time sold.

Based on an analysis of the local market for computer time, the bank feels that it can charge $14 per unit of computer time. Although the bank does not anticipate changing this charge over the 10-year period, it expects the quantity demanded to decline by 5 percent per year after year 1. It is expected that these outside sales of computer time will cost the bank an *additional $40,000 per year* in computer operating costs (including the salary of a computer services representative to handle the new customers). These additional operating costs are expected to increase at a rate of 7 percent annually over the 10-year period.

The bank has a marginal ordinary tax rate of 34 percent. This rate is expected to remain in effect over the life of the project. First Republic uses an after-tax cost of capital of 15 percent to evaluate projects of this risk. This cost of capital was computed based upon the current after-tax cost of equity and debt funds in the bank's capital structure.

Based on the information contained in the case, use the NPV approach to determine if First Republic should acquire the new data processing system.

APPENDIX **10A**

MUTUALLY EXCLUSIVE INVESTMENTS HAVING UNEQUAL LIVES

Replacement Chains

Chapter 10 discusses a number of capital budgeting decision models. When mutually exclusive investments are considered, it is assumed implicitly that the alternative projects have *equal lives.* In actual practice, however, this may not be the case. When two or more mutually exclusive alternatives have *unequal* lives, neither the net present value nor the internal rate of return method yields reliable accept-reject information unless the projects are evaluated for an equal period of time. If, for example, a firm adopts the longer-lived of two projects simply on the basis of net present value or internal rate of return data, it essentially ignores any alternative investment opportunities that might have been available at the end of the shorter-lived project.

Suppose Agrigrow Seed Company is considering two mutually exclusive investments, I and II. Project I requires an initial outlay of $2,000,000 and is expected to generate a 5-year stream of net cash flows of $600,000 per year. Project II also requires an initial outlay of $2,000,000 but is expected to generate a 10-year stream of net cash flows of $375,000 per year. The firm has a 10 percent cost of capital.

Table 10A.1 shows that the net present value of Project I is $274,600 and the net present value of Project II is $304,370. Therefore, the net present value criterion suggests that Project II should be chosen over Project I.

The expected life of Project II is twice as long as that of Project I. Therefore, the two net present values calculated in Table 10A.1 are not really comparable. At this point, Agrigrow must also consider what might happen if Project I were replaced with a similar 5-year life project at the end of 5 years. In other words, it would create a *replacement chain* for the shorter-lived project. Suppose, for example, the firm estimates that replacing Project I with a similar project at the end of five years would cost $2,100,000 and,

TABLE **10A.1**

Cash Flows for Projects I and II: Agrigrow Seed Company

	Project I		Project II	
Year	**Net Investment**	**Net Cash Flow**	**Net Investment**	**Net Cash Flow**
0	$2,000,000	—	$2,000,000	—
1		$600,000		$375,000
2		600,000		375,000
3		600,000		375,000
4		600,000		375,000
5		600,000		375,000
6		—		375,000
7		—		375,000
8		—		375,000
9		—		375,000
10		—		375,000

$NPV_I = -\$2,000,000 + \$600,000(3.791) = \$274,600$ $NPV_{II} = -\$2,000,000 + \$375,000(6.145) = \$304,370$

TABLE 10A.2

Replacement Chain Cash Flows for Project I Compared with Project II: Agrigrow Seed Company

	Project I		Project II	
Year	Net Investment	Net Cash Flow	Net Investment	Net Cash Flow
0	$2,000,000	—	$2,000,000	—
1		$600,000		$375,000
2		600,000		375,000
3		600,000		375,000
4		600,000		375,000
5	2,100,000	600,000		375,000
6		600,000		375,000
7		600,000		375,000
8		600,000		375,000
9		600,000		375,000
10		600,000		375,000

$NPV_I = -\$2,000,000 + \$600,000(6.145) - \$2,100,000(0.621) = \$382,800$ $NPV_{II} = -\$2,000,000 + \$375,000(6.145) = \$304,370$

like Project I, would generate annual net cash flows of $600,000. This results in a new stream of cash flows for Project I, as shown in Table 10A.2. The new net present value for Project I is higher than that for Project II, thus indicating—correctly—that Project I should be chosen over Project II.

Many times it is not possible to get a series of projects (such as Project I with its replacement at the end of five years) that will have an identical time duration to that of the longer-lived project (II). For example, one project might have a life of 15 years, whereas an alternative requires replacement every 8 years. Hence, the shorter-lived project together with its replacement have a 16-year life, whereas the longer-lived project has a 15-year life. Such a comparison will normally be acceptable because the discrepancy occurs for only one year that is 16 years in the future. In present value terms, this will not have much impact.

The importance of time discrepancies such as these depends on the following:

- **The number of years of the discrepancy.** The fewer the years of the discrepancy, the less important it is.
- **The number of years into the future the discrepancy occurs.** The further into the future, the less important the discrepancy is.
- **The relationship between the rate of return on future investments and the cost of capital.** When the rate of return on future investments is equal to the cost of capital, these investments have an NPV = 0. Under these circumstances, the discrepancy can be ignored.

Equivalent Annual Annuities

An alternative approach for dealing with the problem of mutually exclusive investments having unequal lives is to use the equivalent annual annuity approach. This technique can solve the problem of time discrepancies often encountered when using the replacement chain approach.

For example, consider the case of Muncie Tool Company, which needs to replace an aging piece of machinery. One alternative would be to buy new Machine A, having a 9-year life. Another alternative would be to buy new Machine B, with a 5-year life.

In this case, the time discrepancy between A and B is significant—four years. Commonly, this problem is dealt with by developing a string of replacement chains out to a year when both machines would need replacement. The common denominator year in this case is 45 years—indicating nine investments in B and five investments in A.

In cases like this, the equivalent annual annuity approach is often easier to use. In our example, assume the new Machine A will require a net investment of $34,500 and generate net cash flows of $7,000 per year for nine years. Machine B will require a net investment of $25,000 and generate net cash flows of $8,000 per year for five years. Muncie Tool's cost of capital is 10 percent. To make our decision on the basis of the equivalent annual annuity criterion, we use the following three steps:

1. First, compute the net present value of each machine over its original expected economic life:

$$\begin{aligned} NPV_A &= -\$34{,}500 + \$7{,}000(PVIFA_{0.10,9}) \\ &= -\$34{,}500 + \$7{,}000(5.759) \\ &= \$5{,}813 \\ NPV_B &= -\$25{,}000 + \$8{,}000(PVIFA_{0.10,5}) \\ &= -\$25{,}000 + \$8{,}000(3.791) \\ &= \$5{,}328 \end{aligned}$$

   As these calculations indicate, if the possibility of the replacement of Machine B at the end of five years is not considered, Machine A would appear to be the better alternative because of its greater net present value.

2. Next, divide the net present value for each machine computed in step 1 by the PVIFA factor for the project's original life. This gives the *equivalent annual annuity*:

$$\begin{aligned} \text{Equivalent annual annuity (A)} &= \frac{\$5{,}813}{PVIFA_{0.10;9}} \\ &= \frac{\$5{,}813}{5.759} \\ &= \$1{,}009.38 \\ \text{Equivalent annual annuity (B)} &= \frac{\$5{,}328}{PVIFA_{0.10,5}} \\ &= \frac{\$5{,}328}{3.791} \\ &= \$1{,}405.43 \end{aligned}$$

3. The equivalent annual annuity method assumes that each machine will be replaced an infinite number of times into the future and therefore will provide these annual annuities in perpetuity. As perpetuities, these equivalent annual annuities can be valued (at present) by dividing the annuity amount by the cost of capital:[1]

$$\begin{aligned} NPV_A \text{ (assuming infinite replacement)} &= \frac{\$1{,}009.38}{0.10} \\ &= \$10{,}093.80 \\ NPV_B \text{ (assuming infinite replacement)} &= \frac{\$1{,}405.43}{0.10} \\ &= \$14{,}054.30 \end{aligned}$$

   Machine B should be acquired because it has the higher net present value when evaluated over an infinite replacement horizon.

[1]Recall from Chapter 5 that the present value of a perpetuity (PVPER) is equal to the payment (PMT) divided by the interest rate (i). See Equation 5.22.

In general, the equivalent annual annuity method will give the same decision as the replacement chain technique. Its advantage is that it often is computationally simpler, and it simplifies the handling of the time discrepancies that frequently arise in the replacement chain method.

Problems*

CHALLENGE

1. The Smith Pie Company is considering two mutually exclusive investments that would increase its capacity to make strawberry tarts. The firm uses a 12 percent cost of capital to evaluate potential investments. The two projects have the following costs and expected cash flow streams:

Year	Alternative A	Alternative B	Year	Alternative A	Alternative B
0	−$30,000	−$30,000	5	—	$6,500
1	10,500	6,500	6	—	6,500
2	10,500	6,500	7	—	6,500
3	10,500	6,500	8	—	6,500
4	10,500	6,500			

a. Using these data, calculate the net present value for Projects A and B.
b. Create a replacement chain for Alternative A. Assume that the cost of replacing A will be $30,000 and that the replacement project will generate cash flows of $10,500 for years 5 through 8. Using these figures, recompute the net present value for Alternative A.
c. Which of the two alternatives should be chosen, A or B? Why?
d. Use the equivalent annual annuity method to solve this problem. How does your answer compare with the one obtained in Part b?

CHALLENGE

2. BC Minerals is considering a new production process. Two alternative pieces of equipment are available. Alternative P costs $100,000, has a 10-year life, and is expected to generate annual cash inflows of $22,000 in each of the 10 years. Alternative R costs $85,000, has an 8-year life and is expected to generate annual cash inflows of $18,000 in each of the 8 years. BC Minerals's weighted cost of capital is 12 percent. Using the equivalent annual annuity method, which alternative should be chosen?

CHALLENGE

3. Germania Corporation is considering replacing its plant cooling unit. The existing unit has recently "died" and has no salvage value. Of the two competing cooling units, B has a long life but a higher initial cost than the cheaper unit A. The following data are available:

Year	NCF_A	NCF_B	Year	NCF_A	NCF_B
0	−$50,000	−$79,000	3	$25,000	$28,000
1	25,000	28,000	4	—	28,000
2	25,000	28,000	5	—	28,000

The marginal cost of capital is 19 percent. Which cooling unit should be purchased? Why?

*Color blocks behind the numbers denote problems that have check answers provided at the end of the book.

CHALLENGE

Spreadsheet Strategies

4. Turbomachinery Parts Inc. is considering two mutually exclusive equipment investments that would increase its production capacity. The firm uses a 14 percent required rate of return to evaluate capital expenditure projects. The two investments have the following costs and expected cash flow streams:

Year	Investment D	Investment E	Year	Investment D	Investment E
0	−$50,000	−$50,000	4	—	$15,000
1	24,000	15,000	5	—	15,000
2	24,000	15,000	6	—	15,000
3	24,000	15,000			

a. Calculate the net present value for Investments D and E.

b. Create a replacement chain for Investment D. Assume that the cost of replacing D remains at $50,000 and that the replacement project will generate cash inflows of $24,000 for years 4 through 6. Using these figures, recompute the net present value for Investment D.

c. Which of the two investments should be chosen, D or E? Why?

d. Use the equivalent annual annuity method to solve this problem. How does your answer compare with the one obtained in Part b?

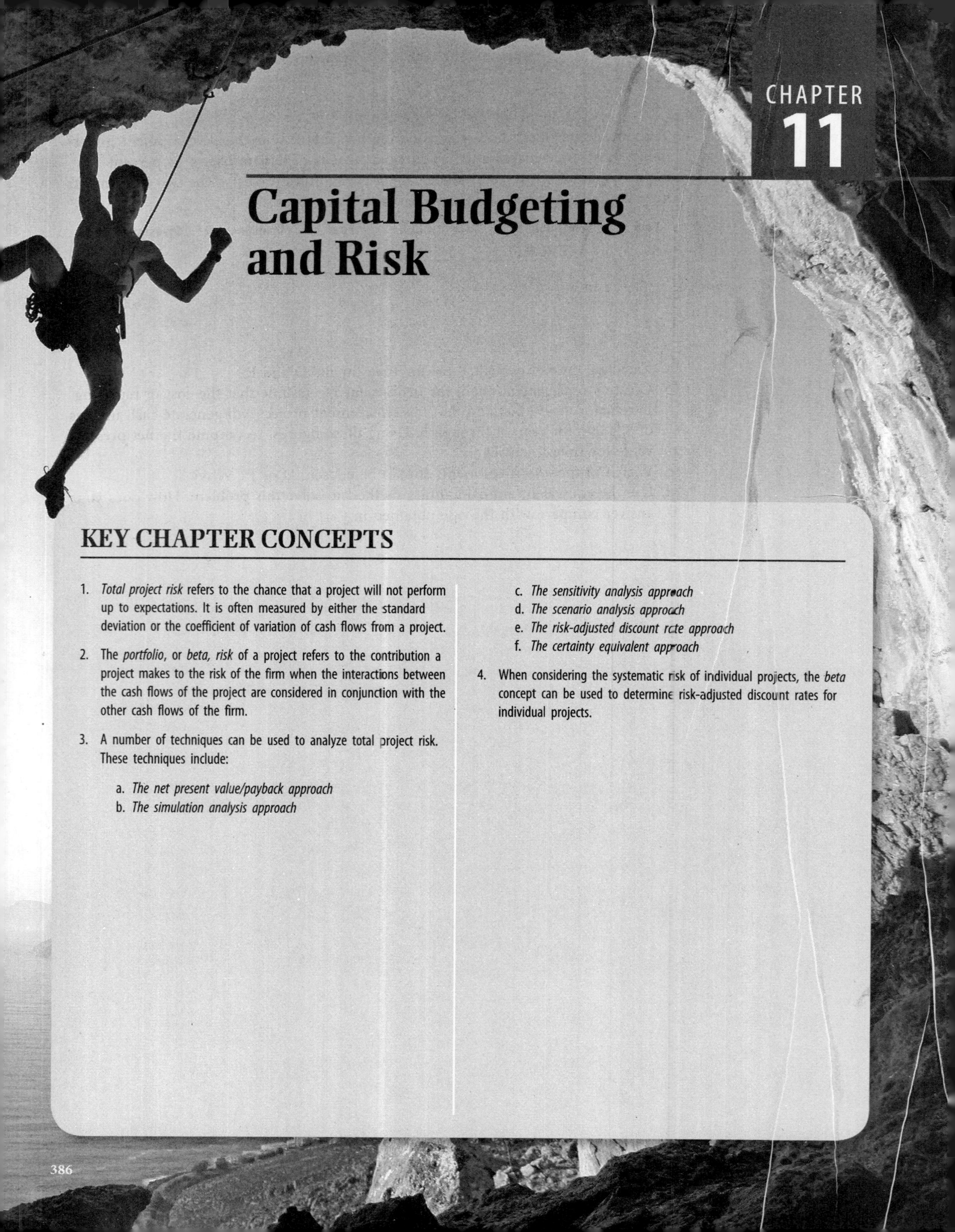

CHAPTER 11

Capital Budgeting and Risk

KEY CHAPTER CONCEPTS

1. *Total project risk* refers to the chance that a project will not perform up to expectations. It is often measured by either the standard deviation or the coefficient of variation of cash flows from a project.
2. The *portfolio*, or *beta, risk* of a project refers to the contribution a project makes to the risk of the firm when the interactions between the cash flows of the project are considered in conjunction with the other cash flows of the firm.
3. A number of techniques can be used to analyze total project risk. These techniques include:
    a. *The net present value/payback approach*
    b. *The simulation analysis approach*
    c. *The sensitivity analysis approach*
    d. *The scenario analysis approach*
    e. *The risk-adjusted discount rate approach*
    f. *The certainty equivalent approach*
4. When considering the systematic risk of individual projects, the *beta* concept can be used to determine risk-adjusted discount rates for individual projects.

FINANCIAL CHALLENGE

Pharmaceutical Risks: Clinical Drug Test Failures

The pharmaceutical industry is characterized by the high profits and high risks associated with bringing new drug compounds to market. For every 1,000 new drug compounds identified by companies, only 30 show promising results. Only three of these compounds get past Phase 1 FDA tests, and only one gets past Phases 2 and 3 and makes it to the market. Some products that make it to the market turn out to be commercial failures even though they are successful in treating a condition or a disease. On average, it takes 12 to 15 years to bring a new compound to the market as an approved drug, and it costs, on average, between $800 million and $1.7 billion. Money invested in unsuccessful compounds is a sunk cost and cannot be recovered. Thus the decision by a pharmaceutical company to invest in a new compound is both very expensive and extremely risky.

Novo Nordisk is a large Danish pharmaceutical company with sales in 2014 of approximately $7.4 billion. Novo Nordisk dominates the worldwide diabetes market, with approximately a 27 percent market share. The company had been working to develop a long-acting, novel insulin product to be marketed under the name Tresiba. Tresiba was believed to have the potential to be a blockbuster drug, with sales that could total $6 billion.

Plans to bring this product to market were dealt a blow by a decision in February 2013 by the Food and Drug Administration (FDA). The FDA was concerned that this new product could increase the risk of cardiovascular events, compared to other products already on the market. The FDA ordered the company to gather "additional cardiovascular data from a dedicated cardiovascular outcomes trial before review of the new drug application can be completed." This requirement for additional tests was expected to delay the launch of the product by at least two years (and cost the company two years' worth of sales and the loss of two years of patent protection). The stock market reaction to this setback was swift and significant. Novo Nordisk's stock declined by 14 percent when the information became public, wiping out $14 billion of the company's market value.

Other recent pharmaceutical clinical trial failures include Sanofi (write-off of $525 million related to the clinical failure of Iniparib, a cancer drug), GlaxoSmithKline (write-off of $246 million related to the clinical failure of Darapladib, a heart disease drug), Merck (write-off of $181 million related to the

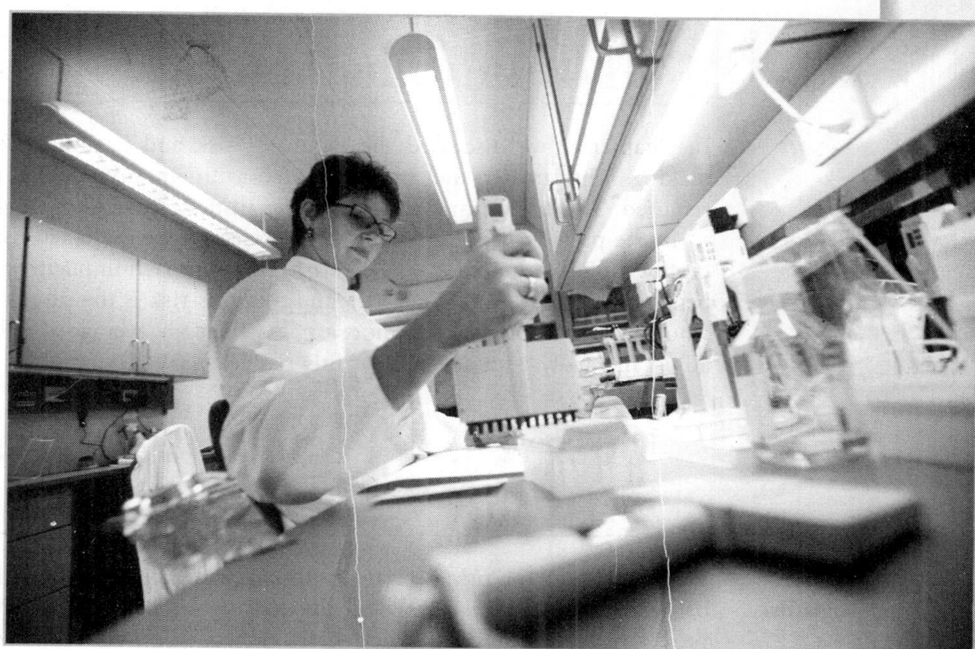

John Mcconnico/Bloomberg/Getty Images

FINANCIAL CHALLENGE — CONTINUED

clinical failure of Preladenant, a Parkinson's disease drug), and Astra Zeneca (write-off of $136 million related to the clinical failure of Fostamatinib, a rheumatoid arthritis drug).

Although risk cannot be eliminated when considering investment projects like these, a capable financial manager should try to determine at the outset what risks are being assumed when a project is undertaken. What is the worst-case outcome? How likely is that outcome? What actions can be taken to reduce the risk? How will investors react to the risk? Given the answers to these questions, risky projects can be evaluated properly. This chapter examines these important questions.

Sources: Pharmaceutical Research and Manufacturers of America, *Pharmaceutical Industry Profile 2009* (Washington, DC: PhRMA, April 2009); "Research and Development in the Pharmaceutical Industry" *A CBO Study* (Washington, DC: Congressional Budget Office, October 2006); Clemens Bomsdorf, "FDA Rebuffs Insulin Drug," *The Wall Street Journal* (February 12, 2013): B1. A. Philippidis, "Top 10 Clinical Trial failures of 2013," www.genengnews.com/insight-and-intelligence/top-10-clinical-trial-failures-of-2013/77900029/?page=2.

CHAPTER OBJECTIVES

Upon completion of this chapter, you should have a clear understanding of the following:

1. The difference between total project risk and portfolio risk
2. The measurement and evaluation of differences in the riskiness of projects
3. The concept of beta risk in capital investment project evaluation

11-1 Introduction

In Chapter 8, we discussed the nature of risk and its influence on financial decision making. The greater the risk associated with an investment, the greater the return required. This basic principle also applies in the capital budgeting area.

In the previous chapter, investment projects were evaluated using the firm's weighted cost of capital (required rate of return). This approach implicitly assumes that all projects being considered are of equal risk and that this risk is the same as that for the firm as a whole. When a project has more or less than an average risk level, it is necessary to adjust the analysis to account for this risk level.

11-2 Total Project Risk Versus Portfolio Risk

beta risk

When analyzing the risk associated with a capital expenditure, it is important to distinguish between the *total project risk* and the *portfolio* or **beta risk** of that investment. By total project risk we mean the chance that a project will perform below expectations—possibly resulting in losses from the project and for the firm. In the worst case, these losses could be so severe as to cause the firm to fail.

HTTP:
The Society for Risk Analysis (SRA) provides current information on risk assessment, communication, and management, and their official publication, *Risk Analysis,* deals with the social, psychological, and theoretical aspects of risk. See:
www.sra.org

In contrast, a project that has a high level of total project risk may not affect the portfolio risk of the firm at all. Consider the case of oil and gas exploration companies. The firms know that any wildcat well they drill will cost about \$2 million and have only a 10 percent chance of success. Successful wells produce profits of \$24 million. Unsuccessful wells produce no profits at all, and the entire investment will be a loss. If each firm only drilled one well, there would be a 90 percent chance the firm would fail (the total project risk would be very high). In contrast, if one firm drilled 100 wildcat wells, the risk of failure from all wells would be very low because of the portfolio risk reduction that results from drilling many wells. In this case, the expected return of the firm would be as follows:

$$\begin{aligned}\text{Expected return} &= \frac{\text{Expected profit per well}}{\text{Investment required per well}}\\ &= \frac{(\text{Probability of success})(\text{Profit}) + (\text{Probability of failure})(\text{Loss})}{\text{Investment required per well}}\\ &= \frac{0.10\ (\$24\text{ million}) + 0.90\ (-\ \$2\text{ million})}{\$2\text{ million}}\\ &= \frac{\$2.4\text{ million} - \$1.8\text{ million}}{\$2\text{ million}}\\ &= 0.30,\text{ or }30\%\end{aligned}$$

This return is achieved with very little risk relative to that facing a firm drilling a single well. As this example illustrates, the risk of drilling any individual well can be diversified away very effectively. Consequently, these risks are not market related, and they should have little, if any, impact on the beta risk of the firm. That risk remains unchanged and approximately equal to the market risk facing other oil and gas exploration companies.

This example has shown that an investment with high total project risk does not necessarily have to possess high beta (systematic) risk. Of course, it is possible for a project to have both high total project risk and high beta risk. For example, a grocery-store chain (which typically has low beta risk) might decide to develop and market a new line of small business computers. Because of the large number of competitors in this business and because of the grocery chain's lack of expertise, this investment can be expected to have a high level of total project risk. At the same time, the beta risk of this investment is likely to be high relative to that of the grocery chain, because business computer sales expand rapidly during boom periods and slow down dramatically during recessions.

From a capital budgeting perspective, the beta risk of a project is certainly important because the beta of a firm influences the returns required by investors in that firm and hence the value of the firm's shares.

Total project risk is also important to consider in most cases for several reasons. There are a number of relatively undiversified investors, including the owners of small firms, for whom total project and total firm risk are important. Also, the total risk of the firm—not just the beta risk—determines the risk of firm failure and potential bankruptcy. Stockholders, creditors, managers, and other employees all are interested in preventing the tragedy (and avoiding the costs) of total firm failure.

Consequently, in the evaluation of an investment project, it is important to consider both the total project risk and the impact of the project on the beta risk of the firm. We continue the chapter with a discussion of a number of techniques that can be used to account for total project risk in the capital budgeting process. In the final section, we examine techniques to use when evaluating the beta risk of a project.

11-3 Adjusting for Total Project Risk

The risk adjustment procedures discussed in this section are appropriate when the firm believes that a project's total risk is the relevant risk to consider in evaluating the project and when it is assumed that the returns from the project being considered are highly positively correlated with the returns from the firm as a whole. Therefore, these methods are appropriate only in the absence of internal firm diversification benefits, which might change the firm's total risk (or the systematic portion of total risk).

Several different techniques are used to analyze total project risk. These include the *net present value/payback approach, simulation analysis, sensitivity analysis, scenario analysis*, the *risk-adjusted discount rate approach*, and the *certainty equivalent approach*. In addition, total project risk can be measured by calculating the standard deviation and coefficient of variation. These calculations are discussed in Chapter 8.

11-3a Net Present Value/Payback Approach

Many firms combine net present value (NPV) with payback (PB) when analyzing project risk. As noted in Chapter 10, the project payback period is the length of time required to recover the net investment. Because cash flow estimates tend to become more uncertain further into the future, applying a payback cutoff point can help reduce this degree of uncertainty. For example, a firm may decide not to accept projects unless they have positive net present values *and* paybacks of less than some stated number of years.

The net present value/payback method is both simple and inexpensive, but it suffers from some notable weaknesses. First, the choice of which payback criterion should be applied is purely subjective and not directly related to the variability of returns from a project. Some investments may have relatively certain cash flows far into the future, whereas others may not. The use of a single payback cutoff point fails to allow for this. Second, some projects are more risky than others during their start-up periods; the payback criterion also fails to recognize this. Finally, this approach may cause a firm to reject some actually acceptable projects. In spite of these weaknesses, however, some firms feel this approach is helpful when screening investment alternatives, particularly international investments in politically unstable countries and investments in products characterized by rapid technological advances. Also, firms that have difficulty raising external capital and thus are concerned about the timing of internally generated cash flows often find a consideration of a project's payback period to be useful.

11-3b Simulation Analysis

Computers have made it both feasible and relatively inexpensive to apply simulation techniques to capital budgeting decisions. The simulation approach is generally more appropriate for analyzing larger projects. A **simulation** is a financial planning tool that models some event. When simulation is used in capital budgeting, it requires that estimates be made of the probability distribution of each cash flow element (revenues, expenses, and so on). If, for example, a firm is considering introducing a new product, the elements of a simulation might include the number of units sold, market price, unit production costs, unit selling costs, the purchase price of the machinery needed to produce the new product, and the cost of capital. These probability distributions are then entered into the simulation model to compute the project's net present value probability distribution.

simulation

Recall from Chapter 10 that net present value is defined as follows (Equation 10.2):

$$\text{NPV} = \sum_{t=1}^{n} \frac{\text{NCF}_t}{(1+\text{k})^t} - \text{NINV}$$

where NCF_t is the net cash flow in period t, NINV is the net investment, and k is the cost of capital. In any period, NCF_t may be computed as follows:

(11.1)
$$NCF_t = [q(p) - q(c + s) - Dep](1 - T) + Dep - \Delta NWC$$

where q is the number of units sold; p, the price per unit; c, the unit production cost (excluding depreciation); s, the unit selling cost; Dep, the annual depreciation; ΔNWC, the change in net working capital; and T, the firm's marginal tax rate. Using Equation 11.1, it is possible to simulate the net present value of the project. Based on the probability distribution of each of the elements that influence the net present value, one value for each element is selected at random.

Assume, for example, that the Wilshire Company is performing a simulation analysis and that the following values for the input variables are randomly chosen: $q = 2{,}000$; $p = \$10$; $c = \$2$; $s = \$1$; $Dep = \$2{,}000$; $\Delta NWC = \$1{,}200$; and $T = 40\%$, or 0.40. Inserting these values into Equation 11.1 gives the following calculations:

$$\begin{aligned} NCF_t &= [2{,}000(\$10)] - 2{,}000(\$2 + \$1) - \$2{,}000](1 - 0.40) + \$2{,}000 - \$1{,}200 \\ &= (\$20{,}000 - \$6{,}000 - \$2{,}000)0.60 + \$2{,}000 - \$1{,}200 \\ &= \$8{,}000 \end{aligned}$$

Assuming that the net investment is equal to the purchase price of the machinery ($10,000, in this example), that the net cash flows in each year of the project's life are identical, except for year 5, when $6,000 of NWC is recovered, that $k = 10\%$,[1] and that the project has a 5-year life, the net present value of this particular iteration of the simulation can be computed as follows:

$$\begin{aligned} NPV &= \frac{\$8{,}000}{(1+0.10)^1} + \frac{\$8{,}000}{(1+0.10)^2} + \frac{\$8{,}000}{(1+0.10)^3} + \frac{\$8{,}000}{(1+0.10)^4} \\ &\quad + \frac{\$14{,}000}{(1+0.10)^5} - \$10{,}000 \\ &= \$8{,}000 \times PVIFA_{0.10,4} + \$14{,}000 \times PVIF_{0.10,5} - \$10{,}000 \\ &= \$8{,}000 \times 3.170 + \$14{,}000 \times 0.621 - \$10{,}000 \\ &= \$24{,}054 \end{aligned}$$

In an actual simulation, the computer program is run a number of different times, using different randomly selected input variables in each instance. Thus, the program can be said to be repeated, or iterated, and each run is termed an *iteration*.[2] In each iteration, the net present value for the project would be computed accordingly. Figure 11.1 illustrates a typical simulation approach.

The results of these iterations are then used to plot a probability distribution of the project's net present values and to compute a mean and a standard deviation of returns.[3] This information provides the decision maker with an estimate of a project's expected returns, as well as its risk. Given this information, it is possible to compute the probability of achieving a net present value that is greater or less than any particular value.

[1]A strong case can be made for using a risk-free rate to discount the cash flows generated in a simulation analysis because the simulation technique directly considers risk by generating a probability distribution of the project's NPV or IRR. To use the cost of capital as the discount rate will result in a double counting of risk. Although this is correct, when a risk-free rate is used as the discount rate, the NPV that results is difficult to interpret. For this reason, many practitioners prefer to use the cost of capital when performing simulation analyses.

[2]Normally, 100 or more iterations of a simulation model are performed.

[3]Regardless of the shape of the probability distribution for the individual variables used in the simulation, the net present value probability distribution will often be normally, or near normally, distributed.

FIGURE 11.1

An Illustration of the Simulation Approach

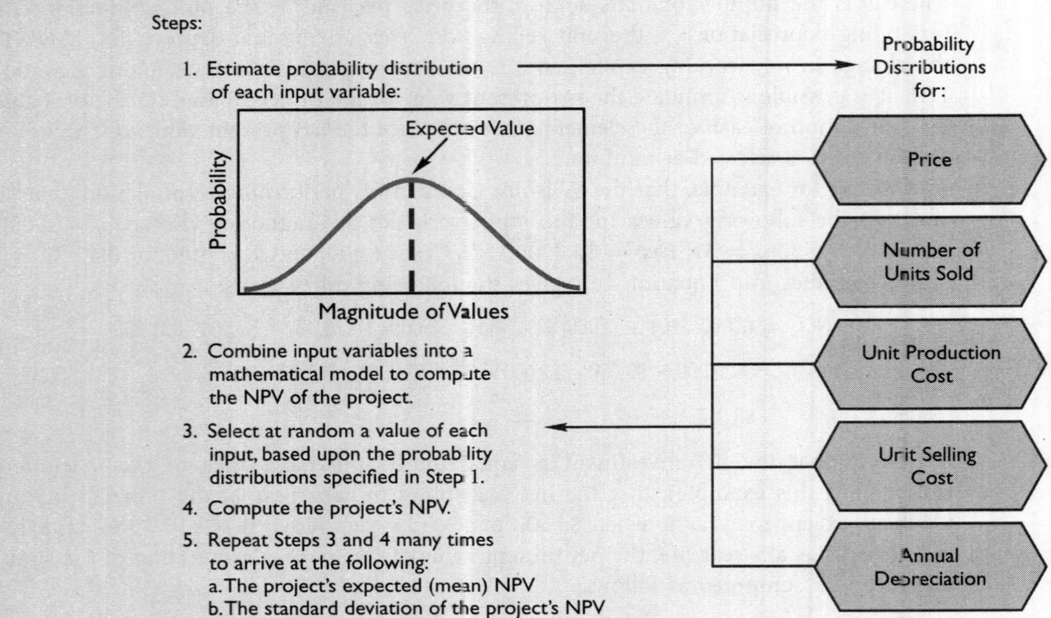

For example, assume that the simulation for the Wilshire Company investment project previously illustrated results in an expected net present value ($\widehat{NPV}$) of $12,000, with a standard deviation (σ) of $6,000. The probability of the project's having a net present value of $0 or less now can be found using the standard normal probability distribution (Table V) and Equation 8.3 from Chapter 8 (substituting NPV for r as the variable of interest). A value of $0 corresponds to:

$$z = \frac{\text{NPV} - \widehat{\text{NPV}}}{\sigma}$$

$$= \frac{\$0 - \$12{,}000}{\$6{,}000}$$

$$z = -2.0$$

or, 2.0 standard deviations *below* the mean on the standard normal probability distribution.

It can be seen from Table V that the probability of a value less than −2.0 standard deviations from the mean is 2.28 percent. Thus, there is a 2.28 percent chance that the actual net present value for this project will be negative. Figure 11.2 shows the probability distribution of this project's net present value. The shaded area under the curve represents the probability that the project will have a net present value of $0 or less.

The simulation approach is a powerful one because it explicitly recognizes all of the interactions among the variables that influence a project's net present value. It provides both a mean net present value and a standard deviation that can help the decision maker

FIGURE 11.2

Wilshire Company: Probability That a Project's Return Will Be Less Than $0

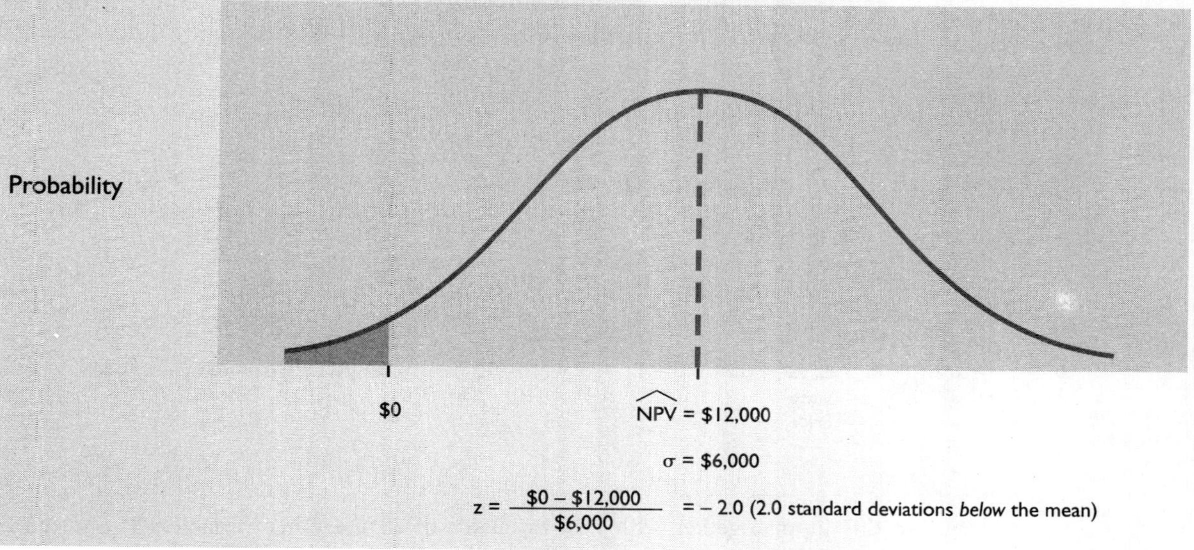

analyze trade-offs between risk and expected return.[4] Unfortunately, it can take considerable time and effort to gather the information necessary for each of the input variables and to correctly formulate the model. This limits the feasibility of simulation to very large projects. In addition, the simulation examples illustrated assume that the values of the input variables are independent of one another. If this is not true—if, for example, the price of a product has a large influence on the number sold—then this interaction must be incorporated into the model, introducing even more complexity.

11-3c Sensitivity Analysis

Sensitivity analysis

Sensitivity analysis is a procedure that calculates the change in net present value given a change in one of the cash flow elements, such as product price. In other words, a decision maker can determine *how sensitive* a project's return is to changes in a particular variable.

Because sensitivity analysis is derived from the simulation approach, it also requires the definition of all relevant variables that influence the net present value of a project. The appropriate mathematical relationships between these variables must be defined, too, in order to estimate the cash flow from the project and compute the net present value. Rather than dealing with the entire probability distribution for each of the input variables, however, sensitivity analysis allows the decision maker to use only the "best estimate" of each variable to compute the net present value.

HTTP:
How do you analyze cash flow sensitivity? Examine the sensitivity of cash flow in a new business at
www.bizfilings.com/toolkit

The decision maker can then ask various what-if questions in which the project's net present value is recomputed under various conditions. For example, the best estimate of a product's price might be $10. The net present value of the project could be computed

[4]Simulation may also be applied to other decision models, such as the internal rate of return or payback approaches. In these cases, the mathematical relationships involved in the simulation have to be respecified.

FIGURE 11.3

Illustrative Sensitivity Curves

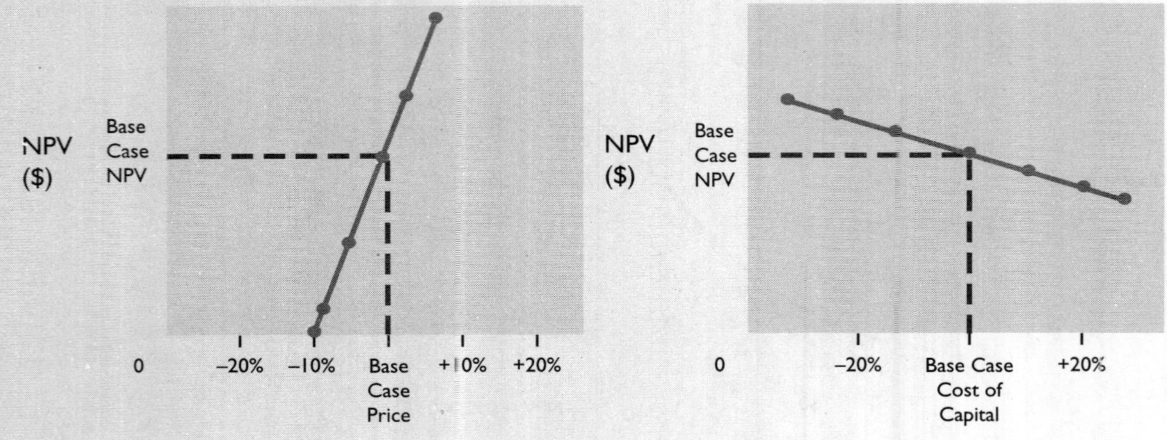

using this input together with best estimates of all the other variables. The next step would involve asking a question like "What if we cannot charge more than $8 per unit?" The net present value could be recomputed using the $8 price and the best estimates for each of the other input variables to determine the effect of the $8 price on the NPV.

Sensitivity analysis can be applied to any variable to determine the effect of changes in one or more of the inputs on a project's net present value. This process provides the decision maker with a formal mechanism for assessing the possible consequences of various scenarios.

It is often useful to construct sensitivity curves to summarize the impact of changes in different variables on the net present value of a project. A sensitivity curve has the project's net present value on the vertical axis and the variable of interest on the horizontal axis. For example, Figure 11.3 shows the sensitivity curves for two variables, sales price and cost of capital for a project.

The steep slope of the price-NPV curve indicates that the net present value is very sensitive to changes in the price for which the product can be sold. If the product price is approximately 10 percent below the base case (or initial analysis) estimate, the net present value of the project drops to $0, and the project becomes unacceptable for further price declines.[5] In contrast, the relatively flat cost-of-capital–NPV curve indicates that the net present value is not very sensitive to changes in the firm's cost of capital. Similar curves could be constructed for project life, salvage value, units sold, operating costs, and other important variables.

Using Spreadsheets for Sensitivity Analysis Spreadsheets, such as Excel, have made the application of sensitivity analysis techniques simple and inexpensive. Once the base case has been defined and entered in the spreadsheet, it is easy to ask hundreds of what-if questions. For example, assume that revenues from a project are expected to be $20,000 in year 1 and to grow by 10 percent annually over the five-year

[5]Notice that sensitivity analysis does not tell the decision maker the actual probability of NPV being negative. The reason for this is that sensitivity analysis uses only the "best estimate" of each variable and not the entire probability distribution.

life of the project. This relationship would be entered into the spreadsheet along with similar relationships for all other factors that go into the determination of the annual net cash flows from the project. The net present value of the base case is computed by the spreadsheet. Now, what if the revenues are estimated to grow only 5 percent annually, instead of 10 percent? Only one change must be made on the spreadsheet (redefine the growth rate to 5 percent), and it automatically recomputes each period's net cash flows and the net present value of the project. This process can be repeated rapidly, literally hundreds of times, to develop a profile of how sensitive the project is to changes in the individual components of the project's cash flows. This allows the decision maker to focus his or her analysis on the key variables that are critical to the project's success. (The CFM Excel models available with this text can be used effectively to illustrate the power of spreadsheets in performing sensitivity analyses.)

11-3d Scenario Analysis

Scenario analysis is another technique that has been used to assess the risk of an investment project. Sensitivity analysis considers the impact of changes in key variables, one at a time, on the desirability of an investment project. In contrast, **scenario analysis** considers the impact of simultaneous changes in key variables on the desirability of an investment project.

scenario analysis

For example, consider the case of Boeing's decision to invest in a new airplane, such as the 787 Dreamliner. The success of this proposed investment project depends on many factors, including the price of the plane, the number of units likely to be demanded, the cost of development, the time period required for development, and the cost of production. When using the scenario analysis technique, the financial analyst might ask the project director to provide various estimates of the project's expected net present value. In addition to what is perceived to be the most likely scenario, the project director might be asked to provide both optimistic and pessimistic estimates. An *optimistic scenario* might be defined by the most optimistic values of each of the most input variables—for example, low development costs, low production costs, high prices, and strong demand. A *pessimistic scenario* would be defined by low prices, project launch delays, soft demand, high development costs, and high production costs. The project manager could also be asked to provide estimates of the probability that the optimistic scenario will result and the probability that the pessimistic scenario will result. With these probability estimates, the financial manager can compute an estimate of the standard deviation of the NPV of the project.

Assume, for example, that the following estimates of the NPV of the 787 project for Boeing have been developed using scenario analysis:

Outcome (j)	NPV_j	Probability (p_j)
Pessimistic	−\$11.4 billion	0.20
Most likely	\$1.3 billion	0.60
Optimistic	\$10.1 billion	0.20

Recall from Chapter 8 that the expected value of a variable, such as net present value, is:

$$\widehat{NPV} = \sum_{j=1}^{n} NPV_j \times p_j$$

The expected NPV of this project would be:

$$\widehat{NPV} = 0.20(-\$11.4) + 0.60(\$1.3) + 0.20(\$10.1) = \$0.52 \text{ billion}$$

Recall also from Chapter 8 that the standard deviation of a variable, such as net present value, is:

$$\sigma = \sqrt{\sum_{j=1}^{n} (NPV_j - \widehat{NPV})^2 p_j}$$

Thus, the standard deviation of net present value can be computed as:

$$\begin{aligned}\sigma &= [(-\$11.4 - \$0.52)^2 0.20 + (\$1.3 - \$0.52)^2 0.60 + (\$10.1 - \$0.52)^2 0.20]^{0.5} \\ &= \$6.87 \text{ billion}\end{aligned}$$

Given the expected NPV of \$0.52 billion and the expected standard deviation of \$6.87 billion (and assuming that the probability distribution is approximately normally distributed), it is now possible to compute the probability that the project will have a negative net present value:

$$\begin{aligned}z &= \frac{0 - \widehat{NPV}}{\sigma} \\ &= \frac{0 - \$0.52}{\$6.87} \\ &= -0.08\end{aligned}$$

From Table V it can be seen that the probability of a value less than −0.08 standard deviations from the mean (\$0.52 billion) is about 46.8 percent. This means that there is a 46.8 percent chance that this project will have a negative NPV.

This example illustrates both the value of scenario analysis and some of its shortcomings. With the aid of spreadsheet programs such as Excel, it is possible to easily estimate the impact of various scenarios on the expected performance of a project. However, scenario analysis techniques normally look only at a limited number of alternative scenarios. Furthermore, the process of assigning probabilities to the outcomes expected from alternative scenarios is difficult and largely subjective.

11-3e Certainty Equivalent Approach

certainty equivalent

Another approach that can be used to deal with total project risk uses certainty equivalents. The **certainty equivalent** approach adjusts the net cash flows in the *numerator* of the NPV equation, in contrast to the risk-adjusted discount rate approach, which involves adjustments to the *denominator* of the NPV equation (as discussed in the next section). A certainty equivalent factor is the ratio of the amount of cash someone would require with certainty at a point in time in order to make him or her indifferent between that certain amount and an amount expected to be received with risk at the same point in time. The project is adjusted for risk by converting the expected risky cash flows to their certainty equivalents and then computing the net present value of the project. The risk-free rate, r_f—not the firm's cost of capital, k—is used as the discount rate for computing the net present value. This is done because the cost of capital is a *risky* rate, reflecting the firm's average risk, and using it would result in a double counting of risk.

Certainty equivalent factors range from 0 to 1.0. The higher the factor, the more certain the expected cash flow. For example, suppose that Thomson Electric Company

(TEC) is evaluating a project that is expected to generate the following cash flows over its five-year life:

Year	Expected NCF	Certainty Equivalent Factor (α_t)	Certainty Equivalent Cash Flows
0	$−10,000	1.0	$−10,000
1	5,000	0.9	4,500
2	6,000	0.8	4,800
3	7,000	0.7	4,900
4	4,000	0.6	2,400
5	3,000	0.4	1,200

The initial outlay of $10,000 is known with certainty. It might be for the purchase price of a piece of equipment. Hence, the certainty equivalent factor for year 0 is 1.0, and the certainty equivalent cash flow is −$10,000 (−$10,000 × 1.0). The $5,000 cash inflow in year 1 is viewed as being somewhat risky. Consequently, the decision maker has assigned a certainty equivalent factor of 0.9 to the net cash flow in year 1. Multiplying $5,000 times the 0.9 certainty equivalent factor yields a certainty equivalent cash flow of $4,500. This means that the decision maker would be indifferent between receiving the promised, risky $5,000 a year from now or receiving $4,500 with certainty at the same time. A similar interpretation is given to the certainty equivalent factors and certainty equivalent cash flows for years 2 through 5.

Algebraically, the certainty equivalent factors, α_t, for the cash flows expected to be received during each time period, t, are expressed as follows:

(11.2)

$$\alpha_t = \frac{\text{Certain return}}{\text{Risky return}}$$

The certainty equivalent factors are used to compute a certainty equivalent net present value as follows:

(11.3)

$$\text{NPV} = -\text{NINV}(\alpha_0) + \sum_{t=1}^{n} \frac{\text{NCF}_t \alpha_t}{(1 + r_f)^t}$$

where:

α_0 = Certainty equivalent factor associated with the net investment (NINV) at time 0

n = Expected economic life of the project

α_t = Certainty equivalent factor associated with the net cash flows (NCF) in each period, t

r_f = Risk-free rate

Note in the TEC example that the certainty equivalent factors decline into the future. This reflects the fact that *most* cash flows are viewed as being more risky the further into the future they are projected to occur.[6] This point is discussed in greater detail in Chapter 8. (See Figure 8.3.) In Table 11.1, we have computed the certainty equivalent net present value for this project assuming an 8 percent risk-free rate. It equals $4,753, and the project therefore is acceptable.

[6]Different individuals may have different certainty equivalent factors, depending on each individual's relative risk aversion. Risk aversion is a function of many factors, including wealth, age, and the nature of a firm's reward structure.

TABLE 11.1

Thomson Electric Company: Calculation of Certainty Equivalent Net Present Value

Year	Expected NCF	Certainty Equivalent Factor (α)	Certainty Equivalent Cash Flow	$PVIF_{0.08,t}$	Present Value of Cash Flows
0	$-10,000	1.0	$-10,000	1.000	$-10,000
1	+5,000	0.9	+4,500	0.926	+4,167
2	+6,000	0.8	+4,800	0.857	+4,114
3	+7,000	0.7	+4,900	0.794	+3,891
4	+4,000	0.6	+2,400	0.735	+1,764
5	+3,000	0.4	+1,200	0.681	+817
			Certainty Equivalent NPV =		+$4,753

The certainty equivalent approach of considering risk is viewed as conceptually sound for the following reasons:

- The decision maker can adjust separately each period's cash flows to account for the specific risk of those cash flows. This normally is not done when the risk-adjusted discount rate approach is applied.[7]
- Decision makers must introduce their own risk preferences directly into the analysis. Consequently, the certainty equivalent net present value provides an unambiguous basis for making a decision. A positive net present value means the project is acceptable to that decision maker, and a negative net present value indicates it should be rejected.

11-3f Risk-Adjusted Discount Rate Approach

risk-adjusted discount rate

The **risk-adjusted discount rate** approach (RADR) adjusts for risk by varying the rate at which the expected net cash flows are discounted when determining a project's net present value. In the risk-adjusted discount rate approach, net cash flows for each project are discounted at a risk-adjusted rate, k_a^*, to obtain the NPV:

$$NPV = \sum_{t=1}^{n} \frac{NCF_t}{(1 + k_a^*)^t} - NINV \quad (11.4)$$

where NCF_t is the net cash flow in period t and NINV is the net investment. The risk-adjusted discount rate, $k_a{}^*$, is the sum of the risk-free rate, r_f, and the appropriate project risk premium. The magnitude of $k_a{}^*$ depends on the relationship between the total risk of the individual project and the overall risk of the firm The *risk-free rate, r_f,* is the required rate of return associated with investment projects characterized by certain cash flow streams. U.S. Treasury securities are good examples of risk-free investments because there is no chance that investors will not get the dollar amount of interest and the principal repayment on schedule. Thus, the yield on U.S. government securities, such as 90-day Treasury bills, is used as the risk-free rate.

Most companies are not in business to invest in risk-free securities; individual investors can do that just as well. Instead, companies assume some amount of risk, expecting to earn higher returns than those available on risk-free securities. The difference between the risk-free rate and the firm's required rate of return (cost of capital) is an *average risk*

[7]It is possible, however, to find a risk-adjusted discount rate that will provide results identical (that is, with the same risk-adjusted net present value) to those obtained from the certainty equivalent approach.

premium to compensate investors for the fact that the company's assets are risky. This relationship is expressed algebraically as follows:

(11.5) $$\theta = k_a - r_f$$

where θ is the average risk premium for the firm; r_f, the risk-free rate; and k_a, the required rate of return for projects of average risk, that is, the firm's cost of capital.

The cash flows from a project having greater than average risk are discounted at a higher rate, k_a*—that is, a risk-adjusted discount rate—to reflect the increased riskiness. Total project risk premiums applied to individual projects are commonly established *subjectively*. For example, some firms establish a small number of *risk classes* and then apply a different *risk premium* to each class. Below-average-risk projects, such as straightforward equipment replacement decisions, might be evaluated at 2 percent *below* the firm's cost of capital (a risk discount). Average-risk projects, such as equipment modification decisions, might be evaluated at the firm's cost of capital; above-average-risk projects, such as facility expansions, might be assigned a risk premium of 3 percent *above* the firm's cost of capital; and high-risk projects, such as investments in totally new lines of business or the introduction of new products, might be assigned a risk premium of 8 percent *above* the firm's cost of capital.

Although the risk-class approach saves time in the analysis stage, it can lead to suboptimal decisions, because the risk premiums themselves are usually determined subjectively and no explicit consideration is given to the variation in returns of the projects assigned to individual classes. In short, the risk-class approach is most useful when evaluating relatively small projects that are repeated frequently. In these cases, much is known about the projects' potential returns, and it is probably not worth the effort to try to compute more "precise" risk premiums. The next section applies the capital asset pricing model to compute risk premia in a more objective way.

11-4 Adjusting for Beta Risk in Capital Budgeting

The *beta* concept introduced in Chapter 8 for security risk analysis can also be used to determine risk-adjusted discount rates (RADR) for individual capital budgeting projects. This approach is appropriate for a firm whose stock is widely traded and for which there is very little chance of bankruptcy. (The probability of bankruptcy is a function of total risk, not just systematic risk.)

HTTP:
You've probably already heard about beta, arbitrage, CAPM, systematic risk, and the efficient frontier. But do you know what deltas, collars, leptokurtosis, swaptions, and inverse floaters are? For a glossary of terms describing financial risks of any type, visit
www.oasismanagement.com

Just as the beta (systematic risk) of a portfolio of securities can be computed as the weighted average of the individual security betas, a firm may be considered as a portfolio of assets, each having its own beta. From this perspective, the systematic risk of the firm is simply the weighted average of the systematic risk of the individual assets.

The risk concepts from the capital asset pricing model (CAPM) can be used to compute an appropriate risk premium to evaluate individual projects. For example, the RADR for any project *j*, may be thought of as the sum of the risk-free rate, r_f, and the risk premium, RP, or:

$$\text{RADR}_j = r_f + \text{RP}_j$$

Applying the CAPM concept of risk, RADR_j is equal to the sum of the risk-free rate, r_f, and the project's beta, β_j, times the market risk premium, r_m (the expected market return) minus r_f, or:

$$\text{RADR}_j = r_f + \beta_j(r_m - r_f)$$

Hence the risk premium for a project from a CAPM perspective is equal to the project's beta times the average market risk premium:

$$\text{RP}_j = \beta_j(r_m - r_f)$$

11-4a The All-Equity Case

For example, consider the security market line shown in Figure 11.4. The firm has a beta of 1.2 and is financed exclusively with internally generated equity capital. The market risk premium is 7 percent. When considering projects of average risk—that is, projects that are highly correlated with the firm's returns on its existing assets and that have a beta similar to the firm's beta (1.2)—the firm should use the computed 13.4 percent cost of equity, or 5% + 1.2 (7%), from Figure 11.4. When considering projects having estimated betas different from 1.2, it should use an equity discount rate equal to the required return calculated from the security market line. For example, if a project's estimated beta is 1.7 and the risk-free rate is 5 percent, the project's required equity return would be 16.9 percent, or 5% + 1.7 (7%), and this would be used as the risk-adjusted discount rate for that project, assuming the project is financed with 100 percent equity.

FIGURE 11.4

Risk-Adjusted Discount Rates and the SML

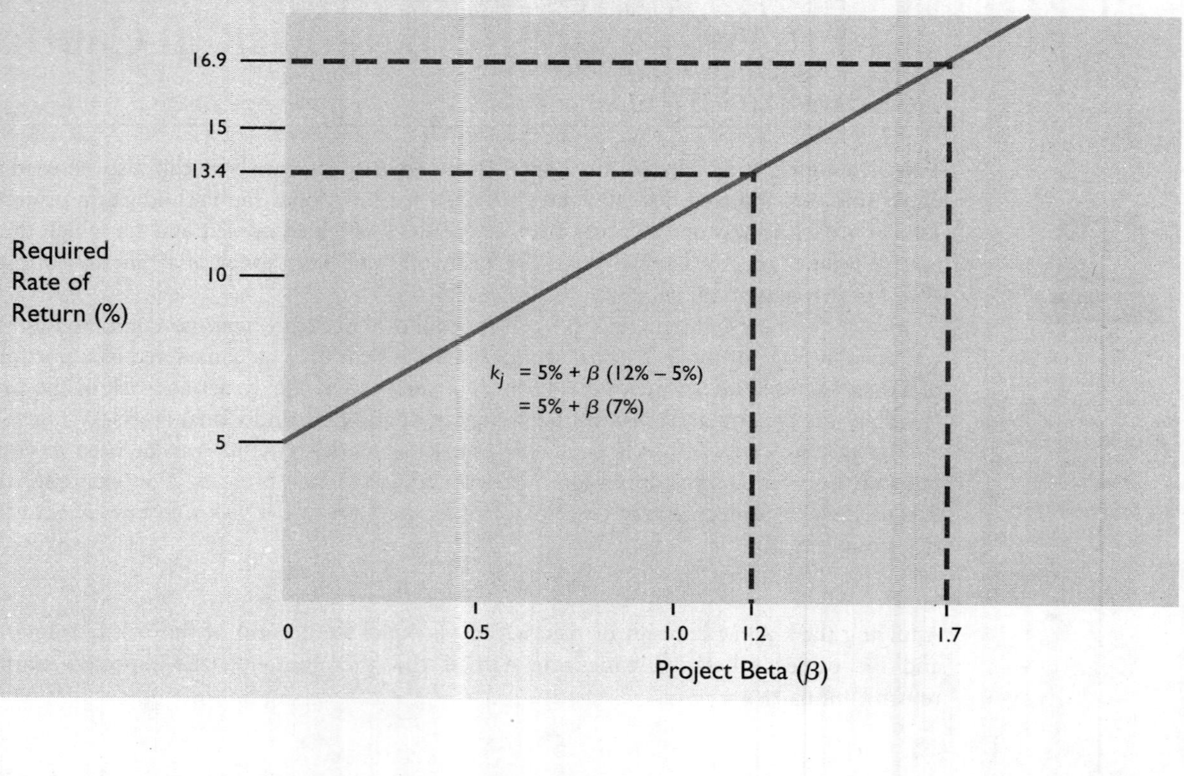

INTERNATIONAL ISSUES

Special Elements of Capital Budgeting Risk

The techniques of risk analysis presented in this chapter will serve a firm well whether it operates only in the United States or multinationally. However, managers of multinational firms need to be aware of special elements of risk when investing abroad.

When evaluating a capital expenditure to be made in another country, the parent firm must be concerned with the cash flows that can be expected to be received by the parent—not the cash flows that will accrue to the overseas subsidiary making the investment. There are several reasons for focusing on cash flows to the parent. First, the host country might block the subsidiary from remitting funds back to the parent. Hence, these "captive" funds are not available to the parent for reinvestment in projects offering the highest rate of return. Second, the parent needs to be concerned with the prospect that its assets in foreign subsidiaries could be taken by the host government with inadequate or no compensation. Third, the parent must consider exchange rate risk between the host country's currency and the dollar. (Exchange rate risk and procedures for managing it are discussed in detail in Chapters 2 and 22.) Related to exchange rate risk is the higher risk of inflation in many countries, particularly developing countries. The risk of highly volatile inflation and the ability of a firm to protect itself from this risk adds additional uncertainty to investments made abroad. Finally, greater uncertainty may be associated with tax rates in the host country than is typical in the United States.

Each of these factors affects the risk of the cash flows that can be expected from investments in other countries. Although multinational firms predominantly use standard capital budgeting procedures, such as NPV and IRR, to evaluate their investments abroad, there is evidence that many multinational firms also use the risk analysis techniques discussed in this chapter. A recent study of the capital budgeting practices of affiliates of U.S.-based multinational firms found that sensitivity analysis and simulation are widely used for assessing project risk.[a] In addition, some financial managers reported that they relied more heavily on their own personal feelings about political and economic events in the host country than on quantitative methods to evaluate project risk.

[a] Lawrence P. Shao, "Capital Investment Evaluation Procedures Utilized by North and Latin American Affiliates," *Multinational Business Review* (Spring 1994): 11–18.

11-4b The Equity and Debt Case

Next, we develop a procedure for computing the risk-adjusted discount rate for projects financed with both debt and equity. To better understand the material in this section, we briefly introduce the concept of a weighted cost of capital, which is developed more extensively in Chapter 12. At this point, it is only necessary to recognize that the required return on the project discussed in this section reflects the project's equity return requirement and the debt return requirement for the funds expected to be used to finance the project.

Consider the example of Vulcan Industries, with a current capital structure consisting of 50 percent debt and 50 percent equity. Vulcan is considering expanding into a new line of business and wants to compute the rate of return that will be required on projects in this area. Vulcan has determined that the debt capacity associated with projects in its new business line is such that a capital structure consisting of 40 percent debt and 60 percent common equity is appropriate to finance these new projects. Vulcan's company beta has been estimated to be 1.3, but the Vulcan management does not believe that this beta risk is appropriate for the new business line. Vulcan's managers must estimate the beta risk appropriate for projects in this new line of business and then determine the risk-adjusted return requirement on these projects.

Because the beta risk of projects in this new business line is not directly observable, Vulcan's managers have decided to rely on surrogate market information. They have identified a firm, Olympic Materials, that competes exclusively in the line of business into which Vulcan proposes expanding. The beta of Olympic has been estimated to be 1.50.

Recall from Chapter 8 that a firm's beta is computed as the slope of its characteristic line and that actual security returns are used in the computations. Accordingly, a firm's computed beta is a measure of both its business risk *and* its financial risk. When a beta is computed for a firm such as Olympic, it reflects both the business and financial risk of that firm. To determine the beta associated with Vulcan's proposed new line of business using the observed beta from another firm (Olympic) that competes exclusively in that business line, it is necessary to convert the observed beta, often called a *leveraged beta*, β_l, into an *unleveraged*, or pure project beta, β_u. This unleveraged beta can then be releveraged to reflect the amount of debt capacity appropriate for this type of project and that will be used by Vulcan to finance it. The following equation can be used to convert a leveraged beta into an unleveraged, or pure project, beta:[8]

(11.6)
$$\beta_u = \frac{\beta_l}{1 + (1 - T)(B/E)}$$

where β_u is the unleveraged beta for a project or firm, β_l is the leveraged beta for a project or firm, B is the market value of the firm's debt, E is the market value of the firm's equity, and T is the firm's marginal tax rate.

The use of this equation can be illustrated for the Vulcan Materials example. The beta, β_l, for Olympic has been computed to be 1.50. Olympic has a capital structure consisting of 20 percent debt and 80 percent common equity and a tax rate of 35 percent. Substituting these values into Equation 11.6 yields:

$$\beta_u = \frac{1.50}{1 + (1 - 0.35)(0.25)} = 1.29$$

The unleveraged, or pure project beta for the proposed new line of business of Vulcan is estimated to be 1.29. Vulcan intends to finance this new line of business with a capital structure consisting of 40 percent debt and 60 percent common equity. In addition, Vulcan's tax rate is 40 percent. Equation 11.6 can be rearranged to compute the leveraged beta associated with this new line of business, given Vulcan's proposed target capital structure for the project:

(11.7)
$$\begin{aligned}\beta_l &= \beta_u[1 + (1 - T)(B/E)] \\ &= 1.29[1 + (1 - 0.4)(0.667)] \\ &= 1.81\end{aligned}$$

With a risk-free rate of 5 percent and a market risk premium of 7 percent, the required return on the equity portion of the proposed new line of business is computed from the security market line as:

$$\begin{aligned}k_e &= 5\% + 1.81(7\%) \\ &= 17.7\%\end{aligned}$$

If the after-tax cost of debt, k_i, used to finance the new line of business is 8 percent, the risk-adjusted required return, k_a^*, on the new line of business, given the proposed capital structure of 40 percent debt and 60 percent equity, is a weighted average of the marginal, after-tax debt and equity costs, or:

$$\begin{aligned}k_a^* &= 0.4(8\%) + 0.6(17.7\%) \\ &= 13.8\%\end{aligned}$$

[8] Robert Hamada, "The Effect of the Firm's Capital Structure on the Systematic Risk of Common Stocks," *Journal of Finance* (May 1972): 435–452.

Therefore, the risk-adjusted required rate of return on the proposed new line of business for Vulcan is 13.8 percent. This number reflects both the pure project risk and the financial risk associated with the project as Vulcan anticipates financing it.

Equations 11.6 and 11.7 provide only an approximation of the effect of leverage on beta. Capital market imperfections, such as the existence of risky debt and uncertainty regarding future levels of debt, introduce error into the beta adjustments just presented. Hence, this procedure should be used with caution. This general procedure is used by many different firms, including Boeing Corporation.

11-4c Computing the Risk-Adjusted Net Present Value

Suppose a company is considering a project whose net investment is $50,000 with expected cash inflows of $10,000 per year for 10 years. Using Equation 11.2, as shown in Table 11.2, the project's NPV is $−1,670 when evaluated at a risk-adjusted discount rate (k_a^*) and $6,500 when evaluated at the weighted average cost of capital (k_a). Assuming that the 16 percent RADR figure has been determined correctly by using the security market line with an accurate beta value, the project should *not* be accepted even though its NPV, calculated using the company's weighted cost of capital, is positive. This new product project is similar to Project 4 in Figure 11.5.

The new product project discussed in the previous paragraph has an internal rate of return of about 15 percent, compared to its 16 percent required return. Therefore, the project should be rejected, according to the IRR decision rule. When the IRR technique

hurdle rate

is used, the RADR given by the SML frequently is called the **hurdle rate**. Some finance practitioners use the term *hurdle rate* to describe any risk-adjusted discount rate.

Figure 11.5 illustrates the difference between the use of a single discount rate, the weighted cost of capital,[9] for all projects regardless of risk level and a discount rate based on the security market line for each project. In the example shown in Figure 11.5, Projects 1, 2, 3, and 4 are being evaluated by the firm. Using the weighted cost of capital approach, the firm would adopt Projects 3 and 4. However, if the firm considered the differential levels of systematic risk for the four alternatives, it would accept Projects 1 and 3 and reject Projects 2 and 4. In general, *the risk-adjusted discount rate approach is considered preferable to the weighted cost of capital approach when the projects under consideration differ significantly in their risk characteristics.*

The one problem remaining with this suggested procedure involves the determination of beta values for individual projects. Thus far, the most workable approach available is

TABLE 11.2

Calculation of NPV at Weighted Average Cost of Capital and Risk-Adjusted Discount Rate

		Weighted Average Cost of Capital ($k_a = .12$)		Risk-Adjusted Discount Rate ($k_a^* = .16$)	
Year t	**Net Cash Flow**	**Interest Factor**	**Present Value**	**Interest Factor**	**Present Value**
0	$−50,000	1.000	$−50,000	1.000	$−50,000
1–10	10,000	5.650	56,500	4.833	48,330
NPV			$ +6,500		$ −1,670

[9]The weighted cost of capital for a firm is defined in greater detail in Chapter 12. It is equal to the marginal cost of equity times the proportion of a common equity in the firm's target capital structure, plus the after-tax marginal cost of debt times the debt proportion in the firm's target capital structure, plus the after-tax marginal cost of preferred stock times its proportion in the firm's target capital structure. In general, the weighted cost of capital is the appropriate discount rate to use when evaluating projects of average risk.

FIGURE 11.5

Risk-Adjusted Discount Rate Versus Weighted Cost of Capital

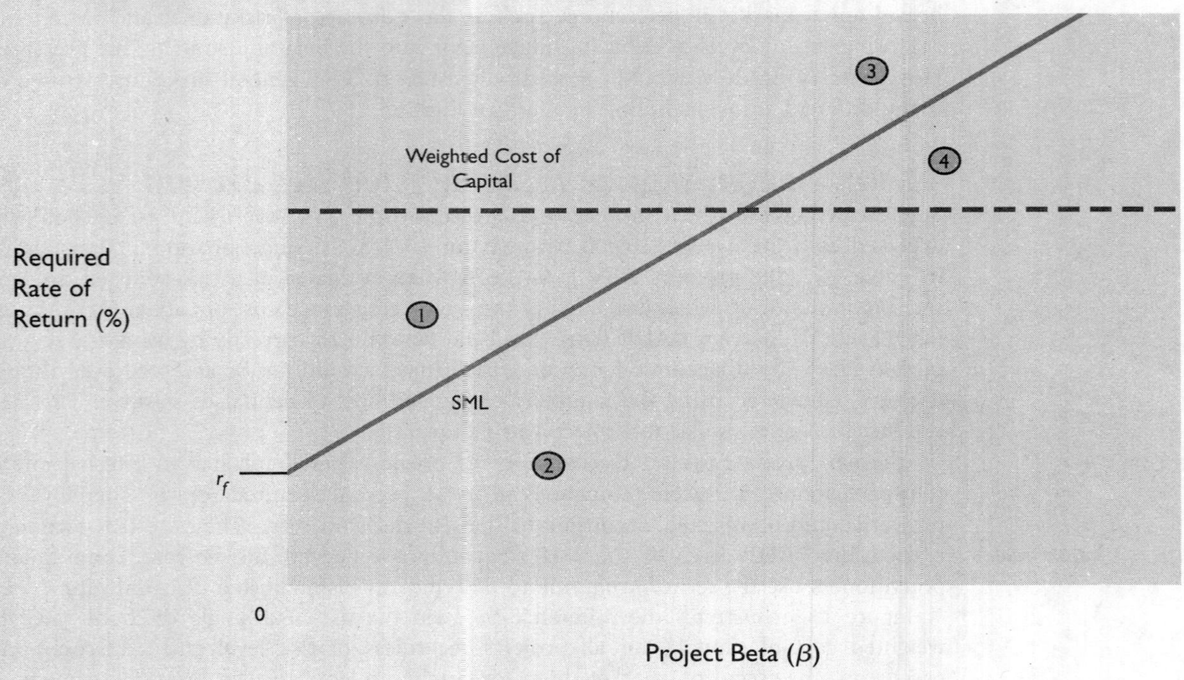

the use of *surrogate market information*, as illustrated in the Vulcan Industries example. For example, if an aluminum firm is considering investing in the leisure-time product industry, the beta for this new project could be computed using the average beta for a sample of firms engaged principally in the leisure product industry. Although the beta for the aluminum firm might be 1.3—resulting in a required equity return on projects of average risk of 14.1 percent, or 5% + (1.3 × 7%), according to Figure 11.4—this would not be the appropriate rate for leisure product projects. Assuming a beta of 0.9 for leisure product firms, the leisure product projects would be required to earn an equity return of only 11.3 percent, or 5% + (0.9 × 7%), because of the lower average level of systematic risk associated with leisure product projects. This assumes that the leisure product projects are financed in the same manner as the firms used to generate the surrogate betas. Otherwise, the beta adjustment procedure in Equations 11.6 and 11.7 must be used.

11-5 Summary

- The *risk* of an investment project is defined in terms of the potential *variability* of its returns. When only one return is possible—for example, as with U.S. government securities held to maturity— there is no risk. When more than one return is possible for a particular project it is risky.
- Risk is also influenced by the possibility of investment *diversification*. If a proposed project's returns are not *perfectly correlated* with the returns from the firm's other investments, the total risk of the firm may be reduced by accepting the proposed project. This is known as the *portfolio effect*.

- A decision maker can adjust for total project risk in capital budgeting in several different ways, including the *net present value/payback approach, simulation analysis, sensitivity analysis, scenario analysis,* the *risk-adjusted discount rate approach,* and the *certainty equivalent approach.* The simulation approach is the most expensive of the techniques discussed in this chapter; it is normally applied only when large projects are being analyzed. The widespread availability of inexpensive and powerful computer software, such as electronic spreadsheets, has made the use of sensitivity analysis far more accessible to small- and medium-size firms than was previously possible.
- The risk-adjusted discount rate approach is widely used by firms that attempt to consider differential project risk in their capital budgeting procedures. It requires that a *risk premium* be computed for each project or group of projects so that an appropriate risk-adjusted discount rate can be applied when evaluating a project's cash flows.
- When a project differs significantly in its systematic risk profile (as measured by *beta*) from the systematic risk of the total firm, a risk-adjusted discount rate appropriate for that project can be computed using the security market line relationship between risk and required return from the capital asset pricing model.
- The decision to employ some risk analysis technique to evaluate an investment project depends on the project's size and the additional cost of applying such a technique as compared with the perceived benefits. For small projects, only the simpler risk adjustment techniques should be used; for major projects that have above- or below-normal risk, it is worthwhile to analyze the project's risk as precisely as possible. Failure to fully analyze the risk of a large project could result in bad investment decisions and even substantial losses.

Important Equations

$$\alpha_t = \frac{\text{Certain return}}{\text{Risky return}}$$

$$\text{NPV} = -\text{NINV}(\alpha_0) + \sum_{t=1}^{n} \frac{\text{NCF}_t \alpha_t}{(1 + r_f)^t}$$

$$\text{NPV} = \sum_{t=1}^{n} \frac{\text{NCF}_t}{(1 + k_a^*)^t} - \text{NINV}$$

$$\beta_u = \frac{\beta_l}{1 + (1 - T)(B/E)}$$

$$\beta_l = \beta_u[1 + (1 - T)(B/E)]$$

11-6 Questions and Topics for Discussion

1. How does the basic net present value model of capital budgeting deal with the problem of project risk? What are the shortcomings of this approach?
2. How would you define *risk* as it is used in a capital budgeting analysis context?
3. Recalling the discussion in Chapter 8, when is the standard deviation of a project's cash flows an appropriate measure of project risk? When is the coefficient of variation an appropriate measure?

4. How does the basic net present value capital budgeting model deal with the phenomenon of increasing risk of project cash flows over time?
5. When should a firm consider the portfolio effects of a new project?
6. What are the primary advantages and disadvantages of applying *simulation* to capital budgeting risk analysis?
7. Computer simulation is used to generate a large number of possible outcomes for an investment project. Most firms invest in a particular project only once, however. How can a computer simulation model be helpful to the typical decision maker who is making a one-time-only investment decision?
8. On average, the expected value of returns from each $1 of premiums paid on an insurance policy is less than $1; this is due to the insurance company's administrative costs and profits. In spite of this fact, why do so many individuals and organizations purchase insurance policies?
9. Describe how certainty equivalent cash flow estimates can be derived for individual project cash flows.
10. Will all individuals apply the same certainty equivalent estimates to the cash flows from a project? Why or why not?

11-7 Self-Test Problems

ST1. Lehigh Products Company is considering the purchase of new automated equipment. The project has an expected net present value of $250,000 with a standard deviation of $100,000. What is the probability that the project will have a net present value less than $50,000, assuming that net present value is normally distributed?

ST2. The Jacobs Company is financed entirely with equity. The beta for Jacobs has been estimated to be 1.0. The current risk-free rate is 4 percent and the expected market return is 10 percent.

a. What rate of return should Jacobs require on a project of average risk?
b. If a new venture is expected to have a beta of 1.6, what rate of return should Jacobs demand on this project?
c. The project in question requires an initial outlay of $9 million and is expected to generate a 10-year stream of annual net cash flows of $1.9 million. Calculate the NPV of the project using Jacobs' required return for projects of average risk.
d. Calculate the NPV of the project using the risk-adjusted rate computed in Part b.

ST3. Homer Stores is considering a new location that is expected to yield the following net cash flows following an initial (year 0), certain outlay (NINV) of $75,000:

Year	Net Cash Flows	Certainty Equivalent Factor
1	$30,000	0.90
2	30,000	0.80
3	30,000	0.65
4	20,000	0.50

a. Compute the NPV of this project at a 15 percent cost of capital.
b. If the risk-free rate is 4 percent, what is the certainty equivalent NPV for the new location?

11-8 Problems*

BASIC

1. Mitchell Auto Parts Inc. has estimated the probability distribution of its annual net cash flows as follows:

Probability	Cash Flow (in Thousands of Dollars)
0.10	$1,000
0.20	1,500
0.40	2,000
0.20	2,500
0.10	3,000

a. Compute the expected annual cash flow.
b. Compute the standard deviation of annual cash flows.
c. Compute the coefficient of variation of annual cash flows.

BASIC

2. A new project has expected annual net cash flows of $400,000 with a standard deviation of $250,000. The distribution of annual net cash flows is approximately normal.
a. What is the probability of the project having negative annual net cash flows?
b. What is the probability that annual net cash flows will be greater than $575,000?

BASIC

3. A proposed factory expansion project has an expected net present value of $100,000 with a standard deviation of $50,000. What is the probability that the project will have a negative net present value, assuming that net present value is normally distributed?

BASIC

4. Two projects have the following expected net present values and standard deviations of net present values:

Project	Expected Net Present Value	Standard Deviation
A	$50,000	$20,000
B	10,000	7,000

a. Using the standard deviation criterion, which project is riskier?
b. Using the coefficient of variation criterion, which project is riskier?
c. Which criterion do you think is appropriate to use in this case? Why?

INTERMEDIATE

5. American Steel Corporation is considering two investments. One is the purchase of a new continuous caster costing $100 million. The expected net present value of this project is $20 million. The other alternative is the purchase of a supermarket chain, also costing $100 million. It, too, has an expected net present value of $20 million. The firm's management is interested in reducing the variability of its earnings.
a. Which project should the company invest in?
b. What assumptions did you make to arrive at this decision?

BASIC

6. Gamma Biosciences is financed entirely with equity. Its beta is 1.5, and its price-earnings ratio is 16. The current risk-free rate is 8 percent, and the expected return on the market is 14 percent.
a. What rate of return should the company require on projects of average risk?
b. If a new project has a beta of 2.0, what rate of return should the company require?

*Color blocks behind the numbers denote problems that have check answers provided at the end of the book.

CHALLENGE **7.** Advanced Systems Company is financed one-third with debt and two-thirds with equity. Its market beta has been estimated to be 1.5. The current risk-free rate is 4 percent, and the expected market return is 11 percent. Advanced Systems' tax rate is 40 percent. Advanced Systems is planning a major research and development (R&D) investment program. Advanced Systems' management believes that these types of projects should be financed conservatively. Specifically, the company plans to finance all R&D investments with 90 percent equity and 10 percent debt.

a. If the pure project beta for the R&D investment is the same as the pure project beta for Advanced Systems' other assets, what rate of return is required on the equity-financed portion of the R&D investment, assuming it is financed 90 percent with equity and 10 percent with debt?

b. Advanced Systems' managers believe this project may have more risk than their other investments. Another firm that invests very heavily in R&D similar to the type proposed by Advanced has been identified. Its capital structure is 80 percent equity and 20 percent debt. Its tax rate is 35 percent, and its market beta is 1.6. Using this information, determine the required return on the equity-financed portion of Advanced Systems' R&D project, assuming it is financed 90 percent with equity and 10 percent with debt.

INTERMEDIATE **8.** Valley Products, Inc. is considering two independent investments having the following cash flow streams:

Year	Project A	Project B
0	−$50,000	−$40,000
1	+20,000	+20,000
2	+20,000	+10,000
3	+10,000	+5,000
4	+5,000	+5,000
5	+5,000	+40,000

Valley uses a combination of the net present value approach and the payback approach to evaluate investment alternatives. It requires that all projects have a positive net present value when cash flows are discounted at 10 percent and that all projects have a payback no longer than three years. Which project or projects should the firm accept? Why?

BASIC **9.** Fox Enterprises is considering expanding into the growing laser copier business. Fox estimates that this expansion will cost $1.8 million and will generate a 20-year stream of expected net cash flows amounting to $400,000 per year. The company's weighted cost of capital is 15 percent.

a. Compute the net present value of the laser copier project using the company's weighted cost of capital and the expected cash flows from the project.

b. Using the risk-adjusted discount rate approach, management has decided that this project has substantially more risk than average and has decided that it requires a 24 percent expected rate of return on projects like this. Recompute the risk-adjusted net present value of this project.

INTERMEDIATE **10.** Apple Jacks Inc. produces wine. The firm is considering expanding into the snack food business. This expansion will require an initial investment in new equipment of $200,000. The equipment will be depreciated on a straight-line basis over a 10-year period to zero. At the end of the project the equipment is estimated to have a salvage value of $50,000. The expansion will also require an increase in working capital for the firm of $40,000. Revenues from the new venture are forecasted at $200,000 per year for the first 5 years and $210,000 per year for years 6 through 10. Operating costs exclusive of depreciation from the new venture are estimated at $90,000 for the first 5 years and $105,000 for years 6 through 10. It is assumed that at the end of year 10, the snack food equipment will be sold for its estimated salvage value. The firm's marginal tax rate is 40 percent. The required return for projects of average risk has been estimated at 15 percent.

a. Compute the project's net present value, assuming that it is an average-risk investment.

b. If management decides that all product line expansions have above-average risk and therefore should be evaluated at a 24 percent required rate of return, what will be the risk-adjusted net present value of the project?

INTERMEDIATE **11.** The Seminole Production Company is analyzing the investment in a new line of business machines. The initial outlay required is $35 million. The net cash flows expected from the investment are as follows:

Year	Net Cash Flow (Million)
1	$5
2	8
3	15
4	20
5	15
6	10
7	4

The firm's cost of capital (used for projects of average risk) is 15 percent.

a. Compute the net present value of this project assuming it possesses average risk.

b. Because of the risk inherent in this type of investment, Seminole has decided to employ the certainty equivalent approach. After considerable discussion, management has agreed to apply the following certainty equivalents to the project's cash flows:

Year	α_t
0	1.00
1	0.95
2	0.90
3	0.80
4	0.60
5	0.40
6	0.35
7	0.30

If the risk-free rate is 9 percent, compute the project's certainty equivalent net present value.

c. On the basis of the certainty equivalent analysis, should the project be accepted?

BASIC **12.** A simulation model similar to the one described in this chapter has been constructed by the Great Basin Corporation to evaluate the largest of its new investment proposals. After many iterations of the model, Great Basin's management has arrived at an expected net present value for Project A of $1.0 million. The standard deviation of the net present value has been estimated from the simulation model results to be $0.8 million.

a. What is the probability that the project will have a negative net present value?
b. What is the probability that the project will have a net present value greater than $2.2 million?

INTERMEDIATE

Spreadsheet Strategies

13. The Buffalo Snow Shoe Company is considering manufacturing radial snow shoes, which are more durable and offer better traction. Buffalo estimates that the investment in manufacturing equipment will cost $250,000 and will have a 10-year economic life. Buffalo will depreciate the equipment on a straight-line basis to a $0 estimated salvage value over a 10-year period. The estimated selling price of each pair of shoes will be $50. Buffalo anticipates that it can sell 5,000 pairs a year at this price. Unit production and selling costs (exclusive of depreciation) will be about $25. The firm's marginal tax rate is 40 percent. A cost of capital of 12 percent is thought to be appropriate to analyze a project of this type. Buffalo has decided to perform a sensitivity analysis of the project before making a decision.

a. Compute the expected net present value of this project.
b. Buffalo's president does not believe that 5,000 pairs of the new snow shoes can be sold at a $50 price. He estimates that a maximum of 3,000 pairs will be sold at this price. How does the change in the estimated sales volume influence the net present value of the project?

INTERMEDIATE

14. Project Alpha offers the following net cash flows following an initial (year 0), certain outlay (NINV) of $70,000:

Year	Net Cash Flow	Certainty Equivalent Factor
1	$30,000	0.91
2	30,000	0.79
3	30,000	0.65
4	20,000	0.52
5	20,000	0.40
6	10,000	0.30

a. Compute the NPV of this project at a 12 percent cost of capital.
b. If the risk-free rate is 4 percent, what is the certainty equivalent NPV for Project Alpha?

CHALLENGE

Spreadsheet Strategies

15. A new project is expected to have an 8-year economic life. The project will have an initial cost of $100,000. Installation and shipping charges for the equipment are estimated at $10,000. The equipment will be depreciated as a 7-year asset under MACRS rules. A working capital investment of $15,000 is required to undertake the project. The revenues from the project in year 1 are expected to be $60,000. These are expected to increase at a compound annual rate of 6 percent. Operating costs exclusive of depreciation are $15,000. These costs are expected to increase at an 8 percent compound annual rate. The firm's marginal tax rate is 40 percent. The expected salvage value of the equipment at the end of year 8 is $20,000.

a. Compute the project's net investment.
b. Compute the annual net cash flows for the project.
c. If the firm's cost of capital is 19 percent, should the project be undertaken?
d. The managers of the firm have also decided to evaluate this project using the certainty equivalent approach. They have established the following certainty equivalent factors for the cash flows forecasted in each year:

Year	α_t
0	1.00
1	0.95
2	0.90
3	0.80
4	0.60
5	0.50
6	0.45
7	0.40
8	0.35

The risk-free rate is 8 percent. Compute the certainty equivalent NPV for this project.

INTERMEDIATE **16.** The managers of U.S. Rubber have analyzed a proposed investment project. The expected net present value (NPV) of the project, evaluated at the firm's weighted cost of capital of 18 percent, has been estimated to be \$100,000. The company's managers have determined that the most optimistic NPV estimate of the project is \$175,000 and the most pessimistic estimate is \$25,000. The most optimistic estimate is a value that is not expected to be exceeded more than 10 percent of the time. The most pessimistic estimate represents a value that the project's NPV is not expected to fall below more than 10 percent of the time. What is the probability that this project will have a negative NPV?

CHALLENGE **17.** U.S. Robotics (USR) has a current (and target) capital structure of 70 percent common equity and 30 percent debt. The beta for USR is 1.4. USR is evaluating an investment in a totally new line of business. The new investment has an expected internal rate of return of 15 percent.

USR wishes to evaluate this investment proposal. If the investment is made, USR intends to finance the project with the same capital structure as its current business. USR's marginal tax rate is 34 percent. USR has identified three firms that are primarily in the line of business into which USR proposes expanding. Their average beta is 1.7, and their average capital structure is 40 percent common equity and 60 percent debt. The marginal tax rate for these three firms averages 40 percent. The risk-free rate is 8 percent, and the expected market risk premium is 8.3 percent. Should USR undertake the project?

INTERMEDIATE **18.** Essex Chemical Company is considering an expansion into a new product line that is more risky than its existing product mix. The new product line requires an investment, NINV, of \$10 million and is expected to generate annual net cash inflows of \$2.0 million over a 10-year estimated economic life. Essex Chemical's weighted cost of capital is 12 percent, and the new product line requires an estimated risk-adjusted discount rate of 17 percent, based upon the security market line and betas for comparable companies engaged in the contemplated new line of business.

a. What is the project's NPV, using the company's weighted cost of capital?

b. What is the project's NPV, using the risk-adjusted discount rate?

c. Should Essex Chemical adopt the project?

INTERMEDIATE **19.** The 3Z Company has estimated that a major project has an expected internal rate of return (IRR) of 18 percent. The most optimistic estimate of the project's IRR is 24 percent, and the most pessimistic estimate is 12 percent. The company expects that its most optimistic estimate of the project's achieved IRR will not be exceeded more than 10 percent of the time. Similarly, 3Z managers do not expect an achieved IRR that is below 12 percent more than 10 percent of the time. The weighted cost of capital is 14 percent. What is the probability that this project will generate returns less than 3Z's weighted cost of capital?

INTERMEDIATE **20.** An investment your firm is considering will cost you $5 million today. You expect to receive $7 million one year from now from the sale of the investment. You also expect to receive $500,000 in income from the investment at the end of one year. The expected sales price of $7 million is normally distributed with a standard deviation of $1 million. If you require a 4 percent rate of return on risk-free projects and a 10 percent rate of return on projects such as this, what contribution will this project make to your firm's value, after considering the riskiness of the projected returns?

BASIC **21.** You have estimated the expected NPV from a project to be $3 million with a standard deviation of $4 million. The distribution of the possible NPVs is approximately normal. If you are willing to accept a 25 percent chance of incurring a negative NPV on the project, should it be undertaken?

CHALLENGE **22.** Albright Properties Inc. (API) has three divisions:

Division	Beta	Proportion of Firm's Assets
Property management	1.1	40%
Land resources	1.6	30
Financial services	—	30

The leveraged beta for API is 1.2. API has a consolidated capital structure consisting of 50 percent debt and 50 percent equity. The Financial Services Division's capital structure is 80 percent debt and 20 percent equity. API is planning to finance new projects in that division with a capital structure of 90 percent debt and 10 percent equity. The risk-free rate is 9 percent, and the market risk premium is 8.3 percent. The pretax cost of debt to API is 19 percent. The tax rate is 40 percent. What discount rate should API apply to the cash flows from "new" projects in the Financial Services Division?

INTERMEDIATE **23.** The management of Greensboro Products has been evaluating the risk of the cash flows associated with a proposed new project. The expected net cash flow for year 1 is $50,000. The most optimistic estimate (not expected to be exceeded more than 10% of the time) of the year 1 net cash flow is $110,000, and the most pessimistic net cash flow estimate for year 1 is –$10,000 (no greater than a 10% chance of a value this low or lower). What is the probability that year 1 net cash flows will be negative?

BASIC **24.** The Carthage Sceptre Corporation is evaluating a possible investment in a new regional distribution warehouse. A careful evaluation of the anticipated net cash flows and net investment expected from the project indicates that the expected net present value (NPV) of this project is $4.5 million. The anticipated standard deviation of this expected NPV is $3 million, and the distribution of the project's NPV is approximately normal. What is the chance that this project will have a positive NPV at least equal to $1 million?

CHALLENGE **25.** The Super Muench Cookie Company is considering a diversification effort that would move it into small retail outlets at major malls around the country. Currently, Super Muench has a capital structure consisting of 30 percent debt and 70 percent equity. Super Muench believes that for the riskier retail outlet portion of its business, a more conservative capital structure of 20 percent debt and 80 percent equity is more appropriate. Super Muench's current pretax cost of debt is 12 percent. The firm's average tax rate is 30 percent, and its marginal tax rate is 40 percent.

Another retail cookie company, Dietz's Dessertery, has been identified. Dietz has a beta (leveraged) of 1.2. Dietz's current capital structure consists of 40 percent debt and 60 percent equity. Dietz's tax rate is 40 percent. The risk-free rate is 7 percent and the market risk premium is 7.4 percent.

Super Muench wants to know what risk-adjusted rate of return is appropriate for investments in its retail outlets.

INTERMEDIATE

26. Worrall's Wahoo Novelties is considering a new venture that would produce golden Wahoo commemorative coins. Worrall has estimated that the net investment required will be $15,000, including a $2,000 investment in net working capital. The project is expected to have a 4-year life. Annual net operating cash flows are estimated to be $10,000 in year 1, $8,000 in year 2, $7,000 in year 3, and $6,000 in year 4. The cost of capital is 12 percent. Worrall's marginal tax rate is 40 percent. The standard deviation of the project's *net present value* is $3,000.

What is the probability that this project will be an acceptable investment?

INTERMEDIATE

HTTP:

27. Use the sensitivity-analysis calculator maintained by SME to perform a cash flow sensitivity-analysis of a firm or project (http://www.smetoolkit.org/smetoolkit/en/content/en/751/Cash-Flow-Sensitivity-Analysis-Worksheet#sthash.OsHBVpjb.dpuf).

CHALLENGE

28. Jeff Himm has recently been hired as a financial analyst for the Bunich Corporation. Bunich has traditionally used the payback method in conjunction with NPV as a way to assess the risk of capital investments that the firm makes. Jeff is a new MBA graduate and is eager to put to work the tools he has learned.

One project that the firm is considering has an expected NPV of $1.5 million. An analysis of the cash flows of the project suggests that the most optimistic estimate of the NPV is $4 million, and the most pessimistic estimate is a negative $1 million. By most optimistic, Jeff explains that it is a value not expected to be exceeded more than 10 percent of the time. By most pessimistic, Jeff explains that it is a value not expected to be less than more than 10 percent of the time. Cash flows are expected to be normally distributed.

a. What is the probability that this project will be acceptable?
b. What is the probability that this project will have an NPV in excess of $1 million?

CHALLENGE

29. Boris' Bucket Works, Inc. (BBW) is the maker of new "easy spill" buckets. These buckets have quickly gained market share and now control 90 percent of the spillable bucket market. BBW is looking to do a product line expansion into the "spill-free" bucket market. The weighted cost of capital for BBW has been estimated to be 16 percent. BBW's beta is 1.3 and the risk-free rate is 6 percent. BBW has a capital structure composed of 40 percent debt and 60 percent equity. The marginal tax rate is 40 percent.

Using pro forma statements prepared by Boris, the expected NPV of this project is –$5 million. The most optimistic estimate of the NPV is $10 million and the most pessimistic estimate is –$20 million. By most optimistic, Boris means a value not likely to be exceeded more than 5 percent of the time. By most pessimistic, he means a value not likely to fall below more than 5 percent of the time. The distribution of NPV is assumed to be normally distributed.

a. What is the probability that this project will be acceptable to BBW, if the goal is to maximize shareholder wealth?
b. What other factors might be important in your analysis? Be specific.

INTEGRATIVE CASE PROBLEM

Capital Budgeting and Risk Analysis

ZeeBancorp is considering the establishment of a contract collection service subsidiary that would provide collection services to small and medium-size firms. Compensation would be in the form of a percentage of the amount collected. For amounts collected up to $100, the fee is 55 percent of the amount collected. For amounts collected between $100 and $500, the fee would be 40 percent of the total amount collected on the account. For amounts collected over $500, ZeeBancorp would receive 35 percent of the total amount collected on the account.

ZeeBancorp expects to generate the following amount of business during the first year of operation of the new subsidiary:

Account Class	Number of Collections	Average Amount Collected for Each Account
Up to $100	4,800	$75
Between $100 and $500	2,100	$325
Over $500	1,250	$850

Over the projected 10-year life of this collection venture, the number of accounts in each group is expected to grow at 6 percent per annum. The average amount collected from each account is expected to remain constant.

To establish the collection subsidiary, ZeeBancorp will have to rent office space at a cost of $250,000 for the first year. (Assume the rent is payable at the *end* of each year.) This amount is expected to grow at a rate of 11 percent per year. Other operating expenses (excluding depreciation) are expected to total $350,000 during the first year and grow at an 11 percent annual rate.

ZeeBancorp will have to invest $150,000 in net working capital if it undertakes this venture. In addition, required new equipment will cost $275,000 to purchase and an additional $25,000 to install. This equipment will be depreciated using the MACRS schedule for a 7-year asset. The salvage value for the equipment is estimated to be $50,000 at the end of 10 years.

The firm's *marginal* tax rate is estimated to be 40 percent over the project's life, and its *average* tax rate is projected to be 35 percent over the project's life. The firm requires a 15 percent rate of return on projects of average risk.

1. Compute the net investment required to establish the collection subsidiary.
2. Compute the annual net cash flows over the 10-year life of the project.
3. Compute the net present value of this project assuming it is an average-risk investment.
4. Should ZeeBancorp invest in the new subsidiary?
5. ZeeBancorp requires all expansion projects such as this to have a payback of four years or less. Under these conditions, should ZeeBancorp invest in the new subsidiary?
6. If management decides that this project has above-average risk and hence the required return is 20 percent, should the investment be made?
7. If collections are only 80 percent of projections and the required return is 20 percent, should the investment be made?
8. If operating (excluding depreciation) and lease expenses are expected to increase at an annual rate of 13 percent, should the collection subsidiary be established, assuming a required return of 20 percent and the original revenue projections?

PART 4

The Cost of Capital, Capital Structure, and Dividend Policy

This part considers three closely related topics: the cost of capital (Chapter 12), capital structure (Chapters 13 and 14), and dividend policy (Chapter 15). The cost of capital is an important input in the capital budgeting decision process. This market-determined cost of funds also directly influences the value of a firm's securities. The cost of capital cannot be considered in isolation. The capital structure of a firm directly affects its cost of capital. A more debt-laden capital structure will at some point increase the risk of the firm's securities and increase the overall cost of capital in the firm. This results in a reduction in the value of the firm. Chapters 13 and 14 look at the determinants of an "optimal" capital structure—one that is consistent with the objective of shareholder wealth maximization. Finally, the dividend policy of a firm (discussed in Chapter 15) impacts a firm's capital structure and provides important information that affects risk and return perceptions of the firm in the eyes of investors.

CHAPTER 12

The Cost of Capital

KEY CHAPTER CONCEPTS

1. The cost of capital is the rate of return required by investors in the firm's securities. The cost of capital determines the rate of return that the firm must earn on its new investments (of average risk) to maximize its value.
2. The required return on any security consists of a risk-free rate of return plus a premium for the risk of that security.
   a. The risk-free rate varies over time and is influenced by the expected rate of inflation and the supply and demand of funds in the overall economy.
   b. The risk premium on a specific security is influenced by the business risk of the firm, the financial risk of the firm, the marketability risk of the security, and the time to maturity of the security.
3. The weighted cost of capital is equal to the after-tax cost of debt times its proportion in the capital structure, plus the after-tax cost of preferred stock times its proportion in the capital structure, plus the cost of common equity times its proportion in the capital structure.
4. The weighted cost of capital is appropriate for determining the return required on projects of average risk.
5. For capital budgeting purposes, the marginal cost of each capital source needs to be calculated.
   a. The after-tax cost of debt is equal to the pretax cost of new debt times one minus the firm's marginal tax rate.
   b. The after-tax cost of a perpetual preferred stock is equal to the annual dividend divided by the net proceeds to the firm from the sale of preferred stock.
   c. The cost of internal equity capital can be computed using a version of the dividend valuation model, the capital asset pricing model, or a risk-premium-over debt approach.
   d. The cost of external equity capital exceeds the cost of internal equity capital by the amount of the issuance costs.
6. The beta concept can also be used to compute divisional costs of capital for firms with several operating divisions that differ substantially with respect to the risks of investments that are made.
7. The optimal capital budget can be determined by comparing the expected project returns to the company's marginal cost of capital schedule.
8. The cost of depreciation-generated funds is equal to the firm's weighted (marginal) cost of capital, before considering new stock issuance costs.

FINANCIAL CHALLENGE

Cost of Equity Capital for SourceGas Distribution LLC

In 1923, the U.S. Supreme Court issued a landmark decision in *Bluefield Water Works and Improvement Company v. Public Service Commission of the State of West Virginia* (262 U.S. 679). Among other things, this ruling set judicial standards regarding the rate of return a public utility is allowed to earn on its invested capital. The Court stated:

> *A public utility is entitled to such rates as will permit it to earn a return on the value of the property which it employs for the convenience of the public equal to that generally being made at the same time ... in other business undertakings which are attended by corresponding risks and uncertainties; ... The return should be reasonably sufficient to assure confidence in the financial soundness of the utility and should be adequate, under efficient and economical management, to maintain and support its credit and enable it to raise the money necessary for the proper discharge of its public duties. A rate of return may be reasonable at one time and become too high or too low by changes affecting opportunities for investment, the money market, and business conditions generally.*

This opinion has been affirmed in many subsequent cases, the most notable one being *Federal Power Commission et al. v. Hope Natural Gas Company* (320 U.S. 591) in 1944.

These decisions establish a number of basic principles that are used when a public utility commission decides on the rate of return a public utility is allowed an opportunity to earn on its equity capital. First, it has been established that the return on equity should be consistent with the opportunity cost principle; that is, the company should be permitted to earn a return equal to that being earned by other companies with similar risks. Second, the return should be sufficient to maintain the financial integrity of the company, maintain its credit, and give it access to the capital markets. Finally, it is recognized that the cost of capital changes depending on business conditions and conditions in the financial markets. The decisions, however, do not establish a methodology for determining the allowed rate of return on common equity to a public utility. In a typical rate case, there is normally extensive controversy regarding the cost of common equity.

Steve Satushek/Stone/Getty Images

SourceGas Distribution LLC is a natural gas distribution company providing residential, commercial, and industrial natural gas services in Colorado, Wyoming, Nebraska, and Arkansas. SourceGas was formerly a part of a larger public company, Kinder Morgan Inc. In a recent major rate case before the Public Service Commission of Wyoming, two witnesses submitted testimony on the cost of equity capital component of the rate case. Their recommendations follow:

- The company's rate of return witness recommended a cost of equity capital in the range of 10.9 percent to 13.8 percent, with a specific point recommendation of 12.0 percent.
- The Office of Consumer Advocate (OCA) also sponsored a rate of return witness who recommended a cost of equity capital range of 5.84 percent to 11.3 percent with a point estimate recommendation of 9.35 percent.

Having considered volumes of conflicting testimony on the issues and having heard at least one full day of live testimony on the question of the cost of equity capital, the Public Service Commission of Wyoming authorized a rate of return on equity capital for the company that was broadly consistent with the recommendations of the OCA witness.

FINANCIAL CHALLENGE — CONTINUED

This chapter develops the principles and models that can be used to compute a firm's cost of debt, preferred stock, and common equity capital. All of the models require the use of some judgment by the analyst. This is particularly true in the case of the cost of common equity. The cost of common equity cannot be computed with the same precision as is possible with debt and preferred stock. However, an analyst who is knowledgeable of the basic principles contained in this chapter can make reasonable estimates of the cost of equity capital for any company.

CHAPTER OBJECTIVES

Upon completion of this chapter, you should have a clear understanding of the following:

1. The calculation of the cost of debt
2. The calculation of the cost of preferred stock
3. The calculation of the cost of common equity
4. The calculation of the weighted average cost of capital
5. The difference between the historical and marginal costs of capital
6. The difference between book value weights and market value weights in calculating the cost of capital

12-1 Introduction

Chapters 9 through 11 considered the capital budgeting decisions of a firm. One of the key variables in capital expenditure analysis is the cost of capital. This chapter discusses the concept of the cost of capital and develops approaches that can be used to measure this important variable.

cost of capital

The cost of capital is concerned with what a firm has to pay for the capital—that is, the debt, preferred stock, retained earnings, and common stock—it uses to finance new investments. It can also be thought of as the rate of return required by investors in the firm's securities. As such, the firm's cost of capital is determined in the capital markets and is closely related to the degree of risk associated with new investments, existing assets, and the firm's capital structure. In general, the greater the risk of a firm as perceived by investors, the greater the return investors will require, and the greater will be the cost of capital.

The cost of capital can also be thought of as the minimum rate of return required on new investments undertaken by the firm.[1] If a new investment earns an internal rate of return that is greater than the cost of capital, the value of the firm increases.

[1]Technically, this statement assumes that the risk of the new investments is equal to the risk of the firm's existing assets. Also, when used in this context, the cost of capital refers to a weighted cost of the various sources of capital used by the firm. The computation of the weighted cost of capital is considered in this chapter.

Correspondingly, if a new investment earns a return less than the firm's cost of capital, the firm's value decreases.

This chapter discusses the weighted cost of capital and its use in the capital budgeting process. The nature of the risk versus required return trade-off made by investors in a firm's securities and the measurement of the cost of individual capital components (debt, common equity, and preferred stock) are also presented. Chapters 13 and 14 continue by considering the relationship between capital structure and the cost of capital.

12-2 Summary of Notation

Before beginning the discussion of the cost of capital, it is helpful to summarize the important elements of notation used throughout this chapter.

r_f = riskless (risk-free) rate of return; the return offered on short-term U.S. Treasury securities

k_d = pretax cost of debt

k_i = after-tax cost of debt

k_p = cost of preferred stock

k_e = cost of internal common equity

k_e' = cost of external common equity

k_a = weighted (marginal) cost of capital

P_0 = the current market price of a security

P_{net} = the net proceeds to the firm from the sale of a security

P_f = market value of a firm's preferred stock

E = market value of a firm's common equity

B = market value of a firm's debt in its capital structure

r_m = expected return on the "market" portfolio

β = the beta (systematic risk) of a company's stock

12-3 Weighted Cost of Capital

weighted cost of capital

Foundation Concept

The *weighted cost of capital* is an extremely important input in the capital budgeting decision process. The **weighted cost of capital** is the discount rate used when computing the net present value (NPV) of a project of *average* risk. Similarly, the weighted cost of capital is the hurdle rate used in conjunction with the internal rate of return (IRR) approach to project evaluation (for a project of average risk).

Thus, the appropriate after-tax cost of capital figure to be used in capital budgeting not only is based on the next (marginal) capital to be raised, but also is weighted by the proportions of the capital components in the firm's long-range target capital structure. Therefore, this figure is called the *weighted*, or *overall, cost of capital.*

The general expression for calculating the weighted cost of capital, k_a, follows:[2]

[2]In the absence of preferred stock in a firm's capital structure, Equation 12.1 can be simplified to:

$$k_a = \left(\frac{E}{E+B}\right)(k_e) + \left(\frac{B}{E+B}\right)(k_d)(1-T)$$

$$k_a = \begin{pmatrix}\text{Equity}\\\text{fraction}\\\text{of}\\\text{capital}\\\text{structure}\end{pmatrix}\begin{pmatrix}\text{Marginal}\\\text{cost}\\\text{of}\\\text{equity}\end{pmatrix} + \begin{pmatrix}\text{Debt}\\\text{fraction}\\\text{of}\\\text{capital}\\\text{structure}\end{pmatrix}\begin{pmatrix}\text{Marginal}\\\text{cost}\\\text{of}\\\text{debt}\end{pmatrix}$$

(12.1)

$$+ \begin{pmatrix}\text{Preferred}\\\text{fraction}\\\text{of}\\\text{capital}\\\text{structure}\end{pmatrix}\begin{pmatrix}\text{Marginal}\\\text{cost}\\\text{of}\\\text{preferred}\\\text{stock}\end{pmatrix}$$

$$= \left(\frac{E}{E+B+P_f}\right)(k_e) + \left(\frac{B}{E+B+P_f}\right)(k_d)(1-T) + \left(\frac{P_f}{E+B+P_f}\right)(k_p)$$

where B is debt, P_f is preferred stock, E is common equity in the target capital structure, k_e is the marginal cost of equity capital, k_d is the marginal pretax cost of debt capital, and k_p is the marginal cost of preferred stock capital.

12-3a Market Value Versus Book Value Weights

When computing the weighted cost of capital for a company, a decision must be made whether to use the proportions of debt, preferred stock, and common equity based on balance sheet values for each of these capital sources, or to use weightings based on market values of debt, preferred stock, and common equity. Although the market value of debt and preferred stock are normally close to their book value, the market value of common equity frequently diverges greatly from the book value of equity. Which weightings are more consistent with the goal of maximizing shareholder value?

It is generally agreed that the preferred weighting to use is the market value weights. Consider the marginal common stock investor. Assume this investor has paid \$20 per share for common stock that was purchased and that the investor's expected rate of return is 12.5 percent (for example, the cost of equity computed using the constant growth dividend valuation model). Assume also that the book value of that share of common stock is currently \$7. When market value weights are used in computing the weighted cost of capital, it is assumed that the marginal investor will be satisfied with a 12.5 percent rate of return on their investment. However, if book values are used, we are assuming that the marginal common stock investor is satisfied with a 12.5 percent return on a book value of \$7. This is clearly incorrect since the appropriate value of the marginal investor's investment is the market price per share of \$20, not the book value of \$7.

Consequently, it is recommended that market value weights be used for the various component costs in the calculation of the weighted cost of capital, especially when there is a significant divergence between book values and market values. However, throughout the discussion that follows and in the problems at the end of the chapter, we present calculations using both book and market value weights for several reasons. First, some firms prefer to use book value weights because market values change daily and it is not practical to calculate a new cost of capital on a daily basis. Second, in the case of privately held firms, book value may have to be used because market prices of the various sources of capital to the private firm are not easily estimated. Many practitioners blend both approaches by combining book values of debt and preferred stock with the market value of common equity. This is done because most firms have several different issues of debt and preferred stock, not all of which are publicly held or traded; consequently, market prices are often unavailable for these securities and book values have to be substituted.

12-3b Gasco Inc.'s Weighted Cost of Capital

Gasco Inc. (GAI), a natural gas company, has a target capital structure consisting of 47 percent common equity, 51 percent debt, and 2 percent preferred stock. The company plans to finance future capital investments in these proportions. All common equity is expected to be derived internally from additions to retained earnings.

The marginal cost of internal common equity has been estimated to be 10.4 percent using the dividend valuation approach. The marginal cost of preferred stock is 8.1 percent and the pretax marginal cost of debt is 8 percent. The marginal tax rate is 40 percent. Using these figures, the weighted cost of capital for GAI can be computed using Equation 12.1 as follows:

$$\begin{aligned} k_a &= 0.47 \times 10.4\% + 0.51 \times 8.0\%(1 - 0.4) + 0.02 \times 8.1\% \\ &= 7.5\% \end{aligned}$$

This is the rate that GAI should use to evaluate investment projects of average risk over the coming year. Table 12.1 illustrates the weighted cost of capital calculation for GAI.

In the following sections, the techniques used to compute each of the component capital costs are presented and illustrated. Then more complex weighted cost of capital schedule calculations are presented.

12-3c The Problem of "Lumpy" Capital

Firms usually raise funds in "lumpy" amounts; for example, a firm may sell $50 million in bonds to finance capital expenditures at one point in time, and it may use retained earnings or proceeds from the sale of stock to finance capital expenditures later on. In spite of this tendency to raise funds in lumpy amounts from various sources at different points in time, the weighted (or composite) cost of funds, not the cost of any particular component of funds, is the cost we are interested in for capital budgeting purposes. Another way of saying this is that *it is generally incorrect to associate any particular source of financing with a particular project*; that is, the investment and the financing decisions should be separate.[3]

TABLE 12.1

Weighted Cost of Capital for Gasco, Inc.

Source of Capital	After-Tax Cost	Target Proportion of Capital	Weighted Cost
Internal common equity	10.4%	0.47	4.89%
Debt	4.8	0.51	2.45
Preferred stock	8.1	0.02	0.16
		1.00	7.50%

[3]This statement is generally true; however, there are exceptions. For example, some projects may possess a higher "debt capacity" than is present for the firm as a whole. This may be due to a different level of business risk. The evaluation of mergers frequently considers the debt capacity of the to-be-acquired firm. Hence, the financing of the project may be considered along with the investment decision itself.

Consider, for example, the case of a firm that is financed 50 percent with debt and 50 percent with equity. The after-tax cost of equity is 16 percent, and the after-tax cost of debt is 10 percent. The firm has two plants, A and B, which are identical in every respect. The manager of Plant A proposes to acquire a new automated packaging machine costing $10 million. A bank has offered to loan the firm the needed $10 million at a rate that will give the firm a 10 percent after-tax cost. The internal rate of return for this project has been estimated to be 12 percent. Because the rate of return exceeds the cost of funds (debt) used to finance the machine, the manager of Plant A argues that the investment should be made.

The manager of Plant B now argues that she, too, should be allowed to make a similar investment. Unfortunately, she is reminded that the firm has a target capital structure of 50 percent debt and 50 percent equity and that her investment will have to be financed with equity in order for the firm to maintain its target capital structure. Because the cost of equity is 16 percent and the project offers only a 12 percent return, the investment is denied for Plant B.

The point of this illustration is that two economically identical projects were treated very differently, simply because the method of financing the projects was tied to the accept-reject decision. To avoid problems of this type, the capital expenditure decision is usually based on a composite capital cost—that is, each project is assumed to be financed with debt and equity in the proportion in which it appears in the target capital structure. In this example, the composite cost of capital is 13 percent, computed as follows:

Source of Capital	After-Tax Cost	Proportion	Composite Cost
Debt	10%	0.5	5%
Equity	16%	0.5	8%
		Weighted cost of capital =	13%

In this example, neither project should be accepted, because the company's weighted cost of capital exceeds the projects' expected rates of return.

Accordingly, as a firm evaluates proposed capital expenditure projects, it normally does not specify the proportions of debt, preferred stock, and common equity financing for each individual project. Instead, each project is presumed to be financed with the same proportion of debt, preferred stock, and equity contained in the company's target capital structure.

12-4 Relative Costs of Capital

Figure 12.1 illustrates the general risk-return trade-off between investors' required rates of return and various sources of funds. As was noted, the risk-free rate, r_f, is usually measured as the rate of return on short-term U.S. Treasury securities. Longer-term U.S. government bonds normally command a higher rate than shorter-term debt because bond prices vary more than prices of shorter-term debt securities over time for equal changes in interest rates. Thus, if interest rates rise, the price of long-term bonds falls, resulting in losses for any investor who must sell the security prior to maturity. Investors normally require a premium to compensate for this interest rate risk.

Long-term debt securities of the U.S. government are always less risky than corporate long-term debt securities of the same maturity. The reason, of course, is the finite probability, however small, that the company will default on its obligation to pay interest and

FIGURE 12.1

General Risk–Required Return Trade-Off

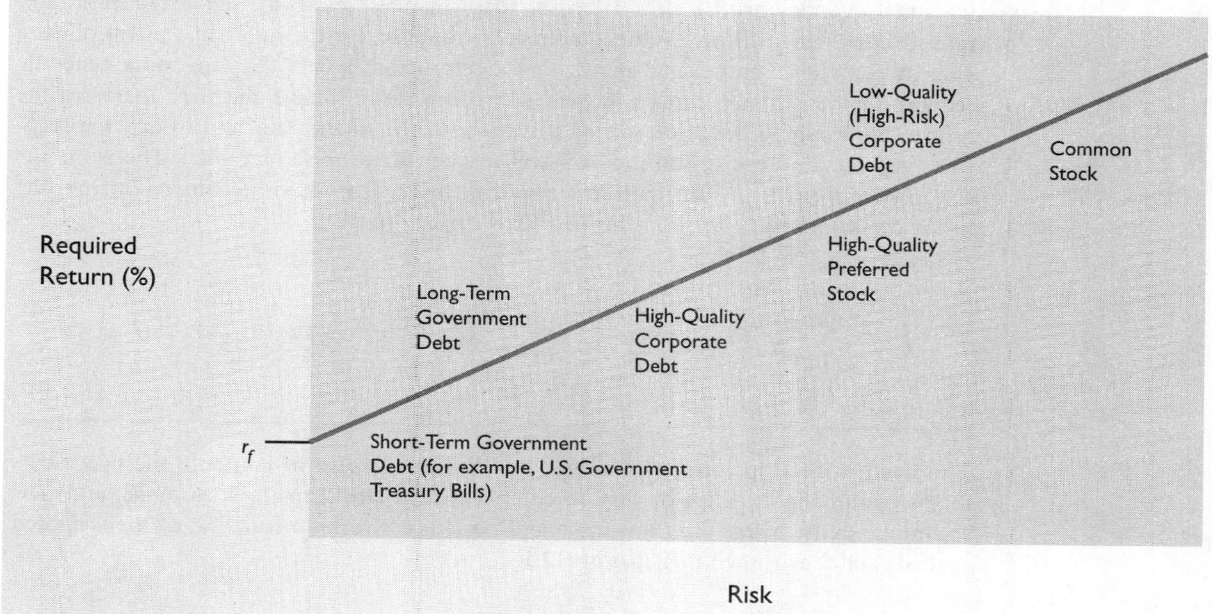

principal. Because the government controls the money supply, it can always meet its nominal financial obligations by printing more money. The actual difference in returns, or yields, between government debt and high-quality corporate debt (AAA rated) is often less than 1 percent and sometimes less than 0.5 percent. In December 2015, the average yield on 10-year AAA corporate bonds was 2.94 percent, and the average yield on 10-year U.S. Treasury bonds was 2.27 percent. Companies with higher default risk must offer high coupon interest rates to investors in order to sell their debt issues because the market recognizes that these higher-default-risk companies are more likely to have difficulty meeting their obligations than lower-default-risk companies. For example, the yield in December 2015 on BBB-rated bonds was 4.14 percent.

HTTP:
For more information on bond yields and interest rate spreads, see

finance.yahoo.com/bonds/composite_bond_rates

Preferred stock is normally riskier than debt. The claims of preferred stockholders on the firm's assets and earnings are junior to those of debt holders. Also, dividends on preferred stock are more likely to be cut or omitted than interest on debt. Consequently, investors usually demand a higher return on a company's preferred stock than on its debt.

Common stock is the riskiest type of security considered here, because dividends paid to common stockholders are made from cash remaining after interest and preferred dividends have been paid. Thus, the common stock dividends are the first to be cut when the firm encounters difficulties. Because there is a greater degree of uncertainty associated with common stock dividends than with the interest on debt or preferred stock dividends, common stock dividends are judged riskier. In addition, the market price fluctuations of common stocks tend to be wider than those of preferred stocks or long-term debt. As a result of this higher risk, investors' required returns on common stock are higher relative to preferred stock and debt. Over the years, the differences between returns realized from long-term corporate debt and common stock of large companies have averaged approximately 5.7 percent.[4]

So far, this section has shown that a particular security's risk affects the return required by investors. The analysis must be taken one important step further, however. If capital markets are to clear (that is, supply equals demand), the firm must offer returns consistent with investor requirements. Suppose, for example, that a firm offers a security for sale in the capital markets at a return that is less than investors generally require. Obviously, not enough buyers will come forth. Unless the firm increases the return (by dropping the price, raising the interest or dividend rate, and so on), the securities will remain unsold, and the firm will not be able to raise its capital. Therefore, *the cost of capital to the firm is equal to the equilibrium rate of return demanded by investors in the capital markets for securities with that degree of risk.*

12-5 Computing the Component Costs of Capital

This section develops and applies methods a firm can use to compute the cost of its major component sources of capital: debt, preferred stock, retained earnings, and new common equity. These are the component costs used in the calculation of the weighted cost of capital as shown in Equation 12.1.

12-5a Marginal Costs

Firms calculate their cost of capital in order to determine a discount rate to use for evaluating proposed capital expenditure projects. Recall that the purpose of capital expenditure analysis is to determine which *proposed* projects the firm should *actually* undertake. Therefore, it is logical that *the capital whose cost is measured and compared with the expected benefits from the proposed projects should be the next or marginal capital the firm raises.*

As we saw in Chapter 9, the capital budgeting process involves an extension of the marginal analysis principle from economics. The marginal revenue (internal rate of return) from a project is compared with the marginal cost of funds needed to finance the project. The marginal cost of funds is the cost of the next increments of capital raised by the firm. Hence, the costs of the various capital funding components (debt, preferred stock, and common equity) must be their marginal costs. Historic *average* capital costs are not relevant for making new (marginal) resource allocation decisions.

When computing the marginal cost of the various component capital sources, companies typically estimate the component costs they anticipate encountering (paying) during the coming year. If capital costs change significantly during the year, it may be necessary to recompute the new capital costs and use the new estimates when evaluating projects from that time forward. Under most circumstances, a semiannual or annual computation of marginal capital costs is sufficient.

12-5b Cost of Debt

The cost of debt capital to the firm is the rate of return required by a firm's creditors. For a debt issue, this rate of return, k_d, equates the present value of all expected future

[4] *Stocks, Bonds, Bills, and Inflation: 2015 Yearbook*™ (Chicago: Morningstar, 2015): Table 6-7.

receipts—interest, I, and principal repayment, M—with the net proceeds, P_{net}, of the debt security (as discussed earlier in Chapter 6):

$$P_{net} = \sum_{t=1}^{n} \frac{I}{(1 + k_d)^t} + \frac{M}{(1 + k_d)^n} \tag{12.2}$$

or

$$P_{net} = I(\text{PVIFA}_{k_d,n}) + M(\text{PVIF}_{k_d,n}) \tag{12.3}$$

The pretax cost of debt, k_d, is calculated in the same way as the yield-to-maturity, shown in Chapter 6. The only difference in the calculation is that when making yield-to-maturity calculations, the price of the bond is the current market price. When computing the pretax cost of debt to a company, the price of the bond is the net proceeds the company receives after considering all issuance costs.

Interest payments made to investors are deductible from the firm's taxable income. Therefore, the *after-tax* cost of debt, k_i, is computed by multiplying the pretax cost of debt, k_d, by 1 minus the firm's marginal tax rate, T:[5]

$$k_i = k_d(1 - T) \tag{12.4}$$

To illustrate the cost-of-debt calculation for GAI, assume that the firm sells $100 million of 20-year 7.8 percent coupon rate bonds. The net proceeds to GAI after issuance costs are $980 for each $1,000 bond. To compute the pretax cost, k_d, of this debt offering, the relationship in Equation 12.3 can be used as follows:

$$\text{Net proceeds} = P_{net} = \$78(\text{PVIFA}_{k_d,20}) + \$1{,}000(\text{PVIF}_{k_d,20})$$

Calculator Solutions

Key	Enter
n	20
i	
PV	−980
PMT	78
FV	1000
	Solution
i	8.00

The calculation of k_d can be done either by trial and error using Tables IV and II at the end of the book or with the aid of a financial calculator.

By trial and error, try 8 percent:

$$\begin{aligned}\$980 &= \$78(9.818) + \$1000(0.215)\\ &\approx \$980\end{aligned}$$

Therefore, the pretax cost of debt is 8 percent.

Assuming a 40 percent marginal tax rate, the after-tax cost of debt is computed using Equation 12.4:

$$\begin{aligned}k_i &= k_d(1 - T)\\ &= 8\%(1 - 0.4)\\ &= 4.80\%\end{aligned}$$

The tax benefits of interest deductibility are available only to firms that are making profits. For a firm losing money, the tax rate in Equation 12.4 is *zero*, and the after-tax cost, k_i, is the same as the pretax cost, k_d.

This procedure works well when a firm is in the process of selling, or has just sold, bonds at the time the cost of capital is being computed. However, in most instances, trips to the capital markets are sporadic. How can the marginal cost of debt be computed in these cases? That is, how can one determine what it would cost a firm to sell debt today (at the time of the cost-of-capital calculation)? This problem has two solutions:

1. If a firm has bonds that are currently outstanding and are being traded in the marketplace, the firm can observe the current market price for those bonds. Given a

[5]The conversion from a pretax to an after-tax cost of debt is accurate when there are no bond issuance costs. When a bond offering entails issuance costs and the bond is sold either at a discount or premium over face value, there will be a small, insignificant error when using Equation 12.4.

current price, the maturity of the bonds, and the coupon rate of interest, the yield-to-maturity on the bond can be computed. This yield-to-maturity may be used as an estimate of the marginal pretax cost of debt, k_d, for the firm.[6]

2. If a firm's outstanding bonds are not traded frequently or are privately held, then the best estimate of the marginal pretax cost of debt can be derived by looking at the pretax cost of debt recently sold by other firms having risk similar to the firm under consideration. For these purposes, having similar risk is normally interpreted to mean that firms have equivalent bond ratings (according to Moody's or Standard & Poor's).

12-5c Cost of Preferred Stock

The cost of preferred stock to the firm is the rate of return required by investors on preferred stock issued by the company. Because many preferred stocks are perpetuities, it is possible to use the simplified preferred stock valuation model developed in Chapter 6.

(12.5)
$$P_0 = \frac{D_p}{k_p}$$

where P_0 is the preferred stock price; D_p, the annual preferred dividend; and k_p, the investors' required rate of return. The cost of preferred stock, k_p, is given by the following equation:

(12.6)
$$k_p = \frac{D_p}{P_{net}}$$

In calculating preferred stock cost, the price that should be used, P_{net}, is the net proceeds to the firm, that is, the proceeds from the sale of the stock after subtracting *issuance costs*.

To illustrate, GAI has just issued 3 million shares of a preferred stock that pay an annual dividend of \$4.05 per share. The preferred stock was sold to the public at a price of \$52 per share. With issuance costs of \$2 per share, the marginal cost of preferred stock is calculated as follows:

$$k_p = \frac{\$4.05}{\$52 - \$2}$$
$$= 0.081 \text{ or } 8.1\%$$

Because payments by the firm to preferred stockholders are in the form of dividends, they are not tax deductible; therefore, the after-tax cost of preferred stock is equal to the pretax rate.

An increasing number of preferred stock issues are callable, have a sinking fund redemption provision, or have a fixed maturity. In these cases, the computation of the cost of preferred stock financing is similar to that for bonds. For example, Progress Energy plans an offering of \$50 par value preferred stock that will pay a \$5.00 dividend per year. The preferred stock is expected to yield Progress net proceeds of \$46.40 per share after all issue costs. The preferred stock must be retired at its par value in 15 years. The cost of this preferred stock issue can be computed by solving for k_p in the following valuation model:

$$P_{net} = \$46.40 = \$5(PVIFA_{k_p,15}) + \$50(PVIF_{k_p,15})$$

[6]This computed yield-to-maturity likely will understate slightly the pretax marginal cost of debt because it does not consider issuance costs.

Calculator Solutions

Key	Enter
n	15
i	
PV	−46.50
PMT	5
FV	50
	Solution
i	11.00

Try:

$$k_p = 11\%$$
$$\$46.40 = \$5(7.191) + \$50(0.209)$$
$$= \$35.95 + \$10.45$$
$$\$46.40 = \$46.40$$

Therefore, k_p equals 11 percent for Progress's anticipated preferred stock offering.

12-5d Cost of Internal Equity Capital

Like the cost of debt and preferred stock, the cost of equity capital to the firm is the equilibrium rate of return required by the firm's common stock investors.

Firms raise equity capital in two primary ways:

- *Internally,* through retained earnings
- *Externally,* through the sale of new common stock

Some analysts and managers incorrectly assume that the cost of internal equity is zero. The opportunity cost concept makes it clear that this is an erroneous assumption. When funds are generated through the earnings of the firm, either managers can pay out these funds as dividends to common stockholders, or the funds can be retained and reinvested in the firm. If the funds were paid out to stockholders, they could reinvest the funds elsewhere to earn an appropriate return, given the risk of the investment. Therefore, if managers decide to retain earnings and reinvest them in the firm, there must be investment opportunities in the firm offering a return equivalent to the returns available to common stockholders, on a risk-adjusted basis, in alternative investments.

The cost of internal equity to the firm is less than the cost of new common stock because the sale of new stock requires the payment of issuance costs. The concept of the cost of internal equity (or simply *equity,* as it is commonly called) can be developed using several different approaches. The first considered here is based on the dividend valuation model.

12-5e Dividend Valuation Model Approach

Briefly reviewing from Chapter 7, the general dividend valuation model (or the *dividend capitalization model,* as it is often referred to) for common stock valuation is as follows:

$$P_0 = \sum_{t=1}^{\infty} \frac{D_t}{(1 + k_e)^t} \tag{12.7}$$

where P_0 is the stock's present value or current market price; D_t, the dividend received in period t; and k_e, the return required by investors. This equation shows that in efficient capital markets, k_e, the required return and thus the cost of equity capital, equates the present value of all expected future dividends with the current market price of the stock. In principle, the cost of equity capital can be calculated by solving Equation 12.7 for k_e. In practice, however, the expected future dividends are not known and cannot be estimated with the same degree of confidence as preferred stock dividends and debt interest. As a result, the general form of the dividend valuation model is not directly useful in calculating the cost of equity capital.

As shown in Chapter 7, if the firm's future per-share dividends are expected to grow each period perpetually at a constant rate, g, the dividend valuation model can be written as follows:

$$P_0 = \frac{D_1}{k_e - g} \tag{12.8}$$

where $D_1 = D_0(1 + g)$ and D_0 is the current period dividend ($t = 0$). Note that in Equation 12.8, k_e must be greater than g, the expected growth rate. As discussed in Chapter 7, the *constant growth valuation model* assumes that a firm's earnings, dividends, *and* stock price will grow at rate g. Thus, g equates to the yearly price appreciation (capital gain). But the total return to stockholders, k_e, is composed of both the price appreciation *and* the dividend yield. Therefore, g cannot be greater than or equal to k_e because it is only one of two components making up k_e.

Equation 12.8 can be rearranged to obtain an expression for calculating the cost of equity, assuming that dividends are expected to grow perpetually at a rate g per year:[7]

$$k_e = \frac{D_1}{P_0} + g \tag{12.9}$$

To illustrate the use of Equation 12.9, suppose GAI's common stock is currently selling for \$56 a share. Its present dividend, D_0, is \$0.20 a share, and the expected long-term earnings and dividend growth rate is 10.0 percent. The cost of internal equity capital, k_e, is calculated as follows:

$$k_e = \frac{\$0.20(1 + 0.10)}{\$56} + 0.10$$

$$= 0.104 \text{ or } 10.4\%$$

Nonconstant Dividend Growth and the Cost of Common Equity The dividend valuation model can also be used to compute the cost of equity for common stocks expected to pay dividends that grow at variable rates in the future. An approach similar to the nonconstant growth dividend valuation model illustrated in Chapter 7 (Equation 7.14) can be used.

For example, Avtec Corporation is a rapidly growing producer of microcircuit boards used in the aerospace industry. Its stock is currently selling for \$10.95 per share. Current dividends, D_0, are \$1.00 per share and are expected to grow at a rate of 10 percent per year over the next 4 years and 6 percent annually thereafter. Avtec's cost of internal equity, k_e, can be found as follows:

$$\$10.95 = \frac{\$1.10}{(1 + k_e)^1} + \frac{\$1.21}{(1 + k_e)^2} + \frac{\$1.33}{(1 + k_e)^3} + \frac{\$1.46}{(1 + k_e)^4} + \frac{1}{(1 + k_e)^4} \times \frac{\$1.55}{k_e - 0.06}$$

$$= \$1.10(\text{PVIF}_{k_e,1}) + \$1.21(\text{PVIF}_{k_e,2}) + \$1.33(\text{PVIF}_{k_e,3})$$

$$+\$1.46(\text{PVIF}_{k_e,4}) + (\text{PVIF}_{k_e,4})\frac{\$1.55}{k_e - 0.06}$$

Note that the last term in this expression, $\$1.55/(k_e - 0.06)$, is equal to the expected stock price at the beginning of year 5 (which is the same as the end of year 4 in time-value terms). Hence it must be discounted back four periods.

[7]The relevant growth rate is the rate expected by investors. This is normally estimated by examining projected future growth rates provided by security analysts, such as Value Line, Merrill Lynch, Zacks, IBES, and Thomson Financial First Call. Analyst earnings forecasts can be found on Yahoo Finance.

The valuation expression must be solved for k_e, the cost of equity capital, using a trial-and-error procedure. A trial value of 17 percent for k_e yields the following:

$$\begin{aligned}\$10.95 &= \$1.10(0.855) + \$1.21(0.731) + \$1.33(0.624) \\ &\quad + \$1.46(0.534) + 0.534\left(\frac{\$1.55}{0.17 - 0.06}\right) \\ &= \$10.95\end{aligned}$$

Thus, Avtec's cost of equity is 17 percent.

In principle, the general dividend valuation model approach can be used to estimate the cost of equity capital for any expected dividend pattern. In practice, many stocks not only have exhibited rather constant growth rates in the past, but look as though they will continue to do so in the future. For these stocks, the constant growth form of the dividend capitalization model is appropriate, and the expected growth rate often can be estimated in the manner discussed in the next section.

12-5f Issues in Implementation

Dividend valuation models (sometimes also referred to as *DCF models*) are frequently used in the calculation of a firm's cost of equity capital. In implementing these models, the analyst must obtain an estimate of the growth rate(s) in earnings and dividends (and stock price) expected by investors. Where can these investor expectations be obtained?

Investors form expectations about future growth rates based upon past realized growth, current earnings and retention rates, expected future earnings rates (such as the return on equity), and conditions in the markets that the firm serves. These factors are often well summarized in the form of analysts' estimates of future growth rates. Analysts' forecasts may be viewed as the best market- and investor-available summary of all of the factors that determine future growth rates. There are two reasons for this. First, a considerable body of research supports the conclusion that analysts' estimates of future earnings growth rates are very accurate—consistently more accurate than estimates provided from any other forecasting model.[8] Second, another body of research has confirmed that analysts' forecasts outperform extrapolative forecasts in explaining share prices.[9]

HTTP:
www.zacks.com
www.thomsonreuters.com/financial

Analyst forecasts are available from a number of sources. As discussed in greater detail in Chapter 7, they can be obtained from individual brokerage houses and investment advisory services, such as Merrill Lynch, Goldman Sachs, and Value Line. In addition, the Thomson Financial First Call summarizes the short- and long-term earnings forecasts made by analysts from major investment firms throughout the United States. Thomson covers the stocks of more than 3,500 firms. Similar growth rate consensus forecasts are available from *Zacks Earnings Estimates*.

12-5g Capital Asset Pricing Model (CAPM) Approach

Capital Asset Pricing Model (CAPM)

Many firms use the **Capital Asset Pricing Model (CAPM)**, discussed in Chapter 8, to compute their cost of common equity. The CAPM formally describes the risk–required

[8] See, for example, L. D. Brown and M. S. Rozeff, "The Superiority of Analyst Forecasts as Measures of Expectations: Evidence from Earnings," *Journal of Finance* (March 1978): 1–16; M. S. Rozeff, "Predicting Long-Term Earnings Growth: Comparisons of Expected Return Models, Submartingales and Value Line Analysts," *Journal of Forecasting* (December 1983): 425–435; R. C. Moyer, R. E. Chatfield, and G. D. Kelley, "The Accuracy of Long-Term Earnings Forecasts in the Electric Utility Industry," *International Journal of Forecasting* 3 (1985): 241–252; and R. C. Moyer, R. E. Chatfield, and P. Sisneros, "The Accuracy of Long-Term Earnings Forecasts for Industrial Firms," *Quarterly Journal of Business and Economics* (Summer 1989): 91–104.

[9] See, for example, J. G. Cragg and B. G. Malkiel, *Expectations and the Structure of Share Prices* (Chicago: University of Chicago Press, 1982); and R. Harris, "Using Analysts' Growth Forecasts to Estimate Shareholder Required Rates of Return," *Financial Management* (Spring 1986): 58–67.

FIGURE 12.2

Security Market Line (SML)

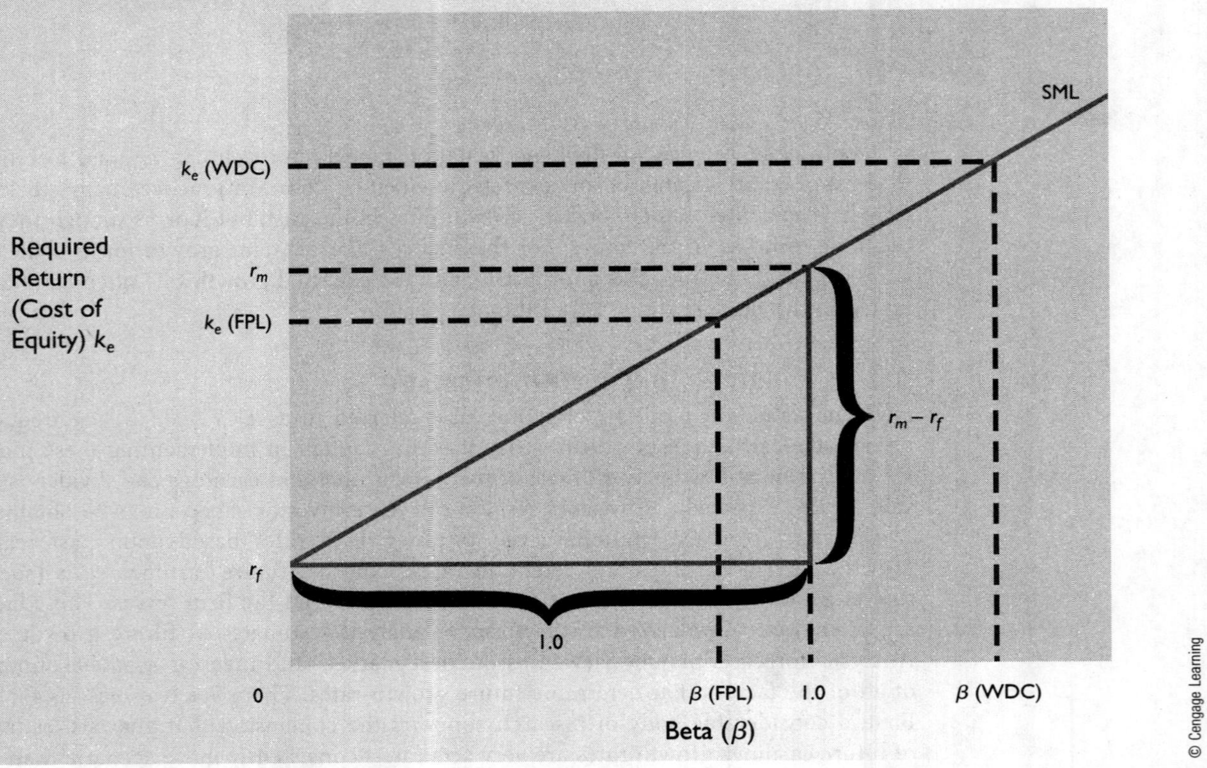

return trade-off for securities. The rate of return required by investors consists of a risk-free return, r_f, plus a premium compensating the investor for bearing the risk. This risk premium varies from stock to stock.

Less risk is associated with an investment in a stable stock, such as FPL Group (FPL), a Florida public utility company, than in the stock of Western Digital (WDC), a medium-size computer components firm. As a result, an investor in Western's stock, WDC, requires a higher return than the FPL investor. Figure 12.2 illustrates the difference in required rates of return (or the cost of internal equity) for the two securities. The relationship illustrated in this figure is the security market line (SML). The SML depicts the risk–required return relationship in the market for all securities.

Recall from Chapter 8 that the security market line is defined as follows:[10]

(12.10)
$$k_j = r_f + \beta_j(r_m - r_f)$$

where k_j = the required rate of return on any security j; r_f = the expected risk-free rate; β_j = the beta (systematic risk) measure for security j; and r_m = the expected return on the market portfolio. Hence, the value $(r_m - r_f)$ equals the market risk premium (the slope of the SML), or the risk premium applicable to a stock of average ($\beta = 1.0$) risk.

[10]In Chapter 8, we used a hat (^) over the r_f and r_m variables to indicate these are *expected* values. For simplicity, the hats are dropped here, but it should be kept in mind that we are still dealing with expected values for these variables.

The SML concept is based on investors' expectations regarding a security's risk and return characteristics. Required returns for any individual security are also dependent on expected future levels of interest rates and the expected return on the market as a whole. These expected values are determined as follows:

- *The risk-free rate* (r_f). The value for r_f that is most frequently used in computing the required return for a security is the 3- or 6-month U.S. Treasury bill rate. (Some practitioners prefer to use a long-term government bond rate instead.)
- *The expected market return* (r_m). The expected market return is the return investors expect to earn in the future on stocks with an average beta of 1.0. The average market risk premium measured relative to 90-day Treasury bill rates has been around 8–9 percent over the past 88 years. The average market risk premium measured relative to long-term government bond income returns has been 7 percent over the same period.[11] Risk premiums such as these may be used for the market risk premium ($r_m - r_f$) in Equation 12.10. Remember that if the market risk premium relative to short-term Treasury bill rate is used, then the risk-free rate (the first term on the right-hand side of Equation 12.10) must be the short-term Treasury bill rate. If the market risk premium relative to long-term government bond rate is used, then the risk-free rate must be the long-term government bond rate, such as the yield on 20-year U.S. government bonds.
- *The firm's* beta (β_j). Beta is normally estimated by using historic values of the relationship between a security's returns and the market returns. In Chapter 8, we illustrated the computation of the beta for Alliance Motors. The *Value Line Investment Survey* and brokerage firms, such as Merrill Lynch, regularly compute and provide betas.[12]

To illustrate, GAI's beta is 0.70. If short-term Treasury bills are yielding 3.05 percent and the short-term market risk premium is assumed to be 8.2 percent, GAI's cost of equity capital may be computed using the short-term SML as follows:

$$\begin{aligned} k_e &= r_f + \beta_j(r_m - r_f) \\ &= 3.05\% + 0.7(8.2\%) \\ &= 8.8\% \end{aligned}$$

If the longer-term version of the SML is used, and the yield on long-term U.S. Treasury bonds is 4.95 percent and the long-term market risk premium is assumed to be 6.6 percent, GAI's cost of equity capital may be computed as:

$$\begin{aligned} k_e &= r_f + \beta_j(r_m - r_f) \\ &= 4.95\% + 0.7(6.6\%) \\ &= 9.6\% \end{aligned}$$

Note the variation between the two SML estimates of GAI's cost of equity and also the variation between these estimates and the 10.4 percent figure derived using the constant growth dividend valuation model earlier in the chapter. Such variation is normal and highlights the fact that estimates of the cost of equity capital are subject to some error.

The SML concept is one more tool that may be used in computing the firm's cost of equity capital, k_e. If all the parameters required of the model are correctly estimated (r_f, $r_m - r_f$, and β_j), the model should give a reasonably accurate estimate of k_e. Many analysts find it useful to compute k_e in more than one way to arrive at a consensus about the rate of return investors require on a security, as is demonstrated in the Financial Challenge at the beginning of this chapter.

---

[11] *Stocks, Bonds, Bills, and Inflation: 2015 Yearbook,*™ Table 6.7.

[12] Because of statistical biases inherent in the historic computation of betas, these reported betas are often adjusted to provide a better estimate of future betas.

INTERNATIONAL ISSUES

Market Equity Risk Premiums Around the World[a]

There remains considerable disagreement among practitioners and academics regarding the best market equity risk premium to use when applying the CAPM model. For example, in 2015, a survey of 1,985 finance and economics professors, analysts, and company managers in the United States yielded an average market risk premium of 5.5 percent. The median value of this risk premium was 5.3 percent. The standard deviation of the expected risk premium was 1.4 percent.

There is considerably more variation in market risk premium estimates when one looks internationally. The surveys, also using responses from professors, analysts, and companies, yielded the following results:

Country	Average Market Risk Premium (%) (2015)
Japan	5.8
Turkey	9.3
South Africa	7.7
China	8.1
India	8.4

The observed variation in market risk premiums suggests that these premiums tend to be lower in major economies and higher in less stable economies. In addition to the observed range of market risk premiums reflected in the table, there is also a considerable range of estimates within most countries. For example, the standard deviation of the estimates of the market risk premium range from 1.2 percent in Switzerland and 1.4 percent in the United States to 5.6 percent in China and 12.3 percent in Argentina.

Country	Average Market Risk Premium (%) (2015)
United States	5.5
Germany	5.3
France	5.6
Spain	5.9
Colombia	8.3
Russia	9.7
Brazil	7.5
Argentina	22.9

Thus, it is apparent from these data that the determination of the CAPM-derived cost of equity capital has considerable variation globally and even within a country.

[a]P. Fernandez, A. Ortiz and J. Acin, "Discount Rate (Risk-Free Rate and Market Risk Premium) Used in 41 Countries in 2015: A Survey" SSRN (November 19, 2015), http://ssrn.com/abstract=2598104

Recall from Chapter 8 that the beta measure of risk considers only the systematic risk or market risk of a stock. Poorly diversified investors may be more interested in total risk than in systematic risk. When this is true, the CAPM may understate returns required by those investors.

12-5h Risk Premium over Debt and Other Approaches for Estimating the Cost of Equity Capital

This section begins by considering a shortcut method of estimating the cost of equity capital based on actual historic returns and ends by discussing non-dividend-paying stocks.

Studies analyzing the historical returns earned by common stock investors have found that the holding period returns from average risk common stock investments over very long time periods have averaged approximately 5.7 percentage points higher than holding period returns on corporate debt issues.[13] Therefore, the cost of equity capital for an average-risk company (a firm with a beta of about 1.0) can be estimated by adding

[13]*Stocks, Bonds, Bills, and Inflation: 2015 Yearbook,*™ Table 6–7.

approximately 5.7 percentage points to the company's current pretax cost of debt. For companies with a less-than-average level of systematic risk, such as electric utilities (electric utility betas average about 0.7), a risk premium over the company's current cost of long-term debt of 3 to 5 percentage points has been found to be approximately correct. For companies with a higher-than-average level of systematic risk, a risk premium in excess of 5.7 percentage points is warranted. Studies have shown that equity risk premiums over a company's debt yields tend to be higher when interest rates are relatively low and lower when interest rates are relatively high. Many analysts use this shortcut method as a reference. Whenever possible, however, the other, more precise methods should be used.

For stocks that do not pay dividends, the dividend capitalization model is obviously an inappropriate valuation model and therefore cannot be used to determine an accurate cost of equity capital. Investors in non-dividend-paying stocks expect to sell the stock in the future at a higher price than the present price, realizing a capital gain. Investors' expectations about the future price are incorporated into the following valuation model:[14]

(12.11)

$$P_0 = \frac{P_t}{(1 + k_e)^t}$$

where P_t is the expected stock price at time t. In principle, a firm could use this valuation model to determine its cost of equity capital. In practice, however, this would be difficult to do, because the company probably has no way of confidently determining the P_t expectations of investors. Instead, the cost of equity capital for non-dividend-paying stocks normally is determined either by using the Capital Asset Pricing Model, the risk premium on debt approach, or by estimating k_e for comparable dividend-paying stocks in their industry.

12-5i Cost of External Equity Capital

The cost of external equity is greater than the cost of internal equity for the following reasons:

- Issuance (flotation) costs associated with new shares are usually high enough that they cannot realistically be ignored.
- The selling price of the new shares to the public is normally set less than the market price of the stock before the announcement of the new issue. Before any announcement, the current market price of a stock usually represents an equilibrium between supply and demand. If supply is increased (all other things being equal), the new equilibrium price will be lower.

In addition, Masulis and Trueman have argued that retained earnings are a cheaper source of funds than the sale of new equity because retention defers the payment of taxable dividends to shareholders and, therefore, reduces the present value of taxes that must be paid by shareholders.[15]

When a firm's future dividend payments are expected to grow at a constant rate of g per period forever, the cost of external equity, k_e', is defined as follows:

(12.12)

$$k_e' = \frac{D_1}{P_{net}} + g$$

[14]If investors in a non-dividend-paying stock expected the company to begin paying dividends at some future date, a form of the dividend capitalization model could be constructed to reflect these expectations.

[15]R. W. Masulis and B. Trueman, "Corporate Investment and Dividend Decisions Under Differential Personal Taxation," *Journal of Financial and Quantitative Analysis* 23 (1988): 369–386.

where P_{net} is the net proceeds to the firm on a per-share basis.[16] To illustrate, consider NICOR Corporation. Its current stock price is $39 per share. NICOR pays a current annual dividend of $1.68 per share. The consensus forecast from security analysts is that earnings and dividends will grow at an annual rate of 6.5 percent per annum for the foreseeable future.

The cost of internal equity capital for NICOR using a constant growth dividend valuation model is:

$$k_e = \frac{\$1.68(1 + 0.065)}{\$39} + 0.065$$

$$= 0.111 \text{ or } 11.1\%$$

The cost of external equity capital, assuming that new shares of stock could be sold to net the company $37 per share, is:

$$k'_e = \frac{D_1}{P_{net}} + g$$

$$= \frac{\$1.68(1 + 0.065)}{\$37} + 0.065$$

$$= 0.113 \text{ or } 11.3\%$$

Because of the relatively high cost of newly issued equity, many companies try to avoid this means of raising capital. The question of whether a firm should raise capital with newly issued common stock depends on its investment opportunities.

Table 12.2 summarizes the cost of capital formulas developed in the preceding sections.

12-6 Divisional Costs of Capital

The approaches already discussed provide an estimate of the return required by equity investors on investment projects of so-called average risk. When some divisions of a company have lower (higher) systematic risk than others, the discount rates for projects adopted by these divisions should be lower (higher) than the discount rate for the firm as a whole.

For example, West Coast Power is an electric utility that has a calculated beta of 0.91. The firm has three divisions: the electric power generation and distribution division, which has 70 percent of the firm's assets; an oil and gas exploration division, which has 20 percent of the assets; and a transportation and barge division, which has 10 percent of the assets. Using surrogate market information—that is, estimating the beta for one or more firms that are purely (or nearly so) engaged in the business of each of West Coast's major divisions (the so-called pure play approach) and using these surrogate betas (after adjusting for leverage differentials using Equations 11.6 and 11.7 that were discussed in the previous chapter)—the beta for each division is estimated as shown here:

[16] An alternative approach to the treatment of issuance costs is to allocate the dollar amount of these costs to individual projects, thus increasing the project cost. When this procedure is used, no adjustment to capital costs is required. This procedure may be superior (from a theoretical perspective) to the cost of capital adjustment procedure, but it is difficult to implement and not widely used.

TABLE 12.2

Formulas for Computing Component Costs

Cost of debt

$$k_i = k_d(1 - T)$$

k_d = Pretax cost of debt

= Yield-to-maturity on a new bond issue when the current price of the bond is set equal to the net proceeds to the issuing company

Cost of preferred stock (for perpetual preferred stock)

$$k_p = \frac{\text{Annual preferred dividend}}{\text{Net proceeds to the company}} = \frac{D_p}{P_{net}}$$

Cost of internal common equity

1. Dividend capitalization model approach, used when dividends grow at a perpetual constant rate:

$$k_e = \frac{\text{Next year's expected dividend}}{\text{Common stock price}} + \text{Expected dividend growth rate} = \frac{D_1}{P_0} + g$$

2. Capital Asset Pricing Model approach:

$$k_e = \text{Risk-free return} + \text{Risk premium} = r_f + \beta_j(r_m - r_f)$$

Cost of external common equity

$$k'_e = \frac{\text{Next year's expected dividend}}{\text{Net proceeds per share to the company}} + \text{Expected dividend growth rate} = \frac{D_1}{P_{net}} + g$$

	Estimated Divisional Beta	Proportion of Firm's Assets	Weighted Average Beta
Electric power	0.75	0.70	0.53
Exploration	1.30	0.20	0.26
Transportation	1.20	0.10	0.12
		Weighted average firm beta =	0.91

Note that the weighted average of the divisional betas is equal to the firm's overall beta—in this case, 0.91.

Conglomerate firms that compete in many different product and geographical markets, such as United Technologies or General Electric, often estimate separate divisional costs of capital. These divisional costs of capital reflect both the differential required returns of equity investors, estimated from the security market line, and the differential debt-carrying capacity of each division. For example, the parent company may have a debt-to-total-assets ratio of 60 percent. Individual divisions within the firm may compete against other firms that typically have higher or lower debt-to-total-assets ratios. In computing each divisional cost of capital, many firms try to reflect both the differential divisional risks and the differential normal debt ratios for each division.

12-7 Determining the Weighted (Marginal) Cost of Capital Schedule

In the beginning of the chapter, the computation of the weighted (marginal) cost of capital was based on the assumption that the firm would get equity funds only from internal sources, that all debt had a single cost, and that all preferred stock had a single cost. The procedure illustrated in that earlier discussion must be modified if the firm anticipates selling new common stock (having a higher component cost) or issuing additional increments of debt securities at successively higher costs to finance its capital budget.

To illustrate, suppose the Major Foods Corporation is developing its capital expenditure plans for the coming year. The company's schedule of potential capital expenditure projects for next year is as follows:

Project	Amount (in Millions of Dollars)	Internal Rate of Return
A	$4.0	13.8%
B	8.0	13.5
C	6.0	12.5
D	5.0	12.0
E	8.0	11.0
F	4.0	10.0

These projects are closely related to the company's present business and have the same degree of risk as its existing assets.

The firm's current capital structure (as well as its targeted future capital structure) consists of 40 percent debt, 10 percent preferred stock, and 50 percent common equity measured on the basis of the current market value of debt, preferred stock, and equity in the capital structure. Table 12.3 shows the current balance sheet for Major Foods. Major Foods can raise up to $5 million in debt funds at a pretax cost of 9 percent; debt amounts exceeding $5 million will cost 10 percent. Preferred stock can be sold at an after-tax cost of 10 percent. Major Foods' marginal tax rate is 40 percent.

Major Foods expects to generate $10 million of retained earnings over the coming year. Its present dividend rate, D_0, is $2 per share. The firm's common stock is now

TABLE 12.3

Balance Sheet for Major Foods (in Millions of Dollars)

Assets		Liabilities and Equity	
Current assets	$100	Current liabilities	$50
Fixed assets	30	Long-term debt	32 (40%)
Total assets	$130	Preferred stock	8 (10%)
		Common equity	40 (50%)
		Total liabilities and equity	$130

selling at $25 per share, and new common stock can be sold to net the firm $24 per share.[17]

Over the past several years, Major Foods' earnings and dividends have grown at an average of 7 percent per year, and this growth rate is expected to continue for the foreseeable future. The company's dividend payout ratio has been, and is expected to remain, more or less constant.

Given this information, Major Foods' weighted (marginal) cost of capital can be calculated for the coming year:

- **Step 1: Calculate the cost of capital for each individual component**—the cost of debt, the cost of preferred stock, and the cost of equity.

Cost of debt:

$$k_i = k_d(1 - T) = 9.0 \times 0.6 = 5.4\% \text{ for the first \$5 million of debt}$$
$$k_i = k_d(1 - T) = 10.0 \times 0.6 = 6.0\% \text{ for debt exceeding \$5 million}$$

Cost of preferred stock:

$$k_p = 10\%(\text{given})$$

Cost of common equity:

Internal (for amounts of retained earnings up to $10 million):

$$k_e = \frac{D_0(1+g)}{P_0} + g$$
$$= \frac{\$2(1.07)}{\$25} + 0.07 = 0.156, \text{ or } 15.6\%$$

External (for amounts of common equity greater than $10 million of retained earnings):

$$k_e' = \frac{\$2(1.07)}{\$24} + 0.07 = 0.159, \text{ or } 15.9\%$$

- **Step 2: Compute the weighted (marginal) cost of capital for each increment of capital raised.** Major Foods should raise funds in proportion to its target capital structure from its lowest-cost sources first. In this case, these sources are retained earnings (15.6% after-tax cost), preferred stock (10% after-tax cost), and the first $5 million in debt (5.4% after-tax cost). When these sources are exhausted, the company should consider using the higher cost sources—external equity (15.9% after-tax cost) and additional debt (6.0% after-tax cost)—together with preferred stock.

How much total financing through combining retained earnings, preferred stock, and debt can be done before the $5 million in low-cost debt is exhausted and Major must acquire additional debt funds at the higher cost? Because we know that the target capital structure consists of 40 percent debt, the total financing, *X*, that this will support is equal to the amount of low-cost debt available divided by the debt fraction in the capital structure:

$$X = \frac{\text{Amount of low-cost debt available}}{\text{Debt fraction of capital structure}}$$
$$= \frac{\$5 \text{ million}}{0.40}$$
$$= \$12.5 \text{ million}$$

This $12.5 million level represents a break point in the marginal cost of capital schedule. *Break points* delineate the levels of financing where the weighted cost of capital increases due to an increase in the cost of one component source of capital; that is, debt, preferred stock, or common equity.

Break points can be determined by dividing the amount of funds available from each financing source at a fixed cost by the target capital structure proportion for that financing source. Thus, we saw in the Major Foods example that the $5 million of debt, with an

[17]The net proceeds per share depend on the number of shares sold. As a very general rule, underwriters are reluctant to sell new shares in an amount that exceeds 10 to 15 percent of a company's existing shares.

INTERNATIONAL ISSUES

The Cost of Capital for Multinational Companies

Multinational companies face a more complex cost of capital problem than purely domestic firms. However, the increased complexity of the problem also offers opportunities to reduce capital costs.

Multinational companies have an opportunity to raise capital in other countries' capital markets, as well as at home, whenever these firms have major operations in foreign countries. One opportunity open to multinational firms is that a host country's government may offer preferential (subsidized) financing terms as an incentive for a firm to locate some of its operations in that country.

Evidence also indicates significant, persistent real differences in the cost of capital between countries. For example, studies of the relative real costs of capital for U.S. and Japanese firms have concluded that during the 1980s, the cost of capital for U.S. firms averaged about 3.3 percentage points higher than for Japanese firms. However, as global capital markets become more integrated and barriers to international capital flows are reduced, opportunities to take advantage of country-to-country differences in capital costs have diminished. Evidence now suggests that differences in capital costs between U.S. firms and firms in most major industrialized countries have all but disappeared.

Most multinational companies raise all or the vast majority of their equity capital in their home country. However, multinational firms commonly raise a substantial portion of their debt capital in the countries in which they maintain significant operations. By doing so, a multinational firm effectively hedges much of the balance sheet risk associated with changes in the value of assets in place due to changes in exchange rates. For example, if Sara Lee builds a plant in France, the accounting value of this investment will decline with decreases in the value of the euro against the U.S. dollar.[a] Offsetting this decline in the accounting value of the French subsidiary's assets is a decline in the value of the debt obligations (when converted to dollars) of the subsidiary. Another advantage of raising a significant portion of a multinational firm's capital in the countries in which it operates is the fact that this insulates the firm from much of the risk of expropriation.

In summary, multinational firms have an opportunity to shop the world for capital that will hedge currency and capital cost risks in the international capital markets.

[a]The value references made here are limited to the accounting value of the assets. The market value of the French assets may actually increase with declines in the value of the euro because the goods produced by the plant will be relatively cheaper when sold for export.

after-tax cost of 5.4 percent, would support total financing of \$12.5 million. Beyond \$12.5 million in total financing, the weighted (marginal) cost of capital will rise because higher-cost debt (6.0%) must now be used. Of this \$12.5 million in total financing, \$5 million will be debt, \$1.25 million (10% of the total) will be preferred stock, and \$6.25 million will be retained earnings. The cost of this first block of funds using Equation 12.1 is as follows:

$$k_a = 0.50 \times 15.6\% + 0.40 \times 5.4\% + 0.10 \times 10\%$$
$$= 10.96\%$$

The amount of available retained earnings also determines a break point. The \$10 million of retained earnings will support total financing of \$20 million (\$10 million/0.5). Therefore, a new break point occurs at a total financing level of \$20 million. Beyond that point, the weighted cost of capital increases due to the higher cost (15.9%) of external equity. Thus, the second block of financing totals \$7.5 million (\$20 million equity break point minus \$12.5 million debt financing break point).

This \$7.5 million block of funds represents the size of the second lowest-cost block of funds. Of this \$7.5 million in financing, \$3.75 million will be retained earnings,

FIGURE **12.3**

Weighted (Marginal) Cost of Capital Schedule for Major Foods

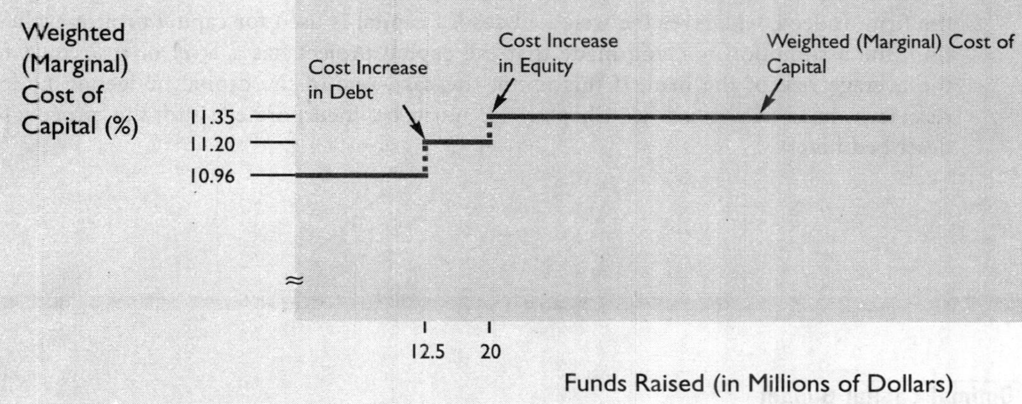

$0.75 million will be preferred stock, and $3 million will be debt. The cost of this second block of funds will be as follows:

$$k_a = 0.50 \times 15.6\% + 0.40 \times 6.0\% + 0.10 \times 10\%$$
$$= 11.20\%$$

Beyond the second block, all additional funds raised will be with high-cost debt, new common stock, and preferred stock. The weighted cost of these funds is as follows:

$$k_a = 0.50 \times 15.9\% + 0.40 \times 6.0\% + 0.10 \times 10\%$$
$$= 11.35\%$$

Figure 12.3 provides a graph of the weighted (marginal) cost of capital schedule for Major Foods.

The weighted (marginal) cost of capital schedule now can be used to determine the optimal capital budget for Major Foods. This procedure is illustrated in the next section.

12-8 Determining the Optimal Capital Budget

optimal capital budget

The **optimal capital budget** can be determined by comparing the expected project returns to the company's marginal cost of capital schedule. This is accomplished by first plotting the returns expected from the proposed capital expenditure projects against the cumulative funds required. The resulting graph is called an **investment opportunity curve**. Next, the previously calculated k_a for the three capital "packages" are combined to

investment opportunity curve

determine the company's *marginal cost of capital curve.* The optimal capital budget is indicated by the point at which the investment opportunity curve and the **marginal cost of capital** curve intersect, as shown in Figure 12.4.

marginal cost of capital

Specifically, the Major Foods Corporation's optimal capital budget totals $23 million and includes Projects A, B, C, and D. Projects E and F are excluded, because their returns are expected to be below the 11.35 percent cost of funds. Acceptance of Projects E and F would result in a decrease in the firm's value. In principle, the optimal capital budget maximizes the value of the firm.

The procedure for determining the optimal capital budget discussed in this section assumes that all projects being considered are equal in risk to the average risk of the firm. Indeed, whenever the weighted cost of capital is used for capital project evaluation, the assumption is being made that the capital project has a level of risk equal to the average risk of the firm. If this is not the case, one of the capital budgeting under risk techniques discussed in Chapter 11 must be incorporated into the procedure described here.

FIGURE 12.4

Determining the Optimal Capital Budget

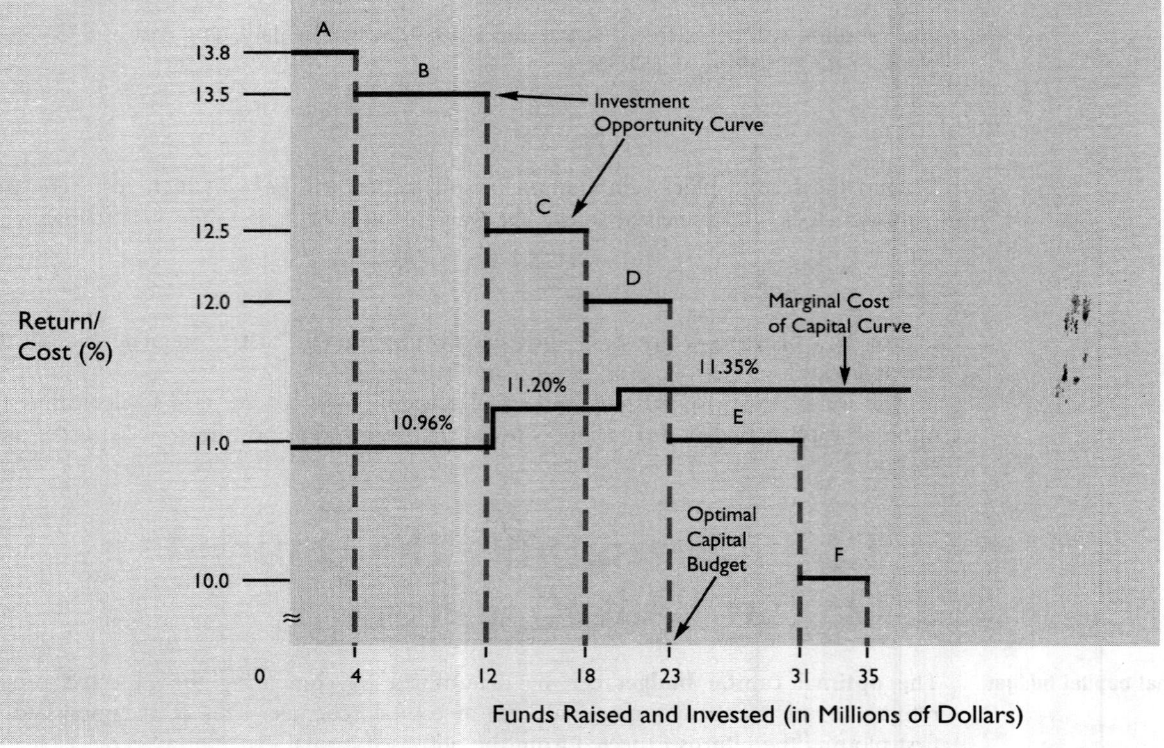

ENTREPRENEURIAL ISSUES

The Cost of Capital

Small firms have a difficult time attracting capital to support their investment programs. Owners of small firms are reluctant to sell common stock because they do not want to lose voting control in the company. When shares are sold, many small firms create two classes of stock, such as Class A and Class B. The Class A stock is the one that is traded most extensively in the capital markets. Class A stock usually receives a higher dividend than Class B. In contrast, Class B stock, often held by the company's founders, has greater voting power than Class A stock. In this way, capital can be raised without losing voting control.

Many firms are so small that it is nearly impossible to raise funds by selling common stock. If stock can be sold, investors will often pay much less for these shares than they would for similar firms that are larger and have their stock traded regularly on an organized exchange or over the counter. Issuance costs for common stock sales of small firms may exceed 20 percent of the issue size. As a consequence, the cost of equity capital tends to be significantly higher for small firms than it is for larger firms. Because of the limited access to the capital markets for new equity, small firms tend to retain a much larger portion of their earnings to fund future growth than larger firms.

Similarly, the sources of debt capital to small firms are also limited. Bonds and debentures cannot be sold publicly until a firm has grown to a relatively large size. Before reaching a size that will permit it to sell securities publicly, the small firm will have to rely upon the following sources for debt funds:

- The owners' own funds and loans from friends
- Loans from commercial banks and savings and loan associations
- Small Business Administration loans
- Commercial finance company loans
- Leasing companies
- Venture capital firms that normally demand some equity interest in the firm through conversion features or warrants (discussed in Chapter 20)
- Private placements of debt issues with insurance companies and large corporations, often with a conversion feature or warrants

Generally, the cost of both debt and equity capital is significantly higher for small firms than for larger firms. The high cost of capital puts small firms at a competitive disadvantage relative to large firms in raising funds needed for expansion.

Conceptually, computing the cost of capital for a small, closely held firm is no different from that for a large, publicly traded firm. The same models of valuation apply to small firms as to large firms. In practice, however, there are often serious difficulties in developing confident estimates of the cost of capital for small firms. Computing the cost of straight debt and preferred stock (nonconvertible and without attached warrants) is relatively easy. However, when debt and preferred stock securities are convertible or have attached warrants, an analyst must make an estimate about the time and conditions under which these securities will be converted into common stock or when the warrants to purchase common stock will be exercised.

In the case of common stock, there is often no ready market for the stock. Hence, it may not be possible to make confident estimates of the stock price when computing the cost of equity. Also, because many small firms pay little or no dividends, applying the dividend valuation model is more difficult. As a consequence, when computing the cost of equity for small firms, analysts must often compute the cost of equity for a group of larger, publicly traded companies in the same line of business and with a similar financial risk (as measured by the capital structure) and then add an additional risk premium reflective of the perceived increased risk due to reduced marketability and liquidity of the small firm's stock and any differential in business and financial risk.

12-9 Cost of Depreciation-Generated Funds

One large source of funds for many firms is funds generated from depreciation. Of course, depreciation per se does not generate cash. Rather, depreciation is simply a non-cash expense charged against income. Therefore, a firm's reported net income will normally understate the amount of cash flow generated by the firm during a given time period. To adjust net income for the cash flow effect of depreciation, the amount of depreciation must be added to net income after taxes. It is in this sense that depreciation represents a source of funds. Also, some firms may generate funds from the sale of assets from time to time. What is the cost of these funds? Because the firm always has the option to either reinvest these funds in the firm or to return them to the stockholders as dividends and to retire outstanding debt, the appropriate opportunity cost of these funds is the firm's weighted (marginal) cost of capital, before considering new stock issuance costs.

With respect to the marginal cost of capital schedule in Figure 12.4, it is generally agreed that these funds have an opportunity cost equal to the first "block" of funds, that is, 10.96 percent. If \$10 million in depreciation-generated funds were available, the first block of funds would increase from \$12.5 million to \$22.5 million, and all other blocks would also be shifted to the right by \$10 million.

12-10 Summary

- A firm's *cost of capital* is defined as the rate the firm has to pay for the debt, preferred stock, common stock, and/or retained earnings it uses to finance its new investments in assets. The cost of capital is the rate of return required by investors in the firm's securities. Cost of capital can also be thought of as the minimum rate of return required on new investments of average risk undertaken by the firm.
- The higher the risk of a security, the higher is the return required by investors. In general, common stock is more risky than preferred stock; preferred stock is more risky than corporate debt securities; and corporate debt securities are more risky than government debt securities. Investors' required returns generally decrease in the same order.
- Firms normally use an after-tax *weighted cost of capital* to evaluate proposed capital expenditure projects. Each project is presumed to be financed with the same proportion of debt, preferred stock, and common equity contained in the company's target capital structure.
- A firm's pretax *cost of debt capital*, k_d, is the rate of return required by investors. The after-tax cost of debt, k_i, is calculated as follows:

$$k_i = k_d(1 - T) = \text{Coupon interest rate } (1 - T)$$

  where T is the firm's marginal tax rate.
- A firm's *cost of preferred stock*, k_p, is the rate of return required by the preferred stock investors. In the case of perpetual preferred stock, the cost is calculated as follows:

$$k_p = \frac{D_p}{P_{net}}$$

  where D_p is the annual preferred dividend and P_{net} is the preferred stock price net of issuance costs on new issues. Preferred stock is used relatively infrequently as a source of capital because its after-tax cost is normally significantly greater than that of debt. This is because interest on debt is a tax-deductible expense for the firm, whereas dividends on stock are not.

- A firm's *cost of equity capital* is defined as the rate of return required by its common stock investors. Equity capital can be raised *internally* through retained earnings and *externally* through the sale of new common stock.
- A firm's *cost of internal equity* can be determined by the dividend valuation model, the Capital Asset Pricing Model (CAPM), using the security market line (SML), or the risk premium on debt approach.
- A firm's *cost of external equity,* k_e', is greater than the cost of internal equity because of issuance expenses.
- The *optimal capital budget* maximizes the value of the firm and occurs at the point where the firm's *investment opportunity curve* and *weighted marginal cost of capital curve* intersect. The investment opportunity curve is obtained by plotting the returns expected from proposed capital expenditure projects against the cumulative funds required.

Important Equations

$$k_a = \begin{pmatrix}\text{Equity}\\ \text{fraction}\\ \text{of}\\ \text{capital}\\ \text{structure}\end{pmatrix}\begin{pmatrix}\text{Marginal}\\ \text{cost}\\ \text{of}\\ \text{equity}\end{pmatrix} + \begin{pmatrix}\text{Debt}\\ \text{fraction}\\ \text{of}\\ \text{capital}\\ \text{structure}\end{pmatrix}\begin{pmatrix}\text{Marginal}\\ \text{cost}\\ \text{of}\\ \text{debt}\end{pmatrix}$$

$$+ \begin{pmatrix}\text{Preferred}\\ \text{fraction}\\ \text{of}\\ \text{capital}\\ \text{structure}\end{pmatrix}\begin{pmatrix}\text{Marginal}\\ \text{cost}\\ \text{of}\\ \text{preferred}\\ \text{stock}\end{pmatrix}$$

$$= \left(\frac{E}{E+B+P_f}\right)(k_e) + \left(\frac{B}{E+B+P_f}\right)(k_d)(1-T) + \left(\frac{P_f}{E+B+P_f}\right)(k_p)$$

$$P_{net} = I(\text{PVIFA}_{k_d,n}) + M(\text{PVIF}_{k_d,n})$$

$$k_i = k_d(1-T)$$

$$k_p = \frac{D_p}{P_{net}}$$

$$k_e = \frac{D_1}{P_0} + g$$

$$P_0 = \frac{P_t}{(1+k_e)^t}$$

$$k_e' = \frac{D_1}{P_{net}} + g$$

$$k_j = r_f + \beta_j\,(r_m - r_f)$$

12-11 Questions and Topics for Discussion

1. How do retained earnings differ from other sources of financing?
2. Does the retained earnings figure shown on a firm's balance sheet necessarily have any relationship to the amount of retained earnings the firm can generate in the coming year? Explain.
3. Why is corporate long-term debt riskier than government long-term debt?
4. Why do investors generally consider common stock to be riskier than preferred stock?
5. Should a firm pay cash dividends in a year in which it raises external common equity?
6. Discuss the meaning of an *optimal* capital budget.
7. Evaluate the statement "Depreciation-generated funds have no explicit cost and therefore should be assigned a zero cost in computing a firm's cost of capital."
8. Describe how to derive the break points in the marginal cost of capital schedule.
9. Discuss the pros and cons of various sources of estimates of future earnings and dividend growth rates for a company.
10. What market risk premium should be used when applying the CAPM to compute the cost of equity capital for a firm if:
    a. The risk-free rate is the 90-day Treasury bill rate?
    b. The risk-free rate is the 20-year government bond rate?
11. What factors determine the required rate of return for any security?
12. What are the similarities and differences in preferred stock and debt as sources of financing for a firm?
13. Why is the marginal cost of capital the relevant concept for evaluating investment projects, rather than a firm's actual, historic cost of capital?

12-12 Self-Test Problems

ST1. Scherr Enterprises has a series of 8 percent coupon bonds outstanding with a $1,000 par value. The bonds mature in 10 years and currently sell for $946. If new bonds are issued, the issuance cost is expected to be $11 per bond. Scherr's marginal tax rate is 40 percent. What is the marginal after-tax cost of debt for Scherr? (Assume annual interest payments.)

ST2. Clarke Equipment currently pays a common stock dividend of $3.50 per share. The common stock price is $60. Analysts have forecast that earnings and dividends will grow at an average annual rate of 6.8 percent for the foreseeable future.

a. What is the marginal cost of retained earnings?

b. What is the marginal cost of new equity if the issuance costs per share are $3?

ST3. Vargo Inc. has a beta estimated by Value Line of 1.3. The current risk-free rate (short-term) is 7.5 percent and the market risk premium is 8.6 percent. What is the cost of equity capital for Vargo?

ST4. Walther Enterprises has a capital structure target of 60 percent common equity, 15 percent preferred stock, and 25 percent long-term debt. Walther's financial analysts have estimated the marginal, after-tax cost of debt, preferred stock, and common equity to be 9 percent, 15 percent, and 18 percent, respectively. What is the weighted marginal cost of capital for Walther?

ST5. Penguin Industries Inc. has a capital structure that currently consists of 40 percent debt and 60 percent common stock, which it considers optimal. Penguin can raise up to \$60 million in long-term debt at a pretax cost of 10 percent. Above \$60 million, the pretax cost of debt is expected to increase to 14 percent. The company's marginal tax rate is 40 percent. Its stock currently sells for \$60 per share and has a beta of 1.20. The company is expected to pay a \$3.60 per share dividend next year, which is expected to grow at a rate of 6 percent per year for the foreseeable future. Penguin expects to generate \$180 million in retained earnings during the coming year. New shares can be sold to net the company \$56 per share. Determine the marginal cost of capital schedule and the break points in the schedule for Penguin.

12-13 Problems*

BASIC **1.** Calculate the after-tax cost of a \$25 million debt issue that Pullman Manufacturing Corporation (40% marginal tax rate) is planning to place privately with a large insurance company. This long-term issue will yield 9.375 percent to the insurance company.

BASIC **2.** Husky Enterprises recently sold an issue of 10-year maturity bonds. The bonds were sold at a deep discount price of \$615 each. After flotation costs, Husky received \$604.50 each. The bonds have a \$1,000 maturity value and pay \$50 interest at the end of each year. Compute the after-tax cost of debt for these bonds if Husky's marginal tax rate is 40 percent.

BASIC **3.** Calculate the after-tax cost of preferred stock for Bozeman-Western Airlines Inc., which is planning to sell \$10 million of \$6.50 cumulative preferred stock to the public at a price of \$50 a share. Issuance costs are estimated to be \$2 a share. The company has a marginal tax rate of 40 percent.

INTERMEDIATE **4.** St. Joe Trucking has sold an issue of \$6 cumulative preferred stock to the public at a price of \$60 per share. After issuance costs, St. Joe netted \$57 per share. The company has a marginal tax rate of 40 percent.

a. Calculate the after-tax cost of this preferred stock offering assuming that this stock is a perpetuity.

b. If the stock is callable in 5 years at \$66 per share and investors expect it to be called at that time, what is the after-tax cost of this preferred stock offering? (Compute to the nearest whole percent.)

INTERMEDIATE **5.** The stock of Alpha Tool sells for \$10.25 per share. Its current dividend rate, D_0, is \$1 per share. Analysts and investors expect Alpha to increase its dividends at a 10 percent rate for each of the next 2 years. This annual dividend growth rate is expected to decline to 8 percent for years 3 and 4 and then to settle down to 4 percent per year forever. Calculate the cost of internal equity for Alpha Tool.

INTERMEDIATE **6.** The Hartley Hotel Corporation is planning a major expansion. Hartley is financed 100 percent with equity and intends to maintain this capital structure after the expansion. Hartley's beta is 0.9. The expected market return is 16 percent, and the risk-free rate is 10 percent. If the expansion is expected to produce an internal rate of return of 17 percent, should Hartley make the investment?

*Color blocks behind the numbers denote problems that have check answers provided at the end of the book.

CHALLENGE

7. Wentworth Industries is 100 percent equity financed. Its current beta is 0.9. The expected market rate of return is 14 percent and the risk-free rate is 8 percent.
   a. Calculate Wentworth's cost of equity.
   b. If Wentworth changes its capital structure to 30 percent debt, it estimates that its beta will increase to 1.1. The after-tax cost of debt will be 7 percent. Should Wentworth make the capital structure change?

INTERMEDIATE

8. The Ewing Distribution Company is planning a $100 million expansion of its chain of discount service stations to several neighboring states. This expansion will be financed, in part, with debt issued with a coupon interest rate of 15 percent. The bonds have a 10-year maturity and a $1,000 face value, and they will be sold to net Ewing $990 after issue costs. Ewing's marginal tax rate is 40 percent.

   Preferred stock will cost Ewing 14 percent after taxes. Ewing's common stock pays a dividend of $2 per share. The current market price per share is $15, and new shares can be sold to net $14 per share. Ewing's dividends are expected to increase at an annual rate of 5 percent for the foreseeable future. Ewing expects to have $20 million of retained earnings available to finance the expansion.

   Ewing's target capital structure is as follows:

Debt	20%
Preferred stock	5
Common equity	75

   Calculate the weighted cost of capital that is appropriate to use in evaluating this expansion program.

INTERMEDIATE

9. Pacific Intermountain Utilities Company has a present capital structure (which the company feels is optimal) of 50 percent long-term debt, 10 percent preferred stock, and 40 percent common equity. For the coming year, the company has determined that its optimal capital budget can be externally financed with $70 million of 10 percent first-mortgage bonds sold at par and $14 million of preferred stock costing the company 11 percent. The remainder of the capital budget will be financed with retained earnings. The company's common stock is presently selling at $25 a share, and next year's common dividend, D_1, is expected to be $2 a share. The company has 25 million common shares outstanding. Next year's net income available to common stock (including net income from next year's capital budget) is expected to be $106 million. The company's past annual growth rate in dividends and earnings has been 6 percent. However, a 5 percent annual growth in earnings and dividends is expected for the foreseeable future. The company's marginal tax rate is 40 percent.

   Calculate the company's weighted cost of capital for the coming year.

CHALLENGE

Spreadsheet Strategies

10. Panhandle Industries Inc. currently pays an annual common stock dividend of $2.20 per share. The company's dividend has grown steadily over the past 9 years from $1.10 to its present level; this growth trend is expected to continue. The company's present dividend payout ratio, also expected to continue, is 40 percent. In addition, the stock presently sells at 8 times current earnings (that is, its P/E multiple is 8).

    Panhandle Industries stock has a beta of 1.15, as computed by a leading investment service. The present risk-free rate is 7.0 percent, and the expected return on the stock market is 13.0 percent.

    a. Suppose an individual investor feels that 12 percent is an appropriate required rate of return for the level of risk this investor perceives for Panhandle Industries. Using the dividend capitalization model and the Capital Asset Pricing Model approaches, determine whether this investor should purchase Panhandle Industries stock.

b. Calculate the company's cost of equity capital using both the dividend capitalization model approach and the Capital Asset Pricing Model approach.

CHALLENGE

Spreadsheet Strategies

11. Colbyco Industries has a target capital structure of 60 percent common equity, 30 percent debt, and 10 percent preferred stock. The cost of retained earnings is 15 percent, and the cost of new equity (external) is 16 percent. Colbyco anticipates having $20 million of new retained earnings available over the coming year. Colbyco can sell $15 million of first-mortgage bonds with an after-tax cost of 9 percent. Its investment bankers feel the company could sell $10 million of debentures with a 9.5 percent after-tax cost. Additional debt would cost 10 percent after tax and be in the form of subordinated debentures. The after-tax cost of preferred stock financing is estimated to be 14 percent.

Compute the marginal cost of capital schedule for Colbyco, and determine the break points in the schedule.

INTERMEDIATE

12. The White Corporation makes small Bozo replicas for sale in the growing Austin market. The firm's capital structure consists of 60 percent common equity, 10 percent preferred stock, and 30 percent long-term debt. This capital structure is believed to be optimal. White is planning to raise funds over the coming year to finance expansion plans. The firm expects to have $40 million of retained earnings available. The cost of retained earnings is 18 percent. Additional common equity can be obtained by selling new common stock at a cost of 19.6 percent. The firm can sell a maximum amount of $20 million of preferred stock at a cost of 15 percent. First-mortgage bonds totaling $25 million can be sold at a pretax cost of 14 percent. Beyond $25 million, the firm would have to sell debentures at a pretax cost of 15 percent. The firm's marginal tax rate is 40 percent.

Identify the size of each block of funds and the cost of the funds in each block. Be sure to identify the *maximum* amount of funds White can acquire.

CHALLENGE

Spreadsheet Strategies

13. Owens Enterprises is in the process of determining its capital budget for the next fiscal year. The firm's current capital structure, which it considers to be optimal, is contained in the following balance sheet:

Balance Sheet

Current assets	$ 40,000,000	Accounts payable	$ 20,000,000
Fixed assets	400,000,000	Other current liabilities	10,000,000
Total assets	$440,000,000	Long-term debt	123,000,000
		Common stock at par	15,500,000
		Paid in capital in excess of par	51,000,000
		Retained earnings	220,500,000
		Total liabilities and stockholders' equity	$440,000,000

Through discussions with the firm's investment bankers, lead bank, and financial officers, the following information has been obtained:

- The firm expects net income from this year to total $80 million. The firm intends to maintain its dividend policy of paying 42.25 percent of earnings to stockholders.
- The firm can borrow $18 million from its bank at a 13 percent annual rate.
- Any additional debt can be obtained through the issuance of debentures (at par) that carry a 15 percent coupon rate.

- The firm currently pays \$4.40 per share in dividends (D_0). Dividends have grown at a 5 percent rate in the past. This growth is expected to continue.
- The firm's common stock currently trades at \$44 per share. If the firm were to raise any external equity, the newly issued shares would net the company \$40 per share.
- The firm is in the 40 percent marginal tax bracket.

Compute Owens' marginal cost of capital schedule.

CHALLENGE

Spreadsheet Strategies

14. Matsumoto Limited (ML), a large conglomerate firm, has a capital structure that currently consists of 20 percent long-term debt, 10 percent preferred stock, and 70 percent common equity. ML has determined that it will raise funds in the future using 40 percent long-term debt, 10 percent preferred stock, and 50 percent common equity.

ML can raise up to \$50 million in the long-term debt market at a pretax cost of 18 percent. Beyond \$50 million, the pretax cost of long-term debt is expected to increase to 20 percent. Preferred stock can be raised at a cost of 19 percent. The limited demand for this security permits ML to sell only \$20 million of preferred stock. ML's marginal tax rate is 40 percent.

ML's stock currently sells for \$40 per share and has a beta of 1.5. ML pays no dividends and is not expected to pay any dividends for the foreseeable future. Investment advisory services expect the stock price to increase from its current level of \$40 per share to a level of \$99.50 per share at the end of 5 years. New shares can be sold to net the company \$38.35. ML expects earnings after taxes and available for common stockholders to be \$60 million.

Compute the marginal cost of capital schedule for ML, and determine the break points in the schedule.

CHALLENGE

Spreadsheet Strategies

15. Rolodex Inc. is in the process of determining its capital budget for the next fiscal year. The firm's current capital structure, which it considers to be optimal, is contained in the following balance sheet:

Rolodex Inc. Balance Sheet (in Millions of Dollars)

Current assets	\$110	Accounts payable	\$ 30
Fixed assets	260	Other current liabilities	20
Total assets	\$370	Long-term debt	128
		Preferred stock	32
		Common stock (20 million shares at par)	20
		Contributed capital in excess of par	30
		Retained earnings	110
		Total liabilities and equity	\$370

Discussions between the firm's financial officers and the firm's investment and commercial bankers have yielded the following information:

- Rolodex can borrow \$40 million from its bank at a pretax cost of 13 percent.
- Rolodex can borrow \$80 million by issuing bonds at a net price of \$687 per bond. The bonds would carry a 10 percent coupon rate and mature in 20 years.
- Additional debt can be issued at a 16 percent pretax cost.
- Preferred stock can be issued at a pretax cost of 16.5 percent.
- Rolodex expects to generate \$140 million in net income and pay \$2 per share in dividends.
- The \$2-per-share dividend (D_1) represents a growth of 5.5 percent over the previous year's dividend. This growth rate is expected to continue for the foreseeable future. The firm's stock currently is trading at \$16 per share.

- Rolodex can raise external equity by selling common stock at a net price of $15 per share.
- Rolodex's marginal tax rate is 40 percent.

a. Compute Rolodex's marginal cost of capital schedule.
b. Given the following investment opportunity schedule, determine Rolodex's optimal capital budget.

Project	Required Investment	Expected Return on Project
A	$140,000,000	17.0%
B	130,000,000	16.0
C	100,000,000	15.0
D	80,000,000	14.2
E	24,000,000	13.0
F	16,000,000	10.9

INTERMEDIATE **16.** The Folske Fan Corporation has four divisions:

Division	Proportion of Firm's Assets
Consumer products	50%
Consulting	10
Industrial products	30
Financial services	10

The (leveraged) beta for Folske has been estimated to be 1.25. The company believes that the (leveraged) beta for consumer products is 1.2; for consulting, 1.3; and for financial services, 1.5. The appropriate capital structure for the industrial products division is 70 percent equity and 30 percent debt (and all projects in that division are currently financed in those proportions). The firm's consolidated capital structure consists of 60 percent equity and 40 percent debt. The risk-free rate is 9 percent, and the market risk premium is 8.6 percent. Folske's marginal tax rate is 40 percent. What is the minimum rate of return that Folske should demand on the equity-financed portion of investments in its industrial products division, assuming these investments continue to be financed with 70 percent equity and 30 percent debt?

INTERMEDIATE **17.** Jenkins Resources Inc. has the following capital structure:

Financing Source	Proportion of Capital Structure
Debentures (9% coupon, $1,000 par value, 12-year maturity)	27%
Preferred stock ($2 dividend, $25 par value)	8
Common equity	65
Total	100%

Jenkins expects to raise future capital in the proportions currently indicated on the balance sheet. The current market price for Jenkins debentures is $1,075. If new debentures were sold, the issuance cost would be $20 per bond. The current market price for the preferred stock is $19. Issuance costs on new preferred stock would be $1 per share for a $25 par value issue. Issuance costs on new equity would be $2.50 per share. The current market price for Jenkins common stock is $40. The stock pays a current (D_0) dividend of $3. This dividend is expected to grow at an annual rate of 47 percent.

What is the weighted (marginal) cost of capital for Jenkins Resources, assuming new capital is raised in the proportions shown here and that all new equity comes from the sale of new shares, new debt comes from the sale of debentures, and new preferred comes from the sale of preferred stock? The firm's marginal tax rate is 40 percent.

INTERMEDIATE

18. Intermountain Resources is a multidivisional company. It has three divisions with the following betas and proportion of the firm's total assets:

Division	Beta	Proportion of Assets
Natural gas pipelines	0.70	50%
Oil and gas production	1.20	30
Oil and gas exploration	1.50	20

The risk-free rate is 7 percent, and the market risk premium is 8 percent.

a. What is the firm's weighted average beta?

b. What required equity rate of return should the firm use for average-risk projects in its natural gas pipeline division?

c. What required equity rate of return should the firm use for average-risk projects in its oil and gas exploration division?

CHALLENGE

Spreadsheet Strategies

19. The current dividend, D_0, of the stock of Sun Devil Corporation is $3 per share. Under present conditions, this dividend is expected to grow at a rate of 6 percent annually for the foreseeable future. The beta of Sun Devil stock is 1.5. The risk-free rate of return is 7 percent, and the expected market rate of return is 14 percent.

a. At what price would you expect Sun Devil common stock to sell?

b. If the risk-free rate of return declines to 6 percent, what will happen to Sun Devil's stock price? (Assume that the expected market rate of return remains at 14 percent.)

c. Sun Devil's management is considering acquisitions in the machine tool industry. Management expects the firm's beta to increase to 1.6 as a result of these acquisitions. The dividend growth rate is expected to increase to 7 percent annually. Would you recommend this acquisition program to management? (Assume the same initial conditions that existed in Part a.)

CHALLENGE

Spreadsheet Strategies

20. Caledonia Minerals has an estimated beta of 1.6. The company is considering the acquisition of another firm that has a beta of 1.2. Both companies are exactly the same size.

a. What is the expected new beta value for the combined firm?

b. The risk-free rate of return is estimated at 7 percent and the market return is estimated as 12 percent. What is your estimate of the required return of investors in Caledonia before and after the merger?

Caledonia Minerals is expected to pay a $1 dividend next year ($D_1 = \$1$). This dividend is expected to grow at a rate of 6 percent per year for the foreseeable future if the merger is not completed. The merger is not expected to change the current dividend rate, but future dividends are expected to grow at a 7 percent rate as a result of the merger.

c. What is the value of a share of stock in Caledonia Minerals prior to the merger?

d. What is the new value of a share of stock, assuming that the merger is completed?

e. Would you recommend that Caledonia go ahead with the merger?

INTERMEDIATE

21. Globe Steel has decided to diversify into the home improvement field. As a result of this expansion, Globe's beta value drops from 1.3 to 0.9, and the expected future long-term growth rate in the firm's dividends drops from 8 to 7 percent. The expected market return is 14 percent; the risk-free rate is 7 percent; and the current dividends per share, D_0, are \$3. Should Globe undertake the planned diversification?

INTERMEDIATE

22. Tucker Manufacturing Company has a beta estimated at 1.0. The risk-free rate is 6 percent and the expected market return is 12 percent. Tucker expects to pay a \$4 dividend next year ($D_1 = \$4$). This dividend is expected to grow at 3 percent per year for the foreseeable future. The current market price for Tucker is \$40.

a. Is the current stock price an equilibrium price, based upon the SML calculation of k_e for Tucker?

b. What do you think the appropriate equilibrium price is? How will that price be achieved?

CHALLENGE

Spreadsheet Strategies

23. Highland Pet Supplies Company forecasts earnings per share of \$2.50 during the coming year. Highland has always paid a dividend equal to 40 percent of its earnings, and it anticipates continuing this practice. Earnings are expected to increase at a rate of 20 percent per year in years 2 and 3, 15 percent in year 4, and 6 percent per year thereafter. The beta of Highland stock is 1.5, the risk-free rate is 7 percent, and the market risk premium has been estimated to be 8 percent.

a. What is the current (time 0) value of a share of Highland stock?

b. What value would you project for a share of stock at the beginning of year 3?

CHALLENGE

24. Del Sarto's Minuteman Novelties Inc. (DSMN) expects its earnings to grow from a current (time 0) level of \$2 per share to \$4 per share over the coming year. After that, earnings are expected to grow at 10 percent per year for 5 years. The current price of the stock of DSMN is \$20 per share. The stock is expected to increase in value by 50 percent over the next 3 years. DSMN's dividend policy is to pay out 50 percent of each year's earnings as dividends. DSMN's marginal tax rate is 40 percent, and its average tax rate is 35 percent. Compute DSMN's cost of internal equity capital.

INTERMEDIATE

25. Access the Thomson consensus earnings forecast report for Mylan Laboratories using data available at www.yahoo.com. From the Yahoo main screen, select "Finance." On the next screen enter the ticker symbol for Mylan (MYL). On the next screen, choose "Analyst Estimates."

HTTP: www.yahoo.com

CHALLENGE

26. Gandha's Pharmaceutical Corporation's beta is 1.5. The current risk-free rate is 4.5 percent and the market risk premium is 9 percent. Gandha currently (time 0) pays a dividend of \$2 per share. This dividend is expected to grow at a rate of 20 percent for the next 3 years. The current stock price is \$30, and the consensus of security analysts is that this price will increase by 50 percent by the end of year 2. Under these circumstances, would you purchase this stock? What do you believe is a fair market price for the stock?

INTEGRATIVE CASE PROBLEM

Cost of Capital

The Marietta Corporation, a large manufacturer of mufflers, tailpipes, and shock absorbers, is currently carrying out its financial planning for next year. In about two weeks, at the next meeting of the firm's board of directors, Frank Bosworth, vice president of finance, is scheduled to present his recommendations for next year's overall financial plan. He has asked Donna Botello, manager of financial planning, to gather the necessary information and perform the calculations for the financial plan.

The company's divisional staffs, together with corporate finance department personnel, have analyzed several proposed capital expenditure projects. The following is a summary schedule of acceptable projects (defined by the company as projects having internal rates of return greater than 8 percent):

Project	Investment Amount (in Millions of Dollars)	Internal Rate of Return
A	$10.0	25%
B	20.0	21
C	30.0	18
D	35.0	15
E	40.0	12.4
F	40.0	11.3
G	40.0	10
H	20.0	9

All projects are expected to have one year of negative cash flow followed by positive cash flows over the remaining years. In addition, next year's projects involve modifications and expansion of the company's existing facilities and products. As a result, these projects are considered to have approximately the same degree of risk as the company's existing assets.

Botello feels that this summary schedule and detailed supporting documents provide her with the necessary information concerning the possible capital expenditure projects for next year. She can now direct her attention to obtaining the data necessary to determine the cost of the capital required to finance next year's proposed projects.

The company's investment bankers indicated to Bosworth in a recent meeting that they feel the company could issue up to $50 million of 9 percent first-mortgage bonds at par next year. The investment bankers also feel that any additional debt would have to be subordinated debentures with a coupon of 10 percent, also to be sold at par. The investment bankers rendered this opinion after Bosworth gave an approximate estimate of the size of next year's capital budget, and after he estimated that approximately $100 million of retained earnings would be available next year.

Both the company's financial managers and its investment bankers consider the present capital structure of the company, shown in the following table, to be optimal (assume that book and market values are equal):

Debt	$ 400,000,000
Stockholders' equity:	
Common stock	150,000,000
Retained earnings	450,000,000
	$1,000,000,000

Botello has assembled additional information, as follows:

- Marietta common stock is currently selling at $21 per share.
- The investment bankers have also indicated that an additional $75 million in new common stock could be issued to net the company $19 per share.
- The company's present annual dividend is $1.32 per share. However, Bosworth feels fairly certain that the board will increase it to $1.415 per share next year.
- The company's earnings and dividends have doubled over the past 10 years. Growth has been fairly steady, and this rate is expected to continue for the foreseeable future. The company's marginal tax rate is 40 percent.

Using the information provided, answer the following questions. (*Note*: Disregard depreciation in this case.)

Spreadsheet Strategies

1. Calculate the after-tax cost of each component source of capital.
2. Calculate the marginal cost of capital for the various intervals, or "packages," of capital the company can raise next year. Plot the marginal cost of capital curve.
3. Using the marginal cost of capital curve from question 2, and plotting the investment opportunity curve, determine the company's optimal capital budget for next year.
4. Should Project G be accepted or rejected? Why?
5. What factors do you feel might cause Bosworth to recommend a different capital budget than the one obtained in question 3?
6. Assume that a sudden rise in interest rates has caused the cost of various capital components to increase. The pretax cost of first-mortgage bonds has increased to 11 percent; the pretax cost of subordinated debentures has increased to 12.5 percent; the company's common stock price has declined to $18; and new stock could be sold to net Marietta $16 per share.
   a. Recompute the after-tax cost of the individual component sources of capital.
   b. Recompute the marginal cost of capital for the various intervals of capital Marietta can raise next year.
   c. Determine the optimal capital budget for next year at the higher cost of capital.
   d. How does the interest rate surge affect Marietta's optimal capital budget?

Spreadsheet Strategies

CHAPTER
13

Capital Structure Concepts

KEY CHAPTER CONCEPTS

1. Capital structure consists of the relative amounts of permanent short-term debt, long-term debt, preferred stock, and common equity used to finance a firm. The optimal capital structure occurs at the point at which the cost of capital is minimized and firm value is maximized.
2. Leverage involves the firm's use of fixed operating costs or fixed capital costs.
3. Business risk is the inherent variability or uncertainty of a firm's operating income. Business risk is caused by many factors, including sales variability and the use of operating leverage.
4. Financial risk is the additional variability of earnings per share and the increased probability of insolvency resulting from the use of fixed-cost sources of capital, such as debt and preferred stock.
5. The value of the firm is independent of capital structure, given perfect capital markets and no corporate income taxes.
6. The optimal capital structure consists entirely of debt if a corporate income tax exists and there are no financial distress costs or agency costs.
7. Given a corporate income tax, financial distress costs, and agency costs, an optimal capital structure consists of some combination of debt and equity.
8. Changes in the capital structure often serve as a signal to outside investors about management's expectations concerning future earnings prospects for the company.
9. According to the pecking order theory, companies prefer internal financing to external financing, and, given that external financing is necessary, they prefer to issue debt securities first and equity securities as a last resort.
10. According to the market timing model, managers raise equity capital when the firm's stock is overvalued. The observed capital structure of the firm is the cumulative result of such equity timing issuances.
11. Financial flexibility is the practice of maintaining a debt ratio that is much lower than the optimal debt ratio.

FINANCIAL CHALLENGE

Apple's $17 Billion Bond Offering Makes History[1]

Headlines like the above were all over the financial pages on May 1, 2013. On that day Apple Inc. floated what was considered to be the largest corporate bond offering in the history of financial markets. The offering consisted of six parts (tranches) ranging in maturity from 3 years to 30 years with varying interest rates as noted in the nearby table.

Besides the size of the offering, what was also remarkable about the debt issue was that this was Apple's first foray into the bond market.[2] Also notable was the fact that Apple had in excess of $140 billion in its cash account at the time of the bond offering. So why did Apple issue this debt? According to management, the proceeds from the debt were to "be used for general corporate purposes, including repurchases of our common stock and payment of dividends under our recently expanded program to return capital to shareholders." Obviously, Apple had enough cash to meet these needs, but most of this cash was tied up in overseas accounts. Bringing it back to the United States would entail significant "repatriation" taxes. Hence, management figured it would be wiser to leave the cash overseas and instead issue debt and use the proceeds to meet their objectives. Much of the press coverage focused on the repatriation tax motivation for the bond issue. Although less focused on, another important feature of the bond issue, in conjunction with the share repurchase, was the impact it would have on Apple's capital structure, which is the subject of this chapter and the subsequent one.

The obvious effect of the bond issue on Apple's capital structure was to increase leverage through the increase in debt. Moreover, by using the proceeds to repurchase shares, Apple further increased its

Pabkov/Shutterstock.com

[1]John Balassi and Josie Cox, "Apple's $17 Billion Bond Offering Makes History," *Huffington Post* (April 30, 2013), www.huffingtonpost.com (accessed February 5, 2016).

[2]Apple issued some debt in 1994 that has long since been paid off.

FINANCIAL CHALLENGE — CONTINUED

leverage by decreasing the value of its outstanding equity. By engaging in this transaction, Apple's management was presumably moving the firm to a more "optimal" capital structure that would maximize value to the firm's shareholders. As a result of the bond offering, Apple's capital ratio moved from 0 percent to 12 percent by the end of fiscal year 2013. On the day of the announcement of the offering, Apple's stock closed at a price of $430.12, an increase of nearly 3 percent from the day before and over 8 percent relative to three days prior. This indicates that shareholders endorsed management's decision to alter the firm's capital structure to one that relies on debt financing as an important part of its capital base.

Apple's reliance on debt financing as a significant part of its capital mix was underscored by its subsequent trips to the debt market in 2014 and 2015 and its use of the proceeds to buy back stock, among other things. Apple raised a total of $55 billion in debt between 2013 and 2015. Its debt-to-capital ratio at the end of fiscal year 2015 was 35 percent. This chapter and the next will provide the reader insights into some of the key factors (including the tax benefits of debt) that Apple's management must have considered in its decision to alter its capital structure.

Principal Amount	Coupon Rate and Maturity
$1,000,000,000	Floating-rate notes due 2016
$2,000,000,000	Floating-rate notes due 2018
$1,500,000,000	0.45% notes due 2016
$4,000,000,000	1% notes due 2018
$5,500,000,000	2.4% notes due 2023
$3,000,000,000	3.85% notes due 2043

Source: Based on information from John Balassi and Josie Cox, "Apple's $17 Billion Bond Offering Makes History," *Huffington Post* April 30, 2013), www.huffingtonpost.com (accessed February 5, 2016); Russ Krull, "Apple's Record Bond Issue," *Motley Fool* (May 6, 2013), www.fool.com (accessed February 5, 2016); Kate Burne and Mike Churney, "Apple's Record Plunge into Pool," *The Wall Street Journal* (April 30, 2013), www.wsj.com (accessed February 5, 2016); and Charles Mead and Sarika Gangar, "Apple Raises $17 Billion in Record Corporate Bond Sales," Bloomberg.com (April 30, 2013), www.bloomberg.com (accessed February 5, 2016). Debt-to-capital ratios were calculated from financial data on www.yahoo.com.

CHAPTER OBJECTIVES

Upon completion of this chapter, you should have a clear understanding of the following:

1. The meaning of business risk and financial risk, and the factors that contribute to them
2. The different theories of capital structure and their implications for optimal capital structure choice

13-1 Introduction

capital structure
financial structure

Capital structure consists of the amounts of permanent short-term debt,[3] long-term debt, preferred stock, and common equity used to finance a firm. In contrast, **financial structure** consists of the amounts of total current liabilities, long-term debt, preferred stock, and common equity used to finance a firm. Thus, capital structure is part of the financial structure, representing the permanent sources of the firm's financing. This chapter deals only with the total permanent sources of a firm's financing; the decision on the proportions of long-term versus short-term financing is considered in Chapter 16.

To illustrate the capital structure concept, suppose that Baker Oil Company currently has $10 million in permanent short-term debt, $40 million in long-term debt outstanding, $10 million in preferred stock, and $40 million in common equity (common stock and retained earnings). In this case, Baker's current capital structure is said to be "50 percent debt, 10 percent preferred stock, and 40 percent common equity."[4] Thus, the capital structure pertains to the permanent debt, preferred stock, and common equity portion of the balance sheet.

target capital structure

The emphasis of capital structure analysis is on the firm's long-range **target capital structure**; that is, the capital structure at which the firm ultimately plans to operate. For most companies, the current and target capital structures are virtually identical, and calculating the target structure is a straightforward process. Occasionally, however, companies find it necessary to change from their current capital structure to a different target. Such a change may be due to an alteration in the company's asset mix (and a resulting change in its risk), or an increase in competition that may imply more risk. For example, in response to increased risk, competition, and deregulation in the electric utility industry, Standard & Poor's, a bond rating agency, reduced the desired proportion of debt in the capital structure of an AA-rated utility from a range of 42–47 percent to a range of 39–46 percent. As a consequence, many utilities have moved toward more conservative capital structures.

Firms may temporarily deviate from their target capital structure for a number of other reasons. For example, in 2009, Pfizer acquired another large pharmaceutical firm, Wyeth, for $68 billion. The firm's assets doubled in size, but its long-term debt more than tripled, causing a significant increase in Pfizer's long-term debt ratio (long-term debt to total capital) from 20 to 37 percent. This increase was due to the additional debt Pfizer issued to make the acquisition; however, it was anticipated that Pfizer would pare the debt down to more normal levels in the coming years. Firms also may deviate from their target capital structure to take advantage of unusually cheap sources of capital. For example, in the post–financial crisis period when the Federal Reserve held rates at a very low level, many companies used the opportunity to raise debt very cheaply. IBM went to the debt market multiple times in 2012 to raise long-term debt at interest rates lower than 2 percent per year. Other companies that raised debt at similarly low rates include Procter & Gamble, McDonalds, and 3M.

[3] *Permanent* short-term debt is contrasted with *seasonal* short-term debt. Short-term debt financing policy is discussed in Chapter 16. In practice, outsiders (for example, analysts) often find it difficult to distinguish permanent short-term debt from other short-term debt. Consequently, in discussions and calculations involving capital structure, permanent short-term debt is typically ignored; that is, capital structure is defined simply as the sum of the long-term debt, preferred stock, and common equity.

[4] Companies normally do not distinguish in their capital structure between whether common equity is obtained by retained earnings or new common stock. In other words, only the *total* common shareholders' equity is considered, not the *relative* amounts in the common stock, contributed capital in excess of par, and retained earnings accounts.

This chapter examines some of the basic concepts and theories used in determining a firm's optimal capital structure. Chapter 14 develops a number of tools of analysis that can assist managers in making actual capital structure decisions.

13-2 Capital Structure Decisions and Maximization of Shareholder Wealth

optimal capital structure

A firm's **optimal capital structure** is the mix of debt, preferred stock, and common equity that *minimizes* the *weighted cost* to the firm *of* its employed *capital*. When the capital structure is such that the weighted cost of capital is minimized, the total value of the firm's securities (and hence the value of the firm) is maximized. As a result, the minimum-cost capital structure is called the *optimal* capital structure.

debt capacity

The amount of debt contained in a firm's optimal capital structure is often referred to as its **debt capacity**. The optimal capital structure and, accordingly, the debt capacity of a firm are determined by such factors as the business risk of the firm, the tax structure, the extent of potential financial distress (for example, bankruptcy) and agency costs, and the role played by capital structure policy in providing signals to the capital markets regarding the firm's performance. Each of these factors is considered in the following sections.

13-2a Assumptions of Capital Structure Analysis

The following analysis is based on some important assumptions. The first is that a firm's investment policy is held constant when we examine the effects of capital structure changes on firm value and particularly on the value of common stock. This assumption means that the level and variability of operating income (EBIT) is not expected to change as changes in capital structure are contemplated. Therefore, capital structure changes affect only the distribution of the operating income between the claims of debt holders, preferred stockholders, and common stockholders.

By assuming a constant investment policy, we also assume that the investments undertaken by the firm do not materially change the debt capacity of the firm. This assumption does not always hold in practice, but for the overwhelming majority of investment projects, it is a realistic assumption that also helps us focus on the key determinants of an optimal capital structure.

13-3 Business Risk

business risk

Two elements of risk are primary considerations in a firm's capital structure decision: business risk and financial risk. Financial risk is discussed in the following section. **Business risk** is the variability or uncertainty of a firm's operating income (EBIT).

Many factors influence a firm's business risk (holding constant the effects of all other important factors), including:

Foundation Concept

1. **The variability of sales volumes over the business cycle.** Firms and industries whose sales fluctuate greatly over the business cycle have more business risk than firms and industries whose sales remain relatively stable over the course of the business cycle. For example, during the U.S. recession that started in late 2007, Ford Motor Company's sales went from \$172 billion in 2007 to \$116 billion in 2009, a drop of over 30 percent. By 2011, when the economy was on the mend, sales had rebounded to \$136 billion, an increase of 17 percent over the 2009 levels. In

contrast, the annual revenues of Johnson & Johnson (a large diversified pharmaceutical company) remained very stable, between $63 billion and $65 billion during this period.

2. **The variability of selling prices.** In some industries, prices are quite stable from year to year, or the firm may be able to increase prices regularly over time. This is true for many consumer products, such as brand-name-prepared food items (for example, Kraft cheese or Nabisco cookies). In contrast, in other industries, price stability is much less certain. One such industry is the airline industry. Because of the fierce competition and fluctuation in jet fuel prices, airlines such as United and Delta have very little pricing power. A comparison of the price index for the processed foods and airline ticket prices would reveal a stable growing index for processed foods but a very volatile pattern for airline ticket prices. Generally, the more price-competitive an industry is, the greater the business risk is for firms in that industry.
3. **The variability of costs.** The more variable the cost is of the inputs used to produce a firm's output, the greater is the firm's business risk. For example, airline companies, such as Delta, American, and United, have been affected significantly by the volatility in the price of jet fuel. Between 2000 and 2015, jet fuel prices have bounced around from a low of approximately $0.50 per gallon in December 2001 to a high of about $4.00 a gallon in July 2008. Prices have jumped as much as 21 percent from one month to the next, while monthly declines have been as much as 31 percent.
4. **The existence of market power.** Market power refers to the ability of a firm to individually dictate the quantity and/or price charged for a product or service. A firm's market power usually stems from controlling a large proportion of the market. For example, Microsoft dominates the market for PC operating systems with a 90 percent share of the market. In 2009, 9 out of 10 PCs were sold with the Microsoft Windows operating system. This dominance has allowed Microsoft to dictate the price it charges for the operating system and thereby reduce its business risk. Market power, however, can be fleeting, as even Microsoft is finding out. Today, tablets, smartphones, and other gadgets are taking over more and more of the functions of the traditional PC. Microsoft is not the dominant player in these new segments. So, viewed more broadly, Microsoft's market power may be diminishing over time.
5. **The extent of product diversification.** All other things held constant, the more diversified a firm's product line is, the less variable its operating income is likely to be. For example, IBM offers a broad array of products and services, including large mainframe computers, servers, semiconductor design and production, computer software and systems, business process outsourcing, and financing. When demand for one of its products or services falters, the related losses in revenue can be offset by sales in other areas. In contrast, Advanced Micro Devices produces primarily various types of semiconductors and processors for the computer industry. It has experienced great volatility in operating earnings over time as demand for its limited product line has fluctuated.
6. **The level and rate of growth.** Rapidly growing firms, such as Amazon.com, often experience great variability in their operating earnings. Rapid growth causes many stresses on the operations of a firm. New facilities must be constructed, frequently with uncertain operating cost characteristics; internal control systems must be expanded and updated; the pool of managerial talent must be increased rapidly; and new products require expensive research and development outlays. These factors often combine to result in high variability of operating income.

7. **The degree of operating leverage (DOL).** Operating leverage involves the use of assets having fixed costs. The airline industry (for example, American Airlines) and the steel industry (for example, U.S. Steel) have high fixed operating costs. The more a firm makes use of operating leverage, the more sensitive EBIT will be to changes in sales. The degree of operating leverage is the multiplier effect resulting from a firm's use of fixed operating costs. The DOL is defined as the *percentage change in EBIT* resulting from (that is, divided by) a given *percentage change in sales (output)*.[5] Thus, if a firm is subject to considerable sales volatility over the business cycle, the variability of EBIT (business risk) can be reduced by limiting the use of assets having fixed costs in the production process. Similarly, if a firm's sales tend to be stable over the business cycle, using a high percentage of fixed-cost assets in the production process will have little impact on the variability of EBIT.

In a sense, the business risk of a firm is determined by the accumulated investments the firm makes over time. These investments determine the industries in which a firm will compete, the amount of the firm's market power, and the extent of fixed costs in the production process. Firms in consumer products industries tend to have low levels of business risk. Examples are grocery retailing (Kroger, for example), food processing (Kraft Heinz), and electric (Duke Energy) and natural gas distribution (Piedmont Natural Gas) utilities. In contrast, firms in durable goods manufacturing (Ford Motor Company), industrial goods manufacturing (U.S. Steel), and airlines (American Airlines) tend to have higher levels of business risk.

13-3a Business Risk: Systematic or Unsystematic?

Business risk possesses both systematic and unsystematic elements. Some of the variability in operating income that results from business risk cannot be diversified away by investors who hold a broad-based portfolio of securities. For example, variability attributable to business cycle behavior is clearly systematic. In contrast, the variability attributable to specific managerial decisions, such as a price promotion campaign, is primarily unsystematic. When analysts attempt to assess the specific total risk of a firm, they must consider both systematic and unsystematic components of that risk. A firm may encounter operating (and financial) difficulty because of both economy-wide factors that impact its operations and because of unique decisions made by its management.

13-4 Financial Risk and Financial Leverage

Financial risk

Foundation Concept

Financial risk is the additional variability of earnings per share *and* the increased probability of insolvency that arises when a firm uses fixed-cost sources of funds, such as debt and preferred stock, in its capital structure.[6] (Insolvency results when a firm is unable to meet contractual financial obligations—such as interest and principal payments on debt, payments on accounts payable, and income taxes—as they come due.) Fixed capital costs represent contractual obligations a company must meet regardless of the EBIT level.[7]

[5]The degree of operating leverage is discussed in greater detail in Chapter 14.

[6]Long-term, noncancelable leases (often called *financial leases*) also represent a significant source of fixed-cost financing for many firms. They are not discussed in this chapter in order to simplify the analysis. See Chapter 19 for a discussion of lease financing.

[7]In financial emergencies, firms can omit preferred dividends, but omitting preferred dividends has many undesirable consequences for the firm (see Chapter 6). Therefore, the payment of preferred dividends is treated here as if it were a contractual obligation similar to interest.

The use of increasing amounts of debt and preferred stock raises the firm's fixed financial costs; this, in turn, increases the level of EBIT that the firm must earn in order to meet its financial obligations and remain in business. A firm accepts the risk of fixed-cost financing to increase the possible returns to stockholders.

financial leverage

The use of fixed-cost financing sources is referred to as the use of **financial leverage**. Financial leverage causes a firm's earnings per share (EPS) to change at a rate greater than the change in operating income (EBIT). For example, if a firm is financed 100 percent by common equity and EBIT increases (or decreases) by 10 percent, EPS will also increase (or decrease) by 10 percent. When financial leverage, such as long-term debt, is used, a 10 percent change in EBIT will result in more than a 10 percent change in EPS. Figure 13.1 illustrates the concept of financial leverage.

- Line A (Firm A) represents the financial leverage used by a firm financed *entirely with common stock.* A given percentage change in EBIT results in the *same* percentage change in EPS.
- Line B (Firm B) represents a firm that uses debt (or other sources of fixed-cost funds) in its capital structure. As a result, the *slope* of the EPS-EBIT line is increased, thus increasing the responsiveness of EPS to changes in EBIT.

FIGURE 13.1

Illustration of Financial Leverage

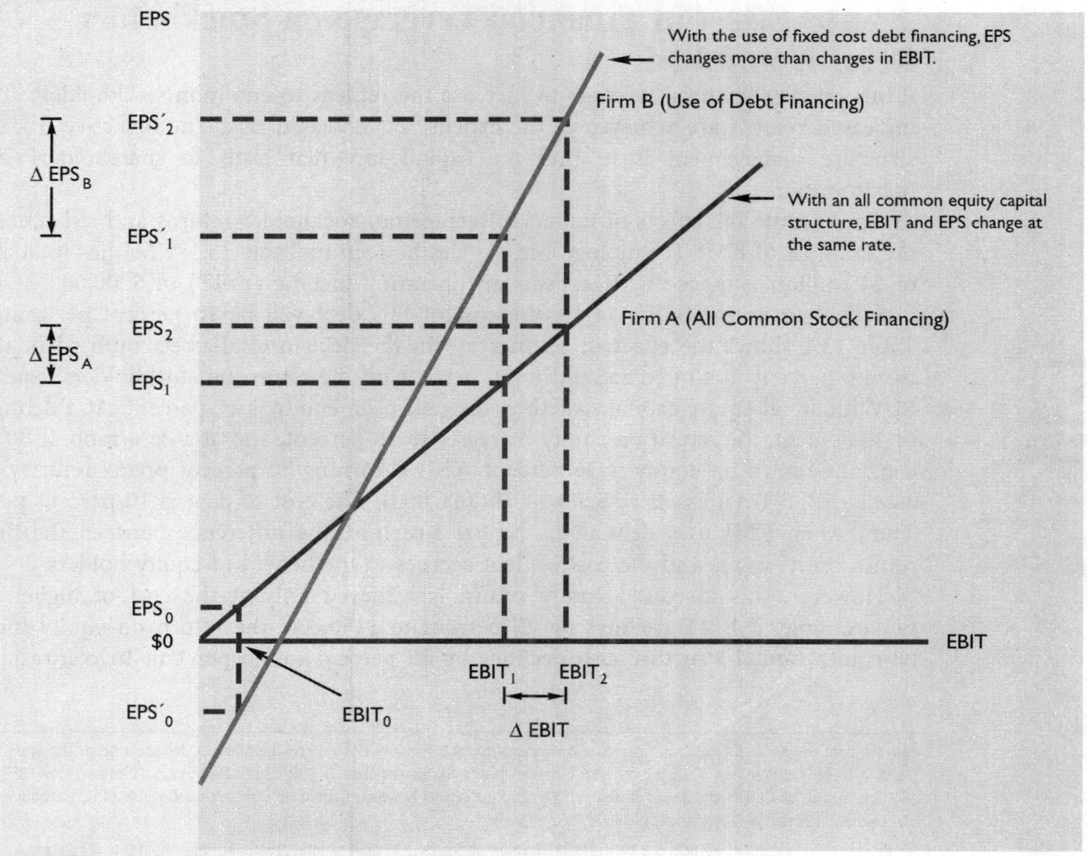

As can be seen in Figure 13.1, a given change in EBIT (ΔEBIT) yields a larger change in EPS if the firm is using debt financing (ΔEPS_B) than if the firm is financed entirely with common stock (ΔEPS_A).

Figure 13.1 also shows that the use of financial leverage magnifies the returns—both positive and negative—to the shareholder. When EBIT is at a relatively high level, such as $EBIT_2$, Firm B's use of financial leverage *increases* EPS above the level attained by Firm A, which is not using financial leverage; that is, $EPS'_2 > EPS_2$. On the other hand, when EBIT is relatively low—for example, at $EBIT_0$—the use of financial leverage *decreases* EPS below the level that would be obtained otherwise; that is, $EPS'_0 < EPS_0$. At $EBIT_0$, the use of financial leverage results in negative EPS for Firm B.

13-4a Financial Risk: Systematic or Unsystematic?

Financial risk, like business risk, contributes to both the systematic and unsystematic risk of a firm's securities. To the extent that the use of *financial leverage* magnifies variations in operating income resulting from unsystematic risk factors, financial leverage contributes to the unsystematic risk of a firm's securities.

Financial researchers have also studied the contribution that financial leverage makes to the systematic risk of a firm's securities.[8] It is well established that systematic risk is a function both of financial risk *and* of operating risk. Hence, security analysts and investors find the measurement of a company's financial risk to be an important element of good financial analysis.

13-4b Effect of Financial Leverage on Stockholder Returns and Risk

Firms employ financial leverage to increase the returns to common stockholders. These increased returns are achieved at the expense of increased risk. The objective of capital structure management is to find the capital mix that leads to shareholder wealth maximization.

To illustrate the effects of financial leverage on stockholder returns and risk, consider the example of KMI Technology Inc. As can be seen in Table 13.1, KMI has total assets of \$1 million. Suppose KMI expects an operating income (EBIT) of \$200,000. If KMI uses debt in its capital structure, the cost of this debt will be 10 percent per annum.[9] Table 13.1 shows the effect of an increase in the debt-to-total-assets ratio (debt ratio) from 0 percent to 40 percent and to 80 percent on the return on stockholders' equity.

HTTP:
To get access to extensive financial information about virtually any company, explore
finance.yahoo.com

With an all-equity capital structure, the return on equity is 12 percent. At a debt ratio of 40 percent, the return on equity increases to 16 percent, and at a debt ratio of 80 percent, the return on equity is 36 percent. KMI is earning 20 percent pretax return on its assets (EBIT/Total assets = \$200,000/\$1,000,000). The cost of debt is 10 percent pretax. Thus, when KMI uses debt in its capital structure, the difference between the pretax return on its assets and the cost of debt accrues to the benefit of equity holders.

However, this increased equity return is achieved only at the cost of higher risk. For example, if EBIT declines by 25 percent to \$150,000, the return on equity for the all-equity capital structure also declines by 25 percent to 9.0 percent. In contrast, at a

[8]An excellent review of the relationship between business risk and financial risk on one hand and systematic risk on the other can be found in C. M. Callahan and F. M. Mohr, "The Determinants of Systematic Risk: A Synthesis," *The Financial Review* (May 1989): 157–181. See also J. M. Gahlon and James A. Gentry, "On the Relationship Between Systematic Risk and the Degrees of Operating and Financial Leverage," *Financial Management* (Summer 1982): 15–23.

[9]In this simplified example, we hold the cost of debt constant as the ratio of debt to total assets increases from 0 to 80 percent. In reality, as the debt ratio increases, the cost of debt can also be expected to increase.

TABLE 13.1

Effect of Financial Leverage on Stockholder Returns and Risk at KMI Technology, Inc.

Leverage Factor (Debt to Total Assets)	**0%**	**40%**	**80%**
Total assets	$1,000,000	$1,000,000	$1,000,000
Debt (at 10% interest)	$ 0	$ 400,000	$ 800,000
Equity	1,000,000	600,000	200,000
Total liabilities and equity	$1,000,000	$1,000,000	$1,000,000
Expected operating income (EBIT)	$ 200,000	$ 200,000	$ 200,000
Interest (at 10%)	0	40,000	80,000
Earnings before tax	$ 200,000	$ 160,000	$ 120,000
Income tax at 40%	80,000	64,000	48,000
Earnings after tax	$ 120,000	$ 96,000	$ 72,000
Return on equity	**12.0%**	**16.0%**	**36.0%**
	Effect of a 25 Percent Reduction in EBIT to $150,000		
Expected operating income (EBIT)	$ 150,000	$ 150,000	$ 150,000
Interest (at 10%)	0	40,000	80,000
Earnings before tax	$ 150,000	$ 110,000	$ 70,000
Income tax at 40%	60,000	44,000	28,000
Earnings after tax	$ 90,000	$ 66,000	$ 42,000
Return on equity	**9.0%**	**11.0%**	**21.0%**
	Effect of a 60 Percent Reduction in EBIT to $80,000		
Expected operating income (EBIT)	$ 80,000	$ 80,000	$ 80,000
Interest (at 10%)	0	40,000	80,000
Earnings before tax	$ 80,000	$ 40,000	$ 0
Income tax at 40%	32,000	16,000	0
Earnings after tax	$ 48,000	$ 24,000	$ 0
Return on equity	**4.8%**	**4.0%**	**0.0%**

40 percent debt ratio, the return on equity declines by 31.25 percent to 11 percent. At an 80 percent debt ratio, the return on equity declines by 41.67 percent to 21 percent.

The effects of a 60 percent reduction in EBIT to $80,000 are even more dramatic. In this case, the pretax return on assets is *less than* the pretax cost of debt. To pay the prior claims of the debt holders, the equity returns are reduced to a level below those that prevail under the all-equity capital structure. In the case of a 40 percent debt ratio, the return on equity is only 4.0 percent, and in the case of an 80 percent debt ratio, the return on equity is 0 percent. Thus it can be seen that the use of financial leverage both increases the potential returns to common stockholders and the risk, or variability, of those returns.

Generally, the greater a firm's business risk is, the less financial leverage that will be used in the optimal capital structure, holding constant all other relevant factors.

13-5 Capital Structure Theory

In this section, we develop some simplified models of the relationship between capital structure, as measured by the ratio of debt to total assets, and the cost of capital (and the value of the firm). These models help isolate the impact of personal and corporate taxes, financial distress costs, and agency costs on the determination of an optimal capital structure. We also consider other factors that influence the choice of long-term financing instruments, including the impact of signaling, information asymmetries, market timing, and financial flexibility.

13-5a Capital Structure Without a Corporate Income Tax

In 1958, two prominent financial researchers, Franco Modigliani and Merton Miller (MM), showed that, under certain assumptions, a firm's overall cost of capital and therefore its value are *independent* of capital structure.[10] These assumptions include:

1. Capital markets are characterized by *perfect* capital market conditions:
   - There are no transaction costs for buying and selling securities.
   - A sufficient number of buyers and sellers exists in the market; so no single investor can have a significant influence on security prices.
   - Relevant information is readily available to all investors and is costless to obtain.
   - All investors can borrow or lend at the same rate.
2. All investors are rational and have homogeneous expectations of a firm's earnings.
3. Firms operating under similar conditions are assumed to face the same degree of business risk. This assumption is called the *homogeneous risk class assumption.*
4. There are no corporate or personal income taxes.

In subsequent work, MM relaxed the last assumption and considered the case when there are corporate taxes (though personal taxes were still assumed to be zero). We illustrate both cases but consider the no-tax first and then the case with taxes.

In the no-tax case, the cost of debt and the overall cost of capital are constant regardless of a firm's financial leverage position, measured as the firm's debt-to-equity ratio, *B/E*. As a firm increases its relative debt level, the cost of equity capital, k_e, increases, reflecting the higher return requirement of stockholders due to the increased risk imposed by the additional debt. The increased cost of equity capital exactly offsets the benefit of the lower cost of debt, k_d, so that the overall cost of capital does not change with changes in capital structure. See Figure 13.2. Because the firm's market value is calculated by discounting its expected future operating income by the weighted (marginal) cost of capital, k_a, the market value of the firm is independent of capital structure.

MM support their theory by arguing that a process of arbitrage will prevent otherwise equivalent firms from having different market values simply because of capital structure differences. **Arbitrage** is the process of simultaneously buying and selling the same or equivalent securities in different markets to take advantage of price differences and thereby make a profit. Arbitrage transactions are risk free. For example, suppose two firms in the same industry differed only in that one was *levered* (that is, it had some debt in its capital structure) and the other was *unlevered* (that is, it had no debt in its capital structure). If the MM theory did not hold, the unlevered firm could increase its market value by simply adding debt to its capital structure. However, in a perfect capital market without transactions costs, MM argue that investors would not reward the firm for increasing its debt. Stockholders could change *their* own financial debt-to-equity structure without cost to receive an equal return. Therefore, stockholders would not increase their opinion of the market value of an unlevered firm just because it took on some debt.

arbitrage

[10] See Franco Modigliani and Merton H. Miller, "The Cost of Capital, Corporation Finance, and the Theory of Investment," *American Economic Review* 48 (June 1958): 261–296. Modigliani and Miller received the Nobel Prize for Economics, though at different times, in part for their pioneering work related to corporate capital structure. Modigliani received the Nobel Prize in 1985 and Miller (along with Harry M. Markowitz and William F. Sharpe) received it in 1990.

FIGURE 13.2

Weighted Cost of Capital: Modigliani and Miller (No Taxes)

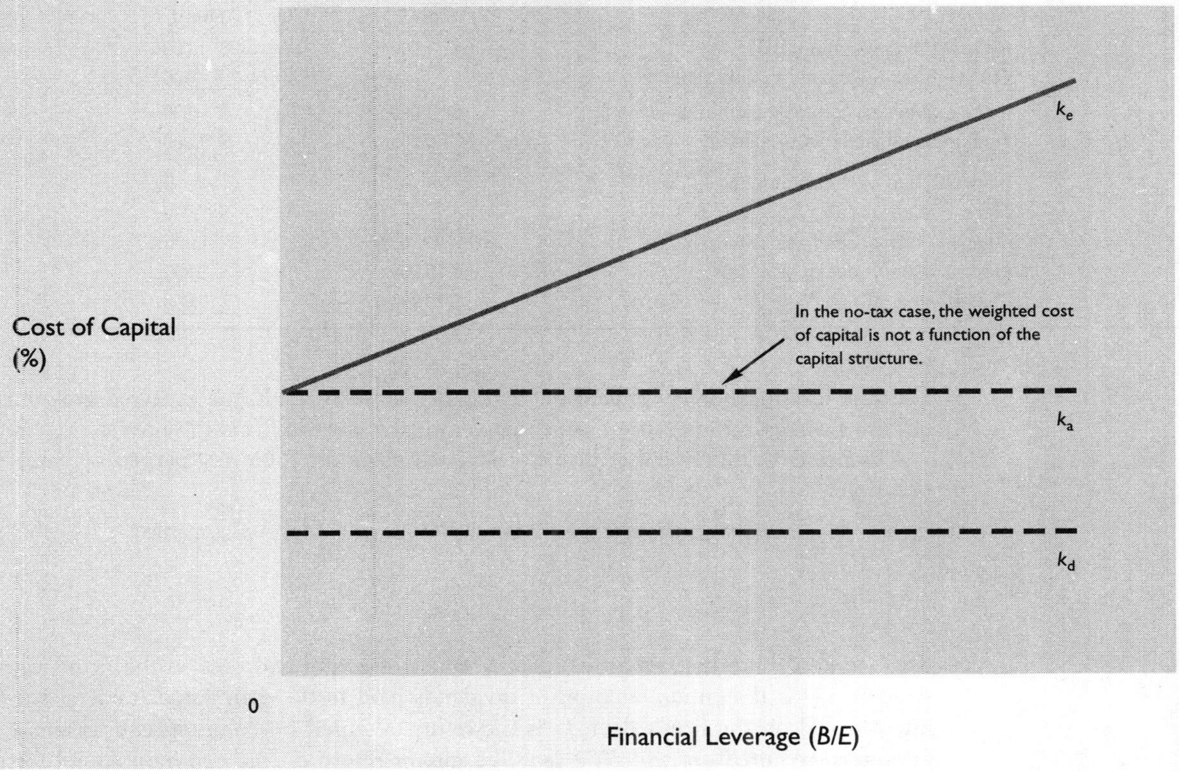

The MM argument is based on the *arbitrage* process. If one of two unlevered firms with identical business risk took on some debt and the MM theory did not hold, its value should increase, and therefore so would the value of its stock. MM suggests that, under these circumstances, investors will sell the overpriced stock of the levered firm. They then can use an arbitrage process of borrowing, buying the unlevered firm's stock, and investing the excess funds elsewhere. Through these costless transactions, investors can increase their return without increasing their risk. Hence, they have substituted their own personal financial leverage for corporate leverage. MM argue that this arbitrage process will continue until the selling of the levered firm's stock drives down its price to the point where it is equal to the unlevered firm's stock price, which has been driven up due to increased buying.

The arbitrage process occurs so rapidly that the market values of the levered and unlevered firms are equal. Therefore, MM conclude that *the market value of a firm is independent of its capital structure in perfect capital markets with no income taxes.*

The MM no-tax theory is illustrated in Table 13.2. The table contains financial data on two firms, U and L, that have equal levels of net operating income (EBIT = \$1,000) and operating risk and that differ only in their capital structures. Firm U is unlevered, and firm L is levered, with a perpetual debt of \$2,000 having a coupon rate (i) of 5 percent in its capital structure. For simplicity, we assume that the income of both firms

TABLE 13.2

Capital Structure Without a Corporate Income Tax: Financial Data of Firms U and L

	Firm U	Firm L
Net operating income (EBIT)	\$ 1,000	\$ 1,000
Less: Interest payments to debt holders, I	—	100
Income available to stockholders (dividends), D	\$ 1,000	\$ 900
Total income available to security holders ($I + D$)	\$ 1,000	\$ 1,000
Required rate of return on debt, k_d	—	5%
Market value of debt, $B = I/k_d$	—	\$ 2,000
Required rate of return on equity, k_e	10%	11.25%
Market value of equity, $E = D/k_e$	\$ 10,000	\$ 8,000
Market value of firm, $E + B$	\$ 10,000	\$10,000

available for stockholders is paid out as dividends. As a result, the expected growth rate of both firms is zero because no income is available for the firms to reinvest.

The present value of either firm is calculated using the following perpetuity valuation equation:[11]

(13.1)

$$\begin{aligned}\text{Market value of firm} &= \text{Market value of equity} + \text{Market value of debt}\\ &= E + B\\ &= \frac{D}{k_e} + \frac{I}{k_d}\end{aligned}$$

where E and B are the respective market values of equity and debt in the firm's capital structure; D is the annual amount of dividends paid to the firm's stockholders; I is the interest paid on the firm's debt; k_e is the return required on common equity; and k_d is the return required on debt. The required rate of return on the common equity for the unlevered firm (U) is 10 percent. Because of the increased financial risk associated with the \$2,000 in debt financing, the required rate of return on the common equity of the levered firm (L) is 11.25 percent. The required return on debt, k_d, is assumed to equal the coupon rate on the debt, i. For firm U, the present value of the expected future cash flows is \$10,000, calculated as follows:

$$\begin{aligned}\text{Market value of firm U} &= \frac{\$1{,}000}{0.10}\\ &= \$10{,}000\end{aligned}$$

For firm L, the present value is also \$10,000, calculated as follows:

$$\begin{aligned}\text{Market value of firm L} &= \frac{\$900}{0.1125} + \frac{\$100}{0.05}\\ &= \$8{,}000 + \$2{,}000\\ &= \$10{,}000\end{aligned}$$

Thus, the market values of firms U and L are equal. This example shows that the market value of the firm is independent of capital structure, assuming that the MM theory holds and no corporate income tax exists.

[11]Recall from Chapter 6 that the value of a perpetual bond (Equation 6.8) is equal to the annual interest payment (I) divided by the required rate of return (k_d). Also, in Chapter 7, the value of a common stock that pays a constant dividend in perpetuity (Equation 7.9) is equal to the annual dividend payment (D) divided by the required rate of return (k_e). Equations 6.8 and 7.9 were developed for the valuation of a single bond or share of stock. The formulas are also applicable to the valuation of the *total* debt (bonds) or equity (stock) of the company.

13-5b Capital Structure with a Corporate Income Tax

Next, the relationship between capital structure and firm market value is considered assuming that a corporate income tax exists. Table 13.3 shows financial data for an unlevered firm (U) and a levered firm (L) assuming a corporate income tax rate, *T*, of 40 percent. The total income available to the security holders of firm U is $600, and, assuming a cost of equity capital equal to 10 percent, the value of firm U is calculated using Equation 13.1:

$$\text{Market value of firm U} = \frac{\$600}{0.10} = \$6{,}000$$

Because interest paid to debtholders is a tax-deductible expense, the total income available to the debt and equity security holders of firm L, shown in Table 13.3, is $640. This amount is greater than the $600 available to the firm U equity security holders by $40.

tax shield

The $40 amount is the **tax shield** caused by the tax deductibility of the interest payments.[12] The annual tax shield amount is calculated using the following equation:

$$\begin{aligned}\text{Tax shield amount} &= i \times B \times T \\ &= 0.05 \times \$2{,}000 \times 0.40 \\ &= \$40\end{aligned} \qquad (13.2)$$

The total market value of firm L is obtained using Equation 13.1:

$$\begin{aligned}\text{Market value of firm L} &= \frac{D}{k_e} + \frac{I}{k_d} \\ &= \frac{\$540}{0.1125} + \frac{\$100}{0.05} \\ &= \$4{,}800 + \$2{,}000 \\ &= \$6{,}800\end{aligned}$$

In this example, the value of firm L is greater than firm U's value by $800. This difference in value is caused by the tax shield. In fact, the difference in value between the

TABLE 13.3

Capital Structure with a Corporate Income Tax: Financial Data on Firms U and L

	Firm U	Firm L
Net operating income (EBIT)	$ 1,000	$ 1,000
Less: Interest payments to debt holders, I	—	100
Income before taxes	$ 1,000	$ 900
Less: Corporate taxes, $T = 40\%$	400	$ 360
Income available to stockholders (dividends), D	$ 600	$ 540
Total income available to security holders, $I + D$	$ 600	$ 640
Required rate of return on debt, k_d	—	5%
Market value of debt, $B = I/k_d$	—	$ 2,000
Required rate of return on equity, k_e	10%	11.25%
Market value of equity, $E = D/k_e$	$ 6,000	$ 4,800
Market value of firm, $E + B$	$ 6,000	$ 6,800

[12]The calculation of the tax shield assumes that a company can take full advantage of the deductibility of interest payments in computing its tax liability. Firms with substantial accumulated losses or firms that can shield income with depreciation may not be able to realize the full amount of the tax savings associated with debt financing.

levered and unlevered firm is equal to the present value of the tax shield from the perpetual debt:

(13.3)
$$\text{Present value of tax shield} = \frac{i \times B \times T}{i} = B \times T$$

In this equation, the annual tax shield amount, iBT, is discounted at a rate, $i(i = k_d)$. In the case of firm L, the present value of the tax shield is \$800, calculated as follows:

$$\text{Present value of tax shield} = \$2{,}000 \times 0.40 = \$800$$

We can now state that the market value of the levered firm is equal to the market value of the unlevered firm plus the present value of the tax shield:

(13.4)
$$\text{Market value of levered firm} = \text{Market value of unlevered firm} + \text{Present value of tax shield}$$

From this equation, we can conclude that the value of the firm increases linearly as the amount of debt in the capital structure increases, as shown in Panel (a) of Figure 13.3. This result implies that a firm should increase its level of debt to the point at which the capital structure consists entirely of debt. In other words, the market value of the firm is maximized and its optimal capital structure is achieved when capital structure is all debt. As shown in Panel (b) of Figure 13.3, the weighted cost of capital k_a declines with increases in financial leverage. This follows from the fact that market value of the firm is inversely related to the firm's weighted cost of capital.[13]

In practice, we do not *normally* observe companies with extremely high levels of debt in their capital structures. In 2015, the average debt-to-capital ratio across all industries was 0.49, or 49 percent.[14] This was nowhere close to the 100 percent debt ratio implied by the MM model with corporate taxes. The one exception involves leveraged buyouts that began in the 1980s, which have resulted in debt ratios of 80 to more than 90 percent. For example, in the leveraged buyout of Warner Music in 2004, the debt ratio went from under 10 percent to over 85 percent following the buyout. Promoters of leveraged buyouts appear to have paid close attention to the advantages of debt financing. However, even in the case of leveraged buyouts, firms rarely approach *and remain* at a 100 percent debt-financed capital structure. Hence, other factors must be influencing the determination of an optimal capital structure. Two of the most important factors are financial distress costs and agency costs, which are considered in the following section.

13-5c Capital Structure with a Corporate Income Tax: Financial Distress Costs and Agency Costs

This section examines the effect of capital structure on the market value of the firm given the existence of a corporate income tax *and* financial distress *and* agency costs.

---

[13]The market value of a firm (sum of the value of debt and equity) with a constant cash flow can be calculated as:

$$\text{EBIT}(1 - T)/k_a$$

This is an alternate formula to Equation 13.1, which also gives you the market value of the firm. The above formula indicates that, holding EBIT$(1-T)$ constant, firm value goes up as k_a decreases and, conversely, firm value goes down as k_a increases.

[14]The debt-to-capital ratio is calculated as the interest bearing debt divided by the sum of interest bearing debt and stockholders' equity. The average was calculated from industry averages presented in Professor Aswath Damodaran's Web site, http://people.stern.nyu.edu/adamodar/New_Home_Page/datacurrent.html (accessed January 27, 2016).

FIGURE 13.3

Market Value of the Firm and Cost of Capital as a Function of Capital Structure (with Corporate Income Tax)

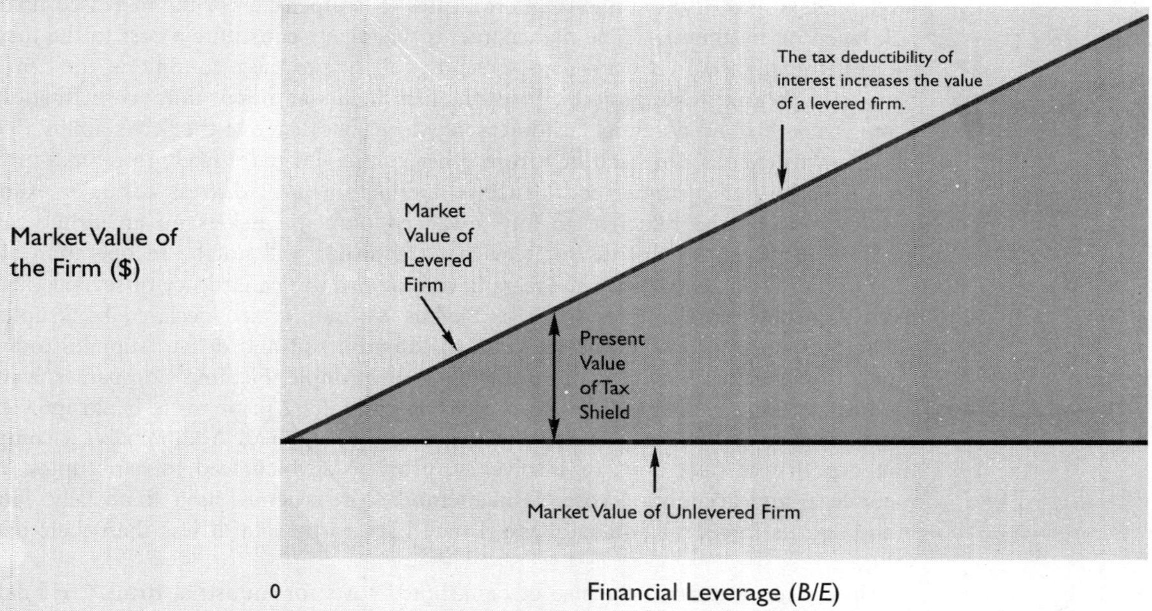

(a) Market Value of the Firm as a Function of Capital Structure

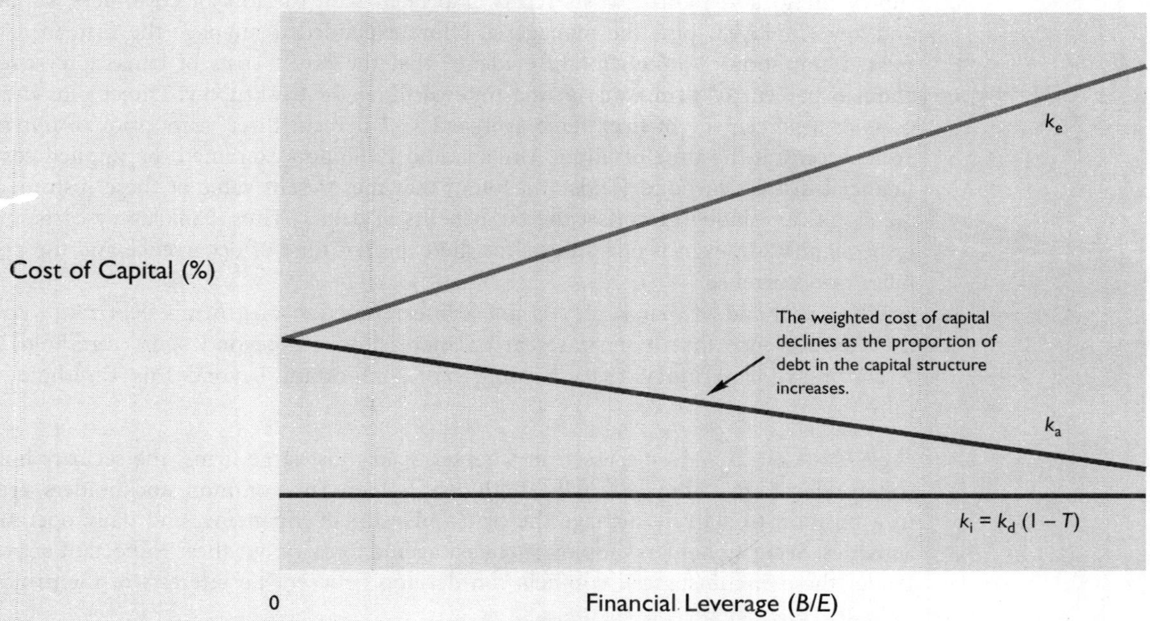

(b) Cost of Capital as a Function of Capital Structure

financial distress costs

Financial Distress Costs From a practical viewpoint, a firm cannot expect to gain the benefits associated with the tax deductibility of interest payments without also increasing certain costs. One significant cost category consists of **financial distress costs**, which include the costs incurred to avoid bankruptcy as well as the direct and indirect costs incurred if the firm files for bankruptcy protection.[15] As a firm increases its debt level, lenders may demand higher interest rates to compensate for the increased financial risk taken on by the firm. The higher interest payments constitute a cost to the firm. In the extreme, lenders may choose not to lend at all. Under these conditions, the firm may have to forgo acceptable projects. Thus, the firm incurs an opportunity cost. In addition, some customers and potential customers may lose confidence in the firm's ability to continue in existence and instead buy from other companies more likely to remain in business. This loss of customer confidence is another financial distress cost. For example, customers would be reluctant to buy advanced purchase tickets on an airline that is experiencing financial distress for fear that the airline will not be in operation at the time of the scheduled travel. Such fears have hastened the bankruptcy of several U.S. airlines, especially smaller ones (such as Skybus Airlines, which declared bankruptcy in 2008). Suppliers, too, would be reluctant to extend credit and deliver supplies to a customer that is experiencing financial distress. For example, Fleming Companies, a major food distributor, cut off supplies to K-Mart in early 2002 prior to its bankruptcy filing out of fear of not being paid for the merchandise supplied. Additionally, a company that experiences cash flow, or insolvency, problems, which lead to bankruptcy, must incur legal and accounting costs as it attempts to restructure itself financially. Finally, if the firm is forced to liquidate, assets may have to be sold at less than their market values.

Altman has measured the size of bankruptcy costs for industrial firms.[16] He defines *bankruptcy costs* as consisting of direct costs (costs paid by debtors in the bankruptcy and restructuring process, such as attorneys' fees and court costs associated with bankruptcy filing) and indirect costs (costs associated with the loss of customers, suppliers, and key employees plus the managerial effort expended to manage the firm in its distressed condition). Altman found evidence that the direct costs of bankruptcy average about 6 percent of firm value at the time of filing for bankruptcy. Direct plus indirect costs as a percentage of firm value averaged 12.1 percent three years prior to filing and 16.7 percent at the time of filing. Almeida and Philippon examined the implied costs of financial distress in bond yields and found that the present value of these distress costs are significant enough to offset the tax benefits of debt.[17] Thus, bankruptcy costs appear to be significant, even if one adjusts for the expected time of occurrence and the probability of occurrence.

The likelihood of bankruptcy is not a linear function of a firm's debt ratio. Rather, there is evidence that it increases at an increasing rate beyond some threshold level. Accordingly, bankruptcy costs become more important beyond this threshold debt ratio.

Agency Costs As discussed in Chapter 1, in most large firms, the security holders (often referred to as the *principals*), both debt holders and common stockholders, are not in a position to actively manage the firm's investment, financing, and daily operational activities. Security holders employ so-called agents to carry out these important activities. Under these circumstances, conflicts can develop between the interests of the principals

[15]Bankruptcy is discussed in greater detail in Chapter 23.

[16]Edward Altman, "A Further Empirical Investigation of the Bankruptcy Cost Question," *Journal of Finance* 39 (1984): 1067–1089.

[17]Heitor Almeida and Thomas Philippon, "The Risk-Adjusted Cost of Financial Distress," *Journal of Finance* 62 (2007), 2557–2586.

and those of the agent. We noted in Chapter 1 that the two most common types of principal- gent conflicts are those that occur between management and shareholders and between creditors and shareholders. The conflict between creditors and shareholders has an important bearing on capital structure choice. In the conflict between creditors and shareholders, the debt holders can be viewed as the principals, and the common stockholders can be viewed as the agents. The common stockholders are in a position to direct the investment and financing decisions of the firm through the elected board of directors and the managers hired by the board.

When debt is used in the capital structure of a firm, common stockholders have incentives to undertake actions that may be detrimental to the interests of the debt holders. Such a conflict results in *agency problems of debt*, one type of which is investing in extremely risky projects or engaging in asset substitution. In an asset substitution, the firm raises money from debt holders, promising to invest the funds in a lower-risk project with a lower interest cost, but instead it invests in a riskier project. The higher expected returns from risky investments accrue to the benefit of stockholders. Also, in the absence of restraints, stockholders are inclined to increase the proportions of debt in the capital structure, thus diminishing the protection afforded the earlier bondholders. The higher risk resulting from these actions may lead to a reduction in a firm's bond ratings. Lower bond ratings translate into lower bond values in the marketplace and thus in a loss in wealth to the bondholders. For example, take the case of the H. J. Heinz Company ("the ketchup company"). In February 2013 it was announced that Heinz was being acquired by a private equity group and Warren Buffett's company, Berkshire Hathaway Inc. At the time it was also announced that the acquisition will involve a significant amount of debt that will be rolled into Heinz's balance sheet once the deal is completed. This would mean that the original bondholders of Heinz will be subject to much higher leverage and higher default risk once the acquisition is completed. Given these prospects, the yields on Heinz bonds went up. For example, the yield on Heinz bonds maturing in 2032 rose from about 4.6 percent to approximately 6.2 percent following the announcement.

Not surprisingly, bondholders will want to take actions that reduce the prospect of this wealth transfer to stockholders. Agency theory argues that the agent will bear the agency costs. Therefore, debt holders can be expected to demand a higher interest rate on the bonds they purchase as compensation for the expected wealth losses. As an alternative, monitoring and bonding expenses can be incurred to reduce not only the incidence of these agency problems, but also the interest rate that will be demanded by bondholders. In the case of bonds, monitoring and bonding expenses take the form of protective covenants in the bond indenture.

Typical protective covenants place restrictions on the payment of dividends, limit the issuance of additional debt, limit the sale of assets, and limit the type of assets that may be acquired. (Protective covenants are discussed in greater detail in Chapters 6 and 19.) However, the more extensive the protective covenants are, the more costly it is to monitor compliance. In addition, increasingly extensive covenants may restrict the operating freedom and efficiency of managers, to the detriment of both stockholders and bondholders.

Thus, the firm can be viewed as having a choice along a continuum. At one extreme, there are no protective covenants, resulting in high interest rates, low or no monitoring costs, and no restrictions placed on the operating freedom of managers. At the other extreme, all decisions of the firm are subject to review by the debt holders—obviously not a feasible condition. *Monitoring and bonding activities should be carried out by the firm up to the point that the reduction in the interest rate charged by debt holders is balanced against the cost of additional monitoring and bonding activities.*

At low debt levels, bondholders do not demand extensive protective covenants and monitoring arrangements, because the risk exposure for the bondholders is viewed as being quite limited. Also, at low debt levels, the interest cost of debt financing will be low. As the amount of debt increases as a proportion of the total capital structure, bondholders find themselves subject to increased risk because managers (acting on behalf of stockholders) may make investments or take financing actions that could harm the current bondholders. Accordingly, monitoring costs are assumed to increase with increases in a firm's financial leverage, resulting in an increase in the *implicit* cost of debt, including the cost of monitoring and lost operating efficiency. This increase in the cost of debt has the effect of reducing the total value of the firm's securities.

In summary, the agency costs of debt are an increasing function of the proportion of debt in the capital structure of a firm. Consequently, agency costs represent another powerful reason why, in addition to the increased probability of financial distress or bankruptcy at higher debt ratios, a firm will choose a value-maximizing capital structure that is less than the 100 percent debt corner solution implied by the MM analysis.

13-5d Value-Maximizing Capital Structure

The preceding discussion of the impact of taxes, bankruptcy costs, and agency costs indicates that the market value of a levered firm can be represented by the following equation:

(13.5)

$$\text{Market value of levered firm} = \begin{pmatrix}\text{Market value}\\ \text{of unlevered}\\ \text{firm}\end{pmatrix} + \begin{pmatrix}\text{Present value}\\ \text{of tax shield}\end{pmatrix} - \begin{pmatrix}\text{Present value}\\ \text{of financial}\\ \text{distress costs}\end{pmatrix} - \begin{pmatrix}\text{Present value}\\ \text{of agency costs}\end{pmatrix}$$

Figure 13.4 illustrates this relationship graphically. As indicated in this figure and in Equation 13.5, the present value of expected financial distress costs and the agency costs associated with debt financing offset the present value of the tax shield accruing from debt. The result is an optimal (value-maximizing) amount of debt, B^*, and an optimal capital structure, B^*/E^*. This approach to determining the optimal capital structure is sometimes referred to as the *static trade-off theory.*[18]

13-5e The Cost of Capital and the Optimal Capital Structure

In this section, we examine the relationship between the cost of capital and the firm's capital structure when corporate taxes, financial distress costs, and agency costs are considered. In the following analysis, for simplicity, we assume that capital structure contains only permanent debt and common equity, that is, no preferred stock financing.

The first step in the analysis considers the relationship between the cost of debt and capital structure. All other things being equal, investors in debt consider the debt less risky if the firm has a low (rather than high) proportion of debt in its capital structure. As the proportion of debt in the capital structure increases, investors require a higher

[18] Stewart C. Myers, "The Capital Structure Puzzle," *Journal of Finance* 39 (July 1984): 575–592; Stewart C. Myers, "Still Searching for Optimal Capital Structure," *Journal of Applied Corporate Finance* 6 (Spring 1993): 4–14.

FIGURE 13.4

Value of the Firm as a Function of Capital Structure (with Corporate Income Tax, Financial Distress Costs, and Agency Costs)

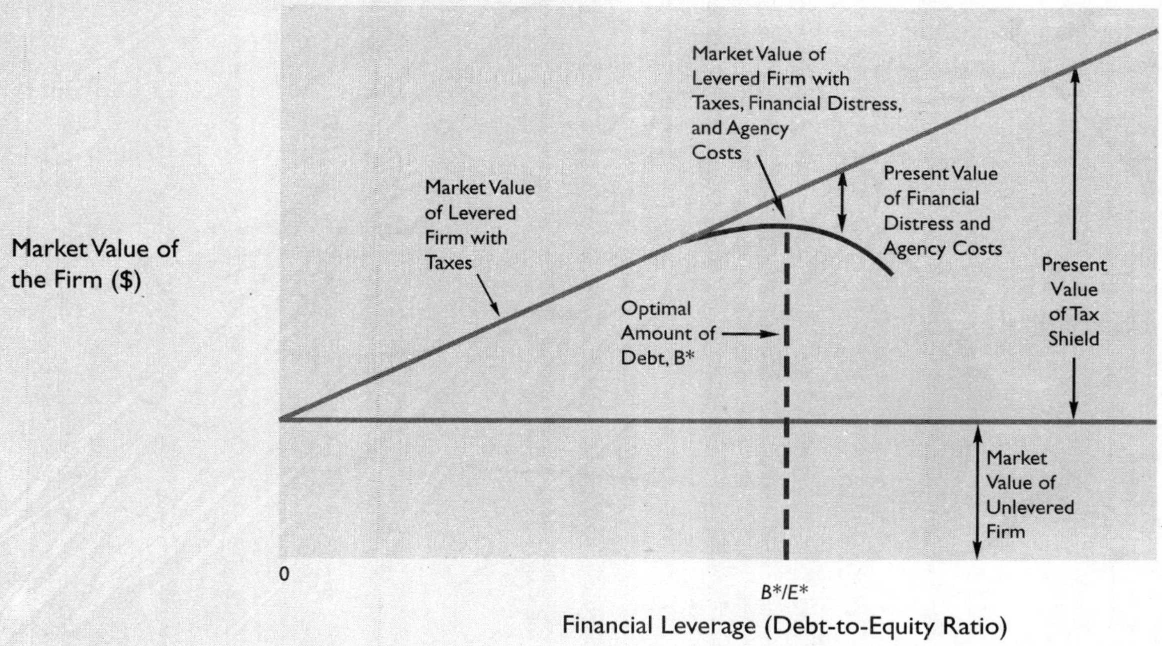

return on the more risky debt. And because the firm's cost of capital is the investor's required return, the cost of debt increases as the proportion of debt increases.

The precise relationship between the cost of debt and the debt ratio is difficult to determine, because observing the cost of debt at two different capital structures (at the same time) for a single firm is impossible. Nevertheless, as discussed earlier, evidence suggests that the cost of debt increases rather slowly for moderate amounts of debt. There is a point at which the capital markets begin to consider any new debt "excessive" and therefore much more risky. The cost of debt curve, k_i, in Figure 13.5 illustrates such a relationship. The actual region where the cost of debt begins to increase more rapidly varies by firm and industry, depending on the firm's level of business risk.

The next step in this analysis focuses on the relationship between the cost of equity capital and capital structure. When a firm has low financial leverage (that is, a low debt-to-equity ratio), any equity employed is less risky than equity used when the firm is financed with a relatively high proportion of debt. Earlier in this chapter, it was shown that the greater the fraction of debt used, the greater the variability in earnings per common share. In addition, the greater the fraction of debt used, the greater the risk of financial distress. Because the returns expected by stockholders in the form of present and future dividends depend partly on current earnings, variability in earnings per common share can result in variability of the returns to investors, that is, greater risk. Therefore, investors' required returns and the cost of equity capital increase as the relative amount of debt used to finance the firm increases.

FIGURE 13.5

Overall Cost of Capital as a Function of Capital Structure

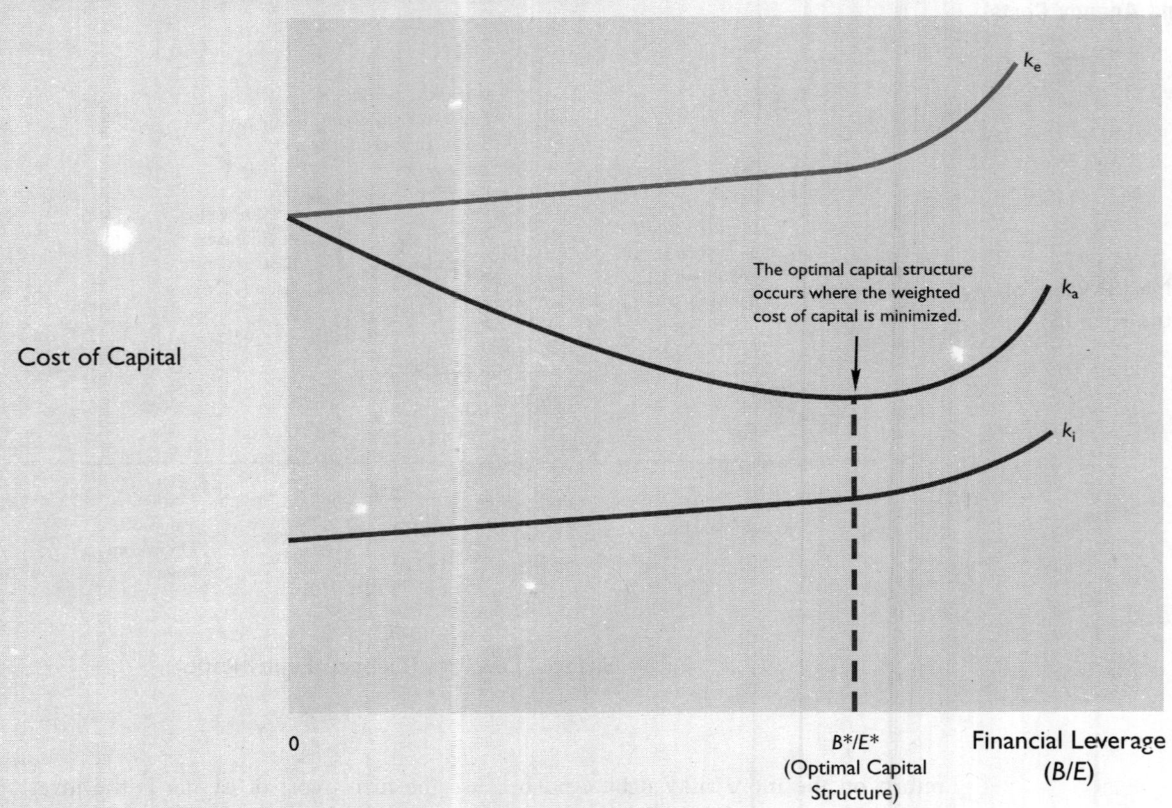

Once again, the exact nature of the relationship between the cost of equity and financial leverage is difficult to determine in practice. However, there is agreement that the cost of equity capital increases at a relatively slow rate as the debt proportion increases up to moderate amounts. Then, in the range where additional debt begins to be viewed as excessive and more risky, the cost of equity increases more rapidly. See Figure 13.5. As is true in the debt illustration, the region where the cost of equity capital, k_e, begins to increase more rapidly varies by firm and industry.

The relationship between the weighted cost of capital, k_a, and financial leverage can now be considered. The following equation is a modified version, without preferred stock in the capital structure, of Equation 12.1 from Chapter 12:

(13.6) $$k_a = \left(\frac{E}{B+E}\right)(k_e) + \left(\frac{B}{B+E}\right)(k_i)$$

This equation can be used to calculate k_a for any level of financial leverage, provided that the values of k_e and k_i at the level of financial leverage are known. (B is the market value of debt, and E is the market value of equity in the firm's capital structure.) Because the relationships between financial leverage and k_i and k_e have been developed, the relationship between k_a and financial leverage follows accordingly. The k_a curve, shown in Figure 13.5, begins at $k_a = k_e$ because, by definition, the weighted cost of capital for an all-equity firm equals the cost of equity. As even small increments of debt are used, k_a becomes lower; as the debt proportion continues to increase from moderate to excessive, k_a "bottoms out" and then begins to increase. The resulting saucer-shaped curve contains a point, B^*/E^*, at which the firm's overall cost of capital is minimized. At B^*/E^*, firm value is also maximized. This point represents the firm's *optimal capital structure*. If the firm is thought of as a cash-flow generator, then the lower the discount rate is (the weighted cost of capital), the higher the firm's value will be.

Figure 13.6 ties together the relationship between the optimal capital structure (with taxes, financial distress costs, and agency costs) with the market value of a firm and its weighted cost of capital. Note that at the optimal capital structure, B^*/E^*, the market value of the firm is maximized and its weighted cost of capital is minimized.

13-5f Other Considerations in the Capital Structure Decision

This section briefly covers some other factors that have an impact on the determination of an optimal capital structure: personal tax effects, industry effects, signaling effects, and managerial preference effects.

Personal Tax Effects The MM tax case led to the conclusion that, in the absence of financial distress costs and agency costs, the firm should attempt to minimize its taxes by employing the maximum amount of debt. However, the MM tax case did not consider the effect of personal income taxes. Miller has extended the tax case analysis to include both corporate and personal income taxes.[19] Miller argued that, although a firm can save taxes by increasing its debt ratio, individual investors would pay greater taxes on their returns from the firm if these returns were predominantly interest, rather than dividends and capital appreciation on common stock. In the extreme case, where investors are not taxed on their common stock earnings but are taxed on their interest income at the same rate as the corporate income tax rate, Miller shows that there is no tax advantage to corporations by issuing debt. In this extreme case, the higher personal tax rate on interest income cancels out the tax shield advantage to corporations of issuing debt. Historically, the tax code has favored capital gains income from stock over interest income because capital gains generally have been taxed at a lower rate than ordinary income (including interest income) and because taxes on capital gains are deferred until the capital gain is realized. Thus, from a tax perspective, investors may prefer to invest in a firm's common stock rather than its debt. Given this scenario, Miller's model indicates that the tax advantage to using debt depends on corporate tax rates being higher than the tax rates of bondholders.

Though Miller's study was of great academic interest, there is very little empirical research that indicates personal taxes affect capital structure choice in practice. In a well-known survey of chief financial officers, personal taxes ranked among the bottom of the list of factors they considered important in determining capital structure policy for the firm.[20]

Industry Effects A number of studies have found significant capital structure differences among industries. For example, a study by Bradley, Jarrell, and Kim show a debt-to-capital ratio (long-term debt divided by sum of long-term debt and market value of equity) for firms in the electric and gas utility industry of 53 percent, compared with 9 percent for firms in the pharmaceutical drug industry. In the same

---

[19]M. H. Miller, "Debt and Taxes," *Journal of Finance* 32 (May 1977): 261–276.

[20]J. Graham and C. Harvey, "How Do CFOs Make Capital Budgeting and Capital Structure Decisions?" *Journal of Applied Corporate Finance* 15, No. 1 (Spring 2002): 8–23.

FIGURE 13.6

Relationship Between the Optimal Capital Structure and the Market Value of a Firm and Its Weighted Cost of Capital

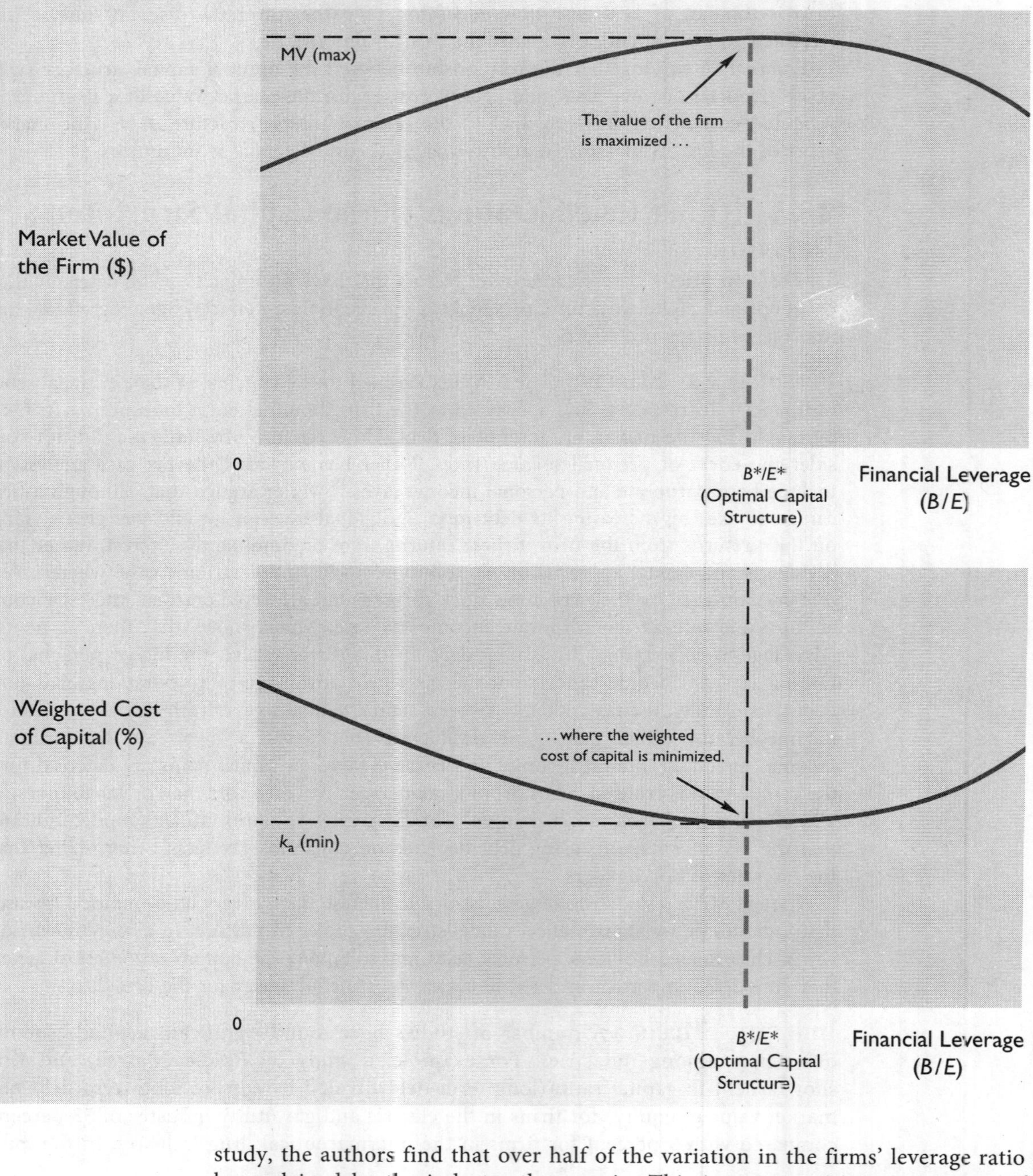

study, the authors find that over half of the variation in the firms' leverage ratio can be explained by the industry they are in. This is not surprising since many of the determinants of debt ratio vary by industry. Several studies find that firm debt ratio is related to the operating risk of the firm, asset composition (amount of fixed asset collateral), growth, and profitability.[21] These factors, to a large degree, vary by industry. For example, the electric utility industry tends to have a lot of fixed assets, and their operating earnings are relatively stable. Consequently, firms in this industry tend to take on more financial leverage. On the other hand, the electronics industry tends to have more volatile earnings, and therefore, firms in this industry tend to have a lower debt ratio.[22]

Signaling Effects Traditional theories of capital structure (e.g., MM model) assume that all investors have access to relevant information concerning a firm's future earnings prospects, but this assumption may not be valid in many cases. Instead, one can argue that the officers and managers of a company, as insiders, have access to information about the expected future earnings and cash flows of the firm that is not available to outside investors. This situation is referred to as **asymmetric information**. When information asymmetry exists, security prices (for example, share prices) may not be correctly valued. Given that managers know more about the firm than do outside investors, changes in a company's investment, financing, or dividend decisions can represent a **signal** to investors concerning management's assessment of the expected future returns and hence the market value of the company. Generally speaking, for the signal to be credible, it must be *costly*. In other words, the consequence of sending a false signal should be severe.

asymmetric information

signal

Thus, the issuance of new securities can be viewed as a signal to the financial marketplace regarding the future prospects of the firm or the future actions planned by the firm's managers.[23] Ross argues that signals provided by capital structure changes are credible because of the potential bankruptcy cost penalty incurred if the implied future cash flows do not occur. In general, studies of capital structure changes have found that new common equity offerings tend to yield *negative* stock price responses and that new debt offerings tend to yield no significant stock price responses.[24] Repurchases of common stock have led to large *positive* announcement returns on the company's common stock. Actions that increase leverage have generally been associated with *positive* stock returns, and actions that decrease leverage are associated with negative stock returns. The results of many studies of capital structure changes are consistent both with direct effects of the change, such as the benefits of greater tax shields, and with indirect information effects. Therefore, when a firm makes capital structure changes, it must be mindful of the potential signal that the proposed transaction will transmit to the marketplace regarding the firm's current and future earnings prospects and the intentions of its managers.[25]

Managerial Preference Effects: The Pecking Order Theory According to the **pecking order theory**, as developed by Myers, a firm may not have a particular target or optimal capital structure.[26] Instead, a company's capital structure changes

pecking order theory

---

[21]See, for example, Murray Z. Frank and Vidhan K. Goyal, "Capital Structure Decisions: Which Factors Are Reliably Important?" *Financial Management* (Spring 2009): 1–37; Paul Marsh, "The Choice Between Equity and Debt: An Empirical Study," *The Journal of Finance* 37 (1982): 121–144.

[22]Michael Bradley, Gregg A. Jarrell, and E. Han Kim, "On the Existence of an Optimal Capital Structure: Theory and Evidence," *The Journal of Finance* 39, No. 3 (July 1984): 857–878.

[23]Stephen Ross, "The Determination of Financial Structure: The Incentive-Signaling Approach," *Bell Journal of Economics* 8 (1977): 23–40.

[24]For a summary of empirical evidence concerning the effects of capital structure changes on security prices, see Thomas E. Copeland and J. Fred Weston, *Financial Theory and Corporate Policy*, 3rd ed. (Reading, MA: Addison-Wesley, 1988): 519–523.

[25]For an excellent discussion and review of the signaling literature as it relates to capital structure decisions, see Ronald W. Masulis, *The Debt/Equity Choice* (Cambridge, MA: Ballinger Publishing, 1988).

[26]See S. Myers, "The Capital Structure Puzzle," *Journal of Finance* 39 (July 1984): 575–592; and S. Myers, "Still Searching for Optimal Capital Structure," *Journal of Applied Corporate Finance* 6 (Spring 1993): 4–14.

when an imbalance between internal cash flows, net of cash dividend payments, and acceptable (that is, NPV > 0) investment opportunities occurs. Firms whose investment opportunities exceed internally generated funds tend to issue more debt securities and hence have higher debt ratios. Conversely, highly profitable firms with limited needs for investment funds tend to have lower debt ratios. In this situation, the firm builds up **financial slack** in the form of highly liquid assets (that is, cash and marketable securities) and unused debt capacity. Financial slack allows a firm to take advantage of attractive future investment opportunities.

financial slack

The pecking order theory indicates that firms prefer internal financing (retained earnings) to external financing (new security issues). This preference for internal financing is based on two considerations. First, because of the flotation costs of new security issues, internal financing is less costly than external financing. Second, according to Myers, because of information asymmetry, managers are likely to issue external securities when they are overvalued, thereby transferring the gains from the new

ETHICAL ISSUES

LBO Stakeholder Impacts

The rapid pace of mergers and acquisitions during the 1980s raised many interesting issues regarding the rights of the various corporate stakeholders in these transactions. Leveraged buyouts (LBOs) result in dramatic increases in the amount of debt used to finance a firm—up to 95 percent of the capital structure in some cases. The use of this large amount of debt permits a small group of investors to acquire ownership and control of a large firm with a relatively small equity investment. By concentrating ownership and control, the equity agency problems associated with the separation of ownership from control are largely eliminated. Also, the heavy burden of fixed charges from the debt financing forces managers to dramatically increase the efficiency of operations of the acquired firm. These benefits from LBOs are well documented.[a]

However, these benefits do not come without significant costs. For example, increased operating efficiency is often achieved by eliminating jobs, reducing other payroll expenses, and closing inefficient plants. The LBO of Safeway resulted in 63,000 managers and workers losing their jobs through store sales and closings. The employees who were reemployed by the new owners of sold stores received significantly lower wages. Many communities lost the substantial civic contributions and support of a formerly generous Safeway.[b]

Bondholders of acquired firms typically experience a loss in the value of their bonds when an LBO is announced.[c]

In the RJR Nabisco acquisition, Metropolitan Life Insurance Company and other bondholders sued KKR because of the loss the RJR bondholders experienced at the time of the takeover.

LBOs raise important ethical questions. How are the competing interests of stakeholders to be resolved in LBOs and other significant financial transactions? Yet these questions rarely have simple answers. Some issues to consider when debating the ethics of LBOs are as follows:

1. Is it in the long-run interest of employees to maintain staffing levels and operate facilities that are inefficient and reduce the company's ability to compete with other enterprises?
2. Are bondholders truly harmed in LBO transactions, considering the bond covenants for which they contracted when they purchased the bonds and the relationship between bond yields and covenant protection?

[a]See, for example, G. D. Bruton, J. K. Keels, and E. L. Scifres, "Corporate Restructuring and Performance: An Agency Perspective on the Complete Buy-out Cycle," *Journal of Business Research* 55 (2002): 709–724.

[b]A Pulitzer Prize–winning discussion of the impact of the Safeway LBO can be found in Susan C. Faludi, "Safeway LBO Yields Vast Profits but Exacts a Heavy Human Toll," *The Wall Street Journal* (May 16, 1990): 1.

[c]For example, see P. Asquith and T. A. Wizman, "Event Risk, Wealth Redistribution and the Return to Existing Bondholders in Corporate Buyouts," *Journal of Financial Economics* (September 1990): 195–214.

INTERNATIONAL ISSUES

Capital Structure

Multinational firms have a more complex capital structure decision than purely domestic firms. Should each foreign subsidiary maintain the same capital structure as the parent's consolidated structure, or should separate capital structures be established for each foreign subsidiary? Most firms tend to pay relatively little attention to establishing uniquely optimal capital structures for their foreign subsidiaries. Rather, the approach is normally one of establishing an optimal capital structure for the multinational firm as a whole and then adjusting foreign subsidiary capital structures to take advantage of local financing opportunities. The objective is to minimize the multinational firm's overall cost of capital.

Factors that determine the specific capital structure that will prevail for each subsidiary include the following:

1. *Exchange rate risk in the host country.* When exchange rate risk is high, the preference is to raise more of the subsidiary's capital in the financial markets of the host country.
2. *Local industry standards.* In some countries, it may be common for firms to have higher debt ratios than in others. Subsidiary capital structures normally reflect these traditions.[a]
3. *Host country requirements.* Some governments place restrictions on the capital structure of multinational firms operating in their country.
4. *Risk of expropriation.* The greater the risk that a multinational firm's subsidiary assets may be expropriated without adequate compensation, the greater will be the incentive for the multinational firm to finance that subsidiary with debt capital, especially debt capital raised in the host country and not guaranteed by the parent firm.
5. *Availability of special, low-cost financing in a host country.* Some host countries make low-cost financing available to multinational firms to stimulate additional investment. When this low-cost financing is available, firms normally take advantage of it.

Other factors that determine the optimal capital structure for a multinational firm as a whole are the increased capital market access for firms operating in several different countries and the extent to which the firm diversifies political and economic country risk. The diversification of political and economic country risk is largely a function of the number and location of foreign subsidiaries of the multinational firm.

[a]J. M. Collins and W. S. Sekely, "The Relationship of Headquarters Country and Industry Classification to Financial Structure," *Financial Management* (Autumn 1983): 45–51.

shareholders to existing shareholders, whom managers are assumed to favor. Also, according to the pecking order theory, dividends are "sticky"; that is, many firms are reluctant to make major changes in dividend payments and only gradually adjust dividend payout ratios to reflect their investment opportunities and thereby avoid the issuance of new securities.[27]

If external financing is required, the "safest" securities—debt—are issued first. As discussed in Chapter 7, the flotation costs of debt securities are generally lower than the costs of equity securities. Also, as noted in the discussion of asymmetric information, the stock market tends to react negatively to announcements of new common stock offerings, whereas debt security announcements tend to have little impact on stock prices. As additional external financing is needed, the firm will work down the pecking order—from safe to more risky debt, then possibly to convertible debt, and finally to common equity as a last resort.

A survey of large (*Fortune* 500) firms suggests that the pecking order theory is more descriptive of how financing decisions are made in practice compared with optimal

[27]This is referred to as a *stable dollar dividend policy.* See Chapter 15.

capital structure theories based on financial distress costs or agency costs.[28] Furthermore, among the respondents expressing a preference for the pecking order theory, approximately 85 percent ranked internal equity (retained earnings) as their first choice for financing new investments. Among external financing sources, respondents ranked straight (that is, nonconvertible) debt highest (most preferred), and external equity (that is, new common stock) was ranked lowest (least preferred).

Managerial Preference Effects: Market Timing Baker and Wurgler[29] suggest that the observed capital structures of firms are the cumulative result of timing equity issuances when they are overvalued. Thus, like the pecking order theory, firms do not have a target capital structure in mind. However, unlike the pecking order theory, according to the market timing model, managers like to issue external equity especially when the stock is overvalued—that is, when the cost of equity is low. The observed capital structure, then, is merely the result of past attempts to time equity issuances. A current low leverage ratio indicates that the firm raised equity funds in the past when it was overvalued, whereas a high leverage indicates that the firm did not time its equity issuance or that it issued equity when it was undervalued. As motivation for their study, Baker and Wurgler point to well-documented evidence that shows that equity issues are preceded by significant run-ups in the firms' stock price. They also point to survey evidence by Graham and Harvey[30] showing that a significant majority of CFOs consider the relative overvaluation of equity as an important or very important factor in the decision to issue equity. Baker and Wurgler find in favor of the market timing model in their empirical examination of observed capital structures of U.S. firms. Subsequent studies by other researchers have produced mixed evidence on the validity of the market timing effect.

Managerial Preference Effects: Financial Flexibility Financial flexibility refers to maintaining unused debt capacity, that is, maintaining a debt ratio that is much lower than the optimal debt ratio. So, if the optimal debt ratio for a firm is 30 percent, financial flexibility dictates that the firm maintain an actual debt ratio of, say, 15 percent. Firms may wish to retain unused debt capacity so that they can tap into it for future expansions or acquisitions. Firms may also want to maintain debt capacity for precautionary reasons such as an unexpected downturn in the business or the economy. Drawing on debt capacity during such periods allows the firm to better weather the downturn and enhance its liquidity. In survey evidence by Graham and Harvey, financial flexibility was cited by 60 percent of the CFOs as being an important or very important determinant in setting their firm's debt policy. This factor was considered more important than all the other factors included in the survey, even earnings volatility and tax savings from debt.

13-6 Managerial Implications of Capital Structure Theory

The rich body of theoretical and empirical capital structure studies provides important insights for financial managers. First, the capital structure decision is clearly one of the

[28] J. Michael Pinegar and Lisa Wilbricht, "What Managers Think of Capital Structure Theory: A Survey," *Financial Management* 18, no. 4 (Winter 1989): 82–91. See also J. Graham and C. Harvey, "How Do CFOs Make Capital Budgeting and Capital Structure Decisions?" *Journal of Applied Corporate Finance* 15, no. 1 (Spring 2002): 8–23.

[29] Malcolm Baker and Jeffrey Wurgler, "Market Timing and Capital Structure," *Journal of Finance* 56 (February 2002): 1–32.

[30] J. R. Graham and C. R. Harvey, "The Theory and Practice of Corporate Finance: Evidence from the Field," *Journal of Financial Economics* 60 (May/June 2001): 187–243.

centrally important decisions facing financial managers. There is little doubt that changes in capital structure result in changes in the market value of the firm. Second, the benefits of the tax shield from debt lead to increased firm value, at least up to the point that increased financial distress and agency costs begin to offset the debt advantage. Third, the optimal capital structure is heavily influenced by the business risk facing the firm. Fourth, when managers make explicit changes in a firm's capital structure, these actions transmit important information to investors about expected future returns and the market value of a company.

13-7 Summary

- *Capital structure* is defined as the relative amount of permanent short-term debt, long-term debt, preferred stock, and common stock used to finance a firm. The capital structure decision is important to the firm because, in practice, a capital structure exists at which the *cost of capital* is minimized. This minimum-cost capital structure is the *optimal* capital structure because the value of the firm is maximized at this point.
- The *business risk* of a firm consists of the variability of a firm's operating income. It is influenced by the variability of sales volumes, prices, and costs over the business cycle. Business risk is also influenced by a firm's market power and its use of operating leverage.
- The *financial risk* of a firm is the additional variability of earnings per share and the increased probability of insolvency that arises when a firm uses fixed-cost sources of funds, such as debt and preferred stock, in its capital structure.
- The use of financial leverage results in an increase in perceived risk to the suppliers of a firm's capital. To offset this increased risk, higher returns are required.
- Modigliani and Miller (MM) showed that the value of the firm is *independent* of capital structure, given perfect capital markets and no corporate income taxes. MM also show that the optimal capital structure consists entirely of debt if a corporate income tax exists.
- Given a corporate income tax, financial distress costs, and agency costs, an optimal capital structure consisting of both debt and equity is shown to exist. Determination of the optimal capital structure involves balancing the present value of the tax shield accruing from debt financing against the present value of the expected financial distress costs and the agency costs associated with debt financing.
- Given that managers have access to better information about a firm's future prospects than do outside investors (*asymmetric information*), capital structure changes often *signal* important information to investors about a firm's future prospects.
- According to the *pecking order theory*, a firm has no particular optimal capital structure. Companies prefer internal financing to external financing, and, given that external financing is necessary, they prefer to issue debt securities first and then equity securities only as a last resort.
- The *market timing model* states that firms do not have a target capital structure. Managers are presumed to issue equity when it is overvalued, that is, when the cost of equity is low. The observed capital structure is simply the cumulative result of past timing of equity issuances.
- *Financial flexibility* refers to the practice of maintaining a debt ratio that is much lower than the optimal debt ratio.

Important Equations

$$\text{Market value of firm} = \text{Market value of equity} + \text{Market value of debt}$$
$$= E + B$$
$$= \frac{D}{k_e} + \frac{I}{k_d}$$

$$\text{Tax shield amount} = i \times B \times T$$

Important Equations (*Continued*)

$$\text{Present value of tax shield} = \frac{i \times B \times T}{i} = B \times T$$

$$\text{Market value of levered firm} = \text{Market value of unlevered firm} + \text{Present value of tax shield}$$

$$\text{Market value of levered firm} = \begin{pmatrix}\text{Market value} \\ \text{of unlevered} \\ \text{firm}\end{pmatrix} + \begin{pmatrix}\text{Present value} \\ \text{of tax shield}\end{pmatrix} - \begin{pmatrix}\text{Present value} \\ \text{of financial} \\ \text{distress costs}\end{pmatrix} - \begin{pmatrix}\text{Present value} \\ \text{of agency costs}\end{pmatrix}$$

13-8 Questions and Topics for Discussion

1. Explain the research results of Modigliani and Miller in the area of capital structure.
2. What is the relationship between the value of a firm and its capital structure without a corporate income tax? With a corporate income tax?
3. What is the relationship between the value of a firm and its capital structure, given the existence of a corporate income tax, bankruptcy costs, and agency costs?
4. What is the *asymmetric information* concept? What role does this concept play in a company's decision to change its financial structure or issue new securities?
5. According to the pecking order theory, if additional external financing is required, which type of securities should a firm issue first? Last?
6. Explain why, according to the pecking order theory, firms prefer internal financing to external financing.
7. What assumptions are required in deriving the proposition that a firm's cost of capital is independent of its capital structure?
8. What role does *signaling* play in the establishment of a firm's capital structure?
9. What is arbitrage? How is it used in deriving the proposition that the value of a firm is independent of its capital structure?
10. Explain the difference between business risk and financial risk.
11. What other factors besides operating leverage can affect a firm's business risk?

13-9 Self-Test Problems

ST1. Ogden Optical Company has estimated the following costs of debt and equity capital (with bankruptcy and agency costs) for various proportions of debt in its capital structure:

Proportion of Debt [B/(B + E)]	Cost of Debt (k_i)	Cost of Equity (k_e)
0.00	—	10.0%
0.10	4.0%	10.1
0.20	4.2	10.3
0.30	4.4	10.8
0.40	4.8	11.4
0.50	5.5	12.5
0.60	6.6	14.5
0.70	8.0	18.0

Determine the firm's optimal capital structure.

ST2. Arizona Minerals, Inc. (AMI) estimated the costs of debt and equity capital with bankruptcy and agency costs for various proportions of debt in its capital structure. Its marginal tax rate is 40 percent.

Debt Ratio [B/(B + E)]	Pretax Cost of Debt (k_d)	Cost of Equity (k_e)	Weighted Average Cost of Capital
0.00	———	———	14.0%
0.10	7.0%	15.0%	———
0.20	———	16.5	———
0.30	10.0	18.5	———
0.40	———	21.5	15.9

a. Fill in the missing entries in the table.
b. Determine the capital structure that minimizes the weighted average cost of capital.

ST3. Citizens Electronics has $25 million in assets. Its expected operating income (EBIT) is $4 million, and its marginal tax rate is 40 percent. If Citizens finances 25 percent of its total assets with debt capital, the pretax cost of funds is 10 percent. If it finances 50 percent of its total assets with debt capital, the pretax cost of funds is 15 percent.

a. Determine the return on equity under three different capital structures: 0 percent, 25 percent, and 50 percent debt ratios.
b. Determine the return on equity under each of the three different capital structures if expected EBIT decreases by 20 percent.
c. Determine the return on equity under the three different capital structures as the result of the 20 percent increase in expected EBIT.

13-10 Problems*

BASIC

1. Referring to Table 13.2, calculate the market value of firm L (without a corporate income tax) if the equity amount in its capital structure decreases to $5,000 and

*Color blocks behind the numbers denote problems that have check answers provided at the end of the book.

the debt amount increases to $5,000. At this capital structure, the cost of equity is 15 percent.

BASIC **2.** a. Referring to Table 13.3, calculate the market value of firm L (with a corporate income tax) if the equity amount in its capital structure decreases to $3,000 and the debt amount increases to $3,000.

b. For firm L (with equity = $3,000 and debt = $3,000), calculate (i) the income available to the stockholders and (ii) the cost of equity.

INTERMEDIATE **3.** Two firms, No Leverage Inc. and High Leverage Inc., have equal levels of operating risk and differ only in their capital structure. No Leverage is unlevered and High Leverage has $500,000 of perpetual debt in its capital structure. Assume that the perpetual annual income of both firms available for stockholders is paid out as dividends. Hence, the growth rate for both firms is zero. The income tax rate for both firms is 40 percent. Assume that there are no financial distress costs or agency costs. You are given the following data:

	No Leverage Inc.	High Leverage Inc.
Equity in capital structure	$1,000,000	$500,000
Cost of equity, k_e	10%	13%
Debt in capital structure	—	$500,000
Pretax cost of debt, k_d	—	7%
Net operating income (EBIT)	$ 100,000	$100,000

Determine the:

a. Market value of No Leverage Inc.

b. Market value of High Leverage Inc.

c. Present value of the tax shield to High Leverage Inc.

INTERMEDIATE **4.** Jersey Computer Company has estimated the costs of debt and equity capital (with bankruptcy and agency costs) for various proportions of debt in its capital structure:

Proportion of Debt	After-Tax Cost of Debt (k_i)	Cost of Equity (k_e)
0.00	—	12.0%
0.10	4.7%	12.1
0.20	4.9	12.5
0.30	5.1	13.0
0.40	5.5	13.9
0.50	6.1	15.0
0.60	7.5	17.0

a. Determine the firm's optimal capital structure, assuming a marginal income tax rate (T) of 40 percent.

b. Suppose that the firm's current capital structure consists of 30 percent debt and 70 percent equity. How much higher is its weighted cost of capital than at the optimal capital structure?

INTERMEDIATE **5.** Piedmont Instruments Corporation has estimated the following costs of debt and equity capital for various fractions of debt in its capital structure.

Debt Fraction	k_i	k_e with Financial Distress Costs and Without Agency Costs	k_e with Financial Distress Costs and Agency Costs
0.00	—	12.00%	12.00%
0.10	4.8%	12.05	12.05
0.30	4.9	12.10	12.20
0.40	5.0	12.20	12.60
0.45	5.2	12.40	13.40
0.50	5.7	12.80	14.80
0.60	7.0	15.00	18.00

a. Based on these data, determine the company's optimal capital structure (i) with financial distress costs and without agency costs and (ii) with financial distress and agency costs.

b. Suppose the company's actual capital structure is 50 percent debt and 50 percent equity. How much higher is k_a at this capital structure than at the optimal value of k_a with financial distress and agency costs?

c. Is it necessary in practice for the company to know precisely its optimal capital structure? Why?

INTERMEDIATE

6. Arrow Technology, Inc. (ATI) has total assets of $10 million and expected operating income (EBIT) of $2.5 million. If ATI uses debt in its capital structure, the cost of this debt will be 12 percent per annum.

a. Complete the following table:

	Leverage Ratio (Debt/Total Assets)		
	0%	25%	50%
Total assets	____	____	____
Debt (at 12% interest)	____	____	____
Equity	____	____	____
Total liabilities and equity	____	____	____
Expected operating income (EBIT)	____	____	____
Less: Interest (at 12%)	____	____	____
Earnings before tax	____	____	____
Less: Income tax at 40%	____	____	____
Earnings after tax	____	____	____
Return on equity	____	____	____
Effect of a 20% Decrease in EBIT to $2,000,000			
Expected operating income (EBIT)	____	____	____
Less: Interest (at 12%)	____	____	____
Earnings before tax	____	____	____
Less: Income tax at 40%	____	____	____
Earnings after tax	____	____	____
Return on equity	____	____	____
Effect of a 20% Increase in EBIT to $3,000,000			
Expected operating income (EBIT)	____	____	____
Less: Interest (at 12%)	____	____	____

	Leverage Ratio (Debt/Total Assets)		
	0%	25%	50%
Earnings before tax	_____	_____	_____
Less: Income tax at 40%	_____	_____	_____
Earnings after tax	_____	_____	_____
Return on equity	_____	_____	_____

b. Determine the percentage change in return on equity of a 20 percent decrease in expected EBIT from a base level of $2.5 million with a debt-to-total-assets ratio of:

i. 0%
ii. 25%
iii. 50%

c. Determine the percentage change in return on equity of a 20 percent increase in expected EBIT from a base level of $2.5 million with a debt-to-total-assets ratio of:

i. 0%
ii. 25%
iii. 50%

d. Which leverage ratio yields the highest expected return on equity?
e. Which leverage ratio yields the highest variability (risk) in expected return on equity?
f. What assumption was made about the cost of debt (that is, interest rate) under the various capital structures (that is, leverage ratios)? How realistic is this assumption?

INTERMEDIATE

7. Colorado Coal Company has estimated the costs of debt and equity capital (with bankruptcy and agency costs) for various proportions of debt in its capital structure.

Debt Ratio $[B/(B+E)]$	Pretax Cost of Debt (k_d)	Cost of Equity (k_e)	Weighted Average Cost of Capital (k_a)
0.00	_____	_____	12.0%
0.15	_____	13.0%	11.68
0.30	8.0%	14.5	_____
0.45	_____	16.5	11.775
_____	14.0	19.0	12.64

The company's income tax rate is 40 percent.

a. Fill in the missing entries in the table.
b. Determine the capital structure (that is, debt ratio) that minimizes the firm's weighted average cost of capital.

CHALLENGE

8. Ohio Quarry Inc. has $12 million in assets. Its expected operating income (EBIT) is $2 million and its income tax rate is 40 percent. If Ohio Quarry finances 20 percent of its total assets with debt capital, the pretax cost of funds is 10 percent. If the company finances 40 percent of its total assets with debt capital, the pretax cost of funds is 15 percent.

a. Determine the rate of return on equity (ROE) under the three different capital structures (0%, 20%, and 40% debt ratios).
b. Which capital structure yields the highest expected ROE?

c. Determine the ROE under each of the three capital structures (0%, 20%, and 40% debt ratios) if expected EBIT decreases by 20 percent.
d. Which capital structure yields the highest ROE calculated in Part c?
e. Determine the percentage change in ROE under each of the three capital structures (that is, debt ratios) as the result of a 20 percent decline in EBIT.
f. Based on the results in Part e, which capital structure yields the highest variability (that is, risk) in ROE?

INTERMEDIATE

9. Washington Paper Company has estimated the costs of debt and equity capital (with bankruptcy and agency costs) for various proportions of debt in its capital structure as follows:

Debt Ratio [$B/(B+E)$]	Pretax Cost of Debt (k_d)	Cost of Equity (k_e)
0.00	—	14.0%
0.10	7.0%	14.2
0.20	7.2	14.6
0.30	7.6	15.4
0.40	8.2	17.0
0.50	9.0	20.0
0.60	10.0	26.0

The firm's marginal (and average) income tax rate is 40 percent. Determine the company's optimal capital structure.

INTERMEDIATE

HTTP:
finance.yahoo.com

10. Visit Yahoo! Finance (finance.yahoo.com) and calculate the debt ratio of an industrial equipment manufacturer, such as Illinois Tool Works, Inc. Then calculate the debt ratio of a service-oriented company, such as Cognizant Technology Solutions. Based on what you learned about leverage in this chapter, what would account for the difference in their debt ratios?

CHAPTER
14

Capital Structure Management in Practice

KEY CHAPTER CONCEPTS

1. The degree of operating leverage (DOL) is defined as the percentage change in EBIT resulting from a 1 percent change in sales.
    a. The degree of operating leverage approaches a maximum as the firm comes closer to operating at its breakeven level of output.
    b. All other things being equal, the higher a firm's DOL, the greater is its business risk.
    c. Business risk, the inherent variability of a firm's EBIT is also influenced by the variability of sales and operating costs over time.
2. The degree of financial leverage (DFL) is defined as the percentage change in earnings per share (EPS) resulting from a 1 percent change in EBIT.
    a. The degree of financial leverage approaches a maximum as the firm comes closer to operating at its loss level, the level where EPS is $0.
    b. All other things being equal, the higher a firm's DFL, the greater its financial risk.
    c. Financial risk, the additional variability of a firm's EPS that results from the use of financial leverage, can also be measured by various financial ratios, such as the debt-to-total-assets ratio and the times-interest-earned ratio.
3. The degree of combined leverage (DCL) is defined as the percentage change in earnings per share resulting from a 1 percent change in sales. It is also equal to the DOL times the DFL. The degree of combined leverage used by a firm is a measure of the overall variability of EPS due to the use of fixed operating and capital costs, as sales levels change.
4. EBIT-EPS analysis is an analytical technique that can be used to help determine the circumstances under which a firm should employ financial leverage. The indifference point in EBIT-EPS analysis is the level of EBIT at which earnings per share are the same regardless of which of two alternative capital structures is used.
5. Cash insolvency analysis can be used to evaluate the impact of a proposed capital structure on the cash position of a firm during a major business downturn.
6. Other factors that are considered when establishing a capital structure policy are industry standards, profitability and the need for funds, lender requirements, managerial risk aversion, and the desire of owners to retain control of the firm.

FINANCIAL CHALLENGE

High-Tech Companies' Love Affair with Debt

According to one report, 24 of the 25 largest software companies utilized some debt financing in their capital structure as of 2010. However, only 7 of them did so in 2002.[1] Here's a sample of a few software/Internet firms and their debt ratios as of 2015:

Salesforce.com	30.5%
Adobe Systems	21.4%
Google	7%
Priceline.com	39%
Microsoft	33%
Oracle	48%
Expedia	45%

About 15 years ago, these same firms had no or negligible amounts of long-term debt. In fact, most of these firms have made their initial trips to the debt market within the last 5–8 years. So, what caused these firms to take up debt? Were they being reckless in taking on this debt? The answer, in brief, is that these firms "matured" or "grew up." Fifteen years ago, most of these firms were much smaller, and the industry or industry segment they operated in was still at the beginning of its lifecycle. Consequently, the firms were subject to high business risk, uncertain growth, limited credit history, and significant bankruptcy risk. It was difficult for firms with that background to obtain debt at a reasonable cost.

Today, these firms and the industries they are in are much more established, have stable growth and cash flows, and have survived through at least one major business cycle or financial crisis event. For example, Microsoft today is a very diversified company with products that encompass many

luchunyu/Shutterstock.com

[1]Ben Wothen, "Tech Firms Bulk Up with Debt," *The Wall Street Journal* (April 20, 2010): B1.

FINANCIAL CHALLENGE — CONTINUED

segments, including operating system software, Internet search, entertainment devices, cloud-based software, consumer and office software, and so forth. Additionally, Microsoft is diversified geographically, with sales throughout the world, and has considerable market power in many of its product segments. All of this translates to low business risk, which means that the firm can afford to take on debt at reasonable cost and avail itself of the benefits of debt, such as the tax shield benefit. The same is true, to varying degrees, of the other companies listed. It is clear that the decision by these firms to alter their preference for debt over time was a result of weighing the costs and benefits of debt and choosing to make the optimal decision based on the particular circumstances.

This chapter presents some of the techniques that will help a firm weigh the costs and benefits of debt and also elaborate on other considerations that may be important in setting an appropriate debt policy for the firm.

CHAPTER OBJECTIVES

Upon completion of this chapter, you should have a clear understanding of the following:

1. The meaning and measurement of operating, financial, and combined leverage
2. The EBIT-EPS framework for analyzing capital structure policy
3. The use of cash insolvency analysis in deciding capital structure policy
4. Other factors considered by managers in setting capital structure policy in practice
5. Operating breakeven analysis and its relation to operating leverage and business risk (covered in the chapter appendix)

14-1 Introduction

This chapter focuses on various tools of analysis that can assist managers in making capital structure decisions that will lead to a maximization of shareholder wealth. The following section develops techniques, derived from accounting data, for measuring operating and financial leverage. As discussed in the previous chapter, operating leverage and financial leverage are important components of a firm's business and financial risk. Other techniques, namely *EBIT-EPS analysis* and *cash insolvency analysis*, can aid management in assessing the risk-versus-return trade-offs associated with the use of debt in a firm's capital structure. The appendix to this chapter discusses *breakeven analysis*, an analytical tool that can provide insights into the business risk a firm faces.

14-2 Operating and Financial Leverage

The concepts of operating and financial leverage were introduced in the previous chapter. In finance, *leverage* is defined as a firm's use of assets and liabilities having fixed costs in an attempt to increase potential returns to stockholders. Specifically, operating leverage involves the use of *assets* having fixed costs, whereas financial leverage involves the use of *liabilities* (and *preferred stock*) having fixed costs.

A firm uses operating and financial leverage in the hope of earning returns in excess of the fixed costs of its assets and liabilities, thereby increasing the returns to common stockholders. Leverage is a double-edged sword, however, because it also increases the *variability* or risk of these returns. If, for example, a firm earns returns that are *less* than the fixed costs of its assets and liabilities, then the use of leverage can actually *decrease* the returns to common stockholders. Thus, leverage magnifies shareholders' potential losses as well as potential gains. Leverage concepts are particularly revealing to the financial analyst in that they highlight the *risk-return trade-offs* of various types of financial decisions, such as those involving the capital structure of the firm.

14-2a Leverage and the Income Statement

Financial statements of the Allegan Manufacturing Company are referred to throughout this section for purposes of illustration. Table 14.1 contains two types of statements for the firm: a traditional format and a revised format. The traditional format shows various categories of costs as separate entries, similar to what you might find in a typical annual report. *Operating costs* include such items as the cost of sales and general, administrative, and selling expenses. Interest charges and preferred dividends, which represent *capital costs*, are listed separately, as are income taxes.

The revised format is more useful in leverage analysis because it divides the firm's operating costs into two categories: *fixed* and *variable.*

14-2b Short-Run Costs

Over the short run, certain operating costs within a firm vary directly with the level of sales, whereas other costs remain constant, regardless of changes in the sales level. Costs that move in close relationship to changes in sales are called **variable costs**. They are tied to the number of units produced and sold by the firm, rather than to the passage of time. They include raw material and direct labor costs, as well as sales commissions.

variable costs

Over the short run, certain other operating costs are independent of sales or output levels. These so-called **fixed costs** are primarily related to the passage of time. Depreciation on property, plant, and equipment; rent; insurance; lighting and heating bills; property taxes; and the salaries of management are all usually considered fixed costs. If a firm expects to keep functioning, it must continue to pay these costs, regardless of the sales level.

fixed costs

A third category, *semivariable costs*, can also be considered. Semivariable costs are costs that increase in a *stepwise* manner as output is increased. One cost that sometimes behaves in a stepwise manner is management salaries. Whereas these costs are generally considered fixed, this assumption is not always valid. A firm may find that it can operate effectively with its current managerial staff even if sales increase by, say, 25 percent, but it may find that further increases in sales may necessitate adding to their managerial staff.

TABLE **14.1**

Traditional and Revised Income Statements

Allegan Manufacturing Company Year Ending December 31, 2016
Traditional Income Statement Format

	Sales		$ 5,000,000
Operating costs	*Less*: Cost of sales	$ 2,500,000	
	Selling, general, and administrative expenses	1,500,000	
	Total operating costs		4,000,000
	Earnings before interest and taxes (EBIT)		1,000,000
Financial costs	*Less*: Interest expense		250,000
	Earnings before taxes (EBT)		750,000
	Less: Income taxes (40% rate)		300,000
	Earnings after taxes (EAT)		450,000
	Less: Preferred stock dividends		150,000
	Earnings available to common stockholders		$ 300,000
	Earnings per share (EPS)—100,000 shares		$ 300

Allegan Manufacturing Company Year Ending December 31, 2016
Revised Income Statement Forma

	Sales		$ 5,000,000
Operating leverage	*Less*: Variable operating costs	$ 3,000,000	
	Fixed operating costs	1,000,000	
	Total operating costs		4,000,000
	Earnings before interest and taxes (EBIT)		1,000,000
Financial leverage	*Less*: Fixed capital costs (interest)		250,000
	Earnings before taxes (EBT)		750,000
	Less: Income taxes (variable), 40% rate		300,000
	Earnings after taxes (EAT)		450,000
	Less: Fixed capital costs (preferred stock dividends)		150,000
	Earnings available to common stockholders		$ 300,000
	Earnings per share (EPS)—100,000 shares		$ 300

Not all costs can be classified as either completely fixed or variable; some have both fixed and variable components. Costs for utilities, such as water and electricity, frequently fall into this category. Whereas part of a firm's utility costs (such as electricity) is fixed and must be paid regardless of the level of sales or output, another part is variable in that it is tied directly to sales or production levels. In the revised format of Allegan's income statement, these are divided into their fixed and variable components and are included in their respective categories of operating costs.

Note that in the revised income statement format, both interest charges and preferred dividends represent fixed capital costs. These costs are contractual in nature and thus are independent of a firm's level of sales or earnings; that is, these charges have to be paid regardless of the firm's sales and earnings performance. Also note that income taxes represent a variable cost that is a function of earnings before taxes.

Panels (a), (b), and (c) of Figure 14.1 show the behavior of variable, fixed, and semivariable costs, respectively, over the firm's output range.

FIGURE 14.1

Behavior of (a) Variable, (b) Fixed, and (c) Semivariable Costs

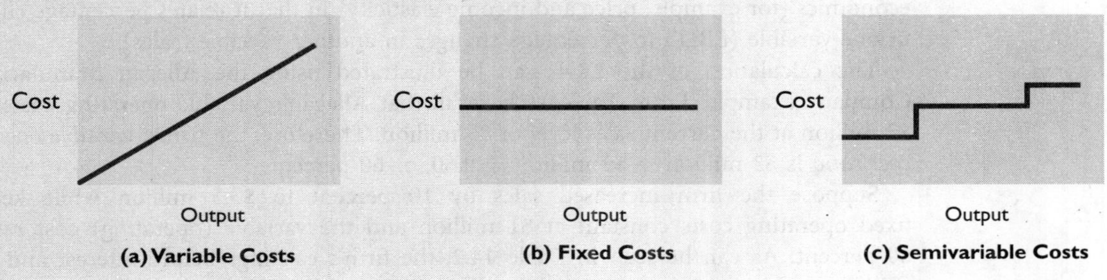

14-2c Long-Run Costs

Over the *long run*, all costs are variable. In time, a firm can change the size of its physical facilities and number of management personnel in response to changes in the level of sales. Fixed capital costs also can be changed in the long run.

14-2d Measurement of Operating and Financial Leverage

Fixed obligations allow a firm to magnify small changes into larger ones, just as a small push on one end of an actual lever results in a large lift at the other end.

degree of operating leverage (DOL)

Operating leverage has fixed operating costs for its fulcrum, so to speak. When a firm incurs fixed operating costs, a change in sales revenue is magnified into a relatively larger change in earnings before interest and taxes (EBIT). The multiplier effect resulting from the use of fixed operating costs is known as the **degree of operating leverage (DOL)**. The greater the proportion of fixed operating costs to total operating costs, the greater the magnifying effect.

degree of financial leverage (DFL)

Financial leverage has fixed capital costs for its fulcrum. When a firm incurs fixed capital costs, a change in EBIT is magnified into a larger change in earnings per share (EPS). The multiplier effect resulting from the use of fixed capital costs is known as the **degree of financial leverage (DFL)**. Similar to the case of operating costs, the greater the use of the fixed capital cost sources of financing in a firm's capital structure, the greater the magnifying effect.

14-2e Degree of Operating Leverage

A firm's *degree of operating leverage* (DOL) is defined as the multiplier effect resulting from the firm's use of fixed operating costs. More specifically, DOL can be computed as the *percentage change* in earnings before interest and taxes (EBIT) resulting from a given *percentage change* in sales (output):

$$\text{DOL at } X = \frac{\text{Percentage change in EBIT}}{\text{Percentage change in sales}}$$

This can be rewritten as follows:

(14.1)
$$\text{DOL at } X = \frac{\frac{\Delta\text{EBIT}}{\text{EBIT}}}{\frac{\Delta\text{Sales}}{\text{Sales}}}$$

where ΔEBIT and ΔSales are the changes in the firm's EBIT and sales, respectively. Because a firm's DOL differs at each sales (output) level, it is necessary to indicate the sales point, X, (in terms of units of output or dollar sales), at which operating leverage is measured. The degree of operating leverage is analogous to the elasticity concept of economics (for example, price and income elasticity) in that it relates percentage changes in one variable (EBIT) to percentage changes in another variable (sales).

The calculation of the DOL can be illustrated using the Allegan Manufacturing Company example. From Table 14.1, recall that Allegan's variable operating costs were \$3 million at the current sales level of \$5 million. Therefore, the firm's *variable operating cost ratio* is \$3 million ÷ \$5 million = 0.60, or 60 percent.

Suppose the firm increased sales by 10 percent to \$5.5 million while keeping fixed operating costs constant at \$1 million and the variable (operating) cost ratio at 60 percent. As can be seen in Table 14.2, the firm's earnings before interest and taxes (EBIT) would increase to \$1.2 million. Substituting the two sales figures (\$5 million and \$5.5 million) and associated EBIT figures (\$1 million and \$1.2 million) into Equation 14.1 yields the following:

$$\text{DOL at } \$5{,}000{,}000 = \frac{\dfrac{(\$1{,}200{,}000 - \$1{,}000{,}000)}{\$1{,}000{,}000}}{\dfrac{(\$5{,}500{,}000 - \$5{,}000{,}000)}{\$5{,}000{,}000}}$$

$$= \frac{\$200{,}000}{\$1{,}000{,}000} \times \frac{\$5{,}000{,}000}{\$500{,}000}$$

$$= 2.0$$

A DOL of 2.0 is interpreted to mean that each 1 percent change in sales from a base sales level of \$5 million results in a 2 percent change in EBIT *in the same direction as the sales change*. In other words, a sales *increase* of 10 percent results in a 10% × 2.0 = 20% *increase* in EBIT. Similarly, a 10 percent *decrease* in sales produces a 10% × 2.0 = 20% *decrease* in EBIT. The greater a firm's DOL, the greater the magnification is of sales changes into EBIT changes.

TABLE 14.2

Effect on Earnings per Share of a 10 Percent Increase in Sales, Allegan Manufacturing Company, Year Ending December 31, 2016

		(1)		(2)	Percentage Change [(2) − (1)] ÷ (1)
Sales		\$ 5,000,000		\$ 5,500 000	+10%
Less: Variable operating costs (0.60 × Sales)	\$3,000,000		\$3,300,000		+10
Fixed operating costs	1,000,000		1,000,000		0
Total operating costs		4,000,000		4,300,000	+8
Earnings before interest and taxes		\$ 1,000,000		\$ 1,200,000	+20
Less: Interest payments (fixed capital cost)		250,000		250,000	0
Earnings before taxes		\$ 750,000		\$ 950,000	+27
Less: *Income taxes* (variable), 40%		300,000		380,000	+27
Earnings after taxes		\$ 450,000		\$ 570,000	+27
Less: Preferred dividends (fixed capital cost)		150,000		150,000	0
Earnings available to common stockholders		\$ 300,000		\$ 420,000	+40
Earnings per share (100,000 shares)		\$ 3.00		\$ 4.20	+40

Equation 14.1 requires the use of two different values of sales and EBIT. Another equation that can be used to compute a firm's DOL more easily is as follows:[2]

(14.2)
$$\text{DOL at } X = \frac{\text{Sales} - \text{Variable costs}}{\text{EBIT}}$$

Inserting data from Table 14.1 on the Allegan Manufacturing Company into Equation 14.2 gives the following:

$$\text{DOL at \$5 million} = \frac{\$5{,}000{,}000 - \$3{,}000{,}000}{\$1{,}000{,}000}$$
$$= 2.0$$

This result is the same as that obtained using the more complex Equation 14.1.

Table 14.3 shows the DOL at various sales levels for Allegan Manufacturing Company. Note that Allegan's DOL is the largest (in absolute value terms) when the firm is operating at the breakeven sales point (that is, where Sales = \$2,500,000 and EBIT = Sales − Variable operating costs − Fixed operating costs = \$2,500,000 − 0.60[\$2,500,000] − \$1,000,000 = \$0).[3] Note also that the firm's DOL is negative below the breakeven sales level. A negative DOL indicates the percentage *reduction* in operating *losses* that occurs as the result of a 1 percent increase in output. For example, the DOL of −1.50 at a sales level of \$1.5 million indicates that, from a base sales level of \$1.5 million, the firm's operating *losses* are *reduced* by 1.5 percent for each 1 percent *increase* in output.

A firm's DOL is a function of the nature of the production process. If the firm employs large amounts of labor-saving equipment in its operations, it tends to have a relatively high DOL, which results in large operating profits (positive EBIT) if sales are high, and large operating losses (negative EBIT) if sales are depressed. Conversely, if a firm's production process primarily relies on labor and the firm has the flexibility to hire and fire employees as needed to meet production requirements, it will tend to have

TABLE **14.3**

DOL at Various Sales Levels, Allegan Manufacturing Company

Sales, TR = P × Q*	Degree of Operating Leverage (DOL)
\$ 500,000	−0.25
1,000,000	−0.67
1,500,000	−1.50
2,000,000	−4.00
2,500,000**	(Undefined)
3,000,000	+6.00
3,500,000	+3.50
4,000,000	+2.67
4,500,000	+2.25
5,000,000	+2.00
5,500,000	+1.83
6,000,000	+1.71

*TR = Total revenue, P = Price, Q = Quantity

**Breakeven sales level.

[2]Equation 14.2 is derived from Equation 14.1. See Problem 4 at the end of this chapter.

[3]Breakeven analysis is covered in Appendix 14A.

a low DOL. In this case, the firm's operating profits will not be as sensitive to changes in sales.

14-2f Degree of Financial Leverage

(EPS)
(EBIT)

A firm's degree of financial leverage (DFL) is computed as the *percentage change* in earnings per share (**EPS**) resulting from a given *percentage change* in earnings before interest and taxes (**EBIT**):

$$\text{DFL at } X = \frac{\text{Percentage change in EPS}}{\text{Percentage change in EBIT}}$$

This can also be written as follows:

$$\text{DFL at } X = \frac{\dfrac{\Delta \text{EPS}}{\text{EPS}}}{\dfrac{\Delta \text{EBIT}}{\text{EBIT}}} \quad (14.3)$$

where ΔEPS and ΔEBIT are the changes in EPS and EBIT, respectively. Because a firm's DFL is different at each EBIT level, it is necessary to indicate the EBIT point, *X*, at which financial leverage is being measured.

Using the information contained in Table 14.4 and shown in Figure 14.2, the degree of financial leverage used by the Allegan Manufacturing Company can be calculated. The firm's EPS level is \$3.00 at an EBIT level of \$1 million. At an EBIT level of \$1.2 million, EPS equals \$4.20. Substituting these quantities into Equation 14.3 yields the following:

$$\begin{aligned}\text{DFL at } \$1{,}000{,}000 &= \frac{\dfrac{(\$4.20 - \$3.00)}{\$3.00}}{\dfrac{(\$1{,}200{,}000 - \$1{,}000{,}000)}{\$1{,}000{,}000}} \\ &= \frac{\$1.20}{\$3.00} \times \frac{\$1{,}000{,}000}{\$200{,}000} \\ &= 2.0\end{aligned}$$

A DFL of 2.0 indicates that each 1 percent change in EBIT from a base EBIT level of \$1 million results in a 2 percent change in EPS *in the same direction as the EBIT change.* In other words, a 10 percent *increase* in EBIT results in a 10% × 2.0 = 20% *increase*

TABLE 14.4

Earnings per Share for Alternative Levels of EBIT, Allegan Manufacturing Company, Year Ending December 31, 2016

EBIT	\$400,000	\$800,000	\$1,000,000	\$1,200,000	\$1,600,000
Less: Interest expenses	250,000	250,000	250,000	250,000	250,000
Earnings before taxes	\$150,000	\$550,000	\$750,000	\$950,000	\$1,350,000
Less: Income taxes	60,000	220,000	300,000	380,000	540,000
Earnings after taxes	\$90,000	\$330,000	\$450,000	\$570,000	\$810,000
Less: Preferred dividends	150,000	150,000	150,000	150,000	150,000
Earnings available to common stockholders	\$–60,000	\$180,000	\$300,000	\$420,000	\$660,000
Earnings per share (EPS)	\$–0.60	\$1.80	\$3.00	\$4.20	\$6.60

FIGURE 14.2

EPS-EBIT Graph for the Allegan Manufacturing Company

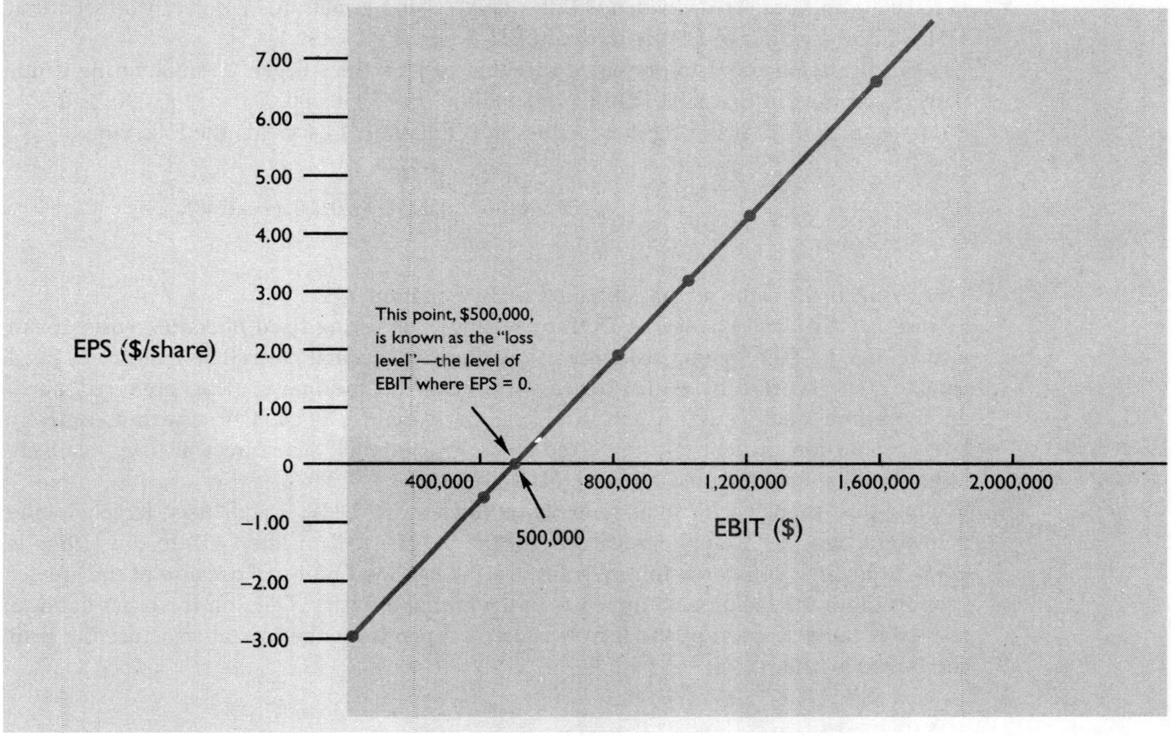

© Cengage Learning

in EPS. Similarly, a 10 percent *decrease* in EBIT produces a 20 percent *decrease* in EPS. The larger the firm's DFL, the greater the magnification is of EBIT changes into EPS changes.

Measuring a firm's DFL using Equation 14.3 is somewhat cumbersome, because it necessitates using two EBIT and EPS projections. Computation is simplified when Equation 14.3 is rewritten as follows:[4]

(14.4)
$$\text{DFL at } X = \frac{\text{EBIT}}{\text{EBIT} - I - D_p/(1 - T)}$$

where I is the firm's interest payments, D_p is the firm's preferred dividend payments, T is the firm's marginal income tax rate, and X is the level of EBIT at which the firm's DFL is being measured.

Unlike interest payments, preferred dividend payments are not tax deductible. Therefore, on a comparable tax basis, a dollar of preferred dividends costs the firm more than

[4]For the firm with no preferred stock, Equation 14.4 becomes the following:

$$\text{DFL at } X = \frac{\text{EBIT}}{\text{EBIT} - I}$$
$$= \frac{\text{EBIT}}{\text{EBT}}$$

where EBT represents earnings before taxes.

a dollar of interest payments. Dividing preferred dividends in Equation 14.4 by $(1 - T)$ puts interest and preferred dividends on an equivalent, *pretax* basis.

As shown in Figure 14.2, Allegan will have EPS = \$0 at an EBIT level of \$500,000. With this level of EBIT, there is just enough operating earnings to pay interest (\$250,000) and preferred dividends (after tax).[5] Using Equation 14.4, it can be seen that DFL will be maximized at that level of EBIT where EPS = \$0.

Consider again the data presented in Table 14.1 on the Allegan Manufacturing Company. According to that table, EBIT = \$1 million, I = \$250,000, D_p = \$150,000, and T = 40 percent, or 0.40. Inserting these values into Equation 14.4 yields the following:

$$\text{DFL at }\$1{,}000{,}000 = \frac{\$1{,}000{,}000}{\$1{,}000{,}000 - \$250{,}000 - \$150{,}000/(1 - 0.40)}$$

$$= 2.0$$

This result is the same as that obtained using Equation 14.3.

Just as a firm can change its DOL by raising or lowering fixed operating costs, it can also change its DFL by increasing or decreasing fixed capital costs. The amount of fixed capital costs incurred by a firm depends primarily on the mix of debt, preferred stock, and common stock equity in the firm's capital structure. Thus, a firm with a relatively large proportion of debt and preferred stock in its capital structure will have relatively large fixed capital costs and a high DFL.

Note that, though a firm has some discretion over its DCL, it is dictated largely by the firm's industry. For example, regardless of the particular firm, the DOL for an airline is going to be high compared to, say, a firm in the fast food industry because of the greater proportion of the fixed operating costs in the airline industry. DFL, on the other hand, is mostly at the discretion of the firm because it depends on the capital structure the firm chooses to adopt.

14-2g Degree of Combined Leverage

Combined leverage occurs whenever a firm employs *both* operating leverage and financial leverage in an effort to increase the returns to common stockholders. It represents the magnification of sales increases (or decreases) into relatively larger earnings per share increases (or decreases), resulting from the firm's use of both types of leverage. The joint multiplier effect is known as the **degree of combined leverage (DCL)**.

degree of combined leverage (DCL)

A firm's degree of combined leverage (DCL) is computed as the percentage change in earnings per share resulting from a given percentage change in sales:

$$\text{DCL at } X = \frac{\text{Percentage change in EPS}}{\text{Percentage change in sales}}$$

This can be rewritten as follows:

(14.5)

$$\text{DCL at } X = \frac{\frac{\Delta\text{EPS}}{\text{EPS}}}{\frac{\Delta\text{Sales}}{\text{Sales}}}$$

where ΔEPS and ΔSales are the changes in a firm's EPS and sales, respectively, and X represents the level of sales at which the firm's combined leverage is measured. The

[5]Recall that preferred dividends are paid from after-tax earnings. Hence, EBIT must be large enough to cover preferred dividends (\$150,000) and the tax (\$100,000) on the pretax earnings needed to pay preferred dividends. For example, if Allegan has EBIT of \$500,000, interest of \$250,000 can be paid (before any taxes are paid), leaving \$250,000 of taxable income. At a 40 percent rate, the tax is \$100,000, leaving \$150,000 for preferred dividends.

degree of combined leverage is also equal to the product of the degree of operating leverage and the degree of financial leverage.[6]

(14.6)
$$\text{DCL at } X = \text{DOL} \times \text{DFL}$$

To simplify matters, Equations 14.2 and 14.4 can be substituted into Equation 14.6 to obtain a new formula for determining the DCL in terms of basic income statement quantities:

$$\text{DCL at } X = \frac{\text{Sales} - \text{Variable costs}}{\text{EBIT}} \times \frac{\text{EBIT}}{\text{EBIT} - I - D_p/(1-T)}$$

or

(14.7)
$$\text{DCL at } X = \frac{\text{Sales} - \text{Variable costs}}{\text{EBIT} - I - D_p/(1-T)}$$

These three formulas for calculating DCL can be illustrated using the Allegan Manufacturing Company example. Equation 14.5 can be used to calculate Allegan's DCL with the data from Tables 14.1 and 14.2. The EPS level was \$3.00 at a sales level of \$5 million and \$4.20 at a sales level of \$5.5 million. Substituting these values into Equation 14.5 yields the following:

$$\text{DCL at } \$5{,}000{,}000 = \frac{\dfrac{(\$4.20 - \$3.00)}{\$3.00}}{\dfrac{(\$5{,}500{,}000 - \$5{,}000{,}000)}{\$5{,}000{,}000}}$$
$$= \frac{\$1.20}{\$3.00} \times \frac{\$5{,}000{,}000}{\$500{,}000}$$
$$= 4.0$$

Substituting Sales = \$5,000,000; Variable costs = \$3,000,000; EBIT = \$1,000,000; I = \$250,000; D_p = \$150,000; and T = 40% (0.40) into Equation 14.7 gives the same value for Allegan's DCL:

$$\text{DCL at } \$5{,}000{,}000 = \frac{\$5{,}000{,}000 - \$3{,}000{,}000}{\$1{,}000{,}000 - \$250{,}000 - \$150{,}000/(1-0.40)}$$
$$= 4.0$$

Also, recall from the earlier discussion of operating and financial leverage for Allegan that DOL = 2.0 and DFL = 2.0. Substituting these values into Equation 14.6 yields a DCL value identical to that just calculated:

$$\text{DCL at } \$5{,}000{,}000 = 2.0 \times 2.0$$
$$= 4.0$$

This DCL is interpreted to mean that each 1 percent change in sales from a base sales level of \$5 million results in a 4 percent change in Allegan's EPS.

The degree of combined leverage used by a firm is a measure of the overall variability of EPS due to fixed operating *and* capital costs as sales levels vary.

---

[6]This follows logically from the definitions of DCL, DOL, and DFL:

$$\frac{\text{Percentage change in EPS}}{\text{Percentage change in sales}} = \frac{\text{Percentage change in EBIT}}{\text{Percentage change in sales}} \times \frac{\text{Percentage change in EPS}}{\text{Percentage change in EBIT}}$$

Equation 14.6 shows that fixed operating and capital costs can be combined in many different ways to achieve a desired DCL. In other words, a number of possible trade-offs can be made between operating and financial leverage. For example, a target DCL of 6.0 can be achieved several different ways: a DOL of 6.0 and a DFL of 1.0, a DOL of 3.0 and DFL of 2.0, a DOL of 2.0 and a DFL of 3.0, etc.

The equation also highlights the fact that DOL and DFL are multiplicative in their effect on DCL. This has important implications for the firm's choice of target capital structure. If a firm has a relatively high DOL, for example, and wishes to achieve a certain DCL, it can offset this high DOL with a lower DFL. Or, if it has a high DFL, it would aim for a lower DOL. To illustrate, assume that a firm is considering purchasing assets that will increase fixed operating costs. To offset this higher DOL, the firm may want to decrease the proportion of debt in its capital structure, thereby reducing fixed financial costs and the DFL.

14-2h Effect of Leverage on Shareholder Wealth and the Cost of Capital

Firms are limited in the amount of combined (that is, operating and financial) leverage that can be used in seeking to increase EPS and shareholder wealth. Recall from Chapter 13 (see Figures 13.4, 13.5, and 13.6) that the use of so-called excessive amounts of *financial* leverage caused the market value of the firm (that is, shareholder wealth) to decline and the cost of capital to rise. Like financial leverage, the use of increasing amounts of combined leverage increases the risk of financial distress. As this risk increases, investors will require higher rates of return on the funds supplied to the firm in the form of preferred and common equity and debt. In other words, because of the financial distress costs and agency costs associated with excessive combined leverage, the firm has to pay higher costs for its funds. These higher costs tend to offset the returns gained from the combined leverage, resulting in a decline in the market value of the firm and a rise in its cost of capital.

14-3 Other Financial Risk Measures

In addition to financial ratios and the degree of combined leverage as measures of the financial risk facing a firm, more formal statements can be made about the financial risk facing a company if the probability distribution of future operating income (EBIT) is approximately normal and if the mean and standard deviation can be estimated. The number of standard deviations, z, that a particular value of EBIT is from the expected value, $\widehat{\text{EBIT}}$, can be computed using an expression similar to Equation 8.3 in Chapter 8:

$$z = \frac{\text{EBIT} - \widehat{\text{EBIT}}}{\sigma} \qquad (14.8)$$

where σ is the standard deviation of EBIT. Equation 14.8, along with the probability values from Table V in the back of the book, can be used to compute the probability that EBIT will be less than (or greater than) some particular value.

For example, consider the case of the Travco Manufacturing Corporation. Given the current capital structure of Travco, the company has interest payment obligations of \$500,000 for the coming year. The company has no preferred stock. The \$500,000 in interest represents the *loss level* for Travco. If EBIT falls below \$500,000, losses will be incurred (EPS will be negative). At EBIT levels above \$500,000, Travco will have positive earnings per share. Based on past experience, Travco's managers have estimated that the expected value of EBIT over the coming year is \$700,000 with a standard deviation of \$200,000 and that the distribution of operating income is approximately normal, as

FIGURE 14.3

Probability Distribution of EBIT, Travco Manufacturing Company

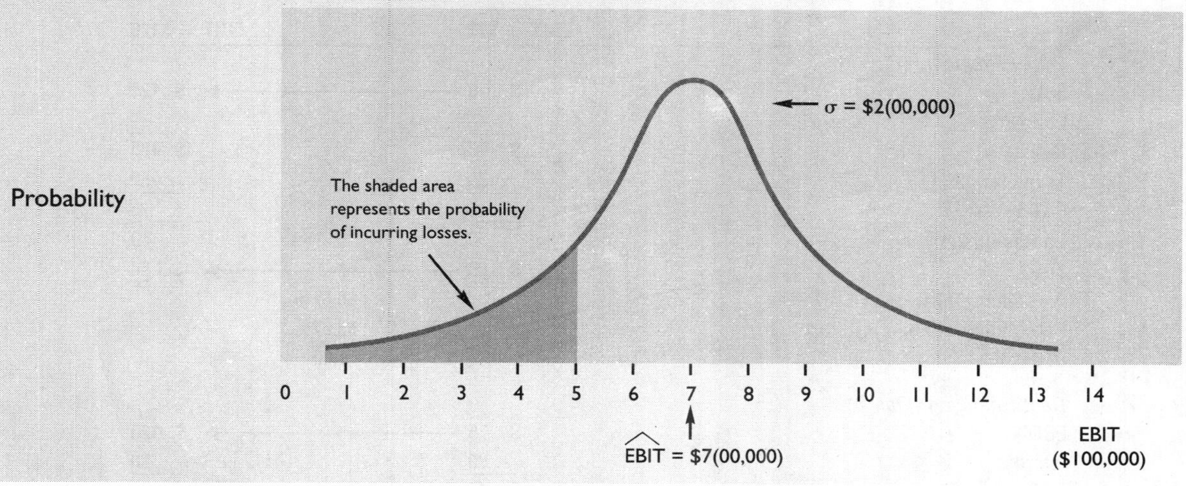

illustrated in Figure 14.3. With this information, it is possible to compute the probability of Travco having either negative or positive earnings per share over the coming year.

Using Equation 14.8, the probability of Travco having negative EPS is equal to the probability of having EBIT below the loss level of $500,000, or:

$$z = \frac{\$500,000 - \$700,000}{\$200,000} = -1.0$$

In other words, a level of EBIT of $500,000 is 1.0 standard deviation below the mean. From Table V, it can be seen that the probability associated with a value that is less than or equal to 1.0 standard deviation below the mean is 15.87 percent. Thus, there is a 15.87 percent chance that Travco will have negative earnings per share (that is, the shaded area in Figure 14.3) with its current capital structure. Conversely, there is an 84.13 percent chance (100 percent less 15.87 percent chance of losses) of having positive earnings per share.

This type of analysis can give a financial manager a better feel for the level of financial risk a firm faces. As we shall see later in the chapter, when a financial manager is considering two or more alternative capital structures, this same kind of analysis can be used to help select the most desirable capital structure.

14-4 EBIT-EPS Analysis

An analytical technique called *EBIT-EPS analysis*[7] can be used to help determine when debt financing is advantageous and when equity financing is advantageous.

Consider the Yuma Corporation, with a present capital structure consisting only of common stock (35 million shares). Assume that Yuma is considering an expansion and evaluating two alternative financing plans.[8] Plan 1, equity financing, would involve the

[7] To review briefly, EBIT is earnings before interest and taxes, or operating earnings; EPS is earnings per share.

[8] Preferred stock is not included in this example because it merely complicates the matter. Because preferred stock is a fixed-income security, it would be treated much like debt in this example.

TABLE 14.5

EBIT-EPS Analysis, Yuma Corporation (All Dollar Figures Except Per-Share Amounts Are in Millions of Dollars)*

	EBIT = \$75		EBIT = \$125
Equity Financing (Plan 1)			
EBIT	\$ 75	→	\$ 125
Interest	—		—
EBT	\$ 75		\$ 125
Taxes (at 40%)	30		50
EAT	\$ 45		\$ 75
Shares outstanding	50		50
EPS	\$ 0.90	→	\$ 1.50
Percentage change in EBIT		+66.67%	
Percentage change in EPS		+66.67%	
DFL		1.00	
Debt Financing (Plan 2)			
EBIT	\$ 75	→	\$ 125
Interest	30		30
EBT	\$ 45		\$ 95
Taxes (at 40%)	18		38
EAT	\$ 27		\$ 57
Shares outstanding	35		35
EPS	\$ 0.77	→	\$ 1.63
Percentage change in EBIT		+66.67%	
Percentage change in EPS		+111.69%	
DFL		1.68	

*EBIT = earnings before interest and taxes; EBT = earnings before taxes; EAT = earnings after taxes; EPS = earnings per share.

sale of an additional 15 million shares of common stock at \$20 each. Plan 2, debt financing, would involve the sale of \$300 million of 10 percent long-term debt.

If the firm adopts Plan 1, it remains totally equity financed. If, however, the firm adopts Plan 2, it becomes partially debt financed. Because Plan 2 involves the use of financial leverage, this financing issue is basically one of whether employing financial leverage is in the best interests of the firm's existing stockholders.

Table 14.5 illustrates the calculation of EPS at two different assumed levels of EBIT for both financing plans. Because the relationship between EBIT and EPS is linear, the two points calculated in Table 14.5 can be used to graph the relationship for each financing plan, as shown in Figure 14.4.

EBIT-EPS indifference point

In this example, earnings per share at EBIT levels less than \$100 million are higher using the equity financing alternative. Correspondingly, at EBIT levels greater than \$100 million, earnings per share are higher with debt financing. The \$100 million figure is called the **EBIT-EPS indifference point**. By definition, the earnings per share for the debt and equity financing alternatives are equal at the EBIT-EPS indifference point:

$$\text{EPS (debt financing)} = \text{EPS (equity financing)} \tag{14.9}$$

This equation may be rewritten as follows:

$$\frac{(\text{EBIT} - I_d)(1 - T) - D_p}{N_d} = \frac{(\text{EBIT} - I_e)(1 - T) - D_p}{N_e} \tag{14.10}$$

FIGURE 14.4

EBIT-EPS Analysis, Yuma Corporation

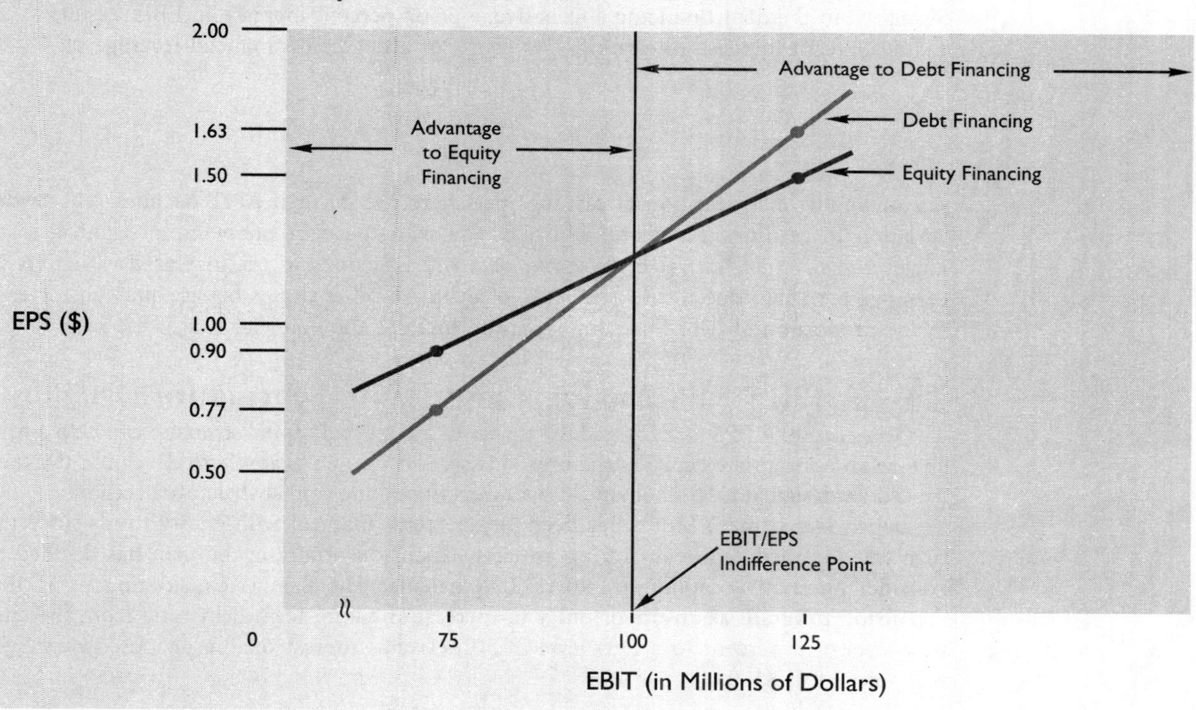

where EBIT is earnings before interest and taxes, I_d is the firm's total interest payments if the debt alternative is chosen, I_e is the firm's total interest payments if the equity alternative is chosen, and N_d and N_e represent the number of common shares outstanding for the debt and equity alternatives, respectively. The firm's effective tax rate is indicated as T, and D_p is the amount of preferred dividends for the firm. This equation may be used to calculate directly the EBIT level at which earnings per share for the two alternatives are equal.[9] The data from the example shown in Table 14.5 yield the EBIT-EPS indifference point:

$$\frac{(\text{EBIT} - \$30)(1 - 0.4) - 0}{35} = \frac{(\text{EBIT} - \$0)(1 - 0.4) - 0}{50}$$

$$50(0.6\ \text{EBIT} - \$18) = 35(0.6\ \text{EBIT})$$

$$30\ \text{EBIT} - \$900 = 21\ \text{EBIT}$$

$$9\ \text{EBIT} = \$900$$

$$\text{EBIT} = \$100(\text{million})$$

Note that in the equity financing alternative, a 66.67 percent increase in EBIT (from \$75 million to \$125 million) results in a 66.67 percent increase in earnings per share (from \$0.90 to \$1.50). By Equation 14.3, the degree of financial leverage is:

[9] An alternative indifference point measure is defined in terms of uncommitted earnings per share. *Uncommitted earnings per share* are defined as earnings after tax and preferred dividends *minus sinking fund obligations* (which are not tax deductible) *on outstanding debt* divided by the number of shares outstanding. Uncommitted earnings per share recognize that sinking fund payments must be made if the firm is to remain solvent. The indifference point based on uncommitted EPS will always be at a higher EBIT level than the indifference point based on EPS.

$$\text{DFL} = \frac{66.67\%}{66.67\%}$$
$$= 1.00$$

Similarly, in the debt financing alternative, a 66.67 percent increase in EBIT results in an 111.69 percent increase in earnings per share, or a degree of financial leverage of:

$$\text{DFL} = \frac{111.69\%}{66.67\%}$$
$$= 1.68$$

A comparable magnification of earnings per share will occur if EBIT declines. This wider variation in earnings per share, which occurs with the debt financing alternative, is an illustration of *financial risk* because *financial risk* is defined as the increased variability in earnings per share due to the firm's use of debt. All other things being equal, an increase in the proportion of debt financing is said to increase the financial risk of the firm.

14-4a EBIT-EPS Analysis and Capital Structure Decisions

The tools of EBIT-EPS analysis and the theory of an optimal capital structure can help a firm choose an appropriate capital structure. This section uses an example to develop a five-step procedure designed to assist financial managers in making capital structure decisions.

Balboa Department Stores has been 100 percent financed with equity funds since the firm was founded. While analyzing a major expansion program, the firm has decided to consider alternative capital structures. In particular, the firm is considering using this expansion program as an opportunity to increase the long-term debt ratio from the current level of 0 percent to a new level of 30 percent. Interest on the proposed new debt will amount to $100,000 per year.

- *Step 1: Compute the expected level of EBIT after the expansion.* Based on Balboa's past operating experience and a projection of the impact of the expansion, the company estimates its expected EBIT to be $500,000 per year under normal operating circumstances.
- *Step 2: Estimate the variability of this level of EBIT.* Based on the past performance of the company over several business cycles, the standard deviation of EBIT is estimated to be $200,000 per year. (EBIT is assumed to be normally distributed or at least approximately so.)
- *Step 3: Compute the indifference point between the two financing alternatives.* This calculation determines whether it is preferable to add debt or to maintain the all-equity capital structure. Using the techniques of EBIT-EPS analysis, the indifference point is computed to be $300,000.
- *Step 4: Analyze these estimates in the context of the risk the firm is willing to assume.* After considerable discussion, management has determined that the method used to finance the expansion must meet two criteria. The firm is willing to accept: (1) a 25 percent chance that EBIT in any year will be below the indifference point (indifference point criterion); and (2) a 5 percent chance that the firm will have to report a loss in any year (loss criterion).

    - *Indifference point criterion.* To complete this analysis, compute the probability that EBIT will be below the indifference point, that is, the probability that EBIT will be less than $300,000, or the area to the left of $300,000 in Panel (a) of Figure 14.5. This is equivalent on the standard normal curve (using Equation 14.8) to the following:

    $$z = \frac{\$300{,}000 - \$500{,}000}{\$200{,}000}$$
    $$= -1.0$$

    or 1.0 standard deviation below the mean. The probability that EBIT will be less than 1.0 standard deviation below the mean is 15.87 percent; again, this is determined from Table V at the end of the book. Therefore, on the basis of the indifference point criterion, the proposed new capital structure appears acceptable.

FIGURE 14.5

Capital Structure Analysis: Balboa Department Stores

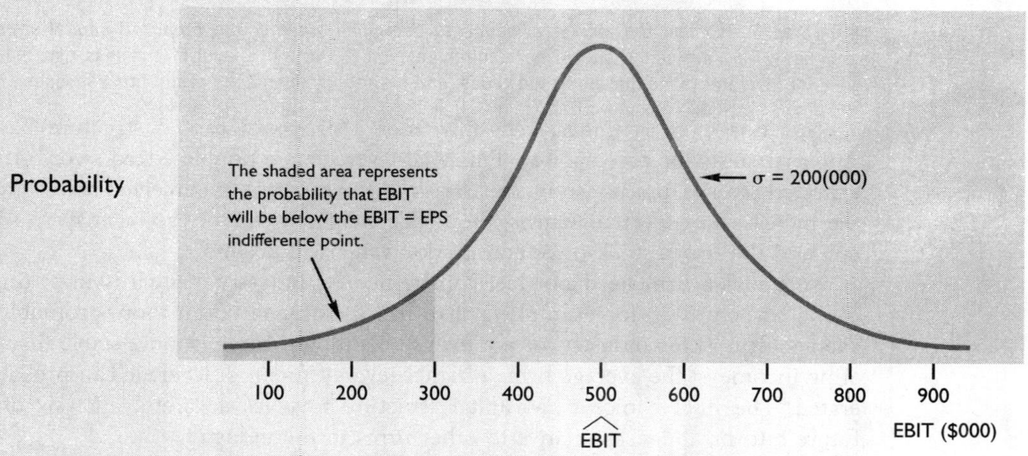

(a) Indifference Point Criterion

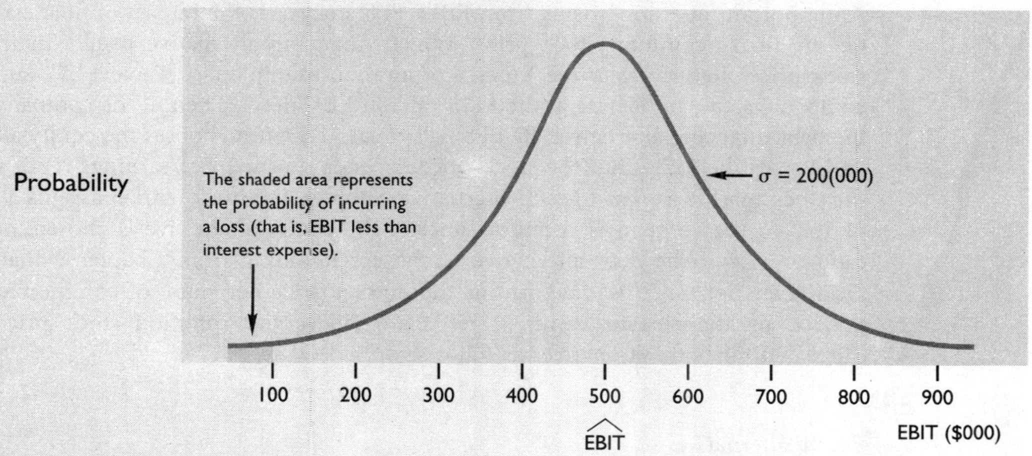

(b) Loss Criterion

- *Loss criterion.* The probability of incurring losses must now be analyzed. This is the probability that EBIT will be less than the required interest payments of $100,000, or the area to the left of $100,000 in Panel (b) of Figure 14.5. On the standard normal curve, this corresponds to the following:

$$z = \frac{\$100{,}000 - \$500{,}000}{\$200{,}000}$$

$$= -2.0$$

or 2.0 standard deviations below the mean. The probability that EBIT will be less than 2.0 standard deviations below the mean is 2.28 percent, as shown in Table V. According to this criterion, the proposed capital structure also seems acceptable.

If either or both of these tests had shown the proposed capital structure to have an unacceptable level of risk, the analysis would have been repeated for lower levels of debt than the proposed 30 percent rate. Similarly, because the proposed capital structure has exceeded the standards set by the firm, management might want to consider even higher levels of debt than the proposed 30 percent.

- *Step 5: Examine the market evidence to determine whether the proposed capital structure is too risky.* This evaluation should be made in relation to the firm's level of business risk, industry norms for leverage ratios and coverage ratios, and the recommendations of the firm's investment bankers.

This final step is undertaken only after a proposed capital structure has met the "internal" tests for acceptability. Financial leverage is a double-edged sword: It enhances expected returns, but it also increases risk. If the increase in perceived risk is greater than the increase in expected returns, the firm's weighted cost of capital may rise instead of fall, and the firm's stock price and market value will decline.

Note that a firm need not feel constrained by industry standards in setting its own capital structure. If, for example, a firm has traditionally been more profitable than the average firm in the industry, or if a firm's operating income is more stable than the operating income of the average firm, a higher level of financial leverage can probably be tolerated. The final choice of a capital structure involves a careful analysis of expected future returns and risks relative to other firms in the industry.

14-4b EBIT-EPS Analysis and Stock Prices

An important question arising from EBIT-EPS analysis is the impact of financial leverage on the firm's common stock price: Which financing alternative results in the higher stock price? Returning to the Yuma Corporation example (see Table 14.5), suppose the company is able to operate at the \$125 million EBIT level. Then, if the company chooses the debt financing alternative, its EPS will equal \$1.63; if it chooses the equity alternative, its EPS will be \$1.50. But the stock price depends on the price/earnings (P/E) ratio that the stock market assigns to each alternative. Suppose the stock market assigns a P/E ratio of 16.0 to the company's common stock if the equity alternative is chosen, and a P/E ratio of 15.4 if the debt alternative is chosen. Recalling from Chapter 3 that the P/E ratio (Equation 3.15) was defined as the market price per share of common stock (P_0) divided by the current earnings per share (EPS), the common stock price can be calculated for both alternatives as follows:

(14.11) $$P_0 = (\text{P/E ratio})(\text{EPS})$$

Equity alternative:

$$P_0 = (16.0)(\$1.50) = \$24.00$$

Debt alternative:

$$P_0 = (15.4)(\$1.63) = \$25.10$$

These calculations show that in this case, the stock market places a higher value on the company's stock if the debt alternative is chosen over the equity alternative. Note that the stock market assigned a slightly lower P/E ratio to the debt alternative. The stock market recognized the increased financial risk associated with the debt alternative, but this increased risk was more than offset by the increased EPS possible with the use of debt.

Let's carry the Yuma Corporation example one important step further. Suppose the company, while operating at the \$125 million EBIT level, chooses an even higher level of debt in its capital structure, which causes its EPS to increase to \$2.25. Suppose further that the stock market feels that this high-debt capital structure significantly increases the company's financial risk—to the point where bankruptcy could occur if EBIT levels turned downward in a recession. If the stock market assigns a P/E ratio of 10.0, for example, the stock price would be \$22.50 (\$2.25 × 10.0), and clearly this change in capital structure would not be desirable.

It is important to emphasize that the P/E ratios in the preceding example are simply assumptions. As an analytical technique, EBIT-EPS analysis does not provide a complete solution to the optimal capital structure question.

In summary, the firm potentially can show increased earnings to its stockholders by increasing its level of financial risk. However, because increases in risk tend to increase the cost of capital (which is analogous to a decrease in the P/E ratio), the firm's management has to assess the trade-off between the higher earnings per share for its stockholders and the higher costs of capital.

14-5 Cash Insolvency Analysis

In Chapter 3, the *times-interest-earned* and *fixed-charge-coverage* ratios were introduced. These ratios provide an indicator of the ability of a firm to meet its interest and other fixed charge obligations (including lease payments, sinking fund payments, and preferred dividends) out of current operating income. Also in that chapter, liquidity ratios, such as the *current ratio* and the *quick ratio*, were introduced. Liquidity ratios provide a simple measure of a firm's ability to meet its obligations, especially in the near term. In that chapter, we also indicated that the best measure of a firm's cash adequacy can be obtained by preparing a detailed cash budget (discussed in greater detail in Chapter 4).

Coverage ratios and liquidity ratios do not provide an adequate picture of a firm's relative solvency. A firm is said to be technically insolvent if it is unable to meet its current obligations. We need a more comprehensive measure of the ability of a firm to meet its obligations if this information is to be used to assist in capital structure planning. Such a measure must consider both the cash on hand and the cash expected to be generated in the future. Donaldson has suggested that a firm's level of fixed financial charges (including interest, preferred dividends, sinking fund obligations, and lease payments), and thus its debt-carrying capacity, should depend on the cash balances and net cash flows that can be expected to be available in a worst-case (recessionary environment) scenario.[10] This analysis requires the preparation of a detailed cash budget under assumed recessionary conditions.

Donaldson defines a firm's net cash balance in a recession, CB_R, to be:

(14.12) $$CB_R = CB_0 + FCF_R$$

where CB_0 is the cash (and marketable securities) balance at the beginning of the recession, and FCF_R is the free cash flows expected to be generated during the recession. *Free cash flow* represents the portion of a firm's total cash flow available to service additional debt, to make dividend payments to common stockholders, and to invest in other projects.

For example, suppose MINECO, a natural resource company, reports a cash (and marketable securities) balance of approximately \$154 million. Suppose also that management anticipates free cash flows of \$210 million during a projected one-year recession. These free cash flows reflect both operating cash flows during the recession and current required fixed financial charges. Under the current capital structure, consisting of

[10]See Gordon Donaldson, "New Framework for Corporate Debt Policy," *Harvard Business Review* 40 (March/April 1962): 117–131; Gordon Donaldson, "Strategy for Financial Emergencies," *Harvard Business Review* 47 (November/December 1969): 67–79.

approximately 32 percent debt, the cash balance at the end of the recession would be \$364 million (\$154 million plus \$210 million). Assume that MINECO's management is considering a change in its capital structure that would add an additional \$280 million of annual after-tax interest and sinking fund payments (that is, fixed financial charges). The effect would be a cash balance at the end of the recession of:

$$CB_R = \$154{,}000{,}000 + \$210{,}000{,}000 - \$280{,}000{,}000 = \$84{,}000{,}000$$

The managers of MINECO must decide whether this projected cash balance of \$84 million leaves them enough of a cushion in a recession.

This analysis can be enhanced if it is possible to specify the probability distribution of expected free cash flows during a recession. For example, if the MINECO managers believe, based on past experience, that free cash flows are approximately normally distributed [see panel (a) of Figure 14.6], with an expected value during a one-year recession (FCF_R) of \$210 million and a standard deviation of \$140 million, they can compute the probability of running out of cash if the new debt is added. The probability of running out of cash is equal to the probability of ending the recession with a cash balance of less than \$0. The probability distribution of MINECO's *cash balance* (Panel [b] of Figure 14.6), will have the same shape (that is, approximately normal with a standard deviation, σ, of \$140 million) as the probability distribution of *free cash flows* (Panel [a]). However, it will be shifted to the left from a mean, FCF_R, of \$210 million to a mean, CB_R, of \$84 million (that is, by the beginning cash balance of \$154 million plus expected free cash flows of \$210 million, less additional fixed financial charges of \$280 million). Employing an expression similar to Equation 14.8, where cash balance CB_R is the variable of interest rather than EBIT, a cash balance of \$0 is equivalent on the standard normal curve to the following:

$$z = \frac{(\$0 - \$84{,}000{,}000)}{\$140{,}000{,}000} = -0.60$$

From Table V, the probability of a z value of -0.60 or less is 27.43 percent. Thus, with an additional \$280 million in fixed financial charges, the probability of MINECO running out of cash during a one-year recession is about 27 percent (shaded area in Panel [b] of Figure 14.6).

The MINECO managers may feel that this is too much risk to assume. If they want to assume only a 5 percent risk of running out of cash during a one-year recession, they can determine the amount of additional interest and sinking fund payments (that is, fixed financial charges) that can be safely added. First, find the number of standard deviations, z, to the left of the mean that gives a 5 percent probability of occurrence in the lower tail of the distribution (the shaded area in Figure 14.7). From Table V, this value of z is found to be approximately -1.65. Next, we calculate the expected cash balance CB_R needed at the end of a one-year recession if the risk of running out of cash is to be held to 5 percent:

$$z = -1.65 = \frac{(\$0 - CB_R)}{\$140{,}000{,}000}$$
$$CB_R = \$231{,}000{,}000$$

Finally, since MINECO expects to enter the recession with \$154 million in cash and to generate \$210 million in free cash flow during a one-year recession, it can take on just \$133 million (that is, \$154,000,000 + \$210,000,000 − \$231,000,000) in additional fixed financial charges.

The willingness of management to assume the risk associated with running out of cash depends on several factors, including:

- Funds available from outstanding lines of credit with banks and the sale of new long-term debt, preferred stock, and common stock.
- The potential funds realized by cutting back on expenses during a business downturn, reducing dividends, and selling assets.

FIGURE **14.6**

Cash Flows and Cash Balance Probability Distributions, MINECO

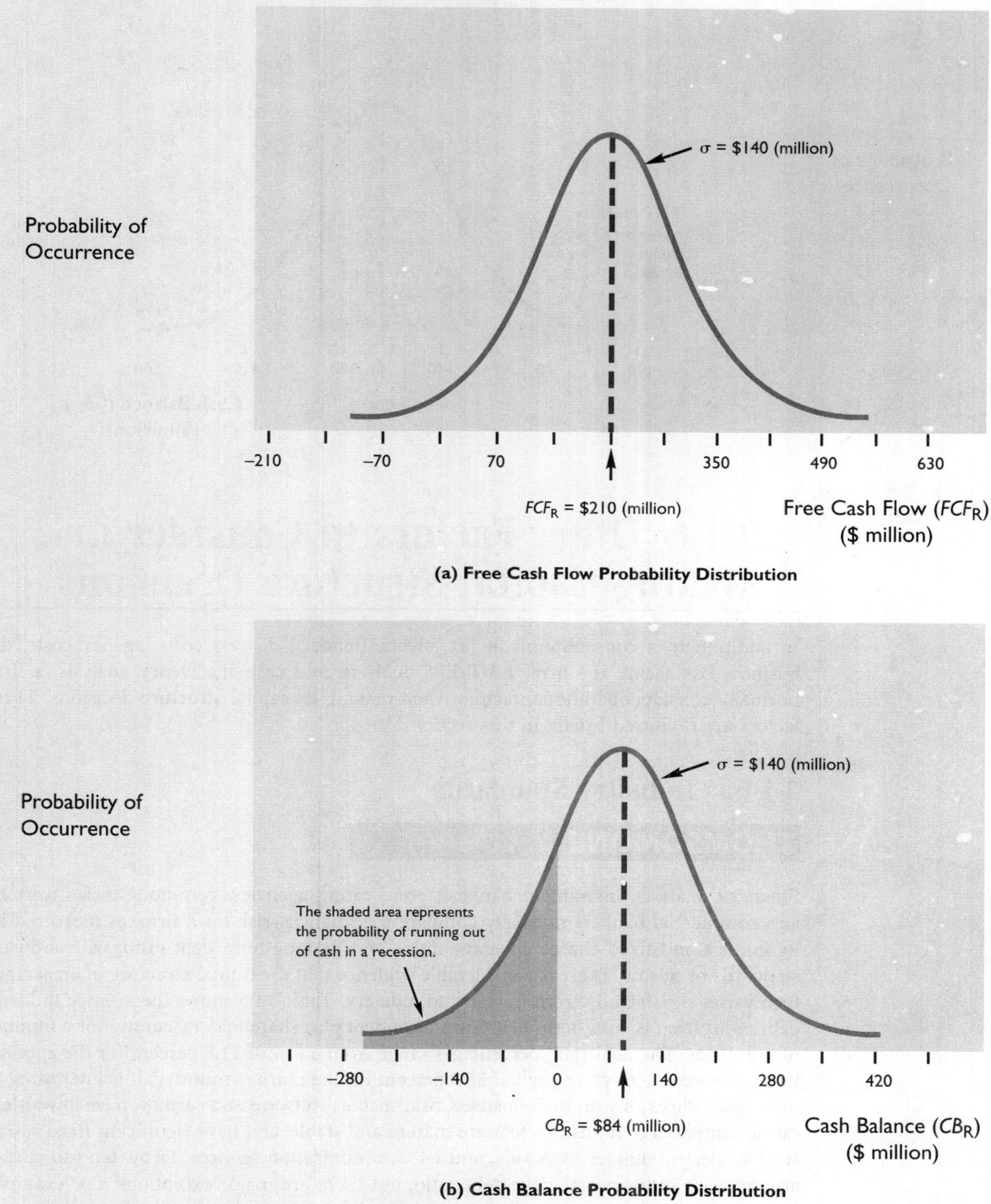

FIGURE 14.7

Cash Balance Probability Distribution, MINECO

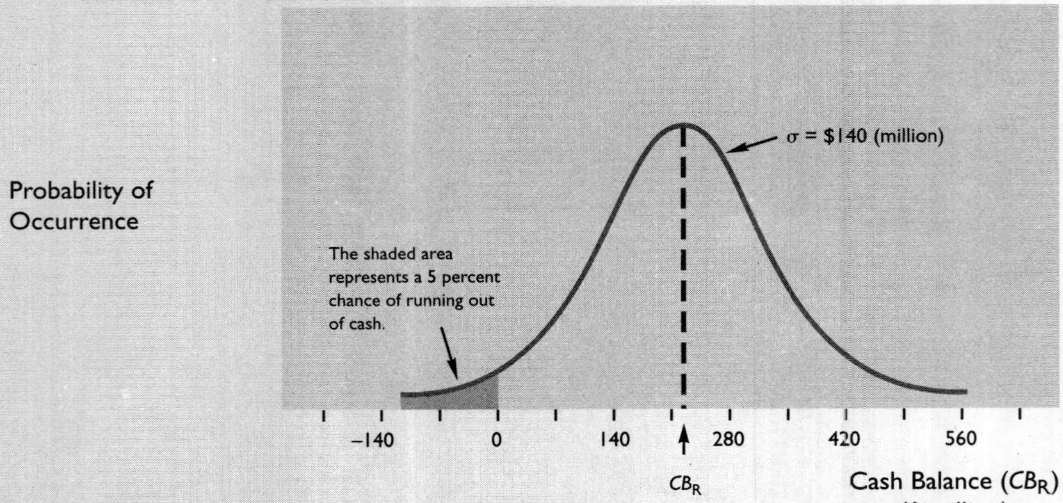

14-6 Other Factors to Consider in Making Capital Structure Decisions

In addition to a consideration of tax effects, financial distress costs, agency costs, the business risk facing the firm, EBIT-EPS analysis, and cash insolvency analysis, a firm normally considers additional factors when making its capital structure decisions. These factors are discussed briefly in this section.

14-6a Industry Standards

THOMSON ONE Business School Edition

Financial analysts, investment bankers, bond rating agencies, common stock investors, and commercial bankers normally compare the financial risk for a firm, as measured by its interest and fixed-charge coverage ratios and its long-term debt ratio, with industry standards or norms. There is considerable evidence that the capital structure of an average firm varies significantly from industry to industry. Table 14.6 shows the average industry debt ratios (that is, long-term debt/long-term debt plus shareholders' equity) for a number of industries. The debt ratio percentages range from a low of 11.8 percent for the application software industry to a high of 55.3 percent for the railroad industry. It is interesting to note that industries with high business risk, such as software and casinos, have lower debt ratios compared to industries that are mature and stable, and have significant fixed assets, such as electric utilities, railroads, and telecommunication services. Firms tend to cluster around their industry's average debt ratio, but there are major exceptions. For example, in the semiconductor manufacturing industry, the debt ratio for Cypress Semiconductors

TABLE 14.6

Leverage Ratios for Selected Industries for 2015

Industry	Debt to Total Capital Ratio (%)
APPLICATION SOFTWARE	11.8
CASINO AND GAMING	14.1
TECHNOLOGY HARDWARE AND EQUIPMENT	15.4
BIOTECHNOLOGY	19.5
HOUSEHOLD PRODUCTS	23.1
SEMICONDUCTOR	23.2
HOTELS, RESTAURANTS, AND LEISURE	25.0
SEMICONDUCTOR EQUIPMENT	27.6
OIL AND GAS DRILLING	27.6
GENERIC PHARMACEUTICALS	27.8
FOOD AND STAPLES RETAILING	31.5
RESTAURANT	33.5
HOMEBUILDING	35.8
AEROSPACE AND DEFENSE	37.4
INDUSTRIAL MACHINERY	38.5
OIL AND GAS PIPELINES	39.2
AUTOMOBILE MANUFACTURING	40.7
WATER UTILITIES	41.1
OIL AND GAS DISTRIBUTION	41.1
GAS UTILITIES	41.3
OIL AND GAS STORAGE AND TRANSPORTATION	41.5
INTEGRATED OIL AND GAS	41.6
PACKAGED FOOD AND MEAT	43.5
TRUCKING	43.9
OIL AND GAS PRODUCTION	44.7
DIVERSIFIED CHEMICALS	44.8
TELECOMMUNICATIONS SERVICES	48.1
FOREST AND PAPER PRODUCTS	50.1
ELECTRIC UTILITIES	50.2
METALS AND MINING	51.6
PAPER MANUFACTURING	55.1
RAILROADS	55.3

Source: calculated from data taken from https://www.capitaliq.comp.

is 53 percent, which is much higher than the industry average of approximately 23 percent. At the other extreme, Synaptics does not use any debt in its capital structure, while Texas Instruments has a debt ratio of 25 percent, close to the industry average. A firm with a capital structure that differs significantly from the industry norms has to convince the financial markets that its business risk is sufficiently different from that of the average firm in the industry to warrant the divergent capital structure. If the firm cannot do so, it may be penalized significantly in its market valuation.

14-6b Profitability and Need for Funds

As noted in the previous chapter, highly profitable firms, with limited needs for funds, tend to have lower debt ratios when compared with less profitable firms. Also, firms that undertake highly leveraged restructurings may temporarily have debt ratios that are

INTERNATIONAL ISSUES

Balancing Operating and Financial Risks at Nestlé

Nestlé is a huge, multinational Swiss foods corporation with operations in at least 150 countries. The overwhelming majority of its sales occur outside Switzerland. Nestlé's various foreign operating subsidiaries enjoy considerable decentralized operational flexibility. Local division managers handle all marketing and production decisions.

In contrast to its decentralized operating policy, Nestlé uses a highly centralized financing strategy. All financing decisions are handled at corporate headquarters. The small corporate finance staff makes all funding decisions for the subsidiaries, establishes the firm's worldwide consolidated capital structure, sets individual subsidiary capital structures, manages worldwide currency exposure risk, and mandates the dividend policy for subsidiaries.

When a subsidiary is first formed, about one-half of the needed financing—the funds used to acquire fixed assets—comes from equity contributions by the parent. The balance of the needed funds, primarily to support working capital investments, is acquired in the host country through the banking system or the sale of commercial paper. In some countries where there is little or no risk of capital expropriation, the parent company may finance working capital needs, depending on the relative cost of funds for the parent compared to the local cost of funds for the subsidiary.

Each subsidiary normally pays a dividend of 100 percent of its profits back to the parent. This guarantees central control over the capital structure of each subsidiary. If additional funds are needed for investment, the parent provides them using the lowest-cost source of capital available. Nestlé manages its overall sources of capital with the objective of maintaining a top credit rating and thereby minimizing its capital costs.

Why does Nestlé follow such a conservative financing strategy? Senior Vice President of Finance Daniel Regolatti states, "Our basic strategy is that we are an industrial company. We have a lot of risks in a lot of countries, so we should not add high financial risks."[a] This strategy recognizes the trade-offs between business risk and financial risk that have been discussed in this chapter.

[a]"The Nestlé Approach to Capital Markets and Innovation," *Business International Money Report* (October 27, 1986): 337; Alan C. Shapiro, *Multinational Financial Management*, 3rd ed. (Needham Heights, MA: Allyn & Bacon, 1989).

significantly above the optimal level until funds from asset sales, new equity issues, or operations can be generated to pay off the debt holders. Hertz Corporation (Hertz Rent-a-Car), for example, had $12.5 billion in total debt in 2005, soon after being bought by a group of private equity investors in a leveraged transaction. However, by the end of 2009, the debt was pared steadily down to $9.9 billion, an amount only slightly higher than what Hertz had prior to being bought out.

14-6c Lender and Bond-Rater Requirements

HTTP:
www.standardandpoors.com/

Lenders and bond rating agencies often impose restrictions on a firm's capital structure choices as a condition for extending credit or for maintaining a bond or preferred stock rating. For example, Standard & Poor's has established the benchmark standards shown in Table 14.7 for rating corporate debt of firms with low ("strong") business risk. These are not the only factors considered when establishing a company's bond rating, but they are very important guidelines that a firm must follow if it wishes to retain or improve its credit rating. A more complete discussion of the factors considered by bond rating agencies is contained in Chapter 6. In a survey of CFOs, Graham and Harvey[11] found that the firm's credit rating was the second most important factor in the choice of their capital structure. General Electric has had a long-standing policy of taking financial

[11]J. R. Graham and C. R. Harvey, "The Theory and Practice of Corporate Finance: Evidence from the Field," *Journal of Financial Economics* 60 (May/June 2001): 187–243.

TABLE 14.7

Standard & Poor's Corporate Bond Rating Standards

Rating Level	Debt Leverage: Total Debt/Capital (%)	Debt/EBITDA(x)
AA	Below 25	Below 1.5
A	25–35	1.5–2.0
A–	35–45	2.0–3.0
BBB	45–50	3.0–4.0
BB	50–60	4.0–5.0
BB–	Greater than 60	Greater than 5

Source: www.standardandpoors.com/prot/ratings/articles/en/us/?articleType=HTML&assetID=1245340716573.

actions consistent with maintaining an AAA rating. General Electric lost this rating and was downgraded one notch below the top rating to a AA+ in 2009 following the U.S. financial crisis that started in late 2007. The company hopes to regain the perfect AAA rating in the future.[12] Johnson & Johnson is another company that takes pride in maintaining its AAA bond rating. Firms may, however, target less than the highest rating. Rolls-Royce Group (known for their jet engines), in its 2015 annual report, noted that "maintaining … an investment grade 'A' credit rating" is one of the firm's objectives with regard to its financial policy.

14-6d Managerial Risk Aversion

Management's willingness to assume risk often has a major impact on the firm's capital structure, although the relative risk aversion of management does not influence the firm's optimal capital structure. Some managers adopt unusually risky or unusually low-risk capital structures. When a suboptimal capital structure is chosen, the financial marketplace will normally penalize a firm for this action.

For example, because of an extremely conservative owner-management financing philosophy, Adolph Coors (the third largest U.S. brewer, which merged with Molson in 2005) did not have any long-term debt in its capital structure until 1990, when the company issued its first long-term debt securities.[13] In 1990, most financial analysts agreed that Coors could safely add a significant amount of debt to its capital structure and thereby lower its overall cost of capital and increase the market value of the firm. Coors was able to sustain this capital structure because the Coors family controlled 100 percent of the company's voting shares. Differences in managerial philosophies regarding the appropriate capital structure for a firm are a major driving force behind many leveraged buyout offers.

14-6e Retention of Control

Some firms use debt or preferred stock financing rather than common stock financing to avoid selling new shares of common stock. When new voting common stock is sold, the relative control position of existing stockholders is diluted. This is especially of concern to smaller firms with significant family ownership. For example, Golf TEC, a golf instruction franchise business, opted for debt rather than additional equity issuance in 2004 in order to expand its business. This was done in part to avoid diluting the ownership stake of the existing investors.

[12]As of the end of 2015, General Electric's bond rating was still AA+.

[13]The issuance of debt securities in 1990 reflected a new management philosophy that came about as the result of a change in top management.

14-7 Summary

- *Leverage* refers to a firm's use of assets and liabilities having fixed costs. A firm uses leverage in an attempt to earn returns in excess of the fixed costs of these assets and liabilities, thus increasing the returns to common stockholders.
- *Operating leverage* occurs when a firm uses assets having fixed operating costs. The *degree of operating leverage* (DOL) measures the percentage change in a firm's EBIT resulting from a 1 percent change in sales (or units of output). As a firm's fixed operating costs rise, its DOL increases.
- *Financial leverage* occurs when a firm makes use of funds (primarily from debt and preferred stock) having fixed capital costs. The *degree of financial leverage* (DFL) measures the percentage change in the firm's EPS resulting from a 1 percent change in EBIT. As a firm's fixed capital costs rise, its DFL increases.
- The *combined leverage* of a firm is equal to the *product* of the degrees of operating and financial leverage. These two types of leverage can be combined in many different ways to achieve a given degree of combined leverage (DCL). The total variability of the firm's EPS is a combination of business risk and financial risk.
- *EBIT-EPS analysis* is an analytical technique that can be used to help determine the circumstances under which a firm should employ financial leverage. Basically, it involves calculating earnings per share at different levels of EBIT for debt and equity financing plans. This information may then be used to graph earnings per share versus EBIT to determine the EBIT levels at which financial leverage is advantageous to the firm.
- The *indifference point* in EBIT-EPS analysis is the level of EBIT at which earnings per share are the same, regardless of which of two alternative capital structures is used. At EBIT levels greater than the indifference level, a more financially levered capital structure will produce a higher level of earnings per share. At EBIT levels lower than the indifference point, a less financially levered capital structure will produce a higher level of earnings per share.
- *Cash insolvency analysis* can provide additional insights about the appropriate capital structure. Cash insolvency analysis evaluates the adequacy of a firm's cash position in a worst-case (recession) scenario.

Important Equations

$$\text{DOL at } X = \frac{\dfrac{\Delta\text{EBIT}}{\text{EBIT}}}{\dfrac{\Delta\text{Sales}}{\text{Sales}}}$$

$$\text{DOL at } X = \frac{\text{Sales} - \text{Variable costs}}{\text{EBIT}}$$

$$\text{DFL at } X = \frac{\dfrac{\Delta\text{EPS}}{\text{EPS}}}{\dfrac{\Delta\text{EBIT}}{\text{EBIT}}}$$

$$\text{DFL at } X = \frac{\text{EBIT}}{\text{EBIT} - I - D_p/(1 - T)}$$

$$\text{DCL at } X = \frac{\dfrac{\Delta\text{EPS}}{\text{EPS}}}{\dfrac{\Delta\text{Sales}}{\text{Sales}}}$$

$$\text{DCL at } X = \text{DOL} \times \text{DFL}$$

Important Equations (*Continued*)

$$\text{DCL at } X = \frac{\text{Sales} - \text{Variable costs}}{\text{EBIT} - I - D_p/(1 - T)}$$

$$z = \frac{\text{EBIT} - \widehat{\text{EBIT}}}{\sigma}$$

$$\frac{(\text{EBIT} - I_d)(1 - T) - D_p}{N_d} = \frac{(\text{EBIT} - I_e)(1 - T) - D_p}{N_e}$$

$$P_0 = (\text{P/E ratio})(\text{EPS})$$

$$CB_R = CB_0 + FCF_R$$

14-8 Questions and Topics for Discussion

1. Define *leverage* as it is used in finance.
2. Define and give examples of the following:
   a. Fixed costs
   b. Variable costs
3. Define the following:
   a. Operating leverage
   b. Financial leverage
4. How is a firm's degree of combined leverage (DCL) related to its degrees of operating and financial leverage?
5. Is it possible for a firm to have a high degree of operating leverage and a low level of business risk? Explain.
6. Is it possible for a firm to have a high degree of combined leverage and a low level of total risk? Explain.
7. What are the major limitations of EBIT-EPS analysis as a technique to determine the optimal capital structure?
8. In practice, how can a firm determine whether it is operating at (or near) its optimal capital structure?
9. Under what circumstances should a firm use *more* debt in its capital structure than is used by the average firm in the industry? When should it use *less* debt than the average firm?
10. Why do public utilities typically have capital structures with about 50 percent debt, whereas major oil companies average about 25 percent debt in their capital structures?
11. What is *cash insolvency analysis,* and how can it help in the establishment of an optimal capital structure?

14-9 Self-Test Problems

ST1. Pinches Salt Company has the following income statement for 2016:

Sales	$ 5,000,000
Variable operating costs	1,000,000
Fixed operating costs	2,000,000
EBIT	$ 2,000,000
Interest	500,000
EBT	$ 1,500,000
Tax (at 40%)	600,000
EAT	$ 900,000
Preferred dividends	100,000
Earnings available to common stockholders	$ 800,000
Shares outstanding	400,000

a. Compute Pinches's DOL, DFL, and DCL.
b. If sales increase to $5,500,000, what is your forecast of EPS?

ST2. Flagstaff Industries Inc. has determined that its EBIT for the coming year is approximately normally distributed with an expected value of $1.75 million and a standard deviation of $1.2 million. Given its current capital structure, Flagstaff has $250,000 in interest obligations due during the coming year. Determine the probability that Flagstaff will have negative EPS.

ST3. The Euclid Corporation has a present capital structure consisting of 100 million shares of common stock. Euclid is considering an expansion program. Two alternative financing plans are under consideration:

- *Plan 1: Equity financing.* Sale of 10 million additional shares of common stock at $15 per share
- *Plan 2: Debt financing.* Sale of $150 million of 12 percent long-term debt (the firm's marginal tax rate is 40 percent)

a. Determine the indifference level of EBIT between the two financing plans.
b. Suppose that Euclid's EBIT is normally distributed with an expected value of $250 million and a standard deviation of $200 million. If the debt alternative is chosen, determine the probability that Euclid will have negative EPS.
c. Determine the probability that the debt financing alternative will produce higher earnings than the equity alternative.

ST4. Buy-Low Distributors has a cash (and marketable securities) balance of $20 million. Free cash flows during a projected one-year recession are expected to be $60 million with a standard deviation of $60 million. (Assume Buy-Low's free cash flows are approximately normally distributed.)

a. Determine the probability that Buy-Low will run out of cash during the recession.
b. Buy-Low is considering a change in its capital structure that would increase its annual fixed charges by $10 million. Determine the probability of running out of cash during the recession if the change in capital structure is undertaken.

14-10 Problems*

INTERMEDIATE

1. The Hurricane Lamp Company forecasts that next year's sales will be $6 million. Fixed operating costs are estimated to be $800,000, and the variable cost ratio (that is, variable costs as a fraction of sales) is estimated to be 0.75. The firm has a $600,000 loan at 10 percent interest. It has 20,000 shares of $3 preferred stock and 60,000 shares of common stock outstanding. Hurricane Lamp is in the 40 percent corporate income tax bracket.

Spreadsheet Strategies

a. Forecast Hurricane Lamp's earnings per share (EPS) for next year. Develop a complete income statement using the revised format illustrated in Table 14.1. Then determine what Hurricane Lamp's EPS would be if sales were 10 percent above the projected $6 million level.

Spreadsheet Strategies

b. Calculate Hurricane Lamp's degree of operating leverage (DOL) at a sales level of $6 million using the following:

i. The definitional formula (Equation 14.1)
ii. The simpler, computational formula (Equation 14.2)
iii. What is the economic interpretation of this value?

Spreadsheet Strategies

c. Calculate Hurricane Lamp's degree of financial leverage (DFL) at the EBIT level corresponding to sales of $6 million using the following:

i. The definitional formula (Equation 14.3)
ii. The simpler computational formula (Equation 14.4)
iii. What is the economic interpretation of this value?

Spreadsheet Strategies

d. Calculate Hurricane Lamp's degree of combined leverage (DCL) using the following:

i. The definitional formula (Equation 14.5)
ii. The simpler computational formula (Equation 14.7)
iii. The degree of operating and financial leverage calculated in Parts b and c
iv. What is the economic interpretation of this value?

INTERMEDIATE

2. The Alexander Company reported the following income statement for 2016:

Sales		$ 15,000,000
Less: Operating expenses		
Wages, salaries, benefits	$ 6,000,000	
Raw materials	3,000,000	
Depreciation	1,500,000	
General, selling, and administrative expenses	1,500,000	
Total operating expenses		12,000,000
Earnings before interest and taxes (EBIT)		$ 3,000,000
Less: Interest expense		750,000
Earnings before taxes		$ 2,250,000
Less: Income taxes		1,000,000
Earnings after taxes		$ 1,250,000
Less: Preferred dividends		250,000
Earnings available to common stockholders		$ 1,000,000
Earnings per share—250,000 shares outstanding		$ 4.00

*Color blocks behind the numbers denote problems that have check answers provided at the end of the book.

Assume that all depreciation and 75 percent of the firm's selling, general, and administrative expenses are *fixed costs* and that the remainder of the firm's operating expenses are *variable costs.*

Spreadsheet Strategies

a. Determine Alexander's fixed costs, variable costs, and variable cost ratio.
b. Based on its 2016 sales, calculate the following for the firm:
   i. DOL
   ii. DFL
   iii. DCL
c. Assume that next year's sales increase by 15 percent, that fixed operating and financial costs remain constant, and that the variable cost ratio and tax rate also remain constant. Use the leverage figures just calculated to forecast next year's EPS.
d. Show the validity of this forecast by constructing Alexander's income statement for next year according to the revised format.
e. Construct an EPS-EBIT graph based on Alexander's 2016 income statement.

CHALLENGE

Spreadsheet Strategies

3. Gibson Company sales for the year 2016 were \$3 million. The firm's variable operating cost ratio was 0.50, and fixed costs (that is, overhead and depreciation) were \$900,000. Its average (and marginal) income tax rate is 40 percent. Currently, the firm has \$2.4 million of long-term bank loans outstanding at an average interest rate of 12.5 percent. The remainder of the firm's capital structure consists of common stock (100,000 shares outstanding at the present time).

a. Calculate Gibson's degree of combined leverage for 2016.
b. Gibson is forecasting a 10 percent increase in sales for next year (2017). Furthermore, the firm is planning to purchase additional labor-saving equipment, which will increase fixed costs by \$150,000 and reduce the variable cost ratio to 0.475. Financing this equipment with debt will require additional bank loans of \$500,000 at an interest rate of 12.5 percent. Calculate Gibson's expected degree of combined leverage for 2017.
c. Determine how much Gibson must reduce its debt in 2017 (for example, through the sale of common stock) to maintain its DCL at the 2016 level.

BASIC

4. Show algebraically that Equation 14.2:

$$\text{DOL at } X = \frac{\text{Sales} - \text{Variable costs}}{\text{EBIT}}$$

is equivalent to Equation 14.1:

$$\text{DOL at } X = \frac{\dfrac{\Delta\text{EBIT}}{\text{EBIT}}}{\dfrac{\Delta\text{Sales}}{\text{Sales}}}$$

BASIC

Spreadsheet Strategies

5. Albatross Airlines' fixed operating costs are \$5.8 million, and its variable cost ratio is 0.20. The firm has \$2 million in bonds outstanding with a coupon interest rate of 8 percent. Albatross has 30,000 shares of preferred stock outstanding, which pays a \$2.00 annual dividend. There are 100,000 shares of common stock outstanding. Revenues for the firm are \$8 million, and the firm is in the 40 percent corporate income tax bracket. Compute the following for the firm:

a. Degree of operating leverage
b. Degree of financial leverage
c. Degree of combined leverage and interpret this value

BASIC

6. Given the following information for Computech, compute the firm's degree of combined leverage (dollars are in thousands except EPS):

	2015	2016
Sales	$ 500,000	$ 570,000
Fixed costs	120,000	120,000
Variable costs	300,000	342,000
Earnings before interest and taxes	80,000	108,000
Interest	30,000	30,000
Earnings per share (EPS)	$ 1.00	$ 1.56

INTERMEDIATE

Spreadsheet Strategies

7. McGee Corporation has fixed operating costs of $10 million and a variable cost ratio of 0.65. The firm has a $20 million, 10 percent bank loan and a $6 million, 12 percent bond issue outstanding. The firm has 1 million shares of $5 (dividend) preferred stock and 2 million shares of common stock ($1 par). McGee's marginal tax rate is 40 percent. Sales are expected to be $80 million.

a. Compute McGee's degree of operating leverage at an $80 million sales level.
b. Compute McGee's degree of financial leverage at an $80 million sales level.
c. If sales decline to $76 million, forecast McGee's earnings per share.

BASIC

8. A firm has earnings per share of $2.60 at a sales level of $5 million. If the firm has a degree of operating leverage of 3.0 and a degree of financial leverage of 5.5 (both at a sales level of $5 million), forecast earnings per share for a 2 percent sales decline.

INTERMEDIATE

9. Blums Inc. expects its operating income over the coming year to equal $1.5 million, with a standard deviation of $300,000. Its coefficient of variation is equal to 0.20. Blums must pay interest charges of $700,000 next year and preferred stock dividends of $240,000. Blums' marginal tax rate is 40 percent. What is the probability that Blums will have negative earnings per share next year? (Assume that operating income is normally distributed.)

INTERMEDIATE

10. A firm has sales of $10 million, variable costs of $5 million, EBIT of $2 million, and a degree of combined leverage of 3.0.

a. If the firm has no preferred stock, what are its annual interest charges?
b. If the firm wishes to reduce its degree of combined leverage to 2.5 by reducing interest charges, what will be the new level of annual interest charges?

INTERMEDIATE

11. Cohen's Bowling Emporium has a degree of financial leverage of 2.0 and a degree of combined leverage of 6.0. The breakeven sales level for Cohen's has been estimated to be $500,000. Fixed costs total $250,000. What effect will a 15 percent increase in sales have on EBIT?

INTERMEDIATE

Spreadsheet Strategies

12. Connely Inc. expects sales of silicon chips to be $30 million this year. Because this is a very capital-intensive business, fixed operating costs are $10 million. The variable cost ratio is 40 percent. The firm's debt obligations consist of a $2 million, 10 percent bank loan and a $10 million bond issue with a 12 percent coupon rate. The firm has 100,000 shares of preferred stock outstanding that pays a $9.60 dividend. Connely has 1 million shares of common stock outstanding, and its marginal tax rate is 40 percent. Compute the following for Connely:

a. Degree of operating leverage
b. Degree of financial leverage
c. Degree of combined leverage
d. EPS if sales decline by 5 percent

INTERMEDIATE

Spreadsheet Strategies

13. McGonnigal Inc. has expected sales of $40 million. Fixed operating costs are $5 million, and the variable cost ratio is 65 percent. McGonnigal has outstanding a $10 million, 10 percent bank loan and $3 million in 12 percent coupon-rate bonds. McGonnigal has outstanding 250,000 shares of a $10 (dividend) preferred stock and 1 million shares of common stock ($1 par value). McGonnigal's average tax rate is 35 percent, and its marginal rate is 40 percent.

a. What is McGonnigal's degree of operating leverage at a sales level of $40 million?
b. What is McGonnigal's current degree of financial leverage?
c. Forecast McGonnigal's EPS if sales drop to $38 million.

INTERMEDIATE

14. Earnings per share (EPS) for Valcor Inc. are $3 at a sales level of $2 million. If Valcor's degree of operating leverage is 2.0 and its degree of combined leverage is 8.0, what will happen to EPS if operating income increases by 3 percent?

CHALLENGE

15. Walker's Gunnery, a small arms manufacturer, has current sales of $10 million and operating income (EBIT) of $450,000. The degree of operating leverage for Walker is 2.5. Next year's sales are expected to increase by 5 percent. Walker has found that, over time, the standard deviation of operating income is $300,000 and operating income is approximately normally distributed about its expected value in any year. Walker's current financial structure contains both debt and preferred stock. Interest payments total $200,000, and preferred stock dividends total $60,000. Walker's marginal tax rate is 40 percent. What is the probability that Walker's Gunnery will report negative earnings per share during the coming year?

INTERMEDIATE

16. Scherr Corporation's current EPS is $5.00 at a sales level of $10 million. At this sales level, EBIT is $2 million. Scherr's DCL has been estimated to be 2.0 at the current level of sales. Sales are forecast to have an expected value of $11 million next year, with a standard deviation of $500,000. The coefficient of variation of sales is equal to 0.045. What is the probability that EPS will be less than $5.00 per share next year, assuming that sales are normally distributed?

INTERMEDIATE

17. Kaufman Industries expects next year's operating income (EBIT) to equal $4 million, with a standard deviation of $2 million. The coefficient of variation of operating income is equal to 0.50. Interest expenses will be $1 million, and preferred dividends will be $600,000. Debt retirement will require principal payments of $1 million. Kaufman's marginal tax rate is 40 percent. If EBIT is normally distributed, what is the probability that Kaufman will have negative EPS next year?

CHALLENGE

Spreadsheet Strategies

18. Emco Products has a present capital structure consisting only of common stock (10 million shares). The company is planning a major expansion. At this time, the company is undecided between the following two financing plans (assume a 40 percent marginal tax rate):

- *Plan 1: Equity financing.* Under this plan, an additional 5 million shares of common stock will be sold at $10 each.
- *Plan 2: Debt financing.* Under this plan, $50 million of 10 percent long-term debt will be sold.

One piece of information the company desires for its decision analysis is an EBIT-EPS analysis.

a. Calculate the EBIT-EPS indifference point.
b. Graphically determine the EBIT-EPS indifference point. (*Hint*: Use EBIT = $10 million and $25 million.)
c. What happens to the indifference point if the interest rate on debt increases and the common stock sales price remains constant?
d. What happens to the indifference point if the interest rate on debt remains constant and the common stock sales price increases?

INTERMEDIATE

19. Two capital goods manufacturing companies, Rock Island and Davenport, are virtually identical in all aspects of their operations—product lines, amount of sales, total size, and so on. The two companies differ only in their capital structures, as shown here:

	Rock Island (millions)	Davenport (millions)
Debt (8%)	$400	$100
Common equity	$600	$900
Number of common shares outstanding	30	45

Each company has $1 billion in total assets.

Capital goods manufacturers typically are subject to cyclical trends in the economy. Suppose that the EBIT level for both companies is $100 million during an expansion and $60 million during a recession. (Assume a 40% tax rate for both companies.)

a. Calculate the earnings per share for both companies during expansion and recession.
b. Which stock is riskier? Why?
c. At what EBIT level are the earnings per share of the two companies identical?
d. Calculate the common stock price for both companies during an expansion if the stock market assigns a price-to-earnings ratio of 10 to Davenport and 9 to Rock Island.

CHALLENGE

Spreadsheet Strategies

20. Morton Industries is considering opening a new subsidiary in Boston, to be operated as a separate company. The company's financial analysts expect the new facility's average EBIT level to be $6 million per year. At this time, the company is considering the following two financing plans:

- *Plan 1: Equity financing.* Under this plan, 2 million common shares will be sold at $10 each.
- *Plan 2: Debt-equity financing.* Under this plan, $10 million of 12 percent long-term debt and 1 million common shares at $10 each will be sold.

Use a 40 percent marginal tax rate in your analysis.

a. Calculate the EBIT-EPS indifference point.
b. Calculate the expected EPS for both financing plans.
c. What factors should the company consider in deciding which financing plan to adopt?
d. Which plan do you recommend the company adopt?
e. Suppose Morton adopts Plan 2, and the Boston facility initially operates at an annual EBIT level of $6 million. What is the times-interest-earned ratio?
f. Suppose Plan 2 is adopted. If the lenders require that the new company maintains a times-interest-earned ratio equal to 3.5 or greater, by how much could the EBIT level drop and the company still be in compliance with the loan agreement?
g. Suppose the expected annual EBIT level of $6 million is normally distributed with a standard deviation of $3 million. What is the probability that the EPS will be negative in any given year if Plan 1 is selected?

INTERMEDIATE

21. High Sky Inc., a hot-air balloon manufacturing firm, currently has the following simplified balance sheet:

	Assets	Liabilities and Capital	
Total assets	$1,100,000	Bonds (10% interest)	$600,000
		Common stock at par ($3), 100,000 shares outstanding	300,000
		Contributed capital in excess of par	100,000
		Retained earnings	100,000
		Total liabilities and capital	$1,100,000

Spreadsheet Strategies

The company is planning an expansion that is expected to cost $600,000. The expansion can be financed with new equity (sold to net the company $4 per share) or with the sale of new bonds at an interest rate of 11 percent. (The firm's marginal tax rate is 40%.)

a. Compute the indifference point between the two financing alternatives.
b. If the expected level of EBIT for the firm is $240,000 with a standard deviation of $50,000, what is the probability that the debt financing alternative will produce higher earnings than the equity alternative? (EBIT is normally distributed.)
c. If the debt alternative is chosen, what is the probability that the company will have negative earnings per share in any period?

INTERMEDIATE

Spreadsheet Strategies

22. The Anaya Corporation is a leader in artificial intelligence research. Anaya's present capital structure consists of common stock (30 million shares) and debt ($250 million with an interest rate of 15%). The company is planning an expansion and wishes to examine alternative financing plans. The firm's marginal tax rate is 40 percent. Two alternatives under consideration are:

- *Plan 1: Common equity financing.* An additional 3 million shares of common stock will be sold at $20 each.
- *Plan 2: Debt financing.* The firm would sell $30 million of first-mortgage bonds with a pretax cost of 14 percent and $30 million of debentures with a pretax cost of 15 percent.

a. Compute the indifference point between these two alternatives.
b. One of Anaya's artificially intelligent financial managers has suggested that the firm might be better off to finance with preferred stock rather than common stock. He suggested that the indifference point be computed between the debt financing alternative and a preferred stock financing alternative. Preferred stock ($60 million) will cost 16 percent after taxes. Which option should be selected on an EPS basis? (No calculations are necessary if you set the problem up and think about the implications.)

INTERMEDIATE

Spreadsheet Strategies

23. The Bullock Cafeteria Corporation has computed the indifference point between debt and common equity financing options to be $4 million of EBIT. EBIT is approximately normally distributed with an expected value of $4.5 million and a standard deviation of $600,000. The coefficient of variation is equal to 0.13.
a. What is the probability that the equity financing option will be superior to the debt option?
b. Under the debt option, Bullock will incur $3 million in interest expenses. What is the chance of Bullock's losing money under the debt option?

INTERMEDIATE

Spreadsheet Strategies

24. Jenkins Products has a current capital structure that consists of $50 million in long-term debt at an interest rate of 10 percent and $40 million in common equity (10 million shares). The firm is considering an expansion program that will cost $10 million. This program can be financed with additional long-term debt at a 13 percent rate of interest, preferred stock at a cost of 14 percent, or the sale of new common stock at $10 per share. The firm's marginal tax rate is 40 percent.

a. Compute the indifference point level of EBIT between the debt financing option and the common stock option.
b. Compute the indifference point level of EBIT between the common stock option and the preferred stock option.
c. Is there an indifference point between the debt and preferred stock options? Why or why not?

INTERMEDIATE

25. The Oakland Shirt Company has computed its indifference level of EBIT to be $500,000 between an equity financing option and a debt financing option. Interest expense under the debt option is $200,000 and $100,000 under the equity option. The EBIT for the firm is approximately normally distributed with an expected value of $620,000 and a standard deviation of $190,000.
a. What is the probability that the equity financing option will be preferred?
b. What is the probability that the firm will incur losses under the debt option?

INTERMEDIATE

26. Lassiter Bakery currently has 3 million shares of common stock outstanding that sell at a price of $25 per share. Lassiter also has $10 million of bank debt outstanding at a pretax interest rate of 12 percent and a private placement of $20 million in bonds at a pretax interest rate of 14 percent. Lassiter's marginal tax rate is 40 percent.

Lassiter is planning entry into a new market area. This project will require Lassiter to raise $30 million. Two alternatives have been proposed:

- *Plan 1: Common equity financing.* Sell new stock at a net proceeds price to Lassiter of $20 per share.
- *Plan 2: Debt-equity financing.* Sell a combination of stock at a net proceeds price to Lassiter of $20 per share and $10 million of long-term debt at a pretax interest rate of 15 percent.

a. Compute the indifference level of EBIT between these two alternatives.
b. If Lassiter's EBIT next year is approximately normally distributed with an expected value of $20 million and a standard deviation of $5 million, what is the probability that Plan 2 will result in higher earnings per share than Plan 1?

INTERMEDIATE

27. Bowaite's Manufacturing has a current cash and marketable securities balance of $50 million. The company's economist is forecasting a two-year recession. Free cash flows during the recession, which are normally distributed, are expected to total $70 million, with a standard deviation of $60 million. The company's marginal tax rate is 40 percent.
a. Under these conditions, what is the probability that Bowaite's will run out of cash during the recession?
b. Bowaite's is considering a major capital expansion project. If the project is undertaken, it will be financed initially with debt totaling $200 million. This debt financing will require after-tax cash outflows for debt service during the two-year recession of $60 million. If Bowaite's is willing to accept a 10 percent chance of running out of cash, should the expansion (with debt financing) be undertaken?

BASIC

28. Next year's EBIT for the Latrobe Company is approximately normally distributed with an expected value of $8 million and a standard deviation of $5 million. The firm's marginal tax rate is 40 percent. Fixed financial charges (interest payments) next year are $1.5 million.
a. What is the probability that Latrobe will have a negative EPS?
b. What is the probability that Latrobe will have a positive EPS?

CHALLENGE

29. Waco Manufacturing Company has a cash (and marketable securities) balance of $150 million. Free cash flows during a projected one-year recession are expected to be $200 million with a standard deviation of $200 million. (Assume that free cash flows are approximately normally distributed.)

a. Determine the probability that Waco will run out of cash during the recession.
b. Waco is considering a change in its capital structure that would add $50 million (after taxes) to its fixed financial charges. Determine the probability of running out of cash if the change in capital structure is undertaken.
c. Determine the maximum additional fixed financial charges that Waco can incur if it is willing to tolerate only a 5 percent chance of running out of cash during the recession.

INTERMEDIATE

Spreadsheet Strategies

30. University Technologies, Inc. (UTI) has a current capital structure consisting of 10 million shares of common stock, $200 million of first-mortgage bonds with a coupon interest rate of 13 percent, and $40 million of preferred stock paying a 5 percent dividend. To expand into Asia, UTI will have to undertake an aggressive capital outlay campaign, expected to cost $200 million. This expansion can be financed either by selling 4 million new shares of common stock at a price of $50 per share or by the sale of $200 million of subordinated debentures at a pretax interest rate of 15 percent. The company's tax rate is 40 percent.
a. Compute the EBIT-EPS indifference point between the equity and debt financing alternatives.
b. If UTI expects next year's EBIT to be $150 million with a standard deviation of $20 million, what is the probability that the equity financing option will produce higher earnings per share than the debt financing option? (Assume that EBIT is normally distributed.)

CHALLENGE

31. EBITDA Inc. a subsidiary of Robinson Enterprises, is considering the purchase of a fleet of new BMWs for the CEO and other senior managers. Currently the firm has a capital structure that consists of 60 percent debt, 30 percent common equity, and 10 percent preferred stock. The pretax interest rate on currently outstanding debt is 9 percent. The dividend yield on the company's preferred stock is 12 percent. Total capitalization is $20 million. This fleet of new cars will cost $1 million, and the company plans to finance the entire purchase with debt at a pretax interest rate of 10 percent. The firm's marginal tax rate is 40 percent. The expected level of EBIT for the firm over the coming year is $1.7 million with a standard deviation of $200,000. (Assume that EBIT is normally distributed.)

If the firm acquires the cars and finances them with debt as proposed, what is the *increase* in the probability of the company's generating losses during the coming year?

INTERMEDIATE

32. Ellington's Cabaret is planning a major expansion that will require $95 million of new financing. Ellington's currently has a capital structure consisting of $400 million of common equity (with a cost of 14 percent and 4 million shares outstanding), $50 million of preferred stock ($50 par, $5 dividend), and $200 million of long-term debt (with a coupon interest rate of 9%). The marginal tax rate is 40 percent, and the average tax rate is 30 percent.

To finance the expansion, Ellington is considering two sources of funding: (1) the sale of new shares of stock at a net price of $95 per share or (2) the sale of debentures at a coupon rate of 10 percent.
a. What is the level of EBIT at the indifference point between these two alternatives? What are the earnings per share at this level?
b. If the expected level of EBIT is $100 million with a standard deviation of $20 million, what is the probability of having unfavorable financial leverage if the debt financing alternative is chosen? (Assume that EBIT is normally distributed.)

INTERMEDIATE

33. Rauchous Resources has traditionally been financed in a most conservative way. The CEO and founder, Rebecca, just does not believe in debt. However, after hearing a consultant discuss the concept of an optimal capital structure, she began to consider new financing options for the company. Rauchous has an expected level of EBIT of $1.5 million, with an estimated standard deviation of $1 million.

a. Given the current capital structure with no debt, what is the probability that Rauchous will have negative earnings per share during the coming year?
b. Rauchous is considering a large share repurchase program to be funded with $10 million of 10 percent debentures. The current price per share of common stock is $50. If this repurchase is undertaken, what is the probability of negative earnings per share during the coming year?

INTERMEDIATE

34. National Value Foods Company (NVFC) is considering opening a new wholly owned subsidiary in Booneville. To finance this investment, NVFC is considering two financing plans: (1) sell 600,000 shares of common stock at $20 each; or (2) sell 200,000 shares of common stock at $20 each and $8 million of 10 percent long-term debt.

a. If NVFC has a marginal tax rate of 40 percent, what is the EBIT-EPS indifference point for this investment?
b. NVFC's expected level of EBIT from this division is $1.0 million with a standard deviation of $400,000. If the firm uses the second financing plan, what is the chance of having unfavorable financial leverage?

APPENDIX **14A**

BREAKEVEN ANALYSIS

Introduction

breakeven analysis

To gain an understanding of the role that operating leverage plays in determining the business risk of a firm, it is useful to develop the fundamentals of **breakeven analysis** (also known as *cost-volume-profit analysis*). Breakeven analysis considers the relationships among a firm's sales, fixed and variable operating costs, and EBIT (operating income) at various output levels.

The term *breakeven analysis* is somewhat misleading, because breakeven analysis is used to answer many questions beyond those dealing with the breakeven (EBIT = 0) output level of a firm or division of a firm. Possible uses include the following:[1]

1. Forecasting the profitability for a firm, division, or product line, given a cost structure and expected sales levels.
2. Analyzing the impact of changes in fixed costs, variable costs, and selling price on operating profits.
3. Analyzing the impact of substituting fixed costs (primarily capital equipment) for variable costs (labor) in a production process.
4. Analyzing the profit impact of a firm's restructuring efforts designed to cut fixed costs.

In addition, we will find that breakeven analysis concepts and an understanding of the relationships among fixed costs, variable costs, prices, and profits are useful when planning the mix of financing sources a firm will use. If a firm, such as American Airlines, already has a high proportion of fixed operating costs that must be covered by sales revenue, it may not be prudent to use large amounts of fixed-cost sources of financing, such as bonds or preferred stock. Many airlines have made this financing error. Some, such as Pan American, Eastern, TWA, and Braniff, were forced into bankruptcy and eventually were liquidated. Others, such as United (Now United Continental) and US Airways, declared bankruptcy and emerged with smaller amounts of debt and interest payments.

Graphic Breakeven Analysis

Breakeven analysis can be developed graphically, algebraically, or as a combination of the two. Figure 14A.1 is an example of a basic linear breakeven analysis chart. Costs and revenues (measured in dollars) are plotted on the vertical axis, and output (measured in units) is plotted on the horizontal axis. The *total revenue* function, TR, represents the total revenue the firm will realize at each output level, given that the firm charges a constant selling price, P, per unit of output. Similarly, the *total* (operating) *cost* function, TC, represents the total cost the firm will incur at each output level. Total cost is computed as the sum of the firm's fixed costs, F, which are independent of the output level, plus the variable costs, which increase at the constant rate, V, per unit of output.

[1] A good illustration of the application of breakeven analysis in finance can be found in U. E. Reinhardt, "Breakeven Analysis for Lockheed's Tri Star: An Application of Financial Theory," *Journal of Finance* 28 (September 1973): 821–838.

FIGURE 14A.1

Linear Breakeven Analysis Chart

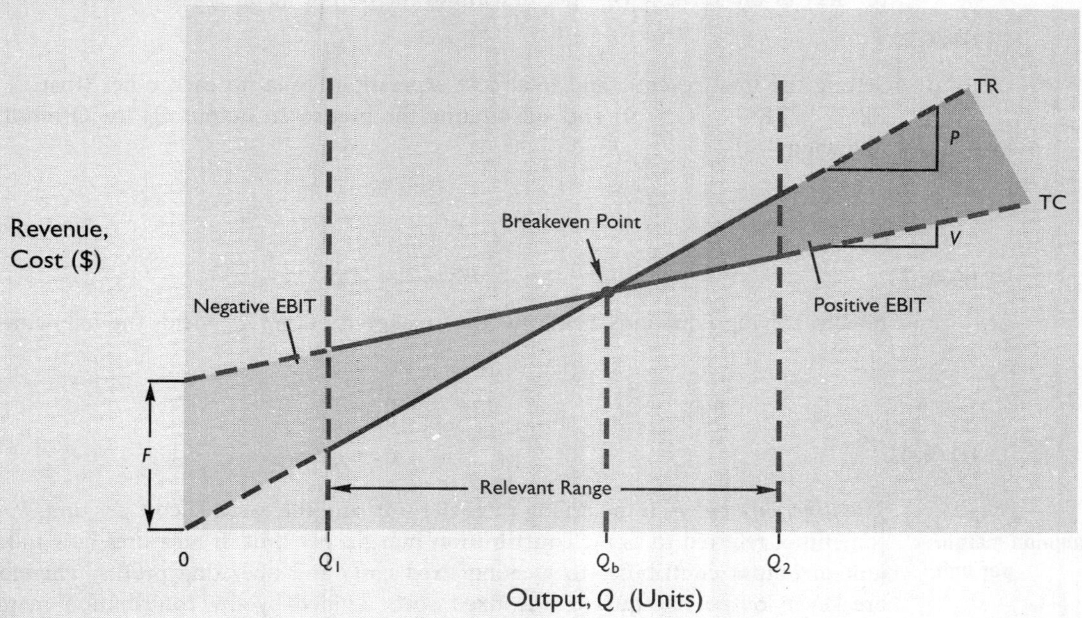

The assumptions of a constant selling price per unit, P, and a constant variable cost per unit, V, yield *linear* relationships for the total revenue and total cost functions. However, these linear relationships are valid only over some *relevant range* of output values, such as from Q_1 to Q_2 in Figure 14A.1.

The breakeven point occurs at point Q_b in Figure 14A.1, where the total revenue and the total cost functions intersect. If a firm's output level is below this breakeven point—that is, if TR < TC—it incurs *operating losses*, defined as a *negative EBIT*. If the firm's output level is above this breakeven point—that is, if TR > TC—it realizes *operating profits*, defined as a *positive EBIT*.

Determining a firm's breakeven point graphically involves three steps:

1. Drawing a line through the origin with a slope of P to represent the TR function
2. Drawing a line that intersects the vertical axis at F and has a slope of V to represent the TC function
3. Determining the point where the TR and TC lines intersect, dropping a perpendicular line to the horizontal axis, and noting the resulting value of Q_b

Algebraic Breakeven Analysis

To determine a firm's breakeven point algebraically, set the total revenue and total (operating) cost functions equal to each other and solve the resulting equation for the breakeven volume.

Total revenue is equal to the selling price per unit times the output quantity:

(14A.1)
$$TR = P \times Q$$

Total (operating) cost is equal to fixed plus variable costs, where the variable cost is the product of the variable cost per unit times the output quantity:

(14A.2)
$$TC = F + V \times Q$$

Setting the total revenue and total cost expressions equal to each other (that is, setting EBIT = TR − TC = 0) and substituting the breakeven output Q_b for Q result in the following:

$$TR = TC$$

or

(14A.3)
$$PQ_b = F + VQ_b$$

Finally, solving Equations 14A.3 for the breakeven output Q_b yields the following:

$$PQ_b - VQ_b = F$$

$$(P - V)Q_b = F$$

(14A.4)
$$Q_b = \frac{F}{P - V}$$

contribution margin per unit

The *difference* between the selling price per unit and the variable cost per unit, $P - V$, is sometimes referred to as the **contribution margin per unit**. It measures how much each unit of output contributes to meeting fixed costs and operating profits. Therefore, the breakeven output is equal to the fixed costs divided by the contribution margin per unit.

Breakeven analysis can also be performed in terms of dollar *sales*, rather than units of output. The breakeven dollar sales volume, S_b, can be determined by the following expression:

(14A.5)
$$S_b = \frac{F}{1 - (V/P)}$$

where V/P is the variable cost ratio (that is, the variable cost per dollar of sales).

Occasionally, the analyst is interested in determining the output quantity at which a *target profit* (expressed in dollars) is achieved. An expression similar to Equation 14A.4 can be used to find such a quantity:

(14A.6)
$$\text{Target volume} = \frac{\text{Fixed cost} + \text{Target profit}}{\text{Contribution margin per unit}}$$

Examples of Breakeven Analysis

Consider again the Allegan Manufacturing Company (see Table 14.1). Assume that the firm manufactures one product, which it sells for \$250 per unit. The current output, Q, is obtained by dividing total dollar sales (\$5 million) by the selling price per unit (\$250) to obtain 20,000 units per year. Its variable (operating) costs per unit, V, are determined by dividing total variable costs (\$3 million) by current output (20,000) to obtain \$150 per unit.

FIGURE 14A.2

Linear Breakeven Analysis Chart for the Allegan Manufacturing Company

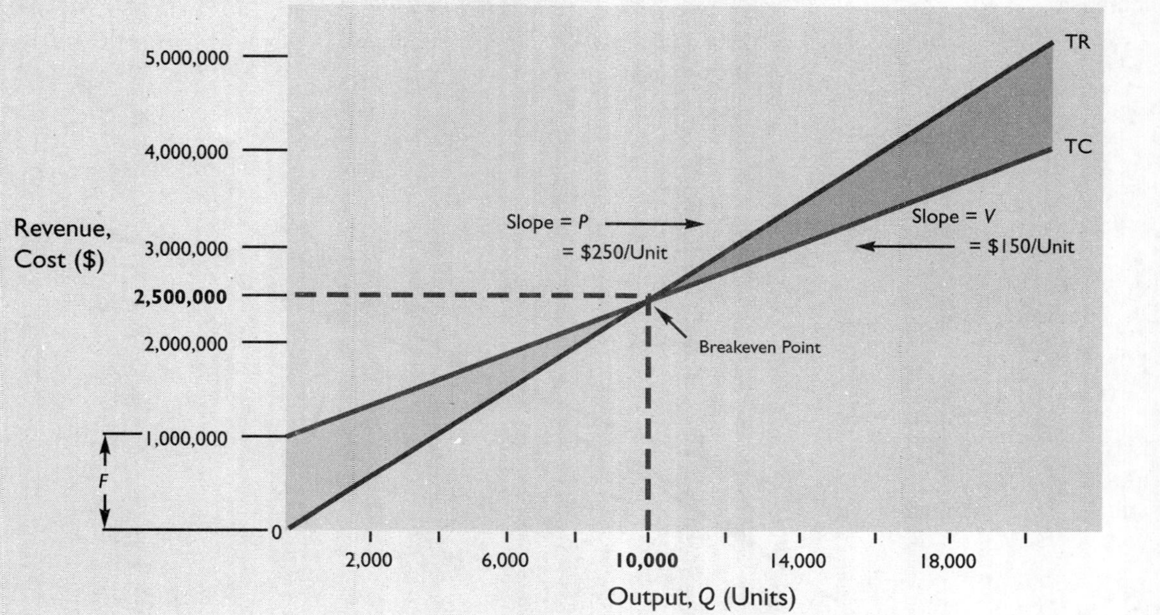

The firm's fixed costs, *F*, are \$1 million. Inserting these figures into Equation 14A.4 yields the following breakeven output:

$$Q_b = \frac{\$1{,}000{,}000}{\$250 - \$150}$$
$$= 10{,}000 \text{ units}$$

Allegan's breakeven output can also be determined graphically, as shown in Figure 14A.2. Also shown in the figure is the breakeven level of dollar sales, \$2.5 million.

Because a firm's breakeven output depends on a number of variables—in particular, the price per unit and variable (operating) costs per unit—managers may wish to analyze the effects of changes in any one of the variables on the breakeven output. For example, they may wish to consider either of the following: (1) changing the selling price; or (2) substituting fixed costs for variable costs.

Assume that Allegan increased the selling price per unit by \$25, to \$275, P'. Inserting this figure into Equation 14A.4 gives a new breakeven output:

$$Q'_b = \frac{\$1{,}000{,}000}{\$275 - \$150} = 8{,}000 \text{ units}$$

Figure 14A.3 graphically shows how an increase in the price per unit increases the slope of the total revenue function, TR′, and reduces the breakeven output.

Rather than increasing the selling price per unit, Allegan's management may decide to substitute fixed costs for variable costs in some aspect of the company's operations. For

FIGURE 14A.3

Linear Breakeven Analysis Chart for the Allegan Manufacturing Company Showing the Effects of a Price Increase

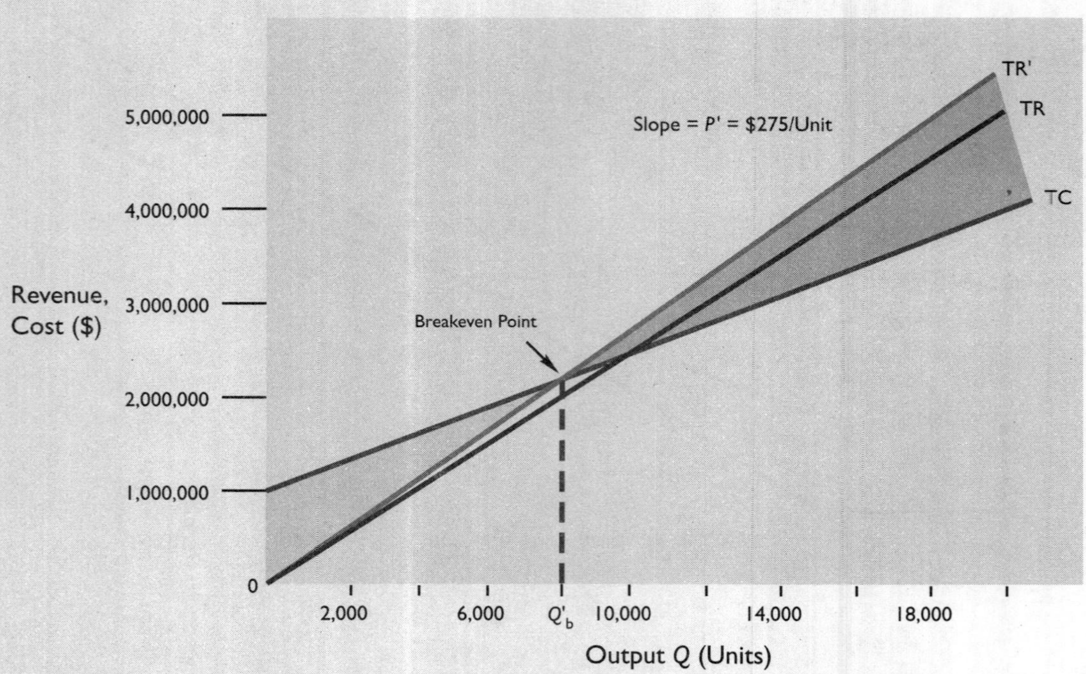

example, as labor wage rates increase over time, many firms seek to reduce operating costs through automation, which in effect represents the substitution of fixed-cost capital equipment for variable-cost labor. Suppose that Allegan determines it can reduce labor costs by $25 per unit by purchasing $1 million in additional equipment. Assume that the new equipment is depreciated over a 10-year life using the straight-line method. Under these conditions, annual depreciation of the new equipment would be $1,000,000 ÷ 10 = $100,000, and the firm's new level of fixed costs, F', would be $1,000,000 + $100,000 = $1,100,000. Variable costs per unit, V', would be $150 – $25 = $125. Substituting P = $250 per unit, V' = $125 per unit, and F' = $1,100,000 into Equation 14A.4 yields a new breakeven output:

$$Q'_b = \frac{\$1{,}100{,}000}{\$250 - \$125}$$
$$= 8{,}800 \text{ units}$$

As Figure 14A.4 shows, the effect of this change in operations is to raise the intercept on the vertical axis, decrease the slope of the total cost function, TC′, and reduce the breakeven output.

FIGURE 14A.4

Linear Breakeven Analysis Chart for the Allegan Manufacturing Company Showing the Effects of Substituting Fixed Costs for Variable Costs

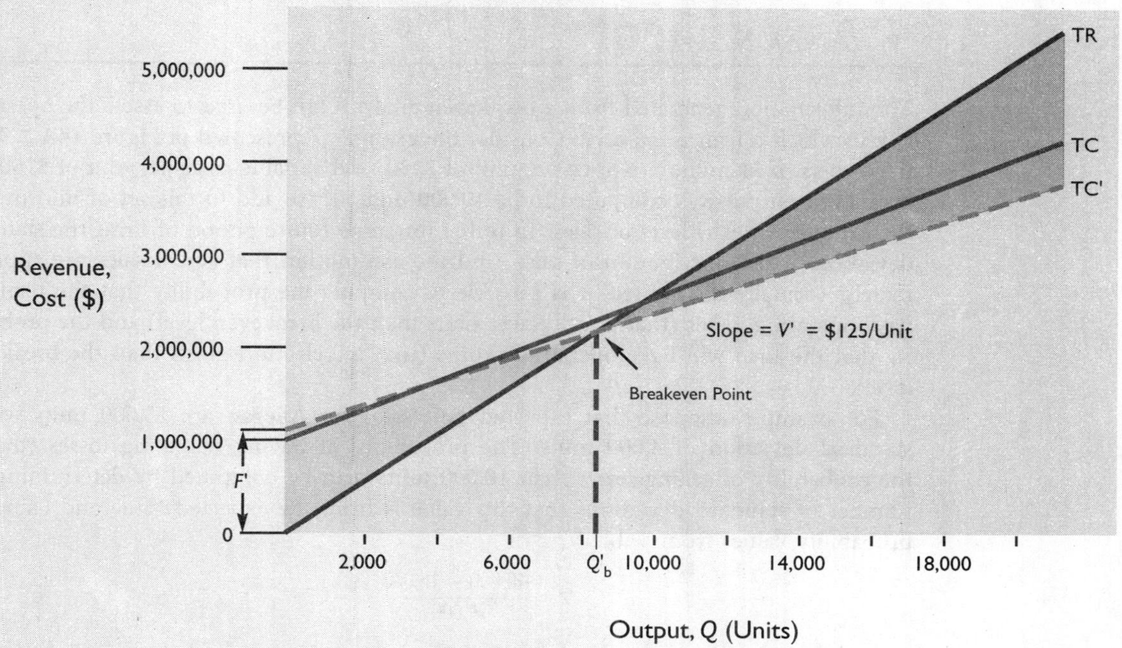

DOL and Breakeven Analysis

The variables defined in the preceding section (TR = total revenue, Q = quantity, P = price per unit, V = variable cost per unit, and F = fixed costs) can also be used to develop a formula for determining a firm's degree of operating leverage, or DOL, at any given output level. Because sales are equivalent to TR (or $P \times Q$), variable cost is equal to $V \times Q$, and EBIT is equal to total revenue (TR) less total (operating) cost, or $(P \times Q) - F - (V \times Q)$, these values can be substituted into Equation 14.2 to obtain the following:

$$\text{DOL at } Q = \frac{(P \times Q) - (V \times Q)}{(P \times Q) - F - (V \times Q)}$$

or

(14A.7)
$$\text{DOL at } Q = \frac{(P - V)Q}{(P - V)Q - F}$$

For example, in the case of Allegan Manufacturing Company, where P = $250/unit, V = $150/unit, and F = $1,000,000, the DOL at an output level of Q = 20,000 units is:

$$\text{DOL at 20,000} = \frac{(\$250/\text{unit} - \$150/\text{unit})20{,}000 \text{ units}}{(\$250/\text{unit} - \$150/\text{unit})20{,}000 \text{ units} - \$1{,}000{,}000}$$
$$= 2.0$$

This is the same value that was obtained in the chapter using Equation 14.1 at a total revenue (TR) of \$5 million (that is, $P = \$250/\text{unit} \times Q = 20{,}000$ units).

Breakeven Analysis and Risk Assessment

The information generated from a breakeven analysis can be used to assess the operating risk to which a firm is exposed. Consider the example represented in Figure 14A.2. With fixed costs of \$1 million, a price per unit of \$250, and variable costs per unit of \$150, the breakeven output was computed to be 10,000 units. If we add to this set of information the *expected* (mean) level of sales (in units) for some future period of time, the standard deviation of the distribution of sales, and the assumption that actual sales are approximately normally distributed, it is possible to compute the probability that the firm will have operating losses (that is, sell fewer units than the breakeven level) and the probability that the firm will have operating profits (that is, sell more units than the breakeven level).

For example, suppose that expected unit sales for Allegan are 15,000 units with a standard deviation of 4,000 units. The probability of having operating losses (that is, the probability of selling fewer than 10,000 units) can be computed by determining the number of standard deviations that this value is from the expected value and using the probability values from Table V:

$$z = \frac{10{,}000 - 15{,}000}{4{,}000} = -1.25$$

In other words, a sales level of 10,000 units is 1.25 standard deviations *below* the mean. Table V indicates that the probability associated with −1.25 standard deviations is 10.56 percent. Therefore, there is a 10.56 percent chance that the firm will incur operating losses and an 89.44 percent (100% minus 10.56%) chance that the firm will record operating profits (that is, sell more than the breakeven number of units of output).

Some Limitations of Breakeven Analysis

Breakeven analysis has a number of limitations. These arise from the *assumptions* that are made in constructing the model and developing the relevant data. The application of breakeven analysis is of value only to the extent that these assumptions are valid.

HTTP:
To download an excellent breakeven analysis Excel template, go to:
www.bankrate.com/brm/news/biz/cashflow_banking/20000414b.asp

Constant Selling Price and Variable Cost per Unit

Recall that in the graphic breakeven analysis model, the assumptions of a constant selling price and variable cost per unit yield linear relationships for the total revenue and total cost functions. In practice, these functions tend to be nonlinear. In many cases, a firm can sell additional units of output only by lowering the price per unit. This results in a total revenue function that is curvilinear, as shown in Figure 14A.5, instead of straight-lined.

In addition, a firm's total cost function may be nonlinear because variable costs per unit initially decrease and then increase. This is also shown in Figure 14A.5. Decreasing

FIGURE 14A.5
Nonlinear Breakeven Analysis Chart

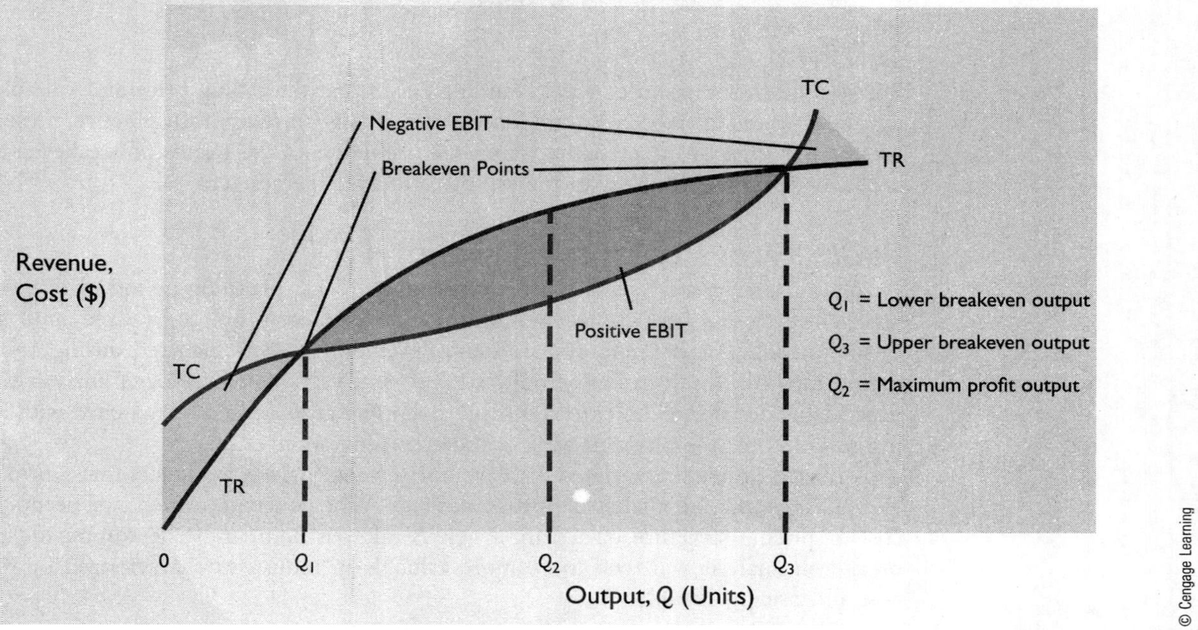

variable costs per unit can occur if, for example, labor specialization results in increased output per labor hour. Increasing variable costs per unit can occur if, for example, a firm uses more costly overtime labor as output approaches production capacity.

Nonlinear TC and TR functions can result in a firm's having more than one breakeven output point. In Figure 14A.5, a breakeven situation occurs at both point Q_1 and point Q_3. This is interpreted to mean that the firm will incur operating losses *below* an output level of Q_1 and *above* an output level of Q_3. The firm's total operating profits are maximized within the range of Q_1-Q_3 at the point where the vertical distance between the TR and TC curves is greatest, that is, at output level Q_2.

In summary, the assumption of a constant selling price and variable cost per unit is probably valid over some relevant range of output levels. However, consideration of output levels outside this range will normally require modifications in the breakeven chart, such as the construction of a new total revenue curve reflecting expected sales levels at each new price.

Composition of Operating Costs

Another assumption of breakeven analysis is that costs can be classified as either fixed or variable. In fact, fixed and variable costs depend on both the time period involved and the output range under consideration. All costs are variable in the long run. In addition, some costs are partly fixed and partly variable. Furthermore, some costs increase in a stepwise manner as output is increased (that is, *semivariable costs*) and are constant only over relatively narrow ranges of output.

Multiple Products

The breakeven model also assumes that a firm is producing and selling either a *single* product or a *constant mix* of different products. In many cases, the product mix changes over time, and problems can arise in allocating fixed costs among the various products.

Uncertainty

Still another assumption of breakeven analysis is that the selling price and variable cost per unit, as well as fixed costs, are known at each level of output. In practice, these parameters are subject to uncertainty. Thus, the usefulness of the results of breakeven analysis depends on the accuracy of the estimates of these parameters.

Short-Term Planning Horizon

Finally, breakeven analysis is normally performed for a planning period of one year or less. However, the benefits received from some costs may not be realized until subsequent periods. For example, research and development costs incurred during a specific period may not result in new products for several years. For breakeven analysis to be a dependable decision-making tool, a firm's operating costs should be matched with resulting revenues for the planning period under consideration.

A related problem associated with the horizon for analysis is the fact that a firm's cost and pricing structure change almost continually. When a significant change occurs in the cost or pricing structure of a firm, a new breakeven point must be computed. Hence, breakeven analysis will tend to be more valuable in industries characterized by relative cost and pricing stability.

Cash Breakeven Point

cash breakeven point

The calculation of a **cash breakeven point** may assist a firm in its financial planning. Some of a firm's fixed operating costs, namely depreciation, are *noncash outlays*. The cash breakeven point is calculated by subtracting the noncash depreciation charges, *Dep*, from the fixed operating costs, *F*, in the numerator of the breakeven equation (Equation 14A.4):

(14A.8)
$$\text{Cash breakeven point} = \frac{F - Dep}{P - V}$$

The cash breakeven point measures the volume of output (units) required to cover the firm's fixed cash operating outlays, such as management salaries, rent, and utilities.

Cash breakeven analysis can also be performed in terms of dollar sales. The cash breakeven dollar sales volume can be determined with the following expression:

(14A.9)
$$\text{Cash breakeven sales} = \frac{F - Dep}{1 - (V/P)}$$

All other things being equal, a firm with a larger proportion of its fixed costs in the form of noncash outlays will have a lower cash breakeven point and be better able to survive during a business downturn than a firm whose fixed costs consist mainly of cash outlays.

Consider the following example. Victor Rodriguez has been offered a new auto dealership, and the manufacturer has provided him with various sales forecasts. As part of a detailed analysis of the proposed dealership, he would like an estimate of the cash breakeven point for new car sales. He estimates that fixed costs will be $2 million a year, including depreciation expense of $300,000 a year. In addition, the new car sales price is expected to be $13,000 per unit, and the new car variable cost is expected to be $11,000 per unit. The estimated cash breakeven point for new car sales can be calculated using Equation 14A.8:

$$\text{Cash breakeven point} = \frac{\$2{,}000{,}000 - \$300{,}000}{\$13{,}000 - \$11{,}000}$$
$$= 850 \text{ units}$$

The cash breakeven sales volume is calculated using Equation 14A.9:

$$\text{Cash breakeven sales} = \frac{\$2{,}000{,}000 - \$300{,}000}{1 - \left(\dfrac{\$11{,}000}{\$13{,}000}\right)}$$
$$= \$11{,}050{,}000$$

Rodriguez can now analyze the manufacturer's marketing data to determine the likelihood of exceeding the estimated cash breakeven point for new car sales.

Questions and Topics for Discussion

1. Explain how a linear breakeven chart is constructed when a firm's selling price, variable costs per unit, and fixed costs are known.
2. What are some of the limitations of breakeven analysis? How can these limitations affect actual financial decision making?
3. Assuming that all other factors remain unchanged, determine how a firm's breakeven point is affected by each of the following developments:
   a. The firm finds it necessary to reduce the price per unit because of competitive conditions in the market.
   b. The firm's direct labor costs increase as a result of a new labor contract.
   c. The Occupational Safety and Health Administration requires the firm to install new ventilating equipment in its plant. (Assume that this action has no effect on worker productivity.)

Self-Test Problems

ST1. Myers Implements is attempting to develop and market a new garden tractor. Fixed costs to develop and produce the new tractor are estimated to be $10 million per year. The variable cost to make each tractor has been estimated at $2,000. The marketing research department has recommended a price of $4,000 per tractor.

a. What is the breakeven level of output for the new tractor?

b. If management expects to generate a target profit of $2 million from the tractor each year, how many tractors must be sold?

ST2. Westerfield Enterprises has determined that the breakeven level of output for its snowblower is 20,000 units. The marketing research department has determined that expected sales will be 22,000 units, with a standard deviation of 4,000 units. What is the probability that Westerfield will incur operating losses from the sale of the snowblower?

Problems*

INTERMEDIATE **1.** East Publishing Company is doing an analysis of a proposed new finance text. Using the following data, answer Parts a through e.

Fixed Costs (per edition):	
Development (reviews, class testing, and so on)	$18,000
Copyediting	5,000
Selling and promotion	7,000
Typesetting	40,000
Total	$70,000
Variable Costs (per copy):	
Printing and binding	$4.20
Administrative costs	1.60
Salespeople's commission (2% of selling price)	.60
Author's royalties (12% of selling price)	3.60
Bookstore discounts (20% of selling price)	6.00
Total	$ 16.00
Projected Selling Price	$ 30.00

The company's marginal tax rate is 40 percent.

a. Determine the company's breakeven volume for this book.

i. In units

ii. In dollar sales

b. Develop a breakeven chart for the text.

c. Determine the number of copies East must sell in order to earn an (operating) profit of $21,000 on this text.

d. Determine total (operating) profits at the following sales levels:

i. 3,000 units

ii. 5,000 units

iii. 10,000 units

e. Suppose East feels that $30.00 is too high a price to charge for the new finance text. It has examined the competitive market and determined that $24.00 would be a better selling price. What would the breakeven volume be at this new selling price?

BASIC **2.** Jenkins Appliances produces microwave ovens. Jenkins has computed its breakeven level of sales to be 60,000 units. An analysis of the market has led Jenkins to *expect* sales of 75,000 units with a standard deviation of 10,000 units. Assume that sales are normally distributed.

a. What is the probability that Jenkins will incur operating losses?

b. What is the probability that Jenkins will operate above its breakeven point?

BASIC **3.** Vargo Industries has computed its breakeven level of output to be 25,000 units. Based on forecasts from its sales force and past experience, expected unit sales are

*Color blocks behind the numbers denote problems that have check answers provided at the end of the book.

32,000, with a standard deviation of 5,200. What is the probability that Vargo will have operating losses? Assume that sales are normally distributed.

INTERMEDIATE

4. Logue Lock Company expects its fixed costs next year to be $750,000. The selling price for its lock is $40. Logue is considering the purchase of new equipment that is expected to reduce unit variable costs from a current level of $25 to a new level of $20. How large could the additional fixed costs from the new equipment be without affecting the breakeven point?

INTERMEDIATE

5. Francis Furniture has current fixed costs of $1 million. Francis's only product, a rolltop desk, sells for $3,000. Variable operating costs per unit are $1,000. Francis plans to buy a new lathe that will produce a more precise roller for the desk. The lathe will add $100,000 in annual fixed costs. Variable operating costs are not expected to change as a result of the lathe purchase. If Francis wishes to leave its breakeven point unchanged, what action must it take?

CHALLENGE

6. Rodney Rogers, a recent business school graduate, plans to open a wholesale dairy products firm. Rogers expects first-year sales to total $5.50 million. He desires to earn a target pretax profit of $1 million during his first year of operation. Variable costs are 40 percent of sales.

a. How large can Rogers's fixed costs be if he is to meet his profit target?

b. What is Rogers's breakeven level of sales at the level of fixed costs determined in Part a?

INTERMEDIATE

7. The current price per unit for shock absorbers produced by Leveland Products is $25. The variable cost per unit is $10. Fixed costs are $600,000.

a. What is the breakeven point in units?

b. What is the DOL at the breakeven point? Explain what this value means conceptually.

INTERMEDIATE

8. The Covington Engine Company is considering opening a new plant facility to build truck engines. As part of a detailed analysis of the proposed facility, Covington's management wants some information on the cash breakeven point. Fixed costs for the facility are expected to be $6 million a year, including depreciation expenses of $800,000 a year. The engines' sales price is expected to be $7,000 per unit, and the variable cost is expected to be $3,000 per unit. Calculate the expected annual cash breakeven point and the expected annual cash breakeven sales.

CHAPTER 15

Dividend Policy

KEY CHAPTER CONCEPTS

1. Dividend policy determines the ultimate distribution of the firm's earnings between retention (that is, reinvestment) and cash dividend payments to shareholders.
2. Factors influencing the firm's choice of a dividend policy are examined, including:
   a. Legal constraints
   b. Restrictive covenants
   c. Tax considerations
   d. Liquidity considerations
   e. Borrowing capacity and access to the capital markets
   f. Earnings stability
   g. Growth prospects
   h. Shareholder preferences
   i. Protection against dilution
3. Alternative dividend policies inc ude:
   a. Passive residual approach
   b. Stable dollar dividend approach
   c. Constant payout ratio approach
   d. Policy of paying a small, regular dividend plus year-end extras
4. Other important topics include:
   a. How dividends are paid
   b. Stock dividends
   c. Stock splits
   d. Share repurchase as a dividend decision

FINANCIAL CHALLENGE

ExxonMobil's Payout Policy

Companies such as ExxonMobil appeal to investors because of their hefty and stable dividend payouts, among other reasons. The large oil companies (e.g., ExxonMobil, Royal Dutch Shell, ConocoPhillips, Total, and Chevron) have been especially known for their generous dividend yields (dividend yield is defined as annualized dividend divided by price per share). Many of these firms pay out dividend yields in the range of 3.4–5.0 percent. These firms are able to afford such payments because they generate substantial cash flows from their operations. Even after accounting for reinvestment needs (exploration, developing new oil wells), the firms are left with significant excess funds, which are used to fund the generous dividends. But dividends are not the only way firms disburse cash to their shareholders. As you will learn from this chapter, firms also disburse funds to their shareholders via share buybacks, that is, they use cash to repurchase shares in the open market. Buybacks have becoming increasingly common in the past 10–15 years.

Among the oil majors, most firms pay out approximately 70–80 percent of their net income to shareholders in the form of dividends and share buybacks, much of it in the form of dividends. ExxonMobil, however, has emphasized buybacks over dividend payments. The company gradually shifted from a focus on dividends to share repurchases over the past 15 years. In recent years, ExxonMobil allocated approximately a third of its shareholder disbursements to dividends and two-thirds to share repurchases. In contrast, the firm spent twice as much on dividends as repurchases in the latter half of the 1990s. While ExxonMobil disbursed a similar proportion of its earnings to its shareholders as its main competitors, the way it did so was very different. As noted, the bulk of the payout was in the form of repurchases, as opposed to their rivals, whose payouts largely come in the form of dividends. This was reflected in the dividend yields. For example, in 2013 ExxonMobil's dividend yield was only 2.5 percent, in contrast to dividend yields of 3.6 percent for Chevron and 5.0 percent for Total.

Katherine Welles/Shutterstock.com

The differential payout policies followed by ExxonMobil and its competitors raise the question of whether repurchases or dividends are a better way to disburse cash to shareholders. As you will learn in this chapter, at a theoretical level, there is no difference between paying out a dollar in the form of a dividend versus a repurchase. However, in practice, there may be considerations that might make one method preferable over the other. For example, research and survey evidence indicate that cutting back on dividends is not viewed favorably by the markets; research shows that announcements of dividend cuts are accompanied by significant drops in share prices. Hence firms need to be careful that the dividends they pay annually can be sustained in the long run with periodic increases over time. However, cutting back on repurchases is not perceived to have the same dire consequence.

This difference in perception between the two types of payout became starkly evident in 2015 when crude oil prices fell dramatically. The resulting drop in operating cash flows to the energy firms made it difficult to sustain the heavy dividend payouts shareholders were used to receiving. Several

FINANCIAL CHALLENGE — CONTINUED

firms had to cut their dividends. In early 2016, ConocoPhillips, Marathon Oil and Anadarko Petroleum announced cuts in dividends ranging from 65 to 80 percent. ExxonMobil, on the other hand, was able to maintain its dividend and even raised it some, though it did announce a suspension of its share buyback program, which it had been curtailing for several quarters. In terms of stock price performance, it appears that ExxonMobil's price dropped considerably less than its peers. Although we cannot necessarily attribute this to differences in the payout policy, it likely had some impact.

The ExxonMobil example above highlights the importance of payout policy including the different types and their potential impact on share price. These and several other aspects of payout policy are discussed in this chapter.

Sources: Bob Ciura, "Are ExxonMobil Corp's Slowing Share Buybacks Reason to Worry?" *Motley Fool* (February 6, 2014), www.fool.com (accessed February 17, 2016); Spencer Jakab, "Exxon Mobil," *The Wall Street Journal* (July 30, 2015), www.wsj.com (accessed February 17, 2016); "Here's Why Exxon Mobil Corporation (XOM) May Be the Best Dividend Investment," *Smarter Analyst* (June 18, 2015), www.smarteranalyst.com (accessed February 17, 2016); and various issues of *Barron's*.

CHAPTER OBJECTIVES

Upon completion of this chapter, you should have a clear understanding of the following:

1. The determinants of dividend policy in practice
2. The impact of dividend policy on firm value
3. Types of dividend policies observed by firms and how dividends are paid
4. Stock dividends and stock splits and why they are declared
5. Stock repurchases and their impact on the firm

15-1 Introduction

The value of a firm is influenced by three types of financial decisions:

- Investment decisions
- Financing decisions
- Dividend decisions

Although each is presented as a separate topic in this and most financial management textbooks,[1] these three types of financial decisions are interdependent in a number of ways. For example, the investments made by a firm determine the level of future earnings and future potential dividends. Capital structure influences the cost of capital, which determines, in part, the number of acceptable investment opportunities. Dividend policy influences the amount of equity capital in a firm's capital structure (via the retained

[1] In this text, investment decisions are dealt with in Chapters 9–11 and 16–18, and financing decisions are discussed in Chapters 6, 7, 13, 14, 16, 19, and 20.

earnings account) and, by extension, influences the cost of capital. In making these interrelated decisions, the goal is to maximize shareholder wealth.

Consider the following dividend decisions:

1. In 2007, Leggett & Platt, a furniture manufacturer, experienced a significant drop in earnings per share to $0.28 from $1.57 in the preceding year. Despite the decline in earnings per share, the firm boosted its dividends per share from $0.67 to $0.78.
2. Monster Beverage Corporation ("Monster Energy" drinks) went public in 1990 and has steadily grown its revenues and profits since then. In 2014 Monster had revenues in excess of $2.4 billion and net income of approximately $480 million. At the end of 2014, the firm had cash and marketable securities of approximately $1.2 billion. Despite its record of profitability and liquidity, Monster to date has chosen not to pay a cash dividend to its stockholders, though it has engaged in share repurchases periodically.
3. In September 2015 Texas Instruments announced a 12 percent increase in its quarterly dividends per share to $0.38 and also announced a $7.5 billion stock buyback program. Texas Instruments is known for regularly raising its dividends per share and, at the same time, announcing significant repurchases of its shares.
4. During 1992, General Motors paid out approximately $990 million ($1.40 per share) in common stock dividends (a *decrease* in stockholders' equity). During the same period, the company sold $2.145 billion in new common stock (an *increase* in stockholders' equity) and incurred $53.625 million in issuance costs.
5. In addition to regular cash dividends, Huntington Bank paid stock dividends (that is, additional shares of common stock) in 20 of the 25 years between 1976 and 2000.

These dividend decisions raise a number of important questions, such as the following:

1. Do you agree with Monster Beverage Corporation's policy of not paying out dividends and choosing, instead, to buy back its own shares?
2. Why did Leggett & Platt pay a common stock dividend in excess of its earnings? Alternatively, would not a reduction of its dividend have been a more prudent strategy because it would conserve cash (that is, reduce cash outflows) during a period of economic difficulty?
3. Why did General Motors pay common stock dividends *and* incur the issuance costs of selling new common stock during the same time period? As an alternative to issuing new common stock, why didn't General Motors reduce its common stock dividend temporarily until it accumulated the amount of equity funds it planned to raise externally?
4. Why does Huntington Bank pay stock dividends when the net effect of these transactions is that total stockholders' equity remains unchanged and each shareholder's proportionate claim on the firm's total earnings remains constant?
5. What are the advantages to Texas Instruments and its shareholders of the $7.5 billion stock repurchase program, compared with paying shareholders an equivalent amount of cash dividends?
6. Finally, on a more fundamental level, does it really matter, with respect to the maximization of shareholder wealth, what amount (or percentage of earnings) a firm pays out in dividends?

In this chapter, we seek to answer dividend policy questions such as these.

This chapter begins by examining the factors that influence a company's choice of dividend policy. Next, it considers the pros and cons of a number of different dividend policies. Finally, it discusses the mechanics of dividend payments, along with stock dividends and share repurchase plans.

15-2 Determinants of Dividend Policy

Dividend policy determines how the earnings of a company are distributed. Earnings are either retained and reinvested in the company or paid out to shareholders. In recent years, the retention of earnings has been a major source of equity financing for private industry. In 2014, corporations retained 49 cents of every dollar of after-tax profits.[2] Retained earnings are the most important source of equity. Retained earnings can be used to stimulate growth in future earnings and as a result can influence future share values. On the other hand, dividends provide stockholders with tangible current returns.

15-2a Industry and Company Variations in Dividend Payout Ratios

Dividend payout policies vary among different industries. As shown in Table 15.1, there is a wide variation in dividend payout ratios among industries, ranging from 3 to

TABLE 15.1

Dividend Payout Ratios for Selected Industries

Industry	2014 Dividend Payout Ratio (%)
Biotechnology	3
Internet software and services	8
Homebuilding	10
Airlines	11
Healthcare	11
Apparel, accessories, & luxury goods	16
Railroads and trucking	16
Communication equipment	20
Aerospace/defense	23
Department and general merchandise stores	24
Movies and entertainment	25
Oil and gas	25
Pharmaceuticals	25
Technology hardware, storage, & peripherals	27
Industrial machinery	27
Casinos and gaming	29
Forest and paper products	33
Apparel retail	35
Chemicals	37
Data processing & outsourced services	43
Restaurant	44
Packaged foods and meat	45
Hotels, resorts, and cruise lines	45
Automobile manufacturers	47
Household products	49
Metals	58
Gas utilities	58
Electric utilities	74

Source: Calculated by the authors from firm data taken from www.netadvantage.standardandpoors.com.

[2]Based on corporate after tax profits and dividend payout data from Bureau of Economic Analysis.

TABLE 15.2

Dividend Payout Ratios for Selected Firms in the Aerospace/Defense Industry

Company	2014 Dividend Payout Ratio*
B/E Aerospace, Inc.	0
Engility Holdings Inc	0
Esterline Technologies Corp.	0
Klx Inc.	0
Moog Inc.–Cl A	0
Taser International Inc.	0
Teledyne Technologies Inc.	0
Textron Inc.	4
Cubic Corp.	9
Huntington Ingalls Ind. Inc.	14
Curtiss-Wright Corp.	15
Raytheon Co.	26
Rockwell Collins Inc.	26
Northrop Grumman Corp.	27
General Dynamics Corp.	30
L-3 Communications Hldgs. Inc.	31
Exelis Inc.	34
United Technologies Corp.	34
Honeywell International Inc.	35
Boeing Co.	39
Lockheed Martin Corp.	48
National Presto Inds. Inc.	132

*Payout ratios will not equal the average shown in Table 15.1 as only values for selected firms are presented here.

74 percent. Likewise, within a given industry, though many firms may have similar dividend payout ratios, there can still be considerable variation. For example, as illustrated in Table 15.2, in the aerospace/defense industry, the dividend payout ratios range from a low of 0 percent to a high of 132 percent.[3] This section examines some of the more important factors that combine to determine a firm's dividend policy.

15-2b Legal Constraints

Most states have laws that regulate the dividend payments a firm chartered in that state can make. These laws basically state the following:

- A firm's capital cannot be used to make dividend payments.
- Dividends must be paid out of a firm's present and past *net* earnings.
- Dividends cannot be paid when the firm is insolvent.

The first restriction is termed the *capital impairment restriction*. In some states, *capital* is defined as including only the par value of common stock; in others, *capital* is more broadly defined also to include the contributed capital in excess of par account (sometimes called *capital surplus*).

For example, consider the following capital accounts on the balance sheet of Johnson Tool and Die Company:

[3]A payout ratio greater than 100 percent means that the firm's dividends exceeded their reported earnings.

Common stock ($5 par; 100,000 shares)	$ 500,000
Contributed capital in excess of par	400,000
Retained earnings	200,000
Total common stockholders' equity	$1,100,000

If Johnson Tool and Die is chartered in a state that defines capital as the par value of common stock, then it can pay out a total of $600,000 ($1,100,000 – $500,000 par value) in dividends. If, however, the company's home state restricts dividend payments to retained earnings alone, then the company could pay dividends only up to $200,000. Regardless of the dividend laws, however, dividends are paid from a firm's *cash* account with an offsetting entry to the *retained earnings* account.

The second restriction, called the *net earnings restriction*, requires that a firm have generated earnings *before* it is permitted to pay any cash dividends. This prevents the equity owners from withdrawing their initial investment in the firm and impairing the security position of any of the firm's creditors.

The third restriction, termed the *insolvency restriction*, states that an insolvent company may not pay cash dividends. When a company is insolvent, its liabilities exceed its assets. The payment of dividends would interfere with the creditors' prior claims on the firm's assets and therefore is prohibited.

These three restrictions affect different types of companies in different ways. New firms, or small firms with a minimum of accumulated retained earnings, are most likely to feel the weight of these legal constraints when determining their dividend policies, whereas well-established companies with histories of profitable performance and large retained earnings accounts are less likely to be influenced by them.

15-2c Restrictive Covenants

Restrictive covenants generally have more impact on dividend policy than the legal constraints just discussed. These covenants are contained in bond indentures, term loans, short-term borrowing agreements, lease contracts, and preferred stock agreements.

These restrictions limit the total amount of dividends a firm can pay. Sometimes they may state that dividends cannot be paid at all until a firm's earnings have reached a specified level. For example, Airgas Inc.'s 6.25 percent senior subordinated notes maturing in 2014 restricted the dividends that can be paid. Most line-of-credit agreements also place limitations on the dividends that can be paid.[4] In a dividend policy study of 80 troubled firms that cut dividends, researchers found that more than half of the firms apparently faced binding debt covenants in the years managers reduced dividends.[5]

In addition, *sinking fund requirements*, which state that a certain portion of a firm's cash flow must be set aside for the retirement of debt, sometimes limit dividend payments. Also, dividends may be prohibited if a firm's net working capital (current assets less current liabilities) or its current ratio does not exceed a certain predetermined level.

15-2d Tax Considerations

At various times, the top personal marginal tax rates on dividend income have been higher than the top marginal tax rates on long-term capital gains income. At other

[4]Line of credit is discussed in Chapter 16.

[5]Harry DeAngelo and Linda DeAngelo, "Dividend Policy and Financial Distress: An Empirical Investigation of Troubled NYSE Firms," *Journal of Finance* (December 1990): 1415–1431.

times, the two top marginal tax rates have been equal. For example, prior to the 1986 Tax Reform Act, the top marginal tax rate on dividend income was 50 percent compared with 20 percent on long-term capital gains income. The 1986 Tax Reform Act eliminated this differential by taxing both dividend and capital gains income at the same marginal rate. The Revenue Reconciliation Act of 1993 created new top marginal tax rates of 39.6 percent for dividend income and 28 percent for capital gains income for individual taxpayers. The Taxpayer Relief Act of 1997 lowered the maximum long-term capital gains rate for individuals to 20 percent, and the Economic Growth and Tax Relief Reconciliation Act of 2001 reduced the top marginal tax rate on dividend income to 38.6 percent for 2002–2003. The 2003 Tax Reduction Act cut the tax rate on dividend income to 15 percent, the same as the new tax rate on capital gains income (this applies to investors who are subject to an ordinary income tax bracket greater than 15 percent, which would be most investors). The American Taxpayer Relief Act of 2012 (signed into law on January 2, 2013, and applying to tax years 2013 and beyond) retained the 15 percent tax rate for dividends and capital gains, except for the highest bracket taxpayers. For taxpayers that fall into the highest ordinary income bracket (39.6 percent, roughly annual incomes greater than $400,000), the capital gains and dividend income tax rate is 20 percent. In addition, these individuals are subject to a Medicare surtax on investment income of 3.6 percent, making the effective capital gains and dividend income tax rate equal to 23.6 percent.

In spite of the equal tax rates on dividend and capital gains income, a tax disadvantage of dividends versus capital gains exists in that dividend income is taxed immediately (in the year it is received), but capital gains income (and corresponding taxes) can be deferred. If a corporation decides to retain its earnings in anticipation of providing growth and future capital appreciation for its investors, the investors are not taxed until their shares are sold. Consequently, for most investors, the *present value* of the taxes on future capital gains income is less than the taxes on an equivalent amount of current dividend income.[6] The deferral of taxes on capital gains can be viewed as an interest-free loan to the investor from the government.

Whereas the factors just explained tend to encourage corporations to retain their earnings, the IRS Code—specifically Sections 531 through 537—has the opposite effect. In essence, the code prohibits corporations from retaining an excessive amount of earnings to protect stockholders from paying taxes on dividends received.

If the IRS rules that a corporation has accumulated excess earnings to protect its stockholders from having to pay personal income taxes on dividends, the firm has to pay a heavy penalty tax on those earnings. It is the responsibility of the IRS to prove this allegation, however. Some companies are more likely to raise the suspicions of the IRS than others. For example, good candidates for IRS review are small, closely held corporations whose shareholders are in high marginal tax brackets, firms that pay consistently low dividends, and those that have large amounts of cash and marketable securities.

15-2e Liquidity and Cash Flow Considerations

Recall from the previous chapter that free cash flow represents the portion of a firm's cash flows available to service new debt, to *make dividend payments* to shareholders, and to invest in other projects. Because dividend payments represent cash outflows, the more liquid a firm is, the better able it is to pay dividends. Even if a firm has a past

[6]The exceptions to this rule are institutional investors (such as pension funds) that pay no income taxes and corporations (such as insurance companies) that pay a lower marginal tax rate on dividend income (10.5%) than on capital gains income (35%). See Appendix 2A for a discussion of corporate income taxes.

record of high earnings that have been reinvested, resulting in a large retained earnings balance, it may not be able to pay dividends unless it has sufficient liquid assets, primarily cash.[7] For example, Corning, which had paid cash dividends continuously since 1945, eliminated its $0.06 per share quarterly dividend during the economic downturn of 2001. The company was faced with a shriveling market for fiber-optic components, massive ($5.1 billion) write-downs of inventory and goodwill, and reduced cash flows. More recently, General Electric in 2009 cut its quarterly dividend from $0.31 to $0.10, or by 68 percent, as a result of cash flow pressures stemming from the global financial crisis of 2008. The company has paid dividends since 1899, but this was the first time it cut the dividends since 1938! As the Corning and General Electric examples illustrate, liquidity is likely to be a problem during a long business downturn, when both earnings and cash flows often decline.

Rapidly growing firms with many profitable investment opportunities also often find it difficult to maintain adequate liquidity and pay dividends at the same time. This is also supported by recent empirical evidence showing that young firms pay little in dividends because their investment opportunities exceed their internal cash flow generation. The evidence also reveals that, as firms evolve into more mature organizations, they pay greater dividends as their internally generated cash flows exceed the investment requirements.[8]

15-2f Borrowing Capacity and Access to the Capital Markets

Liquidity is desirable for a number of reasons. Specifically, it provides protection in the event of a financial crisis. It also provides the flexibility needed to take advantage of unusual financial and investment opportunities. There are other ways of achieving this flexibility and security, however. For example, companies frequently establish lines of credit and revolving credit agreements with banks, allowing them to borrow on short notice.[9] Large well-established firms are usually able to go directly to credit markets with either a bond issue or a sale of commercial paper. The more access a firm has to these external sources of funds, the better able it is to make dividend payments.

A small firm whose stock is closely held and infrequently traded often finds it difficult (or undesirable) to sell new equity shares in the markets. As a result, retained earnings are the only source of new equity. When a firm of this type is faced with desirable investment opportunities, the payment of dividends is often inconsistent with the objective of maximizing the value of the firm.

15-2g Earnings Stability

Most large widely held firms are reluctant to lower their dividend payments, even in times of financial stress. Therefore, a firm with a history of stable earnings is usually more willing to pay a higher dividend than a firm with erratic earnings. Studies have shown that cash flow volatility and dividend payouts are negatively related in the United States and internationally.[10] In a recent survey of financial executives, stability

---

[7]For example, John A. Brittain found that corporate dividend payments are positively related to a firm's liquidity. See John A. Brittain, *Corporate Dividend Policy* (Washington, DC: Brookings, 1966): 184–187.

[8]See, for example, Harry DeAngelo, Linda DeAngelo, and Rene Stulz, "Dividend Policy and the Earned Contributed Capital Mix: A Test of the Lifecycle Theory," *Journal of Financial Economics* (2006): 227–254. Also see David Denis and Igor Isobov, "Why Do Firms Pay Dividends? International Evidence on the Determinants of Dividend Policy," *Journal of Financial Economics* (2008): 62–82.

[9]See Chapters 16 and 19 for a more detailed discussion of this topic.

[10]See, for example, J. B. Chay and Jungwon Suh, "Payout Policy and Cash-Flow Uncertainty," *Journal of Financial Economics* (July 2009): 88–107.

of future earnings was considered to be one of the most important determinants of dividend policy.[11]

15-2h Growth Prospects

A rapidly growing firm usually has a substantial need for funds to finance the abundance of attractive investment opportunities. Instead of paying large dividends and then attempting to sell new shares to raise the equity investment capital it needs, this type of firm usually retains larger portions of its earnings and avoids the expense and inconvenience of public stock offerings. Table 15.3 illustrates the relationship between earnings growth rates and dividend payout ratios for selected companies. Note that the companies with the highest dividend payout ratios tend to have the lowest growth rates and vice versa. For example, Consolidated Edison paid out 65.8 percent of its earnings as dividends in 2015 and had a 10-year compound growth in earnings per share of 2.8 percent, which contrasts with Alphabet's (formerly Google) growth rate of 25.9 percent and a zero dividend payout ratio.

15-2i Shareholder Preferences

In a closely held corporation with relatively few stockholders, management may be able to set dividends according to the preferences of its stockholders. For example, assume

TABLE 15.3

Recent Dividend Payout Ratios and Earnings Growth Rates for Selected Companies

Company (Industry)	2015 Dividend Payout Ratio (%)	10-Year EPS Growth Rate (%)
VeriSign (Internet)	0.0	10.3
Alphabet/Google (Internet)	0.0	25.9
Ross Stores (retail special lines)	19.2	21.8
Disney (entertainment)	22.3	14.5
CVS Health (pharmacy services)	27.2	14.1
Polo Ralph Lauren (apparel)	29.7	9.2
Quest Diagnostics (medical services)	31.0	6.0
Best Buy (retail special lines)	35.0	1.6
Walgreens Boots (pharmacy services)	35.3	9.8
Walmart Stores (retail store)	43.6	5.5
Boeing Company (aerospace)	43.9	13.3
Target (retail store)	45.7	5.7
Hershey Company (food processing)	54.0	6.2
California Water (water utility)	58.3	4.5
Coca-Cola (beverages)	64.4	6.3
Consolidated Edison (electric utility)	65.8	2.8
General Electric (conglomerate)	70.8	−2.8
McDonald's (restaurant)	70.8	9.5
ExxonMobil (petroleum integrated)	71.1	−2.8
Kimberly-Clark (household products)	111.8	−1.8

Source: *Value Line Investment Survey*, various issues, 2015, 2016.

[11]See Alon Brav, John R. Graham, Campbell R. Harvey, and Roni Michaely, "Payout Policy in the 21st Century," *Journal of Financial Economics* (2005): 483–527.

that the majority of a firm's stockholders are in high marginal tax brackets. They probably favor a policy of high earnings retention, resulting in eventual price appreciation, over a high-payout dividend policy. However, high earnings retention implies that the firm has enough acceptable capital investment opportunities to justify the low-payout dividend policy. In addition, recall that the IRS does not permit corporations to retain excessive earnings if they have no legitimate investment opportunities. Also, a policy of high retention when investment opportunities are not available is inconsistent with the objective of maximizing shareholder wealth.

In a large corporation whose shares are widely held, it is nearly impossible for a financial manager to take individual shareholders' preferences into account when setting dividend policy. Some wealthy stockholders who are in high marginal income tax brackets may prefer that a company reinvest its earnings (that is, low payout ratio) to generate long-term capital gains. Other shareholders, such as retired individuals and those living on fixed incomes (sometimes referred to as "widows and orphans"), may prefer a high dividend rate. These shareholders may be willing to pay a premium for common stock in a company that provides a higher dividend yield. Large institutional investors that are in a zero income tax bracket, such as pension funds, university endowment funds, philanthropic organizations (for example, Ford Foundation), and trust funds, may prefer a high dividend yield for reasons different from those of private individual stockholders. First, endowment and trust funds are sometimes prohibited from spending the principal and must limit expenditures to the dividend (and/or interest) income generated by their investments. Second, pension and trust funds have a legal obligation to follow conservative investment strategies, which have been interpreted by the courts to mean investments in companies with a record of regular dividend payments.

clientele effect

It has been argued that firms tend to develop their own "clientele" of investors. This **clientele effect**, originally articulated by Merton Miller and Franco Modigliani, indicates that investors will tend to be attracted to companies that have dividend policies consistent with the investors' objectives.[12] Some companies, such as public utilities, that pay out a large percentage (typically 60 percent or more) of their earnings as dividends have traditionally attracted investors who desire a high dividend yield. In contrast, growth-oriented companies, which pay no (or very low) dividends, have tended to attract investors who prefer earnings retention and greater price appreciation. Empirical studies generally support the existence of a dividend clientele effect.[13]

15-2j Protection Against Dilution

If a firm adopts a policy of paying out a large percentage of its annual earnings as dividends, it may need to sell new shares of stock from time to time to raise the equity capital needed to invest in potentially profitable projects. If existing investors do not or cannot acquire a proportionate share of the new issue, their percentage ownership interest in the firm is *diluted*. Some firms choose to retain more of their earnings and pay out lower dividends rather than risk dilution.

One of the alternatives to high earnings retention, however, involves raising external capital in the form of debt. This increases the financial risk of the firm, ultimately raising the cost of equity capital and at some point lowering share prices.[14] If the firm feels that

[12]Merton Miller and Franco Modigliani, "Dividend Policy, Growth, and the Valuation of Shares," *Journal of Business* 34 (October 1961): 411–433.

[13]See Edwin J. Elton and Martin J. Gruber, "Marginal Stockholder Tax Rates and the Clientele Effect," *Review of Economics and Statistics* (February 1970): 68–74; R. Richardson Pettit, "Taxes, Transactions Costs and the Clientele Effect of Dividends," *Journal of Financial Economics* (December 1977): 419–436; and Mihir A. Desai and Li Jin, "Institutional Tax Clienteles and Payout Policy," *Journal of Financial Economics* (April 2011): 68–84.

[14]See Chapters 13 and 14.

it already has an optimal capital structure, a policy of obtaining all external capital in the form of debt is likely to be counterproductive, unless sufficient new equity capital is retained or acquired in the capital markets to offset the increased debt.

15-3 Dividend Policy and Firm Value

There are two major schools of thought among finance scholars regarding the effect dividend policy has on a firm's value. Although Miller and Modigliani argue that dividend policy does not have a significant effect on a firm's value,[15] Myron Gordon, David Durand, and John Lintner have argued that it does.[16] Each viewpoint is discussed in this section.

15-3a Arguments for the Irrelevance of Dividends

The group led by Miller and Modigliani (MM) contends that a firm's value is determined solely by its investment decisions and that the dividend payout ratio is a mere detail. They maintain that the effect of any particular dividend policy can be exactly offset by other forms of financing, such as the sale of new common equity shares. In essence, MM argue that dividend policy does not alter the total return received by an investor. Dividend policy merely affects the form of the return—dividends or capital gains. Recall from Chapter 2 (Equation 2.2) that the holding period return on a stock investment consists of dividends and the change in price (capital gain or capital loss). MM argue that, for firms that pay out most of their earnings in the form of dividends, the return will largely consist of dividends and a relatively small capital gains component. On the other hand, investors in firms that follow a low dividend payout policy are likely to receive most of their returns in the form of capital gains and relative little in the form of dividends. Given that the total return is unaffected, investors would not be concerned about how the return is split between dividends and capital gains. MM's argument depends on a number of key assumptions, including the following:

- **No taxes.** Under this assumption, investors are indifferent about whether they receive either dividend income or capital gains income.
- **No transaction costs.** This assumption implies that investors in the securities of firms paying small or no dividends can sell at no cost any number of shares they wish in order to convert capital gains into current income.
- **No issuance costs.** If firms did not have to pay issuance costs on the issue of new securities, they could acquire needed equity capital by issuing new common stock at the same cost as equity capital generated internally through retention of earnings. Holding all else constant, firms that pay dividends will need to issue new common stock to meet equity capital requirements for their investments.
- **Existence of a fixed investment policy.** According to MM, the firm's investment policy is not affected by its dividend policy. Furthermore, MM claim that investment policy, not dividend policy, really determines a firm's value.

Informational Content MM realize that there is considerable empirical evidence indicating that changes in dividend policy influence stock prices. As discussed later in this chapter, many firms favor a policy of reasonably stable dividends. An increase in dividends conveys a certain type of *information* to the shareholders, such as an

[15]Miller and Modigliani, "Dividend Policy, Growth, and the Valuation of Shares."

[16]See Myron Gordon, "The Savings, Investment and Valuation of a Corporation," *Review of Economics and Statistics* (February 1962): 37–51; Myron Gordon, *The Investment, Financing and Valuation of the Corporation* (Homewood, IL: Irwin, 1962); David Durand, "Bank Stocks and the Analysis of Covariance," *Econometrica* (January 1955): 30–45; and John Lintner, "Dividends, Earnings, Leverage, Stock Prices and the Supply of Capital to Corporations," *Review of Economics and Statistics* (August 1962): 243–269.

expectation of higher future earnings. Similarly, a cut in dividends may be viewed as conveying unfavorable information about the firm's earnings prospects. MM argue that this **informational content** of dividend policy influences shares prices, *not* the pattern of dividend payments per se.

informational content

Signaling Effects In effect, changes in dividend payments represent a signal to investors concerning management's assessment of the future earnings and cash flows of the company.[17] Management, as an insider, is perceived as having access to more complete information about future profitability than is available to investors outside the company. Dividend changes are thought to provide unambiguous signals about the company's future prospects—information that cannot be conveyed fully through other methods, such as annual reports and management presentations before security analysts. Indeed, many corporate announcements of dividend increases are accompanied by language expressing confidence in the future prospects of the firm. For example, in January 2011, CVS Caremark (the second-biggest U.S. drugstore chain, now known as CVS Health) raised its dividend by 43 percent. The CFO said "this substantial increase reflects our solid financial performance, our optimism with respect to our future growth and our very significant cash-generating capabilities."[18] The signaling effect of changes in dividends is similar to the signaling effect of changes in capital structure (discussed in Chapter 13).

Clientele Effect MM also claim that the existence of clienteles of investors favoring a particular firm's dividend policy should have no effect on share value. They recognize that a firm that changes its dividend policy could lose some stockholders to other firms with a more appealing dividend policy. This, in turn, may cause a temporary reduction in the price of the firm's stock. Other investors, however, who prefer the newly adopted dividend policy will view the firm as being undervalued and will purchase more shares. In the MM world, these transactions occur instantaneously and at no cost to the investor, the net result being that a stock's value remains unchanged.

15-3b Arguments for the Relevance of Dividends

Scholars belonging to the second school of thought argue that share values are indeed influenced by the division of earnings between dividends and retention. Basically, they contend that the MM propositions are reasonable—given MM's restrictive assumptions—but that dividend policy becomes important once these assumptions are removed.

Risk Aversion Specifically, Gordon asserts that shareholders who are risk averse may prefer some dividends over the promise of future capital gains because dividends are regular, certain returns, whereas future capital gains are less certain. This is sometimes referred to as the "bird-in-the-hand" theory. According to Gordon, dividends reduce investors' uncertainty, causing them to discount a firm's future earnings at a lower rate, thereby increasing the firm's value. In contrast, failure to pay dividends increases investors' uncertainty, which raises the discount rate and lowers share prices. Although there is some empirical evidence to support this argument, it is difficult to decide which is more valid—the MM informational content (or signaling effect) of dividends approach, or the Gordon uncertainty resolution approach.

---

[17]Merton H. Miller and Kevin Rock, "Dividend Policy Under Asymmetric Information," *Journal of Finance* (September 1985): 1031–1051; and Paul M. Healy and Krishna G. Palepu, "Earnings Information Conveyed by Dividend Initiations and Omissions," *Journal of Financial Economics* 21 (1988): 149–175.

[18]Shirley A. Lazo, "Speaking of Dividends—The Benefits of CVS," *Barron's* (January 17, 2011): 23.

15-3c Transaction Costs

If the assumption of no transaction costs for investors is removed, then investors care whether they are paid cash dividends or receive capital gains. In the MM world, investors who own stock paying low or no dividends could periodically sell a portion of their holdings to satisfy current income requirements. In practice, however, brokerage charges make such liquidations expensive and imperfect substitutes for regular dividend payments.

15-3d Taxes

Removal of the no-tax assumption also makes a difference to shareholders. As discussed earlier, shareholders in high income tax brackets may prefer low (or no) dividends and reinvestment of earnings within the firm because of the ability to defer taxes into the future (when the stock is sold) on such income. In his study of dividend policy from 1920 to 1960, John A. Brittain found evidence in support of this proposition.[19] In general, he found that rising tax rates tend to reduce dividend payout rates. Moser confirms this for a more recent time period that includes tax rate changes from 1986 to 2004.[20] He found that in periods when the dividend tax penalty increases, firms are less likely to increase dividends, preferring instead to distribute earnings through share repurchases.

15-3e Issuance (Flotation) Costs

The existence of issuance costs on new equity sales also tends to make earnings retention more desirable. Given a firm's investment policy, the payout of earnings the firm needs for investments requires it to raise external equity. External equity is more expensive, however, because of issuance costs. Therefore, the use of external equity will raise the firm's cost of capital and reduce the value of the firm. In addition, the cost of selling small issues of equity to meet investment needs is likely to be prohibitively high for most firms. Therefore, firms with sufficient investment opportunities to profitably use their retained funds tend to favor retention.[21]

15-3f Agency Costs

It has also been argued that the payment of dividends can reduce *agency costs*[22] between shareholders and management.[23] According to this argument, managers are likely to misuse free cash flow (cash flow beyond what is needed to run the business) by investing it in unprofitable projects or diverting it to uses for their private benefit (for example, buy a corporate jet). To avoid this, shareholders demand that excess cash flow be distributed to them. In addition, payment of dividends provides a monitoring benefit. The payment of dividends reduces the amount of retained earnings available for reinvestment and requires the use of more external equity funds to finance growth. Raising external equity funds in the capital markets subjects the company to the scrutiny of regulators

---

[19]Brittain, *Corporate Dividend Policy*, especially Chapter 4.

[20]William J. Moser, "The Effect of Shareholder Taxes on Corporate Payout Choice," *Journal of Financial and Quantitative Analysis* (December 2007): 991–1020.

[21]This argument provides the basis for the passive residual or marginal theory of dividends, discussed later in this chapter.

[22]Agency costs are discussed in Chapter 1.

[23]For a conceptual discussion, see Michael C. Jensen, "Agency Costs of Free Cash Flow, Corporate Finance, and Takeovers," *American Economic Review* 76 (May 1986): 323–329; Frank Easterbrook, "Two Agency Cost Explanations of Dividends," *American Economic Review* 74 (1984): 650–659. For empirical studies, see M. Rozeff, "Growth, Beta and Agency Costs as Determinants of Dividend Payout Ratios," *Journal of Financial Research* (Fall 1982): 249–259; Chinmoy Ghosh and J. Randall Woolridge, "An Analysis of Shareholder Reaction to Dividend Cuts and Omissions," *Journal of Financial Research* (Winter 1988): 281–294; and David J. Denis and Igor Osobov, "Why Do Firms Pay Dividends? International Evidence on the Determinants of Dividend Policy," *Journal of Financial Economics* (July 2008): 62–82.

(such as the SEC) and potential investors, thereby serving as a monitoring function of managerial performance. The agency argument has been used by a number of analysts and investors to pressure several high-tech companies (for example, Apple Inc.) to stop hoarding their excess cash flow and initiate or raise their dividends.[24]

15-3g Conclusions Regarding Dividend Relevance

The empirical evidence as to whether dividend policy affects firm valuation is mixed. Some studies have found that, because of tax effects, investors require higher pretax returns on high-dividend payout stocks than on low-dividend payout stocks.[25] Other studies have found that share prices are unaffected by dividend payout policy.[26]

Many practitioners believe that dividends are important, both for their informational content and because external equity capital is more expensive than retained equity.[27] Thus, when establishing an optimal dividend policy, a firm should consider shareholder preferences along with investment opportunities and the relative cost of retained equity versus externally raised equity.

15-4 Dividend Policies

The previous sections examined a number of practical considerations that influence a firm's board of directors in determining an "optimal" dividend policy. In this section, several alternative dividend strategies are discussed.

15-4a Passive Residual Policy

passive residual policy

The **passive residual policy** suggests that a firm should retain its earnings as long as it has investment opportunities that promise higher rates of return than the required rate. For example, assume that a firm's shareholders could invest their dividends in stocks of similar risk with an expected rate of return (dividends plus capital gains) of 12 percent. This 12 percent figure, then, would constitute the required rate of return on the firm's retained earnings.[28] As long as the firm can invest these earnings to earn this required rate or more, it should not pay dividends (according to the passive residual policy) because such payments would require either that the firm forgo some acceptable investment opportunities or raise necessary equity capital in the more expensive external capital markets.

Interpreted literally, the residual theory implies that dividend payments will vary from year to year, depending on available investment opportunities. There is strong evidence,

[24]Andrew Bary, "Tech's Payout Problem," *Barron's* (September 13, 2010): 19–20.

[25]See Robert H. Litzenberger and Krishna Ramaswamy, "The Effect of Personal Taxes and Dividends on Capital Asset Prices: Theory and Empirical Evidence," *Journal of Financial Economics* (June 1979): 163–196; Litzenberger and Ramaswamy, "Dividends, Short-Selling Restrictions, Tax Induced Investor Clienteles and Market Equilibrium," *Journal of Finance* (May 1980); and Litzenberger and Ramaswamy, "The Effects of Dividends on Common Stock Prices: Tax Effects or Information Effects?" *Journal of Finance* (May 1982): 429–444.

[26]See Fischer Black and Myron Scholes, "The Effects of Dividend Yield and Dividend Policy on Common Stock Prices and Returns," *Journal of Financial Economics* (May 1974): 1–22; and Merton H. Miller and Myron S. Scholes, "Dividends and Taxes: Some Empirical Evidence," *Journal of Political Economy* (December 1983): 1118–1141.

[27]For a survey of chief financial officers' attitudes on dividend policy, see H. Kent Baker, Gail E. Farrelly, and Richard B. Edelman, "A Survey of Management Views on Dividend Policy," *Financial Management* (Autumn 1985): 78–84; and Brav et al., "Payout Policy in the 21st Century," *Journal of Financial Economics* (2005): 483–527.

[28]This is the rate of return that must be earned on the equity-financed portion of new investments. To earn this return on equity, new investments must earn an overall rate of return equal to the weighted cost of capital—reflecting the fact that all investments are made with a mix of debt and equity funds in the proportions of the target capital structure.

however, that most firms try to maintain a rather stable dividend payment record over time. Of course, this does not mean that firms ignore the principles of the residual theory in making their dividend decisions because dividends can be smoothed out from year to year in two ways.[29] First, a firm can choose to retain a larger percentage of earnings during years when funding needs are large. If the firm continues to grow, it can manage to do this without reducing the dollar amount of the dividend. Second, a firm can borrow the funds it needs, temporarily raise its debt-to-equity ratio, and avoid a dividend cut in this way. Because issue costs are lower for large offerings of long-term debt, long-term debt capital tends to be raised in large, lumpy sums. If many good investment opportunities are available to a firm during a particular year, this type of borrowing is preferable to cutting back on dividends. The firm will need to retain earnings in future years to bring its debt-to-equity ratio back in line. A firm that has many good investment opportunities for a number of years may eventually be forced to cut its dividend and/or sell new equity shares to meet financing requirements and maintain an optimal capital structure.

The residual theory also suggests that growth firms will normally have lower dividend payout ratios than firms in mature, low-growth industries. As shown earlier in Table 15.3, companies with low growth rates (such as Consolidated Edison and California Water) tend to have rather high payout ratios, whereas firms with high growth rates (such as Alphabet [formerly Google] and VeriSign) tend to have rather low payout ratios.

15-4b Stable Dollar Dividend Policy

Evidence indicates that most firms—and stockholders—prefer reasonably stable dividend policies. This stability is characterized by a rather strong reluctance to reduce the dollar amount of dividends from one period to the next. Similarly, significant increases in the dollar dividend rate normally are not made until the firm's management is satisfied that future earnings will be high enough to justify the larger dividend. Thus, although dividend rates tend to follow increases in earnings, they also tend to lag behind them to a certain degree.

Figure 15.1 illustrates the relationship between corporate dividends and profits since 1960. It is apparent from this chart that aggregate dividend payments fluctuate much less than corporate earnings. There has been a strong upward trend in the amount of dividends paid, with very few years showing significant reductions. This is in sharp contrast to the more erratic record of corporate earnings.

More specifically, Figure 15.2 shows the dividend and earnings history of Leggett and Platt Inc., a firm that makes box springs and other components for the furniture industry. Although there has been an upward trend in dividends over time, dividend increases tend to lag earnings increases. Annual dividend payments are also more stable than earnings figures. Note, for instance, that despite the significant drop in earnings per share from \$1.57 to \$0.28 in 2007, dividends were not cut back; in fact, the firm raised the dividends from \$0.67 to \$0.78 per share, indicating management's confidence that the decline in earnings in 2007 was temporary. The graph confirms the temporary nature of the earnings decline.

Investors prefer stable dividends for a variety of reasons. For instance, many investors feel that dividend changes possess *informational content*; they equate changes in a firm's dividend levels with profitability. A cut in dividends may be interpreted as a signal that

[29]Robert C. Higgins, "The Corporate Dividend-Saving Decision," *Journal of Financial and Quantitative Analysis* (March 1972): 1531–1538, provides empirical support for the view that each period's dividends are a function of longer-term trends.

FIGURE 15.1

Annual Dividend Payments and Earnings

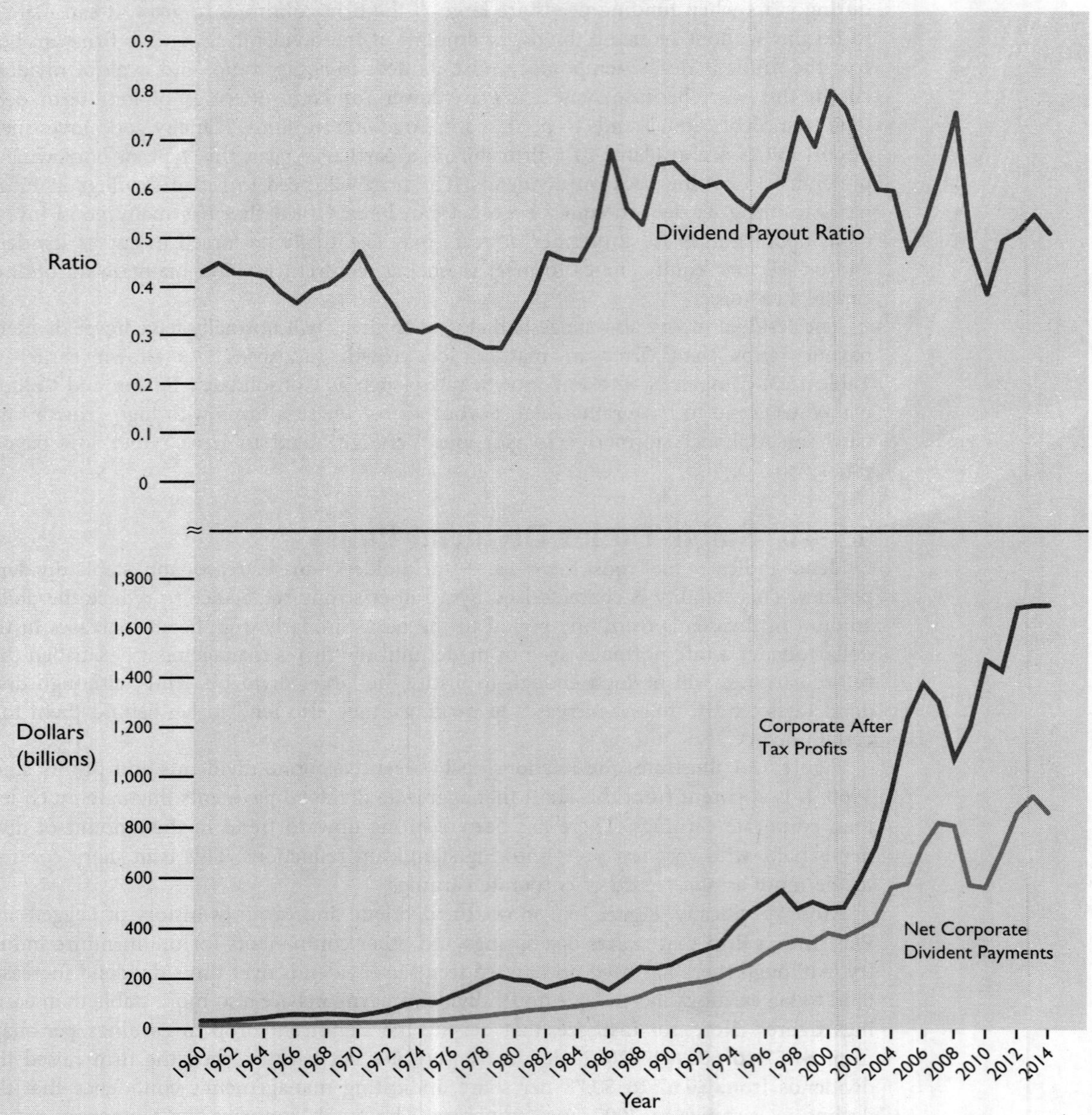

the firm's long-run profit potential has declined. Similarly, a dividend increase is seen as a verification of the expectation that future profits will increase.[30]

In addition, many shareholders need and depend on a constant stream of dividends for their cash income requirements. Although they can sell off some of their shares as an

[30]Sometimes, however, an increase in a firm's dividend payout ratio may be interpreted to mean that the firm no longer has a large number of high-return investment opportunities available to it.

alternative source of current income, associated transaction costs and odd-lot charges make this an imperfect substitute for steady dividend income.

Some managers feel that a stable and growing dividend policy tends to reduce investor uncertainty concerning future dividend streams. They believe investors will pay a higher price for the stock of a firm that pays stable dividends, thereby reducing the firm's cost of equity.

And, finally, stable dividends are legally desirable. Many regulated financial institutions—such as bank trust departments, pension funds, and insurance companies—are limited as to the types of common stock they are allowed to own. To qualify for inclusion in these so-called legal lists, a firm must have a record of continuous and stable dividends. The failure to pay a dividend or the reduction of a dividend amount can result in removal from these lists. This, in turn, reduces the potential market for the firm's shares and may lead to price declines. As shown in Figure 15.2, Leggett and Platt not only continued but increased its per share dividend in 2007, even though its earnings per share was less than the dividends per share.

15-4c Other Dividend Payment Policies

Some firms have adopted a *constant payout ratio* dividend policy. A firm that uses this approach pays out a certain percentage of each year's earnings—for example, 40 percent—as dividends. If the firm's earnings vary substantially from year to year, dividends also will fluctuate. (The late Penn Central Company had adopted this type of dividend payout policy at one time.)

As shown in Figure 15.1, the aggregate dividend payout ratio for U.S. corporations has generally ranged between 35 and 70 percent. This finding supports the notion that firms try to maintain fairly constant payout ratios over time. On a year-to-year basis,

FIGURE 15.2

Dividends and Earnings for Leggett & Platt, Inc.

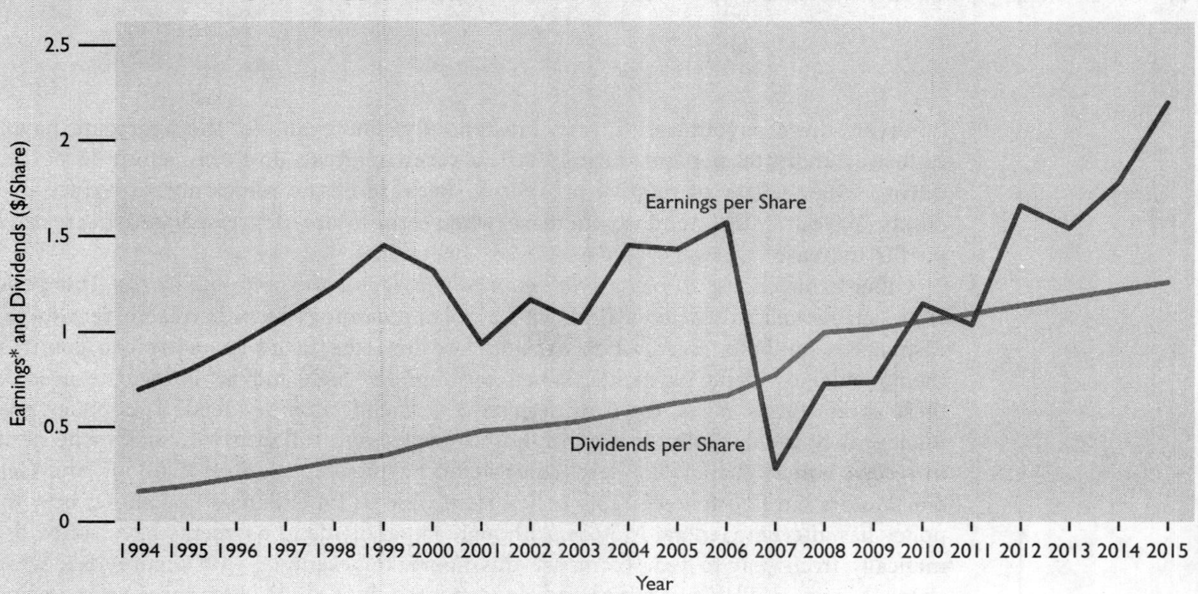

*Excludes nonrecurring gains and losses.

ENTREPRENEURIAL ISSUES

Dividend Policy

Small firms typically differ significantly from larger, more mature firms in terms of the dividend policies they follow. For example, one study of the financial differences between small and large firms found that the average dividend payout ratio for large firms was in excess of 40 percent, whereas the average dividend payout ratio for small firms was less than 3 percent.[a] The study found that the majority of small firms that were planning an initial public stock offering paid no dividends at all in the year prior to their stock offering.

What are the reasons for this dramatic difference in dividend policies between large and small firms? First, it is likely that many small firms are in the rapid growth phase of their business development. During this early phase, the firm is often short of funds needed to finance planned investments and increases in working capital. Another aspect related to the growth phase argument is that small firms typically have restricted access to capital markets, relative to larger firms. A small, closely held firm has no easy way to raise equity capital other than through the retention of earnings. If new shares of stock can be sold, the owners risk a loss of control. In addition, stock offerings for small firms are extremely expensive, both in terms of transactions costs and minority interest discounts (as well as marketability) that investors demand.

Another reason dividend policies differ between small and large firms is that many small firms are closely held by only one or a few owners, and the dividend policy of these firms frequently reflects the income preferences of these individuals. If funds are retained in the firm, taxes are postponed until a distribution is made at some time in the future or until the firm is sold.

As firms mature, their need for funds to support rapid growth declines, and their access to capital markets improves. At this point, they show a tendency to begin or increase dividend payouts. For example, Microsoft, which was founded in 1975, paid no cash dividends until 2003. Since then, the company has been steadily increasing its annual cash dividend payments. In 2012 Microsoft's dividends amounted to approximately half its earnings, suggesting that it is now a "mature" company with limited growth opportunities and little need to accumulate retained earnings.

Clearly, the dividend policies of small and large firms differ significantly. Small firms often pay out a smaller percentage of their earnings than larger firms because small firms tend to be growing rapidly and have limited access to the capital markets for other sources of funds to support their growth.

[a] Ernest W. Walker and J. W. Petty II, "Financial Differences Between Large and Small Firms," *Financial Management* (Winter 1978): 61–68.

however, these payout ratios vary substantially. For example, the aggregate payout ratio was about 68 percent during 2001, a recession year, and only about 35 percent during 1966, a year of relative prosperity. Because of the reluctance to reduce dividends, payout ratios tend to increase when profits are depressed and decrease as profits increase.

Other firms choose to pay a *small quarterly dividend plus year-end extras.* This policy is especially well suited for a firm with a volatile earnings record, volatile year-to-year cash needs, or both. Even when earnings are low, the firm's investors can count on their regular dividend payments. When earnings are high and no immediate need for these excess funds exists, the firm declares a year-end extra dividend. This policy gives management the flexibility to retain funds as needed and still satisfy investors who desire to receive some "guaranteed" level of dividend payments. U.S. Steel, DuPont, and General Motors have all followed this policy from time to time. Figure 15.3 shows how this policy has affected General Motors. Although actual dividend payments have varied dramatically from year to year (compare this figure, for example, with Figure 15.2, which shows Leggett & Platt's earnings and dividends), only in 1993, after three years of huge losses, were dividends cut below $1.20, the regular rate in effect in 1975. Likewise, in

FIGURE 15.3

Dividends and Earnings per Share for General Motors

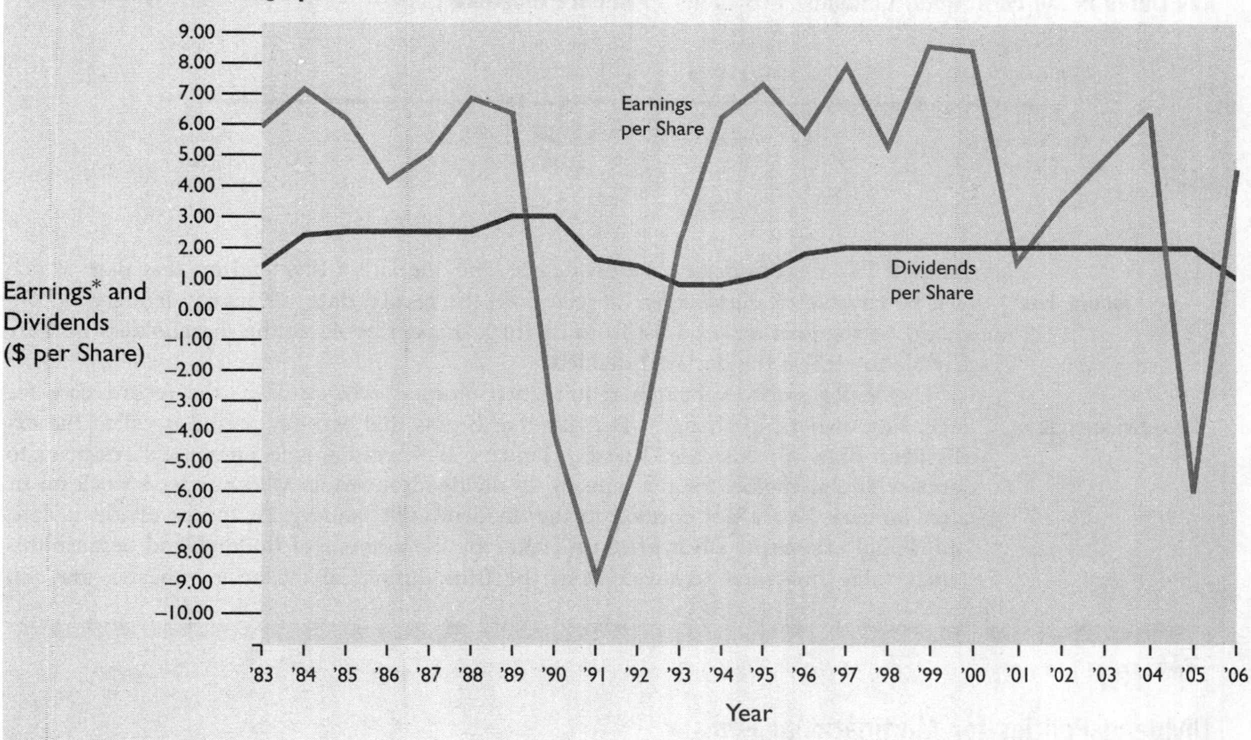

*Excludes nonrecurring gains and losses.

Source: *Value Line Investment Survey* (New York: Value Line, Inc., March 2, 2007).

2006, only after several years of declining market share and massive restructuring changes did General Motors cut in half its regular dividend rate of $2 per share, which had been in effect since 1997.[31]

15-4d How Dividends Are Paid

In most firms, the board of directors holds quarterly or semiannual meetings to evaluate the firm's past performance and decide the level of dividends to be paid during the next period. Changes in the amount of dividends paid tend to be made rather infrequently—especially in firms that follow a stable dividend policy—and only after there is clear evidence that the firm's future earnings are likely to be either permanently higher or permanently lower than previously reported levels.

Most firms follow a dividend declaration and payment procedure similar to that outlined in the following paragraphs. This procedure usually revolves around a *declaration date*, an *ex-dividend date*, a *record date*, and a *payment date*.

declaration date

Figure 15.4 is a time line that illustrates the Ford Motor Company's dividend payment procedure. The firm's board of directors meets on the **declaration date**—Tuesday,

[31]In the aftermath of the financial crisis of 2008, General Motors suspended its dividend and later declared bankruptcy in June 2009. The company emerged from bankruptcy a month later. General Motors resumed payment of dividends in 2014.

FIGURE 15.4

Key Dates in the Ford Motor Company's Dividend Payment Procedure

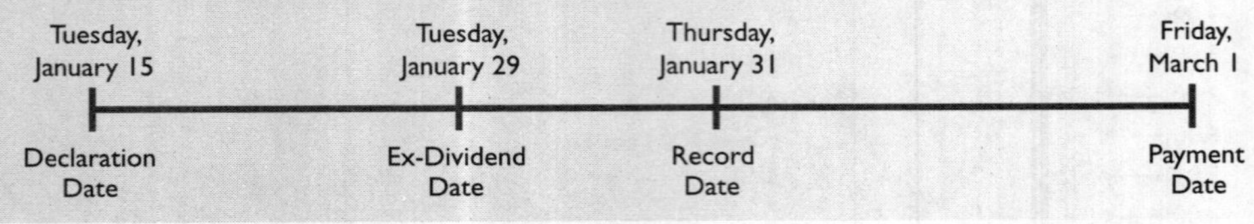

January 15—to consider future dividends. They declare a dividend on that date, which will be payable to *shareholders of record* on the **record date**, Thursday, January 31. On that date, the firm makes a list from its stock transfer books of the shareholders who are eligible to receive the declared dividend.

record date

The major stock exchanges require two *business days* prior to the record date for recording ownership changes. The day that begins this two-day period is called the **ex-dividend date**—in this case, Tuesday, January 29. Investors who purchase stock prior to January 29 are eligible for the January 29 dividend; investors who purchase stock on or after January 29 are not entitled to the dividend. On January 29, the ex-dividend date, one would expect the stock price to decline by the amount of the dividend because this much value has been removed from the firm. Empirical evidence indicates that, on

ex-dividend date

INTERNATIONAL ISSUES

Dividend Policies for Multinational Firms

Dividend payments from foreign subsidiaries represent the primary means of transferring funds to the parent company. Many factors determine the dividend payments that are made back to the parent, including tax effects, exchange risk, political risk, the availability of funds, the financing requirements of the foreign subsidiary, and the existence of exchange controls.[a]

Taxes in the host country play a significant role in determining a multinational subsidiary firm's dividend policy. For example, in Germany, the tax rate on earnings paid out as dividends is much lower than the tax rate on retained earnings. When the parent is located in a country with a strong currency and the subsidiary is located in a country with a weak currency, there will be a tendency to rapidly transfer a greater portion of the subsidiary's earnings to the parent to minimize the exchange rate risk. In the face of high political risk, the parent may require the subsidiary to transfer all locally generated funds to the parent except for funds necessary to meet the working capital and planned capital expenditure needs of the subsidiary.

As is true for domestic enterprises, large and more mature foreign subsidiaries tend to remit a greater proportion of their earnings to the parent, reflecting the reduced growth opportunities and needs for funds that exist in larger firms. Also, when the foreign subsidiary has good access to capital within the host country, it tends to pay larger dividends to the parent because funds needed for future expansion can be obtained locally. Finally, some countries with balance-of-payments problems often restrict the payment of dividends from the subsidiary back to the parent.

Many firms require that the payout ratio for foreign subsidiaries be set equal to the payout ratio of the parent. The argument in favor of this strategy is that it requires each subsidiary to bear an equal proportionate burden of the parent's dividend policy. However, even when this strategy is adopted, it often is modified on a country-by-country basis to reflect the considerations just identified.

[a] A more thorough discussion of these issues is found in Alan C. Shapiro, *Multinational Financial Management*, 6th ed. (Upper Saddle River, NJ: Prentice-Hall, 1999): Chapter 15.

average, stock prices decline by less than the amount of the dividend on the ex-dividend day.[32]

payment date

The **payment date** is normally four weeks or so after the record date—in this case, March 1. On this date, Ford makes dividend payments to the holders of record.

15-4e Dividend Reinvestment Plans

dividend reinvestment plans (DRIPs)

In recent years, many firms have established **dividend reinvestment plans (DRIPs)**. Under these plans, shareholders can have their dividends automatically reinvested in additional shares of the company's common stock. There are two types of dividend reinvestment plans. One type involves the purchase of *existing* stock, and the other type involves the purchase of *newly issued* stock. The first type of plan is executed through a bank that, acting as a trustee, purchases the stock on the open market and then allocates it on a pro rata basis to the participating shareholders. In the second type of plan, the cash dividends of the participants are used to purchase, often at a small discount (up to 5 percent) from the market price, newly issued shares of stock.

This second type of plan enables the firm to raise substantial amounts of new equity capital over time as well as to reduce the cash outflows required by dividend payments. The advantage of a dividend reinvestment plan to shareholders is that it represents a convenient method for them to purchase additional shares of the company's common stock while saving brokerage commissions. The primary disadvantage is that shareholders must pay taxes on the cash dividends reinvested in the company, even though they never receive any cash.[33]

15-5 Stock Dividends and Stock Splits

stock dividend

A **stock dividend** is the payment of additional shares of stock to common stockholders. It involves making a transfer from the retained earnings account to the other stockholders' equity accounts.

For example, the Colonial Copies Company has the following common stockholders' equity:

Pre–Stock Dividend Common Stockholders' Equity

Common stock ($5 par, 100,000 shares)	$ 500,000
Contributed capital in excess of par	1,000,000
Retained earnings	5,000,000
Total common stockholders' equity	$6,500,000

Suppose the firm declares a 10 percent stock dividend and existing shareholders receive 10,000 (10% × 100,000) new shares. Because stock dividend accounting is usually based on the predividend market price, a total of $200,000 (10,000 shares × an assumed market price of $20 per share) is transferred from the firm's retained earnings account to the

[32]See Edwin J. Elton and Martin J. Gruber, "Marginal Stockholder Tax Rates and the Clientele Effect," *Review of Economics and Statistics* (February 1978): 68–74; Avner Kalay, "The Ex-Dividend Behavior of Stock Prices: A Re-examination of the Clientele Effect," *Journal of Finance* (September 1983): 1059–1070; and Jeff Whitworth and Ramesh P. Rao, "Do Tax Law Changes Influence Ex-Dividend Stock Price Behavior? Evidence from 1926–2005," *Financial Management* (Spring 2010): 419–445.

[33]See Richard H. Pettway and R. Phil Malone, "Automatic Dividend Reinvestment Plans of Nonfinancial Corporations," *Financial Management* (Winter 1973): 11–18, for a more detailed discussion of these plans; and Harold Bierman, "The Dividend Reinvestment Plan Puzzle," *Applied Financial Economics* 7 (1997): 267–271.

other stockholders' equity accounts. Of this \$200,000, \$50,000 (\$5 par × 10,000 shares) is added to the common stock account, and the remaining \$150,000 is added to the contributed capital in excess of par account. Following the stock dividend, Colonial has the following common stockholders' equity:

Post–Stock Dividend Common Stockholders' Equity	
Common stock (\$5 par, 110,000 shares)	\$ 550,000
Contributed capital in excess of par	1,150,000
Retained earnings	4,800,000
Total common stockholders' equity	\$6,500,000

The net effect of this transaction is to increase the number of outstanding shares and to redistribute funds among the firm's capital accounts. The firm's total stockholders' equity remains unchanged, and each shareholder's proportionate claim to the firm's earnings remains constant. For example, if Colonial Copies Company has 100,000 shares outstanding prior to a 10 percent stock dividend and its total earnings are \$200,000 (\$2 per share), a stockholder who owns 100 shares has a claim on \$200 of the firm's earnings. Following the 10 percent stock dividend, earnings per share decline to \$1.82 (\$200,000/110,000 shares). The stockholder who originally owned 100 shares now has 110 shares but continues to have a claim on only \$200 (110 shares × \$1.82 per share) of the firm's earnings.

Because each shareholder's proportionate claim on a firm's net worth and earnings remains unchanged in a stock dividend, the market price of each share of stock should decline in proportion to the number of new shares issued. This relationship can be expressed as follows:

$$\text{Post–stock dividend price} = \frac{\text{Pre–stock dividend price}}{1 + \text{Percentage stock dividend rate}} \tag{15.1}$$

In the Colonial Copies example, a \$20 pre–stock dividend price should result in a post–stock dividend price of:

$$\begin{aligned}\text{Post–stock dividend price} &= \frac{\$20}{1 + 0.10}\\ &= \$18.18\end{aligned}$$

If a stockholder's wealth prior to the dividend is \$2,000 (100 shares × \$20 per share), post dividends wealth should also remain at \$2,000 (110 shares × \$18.18 per share).

In essence, all a stock dividend does is increase the number of pieces of paper in the stockholders' hands. Nevertheless, firms declare stock dividends for a number of reasons. First, a stock dividend may have the effect of broadening the ownership of a firm's shares because existing shareholders often sell their stock dividends.[34] Second, in the case of a firm that already pays a cash dividend, a stock dividend results in an effective increase in cash dividends, providing that the per-share dividend rate is not reduced. (It is rare for a firm to declare a stock dividend and reduce its cash dividend rate at the same time.) Finally, the declaration of stock dividends effectively lowers the per-share price of a stock, thereby possibly broadening its investment appeal to more investors, especially individual investors.

HTTP:
Using a search engine such as Google, key in the term *stock split*, and you'll receive thousands of hits. Many of the links are companies announcing their stock splits. As you'll see, splitting stocks is a very common corporate practice.

www.google.com

[34]See C. Austin Barker, "Evaluation of Stock Dividends," *Harvard Business Review* (July/August 1958): 99–114, for an empirical confirmation of this point.

Stock splits

Stock splits are similar to stock dividends in that they have the effect of increasing the number of shares of stock outstanding and reducing the price of each outstanding share. From an accounting standpoint, stock splits are accomplished by reducing the par value of existing shares of stock and increasing the number of shares outstanding. For example, in a two-for-one stock split, the number of shares would be doubled. Although stock splits have an impact similar to stock dividends, they normally are not considered an element of a firm's dividend policy. They are discussed in greater detail in Chapter 7.

15-6 Share Repurchases as Dividend Decisions

In addition to the reasons discussed in Chapter 7 for repurchasing stock, share repurchases can be undertaken as part of the firm's dividend decision. According to the passive residual dividend policy, a firm that has more funds than it needs for investments should pay a cash dividend to shareholders. In lieu of, or in addition to, cash dividends, some firms also repurchase outstanding shares from time to time. For example, for the past few years, Texas Instruments, in addition to paying cash dividends, has spent significant amounts buying back its stock each year.

Since the 1980s, share repurchases have become increasingly popular. One study found that aggregate repurchases represented 26 percent of common stock earnings over the 1983–1997 period, compared with only 3 percent during the 1973–1977 period.[35] In recent years, the tilt in favor of stock repurchases over dividends has become even more pronounced. From 2004 to 2011, companies in the *Standard & Poor's 500* stock index (S&P 500) spent $2.7 trillion on repurchases and only $1.8 trillion on dividends. Thus, repurchases represent a majority of the payout today, at least for the large firms that constitute the S&P 500 index.[36] However, the amount spent on repurchases varies over time, depending on the earnings and liquidity of the firm. In 2007, companies in the S&P 500 stock index bought back a record $590 billion of their shares, more than quadruple the $135 billion bought back in 2003.[37] In 2009, however, repurchases among the S&P 500 companies declined to only $138 billion, reflecting the limited liquidity of the firms in the aftermath of the financial crisis that started in late 2007. However, by 2014, when the economy was in full swing, repurchases by S&P 500 companies bounced back and even exceeded their previous record at S634 billion.[38]

15-6a Procedures for Repurchasing Shares

Firms carry out share repurchase programs in a number of ways. For example, a company may buy directly from its stockholders in what is termed a *tender offer* transaction; it may purchase the stock in the open market, known simply as an *open market repurchase* transaction; or it may privately negotiate purchases from large holders, such as institutions. When a firm initiates a share repurchase program through a tender offer, it is, in effect,

[35]Eugene F. Fama and Kenneth R. French, "Disappearing Dividends: Changing Firm Characteristics or Lower Propensity to Pay?" *Journal of Financial Economics* (April 2001): 3–43.

[36]Nathaniel Popper, "Buybacks Expected to Increase," *The New York Times* (November 27, 2012).

[37]Katrina Brooker, "Buybacks Take a Beating," CNNMoney.com, October 17, 2008.

[38]Chris Brightman, Vitale Kalesnik, and Mark Clements, "Are Buybacks an Oasis or a Mirage," *Research Affiliates* (October 2015), www.researchaffiliates.com (accessed February 7, 2016).

giving shareholders a *put option*—an option to sell their shares at a fixed price above the current market price for a limited period of time. Tender offer repurchases today are rare events; the vast majority of repurchases are undertaken in the open market.

treasury stock

Repurchased shares become known as **treasury stock**. Treasury stock is often used to facilitate mergers and acquisitions; to satisfy the conversion provisions of some preferred stock and debentures, as well as the exercise of warrants; and to meet the need for new shares in executive stock options and employee stock purchase plans. From the stockholders' perspective, share repurchases increase earnings per share for the remaining outstanding shares and also increase stock prices, assuming that investors continue to apply the same *price-to-earnings (P/E) ratio* to the earnings per share before and after repurchase.[39] (Recall from Chapter 3 that the P/E ratio is equal to the price per share divided by the earnings per share. For example, if a stock sells for $40 per share and earns $8 per share, its P/E multiple is 5 [40/8]. The P/E multiple indicates the value placed by investors on a dollar of a firm's earnings. It is influenced by a number of factors, including earnings prospects and investors' perceptions regarding a firm's risk.)

Normally, a firm will announce its intent to buy back some of its own shares so that investors will know why there is sudden additional trading in the stock. An announcement of repurchase is also useful to current shareholders, who may not want to sell their shares before they have had an opportunity to receive any price appreciation expected to result from the repurchase program.

15-6b Share Repurchase Versus Cash Dividend Example

In this section we illustrate the impact of a share repurchase and an equivalent cash dividend on stock price. Suppose that the Hewlett-Packard (HP) Company plans to distribute to its shareholders $750 million in the form of either a one-time extra cash dividend or a share repurchase. The company has expected earnings of $625 million during the coming year and approximately 250 million shares currently outstanding. The current (ex-dividend) market price of HP stock is $50 per share. The company can pay a one-time extra cash dividend of $3 per share ($750 million divided by 250 million shares). Alternatively, it can make a tender offer at $53 per share for 14,150,943 shares ($750 million divided by $53 per share).

If HP decides to declare a one-time extra cash dividend of $3 per share, shareholder wealth would be $53 per share, consisting of the $50 (ex-dividend) share price plus the $3 dividend. The effect on shareholder wealth before and after the stock repurchase is shown in Table 15.4, assuming that the price-to-earnings (P/E) ratio remains the same at 20 ($50 stock price per share divided by $2.50 earnings per share). If HP repurchases $750 million worth of its common stock (at $53 per share), then shareholder wealth is $53 per share, with $3 of this value representing price appreciation. Note that the pretax returns to shareholders are the same under each alternative.

This example illustrates that, ignoring taxes, transaction costs, and other market imperfections, shareholders should be indifferent between equivalent returns from cash dividends and share repurchases. In other words, the value of the firm should not be affected by the manner in which returns (cash dividends versus capital gains) are paid to shareholders. However, empirical studies suggest that share repurchases do increase

[39] If a stock purchase results in a substantial increase in the debt-to-equity ratio, the new P/E ratio may be lower because of increased financial risk.

TABLE 15.4

Hewlett-Packard Company Share Repurchase

	Before Repurchase	After Repurchase
Expected net earnings	$625,000,000	$625,000,000
Shares outstanding	250,000,000	235,849,057
Expected earnings per share	$2.50	$2.65
Price-to-earnings (P/E) ratio	20×	20×
Expected share price (ex-dividend)	$50	$53
Expected dividend	$3	$0

stock prices (that is, value of the firm).[40] Though theoretically there should be no difference between a cash dividend and an otherwise equivalent stock repurchase, in practice stock repurchases and cash dividends are viewed differently. We explore some of the reasons next.[41]

15-6c Tax Considerations

Historically, taxes on capital gains have generally been lower than on dividends, thus favoring stock repurchases over cash dividends. Under the current tax code (2013), the rate for capital gains and dividend income is the same at 15 percent for most investors.[42] However, because taxes on capital gains can be deferred into the future (when the stock is sold), whereas taxes on an equivalent amount of dividend income have to be paid in the current year, firms still have substantial tax reasons to make distributions in the form of share repurchases.

15-6d Financial Flexibility

Substituting discretionary stock repurchases for all or part of regular cash dividends (that is, stable dollar dividend policy) provides a company with greater financial flexibility. Recall that investors associate dividends with informational content and that investors prefer a stable, growing dividend policy to one that involves increasing or decreasing dividends depending on earnings and other needs for the firm's liquidity. With stock repurchases, on the other hand, investors do not generally expect that they will be carried out every year. Thus stock repurchases provide management with greater flexibility so that, when the company has profitable uses for its funds or has fewer earnings, it can defer or scale back the buyback of its stock (and the corresponding cash outflows) until a more appropriate time in the future. Likewise, when the company accumulates excess funds, it can undertake periodic stock repurchases. For example, Pepsi scaled back its stock repurchases in order to pay for a $5.4 billion acquisition of a dairy and beverage company in Russia in 2010.

A recent survey of financial executives indicates that firms increasingly view financial flexibility as a very important consideration in their decision to disburse cash to their

[40]See Larry Y. Dann, "Common Stock Repurchases: An Analysis of Returns to Bondholders and Stockholders," *Journal of Financial Economics* (June 1981): 113–138; and Theo Vermaelen, "Common Stock Repurchases and Market Signaling: An Empirical Study," *Journal of Financial Economics* (June 1981): 139–183.

[41]For a study on the motivations for stock repurchases, see Amy K. Dittmar, "Why Do Firms Repurchase Stock?" *Journal of Business* (July 2000): 331–335. For survey evidence on how financial executives make decisions on cash dividends and stock repurchases, see Brav et al., "Payout Policy in the 21st Century," *Journal of Financial Economics* (2005): 483–527.

[42]Also, see section 15-2d.

shareholders in the form of dividends and/or share repurchases.[43] Research evidence also provides strong support for the role of financial flexibility as a determining factor in the choice between dividends and share repurchases.[44]

15-6e Signaling Effects

Like the signaling effects of cash dividend increases, share repurchases can also have a positive impact on shareholder wealth. A share repurchase may represent a signal to investors that the current share price is undervalued or that management expects the firm to have higher earnings and cash flows in the future.[45] For example, in the aftermath of the 1987 stock market crash, over 900 firms announced stock market repurchase programs in the two weeks following Black Monday, October 19, 1987, when the Dow Jones Industrial Average fell by over 22 percent. In another example, Coach, the largest U.S. maker of luxury handbags, announced in April 2010 the buyback of up to $1 billion of its common stock. The CEO attributed the action to "our confidence in Coach's business outlook."

However, repurchases may also send a negative signal that future growth opportunities are limited. Companies engaging in large buyback programs typically have large cash flows and an insufficient number of positive NPV investments in which to invest. For example, Quaker Oats (acquired by PepsiCo in 2001) repurchased 20 million shares during the late 1980s and early 1990s and was planning the repurchase of an additional 5 million shares. Quaker Oats treasurer Janet K. Cooper explained, "We spend on new products, we make acquisitions, and we raise the dividend, and we still can't soak up all the cash."[46]

15-6f Earnings-per-Share Dilution

One reason stock repurchases are undertaken is to reduce the potential dilution on earnings per share of employee stock option plans and convertible securities. If the firm does not buy back stocks for these needs, it will have to issue new stock, resulting in a dilution effect; that is, the earnings have to be spread over a larger number of shares outstanding, thereby depressing earnings per share and even stock prices. Empirical evidence suggests that the increasing trend in stock repurchases in recent years can be attributed to the growth of stock options and other equity grants in managerial and employee compensation.[47]

15-6g Agency Costs

It has been argued that stock repurchases can reduce agency costs of excess free cash flow. Jensen argues that firms that generate cash flows in excess of what they need to invest profitably may be tempted to misspend the excess cash flow. Jensen suggests that stock repurchases are an efficient mechanism of returning the excess cash flow to stockholders.[48]

[43]See Brav et al. "Payout Policy in the 21st Century," *Journal of Financial Economics* (2005): 483–527.

[44]See, for example, Murali Jagannathan, Clifford P. Stephens, and Michael S. Weisbach, "Financial Flexibility and the Choice Between Dividends and Stock Repurchases," *Journal of Financial Economics* (September 2005): 355–384.

[45]See Vermaelen, "Common Stock Repurchases and Market Signaling: An Empirical Study; and Paul Asquith and David W. Mullins Jr., "Signaling with Dividends, Stock Repurchases, and Equity Issues," *Financial Management* (Autumn 1986): 27–44.

[46]"The Great Buyback Boom of '93," *Business Week* (August 23, 1993): 76.

[47]See Charles J. Cuny, Gerald S. Martin, and John J. Puthenpurackal, "Stock Options and Total Payout," *Journal of Financial and Quantitative Analysis* (April 2009): 391–410.

[48]See Jensen, "Agency Cost of Free Cash Flow, Corporate Finance, and Takeovers," American Economic Review (May 1976): 323–329.

15-6h Advantages and Disadvantages

Let us summarize the advantages and disadvantages of share repurchases as an addition to, or as a substitute for, cash dividends.

Advantages Share repurchases effectively convert dividend income into capital gains income. Shareholders in high (marginal) income tax brackets may prefer capital gains income because of the ability to defer taxes into the future (when the stock is sold). Also, share repurchases provide the firm with greater financial flexibility in timing the payment of returns to shareholders. Finally, share repurchases can represent a signal to investors that the company expects to have higher earnings and cash flows in the future.

Disadvantages A company may overpay for the stock that it repurchases. If the stock price declines, the share repurchase represents an unprofitable use of the company's resources. Also, a share repurchase may trigger IRS scrutiny (and possible tax penalties) if the buyback is viewed as a way for shareholders to avoid taxes on cash dividends. Finally, some current shareholders may be unaware of the share repurchase program and may sell their shares before the expected benefits (that is, price appreciation) occur.

15-7 Summary

- *Dividend policy* determines the ultimate distribution of a firm's earnings between retention (reinvestment) and cash dividend payments to stockholders. Retained earnings provide investors with a source of potential future earnings growth, whereas dividends provide them with a current distribution.
- A number of factors influence a firm's choice of dividend policy. These include the following:

    1. Legal constraints prohibiting dividends that impair capital
    2. Restrictive covenants in bond indentures and other financing agreements
    3. Tax considerations
    4. The need for liquidity
    5. Borrowing capacity and access to the capital markets
    6. Earnings stability
    7. Capital expansion (growth) opportunities

    Shareholders' preferences (*clientele effect*) may also influence a firm's choice of dividend policy. These are determined by stockholders' tax positions and their desire to maintain control of the firm. Some of these factors favor high dividends, whereas others imply a lower payout policy. The board of directors should weigh these factors in each instance and arrive at the best possible dividend policy.
- Under a restrictive set of assumptions articulated by Miller and Modigliani (MM), the value of the firm is dependent solely on its investment decisions. They claim that any observed changes in firm value as a result of dividend decisions are due only to the *informational content* or *signaling effects* of dividend policy. Under these conditions, dividend policy does not affect the value of the firm. After the MM assumptions are removed, dividend policy may affect firm value because of:

    1. Risk-averse behavior of investors
    2. Shareholder transaction costs
    3. Personal taxes
    4. Issuance costs
    5. Agency costs

- A firm may employ any one of a number of alternative dividend policies, including the following:

    1. The passive residual approach
    2. The stable dollar dividend approach
    3. The constant payout ratio approach
    4. The policy of paying a small, regular dividend plus year-end extras

Ample evidence indicates that many firms favor a stable dollar dividend policy.

- *Stock dividends* are sometimes used in lieu of (and in conjunction with) cash dividends. The net effect of stock dividends is to leave the total book value of the firm unchanged while increasing the number of shares outstanding and broadening the ownership base.
- Some firms employ *share repurchase plans* in lieu of (or in addition to) cash dividends. Stock repurchases convert shareholder benefits from ordinary income (dividends) to capital gains income. Theoretically, ignoring taxes, transaction costs, and other market imperfections, share repurchases should have the same effect on shareholder wealth as the payment of cash dividends. However, possibly due to tax considerations (that is, lower tax rates on capital gains income than on dividends and the ability to defer taxes on capital gains income) and signaling effects, share repurchases (via tender offers) are observed to have a positive effect on shareholder wealth.

Important Equation

$$\text{Post-stock dividend price} = \frac{\text{Pre-stock dividend price}}{1 + \text{Percentage stock dividend rate}}$$

15-8 Questions and Topics for Discussion

1. What legal constraints limit the amount of cash dividends that may be paid by a firm?
2. What aspects of U.S. tax laws tend to (a) encourage and (b) discourage large dividend payments by corporations? Explain how.
3. What other "external" factors limit a firm's ability to pay cash dividends?
4. Explain what is meant by the *clientele effect*.
5. Explain what is meant by the *informational content* of dividend policy.
6. Explain what is meant by the *signaling effects* of dividend policy.
7. In the theoretical world of Miller and Modigliani, what role does dividend policy play in the determination of share values?
8. What role do most practitioners think dividend policy plays in determining share values?
9. How can the passive residual view of dividend policy be reconciled with the tendency of most firms to maintain a constant or steadily growing dividend payment record?
10. Why do many managers prefer a stable dollar dividend policy to a policy of paying out a constant percentage of each year's earnings as dividends?
11. Under what circumstances would it make sense for a firm to borrow money to make its dividend payments?
12. Some people have suggested that it is irrational for a firm to pay dividends and sell new stock in the same year because the cost of newly issued equity is greater than the cost of retained earnings. Do you agree? Why or why not?
13. What is a *dividend reinvestment plan*? Explain the advantages of a dividend reinvestment plan to the firm and to shareholders.
14. Why do many firms choose to issue stock dividends? What is the value of a stock dividend to a shareholder?

15. What are the tax limitations on the practice of share repurchases as a regular dividend policy?

16. What effect do share repurchases (undertaken as part of the firm's dividend decision) have on the value of the firm?

17. You are the holder of common stock in the G. Lewis Apartment Renovation Company. Historically, the firm has paid generous cash dividends. The firm has recently announced that it would replace its cash dividend with a 20 percent annual stock dividend. Is this good news, bad news, or is it impossible to tell from the information provided? Explain the reason for your answer.

18. What issues of business ethics may be involved in the establishment of a firm's dividend payment amounts?

15-9 Self-Test Problems

ST1. The board of directors of Complex Computers has decided to declare a 20 percent stock dividend. The company's common stockholders' equity is as follows:

Pre–Stock Dividend Common Stockholders' Equity

Common stock ($1 par, 100,000 shares)	$ 100,000
Contributed capital in excess of par	900,000
Retained earnings	5,000,000
Total common stockholders' equity	$6,000,000

The common stock of Complex Computers is currently trading at $80 a share. The company is growing rapidly and has never paid a cash dividend.

a. Show the company's common stockholders' equity after the stock dividend.
b. Calculate the post–stock dividend price of Complex Computers stock, assuming no other changes occur.

ST2. Sanchez Supermarkets, Inc. (50,000 common shares outstanding) currently has annual earnings before interest and taxes of $1,000,000. Its interest expenses are $200,000 a year, and it pays $100,000 in annual dividends to its stockholders. The company's tax rate is 40 percent, and its common stock's current dividend yield is 2.0 percent.

a. Calculate the company's earnings per share.
b. Calculate the company's dividend payout ratio.
c. Calculate the company's current common stock price.
d. If Sanchez declares and pays a 100 percent stock dividend and then pays an annual cash dividend of $1.10 per share, what is the effective rate by which the dividend has been increased?

15-10 Problems*

BASIC

1. Jacobs Corporation earned $2 million after tax. The firm has 1.6 million shares of common stock outstanding.

a. Compute the earnings per share of Jacobs.

*Color blocks behind the numbers denote problems that have check answers provided at the end of the book.

b. If Jacobs' dividend policy calls for a 40 percent payout ratio, what are the dividends per share?

INTERMEDIATE **2.** Drew Financial Associates currently pays a quarterly dividend of 50 cents per share. This quarter's dividend will be paid to stockholders of record on Friday, February 12, 2016. Drew has 200,000 common shares outstanding. The retained earnings account has a balance of $15 million before the dividend, and Drew holds $2.5 million in cash.

a. What is the ex-dividend date for this quarter?

b. Drew's stock traded for $22 per share the day prior to the ex-dividend date. What would you expect the stock price to open at on the ex-dividend date? Give some reasons why this might not occur.

c. What is the effect of the dividend payment on Drew's cash, retained earnings, and total assets?

BASIC **3.** Winkie Baking has just announced a 100 percent stock dividend. The annual cash dividend per share was $2.40 before the stock dividend. Winkie intends to pay $1.40 per share on each of the new shares. Compute the percentage increase in the cash dividend rate that will accompany the stock dividend.

INTERMEDIATE **4.** Wolverine Corporation plans to pay a $3 dividend per share on each of its 300,000 shares next year. Wolverine anticipates earnings of $6.25 per share over the year. If the company has a capital budget requiring an investment of $4 million over the year and it desires to maintain its present debt to total assets (debt ratio) of 0.40, how much external equity must it raise? Assume that Wolverine's capital structure includes only common equity and debt, and that debt and equity will be the only sources of funds to finance capital projects over the year.

BASIC **5.** Tulia Dairy pays a $2.50 cash dividend and earns $5 per share. The cash dividend has recently been increased to $2.65 per share, *and* a 3 percent stock dividend has been declared. What is the effective rate of increase in the dividends for Tulia as a result of this action?

INTERMEDIATE **6.** The Mori Egg Noodle Company has the following equity accounts on its balance sheet:

Common stock ($10 par, 300,000 shares)	$ 3,000,000
Contributed capital in excess of par	1,500,000
Retained earnings	6,000,000
Total common stockholders' equity	$10,500,000

a. What is the maximum amount of dividends that may be paid by the Mori Company if the capital impairment provisions of state law are limited to the following?

i. The par value of common stock

ii. The par value and the capital in excess of par accounts

b. What other factors may limit Mori's ability to pay dividends?

INTERMEDIATE **7.** Champoux Hair Factory Inc. has earnings before interest and taxes of $200,000. Annual interest amounts to $80,000, and annual depreciation is $80,000. Taxes are computed at a 40 percent rate. Existing bond obligations require the payment of $40,000 per year into a sinking fund.

Champoux wishes to pay a $2-per-share dividend on the existing 20,000 shares. The firm's bond indenture prohibits the payment of dividends unless the cash flow (before dividends and sinking fund payments) is greater than the total of dividends, interest, and sinking fund obligations.

a. Can Champoux pay the proposed dividend?

b. What is the maximum dividend per share that may be paid?

INTERMEDIATE **8.** Lenberg Lens Company believes in the dividends-as-a-residual philosophy of dividend policy. This year's earnings are expected to total $10 million. A very conservative company, Lenberg is financed solely with common stock. The required rate of return on retained earnings is 12 percent, whereas the cost of newly raised capital is 14 percent because of issuance costs.

a. If Lenberg has $6 million of investment projects having expected returns greater than 12 percent, what total amount of dividends should Lenberg pay?

b. If Lenberg has $12 million of investment projects having expected returns greater than 14 percent, what total amount of dividends should Lenberg pay?

c. What factors, other than its belief in the residual theory of dividends, should Lenberg consider in setting its dividend policy in Part b?

CHALLENGE **9.** Phoenix Tool Company and Denver Tool Company have had a very similar record of earnings performance over the past eight years. Both firms are in the same industry and, in fact, compete directly with each other. The two firms have nearly identical capital structures. Phoenix has a policy of paying a constant 50 percent of each year's earnings as dividends, whereas Denver has sought to maintain a stable dollar dividend policy, with changes in the dollar dividend payment occurring infrequently. The record of the two companies follows:

	Phoenix			Denver		
Year	**EPS**	**Dividend**	**Average Market Price**	**EPS**	**Dividend**	**Average Market Price**
2009	$2.00	$1.00	$20	$2.10	$0.75	$18
2010	2.50	1.25	24	2.40	0.75	22
2011	1.50	1.25	15	1.60	0.75	17
2012	1.00	0.50	10	0.90	0.75	14
2013	0.50	0.25	8	0.50	0.50	10
2014	−1.25	nil	8	−1.10	0.50	10
2015	1.00	0.50	10	1.10	0.75	14
2016	1.50	0.75	14	1.45	0.75	17

The president of Phoenix wonders what accounts for Denver's current (2016) higher stock price, in spite of the fact that Phoenix currently earns more per share than Denver and frequently has paid a higher dividend.

a. What factors can you cite that might account for this phenomenon?

b. What do you suggest as an optimal dividend policy for both Phoenix and Denver that might lead to increases in both of their share prices? What are the limitations of your suggestions?

CHALLENGE **10.** The Emco Steel Company has experienced a slow (3 percent per year) but steady increase in earnings per share. The firm has consistently paid out an average of 75 percent of each year's earnings as dividends. The stock market evaluates Emco primarily on the basis of its dividend payout because growth prospects are modest.

Emco's management presents a proposal to the board of directors that would require the outlay of $50 million to build a new plant in the rapidly expanding Florida market. The expected annual return on the investment in this plant is estimated to be in excess of 30 percent, more than twice the current company average. To finance this investment, a number of alternatives are being considered. They include the following:

a. Finance the expansion with externally raised equity.
b. Finance the expansion with 50 percent externally generated equity and 50 percent internally generated equity. This alternative would necessitate a dividend cut for this year only.
c. Finance the expansion with a mix of debt and equity similar to their current relative proportions in the capital structure. Under this alternative, dividends would not be cut. Rather, any equity needs in excess of that which could be provided internally would be raised through a sale of new common stock.

Evaluate these various financing alternatives with reference to their effects on the dividend policy and common stock values of the company.

INTERMEDIATE **11.** The Sweet Times Candy Company has the following equity accounts on its balance sheet:

Common stock ($1 par, 500,000 shares)	$ 500,000
Contributed capital in excess of par	2,000,000
Retained earnings	13,000,000
Total common stockholders' equity	$15,500,000

The current market price of the firm's shares is $50.

a. If the firm declares a 10 percent stock dividend, what will be the impact on the firm's equity accounts?
b. If the firm currently pays no cash dividend, what is the impact of a 10 percent stock dividend on the wealth position of the firm's existing stockholders?
c. If the firm currently pays a cash dividend of $1 per share and this per-share dividend rate does not change after the 10 percent stock dividend, what impact would you expect the stock dividend to have on the wealth position of existing shareholders?

INTERMEDIATE **12.** Striker's Match Company reports the following financial data:

Net earnings	$3,000,000
Shares outstanding	1,000,000
Earnings per share	$3
Market price per share (ex-dividend)	$40
Expected dividend per share	$2

Striker is considering distributing $2 million to existing stockholders, either as cash dividends or through the repurchase of outstanding shares. The repurchase plan is favored by some of the company's wealthiest and most influential stockholders.

If the shares are repurchased, the company would make a tender offer for 47,619 shares at a price of $42. Alternatively, the firm could pay a $2 dividend, after the payment of which each share would sell for $40.

a. Ignoring taxes, what impact does the choice of a dividend payment or share repurchase plan have on the wealth position of the firm's shareholders?
b. If most shareholders are in a very high marginal tax bracket, which alternative is favored?
c. What are the limitations on the repurchase alternative as an element of the firm's dividend policy?

INTERMEDIATE **13.** Concave Systems presently has earnings before interest and taxes of $3 million. Its interest expenses are $500,000 a year, and it pays $600,000 in annual dividends to its shareholders. Concave has 300,000 common shares outstanding, and its tax rate is 40 percent. Its annual capital expenditures are $900,000. Concave's present price-to-earnings ratio is 12.

a. Calculate the company's earnings per share.
b. Calculate the company's dividend payout ratio.
c. Calculate the company's dividend yield.

BASIC **14.** On Friday, August 6, the board of directors of Cisco Industries declares a $0.22 quarterly dividend payable on September 15 to stockholders of record on Tuesday, August 24. When is the ex-dividend date? If you purchase the stock on this date, are you entitled to receive the dividend?

CHALLENGE **15.** Clynne Resources expects earnings this year to be $2 per share. Clynne plans to pay a dividend of $0.70 for the year. During the year, Clynne expects to borrow $10 million in addition to its already outstanding loan balances. Clynne has 10 million shares of common stock outstanding.

a. If all capital outlays are funded from retained earnings and new borrowings and if Clynne follows a residual dividend policy, what capital outlays are planned for the coming year?
b. What is Clynne's target capital structure given these assumptions?

PART 5

Working Capital Management

This part of the book considers the financial management of a firm's current assets and current liabilities, called *working capital management.* Chapter 16 deals with working capital policy, with emphasis on the risk-return trade-offs that are implied. It also looks at current liabilities and the sources of short-term credit. Chapter 17 covers the management of cash and marketable securities. Chapter 18 discusses the management of accounts receivable and inventories. Working capital management influences both the risk of a firm and its expected returns. As such, it is an important determinant of firm value.

CHAPTER

16

Working Capital Policy and Short-Term Financing

KEY CHAPTER CONCEPTS

1. Working capital policy decisions include:
   a. Investment—level of working capital
   b. Financing—proportions of short-term and long-term debt
2. Determination of the optimal level of working capital investment involves profitability versus risk trade-off analysis:
   a. Higher levels of working capital generally reduce profitability.
   b. Higher levels of working capital reduce the risk of financial difficulties.
3. Determination of the optimal proportions of short- and long-term debt involves profitability versus risk trade-off analysis:
   a. Higher proportions of short-term debt increase profitability because of generally lower interest costs.
   b. Higher proportions of short-term debt increase the risk of financial difficulties.
4. Examination of a firm's operating cycle and cash conversion cycle is important in analyzing its liquidity.
5. Overall working capital policy involves analyzing the joint impact of the working capital investment decision and the working capital financing decision on the firm's risk and profitability.
6. *Trade credit*, or *accounts payable*, is the principal source of *spontaneous* short-term credit.
7. *Bank loans*, *commercial paper*, *accounts receivable loans*, and *inventory loans* are the major sources of *negotiated* short-term credit.
8. The cost of trade credit is dependent on the size of any cash discount offered and the lengths of the credit and discount periods.
9. The types of short-term bank credit include *single loans*, *lines of credit*, and *revolving credit agreements.*
10. Commercial paper is a short-term unsecured credit instrument issued by major corporations with good credit ratings.
11. A company can use its accounts receivable to obtain short-term financing. It can either *pledge* the accounts receivable as collateral for a loan or sell (*factor*) the receivables to obtain cash.
12. A company can also use its inventory as collateral for a short-term loan. The lender can either allow the borrower to hold the collateral (under a *floating lien* or *trust receipts* arrangement) or require that a third party hold the collateral (under a *terminal warehouse* or *field warehouse arrangement*).

FINANCIAL CHALLENGE

Freeing Up Cash at Procter & Gamble

Many large companies have instituted more aggressive cash management practices in order to free up funds for expansion and other corporate purposes. One such cash management practice involves the use of trade credit to finance their operations. For example, in the past, Procter & Gamble (P&G) had been paying its suppliers for its purchases within 45 days on average (credit period), which was earlier than the 60 to 90 days that other large companies normally paid their suppliers. The company was seeking to move its payment terms to 75 days. P&G purchases more than $50 billion annually in products and services from about 75,000 different companies (suppliers). This includes such things as plastics, cardboard, fragrances, and chemicals. By increasing the amount of time the company takes to reimburse its suppliers, it was estimated that P&G could free up as much as $2 billion in cash. Other companies, such as Kimberly-Clark, DuPont, and J. C. Penney, were taking similar actions to free up cash.

However, extending the credit period adds to the costs of P&G's suppliers. The suppliers will have to invest more funds in receivables, and they may have to incur more interest expenses to fill the gap between when sales are made and when they are paid by P&G.

In order to help its suppliers with these new payment terms, P&G was working with banks to advance cash to the suppliers after 15 days. Suppliers who wished to get paid before the end of the 75-day credit period would be given a cash advance, less an interest discount. Based on P&G's investment-grade credit rating and lower bank borrowing costs, the interest discount for early payment to the suppliers would be relatively small. Other companies, such as Walmart Stores, Unilever, and Kohl's, were working with banks to offer their suppliers similar financing terms.

This chapter analyzes the risk-return trade-offs associated with the management of working capital. It also illustrates the issues involved when a company is facing financial needs and is seeking

Jonathan Weiss/Shutterstock.com

FINANCIAL CHALLENGE — CONTINUED

to borrow money in the credit markets. The chapter also looks at the various sources and costs of short-term credit, such as the trade credit offered by P&G's suppliers, that can be used to finance a firm's operations.

Source: Serena Ng, "P&G, Big Companies Pinch Suppliers on Payments," *The Wall Street Journal* (April 17, 2013): A1.

CHAPTER OBJECTIVES

Upon completion of this chapter, you should have a clear understanding of the following:

1. The meaning of the term *operating cycle* and its role in determining an appropriate working capital policy
2. The factors that affect working capital policy and the risk-return trade-offs of various working capital policies
3. The costs and benefits of the various sources of short-term credit, including:
   - Trade credit
   - Accrued expenses and deferred income
   - Short-term bank credit
   - Commercial paper
   - Accounts receivable loans
   - Inventory loans

16-1 Introduction

The first half of the chapter deals with the management of working capital, which involves decisions about the optimal overall level of current assets and the optimal mix of short-term and long-term funds used to finance the company's assets. These decisions require an analysis of the risk and expected return trade-offs associated with the various alternative policies.

The second half of the chapter examines the various sources of short-term credit available to the firm.

16-2 Working Capital Policy

Working capital policy involves decisions about a company's current assets and current liabilities—what they consist of, how they are used, and how their mix affects the risk

working capital

net working capital

versus return characteristics of the company. Both the terms **working capital** and **net working capital** normally denote the *difference* between the company's current assets and current liabilities. The two terms are often used interchangeably.

Working capital policies, through their effect on the firm's expected future returns and the risk associated with these returns, ultimately have an impact on shareholder wealth.[1] Effective working capital policies are crucial to a firm's long-run growth and survival. If, for example, a company lacks the working capital needed to expand production and sales, it may lose revenues and profits. Working capital is used by firms to maintain **liquidity**, that is, the ability to meet their cash obligations as they come due. Otherwise, it may incur the costs associated with a deteriorating credit rating, a potential forced liquidation of assets, and possible bankruptcy.

liquidity

Working capital management is a continuing process that involves a number of day-to-day operations and decisions that determine the following:

- The firm's level of current assets
- The proportions of short-term and long-term debt the firm will use to finance its assets
- The level of investment in each type of current asset
- The specific sources and mix of short-term credit (current liabilities) the firm should employ

Working capital differs from *fixed* capital in terms of the time required to recover the investment in a given asset. In the case of fixed capital or long-term assets (such as land, buildings, and equipment), a company usually needs several years or more to recover the initial investment. In contrast, working capital is turned over, or circulated, at a relatively rapid rate. Investments in inventories and accounts receivable are usually recovered during a firm's normal operating cycle, when inventories are sold and receivables are collected.

16-2a Importance of Working Capital

It has already been noted that a firm must have working capital to operate and survive. In many industries, working capital (current assets) constitutes a relatively large percentage of total assets. In the manufacturing sector, for example, current assets comprise about 40 percent of the total assets of all U.S. manufacturing corporations.

Table 16.1 shows the distribution of aggregate assets for several large companies. For the five companies shown, current assets as a percentage of total assets range from about 15 percent to over 42 percent. ExxonMobil, with its relatively high percentage of fixed assets, has a relatively low percentage of current assets. In contrast, IBM has a relatively high percentage of current assets. IBM, which finances customer purchases of some of its products, has over 27 percent of its assets in receivables. Target, a retail store chain, has over 21 percent of its assets in inventories. Because current assets constitute a relatively high percentage of total assets in most businesses, it is important to have effective working capital policies.

In a survey of large industrial corporations, it was found that about 30 percent of the companies have a formal policy for the management of their working capital and another 60 percent have an informal policy.[2] A significantly greater percentage of the

[1]See James A. Gentry, "State of the Art of Short-Run Financial Management," *Financial Management* 17 (Summer 1988): 41–57, for a review of the literature concerning the management of short-run assets and liabilities.

[2]Keith V. Smith and Shirley B. Sell, "Working Capital Management in Practice," in *Readings in the Management of Working Capital*, 2nd ed., Keith V. Smith, ed. (St. Paul, MN: West Publishing Company, 1980).

TABLE 16.1

Distribution of Aggregate Assets in Selected Companies

	ExxonMobil	Walgreens	Merck	Target	IBM
Cash and marketable securities	1.33%	4.36%	15.99%	5.34%	7.21%
Receivables, net	8.01	9.96	6.71	—	27.08
Inventories, net	4.77	12.62	5.67	21.23	1.79
All other current assets	1.02	1.64	5.35	7.46	5.97
Total current assets*	15.14%	28.58%	33.73%	34.02%	42.05%
Fixed Assets, net	72.30	21.91	13.36	62.69	9.16
All other noncurrent assets	12.57	49.51	52.91	3.28	48.79
Total assets*	100.0%	100.0%	100.0%	100.0%	100.0%

*Totals may differ from sums of numbers in column because of rounding.

Source: www.sec.gov/edgar.

larger companies within the sample have a formal policy than do the smaller companies. In almost one-half of the companies that responded to the survey, the financial vice president has responsibility for establishing the company's overall working capital policy. The president and treasurer are the next most frequently mentioned positions as having responsibility for working capital policy. There is considerable variation in the frequency with which companies review their working capital policy. Annual, quarterly, and monthly reviews are mentioned with about the same relative frequency (approximately 14 to 18 percent), whereas approximately one-half of the companies review working capital policy "whenever necessary."

A firm's net working capital position is not only important from an internal standpoint; it is also widely used as one measure of the firm's risk. *Risk*, as used in this context, deals with the probability that a firm will encounter financial difficulties, such as the inability to pay bills on time. All other things being equal, the more net working capital a firm has, the more likely it is to be able to meet current financial obligations. Because net working capital is one measure of risk, a company's net working capital position affects its ability to obtain debt financing. Many loan agreements with commercial banks and other lending institutions contain a provision requiring the firm to maintain a minimum net working capital position. Likewise, bond indentures also often contain such provisions.

HTTP:
Have you ever heard of a working capital revolver? The KBK Capital Corporation will arrange one for you, from $100,000 (peanuts) to $5 million.
www.kbkcapital.com

16-2b Operating Cycle Analysis

A company's operating cycle typically consists of three primary activities: purchasing resources, producing the product, and distributing (selling) the product. These activities create cash flows that are both unsynchronized and uncertain. They are unsynchronized because cash disbursements (for example, payments for resource purchases) usually take place before cash receipts (for example, collection of receivables). They are uncertain because future sales and costs, which generate the respective receipts and disbursements, cannot be forecasted with complete accuracy. If the firm is to maintain liquidity and function properly, it has to invest funds in various short-term assets (working capital) during this cycle. It has to maintain a *cash balance* to pay the bills as they come due. In addition, the company must invest in *inventories* to fill customer orders promptly. And, finally, the company invests in *accounts receivable* to extend credit to its customers.

FIGURE 16.1

Operating Cycle of a Typical Company

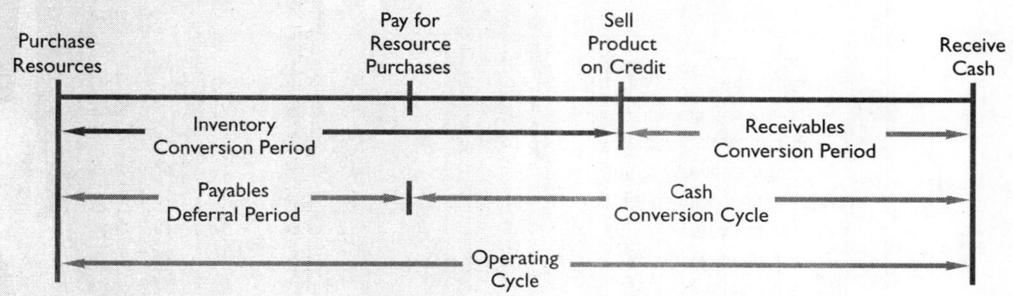

operating cycle

Figure 16.1 illustrates the operating cycle of a typical firm.[3] The **operating cycle** is equal to the length of the inventory and receivables conversion periods:

$$\text{Operating cycle} = \text{Inventory conversion period} + \text{Receivables conversion period} \tag{16.1}$$

inventory conversion period

The **inventory conversion period** is the length of time required to produce and sell the product. It is defined as follows:

$$\text{Inventory conversion period} = \frac{\text{Average inventory}}{\text{Cost of sales}/365} \tag{16.2}$$

receivables conversion period

The **receivables conversion period**, or average collection period, represents the length of time required to collect the sales receipts. It is calculated as follows:

$$\text{Receivables conversion period} = \frac{\text{Average accounts receivable}}{\text{Annual credit sales}/365} \tag{16.3}$$

payables deferral period

The **payables deferral period** is the length of time the firm is able to defer payment on its various resource purchases (for example, materials). The following equation is used to calculate the payables deferral period:[4]

$$\text{Payables deferral period} = \frac{\text{Average accounts payable}}{\text{Cost of sales}/365} \tag{16.4}$$

cash conversion cycle

Finally, the **cash conversion cycle** represents the net time interval between the collection of cash receipts from product sales and the cash payments for the company's various resource purchases. It is calculated as follows:

$$\text{Cash conversion cycle} = \text{Operating cycle} - \text{Payables deferral period} \tag{16.5}$$

[3]The following discussion is based on Verlyn D. Richards and Eugene J. Laughlin, "A Cash Conversion Cycle Approach to Liquidity Analysis," *Financial Management* 9 (Spring 1980): 32–38.

[4]A more precise estimate of the payables deferral period would include other resource purchases, such as wages and taxes, for which payment can be deferred. However, accounting information on such items as salaries, benefits, and payroll taxes payable and selling, general, and administrative expenses frequently are not shown as separate entries on a firm's balance sheet and income statement.

$$\text{Payables deferral period} = \frac{\text{Accounts payable} + \begin{array}{c}\text{Salaries, benefits, and}\\ \text{payroll taxes payable}\end{array}}{\begin{array}{c}(\text{Costs of sales} + \text{Selling, general and}\\ \text{administrative expense})/365\end{array}}$$

TABLE 16.2

Cash Conversion Cycle Analysis for Health and More

	2015	2014
Liquidity ratios:		
Current ratio	1.75	1.82
Quick ratio	0.53	0.52
Cash conversion cycle:		
Inventory conversion period	59.5 days	63.0 days
Receivables conversion period	13.8 days	13.9 days
Operating cycle	73.3 days	76.9 days
Less: Payables deferral period	25.8 days	24.3 days
Cash conversion cycle	47.5 days	52.6 days

The cash conversion cycle shows the time interval over which additional *nonspontaneous* sources of working capital financing must be obtained to carry out the firm's activities.[5] An increase in the length of the operating cycle, without a corresponding increase in the payables deferral period, lengthens the cash conversion cycle and creates further working capital financing needs for the company.

Table 16.2 shows an actual cash conversion cycle analysis for Health & More, a drugstore retailer. Health & More's liquidity, as measured by the current and quick ratios, appears to be almost unchanged from 2014 to 2015, with a small decrease in its current ratio and a small increase in its quick ratio. The reduction of Health & More's cash conversion cycle from 52.6 days in 2014 to 47.5 days in 2015 indicates a more efficient utilization of its working capital. This was due mainly to a decrease in its inventory conversion period and an increase in its payables deferral period.

16-3 Levels of Working Capital Investment

Overall working capital policy considers *both* a firm's level of working capital investment and its financing. In practice, the firm has to determine the *joint* impact of these two decisions upon its profitability and risk. However, to permit a better understanding of working capital policy, the working capital investment decision is discussed in this section, and the working capital financing decision is discussed in the following section. The two decisions are then considered together.

The size and nature of a firm's investment in current assets is a function of a number of different factors, including the following:

- The type of products manufactured
- The length of the operating cycle
- The sales level (because higher sales require more investment in inventories and receivables)
- Inventory policies (for example, the amount of safety stocks maintained; that is, inventories needed to meet higher than expected demand or unanticipated delays in obtaining new inventories)

[5]Spontaneous sources of financing (such as trade credit offered by suppliers) automatically expand (contract) as the company's volume of purchases increases (decreases). Nonspontaneous (or negotiated) sources of financing (such as bank loans), in contrast, do not automatically expand or contract with the volume of purchases. This concept is discussed later in this chapter in the "Short-Term Credit" section.

- Credit policies
- How efficiently the firm manages current assets (Obviously, the more effectively management economizes on the amount of cash, marketable securities, inventories, and receivables employed, the smaller the working capital requirements.)

For the purposes of discussion and analysis, these factors are held constant for the remainder of this chapter. Instead of focusing on these factors, this section examines the risk-return trade-offs associated with alternative levels of working capital investment.

16-3a Profitability Versus Risk Trade-Off for Alternative Levels of Working Capital Investment

Before deciding on an appropriate level of working capital investment, a firm's management has to evaluate the trade-off between expected profitability and the risk that it may be unable to meet its financial obligations. Profitability is measured by the rate of (operating) return on total assets; that is, EBIT/total assets. As mentioned earlier in this chapter, the risk that a firm will encounter financial difficulties is related to the firm's net working capital position.

Consider three alternative working capital policies.[6] Policy C represents a *conservative* approach to working capital management. Under this policy, the company holds a relatively large proportion of its total assets in the form of current assets. Because the rate of return on current assets is normally assumed to be less than the rate of return on fixed assets,[7] this policy results in a *lower expected profitability* as measured by the rate of return on the company's total assets. Assuming that current liabilities remain constant, this type of policy also increases the company's net working capital position, resulting in a *lower risk* that the firm will encounter financial difficulties.

In contrast to Policy C, Policy A represents an *aggressive* approach. Under this policy, the company holds a relatively small proportion of its total assets in the form of lower-yielding current assets and thus has relatively less net working capital. As a result, this policy yields a *higher expected profitability* and a *higher risk* that the company will encounter financial difficulties.

Finally, Policy M represents a *moderate* approach. With this policy, expected profitability and risk levels fall between those of Policy C and Policy A.

These three approaches may be illustrated with the following example. Suppose Burlington Resources has forecasted sales next year to be $100 million and EBIT to be $10 million. The company has fixed assets of $30 million and current liabilities totaling $20 million.

Burlington Resources is considering three alternative working capital investment policies:

- An *aggressive* policy consisting of $35 million in current assets
- A *moderate* policy consisting of $40 million in current assets
- A *conservative* policy consisting of $45 million in current assets

Assume that sales and EBIT remain constant under each policy.[8] Table 16.3 contains the results of the three proposed policies.

---

[6]The relationship between current assets and sales is drawn as a concave *curvilinear* function because it is assumed that economies of scale exist in the holding of current assets. In other words, increases in sales should normally require less than proportionate increases in current assets, particularly for cash and inventories. The amount of the company's *fixed* assets is held constant in the following discussion.

[7]This assumption is based on the principle that the lower an asset's risk, the lower its expected return. Current assets are normally less risky than fixed assets because they can be converted into cash more easily and with less potential loss in value. Therefore, current assets should have lower expected returns.

[8]In practice, however, this assumption may not be completely realistic because a firm's sales are usually a function of its inventory and credit policies. Higher levels of finished goods inventories and a more liberal credit extension policy—both of which increase a firm's investment in current assets—may also lead to higher sales. This effect can be incorporated into the analysis by modifying the sales and EBIT projections under the various alternative working capital policies. Although changing these projections would affect the numerical values contained in Table 16.3, it does not affect the general conclusions concerning the profitability versus risk trade-offs.

TABLE 16.3

Profitability and Risk of Alternative Working Capital Investment Policies for Burlington Resources (in Millions of Dollars)

	Aggressive	Moderate	Conservative
	Relatively Small Investment in Current Assets	Moderate Investment in Current Assets	Relatively Large Investment in Current Assets
Current assets (C/A)	$ 35	$ 40	$ 45
Fixed assets (F/A)	30	30	30
Total assets (T/A)	$ 65	$ 70	$ 75
Current liabilities (C/L)	$ 20	$ 20	$ 20
Forecasted sales	$ 100	$ 100	$ 100
Expected EBIT	$ 10	$ 10	$ 10
Expected rate of return on total assets (EBIT ÷ T/A)	15.38%	14.29%	13.33%
Net working capital position (C/A − C/L)	$ 15	$ 20	$ 25
Current ratio (C/A ÷ C/L)	1.75	2.0	2.25

The aggressive policy would yield the highest expected rate of return on total assets, 15.38 percent, whereas the conservative policy would yield the lowest rate of return, 13.33 percent. The aggressive policy would also result in a lower net working capital position ($15 million) than would the conservative policy ($25 million).

Using net working capital as a measure of risk, the aggressive policy is the riskiest, and the conservative policy is the least risky. The current ratio is another measure of a firm's ability to meet financial obligations as they come due. The aggressive policy would yield the lowest current ratio, and the conservative policy would yield the highest current ratio.

16-3b Optimal Level of Working Capital Investment

The optimal level of working capital investment is the level expected to maximize shareholder wealth. It is a function of several factors, including the variability of sales and cash flows and the degree of operating and financial leverage employed by the firm. Therefore, no single working capital investment policy is necessarily optimal for all firms.

16-4 Proportions of Short-Term and Long-Term Financing

Not only does a firm have to be concerned about the *level* of current assets; it also has to determine the *proportions* of short- and long-term debt to use in financing these assets. This decision also involves trade-offs between profitability and risk.

Sources of debt financing are classified according to their *maturities*. Specifically, they can be categorized as being either *short-term* or *long-term*, with short-term sources having maturities of one year or less and long-term sources having maturities of greater than one year.[9]

[9]In this discussion, the term *long-term financing* includes any *intermediate-term financing*.

16-4a Cost of Short-Term Versus Long-Term Debt

Recall from Chapter 8 that the *term structure of interest rates* is defined as the relationship among interest rates of debt securities that differ in their length of time to maturity. Historically, long-term interest rates have normally exceeded short-term rates.

Also, because of the reduced flexibility of long-term borrowing relative to short-term borrowing, the *effective* cost of long-term debt may be higher than the cost of short-term debt, even when short-term interest rates are equal to or greater than long-term rates. With long-term debt, a firm incurs the interest expense even during times when it has no immediate need for the funds, such as during seasonal or cyclical downturns. With short-term debt, in contrast, the firm can avoid the interest costs on unneeded funds by paying off (or not renewing) the debt. In summary, the cost of long-term debt is generally higher than the cost of short-term debt.

16-4b Risk of Long-Term Versus Short-Term Debt

Borrowing companies have different attitudes toward the relative risk of long-term versus short-term debt than do lenders. Whereas lenders normally feel that risk increases with maturity, borrowers feel that there is more risk associated with short-term debt. The reasons for this are twofold.

First, there is always the chance that a firm will not be able to refinance its short-term debt. When a firm's debt matures, it either pays off the debt as part of a debt reduction program or arranges new financing. At the time of maturity, however, the firm could be faced with financial problems resulting from such events as strikes, natural disasters, or recessions that cause sales and cash inflows to decline. Under these circumstances the firm may find it very difficult or even impossible to obtain the needed funds. This could lead to operating and financial difficulties. The more frequently a firm must refinance debt, the greater is the risk of its not being able to obtain the necessary financing.

Second, short-term interest rates tend to fluctuate more over time than long-term interest rates. As a result, a firm's interest expenses and expected earnings after interest and taxes are subject to greater variation over time with short-term debt than with long-term debt.

16-5 Profitability Versus Risk Trade-Off for Alternative Financing Plans

A company's need for financing is equal to the sum of its fixed and current assets.[10] Current assets can be divided into the following two categories:

- *Permanent* current assets
- *Fluctuating* current assets

fluctuating current assets
permanent current assets

Fluctuating current assets are those affected by the seasonal or cyclical nature of company sales. For example, a firm must make larger investments in inventories and receivables during peak selling periods than during other periods of the year. **Permanent current assets** are those held to meet the company's minimum long-term needs (for example, "safety stocks" of cash and inventories). Figure 16.2 illustrates a typical firm's financing needs over time. The fixed assets and permanent current assets lines are upward sloping, indicating that the investment in these assets and, by extension, financing needs tend to increase over time for a firm whose sales are increasing.

[10]The following discussion assumes a constant amount of equity financing.

FIGURE 16.2

Financing Needs over Time

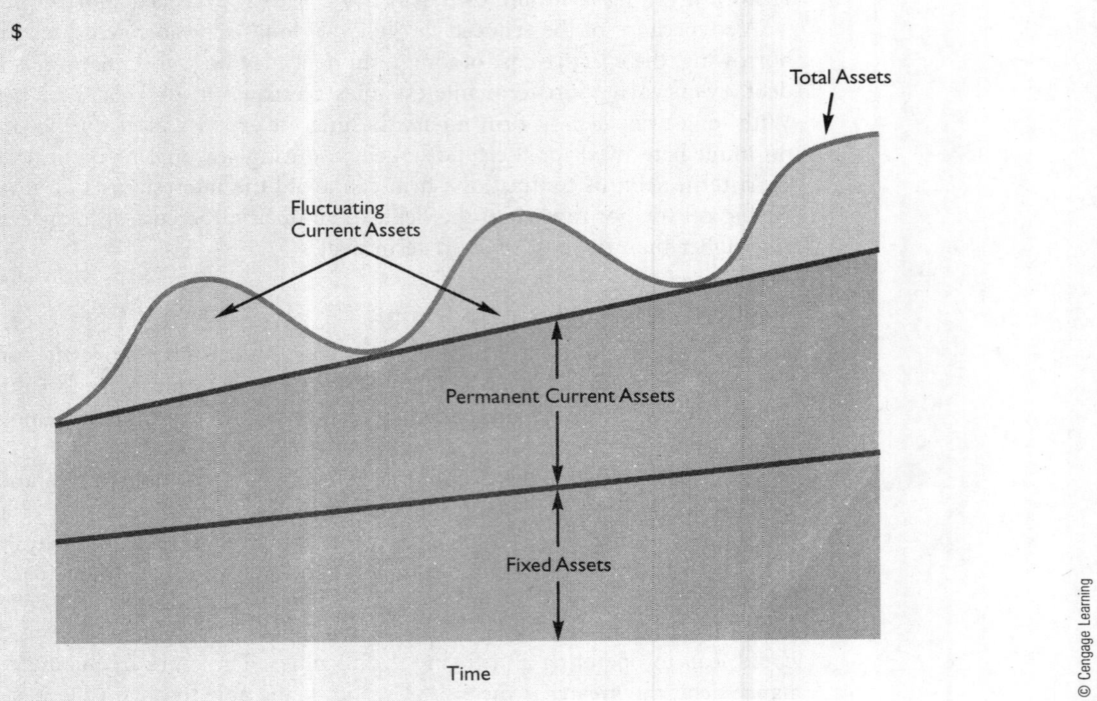

matching approach

One way in which a firm can meet its financing needs is by using a **matching approach** in which the maturity structure of the firm's liabilities is made to correspond exactly to the life of its assets, as illustrated in Figure 16.3. Fixed and permanent current assets are financed with long-term debt and equity funds, whereas fluctuating current assets are financed with short-term debt.[11] Application of this approach is not as simple as it appears, however. In practice, the uncertainty associated with the lives of individual assets makes the matching approach difficult to implement.

Figures 16.4 and 16.5 illustrate two other financing plans. Figure 16.4 shows a *conservative* approach, which uses a relatively high proportion of long-term debt. The relatively low proportion of short-term debt in this approach reduces the risk that the company will be unable to refund its debt, and it also reduces the risk associated with interest rate fluctuations. At the same time, however, this approach cuts down on the expected returns available to stockholders because the cost of long-term debt is generally greater than the cost of short-term debt.

Figure 16.5 illustrates an *aggressive* approach, which uses a relatively high proportion of short-term debt. A firm that uses this particular approach must refinance debt more frequently, and this increases the risk that it will be unable to obtain new financing as needed. In addition, the greater possible fluctuations in interest expenses associated

[11]This analysis does not consider "spontaneous" sources of short-term credit, such as accounts payable. Since spontaneous short-term credit is virtually cost-free when used within reasonable limits, a company will normally employ this type of credit to the fullest extent possible before using "negotiated" sources of short-term credit, such as bank loans. Because none of the conclusions concerning the trade-off between profitability and risk are affected by ignoring spontaneous sources of short-term credit, it need not be considered here.

FIGURE 16.3

Matching Approach to Asset Financing

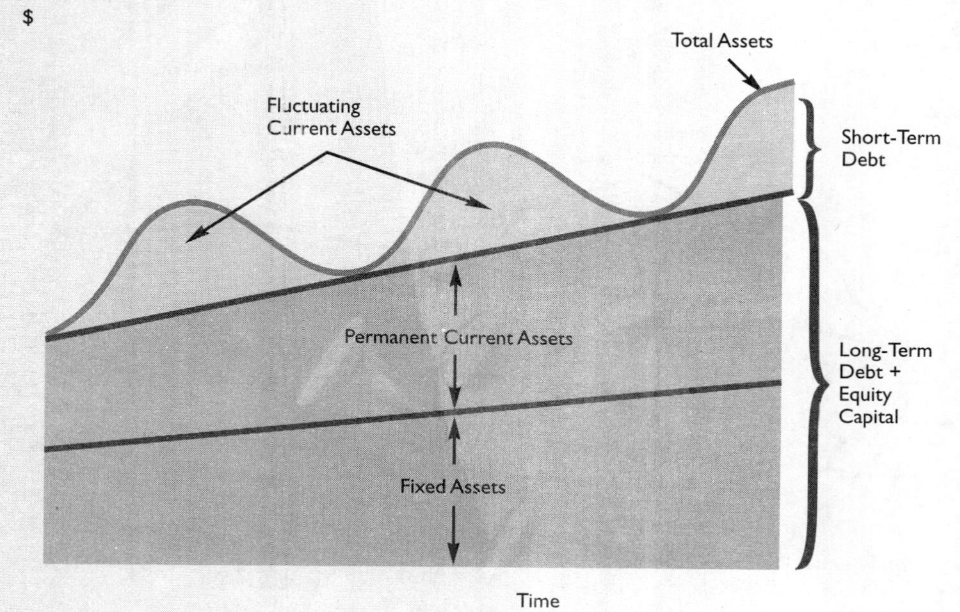

FIGURE 16.4

Conservative Approach to Asset Financing

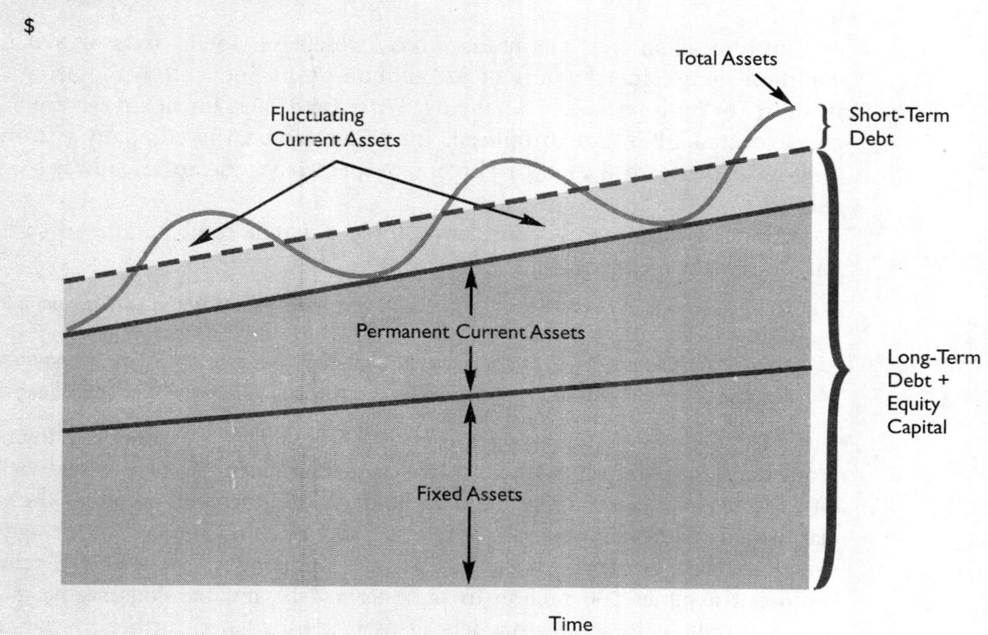

FIGURE 16.5
Aggressive Approach to Asset Financing

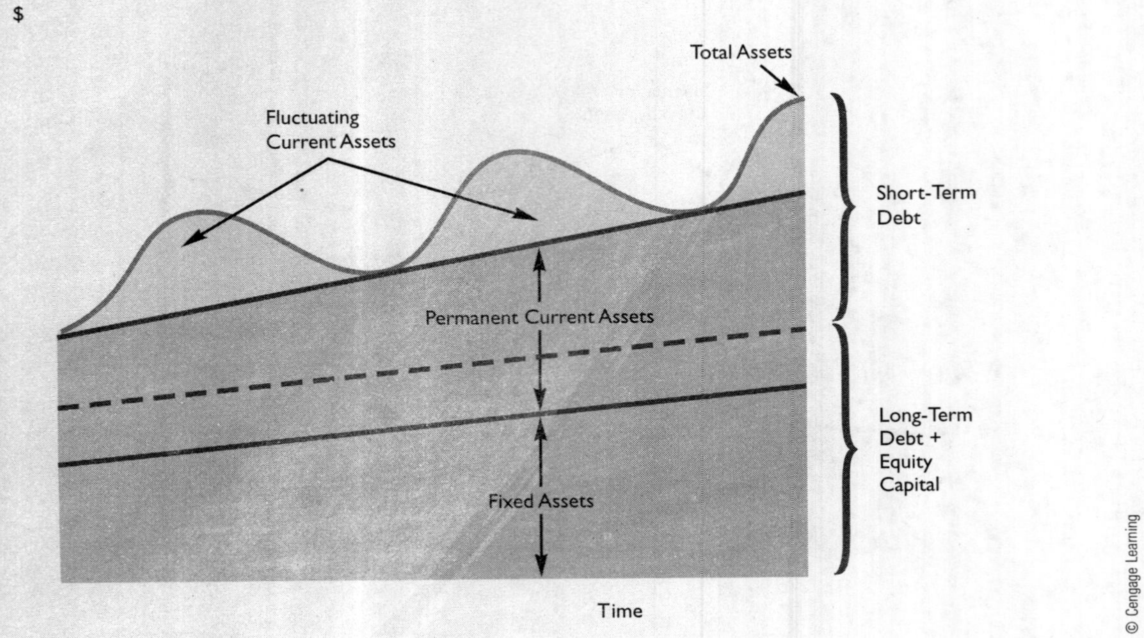

with this financing plan also add to the firm's risk. These higher risks are offset by the higher expected after-tax earnings that result from the normally lower costs of short-term debt.

Consider again Burlington Resources, which has total assets of $70 million and common shareholders' equity of $28 million on its books, thus requiring $42 million in short- or long-term debt financing. Forecasted sales for next year are $100 million and expected EBIT is $10 million. Interest rates on the company's short-term and long-term debt are 8 and 10 percent, respectively, due to an upward-sloping yield curve.

Burlington Resources is considering three different combinations of short-term and long-term debt financing:

- An *aggressive* plan consisting of $30 million in short-term debt (STD) and $12 million in long-term debt (LTD)
- A *moderate* plan consisting of $20 million in short-term debt and $22 million in long-term debt
- A *conservative* plan consisting of $10 million in short-term debt and $32 million in long-term debt

Table 16.4 shows the data for each of these alternative proposed financing plans. From the standpoint of profitability, the aggressive financing plan would yield the highest expected rate of return to the stockholders—13.6 percent—whereas the conservative plan would yield the lowest rate of return—12.9 percent. In contrast, the aggressive plan would involve a greater degree of risk that the company will be unable to refund its debt, because it assumes $30 million in short-term debt and the conservative plan assumes only $10 million in short-term debt. This is substantiated further by the fact that the company's net working capital position and current ratio would be lowest under the

TABLE 16.4

Profitability and Risk of Alternative Financing Policies for Burlington Resources (in Millions of Dollars)

		Aggressive Relatively Large Amount of Short-Term Debt		Moderate Moderate Amount of Short-Term Debt		Conservative Relatively Small Amount of Short-Term Debt
Current assets (C/A)		$ 40		$ 40		$ 40
Fixed assets (F/A)		30		30		30
Total assets (T/A)		$ 70		$ 70		$ 70
Current liabilities (STD)(C/L) (interest rate, 8%)		$ 30		$ 20		$ 10
Long-term liabilities (LTD) (interest rate, 10%)		12		22		32
Total liabilities (60% of T/A)		$ 42		$ 42		$ 42
Common equity		28		28		28
Total liabilities and common equity		$ 70		$ 70		$ 70
Forecasted sales		$ 100		$ 100		$ 100
Expected EBIT		10		10		10
Less Interest:						
STD, 8%	2.4		1.6		0.8	
LTD, 10%	1.2	3.6	2.2	3.8	3.2	4.0
Taxable income		$ 6.4		$ 6.2		$ 6.0
Less Taxes (40%)		2.6		2.5		2.4
Net income after taxes		$ 3.8		$ 3.7		$ 3.6
Expected rate of return on common equity		13.6%		13.2%		12.9%
Net working capital position (C/A − C/L)		$10		$20		$ 30
Current ratio (C/A ÷ C/L)		1.33		2.0		4.0

aggressive plan and highest under the conservative plan—making the degree of risk that the company will be unable to meet financial obligations greater with the aggressive plan. The moderate financing plan represents a middle-of-the-road approach, and the expected rate of return and risk level are between the aggressive and the conservative approaches. In summary, both expected profitability and risk increase as the proportion of short-term debt increases.[12]

16-5a Optimal Proportions of Short-Term and Long-Term Debt

As is the case with working capital investment policy, no one combination of short- and long-term debt is necessarily optimal for all firms. In choosing a financing policy that maximizes shareholder wealth, a firm's financial manager must also take into account various other factors, such as the variability of sales and cash flows, that affect the valuation of the firm.

[12]This example assumes that the costs of short-term and long-term debt would be the same for each of the three financing policies. In practice, however, this would probably not be the case because lenders generally require higher interest rates before making loans involving higher risks. Thus, a company following an aggressive financing policy will probably have to pay slightly higher interest rates on debt than a company following a conservative policy. This effect can be incorporated into the analysis by modifying the interest rates on short-term and long-term debt under the various financing policies. This would affect the numerical values in the example, but it should not affect the general conclusions concerning the profitability versus risk trade-offs.

16-6 Overall Working Capital Policy

Until now, this chapter has analyzed the working capital investment and financing decisions independent of one another in order to examine the profitability-risk trade-offs associated with each, assuming that all other factors are held constant. Effective working capital policy, however, also requires the consideration of the *joint* impact of these decisions on the firm's profitability and risk.

Referring to Burlington Resources again, assume that the company is 60 percent debt financed (both short-term and long-term) and 40 percent financed with common stock. Also, it is evaluating three alternative working capital investment and financing policies. The *aggressive* policy would require a relatively *small* investment in current assets, $35 million, and a relatively *large* amount of short-term debt, $30 million. The *conservative* policy would require a relatively *large* investment in current assets, $45 million, and a relatively *small* amount of short-term debt, $10 million. The firm is also considering a middle-of-the-road approach, which would involve a *moderate* investment in current assets, $40 million, and a *moderate* amount of short-term debt, $20 million.

Table 16.5 shows the data for each approach. The aggressive working capital policy is expected to yield the highest return on shareholders' equity, 15.4 percent, whereas the

TABLE 16.5

Alternative Working Capital Investment and Financing Policies for Burlington Resources (in Millions of Dollars)

	Aggressive Relatively Small Investment in Current Assets; Relatively Large Amount of Short-Term Debt		Moderate Moderate Investment in Current Assets; Moderate Amount of Short-Term Debt		Conservative Relatively Large Investment in Current Assets; Relatively Small Amount of Short-Term Debt	
Current assets (C/A)		$ 35		$ 40		$ 45
Fixed assets (F/A)		30		30		30
Total assets (T/A)		$ 65		$ 70		$ 75
Current liabilities (STD) (C/L) (interest rate, 8%)		$ 30		$ 20		$ 10
Long-term liabilities (LTD) (interest rate, 10%)		9		22		35
Total liabilities (60% of T/A)		$ 39		$ 42		$ 45
Common equity		26		28		30
Total liabilities and common equity		$ 65		$ 70		$ 75
Forecasted sales		$100		$100		$100
Expected EBIT		10		10		10
Less Interest:						
STD, 8%	2.4		1.6		0.8	
LTD, 10%	0.9	3.3	2.2	3.8	3.5	4.3
Taxable income		$ 6.7		$ 6.2		$ 5.7
Less Taxes (40%)		2.7		2.5		2.3
Net income after taxes		$ 4.0		$ 3.7		$ 3.4
Expected rate of return on common equity		15.4%		13.2%		11.3%
Net working capital position (C/A − C/L)		$5		$20		$35
Current ratio (C/A ÷ C/L)		1.17		2.0		4.5

conservative policy is expected to yield the lowest return, 11.3 percent. The net working capital and current ratio are lowest under the aggressive policy and highest under the conservative policy, indicating that the aggressive policy is the riskiest. The moderate policy yields an expected return and risk level somewhere between the aggressive and the conservative policies.

Whereas this type of analysis will not directly yield the optimal working capital investment and financing policies a company should choose, it can give the financial manager some insight into the profitability-risk trade-offs of alternative policies. With an understanding of these trade-offs, the financial manager should be able to make better decisions concerning the working capital policy that will lead to a maximization of shareholder wealth.

16-7 Short-Term Credit

A company normally employs a combination of short- and intermediate-term credit and long-term debt and equity in financing its current and fixed assets. The various sources of long-term financing have already been discussed. This section focuses on the major sources of short-term credit.

Short-term credit includes all of a company's debt obligations that originally were scheduled for repayment within one year.[13] Short-term credit may be either *unsecured* or *secured*.[14] In the case of unsecured short-term debt, a firm obtains credit from the lender without having to pledge any specific assets as collateral, and the lender depends primarily on the cash-generating ability of the firm to repay the debt. If the firm becomes insolvent and declares bankruptcy, the unsecured lender usually stands little chance of recovering all or even a significant portion of the amount owed.

In the case of secured short-term debt, the borrower pledges certain specified assets—such as accounts receivable, inventory, or fixed assets—as collateral.[15] The Uniform Commercial Code, which was adopted by all states during the 1960s, outlines the procedures that must be followed in order for a lender to establish a valid claim on a firm's collateral.

The first step in this process involves the execution of a *security agreement*, which is a contract between the lender and the firm specifying the collateral held against the loan. The security agreement is then filed at the appropriate public office within the state where the collateral is located. Future potential lenders can check with this office to determine which assets the firm has pledged and which are still free to be used as collateral. Filing this security agreement legally establishes the lender's security interest in the collateral. If the borrower defaults on the loan or otherwise fails to honor the terms of the agreement, the lender can seize and sell the collateral to recover the amount owed. Thus, the lender in a secured short-term debt agreement has *two* potential sources of loan repayment: the firm's cash-generating ability and the collateral value of the pledged assets.

Short-term lenders can be classified as either *cash-flow lenders* or *asset-based lenders*, depending upon how they view the two potential sources of loan repayment. Cash-flow lenders look upon the borrower's future cash flows as the *primary* source of loan repayment and the borrower's assets as a *secondary* source of repayment. Asset-based lenders tend to make riskier loans than cash-flow lenders, and as a result, they place much

---

[13]Short-term credit does *not* always correspond exactly to the current liabilities shown on the firm's balance sheet. Current liabilities also include that portion of long-term debt (such as term loans and mortgages) scheduled for repayment during the next year.

[14]Intermediate- and long-term debt may also be either unsecured or secured.

[15]As an alternative to pledging specific assets as collateral for a loan, a company may get a third party to *cosign*, or *guarantee*, the loan. If the borrower defaults, the third party becomes responsible for repayment. Lenders will usually accept only financially sound third parties, such as a stockholder, supplier, or customer who has a vested interest in the company's success.

greater emphasis on the value of the borrower's collateral. Generally, large, low-leveraged companies with good expected cash flows are able to borrow from cash-flow lenders, such as commercial banks, at relatively low rates. Smaller, highly leveraged businesses with more uncertain future cash flows often have to borrow on a secured basis from asset-based lenders, such as commercial finance companies, at relatively high rates.

In general, companies prefer to borrow funds on an unsecured basis because the added administrative costs involved in pledging assets as security raise the cost of the loan to the borrower. In addition, secured borrowing agreements can restrict a company's future borrowing. Many companies, particularly small ones, are not able to obtain unsecured credit, however. For example, a company may be financially weak or too new to justify an unsecured loan, or it may want more credit than the lender is willing to give on an unsecured basis. In any of these circumstances, either the company must provide collateral or it will not receive the loan.

The short-term credit sources available to a company can be either *spontaneous* or *negotiated*. Spontaneous sources, which include *trade credit, accrued expenses,* and *deferred income*, are discussed in upcoming sections. Later sections of this chapter consider the various negotiated sources, such as *bank credit, commercial paper, receivables loans,* and *inventory loans.*

16-8 Cost of Short-Term Funds

Managers need a method to calculate the financing cost for the various sources of short-term financing available to a firm. Equation 5.1 from Chapter 5 gives the amount of interest paid, *I*, on borrowed money:

$$I = PV_0 \times i \times n \tag{16.6}$$

where I = the interest amount in dollars; PV_0 = the principal amount at time 0, or the present value; i = the interest rate per time period; and n = the number of time periods. Solving for i, we obtain:

$$i = \frac{I}{PV_0} \times \frac{1}{n} \tag{16.7}$$

The interest rate, i, is equal to the fractional interest cost per period, I/PV_0, times 1 divided by the number of time periods, or $1/n$.

annual financing cost (AFC)

The equation we use to calculate the **annual financing cost** (AFC) for short-term financing sources is a variation of Equation 16.7:

$$\text{AFC} = \frac{\text{Interest costs} + \text{fees}}{\text{Usable funds}} \times \frac{365}{\text{Maturity (days)}} \tag{16.8}$$

Short-term financing sources may involve fees in addition to the interest costs. Also, the term *usable funds* is used in place of present value because some of the money from a particular short-term financing source may not actually be available for a company to use. The term, 365/Maturity (days), converts the financing cost to an annual rate.

annual percentage rate (APR)

The annual financing cost calculated using Equation 16.8 is only an approximation to the true (effective) **annual percentage rate (APR)**, of a loan. Equation 16.8 does not consider compounding and slightly understates the true APR. Also, Equation 16.8 is normally used for financing sources of one year or less. The following equation gives the true APR for a short-term financing source:

$$\text{APR} = \left(1 + \frac{\text{Interest costs} + \text{fees}}{\text{Usable funds}}\right)^m - 1 \tag{16.9}$$

where *m* is the number of times per year compounding occurs. Equation 16.9 is a variation of Equation 5.27 from Chapter 5. In addition, the APR of a loan is the internal rate of return between the funds received and the funds paid back.

To illustrate the use of Equations 16.8 and 16.9, consider a six-month, $10,000 loan that has $500 of interest. If we assume that principal is paid only at maturity and there are 182 days in the six-month period, the annual financing cost is calculated, using Equation 16.8, as follows:

$$\text{AFC} = \frac{\$500}{\$10{,}000} \times \frac{365}{182}$$
$$= 0.1003 \text{ or } 10.03\%$$

The loan's APR is determined as follows, using Equation 16.9:

$$\text{APR} = \left(1 + \frac{\$500}{\$10{,}000}\right)^{365/182} - 1$$
$$= 0.1028 \text{ or } 10.28\%$$

The annual financing cost percentage approximates the true APR, unless the number of compounding periods is large.

Equation 16.8 is used throughout this chapter to calculate the annual financing cost of the various short-term financing sources available to a firm.

16-9 Trade Credit

Whenever a business receives merchandise ordered from a supplier and is then permitted to wait a specified period of time before having to pay, it is receiving *trade credit.*[16] In the aggregate, trade credit is the most important source of short-term financing for business firms. Smaller businesses in particular usually rely heavily on trade credit to finance their operations because they are often unable to obtain funds from banks or other lenders in the financial markets.

Most trade credit is extended on an *open account* basis. A firm sends a purchase order to a supplier, who then evaluates the firm's creditworthiness using various information sources and decision criteria.[17] If the supplier decides to extend the firm credit, it ships the ordered merchandise to the firm, along with an invoice describing the contents of the shipment, the total amount due, and the terms of sale. When the firm accepts the merchandise shipped by the supplier, it in effect agrees to pay the amount due as specified by the terms of sale on the invoice. Once it has been established, trade credit becomes almost automatic and is subject to only periodic reviews by the supplier. Open account trade credit appears on the balance sheet as *accounts payable.*

promissory note

Promissory notes are sometimes used as an alternative to the open account arrangement. When a company signs a **promissory note**, which specifies the amount to be paid and the due date, it is formally recognizing an obligation to repay the credit. A supplier may require a company to sign a promissory note if it questions the company's creditworthiness. Promissory notes usually appear on the balance sheet as *notes payable.*

[16] If the supplier does not feel the firm is creditworthy, it can require that payment be made either before the goods are shipped (cash before delivery, or CBD) or upon delivery of the merchandise (cash on delivery, or COD). These are cash sales and do not involve an extension of credit.

[17] These sources and criteria are discussed in Chapter 18.

16-9a Credit Terms

Credit terms, or terms of sale, specify the conditions under which a business is required to repay the credit that a supplier has extended to it. These conditions include the *length* and the *beginning date* of the credit period, the *cash discount* (if any) given for prompt repayment, and any *special terms*, such as *seasonal datings.*[18]

16-9b Cost of Trade Credit

Trade credit is considered a *spontaneous* source of financing because it normally expands as the volume of a company's purchases increases. For example, suppose a company experiences increased demand for its products. As a result, the company increases purchases from suppliers by 20 percent, from an average of $10,000 per day to an average of $12,000 per day. Assuming that these purchases are made on credit terms of "net 30" and that the company waits until the last day of the credit period to make payment, its average accounts payable outstanding (trade credit) will automatically increase by 20 percent, from $300,000 ($10,000 × 30) to $360,000 ($12,000 × 30).

Because trade credit is flexible, informal, and relatively easy to obtain, it is an attractive source of financing for virtually all firms, especially new and smaller firms. To make intelligent use of trade credit, however, a firm should consider the associated costs. Unlike other sources of financing, such as bank loans and bonds, which include explicit interest charges, the cost of trade credit is not always readily apparent. It may appear to be "cost-free" because of the lack of interest charges, but this reasoning can lead to incorrect financing decisions.

Obviously, someone has to bear the cost of trade credit. In extending trade credit, the supplier incurs the cost of the funds invested in accounts receivable, plus the cost of any cash discounts that are taken. Normally, the supplier passes on all or part of these costs to its customers implicitly as part of the purchase price of the merchandise, depending on market supply and demand conditions. If a company is in a position to pay cash for purchases, it may consider trying to avoid these implicit costs by negotiating lower prices with suppliers.

If the terms of sale include a cash discount, the firm must decide whether or not to take it. If the firm *takes the cash discount*, it forgoes the credit offered by the supplier beyond the end of the discount period. Assuming that the firm takes the cash discount and wants to make maximum use of the credit offered by suppliers, it should pay its bills on the last day of the discount period. Under these conditions, trade credit does represent a "cost-free" source of financing to the firm (assuming that no additional discounts are available if the firm pays cash on delivery or cash before delivery).

If a company *forgoes the cash discount* and pays bills after the end of the discount period, a definite opportunity cost of trade credit is incurred. In calculating the cost of not taking the cash discount, it is assumed that the company will make maximum use of extended trade credit by paying on the last day of the credit period. Paying after the end of the credit period, or *stretching accounts payable*, subjects the company to certain other costs.

The annual financing cost of forgoing a cash discount is calculated using Equation 16.10. In this application, the AFC is equal to the fractional interest cost per period times the number of borrowing periods per year:

(16.10) $$\text{AFC} = \frac{\text{Percentage discount}}{100 - \text{Percentage discount}} \times \frac{365}{\text{Credit period} - \text{Discount period}}$$

For example, suppose the Benson Company has been extended $150,000 of trade credit from a supplier on terms of "2/10, net 30." As shown in Figure 16.6, the company can

[18]This topic is discussed in Chapter 18.

FIGURE 16.6

Benson Company's Cost of Forgoing the Cash Discount

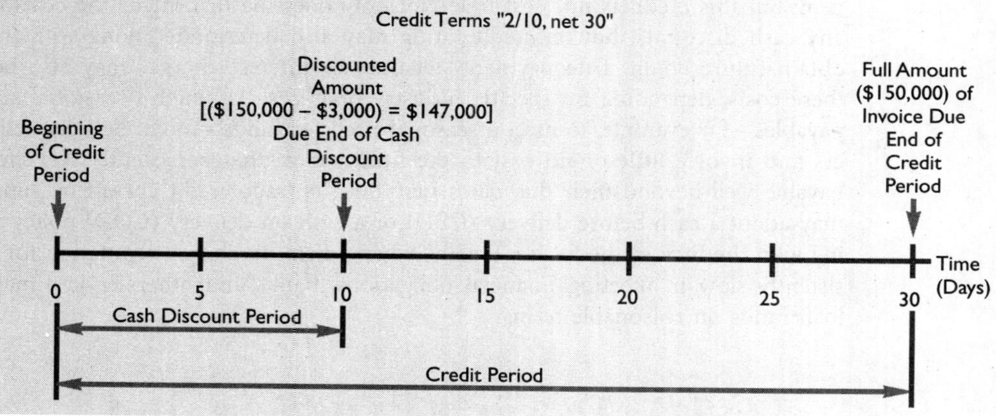

either pay the discounted amount ($147,000) by the end of the discount period (day 10) or pay the full amount of the invoice ($150,000) by the end of the credit period (day 30).

By *not* paying on the 10th day—that is, by forgoing the cash discount—the company has the use of $147,000 (98 percent of the invoice amount) for an additional 20 days and effectively pays $3,000 in interest.[19] Substituting this information into Equation 16.10 yields the following:

$$\begin{aligned} \text{AFC} &= \frac{2}{100-2} \times \frac{365}{30-10} \\ &= \frac{2}{98} \times \frac{365}{20} \\ &= 0.372 \text{ or } 37.2\% \end{aligned}$$

As this example shows, the annual cost of forgoing cash discounts can be quite high. Therefore, when making financing decisions, a company should compare this cost to the costs of other sources of credit.

Also, the company that offers credit terms of "2/10, net 30" should consider the annual financing cost of having the use of funds for an additional 20 days. As the preceding calculation illustrates, the annual financing cost of offering cash discounts when the credit terms are "2/10, net 30" is about 37 percent. Accordingly, a company may want to consider other less expensive methods of encouraging prompt payment of trade credit. However, other benefits may accrue to a company that offers cash discounts. For example, a company may actually increase its sales by offering cash discounts. Or, a company may find that its bad-debt loss ratio is lowered if it offers a discount.

Abuses of cash discounts also exist; for example, a purchaser may deduct the discount amount even when payment is made after the discount period has passed. As a result, the seller has to decide whether to simply accept the lower payment or attempt to collect the unearned cash discount amount. With either alternative, the seller incurs costs.

[19]If a firm does not pay by the cash discount date, it should not pay the invoice until the final date. If the invoice is paid before the final due date, the cost of this financing increases dramatically. For example, assume Benson Company pays on day 11 and does not take the cash discount. The cost of this financing is nearly 745 percent:

$$\left(\frac{2}{98} \times \frac{365}{11-10}\right) = 7.45 \text{ or } 745\%$$

16-9c Stretching Accounts Payable

Rather than pay suppliers within the credit period specified in the terms of sale, a firm can postpone payment of the amount due to beyond the end of the credit period. *Stretching* payments in this manner generates additional short-term financing for the firm, but this credit is not cost-free. Not only does the firm incur the costs of forgoing any cash discounts, but its credit rating may also deteriorate, along with its ability to obtain future credit. Late payment penalties or interest charges may also be added to these costs, depending on specific industry practices. Although occasional stretching of payables—for example, to meet a seasonal need for funds—might be tolerated by suppliers and involve little or no cost to the firm, a firm that persistently stretches accounts payable well beyond their due dates may find its trade credit cut off by suppliers, who may adopt a cash before delivery (CBD) or a cash on delivery (COD) policy when dealing with the firm in the future. Finally, when a firm develops a reputation for being consistently slow in meeting financial obligations, banks and other lenders may refuse to loan funds on reasonable terms.

16-10 Accrued Expenses and Deferred Income

Accrued expenses and deferred income are additional spontaneous sources of unsecured short-term credit.

16-10a Accrued Expenses

Accrued expenses—such as *accrued wages*, *taxes*, and *interest*—represent liabilities for services rendered to the firm that have not yet been paid for by the firm. As such, they constitute an interest-free source of financing.

Accrued wages represent the money a business owes to its employees. Accrued wages build up between paydays and fall to zero again at the end of the pay period, when the employees receive their paychecks. A company can increase the average amount of accrued wages by lengthening the period between paydays. For example, changing from a two-week pay cycle to a four-week pay cycle would effectively double a firm's average level of accrued wages. Also, a company can increase accrued expenses by delaying the payment of sales commissions and bonuses. Legal and practical considerations, however, limit the extent to which a company can increase accrued wages in this manner.

The amounts of *accrued taxes* and *interest* a firm may accumulate is also determined by the frequency with which these expenses must be paid. For example, corporate income tax payments normally are due quarterly, and a firm can use accrued taxes as a source of funds between these payment dates. Similarly, accrued interest on a bond issue requiring semiannual interest payments can be used as a source of financing for periods as long as six months. Of course, a firm has no control over the frequency of these tax and interest payments, so the amount of financing provided by these sources depends solely on the amounts of the payments themselves.

16-10b Deferred Income

Deferred income consists of payments received for goods and services that the firm has agreed to deliver at some future date. Because these payments increase the firm's liquidity and assets—namely, cash—they constitute a source of funds.

Advance payments made by customers are the primary sources of deferred income. These payments are common on large, expensive products, such as jet aircraft. Because these payments are not "earned" by the firm until delivery of the goods or services to the customers, they are recognized on the balance sheet as a liability called *deferred income.*

16-11 Short-Term Bank Credit

Commercial banks are an important source of both secured and unsecured short-term credit. In terms of the aggregate amount of short-term financing they provide to business firms, they rank second behind trade credit. Although trade credit is a primary source of *spontaneous* short-term financing, bank loans represent the major source of *negotiated* short-term funds.

A major purpose of short-term bank loans is to meet the firm's seasonal needs for funds—such as financing the buildup of inventories and receivables. Bank loans used for this purpose are regarded as self-liquidating, because sale of the inventories and collection of the receivables are expected to generate sufficient cash flows to permit the firm to repay the loan prior to the next seasonal buildup.

When a firm obtains a short-term bank loan, it normally signs a promissory note specifying the amount of the loan, the interest rate being charged, and the due date. The loan agreement may also contain various protective covenants.[20] Short-term bank loans appear on the balance sheet under *notes payable.*

prime rate

The interest rate charged on a bank loan is usually related to the **prime rate**, which is the rate banks historically have charged on loans made to their most creditworthy, or *prime*, business customers. The prime rate fluctuates over time with changes in the supply of and demand for loanable funds. During the past 40 years, for instance, the prime rate ranged from as low as 3.25 percent in 2008–2015 during the financial crisis and slow recovery period thereafter to over 20 percent in 1981 during a period of unusually high inflation. In recent years many large, highly profitable companies have been able to borrow at less than the prime rate. Borrowing at rates below the prime rate is partially the result of increased competition among large banks and other suppliers of short-term financing for especially creditworthy borrowers.

London interbank offered rate (LIBOR)

As an alternative to borrowing funds in the United States, large, well-established multinational corporations can borrow short-term funds in the Eurodollar market.[21] The interest rate in the Eurodollar market is usually related to the **London interbank offered rate, or LIBOR**. LIBOR is the interest rate at which banks in the Eurocurrency market lend to each other. For example, large, well-established multinational corporations usually can borrow at about 0.5 percentage points over LIBOR. Because LIBOR is frequently about 1.5 or more percentage points below U.S. bank prime rates, large companies can often borrow in the Eurodollar market at subprime rates. For example, in December 2015, the three-month LIBOR rate was 0.62 percent, compared to an average prime rate of 3.37 percent.[22] However, the LIBOR rate tends to be more volatile over time than the prime rate.

Short-term bank financing is available under three different arrangements:

- Single loans (notes)
- Lines of credit
- Revolving credit agreements

[20]The section on term loans in Chapter 19 discusses these protective covenants.

[21]The Eurocurrency market is discussed in Chapter 2.

[22]"Money Rates—Markets Data Center," www.wsj.com (March 26, 2016).

ETHICAL ISSUES

Interest Rate Manipulation

The London interbank offered rate (LIBOR) is a series of interest rates for different currencies and time periods. A panel of large banks, including Bank of America, Citigroup, and JPMorgan Chase in the United States, make daily submissions to the British Bankers Association of the interest rates they charge other banks, and the average of these rates is reported in the financial press. Other similar rates include the Euro Interbank Offered Rate (EUBOR) and the Tokyo Interbank Offered Rate (TIBOR).

Government regulators found that, beginning in 2006 and continuing through 2010, a number of the submitting banks attempted to manipulate these interest rates. This was done in order to increase the banks' trading profits on securities whose values were linked to the LIBOR rates. According to one estimate, over $300 *trillion* in loans and derivative securities are tied to LIBOR.

Three of the European banks involved in the interest rate rigging have settled the charges against them by agreeing to fines totaling over $2.5 billion—Barclays ($450 million), RBS ($612 million), and UBS ($1.5 billion). A number of executives of these banks lost their jobs, including the CEO of Barclays. In 2015 the alleged ringleader, a former trader for UBS, was found guilty in London of fraud in the plot to manipulate LIBOR and was sentenced to 14 years in prison. A dozen other bankers also faced criminal changes in connection with the rate rigging. Finally, numerous civil lawsuits were filed against the banks involved in setting LIBOR, seeking compensation for alleged financial losses from the interest rate rigging. Estimates of the collective cost to the banks range anywhere from $10 billion to nearly $200 billion.

Sources: Reed Albergotti, "Banks Seek Dismissals of Lawsuits over LIBOR," *The Wall Street Journal* (March 6, 2013); David Enrich et al., "U.S. Wants Criminal Charges for RBS," *The Wall Street Journal* (January 20, 2013): A1; David Enrich and Jean Eaglesham, "UBS Admits Rigging Rates in Epic Plot," *The Wall Street Journal* (December 20, 2012): A1; David Reilly, "Big Banks' $29 Billion Cookie Jar," *The Wall Street Journal* (September 5, 2012): C26; Jean Eaglesham et al., "Rate Probe Keys on Traders," *The Wall Street Journal* (February 7, 2012): C1; Giles Turner and David Enrich, "More Libor Charges on Way," *The Wall Street Journal* (August 5, 2015): C3; Juliet Samuel, "Libor Overseer Chief Was Pushed Out," *The Wall Street Journal* (December 18, 2015): C3.

16-11a Single Loans (Notes)

Businesses frequently need funds for short time periods to finance a particular undertaking. In such a case, they may request a bank loan. This type of loan is often referred to as a *note*. The length of this type of loan can range from 30 days to one year, with most being for 30 to 90 days.

The interest rate a bank charges on an individual loan at a given point in time depends on a number of factors, including the borrower's creditworthiness relative to prime (lowest) credit risks. The interest rate often includes a premium of 1 to 2 or more percentage points above the prime rate, depending on how the bank officer perceives the borrower's overall business and financial risk. If the borrower is in a weak financial position and has overall risk that is thought to be too high, the bank may refuse to make an unsecured loan, regardless of the interest rate. When making the loan decision, the loan officer also considers the size of the checking account balance the company maintains at the bank, the amount of other business it does with the bank, and the rates that competitive banks are charging on similar loans.

The annual financing cost of a bank loan is also a function of when the borrower must pay the interest and whether the bank requires the borrower to maintain a compensating balance.

Interest Payments If the interest on a note is paid at *maturity*, the annual financing cost is equal to the stated annual interest rate. In the case of a **discounted loan**,

discounted loan

however, the bank deducts the interest at the time the loan is made, and thus the borrower does not receive the full loan amount. In other words, the borrower pays interest on funds it does not receive, and the annual financing cost of the loan is greater than the stated annual interest rate.[23]

For example, suppose the Edgewood Flower and Gift Shop receives a six-month (183-day) \$5,000 discounted loan at a stated annual interest rate of 8 percent. The firm pays \$201 interest in advance (0.08 × \$5,000 × 183/365) and receives only \$4,799 (\$5,000–\$201). Using Equation 16.8, the annual financing cost is calculated as follows:

$$\text{AFC} = \frac{\$201}{\$4{,}799} \times \frac{365}{183}$$
$$= 0.084 \text{ or } 8.4\%$$

Discounted bank loans today are relatively uncommon; however, other securities—commercial paper and Treasury bills, for example—are sold on a discount basis.

compensating balance

Compensating Balances A **compensating balance** is a certain percentage, normally in the range of 5 to 20 percent, of a loan balance that the borrower keeps on deposit with a bank as a requirement of a loan made by the bank. The compensating balance requirement is stated either in terms of an *absolute minimum* balance or an *average* balance over some stipulated period; borrowers prefer average balances to minimum balances. A compensating balance increases the return the bank earns on the loan and also provides the bank with a small measure of protection ("right of offset") in the event that the borrower defaults. Compensating balances tend to diminish in importance during periods of slack loan demand.

If the required compensating balance is *in excess* of the amount of funds that normally would be maintained in the company's checking account, the annual financing cost of the loan is greater than the stated interest rate. It can be calculated using Equation 16.8. When a compensating balance is required, the *usable funds* amount in the denominator is the *net* amount of the loan that the company can spend after taking into account the amount borrowed, any required compensating balance, and the balance normally maintained in the bank account.

For example, suppose the Cutler Company obtains a one-year (365-day) \$200,000 bank loan at 9 percent interest but is required to maintain a 20 percent average compensating balance. In other words, the company must maintain a \$40,000 (0.20 × \$200,000) average compensating balance to obtain the loan. If Cutler currently maintains a \$30,000 average balance that can be used to meet the compensating balance requirement, it needs to keep an additional \$10,000 in the account, and thus the loan generates \$190,000 in usable funds. The interest charges on the loan are \$18,000 (\$200,000 × 0.09). Substituting these values into Equation 16.8 yields the following:

$$\text{AFC} = \frac{\$18{,}000}{\$190{,}000} \times \frac{365}{365}$$
$$= 0.095 \text{ or } 9.5\%$$

However, if Cutler currently has no balances in its bank account that can be used to meet the average compensating balance requirement, it has to keep \$40,000 of the

[23]The process for determining the AFC (or APR) of a bank loan is a function of when the loan principal is repaid. The calculations in this section assume that the principal is repaid at maturity. In the case of *installment* loans, principal payments are made periodically (for example, monthly) over the term of the loan.

$200,000 loan in the checking account, and the amount of usable funds is reduced to $160,000. In this case, the annual financing cost becomes significantly higher:

$$\text{AFC} = \frac{\$18{,}000}{\$160{,}000} \times \frac{365}{365}$$
$$= 0.113 \text{ or } 11.3\%$$

16-11b Lines of Credit

line of credit

A firm that needs funds periodically throughout the year for a variety of purposes may find it useful to negotiate a **line of credit** with its bank. A line of credit is an agreement that permits the firm to borrow funds up to a predetermined limit at any time during the life of the agreement. The major advantage of this type of borrowing agreement, as compared with single loans, is that the firm does not have to renegotiate with the bank every time funds are required. Instead, it can obtain funds on short notice with little or no additional justification. Another advantage to establishing a line of credit is that the firm can plan for its future short-term financing requirements without having to anticipate exactly how much it will have to borrow each month.

A line of credit is usually negotiated for a one-year period, with renewals being subject to renegotiation each year. In determining the size of a credit line, a bank will consider a company's creditworthiness, along with its projected financing needs. As part of the application for a line of credit, the company is normally required to provide the bank with a cash budget for the next year, along with current and projected income statements and balance sheets. The interest rate on a line of credit is usually determined by adding to the prime rate a premium based on the borrower's creditworthiness. Because the prime rate normally fluctuates over time, the interest rate charged varies during the life of the agreement.

To illustrate, suppose the Bellevue Candy Company has a $500,000 line of credit at 1 percentage point above the bank's prime rate.[24] During the year, the company borrows, or "draws down," $200,000 on the line, and no compensating balances are in effect during the year. The bank's prime rate is 8.0 percent from January 1 to March 31, and on April 1, the bank raises its prime rate to 8.25 percent, where it remains for the rest of the year. The annual financing cost is calculated as follows using Equation 16.8:

Interest costs (January 1 – March 31):

$$I = \$200{,}000 \times 0.09 \times \frac{90}{365}$$
$$= \$4{,}438.36$$

Interest costs (April 1 – December 31):

$$I = \$200{,}000 \times 0.0925 \times \frac{275}{365}$$
$$= \$13{,}938.36$$

$$\text{Total interest cost} = \$4{,}438.36 + \$13{,}938.36$$
$$= \$18{,}376.72$$

$$\text{AFC} = \frac{\$18.376.72}{\$200{,}000.00} \times \frac{365}{365}$$
$$= 0.0919 \text{ or } 9.19\%$$

A line of credit agreement normally includes certain protective covenants. In addition to possibly including a compensating balance requirement, the loan agreement usually

[24] Finance professionals often refer to this rate as "prime plus one," or "one over prime." In addition, they often write it as "P + 1."

HTTP:
The following Web address provides the largest business capital search engine on the Internet, providing more than 3,600 sources for obtaining business lines of credit:

www.businessfinance.com/business-line-of-credit.htm

contains an annual "cleanup" provision requiring that the company have no loans outstanding under the line of credit for a certain period of time each year, usually 30 to 90 days. This type of policy helps reassure the bank that the company is using the line of credit to finance seasonal needs for funds and not to finance permanent capital requirements. Finally, a line of credit agreement may also contain provisions (similar to those in a term loan agreement) that require the firm to maintain a minimum working capital position, limit total debt and lease financing, and restrict dividend payments.

16-11c Revolving Credit Agreements

Although a line of credit agreement does not legally commit the bank to making loans to the firm under any and all conditions, the bank normally will feel morally obligated to honor the line of credit. Some banks, however, have chosen not to provide financing to a firm when the firm's financial position has deteriorated significantly or when the bank lacks sufficient loanable funds to satisfy all its commitments. If the firm desires a guaranteed line of credit, it must negotiate a committed revolving credit agreement.

ETHICAL ISSUES

Tying Bank Loans to Other Services[a]

In a survey by the Association for Financial Professionals of corporate finance executives, 96 percent of those who responded claimed that they had been pressured by commercial banks to purchase other financial services in exchange for obtaining loans from the banks. These executives included chief financial officers and treasurers of large companies, that is, those with $1 billion or more in annual revenues. Furthermore, almost two-thirds of the respondents indicated that the banks had denied them credit or raised the cost of loans because their corporations did not buy other financial services from the banks.

The reported increase in tying loans to other services is attributed to two primary factors. One is the increased concentration in the banking industry, where three large banks—Citigroup, JPMorgan Chase, and Bank of America—arrange more than 50 percent of the credit lines for large corporations. The other is the repeal of laws that prevented commercial banks from engaging in various investment banking services, such as securities underwriting and merger advice.

Laws enacted in the 1970s made it illegal, with limited exceptions, for commercial banks to explicitly require borrowers to purchase other services, such as insurance, as a requirement for receiving a loan. Such tying arrangements can be anticompetitive because they allow commercial banks to use their dominance in one service, that is, loans, to force companies to buy other services that the companies could purchase, possibly at a lower cost, from other financial institutions.

However, subtler forms of tying are not necessarily illegal. Banks claim that loans to corporate customers are often only marginally profitable. In order for their relationship with corporate clients to be worthwhile, banks feel that they need to include other services. As an official of the American Bankers Association noted, "Everyone who has looked at this has found that relationship banking is part of commerce." Officials at the Justice Department have even claimed that tying can be beneficial because it allows large, knowledgeable corporate borrowers to play one bank off against another in order to obtain the best possible package deal. The Justice Department explained that, "Although tying arrangements can be anticompetitive, overly restrictive laws can also impede legitimate competition." As one industry executive explained, "Banks absolutely should be able to decline to lend if the overall relationship is not sufficiently lucrative." However, "at what point does coercive behavior emerge?"

What factors might cause a commercial banker to seek to coerce a corporate customer to purchase other financial services in addition to loans? What are the possible consequences of such actions for the bank's shareholders? Would more laws help eliminate or minimize such tying arrangements?

[a] Jathon Sapsford, "Executives See Rise in 'Tying' Loans to Other Fees," *The Wall Street Journal* (June 9, 2004): A1.

revolving credit agreement

Under a **revolving credit agreement**, or "revolver," the bank is *legally committed* to making loans to a company up to the predetermined credit limit specified in the agreement. Revolving credit agreements differ from line of credit agreements in that they often require the borrower to pay a *commitment fee* on the unused portion of the funds. This fee is typically in the range of 0.25 to 0.50 percent. Revolving credit agreements are frequently made for periods of up to five years. For example, in April 2007 King Pharmaceuticals (now part of Pfizer) negotiated a new $475 million revolving credit facility with Credit Suisse.[25] This agreement was for a period of five years at a floating interest rate that was 0.875 percent above the LIBOR rate. King agreed to pay a commitment fee of 20 basis points (up to $950,000 annually) on the unused amount of the loan commitment. King was required to maintain an interest coverage ratio of at least 3 to 1. King's net worth had to exceed the sum of $1.5 billion plus 50 percent of positive net income for four previous fiscal quarters. King paid nearly $2 million in fees to arrange this credit facility.

Calculating the annual financing cost of funds borrowed under a revolving credit agreement is slightly more complex than with either a single loan or a line of credit. In addition to the interest rate, commitment fee, compensating balance, and the firm's normal account balance, the annual financing cost of a revolving credit loan also depends on the amount borrowed and the credit limit of the agreement. The annual financing cost can be calculated based on Equation 16.8, as follows:

$$\text{AFC} = \frac{\text{Interest costs} + \text{Commitment fee}}{\text{Usable funds}} \times \frac{365}{\text{Maturity (days)}} \tag{16.11}$$

For example, suppose the Kalamazoo Company has a $4 million revolving credit agreement with its bank to borrow at the prime rate. The agreement requires the company to maintain a 10 percent average compensating balance on any funds borrowed under the agreement, as well as to pay a 0.5 percent commitment fee on the unused portion of the credit line. The prime rate during the year is expected to be 8 percent. Kalamazoo's average borrowing under the agreement during the year is expected to be $2 million. The company maintains an average of $100,000 in its account at the bank, which can be used to meet the compensating balance requirement.

To calculate the annual financing cost of the revolving credit agreement, Kalamazoo must determine the amount of usable funds generated by the loan, the total interest costs, and the commitment fees. Given average borrowing of $2 million during the year, Kalamazoo is required to maintain an average compensating balance of $200,000 (0.10 × $2 million). Because the company currently maintains an average balance of $100,000, $100,000 of the loan is needed to meet the compensating balance requirement. Therefore, the amount of usable funds is $1.9 million. Interest costs on the average amount borrowed are $160,000 (0.08 × $2 million), and the commitment fee on the unused portion of the credit line is $10,000 (0.005 × [$4 million − $2 million]). Substituting these figures into Equation 16.11 yields the following annual financing cost of the loan:

$$\begin{aligned} \text{AFC} &= \frac{\$16{,}000 + \$10{,}000}{\$1{,}900{,}000} \times \frac{365}{365} \\ &= \frac{\$170{,}000}{\$1{,}900{,}000} \times \frac{365}{365} \\ &= 0.0895 \text{ or } 8.95\% \end{aligned}$$

Thus, the annual financing cost of the revolving credit agreement is higher than the stated interest rate.

[25]King Pharmaceuticals 10 Q, first quarter 2007.

Many financially sound companies view revolving credit agreements as a form of financial insurance, and, as a result, these companies frequently have little or no borrowings outstanding against the agreements. For example, in the case of the Ford Motor Company's $11.5 billion, five-year revolving credit agreement, negotiated in 2006, the company had less than $1 billion outstanding through 2008. However, citing the instability of the credit markets and the uncertain state of the global economy, the company in 2009 borrowed the remaining funds available to it under the credit agreement.

16-12 Commercial Paper

commercial paper

Commercial paper consists of short-term unsecured promissory notes issued by major corporations. Only companies with good credit ratings are able to borrow funds through the sale of commercial paper. Purchasers of commercial paper include corporations with excess funds to invest, banks, insurance companies, pension funds, money market mutual funds, and other types of financial institutions. In October 2008, during the credit crisis, the Federal Reserve set up a program (the Commercial Paper Funding Facility [CPFF]) to purchase commercial paper directly from companies. This program supported about one-fifth of the market. Before the CPFF was started, the commercial paper market had undergone a massive reduction of $366 billion during a six-week period. In April 2009, over $1.5 trillion in commercial paper was outstanding, down substantially from a peak of $2.2 trillion in July 2007. After the commercial paper market was stabilized, the Federal Reserve closed the CPFF in February 2010, with all the loans being repaid by the borrowers under the stated terms.

Large finance companies, such as Ford Motor Credit Company, issue sizable amounts of commercial paper on a regular basis, selling it directly to investors like those just mentioned. Large industrial, utility, and transportation firms, as well as smaller finance companies, issue commercial paper less frequently and in smaller amounts; they sell it to dealers who, in turn, sell the commercial paper to investors.

Maturities on commercial paper at the time of issue range from several days to a maximum of nine months. Companies usually do not issue commercial paper with maturities beyond nine months, because these issues must be registered with the Securities and Exchange Commission. The size of an issue of commercial paper can range up to several hundred million dollars. It is usually sold to investors in multiples of $100,000 or more. Large issuers of commercial paper normally attempt to tailor the maturity and amounts of an issue to the needs of investors.

Commercial paper represents an attractive financing source for large, financially sound firms, because interest rates on commercial paper issues tend to be below the prime lending rate. To successfully market commercial paper (and get an acceptable rating from Moody's, Standard & Poor's, or both), however, the company normally must have unused bank lines of credit equal to the amount of the issue.

The primary disadvantage of this type of financing is that it is not always a reliable source of funds. The commercial paper market is impersonal. A firm that is suddenly faced with temporary financial difficulties may find that investors are unwilling to purchase new issues of commercial paper to replace maturing issues. In addition, the amount of loanable funds available in the commercial paper market is limited to the amount of excess liquidity of the various purchasers of commercial paper. During tight money periods, such as during the credit crisis of 2008–2009, enough funds may not be available to meet the aggregate needs of corporate issuers of commercial paper at reasonable rates. As a result, a company should maintain adequate lines of bank credit and recognize the risks of relying too heavily on commercial paper. Finally, a commercial paper issue usually cannot be paid off until maturity. Even if a company no longer needs the funds from a commercial paper issue, it must still pay the interest costs.

Commercial paper is sold on a discount basis; this means that the firm receives less than the stated amount of the note at issue and then pays the investor the full face amount at maturity. The annual financing cost of commercial paper depends on the maturity date of the issue and the prevailing short-term interest rates. In addition to the interest costs, borrowers also must pay a *placement fee* to the commercial paper dealer for arranging the sale of the issue. The annual financing cost can be computed as follows, based on Equation 16.8:

(16.12)
$$\text{AFC} = \frac{\text{Interest costs} + \text{Placement fee}}{\text{Usable funds}} \times \frac{365}{\text{Maturity (days)}}$$

The usable funds are equal to the face amount of the issue less the interest costs and placement fee.

For example, suppose Midland Steel Company is considering issuing $10 million of commercial paper. A commercial paper dealer has indicated that Midland could sell a 90-day issue at an annual interest rate of 9.5 percent. The placement fee would be $25,000. Using Equation 16.12, the annual financing cost of this commercial paper issue is calculated as follows:

$$\text{Interest costs} = \$10{,}000{,}000 \times 0.095 \times \frac{90}{365}$$
$$= \$234{,}247$$
$$\text{AFC} = \frac{\$234{,}247 + \$25{,}000}{\$10{,}000{,}000 - \$234{,}247 - \$25{,}000} \times \frac{365}{90}$$
$$= 0.1079 \text{ or } 10.79\%$$

16-13 Accounts Receivable Loans

Accounts receivable are one of the most commonly used forms of collateral for *secured* short-term borrowing. From the lender's standpoint, accounts receivable represent a desirable form of collateral, because they are relatively liquid and their value is relatively easy to recover if the borrower becomes insolvent. In addition, accounts receivable involve documents representing customer obligations rather than cumbersome physical assets. Offsetting these advantages, however, are potential difficulties. One disadvantage is that the borrower may attempt to defraud the lender by pledging nonexistent accounts. Also, the recovery process in the event of insolvency may be hampered if the customer who owes the receivables returns the merchandise or files a claim alleging that the merchandise is defective. Finally, the administrative costs of processing the receivables can be high, particularly when a firm has a large number of invoices involving small dollar amounts. Nevertheless, many companies use accounts receivable as collateral for short-term financing by either *pledging* their receivables or *factoring* them.

16-13a Pledging Accounts Receivable

pledging accounts receivable

The pledging process begins with a loan agreement specifying the procedures and terms under which the lender will advance funds to the firm. When **pledging accounts receivable**, the firm retains title to the receivables and continues to carry them on its balance sheet. However, the pledged status of the firm's receivables should be disclosed in a footnote to the financial statements. Pledging is an accepted business practice, particularly with smaller businesses. A firm that has pledged receivables as collateral is required to repay the loan, even if it is unable to collect the pledged receivables. In other words, the borrower assumes the default risk, and the lender has *recourse* back to the borrower. Both commercial banks and finance companies make loans secured by accounts receivable.

Once the pledging agreement has been established, the firm periodically sends the lender a group of invoices along with the loan request. Upon receipt of the customer invoices, the lender investigates the creditworthiness of the accounts to determine which are acceptable as collateral. The percentage of funds that the lender will advance against the collateral depends on the quality of the receivables and the company's financial position. The percentage normally ranges from 50 to 80 percent of the face amount of the receivables pledged. The company is then required to sign a promissory note and a security agreement, after which it receives the funds from the lender.

Most receivables loans are made on a *non-notification basis*, which means the customer is not notified that the receivable has been pledged by the firm. The customer continues to make payments directly to the firm. To protect itself against possible fraud, the lender usually requires the firm to forward all customer payments in the form in which they are received. In addition, the borrower is usually subject to a periodic audit to ensure the integrity of its receivables and payments. Receivables that remain unpaid for 60 days or so must usually be replaced by the borrower.

The customer payments are used to reduce the loan balance and eventually repay the loan. Receivables loans can be a continuous source of financing for a company, however, provided that new receivables are pledged to the lender as existing accounts are collected. By periodically sending the lender new receivables, the company can maintain its collateral base and obtain a relatively constant amount of financing.

Receivables loans can be an attractive source of financing for a company that does not have access to unsecured credit. As the company grows and its level of receivables increases, it can normally obtain larger receivables loans fairly easily. And, unlike line of credit agreements, receivables loans usually do not have compensating balance or "cleanup" provisions.

The annual financing cost of a loan in which receivables are pledged as collateral includes both the interest expense on the unpaid balance of the loan and the service fees charged for processing the receivables. Typically, the interest rate ranges from 2 to 5 percentage points over the prime rate, and service fees are approximately 1 to 2 percent of the amount of the pledged receivables. The services performed by the lender under a pledging agreement can include credit checking, keeping records of the pledged accounts and collections, and monitoring the agreement. This type of financing can be quite expensive for the firm.

The following example illustrates the calculation of the annual financing cost of an accounts receivable loan: Port City Plastics Corporation is considering pledging its receivables to finance a needed increase in working capital. Its commercial bank will lend 75 percent of the pledged receivables at 2 percentage points above the prime rate, which is currently 10 percent. In addition, the bank charges a service fee equal to 1 percent of the pledged receivables. Both interest payments and the service fee are payable at the end of each borrowing period. Port City's average collection period is 45 days, and it has receivables totaling $2 million that the bank has indicated are acceptable as collateral. As shown in Table 16.6, the annual financing cost for the pledged receivables is 22.8 percent.

TABLE 16.6

Cost of Pledging Receivables for Port City Plastics Corporation

$$\text{Usable funds} = 0.75 \times \text{Pledgeable receivables}$$
$$= 0.75 \times \$2{,}000{,}000$$
$$= \$1{,}500{,}000$$
$$\text{Interest costs} = \$1{,}500{,}000 \times 0.12 \times \frac{45}{365}$$
$$= \$22{,}192$$
$$\text{Service fee} = \$2{,}000{,}000 \times 0.01$$
$$= \$20{,}000$$
$$\text{AFC} = \frac{\$22{,}192 + \$20{,}000}{\$1{,}500{,}000} \times \frac{365}{45}$$
$$= 0.228 \text{ or } 22.8\%$$

16-13b Factoring Accounts Receivable

factoring

Factoring receivables involves the outright sale of the firm's receivables to a financial institution known as a *factor*. A number of so-called old-line factors, in addition to some commercial banks and finance companies (asset-based lenders), are engaged in factoring receivables. When receivables are factored, title to them is transferred to the factor, and the receivables no longer appear on the firm's balance sheet.

Traditionally, the use of factoring was confined primarily to the apparel, furniture, and textile industries. In other industries, the factoring of receivables was considered an indication of poor financial health. Today, factoring seems to be gaining increased acceptance in other industries.

The factoring process begins with an agreement that specifies the procedures for factoring the receivables and the terms under which the factor will advance funds to the firm. Under the normal factoring arrangement, the firm sends the customer order to the factor for credit checking and approval *before* filling it. The factor maintains a credit department to perform the credit checking and collection functions. Once the factor decides that the customer is an acceptable risk and agrees to purchase the receivable, the firm ships the order to the customer. The customer is usually notified that its account has been sold and is instructed to make payments directly to the factor.

Most factoring of receivables is done on a *nonrecourse* basis; in other words, the factor assumes the risk of default.[26] If the factor refuses to purchase a given receivable, the firm still can ship the order to the customer and assume the default risk itself, but this receivable does not provide any collateral for additional credit.

In the typical factoring agreement, the firm receives payment from the factor at the normal collection or due date of the factored accounts; this is called *maturity factoring*. If the firm wants to receive the funds prior to this date, it can usually obtain an advance from the factor; this is referred to as *advance factoring*. Therefore, in addition to credit checking, collecting receivables, and bearing default risk, the factor also performs a lending function and assesses specific charges for each service provided. The maximum

[26]If the receivables are sold to the factor on a *recourse* basis, the firm is liable for losses on any receivables that are not collected by the factor.

advance the firm can obtain from the factor is limited to the amount of factored receivables *less* the factoring commission, interest expense, and reserve that the factor withholds to cover any returns or allowances by customers. The reserve is usually 5 to 10 percent of the factored receivables and is paid to the firm after the factor collects the receivables.

The factor charges a factoring commission, or service fee, of 1 to 3 percent of the factored receivables to cover the costs of credit checking, collection, and bad-debt losses. The rate charged depends on the total volume of the receivables, the size of the individual receivables, and the default risk involved. The factor normally charges an interest rate of 2 to 5 percentage points over the prime rate on advances to the firm. These costs are somewhat offset by a number of internal savings that a business can realize through factoring its receivables. A company that factors all its receivables does not need a credit department and does not have to incur the administrative and clerical costs of credit investigation and collection or the losses on uncollected accounts. In addition, the factor may be able to control losses better than a credit department in a small- or medium-size company due to its greater experience in credit evaluation. Thus, although factoring receivables may be a more costly form of credit than unsecured borrowing, the net cost may be below the stated factoring commission and interest rates because of credit department and bad-debt loss savings.

HTTP:
For more information on factoring, see the Web site of the International Factoring Association.

www.factoring.org

A Web search at

www.google.com

under the terms "factoring accounts receivable" produces valuable references to many factoring companies.

For example, the Masterson Apparel Company is considering an advance factoring agreement because of its weak financial position and because of the large degree of credit risk inherent in its business. The company primarily sells large quantities of apparel to a relatively small number of retailers, and if even one retailer does not pay, the company could experience severe cash flow problems. By factoring, Masterson transfers the credit risk to the factor, Partners Credit Corporation, an asset-based lender. Partners requires a 10 percent reserve for returns and allowances, charges a 2 percent factoring commission, and will advance Masterson funds at an annual interest rate of 4 percentage points over prime.[27] Assume the prime rate is 10 percent. Factoring receivables will allow the company to eliminate its credit department and save about $2,000 a month in administrative and clerical costs. Factoring will also eliminate bad-debt losses, which average about $6,000 a month. Masterson's average collection period is 60 days, and its average level of receivables is $1 million.

In Table 16.7 the amount of funds Masterson can borrow from the factor and the annual financing cost of these funds are calculated. As the table shows, Masterson can obtain an advance of $859,748, and the annual financing cost is 28.5 percent *before* considering cost savings and elimination of bad-debt losses. *After* considering credit department savings and reductions in bad-debt losses, the annual financing cost drops to 17.2 percent. Masterson can compare the cost of this factoring arrangement with the cost of other sources of funds in deciding whether or not to factor its receivables. This example calculates the factoring cost for a single 60-day period. In practice, if Masterson did enter into a factoring agreement, the agreement would most likely become a continuous procedure.

16-14 Inventory Loans

Inventories are another commonly used form of collateral for secured short-term loans. They represent a flexible source of financing since additional funds can be obtained as the firm's sales and inventories expand. Like receivables, many types of inventories are

[27]Although the reserve for returns is deducted when figuring the amount of usable funds advanced by the factor, it is not part of the cost of factoring, because the factor will return it to Masterson provided that the company's customers make no returns or adjustments.

TABLE 16.7

Cost of Factoring Receivables for Masterson Apparel Company

Calculation of usable funds:		
Average level of receivables		$1,000,000
Less: Factoring commission	0.02 × $1,000,000	−20,000
Less: Reserve for returns	0.10 × $1,000,000	−100,000
Amount available for advance before interest is deducted		$ 880,000
Less: Interest on advance	(0.14 × $880,000 × 60/365)	−20,252
Amount of funds advanced by factor, or *usable* funds		$ 859,748
Interest costs and fees:		
Interest costs		$ 20,252
Fee, or factoring commission		20,000
Total		$ 40,252

Calculation of annual financing cost, *before* considering cost savings and bad-debt losses:

$$AFC = \frac{\$40,252}{\$859,748} \times \frac{365}{60}$$
$$= 28.5\%$$

Calculation of annual financing cost, *after* considering cost savings and bad-debt losses:

Credit department savings, per 60-day period	$ 4,000
Average bad-debt losses, per 60-day period	12,000
Total	$ 16,000

$$AFC = \frac{\$40,252 - \$16,000}{\$859,748} \times \frac{365}{60}$$
$$= 0.172 \text{ or } 17.2\%$$

fairly liquid. Therefore, lenders consider them a desirable form of collateral. When judging whether a firm's inventory would be suitable collateral for a loan, the primary considerations of the lender are the type, physical characteristics, identifiability, liquidity, and marketability of the inventory.

Firms hold three types of inventories: *raw materials*, *work-in-process*, and *finished goods.* Normally, only raw materials and finished goods are considered acceptable as security for a loan. The physical characteristic with which lenders are most concerned is the item's *perishability*. Inventory subject to significant physical deterioration over time is usually not suitable as collateral.

Inventory items also should be *easily identifiable* by means of serial numbers or inventory control numbers; this helps protect the lender against possible fraud and also aids the lender in establishing a valid title claim to the collateral if the borrower becomes insolvent and defaults on the loan. The ease with which the inventory can be *liquidated* and the stability of its *market price* are other important considerations. In the event that the borrower defaults, the lender wants to be able to take possession, sell the collateral, and recover the full amount owed with minimal expense and difficulty.

Both commercial banks and asset-based lenders make inventory loans. The percentage of funds that the lender will advance against the inventory's book value ranges from about 50 to 80 percent and depends on the inventory's characteristics. Advances near the upper end of this range are normally made only for inventories that are standardized, nonperishable, easily identified, and readily marketable. To receive an inventory loan, the borrower must sign both a promissory note and a security agreement describing the inventory that will serve as collateral.

In making a loan secured with inventories, the lender can either allow the borrower to hold the collateral or require that it be held by a third party. If the borrower holds the collateral, the loan may be made under a *floating lien* or *trust receipt* arrangement. If a third party is employed to hold the collateral, either a *terminal warehouse* or a *field warehouse* financing arrangement can be used.

16-14a Floating Liens

floating lien

Under a **floating lien** arrangement, the lender receives a security interest or general claim on *all* of the firm's inventory; this may include both present and future inventory. This type of agreement is often employed when the average value of the inventory items is small, the inventory turns over frequently, or both. Specific items are not identified. Thus, a floating lien does not offer the lender much protection against losses from fraud or bankruptcy. As a result, most lenders will not advance a very high percentage of funds against the book value of the borrower's inventory.

16-14b Trust Receipts

trust receipt

A **trust receipt** is a security agreement under which the firm holds the inventory and proceeds from the sale in trust for the lender. Whenever a portion of the inventory is sold, the firm is required to immediately forward the proceeds to the lender; these are then used to reduce the loan balance.

Some companies engage in inventory financing on a continuing basis. In these cases, a new security agreement is drawn up periodically, and the lender advances the company additional funds using recently purchased inventories as collateral.

All inventory items under a trust receipt arrangement must be readily identified by serial number or inventory code number. The lender makes periodic, unannounced inspections of the inventory to make sure that the firm has the collateral and has not withheld payment for inventory that has been sold.

Businesses that must have their inventories available for sale on their premises, such as automobile and appliance dealers, frequently engage in trust receipt financing, also known as *floor planning*. Many "captive" finance companies that are subsidiaries of manufacturers, such as Ford Motor Credit Company, engage in floor planning for their dealers.

16-14c Terminal Warehouse and Field Warehouse Financing Arrangements

terminal warehouse financing arrangement

Under a **terminal warehouse financing arrangement**, the inventory being used as loan collateral is stored in a bonded warehouse operated by a public warehousing company. When the inventory is delivered to the warehouse, the warehouse company

INTERNATIONAL ISSUES

Foreign Receivables Financing[a]

Small- and medium-size U.S. businesses that sell on credit to customers in foreign countries are faced with additional problems in obtaining loans on these receivables. Because of low profit margins and unfamiliarity with international markets, bank financing of these receivables is often difficult. For example, if a commercial bank does advance funds on the foreign receivables, it may want the seller to use its U.S. assets as additional collateral for the loan.

Alternatively, factors will finance foreign receivables that are insured by the Export-Import Bank. The factor will advance about 85 percent of the amount of the receivables and then remit the remainder, less fees of 1.5 to 3 percent, after the foreign customer's payment is received. Another alternative source of receivables financing is a forfait company, such as London Forfaiting, which will advance funds to the seller before they collect from the buyer. Forfaiters usually want the sales contract guaranteed by a foreign bank or government.

Finally, a trading company can be used to obtain financing. The trading company will take title to the goods and arrange shipment to the foreign buyer. Such companies work with sales contracts that are guaranteed or insured by programs of U.S. and foreign governments. Generally, U.S. exporters that require receivables financing should expect to pay in the range of 2 to 3 percent of the amount of the transaction.

[a]See Bill Holstein, "Exporting: Congratulations Exporter! Now About Getting Paid..." *Business Week* (January 17, 1994): 98.

issues a warehouse receipt listing the specific items received by serial or lot number. The warehouse receipt is forwarded to the lender, who then advances funds to the borrower.

Holding the warehouse receipt gives the lender a security interest in the inventory. Because the warehouse company will release the stored inventory to the firm only when authorized to do so by the holder of the warehouse receipt, the lender is able to exercise control over the collateral. As the firm repays the loan, the lender authorizes the warehouse company to release appropriate amounts of the inventory to the firm.

field warehouse financing agreement

Under a **field warehouse financing agreement**, the inventory that serves as collateral for a loan is segregated from the firm's other inventory and stored on its premises under the control of a field warehouse company. The field warehouse company issues a warehouse receipt, and the lender advances funds to the firm. The field warehouse releases inventory to the firm only when authorized to do so by the lender.

Although terminal warehouse and field warehouse financing arrangements provide the lender with more control over the collateral than it has when the borrower holds the inventory, fraud or negligence on the part of the warehouse company can result in losses for the lender. The fees charged by the warehouse company make this type of financing more expensive than floating lien or trust receipt loans. In a terminal warehouse arrangement, the firm incurs storage charges, in addition to fees for transporting the inventory to and from the public warehouse. In a field warehouse arrangement, the firm normally has to pay an installation charge, a fixed operating charge based on the overall size of the warehousing operation, and a monthly storage charge based on the value of the inventory in the field warehouse.

Overall warehousing fees are generally 1 to 3 percent of the inventory value. The total cost of an inventory loan includes the service fee charged by the lender and the warehousing fee charged by the warehousing company, plus the interest on the funds advanced by the lender. Any internal savings in inventory handling and storage costs that result when the inventory is held by a warehouse company are deducted in computing the cost of the loan.

16-15 Summary

- *Working capital* is the difference between current assets and current liabilities. The term *working capital* is used interchangeably with the term *net working capital.*
- A firm's *operating cycle* is equal to the sum of the inventory and receivables conversion periods. The *cash conversion cycle* is equal to the operating cycle less the payables deferral period.
- *Working capital policy* is concerned with determining the *aggregate amount* and *composition* of a firm's current assets and current liabilities.
- When the level of working capital is increased, both the expected profitability and the risk are lowered. Similarly, when the level of working capital is decreased, both the expected profitability and the risk are increased.
- When the proportion of short-term debt used is increased, both the expected profitability and the risk are increased. Similarly, when the proportion of short-term debt used is decreased, both the expected profitability and the risk are lowered.
- No single working capital investment and financing policy is necessarily *optimal* for all firms. To select the working capital policy that maximizes shareholder wealth, a financial manager should consider additional factors, including the inherent variability in sales and cash flows and the degree of operating and financial leverage employed.
- Short-term credit may be either *secured* or *unsecured.* In the case of secured credit, the borrower pledges certain assets (such as inventory, receivables, or fixed assets) as collateral for the loan. In general, firms prefer to borrow on an unsecured basis, because pledging assets as security generally raises the overall cost of the loan and also can reduce the firm's flexibility by restricting future borrowing.
- *Trade credit, accrued expenses,* and *deferred income* are the primary sources of spontaneous short-term credit. *Bank loans, commercial paper, accounts receivable loans,* and *inventory loans* represent the major sources of *negotiated* short-term credit.
- The *annual financing cost* (AFC) for a short-term credit source is calculated as follows:

$$\text{AFC} = \frac{\text{Intersts costs} + \text{fees}}{\text{Usable funds}} \times \frac{365}{\text{Maturity (days)}}$$

- Trade credit is extended to a firm when it makes purchases from a supplier and is permitted to wait a specified period of time before paying for them. It is normally extended on an *open-account* basis, which means that once a firm accepts merchandise from a supplier, it agrees to pay the amount due as specified by the terms of sale on the invoice.
- Short-term *bank credit* can be extended to the firm under a single loan, a *line of credit,* or a *revolving credit agreement.* A line of credit permits the firm to borrow funds up to a predetermined limit at any time during the life of the agreement. A revolving credit agreement legally commits the bank to provide the funds when the firm requests them.
- *Commercial paper* consists of short-term unsecured promissory notes issued by major corporations with good credit ratings.
- *Accounts receivable loans* can be obtained by either *pledging* or *factoring* receivables. In the case of a pledging arrangement, the firm retains title to the receivables, and the lender advances funds to the firm based on the amount and quality of the receivables. With factoring, receivables are sold to a factor, who takes the responsibility for credit checking and collection of the accounts. With pledging, the lender does not assume credit risk and has *recourse* back to the borrower if payment is not made, whereas factoring is normally a nonrecourse form of financing.

- Several types of *inventory loans* are available. In a *floating lien* or *trust receipt* arrangement, the borrower holds the collateral. In a floating lien arrangement, the lender has a general claim on all of the firm's inventory. In a trust receipt arrangement, the inventory being used as collateral is specifically identified by serial or inventory code numbers. In a *terminal warehouse* and a *field warehouse* arrangement, a third party holds the collateral; in the case of a terminal warehouse arrangement, collateral is stored in a public warehouse, whereas in a field warehouse arrangement, collateral is stored in a field warehouse located on the borrower's premises.
- No one source (or combination of sources) of short-term financing is necessarily optimal for all firms. Many other factors, in addition to the cost of financing, need to be considered when choosing the optimal source or sources of short-term financing. Some of these factors include the availability of funds during periods of financial crisis or tight money, restrictive covenants imposed on the firm, and the nature of the firm's operations and funds requirements. The advantages and disadvantages of the various sources of short-term credit are summarized in Table 16.8.

TABLE **16.8**

Advantages and Disadvantages of Various Sources of Short-Term Credit

Credit Source	Advantages	Disadvantages
Trade credit	Flexible source of financing—expands as firm's purchases increase Relatively easy to obtain	Opportunity cost of forgoing cash discounts can be quite high
Accrued expenses and deferred income	Interest-free source of financing	Limited by legal, contractual, and practical considerations
Short-term bank credit	Flexible source of financing—credit line can be used to meet seasonal needs for funds	May require compensating balance in excess of firm's normal checking-account balance Commitment fees required for guaranteed credit May require "cleanup" provision and other protective covenants that limit firm's financing activities
Commercial paper	Interest rate is often below bank prime rate	Requires unused bank line of credit to issue commercial paper Not always a reliable source of funds—tight credit market conditions or temporary financial difficulties may limit firm's access to this source of funds
Accounts receivable loans	Flexible source of financing—additional financing available as sales and accounts receivable increase Possible credit department and bad-debt loss savings Does not require compensating balance or "cleanup" provisions like line-of-credit borrowing	Service fees can make this source of financing more expensive than unsecured sources Pledging or selling of accounts receivables may weaken firm's financial strength and limit its access to unsecured credit
Inventory loans	Flexible source of financing—additional financing is available as sales and inventories increase Possible savings in inventory handling and storage costs under field warehouse or terminal warehouse agreement Does not require compensating balance or "cleanup" provisions like line-of-credit borrowing	Service fees (fixed and variable costs) for a field warehouse or terminal warehouse agreement can make this source of financing more expensive than unsecured sources

Important Equations

$$\text{Operating cycle} = \text{Inventory conversion period} + \text{Receivables conversion period}$$

$$\text{Inventory conversion period} = \frac{\text{Average inventory}}{\text{Cost of sales}/365}$$

$$\text{Receivables conversion period} = \frac{\text{Average accounts receivable}}{\text{Annual credit sales}/365}$$

$$\text{Payables deferral period} = \frac{\text{Average accounts payable}}{\text{Cost of sales}/365}$$

$$\text{Cash conversion cycle} = \text{Operating cycle} - \text{Payables deferral period}$$

$$\text{AFC} = \frac{\text{Interest costs} + \text{fees}}{\text{Usable funds}} \times \frac{365}{\text{Maturity (days)}}$$

$$\text{APR} = \left(1 + \frac{\text{Interest costs} + \text{fees}}{\text{Usable funds}}\right)^m - 1$$

$$\text{AFC} = \frac{\text{Percentage discount}}{100 - \text{Percentage discount}} \times \frac{365}{\text{Credit period} - \text{Discount period}}$$

16-16 Questions and Topics for Discussion

1. Why does the typical firm need to make investments in working capital?
2. Define and describe the difference between the operating cycle and cash conversion cycle for a typical manufacturing company.
3. Discuss the probability versus risk trade-offs associated with alternative levels of working capital investment.
4. Describe the difference between permanent current assets and fluctuating current assets.
5. Why is it possible for the effective cost of long-term debt to exceed the cost of short-term debt, even when short-term interest rates are higher than long-term rates?
6. Describe the matching approach for meeting the financing needs of a company. What is the primary difficulty in implementing this approach?
7. Discuss the probability versus risk trade-offs associated with alternative combinations of short-term and long-term debt used in financing a company's assets.
8. As the difference between the costs of short- and long-term debt becomes smaller, which financing plan, aggressive or conservative, becomes more attractive?
9. Why is no single working capital investment and financing policy necessarily optimal for all firms? What additional factors need to be considered in establishing a working capital policy?

10. a. Which of the following working capital financing policies subjects the firm to a greater risk?
    i. Financing permanent current assets with short-term debt
    ii. Financing fluctuating current assets with long-term debt
  b. Which policy will produce the higher expected profitability?
11. Define and discuss the function of *collateral* in short-term credit arrangements.
12. How is the annual financing cost for a short-term financing source calculated? How does the annual financing cost differ from the true annual percentage rate?
13. Explain the difference between *spontaneous* and *negotiated* sources of short-term credit.
14. Under what condition or conditions is trade credit *not* a "cost-free" source of funds to the firm?
15. Define the following:
    a. Accrued expenses
    b. Deferred income
    c. Prime rate
    d. Compensating balance
    e. Discounted loan
    f. Commitment fee
16. Explain the differences between a line of credit and a revolving credit agreement.
17. What are some of the disadvantages of relying too heavily on commercial paper as a source of short-term credit?
18. Explain the differences between pledging and factoring receivables.
19. Explain the difference between a floating lien and a trust receipts arrangement.
20. Explain why the annual financing cost of secured credit is frequently higher than that of unsecured credit.
21. Explain why banks normally include a "cleanup" provision in a line of credit agreement.
22. What savings are realized when accounts receivable are factored rather than pledged?
23. Determine the effect of each of the following conditions on the annual financing cost for a line of credit arrangement (assuming that all other factors remain constant):
    a. The bank raises the prime rate.
    b. The bank lowers its compensating balance requirements.
    c. The firm's average bank balance increases as the result of its instituting more stringent credit and collection policies.
24. Under what condition or conditions, if any, might a firm find it desirable to borrow funds from a bank or other lending institution in order to take a cash discount?

16-17 Self-Test Problems

Note: Assume that there are 365 days per year when converting from annual to daily amounts or vice versa.

ST1. The Stowe Manufacturing Company's balance sheet and income statement for last year are as follows:

Balance Sheet (in Millions of Dollars)

Assets		**Liabilities and Equity**	
Cash and marketable securities	$887	Accounts payable	$ 724
Accounts receivable	2,075	Accrued liabilities	
Inventories*	2,120	(salaries and benefits)	332
Other current assets	300	Other current liabilities	1,665
Total current assets	$5,382	Total current liabilities	$2,721
Plant and equipment (net)	3,707	Long-term debt and other liabilities	1,677
Other assets	687	Common stock	296
Total assets	$9,776	Retained earnings	5,082
		Total stockholders' equity	$5,378
		Total liabilities and equity	$9,776

*Assume that average inventory over the year was $2,120 million, that is, the same as ending inventory.

Income Statement (in Millions of Dollars)

Net sales*	$11,990
Cost of sales	6,946
Selling, general, and administrative expenses	2,394
Other expenses	581
Total expenses	$ 9,921
Earnings before taxes	2,069
Taxes	825
Earnings after taxes (net income)	$ 1,244

*All sales are credit sales.

Determine the length of Stowe's:

a. Inventory conversion period
b. Receivables conversion period
c. Operating cycle
d. Payables deferral period
e. Cash conversion cycle

ST2. Cranberry Manufacturing Company is considering the following two alternative working capital investment and financing policies:

	Policy A	**Policy B**
Current assets ÷ Sales	60%	40%
Short-term debt ÷ Total debt	30%	60%

Forecasted sales next year are $150 million. EBIT is projected to be 20 percent of sales. The company's income tax rate is 40 percent. Fixed assets are $100 million. Cranberry wishes to maintain its current capital structure, which consists of 60 percent debt and 40 percent equity. Interest rates on the company's short-term and long-term debt are 10 and 14 percent, respectively.

a. Determine the expected rate of return on equity under each of the working capital policies.
b. Which working capital policy is riskier? Explain.

ST3. Determine the annual financing cost of forgoing the cash discount under each of the following credit terms:

a. 2/10, net 120
b. 2/30, net four months (assume 122 days)

ST4. Determine the annual financing cost of a 9-month (274-day), $25,000 discounted bank loan at a stated interest rate of 10.5 percent, assuming that no compensating balance is required.

ST5. Tarentum Industries Inc. has a revolving credit agreement with its bank under which the company can borrow up to $10 million at an interest rate of 1.5 percentage points above the prime rate (currently 9.5 percent). Tarentum is required to maintain a 10 percent compensating balance on any funds borrowed under the agreement and to pay a 0.50 percent commitment fee on the unused portion of the credit line. Assume that the company has no funds in its account at the bank that can be used to meet the compensating balance requirement. Determine the annual financing cost of borrowing each of the following amounts under the credit agreement:

a. $2 million
b. $7 million

ST6. The Chalfant Company is considering the use of commercial paper to finance a seasonal need for funds. A commercial paper dealer will sell a $25 million issue maturing in 91 days at an annual interest rate of 8.5 percent (deducted in advance). The fee to the dealer for selling the issue is $75,000. Determine Chalfant's annual financing cost of this commercial paper issue.

ST7. The Boone Furniture Company is considering factoring its receivables. Its average level of receivables is $4 million, and its average collection period is 70 days. Boone's bad-debt losses average $9,000 per month. (Assume 30 days per month.) Factoring receivables will save the company $3,000 per month through the elimination of its credit department. The factor charges a 2 percent commission and requires a 10 percent reserve for returns and allowances. Boone can borrow funds from the factor at 3 percentage points over the prime rate, which is currently 9 percent.

a. Determine the amount of usable funds Boone can obtain by factoring its receivables.
b. Calculate the annual financing cost of this arrangement.

16-18 Problems*

Note: Assume that there are 365 days per year when converting from annual or daily amounts or vice versa.

BASIC

1. The Fisher Apparel Company balance sheet for the year ended 2015 is as follows:

December 31, 2015 (in Thousands of Dollars)

Assets		
Cash		$ 3,810
Marketable securities		2,700
Accounts receivable		27,480
Inventories		41,295
Plant and equipment	$64,650	
Less: Accumulated depreciation	17,100	
Net plant and equipment		47,550
Total assets		$122,835

*Color blocks behind the numbers denote problems that have check answers provided at the end of the book.

December 31, 2015 (in Thousands of Dollars)	
Liabilities and Stockholders' Equity	
Accounts payable	$ 14,582
Current portion of long-term debt	3,000
Accrued wages	1,200
Accrued taxes	3,600
Other current liabilities	2,200
Long-term debt	33,000
Common stock ($10 par)	19,500
Capital contributed in excess of par	15,000
Retained earnings	30,753
Total liabilities and stockholders' equity	$122,835

a. What is Fisher's investment in current assets?
b. Determine Fisher's working capital investment.
c. Determine Fisher's current ratio.
d. Determine Fisher's return on stockholders' equity if its 2015 earnings after tax are $10,000(000).

INTERMEDIATE

2. Consider again the comprehensive example involving Burlington Resources (Table 16.5). In this example, it was assumed that forecasted sales and expected EBIT, as well as the interest rates on short-term and long-term debt, were independent of the firm's working capital investment and financing policies. However, these assumptions are not always completely realistic in practice. Sales and EBIT are generally a function of the firm's inventory and receivables policies. Both of these policies, in turn, affect the firm's level of investment in working capital. Likewise, the interest rates on short-term and long-term debt are normally a function of the riskiness of the firm's debt as perceived by lenders and, hence, are affected by the firm's working capital investment and financing decisions. Recompute Burlington's rate of return on common equity under the following set of assumptions concerning sales, EBIT, and interest rates for each of the three different working capital investment and financing policies.

Policy	Forecasted Sales (in Millions of Dollars)	Expected EBIT (in Millions of Dollars)	Interest Rate	
			STD (%)	LTD (%)
Aggressive	$ 98	$ 9.8	8.5	10.5
Moderate	100	10.0	8.0	10.0
Conservative	102	10.2	7.5	9.5

INTERMEDIATE

3. The Garcia Industries balance sheet and income statement for the year ended 2015 are as follows:

Balance Sheet (in Millions of Dollars)

Assets		Liabilities and Stockholders' Equity	
Cash	$ 6.0	Accounts payable	$10.0
Accounts receivable	14.0	Salaries, benefits, and payroll taxes payable	2.0
Inventories*	12.0	Other current liabilities	10.0
Fixed assets, net	40.0	Long-term debt	12.0
	$72.0	Stockholders' equity	38.0
			$72.0

*The average inventory over the past two years also equals $12.0 million.

Income Statement (in Millions of Dollars)	
Net sales	$100.0
Cost of sales	60.0
Selling, general, and administrative expenses	20.0
Other expenses	15.0
Earnings after tax	$ 5.0

a. Determine the length of the inventory conversion period.
b. Determine the length of the receivables conversion period.
c. Determine the length of the operating cycle.
d. Determine the length of the payables deferral period.
e. Determine the length of the cash conversion cycle.
f. What is the meaning of the number you calculated in Part e?

INTERMEDIATE **4.** Wilson Electric Company, a manufacturer of various types of electrical equipment, is examining its working capital investment policy for next year. Projected fixed assets and current liabilities are $20 million and $18 million, respectively. Sales and EBIT are partially a function of the company's investment in working capital—particularly its investment in inventories and receivables. Wilson is considering the following three different working capital investment policies:

Working Capital Investment Policy	Investment in Current Assets (in Millions of Dollars)	Projected Sales (in Millions of Dollars)	EBIT (in Millions of Dollars)
Aggressive (small investment in current assets)	$28	$59	$5.9
Moderate (moderate investment in current assets)	30	60	6.0
Conservative (large investment in current assets)	32	61	6.1

a. Determine the following for each of the working capital investment policies:
   i. Rate of return on total assets (that is, EBIT/total assets)
   ii. Net working capital position
   iii. Current ratio
b. Describe the profitability versus risk trade-offs of these three policies.

INTERMEDIATE **5.** Reynolds Equipment Company is investigating the use of various combinations of short-term and long-term debt in financing its assets. Assume that the company has decided to employ $30 million in current assets, along with $35 million in fixed assets, in its operations next year. Given this level of current assets, anticipated sales and EBIT for next year are $60 million and $6 million, respectively. The company's income tax rate is 40 percent. Stockholders' equity will be used to finance $40 million of its assets, with the remainder being financed by short-term and long-term debt. Reynolds is considering implementing one of the following financing policies:

Financing Policy	Amount of Short-Term Debt (in Millions of Dollars)	Interest Rate	
		LTD (%)	STD (%)
Aggressive (large amount of short-term debt)	$24	8.5	5.5
Moderate (moderate amount of short-term debt)	18	8.0	5.0
Conservative (small amount of short-term debt)	12	7.5	4.5

a. Determine the following for each of the financing policies:
   i. Expected rate of return on stockholders' equity
   ii. Net working capital position
   iii. Current ratio

b. Evaluate the profitability versus risk trade-offs of these three policies.

INTERMEDIATE

6. Superior Brands Inc. wishes to analyze the *joint impact* of its working capital investment and financing policies on shareholder return and risk. The company has $40 million in fixed assets. Also, the firm's financial structure consists of short-term and long-term debt and common equity. Superior wishes to maintain a debt-to-total assets ratio of 50 percent, where debt consists of both short-term and long-term sources. The company's tax rate is 40 percent. The following information was developed for three different policies under consideration:

Working Capital Investment and Financing Policy	Investment in Current Assets (in Millions of Dollars)	Amount of STD (in Millions of Dollars)	Projected Sales (in Millions of Dollars)	EBIT (in Millions of Dollars)	Interest Rate	
					LTD (%)	STD (%)
Aggressive	$56	$48	$118	$11.8	9.5	6.5
Moderate	60	36	120	12.0	9.0	6.0
Conservative	64	24	122	12.2	8.5	5.5

a. Determine the following for each of the three working capital investment and financing policies:
   i. Expected rate of return on stockholders' equity
   ii. Net working capital position
   iii. Current ratio

b. Evaluate the profitability versus risk trade-offs associated with these three policies.

CHALLENGE

7. Educational Toys, Inc. (ETI) has highly seasonal sales and financing requirements. The company's balance sheet on December 31, 2015, is as follows:

Assets (in Millions of Dollars)		Liabilities and Equity (in Millions of Dollars)	
		Short-term debt	$ x
Current assets	$20	Long-term debt	y
Fixed assets	34	Net worth (equity)	30
Total assets	$54	Total liabilities and equity	$54

ETI has made the following projections of its asset needs and net additions to retained earnings (that is, equity) for the next 3 years:

Year	Quarter	Fixed Assets (in Millions of Dollars)	Current Assets (in Millions of Dollars)	Net Additions to Retained Earnings (in Millions of Dollars)
2016	1 (March 31)	$36	$20	$0
	2 (June 30)	36	24	0
	3 (September 30)	36	30	1
	4 (December 31)	36	24	1
2017	1 (March 31)	38	24	0
	2 (June 30)	38	28	0
	3 (September 30)	38	36	1
	4 (December 31)	38	28	2
2018	1 (March 31)	40	28	0
	2 (June 30)	40	32	0
	3 (September 30)	40	38	1
	4 (December 31)	40	30	2

Assuming that ETI does not plan to sell any preferred or new common stock over the next 3 years:

a. Determine ETI's quarterly total assets and *total* (short-term and long-term) *debt requirements* for the next 3 years.

b. Plot the firm's *fixed*, *current*, and *total* assets over time on a graph.

c. Assume that ETI follows a *matching* approach in financing its assets. In other words, long-term debt will be used to finance its fixed and permanent current assets, and short-term debt will be used to finance its fluctuating current assets. The costs of short-term and long-term debt to ETI under this plan are 6 and 8 percent per annum (that is, 1.5 and 2% per quarter), respectively. Using this information, determine the following:

   i. The amount of short-term and long-term debt outstanding each quarter.

   ii. ETI's total interest costs over the 3-year period under this approach

d. ETI is also considering other financing plans. One plan under consideration is a *conservative* policy. Under this policy, the company would determine its *maximum* debt requirements for the coming year and finance this entire amount with long-term debt at an interest rate of 8 percent per annum on December 31 of each year. Any funds in excess of its seasonal (quarterly) needs would be invested in short-term interest-bearing securities to yield a 4 percent per annum rate of return. Using this information, determine the following:

   i. The amount of long-term debt ETI would have to borrow each year

   ii. ETI's net interest costs over the 3-year period under this conservative policy

e. Finally, ETI is also considering an *aggressive* policy. Under this policy, the company would determine its *minimum* debt requirements for the coming year on December 31 of each year and finance one-half of this amount with long-term debt, with the remainder being financed by short-term debt. The costs of short-term and long-term debt under this policy are 6 and 8 percent per annum, respectively. Using this information, determine the following:

i. The amount of short-term and long-term debt outstanding each quarter
ii. ETI's total interest costs over the 3-year period under this aggressive policy

CHALLENGE

8. Greenwich Industries has forecasted its monthly needs for working capital (net of spontaneous sources, such as accounts payable) for 2016 as follows:

Month	Amount	Month	Amount
January	$7,500,000	July	$6,000,000
February	6,000,000	August	7,500,000
March	3,000,000	September	8,500,000
April	2,500,000	October	9,000,000
May	3,500,000	November	9,500,000
June	4,500,000	December	9,000,000

Short-term borrowing (that is, a bank line of credit) costs the company 10 percent, and long-term borrowing (that is, term loans) costs the company 12 percent. Any funds in excess of its monthly needs can be invested in interest-bearing marketable securities to yield 8 percent per annum.

a. Suppose the company follows a *conservative* policy by financing the *maximum* amount of its working capital requirements for the coming year with long-term borrowing and investing any excess funds in short-term marketable securities. Determine Greenwich's *net* interest costs during 2016 under this policy.
b. Suppose the company follows an *aggressive* policy by financing *all* its working capital requirements for the coming year with short-term borrowing. Determine Greenwich's interest costs during 2016 under this policy.
c. Discuss the profitability versus risk trade-offs associated with these conservative and aggressive working capital financing policies.

CHALLENGE

9. Nguyen Enterprises is considering two alternative working capital investment and financing policies. Policy A requires the firm to keep its current assets at 65 percent of forecasted sales and to finance 70 percent of its debt requirements with long-term debt (and 30 percent with short-term debt). Policy B, on the other hand, requires the firm to keep its current assets at 40 percent of forecasted sales and to finance 40 percent of its debt requirements with long-term debt (and 60 percent with short-term debt). Forecasted sales for next year are $20 million. Earnings before interest and taxes are projected to be 15 percent of sales. The firm's corporate income tax rate is 40 percent. Its fixed assets total $10 million. The firm desires to maintain its existing financial structure, which consists of 50 percent debt and 50 percent equity. Interest rates on short- and long-term debt are 12 and 15 percent, respectively.

a. Determine the expected rate of return on equity next year for Nguyen under each of the working capital policies.
b. Which policy is riskier? Cite specific evidence to support this contention.

CHALLENGE **10.** The Hopewell Pharmaceutical Company's balance sheet and income statement for last year are as follows:

Balance Sheet (in Millions of Dollars)

Assets		**Liabilities and Equity**	
Cash and marketable securities	$1,100	Accounts payable***	$900
Accounts receivable*	1,300	Accrued liabilities (salaries and benefits)	300
Inventories**	800	Other current liabilities	700
Other current assets	200	Total current liabilities	$1,900
Total current assets	$3,400	Long-term debt and other liabilities	1,000
Plant and equipment (net)	2,300	Common stock	1,800
Other assets	1,000	Retained earnings	2,000
Total assets	$6,700	Total stockholders' equity	$3,800
		Total liabilities and equity	$6,700

*Assume that average accounts receivable are the same as ending accounts receivable.
**Assume that average inventory over the year was the same as ending inventory.
***Assume that average accounts payable are the same as ending accounts payable.

Income Statement (in Millions of Dollars)

Net sales	$6,500
Cost of sales	1,500
Selling, general, and administrative expenses	2,500
Other expenses	800
Total expenses	$4,800
Earnings before taxes	1,700
Taxes	680
Earnings after taxes (net income)	$1,020

a. Determine Hopewell's cash conversion cycle.

b. Give an interpretation of the value computed in Part a.

INTERMEDIATE **11.** Brakenridge Industries is considering the following two alternative working capital investment and financing policies:

	Policy A	Policy B
Current assets ÷ Sales	50%	40%
Short-term debt ÷ Total debt	40%	50%

Forecasted sales next year are $30 million. EBIT is projected at 25 percent of sales. Fixed assets are $30 million. The firm's income tax rate is 40 percent. Brakenridge desires to maintain its current capital structure, which consists of 50 percent debt and 50 percent equity. Interest rates on the company's short-term and long-term debt are 9 and 12 percent, respectively.

a. Determine the expected rate of return on equity capital under each of the working capital policies.

b. Which working capital policy is riskier? Explain.

INTERMEDIATE **12.** The Butler-Huron Company's balance sheet and income statement for last year are as follows:

Balance Sheet (in Millions of Dollars)

Assets		**Liabilities and Equity**	
Cash and marketable securities	$103	Accounts payable***	$1,166
Accounts receivable*	1,138	Accrued liabilities	
Inventories**	1,827	(salaries and benefits)	536
Other current assets	39	Other current liabilities	493
Total current assets	$3,107	Total current liabilities	$2,195
Plant and equipment (net)	3,523	Long-term debt and other	
Other assets	54	liabilities	2,736
Total assets	$6,684	Common stock	105
		Retained earnings	1,648
		Total stockholders' equity	$1,753
		Total liabilities and equity	$6,684

*Assume that all sales are credit sales and that average accounts receivable are the same as ending accounts receivable.
**Assume that average inventory over the year was the same as ending inventory.
***Assume that average accounts payable are the same as ending accounts payable.

Income Statement (in Millions of Dollars)

Net sales	$13,644
Cost of sales	9,890
Selling, general, and administrative expenses	2,264
Other expenses	812
Total expenses	$12,966
Earnings before taxes	678
Taxes	268
Earnings after taxes (net income)	$ 410

a. Determine Butler-Huron's cash conversion cycle.
b. Determine Butler-Huron's cash conversion cycle assuming that 75 percent of annual sales are credit sales (that is, 25 percent represent cash sales).
c. Determine Butler-Huron's cash conversion cycle assuming that 50 percent of annual sales are credit sales.

BASIC

13. The Milton Company currently purchases an average of $22,000 per day in raw materials on credit terms of "net 30." The company expects sales to increase substantially next year and anticipates that its raw material purchases will increase to an average of $25,000 per day. Milton feels that it may need to finance part of this sales expansion by *stretching* accounts payable.
a. Assuming that Milton currently waits until the end of the credit period to pay its raw material suppliers, what is its current level of trade credit?
b. If Milton stretches its accounts payable an extra 10 days beyond the due date next year, how much *additional* short-term funds (that is, trade credit) will be generated?

INTERMEDIATE

14. Van Buren Resources Inc. is considering borrowing $100,000 for 182 days from its bank. Van Buren will pay $6,000 of interest at maturity, and it will repay the $100,000 of principal at maturity.
a. Calculate the loan's annual financing cost.
b. Calculate the loan's annual percentage rate.
c. What is the reason for the difference in your answers to Parts a and b?

BASIC **15.** Determine the *annual financing cost* of forgoing the cash discount under each of the following credit terms:

a. 2/10, net 60
b. 1½/10, net 60
c. 2/30, net 60
d. 5/30, net four months (assume 122 days)
e. 1/10, net 30

BASIC **16.** Calculate the *annual percentage rate* of forgoing the cash discount under each of the following credit terms:

a. 2/10, net 60
b. 2/10, net 30

BASIC **17.** Determine the *annual financing cost* of forgoing the cash discount if the credit terms are "1/10, net 30" and the invoice is not paid until it is 20 days past due.

BASIC **18.** Determine the annual financing cost of a 1-year (365 day), $10,000 discounted bank loan at a stated annual interest rate of 9.5 percent. Assume that no compensating balance is required.

INTERMEDIATE **19.** The Pulaski Company has a line of credit with a bank under which it can borrow funds at an 8 percent interest rate. The company plans to borrow $100,000 and is required by the bank to maintain a 15 percent compensating balance. Determine the annual financing cost of the loan under each of the following conditions:

a. The company currently maintains $7,000 in its account at the bank that can be used to meet the compensating balance requirement.
b. The company currently has no funds in its account at the bank that can be used to meet the compensating balance requirement.

BASIC **20.** Determine the annual financing cost of a 6-month (182-day) $20,000 discounted bank loan at a stated annual interest rate of 10 percent. Assume that no compensating balance is required.

INTERMEDIATE **21.** Pyramid Products Company has a revolving credit agreement with its bank. The company can borrow up to $1 million under the agreement at an annual interest rate of 9 percent. Pyramid is required to maintain a 10 percent compensating balance on any funds borrowed under the agreement and to pay a 0.5 percent commitment fee on the unused portion of the credit line. Assume that Pyramid has no funds in the account at the bank that can be used to meet the compensating balance requirement. Determine the annual financing cost of borrowing each of the following amounts under the credit agreement:

a. $250,000
b. $500,000
c. $1,000,000

INTERMEDIATE **22.** Wellsley Manufacturing Company has been approached by a commercial paper dealer offering to sell an issue of commercial paper for the firm. The dealer indicates that Wellsley could sell a $5 million issue maturing in 182 days at an interest rate of 8.5 percent per annum (deducted in advance). The fee to the dealer for selling the issue would be $8,000. Determine Wellsley's annual financing cost of this commercial paper financing.

INTERMEDIATE **23.** The Brandt Company has been approached by two different commercial paper dealers offering to sell an issue of commercial paper for the company. Dealer A offered to market an $8 million issue maturing in 90 days at an interest cost of 8.5 percent per annum (deducted in advance). The fee to Dealer A would be $12,000. Dealer B has offered to sell a $10 million issue maturing in 120 days at an interest rate of 8.75 percent per annum (deducted in advance). The fee to Dealer B would be $15,000. Assuming that Brandt wishes to minimize the annual financing cost of issuing commercial paper, which dealer should it choose?

INTERMEDIATE

24. Ranger Enterprises is considering pledging its receivables to finance a needed increase in working capital. Its commercial bank will lend 75 percent of the pledged receivables at 1.5 percentage points above the prime rate, which is currently 12 percent. In addition, the bank charges a service fee equal to 1 percent of the pledged receivables. Both interest and the service fee are payable at the end of the borrowing period. Ranger's average collection period is 50 days, and it has receivables totaling $5 million that the bank has indicated are acceptable as collateral. Calculate the annual financing cost for the pledged receivables.

CHALLENGE

25. Designer Textiles Inc. is considering factoring its receivables. The company's average collection period is 60 days, and its average level of receivables is $2.5 million. Designer's bad-debt losses average $15,000 a month. If the company factors its receivables, it will save $4,000 a month by eliminating its credit department. The factor has indicated that it requires a 10 percent reserve for returns and allowances and charges a 2.5 percent factoring commission. The factor will advance Designer funds at 4 percentage points over prime, which is currently 8 percent.

a. Determine the annual financing cost, *before* considering cost savings and bad-debt losses.
b. Determine the annual financing cost, *after* considering cost savings and bad-debt losses.

INTERMEDIATE

26. The Eaton Company needs to raise $250,000 to expand its working capital and has been unsuccessful in attempting to obtain an unsecured line of credit with its bank. The firm is considering *stretching* its accounts payable. Eaton's suppliers extend credit on terms of "2/10, net 30." Payments beyond the credit period are subject to a 1½ percent per month penalty. Eaton purchases $100,000 per month from its suppliers and currently takes cash discounts. For this problem, assume that a year consists of twelve 30-day months. Assuming that Eaton is able to raise the S250,000 it needs by stretching its accounts payable, determine the following:

a. The firm's annual lost cash discounts
b. Annual penalties
c. The annual financing cost of this source of financing

INTERMEDIATE

27. Which of the following credit terms would you prefer as a customer?

a. 2/10, net 30
b. 1/10, net 40
c. 2/10, net 40
d. 1/10, net 25
e. Indifferent among all options

Explain your choice.

INTERMEDIATE

28. The Odessa Supply Company is considering obtaining a loan from a sales finance company secured by inventories under a field warehousing arrangement. Odessa would be permitted to borrow up to $300,000 under such an arrangement at an annual interest rate of 10 percent. The additional cost of maintaining a field warehouse is $16,000 per year. Determine the annual financing cost of a loan under this arrangement if Odessa borrows the following amounts:

a. $300,000
b. $250,000

INTERMEDIATE

29. Harpo Music Mart needs to raise $300,000 to increase its working capital. The bank, mindful of Harpo's strained financial condition, has refused to loan the firm the needed funds. Harpo is considering *stretching* its accounts payable in order to raise the funds. Current credit terms are "3/10, net 30." Payments beyond the credit period are subject to a 1 percent per month penalty. Harpo purchases $125,000 per month from its suppliers and currently takes cash discounts. If Harpo is able to raise the $300,000 it needs by stretching its accounts payable, determine the annual financing cost of this source of financing. For this problem, assume that a year consists of twelve 30-day months.

INTERMEDIATE **30.** The Kittanning Company has a $2 million line of credit with First Interstate Bank under which it can borrow funds at 1.5 percentage points above the prime rate (currently 9 percent). The company plans to borrow $1.5 million and is required by First Interstate to maintain a 10 percent compensating balance. Determine the annual financing cost of the loan under each of the following conditions:

a. Kittanning currently maintains $100,000 in its account at the bank that can be used to meet the compensating balance requirement.

b. The company currently has no funds in its account at the bank that can be used to meet the compensating balance requirement.

INTERMEDIATE **31.** The Vandergrift Company has a revolving credit agreement with Commerce Bank under which the company can borrow up to $5 million at an annual interest rate of 1 percentage point above the prime rate (currently 9 percent). The company is required to maintain a 10 percent compensating balance on any funds borrowed under the agreement and to pay a 0.4 percent commitment fee on the unused portion of the credit line. Assume that Vandergrift has no funds in its account at Commerce Bank that can be used to meet the compensating balance requirement. Determine the annual financing cost of borrowing each of the following amounts under the credit agreement:

a. $1 million

b. $4 million

INTERMEDIATE **32.** Titusville Petroleum Company is considering pledging its receivables to finance an increase in working capital. Citizens National Bank will lend the company 80 percent of the pledged receivables at 2 percentage points above the prime rate (currently 10 percent). The bank charges a service fee equal to 1.5 percent of the pledged receivables. The interest costs and the service fee are payable at the end of the borrowing period. Titusville has $2 million in receivables that can be pledged as collateral. The average collection period is 45 days. Determine the annual financing cost to Titusville of this receivables-backed loan.

CHALLENGE **33.** DuBois Apparel Company is considering factoring its receivables. The company's average level of receivables is $1.5 million, and its average collection period is 45 days. DuBois's bad-debt losses average $8,000 per month, which it would not incur if it factored its receivables. (Assume 30 days per month.) Also, the company would save $4,000 per month in credit department costs if it factored its receivables. The factor requires a 10 percent reserve for returns and allowances and charges a 2 percent factoring commission. DuBois can borrow funds from the factor at 3 percentage points over the prime rate (currently 9 percent). Determine the *net* annual financing cost of this factoring arrangement.

INTERMEDIATE **34.** The Clearfield Company would be permitted to borrow up to $750,000 secured by inventories under a field warehouse arrangement with a sales finance company. The annual interest rate would be 12 percent. The additional cost of establishing a field warehouse would be $35,000 per year. Determine the annual financing cost to Clearfield under this arrangement if Clearfield borrows:

a. $750,000

b. $500,000

INTEGRATIVE CASE PROBLEM

Working Capital Management

Anderson Furniture Company manufactures furniture and sells its products to department stores, retail furniture stores, hotels, and motels throughout the United States and Canada. The firm has nine manufacturing plants located in Virginia, North Carolina, and Georgia. The company was founded by Edward G. Anderson in 1906 and has been managed by members of the Anderson family since that time. E. G. Anderson III is currently chairman and president of the company. The treasurer and controller of the company is Claire White, who was hired away from a competing furniture company a few years ago. Anderson owns 35 percent of the common stock of the company and (along with the shares of the firm owned by relatives and employees) has effective control over all of the firm's decisions.

Financial data relating to last year's (2015) operations, along with relevant industry comparisons, are shown in Table 16C.1. The firm's overall rates of return on equity and total assets have been around the industry average over the past several years—sometimes slightly above average and sometimes slightly below average. The company is currently operating its plants near full capacity and would like to build a new plant in Georgia at a cost of approximately $7.5 million. White has been exploring various alternative methods of financing this expansion and has been unsuccessful thus far in developing an acceptable plan. The sale of new common stock is not feasible at this time because of depressed stock market prices. Likewise, Anderson's banker has advised the firm that the use of additional long-term debt or lease financing is not possible at this time, given the firm's large amount of long-term debt currently outstanding and its relatively low times interest earned ratio. Anderson has ruled out a cut in the firm's dividend as a means of accumulating the required financing. The only other possible sources of financing available to the firm at this time, according to White, appear to be a reduction in working capital (current assets), an increase in short-term liabilities, or both.

Upon learning of these proposed financing methods, Anderson expressed concern about the effect these plans might have on the liquidity and risk of the firm. White replied that the firm currently follows a very conservative working capital policy and that these financing methods would not increase shareholder risk significantly. As evidence, she cited the firm's relatively high current and quick ratios. Anderson was unconvinced and asked White to provide additional information on the effects of these financing plans on the firm's financial status.

1. Anderson's bank requires a compensating balance of $3 million. How much additional funds can be freed up for investment in fixed assets if the firm reduces its cash balance to the minimum required by the bank?
2. How much additional financing can be obtained from receivables if Anderson institutes more stringent credit and collection policies and is able to reduce its average collection period to the industry average? (Assume that credit sales remain constant at $75 million.)
3. How much additional financing can be obtained for fixed-asset expansion if Anderson is able to increase its inventory turnover ratio to the industry average through tighter control of its raw materials, work-in-process, and finished goods inventories? (Assume that the cost of sales remains constant at $60.75 million.)

TABLE 16C.1

Anderson Furniture Company's Financial Data (in Thousands of Dollars)

			Industry Average
Balance Sheet as of December 31, 2015			
Assets			
Cash	$ 3,690	6.5%	5.0%
Receivables, net	15,000	26.3	21.6
Inventories	20,250	35.5	33.4
Total current assets	$38,940	68.3%	60.0%
Net fixed assets	18,060	31.7	40.0
Total assets	$57,000	100.0%	100.0%
Liabilities and stockholders' equity			
Accounts payable	$ 3,000	5.3%	7.0%
Notes payable (8%)	3,750	6.6	10.0
Total current liabilities	$ 6,750	11.8%	17.0%
Long-term debt (10%)	18,000	31.6	28.0
Stockholders' equity	32,250	56.6	55.0
Total liabilities and equity	$57,000	100.0%	100.0%
Income Statement for the Year Ended December 31, 2015			
Net sales (all on credit)	$75,000	100.0%	
Cost of sales	60,750	81.0	
Gross profit	$14,250	19.0	
Selling and administrative expenses	7,500	10.0	
Earnings before interest and taxes	$ 6,750	9.0	
Interest expense	2,100	2.8	
Earnings before taxes	$ 4,650	6.2	
Income taxes (45.16%)	2,100	2.8	
Earnings after taxes	$ 2,550	3.4%	

Significant ratios	**Anderson**	**Industry Average**
Current	5.76	3.50
Quick	2.77	1.60
Average collection period (days)	73.00	58.803
Inventory turnover (Cost of sales/inventory)	3.00	3.50
Sales to total assets	1.30	1.60
Debt to equity	0.80	0.90
Times interest earned	3.20	4.70
Earnings after tax/sales	3.40%	2.40%
Earnings after tax/equity	7.90%	7.90%

4. Anderson's suppliers extend credit to the firm on terms of "net 30." Anderson normally pays its bills on the last day of the credit period. How much additional financing could be generated if Anderson were to *stretch* its payables 10 days beyond the due date?
5. Prepare a pro forma balance sheet (dollars and percentages) as of December 31, 2016, assuming that Anderson has instituted *all* actions described in Questions 1,

2, 3, and 4, and that the funds generated have been used to build a new plant. (Assume that long-term debt and stockholders' equity at the end of 2016 remain the same as at the end of 2015. In other words, no new long-term debt is issued or old long-term debt retired, and all net income after taxes is paid out in common stock dividends. Also assume that net fixed assets, *except for the new plant*, remain unchanged during 2016. Finally assume that notes payable remain unchanged during 2016.) *Hint*: The *total* amount of funds generated from the reduction of current assets and the increase in current liabilities determined in Questions 1, 2, 3, and 4 is $7.5 million (rounded to the nearest $1,000). Round all figures to the nearest $1,000.

6. Prepare a pro forma income statement for 2016. Assume that sales increase to $87 million as a result of the plant expansion. Also assume that the cost of sales and selling and administrative expense ratios (as a percentage of sales) remain constant. Finally, assume that interest expense and the firm's tax rate remain the same in 2016.
7. Calculate the firm's current, quick, times interest earned, and rate of return on equity ratios based on the pro forma statements determined in Questions 5 and 6. How do these ratios compare with the actual values for 2015 and the industry averages?
8. What considerations might lead Anderson and White to disagree about the desirability of using short-term sources of funds to finance the plant expansion?
9. What other sources of short-term funds might the firm consider using to finance the plant expansion?

CHAPTER 17

The Management of Cash and Marketable Securities

KEY CHAPTER CONCEPTS

1. Companies hold liquid asset balances for several reasons, including:
    a. To conduct transactions
    b. For precautionary reasons
    c. To meet future requirements
    d. For speculative reasons
    e. To compensate banks for various services provided to the firm
2. The optimal liquid asset balance reflects risk and return trade-offs and is a function of the following:
    a. Holding costs, which are the opportunity returns the company could earn on these funds in their next best alternative use
    b. Shortage costs, which include possible lost cash discounts, deterioration of the company's credit rating, higher interest expenses, and financial insolvency
3. The primary objective in controlling cash collections is to reduce the delay between when the customer mails the payment and when it becomes a collected balance in the firm's bank account.
4. Methods for reducing collection time include:
    a. Decentralized collection centers and concentration banks
    b. Lockboxes
    c. Wire transfers and depository transfer checks (DTCs)
    d. Special handling of large remittances
    e. Preauthorized checks (PAC)
5. The primary objective in controlling cash disbursements is to slow payments and keep the firm's funds in the bank as long as possible.
6. Methods of slowing disbursements include:
    a. Scheduling and centralizing payments (zero-balance systems)
    b. Use of drafts rather than checks
    c. Maximizing check-clearing float
    d. Stretching payables
7. Electronic funds transfer systems, including wire transfers, the use of automated clearinghouses, and customer-directed computer movements of funds from one account to another, have the potential to greatly reduce the float in financial transactions.
8. Financial managers need to avoid overstepping the bounds of legal and ethical behavior in making cash collection and disbursement decisions.
9. The primary criteria the firm should use in selecting marketable securities include default risk, marketability (or liquidity), maturity date, and rate of return.

FINANCIAL CHALLENGE

Hunting for "Elephants"

As noted in Chapter 1 Berkshire Hathaway's stated goal is to increase the company's intrinsic value, as measured by its book value, at a faster rate than the market gains of the Standard & Poor's 500-stock index. Despite a 14 percent gain ($24.1 billion) in its book value during 2012, the company fell short of the 16 percent total return on the S&P 500 index. Berkshire Hathaway, a conglomerate with $427 billion in total assets and *$47 billion in cash* at the end of 2012, must invest large sums of money each year in order to generate significant increases in shareholder equity. These funds need to be invested either internally, to expand existing operations, or externally, to acquire new businesses.

During 2012, Berkshire Hathaway spent $2.3 billion to acquire 26 businesses that were merged into its existing businesses. Although these small acquisitions are desirable, they do not lead to significant increases in the company's shareholder equity. In his 2012 letter to shareholders, Warren Buffett, Berkshire Hathaway's CEO, expressed disappointment that the company was unable to make a major acquisition. He refers to these large acquisitions as "elephants." Most of the company's most recent "elephants," such as the purchase of the Burlington Northern Santa Fe (BNSF) railroad for $34 billion in 2010 and Lubrizol for $9.7 billion in 2011, have generated significant returns (earnings and cash flows) for Berkshire Hathaway. As Mr. Buffett noted, "I pursued a couple of elephants [in 2012], but came up empty-handed," and "Charlie [Munger, Vice Chairman] and I have again donned our safari outfits and resumed our search for elephants." Their search paid off in early 2013 with a 50 percent share (along with the Brazilian buyout firm 3G Capital) of the acquisition of H. J. Heinz for $23.4 billion.

iStockPhoto.com/GYI NSEA

Mr. Buffett has indicated that he likes to have a cash balance of $20 billion at all times. During Berkshire Hathaway's 2014 annual meeting, he stated that the company was willing to make a deal up to $50 billion using cash and debt. At the end of the second quarter of 2015, Berkshire Hathaway's cash holdings had grown to nearly $67 billion. Shortly thereafter in August, the company announced the acquisition of Precision Castparts Corporation for $32.4 billion—its largest acquisition to date. Berkshire Hathaway planned to finance the deal using about $23 billion of its own cash plus another $10 billion of debt.

Having a large reserve of liquid assets (cash and marketable securities), and not having to raise new debt or equity capital, allows companies such as Berkshire Hathaway to move quickly in pursuing these large acquisitions. Determining a company's appropriate liquid assets balance involves

FINANCIAL CHALLENGE — CONTINUED

risk-return trade-offs. The factors that must be considered in determining a company's optimal cash and marketable securities balance are examined in this chapter.

Sources: "Warren Buffett's 2012 Letter to Shareholders of Berkshire Hathaway," March 1, 2013; Anupreeta Das and Erik Holm, "Buffett's $24 Billion Gain 'Subpar,'" *The Wall Street Journal* (March 2–3, 2013): B1; Dana Mattioli, Anupreeta Das, and Doug Cameron, "Buffett Pins Growth on Deals," *The Wall Street Journal* (August 10, 2015): H1; Anupreeta Das, "In Precision, Buffett Finds His Type," *The Wall Street Journal* (August 11, 2015): C1.

CHAPTER OBJECTIVES

Upon completion of this chapter, you should have a clear understanding of the following:

1. The reasons for holding liquid asset balance (that is, cash and marketable securities)
2. The methods used in controlling the collection and disbursement of cash, including electronic funds transfer systems
3. The primary criteria used in selecting marketable securities for temporary investments of excess cash

17-1 Introduction

Cash and marketable securities are the most liquid of a company's assets. *Cash* is the sum of the currency a company has on hand and the funds on deposit in bank checking accounts. Cash is the medium of exchange that permits management to carry on the various functions of the business organization. In fact, the survival of a company can depend on the availability of cash to meet financial obligations on time. *Marketable securities* consist of short-term investments a firm makes with its temporarily idle cash. Marketable securities can be sold quickly and converted into cash when needed. Unlike cash, however, marketable securities provide a firm with interest income.

Effective cash and marketable securities management is important in contemporary companies, government agencies, and not-for-profit enterprises. Corporate treasurers continually seek ways to increase the yields on their liquid cash and marketable security reserves. Traditionally, these liquid reserves were invested almost exclusively in negotiable certificates of deposit, Treasury bills, commercial paper, and repurchase agreements (short-term loans backed by Treasury securities). However, in recent years many treasurers have shown a willingness to take some additional risks to increase the return on liquid assets. Financial managers constantly face these types of risk-return trade-offs.

Many firms hold significant cash and marketable securities balances. For example, as seen in the "Financial Challenge" at the beginning of the chapter, Berkshire Hathaway's cash balance was nearly $67 billion in 2015. Large cash balances give firms a cushion to handle economic downturns and the ability to make investments in other firms when the price is attractive. Large cash balances can make firms attractive takeover targets for corporate raiders, who seek to redeploy these surplus funds in more productive ways. For example, Kirk Kerkorian, Chrysler's largest stockholder at the time, made an unsuccessful buyout offer for the company in 1995. He claimed that Chrysler's $7.3 billion cash stockpile was more than the company needed for its operations and that some of this hoard should be paid out to stockholders—either in the form of cash dividends or share repurchases. Chrysler was acquired by Daimler Benz in 1998, although it was sold again by Daimler in 2007. In 2009 during the financial crisis, Chrysler filed for bankruptcy and emerged a couple of months later with Fiat owning a significant interest in the company.

In addition to managing the cash and marketable securities already in the firm's possession, financial managers also aggressively seek to speed up cash collections from customers and to slow down disbursements to suppliers. For example, when Alaska sold its oil leases for $900 million, the state was paid with checks that had to physically reach New York before the state could collect and invest the funds. The state chartered a plane to take the checks to New York, thus saving one day in transit over commercial carriers. The daily interest on these funds at the time was nearly $200,000, and the plane charter cost only $15,000, resulting in $185,000 of additional returns to the state. Cash managers continually look for ways to reduce the collection and clearing time for checks received by the firm so that the funds can be put to work earning a return.

Cash management involves much more than simply paying bills and receiving payments for goods and services. The cash management function is concerned with determining:

- The optimal size of a firm's liquid asset balance
- The most efficient methods of controlling the collection and disbursement of cash
- The appropriate types and amounts of short-term investments a firm should make

Cash management decisions require a firm's managers to consider explicitly the *risk versus expected return* trade-offs from alternative policies. Because cash and marketable securities generally earn low rates of return relative to a firm's other assets, a firm can increase its expected return on assets and common equity by minimizing its investment in cash and marketable securities. However, a firm that carries a bare minimum of liquid assets exposes itself to the risk that it will run out of cash needed to keep the business operating. Also, a firm with extremely low cash balances may not be able to take advantage of unique investment opportunities when they arise.

In this chapter, we review the various cash management decisions that must be made by financial managers. Our analysis considers the risk versus expected return trade-offs characteristic of these decisions.

17-2 Liquid Asset Balance

Firms hold liquid asset balances for a number of reasons, including the following:

- First, because cash inflows and outflows of the day-to-day operations of a firm are not perfectly synchronized, liquid asset balances are necessary to serve as a buffer between these flows. This reason is the *transactions motive*. Liquid asset balances help a firm handle seasonal fluctuations in cash flows. For example, a firm may wish to hold a large amount of liquid assets during surplus months and "draw down" on them during deficit months.
- Second, because future cash flows and the ability to borrow additional funds on short notice are often uncertain, liquid asset balances are necessary to meet unexpected requirements for cash. This is the *precautionary motive*.

- Third, liquid asset balances are held to meet *future requirements,* which include fixed outlays required on specific dates, such as quarterly dividend and tax payments, capital expenditures, and repayments of loans or bond issues. A firm also may hold as liquid assets the proceeds from a new debt or equity securities offering prior to using these funds for expansion.
- Fourth, firms often hold liquid assets for *speculative reasons.* Some firms build up large cash balances in preparation for major acquisitions. For example, as noted in the "Financial Challenge" at the beginning of the chapter, Berkshire Hathaway used its large cash balance to make major acquisitions in 2010, 2011, 2013, and 2015. Large cash balances give companies timing flexibility in pursuing acquisitions.
- Finally, a firm generally has to hold cash balances to compensate its bank (or banks) for the services provided. These are called **compensating balances.**

compensating balances

The following sections consider the importance of cash from a number of perspectives.

17-2a Cash Flows and the Cash Budget

Virtually every activity within a firm generates cash flows. As shown in Figure 17.1, the firm's cash balance is affected by every transaction that involves either a cash inflow or a cash outflow. Cash inflows, or *receipts,* occur when customers pay for their purchases, when a firm obtains bank loans, when it sells new issues of debt and equity securities, and when it sells (or collects interest on) marketable securities. Cash outflows, or disbursements, occur when a firm makes payments to suppliers, when a firm pays wages to employees, taxes to governments, interest and principal to bondholders, and cash dividends to shareholders, and when a firm repays bank loans and purchases marketable securities. Therefore, the cash balance at the end of any given period is the result of many interrelated activities.

Cash flows differ with respect to their degree of *certainty.* In general, future outflows are more certain than future inflows. Most expenditures (outflows) are directly controllable by a firm and, as a result, can be forecasted more easily. For example, outflows for

FIGURE 17.1
Cash Flows Within a Typical Firm*

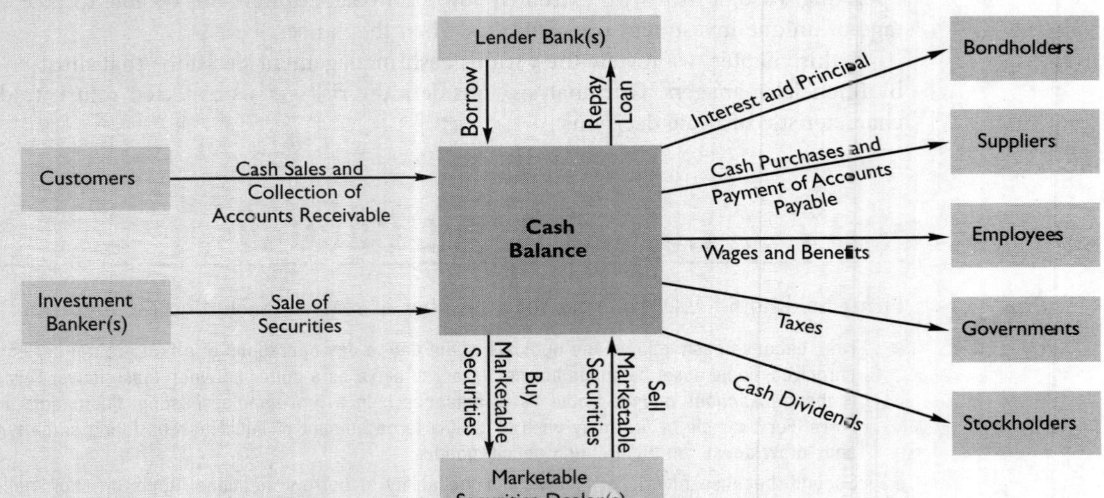

*Arrows indicate the direction of cash flows.

such items as raw materials, labor, dividends, debt repayments, and capital equipment are determined primarily by management decisions and are usually known in advance of their occurrence. Inflows, in contrast, occur partly as a result of decisions made outside a firm and thus are usually more difficult to control and forecast. For example, cash inflows from sales depend primarily on the buying decisions of customers, as well as on when they make their payments.

The first step in efficient cash management is the development of a *cash budget* showing the forecasted cash receipts and disbursements over the planning horizon of the firm.[1] A complete cash budget also contains a forecast of any cumulative cash shortages or surpluses expected during each of the budgeting subperiods—which is the kind of information needed in making cash management decisions. Many larger firms prepare a series of cash budgets, each covering a different time period. For example, a firm may prepare daily cash budgets for the next five working days, weekly cash budgets for the next 10 weeks, and monthly cash budgets for the next 12 months. The daily and weekly forecasts are used in making short-term decisions, such as determining the amount of marketable securities the firm should purchase or sell. The monthly projections are used in longer-range planning, such as determining the amount of bank loans the firm will need. A survey of medium- and large-size companies found that over 80 percent of the respondents relied on cash budgets as a cash forecasting technique.[2]

Knowledge of a potential cash shortage ahead of time gives a financial manager ample opportunity to investigate alternative sources of financing and to choose the least costly one. All other things being equal, lending institutions prefer to make loans to firms that have demonstrated an ability to anticipate their future cash needs. Firms that seem to be faced with frequent cash "emergencies" generally have greater difficulty getting loans. Similarly, advance knowledge of a cash surplus allows the financial manager to invest in appropriate marketable securities.

17-2b Corporate-Bank Relations

A firm's bank provides a variety of both tangible and intangible services. The most significant tangible services include the following:

- Disbursement, wire transfer, direct deposit, and payroll checking accounts
- Collection of deposits—including lockbox, automated collections, depository transfers, and vault services
- Cash management
- Lines of credit, term loans, or both
- Handling of dividend payments
- Registration and transfer of a firm's stock

HTTP:
Wells Fargo will set up and operate a cash management system for you, including lockboxes, faster collections, efficient disbursements, and much more.
https://www.wellsfargo.com/com/

The most important intangible banking service is the availability of future credit if and when the need arises. Other intangible services include the following:

- Supplying credit information
- Providing consultation on such matters as economic conditions, mergers, and international business

A bank is compensated for the services it provides by charging the firm explicit fees and/or requiring the maintenance of a minimum cash balance, or compensating balance, in its checking account. The bank can use this compensating balance to make other loans or investments, and the interest income realized is *compensation* for the various

[1]Chapter 4 contains a discussion of how cash budgets are developed.

[2]R. Kamath, S. Khaksari, H. Meier, and J. Winklepleck, "Management of Excess Cash: Practices and Developments," *Financial Management* (Autumn 1985): 70–77.

services rendered to a firm. Although some banks require firms to maintain *absolute* minimum compensating balances, most stipulate minimum *average* balances.

The monthly account fee that a bank charges a business customer is usually determined by calculating various service charges and then deducting an earnings credit on the account balance. The service charges are computed by multiplying the number of each type of transaction a firm makes per period (such as payroll checks, vendor checks, customer payments, and other deposits) by the bank's charge per item. The earnings credit is computed by multiplying the available balance during the month (which often includes various deductions, such as the bank's reserve requirement) by the earnings credit rate (that is, some specified interest rate). When the total service charges exceed the earnings credit, the bank collects a fee from the customer. Due to competition among banks and differences in the methods used to compute account income and costs, service fees and compensating balance requirements for a given level of account activity vary from bank to bank. As a result, a firm should occasionally do some "comparison shopping" to determine whether its present bank is offering the best fee schedule, compensating balance requirement, and total package of services currently available.

17-2c Optimal Liquid Asset Balance

When a firm holds liquid asset balances, whether in the form of currency, bank demand deposits, or marketable securities, in effect it is investing these funds. To determine the optimal investment in liquid assets, a firm must weigh the benefits and costs of holding these various balances. The determination of an optimal liquid asset balance reflects the classic *risk-versus-return* trade-off facing financial managers. Because liquid assets earn relatively low rates of return, a firm can increase its profitability in relation to its asset base by minimizing liquid asset balances. However, low liquid asset balances expose a firm to the risk of not being able to meet its obligations as they come due. Effective cash management calls for a careful balancing of the risk and return aspects of cash management.

A minimum compensating balance requirement on the part of a bank essentially imposes a *lower limit* on a firm's optimal level of liquid asset balances. When a firm holds liquid assets in excess of this lower limit, it incurs an *opportunity cost*. The opportunity cost of excess liquid assets, held in the form of bank deposits, is the return the firm could earn on these funds in their next best use, such as in the expansion of other current or fixed assets. The opportunity cost of liquid asset balances, held in the form of marketable securities, is the income that could be earned on these funds in their next best alternative use *less* the interest income received on the marketable securities.

Given the opportunity cost of holding liquid asset balances, why would a firm ever maintain a bank balance exceeding the compensating balance requirements? The answer is that these balances help the firm avoid the "shortage" costs associated with inadequate liquid asset balances.

Shortage costs can take many different forms, including the following:

- Forgone cash discounts
- Deterioration of the firm's credit rating
- Higher interest expenses
- Possible financial insolvency

Many suppliers offer customers a cash discount for prompt payment. Having to forgo this cash discount can be quite costly to a firm. In addition, the creditworthiness of a firm is determined at least partially by the current and quick ratios—both of which can be affected by an inadequate liquid asset balance. This, in turn, can cause a firm's credit rating to deteriorate and make loans on favorable terms more difficult to secure in the future. The credit rating also can fall if a firm fails to pay bills on time because of

FIGURE 17.2

Optimal Liquid Asset Balance

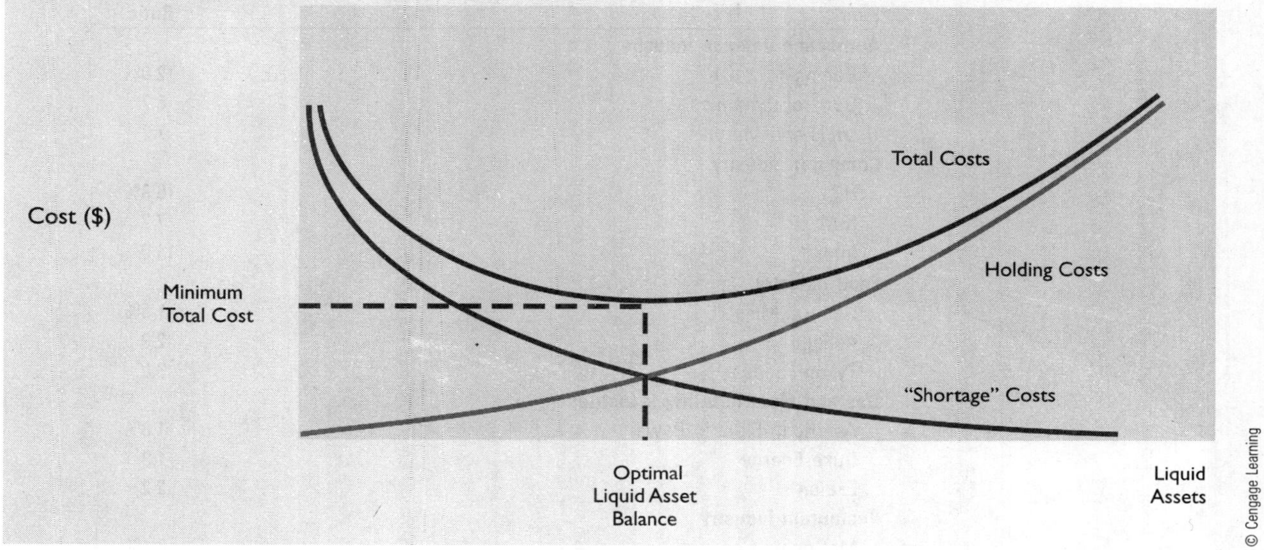

inadequate cash. This can make future credit difficult to obtain from suppliers. If a firm has inadequate liquid asset reserves, it may have to meet unforeseen needs for cash by short-term borrowing, and it may be unable to negotiate for the best terms—including the lowest possible interest rate—if its credit rating is questionable. Inadequate liquid asset balances may cause a firm to incur high transactions costs when converting illiquid assets to cash. Finally, an inadequate liquid asset balance increases a firm's risk of insolvency, because a serious recession or natural disaster would be more likely to reduce the firm's cash inflows to the point where it could not meet contractual financial obligations.

An inverse relationship exists between a firm's liquid asset balance and these shortage costs: the larger a firm's liquid asset balance, the smaller its associated shortage costs. The opportunity holding costs, in contrast, increase as a firm's liquid asset balance is increased. As shown in Figure 17.2, the optimal liquid asset balance occurs at the point where the sum of the opportunity holding costs and the shortage costs is minimized. Admittedly, many of these shortage costs are difficult to measure. Nevertheless, a firm should attempt to evaluate the trade-offs among these costs in order to economize on cash holdings.

Gilmer has performed empirical tests to determine if firms actually do face a U-shaped total cost function associated with the maintenance of liquid asset balances. His results were consistent with the concept of an optimal liquid asset balance as shown in Figure 17.2.[3]

17-2d The Practice of Liquidity Management

In practice, a wide variety of liquidity policies are found to exist among firms. Table 17.1 offers a sample of the liquidity policies practiced by different firms in several industries.

[3]R. H. Gilmer, Jr., "The Optimal Level of Liquid Assets: An Empirical Test," *Financial Management* (Winter 1985): 39–43.

TABLE 17.1

Ratio of Cash and Marketable Securities to Total Assets

Firm	Ratio
Aerospace defense industry	
Boeing	12.0%
General Dynamics	8.7
Lockheed Martin	7.2
Computer industry	
HP	16.3%
IBM	7.2
Intel	14.9
Food industry	
General Mills	1.5%
Kellogg	2.9
Tyson Foods	3.0
Gas and electric utility industries	
American Electric Power	1.8%
Duke Energy	1.3
Exelon	2.2
Restaurant industry	
McDonald's	6.1%
Darden (e.g., LongHorn, Olive Garden, etc.)	8.9
Cheesecake Factory	5.5
Retailing industry	
Macy's	10.5%
Sears Holdings	1.8
Target	5.3

Source: www.sec.gov/edgar.

As the table shows, liquidity practices, as measured by the ratio of cash and marketable securities to total assets, vary significantly among industries and among firms within an industry. Utility firms and food industry companies tend to hold relatively lower liquid asset balances as a proportion of total assets than do firms in the computer industry.

Although this table does not provide data on small- to medium-size firms, in general it can be observed that larger firms tend to hold lower liquid asset balances (relative to total assets) than smaller firms. This is because larger firms tend to have better access to "back up" short-term financing from commercial banks or the commercial paper market. Because smaller firms have more limited credit access, they tend to hold greater liquid asset balances as a cushion against uncertain future needs for funds.

17-3 Controlling the Collection and Disbursement of Cash

The cash collection and disbursement processes provide a firm two areas in which it can economize on cash holdings. For example, suppose that the sales of Briggs & Stratton average about $5 million per business day. If the company can speed up collections by only *one* day, the cash balance will increase by $5 million, and these released funds can be invested in other current assets or in fixed assets. If this additional cash can be invested to yield a 5 percent return, it will generate added income of $250,000 per year (0.05 × $5 million).

Cash collection and disbursement policies are designed to reduce a firm's liquid asset balances (cash and marketable securities) by exploiting imperfections in the collection and payment process. The objective is to speed up collections and slow down disbursements. Financial managers should be aware that policies designed to speed up collections and slow down disbursements are highly competitive. If all firms were to employ the same procedures, the net benefit would be zero. Thus, incremental benefits associated with procedures designed to control collections and disbursements will accrue only to the most aggressive and progressive firms. Similarly, cash managers who do not do at least as much as the average firm in speeding up collections and slowing disbursements will find their firms at a competitive disadvantage.

The primary objective of cash collection involves expediting collections by reducing the lag between the time customers pay their bills and the time the checks are collected. In contrast, the primary objective of cash disbursement is to slow payments so that the firm can keep the funds invested or in the bank as long as possible. Expediting collections and slowing disbursements help increase a firm's cash balance and provide it with funds to use for other profitable investments. Policies designed to control collections and disbursements take advantage of the *float* present in the payment and disbursement system.

17-3a Float

float

A firm's cash balance as shown on the bank's books generally differs from that shown on the firm's own books. This difference is known as **float** and represents the net effect of the delays in the payment of checks a firm writes and the collection of checks a firm receives. Checks written by a firm result in *disbursement*, or *positive*, float; that is, an excess of bank net collected balances over the balances shown on a firm's books. In contrast, *collection float* or *negative float* arises from the delay between the time a customer writes a check to a supplier or other payee and the time the payee actually receives these funds as collected balances (which are spendable). Action being taken by the Federal Reserve System and the rapid progress being made with electronic payment systems means that float will be less important over time. However, until these developments virtually eliminate float, financial managers must understand the sources of float so that they can take legal actions to benefit from it.

There are three primary components, or sources, of float:

1. *Mail float* is the delay between the time a payment is sent to the payee through the mail and the time that payment arrives at the payee's office.
2. *Processing float* represents the delay between receipt of payment from a payer and the deposit of that receipt in the payee's account.
3. *Check-clearing float* is the delay between the time a check is deposited in the payee's account and the time the funds are available to be spent. Checks processed through the Federal Reserve System are "cleared" in two days or less, although the depositor's bank may not make the funds available quite that fast.

17-3b Expediting Collections

Figure 17.3 illustrates the main steps in the cash collection process. The total time involved in this process is a combination of mailing (float) time, company processing (float) time, and check-clearing (float) time, each of which may vary depending on

FIGURE 17.3

Cash Collection Process

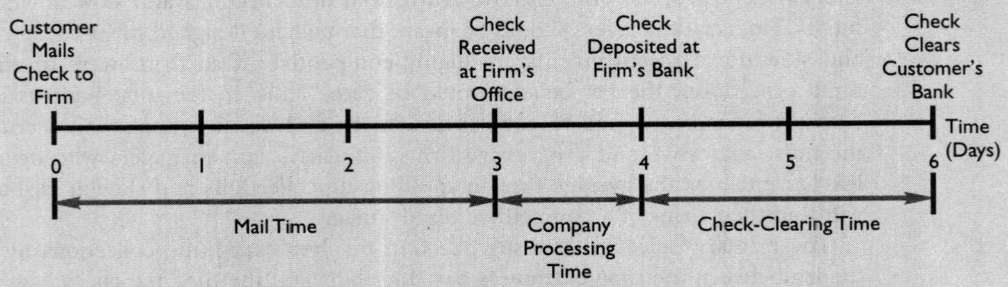

where the firm's customers and their respective banks are located.[4] Some methods available for reducing the collection float are discussed in the following paragraphs.

Decentralized Collection Centers and Concentration Banks Cash collection systems can be either *centralized* or *decentralized.* In the centralized system, customers are instructed to send their payments to the firm's headquarters. In the *decentralized* system, customers mail their payments to a nearby collection center, which is strategically located to minimize mail delay. The collection center then deposits the checks in a local bank and reports this information to the firm's headquarters. Because most of the checks are drawn on banks located in the same geographical area as the collection center, check-clearing float is reduced. Each business day, funds in excess of the amount necessary to compensate the local bank for its services are transferred to an account in a concentration bank, where the firm maintains a disbursement account upon which checks are written. **Concentration banking** is the use of decentralized collection centers and local banks to collect customer payments.

concentration banking

A trade-off exists between the number of collection centers and the potential savings realized. The more collection centers used, the less time is required to convert customers' checks into collected balances. However, these savings from faster collections are offset by the direct fees involved, the opportunity costs of the compensating balances the firm must maintain at each local bank, or both. Financial managers must weigh the trade-offs involved in both savings and costs in deciding on the appropriate number and location of collection centers.

lockbox

Lockboxes Figure 17.4 illustrates a lockbox collection system. A **lockbox** is a post office box maintained by a local bank for the purpose of receiving a firm's remittances. Customers mail payments to this post office box, which is usually no more than a few hundred miles away.[5] The bank empties the box several times each working day, deposits the payments in the firm's account, puts the checks into the clearing system, and sends the firm a list of the payments received each day. Not only does the lockbox reduce

[4]The particular times shown in Figure 17.3 are merely illustrative. Actual times will vary. (This is also true for Figure 17.5.)

[5]Determining the optimal location of lockboxes is a complex problem. For some solutions, see Ferdinand K. Levy, "An Application of Heuristic Problem Solving to Accounts Receivable Management," *Management Science* 12 (February 1966): B-236–B-244; and Robert M. Nauss and Robert E. Markland, "Solving Lock Box Location Problems," *Financial Management* (Spring 1979): 21–31.

FIGURE 17.4
Lockbox Collection System

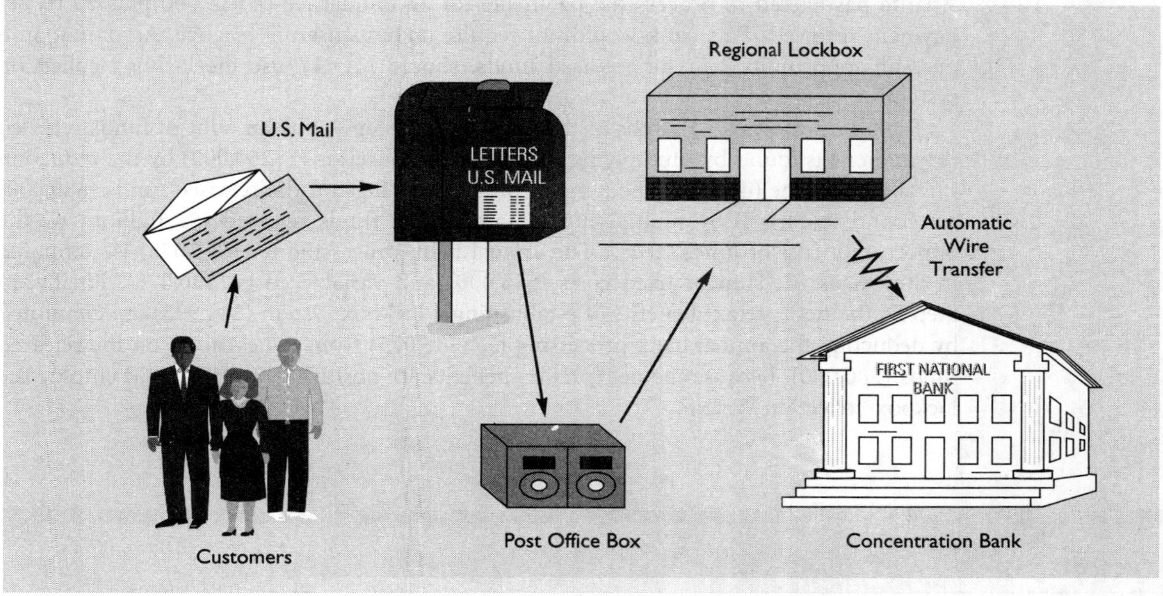

© Cengage Learning

mailing time, but it also eliminates company processing time because the checks are deposited and begin the clearing process *before* the company's accounting department processes the payments received, rather than after processing them. The bank normally charges a fee for this service, requires a compensating balance, or both. Funds in excess of the bank's compensating balance requirement are transferred each day to a master collection account in a concentration bank.

The decision to establish a lockbox collection system requires a comparison of the associated benefits and costs. If the earnings on the funds released by the acceleration of collections exceed the forgone returns on the required compensating balances, the service fees charged by the lockbox bank, or both, the establishment of a lockbox collection system is profitable.

If the number of checks handled is small and the dollar amount of each check is large, a lockbox arrangement is very beneficial to the firm. Under these conditions the bank's workload is light, and the associated service fees, compensating balances, or both, are small. However, when large numbers of checks with small dollar amounts are involved—for example, in the case of oil company credit cards—a lockbox system may not be profitable. Under these conditions, the opportunity costs on the required compensating balances, the service fees, or both may exceed the earnings the firm realizes from having the funds available a few days earlier.

The lockbox decision can be illustrated with the following example. Suppose that the Mutual Life Insurance Company of New York (MONY) currently receives and processes all customer payments at its corporate headquarters in New York City (that is, a *centralized* system). The firm is considering establishing a bank lockbox collection system for seven southeastern states—Florida, North Carolina, South Carolina, Tennessee, Alabama, Georgia, and Mississippi—that would be located in Atlanta. The lockbox would reduce average mailing time for customer payments from 3 days to 1½ days, check-processing time from 2 days to 1 day, and clearing time from 3 days to 1½ days.

Annual collections from the southeastern region are \$91.25 million, and the average number of payments received total 550 per day (assume 365 days per year). A bank in Atlanta has agreed to process the payments for an annual fee of \$15,000 plus \$0.10 per payment received. This bank would not require a compensating balance. Assuming an 8 percent opportunity cost for released funds, should MONY use the lockbox collection system?

Table 17.2 shows an analysis of this decision. In Step A, the amount of funds released (\$1 million) is found by multiplying average daily collections (\$250,000) by the reduction in collection time (4 days). The annual (pretax) earnings on the released funds (\$80,000) are found in Step B by multiplying the amount of funds released (\$1 million) by the opportunity cost of funds (0.08). The annual bank processing fee (\$35,075) is computed in Step C as the sum of fixed costs (\$15,000) and variable costs (\$20,075). Finally, in Step D, the net (pretax) benefits of establishing a lockbox system (\$44,925) are computed by deducting the annual bank processing fee (\$35,075) from the earnings on the released funds (\$80,000). Because the net (pretax) benefits are positive, MONY should employ the lockbox collection system.

TABLE 17.2

Mutual Life Insurance Company of New York (MONY) Analysis of the Decision to Establish a Lockbox Collection System for the Southeastern Region

Step A: Reduction in collection time = Reduction in mailing time + Reduction in processing time + Reduction in check-clearing time
= (3 − 1.5) + (2 − 1) + (3 − 1.5)
= 4 days

Average daily collections = Annual collections ÷ 365
= \$91,250,000 ÷ 365
= \$250,000

Amount of funds released = Average daily collections × Reduction in collection time
= \$250,000 × 4 days
= \$1,000,000

Step B: Annual (pretax) earnings on released funds = Amount of funds released × Interest rate
= \$1,000,000 × 0.08
= \$80,000

Step C: Annual bank processing fee = Fixed cost + Number of payments per year × Variable cost per payment
= \$15,000 + (550 × 365) × \$0.10
= \$15,000 + \$20,075
= \$35,075

Step D: Net (pretax) benefits = Annual (pretax) earnings on released funds − Annual bank processing fee
= \$80,000 − \$35,075
= \$44,925

Wire Transfers and Depository Transfer Checks Once deposits enter the firm's banking network, the objective is to transfer surplus funds (that is, funds in excess of any required compensating balances) from its local (collection) bank accounts to its concentration (disbursement) bank account or accounts. Two methods used to perform this task are *wire transfers* and *depository transfer* checks.

wire transfer

With a **wire transfer**, funds are sent from a local bank to a concentration bank electronically through the Federal Reserve System or a private bank wire system. Wire transfers are the fastest way of moving funds between banks because the transfer takes only a few minutes and the funds become *immediately available* (that is, they can be withdrawn) to the firm upon receipt of the wire notice at the concentration bank. Wire transfers eliminate the mailing and check-clearing times associated with other funds-transfer methods. Some firms leave standing instructions with their local (collection) banks to automatically wire surplus funds on a periodic basis (for example, daily, twice a week, and so on) to their concentration bank. Also, some firms specify in their sales contracts that customers must wire their payments on the due dates.

Wire transfer of funds is available to member banks of the Federal Reserve System and to nonmember banks through their correspondent banks. The cost to corporate customers to send a wire transfer at most banks ranges from \$10 to \$25. A similar charge is made to receive and process a domestic wire transfer. For a firm with multiple collection centers that use wire transfers on a daily basis, the annual costs can be substantial. Consequently, this method of transferring funds should be used only when the incremental value of having the funds immediately available exceeds the additional cost, relative to alternatives, such as depository transfer checks.

depository transfer check (DTC)

A mail **depository transfer check (DTC)** is an unsigned, nonnegotiable check drawn on the local collection bank and payable to the concentration bank. As it deposits customer checks in the local bank each day, the collection center mails a depository transfer check to the concentration bank authorizing it to withdraw the deposited funds from the local bank. Upon receipt of the depository transfer check, the firm's account at the concentration bank is credited for the designated amount. Depository transfer checks are processed through the usual check-clearing process. Although the use of depository transfer checks does not eliminate mailing and check-clearing time, it does ensure the movement of funds from the local collection center banks to the concentration bank in a timely manner. Also, the cost of this method of transferring funds is low; often the only cost involved is postage.

An *electronic depository transfer check* (EDTC) can also be used to move funds from a local bank to a concentration bank. The process of transmitting deposit information to a concentration bank is similar to that for mail DTCs just described, except that the information is sent electronically through an automated clearinghouse, such as the automated clearinghouse (ACH) system of the Federal Reserve (Fedwire) or the Clearing House Interbank Payments System (CHIPS). These systems eliminate the mail float in moving funds from the local bank to a concentration bank. Funds transferred through an automated system are available for use by the firm in one day (or less).

Special Handling of Large Remittances Firms that receive individual remittances in the multimillion-dollar range may find it more profitable to use special courier services to pick up these checks from customers (rather than having their customers mail the checks) and present them for collection to the banks upon which they are drawn.

preauthorized check (PAC)

Use of Preauthorized Checks A **preauthorized check (PAC)** resembles an ordinary check except that it does not require the signature of the person (or firm) on whose account it is being drawn. This system is especially useful for firms that receive a

FIGURE 17.5
Cash Disbursement Process

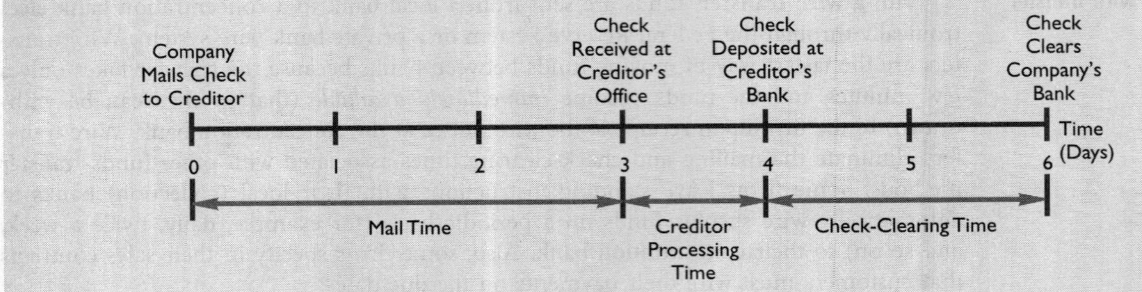

large volume of payments of a fixed amount each period. Insurance companies, savings and loans, charitable institutions, and leasing firms make extensive use of this collection procedure. When preauthorized checks are used, the payer agrees to allow the payee (the firm that is owed the money) to write a check on the payer's account and deposit that check immediately for collection at an agreed-upon time. Preauthorized checks have the advantages of completely eliminating the mail float, reducing billing and collecting expenses, and making the cash flows for both parties highly predictable. Many payers like preauthorized check systems because they do not have to bother to write a check each month.

17-3c Slowing Disbursements

Figure 17.5 illustrates the principal steps involved in the cash disbursement process. Several ways in which a firm can slow disbursements and keep funds in the bank for longer periods of time are discussed in the following paragraphs.

Scheduling and Centralizing Payments A firm should pay bills *on time*—not before or after they are due. There is no significant benefit to be received by paying bills before they are actually due, unless a cash discount is offered for early payment.[6] Payments made ahead of time lower the firm's average cash balance, whereas late payments can impair the firm's credit rating.

Centralizing payments from disbursement accounts maintained at a concentration bank helps minimize the amount of idle funds a firm must keep in local field offices and divisional bank accounts. A number of firms have set up *zero-balance* systems to use disbursement float more effectively. In a **zero-balance system**, a *master*, or *concentration, account* is set up to receive all deposits coming into the zero-balance system. As checks clear through the zero-balance accounts on which they are issued, funds are transferred to these accounts from the master account. These disbursement accounts are called *zero-balance accounts* because exactly enough funds are transferred into them daily to cover the checks that have cleared, leaving a zero balance at the end of the day. In general, all disbursements for accounts payable, payroll, and whatever other purposes the firm desires are issued from these zero-balance accounts. For a zero-balance system

zero-balance system

[6]The cost of not taking cash discounts is discussed in Chapter 16.

to operate effectively, a firm must have a well-developed network for reporting deposits and disbursements, as well as a close working relationship with its bank. In making the decision to put into effect a more efficient cash disbursement system, such as a zero-balance system, a company's financial managers need to compare the returns that can be earned on released funds to the cost of implementing the system.

drafts

Drafts A draft is similar to a check, except that it is not payable on demand. Instead, when a draft is transmitted to a firm's bank for collection, the bank must present the draft to the firm for acceptance before making payment. In practice, individual drafts are considered to be legally paid automatically by the bank on the business day following the day of presentation to the firm, unless the firm returns a draft and explicitly requests that it not be paid. Once the draft has been presented, the firm must immediately deposit the necessary funds to cover the payment.

The use of drafts rather than checks permits a firm to keep smaller balances in its disbursement accounts because funds do not have to be deposited in them until the drafts are presented for payment. Normally, drafts are more expensive to use than checks. The lower account balances and higher processing costs cause banks to impose

ETHICAL ISSUES

Cash Management

Financial managers are confronted with legal and ethical issues as they make cash collection and disbursement decisions. For example, a large firm, such as General Motors (GM) might be tempted to systematically be a few days late in making payments to a small supplier. GM managers may be confident that the small firm will not risk damaging its supply relationship with GM over payment delays of a few days.

Similarly, a cash manager may take advantage of weak control mechanisms in its banks and make short-term investments using uncollected funds. E.F. Hutton's managers got into a lot of trouble with this type of activity. In 1985, E.F. Hutton & Company, a large securities brokerage firm (now part of Morgan Stanley Wealth Management), pleaded guilty to federal fraud charges involving the operation of a massive check-writing scheme to obtain money from many of its 400 banks without paying interest. The firm pleaded guilty to 2,000 counts of mail and wire fraud and agreed to pay more than $10 million in criminal fines and restitution to the banks. According to the Justice Department, Hutton systematically overdrew hundreds of its own accounts in banks throughout the country and intentionally moved money between banks to artificially delay the collection of funds. The scheme involved checks totaling more than $4 billion. By doing this, Hutton was able to use as much as $250 million in interest-free money on some days.

According to Justice Department documents, Hutton officials frequently misused bank accounts of its branches by writing checks for amounts in excess of the volume of customer funds deposited in these accounts. Hutton also pleaded guilty to extending the float time during which checks are cleared by setting up a chain of transfers between branch accounts. These transactions, according to the Justice Department, resembled a check-kiting scheme and were carried out illegally without the prior agreement or consent of the banks involved. Indeed, the banks generally did not realize they were victims until they were told by officials from the government.

A good financial manager should be mindful of the legal and ethical effects of the firm's actions. Legal violations can result in costly fines, embarrassment, and, in some cases, prison terms. Violations of business contracts and the trust built in business transactions may be very costly to a firm's reputation and its future business relationships. In the Hutton case, not only were key employees prosecuted, but also the firm's reputation was so damaged that it was forced to combine with another investment bank to avert failure.

service charges on firms using drafts; this cost must be included in the analysis of the benefits and costs of using drafts to pay bills.

Drafts are now used primarily to provide for centralized control over payments authorized in field offices, rather than as a means of slowing disbursements. For example, a claims agent for Nationwide Insurance might issue a draft to provide for quick settlement of an insurance claim. The claims agent does not have the authority to write a check against Nationwide's checking accounts. The issuing of a draft makes it possible to maintain centralized control over these disbursements. The Federal Reserve System requires a firm to transfer funds to the bank through which payment is to be made as soon as the drafts are presented to the firm.

Maximizing Check-Clearing Float Some firms make payments to suppliers from checking accounts located a long distance from the supplier. For example, an East Coast supplier might be paid with checks drawn on a West Coast bank; this increases the time required for the check to clear through the banking system. Some firms maintain an intricate network of disbursing accounts. Checks are issued from the account most distant from the payee, thereby maximizing check-clearing float.

17-4 Electronic Funds Transfer

The previous discussion of methods to speed up collections and slow disbursements assumes that virtually all transactions involve the transfer of paper (checks) between the payer and the payee. These methods to control collections and disbursements are designed to reduce the float involved in financial transactions. The increasing use of electronic funds transfer (EFT) system and other developments in check processing are reducing opportunities to play the "float" game.

Checks, for example, no longer have to be written and signed physically. Businesses and consumers may now issue "checks by phone" or "eChecks" (electronic checks). In both cases the issuer provides information on the amount of the payment and the checking account to be debited, and the check is electronically generated and presented to the issuing bank. This practice reduces the mail float and also reduces the check-clearing float.

Many consumers now have automatic teller cards that give them access to cash 24 hours a day, seven days a week. In addition, banking customers can use automatic tellers to transfer funds between accounts. Special credit cards, called *debit cards*, are used by many consumers. When a debit card is used, funds are transferred from the consumer's bank account electronically to the account of the retailer. The retailer no longer must be concerned whether a check will be good when it is deposited.

Large payments can be made by wire transfers or through an automated clearinghouse. The automated clearinghouse (ACH) system is a computer-based alternative to the paper-check collection and clearing system. The ACH sorts check-like electronic images and exchanges electronic records of payment and receipt. Although acceptance of electronic checking was initially slow, growth has increased dramatically in recent years.

Additionally, it is now common for companies and other organizations to use direct deposits for high volume, periodic payments such as payroll and dividends. In a direct deposit, the bank debits the employer's bank and electronically transmits the payroll check to the employee's bank via the ACH system. The U.S. government also uses direct deposit to process various transfer payments (for example, social security checks).

EFT mechanisms are profoundly changing the nature of the cash management function. Although paper checks, with their associated mail and processing float, will not disappear completely for some time (if ever), the importance of developing elaborate mechanisms to manage float will be reduced greatly as increased volumes of payments are made electronically. Increased reliance on EFT as the mechanism for payment will free up some of the cash invested in accounts receivable for more productive uses.

17-4a Check Clearing for the 21st Century Act

Also known as the "Check 21" act, this federal law took effect on October 28, 2004. It dramatically altered the way checks are processed. Prior to the new law taking effect, the check-clearing process required that physical exchanges of checks take place. Under the Check 21 act, banks may present copies of the original checks, called "substitute checks" or "image replacement documents (IRDs)." Because IRDs may be transmitted electronically, they reduce check-clearing time, especially for out-of-state checks. It is expected that these out-of-state checks will clear now in less than 24 hours where they used to take as long as 3–4 days. For consumers and businesses, they can expect their disbursement float will be shortened. It also means that adequate precaution should be exercised to ensure that checks are written against adequate reserves in their checking account; otherwise they are liable to incur nonsufficient funds (NSF) charges or overdraft charges.

17-5 Investing in Marketable Securities

Rather than let their cash reserves build up in excess of daily cash requirements, many firms invest in interest-bearing short-term marketable securities. Determining the level of liquid assets that should be invested in marketable securities depends on several factors, including:

- The interest to be earned over the expected holding period
- The transaction costs involved in buying and selling the securities
- The variability of the firm's cash flows

Various quantitative models have been developed for determining the optimal division of a firm's liquid asset balance between cash and marketable securities.[7] These models vary in complexity, depending partly on the assumptions made about the firm's cash flows. The simpler *deterministic* models assume that cash payments occur at a *uniform certain rate* over time. The more complex *probabilistic* or *stochastic* models assume that cash balances fluctuate from day to day in a *random* or unpredictable manner. Although these models provide the financial manager with useful insights into the cost trade-offs involved in effective cash management, they have not been widely implemented in actual decision-making situations.

17-5a Choosing Marketable Securities

A firm may choose among many different types of securities when deciding where to invest excess cash reserves. In determining which securities to include in its portfolio, the firm should consider a number of criteria, including the following:[8]

---

[7]Inventory models were first applied to cash management by William J. Baumol in "The Transactions Demand for Cash: An Inventory Theoretic Approach," *Quarterly Journal of Economics* 66 (November 1952): 545–556. See Terry S. Maness and John T. Zietlow, *Short-Term Financial Management*, 2nd ed. (Cincinnati, OH: Thomson Learning/South-Western, 2002), Chapter 15, for a discussion of the cash and marketable securities allocation decision.

[8]Another criterion is *tax considerations*. Interest received by corporations on municipal securities is exempt from federal (and some state) income taxes. Likewise, a large proportion (70 percent) of intercompany dividends is exempt from federal income taxes. Thus, when comparing yields (or rates of return) on alternative marketable securities, it is important that this be done on an after-tax basis.

- Default risk
- Marketability
- Maturity date
- Rate of return

Notice that the first three criteria deal with risk and the last one deals with return.

Default Risk

default risk

Most firms invest only in marketable securities that have little or no **default risk** (the risk that a borrower will fail to make interest and/or principal payments on a loan). U.S. Treasury securities have the lowest default risk, followed by securities of other U.S. government agencies and, finally, by corporate and municipal securities. Various financial reporting agencies, including Moody's Investors Service and Standard & Poor's, compile and publish information concerning the safety ratings of the various corporate and municipal securities. Given the positive relationship between a security's expected return and risk and the desire to select marketable securities having minimal default risk, a firm has to be willing to accept relatively low expected yields on its marketable securities investments.

Marketability

A firm usually buys marketable securities that can be sold on short notice without a significant price concession. Thus, there are two dimensions to a security's marketability: the time required to sell the security and the price realized from the sale relative to the last quoted price. If a long period of time, a high transaction cost, or a significant price concession is required to dispose of a security, the security has poor marketability and generally is not considered suitable for inclusion in a marketable securities portfolio. Naturally, a trade-off is involved here between risk and return. Generally, a highly marketable security has a small degree of risk that the investor will incur a loss, and consequently, it usually has a lower expected yield than one with limited marketability.

Maturity Date

Firms usually limit their marketable securities purchases to issues that have relatively short maturities. Recall that prices of debt securities decrease when interest rates rise and increase when interest rates fall. For a given change in interest rates, prices of long-term securities fluctuate more widely than prices of short-term

ENTREPRENEURIAL ISSUES

Cash Management

Following efficient cash management policies is important for all firms, government agencies, and not-for-profit enterprises. However, effective cash management is particularly important for entrepreneurial firms for several reasons. First, entrepreneurial businesses do not have the same extensive access to the capital markets as do larger firms. A major source of capital funds to small firms is commercial banks. However, bankers require borrowers to present detailed analyses of their anticipated cash needs. To do this, a firm must have efficient cash management procedures in place. Second, because of an entrepreneurial firm's limited access to capital, a cash shortage problem is both more difficult and more costly for an entrepreneurial firm to rectify than for a large firm. Third, because many entrepreneurial firms are growing rapidly, they have a tendency to run out of cash. Growing sales require increases in inventories and accounts receivable, thereby using up cash resources. Finally, entrepreneurial firms frequently operate with only a bare minimum of cash resources because of the high cost of, and limited access to, capital. As a result, it is imperative that financial managers of entrepreneurial firms use their firm's scarce cash resources in the most efficient way possible.

securities with equal default risk. Thus, an investor who holds long-term securities is exposed to a greater risk of loss if the securities have to be sold prior to maturity. This is known as *interest rate risk.*[9] For this reason, most firms generally do not buy marketable securities that have more than 180 to 270 days remaining until maturity, and many firms restrict most of their temporary investments to those maturing in less than 90 days. Because the yields on securities with short maturities are often lower than the yields on securities with longer maturities, a firm has to be willing to sacrifice yield to avoid interest rate risk.

Rate of Return Although the rate of return, or yield, is also given consideration in selecting securities for inclusion in a firm's portfolio, it is less important than the other three criteria just described. The desire to invest in securities that have minimum default and interest rate risk and that are readily marketable usually limits the selection to those having relatively low yields.

17-5b Types of Marketable Securities

Firms normally confine their marketable securities investments to "money market" instruments, that is, those high-grade (low default risk), short-term debt instruments having original maturities of one year or less. Money market instruments that are suitable for inclusion in a firm's marketable securities portfolio include U.S. Treasury issues, other federal agency issues, municipal securities, negotiable certificates of deposit, commercial paper, repurchase agreements, bankers' acceptances, Eurodollar deposits, auction rate securities, money market mutual funds, and bank money market accounts. (In some cases, firms will also use long-term bonds having one year or less remaining to maturity as "marketable" securities and treat them as money market instruments.)

Table 17.3 lists the characteristics and yields of various money market instruments. As can be seen in the last three columns of the table, yields on these securities vary considerably over time. Yields were near their historic highs in August 1981, during a period of relatively high inflation. Following the financial crisis of 2008–2009, yields were near their lowest levels in decades. Yields are a function of a number of factors, including the state of the economy, the rate of inflation, and government monetary and fiscal policies.

U.S. Treasury Issues U.S. Treasury bills are the most popular marketable securities. They are sold at weekly auctions through Federal Reserve Banks and their branches and have standard maturities of 91 days, 182 days, and one year. Treasury bills are issued at a discount and then redeemed for the full face amount at maturity. Once they are issued, Treasury bills can be bought and sold in the secondary markets through approximately 40 government securities dealers. There is a large and active market for Treasury bills, which means that a firm can easily dispose of them when it needs cash. The smallest denomination of Treasury bills is $10,000 of maturity value.

The advantages of Treasury issues include short maturities, a virtually default-free status, and ready marketability. Their primary disadvantage lies in the fact that their yields normally are the lowest of any marketable security.

The Treasury also issues notes that have original maturities from 2 to 10 years and bonds that have maturities over 10 years. As these securities approach their maturity dates, they become, in effect, short-term instruments that are then suitable for inclusion in a firm's marketable securities portfolio. Treasury bonds and notes pay interest semiannually. Minimum Treasury bond denominations are $1,000.

[9] Interest rate risk is discussed in Chapter 7.

TABLE 17.3

Characteristics and Yields of Selected Money Market Instruments

Instrument	Issuer	Denominations	Maturities
U.S. Treasury bills	U.S. Treasury	Various denominations from $10,000 to $1,000,000	91 days, 182 days, 52 weeks
Federal agency issues	Government-sponsored enterprises (GSEs)	Various denominations from $5,000 to $1,000,000	Wide variation in maturities, from several days to more than 10 years
Short-term municipal securities	State and local government and their agencies	$5,000 to $5,000,000	1 month to 1 year
Negotiable certificates of deposit	Commercial banks	$100,000 to $1,000,000	7 days to 18 months or more
Commercial paper	Larger corporations and finance companies with strong credit ratings	$100,000 or more	2 or 3 days to 270 days
Repurchase agreements	Banks and securities dealers	Varying amounts; no standard denominations	1 day to several months
Bankers' acceptances	Commercial banks	Varying amounts, depending on the size of commercial transaction	30 to 180 days
Eurodollar deposits	Foreign banks	$1,000,000	1 day to 6 months (or more)
Auction rate securities	Investment banks	$25,000 for debt securities and $100,000 for preferred stock	7 days to 1 year
Money market mutual funds	Securities dealers and mutual fund companies	Minimum of $1,000 is usually required; no standard denominations	Redeemable at any time
Bank money market accounts	Commercial banks	Minimum of $2,500 required	Normally redeemable at any time (by law, banks reserve the right to require 7 days' written notice for withdrawals)

*n.a.—not available.

Source: *Federal Reserve Statistical Release,* H. 15, Various issues, www.federalreserve.gov/releases.

Marketability		Yields* (%) Aug. 1981	May 2007	Feb. 2016
Highly organized secondary market	(3 months)	15.51	4.85	0.26
	(6 months)	15.52	4.98	0.43
	(1 year)	14.70	4.91	0.52
Well-established secondary market for short-term securities		—	—	—
Not as good as U.S. Treasury and federal agency issues		—	—	—
Fairly good secondary market	(1 month)	17.91	5.28	n.a.
	(3 months)	17.96	5.31	n.a.
	(6 months)	17.98	5.31	n.a.
Weak secondary market	(1 month)	17.58	5.22	0.38
	(3 months)	17.23	5.17	0.57
	(6 months)	16.62	n.a.	n.a.
Limited, but borrower agrees to repurchase securities at a fixed price on a fixed date		—	—	—
Good, although less extensive than for most other instruments	(3 months)	17.22	n.a.	n.a.
	(6 months)	16.56	n.a.	n.a.
Developing a secondary market	(3 months)	18.79	5.32	0.70
Saleable at auction periodically		—	—	—
Good, because the fund agrees to redeem shares at any time		Yields vary from fund to fund, but usually exceed the yield available on Treasury bills		
Excellent, but not available to all business firms		Yields vary significantly from bank to bank, but usually are below Treasury bill yields		

HTTP:
Information on Treasury securities is available at

www.treasurydirect.gov

Additional material on other federal agency issues can be found at their home pages, such as

www.fhlb.com

or

www.fanniemae.com

Other Federal Agency Issues A number of federal government-sponsored enterprises have been formed to improve the flow of credit to targeted sections of the economy, such as housing and agriculture. These GSEs, including the Federal Home Loan Banks, Federal National Mortgage Association (Fannie Mae), Federal Home Loan Mortgage Corporation (Freddie Mac), and CoBank (agricultural loans), issue their own securities. Although these GSE securities do not constitute a legal obligation of the U.S. government, there is an implicit guarantee that the government will not allow these institutions to fail and default on their debt. This implicit guarantee was tested during the subprime mortgage crisis, when the government bailed out and put Fannie Mae and Freddie Mac into conservatorship in September 2008. As a consequence of this implicit guarantee, most investors consider these debt securities to be very low-risk securities, and they sell at yields slightly above U.S. Treasury securities but below other money market instruments. Because these securities are traded in the secondary markets through the same dealers who handle U.S. Treasury securities, they are readily marketable should a firm need to dispose of them before maturity. Minimum denominations are generally $5,000.

Municipal Securities State and local governments and their agencies issue various types of interest-bearing securities. Short-term issues are suitable for inclusion in a firm's marketable securities portfolio. The yields on these securities vary with the creditworthiness of the issuer. The pretax yields on these securities are generally lower than the yields on Treasury bills because the interest is exempt from federal (and some state) income taxes. The secondary market for municipal issues is not as strong as that for Treasury and other federal agency issues. Municipal (tax-exempt) money market mutual funds are also available.

Negotiable Certificates of Deposit Commercial banks are permitted to issue certificates of deposit (CDs), which entitle the holder to receive the amount deposited plus accrued interest on a specified date. At the time of issue, maturities on these instruments range from seven days to 18 months or more. Once issued, CDs become *negotiable*, meaning they can be bought and sold in the secondary markets. Because CDs of the largest banks are handled by government securities dealers, they are readily marketable and thus are suitable for inclusion in a firm's marketable securities portfolio. Yields on CDs are generally above the rates on federal agency issues having similar maturities.

commercial paper

Commercial Paper **Commercial paper** consists of short-term unsecured promissory notes issued by large, well-known corporations and finance companies with strong credit ratings. Some finance companies—such as Ford Credit Company—which issue large amounts of commercial paper regularly sell it directly to investors. Industrial, utility, and transportation firms and smaller finance companies, which issue commercial paper less frequently and in smaller amounts, sell their commercial paper through commercial paper dealers. Maturities on commercial paper at the time of issue range from 2 or 3 days to 270 days. As noted in Chapter 16, the amount of commercial paper outstanding declined significantly in 2008 during the financial crisis.

The secondary market for commercial paper is weak, although it is sometimes possible to make arrangements with the issuer or commercial paper dealer to repurchase the security prior to maturity. This weak secondary market combined with a somewhat higher default risk results in higher yields on commercial paper than on most other money market instruments.

repurchase agreement

Repurchase Agreements A **repurchase agreement**, or repo, is an arrangement with a bank or securities dealer in which the investor acquires certain short-term

INTERNATIONAL ISSUES

Cash Management

The goals of cash management in a multinational company (MNC) parallel the cash management goals of purely domestic corporations. That is, MNCs attempt to speed up collections, slow disbursements, and make the most efficient use of the firm's cash resources by minimizing excess balances and investing balances to earn the highest possible return, consistent with liquidity and safety constraints. However, there are some unique elements of cash management for an MNC.

First, cash management is complicated by difficulties and costs associated with moving funds from one country (and currency) to another. It is costly to convert cash from one currency to another. Second, there is a general lack of integrated international cash transfer facilities, such as exist in the United States and most other Western nations. The absence of this capability makes it difficult to move funds quickly from one country to another. Third, investment opportunities for temporary excess cash balances are much broader for an MNC than for a domestic firm. MNCs must consider short-term investment options in many different countries—a process further complicated by exchange rate risk. Fourth, the host government may place restrictions on the movement of cash out of the country.

Practicing MNC cash managers have developed a number of techniques designed to optimize the process of international cash management in the face of these difficulties. First, there is general agreement that the cash management function for an MNC should be centralized with respect to the information-gathering and decision-making process. The parent normally maintains an international cash manager who has the expertise and responsibility to keep track of the firm's cash balances around the world and to identify the best sources for short-term borrowing and lending.

Second, many MNCs have instituted a process called *multilateral netting.* **Multilateral netting** is designed to minimize the cost associated with misdirected funds. **Misdirected funds** are funds that cross an international border unnecessarily. It is costly to convert funds from one currency to another, hence it is desirable to minimize unnecessary transactions. For example, consider an MNC that has subsidiaries operating in Spain, England, and Switzerland. Each subsidiary purchases supplies from the other subsidiaries. If the English unit purchases $10 million from the unit in Spain, and the Spanish unit purchases $8 million from the English unit, the transaction cost associated with transferring funds from the English unit to the Spanish unit can be reduced if these payments are *netted out* against each other. Thus, instead of the English unit converting $10 million in funds to send to the Spanish unit, it will net out the Spanish unit's purchases from the English unit and simply send a $2 million payment. The greater the number of subsidiaries an MNC has, the more complex is the process of managing a multilateral netting system. At the same time, the potential cost savings are greatly increased.

multilateral netting

misdirected funds

securities subject to a commitment from the bank or dealer to repurchase the securities on a specified date. Securities used in this agreement can be government securities, CDs, or commercial paper. Their maturities tend to be relatively short, ranging from one day to several months, and are designed to meet the needs of the investor.

The yield on a repo is slightly less than the rate that can be obtained from outright purchase of the underlying security. The repo rate approximates the rate on federal funds, which is the rate used when banks borrow from other banks. Although repos generally are considered very safe investments, a number of investors did incur losses when several small government securities dealers (which were active in the repo market) failed.

bankers' acceptance

Bankers' Acceptances A **bankers' acceptance** is a short-term debt instrument issued by a firm as part of a commercial transaction. Payment is guaranteed by a commercial bank. Bankers' acceptances are commonly used financial instruments in international trade, as well as in certain lines of domestic trade.

These instruments vary in amount, depending on the size of the commercial transactions. A secondary market exists in which these acceptances can be traded should a bank or investor choose not to hold them until maturity, which usually ranges between 30 and 180 days at the time of issue. Bankers' acceptances are relatively safe investments because both the bank and the borrower are liable for the amount due at maturity. Their yields are comparable to the rates available on CDs.

Eurodollar Deposits Eurodollar deposits are dollar-denominated deposits in banks or bank branches located outside the United States. These deposits usually have slightly higher yields than on corresponding deposits in domestic banks because of the additional risks. Eurodollar CDs issued by London banks are negotiable, and a secondary market is developing for them.

auction rate securities

Auction Rate Securities A number of large investment banks issue, on behalf of their clients, **auction rate securities**, a type of security (debt or preferred stock), that is a suitable investment for excess corporate funds. The yield on these securities is adjusted periodically, typically every 7, 28, or 35 days for debt securities and every 49 days for preferred stocks. At each of these points in time, investors can exchange these securities for cash. Broker-dealers may also provide a secondary market for these securities between auctions. Minimum investments typically are $25,000 for debt securities and $100,000 for preferred stocks.

Auction rate securities were sold by investment banks as a safe but slightly higher-yielding alternative to money market funds. The auctions ran smoothly for years until February 2008, when the credit crisis scared bidders away, and more than $300 billion of these securities became illiquid. As a result of the threat of lawsuits and government pressure, most of the largest issuers of these securities, such as UBS and Merrill Lynch, agreed to buy back these securities from their customers. Investors learned that these securities were not as marketable as they had been led to believe.

Money Market Mutual Funds Many of the higher-yielding marketable securities described earlier are available only in relatively large denominations. For example, negotiable CDs usually come in amounts of $100,000 or more. As a result, a smaller firm that has limited funds to invest at any given time is often unable to obtain the higher yields offered on these securities. An alternative is a *money market mutual fund* that pools the investments of many other small investors and invests in large-denomination money market instruments. By purchasing shares in a money market fund, such as Dreyfus Liquid Assets or Vanguard Prime Money Market, a smaller firm can approach the higher yields offered on large-denomination securities. In addition, most of these funds offer check-writing privileges, which provide liquidity and enable firms to earn interest on invested funds until their checks clear.

HTTP:
Contingency Analysis maintains a glossary that defines and discusses financial terms such as repos, reverse repos, liquidity, payment netting, reinvestment risk, and much more.
www.contingencyanalysis.com

Money market mutual funds are considered among the safest places to invest short-term funds. However, they are not completely risk free, as some investors found out during the financial crisis of 2008–2009. Reserve Management's $62 billion money market fund "broke the buck" in September 2008 when the fund's asset value fell below $1 per share and investors were unable to redeem their money. This default occurred because the fund held $785 million in Lehman Brothers securities when Lehman filed for bankruptcy. Investors in Reserve Management's money market fund got back approximately 99 cents on each dollar invested. This episode has led to greater regulation of money market mutual funds.

Bank Money Market Accounts Banks are permitted to offer checking accounts with yields comparable to those on money market mutual accounts with limited check-writing privileges. These accounts provide yields that are comparable to those on money market mutual funds.

17-6 Summary

- A firm holds liquid asset balances for the following primary reasons:
  1. To conduct transactions
  2. For precautionary purposes
  3. To meet future requirements
  4. For speculative reasons
  5. To compensate its bank or banks for various services rendered
- To manage cash effectively, a firm must first develop a *cash budget* showing all of the forecasted cash inflows and outflows over the planning horizon.
- A firm's optimal liquid asset balance reflects risk and return trade-offs and depends on both the opportunity cost of holding excess balances and the "shortage" costs associated with not having enough needed cash available.
- The primary objective in controlling cash collections is to reduce the delay between the time when the customer mails the payment and when it becomes a collected balance. Methods for reducing collection time include decentralized collection centers and concentration banks, lockboxes, wire transfers, depository transfer checks, special handling of large remittances, and the use of preauthorized checks.
- The primary objective in controlling cash disbursements is to slow payments and keep the firm's funds in the bank as long as possible. Techniques for slowing disbursements include scheduling and centralizing payments (zero-balance systems), using drafts rather than checks, maximizing check-clearing float, and stretching payables.
- Electronic funds transfer mechanisms, including the use of wire transfers and automated check clearinghouses, increasingly will reduce the importance of float management techniques.
- The primary criteria a firm should use in selecting *marketable securities* include *default risk, marketability* (or *liquidity*), *maturity date,* and *rate of return.*

17-7 Questions and Topics for Discussion

1. Define the following terms:
   a. Demand deposits
   b. Compensating balance
   c. Disbursement float
   d. Deposit float
   e. Lockbox
   f. Wire transfer
   g. Depository transfer check
   h. Zero-balance system
   i. Draft
   j. Automated clearinghouse
2. What are the primary reasons a firm holds a liquid asset balance?
3. Describe the cost trade-offs associated with maintaining the following:
   a. Excessive liquid asset balances
   b. Inadequate liquid asset balances
4. Define *float* and describe the difference between *disbursement* float and *deposit* float.

5. Describe the primary services a bank provides to a firm. How is the bank compensated for these services?
6. Describe the methods available to a firm for expediting the collection of cash.
7. Describe the techniques available to a firm for slowing disbursements.
8. Explain the trade-offs involved in determining the number of collection centers that a firm should use.
9. What factors should the firm consider in deciding whether to establish a lockbox collection system?
10. What are the primary criteria in selecting marketable securities for inclusion in a firm's portfolio?
11. What types of marketable securities are most suitable for inclusion in a firm's portfolio? What characteristics of these securities make them desirable investments for temporarily idle cash balances?
12. What is multilateral netting? Give an example of how this would work for a multinational firm.
13. What measures can the board of directors of a corporation take to discourage unethical (and illegal) behavior, such as the mail and wire fraud by E. F. Hutton managers described in the chapter?

17-8 Self-Test Problems

Note: When converting from annual data to daily data or vice versa, assume there are 365 days per year.

ST1. The White Oak Company's annual sales are $219 million. An average of 9 days elapses between when a customer mails its payment and when the funds become usable by the firm.

a. If the company could speed up the collection of funds by 2 days, what would be the increase in the firm's average cash balance?
b. Assuming that these additional funds can be invested in marketable securities that yield 7 percent per year, determine the increase in White Oak's annual (pretax) earnings.

ST2. Builders Circle, a hardware and building supplies company, processes all its customer credit card payments at its Atlanta headquarters. A Boston bank has offered to process the payments from Builders Circle customers located in the New England region for $50,000 per year plus $0.20 per payment. No compensating balance will be required. Under this lockbox arrangement, the average mailing time for payments would be reduced from 3 days to 1.5 days. Check processing and clearing time would be reduced from 5 days to 2 days. Annual collections from the New England region are $292 million. The total number of payments received annually is 600,000 (an average of 50,000 credit card holders × 12 payments per year). Assume that any funds released by this lockbox arrangement can be invested by Builders Circle to earn 10 percent per year before taxes. The establishment of a lockbox system for the New England region will reduce payment processing costs at its Atlanta headquarters by $40,000 per year. Using this information, determine:

a. The amount of funds released by this lockbox arrangement
b. The annual (pretax) earnings on the released funds
c. The annual fee that Builders Circle must pay the Boston bank for processing the payments

d. The annual *net* (pretax) benefits Builders Circle will receive by establishing this lockbox arrangement with the Boston bank

17-9 Problems*

Note: When converting annual data to daily data or vice versa in these problems, assume there are 365 days per year.

BASIC

1. Dexter Instrument Company's sales average $3 million per day.

a. If Dexter could reduce the time between customers' mailing their payments and the funds becoming collected balances by 2.5 days, what would be the increase in the firm's average cash balance?

b. Assuming that these additional funds can be invested in marketable securities to yield 8.5 percent per annum, determine the annual increase in Dexter's (pretax) earnings.

BASIC

2. Exman Company performed a study of its billing and collection procedures and found that an average of 8 days elapses between the time when a customer's payment is received and when the funds become usable by the firm. The firm's *annual* sales are $540 million.

a. Assuming that Exman could reduce the time required to process customer payments by 1.5 days, determine the increase in the firm's average cash balance.

b. Assuming that these additional funds could be used to reduce the firm's outstanding bank loans (current interest rate is 8 percent) by an equivalent amount, determine the annual pretax savings in interest expenses.

CHALLENGE

3. Great Lakes Oil Company currently processes all its credit card payments at its domestic headquarters in Chicago. The firm is considering establishing a lockbox arrangement with a Los Angeles bank to process its payments from 10 western states. Under the arrangement, the average mailing time for customer payments from the western region would be reduced from 3 days to 1.5 days, whereas check processing and clearing time would be reduced from 6 days to 2.5 days. Annual collections from the western region are $180 million. The total number of payments received annually is 4.8 million (an average of 400,000 credit card customers × 12 payments per year). The Los Angeles bank will process the payments for an annual fee of $75,000 plus $0.05 per payment. No compensating balance will be required. Assume that the funds released by the lockbox arrangement can be invested elsewhere in the firm to yield 10 percent before taxes. The establishment of a lockbox system for the western region will reduce payment-processing costs at the Chicago office by $50,000 per year. Using this information, determine the following:

a. The amount of funds released by the lockbox arrangement

b. The annual (pretax) earnings on the released funds

c. The annual fee Great Lakes Oil must pay to the Los Angeles bank for processing the payments

d. The annual *net* (pretax) benefits Great Lakes Oil will receive by establishing this lockbox arrangement with the Los Angeles bank

Great Lakes Oil has also received a proposal from a Salt Lake City bank to set up a lockbox system for the firm. Average mailing time for checks in the western region would be reduced to 2 days under the proposal from the Salt Lake City bank, and check processing and clearing time would average 2.5 days. The Salt Lake City bank

*Color blocks behind the numbers denote problems that have check answers provided at the end of the book.

would not charge any fees for processing the payments, but it would require Great Lakes Oil to maintain a $1.5 million average compensating balance with the bank—funds that normally would be invested elsewhere in the firm (yielding 10 percent) and not kept in a non-interest-bearing checking account.

e. Determine the annual *net* (pretax) benefits to Great Lakes Oil of establishing a lock-box system with the Salt Lake City bank.

f. Which of the two lockbox systems (if any) should the firm select?

INTERMEDIATE

4. Japanese Motors, a major importer of foreign automobiles, has a subsidiary (Japanese Motor Credit Company, or JMCC) that finances dealer inventories, as well as retail installment purchases of the company's cars. With respect to the financing of retail purchases, JMCC currently employs a centralized billing and collection system. Once a customer's credit has been approved at one of the subsidiary's 50 local branch offices, the information is forwarded to JMCC headquarters (located in Los Angeles) and the customer is issued a book of payment coupons. Each month during the life of the installment contract, the customer mails a coupon stub along with the payment to the Los Angeles office. The average mailing, processing, and check-clearing time with the present collection system is 8 days.

In an effort to reduce this collection time, JMCC is considering establishing a decentralized collection system. Under this system, customers would be instructed to mail their payments to the nearest local branch office, which would then deposit the checks in a local bank and report this information to JMCC headquarters in Los Angeles. As the checks clear in the local banks, funds would be sent each day to JMCC's central bank in Los Angeles. This decentralized collection system would reduce both mailing time and check-clearing time and reduce the average collection time to 5 days.

JMCC's annual installment collections are $900 million. Implementation of the decentralized collection system is expected to reduce collection costs at the Los Angeles headquarters by $100,000 a year compared with the currently employed centralized collection system. However, branch office collection costs are expected to rise by $225,000 if the decentralized system is implemented. JMCC's Los Angeles bank currently requires the firm to maintain a $250,000 balance as compensation for depositing customer payments. Compensating balances at the 50 local banks that JMCC would employ with the decentralized collection system are expected to total $500,000. Any funds released under the decentralized collections system would be used to reduce the firm's debt, which currently carries an interest rate of 7.5 percent.

Using this information, determine the annual *net* pretax benefits JMCC would realize by implementing a decentralized collection system.

INTERMEDIATE

5. J-Mart, a nationwide department store chain, processes all its credit sales payments at its suburban Detroit headquarters. The firm is considering the implementation of a lockbox collection system with an Atlanta bank to process monthly payments from its southeastern region. Annual credit sales collections from the region are $60 million. The establishment of the lockbox system would reduce mailing, processing, and check-clearing time from 8 days currently to 3.5 days, reduce company processing costs by $25,000 per year, and reduce the compensating balance of its Detroit bank by $200,000. The Atlanta bank would not charge any fee for the lockbox service but would require J-Mart to maintain a $500,000 compensating balance. Funds released by the lockbox arrangement could be invested elsewhere in the firm to earn 15 percent before taxes. Determine the following:

a. The amount of funds released by the lockbox arrangement

b. The annual (pretax) earnings on the released funds

c. The annual *net* (pretax) benefits to J-Mart of establishing the lockbox system with the Atlanta bank

INTERMEDIATE

6. Peterson Electronics uses a decentralized collection system whereby customers mail their payments to one of six regional collection centers. The checks are deposited each working day in the collection center's local bank, and a depository transfer check for the amount of the deposit is *mailed* to the firm's concentration bank in New York. On average, 5 days elapse between the time the checks are deposited in the local bank and the time the funds become collected funds (and available for disbursements) at the concentration bank. Peterson is considering using wire transfers instead of depository transfer checks in moving funds from the six collection centers to its concentration bank. Wire transfers would reduce the elapsed time by 3 days. Depository transfer checks cost $0.50 (including postage), and wire transfers cost $10. Assume there are 250 working days per year. Peterson can earn 7 percent before taxes on any funds that are released through more efficient collection techniques. Determine the net (pretax) benefit to Peterson of using wire transfers if annual sales are:

a. $15 million
b. $75 million

Suppose Peterson is considering using *electronic* depository transfer checks, rather than mail depository transfer checks, to move funds from its six collection centers to its concentration bank. Electronic depository transfer checks would *reduce* collection time by 2 days and would cost $2.50 each. Determine the net (pretax) benefit to Peterson of using electronic depository transfer checks if annual sales are

c. $15 million
d. $75 million

CHALLENGE

7. Wisconsin Paper Company is considering establishing a zero-balance system for its payroll account. The firm pays its employees every 2 weeks on Friday (that is, 26 pay periods per year). Currently, the firm deposits the necessary funds in the payroll account on Friday to cover the total amount of the checks written each pay period, which averages $1 million. However, the firm has found that the majority of the checks did not clear the payroll account until the following week. A typical distribution of when the checks clear the payroll account is as follows:

Day	Amount of Funds Clearing Payroll Account
Friday	$ 300,000
Monday	450,000
Tuesday	150,000
Wednesday	100,000
Total	$1,000,000

Assume that the firm can earn 6 percent on any funds released from its payroll account using a zero-balance system.

a. Determine the annual pretax returns the firm would realize from the use of a zero-balance system for its payroll account.
b. What additional information is necessary to make a decision concerning the desirability of establishing such a system?

INTERMEDIATE

8. The High-Rise Construction Company, located in Houston, receives large remittances (that is, progress payments) from customers with whom it has contracts. These checks are frequently drawn on New York City banks. If the checks are deposited in High-Rise's Houston bank, the funds will not become collected balances and usable by the firm until 2 *business* days later. In other words, deposits made on Monday become available for use on Wednesday, and deposits made on Friday become available to the firm on the following Tuesday. However, if High-Rise sends an employee to New York with the check and she presents it for payment at the bank upon which it is drawn, the funds will be available immediately (that is, the same day) to the firm. Assuming that High-Rise can earn 6 percent on short-term investments and that the cost of sending an employee to New York to present the check for payment is $350, determine the following:

a. The net (pretax) benefit to the firm of using this special handling procedure for a $1 million check received on the following days:
   i. Monday
   ii. Friday

Why do the answers to Parts i and ii differ?

b. The amount of a check on which the firm just "breaks even" (that is, the net pretax benefit equals zero) using the special handling procedure, assuming that the check is received on the following days:
   i. Monday
   ii. Friday

INTERMEDIATE

9. Jackson's Thriftway currently processes all of its credit sales at its Seguin, Texas, headquarters. The firm is considering establishing a lockbox arrangement with a Chicago bank to process payments from customers in 12 midwestern states. Average mailing time for customers from this region is currently 4 days. It is expected that the system will reduce this to 2.5 days. Check processing and clearing time would be reduced from 4 days to 1.5 days with the lockbox arrangement. Annual collections from this region are $200 million. The lockbox arrangement would reduce the compensating balance requirement at the firm's Seguin bank by $400,000 and reduce annual payment processing costs at the Seguin office by $25,000. Funds released by the lockbox arrangement can be invested elsewhere in the firm to earn 14 percent before taxes.

a. The Chicago bank has agreed to process Jackson's customer payments for an annual fee of $130,000. Determine the annual net pretax benefits to Jackson's of establishing a lockbox system with the Chicago bank.

b. The Chicago bank has agreed to process Jackson's customer payments "free of charge" if the firm maintains a minimum compensating balance of $2 million in its account at the bank. Determine the annual net pretax benefits to Jackson's of establishing the lockbox system under these conditions.

CHALLENGE

10. Two banks, First Fidelity Bank and First Union Bank, have offered to process Zack's retail charge card payments. First Fidelity will process the payments for a fee of $0.15 per payment with no compensating balance required. First Union will process the payments "free of charge," provided that Zack's maintains a compensating balance of $3 million at the bank. Zack's averages 125,000 payments per month from its credit card holders. The company can earn 8 percent before taxes on any available funds.

a. Determine which of the two payment processing proposals Zack's should accept if the objective is to minimize costs.

b. Determine the rate of return (that is, Zack's opportunity cost of funds) at which the costs of the two proposals would be equal.

c. Determine the number of payments per month at which the costs of the two proposals would be equal, assuming that the processing fees ($0.15) and compensating balances ($3,000,000) remain constant.

CHALLENGE

11. World Telephone & Telegraph (WTT) is considering the establishment of a zero-balance system for its dividend payment account. The firm pays common stockholders quarterly dividends. Currently, WTT deposits the necessary funds to cover the dividend payments on the day the checks are mailed to shareholders. A typical distribution of when the checks clear the dividend account is as follows:

	Day	Amount of Funds Clearing Dividend Account (in Millions of Dollars)
	Friday (checks mailed)	—
Week 1	Monday	$ 3
	Tuesday	15
	Wednesday	18
	Thursday	14
	Friday	8
Week 2	Monday	6
	Tuesday	5
	Wednesday	3
	Thursday	1
	Friday	1
	Total	$74

WTT can earn 7.5 percent per annum on any funds released from its dividend payment account using a zero-balance system.

a. Determine the annual pretax returns the firm would earn on the funds released from a zero-balance system.
b. What other considerations need to be examined in making a decision about the desirability of establishing such a system?

CHALLENGE

12. Tokyo Electric Company (TEC) sells most of its products in the United States through 50 large distributors and retail chains (for example, Sears, Kmart). Currently, TEC's customers mail their payments, which are due monthly, to the company. The company is considering having its customers make payments by wire transfer on the dates payments are due. TEC's financial analysts expect this method of payment would reduce average mailing and check-clearing time by 5 days. Any funds released by this system could be reinvested in the firm to earn 8 percent before taxes. The cost to TEC (including a $15 per payment rebate to customers) would be $30 per payment. Determine the net (pretax) benefits to TEC of using a wire transfer payment system if monthly payments from each customer average:

a. $25,000
b. $50,000

CHAPTER 18

The Management of Accounts Receivable and Inventories

KEY CHAPTER CONCEPTS

1. *Accounts receivable management* refers to the decisions a business makes regarding its overall credit and collection policies and the evaluation of individual credit applicants.
2. In formulating an optimal credit policy, a company's financial managers must analyze the marginal benefits and costs associated with changes in each of the following variables:
   a. Credit standards
   b. Credit terms
   c. Collection effort
3. The evaluation of individual credit applicants consists of the following three principal steps:
   a. Gathering relevant information on the credit applicant
   b. Analyzing the information obtained to determine the applicant's creditworthiness
   c. Deciding whether to extend credit to the applicant and, if so, determining the amount of the line of credit
4. The determination of the optimal level of inventory investment requires that the benefits and costs associated with alternative levels be measured and compared.
5. Inventory-related costs include:
   a. Ordering costs
   b. Carrying costs
   c. Stockout costs
6. The use of inventory control models can aid in efficiently managing a company's level of inventory investment.
7. The economic order quantity model permits determination of the quantity of an inventory item that should be ordered to minimize total inventory costs.

FINANCIAL CHALLENGE

Inventories and Political Risks

Manufacturing companies hold inventories as a buffer between the various phases of the procurement-production-sales cycle. There are costs and benefits of holding inventories. Costs include the cost of funds invested in inventories. Benefits include the avoidance of stockouts, that is, the costs associated with the inability to meet demand for the product. Stockouts can occur due to factors such as erroneous forecasts of future demand for the product and unforeseen delays in the procurement of raw materials and production of the product.

Political risks can have an impact on the inventories held by companies. For example, the inventory decisions of such companies as Boeing and United Technologies were affected by the tensions that rose in 2014 between Russia and the United States over Russia's move to annex the Ukrainian region of Crimea. Both companies bought a significant share of their titanium from a Russian company, VSMPO-Avisma, which was the world's largest titanium producer, supplying about 30 percent of the titanium used in the aerospace industry. VSMPO had financial ties to Rostec State Corporation, which is owned by the Russian government. Additionally, the Ukraine provided almost all of the titanium concentrate used by VSMPO. Boeing and United Technologies, in order to minimize the risk of stockouts, began stockpiling titanium—a critical element used in the production of jet airplanes and engines. Besides their regular titanium purchases, both companies reportedly began stockpiling an additional six months' supply of titanium forgings. As an official from Boeing said, "We are taking all appropriate actions to insure that we have a necessary supply of titanium forgings. This includes increasing inventory and exploring all available sources of supply." On the other hand, Airbus, which buys 60 percent of its titanium from Russia, reportedly did not seek to build a stockpile of the metal. As the CEO of Airbus stated, "I do not expect the flow of [titanium] will be cutoff short of all-out war."

Companies make inventory investment decisions based on the costs and benefits of holding inventory. The second part of this chapter focuses on inventory management.

Source: John Ostrower and Andy Pasztor, "Boeing, United Technologies Stockpile Titanium Parts," *The Wall Street Journal* (August 7, 2014), www.wsj.com.

CHAPTER OBJECTIVES

Upon completion of this chapter, you should have a clear understanding of the following:

1. The methods used for establishing optimal credit and collection policies
2. The procedures for evaluating individual credit applicants
3. The measurement of the various types of inventory-related costs
4. The models and procedures for determining a firm's optimal level of inventory investment

18-1 Introduction

Accounts receivable and inventories constitute important investments for most companies. As we saw earlier in Table 16.1, these two current assets represent sizable proportions of the total assets of firms in a wide variety of industries. In the next two sections, we discuss the management of accounts receivable. We examine inventory management in the remainder of the chapter.

18-2 Accounts Receivable Management

Accounts receivable consist of the credit a business grants its customers when selling goods or services.[1] They take the form of either *trade credit*, which the company extends to other companies, or *consumer credit*, which the company extends to its ultimate consumers.[2] The effectiveness of a company's credit policies can have a significant impact on its total performance. For example, Monsanto's credit manager has estimated that a reduction of only one day in the average collection period for the company's receivables increases its cash flow by $10 million and improves pretax profits by $1 million.

For a business to grant credit to its customers, it has to do the following:

- Establish credit and collection policies
- Evaluate individual credit applicants

In this section we develop the establishment of optimal credit and collection policies. In the following section, we discuss procedures for evaluating individual credit applicants.

[1] From the *customer's* perspective, credit represents a form of short-term financing known as accounts payable. This is discussed in greater detail in Chapter 16.

[2] Some companies use their accounts receivable to obtain short-term financing. For example, a company that is somewhat weak financially might be unable to borrow short-term funds without putting up collateral for the loan. In such a case, the company might use its accounts receivable as the collateral by *pledging* them to the bank. Alternatively, the company might consider selling, or *factoring*, its accounts receivable to obtain cash. Accounts receivable pledging and factoring are discussed in Chapter 16.

18-2a Shareholder Wealth and Optimal Investments in Accounts Receivable

When a company decides to extend credit to customers, it is making an investment decision, namely, an investment in accounts receivable, a *current asset*. As with the decision to invest in *long-term assets*, the primary goal is the maximization of shareholder wealth. Recall from the discussion of the basic framework for capital budgeting decisions in Chapter 9 that the optimal capital budget is determined by accepting all investment projects whose marginal returns, as measured by the internal rate of return, are greater than or equal to the marginal costs of the funds invested in the projects, as measured by the marginal cost of capital. Such a decision rule maximizes shareholder wealth because the projects accepted will earn a return greater than or equal to cost of the funds to the owners of the firm. Following similar reasoning, a company will maximize shareholder wealth by investing in accounts receivable as long as the expected marginal returns obtained from each additional dollar of receivables investment exceed the associated expected marginal costs of the investment, *including the cost of the funds invested.*

The establishment of an *optimal credit extension policy* requires the company to examine and attempt to measure the *marginal costs* and *marginal returns* (benefits) associated with alternative policies. What are the marginal returns and costs associated with a more liberal extension of credit to a company's customers? With respect to returns, a more liberal extension presumably stimulates sales and leads to increased gross profits, assuming that all other factors (such as economic conditions, prices, production costs, and advertising expenses) remain constant. Offsetting these increased returns are several types of credit-related marginal costs, including the opportunity costs of the additional capital funds employed to support the higher level of receivables. Any increase in sales resulting from a more liberal credit extension policy may also result in increased inventory levels and associated inventory investment costs. Checking new credit accounts and collecting the higher level of receivables also results in additional costs. And finally, a more liberal credit policy frequently results in increased bad-debt expenses because a certain number of new accounts are likely to fail to repay the credit extended to them.

In determining an optimal credit extension policy, a company's financial managers must consider a number of major controllable variables that can be used to alter the level of receivables, including the following:

- Credit standards
- Credit terms
- Collection effort

The remainder of this section discusses each of these variables in greater detail.

18-2b Credit Standards

Credit standards are the criteria a company uses to screen credit applicants in order to determine which of its customers should be offered credit and how much. The process of setting credit standards allows the firm to exercise a degree of control over the "quality" of accounts accepted.[3] The quality of credit extended to customers is a multidimensional concept involving the following:

- The time a customer takes to repay the credit obligation, *given that it is repaid*
- The probability that a customer will fail to repay the credit extended to it

[3]Complete control over the quality of accounts accepted is generally impossible due to uncertainty about future events (for example, a recession or a strike) that could make it difficult or even impossible for a customer to repay its account.

average collection period The **average collection period** serves as one measure of the promptness with which customers repay their credit obligations. It indicates the average number of days a company must wait after making a credit sale before receiving the customer's cash payment. Obviously, the longer the average collection period, the higher a company's receivables investment and, by extension, its cost of extending credit to customers.

bad-debt loss ratio The likelihood that a customer will fail to repay the credit extended to it is sometimes referred to as *default risk*. The **bad-debt loss ratio**, which is the proportion of the total receivables volume a company never collects, serves as an overall, or aggregate, measure of this risk. A business can estimate its loss ratio by examining losses on credit that has been extended to similar types of customers in the past.[4] The higher a firm's loss ratio, the greater the cost of extending credit.

For example, suppose that Bassett Furniture Industries is considering making a change in its credit standards. Before reaching any decision, the company first must determine whether such a change would be profitable. The first step in making this decision involves an evaluation of the overall creditworthiness of the company's existing and potential customers (retailers) using various sources of information.[5] Table 18.1 illustrates the credit sales, average collection period, and loss ratio data for various credit risk groups of the company's customers in its northwest region.

Under its current credit policy, Bassett extends unlimited credit to all customers in Credit Risk Groups 1, 2, and 3, and no credit to customers in Groups 4 and 5, meaning that the customers in these latter two groups must submit payment along with their orders. As a result of this policy, Bassett estimates that it "loses" $300,000 per year in sales from Group 4 customers and $100,000 per year in sales from Group 5 customers.[6]

variable cost ratio Bassett also estimates that its *variable* production, administrative, and marketing costs (including credit department costs) are approximately 75 percent of total sales; that is, the **variable cost ratio** is 0.75.[7] Thus, the profit contribution ratio per dollar of sales is 1.0 − 0.75 = 0.25, or 25 percent. The company's required pretax rate of return (that is, the opportunity cost) on its current assets investment is 20 percent.

TABLE 18.1

Credit Evaluation Data Compiled by Bassett Furniture Industries

Credit Risk Group	Credit Sales ($)	Average Collection Period (Days)	Bad-Debt Loss Ratio (%)
1	900,000	25	—
2	1,100,000	30	0.5
3	400,000	45	3
4	300,000*	60	7
5	100,000*	90	13

*Estimated lost sales due to the fact that no credit is extended to customers in these risk categories.

[4]This estimation procedure assumes that the loss ratio does not change significantly over time because of changing economic conditions. Otherwise, the loss ratio should be adjusted to take account of expected future economic changes. This procedure also assumes that credit extension and repayment information is available on a sufficiently large sample of accounts to provide a company with a reliable estimate of its loss ratio. Without this information, the financial manager simply has to make an "educated guess" as to the size of the loss ratio.

[5]Some of these sources of information are described later in this chapter.

[6]Throughout the chapter, *estimates* of variables, such as sales, the average collection period, and the bad-debt loss ratio, are used in the analysis of credit policy decisions. These estimates are subject to uncertainty. *Sensitivity analysis* (described in Chapter 11) can be performed to determine the effect on profitability of different estimates of one (or more) of these variables.

[7]This analysis assumes that the collection costs for Credit Risk Group 4 customers are the same as for customers in the other groups and are included in credit department costs.

One alternative Bassett is considering is to relax credit standards by extending full credit to Group 4 customers. Bassett estimates that an additional inventory investment (that is, raw materials, work-in-process, and finished goods) of $120,000 is required to expand sales by $300,000. In evaluating this alternative, the financial manager has to analyze how this policy would affect pretax profits. If the marginal returns of this change in credit standards exceed the marginal costs, pretax profits would increase, and the decision to extend full credit to the Group 4 customers would increase shareholder wealth.

Table 18.2 contains the results of this analysis. In Step A, the marginal profitability of the additional sales, $75,000, is calculated. Next, the cost of the additional investment in receivables, $9,863, is calculated in Step B.[8] In Step C, the additional bad-debt loss, $21,000, is computed. Then, the cost of the additional investment in inventory, $24,000, is calculated in Step D. Finally, in Step E, the net change in pretax profits is determined by deducting the marginal costs computed in Steps B, C, and D from the marginal returns found in Step A. Because this expected net change is a positive $20,137, the analysis indicates that Bassett should relax its credit standards by extending full credit to the Group 4 customers.

This analysis contains a number of explicit and implicit assumptions of which the financial manager must be aware. One assumption is that *the company has excess capacity* and thus could produce the additional output at a *constant variable cost ratio* of 0.75. If the company is currently operating at or near full capacity, and additional output could be obtained only by paying more costly overtime rates and/or investing in new facilities, this analysis would have to be modified to take account of these incremental costs. This analysis also assumes that the average collection period of the customers in Groups 1, 2, and 3 would *not increase* once the company began extending credit to Group 4 customers. If it became known that the Group 4 customers had 60 days or more to pay their bills with no penalty involved, the Group 1, 2, and 3 customers, who normally pay their bills promptly, might also start delaying their payments. If this occurred, the analysis would have to be modified to account for such shifts. It was also assumed that the required rate of return on the investment in receivables and inventories for Group 4 *does not change* as a result of extending credit to these more risky accounts. A case can be made for increasing the required rate of return to compensate for the increased risk of the new accounts. Finally, this example assumes that an increase in inventory investment is necessary as a result of changes in the firm's credit policy. In summary, for this type of analysis to be valid and to lead to the correct decision, it must include *all* the marginal costs and benefits that result from the decision.

[8]Note that we have chosen to use sales value in determining the (opportunity) cost of the additional receivables investment. Disagreement exists in the finance literature concerning the measurement of the incremental investment in accounts receivable (and its associated opportunity cost) arising from a change in credit standards. Some authors contend that the relevant measure of investment is the dollar *cost* the firm has tied up in the new accounts receivable, rather than the total *sales value*. The rationale for this approach is that the "profit" on the sale—that is, the difference between the amount of the accounts receivable and their associated cost—would be nonexistent without the change in credit standards. Hence, no opportunity cost is incurred on this uncollected "profit." Advocates of this approach use variable cost or total cost as a measure of the amount of funds invested in accounts receivable. Other authors claim that the total sales value of the new accounts receivable is indeed the relevant measure of investment in accounts receivable because the opportunity cost of the increased level of accounts receivable is the return a company could earn if it reduced accounts receivable back to its original level. In other words, considerations of symmetry require that the opportunity cost of increasing accounts receivable by a given amount should be equal to the returns that could be earned on the funds released from decreasing accounts receivable by the same amount. The interested reader should consult the following references for a more complete discussion of the issues involved: John S. Oh, "Opportunity Cost in the Evaluation of Investment in Accounts Receivable," *Financial Management* 5 (Summer 1976): 32–35; Edward A. Dyl, "Another Look at the Evaluation of Investment in Accounts Receivable," *Financial Management* 6 (Winter 1977): 67–70; Joseph C. Atkins and Yong H. Kim, "Comment and Correction: Opportunity Cost in the Evaluation of Investment in Accounts Receivable," *Financial Management* 6 (Winter 1977): 71–74; Tirlochan S. Walia, "Explicit and Implicit Cost of Changes in the Level of Accounts Receivable and the Credit Policy Decision of the Firm," *Financial Management* 6 (Winter 1977): 75–80; and J. Fred Weston and Pham D. Tuan, "Comment on Analysis of Credit Policy Changes," *Financial Management* 9 (Winter 1980): 59–63.

TABLE 18.2

Bassett Furniture Industries' Analysis of the Decision to Relax Credit Standards by Extending Full Credit to Customers in Credit Risk Group 4

Step A: Additional sales	$300,000	
Marginal profitability of additional sales		
= Profit contribution ratio × Additional sales		
= 0.25 × $300,000		$75,000
Step B: Additional investment in receivables		
= Additional average daily sales*		
× Average collection period		
$= \frac{\text{Additional annual sales}}{365} \times 60$		
$= \frac{\$300{,}000}{365} \times 60$	$ 49,315	
Cost of the additional investment in receivables		
= Additional investment in receivables		
× Required pretax rate of return		
= $49,315 × 0.20		$ 9,863
Step C: Additional bad-debt loss		
= Bad-debt loss ratio × Additional sales		
= 0.07 × $300,000		$21,000
Step D: Additional investment in inventory	$120,000	
Cost of the additional investment in inventory		
= Additional investment in inventory		
× Required pretax rate of return		
= $120,000 × 0.20		$24,000
Step E: Net change in pretax profits		
= Marginal returns – Marginal costs		
= A – (B + C + D)		
= $75,000 – ($9,863 + $21,000 + $24,000)		+$20,137

*Standard practice is to assume that there are 365 days per year.

HTTP:
Inc. Magazine maintains an "archives" link at its home page enabling you to search back issues for articles about a particular topic. Try keying in a few terms learned in this chapter (or any chapter) and see what *Inc. Magazine* advises about your choices.

www.inc.com

18-2c Credit Terms

A company's *credit terms*, or terms of sale, specify the conditions under which the customer is required to pay for the credit extended to it. These conditions include the *length of the credit period* and the *cash discount* (if any) given for prompt payment plus any special terms, such as *seasonal datings*. For example, credit terms of "net 30" mean that the customer has 30 days from the invoice date within which to pay the bill and that no discount is offered for early payment.

credit period

Credit Period

The length of a company's **credit period** (the amount of time a credit customer has to pay the account in full) is frequently determined by industry customs, and thus it tends to vary among different industries. The credit period may be as short as seven days or as long as six months. Variation appears to be positively related to the length of time the merchandise is in the purchaser's inventory. For example, manufacturers of goods having relatively low inventory turnover periods, such as jewelry, tend to offer retailers longer credit periods than distributors of goods having higher inventory turnover periods, such as food products.

A company's credit terms can affect its sales. For example, if the demand for a particular product depends in part on its credit terms, the company may consider lengthening the credit period to stimulate sales. For example, in the 1980s, IBM apparently tried to stimulate declining sales of its PCjr home computer by extending the length of the credit period in which dealers had to pay for the computers. In making this type of decision, however, a company must also consider its closest competitors. If they lengthen their credit periods, too, every company in the industry may end up having about the same level of sales, a much higher level of receivables investments and costs, and a lower rate of return.

Analyzing the possible effects of an increase in a company's credit period involves comparing the profitability of the increased sales that are expected to occur with the required rate of return on the additional investment in receivables and inventories. Additional bad-debt losses must also be considered. If a company continues to accept the same quality of accounts under its lengthened credit terms, no significant change in the bad-debt loss ratio should occur.

For example, suppose that Nike, a distributor of athletic shoes and sportswear, is considering changing its credit terms from "net 30" to "net 60" in its western Michigan sales territory. The company expects sales (all on credit) to increase by about 10 percent from a current level of $2.2 million, and it expects its average collection period to increase from 35 days to 65 days. The bad-debt loss ratio should remain at 3 percent of sales. The company also estimates that an additional inventory investment of $50,000 is required for the expected sales increase. The company's variable cost ratio is 0.75, which means that its profit contribution ratio (per dollar of sales) is $1.00 - 0.75 = 0.25$. Nike's required pretax rate of return on investments in receivables and inventories is 20 percent.

Table 18.3 contains an analysis of Nike's decision. Many of the calculations in this table are similar to those in Table 18.2, which analyzed the effects of a change in credit standards. The marginal returns ($55,000) computed in Step A represent the marginal profitability of the additional sales generated by the longer credit period. The marginal costs (obtained in Steps B, C, and D) consist of the cost of the additional receivables investment ($44,000), the additional bad-debt losses ($6,600), and the cost of the additional inventory investment ($10,000). The net increase in pretax profits (Step E) that would result from the decision to lengthen the credit period is −$5,600. Therefore, the decision does not appear to be worthwhile.

cash discount

Cash Discounts

A **cash discount** is a discount offered on the condition that the customer will repay the credit extended within a specified period of time. A cash discount is normally expressed as a percentage discount on the net amount of the cost of goods purchased (usually excluding freight and taxes). The length of the discount period is also specified when discount terms are offered. For example, credit terms of "2/10, net 30" mean that the customer can deduct 2 percent of the invoice amount if payment is made within 10 days from the invoice date. If payment is not made by this time, the full invoice amount is due within 30 days from the invoice date. (In some cases, the discount period may begin with the date of shipment or the date of receipt by the customer.) Like the length of the credit period, the cash discount varies among different lines of business.

Cash discounts are offered (or increased) to speed up the collection of accounts receivable and, by extension, reduce a company's level of receivables investment and associated costs.[9] Offsetting these savings or benefits is the cost of the discounts

[9]Offering a cash discount may also increase demand and sales because some potential customers may view it as a form of price cut and be willing to purchase the product at this new "lower" price. Throughout the ensuing analysis, it is assumed that the cash discount is *not* perceived as a price cut and that there is no resulting increase in demand. It is also assumed that offering cash discounts will not reduce bad-debt losses by any measurable amount.

TABLE **18.3**

Nike's Analysis of the Decision to Change Its Credit Terms from "Net 30" to "Net 60"

Step A: Additional sales		
= Percent increase × Present sales		
= 0.10 × $2,200,000	$220,000	
Marginal profitability of additional sales		
= Profit contribution ratio × Additional sales		
= 0.25 × $220,000		$55,000
Step B: Additional investment in receivables		
= New average balance − Present average balance		
$= \frac{\text{New annual sales}}{365} \times \text{New average collection period}$		
$- \frac{\text{Present annual sales}}{365} \times \text{Present average collection period}$		
$= \frac{\$2{,}420{,}000}{365} \times 65 - \frac{\$2{,}200{,}000}{365} \times 35$		
= $430,959 − $210,959	$220,000	
Cost of the additional investment in receivables		
= Additional investment in receivables		
× Required pretax rate of return		
= $220,000 × 0.20		$44,000
Step C: Additional bad-debt loss		
= Bad-debt loss ratio × Additional sales		
= 0.03 × $220,000		$ 6,600
Step D: Additional investment in inventory	$ 50,000	
Cost of the additional investment in inventory		
= Additional investment in inventory		
× Required pretax rate of return		
= $50,000 × 0.20		$10,000
Step E: Net change in pretax profits		
= Marginal returns − Marginal costs		
= A − (B + C + D)		
= $55,000 − ($44,000 + $6,600 + $10,000)		−$ 5,600

that are taken, which is equal to the lost dollar revenues from the existing unit sales volume.

For example, suppose that Sony Music (a subsidiary of the Sony Corporation) is considering instituting a cash discount. The company currently sells to distributors on credit terms of "net 30" and wants to determine the effect on pretax profits of offering a 1 percent cash discount on terms of "1/10, net 30" to distributors in its southwestern Ohio region. The company's average collection period is now 50 days and is estimated to decrease to 28 days with the adoption of the 1 percent cash discount policy. It also is estimated that approximately 40 percent of the company's customers will take advantage of the new cash discount. Sony's annual credit sales in the southwest region are $2.5 million, and the company's required pretax rate of return on receivables investment is 20 percent.

TABLE 18.4

Sony Music: Analysis of the Decision to Offer a 1 Percent Cash Discount

Step A: Decrease in average receivables balance

$= \text{Present average balance} - \text{New average balance}$

$= \dfrac{\text{Annual sales}}{365} \times \text{Present average collection period}$

$- \dfrac{\text{Annual sales}}{365} \times \text{New average collection period}$

$= \dfrac{\$2{,}500{,}000}{365} \times 50 - \dfrac{\$2{,}500{,}000}{365} \times 28$

$= \$342{,}466 - \$191{,}781$ — $150,685

Earnings on the funds released by the decrease in receivables

$= \text{Decrease in receivables} \times \text{Required pretax rate of return}$

$= \$150{,}685 \times 0.20$ — $30,137

Step B: Cost of cash discount

$= \text{Annual sales} \times \text{Percentage taking discount}$

$\times \text{Percentage discount}$

$= \$2{,}500{,}000 \times 0.40 \times 0.01$ — $10,000

Step C: Net change in pretax profits

$= \text{Marginal returns} - \text{Marginal costs}$

$= A - B$

$= \$30{,}137 - \$10{,}000$ — +$20,137

Table 18.4 contains an analysis of Sony's proposed cash discount policy. The marginal returns ($30,137) computed in Step A represent the earnings Sony expects to realize on the funds released by the decrease in receivables. The marginal costs ($10,000) found in Step B represent the cost of the cash discount. Subtracting the marginal costs from the marginal returns (Step C) yields a net increase in pretax profits of $20,137, indicating that Sony should offer the proposed 1 percent cash discount, if it is confident about the accuracy of the estimates used in this analysis.

seasonal datings

Seasonal Datings **Seasonal datings** are special credit terms that are sometimes offered to retailers when sales are highly concentrated in one or more periods during the year. Under a seasonal dating credit arrangement, the retailer is encouraged to order and accept delivery of the product well ahead of the peak sales period and then to remit payment shortly after the peak sales period. The primary objective of seasonal dating is to increase sales to retailers who are unable to finance the buildup of inventories in advance of the peak selling period because of a weak working capital position, limited borrowing capacity, or both.

For example, O. M. Scott & Sons, manufacturers of lawn and garden products, has used a seasonal dating plan that is tied to the growing season. Payments for winter and early spring shipments are due at the end of April and May, depending on the geographical area, and payments for shipments during the summer months are due in October or November. Payments for purchases made outside the two main selling seasons are due on the 10th of the second month following shipment. A cash discount of 0.6 percent per month is offered to encourage payments in advance of these seasonal dates. The arrangement enables and encourages dealers of lawn and garden products to be fully stocked with Scott products in advance of the peak selling periods.

18-2d Collection Effort

The collection effort consists of the methods a business employs in attempting to collect payment on past-due accounts. Some commonly used methods include the following:

- Sending notices or letters informing the customer of the past-due status of the account and requesting payment
- Telephoning and/or visiting the customer in an effort to obtain payment
- Employing a collection agency
- Taking legal action against the customer

Another approach, which is also effective in some cases, is for the firm to refuse to make new shipments to the customer until the past-due bills are paid. Although the objectives of the collection effort are to speed up past-due payments and reduce bad-debt losses, a company must also avoid antagonizing normally creditworthy customers who may be past due for some good reason—for example, because of temporary liquidity problems. A collection effort that is too aggressive may reduce future sales and profits if customers begin buying from other businesses whose collection policies are more lenient.

When determining which methods to use in its collection effort, a company has to consider the amount of funds it has available to spend for this purpose. If the firm has a relatively small amount of money available for collecting past-due accounts, it must confine itself to less costly (and less effective) methods, such as sending letters and making telephone calls. If it has a larger budget, the firm can employ more aggressive procedures, such as sending out representatives to personally contact past-due customers. In general, the larger the company's collection expenditures, the shorter its average collection period and the lower its level of bad-debt losses. The benefits of additional collection efforts, however, are likely to diminish rapidly at extremely high expenditure levels.

The marginal benefits of the decision to increase collection expenditures consist of the earnings on the funds released from the receivables investment as a result of the shorter average collection period, plus the reduction in bad-debt losses. A business should increase its collection expenditures only if these marginal benefits are expected to exceed the amount of the additional collection expenditures.

18-2e Monitoring Accounts Receivable

For a company to effectively control its receivables investment, the credit manager must monitor the status and composition of these accounts. An *aging of accounts* is a useful monitoring technique.[10] In an aging analysis, a company's accounts are classified into different categories based on the number of days they are past due. These classifications show both the aggregate amount of receivables and the percentage of the total receivables outstanding in each category. Aging of accounts receivable provides more information than such summary ratios as, for example, the average collection period. Comparing aging schedules at successive points in time (for example, monthly, quarterly, or semiannually) can help the credit manager monitor any changes in the "quality" of the company's accounts.

[10] Aging schedules are also discussed in Chapter 3.

18-3 Evaluating Individual Credit Applicants

Once a company has established its credit and collection policies, it can use them as a basis for evaluating individual credit applicants.[11] In general, the credit evaluation process consists of these main steps:

- Gathering relevant information on the credit applicant
- Analyzing the information obtained to determine the applicant's creditworthiness
- Deciding whether to extend credit to the applicant and, if so, determining the amount of the line of credit

The credit evaluation process is limited by both time and cost. Often a business may have only a few days—or, in some cases, only a few hours—in which to evaluate a credit request. Delaying this decision too long may result in the loss of a potential customer's order.

The credit evaluation process is also limited by the amount of resources the credit department has available. The amount of time and money a company spends on evaluating a customer's request for credit should depend on the size of the losses the company would experience if it made an incorrect decision. These potential losses stem from either denying credit to a creditworthy customer or offering credit to a customer who is not creditworthy. The larger the potential losses, the more time and money a business should spend on evaluating the credit applicant.

18-3a Gathering Information on the Credit Applicant

Information for evaluating the creditworthiness of a customer is available from a variety of sources, including the following:

- Financial statements submitted by the customer
- Credit reporting organizations
- Banks
- The company's own prior experience with the customer

These sources differ with respect to their costs and the reliability of the information they provide.

Financial Statements A company can ask a credit applicant to supply various kinds of financial information, such as income statements and balance sheets (preferably audited ones), and possibly even a forecasted budget. This information can be used to evaluate the applicant's financial strength—and the applicant's ability to repay credit obligations. Unwillingness on the part of the applicant to supply financial statements may indicate financial weakness and suggest the need for more detailed checking, the outright refusal to extend credit, or both.

HTTP:
www.dnb.com

Credit-Reporting Organizations A number of national and local organizations collect information on the financial position and credit standing of businesses. Companies and lending institutions that are considering extending credit to a company may obtain information about it from these organizations, usually for a fee. The most widely known credit-reporting organization is Dun & Bradstreet Credit Services, which provides its subscribers with online credit reports on individual businesses.

[11]Once these policies are established, however, they do not have to remain static over time. The credit manager should review them periodically, making appropriate modifications as dictated by changing economic conditions (for example, rising interest rates) or other circumstances.

HTTP:
www.nacm.org

A typical report contains a summary of trade credit payments to existing suppliers, which can be extremely valuable to companies that are considering extending credit to a particular company. Also included in a typical report are financial data from the firm's balance sheet and income statement, a review of its banking relationships, historical information about the owners, and a description of its operations, including the location of facilities and the kinds of products sold.[12]

The National Association of Credit Management also fills requests for information on the repayment patterns of specific companies. In addition, a number of other organizations collect and disseminate credit information within given industries, such as the toy and furniture industries, as well as within given geographical areas, such as Chicago and New York.

Banks Many banks will assist their business customers in obtaining information on the creditworthiness of other businesses. Through its contacts with other banks, a customer's bank can often obtain detailed information on the payment patterns and financial status of the company under investigation and pass this information on to a customer.

Prior Experience with the Customer A company's experience with a credit customer can be extremely useful when deciding whether to continue extending credit, increase the amount of credit it currently grants to the customer, or both. If, for example, the customer tends to remit payments well beyond the due date and/or if the company must employ expensive collection methods in obtaining payments, the credit analyst should weigh this unfavorable information in making the credit extension decision.

18-3b Analyzing Creditworthiness and Making the Credit Decision

Credit analysts ideally should obtain information about an applicant from as many sources as possible, but they should also consider the time and costs involved. Specifically, analysts should weigh the expected returns to be derived from any additional information against the cost involved in obtaining it.

A good way to structure information collection is to proceed *sequentially*, beginning with the least costly and least time-consuming sources. If the results of this initial check indicate that more information is needed, the analyst can proceed to additional sources. For example, the analyst may begin by consulting the customer's past credit history with the company. If further information is needed, the analyst can then check with Dun & Bradstreet and/or ask the applicant to supply financial statements and a list of companies that have extended trade credit to it in the past. Finally, if still more information is needed, the credit analyst can request credit checks through banks and the applicant's trade creditors.

Because a great deal of information is usually available about a credit applicant, the credit manager must be able to sort through this information and extract the key elements that will enable a reliable overall assessment of the applicant's creditworthiness to be made. There are no magic formulas for making unerring credit decisions, but there are some traditional guidelines that can serve as a framework for analysis. These guidelines are called the "five Cs of credit":

- *Character* refers to the applicant's willingness or desire to meet credit obligations. Past payment patterns are useful in gauging this aspect of creditworthiness.
- *Capacity* refers to the applicant's ability to meet financial obligations. A reasonable estimate of an applicant's capacity can usually be obtained by examining its liquidity position and projected cash flows.

[12]The reliability and comprehensiveness of this type of report depends in part on how willing a business is to supply D&B with pertinent information.

- *Capital* refers to the applicant's financial strength, particularly with respect to net worth. Evidence about a company's capital can usually be obtained by evaluating the balance sheet using financial ratios.
- *Collateral* represents the assets that the applicant may pledge as security for the credit extended to it. However, collateral is often not a critical consideration because the primary concern for the company offering trade credit is the timely repayment of the credit, not foreclosing on the pledged assets.
- *Conditions* refer to the general economic climate and its effect on the applicant's ability to pay. A good credit risk in prosperous times might be unable to make payments during a recession.

Many credit analysts feel that the first two *C*s, character and capacity, are the most important insofar as they help to ensure that the firm considering extending credit will not leave anything important out of the analysis.

Numerical credit scoring systems are another technique that has been found useful, particularly in the area of consumer credit. This technique allows the credit-granting business to quantitatively rate various financial and personal characteristics of the applicant, such as the length of the time in business, its D&B credit rating, and its current ratio. The total credit score can then be computed based on the characteristics thought to be related to creditworthiness. The applicant's credit score is next compared with those of other applicants, or with a minimally acceptable cutoff score. Although numerical credit scoring systems can be beneficial in credit screening, they can be difficult and expensive to install.

Guidelines and techniques such as these can aid in the analysis of an applicant's creditworthiness; the ability to make sound credit decisions, however, ultimately depends on the decision maker's experience and judgment in evaluating the available information.

18-4 Inventory Management

HTTP:
Visit Inventory Management's Web site to link to their many blog articles on inventory management.

www.inventorymanagement.com/index.html

Inventories serve as a buffer between the various phases in the procurement-production-sales cycle of a manufacturing firm.[13] They uncouple the various phases by giving the firm flexibility with respect to timing the purchase of raw materials, scheduling production facilities and employees, and meeting fluctuating and uncertain demand for the finished product. Inventories also serve similar purposes in the procurement-sales cycle of a wholesaling or retailing firm.

The remainder of this chapter explores the various types of inventories and their functions, along with the different categories of inventory-related costs. It also develops some models and procedures that can be used in efficiently managing a firm's level of inventory investment. Although financial managers usually do not have primary responsibility for managing a company's inventories, they are responsible for seeing that funds are invested in a manner consistent with shareholder wealth maximization. (Normally, production and/or marketing management has primary responsibility for determining the specific quantities of the various types of inventories that the firm holds.) To perform this function, financial managers must have a good working knowledge of inventory control techniques.

Like any other asset, the holding of inventories constitutes an investment of funds. Determining the optimal level of inventory investment requires that the benefits and costs, *including the opportunity cost of the funds invested,* associated with alternative levels be measured and compared. To do this, it is necessary to determine the specific benefits associated with holding the various types of inventories.

[13]Inventories are sometimes used as collateral for short-term loans. This topic is discussed in detail in Chapter 16.

18-4a Benefits of Holding Inventories

Manufacturing firms generally hold three types of inventories:

- Raw materials inventories
- Work-in-process inventories
- Finished goods inventories

Raw Materials Inventories Raw materials inventory consists of items a business purchases for use in its production process. It may consist of basic materials (for example, iron ore for a steel-making operation), manufactured goods (for example, memory chips for a computer assembly operation), or both. Maintaining adequate raw materials inventories provides a company with advantages in both purchasing and production. Specifically, the purchasing department benefits by being able to buy needed items in large quantities and take advantage of *quantity discounts* offered by suppliers. In addition, if rising prices, shortages of specific items, or both are forecasted for the future, maintaining a large stock of raw materials ensures that the company will have adequate supplies at reasonable costs.

Knowing that adequate stocks of raw materials will be available when needed permits the production department to meet production schedules and make the most efficient use of its personnel and facilities. Therefore, there are a number of valid reasons why a company's purchasing and production departments will want to maintain large inventories of raw materials.

Work-in-Process Inventories Work-in-process inventory consists of all items that are presently in the production cycle at some intermediate stage of completion. For example, they may be currently undergoing some type of operation (such as assembly or painting); they may be in transit between operations; or they may be stored somewhere, awaiting the next step in the production cycle.

Work-in-process inventories are a necessary part of modern industrial production systems because they give each operation in the production cycle a certain degree of independence. This, in turn, aids in the efficient scheduling of the various operations and helps minimize costly delays and idle time. For these reasons, a company's production department will want to maintain reasonable work-in-process inventories. In general, the longer a firm's production cycle, the larger its work-in-process inventory.

Finished Goods Inventories Finished goods inventory consists of those items that have completed the production cycle and are available for sale. With the exception of large-scale, specialized types of equipment—such as industrial machinery, military armaments, jet airplanes, and nuclear reactors, which are normally contracted for *before* they are produced—most consumer and industrial products are manufactured and stored in inventory to meet forecasted future sales.

Keeping enough finished goods inventories on hand provides significant benefits for both the marketing and the production departments. From marketing's perspective, large finished goods inventories enable it to fill orders promptly, minimize lost sales, and avoid shipment delays due to stockouts. From production's standpoint, maintaining a large finished goods inventory permits items to be manufactured in large production runs, which helps keep unit production costs low by spreading fixed setup expenses over large volumes of output.

18-4b Inventory-Related Costs

At the same time that a number of benefits are to be realized from holding inventories, a number of costs also must be considered, including the following:

- Ordering costs
- Carrying costs
- Stockout costs

ordering costs

Ordering Costs

Ordering costs represent all the costs of placing and receiving an order. They are stated in dollars per order. When a company is ordering from an external source, these include the costs of preparing the purchase requisition, expediting the order (for example, long-distance calls and follow-up letters), receiving and inspecting the shipment, and handling payment. Such factors as an item's price and engineering complexity also affect its ordering costs. When an order is placed for an item that is manufactured *internally* within a company, ordering costs consist primarily of *production setup* costs, which are the expenses incurred in getting the plant and equipment ready for a production run.

In practice, the cost per order generally contains both fixed and variable components because a portion of the cost—such as that of receiving and inspecting the order—normally varies with the quantity ordered. However, many simple inventory control models, such as the EOQ model (which is described later in this chapter), treat cost per order as fixed by assuming that these costs are independent of the number of units ordered.

carrying costs

Carrying Costs

Carrying costs constitute all the costs of holding items in inventory for a given period of time. They are expressed either in dollars per unit or as a percentage of the inventory value per period. Components of this cost include the following:

- Storage and handling costs
- Obsolescence and deterioration costs
- Insurance
- Taxes
- The cost of the funds invested in inventories

Storage and handling costs include the cost of warehouse space. If a company leases warehouse space, this cost is equal to the rent paid. If a company owns the warehouse, this cost is equal to the value of the space in its next-best alternative use (that is, the opportunity cost). These costs also include depreciation on the inventory handling equipment, such as conveyors and forklift trucks, and the wages and salaries paid to warehouse workers and supervisors.

Inventories are valuable only if they can be sold. *Obsolescence* costs represent the decline in inventory value caused by technological or style changes that make the existing product less saleable. *Deterioration costs* represent the decline in value caused by changes in the physical quality of the inventory, such as spoilage and breakage.

Another element of carrying cost is the *cost of insuring* the inventory against losses due to theft, fire, and natural disaster. In addition, a company must pay any *personal property taxes* and *business taxes* required by local and state governments on the value of its inventories.

The *cost of funds invested in inventories* is measured by the *required rate of return* on these funds. Because inventory investments are likely to be of "average risk," the overall weighted cost of capital should be used to measure the cost of these funds. If it is felt that inventories constitute an investment with either an above-average or below-average risk,

TABLE 18.5

Inventory Carrying Costs (as a Percentage of Inventory Value)

Cost Category	Low	High
Storage costs	1.0%	4.0%
Obsolescence and physical loss	5.0	10.0
Insurance costs	1.0	3.0
Property taxes	1.0	3.0
Cost of money	12.0	25.0

Source: W. E. Dollar, *Effective Purchasing and Inventory Control for Small Business* (Boston: Inc./CBI Publications, 1983): 71.

some adjustment in the weighted cost of capital may be necessary to account for this difference in risk.[14]

Some firms incorrectly use the rate of interest on borrowed funds as a measure of this cost. This tends to understate the true cost because a given amount of lower-cost debt must be balanced with additional higher-cost equity financing. Inventory investment cost constitutes an opportunity cost in that it represents the return a firm forgoes as a result of deciding to invest its limited funds in inventories rather than in some other asset. Therefore, for most inventory decisions, the appropriate opportunity cost is the firm's weighted cost of capital.

The cost of carrying inventories can represent a significant cost of doing business. Table 18.5 contains some ranges on annual inventory carrying costs, expressed as a percentage of inventory value. This study found that *total* annual carrying costs were in the range of 20 to 45 percent for most of the businesses surveyed.

Like ordering costs, inventory carrying costs contain both fixed and variable components. Most carrying costs vary with the inventory level, but a certain portion of them—such as warehouse rent and depreciation on inventory handling equipment—are relatively fixed over the short run. Most of the simple inventory control models, such as the EOQ model, treat the entire carrying cost as variable.

stockout costs

Stockout Costs **Stockout costs** are incurred whenever a business is unable to fill orders because the demand for an item is greater than the amount currently available in inventory. When a stockout in raw materials occurs, for example, stockout costs include the expenses of placing special orders (back ordering) and expediting incoming orders, in addition to the costs of any resulting production delays. A stockout in work-in-process inventory results in additional costs of rescheduling and speeding production within the plant, and it also may result in lost production costs if work stoppages occur. Finally, a stockout in finished goods inventory may result in the immediate loss of profits if customers decide to purchase the product from a competitor, and in potential long-term losses if customers decide to order from other companies in the future.

18-5 Inventory Control Models

Given the significance of the benefits and costs associated with holding inventories, it is important that the firm efficiently control the level of inventory investments. A number of inventory control models are available that can help in determining the optimal

[14] Chapters 8 and 11 discuss the determination of risk-adjusted discount rates.

inventory level of each item. These models range from the relatively simple to the extremely complex. Their degree of complexity depends primarily on the assumptions made about the demand or use for the particular item and the **lead time** required to secure additional stock.

lead time

A related question involves the extent of control and the type of inventory model that should be applied to different inventory items. A technique called *ABC inventory classification* can be helpful in this regard. The **ABC inventory classification** method divides a company's inventory items into three groups. Group A consists of those items with a relatively large dollar value but a relatively small percentage of the total items, whereas group C contains those items with a small dollar value but a large percentage of the total items. Group B contains the items which are in between groups A and C. A typical result of an ABC analysis is that group A contains roughly 1 to 10 percent of the total number of items carried in inventory, but these items may represent as high as 80 to 90 percent of the total dollar value of the inventory. On the other hand, group C may contain about 50 percent of the total number of items, but these items may constitute less than 10 percent of the inventory's total dollar value. Group B contains the remaining items. Even though the actual cutoff between the groups is somewhat arbitrary, the ABC method provides management with information that can be used to determine how closely different inventory items should be controlled.

ABC inventory classification

As an example, consider the Toro Company, which manufactures lawn mowers. It purchases gasoline motors from another company for use in these mowers. Because of their cost, the motors might be classified as group A items. As a result, Toro management might determine the inventory costs associated with the motors and use a detailed model to calculate the economic order quantity. On the other hand, Toro might classify all nuts and bolts it uses as a group C item. As a result, the company's policy on nuts and bolts might consist of little more than simply keeping an ample supply on hand.

In the "classic" inventory models, which include both the simpler *deterministic* models and the more complex *probabilistic* models, it is assumed that demand is either uniform or dispersed and *independent* over time.[15] In other words, demand is assumed either to be *constant* or to fluctuate over time due to *random* elements. These types of demand situations are common in retailing and some service operations.

The simpler deterministic inventory control models, such as the **economic order quantity** *(EOQ) model*, assume that both demand and lead times are *constant* and known with *certainty*. Thus, deterministic models eliminate the need to consider stock-outs. The more complex probabilistic inventory control models assume that demand, lead time, or both are *random variables with known probability distributions*.[16]

economic order quantity

18-5a Basic EOQ Model

In its simplest form, the EOQ model assumes that the annual demand or usage for a particular item is known with certainty. It also assumes that this demand is stationary or uniform throughout the year. In other words, seasonal fluctuations in the rate of demand are ruled out. Finally, the model assumes that orders to replenish the inventory

[15]*Dependent* demand models, in contrast, assume that demand tends to be "lumpy," or to occur at specific points in time. Dependent demand tends to occur when products are manufactured in lots, because all the items required to produce the lot are usually withdrawn from inventory at the same time, rather than unit by unit. Dependent demand is a direct result of the demand for a "higher level" item. Material requirements planning (MRP) models have been developed to deal with the case of dependent demand. See Norman Gaither and Greg Frazier, *Production and Operations Management*, 8th ed. (Cincinnati, OH: South-Western College Publishing, 1999), Chapter 11, for a discussion of MRP.

[16]Rather than survey all the various inventory control models in depth, this chapter develops the deterministic EOQ model to illustrate the cost trade-offs involved in determining the optimal inventory level. It then examines the factors that must be considered and the cost trade-offs involved in developing a probabilistic model, without using mathematical analysis or formal solution techniques.

FIGURE 18.1

Certainty Case of the Inventory Cycle

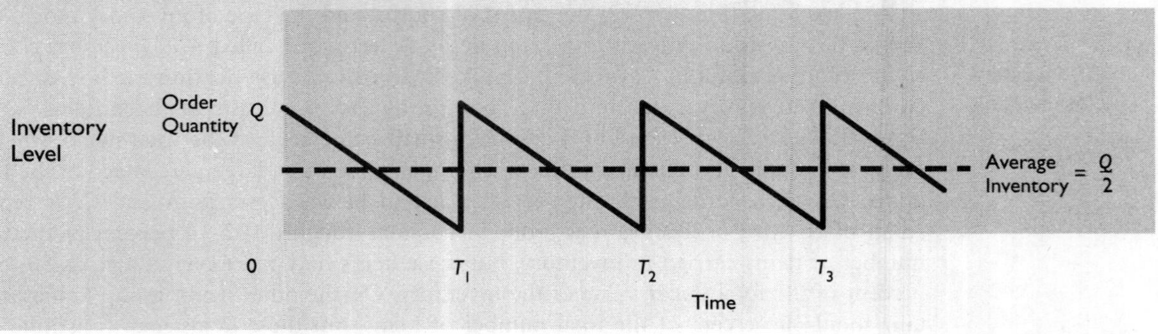

of an item are filled instantaneously. Given a known demand and a zero lead time for replenishing inventories, there is no need for a company to maintain additional inventories, or safety stocks, to protect itself against stockouts.

The assumptions of the EOQ model yield the saw-toothed inventory pattern shown in Figure 18.1. The vertical lines at the 0, T_1, T_2, and T_3 points in time represent the instantaneous replenishment of the item by the amount of the order quantity, Q, and the negatively sloped lines between the replenishment points represent the use of the item. Because the inventory level varies between 0 and the order quantity, average inventory is equal to one-half of the order quantity, or $Q/2$.

This model assumes that the costs of placing and receiving an order are the same for each order and independent of the number of units ordered. It also assumes that the annual cost of carrying one unit of the item in inventory is constant, regardless of the inventory level. Total annual inventory costs, then, are the sum of ordering costs and carrying costs.[17] The primary objective of the EOQ model is to find the order quantity, Q, that minimizes total annual inventory costs.

Algebraic Solution In developing the algebraic form of the EOQ model, the following variables are defined:

Q = The order *quantity*, in units

D = The annual *demand* for the item, in units

S = The cost of placing and receiving an order, or *setup* cost

C = The annual cost of *carrying* one unit of the item in inventory

Ordering costs are equal to the number of orders per year multiplied by the cost per order, S. The number of orders per year is equal to annual demand, D, divided by the order quantity, Q. Carrying costs are equal to average inventory, $Q/2$, multiplied by the annual carrying cost per unit, C.

The total annual cost equation is as follows:

$$\text{Total costs} = \text{Ordering costs} + \text{Carrying costs} \tag{18.1}$$

[17]The *actual* cost of the item (that is, the price paid for items purchased externally or the production cost for items manufactured internally) is excluded from this analysis because it is assumed to be constant regardless of the order quantity. This assumption is relaxed when quantity discounts are considered.

By substituting the variables just defined into Equation 18.1, the following expression is obtained:

(18.2)
$$\text{Total costs} = (\text{Number of orders per year} \times \text{cost of order}) + (\text{Average inventory} \times \text{Annual carrying cost per unit})$$

or, in algebraic terms,

(18.3)
$$\text{Total costs} = \left(\frac{D}{Q} \times S\right) + \left(\frac{Q}{2} \times C\right)$$

The EOQ is the value of Q that minimizes the total costs given in Equation 18.3. The standard procedure for finding this value of Q involves calculus.[18] The optimal solution, or EOQ, is equal to the following:

(18.4)
$$Q^* = \sqrt{\frac{2SD}{C}}$$

Another item of information that is sometimes useful for planning purposes is the optimal length of one inventory cycle, that is, the time between placements of orders for the item. The optimal length of one inventory cycle, T^*, measured in days, is equal to the economic order quantity, Q^*, divided by the average daily demand, $D/365$ (assuming 365 days per year), as follows:

(18.5)
$$T^* = \frac{Q^*}{D/365}$$

This equation can be rewritten as follows:

(18.6)
$$T^* = \frac{365 \times Q^*}{D}$$

The following example illustrates the use of the EOQ model. Suppose Macy's sells Simmons mattresses through its department stores located in the Chicago metropolitan area. All inventories are maintained at the firm's centrally located warehouse. Annual demand for the Simmons standard-size mattress is 3,600 units and is spread evenly throughout the year. The cost of placing and receiving an order is $31.25.

Macy's annual carrying costs are 20 percent of the inventory value. Based on a wholesale cost of $50 per mattress, the annual carrying cost per mattress is 0.20 × $50 = $10. Because Simmons maintains a large regional distribution center in Chicago, Macy's can replenish its inventory virtually instantaneously. The company wishes to determine the number of standard-size mattresses it should periodically order from Simmons in order to minimize the total annual inventory costs. Substituting $D = 3{,}600$, $S = \$31.25$, and $C = \$10$ into Equation 18.4 yields the following EOQ:

$$Q^* = \sqrt{\frac{2 \times \$31.25 \times 3{,}600}{\$10}}$$
$$= 150 \text{ mattresses}$$

Using Equation 18.3, we can calculate the total annual inventory costs of this policy:

$$\text{Total costs}^* = \frac{3{,}600}{150} \times \$31.25 + \frac{150}{2} \times \$10$$
$$= \$1{,}500$$

[18]Specifically, the first derivative of Equation 18.3 with respect to Q is set equal to 0, and the equation is solved for Q.

FIGURE 18.2

Graphic Solution of the EOQ Model

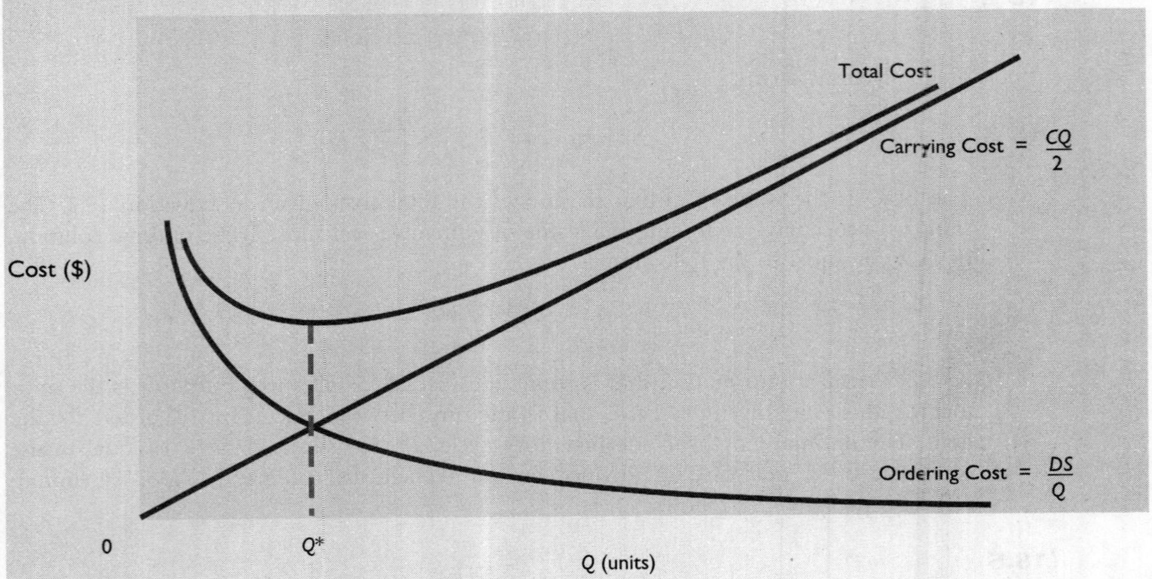

Finally, Equation 18.6 can be used to determine Macy's optimal inventory cycle for these mattresses:

$$T^* = \frac{365 \times 150}{3{,}600}$$
$$= 15.2 \text{ days}$$

Thus, the EOQ of 150 mattresses and the optimal inventory cycle of 15.2 days for this item indicate that Macy's should place an order for 150 mattresses every 15.2 days.

Graphic Solution The order quantity that minimizes total annual inventory costs can be determined graphically by plotting inventory costs (vertical axis) as a function of the order quantity (horizontal axis). As we can see in Figure 18.2, annual ordering costs, DS/Q, vary *inversely* with the order quantity, Q, because the number of orders placed per year, D/Q, decreases as the size of the order quantity increases. Carrying costs, $CQ/2$, vary *directly* with the order quantity, Q, because the average inventory, $Q/2$, increases as the size of the order quantity increases.

The total inventory cost curve is found by vertically summing the heights of the ordering cost and carrying cost functions. The order quantity corresponding to the lowest point on the total cost curve is the optimal solution—that is, the economic order quantity, Q^*.

18-5b Extensions of the Basic EOQ Model

The basic EOQ model makes a number of simplifying assumptions, including those pertaining to replenishment lead time and demand for the item. In practical applications of inventory control models, however, some of these assumptions may not be valid. Thus, it is important to understand how different assumptions affect the analysis and the optimal order quantity. The following discussion examines what occurs when some of these assumptions are altered.

Nonzero Lead Time The basic EOQ model assumes that orders to replenish the inventory of an item are filled instantaneously; that is, the lead time is zero. In practice, however, some time usually elapses between when a purchase order is placed and when the item actually is received in inventory. This lead time consists of the time it takes to manufacture the item, the time it takes to package and ship the item, or both.

If the lead time is *constant* and *known with certainty*, the optimal order quantity, Q^*, is not affected, although the time when an order should be placed is. Specifically, a company should not wait to reorder until the end of the **inventory cycle**, when the inventory level reaches zero—such as at points T_1, T_2, and T_3 in Figure 18.3. Instead, it should place an order n days *prior* to the end of each cycle, n being equal to the replenishment lead time measured in days. The **reorder point** is defined as the inventory level at which an order should be placed for replenishment of an item. Assuming that demand is constant over time, the reorder point, Q_r, is equal to the lead time, n (measured in days), multiplied by daily demand:

inventory cycle

reorder point

$$Q_r = n \times \frac{D}{365} \tag{18.7}$$

where $D/365$ is daily demand (based on 365 days per year).

For example, if the lead time for standard-size mattresses ordered by Macy's (discussed earlier in this section) is five days and annual demand is 3,600 mattresses, an order for 150 mattresses (that is, the economic order quantity) should be placed when the inventory level reaches the following:

$$\begin{aligned} Q_r &= 5 \times \frac{3{,}600}{365} \\ &= 49.3 \text{ mattresses} \end{aligned}$$

FIGURE 18.3

Nonzero Replenishment Lead Time Case of an Inventory Cycle

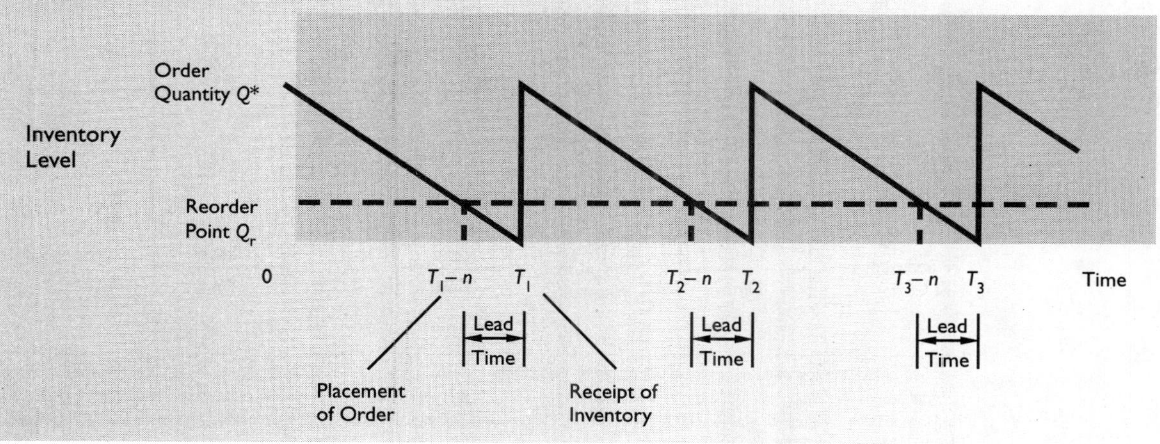

which occurs during the 10th day of each inventory cycle. Five days later, during the 15th day of the inventory cycle—when the inventory level falls to zero—Macy's will receive the order and the inventory level will again rise to 150.

Probabilistic Inventory Control Models Thus far, the analysis has assumed that demand or usage is uniform throughout time and known with certainty, as well as that the lead time necessary to procure additional inventory is also a fixed, known value. However, in most practical inventory management problems, either (or both) of these assumptions may not be strictly correct. Typically, demand fluctuates over time due to seasonal, cyclical, and "random" influences, and imprecise forecasts of future demands are often all that can be made. Similarly, lead times are subject to uncertainty because of such factors as transportation delays, strikes, and natural disasters. Under these conditions, the possibility of stockouts exists. To minimize the possibility of stockouts and the associated stockout costs, most companies use a standard approach of adding a *safety stock* to their inventory. A safety stock is maintained to meet unexpectedly high demand during the lead time, unanticipated delays in the lead time, or both.

Figure 18.4 shows the inventory pattern characterized by these more realistic assumptions. During the first inventory cycle ($0 - T_2$), an order to replenish the inventory is placed at T_1, when the inventory level reaches the predetermined order point. The order is then received at T_2. The second cycle ($T_2 - T_4$) is similar to the first, except that demand exceeds the normal inventory of the item and part of the safety stock is consumed during the lead time prior to receipt of the order at T_4. During the third cycle ($T_4 - T_6$), demand exceeds the normal inventory plus the safety stock and, as a result, a stockout occurs during the lead time prior to receipt of the order at T_6.

Determining the optimal safety stock and order quantities under these more realistic conditions is a fairly complex process that lies beyond the scope of this text.[19] However,

FIGURE 18.4

Uncertainty Case of the Inventory Cycle

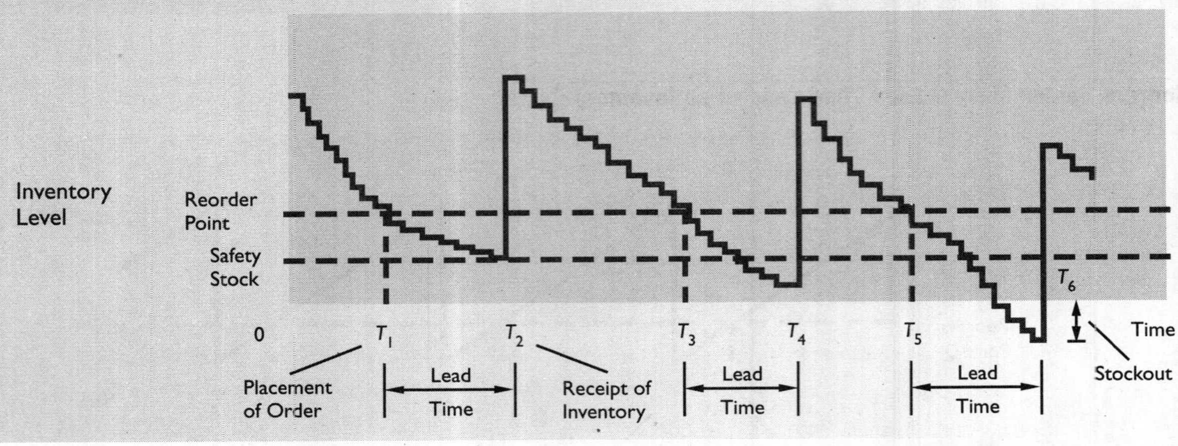

[19]See any of the following books for a discussion of these more complex models: H. M. Wagner, *Principles of Operations Research: With Applications to Managerial Decision*, 2nd ed. (Englewood Cliffs, NJ: Prentice-Hall, 1975); Gaither and Frazier, *Production and Operations Management*, Chapter 10; and Richard I. Levin, Joel P. Stinson, and Everette S. Gardner, Jr., *Quantitative Approaches to Management*, 7th ed. (New York: McGraw-Hill, 1989).

the factors that have to be considered in this type of analysis can be identified briefly. All other things being equal, the optimal safety stock increases as the uncertainty associated with the demand forecasts and lead times increases. Likewise, all other things being equal, the optimal safety stock increases as the cost of stockouts increases. Determining the optimal safety stock involves balancing the *expected* costs of stockouts against the cost of carrying the additional inventory.

18-5c Just-in-Time Inventory Management Systems

just-in-time inventory management systems

Just-in-time inventory management systems are part of a manufacturing approach that seeks to reduce the company's operating cycle and associated costs by eliminating wasteful procedures. Just-in-time inventory systems are based on the idea that all required inventory items should be supplied to the production process at exactly the right time and in exactly the right quantities. This approach was first developed by the Toyota Motor Corporation in the 1950s. In contrast, inventory models used in many plants, which rely on safety stocks, are sometimes referred to as "just-in-case" models.

The just-in-time approach works best for companies engaged in repetitive manufacturing operations. A key part of just-in-time techniques is the replacement of production in large batches with a continuous flow of smaller quantities. The use of a just-in-time inventory system requires close coordination between a company and its suppliers, because any disruption in the flow of parts and materials from the supplier can result in costly production delays and lost sales. For example, the March 2011 earthquake, tsunami, and nuclear reactor meltdown, which devastated northern Japan, caused major worldwide disruptions in the automobile parts supply chain. Toyota, Nissan, and Honda were forced to slow production or temporarily close their assembly plants in North America, Europe, and Asia. General Motors and Ford also encountered minor disruptions due to parts shortages.

Businesses have reported significant reductions in production time and inventory costs resulting from the use of just-in-time techniques. For example, Sharp Corporation, a major LCD television manufacturer, sought to streamline production by moving 17 outside suppliers and service vendors inside a massive $11 billion production facility it opened in 2009 in Sakai, Japan—a kind of hyper just-in-time delivery system.[20] Analysts estimated that this massive plant could result in 5 to 10 percent savings to Sharp. Also, Corning, the world's largest maker of glass used in LCD televisions, built a factory next to the Sharp plant. The proximity of the two plants, in addition to reducing the risk of damage in transporting the large glass sheets on trucks, reduced Corning's order cycle time from an average of two weeks to just a few hours.

18-6 Summary

- A company should change its credit extension policy only if the expected *marginal benefits* of the change will exceed the expected *marginal costs*. A more liberal credit policy normally leads to increased sales and generates marginal benefits in the form of higher gross profits. The marginal costs of this type of policy, however, include the cost of the additional funds invested in accounts receivable and inventories, any additional credit checking and collection costs, and increased bad-debt expenses.

[20]Daisuke Wakabayashi, "Sharp's New Plant Reinvents Japan Manufacturing Model," *The Wall Street Journal* (November 30, 2009): B1.

- A financial manager can exercise control over the company's level of receivables investment through three credit policy variables: *credit standards, credit terms,* and the *collection effort.* All three variables can be used to control the average collection period and bad-debt loss ratio.

  1. Credit standards are the criteria a business uses to screen its credit applicants.
  2. Credit terms are the conditions under which customers are required to repay the credit extended to them. Credit terms specify the length of the credit period and the cash discount (if any) given for early payment.
  3. The collection effort represents the methods used in attempting to collect payment from past-due accounts.

- Evaluating individual credit applicants involves *gathering information* about the applicant, *analyzing this information* to determine the applicant's creditworthiness, and then *making the credit decision.*
- The five *Cs* of credit, which are *character, capacity, capital, collateral,* and *conditions,* can be used as credit-screening guidelines to help ensure that a company will consider most of the relevant factors in the analysis and decision-making process.
- Inventories serve as a *buffer* between the various stages of the manufacturing firm's procurement-production-sales cycle. By uncoupling the various phases of the firm's operations, inventories provide the firm with flexibility in timing purchases, scheduling production, and meeting fluctuating, uncertain demand for the finished product.
- Inventory-related costs include *ordering costs, carrying costs,* and *stockout costs.* Ordering costs include all the costs of placing and receiving an order. Carrying costs include the various costs of holding items in inventory, including the cost of funds invested in inventory. Stockout costs are the costs incurred when demand exceeds available inventory, such as lost profits.
- Inventory control models are usually classified into two types: *deterministic,* if demand and lead time are known with *certainty,* and *probabilistic,* if demand and/or lead time are *random variables* with known probability distributions.
- The objective of the deterministic *economic order quantity (EOQ) model* is to find the order quantity that minimizes total inventory costs.
- The economic order quantity Q^* is equal to $\sqrt{2SD/C}$ where D is the annual demand; S, the fixed cost per order; and C, the annual carrying cost per unit.
- Probabilistic inventory control models require consideration of the possibility of *stockouts.* One approach used to handle this problem is to add a *safety stock* to the inventory.
- *Just-in-time inventory models* are based on the concept that required inventory items are supplied exactly as needed by production. Successful implementation of just-in-time models can reduce inventory investment.

Important Equations

$$\text{Total cost} = \left(\frac{D}{Q} \times S\right) + \left(\frac{Q}{2} \times C\right)$$

$$Q^* = \sqrt{\frac{2SD}{C}}$$

$$T^* = \frac{Q^*}{D/365}$$

18-7 Questions and Topics for Discussion

1. What are the marginal returns and costs associated with a more liberal extension of credit to a firm's customers?
2. What are the major credit policy variables a firm can use to control its level of receivables investment?
3. Define the following terms:
   a. Average collection period
   b. Bad-debt loss ratio
   c. Aging of accounts
4. Discuss at least two reasons why a firm might want to offer seasonal datings to its customers.
5. Describe the marginal costs and benefits associated with each of the following changes in a firm's credit and collection policies:
   a. Increasing the credit period from 7 to 30 days
   b. Increasing the cash discount from 1 to 2 percent
   c. Offering a seasonal dating credit plan
   d. Increasing collection expenditures (and effort)
6. Describe the three steps involved in evaluating credit applicants.
7. What are the primary sources of information about the creditworthiness of credit applicants?
8. Describe the five *Cs* of credit used in evaluating the creditworthiness of a credit applicant.
9. How does a firm's required rate of return on investment enter into the analysis of changes in its credit and collection policies?
10. A firm is currently selling on credit terms of "net 30," and its accounts receivable average 30 days past due (that is, the firm's average collection period is 60 days). What credit policy variables might the firm consider changing to reduce its average collection period?
11. "The objective of the firm's credit and collection policies should be to minimize its bad-debt losses." Do you agree or disagree with this statement? Explain.
12. Discuss how each of the following factors would tend to affect a firm's credit extension policies:
    a. A shortage of working capital
    b. An increase in output to the point where the firm is operating at full production capacity
    c. An increase in the firm's profit margin (that is, its profit contribution ratio)
    d. An increase in interest rates (that is, borrowing costs)
13. Describe the benefits of holding the following:
    a. Raw materials inventories
    b. Work-in-process inventories
    c. Finished goods inventories
14. Describe the components of carrying costs.
15. How do ordering costs for items purchased externally differ from ordering costs for items manufactured internally within the firm?
16. Describe the nature of stockout costs associated with a stockout in the following:
    a. Raw materials inventories
    b. Work-in-process inventories
    c. Finished goods inventories

17. What is ABC inventory classification? How can this method be useful to a business?
18. Describe the assumptions underlying the basic EOQ model.
19. In general terms, describe how to deal with each of the following conditions when determining the optimal inventory level:
a. Constant (nonzero) replenishment lead time known with certainty
b. Demand and replenishment lead time subject to uncertainty
20. How does the firm's required rate of return on investment enter into inventory decisions?
21. What are just-in-time inventory models?
22. Define the following terms:
a. Stockout
b. Deterministic inventory control models
c. Probabilistic inventory control models
d. Safety stock
e. Lead time

18-8 Self-Test Problems

Note: When converting from annual data to daily data or vice versa, assume there are 365 days per year.

ST1. Taiwan Electronic Company sells on terms of "net 30." Annual credit sales are $54.75 million, and its accounts receivable average 10 days overdue.
a. Determine Taiwan Electronic Company's investment in receivables.
b. Suppose that, as the result of a recession, annual credit sales decline by 15 percent and customers delay their payments to an average of 25 days past due. Determine the company's new level of receivables investment.

ST2. Plant Nutrients Inc. (PNI) sells fertilizers and pesticides to various retail hardware and nursery stores on terms of "2/10, net 30" The company currently does not grant credit to retailers with a 3 (fair) or 4 (limited) Dun & Bradstreet Composite Credit Appraisal. An estimated $5,475,000 in additional sales per year could be generated if PNI extended credit to retailers in the "fair" category. The estimated average collection period for these customers is 75 days, and the expected bad-debt loss ratio is 5 percent. The company also estimates that an additional inventory investment of $800,000 is required for the anticipated sales increase. Approximately 10 percent of these customers are expected to take the cash discount. PNI's variable cost ratio is 0.75, and its required pretax rate of return on investments in current assets is 18 percent. Determine the following:
a. Marginal profitability of additional sales
b. Cost of additional investment in receivables
c. Additional bad-debt loss
d. Cost of additional investment in inventory
e. Additional cash discounts
f. Net change in pretax profits

ST3. Blackhawk Supply Company sells $21.9 million of its products to wholesalers on credit terms of "net 30." Currently, the firm's average collection period is 55 days. Blackhawk is considering offering a 2 percent discount to customers who pay their bills within 10 days. The firm expects 50 percent of its customers to take the discount and its average collection period to decline to 35 days. Blackhawk's required pretax return on receivables investment is 18 percent. Determine the net effect on Blackhawk's pretax profits of offering a 2 percent cash discount.

ST4. SportsMart, a chain of sporting goods stores, sells 360,000 baseballs per year. (Assume that sales are uniform throughout the year.) The baseballs cost SportsMart \$15 per dozen (\$1.25 each). Annual inventory carrying costs are 20 percent of inventory value. The costs of placing and receiving an order are \$72. Assume that inventory replenishment occurs virtually instantaneously. Determine the following:

a. Economic order quantity
b. Total annual inventory costs of this policy
c. Optimal ordering frequency

18-9 Problems*

Note: When converting annual data to daily data or vice versa in these problems, assume there are 365 days per year.

BASIC

1. Miranda Tool Company sells to retail hardware stores on credit terms of "net 30." Annual credit sales are \$18 million and are spread evenly throughout the year. The company's variable cost ratio is 0.70, and its accounts receivable average \$1.9 million. Using this information, determine the following for the company:

a. Average daily credit sales
b. Average collection period
c. Average investment in receivables

BASIC

2. Drake Paper Company sells on terms of "net 30." The firm's variable cost ratio is 0.80.

a. If annual credit sales are \$20 million and its accounts receivable average 15 days *overdue*, what is Drake's investment in receivables?
b. Suppose that, as the result of a recession, annual credit sales decline by 10 percent to \$18 million, and customers delay their payments to an average of 25 days *past the due date*. What will be Drake's new level of receivables investment?

INTERMEDIATE

3. Looking back at Tables 18.1 and 18.2, evaluate the impact on Bassett's pretax profits of extending full credit to the customers in Credit Risk Group 5. Assume that Bassett's pretax required rate of return on inventory investments is 20 percent and that an additional inventory investment of \$40,000 is required due to the anticipated sales increase from customers in Credit Risk Group 5.

INTERMEDIATE

4. Once again, consider the Bassett Furniture Industries example (Tables 18.1 and 18.2). Assume that rising labor and interest costs have increased Bassett's variable cost ratio from 0.75 to 0.80 and its required pretax rate of return on receivables and inventory investments from 20 to 25 percent. Reevaluate the effect of Bassett's pretax profits of extending full credit to the customers in Credit Risk Group 4.

INTERMEDIATE

Spreadsheet Strategies

5. Epstein Company, a wholesale distributor of jewelry, sells to retail jewelry stores on terms of "net 120." Its average collection period is 150 days. The company is considering the introduction of a 4 percent cash discount if customers pay within 30 days. Such a change in credit terms is expected to reduce the average collection period to 108 days. Epstein expects 30 percent of its customers to take the cash discount. Annual credit sales are \$6 million. Epstein's variable cost ratio is 0.667, and its required pretax return on receivables investment is 15 percent. The company

*Color blocks behind the numbers denote problems that have check answers provided at the end of the book.

does not expect its inventory level to change as a result of the change in credit terms. Determine the following:

a. The funds released by the change in credit terms
b. The net effect on Epstein's pretax profits

INTERMEDIATE

Spreadsheet Strategies

6. In an effort to speed up the collection of receivables, Hill Publishing Company is considering increasing the size of its cash discount by changing its credit terms from "1/10, net 30" to "2/10, net 30." Currently, the company's collection period averages 43 days. Under the new credit terms, it is expected to decline to 28 days. Also, the percentage of customers who will take advantage of the cash discount is expected to increase from the current 50 percent to 70 percent with the new credit terms. Bad-debt losses currently average 4 percent of sales and are not expected to change significantly if Hill changes its credit policy. Annual credit sales are $3.5 million, the variable cost ratio is 60 percent, and the required pretax rate of return (that is, the opportunity cost) on receivables investment is 14 percent. The company does not expect its inventory level to change as a result of its proposed change in credit terms. Assuming that Hill does decide to increase the size of its cash discount, determine the following:
   a. The earnings on the funds released by the change in credit terms
   b. The cost of the additional cash discounts taken
   c. The net effect on Hill's pretax profits

CHALLENGE

7. The North Carolina Furniture Company (NCFC) manufactures upholstered furniture, which it sells to various small retailers in the Northeast and Midwest on credit terms of "2/10, net 60." The company currently does not grant credit to retailers with a 3 (fair) or 4 (limited) Dun & Bradstreet Composite Credit Appraisal. If NCFC were to extend credit to retailers in the "fair" category, an estimated additional $1.2 million per year in sales could be generated. The estimated average collection period for these customers is 90 days, and the expected bad-debt loss ratio is 6 percent. Approximately 20 percent of these customers are expected to take the cash discount. NCFC's variable cost ratio is 0.70, and its required pretax rate of return on current assets investments is 20 percent. The company also estimates that an additional investment in inventory of $350,000 is necessary for the anticipated sales increase. Determine the net change in NCFC's pretax profits from extending credit to retailers in the "fair" category.

CHALLENGE

8. Michigan Pharmaceuticals Inc. a wholesale distributor of ethical drugs to local pharmacies, has been experiencing a relatively long average collection period because many of its customers face liquidity problems and delay their payments well beyond the due date. In addition, its bad-debt loss ratio is high because a number of pharmacies have closed due to financial difficulties. To avoid these problems in the future, Michigan Pharmaceuticals is considering a plan to *institute more stringent credit standards* to keep the average collection period and bad-debt losses from rising beyond acceptable limits. Specifically, the firm plans to refuse to grant additional credit to any current customers more than 15 days past due on their payments. Such a change in credit policy is expected to reduce current annual sales of $6.5 million by 20 percent, *reduce* the average collection period from 110 days to 75 days, and lower bad-debt losses from 8 to 4 percent. Due to the expected decrease in sales, the company estimates that its inventories will decrease by $250,000. The firm's variable cost ratio is 0.75, and its required pretax return on investments in receivables and inventories is 15 percent. Determine the net effect of this plan on the pretax profits of Michigan Pharmaceuticals.

INTERMEDIATE

9. Swenson Electric Company sells on terms of "net 30." Given the following information on its receivables, construct an aging of accounts schedule as of September 1, showing the percentage of accounts that are current, 1 to 30 days past due, 31 to

60 days **past** due, 61 to 90 days past due, and over 90 days past due. (Assume 30 days in each month.)

Account Number	Invoice Date	Amount Due
1311	August 15	$1,315
1773	July 14	721
1217	July 25	677
1319	August 14	1,711
1814	April 10	325
1713	August 5	917
1443	May 8	493
1144	June 28	211
1972	May 5	755
1011	April 21	377
1619	August 28	1,550
1322	August 13	275
1173	March 5	675
1856	August 12	695
1317	June 10	720

CHALLENGE

10. Creole Industries Inc. estimates that if it spent an additional $20,000 to hire another collection agent in its credit department, it could lower its bad-debt loss ratio to 3.5 percent from a current rate of 4 percent and also reduce its average collection period from 50 to 45 days. (Assume that sales and inventory remain unchanged if the agent is hired.) Creole's annual credit sales are $5 million, and its variable cost ratio is 0.75. The firm's required pretax rate of return on receivables investment (that is, the opportunity cost) is 18 percent. Determine the net effect on Creole's pretax profits of hiring the additional collection agent.

CHALLENGE

Spreadsheet Strategies

11. Jenkins Supply Corporation sells $120 million of its products to wholesalers on terms of "net 50." Currently, the firm's average collection period is 65 days. In order to speed up the collection of receivables, Jenkins is considering offering a 1 percent cash discount if customers pay their bills within 15 days. The firm expects 40 percent of its customers to take the discount and its average collection period to decline to 40 days. The firm's required pretax return on receivables investments is 20 percent. Determine the net effect on Jenkins' pretax profits of offering a 1 percent cash discount.

CHALLENGE

Spreadsheet Strategies

12. The Bimbo Corporation has been experiencing a decline in sales relative to its major competitors. Because Bimbo is confident about the quality of its products, it suspects that this sales loss may reflect its relatively stringent credit standards and terms. The firm currently has credit sales of $50 million annually. With current credit terms of "net 20," its average collection period is now 25 days. Bad-debt losses are 2 percent of credit sales. The firm's variable cost ratio is 0.80, and its required pretax return on receivables and inventory investments is 20 percent.

Bimbo plans to change its credit terms to "2/10, net 30." It expects 20 percent of its customers to take advantage of the cash discount. Bimbo also plans to relax credit standards and take on riskier accounts. This action is expected to increase credit sales by 30 percent. Bad-debt losses are expected to increase to 3 percent of credit sales, and the average collection period is expected to become 30 days. The company also estimates that an additional investment in inventory of $3 million is required because of the anticipated sales increase. Determine the net effect of this plan on the pretax profits of Bimbo.

CHALLENGE

13. Allied Apparel Company received a large order from Websters Department Stores, which operates a chain of approximately 300 popular-priced department stores located primarily in the New England–Middle Atlantic states. Allied is considering extending trade credit to Websters. As part of its credit check, Allied obtained Websters' balance sheets and income statements for the last three years. A check of several of Websters' trade creditors has revealed that the firm generally takes any cash discounts when they are offered but averages about 30 days overdue on its payments to two suppliers whose credit terms are "net 30."

A Dun & Bradstreet publication entitled *Key Business Ratios* yielded the following information concerning the "average" financial ratios for firms in the same line of business as Websters:

Current assets to current liabilities	2.82
Earnings after taxes to sales	1.89%
Earnings after taxes to stockholders' equity	5.65%
Total liabilities to stockholders' equity	1.48

Websters Department Stores Balance Sheet (in Thousands of Dollars)

	2014	2015	2016
Assets			
Current assets:			
Cash and marketable securities	$ 9,283	$ 13,785	$ 23,893
Accounts receivable (net)	162,825	179,640	140,543
Inventories	119,860	135,191	120,707
Other	1,994	2,190	1,956
Total current assets	$293,962	$ 330,806	$296,099
Long-term assets:			
Building and equipment (net)	$ 27,426	$ 30,295	$ 30,580
Other	11,821	14,794	16,687
Total long-term assets	$ 39,247	$ 45,089	$ 47,267
Total assets	$333,209	$ 375,895	$343,366
Liabilities and stockholders' equity			
Current liabilities:			
Accounts payable	$ 23,637	$ 21,861	$ 15,020
Notes payable	117,010	135,929	165,299
Other	49,273	49,229	29,653
Total current liabilities	$189,920	$ 207,019	$209,972
Long-term liabilities:			
Debentures	$ 38,001	$ 36,101	$ 35,201
Term loan	—	28,440	29,701
Other	4,986	853	655
Total long-term liabilities	$ 42,987	$ 65,394	$ 65,557
Stockholders' equity:			
Common stock	$ 5,576	$ 5,576	$ 5,576
Preferred stock	2,580	2,580	2,580
Retained earnings	92,146	95,326	59,681
Total stockholders' equity	$100,302	$ 103,482	$ 67,837
Total liabilities and stockholders' equity	$333,209	$ 375,895	$343,366

Websters Department Stores Income Statement (in Thousands of Dollars)

	2014	2015	2016
Sales	$494,550	$556,132	$ 529,857
Cost of sales	337,580	384,899	390,980
Gross profit	$156,970	$171,233	$ 138,877
Selling, general, and administrative expenses	133,330	155,494	187,926
Earnings before taxes	$ 23,640	$ 15,739	$ −49,049
Income taxes	7,715	6,222	−14,741
Earnings after taxes	$ 15,925	$ 9,517	$ −34,308
Dividends	6,343	6,337	1,337
Additions to retained earnings	$ 9,582	$ 3,180	$ −35,645

In evaluating Websters' application for trade credit, answer the following questions:

a. What positive financial factors would lead Allied to decide to extend credit to Websters?

b. What negative financial factors would lead Allied to decide *not* to extend credit to Websters?

c. What additional information about Websters would be useful in performing the analysis?

CHALLENGE **14.** Saccomanno Industries Inc. is considering whether to discontinue offering credit to customers who are more than 10 days overdue on repaying the credit extended to them. Current annual credit sales are $10 million on credit terms of "net 30." Such a change in policy is expected to reduce sales by 10 percent, cut the firm's bad-debt losses from 5 to 3 percent, and reduce its average collection period from 72 days to 45 days. The firm's variable cost ratio is 0.70 and its required pretax return on receivables and inventory investments is 25 percent. Because of the anticipated decrease in sales, the company expects its inventories to decrease by $200,000. Determine the net effect of this credit-tightening policy on the pretax profits of Saccomanno Industries.

CHALLENGE **15.** The Blawnox Company is concerned about its bad-debt losses and the length of time required to collect receivables. Current sales are $43.8 million per year. Bad-debt losses are currently 3.5 percent of sales, and the average collection period is 68 days (credit terms are "net 30"). One plan under consideration is to tighten credit standards by refusing to grant additional credit to any customers who are more than 15 days past due on their payments. This change in credit policy is expected to reduce sales by 10 percent but also reduce bad-debt losses to 2.5 percent of sales and reduce the average collection period to 40 days. The firm's variable cost ratio is 70 percent, and its required pretax rate of return on current assets investments is 18 percent. The company also expects its inventory investment to decrease by $1 million due to the anticipated decrease in sales. Determine the net effect of this plan on Blawnox's pretax profits.

INTERMEDIATE **16.** Allstar Shoe Company produces a wide variety of athletic-type shoes for tennis, basketball, and running. Although sales are somewhat seasonal, production is uniform throughout the year. Allstar's production and sales average 1.92 million pairs of shoes per year. The company purchases shoelaces for its entire product line. Shoelaces are bought in lots of 10,000 pairs at a price of $800 per lot. Ordering costs are $20, including the cost of preparing the purchase order and inspecting the shipment when it arrives at the company's warehouse. Annual inventory carrying costs average 15 percent of the inventory value. Assuming that the shoelace manufacturer is located nearby and that orders are filled on the same day they are placed (that is, virtually instantaneously), determine the following:

a. The EOQ for shoelaces
b. The total annual inventory costs of this policy
c. The frequency with which Allstar should place its orders for shoelaces

INTERMEDIATE **17.** Quick-Copy Duplicating Company uses 110,000 reams of standard-size paper a year at its various duplicating centers. Its current paper supplier charges $2.00 per ream. Annual inventory carrying costs are 15 percent of inventory value. The costs of placing and receiving an order of paper are $41.25. Assuming that inventory replenishment occurs virtually instantaneously, determine the following:

a. The firm's EOQ
b. The total annual inventory costs of this policy
c. The optimal ordering frequency
d. Compute and plot ordering costs, carrying costs, and total inventory costs for order quantities of 2,000, 4,000, 5,000, 5,500, 6,000, 7,000, and 9,000 reams. Connect the points on each function with a smooth curve, and determine the EOQ from the graph (and the table used in constructing the graph).

INTERMEDIATE **18.** Southeast Publishing Company employs a high-speed printing press in its operations. A typical production run of 5,000 to 50,000 copies of a textbook can be produced in less than one day. The manager of the business textbook division is attempting to determine the optimal number of copies of the seventh editions of its financial management and managerial economics textbooks to produce. Expected annual demand for the two books are 50,000 and 22,500 copies, respectively. Furthermore, the manager does not want to produce more than a 3-year supply of either book because these textbooks are normally revised after the third year. Setup costs of getting the printing press (and bindery) ready for a production run of a given textbook are $2,500 and $2,000, respectively, for the two books. Annual carrying costs are $0.80 per copy (16 percent annual carrying charge times the $5.00 production cost per copy). For each textbook, determine the following:

a. The economic order quantity
b. The total annual inventory costs
c. The optimal ordering frequency

19. Arizona Instruments uses integrated circuits (ICs) in its business calculators. Its annual demand for ICs is 120,000 units. The ICs cost Arizona Instruments $10 each. The company has determined that the EOQ is 20,000 units. It takes 18 days between when an order is placed and when the delivery is received. Carrying costs are 20 percent of the inventory value. Determine the following:

a. The optimal ordering frequency
b. The average inventory and annual carrying costs
c. The reorder point

INTERMEDIATE **20.** General Cereal Company purchases various grains (for example, wheat and corn) that it processes into ready-to-eat cereals. Its annual demand for wheat is 250,000 bushels. Assume that demand is uniform throughout the year. The average price of wheat is $3.0625 per bushel (delivered). Annual inventory carrying costs are 16 percent of inventory value. The costs of placing and receiving an order are $98. Assume that inventory replenishment occurs virtually instantaneously. Determine the following:

a. Economic order quantity
b. Total annual inventory costs of this policy
c. Optimal ordering frequency

CHALLENGE

21. Books, etc., a nationwide chain of bookstores, anticipates that annual demand for the paperback version of a best-selling novel will be 150,000 copies. The books cost the firm $2 each. Books, etc. has determined that the optimal order quantity (EOQ) is 30,000 copies. It takes 20 days between when an order is placed and when the delivery is received. Carrying costs are 15 percent of the inventory value. Determine the following:

a. Optimal ordering frequency
b. Average inventory and annual carrying costs
c. Reorder point

Books, etc. decides that it wants to maintain a 60-day safety stock of the novel to meet unexpected demand and possible shipment delays from the publisher. Determine the following:

d. Amount of safety stock, in units
e. Average inventory and annual carrying costs
f. Reorder point

PART 6

Additional Topics in Contemporary Financial Management

Part 6 looks at a number of additional topics that are important for financial managers. Chapter 19 deals with leasing and other intermediate-term financing alternatives. Chapter 20 discusses derivative financial instruments including options and option-related financing instruments and strategies. Puts, calls, convertible securities, warrants, rights, and swaps are all discussed. Chapter 21 examines various risk-management techniques. Chapter 22 covers advanced international finance topics including parity conditions and international risk hedging. Chapter 23 focuses on corporate restructuring, with emphasis on mergers, liquidations, spin-offs, and failure and reorganization. Each of the decision areas covered in this part offers significant opportunities for adding to shareholders' wealth.

CHAPTER
19

Lease and Intermediate-Term Financing

KEY CHAPTER CONCEPTS

1. A *lease* is a contract that allows an individual or a firm to make economic use of an asset for a stated period of time without obtaining an ownership interest in the asset.
2. The major parties to a lease are the *lessor* and the *lessee*.
    a. The lessor is the owner of the asset and the party who receives the lease payments.
    b. The lessee is the user of the asset and the party who makes the lease payments.
3. There are several different classifications of leases.
    a. *Operating leases* are cancelable, period-by-period leases.
    b. *Financial* or *capital leases* are not cancelable. The lease payments under a financial lease are sufficient to fully amortize the cost of the asset plus provide a return to the lessor.
    c. *Leveraged leases* are special financial leases involving three parties: the lessor, the lessee, and a group of lenders. Leveraged leases are especially important to firms that cannot take advantage of the tax benefits of ownership.
4. Leasing decisions are often influenced by the tax and accounting treatment of the transaction.
5. An asset should be leased rather than owned if the present value cost of leasing is less than the present value cost of owning.
6. Term loans are debt obligations having an initial maturity between 1 and 10 years.
    a. The major suppliers of term loans are banks, insurance companies, pension funds, and equipment suppliers.
    b. Term loans are usually amortized over the life of the loan.
    c. The interest rate on term loans obtained from commercial banks is normally greater than the bank's prime rate.
    d. Some term loans from banks require that a compensating balance be maintained at the bank. Other term loans contain a provision that gives the lender an equity participation in the borrowing company.
    e. Most term loans are secured. The loan agreement contains affirmative, negative, and restrictive covenants. In addition, the conditions that determine when a default on the loan has occurred are detailed in the loan agreement.
7. Equipment financing loans are commonly made for equipment that is readily marketable. These loans are normally secured with a *conditional sales contract* or a *chattel mortgage*.

FINANCIAL CHALLENGE

Sears Does a $2.5 Billion Sale-and-Leaseback

Sears is an iconic name in American retailing, with a history that dates back to 1886. The current company, known as Sears Holdings, has two major segments, Sears Domestic and Kmart. In the past two decades, the retailing sector, where Sears used to be a dominant player, has undergone dramatic changes. New competitors such as Lowe's and Home Depot have challenged Sears' former domination of the household appliances business. Internet sales have also cut into the traditional markets for Sears, especially the catalog business. The Kmart sector of the business, once a leader of the discount, big-box discount department store business, has been decimated by competition from Walmart.

In the face of this new competition, Sears' financial performance has been dreadful. Its stock price declined from a high in 2011 of over $86 per share to $19.73 near the end of 2015. Total revenue was $39.8 billion for the year ending February 2, 2013. By January 2015, total revenue had declined to $31.2 billion, and it continued to decline into 2015. In the year ending February 2, 2013, Sears posted net losses of $930 million. These losses grew to $1.36 billion in the year ending on February 2, 2014, and $1.68 billion in the year ending on January 31, 2015. The company's cash balances slipped dramatically during this same period.

Faced with deteriorating operating performance and declining liquidity, Sears looked for ways to "unlock" cash from its balance sheet. The largest asset item on Sears' balance sheet was "property, plant and equipment," dominated by the value of Sears and Kmart stores. In order to covert these fixed assets into cash, Sears formed a real estate investment trust (REIT), Seritage Growth Properties, which was spun off to shareholders in July 2015. The REIT acquired 235 of the company's wholly owned properties and 31 joint venture properties with over 42 million square feet across 49 states and Puerto Rico. Sears entered into agreements to lease back these properties from Seritage. As a result of this transaction, Sears received nearly $3 billion of proceeds that could be used to fund the $1+ billion per year of operating losses that Sears was expected to generate in the coming years, until it can find a business model that can return the company to solid profitability.

Sale and leaseback transactions such as this are not uncommon when owners of assets are not in a financial position to take advantage of the tax deductions associated with property ownership. Other firms, such as airlines, lease airplanes because lease financing is easy to arrange and also lets the lessor take advantage of the tax benefits of ownership if the airline cannot.

This chapter examines the factors that a firm must consider when it decides whether to own or lease assets. The pros and cons of leasing are considered from the perspective of both the lessee (the asset user) and the lessor (the asset owner).

Source: "Sears' Shares Plunge After Dismal Same-Store Sales," *Reuters* (August 3, 2015). www.reuters.com/article/us-sears-holdings-stocks-idUSKCN0Q820H20150803; N. Callahan, "Sears to Form REIT for $2.5-Billion Sale-and-Leaseback Deal," *The Globe and Mail* (April 1, 2015), www.theglobeandmail.com; *Bloomberg News*, April 1, 2015; "Seritage Growth Properties Announces Third Quarter 2015 Earnings Release Date," *The Wall Street Journal*, October 29, 2015.

digitalreflections/Shutterstock.com

CHAPTER OBJECTIVES

Upon completion of this chapter, you should have a clear understanding of the following:

1. The difference between lease financing and ownership, including the benefits and disadvantages of each
2. The different classifications of leases and why these classifications matter
3. How to determine whether an asset should be leased or owned
4. The various sources of term loan financing

19-1 Introduction

The first half of this chapter deals with lease financing from the perspective of both the owner and the user of an asset. The second half of the chapter deals with other types of intermediate-term financing, such as term loans and equipment loans.

19-2 Leasing

Leasing

lease

lessor

lessee

A promotional brochure from the Warner and Swasey Financial Corporation states, "The value of a machine is in the use, not its ownership." This is true in the sense that a firm may wish to acquire the use of an asset needed in the production of goods and the providing of services, but finds it unnecessary to acquire legal title to the asset. **Leasing** is a means of obtaining economic use of an asset for a specific period of time without obtaining an ownership interest in the asset. In the **lease** contract, the property owner (**lessor**) agrees to permit the property user (**lessee**) to make use of the property for a stated time. In return, the lessee agrees to make a series of periodic payments to the lessor.

Leasing as a source of intermediate- and long-term financing has become increasingly popular since World War II. Prior to that time, most lease contracts were written for real estate and farm property. Today, few major firms are not involved in leasing. Leased assets range from transportation equipment (such as railroad rolling stock, trucks, automobiles, airplanes, and ships) to computers, medical equipment, specialized industrial equipment, energy transmission equipment, and mining equipment. Some firms lease entire power-generating plants and aluminum reduction mills. In the hotel and motel industry, leases may even include bathroom fixtures, paintings, furniture, and bedding.

Estimated business fixed investment in plant, equipment and software in 2015 was $1.58 trillion in 2015. Of this total, more than 65 percent was financed through loans, leases, and lines of credits.[1] (These totals exclude business leases of facilities, such as offices and manufacturing plants.) Leasing transactions are common in the airline, rail, real estate, agriculture, construction, manufacturing, computer, medical equipment, trucking, and oil and gas industries.

[1]"Monthly Leasing and Finance Index," *Equipment Leasing and Finance Index* (December 2015), (www.elfaonline.org).

Many types of firms originate leases: commercial banks, savings and loan institutions, finance companies, insurance companies, investment banks, equipment manufacturing companies (often through captive leasing subsidiaries), and independent leasing companies.

Because of the growing importance and widespread acceptance of lease financing, the contemporary financial manager should have a good understanding of this financing method. The following sections discuss the characteristics of various types of leases and develop a lease analysis model from the perspective of the lessor. Later sections consider the tax and accounting treatment of leases and the advantages and disadvantages of leases. Finally, a lease analysis model is developed from the perspective of the lessee.

19-3 Types of Leases

Leases are classified in a number of ways. "True leases," which are the primary focus of this chapter, are traditional leases in which the lessor is considered to hold the legal title to the leased asset. The asset user, the lessee, has no ownership interest in the asset. *Operating leases* and various types of *financial*, or *capital*, *leases* are subcategories of true leases.

19-3a Operating Leases

operating lease

An **operating lease**, sometimes called a *service* or *maintenance lease*, is an agreement that provides the lessee with use of an asset on a period-by-period basis. Normally, the payments under an operating lease contract are insufficient to recover the full cost of the asset for the lessor. As a result, the contract period in an operating lease tends to be somewhat less than the usable economic life of the asset, and the lessor expects to recover the costs (plus a return) from renewal rental payments, the sale of the asset at the end of the lease period, or both.

The most important characteristic of an operating lease is that it may be canceled at the option of the lessee as long as the lessor is given sufficient notice. Even though the lessee may be required to pay a penalty to the lessor upon cancellation, this is preferable to being compelled to keep an asset that is expected to become obsolete in the near future. For example, many firms lease their computers under an operating lease arrangement. (Of course, the lessor charges a rental fee that is consistent with expectations of the asset's economic life.)

HTTP:
The Equipment Leasing Association maintains an extensive directory of leasing companies at
www.ELFAonline.org

Most operating leases require the lessor to maintain the leased asset. In addition, the lessor is normally responsible for any property taxes owed on the asset and for providing appropriate insurance coverage. The costs of these services are built into the lease rate.

19-3b Financial or Capital Leases

financial lease

A **financial lease**, also termed a *capital lease*, is a noncancelable agreement.[2] The lessee is required to make payments throughout the lease period, whether or not the asset continues to generate economic benefits. Failure to make payments has serious financial consequences and could eventually force the lessee into bankruptcy.

With financial leases, the lessee is generally responsible for maintenance of the asset. The lessee may also have to pay insurance and property taxes. The total payments over the lease period are sufficient to amortize the original cost of the asset and provide a

[2] This chapter focuses primarily on financial leases, rather than operating leases, because financial leases represent more permanent obligations. The analysis techniques discussed later in this chapter, however, are equally applicable to both operating and financial leases.

return to the lessor. Some financial leases provide for a renewal or repurchase option at the end of the lease; these renewal and repurchase options are subject to IRS regulations.

A financial lease may originate either as a *sale and leaseback* or as a *direct lease*.

sale and leaseback

Sale and Leaseback A **sale and leaseback** occurs when a company sells an asset to another firm and immediately leases it back for its own use. In this transaction, the lessor normally pays a price close to the asset's fair market value. The lease payments are set at a level that will return the full purchase price of the asset to the lessor, plus provide a reasonable rate of return. The sale and leaseback is advantageous to the lessee for the following reasons:

- The lessee receives cash from the sale of the asset, which may be reinvested elsewhere in the firm or used to increase the firm's liquidity.
- The lessee can continue using the asset, even though it is owned by someone else.

A good illustration of a sale and leaseback transaction was Public Service of New Mexico's decision to sell and lease back its partial interest in Palo Verde Nuclear Plant Unit 1 for $325 million. This transaction reduced its annual mortgage payments by one-half, to $40 million per year for the next 15 years, and its total cost by $375 million. Many small and medium-sized companies have raised capital by entering into a sale and leaseback agreement with financial institutions such as GE Capital.

direct lease

Direct Lease A **direct lease** is initiated when a firm acquires the use of an asset that it previously did not own. The lessor may be the manufacturer of the asset or a financial institution. In the latter instance, the user-lessee first determines the following:

- What equipment will be leased
- Which manufacturer will supply the equipment
- What options, warranties, terms of delivery, installment agreements, and service agreements will have to be made
- What price will be paid for the asset

The lessee then contacts a financial institution and works out the terms of the lease, after which the institution (which then becomes the lessor) acquires the asset for the lessee and the lessee starts making the lease payments. Under this arrangement, the lessee is usually responsible for taxes, insurance, and maintenance.

19-3c Leveraged Leases

A large proportion of all financial leases currently written in the United States are leveraged leases. Also known as *third-party equity leases* and *tax leases*, leveraged leases are designed to provide financing for assets that require large capital outlays (generally greater than $300,000) and have economic lives of five years or more. Leveraged leases are usually tax motivated because the asset user (lessee) is not in a tax position where it can make use of the accelerated depreciation tax shields if the asset is owned instead of leased.

leveraged lease

A **leveraged lease** is a three-sided agreement among the lessee, the lessor, and the lenders. The *lessee* selects the leased asset, receives all the income generated from its use, and makes the periodic lease payments. The *lessor* (normally a financial institution, such as a leasing company or a commercial bank) acts either for itself or as a trustee for an individual or a group of individuals to provide the equity funds needed to purchase the asset. The *lenders* (usually banks, insurance companies, trusts, pension funds, or foundations) lend the funds needed to make up the asset's full purchase price. Specifically, the lessor normally supplies 20 to 40 percent of the purchase price, and the lenders provide the remaining 60 to 80 percent. For example, in the Public Service

Company of New Mexico sale and leaseback of the Palo Verde Nuclear Plant discussed earlier, the lessors (Chrysler Capital, Drexel Burnham Leasing, and Mellon Financial Services) borrowed approximately 80 percent of the purchase price of the facilities.

Figure 19.1 is an announcement of a leveraged lease that was arranged by Salomon Brothers for Kansas City Southern Lines. In this case, the Ford Motor Credit Company acted as the lessor and provided equity funds of $4,728,974 to acquire 450 boxcars, which were leased to Kansas City Southern Lines. Debt funds of $10,072,198 were provided by a number of institutional lenders.

In a leveraged lease, the long-term money is supplied to the lessor by the lenders on a nonrecourse basis; that is, the lenders cannot turn to the lessor for repayment of the debt in the event of default. Normally, the lender receives mortgage bonds secured by the following:

- A first lien on the asset
- An assignment of the lease
- An assignment of the lease rental payments
- Occasionally, a direct guarantee from the lessee or a third party (such as the government, in the case of merchant vessel financing)

FIGURE 19.1

Announcement of a Leveraged Lease Financing Arrangement

This announcement appears as a matter of record only

KANSAS CITY SOUTHERN Lines

$14,801,172

Kansas City Southern Lines

15 Year Leveraged Lease of 450 Boxcars
Equity Funds of $4,728,974 were provided by

Ford Motor Credit Company

Debt Funds of $10,072,198 were provided by
various institutional lenders.

The undersigned arranged the financing for
this leveraged lease transaction.

Salomon Brothers ITEL CORPORATION

Source: Salomon Brothers.

In the example mentioned earlier of the Public Service Company of New Mexico nuclear plant sale and leaseback, the public debt used to finance the transaction was indirectly secured by the facilities and was payable from rental payments due by the utility under the leases. The debt was structured to have principal and interest payments that correspond to the receipt of rental payments. Because the lenders do not have recourse to the lessor in the event of default, the lessor's risk is limited to the 20 to 40 percent equity contribution.

As the owner of the asset, the lessor reports the lease payments as gross income. The lessor receives benefits from the tax-deductible interest and accelerated depreciation. As a result, the lessor incurs large tax losses and receives large cash inflows during the early years of the lease.

Because the lessor receives the entire accelerated depreciation tax shield although making a relatively small equity investment, the lessor can provide an attractive lease rate to the lessee. Lease rates of 4 to 6 percent are not uncommon when AAA-rated bonds are yielding from 9 to 10 percent. Figure 19.2 is a diagram of a typical leveraged lease arrangement.

Lessees who anticipate that their taxable income will not be sufficient to allow them to take advantage of the tax benefits of ownership are most likely to use leveraged leases for large transactions. These include firms with low profit levels, large tax-loss carryforwards,

FIGURE 19.2

Diagram of a Typical Leveraged Lease

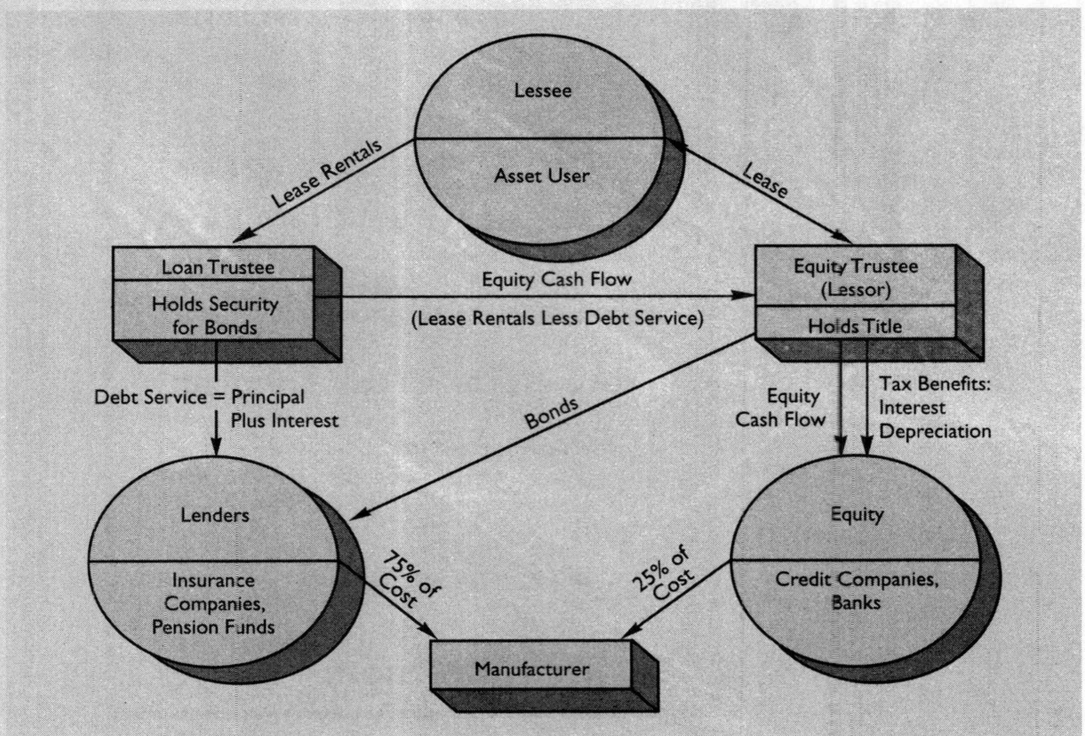

or large amounts of tax-exempt income. The lessee effectively gives up the tax benefits of ownership in exchange for more favorable lease rates.

19-4 Advantages and Disadvantages of Leasing

Leasing offers a number of potential advantages. However, the prudent financial manager should also be aware of the disadvantages.

19-4a Advantages

Perhaps the major advantage of leasing is that it provides *flexible financing*. Most lease arrangements tend to have fewer restrictive covenants than loan agreements. In addition, leasing is well suited to piecemeal financing. A firm that is acquiring assets over time may find it more convenient to lease them than to negotiate term loans or sell securities each time it makes a new capital outlay.

In the case of real estate leasing, the lessee may *effectively be able to depreciate land*. Because the lease payments will reflect both the lessor's investment in any buildings *and* the cost of the land, the lessee is able to effectively depreciate the land by deducting the full amount of the lease payment for tax purposes. To keep this benefit in perspective, however, it should be noted that the lessee also loses any salvage value associated with the property at the end of the lease.

The lessee may also be able to make *lower payments* because of the tax benefits enjoyed by the lessor. This is especially important in the case of a leveraged lease, when the lessee is a firm with insufficient taxable income to take advantage of the tax benefits of ownership. In fact, the majority of lease transactions made are tax motivated.

In addition, it *may* be possible for the lessee to *avoid some of the risks of obsolescence* associated with ownership. This is the second most cited reason why lessees choose lease financing. The lessor will charge a lease rate intended to provide a specified return on the required net investment. The net investment is equal to the cost of the asset minus the present value of the expected salvage value at the end of the lease. If the actual salvage is less than originally expected, the lessor bears the loss.

For the small or marginally profitable firm, *leasing is often the only available source of financing* because the title to leased property remains with the lessor and reduces the lessor's risk in the event of failure. If the lessee does fail, the lessor can recover the leased property more quickly than a secured lender.[3] For example, Ethiopian Airlines partnered with ILFC, the global jet leasing company, to acquire 13 Boeing 787 Dreamliners by 2015. It is doubtful that the airline could have found traditional lenders willing to fund these aggressive aircraft investments.

Leasing tends to *smooth out expenses* for the lessee. Because lease payments are a constant annual outlay, whereas MACRS depreciation expenses are large in the early years of ownership and less in later years, earnings tend to appear more stable when assets are leased rather than owned. In addition, reported earnings per share normally may be higher in the early years of a lease, compared with ownership, because of the use of MACRS depreciation when the asset is owned.

Leasing is said to provide *100 percent financing*, whereas most borrowing requires a down payment. This is the major reason cited by lessees for why they choose lease

[3]For a more complete discussion of the bankruptcy implications of leasing, see V. S. Krishnan and R. C. Moyer, "Bankruptcy Costs and the Financial Leasing Decision," *Financial Management* (Summer 1994).

ENTREPRENEURIAL ISSUES

Leasing by Small Businesses[a]

During business downturns, many small businesses find it difficult to get small business loans from banks. For example, when Nun-Lo Corporation of Ballwin, Missouri, sought bank financing to acquire a new $20,000 printing press, its bankers said no because of the firm's $60,000 in outstanding debt. Nun-Lo ended up leasing the press instead, for $550 per month over a 36-month period.

Many firms that are in the same position as Nun-Lo have sought lease financing as an alternative to traditional bank financing. In addition to its greater availability, firms that have made use of lease financing cite the following advantages:

1. Less cash required up-front
2. Better protection against obsolescence at the end of the lease term
3. Quicker approvals from lessors than from lenders
4. Fewer restrictive covenants from lessors than from lenders
5. Easier access to capital

However, these advantages do not come cheap. Lease financing often entails high effective financing costs relative to borrowing. One firm that chose to lease an asset rather than borrow to buy it found that the effective cost on the lease was 15.4 percent, nearly double the bank's loan rate. In addition, the lessee had to give up all of the tax benefits of ownership—notably the depreciation tax shields arising from the new equipment.

Thus, while leasing has gained favor among small firms as a quick and flexible financing alternative, these benefits have typically come at a high cost.

[a]Based on "Many Small Businesses Are Sold on Leasing," *The Wall Street Journal* (October 27, 1993): B2.

financing. However, because lease payments are normally made in advance of each period, this 100 percent financing benefit is diminished by the amount of the first required lease payment.

From the lessee's perspective, leases can *increase a firm's liquidity*. For example, a sale and leaseback transforms some of a firm's fixed assets into cash in exchange for an obligation to make a series of fixed future payments. This has been the primary motivation for sale and leaseback transactions undertaken by several troubled airlines.

Finally, leasing gives some plant or divisional managers additional *flexibility in acquiring assets* if lease agreements are not subject to internal capital expenditure constraints. In recent years, local school districts, municipalities, and the U.S. Navy, among other organizations, have used leasing to circumvent capital outlay restrictions.

19-4b Disadvantages

The primary disadvantage of leasing is *cost*. For a firm with a strong earnings record, good access to the credit markets, and the ability to take advantage of the tax benefits of ownership, leasing is often a more expensive alternative. Of course, the actual cost difference between ownership and leasing depends on a number of factors and varies from case to case.

Another disadvantage of leasing is the *loss of the asset's salvage value*. In real estate, this loss can be substantial. A lessee may also have *difficulty getting approval to make property improvements* on leased real estate. If the improvements substantially alter the property or reduce its potential range of uses, the lessor may be reluctant to permit them.

In addition, if a leased asset (with a financial lease) becomes obsolete or if the capital project financed by the lease becomes uneconomical, the *lessee may not cancel the lease without paying a substantial penalty*.

Also, in bankruptcy, lease payments normally must be made, whereas interest and principal payments are suspended.

19-5 Tax and Accounting Aspects of Leases

Leasing assets involves a number of tax and accounting considerations, which are examined in this section.

19-5a Tax Status of True Leases

Annual lease payments are tax deductible for the lessee if one crucial criterion is met: The IRS must agree that a contract truly is a lease and not just an installment loan called a lease. Before embarking on a lease transaction, all involved parties should obtain an opinion from the IRS regarding the tax status of the proposed lease. The opinion of the IRS normally revolves primarily around the following general rules:

- The remaining useful life of the equipment at the end of the lease term must be the greater of 1 year or 20 percent of its originally estimated useful life.
- Leases in excess of 30 years are *not* considered to be leases for tax purposes.
- The lease payments must provide the lessor with a fair market rate return on the investment. This profit potential must exist apart from the transaction's tax benefits.
- Renewal options must be reasonable, that is, the renewal rate must be closely related to the economic value of the asset for the renewal period.
- If the lease agreement specifies a purchase option at the end of the lease period, the purchase price must be based on the asset's fair market value at that time.
- The schedule of lease payments should not be very high early in the lease and very low thereafter. Such a payment schedule suggests that the lease structure is being used merely to avoid taxes.
- In the case of a leveraged lease, the lessor must provide a minimum of 20 percent equity.
- Limited-use property (valuable only to the lessee) may not be leased.

If the IRS does not agree that a contract is truly a lease, taxes are applied as if the property had been sold to the lessee and pledged to the lessor as security for a loan. The reason for the IRS restrictions previously cited is that the IRS wants to prohibit lease transactions set up purely to speed up tax deductions. For example, a building would normally be depreciated over 39 years under MACRS depreciation rules. It would be possible to set up a lease over a three-year period that allowed the lessee to effectively write off the cost of the building for tax purposes over three years. This would increase tax deductions for the lessee at the expense of tax receipts to the U.S. Treasury. These IRS guidelines are designed to prevent this type of abuse.

19-5b Leases and Accounting Practices

In recent years, firms have tended to disclose more information regarding lease obligations.

In November 1976, the Financial Accounting Standards Board (FASB) issued *Standard No. 13*, which *requires* lessees to capitalize certain types of leases, primarily financial or capital leases. The capitalized value of a lease is determined by computing the present value of all required lease payments, discounted at a rate equal to the lessee's incremental borrowing rate for a secured loan over a term similar to the lease.[4] Table 19.1 illustrates this procedure.

[4]In certain circumstances, it is possible for a firm to use a lower rate. See FASB *Standard No. 13* for a more detailed discussion.

TABLE 19.1

Accounting Treatment of Leases

Assets		Liabilities	
Leased property under capital		Current:	
leases less accumulated amortization	$1,500	Obligations under capital leases*	$ 150
	$1,500	Long term:	
		Obligations under capital leases*	$1,350
			$1,500

*The $150 represents lease payments due during the next year. The $1,350 represents the present value of lease payments due beyond one year in the future.

In addition to making these balance sheet adjustments, a firm must show the following in the footnotes to the financial statements:[5]

- For financial leases:
  1. The gross amount of assets by major classes according to nature or use reported under financial leases as of the date of the balance sheet
  2. The amount of accumulated lease amortization
  3. Future minimum lease payments as of the date of the latest balance sheet presented, in total and for each of the next five fiscal years
- For operating leases:
  1. Future minimum rental payments required as of the date of the latest balance sheet presented, in total and for each of the following five fiscal years
  2. The rental expense for each period for which an income statement is presented

The lessee must also indicate in the notes to the financial statements the existence and terms of renewal or repurchase options and escalation clauses, any restrictions imposed by leases (such as restrictions on dividends, additional debt, or further leasing), and any contingent rental obligations. Figure 19.3 illustrates how these lease disclosure requirements affected Darden Restaurants Inc. as reported in their 2015 annual report.

The effect of these disclosure requirements is to lower a firm's reported return on investment and to increase the reported debt-to-equity ratios of a firm that has acquired a portion of its assets through leasing. In the past, some analysts argued that one of the advantages of leasing was that it provided "off-balance sheet" financing and tended to increase a firm's capacity to borrow. Whether or not this was true, the lease-reporting requirements help to eliminate this distortion, facilitate clearer analysis of a firm's financial condition, and make it easier to make comparisons among firms.

19-6 Determining Lease Payments: The Lessor's Perspective

Suppose that the Dole Company (lessee) desires to lease a piece of farm equipment valued at $100,000 from Deere & Company (lessor) for a period of five years. Under the terms of the lease, payments are to be made at the beginning of each of the five years. Deere expects to depreciate the asset on a straight-line basis of $20,000 per year down to

[5]The requirements presented here are not all inclusive; they merely summarize the most significant disclosures.

FIGURE 19.3

Lease Disclosure for Darden Restaurants' 2015 Annual Report

An analysis of rent expense incurred related to restaurants in continuing operations is as follows:

(in millions)		**Fiscal Year**	
	2015	**2014**	**2013**
Restaurant minimum rent	$ 167.0	$ 146.4	$ 128.8
Restaurant rent averaging expense	16.7	26.9	24.2
Restaurant percentage rent	7.7	6.6	6.0
Other	3.5	5.5	5.6
Total rent expense	$ 194.9	$ 185.4	$ 161.6

Total rent expense included in discontinuec operations was $6.2 million, $36.2 million and $34.6 million for fiscal 2015, 2014 and 2013, respectively. These amounts include restaurant minimum rent of $5.8 million, $33.0 million and $31.8 million for fiscal 2015, 2014 and 2013, respectively.

The annual future lease commitments under capital lease obligations and noncancelable operating and financing leases, including those related to restaurants reported as discontinued operations, for each of the five fiscal years subsequent to May 31, 2015 and thereafter is as follows:

(in millions)

Fiscal Year	**Capital**	**Financing**	**Operating**
2016	$ 5.7	$ 6.6	$ 189.8
2017	5.9	6.8	180.1
2018	6.0	6.9	165.6
2019	6.1	7.0	147.2
2020	6.1	7.2	128.7
Thereafter	55.0	117.7	360.9
Total future lease commitments	$ 84.8	$ 152.2	$ 1,172.3
Less imputed interest (at 6.5%), (various)	(30.3)	(76.9)	
Present value of future lease commitments	$ 54.5	$ 75.3	
Less current maturities	(2.4)	(1.2)	
Obligations under capital and financing leases, net of current maturities	$ 52.1	$ 74.1	

During fiscal 2015 we began marketing selected properties for individual sale-leaseback transactions through which we sell the assets at fair value and subsequently lease them back. The resulting leases generally qualify and are accounted for as operating leases. The operating leases that resulted from the completed transactions are included in the above table.

a book salvage value of $0. Actual salvage value is expected to be $10,000 at the end of five years. This salvage value will be treated as a recapture of depreciation and taxed at Deere's marginal tax rate of 40 percent. Thus, the after-tax salvage value will be $6,000 ($10,000 actual salvage less $4,000 tax on depreciation recapture). If Deere requires an 11 percent after-tax rate of return on the lease, what will be the annual lease payments?

- **Step 1: Compute the lessor's amount to be amortized.** In this case, it is the $100,000 initial outlay minus the present value of the after-tax salvage at the end of year 5 minus the present value of the after-tax depreciation tax shield for each year. (Recall that depreciation reduces taxable income by the amount of the depreciation and thus reduces a firm's cash outflow for tax payments by an amount equal to the depreciation times the company's marginal ordinary tax rate.)

Initial outlay	$100,000
Less: Present value of $6,000 after-tax salvage at 11%	
($6,000 × $PVIF_{0.11,5}$) = $6,000 × 0.593	3,558
Less: Present value of annual depreciation tax shield	
($20,000 × 0.4 × $PVIFA_{0.11,5}$) = $8,000 × 3.696	29,568
Amount to be amortized	$ 66,874

(If an accelerated depreciation method, such as MACRS, was used by the lessor, the present value of the annual depreciation tax shield would have to be done using a series of Table II PVIF factors, because the annual depreciation tax shield normally will change most years under accelerated depreciation methods.)

- **Step 2: Compute the annual *after-tax* lease income.**[6] This is the income that the lessor must receive in order to earn the needed 11 percent return. Remember that lease payments received by a lessor are treated as taxable, ordinary income. These payments can be computed using the appropriate interest factor for the present value of an annuity (PVIFA from Table IV). Because lease payments are normally made at the beginning of each year, they constitute an *annuity due*. Thus, the last four payments, which occur at the ends of years 1 through 4, are discounted, whereas the present value of the first payment, made at the *beginning* of year 1, is not discounted. Recall from Chapter 5 that taking the PVIFA for 11 percent and five years and multiplying by (1 + 0.11) gives the required PVIFA for an annuity due. If *PMT* is the annual after-tax lease income to the lessor, the present value of the lease income may be set equal to the amount to be amortized to determine the required *PMT*, as follows:

Calculator Solutions

Key	Enter
n	5
i	11
PV	−66,874
PMT	
FV	
	Solution
PMT	16,301

$$\text{Amount to be amortized} = PMT(PVIFA_{0.11,5})(1 + 0.11)$$

$$\$66{,}874 = PMT(3.696)(1.11)$$

$$\$66{,}874 = PMT(4.103)$$

$$PMT = 16{,}299$$

Therefore, Deere & Company needs to receive five beginning-of-the-year, after-tax lease income amounts of $16,301 (calculator accuracy) in order to earn an 11 percent after-tax return on the lease.

- **Step 3: Convert the lease income requirement of the lessor to a lease payment requirement of the lessee.** Recalling that lease payments received by the lessor from the lessee are taxed as ordinary income, we can convert the after-tax lease income requirement of the lessor into a lease payment requirement for the lessee as follows:

$$\begin{array}{c}\text{Lease payment required}\\\text{from the lessee}\end{array} = \frac{\begin{array}{c}\text{Lessee income required}\\\text{by the lessor (after tax)}\end{array}}{\begin{array}{c}\text{1 minus lessor's marginal}\\\text{tax rate}\end{array}}$$

$$= \frac{\$16{,}301}{1 - 0.4} = \$27{,}168$$

Therefore, the Dole Company will have to make an annual lease payment of $27,168 to Deere & Company at the beginning of each year.

19-7 Lease-Buy Analysis: The Lessee's Perspective

Financial theorists and model builders have devoted a substantial amount of time and effort to developing an analytical framework within which the differential costs

[6]This problem must be solved with the calculator in the beginning-of-period payment mode. The difference between the interest table solution and the calculator solution is due to rounding.

associated with leasing versus buying can be compared. At least 15 different approaches to the problem have been suggested, and there is considerable disagreement as to which one is the best.[7] In spite of this abundance of models, the perplexed financial manager can take some comfort in the fact that the practical effects resulting from the differences in the models tend to be small because few real-world decisions are changed as a result of which lease-buy model is chosen.

One of the most commonly used approaches to the analysis of a lease versus purchase decision assumes that the appropriate comparison should be between *leasing* and *borrowing to buy*. Advocates of this approach argue that a financial lease is much like a loan in that it requires a series of fixed payments. Failure to make lease payments, like failure to make loan payments, may result in bankruptcy.

The basic approach of the lease-buy analysis model is to compute the *net advantage to leasing* (NAL). The net advantage to leasing compares the present value cost of leasing with the present value cost of owning the asset. If the cost of owning the asset is greater than the cost of leasing the asset, the NAL is positive and the model indicates that the asset should be leased.

The *net advantage to leasing* calculation is as follows:

	Installed cost of the asset
Less:	Present value of the after-tax lease payments
Less:	Present value of depreciation tax shield
Plus:	Present value of after-tax operating costs incurred if owned but not if leased
Less:	Present value of the after-tax salvage value
Equals:	Net advantage to leasing

The installed cost of the asset equals the purchase price plus installation and shipping charges. The installed cost forms the basis on which depreciation is computed.

The present value of the after-tax lease payments that are made if the asset is leased reduces the NAL; hence, they are subtracted when computing the NAL. These lease payments are discounted at the firm's after-tax marginal cost of borrowing to reflect the fact that lease payments are contractually known in advance and thus are not subject to much uncertainty. The present value of the depreciation tax shield is equal to the depreciation claimed each year if the asset is owned times the firm's marginal tax rate. The depreciation tax shield reduces the cost of ownership and hence is subtracted when computing the NAL. Because the depreciation amounts are also known with relative certainty, they are also discounted at the firm's after-tax marginal cost of borrowing.[8]

Sometimes operating costs are incurred if the asset is owned but not if it is leased. These may include property tax payments, insurance, or some maintenance expenses. If these do exist, they represent a benefit of leasing and increase the NAL. Hence, the after-tax amount of these costs is added in the NAL calculation. These operating cost savings are also discounted at the after-tax marginal cost of borrowing, reflecting their relative certainty. Finally, if the asset is owned, the owner will receive the after-tax salvage value. This is lost if the asset is leased. Hence the after-tax salvage reduces the NAL and must be subtracted when calculating the NAL. Because asset salvage values are

[7]Basically, the various models differ as to which discount rate should be used to evaluate various components of the cash flows and which cash flows should be considered.

[8]The depreciation amounts are known with certainty, but the tax shield from depreciation may not be certain because of potential future changes in the marginal corporate tax rate, which may alter the value of the tax shield. Also, there is always the chance that a company will not have sufficient taxable income to take advantage of the depreciation tax shield.

generally subject to substantial uncertainty, they are normally discounted at a rate equal to the firm's weighted (marginal) cost of capital.

19-7a Example of Lease-Buy Analysis

Consider the following example to illustrate the lease-buy analysis procedure just described. Suppose that the Gamma Corporation is trying to decide whether it should purchase or lease a new heavy-duty Ford truck. (The firm has already computed the net present value of this proposed asset acquisition and found the project to be acceptable.) The truck can be purchased for $50,000, including delivery. Alternatively, the truck can be leased from Ford Motor Credit for a six-year period at a beginning-of-the-year lease payment of $10,000. If purchased, Gamma could borrow the needed funds from PNC Bank at an annual interest rate of 10 percent. If the truck is purchased, Gamma estimates that it will incur $750 per year of expenses to cover insurance and a maintenance contract. These expenses would not be incurred if the truck is leased. The truck will be depreciated under MACRS guidelines as a five-year asset. Gamma expects the actual salvage value to be $20,000 at the end of six years. Gamma's marginal tax rate is 40 percent, and its weighted after-tax cost of capital is 15 percent. Which alternative—leasing or buying—should be chosen? In order to answer this question, we need to compute the NAL. This is shown in Table 19.2. The calculation in Table 19.2 indicates a net advantage to leasing of –$1,296. Because the NAL is negative, the asset should be owned rather than leased.[9]

This procedure can be used to evaluate any lease versus buy decision only after it has been determined by standard capital budgeting techniques that an asset should be acquired, that is, it has a positive net present value.

19-8 Term Loans

term loan

A **term loan**, or *intermediate-term credit*, is defined as any debt obligation having an initial maturity between 1 and 10 years. It lacks the permanency characteristic of long-term debt. Term loans are well suited for financing small additions to plant facilities and equipment, such as a new piece of machinery. These loans can also be used to finance a moderate increase in working capital when:

- The cost of a public offering of bonds or stock is too high.
- The firm intends to use the term debt only until its earnings are sufficient to amortize the loan.
- The desired increase is relatively long-term but not permanent.

Term loans are often preferable to short-term loans because they provide the borrower with a certain degree of security. Rather than having to be concerned about whether a short-term loan will be renewed, the borrower can have a term loan structured in such a way that the maturity coincides with the economic life of the asset being financed. Thus, the cash flows generated by the asset can service the loan without putting any additional financial strain on the borrower.

Term loans also offer potential cost advantages over long-term sources of financing. Because term loans are privately negotiated between the borrowing firm and the lending institution, they are less expensive than public offerings of common stock or bonds. The

[9]The lease-buy analysis procedure used here implicitly assumes that the leasing alternative and the borrowing-to-buy alternative have the same impact on the company's debt capacity. This is desirable because leasing and borrowing both represent fixed obligations that are treated by financial analysts as equivalent to debt. Lease-buy analysis also assumes that the asset satisfies the lessee's normal capital investment criteria, such as NPV.

TABLE 19.2

Calculation of the Net Advantage to Leasing for Gamma Corporation

End of Year (1)	Installed Asset Cost (2)	Lease Payment After-Tax* (3)	Depreciation** (4)	Depreciation Tax Shield† (5)	Additional Operating Costs if Owned After-Tax†† (6)	NAL Cash Flows Except Salvage‡ (7) = (2) − (3) − (5) + (6)
0	$50,000	$6,000	—	—	—	$44,000
1	—	6,000	$10,000	$4,000	$450	−9,550
2	—	6,000	16,000	6,400	450	−11,950
3	—	6,000	9,600	3,840	450	−9,390
4	—	6,000	5,760	2,304	450	−7,854
5	—	6,000	5,760	2,304	450	−7,854
6	—	—	2,880	1,152	450	−702

PVIF @6%‡‡ (8)	Present Value§ (9) = (7) × (8)	After-Tax Salvage§§ (10)	PVIF @15% (11)	Present Value Salvage¶ (12) = (10) × (11)	NAL¶¶ (13) = (9) − (12)
1.000	$44,000	—	—	—	$44,000
0.943	−9,006	—	—	—	−9,006
0.890	−10,636	—	—	—	−10,636
0.840	−7,888	—	—	—	−7,888
0.792	−6,220	—	—	—	−6,220
0.747	−5,867	—	—	—	−5,867
0.705	−495	$12,000	0.432	$5,184	−5,679
				Net Advantage to Leasing =	−$1,296

*The after-tax lease payment equals the total lease payment ($10,000) times 1 minus Gamma's marginal tax rate (40%). The benefit of the tax deductibility of lease payments is assumed to be received at approximately the same time the lease payments are made, reflecting the quarterly payment of taxes.

**MACRS depreciation is computed using the 5-year MACRS rates times the asset cost. The MACRS rates are 20%, 32%, 19.2%, 11.52%, 11.52%, and 5.76%, respectively, over the six years.

†The depreciation tax shield is equal to the depreciation in column (4) times Gamma's marginal tax rate (40%).

††Column (6) is equal to $750 pretax cost times 1 minus Gamma's marginal tax rate (40%).

‡Column (7) is the total of the cash flows needed to compute the NAL that are discounted at the after-tax cost of debt for Gamma. It is equal to the asset cost (2), less the after-tax lease payments (3), less the depreciation tax shield (5), plus the additional after-tax operating costs incurred if the asset is owned (6).

‡‡The after-tax cost of debt is 6 percent (10% pretax cost times 1 minus Gamma's marginal tax rate [40%]).

§The present value of column (9) is equal to the cash flows in column (7) times the PVIF factors in column (8).

§§The after-tax salvage is equal to the pretax salvage ($20,000) times 1 minus Gamma's marginal tax rate (40%).

¶The present value of the salvage is equal to the after-tax salvage times the PVIF for 15 percent and six years, where the 15 percent represents Gamma's weighted cost of capital.

¶¶The NAL is equal to the sum of the present value cash flows from column (9) minus the present value of the after-tax salvage from column (12).

issuing firm in a public offering must pay the registration and issue expenses necessary to sell the securities. For small- to moderate-size offerings, these expenses can be large in relation to the funds raised.[10]

19-8a Repayment Provisions

A term loan agreement usually requires that the principal be amortized over the life of the loan, which means that the firm is required to pay off the loan in installments, rather than in one lump sum. Amortizing has the effect of reducing the risk to the lender that the borrower will be unable to retire the loan in one lump sum when it comes due.

[10]See Chapter 7 for a discussion of the costs of issuing new debt and equity (common stock) securities.

Amortization of principal is also consistent with the idea that term loans are not a permanent part of a firm's capital structure.

amortization schedule

The **amortization schedule** of a term loan might require the firm to make equal quarterly, semiannual, or annual payments of principal and interest. For example, assume that Arrow Envelope Company borrows $250,000 payable over five years, with an interest rate of 10 percent per annum on the unpaid balance. The repayment schedule calls for five equal annual payments, the first occurring at the end of year 1.

Recall from Chapter 5 that the annual payment (*PMT*) required to pay off a loan can be computed using Equation 5.19:

$$\text{PVAN}_0 = PMT(\text{PVIFA}_{i,n}) \tag{19.1}$$

or

$$PMT = \frac{\text{PVAN}_0}{\text{PVIFA}_{i,n}}$$

In this example, substituting the present value of the annuity (PVAN_0) = $250,000, the number of time periods (n) = 5, the interest rate (i) = 10 percent, and the $\text{PVIFA}_{0.10,\,5} = 3.791$ from Table IV into this equation yields an approximate annual payment of $65,945.66. A more accurate solution, obtained with a financial calculator, is $65,949.37.[11]

By making five annual payments of $65,949.37 to the lender, Arrow will just pay off the loan and provide the lender with a 10 percent return. Panel (a) of Table 19.3 shows the amortization schedule for this term loan.

Over the life of this loan, Arrow will make total payments of $329,746.85. Of this amount, $250,000 is the repayment of the principal, and the other $79,746.85 is interest. It is important to know what proportions of a loan payment are principal and interest because interest payments are tax deductible.

Calculator Solutions

Key	Enter
n	5
i	10
PV	−250,000
PMT	
FV	
	Solution
PMT	65,949.37

In this example, the repayment schedule calls for equal periodic payments to the lender consisting of both principal and interest. Other types of repayment schedules are also possible, including the following:

- The borrower might be required to make equal reductions in the principal outstanding each period, with the interest being computed on the remaining balance for each period. Panel (b) of Table 19.3 illustrates such a repayment schedule, where Arrow is required to repay $50,000 of the principal each year.
- The borrower might be required to make equal periodic payments over the life of the loan that only partially amortize the loan, leaving a lump sum payment that falls due at the termination of the loan period, called a **balloon loan**. Panel (c) of Table 19.3 shows a repayment schedule requiring Arrow to repay one-half ($125,000) of the term loan over the first four years with the balance ($125,000) due at the end of the fifth year.

balloon loan

bullet loan

- The borrower might be required to make a single principal payment at maturity while making periodic (usually quarterly) interest payments only over the life of the loan, called a **bullet loan**. Panel (d) of Table 19.3 lists the payments required to pay off this loan, given that Arrow is required to make only annual interest payments over the first four years of the loan with the principal ($250,000) plus an annual interest payment due at maturity.

19-8b Interest Costs

The interest rate charged on a term loan depends on a number of factors, including the general level of interest rates in the economy, the size of the loan, the maturity of the loan, and the borrower's credit standing. Generally, interest rates on intermediate-term loans tend to be slightly higher than interest rates on short-term loans because of the

[11]The solution obtained from Table IV differs slightly from the true payment because of rounding errors—the table is accurate to only three decimal places.

TABLE 19.3

Loan Amortization Schedules for Arrow Envelope Company

	End of Year (1)	Annual Payment (2)	Interest* (3)	Principal Reduction** (4)	Remaining Balance[†] (5)
(a) Equal Annual Payments	0	$ —	$ —	$ —	$250,000.00
	1	65,949.37[††]	25,000.00	40,949.37	209,050.63
	2	65,949.37	20,905.06	45,044.31	164,006.32
	3	65,949.37	16,400.63	49,548.74	114,457.58
	4	65,949.37	11,445.76	54,503.61	59,953.97
	5	65,949.37	5,995.40	59,953.47	0.00
	Total	$329,746.85	$79,746.85	$250,000.00	
(b) Equal Annual Reductions in Principal ($50,000 each year)	0	$ —	$ —	$ —	$250,000
	1	75,000	25,000	50,000	200,000
	2	70,000	20,000	50,000	150,000
	3	65,000	15,000	50,000	100,000
	4	60,000	10,000	50,000	50,000
	5	55,000	5,000	50,000	0
	Total	$325,000	$ 75,000	$ 250,000	
(c) Balloon Loan ($125,000 due at maturity)	0	$ —	$ —	$ —	$250,000.00
	1	51,933.85[‡]	25,000.00	26,933.85	223,066.15
	2	51,933.85	22,306.62	29,627.23	193,438.91
	3	51,933.85	19,343.89	32,589.96	160,848.95
	4	51,933.85	16,084.90	35,848.95	125,000.00
	5	137,500.00	12,500.00	125,000.00	0.00
	Total	$345,235.40	$95,235.41	$249,999.99[‡‡]	
(d) Bullet Loan ($250,000 due at maturity)	0	$ —	$ —	$ 0	$250,000
	1	25,000	25,000	0	250,000
	2	25,000	25,000	0	250,000
	3	25,000	25,000	0	250,000
	4	25,000	25,000	0	250,000
	5	275,000	25,000	250,000	0
	Total	$375,000	$125,000	$ 250,000	

*Interest each year is equal to 0.10 times the remaining balance from the previous year.

**Principal reduction each year equals the annual payment minus interest.

[†]Remaining balance each year is equal to the previous year's remaining balance minus principal reduction.

[††]$PMT = \$250{,}000/3.790786769 = \$65{,}949.37$.

[‡]$PMT = \$125{,}000/3.169865446 + \$125{,}000 \times 0.10 = \$51{,}933.85$.

[‡‡]Differs from $250,000 because of rounding error. If fractional cents were used, no rounding would be necessary.

higher risk assumed by the lender. Also, large term loans tend to have lower rates than small term loans because the fixed costs associated with granting and administering a loan do not vary proportionately with the size of the loan. In addition, large borrowers often have better credit standings than small borrowers. An interest rate between 0.25 and 2.5 percentage points above the prime rate is common for term loans obtained from banks, or LIBOR + 200 to 500 basis points.

The interest rate on a small term loan is sometimes the same throughout the loan's lifetime. In contrast, most larger term loans specify a *variable* interest rate, which depends on the bank's prime lending rate or on LIBOR. For example, if a loan is initially made at 0.5 percentage points above the prime rate, the loan agreement might specify that the interest charged on the remaining balance will continue to be 0.5 percentage points above the prevailing rate. Thus, whenever the prime rate is increased, the loan rate also increases; if the prime rate declines, so does the interest rate on the loan.

Compensating Balances It is not uncommon for a bank to require a borrowing firm to keep a percentage of its loan balance—for example, 10 percent—on deposit as a compensating balance. If this balance is greater than the amount the firm would normally keep on deposit with the bank, this requirement effectively increases the firm's cost of the loan. Compensating balance requirements and their effect on the cost of a loan are discussed in Chapter 16.

Equity Participations The interest rate charged on a term loan may also be influenced by a desire on the part of the lending institution to take an equity position (often called a "kicker") in the company as an additional form of compensation. This is usually accomplished through the issuance of a *warrant* by the borrower to the lender. A **warrant** is an option to purchase a stated number of shares of a company's common stock at a specified price sometime in the future. If the company prospers, the lending institution shares in this prosperity on an equity basis. The issuance of warrants in conjunction with a term loan is common when the loan has an above-normal level of risk but the lending institution feels the borrower has promising growth potential. Alternatively, the borrower may issue warrants to secure a more favorable lending rate. Warrants are discussed in detail in Chapter 20.

warrant

19-9 Security Provisions and Protective Covenants

The security provisions and protective covenants specified by a term loan agreement are often determined by the borrower's credit standing: the weaker the credit standing, the more restrictive the protective covenants.

19-9a Security Provisions

In general, security requirements apply more often to intermediate-term loans than to short-term loans, due to the fact that longer-term loan contracts tend to have more default risk. Security provisions are also dependent on the size of the borrowing firm. For example, term loans to small firms tend to be secured more often than term loans to large firms, although there is an increasing tendency for all bank-oriented term loans to be secured.

The sources of security for a term loan include the following:

- An assignment of payments due under a specific contract
- An assignment of a portion of the receivables or inventories
- The use of a floating lien on inventories and receivables
- A pledge of marketable securities held by the borrower
- A mortgage on property, plant, or equipment held by the borrower
- An assignment of the cash surrender value of a life insurance policy held by the borrower for its key executives

19-9b Affirmative Covenants

affirmative loan covenant

An **affirmative loan covenant** is a portion of a loan agreement that outlines actions the borrowing firm *agrees to take* during the term of the loan. Typical affirmative covenants include the following:

- The borrower agrees to furnish periodic financial statements to the lender, including a balance sheet, income statement, and a statement of cash flows. These may be furnished monthly, quarterly, or annually and frequently are required to be audited. Pro forma cash budgets and projections of the costs needed to complete contracts on hand may also be required.
- The borrower agrees to carry sufficient insurance to cover insurable business risk.
- The borrower agrees to maintain a minimum amount of net working capital (current assets less current liabilities).
- The borrower agrees to maintain management personnel who are acceptable to the financing institution.

19-9c Negative Covenants

negative loan covenant

A **negative loan covenant** outlines actions that the borrowing firm's management *agrees not to take* without prior written consent of the lender. Typical negative covenants include the following:

- The borrowing firm agrees not to pledge any of its assets as security to other lenders, as well as not to factor (sell) its receivables. This type of agreement, called a *negative pledge clause*, is found in nearly all unsecured loans. It is designed to keep other lenders from interfering with the immediate lender's claims on the assets of the firm.
- The borrower is prohibited from making mergers or consolidations without the lender's approval. In addition, the borrower may not sell or lease a major portion of its assets without written approval of the lender.
- The borrower is prohibited from making or guaranteeing loans to others that would impair the lender's security.

19-9d Restrictive Covenants

restrictive loan covenants

Rather than requiring or prohibiting certain actions on the part of the borrower, **restrictive loan covenants** merely *limit their scope*. These are typical restrictive covenants:

- Limitations on the amount of dividends a firm may pay
- Limitations on the level of salaries, bonuses, and advances a firm may give to employees

These restrictions, in essence, force the firm to increase its equity capital base, thereby increasing the security for the loan.

Other restrictive covenants might include the following:

- Limitations on the total amount of short- and long-term borrowing the firm may engage in during the period of the term loan
- Limitations on the amount of funds the firm may invest in new property, plant, and equipment (this restriction usually applies only to those investments that cannot be financed from internally generated funds)

And, finally, a firm that has outstanding long-term debt may be restricted as to the amount of debt it can retire without also retiring a portion of the term loan.

These restrictions are quite common, but the list is not all-inclusive. For example, a standard loan agreement checklist published by a large New York City bank lists 34 commonly used covenants. In general, covenants included in a loan agreement are determined by the particular conditions surrounding the granting of the term loan, including the credit record of the borrower and the maturity and security provisions of the loan.

19-9e Default Provisions

All term loans have *default provisions* that permit the lender to insist that the borrower repay the entire loan immediately under certain conditions. The following are examples:

- The borrower fails to pay interest, principal, or both as specified by the terms of the loan.
- The borrower materially misrepresents any information on the financial statements required under the loan's affirmative covenants.
- The borrower fails to observe any of the affirmative, negative, or restrictive covenants specified within the loan.

A borrower who commits any of these common acts of default will not necessarily be called on to repay a loan immediately, however. Basically, a lender will use a default provision only as a last resort, seeking in the meantime to make some agreement with the borrower, such as working out an acceptable modified lending plan with which the borrower is better able to comply. Normally, a lender will call a loan due only if no reasonable alternative is available or if the borrower is facing near-certain failure.

19-10 Suppliers of Term Loans

There are numerous sources of term loans, including commercial banks, insurance companies, pension funds, commercial finance companies, government agencies, and equipment suppliers. Many of these sources are discussed in the following subsections.

19-10a Commercial Banks and Savings and Loan Associations

Many commercial banks and some savings and loan associations are actively involved in term lending. For example, about one-third of all commercial and industrial loans made by commercial banks are term loans. However, the market share of commercial banks has declined as more firms have issued "junk" bonds, either publicly or in private placements.

In spite of this level of activity, banks generally tend to favor loans having relatively short maturities—that is, less than five years—although some banks will make loans having maturities as long as 10 years or more. In addition, some banks limit their term lending to existing customers. Often banks will form *syndicates* to share larger term loans; this not only limits the risk exposure for any one bank but also complies with regulations that limit the size of *unsecured* loans made to single customers.

19-10b Life Insurance Companies and Pension Funds

Whereas commercial banks tend to prefer shorter-term loans, insurance companies and pension funds are more interested in longer-term commitments, for example, 10 to 20 years. As a result, it is common for a bank and an insurance company to share a term loan commitment. Under this type of arrangement, the bank might agree to finance the first five years of a loan with the insurance company financing the loan for the remaining years. This arrangement also can be advantageous to the borrower because banks generally can charge a lower rate of interest for loans having shorter maturities.

From the borrowing firm's perspective, term loan agreements with pension funds and insurance companies have one significant limitation. If a firm decides to retire a term loan with a bank, it usually may do so without penalty. Because insurance companies are interested in having their funds invested for longer periods of time, however, prepayment of an insurance company term loan may involve some penalties.

Term loans from insurance companies and pension funds usually are secured, often with a mortgage on an asset, such as a building. These mortgage-secured loans are rarely made for amounts greater than 65 to 75 percent of the value of the collateral, however.

Finally, term loans from life insurance companies and pension funds tend to have slightly higher stated rates of interest than bank term loans; this is because (1) they are generally made for longer maturities, and (2) there are no compensating balance requirements.

19-10c Small Business Administration (SBA)

The Small Business Administration (SBA), an agency of the federal government, was established in 1953 to make credit available to small businesses that cannot reasonably obtain financing from private sources. SBA loans are normally made available through commercial banks, with the SBA providing the bank with a guarantee for all or a part of the loan.

SBA-guaranteed loans are made available through several programs, including SBA Express (an expedited program for small businesses with a maximum loan ceiling of $350,000). SBA 7(a) term loans have a loan ceiling of $5 million. SBA 504 term loans offer credit amounts between $150,000 and $6.0 million.

19-10d Small Business Investment Companies (SBICs)

HTTP:
Capital South Partners is a large SBIC headquartered in Charlotte, North Carolina.
www.capitalsouthpartners.com

Small business investment companies (SBICs) are licensed by the government to make both equity and debt investments in small firms. They raise their capital by borrowing from the SBA and other sources and by raising equity from private investors.

The SBICs take an equity interest in the small firms they loan funds to, hoping to profit from their growth and prosperity. Unlike SBA loans, which are made to any eligible creditworthy small business, SBICs specialize in providing funds to firms that have above-average growth potential. Naturally, these firms often have above-average risk as well. Thus, the interest charge on an SBIC loan is generally somewhat higher than that on a normal bank term loan. SBIC loans have maturities as long as 10 to 20 years.

19-10e Industrial Development Authorities (IDAs)

Many states and municipalities have organized industrial development authorities (IDAs) to encourage new firms to locate in their area or to assist existing firms with expansion plans. In a typical financing plan, a local IDA sells tax-exempt municipal revenue bonds and uses the proceeds to build a firm's new facility. It then leases the plant to the firm, collecting lease payments from the firm that are large enough to pay the principal and interest on the municipal revenue bonds. Because bonds of this nature are tax exempt, the interest on them is generally lower than the interest on bonds issued directly by a private corporation. As a result, an IDA can charge a firm an attractively low lease rate.

The growing need to finance pollution control expenditures has led to the development of *pollution control revenue bonds*, which are issued by municipalities. Proceeds from these bonds are used to acquire pollution control equipment, which is then sold or leased to local industries. Because interest payments on pollution control revenue bonds are tax-free to investors, a firm's cost is much lower than it would be if these investments had to be financed with conventional debt or equity.

19-11 Equipment Loans

When a firm procures a loan to finance new equipment, it may use the equipment itself as collateral for an intermediate-term loan. These loans are called *equipment financing loans*. Equipment financing loans are commonly made for readily marketable equipment. These loans are normally made for somewhat less than the market value of the equipment, and the difference provides a margin of safety for the lender. This difference may range between 20 and 30 percent for readily marketable and mobile equipment, such as trucks or cars. The amortization schedule for an equipment financing loan is usually tied closely to the asset's economic life.

There are several potential sources of equipment financing, including commercial banks, sales finance companies, equipment sellers, insurance companies, and pension funds. Commercial banks are often the least expensive source of such financing—especially when compared with sales finance companies. The equipment seller may provide financing either directly or through a captive finance subsidiary (that is, the seller's own financing subsidiary). Although at first glance, an equipment seller may appear to charge a very modest interest rate, it often is difficult to make a meaningful comparison between the rates charged by a supplier and other financing sources, such as commercial banks. The reason is because the selling firm might price the equipment in such a way as to conceal part of the cost of carrying its credit customers; that is, noncash customers may pay relatively higher prices than cash customers.

There are two primary security instruments used in connection with equipment financing loans; the *conditional sales contract* and the *chattel mortgage*. Each of these is discussed in the following subsections.

19-11a Conditional Sales Contract

conditional sales contract

When a **conditional sales contract** (sometimes called a *purchase money mortgage*) is used in an equipment financing transaction, the seller retains title until the buyer has made all payments required by the financing contract. Conditional sales contracts are used almost exclusively by equipment sellers. At the time of purchase, the buyer normally makes a down payment to the seller and issues a promissory note for the balance of the purchase price. The buyer then agrees to make a series of periodic payments (usually monthly or quarterly) of principal and interest to the seller until the note has been paid off. When the last payment has been made, the title to the equipment passes to the buyer. In the case of default, the seller may repossess the asset.

19-11b Chattel Mortgage

chattel mortgage

A **chattel mortgage** is a lien on property other than real estate. Chattel mortgages are most common when a commercial bank or sales finance company makes a direct equipment financing loan. It involves the placement of a lien against the property by the lender. Notification of the lien is filed with a public office in the state where the equipment is located. Given a valid lien, the lender may repossess the equipment and resell it if the borrower defaults on the loan payment.

19-12 Summary

- A *lease* is a written agreement that permits the *lessee* to use a piece of property owned by the *lessor* in exchange for a series of periodic lease or rental payments.
- An *operating lease* provides the lessee with the use of an asset on a period-by-period basis. An operating lease *may be canceled* at the lessee's option. Most operating leases are written for a relatively short period of time, normally less than five years.
- A *financial lease* is a *noncancelable* agreement that obligates the lessee to make payments to the lessor for a predetermined period of time. There are two major types of financial leases: *sale and leaseback*

agreements and *direct leases. Leveraged leases,* also called *tax leases,* have become increasingly common. Approximately 85 percent of the financial leases written today are leveraged leases.

- Subject to a series of IRS guidelines, firms that lease a portion of their assets may deduct the full amount of the lease payment for tax purposes.
- Decisions by the Financial Accounting Standards Board (FASB) require that many financial leases be capitalized and shown on the lessee's balance sheet.
- Leasing offers a number of potential advantages, including flexibility, the effective depreciation of land, and tax benefits (in some cases). It may also be the only source of financing available to many marginally profitable firms. It has a number of potential disadvantages, too. For example, leasing tends to be more costly than ownership for a firm with a good earnings record and good access to the capital markets.
- A number of analytical models are available to assist the lessor in determining what lease payments to charge. Other models are available to assist the lessee in determining which is the less expensive source of financing—leasing or borrowing to buy.
- *Term loans,* or *intermediate-term credit,* include any debt obligation having an initial maturity between 1 and 10 years. Term loans are usually amortized by a series of installments. The interest rate normally ranges between 0.25 and 2.5 percent above the prime rate. Many term loan agreements require that some specific asset be pledged as *security.* In addition, the borrowing firm may have to agree to certain *affirmative, negative,* and *restrictive covenants* governing its actions during the loan period.
- Term loans that are secured by a lien on a piece of equipment are called *equipment financing loans.* The two primary security instruments used in equipment financing are the *conditional sales contract* and the *chattel mortgage.*

19-13 Questions and Topics for Discussion

1. What are the primary differences between operating leases and financial leases?
2. How does a leveraged lease differ from a nonleveraged financial lease? What type of firm or organization is most likely to take advantage of the leveraged lease financing option? What type of individual or financial institution is most likely to act as the lessor in a leveraged lease?
3. From a tax perspective, what primary requirements in a lease transaction must be met in order for the IRS to consider the transaction a genuine lease? Why is a favorable IRS ruling regarding the tax status of a lease important to both the lessor and the lessee?
4. One advantage that has often been claimed of lease financing is that it creates "off-balance sheet" financing. Evaluate this benefit in light of FASB *Standard No. 13.*
5. How can leasing allow a firm to effectively "depreciate" land?
6. What effect does leasing have on the stability of a firm's reported earnings?
7. It has been argued that leasing is almost always more expensive than borrowing and owning. Do you think this is true? Why or why not? Under what circumstances is leasing likely to be more desirable than direct ownership?
8. Why do you think it is easier for firms with weak credit positions to obtain lease financing than bank loan financing?
9. Under what circumstances might a firm prefer intermediate-term borrowing to either long- or short-term borrowing?
10. Discuss the advantages and disadvantages of the following types of term loans:
    a. Those that require equal periodic payments
    b. Those that require equal periodic reductions in outstanding principal
    c. Balloon loans
    d. Bullet loans

11. What are the major factors that influence the effective cost of a term loan?
12. Define the following and give an example of each:
a. Affirmative covenants
b. Negative covenants
c. Restrictive covenants
13. What institutions are the primary suppliers of business term loans?
14. Define the following:
a. A conditional sales contract
b. A chattel mortgage
15. Under what conditions would a firm prefer the following?
a. A "fixed-rate" term loan from a bank
b. A "floating-rate" term loan, with the rate tied to the bank's prime rate

19-14 Self-Test Problems

ST1. PepsiCo is planning to acquire a fleet of trucks to support its new Pepsi Express distribution system in the Omaha area. The installed cost of the trucks is $777,000. The salvage value at the end of five years is expected to be $75,000 after-tax. The present value of the expected salvage is $42,600, after discounting at PepsiCo's cost of capital. The present value (using PepsiCo's after-tax cost of debt as the discount rate) of the depreciation tax shield from this project is $210,000. The present value of the after-tax lease payments (also using PepsiCo's after tax cost of debt as the discount rate) is $575,000. PepsiCo will incur (in present value terms) operating costs of $140,000 more, after-tax, if the trucks are owned than if they are leased.
What is the net advantage of leasing in this case? What should PepsiCo do?

ST2. Deseret Resources has received approval for a 5-year term loan from a commercial bank for $2 million at a stated interest rate of 8 percent. The loan requires that interest be paid at the end of each year on the balance remaining at the beginning of each year. In addition, a principal payment of $250,000 must be paid at the end of each of the first four years, with the remaining balance being paid off at the end of five years. The bank will charge Deseret a $50,000 loan-processing fee.
a. What payments are required at the end of each of the five years?
b. What is the effective, pretax cost of this loan?

ST3. MB Leasing has been asked to quote a lease rate for a new computer system for Hastings Distribution Company. The system will cost $385,000 and will be leased by MB Leasing for 5 years. Lease payments will be made at the beginning of each year. MB Leasing will depreciate the system on a straight-line basis of $77,000 per year down to a book salvage value of $0. Actual salvage value at the end of 5 years is estimated to be $52,500. MB Leasing's marginal tax rate is 40 percent. MB Leasing requires a 12 percent after-tax rate of return on this lease. Determine the required annual beginning-of-the-year lease payments.

19-15 Problems*

BASIC

1. MacKenzie Corporation is considering leasing a new asset. The lease would run for eight years and require eight *beginning-of-year* payments of $100,000 each. If MacKenzie capitalizes this lease for financial reporting purposes at a 10 percent rate,

*Color blocks behind the numbers denote problems that have check answers provided at the end of the book.

what asset amount will be reported initially on its balance sheet? What liability amount will be reported on its balance sheet? (Remember, lease payments are made at the beginning of each year, making them an annuity due.)

INTERMEDIATE **2.** Ajax Leasing Services has been approached by Gamma Tools to provide lease financing for a new automated screw machine. The machine will cost \$220,000 and will be leased by Gamma for five years. Lease payments will be made at the beginning of each year. Ajax will depreciate the machine on a straight-line basis of \$44,000 per year down to a book salvage value of \$0. Actual salvage value is estimated to be \$30,000 at the end of five years. Ajax's marginal tax rate is 40 percent. Ajax desires to earn a 12 percent after-tax rate of return on this lease. What are the required annual beginning-of-year lease payments?

INTERMEDIATE **3.** The First National Bank of Springer has established a leasing subsidiary. A local firm, Allied Business Machines, has approached the bank to arrange lease financing for \$10 million in new machinery. The economic life of the machinery is estimated to be 20 years. The estimated salvage value at the end of the 20-year period is \$0. Allied Business Machines has indicated a willingness to pay the bank \$1 million per year at the *end* of each year for 20 years under the terms of a financial lease.

a. If the bank depreciates the machinery on a straight-line basis over 20 years to a \$0 estimated salvage value and has a 40 percent marginal tax rate, what *after-tax* rate of return will the bank earn on the lease?

b. In general, what effect would the use of MACRS depreciation by the bank have on the rate of return it earns from the lease?

CHALLENGE **4.** Jenkins Corporation wants to acquire a \$200,000 computer. Jenkins has a 40 percent marginal tax rate. If owned, the computer would be depreciated on a straight-line basis to a *book* salvage value of \$0. The actual cash salvage value is expected to be \$20,000 at the end of 10 years. If the computer is purchased, Jenkins could borrow the needed funds at an annual pretax interest rate of 10 percent. If purchased, Jenkins will incur annual maintenance expenses of \$1,000. These expenses would not be incurred if the computer is leased. The lease rate would be \$28,000 per year, payable at the beginning of each year. Jenkins' weighted after-tax cost of capital is 12 percent.

a. Compute the *net advantage* to leasing.

b. In general, what effect would the use of accelerated depreciation, such as MACRS, have on the answer to Part a?

c. What alternative, leasing or owning, should be chosen?

INTERMEDIATE **5.** The following stream of after-tax cash flows are available to you as a potential equity investor in a leveraged lease:

End of Year	Cash Flow (After-Tax)	End of Year	Cash Flow (After-Tax)
0	\$−50	6	\$ 0
1	+30	7	−5
2	+20	8	−10
3	+15	9	−15
4	+10	10	+10
5	+5		

The cash flow in year 0 represents the initial equity investment. The positive cash flows in years 1 to 5 result from the tax shield benefits from accelerated depreciation and interest deductibility on the nonrecourse debt. The negative cash flows in years

7 to 9 are indicative of the cash flows generated in a leveraged lease after the earlier-period tax shields have been used. The positive cash flow occurring in year 10 is the result of the asset's salvage value.

a. What problems would you encounter in computing the equity investor's rate of return on this investment?

b. If, as a potential equity investor, you require an 8 percent after-tax rate of return on investments of this type, should you make this investment?

INTERMEDIATE

6. The Jacobs Company desires to lease a numerically controlled milling machine costing \$200,000. Jacobs has asked both First Manufacturers Bank Leasing Corporation and Commercial Associates, Inc. (a commercial finance company) to quote an annual lease rate. Both leasing companies now require a 20 percent *pretax* rate of return on this type of lease. Suppose First Manufacturers estimates the machine's salvage value at the end of the lease to be \$30,000 and Commercial Associates estimates salvage to be \$80,000. Based on this information, what annual (beginning-of-year) lease payments will each leasing company require if the lease term is 5 years? (*Note:* Because the required rate of return of both the bank and the finance company is stated on a pretax basis, you need not consider depreciation or the tax effects of salvage.)

INTERMEDIATE

7. The First National Bank of Great Falls is considering a leveraged lease agreement involving some mining equipment with the Big Sky Mining Corporation. The bank (40 percent tax bracket) will be the lessor; the mining company, the lessee (0 percent tax bracket); and a large California pension fund, the lender. Big Sky is seeking \$50 million, and the pension fund has agreed to lend the bank \$40 million at 10 percent. The bank has agreed to repay the pension fund \$4 million of principal each year plus interest. (The remaining balance will be repaid in a balloon payment at the end of the 5th year.) The equipment will be depreciated on a straight-line basis over a 5-year estimated useful life with no expected salvage value. Assuming that Big Sky has agreed to annual lease payments of \$10 million, calculate the bank's initial cash outflow and its first 2 years of cash inflows.

CHALLENGE

8. As a financial analyst for Muffin Construction, you have been asked to recommend the method of financing the acquisition of new equipment needed by the firm. The equipment has a useful life of 8 years. If purchased, the equipment, which costs \$700,000, will be depreciated under MACRS rules for 7-year class assets. If purchased, the needed funds can be borrowed at a 10 percent pretax annual rate. Muffin's weighted after-tax rate of capital is 12 percent. The *actual* salvage value at the end of 8 years is expected to be \$50,000. Muffin's marginal ordinary tax rate is 40 percent. Annual, beginning-of-year lease payments would be \$160,000.

a. Compute the net advantage to leasing.

b. Should Muffin lease or own the equipment?

CHALLENGE

Spreadsheet Strategies

9. Darling Leasing is considering the lease to Major State University of a piece of equipment costing \$100,000. The period of the lease will be 8 years. The equipment will be depreciated under MACRS rules for 7-year class assets. Darling's marginal tax rate is 40 percent. Annual (end-of-year) lease payments will be \$20,000. Estimated salvage is \$10,000. If Darling requires a 20 percent after-tax return on equipment it leases, should the lease be made?

BASIC

Spreadsheet Strategies

10. Lobo Banks normally provides term loans that require repayment in a series of equal annual installments. If a \$10 million loan is made, what would be the annual end-of-year payments, assuming the following?

a. A 10 percent loan for 12 years

b. A 10 percent loan for 9 years

c. A 6 percent loan for 8 years

Spreadsheet Strategies INTERMEDIATE **11.** Set up the amortization schedule for a 5-year, $1 million, 9 percent term loan that requires equal annual end-of-year payments. Be sure to distinguish between the *interest* and the *principal* portion of each payment. What is the *effective* interest cost of this loan?

CHALLENGE **12.** Set up the amortization schedule for a 5-year, $1 million, 9 percent loan that requires equal annual end-of-year *principal* payments plus interest on the unamortized loan balance. What is the *effective* interest cost of this loan?

Spreadsheet Strategies CHALLENGE **13.** Set up the amortization schedule for a 5-year, $1 million, 9 percent bullet loan. How is the principal repaid in this type of loan? What is the *effective* interest cost of this loan?

CHALLENGE **14.** A firm receives a $1 million, 5-year loan at a 10 percent interest rate. The loan requires annual payments of $125,000 per year (at the end of each year) for years 1 to 4.

a. What payment is required at the end of year 5?

b. What would you call this type of loan?

c. How does it differ from the loan in Problem 11?

d. What is the *effective* interest cost of this loan?

Spreadsheet Strategies CHALLENGE **15.** A $10 million, 5-year loan bears an interest rate of 7 percent. The loan repayment plan calls for five annual end-of-year payments. Each payment is to include an equal amount of principal repayment ($2 million per year) plus accrued interest. Set up the amortization schedule for this loan. Be sure to distinguish between the *interest* and the *principal* portions of each annual payment. What is the *effective* interest cost of this loan?

INTERMEDIATE **16.** Huskie Bank has provided the Mucklup Manufacturing Company with a 2-year term loan for $200,000 at a stated annual rate of interest of 10 percent. Interest for the entire 2-year period must be prepaid; that is, the loan's total interest payments must be made at the same time the loan is granted. Mucklup is required to repay the entire $200,000 principal balance at the end of the 2-year period. Compute the *effective* annual percentage rate of the loan.

CHALLENGE **17.** The James Company has been offered a 4-year loan from its bank in the amount of $100,000 at a stated interest rate of 10 percent per year. The loan will require four equal end-of-year payments of principal and interest plus a $30,000 balloon payment at the end of the fourth year.

a. Compute the amount of each of the end-of-year payments.

b. Prepare a loan amortization schedule detailing the amount of principal and interest in each year's payment.

c. What is the *effective* interest rate on this loan? Prove your answer.

Spreadsheet Strategies CHALLENGE **18.** A $1 million loan requires five end-of-year equal payments of $284,333.

a. Calculate the *effective* interest rate on this loan.

b. How much interest (in dollars) is paid over the life of this loan?

INTERMEDIATE **19.** U.S. Fax has been granted a loan from a commercial finance company for $1 million at a stated interest rate of 10 percent. The loan requires that interest payments be made at the end of each of the next 5 years. At the end of 5 years, the entire loan balance must be repaid. The finance company requires U.S. Fax to pay a $25,000 loan-processing fee at the time the loan is approved. What is the *effective* cost of this loan?

CHALLENGE **20.** A $10 million principal amount, 3-year, term loan carries an interest rate of 10 percent. All interest payments (which would normally be due at the end of each year) are deferred until the end of 3 years. The unpaid interest amount compounds at a 10 percent annual rate during the period(s) it remains unpaid. At the end of 3 years, the borrower must repay the principal amount, the deferred interest, plus interest on the deferred interest. The lender also charges a front-end loan origination fee on this loan of $100,000. Compute the *effective* cost of this loan.

BASIC **21.** Suppose your firm has decided to build a 10-story office building and, just as Sears leased the Sears Tower in Chicago, your firm has decided to contract a professional lessor to build the building and then lease it to you on a 30-year lease. Using a major search engine, find three leasing companies that provide such real estate leasing.

INTEGRATIVE CASE PROBLEM

Lease and Term Loan Analysis

Suppose that FedEx Kinko's has decided to install personal computers and printers in its Pittsburgh store that will be rented to customers on an hourly basis. FedEx Kinko's management has called in consultants from a number of computer suppliers to assist it in designing a system. After considering a number of alternatives, FedEx Kinko's decided that an Apple computer system consisting of eight iMac computers and two printers best meets its current and projected future needs. FedEx Kinko's evaluated the desirability of the acquisition of the Apple computer system using its normal capital budgeting procedures. It found that the computer system has a large positive expected net present value.

Jim Horn, a new management trainee in the financial planning office, has recently been reading about the boom in the leasing industry. He feels that if leasing is growing as rapidly as it seems, there must be some significant advantages to the leasing alternative compared to ownership.

If purchased, the new computer system will cost $50,000 installed. The computer system has an estimated economic life of six years. FedEx Kinko's would depreciate the computer system as a 5-year class asset under MACRS rules to a $0 estimated salvage value. If purchased, FedEx Kinko's could borrow the needed funds from PNC Bank at a 10 percent pretax annual percentage rate of interest.

If FedEx Kinko's decides to lease the computer system, it will be required to make six beginning-of-year lease payments of $11,000 each. FedEx Kinko's weighted cost of capital is 12 percent (after-tax), and its marginal tax rate is 40 percent.

Under both the lease alternative and the borrow-and-buy alternative, FedEx Kinko's will contract with a computer service company to handle the estimated annual service and maintenance costs.

1. Compute the net advantage to leasing.
2. Which alternative should FedEx Kinko's accept? What other factors might be considered?
3. If the computer system is owned and FedEx Kinko's borrows the needed funds from PNC in the form of a bullet loan carrying a 10 percent interest rate instead of an equal payment loan at 10 percent, what effect would this have on the decision to lease or buy?
4. What effect would the use of straight-line depreciation have on the lease-buy decision? (Answer verbally; no calculations are needed. Ignore the bullet loan assumption in Question 3.)
5. If, at the end of 6 years, the computer system is expected to have an actual salvage value of $5,000, what would be the impact on the net advantage of leasing?

CHAPTER 20

Financing with Derivatives

KEY CHAPTER CONCEPTS

1. To manage long-term funding sources effectively, financial managers must understand the different types of securities the firm can issue.
2. An *option* is one type of *derivative* security giving the right to buy or sell an asset at a set price during a specified time period.
   a. A *call* option is an option to *buy* an asset at a set price.
   b. A *put* option is an option to *sell* an asset at a set price.
3. The value of a call option is dependent upon four variables:
   a. The relationship between the option's exercise price and the price of an underlying stock
   b. The time remaining until the option expires
   c. The level of interest rates
   d. The expected volatility of the underlying stock's price
4. Several formal option valuation models are available to compute the value of options, including the Black-Scholes model, which is presented and illustrated in Appendix 20A.
5. A convertible security is a fixed-income security, such as a debenture or a share of preferred stock, that may be exchanged for the company's common stock at the holder's option.
6. A warrant is an option issued by a company to purchase shares of the company's common stock for a particular price during a specified period of time.
7. In a rights offering, common stockholders receive an option to purchase additional shares of the company's common stock, in proportion to the shares they currently own, at a price below the market value.
8. *Swaps* can be used to manage certain types of financial risk.
9. Companies that issue bonds often include a call option in the bond indenture, permitting the company to refund the bonds if interest rates decline. The bond refunding process is detailed in Appendix 20B.

FINANCIAL CHALLENGE

A "Whale" of a Loss for JPMorgan Chase

The chief investment officer (CIO) at JPMorgan Chase was responsible for managing a $370 billion portfolio, which represented about 17 percent of the bank's $2.2 trillion in assets. A group of traders at the London office of the CIO traded complex derivative securities on indexes that tracked high-yield corporate bonds. The stated purpose of these trades was to protect the bank against losses (defaults) on its loan portfolio in the event of a recession in Europe. However, many of these trading positions became hard to unwind and led to losses starting in January 2012. In May 2012, the bank reported losses of more than $2 billion and, by the end of the year, the losses rose to over $6 billion. Brono Iksil, a trader at the London office, known as the "London whale," was at the center of these losses. This trader and the London office had a reputation for making big trades with large upside and downside potential.

JPMorgan claimed that the trades were meant to hedge risks in its loan portfolio, but that the hedges were poorly executed and that management failed to monitor them properly. The bank's CEO (James Dimon) testified before a congressional committee that "We don't gamble" but "We do make mistakes." However, due to the large size and complexity of these trades, some observers believed that the goal of the bank was to generate short-term profits rather than just to protect the bank's large corporate loan portfolio and other investments from losses.

The bank, along with a number of its executives and traders, suffered significant fallout from the episode. As part of the settlement with U.S. and British regulators, JPMorgan paid over $1 billion in civil fines and penalties. The bank also admitted to wrongdoing. This was a departure from typical settlements with the Securities and Exchange Commission, which often allow firms to settle the charges without either admitting or denying guilt. Admitting to having deficient internal controls and disclosing incorrect information related to the trades tarnished JPMorgan's reputation for having the best risk management on Wall Street. With respect to the individual bankers, U.S. prosecutors filed criminal charges against two former traders in the bank's London office. The charges included conspiracy, wire fraud, faking books and records, and causing JPMorgan to make "false and misleading" statements in two securities filings. The "London whale" (Mr. Iksil) avoided prosecution by helping investigators build the case against the other two traders. Lastly, the bank's CEO (Mr. Dimon) saw his 2012 compensation cut in half despite record earnings by the bank.

This chapter discusses the use of derivative instruments, their valuation, and their role in the financing plans of a company.

iStockphoto.com/Henk Badenhorst

Sources: Katy Burne et al., "Hedge or Bet? Parsing a Trade," *The Wall Street Journal* (May 16, 2012): C1; Gregory Zuckerman, "From Caveman to Whale," *The Wall Street Journal* (May 17, 2012): C1; Gregory Zuckerman and Dan Fitzpatrick, "J. P. Morgan Unit Shifts Operations," *The Wall Street Journal* (June 25, 2012): C1; Monica Langley and Dan Fitzpatrick, "Claw Is Out for 'Whale' Officials," *The Wall Street Journal* (July 11, 2012): C1; Dan Fitzpatrick and Joann Lublin, "Regulatory 'Whale' Hunt Advances," *The Wall Street Journal* (December 21, 2012): C1; Dan Fitzpatrick et al., "J. P. Morgan Ordered to Fix Lapses," *The Wall Street Journal* (January 15, 2013): C1; Dan Fitzpatrick et al., "Senate Slams 'Whale' Trades," *The Wall Street Journal* (March 15, 2013): A1; Andrew Akerman et al, "J. P. Morgan Set to Agree to Big Fine for 'Whale'" *The Wall Street Journal* (September 17, 2013) A1; Scott Peterson, "'Whale' Fine Set by CFTC," *The Wall Street Journal* (October 16, 2013): C1.

CHAPTER OBJECTIVES

Upon completion of this chapter, you should have a clear understanding of the following:

1. The methods used to value short-term options and the models used in their valuation, such as the Black-Scholes model
2. The use and valuation of convertible securities, such as convertible bonds and preferred stocks
3. The uses and valuation of warrants
4. The uses and valuation of rights offerings
5. The uses of interest rate swaps and credit default swaps in the financing activities of the firm
6. The procedure for determining whether to call a bond issue

20-1 Introduction

derivative

Options and option-related financing play an important role in the management of a firm's assets and liabilities. Options are one of two important classes of so-called **derivative** securities—that is, securities whose value is derived from another asset. Another important class of derivative securities is forward-type contracts, such as futures contracts and forward contracts. Swaps are another important class of derivative securities. A wide array of securities contain option features, including:

1. *Short-term options* on common stocks, stock market indexes (for example, *Standard & Poor's 500* Stock Price Index), 30-year Treasury bonds (for example, interest rate options), and foreign currency options (for example, on the British pound and Japanese yen). These options are traded on organized exchanges, such as the Chicago Mercantile Exchange and the Chicago Board Options Exchange.[1]
2. *Convertible fixed-income securities*, such as debentures or preferred stocks, that may be exchanged for the company's common stock at the holder's option. By giving the fixed-income security holder an opportunity to share in any increase in its common stock value, the firm is able to reduce potential conflicts between the fixed-income security holders and stockholders, resulting in lower agency costs.
3. *Warrants*, which are options issued by a company to purchase shares of the company's common stock at a particular price during a specified period of time. Warrants are frequently sold to investors as part of a *unit* that consists of a fixed-income security with a warrant attached. As a result, warrants are issued by firms for similar reasons as convertible securities.
4. A *rights offering* occurs when common stockholders are given an option to purchase additional shares of the company's common stock, in proportion to the fraction they currently own, at a price below the market value.

[1]See, for example, Charles W. Smithson and Clifford W. Smith, *Managing Financial Risk* (New York: McGraw-Hill, 1998), for a discussion of many of these instruments. See also Robert Jarrow and Stuart Turnbull, *Derivative Securities* (Cincinnati, OH: South-Western, 1996); and R. L. McDonald, *Derivatives Markets* (Boston: Addison Wesley, 2003).

5. *Swaps* are contracts between financial institutions or companies to exchange cash payments at specified points in time based on the value of an underlying asset.

Also, as we will see in the next section, a firm's common stock can be understood more fully using an options framework.

This chapter examines the characteristics and valuation of options and option-related financing. An understanding of these concepts is necessary to evaluate the impact that decisions to issue or purchase these types of securities have on shareholder wealth.

20-2 Options

option An **option** is a security that gives its holder the right, but not the obligation, to buy or sell an asset at a set price (the *exercise price*) during a specified time period. Options are

call classified as either *call* or *put* options. A **call** is an option to *buy* a particular asset,

put whereas a **put** is an option to *sell* it.

20-2a Option Valuation Concepts

Suppose an investor is offered an opportunity to purchase a call option on one share of McKean Company stock. Consider the following sets of conditions:

1. The option's exercise price is \$25; the McKean stock price is \$30 a share; and the option's expiration date is today. Under these conditions, the investor is willing to pay \$5 for the option. In other words, the value of a call option at expiration is equal to the stock price minus the exercise price, or:

(20.1)
$$\begin{matrix}\text{Value of a call}\\ \text{option at expiration}\end{matrix} = \text{Stock price} - \text{Exercise price}$$

2. The option's exercise price is \$25; the McKean stock price is \$30 a share; and the option expires in six months. Given these conditions, the investor is willing to pay more than \$5 for the option because of the chance that the stock price will increase, thereby also causing the option to increase in value. Therefore,

(20.2)
$$\begin{matrix}\text{Value of a call}\\ \text{option prior}\\ \text{to expiration}\end{matrix} > \text{Stock price} - \text{Exercise price}$$

3. The option's exercise price is \$0.01; the McKean stock price is \$30; and the option expires in six months. Under these somewhat unusual conditions, the option investor is willing to pay *almost as much as the stock price.* However, under no conditions should the investor be willing to pay more than the stock price. Therefore,

(20.3)
$$\begin{matrix}\text{Maximum value}\\ \text{of a call option}\end{matrix} = \text{Stock price}$$

4. The option's exercise price is \$25; the McKean stock price is \$0.01; and the option expires today. The investor most likely is willing to pay nothing for the option given these conditions, but the investor also is not willing to pay someone to take the option "off his hands," because it is an option and can be allowed to expire with no additional cost. Therefore,

(20.4)
$$\begin{matrix}\text{Minimum value}\\ \text{of a call option}\end{matrix} = 0$$

FIGURE 20.1

McKean Company: Call Option Valuation at Different Stock Prices*

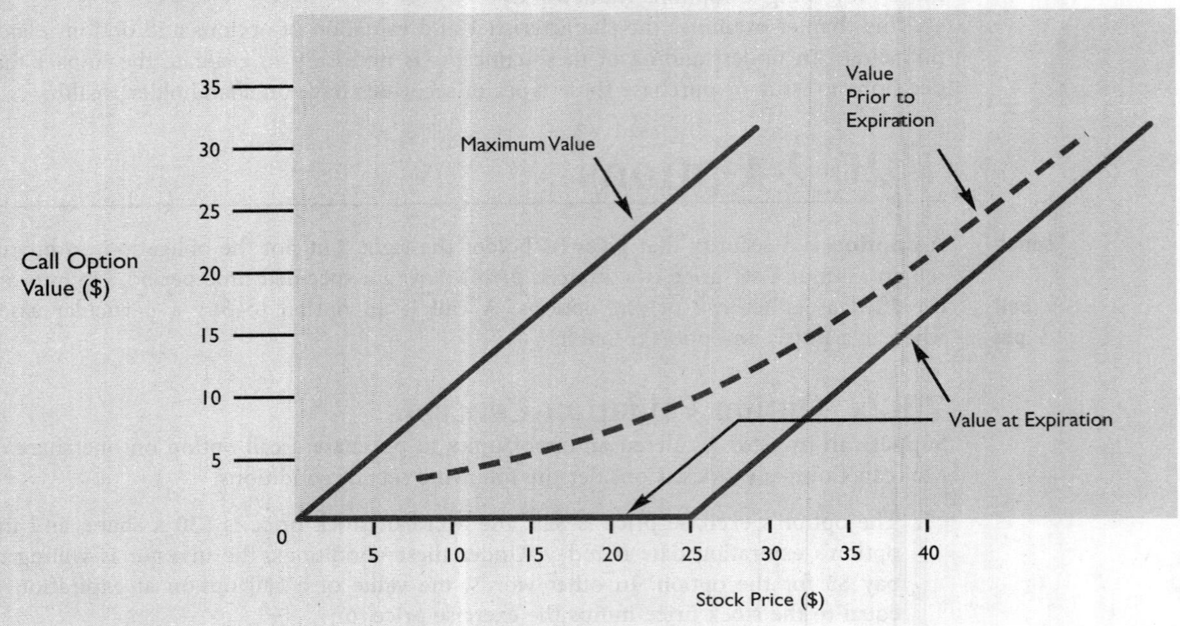

*Exercise price = $25.

The results of these sets of conditions are shown in Figure 20.1.[2]

20-2b Variables Affecting Call Option Valuation

The examples in the previous section illustrate that the value of a call option is dependent on the relationship between the option's exercise price, the price of the underlying stock, and the length of time before the option's expiration date. Two other variables that influence the value of a call option are the level of interest rates and the expected volatility of the underlying stock's price. A discussion of these four variables follows.[3]

Relationship Between the Exercise Price and the Stock Price The effect of the exercise, or strike, price on option value is seen by examining Table 20.1, which lists a number of options quotations for Apple Corporation (formerly Apple Computer). At the time (February 19, 2016) Apple's stock was selling at $96.04 a share. For options expiring on June 17, 2016, the call option with a $100 exercise price sold at a higher price ($4.60) than the option with a $105 exercise price ($2.85) because buyers have to pay more money to exercise options with higher exercise prices. Thus, these options have less value to potential buyers. Therefore, *the higher the exercise price, given the stock price, the lower the call option value*, all other things being equal.

[2]Figure 20.1 shows a $25 exercise price. Technically, Figure 20.1 shows only the results of conditions 1, 2, and 4.

[3]A model for determining the equilibrium value of an option as a function of these variables is developed in Fischer Black and Myron Scholes, "The Pricing of Options and Corporate Liabilities," *Journal of Political Economy* 81 (May/June 1973): 637–654. The Excel templates available with the text include a Black-Scholes option pricing model. The Black-Scholes option pricing model is presented and illustrated in Appendix 20A.

TABLE 20.1

Selected Call Option Prices for Apple Corporation*

	Expiration Date		
Exercise Price	**June 17, 2016**	**October 21, 2016**	**January 20, 2017**
$95	$6.95	$9.70	$11.19
100	4.60	7.30	8.90
105	2.85	5.55	7.03
110	1.68	3.95	5.40

**Note*: Apple's stock was selling at $96.04 a share. The date of the option prices is February 19, 2016; www.finance.yahoo.com.

contingent claim

Because an option's value (payoff) is dependent, or *contingent*, on the value of another security (in this case, the underlying stock), an option is said to be a **contingent claim**.

Time Remaining Until Expiration Date The figures in Table 20.1 show that an option with a $100 exercise price expiring on January 20, 2017, has a higher value ($8.90) than an option with an October 21, 2016 expiration date ($7.30) because investors realize that Apple's stock has a greater chance to increase in value with three additional months before expiration. Thus, *the longer the time remaining before the option expires, the higher the option value,* all other things being equal. Because of this, an option is sometimes referred to as a "wasting asset."

Interest Rates The buyer of common stock incurs either interest expense (explicit cost) if the purchase funds are borrowed or lost interest income (implicit cost) if existing funds are used for purchase. In either case, an interest cost is incurred.[4]

Buying a call option is an alternative to buying stock, and by buying an option, the interest cost associated with holding stock is avoided. Because options are an alternative to ownership, option values are affected by the stock ownership interest costs. As a result, *the higher the level of interest rates* (and, hence, the interest cost of stock ownership), *the higher the call option's value,* all other things being equal.

Expected Stock Price Volatility Suppose an investor has a choice of buying a call option on either stock S or stock V. Both stocks currently sell at $50 a share, and the exercise price of both options is $50. Stock S is expected to be the more stable of the two—its value at the time the option expires has a 50 percent chance of being $45 and a 50 percent chance of being $55 a share. In valuing the call option on stock S, the investor considers only the $55 price and its probability because if the stock goes to $45 a share, the call option with a $50 exercise price becomes worthless.

Stock V is expected to be more volatile; its expected value at the time of option expiration has a 50 percent probability of being $30 and a 50 percent probability of being $70 a share. Similarly, in valuing the call option on stock V, the investor considers only the $70 price and its probability.

The investor now has sufficient information to conclude that the call option on stock V is more valuable than the call option on stock S because a greater return can be earned by investing in an option that has a 50 percent chance of being worth $20 at expiration (stock price − exercise price = $70 − $50 = $20) than an option that has a 50 percent

[4]The interest cost is offset by any dividends received.

HTTP:
Option valuation using the Black-Scholes model is easy using the option calculator available at
www.numa.com

probability of being worth \$5 at expiration (stock price − exercise price = \$55 − \$50 = \$5). Therefore, the *greater the expected stock price volatility, the higher the call option value*, all other things being equal.

20-2c Option Valuation Models

Financial researchers have made considerable progress in developing formal models to value options. Appendix 20A illustrates the popular Black-Scholes option pricing model.

20-2d Call Options on Bonds

Many corporate bonds have a call feature included in the bond indenture. This call option gives the issuing company the right to redeem (call) the bonds prior to their scheduled maturity, usually with the payment of a premium, above the bond's face value, to the bondholder. The most common circumstances that lead to the exercise of the call option by the bond issuer are (1) interest rates have fallen such that the issuer can sell new bonds at a lower interest rate (see Appendix 20B); or (2) the bonds are called as a way to force conversion of the bonds to common stock by the bondholders.

20-2e Common Stock in an Options Framework

Any firm with debt can be analyzed in an options framework.[5] Suppose a start-up firm raises equity capital and also borrows \$7 million, due two years from now. Then, suppose further that the firm undertakes a risky project to develop new computer parts. In two years, the firm must decide whether or not to default on its debt repayment obligation.

Consider this example in an options context. The stockholders can be viewed as having sold this firm to the debtholders for \$7 million when they borrowed the \$7 million. But the stockholders retained an option to buy back the firm. The stockholders have the right to exercise their option by paying off the debt claim at maturity. Whether they do depends on the value of the firm at the time the debt is due. If the value of the firm is greater than the debt claim, the stockholders will exercise their option by paying off the debt. But if the value of the firm is less than the debt claim, the stockholders will let their option expire by not repaying the debt.

This simplified example has interesting implications. Earlier in the options discussion, we showed that the greater the expected stock price volatility, the higher the call option value will be. Therefore, if the stockholders choose high-risk projects with a chance of very large payoffs, they increase the value of their option. But, at the same time, they also increase the likelihood of defaulting on the debt, thereby decreasing its value. Thus it is easy to see how potential conflicts between stockholders and debtholders can occur. These potential conflicts are discussed further in the next section on convertible securities. In fact, we shall see that giving the bondholders an equity stake in the firm decreases the potential for conflicts between stockholders and debtholders.

20-3 Convertible Securities

Both debentures and preferred stock can have convertibility or conversion features. When a company issues convertible securities, its usual intention is the future issuance

[5]The following discussion is based on Scott P. Mason and Robert C. Merton, "The Role of Contingent Claims Analysis in Corporate Finance," in *Recent Advances in Corporate Finance*, Edward I. Altman and Marti G. Subrahmanyam, eds. (Homewood, IL: Richard D. Irwin, 1985).

of common stock. To illustrate, suppose the Beloit Corporation issues 2 million shares of convertible preferred stock at a price of \$50 a share. After the sale, the company receives gross proceeds of \$100 million. Because of the convertibility feature, the company can expect to issue shares of common stock in exchange for the redemption of the convertible preferred stock over some future time period. As a result, convertibles are sometimes described as a deferred equity offering. In the case of Beloit's convertible preferred, each \$50 preferred share can be exchanged for two shares of common stock; that is, the holder has a call option to buy two shares of the company's common stock at an exercise price of \$25 a share. Therefore, if all the preferred shares are converted, the company in effect will have issued 4 million new common shares, and the preferred shares will no longer appear on Beloit's balance sheet. No additional funds are raised by the company at the time of conversion.

20-3a Features of Convertible Securities

Convertible securities

conversion price

As an introduction to the terminology and features of convertible securities, consider the \$115 million, 25-year issue of $6\frac{1}{8}$ percent convertible subordinated debentures sold by Advanced Research Inc. (ARI), a computer software company. **Convertible securities** are exchangeable for common stock at a stated **conversion price**. In the case of the ARI issue, the conversion price at the time of issue was \$84. This means that each \$1,000 debenture was convertible into common stock at \$84 a share.

conversion ratio

The number of common shares that can be obtained when a convertible security is exchanged is determined by the **conversion ratio**, which is calculated as follows:

$$\text{Conversion ratio} = \frac{\text{Par value of security}}{\text{Conversion price}} \quad (20.5)$$

In the case of ARI's convertible subordinated debentures, the conversion ratio at the time of issue was the following:

$$\text{Conversion ratio} = \frac{\$1{,}000}{\$84} = 11.9048$$

HTTP:
Valuing convertible securities and their embedded options is easy using the convertible bond calculator available at
www.numa.com

Thus, each \$1,000 ARI debenture could be exchanged for 11.9048 shares of common stock. Although the conversion ratio may change one or more times during the life of the conversion option, it is more common for it to remain constant.

Normally, the conversion price is set about 15 to 30 percent above the common stock's market price prevailing at the time of issue. For example, at the time ARI issued its convertible debentures, the market price of its common stock was about \$65 a share. The \$19 difference between the conversion price of \$84 and the market price represents a 29 percent premium.

Holders of convertible securities are protected against dilution by the company. For example, suppose ARI were to split its common stock two for one. The conversion price (and therefore, the conversion ratio) would be adjusted so that the holders would not be disadvantaged by the split. Specifically, in the ARI case, the new conversion price would be $\$84 \div 2 = \$42$, and the new conversion ratio would be $11.9048 \times 2 = 23.8096$.

20-3b Managing Long-Term Funding with Convertibles

As a general rule, relatively small, risky companies whose common stock is publicly traded are the principal issuers of convertibles. These companies, for the most part, are rapidly growing and in need of funds to finance their growth. Investors, on the other hand, are frequently reluctant to lend money to small, risky companies without promises of high interest payments and assurances from the company that it will properly manage the debt.

Recall that in Chapter 1 we introduced agency problems and discussed the conflicts that can occur between a firm's stockholders and its creditors. We said that creditors, to protect their interests, often insist on certain protective covenants in the company's bond indentures. The agency costs to properly implement and monitor the covenants can be high, particularly for small, risky companies. As a result, because of potential conflicts between shareholders and bondholders and the associated agency costs, it is usually easier and cheaper to offer the bondholders an equity stake in the company—that is, a convertible security. With an equity stake, bondholders are less concerned about any company attempts to increase the returns to the shareholders by means of risky projects.

In addition to agency costs, there are several other reasons for issuing convertibles. One is that cash flow benefits accrue to the issuing company in the form of lower interest payments or dividends; this occurs because investors are willing to accept the conversion privilege as part of their overall return. As an example, consider again the ARI 6⅛ percent convertible subordinated debentures. At the time ARI sold those convertibles, the company would have had to pay about 9 percent interest on any nonconvertible debt it issued. Thus, the convertibility feature is saving ARI about $2.9 million a year ([0.09 − 0.06125] × $100 million) in interest expense. Typically, firms can issue convertible securities with interest rates or dividend yields about 3 percentage points below similar, nonconvertible issues; that is, issues without convertibility features.

Another reason firms issue convertible securities is to sell common stock at a higher price than the prevailing market price at the time of issue. Suppose a company needs additional equity financing because of a relatively high proportion of fixed-income securities in its capital structure. If the company's management feels the price of its common stock is temporarily depressed, one alternative is to consider issuing a convertible security. With the conversion price typically set about 15 to 30 percent above the market price at the time of issue, the use of a convertible security effectively gives the issuing company the potential for selling common stock above the existing market price. However, for the sale to be successful, conditions in the future must be such that investors will want to exercise their conversion option. Also, if the market price rises considerably above the conversion price, it may turn out that the company would have been better off to wait and sell common stock directly, rather than sell the convertible issue at all.

A final reason for issuing convertible securities centers around the fact that the earnings resulting from projects funded by a particular external financing issue may not begin for some time after financing occurs. For example, the construction and start-up period for a major expansion may be several years. During this period, the company may desire debt or preferred stock financing. Eventually, once the expansion is fully operational and producing income, the company may want to achieve its original goal of additional common stock financing. The deferred issue of common stock minimizes the dilution in earnings per share that results from the immediate issuance of common stock.

20-3c Valuation of Convertible Securities

Because convertible securities possess certain characteristics of both common stock and fixed-income securities, their valuation is more complex than that of ordinary nonconvertible securities. The actual market value of a convertible security depends on both the *common stock value*, or *conversion value*, and the value of a fixed-income security, or *straight-bond* or *investment value*. Each of these is discussed here.[6]

Conversion Value The conversion value, or stock value, of a convertible bond is defined as the conversion ratio times the common stock's market price:

(20.6)
$$\text{Conversion value} = \text{Conversion ratio} \times \text{Stock price}$$

To illustrate, assume that a firm offers a convertible bond that can be exchanged for 40 shares of common stock. If the market price of the firm's common stock is $20 per share, the conversion value is $800. If the market price of the common stock rises to $25 per share, the conversion value becomes $1,000. And if the stock price rises to $30 per share, the conversion value becomes $1,200.

In the case of ARI's convertible bonds, the conversion value was 11.9048 × $65 (the price per common share at the time of issue), $773.81 or $774.

straight-bond value

Straight-Bond Value The **straight-bond value**, or investment value, of a convertible debt issue is the value it would have if it did not possess the conversion feature (option). Thus, it is equal to the sum of the present value of the interest annuity plus the present value of the expected principal repayment:

(20.7)
$$\text{Straight-bond value} = \sum_{t=1}^{n} \frac{\text{Interest}}{(1 + k_d)^t} + \frac{\text{Principal}}{(1 + k_d)^n}$$

where k_d is the current yield to maturity for *nonconvertible* debt issues of similar quality and maturity; *t*, the number of years; and *n*, the time to maturity.

Considering again ARI's 6⅛ percent, 25-year convertible debentures, the bond value at the time of issue is calculated as follows, assuming that 9 percent is the appropriate discount rate (and that interest is paid annually):

$$\begin{aligned}\text{Straight-bond value} &= \sum_{t=1}^{25} \frac{\$61.25}{(1.09)^t} + \frac{\$1{,}000}{(1.09)^{25}} \\ &= \$61.25(\text{PVIFA}_{0.09,\,25}) + \$1{,}000(\text{PVIF}_{0.09,\,25}) \\ &= \$61.25(9.823) + \$1{,}000(0.116) \\ &= \$717.66 \text{ or } \$718\end{aligned}$$

Market Value The market value of a convertible debt issue is usually somewhat above the higher of the conversion or the straight-bond value; this is illustrated in Figure 20.2.

conversion premium

The difference between the market value and the higher of the conversion or the straight-bond value is the **conversion premium** for which the issue sells. This premium tends to be largest when the conversion value and the straight-bond value are nearly identical. This set of circumstances allows investors to participate in any common stock appreciation while having some degree of downside protection because the straight-bond value can represent a "floor" below which the market value will not fall.[7] The ARI convertible debentures described in this section were offered to the public at $1,000 per bond and quickly were bought up by investors. In this case, investors were willing to pay $1,000 for an issue having a conversion value of approximately $774 and a bond value of $718. The $1,000 market value contained a premium of $226 over the conversion value (which was higher than the bond value). This premium can be thought of as

[6] For simplicity, only convertible debt is considered in this discussion, although the principles apply to convertible preferred stock as well.

[7] The straight-bond value may fall if long-term interest rates rise or if the perceived risk of the firm increases.

FIGURE 20.2

Advanced Research: Convertible Debenture Valuation at Different Stock Prices*

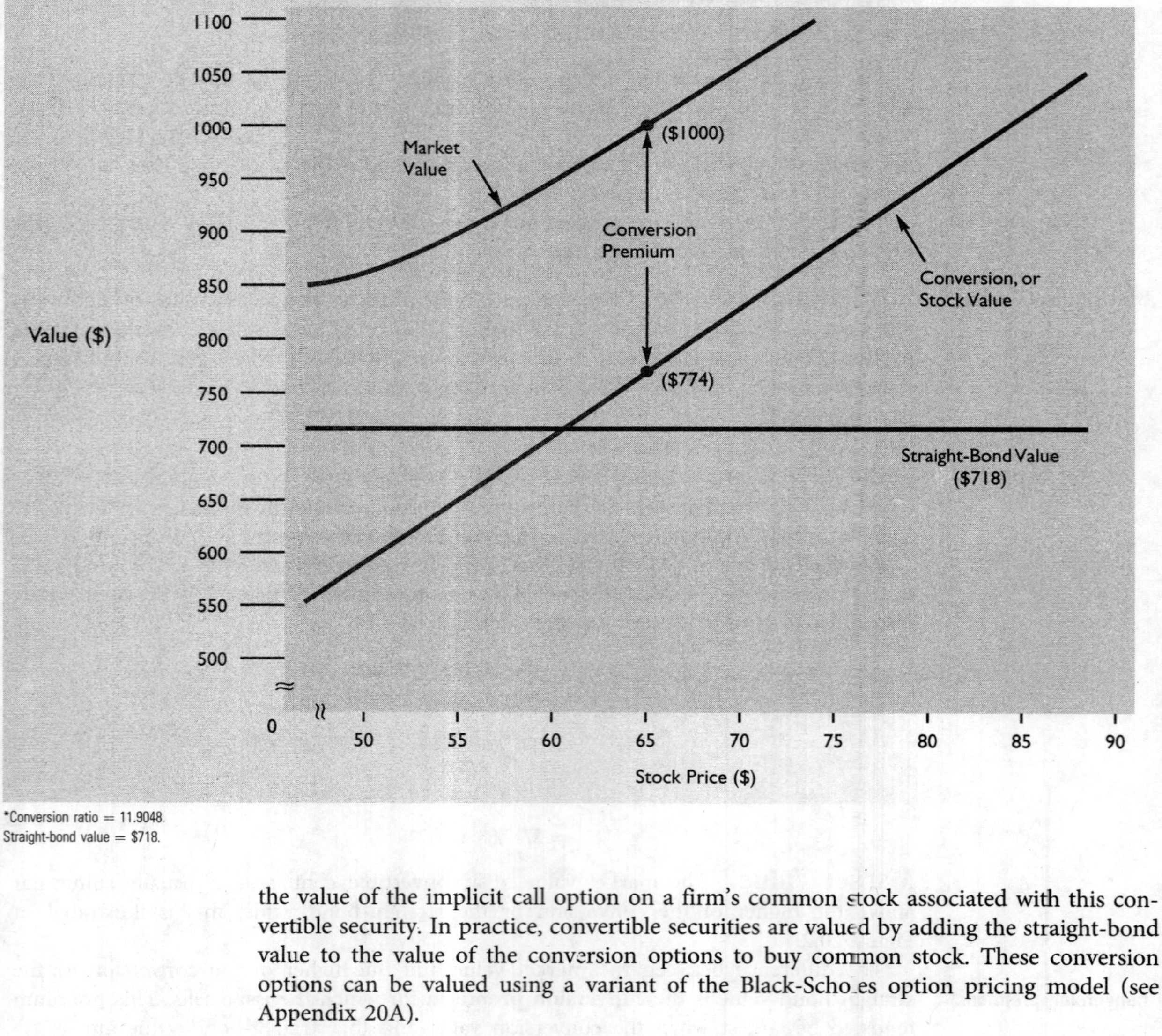

*Conversion ratio = 11.9048.
Straight-bond value = $718.

the value of the implicit call option on a firm's common stock associated with this convertible security. In practice, convertible securities are valued by adding the straight-bond value to the value of the conversion options to buy common stock. These conversion options can be valued using a variant of the Black-Scholes option pricing model (see Appendix 20A).

20-3d Converting Convertible Securities

Conversion can occur in one of two ways:

- It may be *voluntary* on the part of the investor.
- It can be effectively *forced* by the issuing company.

Whereas voluntary conversions can occur at any time prior to the expiration of a conversion feature, forced conversions occur at specific points in time.

The method most commonly used by companies to force conversion is the exercise of the *call* privilege on the convertible security. For example, consider the Compaq Computer (now part of Hewlett-Packard Company) convertible bonds maturing in 2012, which the company decided to call for redemption in 1988. The bonds had a conversion ratio of 25.22, and the market price of the Compaq common stock at the time of the call was $61.25 per share. Therefore, the conversion value was approximately $1,545 per bond. The call price—which was set and agreed upon by both the borrower and the lender at the time of the original issue—was $1,047.25 per bond.

Holders of the Compaq convertibles had two alternatives under these circumstances:

- Conversion, in which case the holder would receive common stock having a market value of $1,545 per bond
- Redemption, in which case the holder would receive $1,047.25 in cash for each bond

The conversion alternative was the obvious choice because even those investors who did not wish to hold the common stock could sell it upon conversion for more money than they would receive from redemption. By calling the bonds, Compaq was able to remove $150 million in long-term debt from its balance sheet without having to redeem the bonds for cash, and was able to save $7.9 million a year in interest expense.

Another way in which a company can encourage conversion is by raising its dividend on common stock to a high enough level that holders of convertible securities are better off converting them and receiving the higher dividend.

20-3e Convertible Securities and Earnings Dilution

If a convertible security (or warrant) issue is ultimately exchanged for common stock, the number of common shares will increase and earnings per share will be reduced (that is, diluted), all other things being equal. Companies are required (by Accounting Principles Board Opinion 15) to disclose this potential dilution by reporting both primary and fully diluted earnings per share. Primary earnings per share are calculated based on the number of common shares outstanding plus common stock equivalents. A common stock equivalent must meet certain tests, but it basically includes any convertible security that derives its value primarily from the common stock into which it can be converted. Fully diluted earnings per share are calculated based on the assumption that *all* dilutive securities are converted into common shares. In calculating primary or fully diluted earnings per share, earnings must be adjusted for the interest or preferred dividends saved as the result of conversion.

20-4 Warrants

warrant

As mentioned earlier in this chapter, a **warrant** is a company-issued option to purchase a specific number of shares of the issuing company's common stock at a particular price during a specified time period. Warrants are frequently issued in conjunction with an offering of debentures or preferred stock. In these instances, like convertibles, warrants tend to lower agency costs.

In addition, during the 1980s, the various ways in which warrants were used as a financing device seemed to expand. For example, warrants were used in conjunction with bond swaps, equity offerings, and debt restructurings. In the 1987 bankruptcy reorganization of Global-Marine, now part of Transocean, an off-shore operator of oil and gas drilling rigs, warrants were issued to preferred and common stockholders (along with a small percentage of the new common stock). More recently, as part of its bankruptcy settlement in 2009, General Motors' bondholders forgave $27 billion of debt in exchange for common stock and warrants in the new company. Also, small, high-risk companies in need of additional financing may offer warrants to prospective lenders in order to give the potential for high expected returns as compensation for the loan's high risk.

20-4a Features of Warrants

To understand some of the features of financing with warrants, consider Owens Corning, which in 2006 issued 7.8 million Series B warrants in conjunction with the company's emergence from bankruptcy. Each warrant allowed the purchase of one common share at $45.25. The **exercise price** of a warrant is the price at which the holder can purchase common stock of the issuing company. The exercise price of Owens Corning Series B warrants was $45.25, approximately 64 percent above the $27.60 per-share market price of the common stock at the time of issue. The exercise price normally remains constant over the life of the warrant. Exceptions to this rule include stock splits and dividend payments. When this occurs, the exercise price of the warrant is adjusted to reflect the new number of shares and share price. For example, Ford Motor Company's warrants, issued December 9, 2009, were adjusted to reflect the payment of a $0.05 per share cash dividend in the fourth quarter of 2012. The price of each warrant was reduced from $9.05 to $9.01. Also, the number of shares to be received upon exercising one warrant was increased from 1.0167 shares to 1.0212 shares. Typically, the life of a warrant is between 5 and 10 years, although on occasion the life can be longer or even perpetual.

exercise price

When the management of Owens Corning issued the warrants, they hoped the common share price would rise above the $45.25 level and remain there, especially after the warrants expired, because this would mean that the company could reasonably expect holders to exercise their warrants. If this happened, Owens Corning would realize its goal of raising additional capital totaling approximately $353 million at expiration (7.8 million warrants × $45.25 per warrant). In contrast, with convertible securities such as convertible bonds or preferred stock, the company does not receive additional funds at the time of conversion.

If a warrant is issued as part of a "unit" with a fixed-income security, the warrant is usually *detachable* from the debenture or preferred stock; this means that purchasers of the units have the option of selling the warrants separately and continuing to hold the debenture or preferred stock. As a result, other investors can purchase and trade warrants.

Prior to 1970, warrants were not usually used as a financing vehicle by large, well-established firms. In April of that year, however, AT&T sold $1.6 billion of 30-year debentures with warrants to buy 31.4 million common shares at $52 each through May 15, 1975. The use of warrant financing by AT&T undoubtedly caused other large firms to consider warrants. Also, before 1970, warrants were normally either listed on the American Stock Exchange (now known as NYSE MKT LLC) or traded over the counter because the New York Stock Exchange would not list them. However, with the AT&T warrants, the NYSE changed its policy and began to list warrants of NYSE companies if the warrants met certain requirements, including a life greater than five years. Since then, various other companies—including Travelers, Zale, Ford, General Motors, Kinder Morgan, and Raytheon—have had their warrants trade on the NYSE.

Holders of warrants do not have the rights of common stockholders, such as the right to vote for directors or receive dividends, until they exercise their warrants.

20-4b Reasons for Issuing Warrants

The primary reason for issuing warrants with a fixed-income security offering is to lower agency costs. In addition, just as with convertible securities, warrants can permit a company to sell common stock at a price above the price prevailing at the time of original issue. Warrants also allow a company to sell common stock in the future without incurring significant issuance costs at the time of sale.

20-4c Valuation of Warrants

In general, the value of a warrant depends upon the same variables that affect call option valuation. Because a warrant's value depends upon the price of the issuing company's stock, it is a contingent claim, just like an option. In this connection, the formula value of a warrant (also called "the value at expiration") is defined by the following equation:

$$\begin{matrix}\text{Formula} \\ \text{value of a} \\ \text{warrant}\end{matrix} = \text{Max}\left\{\$0;\ \left(\begin{matrix}\text{Common stock} \\ \text{market price} \\ \text{per share}\end{matrix} - \begin{matrix}\text{Exercise} \\ \text{price} \\ \text{per share}\end{matrix}\right) \times \begin{matrix}\text{Number of shares} \\ \text{obtainable with} \\ \text{each warrant}\end{matrix}\right\} \quad \textbf{(20.8)}$$

At the time of issue, a warrant's exercise price is normally greater than the common stock price. Even though the calculated formula value may be negative, it is considered to be zero because securities cannot sell for negative amounts. For example, at the time of issue (October 2006), the Owens Corning warrants had an exercise price of \$45.25, and the firm's common stock price was \$27.60 per share. Each warrant entitled the holder to one share, and the formula value was zero:

$$\begin{aligned}\text{Formula value} &= \text{Max}\{\$0;\ (\$27.60 - \$45.25)\ (1)\} \\ &= \$0\end{aligned}$$

If the stock price rises above the exercise price of the warrant, the formula value will be greater than zero. For example, if Owens Corning's stock price is \$60 and if the warrant price is \$19.32, then the formula of the warrant would be:

$$\begin{aligned}\text{Formula value} &= \text{Max}\{\$0;\ (\$60 - \$45.25)\ (1)\} \\ &= \$14.75\end{aligned}$$

HTTP:
Valuing warrants is easy using the warrant calculator available at
www.numa.com

and the warrant would be selling for 31 percent above the formula value. Prior to the warrant's expiration, we see that the expected market price of the warrant is greater than the formula value, just as we discussed in the case of options.

On the expiration date of a warrant, the expected market price of the warrant would be equal to the formula value, as was the case for options (discussed earlier). For the Owens Corning warrants, which expired on October 31, 2013, the market price of the stock was \$35.93 on this date, and the market price of the warrants was equal to the formula value, \$0.

$$\begin{aligned}\text{Formula value} &= \text{Max}\{\$0;\ (\$35.93 - \$45.25)\ (1)\} \\ &= \$0\end{aligned}$$

As a result, the warrants expired and were not exercised and Owens Corning did not issue any additional common stock at that time.

20-4d Comparison of Convertible Securities and Warrants

Having covered the characteristics and valuation of convertible securities and warrants, we now summarize the similarities of and differences between these types of securities. In this comparison, we are assuming that the warrants are issued as part of a fixed-income security offering. The similarities include the following:

1. Both convertibles and warrants tend to lessen potential conflicts between fixed-income security holders and stockholders, thereby reducing agency costs.
2. The intention is the deferred issuance of common stock at a price higher than that prevailing at the time of the convertible or warrant issue.

3. Both the convertibility option and the attachment of warrants result in interest expense or preferred dividend savings for the issuing company, thereby easing potential cash flow problems.

Some of the differences include the following:

1. The company receives additional funds at the time warrants are exercised, whereas no additional funds are received at the time convertibles are converted.
2. The fixed-income security remains on the company's books after the exercise of warrants; in the case of convertibles, the fixed-income security is exchanged for common stock and taken off the company's books.
3. Because of the call feature, convertible securities potentially give the company more control than warrants over when the common stock is issued.

20-5 Analysis of Rights Offerings

In addition to the sale of new common stock through underwriters, new equity capital can be raised using another option-based financing approach called a *rights offering*. In a **rights offering**, the firm's existing stockholders are given an *option* to purchase a fraction of the new shares equal to the fraction they currently own, thereby maintaining their original ownership percentage.

rights offering

Hence, rights offerings are used in equity financing by companies whose charters contain the *preemptive right*. In addition, rights offerings *may* be used as a means of selling common stock in companies in which preemptive rights do not exist. The number of rights offerings has gradually declined over the years.

The following example illustrates what a rights offering involves. The Miller Company has 10 million shares outstanding and plans to sell an additional 1 million shares via a rights offering. In this case, each right entitles the holder to purchase 0.1 share, and it takes 10 rights to purchase 1 share. (The **rights** themselves really are the documents describing the offer. Each stockholder receives one right for each share currently held.) The company has to decide on a *subscription price*, which is the price the right holder will have to pay per new share. The subscription price has to be less than the market price, or right holders will have no incentive to subscribe to the new issue. As a general rule, subscription prices are 5 to 20 percent below market prices. If the Miller Company's stock is selling at $40 per share, a reasonable subscription price might be $35 per share.

rights

20-5a Valuation of Rights

Because a right represents an opportunity to purchase stock below its current market value, the right itself has a certain value, which is calculated under two sets of circumstances:

- The *rights-on* case
- The *ex-rights* case

rights-on
ex-rights

A stock is said to "trade with **rights-on**" when the purchasers receive the rights along with the shares they purchase. In contrast, a stock is said to "trade **ex-rights**" when the stock purchasers no longer receive the rights.

For example, suppose the Miller Company announced on May 15 that shareholders of record as of Friday, June 20, will receive the rights. This means that anyone who purchased stock on or before Wednesday, June 18, will receive the rights, and anyone who purchased stock on or later than June 19 will not.[8] The stock trades with rights-on up to and including June 18 and goes ex-rights on June 19, the *ex-rights date*. On that date, the stock's market value falls by the value of the right, all other things being equal.

The formula (or terminal) value of a right for the rights-on case can be calculated using the following equation:

(20.9)
$$R = \frac{M_o - S}{N + 1}$$

where R is the formula value for the right; M_o, the rights-on market price of the stock; S, the subscription price of the right; and N, the number of rights necessary to purchase one new share. In the Miller Company example, the right's formula value is:

$$R = \frac{\$40 - \$35}{10 + 1}$$
$$= \$0.455$$

The formula value of a **right** when the stock is trading ex-rights can be calculated by using the following equation:

(20.10)
$$R = \frac{M_e - S}{N}$$

where M_e is the ex-rights market price of the stock; S, the subscription price of the right; and N, the number of rights necessary to purchase one new share. If the Miller stock were trading ex-rights, the formula value of a right would be as follows:

$$R = \frac{\$39.545 - \$35}{10}$$
$$= \$0.455$$

(Note that M_e is lower than M_o by the amount of the right; that is, \$40 versus \$39.545.)

Some shareholders may decide not to use their rights because of lack of funds or some other reason. These stockholders can sell their rights to other investors who wish to purchase them. Thus, a market exists for the rights, and a market price is established for them. Generally, the market price is higher than the formula value until the time of expiration. The same factors discussed previously, which determine the value of a call option, also determine the value of a right, since a right is simply a short-term call option on the stock. As with call options, investors can earn a higher return by purchasing the rights than by purchasing the stock because of the leverage rights provide. In general, the premium of market value over formula value decreases as the rights expiration date approaches. A right is worthless after its expiration date.

One can demonstrate that there is no net gain or loss to shareholders either from exercising the right or from selling the right at the formula value.[9] For example, suppose an investor owns 100 shares of the Miller Company common stock discussed earlier. The investor is entitled to purchase 10 (0.1 × 100) additional shares at \$35 per share. Prior to the rights offering, the 100 shares of Miller Company are valued at \$4,000 (100 shares × \$40 per share). *Exercise* of the rights will give the investor 10 additional shares at a cost of \$35 per share, or a total of \$350. These 110 shares will be valued at \$4,350 (110 × \$39.545). Deducting the cost of these additional shares (\$350) from the total value of the shares (\$4,350), one obtains the same value (\$4,000) as before the rights offering. Sale of the rights will yield \$45.50 (100 × \$0.455) to the investor. Combining this value

---

[8]A stock purchaser becomes a shareholder of record two *trading* days after purchase.

[9]This analysis ignores any brokerage fees incurred in the sale of the rights.

with the \$3,954.50 (100 × \$39.545) value of the 100 shares still owned, one also obtains the same value (\$4,000) as before the rights offering.

20-6 Swaps[10]

swap

Swaps are another type of financial derivative that can be used in the financing activities of a firm. A **swap** is a contract between financial institutions or companies to exchange cash payments at specified points in time based on the value of an underlying asset, such as a currency (exchange rates), debt instrument (interest rates), commodity, or stock. Many financial institutions such as investment banks, commercial banks, insurance companies, and hedge funds act as intermediaries in arranging swaps. Some intermediaries act as brokers and receive commissions for finding counterparties for the transaction. Other intermediaries act as dealers or market makers by themselves as counterparties to swap contracts. This section focuses on swaps related to debt instruments—namely, *interest rate swaps* and *credit default swaps.*

20-6a Interest Rate Swaps

Interest rate swaps can be used to protect a financial institution or business against fluctuations in interest rates.[11] Like futures contracts, swaps can be used to hedge against interest rate risk. Although futures contracts are more effective in hedging against short-term risks (less than one year), swaps are more effective in hedging against long-term risks (up to 10 years or even longer). It was estimated that \$320 *trillion* (notional value[12]) of interest rate swap contracts were outstanding in June 2015.[13]

interest rate swaps

Of the many and various types of **interest rate swaps**, the most basic is one in which a party is seeking to exchange floating rate interest payments for fixed rate interest payments, or vice versa. Consider the case of a finance company (for example, Ford Credit) with floating rate debt (for example, floating rate bonds) and fixed rate loans (for example, automobile installment loans) that wants to protect itself against an increase in interest rates. The finance company can enter into a swap contract with another party who agrees to pay the interest costs in excess of a specified rate (for example, 7.5 percent) for a given period of time (for example, three years). Should interest rates increase in the future, the finance company will receive rising payments from the other party to the swap agreement to cover its losses.

The other party to the swap agreement could be a bank, which borrows at fixed interest rates (for example, certificates of deposit) and lends money to corporations at floating rates. The bank may desire to protect itself against a decline in interest rates. Should interest rates decline in the future, the bank will continue receiving fixed interest payments from the other party to the swap agreement. This swap is illustrated in Figure 20.3. In most interest rate swaps, the floating rate used in computing the payments between the parties to the swap is tied to the London Interbank Offered Rate (LIBOR). (LIBOR is discussed in Chapter 2.) In this example, it is 2.5 percentage points

HTTP:
Information on swaps can be found at the Web site maintained by the Chicago Board of Trade.

www.cmegroup.com/company/cbot.html
www.numa.com

[10] See John F. Marshall and Kenneth R. Kapnes, *Understanding Swap Finance* (Cincinnati, OH: South-Western, 1990), for a more detailed discussion of interest rate swaps.

[11] Futures contracts are discussed in Chapter 2.

[12] *Notional value* refers to the total amount of the debt instrument, not the amount of the payments exchanged between the counterparties to the swap contract.

[13] "Semiannual OTC Derivatives Statistics" (December 6, 2015), Bank for International Settlements, www.bis.org.

FIGURE 20.3

Interest Rate Swap

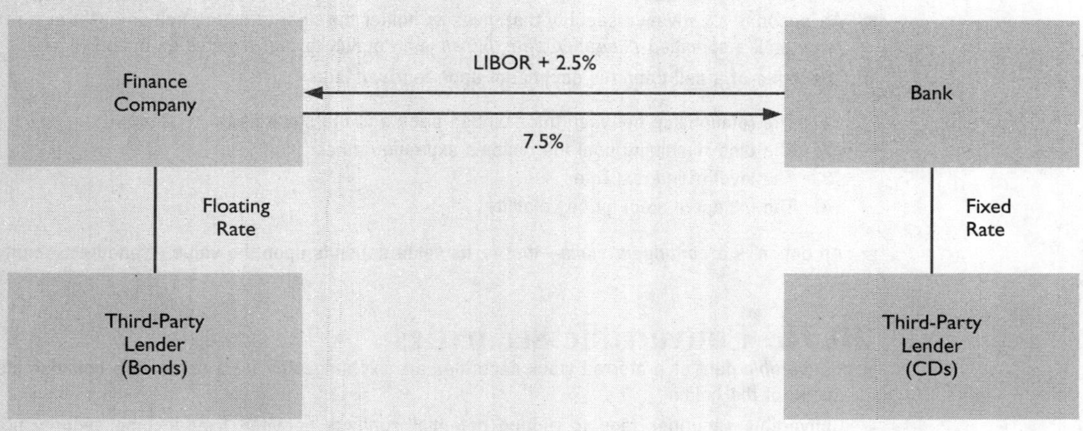

above LIBOR. Generally, in a swap agreement, the parties exchange only the interest differential, not the principal or actual interest payments.

20-6b Credit Default Swaps

credit default swap

A **credit default swap** is a type of credit insurance contract in which one party pays another party a fee (premium) to protect itself from the risk of default on a debt instrument. These debt instruments include bonds, bank loans, and mortgages. If the borrower defaults on the debt instrument, then the insurer compensates the holder of the debt instrument for the loss. The insurer is required to post collateral to support its payment obligation. The estimated size of the credit default swap market was nearly $14.6 *trillion* (notional value) in June 2015.[14]

The market for the various types of swaps was largely unregulated prior to the financial crisis of 2008–2009. Unlike other derivative contracts that are traded on organized exchanges, such as those for options and futures contracts, there was no clearinghouse to guarantee fulfillment of the contracts. The issuers of these swap contracts got into financial trouble when the housing market collapsed, causing massive defaults on these securities. Without adequate collateral, a number of the financial institutions that issued these contracts were forced to declare bankruptcy, such as Lehman Brothers, or to accept government bailouts, such as American International Group (AIG).

Following the financial crisis, the United States and most of the major European Union (EU) countries instituted new regulations designed to curb some of the abuses that contributed to the crisis. With respect to derivative securities, central clearinghouses were to be established to standardize and guarantee payment of the contracts. The regulations were designed to make the markets more liquid and transparent and hence less likely to lead to the problems encountered during the crisis.

[14]"Semiannual OTC Derivatives Statistics" (December 6, 2015), Ibid.

20-7 Summary

20-7a Options

- An *option* is a derivative security that gives its holder the right to buy or sell an asset at a set *exercise price* until a specified *expiration date.* A *call* is an option to *buy,* a *put* is an option to *sell.*
- The value of a call option is dependent upon four variables:

  1. The relationship between the exercise price and the stock price
  2. The time remaining until the option's expiration date
  3. The level of interest rates
  4. The expected stock price volatility

- An option is a *contingent claim*—that is, its value depends upon the value of another security.

20-7b Convertible Securities

- *Convertible* debt or preferred stock securities are exchangeable for a company's common stock at the option of the holder.
- Convertible securities tend to reduce potential conflicts between fixed-income security holders and stockholders, resulting in reduced agency costs.
- The price at which a convertible security is exchangeable for a common stock is the *conversion price.*
- The number of common shares that can be obtained when a convertible security is exchanged is the *conversion ratio,* which is calculated by dividing the par value of the security by the conversion price.
- At the time of issue, the conversion price normally exceeds the market price of the common stock by about 15 to 30 percent.
- Convertible securities possess characteristics of both common stock and fixed-income securities. Their market value is a function of both their stock, or conversion, value and their value as a fixed-income security. The *conversion value* is calculated by multiplying the conversion ratio by the current stock price.

20-7c Warrants

- A *warrant* is an option issued by a company to purchase shares of the company's common stock at a particular price during a specific time period. Warrants are frequently issued as part of a fixed-income security offering.
- The *exercise price* of a warrant is the price at which the holder can purchase common stock of the issuing company.
- The primary reason for issuing a warrant with a fixed-income security offering is that warrants tend to lower agency costs.
- The *formula value* of a warrant depends on the number of common shares each warrant is entitled to receive when exercised and the difference between the common stock market price and the warrant exercise price. Warrants normally sell at a premium over their formula value.

20-7d Rights Offering

- In a *rights offering,* common stockholders receive stock purchase rights, which entitle them to purchase additional shares of the company's common stock, in proportion to the shares they currently own, at a price below the market value.
- In a rights offering, there is no gain or loss to shareholders from either exercising the rights or selling the rights at the formula value.

20-7e Swaps

- A *swap* is a contract between financial institutions or companies to exchange cash payments at specified points in time based on the value of an underlying asset.
- An *interest rate swap* can be used to hedge against fluctuations in interest rates.
- A *credit default swap* can be used to protect against the risk of default on a debt instrument.

Important Equations

$$\text{Value of a call option at expiration} = \text{Stock price} - \text{Exercise price}$$

$$\text{Value of a call option prior to expiration} > \text{Stock price} - \text{Exercise price}$$

$$\text{Maximum value of a call option} = \text{Stock price}$$

$$\text{Minimum value of a call option} = 0$$

$$\text{Conversion ratio} = \frac{\text{Par value of security}}{\text{Conversion price}}$$

$$\text{Conversion value} = \text{Conversion ratio} \times \text{Stock price}$$

$$\text{Straight-bond value} = \sum_{t=1}^{n} \frac{\text{Interest}}{(1 + k_d)^t} + \frac{\text{Principal}}{(1 + k_d)^n}$$

$$\text{Formula value of a warrant} = \text{Max}\left\{ \$0; \left(\begin{matrix}\text{Common stock}\\ \text{market price}\\ \text{per share}\end{matrix} - \begin{matrix}\text{Exercise}\\ \text{price}\\ \text{per share}\end{matrix} \right) \times \begin{matrix}\text{Number of shares}\\ \text{obtainable with}\\ \text{each warrant}\end{matrix} \right\}$$

$$R = \frac{M_o - S}{N + 1}$$

$$R = \frac{M_e - S}{N}$$

20-8 Questions and Topics for Discussion

1. Define the following terms:
   a. Option
   b. Call
   c. Put
   d. Contingent claim
2. What are the similarities and differences between options and warrants?
3. What variables are important in determining call option prices?
4. Will call option values generally be higher at a time when interest rates are relatively high, compared with a time when interest rates are relatively low, all other things being equal?
5. How does a stock's expected price volatility affect the value of a call option on it?
6. In what ways are convertible securities and warrants similar? Dissimilar?
7. Why do companies issue convertible securities?
8. What is the relationship between conversion value, bond value, and market value for a convertible security?
9. How can a company effectively force conversion of a convertible security?
10. What is the *preemptive right* of common stockholders? In what type of company is the preemptive right important? Unimportant?
11. Why would a firm use an interest rate swap as part of its financing strategy?

20-9 Self-Test Problems

ST1. The Bradford Company has debentures outstanding (par value = $1,000) that are convertible into common stock at a price of $40 per share. The convertible bonds have a coupon interest rate of 8 percent and mature in 20 years. The convertible bonds are callable at 102 percent of par value. The company has a marginal tax rate of 40 percent.

a. Calculate the conversion value of the bonds if Bradford's common stock is selling for $35 per share.
b. Calculate the straight-bond value, assuming that straight debt of equivalent risk and maturity is yielding 11 percent.
c. Determine the conversion premium if the market value of the bonds is $925.
d. Determine the conversion value of the bonds if the company's common stock price increases to $55 per share.
e. Given the information in Part d, what is a realistic estimate of the market price of the convertible bond issue? (No numerical calculations are necessary for this part of the problem.)

ST2. The Somerset Company has warrants outstanding that expire in three years. Each warrant entitles the holder to purchase one share of common stock at an exercise price of $40 per share. Determine the formula value and premium over the formula value if the respective prices of common stock and warrants are:

a. $32 per share and $1.50 per warrant
b. $40 per share and $3.50 per warrant
c. $48 per share and $10 per warrant

ST3. The Seven Springs Company plans to sell an additional 2 million shares of common stock through a rights offering. The company currently has 20 million shares outstanding. Each shareholder will receive one right for each share currently held. Therefore, each right will enable shareholders to purchase 0.10 shares. Seven Springs common stock currently is selling for $25 per share and the subscription price of the rights will be $22 per share.

a. Calculate the formula value of the right for both the *rights-on* and *ex-rights* cases.

b. Determine the amount that the market price of the company's stock is expected to drop on the ex-rights date, assuming all other things are equal.

c. If the market price of Seven Springs common stock increases to $30 per share, determine the formula value of the rights (*rights-on* case).

20-10 Problems*

BASIC

1. The BWS Corporation stock is selling at $50 a share today.

a. Calculate the value of a BWS call option if its exercise price is $40 and it expires today.

b. What can you say about the value of a BWS call option if its exercise price is $40 and it expires in six months?

c. Calculate the value of a BWS call option if its exercise price is $60 and it expires today.

d. What can you say about the value of a BWS call option if its exercise price is $60 and it expires in six months?

BASIC

2. The BWS Corporation stock is selling at $50 a share today.

a. Calculate the value of a BWS put option if its exercise price is $40 and it expires today.

b. What can you say about the value of a BWS put option if its exercise price is $40 and it expires in six months?

c. Calculate the value of a BWS put option if its exercise price is $60 and it expires today.

d. What can you say about the value of a BWS put option if its exercise price is $60 and it expires in six months?

INTERMEDIATE

3. The LeMonde Corporation has debentures outstanding (par value = $1,000) that are convertible into the company's common stock at a price of $25 per share. The convertibles have a coupon interest rate of 6 percent and mature 20 years from now. In addition, the convertible debenture is callable at 107 percent of par value. The company has a marginal tax rate of 40 percent.

a. Calculate the conversion value if LeMonde's common stock is selling at $25 a share.

b. Calculate the bond value, assuming that straight debt of equivalent risk and maturity is yielding 9 percent.

c. Using the answers from Parts a and b, what is a realistic estimate of the market value of the convertible debentures? (No calculation is necessary for this part of the problem.)

d. What is the conversion value if the company's common stock price increases to $35 a share?

---

*Color blocks behind the numbers denote problems that have check answers provided at the end of the book.

e. Given the situation presented in Part d, what is a realistic estimate of the market value of the convertible debenture? (No calculation is necessary for this part of the problem.)

f. What is the minimum common stock price that will allow LeMonde management to use the call feature of the debentures to effectively force conversion?

g. Suppose that increased expectations concerning inflation cause the yield on straight debt of equivalent risk and maturity to reach 10 percent. How will this affect the bond value of the convertible?

INTERMEDIATE **4.** Automatic Data Processing issued $150 million of 6½ percent convertible debentures maturing in 2020. The debentures are convertible into common stock at $83.45 a share. The company's common stock was trading at about $67 a share when the convertibles were issued.

a. How many shares of common stock can be obtained by converting one $1,000 par value debenture; that is, what is the conversion ratio?

b. What was the conversion value of this issue when these debentures were originally issued?

c. By what percentage was the conversion price above the stock price when these debentures were originally issued?

BASIC **5.** The Manchester Corporation has warrants presently outstanding, and each warrant entitles the holder to purchase one share of the company's common stock at an exercise price of $20 a share. If the market price of the warrants is $8 and the common stock price is $24 a share, what is the premium over the formula value for the warrants?

BASIC **6.** Horizon Corporation has warrants to purchase common stock outstanding. Each warrant entitles the holder to purchase one share of the company's common stock at an exercise price of $20 a share. Suppose the warrants expire on September 1, 2020. One year prior to expiration, when the company's common stock was trading at about $21.50 a share, the warrants were trading at $5 each.

a. What was the formula value of the warrants one year prior to expiration?

b. What was the premium over the formula value one year prior to expiration?

c. What are the reasons investors were willing to pay more than the formula value for these warrants one year prior to expiration?

d. Suppose that in August 2020 the Horizon common stock is still trading at $21.50 a share. What do you think the warrant price would be then? Why?

e. Horizon paid an annual dividend of $1 a share, as of one month ago, to its common shareholders. Do warrant holders receive dividends?

INTERMEDIATE **7.** Shaw Products Company, whose present balance sheet is summarized here, is considering issuing $100 million of 6 percent subordinated debentures (par value = $1,000), which are convertible into common stock at a price of $40.

Balance Sheet (in Millions of Dollars)

Current assets	$200	Current liabilities	$100
Fixed assets, net	300	Long-term debt	150
Total assets	$500	Common equity	250
		Total liabilities and equity	$500

a. Show the pro forma balance sheet for the issuance of the convertibles prior to conversion. Assume the proceeds are invested in new plant and equipment, and disregard issuance costs.

b. Show the pro forma balance sheet, assuming conversion of the entire issue.

c. How much additional money will the company raise at the time of conversion?

INTERMEDIATE **8.** The capital structure of Whitefield Mills Inc. is as follows:

Long-term debt	$250 million
Common stock, $1 par	25 million
Contributed capital in excess of par value	150 million
Retained earnings	350 million
Total capitalization	$775 million

The company has decided to raise additional capital by selling $75 million of 8 percent debentures with warrants attached. Each $1,000 debenture will have 25 warrants attached, and each warrant will entitle the holder to purchase one share of common stock at $30.

a. Show the company's new capital structure after the sale of debentures and the exercise of all the warrants. Assume that no other changes in capital structure occur between now and the time the warrants are exercised.
b. What condition is necessary for the warrants to be exercised?
c. How much total money will the company raise as a result of this security issue, if all warrants are exercised?

INTERMEDIATE **9.** You own 10 Bitterroot Industries Inc. 8 percent convertible debentures maturing in 2030. The conversion ratio of the debentures is 30, and the debentures are callable at $1,070 each. You bought the debentures when they were originally issued in 2000 for $1,000 each. At that time, Bitterroot common stock was selling at $28.50 a share, and now it is up to $44 a share. The convertible debentures are now selling at $1,320 each. Last week, you received a notice from Bitterroot Industries stating that the company is calling the debentures.

a. What are your alternatives?
b. Which alternative should you choose?

CHALLENGE **10.** Calculate the after-tax component cost of capital, k_c, for a 7.5 percent convertible debenture sold at par and due to mature in 25 years. The conversion ratio is 25, and conversion is expected to occur at the end of 10 years, when the common stock price is expected to be $54 a share. The company has a 40 percent marginal tax rate. Is there any reason for you to believe that this estimate may be biased up or down?

INTERMEDIATE **11.** Oswego Manufacturing Company has decided to sell additional common stock through a rights offering. The company has 50 million shares outstanding and plans to sell an additional 5 million shares through the rights offering. Each shareholder will receive one right for each share currently held, and thus each right will entitle shareholders to purchase 0.1 shares. Oswego's common stock is currently selling at $50 a share, and the subscription price of the rights will be $45 a share.

a. Calculate the formula value of the right for both the *rights-on* and the *ex-rights* cases.
b. How much is the market price of the company's stock expected to drop on the ex-rights date, all other things being equal? Why?
c. If the market price of Oswego's common stock increases to $52 a share, what will the formula value of the right be (*rights-on* case)?
d. Discuss the trend of the right's market price over its life, assuming the company's common stock continues to trade in the $50 range. (No numerical calculations are necessary for this part of the problem.)

INTERMEDIATE **12.** The Oil City Company plans to sell an additional 1 million shares of common stock through a rights offering. The company currently has 12 million shares outstanding.

Each shareholder will receive one right for each share currently held. Therefore, each right will enable shareholders to purchase 0.0833 shares. Oil City's common stock is currently selling for $30 per share, and the subscription price of the rights will be $25 per share.

a. Calculate the formula value of the right for both the *rights-on* and *ex-rights* cases.
b. Determine the amount that the market price of the company's stock is expected to drop on the ex-rights date, assuming that all other things are equal.
c. If the market price of Oil City's common stock increases to $40 per share, what is the formula value of the rights (rights-on case)?

INTERMEDIATE **13.** The Monroeville Company has warrants outstanding that expire in five years. Each warrant entitles the holder to purchase 0.5 shares of common stock at an exercise price of $32 per share. Determine the formula value and premium over the formula value if the respective prices of common stock and warrants are:

a. $30 per share and $1 per warrant
b. $32 per share and $2 per warrant
c. $38 per share and $3.50 per warrant

CHALLENGE **14.** The Findlay Company has debentures outstanding (par value = $1,000) that are convertible into common stock at a price of $50 per share. The convertible bonds have a coupon interest rate of 9 percent and mature in 18 years. The convertible bonds are callable at 103 percent of par value. The company has a marginal tax rate of 40 percent.

a. Calculate the conversion value of the bonds if Findlay's common stock is selling for $45 per share.
b. Calculate the straight-bond value, assuming that straight debt of equivalent risk and maturity is yielding 12 percent.
c. Determine the conversion premium if the market value of the bonds is $935.
d. Determine the conversion value of the bonds if the company's common stock price increases to $65 per share.
e. Given the information in part d, what is a realistic estimate of the market price of the convertible bond issue? (No calculations are required for this part of the problem.)

INTERMEDIATE **15.** The Wolverine Corporation has a convertible preferred stock outstanding. The par value of this preferred stock is $100, and it pays a $10 dividend. The preferred stock is callable at 103 percent of par value. It has 10 years remaining until maturity and is convertible into 2.5 shares of common stock. The current common stock price is $42. Similar (quality and maturity) nonconvertible preferred stock sells at a price to yield 9 percent.

a. What is the conversion value of this preferred stock?
b. What is the straight (nonconvertible) preferred stock value of this security?
c. If interest rates decline such that similar (quality and maturity) nonconvertible preferred stock sells at a price to yield 7 percent and the price of Wolverine's common stock increases to $44, for how much will this convertible security sell?

CHALLENGE **16.** Five years ago, in conjunction with a financial restructuring, Laurenberg Electric sold a $100 million issue of bonds at a coupon interest rate of 12 percent. Each bond came with 30 detachable warrants. Each warrant entitled the holder to purchase one share of Laurenberg's common stock at $15 per share. The warrants were set to expire 25 years from the date of issue. When Laurenberg's stock sold for $7 per share, the value of a warrant in the marketplace was $0.50.

a. What is the formula value of each warrant under these conditions?
b. What factors influence this value?

At a stock price of $15, the market price of each warrant was $3. At a stock price of $20, the market price of each warrant was $6.50. At a stock price of $25, the market price of each warrant was $10.50.

c. If an investor purchases the stock and the warrant when the stock price is $15, what holding period return will be earned on both, assuming that the stock and the warrant are sold when the stock price reaches $20?

d. If an investor purchases the stock and the warrant when the stock price is $20, what holding period return will be earned on both, assuming that the stock and the warrant are sold when the stock price reaches $25?

What happens to the rate of return from the warrant as the stock price rises? Why do you think this happens?

CHALLENGE

17. Nullcom Inc. has debentures (face value = $1,000) outstanding that are convertible into common stock at a price of $40 per share. The debentures pay an interest rate of 9 percent per annum and have a remaining life of 10 years. Nonconvertible debentures of a similar credit rating and maturity are selling at a price to yield 11 percent. The current price of a share of Nullcom's stock is $35.

a. Compute the straight bond value of each of these debentures.

b. Compute the conversion value of each of these debentures.

c. What is the absolute minimum price for one of these debentures today? What price would you expect to pay for one of these debentures?

d. If the debentures are called at 105 today and you own 10 of these debentures, what action should you take?

• APPENDIX **20A**

THE BLACK-SCHOLES OPTION PRICING MODEL

The Foundations of Option Valuation

In Chapter 20, the valuation of a call of option was determined to be a function of the following variables:

- The current price of the asset underlying the option. In the case of stock options, this is the price of the common stock on which the option has been written.
- The exercise price of the option.
- The time remaining until the option expires.
- The risk-free rate of interest.
- The volatility of the underlying asset, for example, the share of stock on which the option was written.

Financial research has made great strides in the formal valuation of options. A path-breaking paper by Fischer Black and Myron Scholes[1] developed a formal model for option valuation that is widely used today. The Black-Scholes model was developed from the premise that a strategy of borrowing to buy stock can exactly equal the risk associated with the purchase of a call option. Because the price of a common stock is readily observable, as is the borrowing rate, they showed that it is possible to derive the theoretically correct value for a call option.

The Black-Scholes model is based on the following assumptions:

1. The stock pays no dividends during the life of the option. Although this might seem like a serious limitation of the model, other models have been developed that take dividends into account. A common way of adjusting the Black-Scholes model for the effect of dividends is to subtract the present value of expected dividend payments during the life of the option from the stock price variable in the model.
2. The call option is a European option. European options can be exercised only at expiration, whereas American options can be exercised at any time up until the expiration date. This assumption is not important because few options are exercised prior to expiration. When an option is exercised prior to expiration, the option holder loses the value of any premium (the difference between the market value of the option and the option's intrinsic value, which is defined as the difference between the stock price and the exercise price) that is contained in the option price.
3. Stock prices are assumed to follow a random walk. Investors are assumed not to be able to predict the direction of the overall market or of any particular stock.
4. There are no transaction costs in the buying and selling of options. This assumption is violated in reality, but transaction costs are low enough that this assumption is not a serious limitation of the model.
5. The probability distribution of stock returns is normally distributed.
6. Short-term, risk-free interest rates are assumed to be known and constant over the life of the option contract. The discount rate on 30-day U.S. government Treasury bills is often used as the risk-free rate in the Black-Scholes model.
7. The variance of returns on the underlying stock is assumed to be constant and known to investors over the option's life.

[1]Fischer Black and Myron Scholes, "The Pricing of Options and Corporate Liabilities," *Journal of Political Economy* (May–June 1973): 637–654.

With these assumptions, the "correct" market value of an option can be determined. If the price of an option differs from this theoretically "correct" value, it is possible for investors to set up a risk-free arbitrage position and earn a rate of return in excess of the risk-free rate. Hence, it can be said that there are powerful market forces at work to keep actual market values of options consistent with their theoretical values.

The Black-Scholes Option Pricing Model

The Black-Scholes model defines the equilibrium value of a call option to buy one share of a company's common stock as:

(20A.1)
$$C = P_s N(d_1) - \frac{E}{e^{rt}} N(d_2)$$

where:

P_s = current stock price

t = time in years until the expiration of the option

E = exercise price of the call option

r = short-term annual, continuously compounded, risk-free rate of interest

$N(d)$ = the value of a cumulative normal density function; the probability that a standardized, normally distributed random variable will be less than or equal to the value d

e = the exponential value (2.71828)

$$d_1 = \frac{ln(P_s/E) + \left(r + \frac{\sigma^2}{2}\right)t}{\sigma\sqrt{t}}$$

$d_2 = d_1 - \sigma\sqrt{t}$

σ = the standard deviation per year in the continuous return on the stock

ln = natural logarithm

Equation 20A.1 is a rather intimidating-looking formula. Fortunately, applying this formula to actual data is relatively easy, as illustrated in the next section.

Applying the Black-Scholes Model

Consider the case of Queen Pharmaceuticals Inc. Based on an analysis of past returns for Queen's common stock, the standard deviation of its stock returns has been estimated to be 0.3, or 30 percent. As of January 14, Queen's stock price was $P_s = \$30$. The exercise price of its call options was $E = \$29$. The short-term annual, continuously compounded interest rate was $r = 0.06$, and the time to expiration of the call option was $t = 0.5$ or one-half year. With this information, we can now compute the equilibrium value of one of these call options.

- **Step 1**: Compute the values for d_1 and d_2.

$$d_1 = \frac{ln(P_s/E) + \left(r + \frac{\sigma^2}{2}\right)t}{\sigma\sqrt{t}}$$

$$= \frac{ln\left(\frac{30}{29}\right) + \left(0.06 + \frac{(0.3)^2}{2}\right)0.5}{0.3\sqrt{0.5}}$$

$$= \frac{0.0339 + .0525}{0.2121}$$

$$= 0.4074$$

$$d_2 = d_1 - \sigma\sqrt{t}$$

$$= 0.4074 - 0.3\sqrt{.5}$$

$$= 0.1953$$

- **Step 2**: Compute N(d_1) and N(d_2).

  To compute the values for N(d_1) and N(d_2) we need to answer the following type of question: What is the probability that a value from a standardized normal distribution will be below a specific value, such as d_1 or d_2?

  This question can be easily answered using Table V at the back of the book. Recall that the values in Table V are the probabilities of having a value greater than z (for positive standard normalized values such as d_1 or d_2 in this example) or less than z (for negative standard normalized values). Because d_1 and d_2 are both positive, we can find the probability of a value greater than d_1 or d_2 directly from Table V and then subtract this probability from 1.0 to get the probability of a value less than d_1 or d_2, as is required in the Black-Scholes model.

  From Table V, the probability of a value greater than d_1 (rounded to 0.41) is 0.3409. Hence the value for N(d_1) will be 1.0 – 0.3409 or 0.6591. Similarly, the probability of a value greater than d_2 (rounded to 0.20) is 0.4207. Hence the value for N(d_2), that is, the probability of a value less than d_2, will be 1.0 – 0.4207 = 0.5793.

- **Step 3**: Calculate the value of C, the call option for Queen Pharmaceuticals stock.

$$C = P_s N(d_1) - \frac{E}{e^{rt}} N(d_2)$$

$$= 30(0.6591) - \frac{29}{e^{(0.06)(0.5)}}(0.5793)$$

$$= \$3.47$$

Therefore, the Black-Scholes model indicates that an option to purchase one share of Queen Pharmaceuticals stock is worth approximately $3.47, given the assumptions presented here. Option values are especially sensitive to the estimates of stock return volatility that are input in the model.

HTTP:

These calculations can be simplified by using one of the many free option price calculators available on the Web, such as www.numa.com or www.freeoptionpricing.com or www.optionvue.com.

Problems

1. Targezept Bionics Inc. has a common stock outstanding that sells for $21 per share. A call option on the stock has an exercise price of $20 and will expire in three months. Based on an analysis of the stock's past volatility, you have estimated the

standard deviation of returns to be 0.6. The short-term interest rate is now 5 percent and you expect that to remain constant over the next six months.

Use the Black-Scholes option pricing model to estimate the value of this option.

2. Use the option price calculator that can be found at www.numa.com, or another option price calculator, to test the sensitivity of option values to changes in the key input variables. Use the data from Problem 1 as the base case and vary the values for the interest rate, time to maturity, and stock return volatility to see what happens to the value of the call option on the stock of Targezept.

APPENDIX 20B

BOND REFUNDING ANALYSIS

The Bond Refunding Process

Bond refunding occurs when a company exercises its option to redeem a callable issue and sells a lower-cost issue to take its place.[1] The decision of whether to refund a particular debt issue is usually based on a capital budgeting (present value) analysis. The principal benefit, or cash inflow, is the present value of the after-tax interest savings over the life of the issue. The principal investment, or cash outflow at the time of refunding, consists primarily of the call premium and the issuance (flotation) cost of the new debt.

Bond refunding differs from other capital expenditure projects in one very important way: The cash inflows are known with considerably greater certainty than the cash flows from a typical capital expenditure project and thus are less risky. As a result, the weighted cost of capital is not used. Instead, the *after-tax cost of the new debt* is believed to be a more appropriate discount rate for bond refunding analysis.[2]

Bond refunding becomes an important decision facing many firms whenever interest rates decline substantially from earlier levels. For example, firms that had issued bonds with coupon rates of 13 percent or more during the period of high inflation and high interest rates in the early 1980s found that they could refund these issues at rates under 9 percent during the early 2000s.

As an illustration of bond refunding, consider the following example. The APCO Company issued $100 million of 30-year, 13 percent debt five years ago. In the meantime, interest rates have declined, and the firm's management feels the decline has bottomed out. The debt issue is now callable at 107 percent of par. The company could refund the old issue with a new 25-year, 10 percent, $100 million issue. Issuance costs on the new issue would be 0.5 percent, or $500,000, whereas the unamortized issuance costs on the old issue are $450,000. If APCO decided to call the old issue and refund it, both issues would be outstanding for a three-week period, resulting in overlapping interest payments. The company's marginal tax rate is 40 percent. For purposes of discounting, the after-tax cost of new debt is $0.10 \times (1 - 0.4) = 0.06$.

To determine whether APCO should refund the old issue, a bond refunding analysis is carried out.

Step 1: Calculate the interest savings (cash inflows).[3]

(20B.1) $$\text{Annual interest, after-tax} = \text{Issue size} \times \text{Interest rate} \times (1 - \text{Tax rate})$$

$$\text{Annual interest, old issue} = \$100 \text{ million} \times 13\% \times 0.6 = \$7.8 \text{ million}$$

$$\text{Annual interest, new issue} = \$100 \text{ million} \times 10\% \times 0.6 = \$6.0 \text{ million}$$

$$\text{Annual after-tax interest savings} = \$1.8 \text{ million}$$

$$\begin{aligned}\text{Present value of interest savings} &= \text{Annual after-tax interest savings} \times PVIFA_{0.06,25}\\ &= \$1.8 \text{ million} \times 12.783\\ &= \$23.009 \text{ million}\end{aligned}$$

[1]Callable preferred stock can also be refunded. The same consideration and analysis apply to both debt and preferred stock.

[2]See Chapter 12 for a discussion of the cost of capital.

[3]This calculation assumes that interest is received once a year at year end. Actually, interest is paid every six months. However, the two results are not materially different.

- Step 2: Calculate the net investment (net cash outflow at time 0). This involves computing the after-tax call premium, the issuance cost of the new issue, the issuance cost of the old issue, and the overlapping interest.

The after-tax call premium is calculated as follows:

(20B.2)
$$\begin{aligned}\text{Call premium, after-tax} &= \text{Call premium} \times (1 - \text{Tax rate})\\ &= \$7 \text{ million} \times (1 - 0.4) = \$4.2 \text{ million}\end{aligned}$$

The call premium is a cash outflow.

The issuance cost on the new issue is 0.5 percent, or $500,000. This amount cannot be deducted from APCO's current period income for tax purposes. Instead, it must be capitalized and amortized over the life of the debt issue because the benefits that accrue to a firm as a result of an issuance cost expenditure occur over the life of the issue. Thus,

(20B.3)
$$\begin{aligned}\begin{array}{l}\text{Present value of}\\ \text{issuance cost}\\ \text{of new issue}\end{array} &= \text{Issuance cost} - \text{Present value tax effect}\\ &= \text{Issuance cost} - \left(\begin{array}{c}\text{Annual after-tax}\\ \text{savings from}\\ \text{amortization}\end{array} \times \text{PVIFA}_{0.06,25}\right)\\ &= \text{Issuance cost} - \left(\frac{\text{Issuance cost}}{\text{Number of years}} \times \text{Tax rate} \times \text{PVIFA}_{0.06,25}\right)\\ &= \$500{,}000 - \left(\frac{\$500{,}000}{25} \times 0.4 \times 12.783\right)\\ &= \$500{,}000 - \$102{,}264\\ &= \$397{,}736\end{aligned}$$

The present value of the issuance cost of the *new* issue is a net cash outflow.

APCO has been amortizing the issuance cost of the old issue over its life. If it refunded the issue, the company would no longer receive the benefits from the old issue's issuance cost and therefore could write off the remaining unamortized issuance cost at the time of refunding. Because of the write-off, however, APCO would lose the benefits of the old issuance cost over the remaining life of the issue. Thus,

(20B.4)
$$\begin{aligned}\begin{array}{c}\text{Present value of}\\ \text{issuance cost of}\\ \text{old issue}\end{array} &= \begin{array}{c}\text{Present value,}\\ \text{lost benefits}\\ \text{old issuance cost,}\\ \text{after tax}\end{array} - \begin{array}{c}\text{Present value,}\\ \text{write-off old}\\ \text{issuance cost,}\\ \text{after tax}\end{array}\\ &= \left(\frac{\text{Old issuance cost}}{\text{Number of years}} \times \text{Tax rate} \times \text{PVIFA}_{0.06,25}\right)\\ &\quad - (\text{Old issuance cost} \times \text{Tax rate})\\ &= \left(\frac{\$450{,}000}{25} \times 0.4 \times 12.783\right) - (\$450{,}000 \times 0.4)\\ &= \$92{,}038 - \$180{,}000\\ &= -\$87{,}962\end{aligned}$$

The issuance cost effect of the old issue is a net cash inflow at the time of refunding.

In most bond refundings, it is necessary for a firm to sell the new issue and receive the proceeds before paying off the old lenders. Both issues are usually outstanding for less than a month. Thus, the interest expense on the old issue during the overlapping period is considered a cost, or part of the refunding investment. In APCO's case, this expense is calculated as follows:

(20B.5)

$$\text{Overlapping interest} = \text{Size of issue} \times \text{Annual interest rate of old issue, after tax} \times \text{Fraction of year both issues outstanding}$$

$$= \$100\text{ million} \times 0.078 \times \frac{3}{52}$$

$$= \$450{,}000$$

The overlapping interest is a cash outflow.[4]

In summary, the net investment is calculated as follows:

Call premium	$4,200,000
Present value of issuance cost, new issue	397,736
Present value of issuance cost, old issue	–87,962
Overlapping interest	450,000
Net investment (cash outflow)	$4,959,774

- **Step 3: Finally, calculate the net present value of refunding.**

(20B.6)

$$\text{Net present value of refunding} = \text{Present value, interest savings} - \text{Present value, net investment}$$

$$= \$23.009\text{ million} - \$4.960\text{ million}$$

$$= \$18.049\text{ million}$$

Because the net present value is positive, APCO should call its old issue and refund it with the new one.[5]

Problems*

CHALLENGE

1. The Warren Electric Company is considering refunding its $150 million, 12 percent debt issue with a 10 percent, 20-year debt issue. The existing (old) issue also matures in 20 years and now is callable at 105 percent of par. The unamortized issuance cost on the old issue is $600,000, and the issuance cost of the new issue is 0.4 percent. Both the new and old debt issues will be outstanding for 4 weeks, resulting in overlapping interest. Warren Electric's weighted cost of capital is 10 percent and its marginal tax rate is 40 percent. The company's treasurer feels that the decline in interest rates has bottomed out. Determine the net present value of refunding the old bond issue.

[4]Normally, during the period of the overlap, the proceeds from the sale of the new issue are temporarily invested in short-term securities. The interest earned will offset part of the overlapping interest expense. For simplification, this offset against the overlapping interest expense has not been considered in this example.

[5]Financial analysts normally can determine the *approximate* net present value of refunding by comparing the present value of the interest savings with the after- tax cost of the call premium. However, as is true with any shortcut method, caution should be exercised.

*Color blocks behind the numbers denote problems that have check answers provided at the end of the book.

CHALLENGE

Spreadsheet Strategies

2. The Springfield Gas and Electric Company is considering refunding $50 million of 11 percent debt with an 8 percent, 20-year debt issue. The existing, or old, issue also matures in 20 years and now is callable at 108 percent of par. The unamortized issuance cost on the old issue is $400,000, and the issuance cost of the new issue is 0.875 percent. The company estimates that both issues will be outstanding for four weeks, resulting in overlapping interest. The company has a weighted cost of capital of 10 percent and a 40 percent marginal tax rate. In addition, the company's financial management feels as though the present interest rate decline has nearly bottomed out. Calculate the net present value of the refunding and make a recommendation to management on whether to refund the bonds. (*Note*: $PVIFA_{0.048,20}$ can be determined using Equation 5.18 from Chapter 5.)

CHALLENGE

Spreadsheet Strategies

3. The Phillipsburg Power Company is considering refunding its $250 million, 11.5 percent debt issue with a 10 percent, 15-year debt issue. The existing (old) issue also matures in 15 years and now is callable at 103.5 percent of par. The unamortized issuance cost on the old issue is $937,500, and the issuance cost of the new issue is 0.5 percent. Both the new and old debt issues will be outstanding for three weeks, resulting in overlapping interest. Phillipsburg's weighted cost of capital is 10 percent, and its marginal tax rate is 40 percent. The company's chief financial officer feels that the decline in interest rates has bottomed out. Determine the net present value of refunding the old bond issue.

CHALLENGE

Spreadsheet Strategies

4. The Altoona Electric Company is considering refunding its $200 million, 12.5 percent debt issue with a 10 percent, 10-year debt issue. The existing (old) issue also matures in 10 years and now is callable at 104 percent of par. The unamortized issuance cost on the old issue is $666,667, and the issuance cost of the new issue is 0.4 percent. Both the new and old debt issues will be outstanding for four weeks, resulting in overlapping interest. Altoona Electric's weighted cost of capital is 10 percent, and its marginal tax rate is 40 percent. The company's treasurer feels that the decline in interest rates has bottomed out. Determine the net present value of refunding the old bond issue.

CHAPTER 21

Risk Management

KEY CHAPTER CONCEPTS

1. Risk is the possibility that the actual cash flows from an investment or any other business transaction will be different from the expected cash flows.
2. There are several reasons why a firm may choose to employ risk management techniques, including reducing the chance of financial distress, assuring that the firm will have adequate cash flows to make needed investments in times of financial difficulty, and helping management to focus on issues that are key to the performance of the firm and are under management's control.
3. Nonhedging strategies that can be used to manage business risk include the acquisition of additional information, diversification, insurance, the use of patents and copyrights, and the limited use of firm-specific assets.
4. Hedging strategies for reducing risk involve taking offsetting positions in the ownership of an asset or security through the use of derivative securities such as forward contracts, futures contracts, and options to counter risk exposure in the cash market.
5. Long hedges involve the purchase of a forward or futures contract to cover required future purchases of a commodity or currency. Short hedges involve the sale of a forward or a futures contract to cover a required future sale of a commodity or currency. Call options can be used to hedge future purchase requirements, and put options can be used to hedge future sales commitments.

FINANCIAL CHALLENGE

Hedging and Hershey's Sweet Success

The Hershey Company is one of the leading chocolate and confectionary manufacturers in the world. Most of us are familiar with their chocolate products, including Hershey's Kisses, KitKat, and Reese's. Though the business appears to be a simple one, it is fraught with a number of risks that if not managed properly can lead to financial difficulty, even failure. You may be wondering: How difficult is it to run a business whose core product essentially involves mixing a bunch of ingredients including cocoa and sugar and turning it into chocolate bars? Although the product itself is not high tech, the risks inherent in the business are anything but simple.

We highlighted two key ingredients in the manufacturing process: cocoa and sugar. Both are major commodity products that are affected by global factors including agricultural land devoted to production, weather, agricultural subsidies, geopolitical risk, fuel prices, import restrictions, and so forth. In fact, cocoa and sugar prices can be very volatile. For instance, the world market spot price for cocoa has varied between $1,530 and $3,522 per metric ton in the period between January 2006 and December 2015. It is not uncommon for the price to change by $200 per metric ton from one month to the next. Similar volatility is exhibited in the sugar market. The spot price for sugar in the United States has varied between 19.6 and 40.4 cents per pound over the same period. Price jumps of 25 percent in a matter of months are not uncommon.

Despite this volatility, Hershey has managed to keep its cost of goods sold and, therefore, its gross profit at a very stable level. For example, the cost of goods averaged 56.4 percent between 2010 and 2014 and has been within 2 percent from the average in any given year. Given that cocoa, sugar, and other commodities (e.g., dairy, nuts) make up a significant portion of the cost of production, it is remarkable that the company has been able to maintain fairly stable production costs in the face of very volatile input prices. How is Hershey able to do this? Very simply, the firm does an excellent job of managing its risks. Among other things, they make use of the derivative markets to hedge their input prices. Hershey's use of derivatives to manage its risk extends beyond input factors and includes managing financial risks such as interest rates and currency fluctuations. Their

iStockPhoto.com/Roel Smart

FINANCIAL CHALLENGE — CONTINUED

use of derivatives to manage risk is captured in the following quote from Hershey's 2014 10-K annual report:

> We use certain derivative instruments to manage our interest rate, foreign currency exchange rate, and commodity price risks. We monitor and manage these exposures as part of our overall risk management program.
>
> We enter into interest rate swap agreements and foreign currency forward exchange contracts and options for periods consistent with related underlying exposures. We enter into commodities futures and options contracts and other derivative instruments for varying periods. These commodity derivative instruments are intended to be, and are effective as, hedges of market price risks associated with anticipated raw material purchases, energy requirements and transportation costs.

In this chapter we illustrate some of the basic hedging techniques that a firm like Hershey may use to mitigate volatility.

Sources: The Hershey Company 2014 10-K Annual Report; Steven M. Sears, "The Sweet Smell of Success at Hershey," *Barron's* (February 8, 2011), http://online.barrons.com/article/SB50001424052970203926004576132121910239328.html.

CHAPTER OBJECTIVES

Upon completion of the chapter, you should have a clear understanding of the following:

1. The meaning and importance of risk management
2. Nonhedging strategies for managing risk
3. Hedging strategies for risk management

21-1 Introduction

This chapter explores the important area of corporate risk management. As you will recall from Chapter 8, the concept of risk refers to the variability of possible future returns from an investment or, more generally, from any business transaction. Risk is the possibility that the actual cash flows from an investment or any other business transaction will be different from the expected cash flows. There are a number of techniques that companies can use to control and/or eliminate risk. In this chapter, we consider when it is desirable to manage risk using these techniques. Next we look at alternative strategies for managing risk, including the use of derivatives, such as forward contracts, futures contracts, and options. Each of these derivative risk-management products is illustrated with an example.

HTTP:
The Energy Information Administration discusses how the use of derivatives can affect the level and type of investment in energy-related businesses.

www.eia.doe.gov/oiaf/servicerpt/derivative/chapter8.html

21-2 Why Manage Risk?[1]

Individuals and companies make choices every day about which risks and how much risk they are willing to assume at any point in time. For example, most individuals buy car insurance that has a deductible limit for the various coverage elements, such as collision insurance. Some individuals have a $500 deductible policy, while others may choose a $2,500 deductible policy. This means that the policyholder is responsible for the first $500 or $2,500 of damage to a vehicle in a collision, and the insurance company is responsible only for amounts above the deductible. Why do some individuals choose the $500 limit, others choose $2,500, and still others choose not to carry any collision insurance coverage at all—that is, they self-insure?

Similarly, some firms that sell their products extensively in international export markets or import significant quantities of raw materials and/or finished goods take actions designed to protect themselves from unfavorable currency exchange rate swings. Other firms simply accept this risk as an ordinary risk of doing business. It can be argued, for example, that currency and commodity price volatility is primarily a component of unsystematic risk that investors can effectively eliminate by holding well-diversified portfolios of stocks. If that is the case, why should a company care about this risk?

There are good reasons to seek to eliminate some of these risks by engaging in hedging transactions. When a company hedges a transaction, it assumes offsetting risks that neutralize the original risk. Perhaps the most important reason to hedge a business risk is to reduce the chance of financial distress. Because financial distress is costly and may ultimately lead to the forced liquidation of the firm, it is desirable to reduce the risk of financial distress. Hence, if a transaction is large enough that potential, but unanticipated, price swings for raw materials could lead the firm to financial distress and/or bankruptcy, it is probably worthwhile for the firm to seek to hedge against this risk. For example, a company that sells diesel fuel under long-term, fixed-price contracts is well advised to develop hedging strategies to protect against potential increases in oil prices. A collateral benefit of reducing the probability of financial distress through hedging is the fact that firms engaging in effective risk-management strategies will normally have an enhanced debt capacity in their capital structure, resulting in a reduced weighted cost of capital.

Another reason why firms engage in hedging transactions to manage their risks is to assure that they will have adequate cash flows to make needed investments. For example, a pharmaceutical company normally has large ongoing R&D investment obligations. These investments are the lifeblood of the company. If a firm has extremely volatile cash flow streams because of international currency risk exposure or some other factor, the time may come when there might be a shortfall in the cash needed to sustain these investments. One might argue that the firm could always go to the external capital marketplace to get the necessary funds. Although that is sometimes possible, external capital suppliers may be reluctant to provide funds for intangible asset investments such as R&D at a time when the firm is having difficulty generating operating cash flows.

Finally, it may be advantageous for a firm to hedge some of its largest risks, such as exchange rate risk or future raw material price risk, so that the focus of management's attention is properly placed on issues under management's control. Because exchange rate risk and prices of raw materials are largely outside the control of management, it

[0]An excellent discussion of the rationale for hedging is found in "Why Manage Risk," *Harvard Business School Teaching Note No. 294107-HCB-ENG*, February 23, 2001.

may be desirable to hedge to eliminate these risks, so that management attention can be directed toward day-to-day operating matters that are under their control. A related benefit of hedging these external risks is that it focuses managerial performance appraisal and the determination of incentive compensation on factors that are under management's control, rather than on things outside of their control. For example, spikes and volatility in several agricultural commodity prices have prompted a number of food industry firms to actively institute commodity risk management into their businesses. Examples of such companies are Hershey's (see this chapter's Financial Challenge), a chocolate manufacturer; Pilgrim's Pride, a producer of processed chicken products; and Starbucks, a popular chain of coffeehouses.

It is true that many business risks can theoretically be hedged by individual investors and hence do not need to be hedged by the company. However, in practice this is quite difficult for individual investors to do. First, individual investors rarely have enough detailed information about the operational aspects of a company's performance to allow them to implement effective hedging strategies across the myriad risks faced by a typical company. In addition, there are large economies of scale in implementing hedging strategies, and the company has a huge comparative advantage in hedging because of these economies.

21-3 Nonhedging Risk-Management Strategies

There is a wide range of strategies available to managers seeking to reduce the level of risk encountered in the operation of their enterprise. Some of these strategies make use of derivative securities and well-developed hedging strategies. Before turning to hedging strategies, we review other approaches open to managers seeking to control risk.

21-3a Acquisition of Additional Information

In many cases, the risk facing a manager arises because of a lack of information. For example, when making the decision to develop and market a new product, there is considerable risk regarding the market's acceptance of the new product. To reduce this risk, many firms "test-market" the product in a limited area or present the product to panels of consumers for their evaluation. These tactics provide important information to the company as it seeks to assess the probability of success of the new product.

Information can also be purchased from individuals or firms that possess the knowledge the decision maker seeks. For example, a wildcat oil-drilling firm will employ the services of petroleum geologists as it attempts to determine where to drill exploratory wells. Similarly, companies that plan to sell new debt securities often pay to have their bonds "rated" by one of the bond-rating services, such as Moody's or Standard & Poor's. The ratings applied to the bonds reduce the risk of determining the yield that will have to be offered to investors when the bonds are sold.

Because collecting additional information is costly, wealth-maximizing firms will pay for the additional information as long as the marginal value of that information is expected to exceed the marginal cost of acquiring it. For example, securing a bond rating from Moody's or Standard & Poor's is a relatively low-cost process. The benefits of reduced risk uncertainty in the minds of bond investors often save a company many millions of dollars in their borrowing costs.

21-3b Diversification

We saw in Chapter 8 that there is considerable value in diversifying a portfolio of assets, because the risk of that portfolio will normally be less than the weighted average risk of the assets in the portfolio. This principle is widely applied by individual investors as they make their stock and bond investment decisions. Diversification can also have value for individual firms. Many firms work to diversify their customer and supplier base so that they will not be severely impacted by negative developments at a single customer or supplier. Firms arrange for multiple supply sources of key resources. Similarly, they seek to expand the customer base to diversify away some customer risk. Without a diversified customer and/or supplier base, it is conceivable that the long-term viability of a company could be threatened by the failure of a single customer or supplier.

Although this type of within-company diversification is prudent, some firms have carried the concept of prudent diversification to counterproductive ends. During the 1960s and 1970s, many firms such as ITT, Sears, LTV, Mobil, and Litton Industries attempted to reduce the risk of their operations by diversifying into a wide range of often unrelated industries. The rationale that was made for these far-flung acquisitions was to reduce the inherent operating risk of the enterprise. For example, Mobil acquired Montgomery Ward (a national department store chain) because of the cyclical risk of the oil industry. Ford Motor acquired a network of savings and loan institutions, and Sears diversified into insurance (Allstate), real estate brokerage (Coldwell Banker), and investment brokerage (Dean Witter) businesses.

It soon became apparent that acquisitions such as these made little sense. If investors wanted to diversify their portfolios, they could do so much more cheaply than companies, who often paid acquisition premiums of 25 to 75 percent. Second, these acquisitive firms had little expertise in running such far-flung enterprises. What do the executives at Mobil know about running Montgomery Ward, a department store chain? As it grew increasingly apparent that this type of diversification outside of management's areas of expertise was not value enhancing, many of these firms subsequently sold off their unrelated businesses, often at a significant loss, and returned to their core business.

Hence, we can conclude that diversification of the customer and supplier base within its core business can often be a value-enhancing strategy, but diversification into unrelated businesses often results in the destruction of value.

21-3c Insurance

When a firm makes a premium payment to an insurance company, the firm is exchanging the premium payment for protection against specified losses, up to the limits identified in the policy. Insurance is commonly available for losses due to fires, natural disasters, accidents occurring in the workplace, the death of key employees, fraud, product liability, thefts, certain unforeseen business interruptions, and potential liabilities of officers and directors that may arise in the course of exercising their fiduciary responsibilities to the firm. Some financial instruments such as corporate bonds are backed by insurance that guarantees the payment of principal and interest.

When deciding which risks should be insured externally, and which should be self-insured, managers are confronted with a trade-off between a certain, small, periodic cost (the insurance premium) and the uncertainty of bearing the full cost of a large loss from time to time. The willingness of managers to assume some insurable risk, the cost of the insurance, the severity of the consequences of experiencing an uninsured risk (could it lead to financial distress?), and the competitiveness of the pricing for any insurance product all determine whether insurance is purchased. For these reasons, it is common to find that large companies generally buy insurance against events that can lead to losses large enough to cause financial distress. At the same time, these companies typically self-insure against smaller, more routine losses. They reason that these small losses are not of the size to have a material impact on the performance and viability of the firm. Hence, there is no reason to pay the administrative costs associated with the pricing of insurance products.

21-3d Gaining Control over the Operating Environment

Some business risks can be reduced by actions designed to gain control over the operating environment. For example, to ensure adequate outlets for its products, a firm may establish a network of exclusive dealerships, such as is common in the automotive marketplace. If access to raw materials is uncertain, a firm may integrate backwards to the source of supplies. The use of patents and copyrights can protect a firm against immediate competition. Patents are the backbone of several major industries such as the branded, prescription pharmaceutical industry. These patents secure the intellectual property rights of the developer (inventor) and provide a strong incentive for continued innovation and the associated economic gains to society from continued technological and innovative progress.

HTTP:
Read a white paper on risk management and derivatives from Strategies & Tactics, a portfolio and risk-management consulting firm.
www.strategies-tactics.com/derivatives.htm

Legal action is often used to enforce rights under patents and copyrights. For example, in 2011, Apple sued Samsung for violating several of its intellectual patents having to with the "design and feel" of its iPhone and iPad products. Apple has a history of jealously guarding its intellectual property, including prior suits against Motorola and Microsoft.[2] Legal action of this type is often required to secure intellectual property rights under patent and copyright laws.

21-3e Limited Use of Firm-Specific Assets

If a firm builds a plant that can only be used to produce its specific product, that firm has effectively limited its options should the product prove to be unsuccessful. The more general the purpose of the assets employed by a firm, the greater flexibility that firm has to redeploy these assets to other uses. A trade-off exists between the use of firm- or product-specific assets, which are likely to be more efficient, and the use of more general-purpose assets, which give the firm increased future flexibility. When planning new investments, this trade-off must be carefully evaluated.

The case for using more general-purpose assets is well-illustrated in recent trends in the manufacture of automobiles. In the past, car companies built plants that had the capacity to produce only one type of vehicle. It usually took up to two years to convert a plant from making cars to making small SUVs. In recent years, most automakers have aggressively pursued flexible manufacturing techniques. For example, Ford as of 2012 had the only plant in the world that was capable of building gas-powered, hybrid, plugin hybrid, and electric cars all on the same production line.[3]

[2]Connie Guglielmo, "The Apple vs. Samsung Dispute: 20 Talking Points," *Forbes* (August 21, 2012), www.forbes.com (accessed April 7, 2013); Charlie Osborne, "Apple vs. Samsung Timeline: The Guide to What's Happening," *ZDNet* (August 14, 2012), www.ZDnet.com (accessed April 7, 2013); and Nick Wingfield, "Jury Awards $1 Billion to Apple in Samsung Patent Case," *The New York Times* (August 24, 2012), online edition (accessed April 7, 2013).

[3]"Ford Uses New Flexible Michigan Plant to Build 'Wild Focus,' C-Max Energi Plug-in Hybrids," *New York Daily News* (November 8, 2012), www.nydailynews/autos (accessed April 7, 2013).

21-4 Hedging Strategies for Risk Management

hedge

A **hedge** is a transaction that limits the risk associated with fluctuations in the price of a commodity, currency, or financial instrument. A hedge is accomplished by taking offsetting positions in the ownership of an asset or security through the use of derivative securities, such as buying or selling a forward contract, a futures contract, or an option to offset risk exposure in the cash market.

21-4a Forward Contracts

forward contract

A **forward contract** is an agreement to buy or sell an asset at some point in time in the future at a specified price agreed to at the time the contract is purchased or sold. The specified price is called the *delivery price*, and it remains fixed during the term of the contract. The party that agrees to buy the asset in the future is said to have taken a *long* position, whereas the party that agrees to sell the asset has a *short* position. The *spot price* is the current price of the asset. A rise (fall) in the spot price generates a profit (loss) for the holder of the long position and a loss (profit) for the holder of the short position. In a typical forward contract, cash flows are exchanged between the buyer and the seller only on the maturity date of the contract. Because forward contracts can be executed for any quantity of an asset and for any maturity date, they are generally not liquid, that is, there is no organized market for the purchase and sale of forward contracts. Also, because no cash flows exchange hands until maturity, forward contracts are said to possess *performance risk*. Performance risk is the risk that at maturity, the party that has losses from the contract may fail to make the necessary payments to the party with the gains from price movements in the contract.

Forward contracts are most common in the foreign currency markets. Figure 21.1 shows foreign currency exchange rates for a number of countries. This table also shows forward rates of exchange between the dollar and several key currencies including the Australian dollar, the Japanese yen, the Swiss franc, and the U.K. pound. From the figure, note the potential for considerable volatility in exchange rates. For example, in the two-month year-to-date (YTD) period from January 1 to February 24, 2016, the Argentine peso-U.S. dollar exchange rate had changed by 18.6 percent. The use of forward foreign exchange rate contracts to hedge business transactions denominated in a foreign currency is illustrated in Chapter 22.

21-4b Futures Contracts

futures contract

A **futures contract** is a standardized contract, traded on an organized exchange, to buy or sell an asset at a specified future time at a specified price. The specified price is known as the *delivery price*. The party that agrees to buy a futures contract is said to have a *long* position, and the party that agrees to sell a futures contract is said to have a *short* position. The current price of the asset in question is known as the *spot price*. Hence, a rise in the spot price leads to a profit for those holding a long position in the futures contract and a loss for those holding a short position.

Futures contracts require daily settlement between the buyer and seller for gains and losses. For example, assume that Cone Mills buys a futures contract for the delivery of 50,000 pounds of cotton, three months hence, at a price of 70 cents per pound. As the buyer of the contract, if the price of cotton rises to 71 cents per pound the day after the

FIGURE 21.1

Forward and Spot Foreign Currency Exchange Rates (February 24, 2016)

Country/currency	US$ equiv Wednesday	US$ equiv Tuesday	US$ vs. 1-day % chg	US$ vs. YTD % chg
Americas				
Argentina peso	0.0652	0.0653	0.14	18.6
Brazil real	0.2526	0.2527	0.06	unch
Canada dollar	0.7297	0.7249	−0.66	−1
Mexico peso	0.0549	0.0549	0.01	5.9
Asia-Pacific				
Australian dollar	0.7196	0.7204	0.11	1.3
1 month forward rate (3/29/2016)	0.7168			
2 month forward rate (4/26/2016)	0.7159			
3 month forward rate (5/26/2016)	0.7149			
China yuan	0.1532	0.1532	0.04	0.5
Hong Kong dollar	0.1287	0.1287	0.01	0.2
India rupee	0.01461	0.01459	−0.19	3.4
Indonesia rupiah	0.0000747	0.0000745	−0.28	−3.2
Japan yen	0.00891	0.00892	0.06	−6.8
1 month forward rate (3/29/2016)	0.00898			
2 month forward rate (4/26/2016)	0.00899			
3 month forward rate (5/26/2016)	0.00900			
Malaysia ringgit	0.237	0.2369	−0.07	−2
New Zealand dollar	0.666	0.6641	−0.29	2.6
Singapore dollar	0.7116	0.7106	−0.14	−0.9
South Korea won	0.0008112	0.0008117	0.05	4.8
Taiwan dollar	0.03004	0.03004	0.02	1.1
Thailand baht	0.02803	0.028	−0.14	−1
Europe				
Euro area euro	1.1015	1.102	0.05	−1.4
1 month forward rate (3/29/2016)	1.1030			
2 month forward rate (4/26/2016)	1.1040			
3 month forward rate (5/26/2016)	1.1049			
Russia ruble	0.01319	0.01311	−0.6	5.4
Sweden krona	0.1178	0.1178	0.02	0.5
Switzerland franc	1.0113	1.0088	−0.25	−1.3
1 month forward rate (3/29/2016)	1.0154			
2 month forward rate (4/26/2016)	1.0170			
3 month forward rate (5/26/2016)	1.0187			
Turkey lira	0.3406	0.3397	−0.25	0.6
U.K. pound	1.3927	1.4022	0.68	5.8
1 month forward rate (3/29/2016)	1.3935			
2 month forward rate (4/26/2016)	1.3937			
3 month forward rate (5/26/2016)	1.3939			
Middle East/Africa				
Bahrain dinar	2.6544	2.6539	−0.02	−0.1
Egypt pound	0.1278	0.1277	−0.03	unch
Israel shekel	0.2553	0.2557	0.14	0.6
Saudia Arabia riyal	0.2666	0.2666	unch	−0.1
South Africa rand	0.0641	0.0656	2.39	0.8

Source: Spot rates are from wsj.com (February 24, 2016). Forward rates are from Bloomberg (February 24, 2016)

contract has been purchased, Cone Mills has a profit of 1 cent per pound, or $500. The seller of the contract, Texas Cotton Cooperative, has an identical loss. Under the rules of the ICE Futures U.S. exchange, where cotton futures are traded, the losers must pay the winners each day. This is called *marking to market*. Performance on a contract is guaranteed both by the requirement to mark to market and by the requirement that both parties maintain a *margin account*, or performance bond with their broker. The funds placed in the margin account are used to assure that losers have sufficient resources to pay the winners each day. If the amount in the margin account slips below the minimum required, the broker will demand that more funds be added to the account. If that is not done immediately, the broker will liquidate the position of the account holder. A "clearinghouse" operated by the exchange handles all payments between buyers and sellers over the life of the contract. In essence, all contracts are purchased from the clearinghouse or sold by the clearinghouse. The combination of the clearinghouse and margin accounts assures performance under the terms of all futures contracts.

When a futures contract matures, the buyer of the contract has the option of either taking delivery of the commodity underlying the contract or reversing its position by making an offsetting transaction. Only rarely do contract buyers (long position) take delivery. It is much more common for them to reverse their positions just prior to expiration by selling an identical contract. Because the buyer has purchased a contract (the original transaction) and sold an identical contract (normally just prior to expiration), the clearinghouse recognizes these transactions as offsetting each other. The opposite is true of the seller (short position) of the contract. The seller will have to purchase a contract to offset their short position.

21-4c A Long Hedge

Figure 21.2 is a table of metal futures prices traded on the Commodity Exchange Inc. (COMEX), a division of the New York Mercantile Exchange, as of February 10, 2016. As can be seen, copper contracts are for 25,000 pounds of copper, and the prices are quoted in dollars per pound. The column headed as "Settle" is the closing price of the contract for that day. The column headed as "Open Int" indicates the number of contracts that have been bought and sold and remain outstanding.

Suppose that on February 10, 2016, Halstead Industries anticipates the need for 100,000 pounds of copper in mid-August 2016 to meet its obligations under a contract to deliver copper tubing to an appliance manufacturer. Halstead has a number of choices. First, it could simply wait until August and buy the copper it needs. This choice, however, poses a risk that copper prices will rise, reducing the profitability of the contract with the appliance manufacturer. A second alternative is to buy today the copper it needs to fulfill the contract and store it until it is needed in August. The disadvantage of this alternative is the fact that Halstead will have a considerable amount of money tied up in this raw materials inventory, plus Halstead would have to pay to store the copper.

Alternatively, Halstead could execute what is called a *long hedge*; that is, Halstead could buy four copper futures contracts for August delivery at the August futures price, as of February 10, 2016. Assume that the purchase occurred at the closing price of the August contract of $2.037 per pound. The futures price represents a market-determined expectation of what the price of copper will be in mid-August. As time passes leading up to August, assume that the price of copper has risen to $2.65 per pound, because of a worldwide economic recovery and developing shortages of copper. If Halstead had remained unhedged, it would have had a loss of $0.613 or 61.3 cents per pound ($2.65 minus $2.037), or $61,300. Because

FIGURE 21.2

Selected Metal Futures Contract Prices

Wednesday, February 10, 2016

						LIFETIME		
	Open	**High**	**Low**	**Settle**	**Chg**	**High**	**Low**	**Open Int**
Copper-High (CMX)-25,000 lbs.; $ per lb.								
16-Feb	2.024	2.026	2.003	**2.025**	−0.0135	2.1335	1.941	1,026
16-Mar	2.041	2.043	1.999	**2.027**	−0.0125	2.1395	1.9355	86,867
16-Apr	2.0445	2.0445	2.0025	**2.029**	−0.0125	2.1405	1.9415	1,303
16-May	2.0435	2.046	2.0025	**2.03**	−0.013	2.1435	1.944	63,685
16-Jun	2.0425	2.0425	2.007	**2.0335**	−0.013	2.1445	1.954	1,201
16-Jly	2.0455	2.048	2.0075	**2.0335**	−0.013	2.148	1.958	20,062
16-Aug	2.048	2.048	2.0245	**2.037**	−0.013	2.146	1.976	343
16-Sep	2.027	2.0395	2.009	**2.0345**	−0.013	2.147	1.969	8,313
16-Oct	2.0235	2.0235	2.0235	**2.036**	−0.0135	2.148	1.973	373
16-Dec	2.028	2.0475	2.0195	**2.036**	−0.0135	2.148	1.971	5,030
17-Feb	2.026	2.026	2.026	**2.039**	−0.0135	2.1155	1.978	49
17-Mar	2.032	2.032	2.0255	**2.037**	−0.0135	2.113	1.978	1,151
17-May	2.027	2.027	2.027	**2.037**	−0.135	2.114	1.9745	440
17-Jly	2.0285	2.0285	2.0285	**2.0385**	−0.0135	2.118	1.9855	190
17-Sep	2.03	2.03	2.0285	**2.0395**	−0.135	2.066	1.989	91
17-Dec	2.0325	2.033	2.0325	**2.0415**	−0.135	2.0415	2.01	194
Est vol 75,044; vol n.a. n.a.; open int, 190,847, n.a..								
Gold (CMX)-100 troy oz.; $ per troy oz.								
16-Feb	1189.8	1197.7	1182.1	**1194.7**	−4	1200.4	1061	2,057
16-Mar	1189.5	1197.6	1181.5	**1194.3**	−4.1	1201.1	1062.5	1,895
16-Apr	1189.7	1198.1	1181.6	**1194.6**	−4	1201.4	1061.9	2,96,735
16-Jun	1191.1	1198.4	1182.2	**1195.1**	−4	1200.9	1063	59,202
16-Aug	1190.7	1198.8	1183.1	**1195.7**	−4	1200.6	1065.7	13,467
16-Oct	1184	1199.5	1184	**1196.2**	−4.1	1200.1	1066.2	3,849
16-Dec	1192	1200.1	1184.5	**1196.8**	−4.1	1203.4	1066	15,729
17-Feb	1194.4	1197	1194.1	**1197.5**	−4.1	1200.5	1076.6	1,959
17-Jun	1197.8	1197.8	1197.8	**1199.1**	−4.1	1203.6	1078.8	5,341
17-Dec	1190.5	1190.5	1188.8	**1201.7**	−4.1	1205	1083	5,621
Est vol 174,076; vol n.a. n.a.; open int, 414,305, n.a..								
Palladium (NYM) - 50 troy oz.; $ per troy oz.								
16-Feb	492	492	492	**525**	7.2	547.8	460	1
16-Mar	515.75	525.25	507.6	**524.7**	7.85	563.3	451.5	21,443
16-Jun	520	526	509.9	**525.5**	7.9	551.45	458.6	5,568
Est vol 9,047; vol n.a. n.a.; open int, 27,198, n.a..								
Platinum (NYM)-50 troy oz.; $ per troy oz.								
16-Feb	929.2	929.2	929.2	**933.3**	−4.4	933.3	815.8	3
16-Mar	932.8	935	924.7	**933.7**	−4.8	935	817.3	11
16-Apr	932.7	937.1	922.9	**934.2**	−5.2	939.9	811.4	59,672
16-Jly	930.3	937	925.9	**934.6**	−5.3	938.6	812.4	5,622
16-Oct	938.2	938.2	936	**935.9**	−5.2	938.3	815.7	114
Est vol 12,154; vol n.a. n.a.; open int, 65,426, n.a..								

FIGURE 21.2

Selected Metal Futures Contract Prices *(Continued)*

Wednesday, February 10, 2016

	Open	High	Low	Settle	Chg	LIFETIME High	LIFETIME Low	Open Int
Silver (CMX)-5,000 troy oz.; $ per troy oz.								
16-Feb	15.3	15.3	15.3	**15.277**	−0.167	15.42	13.735	20
16-Mar	15.285	15.325	15.11	**15.282**	−0.167	15.48	13.73	90,156
16-Apr	15.15	15.15	15.15	**15.293**	−0.169	15.48	14.205	57
16-May	15.305	15.345	15.125	**15.302**	−0.171	15.5	13.76	43,866
16-Jly	15.325	15.335	15.18	**15.326**	−0.172	15.525	13.81	9,768
16-Sep	15.345	15.36	15.215	**15.348**	−0.172	15.505	13.93	5,940
16-Dec	15.345	15.395	15.21	**15.381**	−0.174	15.58	13.865	10,305
17-Mar	15.38	15.425	15.38	**15.418**	−0.174	15.425	14.26	64
17-Dec	15.555	15.555	15.555	**15.539**	−0.175	15.715	14.14	1,176
18-Dec	15.685	15.685	15.685	**15.697**	−0.18	15.87	15.685	177

Est vol 78,549; vol n.a. n.a.; open int, 164,666, n.a.

Source: wsj.com

of the purchase of the copper futures contracts, this loss in the cash market is offset by profits in the futures market. This is illustrated in Table 21.1.

21-4d A Short Hedge

Another type of hedge transaction is called a *short hedge*. Consider the case of the Battle Mountain Copper Company. Battle Mountain has agreed on February 10, 2016, to sell 50,000 pounds of copper that it has not yet produced to Ford Motor Company for delivery in mid-June 2016 at an expected price of $2.0335 per pound, the price of June copper futures contracts. Battle Mountain knows that this will be a profitable transaction because its cost of production is less than the expected sales price. However, it is possible that between February and June, the spot price of copper may decline, such that Battle Mountain would be forced to sell the copper at a loss. To protect against this possibility, Battle Mountain could use the copper futures market to set up a short hedge. A short hedge in copper is illustrated in Table 21.2.

TABLE 21.1

Long Hedge in Copper

Cash Market	**Futures Market**
February 10, 2016	
Halstead anticipates a need for 100,000 pounds of copper in mid-August 2016 and anticipates paying $2.037 per pound, or $203,700.	Halstead buys four 25,000-pound August futures contracts at $2.037 per pound, or a total cost of $203,700.
August 15, 2016—the spot price of copper has risen to $2.65 per pound.	
Halstead buys 100,000 pounds of copper from a local metals dealer at $2.65 per pound for a total cost of $265,000.	Halstead sells four 25,000-pound August futures contracts at $2.65 per pound, or a total of $265,000.
Loss in cash market: $61,300	**Profit in futures market: $61,300**

TABLE 21.2

Short Hedge in Copper

Cash Market	Futures Market
February 10, 2016	
Battle Mountain anticipates the sale of 50,000 pounds of copper in mid-June 2016 and expects to receive $2.0335 per pound, or $101,675.	Battle Mountain sells two 25,000-pound June futures contracts at $2.0335 per pound, or $ 101,675.
June 15, 2016—the spot price of copper has fallen to $1.70 per pound.	
Battle Mountain sells 50,000 pounds of copper to Ford Motor Company at the June spot price of $1.70 per pound for a total of $85,000.	Battle Mountain buys two 25,000-pound June futures contracts at $1.70 per pound, or total cost of $85,000.
Loss in cash market: $16,675	**Profit in futures market: $16,675**

As this example illustrates, the short hedge has protected Battle Mountain from the unanticipated price decline for copper between February and June. Although both of these examples illustrate perfect hedges, in real-world hedging situations it is extremely difficult to perfectly hedge the risks illustrated here. Hedging is difficult to do perfectly because: (1) the available futures contract sizes may not match the hedging needs of the firm; and (2) there may be a change in the relationship between the futures price and the local spot price, so-called basis risk. Nevertheless, it is often possible to set up effective hedges of price risk using these hedging strategies.

21-5 Hedging Price Risk with Options

In the previous examples, the hedges were effectively perfect because the long and short hedges that were put in place locked in the effective purchase price (the long hedge) and selling price (the short hedge) for copper. Reconsider the case of Battle Mountain Copper Company and its plans to sell 50,000 pounds of copper to Ford Motor Company in mid-June 2016. Earlier, we showed what would have happened to Battle Mountain if the price of copper had declined between February 10, 2016, and June 15, 2016. The losses the company would have experienced in the cash market were offset by gains in the futures market. But what if the price of copper had risen during that time period from $2.0335 pound to $2.45 per pound? The managers who set up this hedge might have had a tough time explaining to their superiors why the company was only getting $2.0335 per pound instead of the $2.45 price that was prevailing in June.

Is it possible for Battle Mountain to protect itself against price declines and at the same time be in a position to benefit from price increases? The answer is yes, but this type of one-sided insurance comes at a price. Recall from the previous chapter that a *call option* gives the buyer the right to purchase something, such as a share of stock or an amount of copper, at the exercise price of the option up until the time the option expires (in the case of American options), or at expiration (in the case of European options). Similarly, a *put option* gives the buyer the right to sell something at the exercise price of the option up until the time the option expires (in the case of American options), or at expiration (in the case of European options). Which option should Battle

TABLE 21.3

Impact of Put Option Hedge for Battle Mountain Copper

Price of copper increases from $2.0335 to $2.45 per pound:

Sell copper to Ford Motor Company for $2.45 per pound in June 2016.

Let put options purchased in February expire for a loss of the option premium of 4.65 cents ($0.0465) per pound.

Net proceeds received from the sale of copper to Ford Motor Company:
$2.45 minus $0.0465 = $2.4035 per pound

Price of copper falls from $2.0335 to $1.70 per pound:

Sell copper to Ford Motor Company for $1.70 per pound in June 2016.

Sell put options at their expiration value of $0.30 per pound in June 2016. (Expiration value equals the difference between the exercise price of $2.00 and the final spot price for copper of $1.70.)

Earn net profit on options of $0.30 less the initial option premium of $0.0465, or $0.2535 per pound.

Net proceeds received from the sale of copper to Ford Motor:
$1.70 pound plus $0.2535 per pound, or $1.9535 per pound.

Mountain use in this example? Because Battle Mountain wants to *sell* copper to Ford Motor Company, it should buy put options on copper with an expiration date in June 2016.

Recall also from our discussion of options that, unlike futures contracts, options require the payment of a premium that is dependent on several factors, including the time remaining to expiration, the level of interest rates, and the volatility of the underlying asset (in this case, the price of copper). Suppose a June put option is available for copper with an exercise price of $2.00 per pound and the price of that option (the premium) is 4.65 cents ($0.0465) per pound. If the price of copper rises from an expected level of $2.0335 to $2.45, Battle Mountain would simply let its put options on copper expire and sell the copper to Ford for $2.45 per pound. But if the price declined to $1.70 per pound, Battle Mountain could exercise its put options and sell the copper at the exercise price of $2.00 per pound. This one-side protection comes at a price, however, and that price is the option premium of 4.65 cents ($0.0465) per pound paid when the option was purchased. Table 21.3 illustrates the profits and losses from the option strategy discussed here.

It is apparent in this table that the options hedging strategy allows Battle Mountain to benefit from price increases, and it provides protection from price declines. There is a cost to this protection, however, and that cost is the option premium, which in this case was $0.0465 per pound.

21-5a Final Comments Regarding Risk-Management Strategies

This chapter has provided a brief introduction to some of the risk-management strategies available to managers who want to reduce or eliminate some of the important operating and financial risks facing them. Risk is one of the most important variables that managers must deal with as they seek to maximize shareholder wealth. Choosing the proper risk-management techniques can make the difference between success and failure. The financial crisis of 2008 and the prospect of new and additional regulations to curb risky practices (especially among financial institutions) will ensure that risk management at firms will take on greater significance going forward. Risk management will become an enterprise-wide function. This trend has already begun, as evidenced by the appointment

ETHICAL ISSUES

AIG, the Financial Crisis of 2008, and the Failure of Risk Management[a]

The board of directors of the beleaguered AIG in September 2008 accepted a deal from the U.S. government. It was a deal they could not reject: an $85 billion loan in return for surrendering control of AIG. By March 2009, the AIG bailout costs stood at $170 billion and were rising even further.

AIG's businesses included life and property-casualty insurance policies across 100 countries. With employee strength of 100,000, AIG had a diversified portfolio of businesses, including companies that made consumer loans and leased aircraft. AIG also engaged in selling credit protection against the possibility of default in a variety of assets, including subprime mortgages. In these contractual agreements or protections, called credit default swaps (CDSs), the counterparties agreed to make regular payments to AIG, which in turn agreed to compensate the counterparties if the underlying securities defaulted. AIG also posted collateral, such as cash or government bonds, to its counterparties if market prices of the swaps moved against AIG. If they did move against AIG, the underlying securities became more risky.

AIG was aggressively selling CDSs to numerous financial institutions and companies around the world, including Wall Street firms and industrial corporations, using its huge balance sheet and strong credit ratings. AIG believed that having a huge balance sheet and strong credit rating would shield the counterparties from bond defaults. As of June 30, 2008, AIG had CDSs of $441 billion in debt, such as corporate bonds and mortgage bonds.

While AIG's core businesses were healthy, problems began to manifest themselves in the Financial Products Group, a unit within AIG that sold the complex CDSs. The exposure to CDSs tied AIG's fortunes closely to the fate of the housing and credit markets. When the housing market started tumbling, the value of those contracts plunged forcing counterparties to demand more collateral. AIG had to pay the collateral or face bankruptcy. AIG's bankruptcy could have cascaded into a string of bank failures around the world, posing a systemic threat to the global financial enterprise. This prompted the eventual bailout of AIG by the U.S. government.

The AIG episode shows that improperly handled risk management could have implications not only for one firm but, for all counterparties dealing with it. AIG believed that the value of the CDSs would never fall in value and got drawn into the false impression that it could keep collecting the fixed payments. AIG thought it understood all the risk ramifications of the CDS instruments, but after the fact it became clear it had not. AIG also failed to hedge its own risk while it was busy acting as a counterparty in somebody else's hedging strategy. In AIG's case, the counterparties were spread far and wide, which further exacerbated the threat to the global financial system.

---

[a]Written by Subbu Iyer (University of New Mexico).

Sources: Mathew Karnitschnig, Liam Pleven, and Serena Ng, "AIG Faces Cash Crisis as Stock Dives 61%," *The Wall Street Journal* (September 16, 2008): A1; Mathew Karnitschnig, Deborah Solomon, Liam Pleven, and Jon E. Hilsenrath, "U.S. to Take Over AIG in $85 Billion; Central Banks Inject as Credit Dries Up—Emergency Loan Effectively Gives Government Control of Insurer: Historic Move Would Cap 10 Days That Reshaped U.S. Finance," *The Wall Street Journal* (September 17, 2008): A1; Serena Ng, "The Financial Crisis: AIG at Risk: Financial Firms Gird for Backlash from Weakened AIG," *The Wall Street Journal* (September 17, 2008): A10; Monica Langley, Deborah Solomon, and Matthew Karnitschnig, "Bad Bets and Cash Crunch Pushed Ailing AIG to Brink," *The Wall Street Journal* (September 18, 2008): A1; Lucian Bebchuk, "AIG Still Isn't Too Big to Fail," *The Wall Street Journal* (March 20, 2009).

of chief risk officers (CROs) at many firms. Universities have also begun to offer specializations at the undergraduate and graduate levels in risk management. However, it is important to note that, as the nearby story of AIG illustrates, risk management cannot consider every eventuality and is subject to the assumptions underlying the model used to control risk. The discussion in this chapter has just scratched the surface of this important topic. In advanced courses, you will learn how a wide range of financial derivatives can be used to help manage a wide variety of risks, from currency risks (illustrated in greater detail in Chapter 22), to interest rate risks, and various aspects of pricing risk.

21-6 Summary

- Risk management encompasses a range of strategies and techniques that can be used to reduce the variability of possible future returns from any business transaction. The goal is to reduce the variability of a firm's expected cash flows.
- The most important reason for firms to use risk-management techniques is to reduce the chance of catastrophic financial distress. Other reasons include assuring that adequate cash flows will be available to make needed investments, even in challenging business environments, and helping management focus attention on issues more directly under its control.
- Nonhedging strategies that managers use to control risk include the acquisition of additional information; diversification; the purchase of insurance; the use of patents, copyrights, and other forms of legal protection of intellectual property; and the limited use of firm-specific assets.
- A hedge is a transaction that limits the risk associated with fluctuations in the price of a commodity, currency, or financial instrument. A hedge is accomplished by taking offsetting positions in the ownership of an asset or security through the use of derivative securities, such as forward contracts, futures contracts, and options.
- A forward contract is an agreement to buy or sell an asset at some point in time in the future at a price agreed to at the time the forward contract is purchased or sold. Forward contracts can be executed for any quantity of any asset for any maturity date. Consequently, they are not highly liquid. Forward contracts frequently have an element of performance risk from the counterparty to the contract.
- A futures contract is a *standardized* contract, traded on an organized exchange, to buy or sell an asset at a specified future time at a specified price. Because it is standardized with respect to quantity, quality, and delivery date and place, futures contracts are highly liquid. Exchange procedures eliminate performance risk from the counterparty to the contract.
- A long hedge involves the purchase of a forward or futures contract to cover required future purchases of a commodity or currency. Short hedges involve the sale of a forward or a futures contract to cover a required future sale of a commodity or currency. Call options can be used to hedge future purchase requirements, and put options can be used to hedge future sales commitments.

21-7 Questions and Topics for Discussion

1. What types of risks should shareholder wealth-maximizing managers seek to offset in a firm they are managing? Why?
2. How can the acquisition of additional information be an effective tool of risk management? Give an original example of the use of this technique.
3. What role does diversification play in risk-management strategies?
4. Against what types of risks should a wealth-maximizing firm try to purchase insurance? What types of risks should be self-insured?
5. How can patents, copyrights, and legal challenges be used to manage business risk?
6. What are the primary differences between forward contracts and futures contracts?
7. Options can protect a firm against the downside risk of a business transaction while preserving the upside potential from the transaction. In contrast, forward and futures contracts normally protect against the downside risk but forfeit the upside potential. Why, then, don't firms always use options to hedge their risks instead of forward and futures contracts?

21-8 Self-Test Problems

ST1. Shining Rock Mining is a gold-mining firm that is concerned about controlling the volatility of its revenues. The current price of gold is $1,625 per ounce, but over the past year it has traded for as little as $1,450 and as much as $1,750. These price swings have been known to occur in as little as one month. Shining Rock expects to have 5,000 ounces of gold available for sale over the coming month.

a. If Shining Rock does not hedge these sales, what is the maximum amount of total revenue they could hope to receive based on prices over the past year? What is the minimum amount of total revenue they could hope to receive?

b. The futures price for gold delivered in one month is $1,630. If Shining Rock sells its gold in the futures market, what will be its total revenue?

c. If Shining Rock buys a put option to sell gold in one month at $1,630, and the put option costs $4.25 per ounce, what will its total revenues be?

ST2. Independence Airline anticipates the need to buy 1 million gallons of jet fuel in 3 months. The current price of jet fuel is $3.30 per gallon. The 3-month futures price for jet fuel is $3.45 per gallon. Independence is concerned that unrest in the Middle East could cause the price of jet fuel to rise well above $3.45. If the price of jet fuel actually increases to $4.00 over the next 3 months, compare the company's cost of jet fuel if it remains unhedged versus the cost if it buys jet fuel futures contracts to cover its jet fuel purchases in 3 months.

21-9 Problems*

BASIC

1. California Plastics uses crude oil as one of its major raw material inputs. The current price of crude oil is $95 per barrel. The company is concerned that significant increases in the price of crude oil could jeopardize its profits. Each $1 increase in the price of crude oil reduces the company's earnings per share by about $0.02. How can California Plastics use futures contracts and/or options to protect itself against unfavorable price movements?

INTERMEDIATE

2. In February, Tech Components Inc. (TCI), a manufacturer of specialized electronic components, was negotiating a supply agreement with a major auto manufacturer to supply specialized electronic components for delivery in 6 months. One of the key inputs into the making these specialized components is silver. The current spot price of silver is $25.15 per troy ounce. The 6-month futures price for silver is $26.90.

a. What silver price should TCI use as it establishes a price to quote to the auto manufacturer—the current price or the 6-month futures price?

b. Set up a hedge using the futures market for silver that will protect TCI against increases in the price of silver over the coming 6 months.

c. How could TCI use options to hedge this risk? Which type of options should be used—puts or calls?

BASIC

3. Jenkins Electronics has purchased a large quantity of electronic components from a Japanese firm for use in its new DVD players. The Japanese supplier has agreed to give Jenkins payment terms of net 90. The Japanese firm insists that payments be made in yen. The current exchange rate between the dollar and the yen is 108 yen per dollar. The 3-month forward exchange rate is 105 yen per dollar. What strategy would you recommend to Jenkins if it wants to protect itself against increases in the value of the yen over the next 90 days?

INTERMEDIATE

4. Disher Cotton Farms is a large cotton producer located near Lubbock, Texas. Each year Disher plants its fields in cotton and then waits until the fall before the cotton is picked and sold. Disher knows that its cost of producing cotton is about $0.75 per

*Color blocks behind the numbers denote problems that have check answers provided at the end of the book.

pound. In April when the cotton is planted, the current market price for cotton is \$0.83. The October futures price is \$0.81. Disher expects to produce 250,000 pounds of cotton this season.

a. If Disher does not hedge its cotton crop, what total revenue can it expect to receive in October?
b. If Disher does hedge its cotton crop in the futures market, what total revenue can it expect to receive in October? What type of hedge is this called?
c. Which alternative (a or b) is preferred, and why?
d. What risks does Disher face if it sells its entire expected cotton crop in the futures market?

CHALLENGE

5. One of the most important operating expenses for the Olde Virginia Brick Company is natural gas, which is used to bake and dry the bricks. Natural gas prices have recently been quite volatile, now approaching \$4 per mcf (1,000 cubic feet). Olde Virginia is bidding on a contract for a large quantity of bricks to be provided for a new mall project that is under construction. The bricks must be delivered in 6 months. Olde Virginia has estimated that it can make a nice profit on the order at the current price of natural gas. If natural gas prices increase to \$4.50 per mcf, Olde Virginia will just break even on the order. The 6-month futures contract price for natural gas is \$3.75 per mcf. The cost of a call option to buy natural gas at \$3.75 is \$0.15 per mcf.

a. If Olde Virginia does not hedge the cost of its natural gas inputs, what is the expected cost of the gas to produce this large order?
b. If Olde Virginia hedges the cost of its natural gas inputs in the futures market, what is the expected cost of the gas for this order?
c. If Olde Virginia hedges the cost of its natural gas inputs by buying call options at a strike price of \$3.75, what is the expected cost of the gas for this order?
d. Which strategy would you suggest, and why?

CHAPTER 22

International Financial Management

KEY CHAPTER CONCEPTS

1. The theory of *interest rate parity* states that the percentage differential between the spot and the forward rate for a currency is equal to the approximate difference in interest rates in the two countries over the same time horizon.
2. The theory of *relative purchasing power parity* states that in comparison to a period when exchange rates between two countries are in equilibrium, changes in differential rates of inflation between the countries will be offset by equal but opposite changes in the future spot currency rate.
3. The forward rate is often considered to be an unbiased estimator of the future spot currency rate.
4. The *Fisher effect* states that nominal interest rates are approximately equal to the sum of the real interest rate and the expected inflation rate.
5. The *international Fisher effect* theory states that differences in interest rates between two countries should be offset by equal but opposite changes in the future spot rate.
6. Three important categories of foreign exchange risk are (1) transaction exposure, (2) economic exposure, and (3) translation exposure.
7. A hedge is an offsetting transaction designed to reduce or avoid risk. Forward and futures exchange hedges and money market hedges are used to reduce transaction exposure. Financing with debt denominated in the same currency as foreign assets is a means of hedging against translation and economic exposure.

FINANCIAL CHALLENGE

Lexus Comes to the United States

Japan is one of the largest trading partners with the United States. In 2012, the United States exported more than \$60 billion worth of goods to Japan and imported more than \$125 billion from Japan. One large component of the trade figure is the import of automobiles from Japan to the United States. Although several Japanese auto firms have moved final production of many of their cars to plants in the United States (Toyota, Nissan, Subaru, and Honda, for example), many products are still being made in Japan and imported as finished goods into the United States. By manufacturing cars in Japan, and incurring production costs in Japanese yen (JPY), a company is exposed to the risk of currency fluctuations between the JPY and the dollar.

Courtesy of Toyota Motor Corporation

For example, assume that Toyota's Lexus division can produce a Lexus ES sedan for 5 million JPY (including the desired profit margin and transportation costs). If the exchange rate is 100 JPY to the dollar, this translates into a U.S. price of \$50,000. This price is competitive with other similar luxury cars sold in the United States. Now assume that the JPY increases in value so that it takes only 75 JPY to buy \$1. If the Lexus is still sold in the United States for \$50,000 (because that is the price point for the products with which it competes), Toyota will receive only 3,750,000 JPY (\$50,000 × 75 JPY/dollar), well below the desired 5 million JPY. On the other hand, if the value of the JPY weakens relative to the dollar, so that it takes 140 JPY to buy \$1, then Toyota will receive 7 million JPY—well above its target of 5 million yen. Thus, it can be seen that the profits of the Lexus division can fluctuate substantially from year to year, based not only on sales volumes, but also on changes in the exchange rate.

Over the years there has been substantial variation in the JPY-to-dollar exchange rate. Some selected exchange rates going back to the late 1990s are as follows:

Year	JPY/Dollar
1998	144.75
2002	134.87
2008	110.17
2012	75.93
2013	99.47
2015	122.94

Faced with this substantial volatility in exchange rates, a company like Toyota has several options open to it to maintain its competitive position and to avoid drastic fluctuations in financial

FINANCIAL CHALLENGE — CONTINUED

performance. In the relatively short term, Toyota can use currency futures markets to hedge changes in exchange rates. In the longer term, it can aggressively work to cut manufacturing costs in Japan so that it can continue to offer its products in the United States at dollar-denominated competitive prices while making adequate profits in Japan on these sales. Finally, the company can reduce the exchange rate risk of producing cars for the U.S. market by incurring more of its costs in dollars, rather than in JPY. Most often, this is accomplished by moving the manufacture of all or a substantial portion of the cars to the market where the car is being sold, in this case to the United States.

In April 2013, Toyota announced plans to invest more than $350 million to expand its Georgetown, Kentucky, plant to give it the capacity to build Lexus ES sedans. Toyota received tax incentives from the Commonwealth of Kentucky of $146.5 million. The plant produced its first Lexus E350 in October 2015. The plant expansion brought 750 new jobs to the Georgetown plant. Luxury car sales have been growing rapidly in the United States, and competition among producers is stiff. The U.S. production location will enable Lexus to remain competitive in this market. Nissan has also recently announced plans to build its first Infiniti luxury car at its Tennessee plant.

This chapter examines the major factors that affect exchange rates, the meaning and rationale for international exchange rate parity relationships, the techniques to forecast exchange rates, and the nature and management of exchange rate risk.

CHAPTER OBJECTIVES

Upon completion of this chapter, you should have a clear understanding of the following:

1. The major factors that affect exchange rates
2. The rationale for each of the international parity relationships
3. Techniques that can be used to forecast future exchange rates
4. The major categories of foreign exchange risk:
   - Transaction exposure
   - Economic exposure
   - Translation exposure

22-1 Introduction

As the world economy has become more globally integrated, virtually every firm and individual is affected by developments in the economies of countries other than their own. Recently, the debates in Europe about how to deal with weaker Eurozone countries, notably Greece, Italy, Portugal, Spain, and Cyprus, have impacted the economic climate around the world. Individuals are affected by global economic conditions as multinational firms seek the cheapest place to produce their products—resulting in employment winners and losers. A textile firm may move to Mexico from North Carolina at the same time that Lexus announces the construction of a new plant in Kentucky. In making plant location decisions, managers consider wage costs, the quality of the workforce, transportation costs, economic incentives, the cost of raw materials, exchange rate levels and risks, and political risk (such as the risk of expropriation or the blocking of funds). In addition, firms may decide to locate in multiple countries to gain quicker access to new technologies as they develop. Some international plant location decisions are designed, at least in part, to avoid political and regulatory barriers. For example, Japanese and German auto firms, including Toyota, Nissan, Subaru, Mercedes, BMW, and Honda, have built large assembly plants in the United States to reduce the currency risk and labor cost risk associated with a one-country location strategy.

Financial managers willing to venture into the global financial marketplace may find lower-cost financing alternatives than are available in their home country. With trade barriers being lowered around the world, the managers of tomorrow cannot limit their knowledge to "Island America." Rather, these managers will find that understanding the functioning of the global financial marketplace is a key element of their knowledge and skill base.

This chapter continues the discussion of international finance that was begun in Chapter 2. Here we explore the factors that determine exchange rates, look at ways to forecast future exchange rates, and consider various aspects of foreign exchange risk and ways of managing that risk.

22-2 Factors That Affect Exchange Rates

Exchange rates between currencies vary over time, reflecting supply and demand considerations for each currency. For example, the demand for British pounds comes from a number of sources, which include foreign buyers of British exports who must pay for their purchases in pounds, foreign investors who desire to make investments in physical or financial assets in Britain, and speculators who expect British pounds to increase in value relative to other currencies. The British government may also be a source of demand if it attempts to keep the value of the pound (relative to other currencies) from falling by using its supply of foreign currencies or gold to purchase pounds in the market.

Sources of supply include British importers who need to convert their pounds into foreign currency to pay for purchases, British investors who desire to make investments in foreign countries, and speculators who expect British pounds to decrease in value relative to other currencies.

Exchange rates are also affected by economic and political conditions that influence the supply of, or demand for, a country's currency. Some of these conditions include differential inflation and interest rates among countries, the government's trade policies, and the government's political stability. A high rate of inflation within a country tends to lower the value of its currency with respect to the currencies of other countries experiencing lower rates of inflation. The exchange rate will tend to decline as holders sell or exchange the country's currency for other currencies whose purchasing power is not declining at as high a rate. In contrast, relatively high interest rates within a country tend to increase the value of a currency as foreign investors seek to convert their currencies and purchase these higher-yielding securities.

Government trade policies that limit imports—such as the imposition of tariffs, import quotas, and restrictions on foreign exchange transactions—reduce the supply of the country's currency in the foreign exchange market. This, in turn, tends to increase the value of the country's currency with respect to other currencies and thus to increase exchange rates.

Finally, the political stability of the government affects the risks perceived by foreign investors and companies doing business in the country. These risks include the possible expropriation of investments or restrictions on the amount of funds (such as returns from investments) that may be taken out of the country.

In the following sections, we develop the important relationships among spot rates, forward rates, interest rates, and inflation rates as they impact foreign currency exchange rates.

22-2a Covered Interest Arbitrage and Interest Rate Parity

HTTP:
Foreign exchange actually includes spot contracts, forward contracts, futures, options, swaps, foreign currency loans/ deposits, etc. Visit XE's Web site for a comprehensive listing of important foreign exchange terminology.
www.xe.com/currencytrading/terms.php

There is a close relationship between the interest rates in two countries and the forward exchange rate premium or discount. Consider a U.S. investor with $1.2 million to invest who notes that the interest rate on 90-day certificates of deposit (CDs) available at Swiss banks is 1.0 percent for 90 days. At the same time, the 90-day CD rate in the United States is only 0.25 percent. Assume that the spot rate of the Swiss franc (CHF) is $0.90/CHF and the 90-day forward rate is also $0.90. As an investor, you know that you can immediately convert $1.2 million into CHF1.3333 million at today's spot rate of $0.90 with no risk. You can also lock in the 1.0 percent Swiss interest rate for 90 days by purchasing a Swiss CD with your CHF1.3333 million. However, there is risk regarding the exchange rate at which you will be able to convert CHF back to dollars at the end of 90 days. You can guarantee this rate by selling 1.333 million CHF (plus the interest you will receive on your Swiss CD) in the 90-day forward market at today's forward rate of $0.90. This transaction will guarantee you a risk-free profit. Consider the following steps in this transaction:

1. Convert $1.2 million into CHF1.3333 million at today's spot rate of $0.90/CHF.
2. Buy a 90-day CD at a Swiss bank yielding 1.0 percent every 90 days.
3. Simultaneously sell CHF1.3466 million forward (original CHF1.3333 million plus CHF13,333 in interest) at $0.90 to net you $1,211,970.
4. This compares favorably with the $1,203,000 ($1.2 million plus interest at 0.25%) you could have received from investing in a U.S. CD.

This risk-free transaction enabled you to earn an additional return of $8,970 over what would be available by investing in the United States. Because there are virtually no barriers to prevent individuals from engaging in this transaction called **covered interest arbitrage**, it can be expected that opportunities to earn risk-free additional returns such as these will not persist very long. The demand by American investors for CHF will put upward pressure on the spot price of CHF, to a price greater than $0.90/CHF. At the same time, as American investors sell CHF forward to cover their position, this will put downward pressure on the forward rate of the CHF to a price less than $0.90. Furthermore, as funds leave the United States for Switzerland, the reduced supply of funds will tend to increase U.S. interest rates. The increased supply of funds in Switzerland, on the other hand, will tend to lower Swiss interest rates.

covered interest arbitrage

The net effect of these transactions and market pressures will be an equilibrium condition where covered interest arbitrage transactions are not possible. This relationship is called **interest rate parity** (IRP). When IRP exists, the forward rate will differ from the spot rate by just enough to offset the interest rate differential between the two currencies. The IRP condition states that the home (or domestic) interest rate must be higher (lower) than the foreign interest rate by an amount equal to the forward discount (premium) on the home currency. In other words, the forward premium or discount for a currency quoted in terms of another currency is approximately equal to the difference

interest rate parity

in interest rates prevailing between the two countries. Thus, if interest rates in Switzerland are higher than interest rates in the United States, then the IRP condition indicates that the dollar can be expected to increase in value relative to the CHF. The exact IRP relationship is:

(22.1)
$$\text{IRP}: \left(\frac{F - S_0}{S_0}\right) = \left(\frac{i_h - i_f}{1 + i_f}\right)$$

HTTP:
A handy currency conversion tool can be found at
www.xe.com/ucc

where i_h is the home (U.S.) interest rate, i_f is the comparable foreign (Swiss) interest rate, F is the *direct quote* forward rate, and S_0 is the *direct quote* spot rate.[1] (Note that the interest rates in Equation 22.1 are the interest rates for the same period of time as the number of days in the forward price, not necessarily annualized interest rates.) The relationship in Equation 22.1 can be simplified to:

(22.2)
$$\text{IRP}: \frac{F}{S_0} = \frac{1 + i_h}{1 + i_f}$$

An approximation of the IRP relationship is:

(22.3)
$$\text{Approximate IRP}: \left(\frac{F - S_0}{S_0}\right) \approx (i_h - i_f)$$

Equation 22.3 indicates that when interest rate parity exists, differences in interest rates between two countries will be (approximately) offset by changes in the relative value of the two currencies.

To illustrate, assume that the 90-day interest rate is 1.5 percent in the United States and 2.5 percent in Switzerland, and the current spot exchange rate between dollars and CHF is \$0.90. If IRP holds, what will the 90-day forward rate be (using the exact relationship in Equation 22.2)?

$$(F/\$0.90) = (1 + 0.015)/(1 + 0.025)$$
$$F = \$0.8912$$

In this case, the dollar has increased in value relative to the CHF (that is, it takes fewer dollars to buy each CHF). Why do you think this should occur?

22-2b Purchasing Power Parity

When there are no significant costs or other barriers associated with moving goods or services between markets, then the price of each product should be the same in each market. In economics, this is known as the *law of one price*. When the different markets represent different countries, the law of one price says that prices will be the same in each country after making the appropriate conversion from one currency to another. Alternatively, one can say that exchange rates between two currencies will equal the ratio of the price indexes between the countries. In international finance and trade, this relationship is known as the absolute version of *purchasing power parity*.

In reality, we know that this relationship does not hold because of the costs of moving goods and services and the existence of tariffs and other trade barriers. For example, *The Economist*, in a lighthearted look at the law of one price, regularly reports on the price of Big Mac hamburgers in various countries. When the price of a Big Mac in July 2015 was \$4.79 in the United States, it cost (after converting currencies) \$4.05 in France, \$2.09 in South Africa, \$3.15 in Brazil, \$2.99 in Japan, and \$5.65 in Norway.[2] It is obviously not possible to buy Big Macs in Cape Town and ship them to New York for sale, for

[1]Recall that a *direct quote* is the home currency price of a unit of foreign currency, such as \$/CHF (from the perspective of an American).

[2]D.H. and L.D., "The Big Mac Index," *The Economist* (July 16, 2015), www.economist.com/content/big-mac-index.

example. Hence the law of one price does not hold for Big Macs. On the other hand, for goods that are standardized and somewhat easier to move and store, such as gold or crude oil, one would expect only minor violations of the law of one price.

relative purchasing power parity

A less restrictive form of the law of one price is known as **relative purchasing power parity** (PPP). The relative PPP principle states that in comparison to a period when exchange rates between two countries are in equilibrium, changes in the differential rates of inflation between two countries will be offset by equal but opposite changes in the future spot exchange rate. For example, if prices in the United States rise by 4 percent per year and prices in Switzerland rise by 6 percent per year, then relative PPP holds if the Swiss franc (CHF) weakens relative to the U.S. dollar by approximately 2 percent.

The exact relative purchasing power parity relationship is:

(22.4)
$$\text{Relative PPP:} \left(\frac{S_1 - S_0}{S_0}\right) = \left(\frac{\pi_h - \pi_f}{1 + \pi_f}\right)$$

where S_1 is the expected future (direct quote) spot rate at time period 1, S_0 is the current (direct quote) spot rate, π_h is the expected home country (U.S.) inflation rate, and π_f is the expected foreign country inflation rate.[3] This relationship can be simplified to:

(22.5)
$$\text{Relative PPP:} \left(\frac{S_1}{S_0}\right) = \left(\frac{1 + \pi_h}{1 + \pi_f}\right)$$

Using the previous example, if U.S. prices are expected to rise by 4 percent over the coming year, prices in Switzerland are expected to rise by 6 percent during the same time, and the current spot exchange rate (S_0) is \$0.90/CHF, then the expected spot rate in one year (S_1), will be:

$$S_1/\$0.90 = (1 + 0.04)/(1 + 0.06)$$
$$S_1 = \$0.8830$$

The higher Swiss inflation rate can be expected to result in a decline in the future spot value of the CHF relative to the dollar by about 1.89 percent.

The market forces that support the relative PPP relationship operate in the following way. If one nation has a higher inflation rate than another, its goods and services will become relatively more expensive, making its exports less price competitive and imports more price competitive. The resulting deficit in foreign trade will place downward pressure on the currency value of the high-inflation country until a new, lower equilibrium value is established. The opposite will be true for the country with the lower inflation rate. For example, if the United States has a lower inflation rate than its major trading partners, relative PPP indicates that the value of the dollar can be expected to increase relative to the value of the currencies of these other trading partners.

Tests of relative PPP indicate that the relationship holds up reasonably well over long periods, but it is a less accurate indicator of short-term currency value changes. Also, the relative PPP relationship is stronger for those countries experiencing high rates of inflation. Tests of the strength of the PPP relationship are hampered by the use of noncomparable price indexes between countries and government interference in commodity and currency markets. Nevertheless, the general relationship between inflation rates and currency values is widely accepted, even if it is difficult to measure properly.

HTTP:
To more accurately estimate the true living standards in developing countries, the IMF and many other multilaterals use PPP analyses.
www1.oecd.org/

[3]The relationship in Equation 22.4 can be approximated as

$$\frac{S_1 - S_0}{S_0} \approx \pi_h - \pi_f$$

22-2c Expectations Theory and Forward Exchange Rates

If foreign currency markets are efficient, the forward rate should reflect what market participants expect the future spot rate for a currency to be. For example, if market participants expected the one-year future spot rate (S_1) for CHF to be $0.88, then what would the one-year forward rate (F_1) have to be? It would also have to be $0.88. If the forward rate were lower than this amount, market participants would want to buy CHF forward, thereby placing upward price pressure on the CHF until an equilibrium is reached where the forward rate equals the expected future spot rate.

If the expected future spot rate is equivalent to the forward rate, we can say that the forward rate is an *unbiased* estimator of the future spot rate. It is important to recognize that this does not mean that the forward rate will always be equal to the actual future spot rate. Rather, it means that the estimates of the future spot rate provided by the forward rate will not systematically overshoot or undershoot the actual future spot rate, but will equal it *on average.*

Evidence regarding the expectations theory of forward exchange rates indicates that, in general, the forward rate is an unbiased estimate of expected future spot rates, if risk in the currency markets is ignored.[4] There is some evidence, however, that when the forward rate implies a large change from the current spot rate, these forecasts tend to overshoot the actual future spot rate.

Forward rates as unbiased estimates of expected future spot rates have important implications for managers. First, managers should not spend the firm's resources to buy forecasts of future exchange rates since unbiased forecasts are provided free in the marketplace. Second, managers will find that hedging their future foreign currency risk by making use of the forward market should be a cost-effective way of limiting this risk exposure. In the following sections, some of these hedging techniques are considered.

22-2d The International Fisher Effect

The final piece in the international currency market puzzle is the relationship between interest rates and future spot currency rates. In his 1930 book, *The Theory of Interest,* Irving Fisher established that in equilibrium lenders will receive a nominal rate of interest equal to a real interest rate plus an amount sufficient to offset the effects of expected inflation. *Nominal interest rates* are market rates stated in current, not real, terms, such as the rates quoted in financial publications like *The Wall Street Journal.* Real rates of return are not directly observable. The real rate of return is the rate at which borrowing and lending in the financial markets are in equilibrium. The real rate of return is equal to the real rate of growth in the economy, and it reflects the time preference of market participants between present and future consumption. The relationship between nominal (risk-free) rates of return, real rates of return, and expected inflation is:

$$(1+i) = (1+i_R)(1+\pi)$$

or

(22.6)
$$i = i_R + \pi + i_R\pi$$

where i is the nominal (and risk-free) rate of interest, i_R is the real rate of return, and π is the expected inflation rate. This relationship is often referred to as the *Fisher effect.*[5]

---

[4]Lars P. Hansen and Robert J. Hodrick, "Forward Exchange Rates as Optimal Predictors of Future Spot Rates: An Econometric Analysis," *Journal of Political Economy* 88, no. 5 (October 1980): 829–853.

[5]This relationship can be approximated as:

$$i \approx i_R + \pi$$

For example, if the annual real rate of return in Hong Kong was 3 percent and the expected annual inflation rate was 8 percent, the nominal interest rate would be:

$$i = 0.03 + 0.08 + (0.03)(0.08) = 0.1124 \text{ or } 11.24\%$$

Fisher argues that in the absence of government interference and holding risk constant, real rates of return across countries will be equalized through a process of arbitrage. If real rates of return are higher in the United States than in Japan, for example, capital will flow to the United States from Japan until an equilibrium is reached. The assumption of equal real rates of return across countries ignores differences in risk and attitudes toward risk that may exist in different cultures. Also, to the extent that there are barriers to the movement of capital between countries, real rates of return may be different between countries. In spite of these limitations, the assumption of equal real returns is useful because (1) it is a reasonable representation of reality among the major industrialized countries, and (2) as capital markets become increasingly internationalized and barriers to capital flows fall, differences in real rates of return can be expected to decrease.

If real rates of return tend to be equalized across countries, it follows that differences in observed nominal rates between countries must be due primarily to different inflation expectations. Incorporating the equilibrium condition for real interest rates with relative PPP leads to what has been called the **international Fisher effect (IFE)**. The IFE states that differences in interest rates between two countries should be offset by equal but opposite changes in the future spot exchange rate. For example, if one-year nominal interest rates are 3 percent in the United States and 5 percent in Hong Kong, then IFE predicts that the Hong Kong dollar (HKD) should decrease in value relative to the U.S. dollar by approximately 2 percent.

international Fisher effect (IFE)

The exact IFE relationship is:

(22.7)

$$\text{IFE}: \left(\frac{S_1 - S_0}{S_0}\right) = \left(\frac{i_h - i_f}{1 + i_f}\right)$$

where S_1 is the expected future (direct quote) spot rate at time period 1, S_0 is the current (direct quote) spot rate, i_h is the home country (U.S.) nominal interest rate, and i_f is the foreign country nominal interest rate.[6] This relationship can be simplified to:

(22.8)

$$\text{IFE}: \left(\frac{S_1}{S_0}\right) = \left(\frac{1 + i_h}{1 + i_f}\right)$$

Using the previous example, if one-year U.S. nominal interest rates are 3 percent, one-year Hong Kong nominal interest rates are 5 percent, and the current spot exchange rate, S_0, is \$0.129/HKD, then the expected spot rate in one year, S_1, will be:

$$S_1/\$0.129 = (1 + 0.03)/(1 + 0.05)$$
$$S_1 = \$0.1265$$

The higher nominal Hong Kong interest rate results in an expected decrease in the value of the HKD (increase in the value of the \$) from \$0.129/HKD to \$0.1265/HKD.

22-2e An Integrative Look at International Parity Relationships

Figure 22.1 provides an integrative look at international parity relationships. Beginning with the lower box in the figure, suppose one observes that the one-year nominal interest rate is 10 percent in the United States and 5 percent in Switzerland. This implies,

---

[6]This relationship can be approximated as:

$$\frac{S_1 - S_0}{S_0} \approx i_h - i_f$$

FIGURE 22.1

International Parity Conditions: An Integrative Look

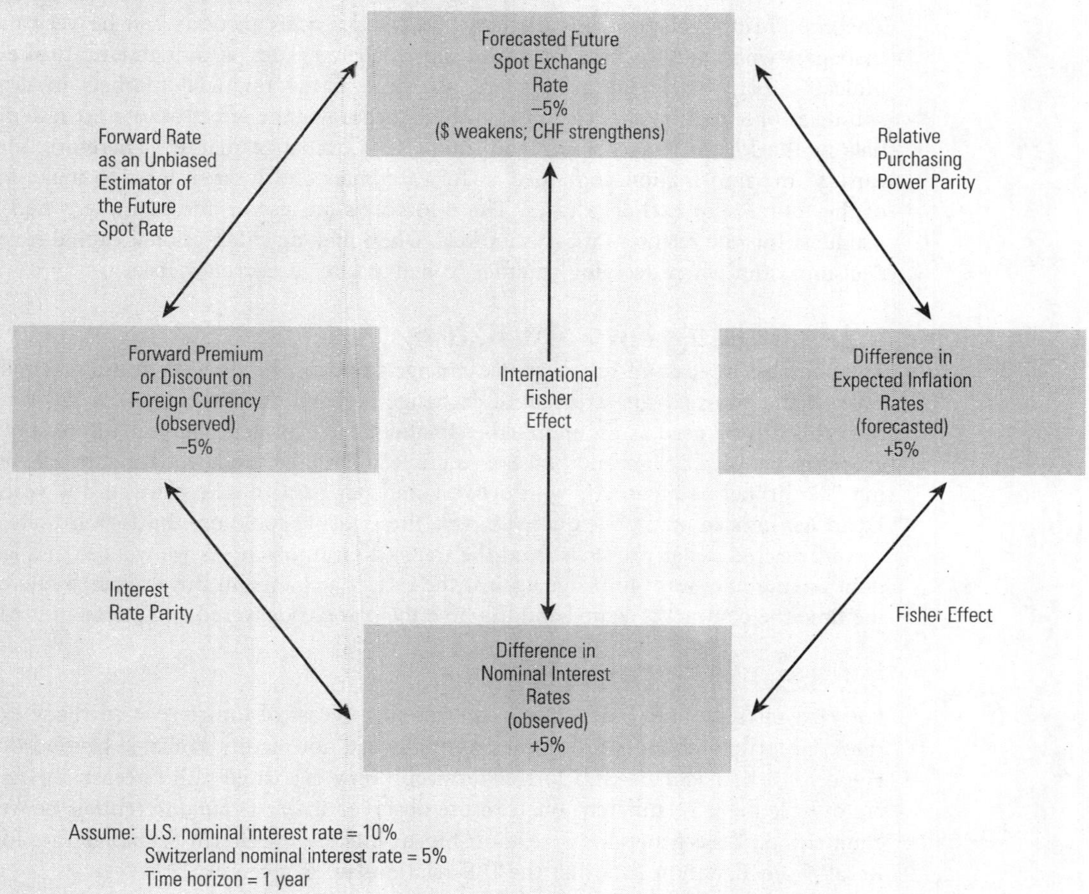

according to the Fisher effect, that the difference in expected inflation rates between the United States and Switzerland is also 5 percent because real rates of return are assumed to be equal between the United States and Switzerland. The 5 percent inflation differential means that the one-year future spot rate of exchange between dollars and CHF can be expected to change such that the dollar will weaken by 5 percent relative to the CHF. This condition is expected from the purchasing power parity relationship.

The 5 percent differential in interest rates also implies that the dollar will sell at a 5 percent discount in the one-year forward market relative to the CHF. This expectation arises from the interest rate parity relationship. If the forward rate is an unbiased estimator of future spot rates, then the one-year future spot rate of exchange between dollars and CHF can be expected to change such that the dollar will weaken by 5 percent relative to the CHF.

Finally, the international Fisher effect implies that if one-year nominal interest rates are 5 percent higher in the United States than in Switzerland, then the one-year future spot rate of exchange between the dollar and the CHF will change such that the dollar will weaken by 5 percent relative to the CHF.

22-3 Forecasting Future Exchange Rates

The equilibrium relationships discussed in the previous sections can be very useful to managers who need forecasts of future spot exchange rates. Although empirical evidence indicates that these relationships are not perfect, the financial markets in developed countries operate in a way that efficiently incorporates the effect of interest rate differentials in the forward market and the future spot exchange market. Therefore, managers can use the information contained in forward rates and interest rates to make forecasts of the future spot exchange rates. These forecasts are useful, for example, when pricing products for sale in international markets, when making international capital investment decisions, and when deciding whether to hedge foreign currency risks.

22-3a Using Forward Rates

The simplest forecast of future spot exchange rates can be derived from current forward rates. If the one-year forward rate of exchange between dollars and yen is 110 yen/dollar, then this can be used as an unbiased estimate of the expected one-year future spot rate of exchange between dollars and yen. For example, if Boeing were negotiating the sale of a Boeing 737 airliner to Japan Air with delivery and payment to take place in one year, and if Japan Air insisted on a price quoted in yen, then Boeing could use this forward rate to convert its desired dollar proceeds from the transaction into yen. As we will see in a later section, Boeing may want to hedge against the risk of a change in this exchange rate between the time the contract is signed and the time the plane is delivered and payment is received.

22-3b Using Interest Rates

Forward rates provide a direct and convenient forecast of future spot currency exchange rates. Unfortunately, forward quotes normally are not readily available beyond one year. Hence, if a manager needs a longer-term currency exchange rate forecast, forward rates are of little help. Fortunately, one can use observed interest rate differentials between two countries and the general IFE relationship to make longer-term exchange rate forecasts. Recall from Equation 22.8 that the IFE relationship is given as:

$$\left(\frac{S_1}{S_0}\right) = \left(\frac{1+i_h}{1+i_f}\right)$$

This relationship can be modified to cover more than one period into the future as follows:

(22.9)
$$\left(\frac{S_n}{S_0}\right) = \frac{(1+i_h)^n}{(1+i_f)^n}$$

For example, assume that the annual nominal interest rate on five-year U.S. Treasury bonds is 6 percent and the annual nominal interest rate on five-year Swiss government bonds is 4.5 percent. Also, assume that the current spot exchange rate between dollars and Swiss francs (CHF) is \$0.9000/CHF. What is the expected future spot rate in five years? It can be calculated using Equation 22.9 as follows

$$S_5/\$0.9000 = (1+0.06)^5/(1+0.045)^5$$
$$S_5 = \$0.9665$$

The IFE relationship predicts that the dollar will lose value relative to the CHF. The expected spot exchange rate in five years is \$0.9665/CHF.

One could also use the PPP relationship to forecast future exchange rates. However, the advantage of the IFE relationship is that interest rates between two countries are readily observable for almost any maturity, whereas differential levels of future inflation are not. In order to use PPP to make exchange rate forecasts, one would first have to forecast the inflation rates in both countries. Hence it is normally desirable to use the IFE relationship when making longer-term exchange rate forecasts, such as might be needed when evaluating foreign long-term investment projects with cash flows extending several years into the future.

22-4 Foreign Exchange Risk[7]

Foreign exchange risk is said to exist when a portion of the cash flows expected to be received by a firm are denominated in foreign currencies. As exchange rates change, there is uncertainty about the amount of domestic currency that will be received from a transaction denominated in a foreign currency. There are three primary categories of foreign exchange risk that multinational firms must consider:

1. Transaction exposure (short-term)
2. Economic (operating) exposure (long-term)
3. Translation (accounting) exposure

22-4a Transaction Exposure

transaction exposure

Most firms have contracts to buy and sell goods and services, with delivery and payment to occur at some time in the future. If payments under the contract involve the use of foreign currency, additional risk is involved. The potential for change in value of a foreign currency–denominated transaction due to an exchange rate change is called **transaction exposure**.

For example, General Electric is a major producer of locomotives. Suppose that General Electric contracts with the Brazilian government to sell 100 locomotives for delivery one year from now. General Electric wants to realize $400 million from this sale. The Brazilian government has indicated that it will only enter into the contract if the price is stated in Brazilian reals (BRL). The one-year forward rate is BRL4.0/$. Hence General Electric quotes a price of BRL1,600,000,000. Once the contract has been signed, General Electric faces a significant transaction exposure. Unless General Electric takes actions to guarantee its future dollar proceeds from the sale—that is, unless it hedges its position, for example, by selling BRL1,600,000,000 in the one-year forward market—it stands to lose on the transaction if the value of the BRL weakens. Suppose that over the coming year the inflation rate in Brazil rises significantly beyond what was expected at the time the deal was signed. According to relative PPP, the value of the BRL can be expected to decline, say to BRL5/$. If this happens, General Electric will receive only $320 million (BRL1,600,000,000/BRL5/$) rather than the $400 million it was expecting.

One well-documented example of the potential consequences of transaction exposure is the case of Laker Airlines. In the late 1970s, in the face of growing demand from British tourists traveling to the United States, Laker purchased several DC-10 aircraft and

[0]See Jeff Madura, *International Financial Management*, 12th ed. (Cincinnati, OH: Cengage Learning, 2015) for further discussions of the management of foreign exchange risk.

financed them in U.S. dollars. This transaction ultimately led to Laker's bankruptcy because Laker's primary source of revenue was pounds sterling, whereas its debt costs were denominated in dollars. Over the period from the late 1970s to 1982, when Laker failed, the dollar strengthened relative to the pound sterling. This had a devastating effect because (1) the strong dollar discouraged British travel to the United States, and (2) the pound sterling cost of principal and interest payments on the dollar-denominated debt increased.

Managing Transaction Exposure A number of alternatives are available to a firm faced with transaction exposure. First, the firm may choose to do nothing and simply accept the risk associated with the transaction. Doing nothing works well for firms with extensive international transactions that may tend to cancel each other out. For example, if General Electric has purchased goods or services from Brazilian firms that require the payment in approximately the same number of BRL as it expects to receive from the sale of the locomotives, then it is not necessary to do anything to counter the risk arising from a loss in value of the BRL relative to the dollar.

A second alternative is to invoice all transactions in dollars (for a U.S.-based firm). This avoids any transaction risk for the U.S. firm, but shifts this risk to the other party. For example, in September 1992, in a period of extreme volatility of European currencies, Dow Chemical announced that it would use the German mark as the common currency for all its European business transactions. This action shifted currency risks from Dow to its customers who did business in other currencies. When a firm is considering this alternative, it needs to determine whether this strategy is competitively possible, or whether parties on the other side of the transaction may resist or perhaps insist on a lower price if they are forced to bear all the transaction risk. In Dow's case, analysts and competitors doubted that customers would be willing to bear all of the exchange rate risk and felt that Dow would ultimately abandon this strategy.

Two hedging techniques that are possible for a U.S. company to protect itself against transaction exposure are:

- Execute a contract in the forward exchange market or in the foreign exchange futures market.
- Execute a *money market hedge.*

Consider a situation in which DuPont purchases materials from a British supplier, Commonwealth Resources, Ltd. Because the amount of the transaction (£2 million) is stated in pounds, DuPont bears the exchange risk. This example of transaction exposure is illustrated in Table 22.1. Assume that Commonwealth Resources extends 90-day trade credit to DuPont and that the value of the pound unexpectedly increases from $1.69/pound on the purchase date to $1.74 per pound on the payment date. If DuPont takes the trade credit extended to it, the cost of the purchase effectively increases from $3.38 million to $3.48 million (that is, £2,000,000 × $1.74/pound).

TABLE 22.1

Example of Transaction Exchange Rate Risk: DuPont

		Amount of Transaction	
Date	**Exchange Rate**	**U.S. Dollars**	**British Pounds**
Purchase date	$1.69/pound	$3,380,000	£2,000,000
Payment date	$1.74/pound	$3,480,000	£2,000,000

First, DuPont could execute a contract in the forward exchange market to buy £2 million at the *known* 90-day forward rate, rather than at the *uncertain* spot rate prevailing on the payment date. This is referred to as a *forward market hedge.* Assume, for example, that the 90-day forward rate is \$1.70/pound. Based on this rate, DuPont effectively would be able to exchange \$3.4 million (that is, £2,000,000 × \$1.70/pound) 90 days later on the payment date when it is required to pay for the materials. Thus, DuPont would be able to take advantage of the trade credit and, at the same time, hedge against foreign exchange risk.

A second hedging technique, called a *money market hedge,* involves DuPont borrowing funds from its bank, exchanging them for pounds at the spot rate, and investing them in interest-bearing British securities to yield £2 million in 90 days. By investing in securities that mature on the same date the payment is due to Commonwealth Resources (that is, 90 days after the purchase date), DuPont will have the necessary amount of pounds available to pay for the materials. The net cost of this money market hedge to DuPont will depend on the interest rate on the funds it borrows from its bank relative to the interest rate on the funds it invests in securities. If the conditions of interest rate parity are satisfied, these two hedging techniques are equivalent.

Other transaction risk reduction strategies include the use of options on foreign currencies (discussed in Chapters 20 and 21) and negotiating a risk-sharing contract between the two parties to a transaction in which both parties agree in advance to share in some way the financial consequences of changes in value between the affected currencies.

For large multinational companies, there will be many international transactions involving many different currencies. Attempting to hedge separately the transaction exposure for each international transaction would be time-consuming and inefficient. For example, consider Sara Lee Corporation, which has operations in both the United Kingdom and France. The British subsidiary makes purchases in France that require euros. At the same time the French subsidiary makes purchases in the United Kingdom that require pounds sterling. To the extent that these transactions offset, no hedge is necessary. Multinational firms often make thousands of overlapping transactions using different currencies. Thus it is a complex matter to keep track of *net* currency exposures and avoid hedging against risks that do not really exist when one takes the consolidated corporate view, rather than the narrow subsidiary view of exchange risk.

22-4b Economic Exposure

economic (or operating) exposure

Economic (or operating) exposure refers to changes in a firm's operating cash flows (and hence the firm's value) that come about because of *real* rather than *nominal* changes in exchange rates. Real exchange rate changes occur when there are deviations from purchasing power parity (PPP). Under relative PPP, exchange rates should vary to reflect changes in the price level of goods and services in one country relative to another. For example, if the inflation rate in Mexico is 5 percent higher per year than in the United States, relative PPP says that the value of the Mexican peso can be expected to decline by about 5 percent relative to the dollar. Thus goods purchased in the United States from Mexico will cost the same as they did before the increase in Mexican inflation, after adjusting for the decline in the value of the peso.

Real exchange rate changes can affect the way competing companies in two countries do business and can impact the business conditions in the countries. For example, in April 1995, \$1 equaled about ¥83. In December 2015, \$1 equaled about ¥123. In relative terms, the dollar was "weak" and the yen was "strong" in April 1995, whereas in January 2002, the dollar was "strong" and the yen was "weak."

The weakening of the dollar and the strengthening of the yen (¥) can have a dramatic impact on firms doing business in the United States and Japan. The showcase example of these effects is the relative performance of the Japanese and American automobile industries. In the mid-1980s, Japanese products were generally cheaper (and of better quality) than their American counterparts. The Japanese share of the U.S. auto market was growing, restrained only by voluntary import restrictions agreed to by the Japanese. By 1995, the increased value of the yen relative to the dollar had reversed the fortunes of automakers in both countries. Japanese autos were selling for several thousand dollars more in 1995 than comparable U.S. products. American firms reported significant increases in U.S. market share at the expense of the Japanese. Japanese auto firms were experiencing significant financial difficulties at a time when U.S. auto firms were reporting substantial increases in profit. U.S. firms had also begun exporting vehicles to Japan.

In an attempt to offset the impact of their significant economic exposure in the United States, Japanese firms have aggressively moved to establish manufacturing and assembly operations in the United States and some European countries, so that many of their costs will be denominated in the same currency as their revenues. (See the Financial Challenge at the beginning of the chapter.) Also, by locating plants in many different countries, multinational firms have the flexibility to shift production from one location to another in order to offset unfavorable economic exposure.

Managing Economic Exposure Economic exposure is much more difficult and expensive to manage than the shorter-term transactions exposure already discussed. Strategies to manage the impact of real changes in exchange rates in countries where a multinational firm operates include:

1. **Shift production from high-cost (exchange-rate adjusted) plants to lower-cost plants**—for example, moving labor-intensive sewing operations from U.S. textile plants to plants in Mexico.
2. **Increase productivity**—adopt labor-saving technologies, implement flexible manufacturing systems, reduce product cycles, make use of benchmarking; that is, copy your strongest competitors.
3. **Outsource the supply of many of the components needed to produce a product to lower-cost locations**—for example, some U.S. publishing houses have outsourced typesetting to areas in the Far East with lower labor costs.
4. **Increase product differentiation to reduce the price sensitivity in the market**—for example, the Japanese have moved more to the luxury car market as the yen has strengthened because of the greater price flexibility the luxury market provides relative to the economy car market.
5. **Enter markets with strong currencies and reduce involvement in competitive markets with weak currencies**—U.S. firms have become increasingly aggressive in entering the Japanese market as the yen has increased in value relative to the dollar.

22-4c Translation Exposure

translation exposure

When a multinational firm (parent) has one or more foreign subsidiaries with assets and liabilities denominated in a foreign currency, it faces **translation exposure**. For example, if a U.S.-based multinational firm operates a subsidiary in South Africa, the value of the subsidiary's assets and liabilities in rands must be translated into the home (U.S. $)

ETHICAL ISSUES

Payment of Bribes Abroad[a]

Managers of multinational firms often must deal with the problem of making bribes or "grease" payments abroad in order to facilitate a transaction. Customs with respect to the acceptability and need for such payments vary greatly in different countries. The issue of questionable payments is especially important to managers of U.S. firms because of the Foreign Corrupt Practices Act (FCPA) of 1977 as amended in the Omnibus Trade and Competitiveness Act of 1988 and amended again in 1998. The provisions of this act declare payments in the form of phony discounts, fake invoices, and inflated expense accounts illegal.

A study of 400 firms by the Securities and Exchange Commission (SEC) in the mid-1970s revealed that these firms had made over $300 million in questionable payments to officials of foreign governments, politicians, agents, and others to secure business abroad. Exxon, for example, disclosed that it had made nearly $60 million in such payments. These payments have been most common in capital-intensive industries such as aerospace, construction, and energy, which deal with large projects or contracts.

A 2009 study completed by Transparency International found that in developing and transition countries alone, bribes and corruption in the awarding of development contracts total as much as $40 billion annually. International price fixing cartels cost consumers $300 billion per year.

In spite of the FCPA, U.S.-based firms have continued to make "grease" payments abroad. U.S. companies, including Dow Chemical, Xerox, Tyco, Accenture, IBM, Monsanto, Titan, and Enron, have been implicated in overseas bribery cases in recent years. A global survey conducted by PriceWaterhouseCoopers found that 49 percent of companies surveyed were required to offer or pay a bribe at least four times.

Since passage of the FCPA, the U.S. government has attempted to extend the anticorruption laws to foreign companies. Initially, these efforts were viewed as naive by overseas companies and governments. However, more recently, the 29 countries in the Organisation for Economic Co-operation and Development (OECD) have been working on a treaty to ban illegal payments to government officials. Dozens of multinational companies have supported this effort. For example, many large European companies, including Petrofina SA of Belgium, Pirelli SpA of Italy, and Robert Bosch GmbH of Germany, have pledged to abstain from bribery.

Both ethical standards and U.S. law prohibit the payment of bribes to obtain business abroad. However, in many countries the receipt of bribes is not only permitted, but also expected. How can managers reconcile this conflict between domestic ethical standards and traditional foreign business practice?

[a]This ethical issue is based on "Corporate Crime and Abuse," Center for Corporate Policy, www.corporatepolicy.org/issues/FCPA.htm. See also Transparency International, "Global Corruption Report," 2009, www.transparency.org.

currency when the parent firm prepares its consolidated financial statements. When the translation occurs, there can be gains or losses, which must be recognized in the financial statements of the parent.

Current accounting standards are set forth in *Statement of Financial Accounting Standards Number 52.* The major provisions of this standard are:

- Current assets, unless covered by forward exchange contracts, and fixed assets are translated into dollars at the rate of exchange prevailing on the date of the balance sheet.
- Current and long-term liabilities payable in foreign currency are translated into dollars at the rate of exchange prevailing on the date of the balance sheet.
- Income statement items are translated either at the rate on the date of a particular transaction or at a weighted average of the exchange rates for the period of the income statement.
- Dividends are translated at the exchange rate on the date the dividend is paid.
- Equity accounts, including common stock and contributed capital in excess of par value, are translated at historical rates.

TABLE 22.2

Effect of a Decrease in the Exchange Rate on American Products' Balance Sheet

	Exchange Rate			
	$0.80 (U.S.) = $1.00 (Canadian)		$0.75 (U.S.) = $1.00 (Canadian)	
	$(Canadian)	$(U.S.)	$(Canadian)	$(U.S.)
Assets	$12,000,000	$9,600,000	$12,000,000	$9,000,000
Liabilities	8,000,000	6,400,000	8,000,000	6,000,000
Net equity position	$ 4,000,000	$3,200,000	$ 4,000,000	$3,000,000

- Gains and losses to the parent from translation are not included in the parent's calculation of net income, nor are they included in the parent's retained earnings. Rather, they are reported in a separate equity account named "Cumulative foreign currency translation adjustments" or a similar title. Gains or losses in this account are not recognized in the income statement until the parent's investment in the foreign subsidiary is sold or liquidated.

A decline in the value of a foreign currency relative to the U.S. dollar reduces the conversion value of the foreign subsidiary's liabilities as well as its assets. Therefore, the parent company's risk exposure depends on the foreign subsidiary's net equity position (that is, assets minus liabilities). Thus, on the books of the parent company, the subsidiary's creditors in effect bear part of the decline in the value of the subsidiary's assets.

The impact of a decrease in the exchange rate on the firm's balance sheet can be illustrated with the following example. American Products has a subsidiary, Canadian Products, with total assets of $12 million (Canadian) and total liabilities of $8 million (Canadian). Based on an exchange rate of $0.80 (U.S.) per dollar (Canadian), the net equity position of the Canadian subsidiary on American Products' balance sheet as shown in Table 22.2 is $3.2 million (U.S.). Suppose now that the exchange rate declines to $0.75 (U.S.) per dollar (Canadian) and all other things remain the same. As can be seen in the table, the net equity position of the Canadian subsidiary on American Products' balance sheet declines to $3 million (U.S.), resulting in a $200,000 currency exchange loss.

Managing Translation Exposure In general, when a foreign subsidiary's assets are greater than its liabilities, currency exchange losses will occur when the exchange rate decreases. The opposite effects are true for increases in the exchange rate. A company can hedge and manage its balance sheet translation exposure by financing its foreign assets with debt denominated in the same currency.

For example, in September 1993, Dow Chemical issued 4.625 percent Eurobonds. Instead of being denominated in U.S. dollars, as is usual for securities of U.S. companies, these bonds are denominated in Swiss francs. The Dow Chemical debt issue totaled 150,000,000 Swiss francs, or about $103,000,000, based on the exchange rate between the U.S. dollar and the Swiss franc at the time of issuance.

Dow Chemical's financial managers apparently had a choice between whether to issue Swiss franc–denominated or U.S. dollar–denominated debt. One possible reason for issuing Swiss franc–denominated debt may have been to hedge the company's Swiss assets. For example, if the value of the Swiss franc drops compared to the U.S. dollar value, presumably the U.S. dollar value of Dow Chemical's Swiss assets also decreases. However, if this happens, the U.S. dollar amount of both the interest and principal that Dow Chemical has to pay also decreases.

A multinational company can also minimize its exchange rate risk, as well as the risk of expropriation or nationalization of its assets by a foreign government, by developing a *portfolio* of foreign investments. Rather than making all its direct investments in foreign subsidiaries that are located in one particular country, the firm can spread its foreign investments among a number of different countries, thus limiting the risk of incurring large losses within any one country.

22-5 Summary

- The theory of *interest rate parity* states that the percentage differential between the spot and the forward rates for a currency quoted in terms of another currency is equal to the approximate difference in interest rates in the two countries over the same time horizon.
- The theory of *relative purchasing power parity* states that in comparison to a period when exchange rates between two countries are in equilibrium, changes in differential rates of inflation between two countries will be offset by equal but opposite changes in the future spot currency rate.
- The forward rate is often taken as an *unbiased estimator* of the future spot currency rate.
- The nominal rate of interest is approximately equal to the sum of the real rate of interest and the expected inflation rate. This relationship is known as the *Fisher effect*.
- The *international Fisher effect* theory states that differences in interest rates between two countries will be offset by equal but opposite changes in the future spot rate.
- Forecasts of future spot exchange rates can be derived from forward rates, if available, or from observed interest rates between two countries in conjunction with the international Fisher effect theory.
- Firms that compete in a global economy face three categories of foreign exchange risk:

    1. Transaction or short-term exposure
    2. Economic (operating) or long-term exposure
    3. Translation (accounting) exposure

- Many risk-reducing strategies are available to firms facing these risks, including the use of various hedges, such as a forward hedge and a money market hedge.

Important Equations

$$\text{IRP}: \frac{F}{S_0} = \frac{1 + i_h}{1 + i_f}$$

$$\text{Relative PPP}: \left(\frac{S_1}{S_0}\right) = \left(\frac{1 + \pi_h}{1 + \pi_f}\right)$$

$$\text{IFE}: \left(\frac{S_1}{S_0}\right) = \left(\frac{1 + i_h}{1 + i_f}\right)$$

$$\left(\frac{S_n}{S_0}\right) = \frac{(1 + i_h)^n}{(1 + i_f)^n}$$

22-6 Questions and Topics for Discussion

1. What is the theory of interest rate parity?
2. What is covered interest arbitrage?
3. Describe two techniques that a company can use to hedge against transaction exchange risk.
4. Describe the factors that cause exchange rates to change over time.
5. What are the advantages to a U.S. firm of financing its foreign investments with funds raised abroad?
6. Describe how the concepts of relative purchasing power parity, interest rate parity, and the international Fisher effect are related.

22-7 Self-Test Problems

ST1. Assume that the annualized discount on forward Canadian dollars is 3 percent. The annualized U.S. interest rate is 8 percent, and the comparable Canadian interest rate is 12 percent. How can a U.S. trader use covered interest arbitrage to take advantage of this situation?

ST2. Chrysler is planning to sell its new minivan in Japan. Chrysler receives $12,000 for each van sold in the United States and wants to get the same net proceeds from its export sales.

a. If the exchange rate of Japanese yen for U.S. dollars is ¥140 = $1, what price must Chrysler charge in Japan (in yen)?

b. What price will Chrysler have to charge in Japan if the value of the dollar falls to 120 yen?

ST3. The annualized yield on 3-year maturity U.S. government bonds is 4 percent, while the yield on similar maturity Swiss bonds is 5 percent. The current spot exchange rate between the dollar and the Swiss franc (CHF) is $0.61/CHF. What is the expected future spot rate for the CHF in 3 years?

22-8 Problems*

BASIC

1. If the 1-year U.S. Treasury bill rate is 7.0 percent, the spot rate between U.S. dollars and British pounds is £1 = $1.69, and the 90-day forward rate is £1 = $1.68, what rate of interest is expected on British Treasury bills, assuming that interest rate parity between the dollar and pound exists?

INTERMEDIATE

2. Suppose the British short-term interest rate is 13 percent and the corresponding U.S. rate is 8 percent. Suppose at the same time that the discount on forward pounds is 3 percent per year. Do these conditions present an opportunity for covered interest arbitrage? If so, what steps should a trader in New York take? What annual rate will the trader earn?

*Color blocks behind the numbers denote problems that have check answers provided at the end of the book.

INTERMEDIATE

3. Mammouth Mutual Fund of New York has $5 million to invest in certificates of deposit (CDs) for the next six months (180 days). It can buy either a Philadelphia National Bank (PNB) CD with an annual yield of 4 percent or a Zurich (Switzerland) Bank CD with a yield of 6 percent. Assume that the CDs are of comparable default risk. The analysts of the mutual fund are concerned about exchange rate risk. They were quoted the following exchange rates by the international department of a New York City bank:

Switzerland (CHF)	
Spot	$1.000
30-day forward	0.995
90-day forward	0.998
180-day forward	0.980

a. If the Zurich Bank CD is purchased and held to maturity, determine the net gain (loss) in U.S. dollars relative to the PNB CD, assuming that the exchange rate in 180 days equals today's spot rate.
b. Suppose the Swiss CHF declines in value by 5 percent relative to the U.S. dollar over the next 180 days. Determine the net gain (loss) of the Zurich Bank CD in U.S. dollars relative to the PNB CD for an uncovered position.
c. Determine the net gain (loss) from a covered position.
d. What other factor or factors should be considered in the decision to purchase the Zurich Bank CD?

BASIC

4. Last year, the French marketing subsidiary of International Pharmaceuticals Corporation (IPC), a New Jersey–based drug manufacturer, earned 700,000 euros. This year, partly due to a weaker U.S. dollar, the French subsidiary will earn 900,000 euros. Last year, the exchange rate was 1.2 euros per dollar, and this year, it is 1.0 euro per dollar. Calculate how many U.S. dollars the French subsidiary contributes to IPC's earnings in each year.

INTERMEDIATE

5. As of today, the following information is available:

	United States	Israel
Real rate of interest required by investors	2.0%	2.0%
Nominal interest rate	3.0%	7.0%
Spot rate	$0.20/shekel	
1-year forward rate	$0.19/shekel	
Call option premium at a strike price of $0.20	2.0%	

Using this information, make three *independent* forecasts of the 1-year future spot rate for the Israeli shekel. (Use exact, not approximation, relationships.)

INTERMEDIATE

6. Shoesmith Wave Inc., a new and largely unproven economic forecasting service, expects the inflation rate in South Korea to average 9 percent per year over the next 5 years. In comparison, Shoesmith expects a U.S. inflation rate over this same period to be 3 percent per year. The yield on 5-year U.S. government bonds is 6 percent per year. The yield on 5-year Korean government bonds is 11 percent per year. One percentage point of this yield differential can be accounted for by political risk differences between the United States and South Korea, with the United States perceived as having the lower political risk. The current exchange rate is 350 won per dollar.

Forecast the future 5-year spot rate for the won (versus the dollar) using the Shoesmith Wave forecast and the forecast from the financial markets.

CHALLENGE **7.** The Jennette Corporation, a firm based in Mt. Pleasant, South Carolina, has an account payable with a British firm coming due in 180 days. The payable requires Jennette to pay £200,000. Winthrop Jennette, the firm's founder and CEO, is an astute manager. He has asked his CFO, Artis Montgomery, to advise him on the various options for dealing with the exchange risk inherent in this payable. He wishes to know the expected dollar cost of (1) a forward hedge, (2) a money market hedge, and (3) remaining unhedged.

The following information is available to Artis. The spot rate of the pound today is $1.50. The current 180-day forward rate of the pound is $1.47. Interest rates are as follows:

	United Kingdom	United States
180-day deposit rate	4.5%	4.5%
180-day borrowing rate	5.0%	5.0%

a. What is the expected dollar cost of the forward hedge?
b. What is the expected dollar cost of the money market hedge?
c. What is the expected dollar cost of remaining unhedged?
d. Which alternative do you recommend? What are the risks associated with this recommendation?

INTERMEDIATE **8.** On January 1, the cost of borrowing Hong Kong dollars (HKD) for 1 year was 18 percent. During the year the U.S. inflation rate was 2 percent and the Hong Kong inflation rate was 9 percent. The exchange rate on January 1 was HKD7/$. On December 31, the exchange rate was HKD8/$. If you borrowed HKD100,000 on January 1, converted this to dollars and used these funds for one year, and then paid off the HKD loan on December 31, what was the *real* cost of borrowing HKD for one year?

CHALLENGE **9.** The Vaderson Forecasting Associates sells a broad range of economic forecasting services to businesses and government agencies. One of its primary products is the Vaderson Exchange Rate Seer, a model that forecasts future spot exchange rates.

Finley Incorporated, a maker and exporter of Fightin' Blue Hen paraphernalia, has just received a large order from Kruse, AG, a large Swiss retailing chain. Delivery of the merchandise would occur in 2 years, and Finley wishes to determine the price in Swiss francs (CHF) to charge for the order. If the items were being sold for delivery today, Finley would want to receive $1.4 million, an amount that would recover all variable costs and make an acceptable contribution to overhead and profit. The current exchange rate between the dollar and the Swiss franc is $0.66/CHF. Finley expects that its (dollar) costs will rise at about 3 percent per year over the coming 2 years and would like to recover these cost increases in proportional increases in the contract price. The annual yield on 2-year Treasury bonds is 5.5 percent in the United States. Similar risk bonds sell to yield 4.5 percent annually in Switzerland. Vaderson forecasts that the spot rate of exchange between the $ and the CHF will be $0.64/CHF.

If you had to make a recommendation regarding the pricing of this order, what is the *best* estimate of the price (in CHF) you can recommend that management charge if it wants to just cover its costs and profit objectives?

INTERMEDIATE

10. The Swiss franc (CHF) is currently trading in the spot market at \$0.5800/CHF. The 180-day forward rate is \$0.5743/CHF. The U.S. Treasury bill rate for 180 days is 3.1 percent in the United States. What do you expect is the 180-day Swiss government security rate? Why?

CHAPTER 23

Corporate Restructuring

KEY CHAPTER CONCEPTS

1. Reasons a company may choose external growth by merger or acquisition over internal growth can include the following:
   a. The availability of lower-cost assets
   b. Greater economies of scale
   c. The availability of more secure raw material supplies and additional end-product markets
   d. The possibility of more rapid growth
   e. Greater diversification
   f. Tax considerations
2. The valuation of merger/acquisition candidates involves the application of capital budgeting principles. A merger/acquisition is an acceptable project if the present value of its expected free cash inflows exceeds the acquisition cost.
3. The acquisition of a company with a higher P/E ratio than that of the acquirer causes the earnings per share figure of the acquiring company to decrease if the exchange ratio is based on current stock market prices and no synergy exists. Similarly, the acquisition of a company with a lower P/E ratio causes the earnings per share figure of the acquiring company to increase.
4. In the pooling of interests method of accounting for mergers, the acquired assets are recorded at their original cost. In the purchase method, acquired assets are recorded at their fair market values, and any additional amount paid is listed as goodwill, which must then be amortized.
5. In a financial context, a firm is
   a. *Technically insolvent* when it is unable to meet its current obligations as they come due, even though the value of the assets exceeds its liabilities
   b. *Legally insolvent* if the recorded value of its assets is less than the recorded value of its liabilities
   c. *Bankrupt* if it is unable to pay its debts and it files a bankruptcy petition in accordance with the federal bankruptcy laws
6. The primary causes of business failures are economic factors and lack of experience on the part of the owners of the business.
7. A failing company can either:
   a. Attempt to resolve its difficulties with its creditors on a voluntary, or informal, basis or
   b. Petition the courts for assistance and formally declare bankruptcy
8. In a bankruptcy proceeding, if the going-concern value of the firm is greater than its liquidation value, it is reorganized; otherwise, it is liquidated.
   a. A reorganization plan is carried out under Chapter 11 of the Bankruptcy Reform Act.
   b. A liquidation is carried out under Chapter 7 of the Bankruptcy Reform Act.
9. Other important topics include:
   a. Leveraged buyouts
   b. Divestitures and restructuring
   c. Antitakeover measures

FINANCIAL CHALLENGE

Did Facebook Overpay for Its Acquisition of WhatsApp?[1]

On February 19, 2014, Facebook announced its acquisition of WhatsApp, a popular smartphone messaging app. During 2013 WhatsApp brought in approximately $10 million in revenues and had a net loss of over $100 million for the year.[2] Despite the fact that WhatsApp was not generating much revenue and was operating at a loss, Facebook was willing to pay a considerable amount for the company. The mix of cash, Facebook stock, and restricted shares that Facebook used to acquire WhatsApp was valued at more than $19 billion at the time the acquisition was announced. During the three days surrounding the announcement of the acquisition, the price of Facebook's stock increased by 4.0 percent. By the end of trading on October 6, which is when the deal was closed, the value of Facebook's stock had increased by an additional 11.4 percent. Why would Facebook be willing to pay so much for a company that operated at a loss and generated relatively insignificant revenues? Likewise, why would the market's reaction suggest that the deal was a good one for Facebook?

When one company is looking to acquire another company, one of the main drivers of how much the acquiring company is willing to pay is its estimate of the present value of all of the future cash flows of the potential target company. During the conference call accompanying the announcement of the acquisition, Facebook's CEO, Mark Zuckerberg, seemed more concerned with WhatsApp's user growth than its near-term profitability. The Facebook CEO stated that, "we believe that once we get to being a service that has [a] billion, two billion, maybe even three billion people one day, that there are many clear ways to monetize, but the right strategy we believe is to continue focusing on growth."[3] Clearly, Zuckerberg believed that WhatsApp had the ability to continue to grow rapidly and that Facebook would eventually be able to monetize WhatsApp, and the market agreed. At the time the acquisition was announced, WhatsApp reportedly had more than 450 million users, and was adding approximately 1 million new users each day.[4] By February 1, 2016, WhatsApp was reporting that it had broken 1 billion users.[5] Importantly, the acquisition also indirectly allowed Facebook to increase its presence in China.[6] While Facebook is banned in China, WhatsApp is not. The acquisition potentially gave Facebook greater access to a huge market.

catwalker/Shutterstock.com

Another driver of the value of a merger or acquisition is through potential synergy. Synergy is simply the notion that the value of two companies, when combined, can be greater than the sum of the values of each separate company. At the time of the acquisition, one potential synergy was between Facebook's own

[1]Financial Challenge written by Anil P. Rao.

[2]*WhatsApp Inc. Financial Statements, Years Ended December 31, 2013 and 2012*, http://www.sec.gov/Archives/edgar/data/1326801/000132680114000047/exhibit991auditedwhatsappi.htm.

[3]"Facebook's CEO Describes Acquisition of WhatsApp (Transcript)" (February 30, 2014), http://seekingalpha.com/article/2035153-faceboooks-ceo-discusses-acquisition-of-whatsapp-transcript.

[4]Adrian Covert, "Facebook Buys WhatsApp for $19 Billion," *CNN Money* (February 19, 2014), http://money.cnn.com/2014/02/19/technology/social/facebook-whatsapp/.

[5]"One Billion," *WhatsApp* (blog), https://blog.whatsapp.com/616/One-billion.

[6]Ibid. 4.

FINANCIAL CHALLENGE — CONTINUED

existing messaging app, dubbed Facebook Messenger, and WhatsApp. During the conference call to announce the WhatsApp acquisition, Zuckerberg stated his belief that WhatsApp and Facebook Messenger are complementary; the former is a replacement for SMS (text) messaging, while the latter is often used to chat with Facebook friends and for sending messages that are not seen in real time.[7] Although Zuckerberg also noted that WhatsApp would largely be run independently, it seems obvious that there is potential for synergies between the two apps down the road. Since ultimately both apps deal in messaging and communication, it seems likely that technology developed for one app could potentially be used or modified for use in the other app. Facebook Messenger could potentially make use of software developed by WhatsApp, implement tools developed by WhatsApp, or utilize data gathered by WhatsApp, and vice versa. These synergies could potentially make Facebook Messenger and WhatsApp each more valuable than they would be as stand-alone entities.

CHAPTER OBJECTIVES

Upon completion of this chapter, you should have a clear understanding of:

1. What mergers are, the different types, why they occur, and how they are valued
2. Divestitures and other forms of corporate restructuring
3. Antitakeover measures and their purpose
4. Leveraged buyouts
5. Business failures, bankruptcy, and liquidation

23-1 Introduction

Corporate restructuring encompasses a broad array of activities that include changes in the ownership, asset structure, and/or capital structure of a company. The goal of any corporate restructuring should be to maximize shareholder wealth. Some aspects of corporate restructuring have already been examined, such as share repurchases discussed in Chapter 15. This chapter focuses on a number of other forms of corporate restructuring, including external expansion (mergers/acquisitions) and business failure (bankruptcy). The next section examines mergers, and the final section discusses bankruptcy.

23-2 Mergers and Acquisitions

Businesses grow *externally* by acquiring, or merging with, other ongoing businesses; this is in contrast to *internal* growth, which is achieved by purchasing individual assets, such

[7]Facebook WhatsApp acquisition conference call transcript http://seekingalpha.com/article/2035153-facebooks-ceo-discusses-acquisition-of-whatsapp-transcript.

as those evaluated in the discussion of capital expenditures in Chapters 9 through 11. When two companies combine, the acquiring company generally pays for the acquired business either with cash or with its own securities, and the acquired company's liabilities and assets are transferred to the acquiring company.

23-2a Mergers Defined

merger

consolidation

A **merger** is technically a combination of two or more companies in which all but one of the combining companies legally cease to exist and the surviving company continues in operation under its original name. A **consolidation** is a combination in which all of the combining companies are dissolved and a new firm is formed. The term *merger* is generally used to describe both of these types of business combinations. *Acquisition* is also used interchangeably with *merger* to describe a business combination. In the following discussion, the term *merger* is used, and it is assumed that only two companies are involved—the acquiring company and the merger candidate.[8]

23-2b Merger Statistics

Table 23.1 and Figure 23.1 present data on the number and dollar value of merger deals in the United States for the period 1985 to 2015. The table and, especially, the figure show that mergers occur in waves. Merger activity ebbs and flows with the state of the economy. Merger activity expanded greatly during the mid to late 1980s, reaching a high in 1988 (in deal value). In that year, total deal value amounted to nearly $600 billion. During the recession of the early 1990s, the aggregate value of mergers declined to a low of approximately $190 billion in 1991–1992. Beginning in 1993, during a period of relative prosperity, the aggregate value of mergers increased each year for the next six years, reaching a peak of $2.1 *trillion* in 1999. The number of deals followed a similar pattern. During the subsequent downturn in the economy beginning in 2001, merger activity dropped to $521 billion in 2002. As the economy began expanding again, merger activity peaked to $2.0 *trillion* in 2007, representing more than 14,000 deals; but, following the recession and financial crisis that started in 2008, merger activity declined to $875 billion in 2009. Since then merger activity has once again picked up. In 2015 total merger activity amounted to nearly $2.4 trillion, an all-time high in dollar terms. Table 23.2 contains a listing of some of the largest mergers involving U.S. companies. Many transactions are international in scope—that is, they involve both U.S. and foreign companies. Some of the acquisitions involve the purchase of U.S. companies by foreign companies, such as the Belgian firm InBev's purchase of Anheuser-Busch and the German firm Daimler-Benz's purchase of Chrysler. Table 23.1 only shows completed mergers. Not all mergers that are announced end up being completed. For example, AT&T's proposed acquisition of T-Mobile USA for $39 billion in 2011 failed because of government regulatory issues.

23-2c Types of Mergers

horizontal merger

Mergers are generally classified according to whether they are *horizontal*, *vertical*, or *conglomerate*. A **horizontal merger** is a combination of two or more companies that

---

[8]In some instances, merger candidates may be referred to as "takeover candidates," "to-be-acquired companies," "acquired companies," or "target companies."

TABLE 23.1

Merger Statistics, United States

Year	Number of Deals	Deal Value ($ billion)
1985	2,807	316
1986	3,794	359
1987	4,081	370
1988	5,047	597
1989	6,919	482
1990	6,934	265
1991	6,715	189
1992	6,898	190
1993	8,038	323
1994	9,434	422
1995	11,204	676
1996	12,620	752
1997	13,876	1,119
1998	15,453	1,817
1999	13,818	2,139
2000	14,166	1,970
2001	9,722	1,012
2002	8,675	521
2003	9,378	669
2004	10,790	1,004
2005	11,514	1,344
2006	13,173	1,862
2007	14,220	1,974
2008	11,961	1,219
2009	9,681	875
2010	10,456	985
2011	10,762	1,256
2012	10,840	993
2013	11,012	1,213
2014	12,403	2,145
2015	11,956	2,380

Source: Institute for Mergers, Acquisitions, and Alliances

compete directly with one another: for example, the acquisition of Wyeth by Pfizer in 2009—both large pharmaceutical companies—was a horizontal merger. The U.S. government has vigorously enforced antitrust legislation in an attempt to stop large horizontal combinations, and this effort has been effective. For example, in 2011 the Department of Justice, responsible for enforcing antitrust laws, disallowed the merger between AT&T and T-Mobile USA because the combination would result in too much concentration in the cell phone industry. However, horizontal combinations in which one of the firms is failing are often viewed more favorably. An example of this is the merger between then-bankrupt American Airlines and US Airways in 2013. This type of merger is also common in the banking sector, especially following the financial crisis of 2008. For example, JPMorgan Chase acquired the failing Washington Mutual Bank in 2008. Also, mergers that allow the companies to compete effectively in world markets are viewed more

FIGURE 23.1
Mergers & Acquisitions United States

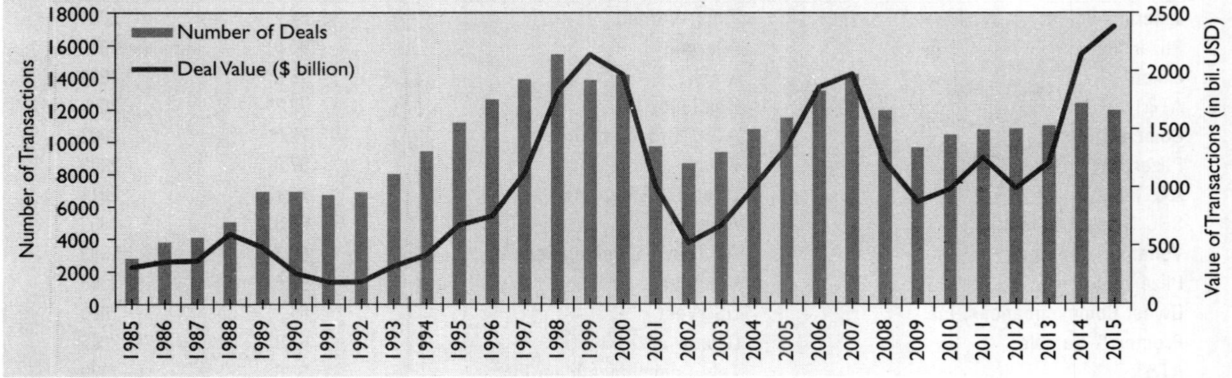

Source: Institute for Mergers, Acquisitions, and Alliances

favorably; the acquisition of McDonnell Douglas by Boeing was an example of this type of horizontal merger.

vertical merger

A **vertical merger** is a combination of companies that may have a buyer-seller relationship with one another. You can also think of it as a merger between firms operating at different stages of production. For example, ArcellorMittal, one of the leading integrated steel and mining companies in the world, started out as a steel manufacturer but over time acquired a number of iron ore companies to achieve vertical integration.[9] This type of business combination has gradually declined in importance in recent years.

conglomerate merger

A **conglomerate merger** is a combination of two or more companies in which neither competes directly with the other and no buyer-seller relationship exists. For example, General Motors' acquisition of the data processing company Electronic Data Systems in 1984 was a conglomerate merger. The 2009 purchase of one of the largest railroad companies in the United States—Burlington Northern Santa Fe (BNSF)—by Berkshire Hathaway is another example of a conglomerate merger.

23-2d Form of Merger Transactions

A merger transaction may be a stock purchase or an asset purchase. In a *stock purchase*, the acquiring company buys the stock of the to-be-acquired company and assumes its liabilities. In an *asset purchase*, the acquiring company buys only the assets (some or all) of the to-be-acquired company and does not assume any of its liabilities.

Normally, the buyer of a business prefers an asset purchase rather than a stock purchase, because unknown liabilities, such as any future lawsuits against the company, are not incurred. In addition, an asset purchase frequently allows the acquiring company to depreciate its new assets from a higher basis than is possible in a stock purchase. As a result of the unknown liability question, many large companies that acquire small companies refuse to negotiate on any terms other than as an asset purchase.

[9]ArcellorMittal also engaged in a number of horizontal mergers over its history.

TABLE 23.2

Large Mergers and Acquisitions Involving U.S. Companies

Purchaser	Company Acquired	Purchase Price ($ Billion)	Year
America Online	Time Warner	$164.7	2001
Pfizer Inc.	Allergan	160.0	2015
Exxon	Mobil	78.9	1999
AT&T	BellSouth	72.7	2006
Comcast	AT&T Broadband	72.0	2002
Pfizer Inc.	Wyeth	67.3	2009
AT&T Inc.	DirectTV Group Inc.	67.1	2014
SBC Communications	Ameritech	62.6	1999
Vodafone Group	Air Touch Communication	60.3	1999
Pfizer Inc.	Pharmacia	59.5	2003
Qwest Communications, Inc.	US West	56.3	2000
Procter & Gamble	Gillette	54.9	2005
AT&T	Tele-Communications, Inc.	53.6	1999
Bell Atlantic	GTE	53.4	2000
InBev NV	Anheuser-Busch Cos. Inc.	52.2	2008
AT&T	MediaOne Group	49.3	2000
British Petroleum	Amoco	48.2	1998
Roche Holding AG	Genentech Inc.	46.7	2009
Chevron	Texaco	42.9	2001
WorldCom	MCI Communications	41.9	1998
JDS Uniphase	SDL	41.1	2001
Cingular Wireless	AT&T Wireless	41.0	2004
Daimler-Benz	Chrysler	40.5	1998
Berkshire Hathaway	Burlington Northern Santa Fe	36.7	2010
Viacom	CBS	39.4	2000
Sprint	Nextel Communications	39.0	2005
Merck & Co. Inc.	Schering-Plough Corp.	38.4	2009
ExxonMobil	XTO Energy	40.3	2010
ConocoPhillips	Burlington Resources	35.8	2006
Bain Capital, Kohlberg Kravis Roberts, Merrill Lynch Global Private Equity, and Thomas Frist (LBO)	HCA	32.9	2006
Investor Group	TXU Corp	32.1	2007
Deutsche Telekom	Voice Stream Wireless	30.0	2001
Express Scripts	Medco Health Solutions	29.4	2012
Facebook, Inc.	WhatsApp Inc.	19.4	2014

Source: Various issues of *Mergers and Acquisitions*, *Forbes*, and *The Wall Street Journal.*

23-2e Holding Companies

holding company

One form of business combination is the **holding company**, in which the acquiring company simply purchases all or a controlling block of another company's common shares. The two companies then become *affiliated*, and the acquiring company becomes the holding company in this *parent-subsidiary* relationship. Many large banks are organized as holding companies with subsidiaries offering various types of financial products and services. For example, Mellon Financial Corporation (which merged with Bank of New York) has a number of subsidiaries, including The Dreyfus Company (mutual funds), and The Boston Company (trust and money management). Many conglomerates are structured as holding companies. An example is Berkshire Hathaway, a firm led by the legendary investor Warren Buffett. Berkshire Hathaway owns several dozen different businesses ranging from insurance (GEICO) to railroads (BNSF).

23-2f Joint Ventures

joint venture

Another form of business combination is a **joint venture**, in which two (unaffiliated) companies contribute financial and/or physical assets, as well as personnel, to a new company formed to engage in some economic activity, such as the production or marketing of a product. The Dow Corning Company (manufacturer of silicone-based products) is an example of a joint venture established by Dow Chemical and Corning in 1943 that continues to exist to this day as a joint venture. Dow Chemical and Corning each have a 50 percent interest in the company. More recently in 2012, Starbucks and Tata Global Beverages formed a 50-50 joint venture to operate a chain of coffeehouses in India. Starbucks is the largest coffeehouse chain in the world, while Tata Global Beverages is the second largest seller of teas in the world. Joint ventures are often international in scope, such as the agreement between Samsung (Korea) and Sony (Japan) in 2004 to produce LCD panels for their respective LCD television models. The joint venture enabled the two companies to share the heavy capital costs associated with building a factory to produce LCD panels.

23-2g Leveraged Buyouts

leveraged buyout (LBO)

One frequently used method to buy a company or a division of a large company is a **leveraged buyout (LBO)**. In a typical LBO, the buyer borrows a large amount of the purchase price, using the purchased assets as collateral for a large portion of the borrowings. The buyers are usually private equity firms and, frequently, include the managers of the division or company being sold.[10] It is anticipated that the earnings (and cash flows) of the new company will be sufficient to service the debt and permit the new owners to earn a reasonable return on their investment. In some cases, sales of assets are used to help pay off the debt. The LBO of a publicly held company is sometimes referred to as *going private* because the entire equity in the company is purchased by a small group of investors and is no longer publicly traded.

The majority of LBOs involve relatively small companies. However, a number of LBOs involving large companies have occurred. For example, in the largest merger or acquisition ever undertaken up to that time, the private equity firm of Kohlberg Kravis Roberts used an LBO to purchase RJR Nabisco for $24.7 billion in 1989. However, by the early 1990s, the number of LBO transactions had declined sharply, partly because many existing LBOs were experiencing difficulties servicing their large debt loads. Because LBOs rely on significant debt financing, their popularity is tied to low interest rates and ease of availability of credit. In the years leading up to the financial crisis of 2008, LBOs were very popular because of the prevailing low interest rates and ease of credit availability. In the aftermath of the financial crisis, LBOs dropped to a trickle in 2009. Many that had been in the process of being acquired

[10] A private equity firm is an investment fund that pools money from large institutions (for example, pension funds, endowment funds) and wealthy individuals and buys public and private companies that are undervalued or distressed. The private equity firm makes money by improving the operations of the company and then taking it public through an initial public offering or by selling the company to another firm. Some of the largest private equity firms include Kohlberg Kravis Roberts, Bain Capital, TPG Capital, and The Carlyle Group.

were cancelled because credit availability from banks and other financial institutions became scarce. LBO activity has gone up sharply since 2009 as a result of the stabilizing economy and improved availability of credit at extremely low interest rates. One recent example is the $25 billion leveraged buyout of Dell, Inc. by its CEO-founder, Michael Dell, and private equity firm, Silver Lake Management LLC, that took place in 2013.

23-2h Divestitures and Restructurings

Divestitures and *restructurings* can be an important part of a company's merger and acquisition strategy. After an acquiring company completes an acquisition, it frequently examines the various assets and divisions of the recently acquired company to determine whether all the acquired company's pieces fit into the acquiring company's future plans. If not, the acquiring company may sell off, or *divest*, a portion of the acquired company. In so doing, the acquiring company is said to be *restructuring* itself.

Divestitures and restructurings, however, are frequently not associated directly with a company's acquisitions. A company may divest itself of certain assets because of a change in overall corporate strategy. For example, Citigroup (parent of Citibank) decided to get out of the insurance business in 2005 and sold its Travelers Life & Annuity subsidiary to MetLife. As a result, Citibank changed, or restructured, the asset side of its balance sheet; this is called an *operational restructuring*. In addition, a company can change its capital structure and thereby carry out a *financial restructuring*. For example, Georgia Gulf Corporation halved its long-term debt in 2009 from 83 percent to 44 percent of total assets by exchanging its long-term debt for convertible preferred and common stock. This restructuring saved Georgia Gulf from likely bankruptcy.

Instead of selling a part of the company for cash, divestitures can be accomplished through a spin-off or an equity carve-out. In a *spin-off*, common stock in a division or subsidiary is distributed to shareholders of the parent company on a pro rata basis. The subsidiary or division becomes a separate company. Owners of the parent company who receive common stock in the new company can keep the shares or sell them to other investors. An example of such a divestiture was the spin-off by eBay of its PayPal subsidiary. eBay, a leading online auction and shipping website, acquired the digital payments processing firm, PayPal, in 2002. eBay spun-off PayPal in July 2015, so each could focus on their respective businesses and thereby realize their full potential. In the spin-off, an owner of a share of eBay received one share of PayPal. In an equity carve-out, or partial public offering, common stock in the subsidiary or division is sold directly to the public, with the parent company usually retaining a controlling interest in the shares outstanding. For example, in 1993 Sears sold a 20 percent stake in its Allstate insurance subsidiary through an initial public offering, while retaining an 80 percent interest in the unit. Two years later, in 1995, Sears spun off the remaining 80 percent interest in Allstate through a special tax-free dividend to its common stockholders.

Spin-offs and equity carve-outs can be used by large, diversified companies to remove either an underperforming unit that is hurting the overall firm or a healthy subsidiary that is buried among underperforming units. In the 1990s and later, spin-offs were used to achieve the same results that leveraged buyouts did in the 1980s, namely, more focused and efficient companies.

An alternative to either selling or spinning off a division is to issue a *tracking stock*. A tracking stock enables a large company that has a subsidiary in a high-growth business, which is buried within the organization, to capture the value of this business. The theory is that the sum of the values of the tracking stock of the high-growth business and the parent company's stock, which are traded separately, will be worth more than the single stock of the parent company.

Tracking stocks were first issued in the mid-1980s when General Motors created separate stocks for two of its high-growth subsidiaries: Electronic Data Systems and Hughes Electronics. Other companies, such as AT&T and Circuit City, also issued tracking stocks for their faster-growing subsidiaries Liberty Media and CarMax, respectively. Tracking stocks have lost their popularity in recent years.

23-2i Tender Offers

Although many mergers are the result of a friendly agreement between the two companies, a company may wish to acquire another company even when the combination is opposed by the management or board of directors of the merger candidate company. In such a case, the acquiring company makes a *tender offer* for common shares of the merger candidate. In a **tender offer**, the acquiring company effectively announces that it will pay a certain price above the current market price for any of the merger candidate's shares that are "tendered" (that is, offered to it) before a particular date. Often, tender offers are revised upward and the dates extended, especially if the initial response looks promising or the target management expresses dissatisfaction with the initial tender offer price. For example, Roche Holdings' initial tender offer for Genentech in February 2009 was $86.50, which included a premium of roughly $6.50 over what the Genentech stock traded for two months earlier. Genentech's management initially said it was not in favor of being acquired and indicated that the tender offer price was too low. Eventually, Roche raised the tender offer price and acquired Genentech at $95 per share.

tender offer

23-2j Rationale for Restructuring

A number of reasons have been suggested for the increased corporate restructuring activity during the later part of the twentieth century and first part of the twenty-first century. According to Jensen, the most important reasons are the failure of internal control mechanisms to prevent unproductive capital investment (that is, overinvestment) and organizational inefficiencies (overstaffing) by many large U.S. corporations.[11] He claims that this control system—the internal management supervised by a board of directors—breaks down in mature companies with large cash flows and few good investment opportunities. Firms in the oil, tobacco, food processing, and retailing industries have been notable in this regard. These inefficiencies allow acquirers to pay a large premium over the pretakeover market value of the company and earn high returns on their investment by using the acquired company's resources more efficiently.

A second reason cited is the emergence of private equity investors, such as Kohlberg Kravis Roberts, Blackstone Group, Texas Pacific Group, Carlyle Group, and Merrill Lynch Global Private Equity, who take large equity positions or purchase entire companies. Several of these private equity investors have raised $15 billion or more to use in acquiring companies. In some cases, such as the LBO of TXU, several private equity funds join together to purchase a company. Unlike comparatively passive institutional investors, such as pension funds, private equity investors take an active role in setting the strategic direction and monitoring the performance of the companies. Usually these investors install their own management team and give them significant equity positions in the companies as incentives to operate efficiently and increase shareholder value.

[11]Michael Jensen, "Corporate Control and the Politics of Finance," *Journal of Applied Corporate Finance* (Summer 1991): 13–33.

Typically, private equity buyers use their own funds to pay for 20 percent or so of the purchase price and finance the remaining amount with junk bonds and bank debt.[12] In the case of highly leveraged transactions, large debt service payments put pressure on management to reduce costs and make better capital investment decisions.

A third reason for the corporate restructuring boom is the ready availability and relatively low cost of credit to finance these transactions. Junk bond financing, as well as financing provided by commercial banks, insurance companies, and pension funds, provide the debt capital that permits private equity investors to leverage their purchases.

23-2k Antitakeover Measures

In response to the merger and acquisitions boom of the late 1980s, many companies adopted various measures designed to discourage unfriendly takeover attempts. These antitakeover measures, sometimes referred to as *shark repellents*, are as follows:

1. *Staggered board.* Stagger the terms of the board of directors over several years instead of having the entire board come up for election at one time. Thus, the acquiring firm will have difficulty electing its own board of directors to gain control.
2. *Golden parachute contracts.* Give key executives employment contracts under which the executives will receive large benefits if they are terminated without sufficient cause after a merger. Corporate takeovers often raise serious agency problems between stockholders and managers. A takeover at a large premium over the current market price of the firm's stock is beneficial to stockholders. At the same time, the offer may be detrimental to managers because they may lose their jobs if the takeover is successful and the new owners replace them. Golden parachute contracts are used to encourage management to act in the interests of stockholders in any takeover attempt.
3. *Supermajority voting rules.* Insert in the corporate charter voting rules that require a supermajority of shares (for example, 80 percent) to approve any takeover proposals.
4. *Poison pills.* Also known as shareholders rights plans, the "pill" or "right" is usually triggered when a shareholder (bidder) gains significant ownership in a firm (target). The trigger allows non-bidder shareholders to buy additional shares at a steep discount with the effect of diluting the ownership percentage of the bidder and raising the cost to the bidder of acquiring these additional shares.

Once an unfriendly takeover attempt has been initiated, the target company's management can employ various other antitakeover measures to deter a takeover, including the following:

1. *White knight.* The target company's management can try to find another, more friendly acquiring company that is willing to enter into a bidding war with the company making the first offer.
2. *Standstill agreement.* The target company's management can attempt to negotiate an agreement with the bidder whereby the bidder agrees to limit its holdings in the target company.
3. *Pacman defense.* Named after the video game, the target company can make a takeover bid for the stock of the bidder.
4. *Litigation.* Legal action (that is, suits and appeals in state and federal courts) can be used to delay a takeover attempt.
5. *Asset and/or liability restructuring.* A target company can sell assets that the bidder wants to another company, or it can issue larger amounts of debt and use the

[12] Dennis K. Berman and Henry Sender, "Big Deal: Records Were Meant to Be Broken," *The Wall Street Journal* (January 9, 2006): C1.

proceeds to repurchase its common stock. These actions make the target company less desirable to the bidder.

6. *Greenmail.* The takeover candidate can attempt to buy back its shares, at a premium over the shares' market price, from the company or investor who initiated the unfriendly takeover attempt. The amount of the premium is referred to as "greenmail."

More recently, institutional investors, who often control a significant block of a company's stock, have become increasingly active participants in battles for control in many firms. Pension funds such as the California Public Employees Retirement System (CalPERS) and the college teachers' retirement fund, TIAA-CREF, as well as other institutions (even individuals), have sponsored numerous shareholder proposals in firms in which they own stock to rescind various antitakeover measures and undertake other actions to improve corporate governance in the firms. Shareholder proposals are basically proposals that shareholders put forth for consideration at the firm's annual meeting and are voted on by shareholders. Though shareholder proposals are only advisory in nature and firms are not legally required to abide by them, a majority vote in favor of a shareholder proposal sends a strong message to the board of directors and management that if the proposal is not adopted, stockholders may not be sympathetic to management and the board and may even replace them in future board elections. Such institutional pressures have resulted in many firms rescinding a number of antitakeover measures such as poison pills and staggered elections of board members.[13]

23-21 Reasons for Mergers

The following are some of the reasons why a firm might consider acquiring another firm, rather than choosing to grow internally:

- A firm may be able to acquire certain desirable assets at a lower cost by combining with another firm than it could if it purchased the assets directly. For example, Google's purchase of Motorola Mobility in 2012 gave it quick access to the technology and production of cell phones, which it did not have. Building this capability on its own would have been far more expensive and time-consuming
- A firm may be able to achieve greater economies of scale by merging with another firm; particularly in the case of a horizontal merger. When the net income for the combined companies after merger exceeds the sum of the net incomes prior to the merger, *synergy* is said to exist. The synergy benefits may come through increased sales, decreased costs, or both. For example, in its proposed 2013 acquisition of American Airlines (AMR Corporation), US Airways estimated $1.4 billion annual cost savings on $40 billion in revenue.
- A firm that is concerned about its sources of raw materials or end-product markets might acquire other firms at different stages of its production or distribution processes. These are vertical mergers. For example, in 1984 Mobil Corporation (now part of ExxonMobil), a major international oil company considered strong in refining and marketing but somewhat "crude poor," acquired Superior Oil Company, which owned large oil and gas reserves and had no refining and marketing operations. The acquisition resulted in Mobil becoming a better balanced oil company.
- A firm may wish to grow more rapidly than is possible through internal expansion. Acquiring another company may allow a growing firm to move more rapidly into a geographic or product area in which the acquired firm already has established markets, sales personnel, management capability, warehouse facilities, and so on, than would be possible by starting from scratch.
- A firm may desire to diversify its product lines and businesses in an attempt to reduce its business risk by smoothing out cyclical movements in its earnings. For example, a capital equipment manufacturer might achieve steadier earnings by expanding into the replacement parts business. During a

[13]R. Romano, "Less Is More: Making Investor Activism a Valuable Mechanism of Corporate Governance," *Yale Journal of Regulation* 18 (Summer 2001): 174–251; R. S. Thomas and J. F. Cotter, "Shareholder Proposals in the New Millennium: Shareholder Support, Board Response, and Market Reaction," *Journal of Corporate Finance* 13 (June 2007): 368–381.

recession, expenditures for capital equipment may slow down, but expenditures on maintenance and replacement parts may increase. This reason is of questionable benefit to the company's shareholders because most investors can diversify their holdings (through the securities markets) more easily and at a lower cost than the company can.

- A firm that has suffered losses and has a tax-loss carry-forward may be a valuable merger candidate to a company that is generating taxable income. If the two companies merge, the losses may be deductible from the profitable company's taxable income and hence lower the combined company's income tax payments. This was a factor in the 1980s acquisition of American Motors Corporation (AMC) by Chrysler. AMC's huge accumulated losses allowed Chrysler to shield its significant profits from taxes for several years.

This list, although not exhaustive, indicates the principal reasons why a firm may choose external expansion over internal growth.

If one firm wishes to acquire all or a portion of another firm, it is important to question whether the acquisition will be anything more than a zero net present value project in an efficient capital market. If it is, this excess value must result from the acquiring firm's access to superior managerial and labor talents at costs not fully reflective of their marginal value, from access to raw material and other necessary inputs at lower costs, from an ability to price the product in a more profitable way (perhaps because of an established brand name), from operating synergies in the production and/or distribution areas, from access to capital at a lower cost, from generally more efficient operations due to lower agency costs in the acquiring firm compared to those in the acquired firm, or from some other source. Each of these possible reasons is suggestive of an inefficiency in a factor, product, or portion of the capital markets.

A number of empirical studies have examined the returns to the stockholders of the merger candidate and the acquiring company in a takeover.[14] Because the acquiring company must pay a premium over the current market price to obtain the merger candidate, one would expect to see positive returns to the acquired firm's shareholders. This is the case, with average returns of 20 percent or more in successful mergers.[15] For the acquiring company's shareholders, the returns are not as good, averaging 5 percent or less in successful mergers.[16]

23-2m Accounting Aspects of Mergers

purchase method

Historically (prior to July 1, 2001), two basic methods have been used to account for mergers: either the *purchase method* or the *pooling of interests method.* In the **purchase method**, the total value paid or exchanged for the acquired firm's assets is recorded on the acquiring company's books. The tangible assets acquired are recorded at their fair market values, which may or may not be more than the amount at which they were carried on the acquired firm's balance sheet prior to the merger.

goodwill

The excess of the total value paid over the fair market value of the acquired assets is an intangible asset termed **goodwill**. Firms are allowed to amortize the goodwill over a useful life not to exceed 40 years.[17] The intangible asset of goodwill can be quite

[14]See J. Fred Weston, Kwang S. Chung, and Susan E. Hoag, *Mergers, Restructuring, and Corporate Control* (Englewood Cliffs, NJ: Prentice-Hall, 1990), Chapter 10, for a summary of the empirical studies relating to the returns associated with corporate restructuring. See also Steven Kaplan, "The Effects of Management Buyouts on Operating Performance and Value," *Journal of Financial Economics* (October 1989): 217–254.

[15]Weston, Chung, and Hoag, *Mergers, Restructuring, and Corporate Control*: 257.

[16]Weston, Chung, and Hoag, *Mergers, Restructuring, and Corporate Control*: 259.

[17]The expression *goodwill* rarely appears on the balance sheet; instead, we often find "investment in consolidated subsidiaries in excess of net assets at date of acquisition, less amortization." The allowable length of amortization has varied over time. Starting in mid-2001, amortization was no longer permitted. However, firms are required to annually test for impairment and any decreases had to be reported as a loss in the income statement and subtracted from the asset side of the balance sheet. It should also be noted that starting on July 1, 2001, pooling was no longer permitted, and firms had to use the purchase method of accounting.

TABLE 23.3

Comparison of the Purchase and the Pooling of Interests Methods of Accounting for Mergers ($ Millions)*

	Before Acquisition		Company B (After Acquisition of Company A)	
	Company A	Company B	Purchase Method	Pooling of Interests Method
Total assets, book value	$10	$50	$63	$60
Liabilities, book value	3	15	18	18
Stockholders' equity, book value	7	35	45	42

*Terms of merger: Company B acquires common stock of Company A for $10 million.

significant for many companies. For example, when Philip Morris purchased Kraft Inc. in 1988 for $12.9 billion, the fair market value of Kraft's physical assets was about $1.3 billion. The difference of $11.6 billion, or 90 percent of the purchase price, represented the intangible asset of goodwill (that is, Kraft brands and consumer loyalty).

pooling of interests method

In the **pooling of interests method**, the acquired company's assets are recorded on the acquiring company's books at their cost (net of depreciation) when originally acquired. Thus, any difference between the purchase price and the book value is not recorded on the acquiring company's books, and no goodwill account is created.

The pooling of interests method has certain advantages over the purchase method. All other things being equal, reported earnings will be higher under the pooling method, primarily because depreciation will not be more than the sum of the depreciation charges prior to the merger. In addition, because goodwill is not created on the balance sheet in a pooling, it cannot appear as an amortization charge on the acquiring firm's income statement.

For example, suppose that Company B acquires Company A's outstanding common stock for $10 million. The book value of the acquired shares is $7 million. Table 23.3 shows the results of this merger, according to both the purchase and pooling of interests methods.

In the pooling of interests method, the two balance sheets are combined, and the $3 million difference between the purchase price and the book value of Company A's stock is not considered. In the purchase method, in contrast, the $3 million difference between the purchase price and the book value is recorded on both sides of Company B's postmerger balance sheet as an increase in total assets and as stockholders' equity.

The book value of Company A's *assets* is $10 million. Suppose that the market value of Company A's assets at the date of acquisition is $11 million. Company B paid $3 million above the book value of *stockholders' equity*. Of this $3 million, the $1 million difference between the assets' market value and book value is recorded on the balance sheet in the appropriate tangible assets accounts. The other $2 million is recorded as goodwill.

Despite its popularity, the Financial Accounting Standards Board voted to eliminate the pooling of interests method starting July 1, 2001. The objective of this change was to create more compatible financial statements among companies that make acquisitions. Also, this decision is more consistent with international accounting standards, which generally do not allow the pooling of interests method.

23-2n Tax Aspects of Mergers

Taxes can play an important role in determining how an acquired company's shareholders receive compensation for their shares. Merger transactions that are effected through the use of voting equity securities (either common stock or *voting* preferred stock) are tax-free. For example, if an acquired company's stockholders have a gain on the value of their shares at the time of the merger, the gain is not recognized for tax purposes if these shareholders receive voting equity securities of the acquiring company; any gains are not recognized until the newly acquired shares are sold.

In contrast, if the acquired company's shareholders receive cash or *nonvoting* securities (such as debt securities, *nonvoting* preferred stock, or warrants) in exchange for their shares, any gains are taxable at the time of the merger. When a partial cash down payment is made, however, the exchange can be treated as an installment purchase, and the seller can spread the tax liability that is created over the payment period.

23-2o Valuation of Merger Candidates

In principle, the valuation of merger candidates is an application of the capital budgeting techniques described in Chapters 9 through 11. The purchase price of a proposed acquisition is compared to the present value of the expected future cash inflows from the merger candidate. If the present value of the cash inflows exceeds the purchase price, the merger project has a positive net present value and is acceptable.

In the case of an acquisition candidate whose common stock is actively traded, the market value of the stock is a key factor in the valuation process. To induce the stockholders of the acquisition candidate to give up their shares for the cash and/or securities of the acquiring firm, they have to be offered a premium over the market value of the stock prior to the merger announcement. Generally, a 10 to 20 percent premium is considered a minimum offer. Even then, in many situations, stockholders may hold out for much better offers, either from the company making the initial offer or from other interested companies.

23-2p Valuation Techniques

Two major methods are typically used to value merger candidates: the discounted cash flow method and the comparative multiples method.

discounted cash flow (DCF) method

Discounted Cash Flow Method

The **discounted cash flow (DCF) method** for valuing merger candidates is similar to calculating the net present value in a capital budgeting problem except that we are calculating the value of a firm rather than a specific project. The DCF value of a target firm or potential merger candidate is equal to the present value of all future expected cash flows (after the merger) discounted at the appropriate cost of capital. Thus, the two key elements for determining the DCF value of a target firm are (1) proper forecasting of postmerger cash flows and (2) determining an appropriate postmerger discount rate for the cash flows. Of the two requirements, forecasting future cash flows is more difficult. Forecasts should consider the impact of the merger on sales following the merger and synergy benefits. Assessing the benefits of a merger on sales and operating and other synergies can be tricky. Acquiring firms often overestimate the sales and synergy benefits, leading to overpayment for the target firm and subsequent failure of the merger.

Table 23.4 illustrates the application of the DCF method to the valuation of a potential target firm. In its desire to cater to the green movement, Toro Lawn Tractors is interested in expanding its offering of traditional gasoline-powered lawn mowers to include solar-powered lawn mowers. Green Mowers, Inc., is a small privately owned company that specializes in manufacturing lawn mowers that run on solar-powered batteries. The firm is profitable, but the owners have limited capital and feel that a bigger company can provide the capital needed to expand the business nationally. In addition, the owners are getting on in age and desire to retire. Toro, on the other hand, is a large firm with access to relatively cheap capital and has distributors nationwide. Thus, the

TABLE 23.4

Five-Year Projected Postmerger Cash Flows for Green Mowers

	Year 1	Year 2	Year 3	Year 4	Year 5
1. Sales[a]	$2,000,000	$2,200,000	$2,420,000	$2,662,000	$2,928,200
2. Cost of goods sold[b]	1,000,000	1,100,000	1,210,000	1,331,000	1,464,100
3. Selling, general, and administrative expenses[c]	400,000	440,000	484,000	532,400	585,640
4. Depreciation expense[d]	100,000	110,000	121,000	133,100	146,410
5. Earnings before interest and taxes (EBIT)	500,000	550,000	605,000	665,500	732,050
6. Taxes (40%)	200,000	220,000	242,000	266,200	292,820
7. Earnings after taxes	300,000	330,000	363,000	399,300	439,230
8. Add back depreciation expense	100,000	110,000	121,000	133,100	146,410
9. Cash flow	400,000	440,000	484,000	532,400	585,640
10. Retentions for capital expenditure and net working capital[e]	140,000	154,000	169,400	186,340	204,974
11. Net cash flow to acquiring firm	$ 260,000	$ 286,000	$ 314,600	$ 346,060	$ 380,666

[a]Sales are assumed to grow at 10 percent annually until year 5.

[b]Cost of goods sold are estimated to be 50 percent of sales.

[c]Selling, general, and administrative expenses are estimated to equal 20 percent of sales.

[d]Depreciation expense is assumed to equal 5 percent of sales.

[e]Retentions for capital expenditures and net working capital are projected to equal 7 percent of sales.

potential acquisition of Green Mowers by Toro could be a mutually beneficial one. Toro feels that it can easily double the sales of Green Mowers to $2 million in the year after the acquisition and then grow the business at a rate of 10 percent per year for four more years until year 5 of the projection period.

- Line 1 of Table 23.4 shows sales projections for the target firm after the takeover by Toro.
- Lines 2 and 3 show the cost of goods sold and selling, general, and administrative expenses. These are assumed to reflect potential synergy benefits from the merger. For example, the projections assume that cost of goods sold equals 50 percent of sales and selling, general, and administrative expenses equal 20 percent of sales. Both percentages are assumed to be lower than the current percentages for Green Mowers. The greater buying power of Toro is likely to result in lower cost of production, which is reflected in the cost of goods sold projections. Similarly, the selling, general, and administrative expenses should reflect lower overhead and savings in marketing expenses once Green Mowers becomes a part of the larger Toro organization.
- Line 4 contains the projected depreciation expense, which is assumed to equal 5 percent of sales for purposes of the exercise. Although depreciation expense is not normally considered to vary directly with sales, for ease of presentation we have assumed it to vary directly with sales.
- Line 5 shows the earnings before interest and taxes (EBIT). We then subtract taxes in line 6 at a 40 percent rate to give us earnings after taxes, or net income, which is shown in line 7. Note that we did not subtract any interest expense. This is similar to capital budgeting, where we ignore interest expenses in determining the project's cash flows because the discount rate used—the firm's cost of capital—includes the cost of financing from debt. Recall from Chapter 12 the firm's cost of capital is the weighted average cost of all sources of capital used by the firm, including debt and equity. Subtracting interest expense when discounting by the cost of capital will lead to double-counting the effect of debt financing.
- Depreciation is added back in line 8 to give us cash flow in line 9.
- Next, retentions for capital expenditure and net working capital are subtracted in line 10. These expenditures are assumed to be needed for the sustainability and growth of the business. Retentions are assumed to equal 7 percent of sales.
- The resulting net cash flow is shown in line 11.

Table 23.4 shows projections for the first five years of the postmerger period. Beyond year 5, Toro believes net cash flows will grow at a constant rate of 5 percent. Thus the present value of the cash flows beyond year 5 (terminal value) can be calculated using the constant growth formula:

(23.1)

$$\text{Terminal value in year 5} = \frac{\text{Net cash flow in year 6}}{k - g}$$

Net cash flow in year 6 is given by:

$$\text{Net cash flow in year 5} \times (1 + g) \text{ or } \$380{,}666\,(1 + 0.05) = \$399{,}699.30.$$

Toro believes that it is appropriate to discount postmerger flows at its cost of capital of 12 percent. This is appropriate since Toro expects to finance the acquisition using a similar mix of debt and equity as currently contained in its capital structure and because the business risk associated with producing and selling the newly acquired line of mowers is similar to those currently being produced and sold by Toro.[18] Plugging the relevant values into Equation 23.1 yields:

$$\begin{aligned}\text{Terminal value in year 5} &= \frac{\$399{,}699.30}{0.12 - 0.05}\\ &= \$5{,}709{,}990\end{aligned}$$

This terminal value represents the present value of all net cash flows beyond year 5 as of the end of year 5.

Now that we have the annual cash flows and the terminal value, we can calculate the value of the target firm to Toro. This is simply the present value of the annual cash flows in years 1 to 5 plus the terminal value at the end of year 5, all discounted at the cost of capital of 12 percent:

$$\begin{aligned}\text{Target firm value} &= \frac{\$260{,}000}{(1+0.12)^1} + \frac{\$286{,}000}{(1+0.12)^2} + \frac{\$314{,}600}{(1+0.12)^3} + \frac{\$346{,}060}{(1+0.12)^4} + \frac{\$380{,}666}{(1+0.12)^5} + \frac{\$5{,}709{,}990}{(1+0.12)^5}\\ &= \$4{,}359{,}995.54\end{aligned}$$

Based on the projections, the target firm, Green Mowers, is worth approximately $4.36 million to Toro. Obviously Toro should try to negotiate a lower price if possible. At this price ($4.36 million), the expected postmerger cash flows will yield a return equal to the cost of capital, that is, 12 percent. Thus, the NPV is 0. To generate a positive NPV on this investment, Toro should pay less than $4.36 million.

Note that the $4.36 million value is the total value of the target firm. If the target firm has debt (for example, bank loans or bonds), these will have to be subtracted to arrive at the value of the equity. Assuming Green Mowers has bank debt outstanding of $1 million, the value of the equity is equal to $3.36 million. This is the amount Toro would be willing to offer to the equity owners of Green Mowers. In practice, the acquisition price for the equity is quoted in price per share. If Green Mowers has 100,000 shares outstanding, the offer price would equal $3.36 million/100,000, or $33.60 per share.

comparative multiples method

Comparative Multiples Method The **comparative multiples method** values the target firm using price multiples paid for other merger candidates that are comparable to the company being valued. Multiples can be based on sales; earnings before interest, taxes, depreciation, and amortization; net income; and earnings per share. For example, if two companies similar to Green Mowers were recently acquired at an average price-to-sales multiple of 5.2, the comparative multiples method suggests that a

[18] The discount rate/cost of capital should reflect the financing used for the acquisition and the risk of the acquired firm's cash flows. That is, if the merger candidate's business is riskier than the acquiring firm's cash flows, then a higher discount rate than the acquiring firm's current cost of capital should be used. Similarly, if the acquisition will be financed by a mix of debt and equity that is different from that contained in the acquiring firm's target capital structure, then a discount rate that reflects the acquisition financing mix should be used.

reasonable valuation for Green Mowers should be 5.2 times its current sales (assume current sales are \$1.0 million per year): \$1.0 million × 5.2 = \$5.2 million. Financial analysts who use this method should exercise caution and determine whether the companies being compared are indeed similar. This method, which focuses on the current income statement, may not be useful if multiples of recent, similar mergers vary widely.

Of the two methods, the discounted cash flow method is the more accurate because it takes into account the target firm's expected cash flows following the merger. It should be borne in mind that the quantitative assessments of value should be supplemented by other considerations in evaluating the desirability of a merger or an acquisition. The eventual success of a merger also depends on such factors as the merger candidate's management quality, complete disclosure, and quality of all relevant information and financial statements, liability issues, corporate culture, and corporate reputation.

23-2q Analysis of a Merger: Earnings per Share and P/E Effects

The following merger examples illustrate some of the steps and considerations involved in typical mergers. The focus is on the impact mergers have on postmerger earnings per share and the potential valuation consequences using the P/E multiple. Diversified Industries Inc. is considering acquiring either High-Tech Products Inc. or Stable Products Inc. High-Tech Products has a high expected growth rate and sells at a higher P/E ratio than Diversified. Stable Products, on the other hand, has a low expected growth rate and sells at a lower P/E ratio than Diversified. Table 23.5 contains financial statistics on Diversified and the two merger candidates.

The possible merger of Diversified with Stable Products is considered first. To entice Stable Products' present stockholders to tender their shares, Diversified would probably have to offer them a premium of at least 10 to 20 percent over Stable Products' present stock price. Suppose Diversified decides to offer a price of \$24 per share and Stable Products accepts. The exchange is on a stock-for-stock basis. As a result, because Diversified's stock price is \$30 a share, Stable Products' shareholders receive 0.8 share of Diversified common stock for every share of Stable Products stock they hold; in other words, the *exchange ratio* is 0.8. The **exchange ratio (ER)** is the number of acquiring company shares received per share of acquired company stock owned.

exchange ratio (ER)

Next, the possible merger of Diversified with High-Tech Products is considered. If Diversified decides to offer \$60 a share and High-Tech Products accepts, the High-Tech Products' shareholders would receive 2 shares of Diversified common stock for every share of High-Tech Products stock they hold; in other words, the exchange ratio would be 2.0.

TABLE 23.5

Selected Financial Data: Diversified Industries and Two Merger Candidates

	Diversified Industries	Stable Products	High-Tech Products
Sales	\$1,200 million	\$130 million	\$100 million
Earnings after taxes (EAT)	\$120 million	\$12 million	\$16 million
Number of shares outstanding, NS	40 million	4 million	4 million
Earnings per share, EPS	\$3.00	\$3.00	\$4.00
Dividends per share, D_0	\$1.65	\$1.50	\$0.80
Common stock market price, P_0	\$30.00	\$21.00	\$52.00
Price–earnings (P/E) ratio	10.0	7.0	13.0
Expected annual growth rate, g	7%	5%	14%

TABLE 23.6

Diversified Industries: Pro Forma Financial Statement Summary Assuming Separate Mergers*

	Before Merger	After Merger with Stable Products	After Merger with High-Tech Products
Sales	$1,200 million	$1,330 million	$1,300 million
Earnings after taxes, EAT	$120 million	$132 million	$136 million
Common shares outstanding, NS	40 million	43.2 million	48 million
Earnings per share, EPS	$3.00	$3.06	$2.83

*The exchange ratio is 0.8 share of Diversified common stock for each 1.0 share of Stable Products and 2.0 shares of Diversified for each 1.0 share of High-Tech Products. The net income figure for Diversified Industries (after merger) assumes that no economies of scale or synergistic benefits are realized as a result of either proposed merger.

Table 23.6 shows the pro forma financial statement summary for Diversified, assuming separate mergers with each of the merger candidates. The following equation is used to calculate the postmerger earnings per share for the combined companies, EPS_c:

(23.2)
$$EPS_c = \frac{EAT_1 + EAT_2 + EAT_{1,2}}{NS_1 + NS_2(ER)}$$

where EAT_1 and EAT_2 are the earnings after taxes of the acquiring and acquired companies, respectively, $EAT_{1,2}$ is the immediate synergistic earnings from the merger, and NS_1 and NS_2 are the number of shares outstanding of the acquiring and acquired companies, respectively. For the acquisition of Stable Products by Diversified, EPS_c is calculated as follows:

$$EPS_c = \frac{\$120 \text{ million} + \$12 \text{ million} + 0}{40 \text{ million} + [(4 \text{ million})(0.8)]}$$
$$= \$3.06$$

As a result of a merger with Stable Products, Diversified has earnings per share of $3.06, as compared with $3.00 without the merger. In other words, the merger transaction can cause Diversified's earnings to change, due to P/E differences between the merging companies. Specifically, if the exchange ratio is based on current stock market prices and no synergy exists, *the acquisition of a company with a lower P/E ratio causes the earnings per share figure of the acquiring company to increase. Similarly, the acquisition of a company with a higher P/E ratio causes the earnings per share figure to decrease*. This short-term change in earnings per share is caused solely by the merger transaction, and a rational stock market does not perceive this change to be *real* growth or *real* decline.

A more important question remains: What will happen to the price and the P/E ratio of Diversified's stock after a merger has been accomplished? Obviously, it can go up, stay the same, or go down. Normally, the stock market seems to view mergers rationally, recognizing that the postmerger P/E ratio is a weighted average of the two premerger P/E ratios. As a result, the postmerger share price of the acquiring company is usually in the same range as prior to the merger, unless significant economies of scale or synergistic benefits are achieved in the merger.

With regard to a possible merger with Stable Products, suppose Diversified's management is not willing to incur an initial dilution in its earnings per share. What are the maximum price and exchange ratio that Diversified should agree to under this criterion? The maximum price is calculated using the following equation:

(23.3)
$$P_{max} = (P/E)_1(EPS_2)$$

where P_{max} is the maximum offering price without incurring an initial EPS dilution, $(P/E)_1$ is the price-to-earnings ratio of the acquiring company, and EPS_2 is the earnings per share for the to-be-acquired company. Diversified can offer up to $30 a share for Stable Products without diluting its EPS:

$$P_{max} = (10)(\$3.00) \\ = \$30$$

A price of $30 a share in this example results in an exchange ratio of 1.0, because Diversified's stock is also selling at $30 a share.

Suppose Diversified Industries merges with High-Tech Products and initially dilutes its EPS to $2.33 from its present $3.00 level, assuming no immediate synergy. Diversified's managers may want to know how long it will take the expected EPS of the combined companies to equal the expected EPS of Diversified without the acquisition. To answer this question, we have to consider the expected growth rates of the individual companies given in Table 23.5. Without a merger, Diversified's earnings, dividends, and assets are expected to grow at an annual rate of 7 percent, and High-Tech Products' earnings are expected to grow at 14 percent a year. Assume that the combined companies grow at 9 percent a year. The expected EPS growth for Diversified with and without merger is shown in Figure 23.2. Based on expected growth rates, the EPS of Diversified with the merger will be equal to its EPS without the merger in about three years.[19] This information will be used by the Diversified management in its decision as to whether to acquire High-Tech Products.

23-3 Business Failure

The remainder of this chapter considers what happens when businesses experience severe and extended problems that might cause failure. The purpose is to present an overview of business failure and the alternatives available to the failing firm. In this section, we define business failure and discuss its frequency and causes. The section also examines the various alternatives available to failing firms, including the procedures involving the federal bankruptcy laws.

23-3a Definitions of Business Failure

Business failure can be considered from both an *economic* and a *financial* viewpoint. In an economic sense, *business success* is associated with firms that earn an adequate return (equal to or greater than the cost of capital) on their investments. Similarly, *business failure* is associated with firms that earn an inadequate return on their investments. An important aspect of business failure involves the question of whether the failure is *permanent* or *temporary*. For example, suppose a company has $1 million invested in assets and generates operating earnings of only $10,000. Obviously, this 1 percent return on investment is inadequate. However, the appropriate course of action depends to some extent on whether this business failure is judged to be permanent or temporary. If it is permanent, the company should probably be liquidated. If failure is temporary, the company should probably attempt to "ride out the storm," especially if steps can be taken to speed the company's return to business success. From an economic standpoint, business

[19]The number of years, n, for the two alternatives to produce equal EPS levels is calculated using the following equation:

$$EPS_1(1+g_1)^n = EPS_2(1+g_2)^n$$

where EPS_1 and EPS_2 are the initial EPS values for the alternatives, and g_1 and g_2 are the expected annual growth rates for the alternatives.

FIGURE 23.2

Diversified Industries' Expected EPS Growth with and without the High-Tech Products Acquisition

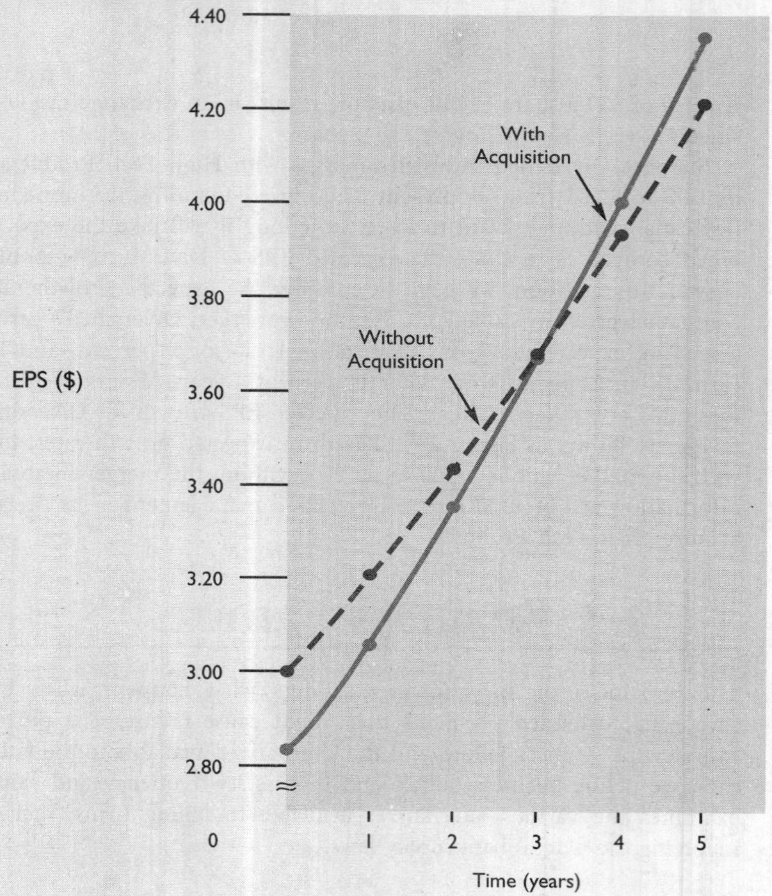

failure is also said to exist when a firm's revenues are not sufficient to cover the costs of doing business.

It is more common, however, for business failure to be viewed in a *financial context*, as a *technical insolvency*, a *legal insolvency*, or a *bankruptcy*. A firm is said to be **technically insolvent** if it is unable to meet its current obligations as they come due, even though the value of its assets exceeds the value of its liabilities.[20] A firm is **legally insolvent** if the recorded value of its assets is less than the recorded value of its liabilities. A firm is **bankrupt** if it is unable to pay its debts and files a bankruptcy petition in accordance with the federal bankruptcy laws.

technically insolvent

legally insolvent

bankrupt

HTTP:
For information on firms that have declared bankruptcy, see
www.bankruptcydata.com

23-3b Business Failure Statistics

Over the period from 2001 to 2015, approximately 38,000 businesses filed for bankruptcy each year in the United States. The failure rate is generally cyclical, with more

[20]A firm that is technically insolvent can also be said to be illiquid.

bankruptcies occurring during recessionary periods than during periods of strong economic activity. For example, in 2007, before the financial crisis started, there were about 28,000 business bankruptcies. The numbers jumped to approximately 43,500 in 2008 and to 60,800 in 2009 when the economy experienced the brunt of the financial crisis. By 2015 the number of business bankruptcies declined to just under 25,000.[21]

Another interesting characteristic involves the ages of failed businesses. As shown in Table 23.7, about 30 percent of all companies that failed had been in business three years or less, and about 50 percent had been in business five years or less. Only about one-quarter had been in business more than 10 years.

Table 23.8 lists the largest bankruptcy filings through 2015. A number of these companies, such as Federated Department Stores and General Motors Corporation, have successfully reorganized themselves while in bankruptcy and have emerged to become profitable again. Other companies, such as Adelphia Communications, were liquidated and ceased to exist. For a number of companies, the outcome is pending and may not be known for some time. There can be considerable variation in the length of time a firm is in bankruptcy. For example, when US Airways filed for bankruptcy the first time in August 2002, it emerged less than a year later in March 2003. On the other hand, in the case of Penn Central railroad (not shown in the table), it took the company more than eight years to emerge from bankruptcy.

23-3c Causes of Business Failure

Table 23.9 shows the causes of business failure for companies that have failed. Although businesses fail for a number of reasons, most failures seem to be due at least in part to economic factors, financial causes, and lack of experience on the part of the owners of the businesses.

When businesses experience problems such as inadequate sales and heavy operating expenses, they frequently encounter cash flow problems as well. As a result of the cash flow problems, these businesses often increase their short-term borrowings. If the problems persist, the cash flow difficulties can become more acute, and the business may not be able to meet its obligations to its creditors on a timely basis.

Many of these characteristics of failing firms were measured by the financial ratios used in the Altman bankruptcy prediction model discussed in Chapter 4. Such financial

TABLE 23.7

Failures by Age of Business

One year or less	9.0%
Two years	11.2
Three years	11.2
Total three years or less	31.4%
Four years	10.0
Five years	8.4
Total five years or less	49.8%
Total six to ten years	24.3
Total over ten years	25.9
	100.0%

Source: The Dun & Bradstreet Corporation, Economic Analysis Department, March 1991.

[21]Based on Table F-2 U.S. Bankruptcy Courts, http://www.uscourts.gov.

TABLE 23.8

Largest Public Company Filings of All Time by Assets, Excluding Primarily Financial Companies

Company	Assets (in Billions of Dollars)	Bankruptcy Date
WorldCom, Inc.	$103.91	7/21/2002
General Motors Corporation	91.05	6/1/2009
Enron Corp.	65.50	12/2/2001
Energy Future Holdings Corp. (formerly TXU Corp.)	40.97	4/29/2014
Chrysler LLC	39.30	4/30/2009
Pacific Gas and Electric Company	36.15	4/6/2001
Texaco, Inc.	34.94	4/12/1987
Global Crossing, Ltd.	30.19	1/28/2002
General Growth Properties, Inc.	29.56	4/16/2009
Lyondell Chemical Company	27.39	1/6/2009
Calpine Corporation	27.22	12/20/2005
UAL Corporation	25.20	12/9/2002
AMR Corp (American Airlines)	25.10	11/29/2011
Delta Air Lines, Inc.	21.80	9/14/2005
Adelphia Communications Corp.	21.50	6/25/2002
Mirant Corporation	19.42	7/14/2003
NTL Incorporated	16.83	5/8/2002
Delphi Corporation	16.59	10/8/2005
Kmart Corporation	14.63	1/22/2002
Northwest Airlines Corporation	14.04	9/14/2005
Charter Communications, Inc.	13.88	3/27/2009
Tribune Company	13.15	12/8/2008
R.H. Donnelley Corp	11.88	5/28/2009
Caesars Entertainment Operating Co.	11.68	1/15/2015
NRG Energy, Inc.	10.88	5/14/2003
Federal-Mogul Corporation	10.15	10/1/2001
Dana Corporation	9.05	3/3/2006
Comdisco, Inc.	8.75	7/16/2001
United Pan-Europe Communications NV	8.48	12/3/2002
US Airways Group, Inc. (2004)	8.35	9/12/2004
US Airways Group, Inc. (2002)	8.03	8/11/2002
XO Communications, Inc.	7.93	6/17/2002
Federated Dept. Stores	7.91	1/15/1990

Source: Kerry Mastroianni, ed., *The 2007 Bankruptcy Yearbook and Almanac* (Boston: New Generation Research, Inc., 2007); www.bankruptcydata.com.

variables as sales, operating expenses (through the effect on EBIT), short-term borrowings (debt), and cash flow (through its effect on net working capital) were all components of one or more of the ratios used to forecast failure.

23-3d Alternatives for Failing Businesses

Once a firm begins encountering these difficulties, the firm's owners and management have to consider the alternatives available to failing businesses. In general, a failing company has two alternatives:

1. It can attempt to resolve its difficulties with its creditors on a *voluntary*, or *informal*, basis.
2. It can petition the courts for assistance and *formally* declare *bankruptcy*.

TABLE 23.9

Causes of Business Failures

Underlying Causes	Percentage*
Economic factors (e.g., industry weakness, insufficient profits)	41.0%
Finance factors (e.g., heavy operating expenses, insufficient capital)	32.5
Experience factors (e.g., lack of business knowledge, lack of line experience, lack of management experience)	20.6
Neglect (e.g., poor work habits, business conflicts)	2.5
Fraud	1.2
Disaster	1.1
Strategy factors (e.g., receivables difficulties, overexpansion)	1.1
	100.0%

*Results are based on primary reason for failure.

Source: The Dun & Bradstreet Corporation, Economic Analysis Department, March 1991.

A company's creditors may also petition the courts, and this may result in the company's being involuntarily declared bankrupt.

Regardless of whether a business chooses informal or formal methods to deal with its difficulties, eventually the decision has to be made whether to *reorganize* or *liquidate* the business. Before this decision can be made, both the business's liquidation value and its going-concern value have to be determined. *Liquidation value* equals the proceeds that would be received from the sale of the business assets minus liabilities. **Going-concern value** equals the capitalized value of the company's operating earnings minus its liabilities. Basically, if the going-concern value exceeds the liquidation value, the business should be reorganized; otherwise, it should be liquidated. However, in practice, the determination of the going-concern and liquidation values is not an easy matter. For example, problems may exist in estimating the price that the company's assets will bring at auction. In addition, the company's future operating earnings and the appropriate discount rate at which to capitalize the earnings may be difficult to determine. Also, management understandably is not in a position to be completely objective about these values.

going-concern value

23-3e Informal Alternatives for Failing Businesses

Regardless of exactly why a business begins to experience difficulties, the result is often the same: cash flow problems.

Frequently, the first steps taken by the troubled company involve stretching its payables. In some cases, this action can buy the troubled company up to several weeks of needed time before creditors take action.

If the difficulties are more than just minor and temporary, the company may next turn to its bankers and request additional working capital loans. In some situations, the bankers may make the additional loans, especially if they perceive the situation to be temporary. Another possible action the company's bankers and creditors may take is to restructure the company's debt.

Debt restructuring by bankers and other creditors can be quite complex. However, debt restructuring basically involves either extension, composition, or a combination of these two approaches. In an **extension**, the failing company tries to reach an agreement with its creditors that will permit it to lengthen the time it has to meet its obligations. In a **composition**, the firm's creditors accept some percentage amount less than their actual original claims, and the company is permitted to discharge its debt obligations by paying

extension

composition

less than the full amounts owed. The percentage a company's creditors will agree to in the event of a composition is usually greater than the percentage they could net if the company had to sell its assets to satisfy their claims. If a company's creditors feel that the company can overcome its financial difficulties and become a valuable customer over the long run, they may be willing to accept some form of composition.

Debt restructuring by lenders can involve deferment of both interest and principal payments for a time. Before lenders will agree to these deferments, they often require the troubled company's suppliers to make various concessions as well. In addition, the lenders frequently demand and receive *warrants* in return for making their deferment concessions.

Large companies that experience cash flow difficulties often sell off real estate, various operating divisions, or both to raise needed cash. For example, Pan American Airlines, which incurred over $1 billion in losses during the 1980s, sold its New York headquarters building, its Intercontinental Hotels subsidiary, its Pacific route system, and various aircraft during this period to raise the cash needed to stay in business. These asset sales continued into 1991 when the company essentially liquidated itself.

Another method often used by failing companies to raise needed cash is the sale and leaseback of its land and buildings. Some companies also resort to more unusual methods of conserving cash, such as offering preferred stock to certain employees in exchange for a portion of their salary.

Frequently, failing companies voluntarily form a *creditors' committee* that meets regularly and attempts to help the company out of its predicament. The creditors are usually requested to accept deferred payments, and in return, the creditors usually request that the company cut various expenditures. If the company and its creditors are able to reach an agreement on the appropriate actions to take, the legal and administrative expenses associated with formal bankruptcy procedures are not incurred. Accordingly, both the company and creditors may be better off as a result.

assignment

Liquidation can also occur outside the bankruptcy courts. The process is called an **assignment**. Usually a trustee, who is probably one of the major creditors, is assigned the assets. The trustee then has the responsibility of selling the assets and distributing the proceeds in the best interest of the creditors.

23-3f Formal Alternatives for Failing Businesses Under the Bankruptcy Laws

Bankruptcy Reform Act of 1978

The **Bankruptcy Reform Act of 1978** states the basic mechanics of the bankruptcy procedure.[22] Either the failing company or its unsecured creditors may initiate bankruptcy procedures by filing a claim in bankruptcy court. When the debtor company files for bankruptcy, it is termed a *voluntary* petition. A bankruptcy proceeding may also be initiated by a group of three or more of the company's unsecured creditors that have aggregate claims of at least $500. The unsecured creditors filing the claim must assert that the debtor company is not paying its present debts as they come due. Such a claim is termed an *involuntary* petition.

After the initial bankruptcy petition has been filed, both the failing company and its creditors receive protection from the courts. The company itself is protected from any further actions on the part of the creditors while it attempts to work out a *plan of*

[22]The Bankruptcy Reform Act of 1978, in general, streamlined the U.S. bankruptcy procedures and increased the number of bankruptcy courts. The Reform Act contains eight odd-numbered chapters, 1 through 15, which are labeled with Arabic numerals instead of the roman numerals used in the old Bankruptcy Act. The act has been amended several times since 1978, including changes enacted in 2005 through the Bankruptcy Abuse Prevention and Consumer Protection Act of 2005. The 2005 changes largely affected bankruptcy filings by individuals, making it more difficult to file bankruptcy.

reorganization. The debtor company has 120 days to work out a plan of reorganization. After that, the creditors may file a plan of their own. The court has considerable latitude in a bankruptcy case. For example, depending on the nature of the case, it may decide to appoint a *trustee* who will be responsible for running the business and protecting the creditors' interests. Normally, the troubled company is allowed to continue operations. If there is reason to believe that continuing operations will result in further deterioration of the creditors' position, however, the court can order the firm to cease operating.

A new development and alternative for firms considering bankruptcy is the prepackaged bankruptcy. Prepackaged bankruptcy filings must be agreed to by more than 50 percent of the creditors who hold at least two-thirds of the debt before filing for bankruptcy. Prepackaged filings can speed a firm through the process in a few months (for example, four months for Southland, owner of the 7-Eleven chain, and only one month in the case of General Motors), compared to the many years in which traditional filings last. For example, Revco Drugstores declared bankruptcy in 1988 and did not emerge from bankruptcy until 1992. Revco incurred over $40 million in legal and accounting fees associated with resolving its bankruptcy.

An important aspect of the bankruptcy procedures involves what to do with the failing firm. Just as in the case of the informal alternatives, a decision has to be made about whether a firm's value as a *going concern* is greater than its *liquidation* value. Generally, if this is the case and a suitable plan of reorganization can be formulated, the firm is reorganized; otherwise, it is liquidated.

23-3g Reorganization

Chapter 11 of the Bankruptcy Reform Act

During **Chapter 11** proceedings, the failing company presents its current financial status and its proposed plan of reorganization. This plan of reorganization is normally similar to either composition or extension.

The bankruptcy court and the Securities and Exchange Commission (SEC) review the plan of reorganization for fairness and feasibility. The term *fairness* means that the claims are to be settled in the order of their priority. The priority of claims is discussed in detail in the next section on liquidation. A *feasible* plan of reorganization is one that gives the business a good chance of reestablishing successful operations. For example, the plan must provide an adequate level of working capital, a reasonable capital structure and debt-to-equity ratio, and an earning power sufficient to reasonably cover interest and dividend requirements. Often a recapitalization may result in fewer fixed charges for the reorganized company and thereby afford it a better chance of succeeding. The reorganization may also involve an extension of the debt maturities, which would help the company's cash flow by causing the debt's principal retirement to occur at later dates.

After the bankruptcy court and the SEC have reviewed the reorganization plan, it is submitted to the firm's creditors for approval. Creditors vote by class (for example, unsecured creditors, secured creditors, common stockholders) on the reorganization plan (or plans, in the case where more than one plan is submitted for approval). The plan must be approved by a simple majority (that is, 50 percent) of the creditors voting in each class and by creditors representing two-thirds (that is, 66.7 percent) of the total amount of claims voting in each class. Once the bankrupt company obtains approval from the bankruptcy court and its creditors, it can leave Chapter 11. At this point, the court-appointed trustee's task is to implement the plan.

An example of a company that went through a Chapter 11 reorganization is Global-Marine, an offshore oil drilling company.[23] Faced with reduced revenues because of the

[23] *BusinessWeek* (March 13, 1989): 44.

TABLE 23.10

Reorganization of Global-Marine, Inc.

Creditor Group	Amount Owed	Amount Received
Secured creditors	$700 million	$95 million in cash $400 million in debt 60% of the common stock
Senior unsecured creditors	$154 million	$17 million in debt 30% of the common stock
Subordinated bondholders	$400 million	7.5% of the common stock
Preferred shareholders	—	0.7% of the common stock
Common shareholders	—	1.8% of the common stock

Source: Reprinted from the March 13, 1989, issue of *BusinessWeek* by special permission, copyright © 1989 by the McGraw-Hill Companies.

decline in oil prices and with $1.3 billion in debt, the company filed for bankruptcy in January 1986. Over the next three years, under the supervision of the bankruptcy court, Global cut its workforce from a high of 3,047 to 1,506 employees. It reduced its yearly overhead from $59 million to $25 million. In February 1989, Global-Marine emerged from bankruptcy. Between 1984 and 1988, the company lost $874 million. Over the next five years (1989 to 1993), after it emerged from bankruptcy, its losses narrowed to $161 million. Beginning in 1994, Global-Marine had a positive net income during each of the next seven years, before merging in 2001 with Santa Fe International to form Global Santa Fe Corporation in 2001.

The reorganization plan is shown in Table 23.10. About 40 senior creditors received a combination of cash, debt securities, and 90 percent of the common stock of the reorganized company. Subordinated debt holders received 7.5 percent of the common stock. Global's negative net worth of $116 million virtually wiped out preferred and common shareholders. They received only 2.5 percent of the common stock of the reorganized company, valued at about $3.7 million, plus warrants.

23-3h Liquidation

Chapter 7 of the Bankruptcy Reform Act

If for some reason reorganization is judged unfeasible, a legally declared bankrupt company may be liquidated. The liquidation procedures are described in **Chapter 7 of the Bankruptcy Reform Act**. In the liquidation procedure, a *referee* is normally appointed to handle the administrative aspects of the bankruptcy procedure. The referee then arranges for a meeting of the creditors, and they in turn select a *trustee*, who liquidates the business and pays the creditors' claims according to the priority of claims set forth in Chapter 7.

absolute priority rule

The **absolute priority rule** states that, in general, secured debts are satisfied first from the sale of the secured assets and that all claims of creditors must be satisfied before any claims by stockholders. The following list specifies the order of priority in which unsecured debts must be paid:

1. The expenses involved in the administration of the bankruptcy
2. Business expenses incurred after an involuntary petition has been filed but before a trustee has been appointed
3. Wages owed for services performed during the three months prior to the bankruptcy proceedings
4. Certain unpaid contributions to employee benefit plans

TABLE 23.11

Balance Sheet, Failures Galore, Inc.*

Assets		Liabilities and Equity	
Current assets	S 6,000,000	Accounts payable	$ 2,000,000
Fixed assets, net	6,500,000	Bank notes payable	2,000,000
		Accrued wages	200,000
		Accrued taxes	300,000
		Mortgage bonds	2,000,000
		Debentures	2,000,000
		Subordinated debentures	2,000,000
		Preferred stock	1,000,000
		Common equity	1,000,000
Total assets	$12,500,000	Liabilities and equity	$12,500,000

*The subordinated debentures are subordinate to the bank notes payable. Assume that all the accrued wages can be paid out of the liquidation proceeds.

5. Certain customer layaway deposits
6. Taxes owed to federal, state, and local governments
7. Claims of general and unsecured creditors
8. Preferred stockholders, who receive an amount up to the par value or stated value of the preferred stock
9. Common stockholders, who share any remaining funds equally on a per-share basis

To illustrate the absolute priority rule in a liquidation, consider the balance sheet prior to the liquidation of Failures Galore Inc. shown in Table 23.11.[24] Suppose the total proceeds of the liquidation are $6.8 million. The distribution of these proceeds is shown in Table 23.12. The proceeds have been distributed in accordance with the absolute priority rule. Each general and unsecured creditor receives a settlement percentage of the funds owed after priority claims have been settled. As shown in Table 23.12, these priority claims are bankruptcy administration expenses, wages, and taxes owed. In addition, mortgage bondholders receive $1.5 million from the sale of secured assets; this leaves the mortgage bondholders as general creditors for the balance of their claim ($500,000). After these priority claims have been met, $4.25 million in assets is left to meet the remaining creditor claims of $8.5 million. Each general creditor receives 50 percent of the claim, except bank notes. Because the subordinated debentures are subordinate to bank notes, the bank notes receive the proportionate claim of the subordinated holders ($1 million in this case) in addition to the $1 million directly due the bank notes. Hence, because of the subordination provision in the debentures, the bank notes are paid off in full.

The absolute priority rule is also used in bankruptcy reorganizations. However, in reorganization proceedings, deviations from the absolute priority rule by the courts have been observed. In a detailed study of 30 bankruptcy cases filed subsequent to the effective date of the 1978 Bankruptcy Reform Act, 23 cases resulted in shareholders being awarded more than they were entitled to under strict adherence to the absolute priority rule.[25] The excess amount received by the shareholders averaged 7.6 percent for

[24]Assume that this liquidation is a voluntary petition, that no unpaid contributions to employee benefit plans exist, and that no customer layaway deposits are involved. In other words, items 2, 4, and 5 in the priority of claims do not apply to this example.

[25]Allan C. Eberhart, William T. Moore, and Rodney L. Roenfeldt, "Security Pricing and Deviations from the Absolute Priority Rule in Bankruptcy Proceedings," *Journal of Finance* (December 1990): 1457–1469.

TABLE 23.12

Distribution of the Proceeds from the Liquidation of Failures Galore, Inc.

Total liquidation proceeds	$6,800,000
1. Bankruptcy administration expenses	$ 550,000
2. Wages owed to employees	200,000
3. Taxes owed to governments	300,000
Total priority claims	$1,050,000
Funds available for claims of creditors	$5,750,000
4. Payment to mortgage bondholders (proceeds from sale of secured assets)	1,500,000
Funds available for claims of general and unsecured creditors	$4,250,000

$$\text{Settlement percentage for general and unsecured creditors} = \frac{\text{Funds available for general and unsecured creditors}}{\text{Total claims of general and unsecured creditors}}$$

$$= \frac{4{,}250{,}000}{8{,}500{,}000}$$

$$= 50\%$$

	Total Claim	Settlement, 50% of Claim (Before Subordination Adjustment)	Settlement, 50% of Claim (After Subordination Adjustment)
Accounts payable	$2,000,000	$1,000,000	$1,000,000
Bank notes payable	2,000,000	1,000,000	2,000,000
Mortgage bonds	500,000	250,000	250,000
Debentures	2,000,000	1,000,000	1,000,000
Subordinated debentures	2,000,000	1,000,000	0
	$8,500,000	$4,250,000	$4,250,000
Funds available for preferred and common stockholders		$ 0	

the 30 cases. Two of the major reasons for the deviations are that the creditors may lack adequate information about the firm's value or that they may be willing to compromise because of the potential cost of a lengthy reorganization.

23-4 Summary

- Technically, a *merger* is a combination of two or more companies in which all but one of the companies legally cease to exist and the surviving company continues operation under its original name. A *consolidation* is a combination in which all the companies are dissolved and a new company is formed. The term *merger* is used to describe both of these types of business combinations.
- Mergers are classified according to whether they are *horizontal, vertical,* or *conglomerate.* In a horizontal merger, the combining companies are direct competitors. In a vertical merger, the companies have a buyer-seller relationship. In a conglomerate merger, neither company competes directly with the other, and no buyer-seller relationship exists.
- A *holding company* owns controlling interest in another legally separate company, and the relationship between these affiliated companies is called a *parent-subsidiary* relationship.
- In a *leveraged buyout,* the buyer of a company borrows a large portion of the purchase price, using the purchased assets as partial collateral for the loans.

- Companies choose external growth over internal growth for a number of reasons, including the following:

  1. The availability of lower-cost assets
  2. Greater economies of scale
  3. The availability of more secure raw material supplies and additional end-product markets
  4. The possibility of more rapid growth
  5. Greater diversification
  6. Tax considerations

- In the *pooling of interests* method of accounting for mergers, the acquired assets are recorded at their cost when acquired. In the *purchase* method, acquired assets are recorded at their fair market values, and any additional amount paid is listed as *goodwill*, which must then be amortized. The pooling of interest method is no longer allowed by the Financial and Accounting Standards Board.
- Two major methods are used to value merger candidates: the *discounted cash flow method* and the *comparative multiples method*. The discounted cash flow method, which is an application of capital budgeting techniques, is the most theoretically correct valuation method.
- A firm is *bankrupt* if its total liabilities exceed the value of its total assets. A firm is *technically insolvent* if it cannot meet its current obligations as they come due, even though the value of its assets exceeds its liabilities.
- Failing firms have two basic alternatives:

  1. They can attempt to resolve the difficulties with their creditors on an *informal*, voluntary basis.
  2. They can petition the courts for assistance and *formally* declare *bankruptcy*. In addition, the creditors may petition the courts, and the firm may be involuntarily declared bankrupt.

- Legal bankruptcy proceedings focus on the decision of whether the failing firm should be *reorganized* or *liquidated*. If its going-concern value is greater than its liquidation value, the business will usually be reorganized; otherwise, it will be liquidated.
- The Bankruptcy Reform Act contains two chapters that outline different bankruptcy procedures. In a Chapter 11 proceeding, the troubled company seeks court protection from its creditors while it works out a *reorganization plan*. If reorganization is judged not feasible, the bankrupt company is liquidated. The liquidation procedures are set forth in Chapter 7 of the act.

Important Equation

$$EPS_c = \frac{EAT_1 + EAT_2 + EAT_{12}}{NS_1 + NS_2(ER)}$$

23-5 Questions and Topics for Discussion

1. Define the following terms:
   a. Merger
   b. Consolidation
   c. Holding company
2. Describe some of the measures used by companies to discourage unfriendly takeover attempts.
3. What is the difference between an asset purchase and a stock purchase?
4. What is the difference between an operational restructuring and a financial restructuring?

5. Discuss the differences between the following types of mergers:
   a. Horizontal mergers
   b. Vertical mergers
   c. Conglomerate mergers
6. What are some of the reasons why firms merge with other firms?
7. What methods do financial analysts use to value merger candidates? What are the limitations of each method?
8. Explain what happens to the postmerger earnings-per-share figure when a company with a relatively high P/E ratio acquires a company with a lower P/E ratio, assuming that the exchange ratio is based on current stock market prices and no synergy exists.
9. What are the differences between the *purchase* method and the *pooling of interests* method of accounting for mergers?
10. What is a *leveraged buyout*? What is *mezzanine financing*? (Use Google in getting your answer.)
11. What is a *tax-free merger*?
12. Explain the difference between the economic and financial definitions of business failure.
13. Explain the differences among the following terms related to financial failure:
    a. Technical insolvency
    b. Legal insolvency
    c. Bankruptcy
14. What alternatives are available to the failing firm?
15. Basically, what determines whether a bankrupt company is reorganized or liquidated?
16. In a debt reorganization, explain the difference between a *composition* and an *extension*.
17. Explain why an informal settlement may be preferable to declaring bankruptcy for both the failing firm and its creditors.
18. What are the differences between Chapter 7 and Chapter 11 of the Bankruptcy Reform Act?
19. In connection with reorganization plans, what do *fairness* and *feasibility* mean?
20. Explain how a firm that has failed can be reorganized to operate successfully.
21. Rank in order of priority (highest to lowest) the following claims on the proceeds from the liquidation of a bankrupt firm:
    - Taxes owed to federal, state, and local governments
    - Preferred stockholders
    - Common stockholders
    - Expenses of administering the bankruptcy
    - Secured creditors
    - Unsecured creditors
    - Wages in three months before bankruptcy
    - Customer deposits
    - Expenses incurred after the bankruptcy petition is filed and before a trustee is appointed
    - Contributions to employee benefit plans

23-6 Self-Test Problems

ST1. Zenith Industries is considering the acquisition of the Nadir Corporation in a stock-for-stock exchange. (The expression *stock-for-stock exchange* means that the common stock of one company is exchanged for the common stock of another.) Assume that no immediate synergistic benefits are expected. Selected financial data on the two companies are shown here:

	Zenith	Nadir
Sales (millions)	$500	$ 100
Earnings after taxes (millions)	$ 30	$ 12
Common shares outstanding (millions)	6	2
Earnings per share	$ 5	$ 6
Common stock price per share	$ 50	$ 40
Dividends per share	$ 2	$ 1.50

a. If Zenith is not willing to incur an initial dilution in its earnings per share—that is, not have the postmerger earnings per share be below $5 per share—and if Zenith also feels that it will have to offer the Nadir shareholders a minimum of 25 percent over Nadir's current market price, what is the relevant range of Nadir per-share stock prices with which Zenith is working?

b. Calculate Zenith's postmerger earnings per share if the Nadir stockholders accept an offer by Zenith of $50 a share in a stock-for-stock exchange.

ST2. Melissa's Kitchen Inc. is considering acquiring Takeshi's Takeout Corporation, a small local restaurant chain in Denver, Colorado. Expected net cash flows from the acquisition for the first 4 years of the postmerger period follow. After 4 years, the net cash flows are expected to grow at a constant rate of 5 percent per year. If the appropriate discount rate is 14 percent, what is the most Melissa's Kitchen should pay for Takeshi's Takeout?

	Year 1	Year 2	Year 3	Year 4
Net cash flows	$350,000	$400,000	$475,000	$550,000

23-7 Problems*

INTERMEDIATE

1. The Blue Oil Corporation and the Grey Plastics Company have agreed to a merger. The Grey Plastics stockholders will receive 0.75 shares of Blue for each share of Grey held. Assume that no synergistic benefits are expected.

a. Complete the following table:

	Blue Oil	Grey Plastics	Combined Companies
Sales (millions)	$500	$125	______
Earnings after taxes (millions)	$ 60	$ 13	______
Common shares outstanding (millions)	16	4	______
Earnings per share	$ 3.75	$ 3.25	______
Common stock (price per share)	$ 41.25	$ 26	______
Price/earnings ratio	______	______	10.0

*Color blocks behind the numbers denote problems that have check answers provided at the end of the book.

b. Calculate the premium percentage received by the Grey stockholders.

Assume *both* that immediate synergistic earnings of $3 million per year will occur as a result of the merger and that the P/E ratio of the combined companies is 10.5.

c. Rework Part a.

d. Rework Part b.

CHALLENGE

2. The McPherson Company is considering acquiring the McAlester Company. Selected financial data for the two companies are shown here:

	McPherson	McAlester
Sales (millions)	$250	$30
Earnings after taxes (millions)	$ 20	$ 2.25
Common shares outstanding (millions)	5	1
Earnings per share	$ 4.00	$ 2.25
Dividends per share	$ 1.20	$ 0.40
Common stock (price per share)	$ 40	$18

Both companies have 40 percent marginal tax rates. Assume that no synergistic benefits are expected.

a. Calculate the McPherson Company's postmerger earnings per share if the McAlester stockholders accept an offer of $20 a share in a stock-for-stock exchange. (The expression *stock-for-stock exchange* means that the common stock of one company is exchanged for the common stock of another company.)

b. Recalculate Part a, assuming that the McPherson common stock price is $42 a share. (All other figures remain constant.)

c. Calculate McPherson's earnings per share if the McAlester stockholders accept one $6 convertible preferred share (stated value, $100) for each 5 shares of McAlester stock held.

d. Calculate McPherson's earnings per share if each group of 50 shares of McAlester stock is exchanged for one 8 percent, $1,000 debenture.

e. Compare the premerger expected dividend return on the McAlester stock with the expected postmerger dividends or interest available with the exchanges described in Parts a, c, and d. (Undoubtedly, at the time of acquisition, McPherson would have pointed out these expected increases in yield to the McAlester stockholders.) Assume that an investor initially holds 100 shares of McAlester stock.

f. What can be said about comparing the expected total postmerger return (dividends plus price appreciation) on the McAlester stock versus the expected total postmerger return on the McPherson securities?

INTERMEDIATE

3. Ball Industries is considering acquiring the Keyes Corporation in a stock-for-stock exchange. Selected financial data on the two companies follow:

	Ball	Keyes
Sales (millions)	$600	$75
Earnings after taxes (millions)	$ 30	$10
Common shares outstanding (millions)	6	4
Earnings per share	$ 5	$2.50
Common stock (price per share)	$ 50	$20

Assume that no synergistic benefits are expected.

a. What is the maximum exchange ratio Ball should agree to if one of its acquisition criteria is no initial dilution in earnings per share?

b. Suppose an investor had purchased 100 shares of Keyes common stock 5 years ago at $12 a share. If the Keyes stockholders accept an offer of $24 a share in a stock-for-stock exchange, how much capital gains tax would this investor have to pay at the time the Keyes shares are exchanged for the Ball shares? (Assume a capital gains tax rate of 28 percent for this investor.)

Assume that immediate synergistic earnings of $4 million will occur as a result of the acquisition.

c. Calculate the postmerger earnings per share if the Keyes stockholders accept an offer by Ball of $24 a share in a stock-for-stock exchange.

INTERMEDIATE

4. Looking back at Tables 23.5 and 23.6, assume that Diversified Industries acquires High-Tech Products in a stock-for-stock transaction and no immediate synergistic benefits are expected. How long will it take the expected EPS of the combined companies to equal the expected EPS of Diversified without the merger if Diversified is expected to grow at an annual rate of 7 percent without the merger and the combined companies are expected to grow at 8 percent a year?

INTERMEDIATE

5. Consider Failures Galore Inc. (Tables 23.11 and 23.12).

a. If total liquidation proceeds are $5.95 million, what is the distribution of these proceeds among the various creditors of Failures Galore?

b. If total liquidation proceeds are $7.65 million, what is the distribution of these proceeds among the various creditors of Failures Galore?

CHALLENGE

6. Go-for-Broke Company is being liquidated under Chapter 7 of the bankruptcy code. When it filed for bankruptcy, its balance sheet was as follows:

Assets		**Liabilities and Equity**	
Current assets	$14,500,000	Accounts payable	$12,145,000
Fixed assets		Accrued wages*	2,030,000
Land and buildings (net)	6,525,000	Accrued taxes	1,160,000
Equipment	7,975,000	Notes payable (bank)**	1,350,000
Total assets	$29,000,000	Total current liabilities	$16,685,000
		Mortgage bonds***	4,775,000
		Debentures	2,450,000
		Stockholders' equity	5,090,000
		Total liabilities and equity	$29,000,000

*All accrued wages must be paid out of the liquidation proceeds.
**The bank loan is unsecured.
***Mortgage bonds are secured by land and buildings.

Assume that the liquidation is a voluntary petition, that no unpaid contributions to employee benefit plans exist, and that no customer layaway deposits are involved. The proceeds from the liquidation of the company's assets are as follows:

Current assets	$9,425,000
Land and buildings	3,045,000
Equipment	4,130,000
Total	$16,600,000

Bankruptcy administration charges are $643,750.

a. Determine the distribution (dollar amount and percentage) of the liquidation proceeds among the various creditors of Go-for-Broke.
b. Assume that the debentures ($2.45 million) are subordinated to bank notes payable. Determine the distribution (dollar amount and percentage) of the liquidation proceeds among the various creditors of Go-for-Broke.

INTERMEDIATE **7.** Wilson Industries is considering the acquisition of the Blanchard Company in a stock-for-stock exchange. Selected financial data for the two companies are shown next. An immediate synergistic earnings benefit of $1 million is expected in this merger, due to cost savings.

	Wilson	Blanchard
Sales (millions)	$150	$30
Earnings after taxes (millions)	$ 25	$ 3.5
Common shares outstanding (millions)	8	2
Earnings per share	$ 3.125	$ 1.75
Dividends per share	$ 1.50	$ 0.75
Common stock price per share	$ 40	$19.50

Calculate the postmerger earnings per share if the Blanchard shareholders accept an offer of $22 per share in a stock-for-stock exchange.

BASIC **8.** Apex Corporation is considering the purchase of Pinnacle Company in a stock-for-stock exchange. Selected data on the two companies are shown in the following table:

	Apex	Pinnacle
Sales (millions)	$750	$175
Earnings after taxes (millions)	$100	$ 20
Common shares outstanding (millions)	50	20
Share price	$ 40	$ 15
Earnings per share	$ 2.00	$ 1.00
Dividends per share	$ 1.00	$ 0.40
P/E ratio	20	15
Dividend payout ratio	50%	40%

Assume that there are no synergistic benefits as the result of the merger. Determine EPS for the combined company if Apex offers a:

a. 20 percent premium for Pinnacle
b. 40 percent premium for Pinnacle
c. 50 percent premium for Pinnacle

BASIC **9.** Consider Problem 8 again. Assume that there are immediate synergistic benefits of $4 million if Apex and Pinnacle merge. Answer Parts a, b, and c of Problem 8 under these conditions.

INTERMEDIATE **10.** A financial analyst with MTC International has estimated the annual after-tax net cash flow from a proposed merger to be $1.5 million. This cash flow is expected to continue for 10 years. For the following 5 years, the net cash flow is estimated to be $0.7 million per year. MTC International feels that the appropriate risk-adjusted discount rate is 16 percent. Calculate the present value of the expected net cash flows from the proposed merger through year 15.

INTERMEDIATE **11.** Jeff's Powerwash Inc. which operates in Texas, is considering acquiring Frank's Superior Carworks chain of car washes in Maryland. The expected net cash flows from the acquisition for the first 3 years of the postmerger period follow. After 3 years, the net cash flows are expected to grow at a constant rate of 4 percent per year. If the appropriate discount rate is 10 percent, what is the most Jeff's Powerwash should pay for Frank's Superior Carworks?

	Year 1	**Year 2**	**Year 3**
Net cash flows	$550,000	$650,000	$750,000

INTERMEDIATE **12.** In Problem 11, assume Frank's Superior Carworks has $1.5 million in debt and 500,000 shares outstanding. Based on your answer to Problem 11, how much would Jeff's Powerwash be willing to pay for each share of Frank's Superior Carworks?

INTERMEDIATE **13.** NPR MedTech Corporation is considering acquiring IV Pumps Inc. a relatively small company that manufactures intravenous pumps for use by hospitals. NPR MedTech believes it can grow IV Pumps' sales by 30 percent per year for the first 5 years after it acquires the firm. In the year just ended, IV Pumps' sales were $1 million. Operating expenses (cost of goods *plus* selling, general, and administrative expenses) are projected to equal 60 percent of sales. Depreciation expense is forecasted to be $100,000, $150,000, $175,000, $200,000, and $225,000, respectively, for the next 5 years. Retentions to sustain the business are expected to equal $225,000 per year for the next 5 years. After 5 years, net cash flows are expected to grow at a constant rate of 6 percent. NPR MedTech's tax rate is 40 percent. Assuming that the appropriate cost of capital for discounting the cash flow is 12 percent, what is the maximum NPR MedTech should pay for IV Pumps?

HTTP: BASIC **14.** Using a search engine, find out how many business bankruptcies occurred in the United States during the last calendar year. Then try to break down these bankruptcies by type (retail, restaurant, etc.). Finally, find out whether the trend for bankruptcies (both in absolute number and as a percentage of businesses in existence) is up or down.

HTTP: BASIC **15.** Find a business for sale in each of three major industries of your choice, as listed on the MergerNetwork Website (www.mergernetwork.com) under "Large U.S. Sellers." Then select the "dream" business you'd love to own (consulting? restaurant? manufacturing? ...).

INTEGRATIVE CASE PROBLEM

Mergers and Acquisitions

Admiral Foods Corporation is a diversified food processing and distributing company that has shown excellent growth over the past 10 years as a result of a balanced program of acquisitions and internal growth.

One segment of the food business in which Admiral has only recently begun to compete, however, is the fast-food business. The present top management of Admiral Foods feels that good future growth in the fast-food business is still possible, regardless of the rapid expansion of the last two decades. During the past year, members of the Admiral staff have examined and analyzed a number of independent fast-food firms. One company that the analysis indicated as potentially suitable for acquisition by Admiral is Favorite Food Systems Inc.

Favorite Food Systems Inc. which was founded by John Favorite in 1994, is a West Coast chain with current annual sales of approximately $75 million. Favorite's history can best be described as up and down, with the general trend up. The company survived several brief shaky periods during the late 1990s. In 2003, the company went public. (The Favorite family now controls about 57 percent of the common stock.) By 2006, Favorite Foods was recommended by two brokerage firms and was touted by one investment service as "another potential McDonald's." This and other predictions never came true. In fact, Favorite Food Systems' growth rate has slowed appreciably during the past five years. One reason frequently given in the trade for Favorite's growth slowdown is Mr. Favorite's apparent indecision regarding expansion. As a result, the competition has increasingly gotten the jump on Favorite with the best locations in new residential growth areas.

The following table shows last year's balance sheets and income statements for both Admiral and Favorite.

Admiral Foods Corporation Balance Sheet (in Millions of Dollars)

Current assets	$225	Current liabilities	$101
Fixed assets, net	307	Long-term debt	106
		Common equity (10,000,000 shares)	325
Total assets	$532	Total liabilities and equity	$532

Admiral Foods Corporation Income Statement (in Millions of Dollars)

Sales	$1,261.0
Less: Expenses, excluding depreciation	1,118.2
Less: Depreciation	36.0
Earnings before interest and taxes	$ 106.8
Less: Interest	12.8
Earnings before taxes	$ 94.0
Less: Taxes (40%)	37.6
Earnings after taxes	$ 56.4

Favorite Food Systems, Inc. Balance Sheet (in Millions of Dollars)

Current assets	$10.6	Current liabilities	$ 6.5
Fixed assets, net	12.1	Long-term debt	2.2
		Common equity	
Total assets	$22.7	(2,000,000 shares)	14.0
		Total liabilities and equity	$22.7

Favorite Food Systems, Inc. Income Statement (in Millions of Dollars)

Sales	$75.2
Less: Expenses, excluding depreciation	65.4
Less: Depreciation	1.4
Earnings before interest and taxes	$ 8.4
Less: Interest	0.4
Earnings before taxes	$ 8.0
Less: Taxes (40%)	3.2
Earnings after taxes	$ 4.8

Additional Information

	Admiral Foods Corporation	Favorite Food Systems
Dividends per share	$ 2.50	$ 0.60
Common stock (price per share)	$50	$15

Marie Harrington received her BBA degree in finance three years ago and went to work for Admiral Foods as a financial analyst in the corporate budget department. Recently, she became a senior financial analyst responsible for analyzing mergers and major capital expenditures. One of her first assignments is to prepare a financial analysis of the proposed Favorite acquisition. It is the conservative policy of Admiral Foods to analyze acquisitions assuming that no synergistic benefits will occur. Admiral Foods has found that the amount of synergy in a merger is relatively difficult to forecast. During Harrington's discussions with her supervisor, they decided that the analysis should contain the following items:

1. Calculate the exchange ratios, based on the common stock market value and earnings per share.
2. Mr. Favorite has suggested an exchange ratio based on a 25 percent increase over Favorite's current market price. Calculate this exchange ratio.
3. What is the maximum exchange ratio Admiral Foods should agree to if one of its acquisition criteria specifies no initial dilution in earnings per share? What per-share price for Favorite Food Systems does this exchange ratio represent?
4. Even though Harrington's assignment is primarily financial in nature, what other considerations are important in a merger such as this?
5. Calculate the Admiral Foods postmerger earnings per share, assuming each share of Favorite stock is exchanged for 0.40 shares of Admiral stock.

6. In discussions with Admiral, Mr. Favorite has stated that he would prefer to exchange his Favorite shares for either Admiral common stock or a convertible preferred rather than cash or debentures. Why?
7. Based on the information given in the case and your analysis, what do you feel is a fair exchange ratio?

Reference Materials

See www.cengagebrain.com for these additional reference files:

Table I: Future Value Interest Factor (FVIF)
Table II: Present Value Interest Factor (PVIF)
Table III: Future Value of an Annuity Interest Factor (FVIFA)
Table IV: Present Value of an Annuity Interest Factor (PVIFA)
Problem Solving Using Financial Calculators:
Future Value
Present Value
Future Value of an Ordinary Annuity
Present Value of an Ordinary Annuity

TABLE I

Future Value Interest Factor (FVIF) ($1 at i % per period for n periods); FVIF = $(1 + i)^n$; $FV_n = PV_0\ (FVIF_{i,n})$

Period, n	1%	2%	3%	4%	5%	6%	7%	8%	9%	10%	11%	12%	13%
0	1.000	1.000	1.000	1.000	1.000	1.000	1.000	1.000	1.000	1.000	1.000	1.000	1.000
1	1.010	1.020	1.030	1.040	1.050	1.060	1.070	1.080	1.090	1.100	1.110	1.120	1.130
2	1.020	1.040	1.061	1.082	1.102	1.124	1.145	1.166	1.188	1.210	1.232	1.254	1.277
3	1.030	1.061	1.093	1.125	1.158	1.191	1.225	1.260	1.295	1.331	1.368	1.405	1.443
4	1.041	1.082	1.126	1.170	1.216	1.262	1.311	1.360	1.412	1.464	1.518	1.574	1.630
5	1.051	1.104	1.159	1.217	1.276	1.338	1.403	1.469	1.539	1.611	1.685	1.762	1.842
6	1.062	1.126	1.194	1.265	1.340	1.419	1.501	1.587	1.677	1.772	1.870	1.974	2.082
7	1.072	1.149	1.230	1.316	1.407	1.504	1.606	1.714	1.828	1.949	2.076	2.211	2.353
8	1.083	1.172	1.267	1.369	1.477	1.594	1.718	1.851	1.993	2.144	2.305	2.476	2.658
9	1.094	1.195	1.305	1.423	1.551	1.689	1.838	1.999	2.172	2.358	2.558	2.773	3.004
10	1.105	1.219	1.344	1.480	1.629	1.791	1.967	2.159	2.367	2.594	2.839	3.106	3.395
11	1.116	1.243	1.384	1.539	1.710	1.898	2.105	2.332	2.580	2.853	3.152	3.479	3.836
12	1.127	1.268	1.426	1.601	1.796	2.012	2.252	2.518	2.813	3.138	3.498	3.896	4.335
13	1.138	1.294	1.469	1.665	1.886	2.133	2.410	2.720	3.066	3.452	3.883	4.363	4.898
14	1.149	1.319	1.513	1.732	1.980	2.261	2.579	2.937	3.342	3.797	4.310	4.887	5.535
15	1.161	1.346	1.558	1.801	2.079	2.397	2.759	3.172	3.642	4.177	4.785	5.474	6.254
16	1.173	1.373	1.605	1.873	2.183	2.540	2.952	3.426	3.970	4.595	5.311	6.130	7.067
17	1.184	1.400	1.653	1.948	2.292	2.693	3.159	3.700	4.328	5.054	5.895	6.866	7.986
18	1.196	1.428	1.702	2.026	2.407	2.854	3.380	3.996	4.717	5.560	6.544	7.690	9.024
19	1.208	1.457	1.754	2.107	2.527	3.026	3.617	4.316	5.142	6.116	7.263	8.613	10.197
20	1.220	1.486	1.806	2.191	2.653	3.207	3.870	4.661	5.604	6.728	8.062	9.646	11.523
24	1.270	1.608	2.033	2.563	3.225	4.049	5.072	6.341	7.911	9.850	12.239	15.179	18.790
25	1.282	1.641	2.094	2.666	3.386	4.292	5.427	6.848	8.623	10.835	13.585	17.000	21.231
30	1.348	1.811	2.427	3.243	4.322	5.743	7.612	10.063	13.268	17.449	22.892	29.960	39.116
40	1.489	2.208	3.262	4.801	7.040	10.286	14.974	21.725	31.409	45.259	65.001	93.051	132.782
50	1.645	2.692	4.384	7.107	11.467	18.420	29.457	46.902	74.358	117.391	184.565	289.002	450.736
60	1.817	3.281	5.892	10.520	18.679	32.988	57.946	101.257	176.031	304.482	524.057	897.597	1,530.05

Period, n	14%	15%	16%	17%	18%	19%	20%	24%	28%	32%	36%	40%
0	1.000	1.000	1.000	1.000	1.000	1.000	1.000	1.000	1.000	1.000	1.000	1.000
1	1.140	1.150	1.160	1.170	1.180	1.190	1.200	1.240	1.280	1.320	1.360	1.400
2	1.300	1.322	1.346	1.369	1.392	1.416	1.440	1.538	1.638	1.742	1.850	1.960
3	1.482	1.521	1.561	1.602	1.643	1.685	1.728	1.907	2.067	2.300	2.515	2.744
4	1.689	1.749	1.811	1.874	1.939	2.005	2.074	2.364	2.684	3.036	3.421	3.842
5	1.925	2.011	2.100	2.192	2.288	2.386	2.488	2.932	3.436	4.007	4.653	5.378
6	2.195	2.313	2.436	2.565	2.700	2.840	2.986	3.635	4.398	5.290	6.328	7.530
7	2.502	2.660	2.826	3.001	3.185	3.379	3.583	4.508	5.629	6.983	8.605	10.541
8	2.853	3.059	3.278	3.511	3.759	4.021	4.300	5.590	7.206	9.217	11.703	14.758
9	3.252	3.518	3.803	4.108	4.435	4.785	5.160	6.931	9.223	12.166	15.917	20.661
10	3.707	4.046	4.411	4.807	5.234	5.695	6.192	8.594	11.806	16.060	21.647	28.925
11	4.226	4.652	5.117	5.624	6.176	6.777	7.430	10.657	15.112	21.199	29.439	40.496
12	4.818	5.350	5.926	6.580	7.288	8.064	8.916	13.215	19.343	27.983	40.037	56.694
13	5.492	6.153	6.886	7.699	8.599	9.596	10.699	16.386	24.759	36.937	54.451	79.372
14	6.261	7.076	7.988	9.007	10.147	11.420	12.839	20.319	31.961	48.757	74.053	111.120
15	7.138	8.137	9.266	10.539	11.974	13.590	15.407	25.196	40.565	64.359	100.712	155.568
16	8.137	9.358	10.748	12.330	14.129	16.172	18.488	31.243	51.923	84.954	136.969	217.795
17	9.276	10.761	12.468	14.426	16.672	19.244	22.186	38.741	66.461	112.139	186.278	304.914
18	10.575	12.375	14.463	16.879	19.673	22.901	26.623	48.039	85.071	148.023	253.338	426.879
19	12.056	14.232	16.777	19.748	23.214	27.252	31.948	59.568	108.890	195.391	344.540	597.630
20	13.743	16.367	19.461	23.106	27.393	32.429	38.338	73.864	139.380	257.916	468.574	836.683
24	23.212	28.625	35.236	43.297	53.109	65.032	79.497	174.631	374.144	783.023	1,603.00	3,214.20
25	26.462	32.919	40.874	50.658	62.669	77.388	95.396	216.542	478.905	1,033.59	2,180.08	4,499.88
30	50.950	66.212	85.850	111.065	143.371	184.675	237.376	634.820	1,645.50	4,142.07	10,143.0	24,201.4
40	188.884	267.864	378.721	533.869	750.378	1,051.67	1,469.77	5,455.91	19,426.7	66,520.8	219,562	700,038
50	700.233	1,083.66	1,670.70	2,566.22	3,927.36	5,988.91	9,100.44	46,890.4	229,350	*	*	*
60	2,595.92	4,384.00	7,370.20	12,335.4	20,555.1	34,105.0	56,347.5	402,996	*	*	*	*

*These interest factors exceed 1,000,000

TABLE II

Present Value Interest Factor (PVIF) ($1 at *i* % per period for *n* periods);

$$\text{PVIF} = \frac{1}{(1+i)^n};\ \text{PV}_0 = \text{FV}_n(\text{PVIF}_{i,n})$$

Period, *n*	1%	2%	3%	4%	5%	6%	7%	8%	9%	10%	11%	12%	13%
0	1.000	1.000	1.000	1.000	1.000	1.000	1.000	1.000	1.000	1.000	1.000	1.000	1.000
1	0.990	0.980	0.971	0.962	0.952	0.943	0.935	0.926	0.917	0.909	0.901	0.893	0.885
2	0.980	0.961	0.943	0.925	0.907	0.890	0.873	0.857	0.842	0.826	0.812	0.797	0.783
3	0.971	0.942	0.915	0.889	0.864	0.840	0.816	0.794	0.772	0.751	0.731	0.712	0.693
4	0.961	0.924	0.889	0.855	0.823	0.792	0.763	0.735	0.708	0.683	0.659	0.636	0.613
5	0.951	0.906	0.863	0.822	0.784	0.747	0.713	0.681	0.650	0.621	0.593	0.567	0.543
6	0.942	0.888	0.838	0.790	0.746	0.705	0.666	0.630	0.596	0.564	0.535	0.507	0.480
7	0.933	0.871	0.813	0.760	0.711	0.665	0.623	0.583	0.547	0.513	0.482	0.452	0.425
8	0.923	0.853	0.789	0.731	0.677	0.627	0.582	0.540	0.502	0.467	0.434	0.404	0.376
9	0.914	0.837	0.766	0.703	0.645	0.592	0.544	0.500	0.460	0.424	0.391	0.361	0.333
10	0.905	0.820	0.744	0.676	0.614	0.558	0.508	0.463	0.422	0.386	0.352	0.322	0.295
11	0.896	0.804	0.722	0.650	0.585	0.527	0.475	0.429	0.388	0.350	0.317	0.287	0.261
12	0.887	0.788	0.701	0.625	0.557	0.497	0.444	0.397	0.356	0.319	0.286	0.257	0.231
13	0.879	0.773	0.681	0.601	0.530	0.469	0.415	0.368	0.326	0.290	0.258	0.229	0.204
14	0.870	0.758	0.661	0.577	0.505	0.442	0.388	0.340	0.299	0.263	0.232	0.205	0.181
15	0.861	0.743	0.642	0.555	0.481	0.417	0.362	0.315	0.275	0.239	0.209	0.183	0.160
16	0.853	0.728	0.623	0.534	0.458	0.394	0.339	0.292	0.252	0.218	0.188	0.163	0.141
17	0.844	0.714	0.605	0.513	0.436	0.371	0.317	0.270	0.231	0.198	0.170	0.146	0.125
18	0.836	0.700	0.587	0.494	0.416	0.350	0.296	0.250	0.212	0.180	0.153	0.130	0.111
19	0.828	0.686	0.570	0.475	0.396	0.331	0.276	0.232	0.194	0.164	0.138	0.116	0.098
20	0.820	0.673	0.554	0.456	0.377	0.312	0.258	0.215	0.178	0.149	0.124	0.104	0.087
24	0.788	0.622	0.492	0.390	0.310	0.247	0.197	0.158	0.126	0.102	0.082	0.066	0.053
25	0.780	0.610	0.478	0.375	0.295	0.233	0.184	0.146	0.116	0.092	0.074	0.059	0.047
30	0.742	0.552	0.412	0.308	0.231	0.174	0.131	0.099	0.075	0.057	0.044	0.033	0.026
40	0.672	0.453	0.307	0.208	0.142	0.097	0.067	0.046	0.032	0.022	0.015	0.011	0.008
50	0.608	0.372	0.228	0.141	0.087	0.054	0.034	0.021	0.013	0.009	0.005	0.003	0.002
60	0.550	0.305	0.170	0.095	0.054	0.030	0.017	0.010	0.006	0.003	0.002	0.001	0.001

Period, *n*	14%	15%	16%	17%	18%	19%	20%	24%	28%	32%	36%	40%
0	1.000	1.000	1.000	1.000	1.000	1.000	1.000	1.000	1.000	1.000	1.000	1.000
1	0.877	0.870	0.862	0.855	0.847	0.840	0.833	0.806	0.781	0.758	0.735	0.714
2	0.769	0.756	0.743	0.731	0.718	0.706	0.694	0.650	0.610	0.574	0.541	0.510
3	0.675	0.658	0.641	0.624	0.609	0.593	0.579	0.524	0.477	0.435	0.398	0.364
4	0.592	0.572	0.552	0.534	0.516	0.499	0.482	0.423	0.373	0.329	0.292	0.260
5	0.519	0.497	0.476	0.456	0.437	0.419	0.402	0.341	0.291	0.250	0.215	0.186
6	0.456	0.432	0.410	0.390	0.370	0.352	0.335	0.275	0.227	0.189	0.158	0.133
7	0.400	0.376	0.354	0.333	0.314	0.296	0.279	0.222	0.178	0.143	0.116	0.095
8	0.351	0.327	0.305	0.285	0.266	0.249	0.233	0.179	0.139	0.108	0.085	0.068
9	0.308	0.284	0.263	0.243	0.225	0.209	0.194	0.144	0.108	0.082	0.063	0.048
10	0.270	0.247	0.227	0.208	0.191	0.176	0.162	0.116	0.085	0.062	0.046	0.035
11	0.237	0.215	0.195	0.178	0.162	0.148	0.135	0.094	0.066	0.047	0.034	0.025
12	0.208	0.187	0.168	0.152	0.137	0.124	0.112	0.076	0.052	0.036	0.025	0.018
13	0.182	0.163	0.145	0.130	0.116	0.104	0.093	0.061	0.040	0.027	0.018	0.013
14	0.160	0.141	0.125	0.111	0.099	0.088	0.078	0.049	0.032	0.021	0.014	0.009
15	0.140	0.123	0.108	0.095	0.084	0.074	0.065	0.040	0.025	0.016	0.010	0.006
16	0.123	0.107	0.093	0.081	0.071	0.062	0.054	0.032	0.019	0.012	0.007	0.005
17	0.108	0.093	0.080	0.069	0.060	0.052	0.045	0.026	0.015	0.009	0.005	0.003
18	0.095	0.081	0.069	0.059	0.051	0.044	0.038	0.021	0.012	0.007	0.004	0.002
19	0.083	0.070	0.060	0.051	0.043	0.037	0.031	0.017	0.009	0.005	0.003	0.002
20	0.073	0.061	0.051	0.043	0.037	0.031	0.026	0.014	0.007	0.004	0.002	0.001
24	0.043	0.035	0.028	0.023	0.019	0.015	0.013	0.006	0.003	0.001	0.001	0.000
25	0.038	0.030	0.024	0.020	0.016	0.013	0.010	0.005	0.002	0.001	0.000	0.000
30	0.020	0.015	0.012	0.009	0.007	0.005	0.004	0.002	0.001	0.000	0.000	0.000
40	0.005	0.004	0.003	0.002	0.001	0.001	0.001	0.000	0.000	0.000	0.000	0.000
50	0.001	0.001	0.001	0.000	0.000	0.000	0.000	0.000	0.000	0.000	0.000	0.000
60	0.000	0.000	0.000	0.000	0.000	0.000	0.000	0.000	0.000	0.000	0.000	0.000

TABLE III

Future Value of an Annuity Interest Factor (FVIFA) ($1 per period at i% per period for n periods);

$$\text{FVIFA} = \frac{(1+i)^n - 1}{i}; \text{FVAN}_n = PMT(\text{FVIFA}_{i,n})$$

Period, n	1%	2%	3%	4%	5%	6%	7%	8%	9%	10%	11%	12%	13%
1	1.000	1.000	1.000	1.000	1.000	1.000	1.000	1.000	1.000	1.000	1.000	1.000	1.000
2	2.010	2.020	2.030	2.040	2.050	2.060	2.070	2.080	2.090	2.100	2.110	2.120	2.130
3	3.030	3.060	3.091	3.122	3.152	3.184	3.215	3.246	3.278	3.310	3.342	3.374	3.407
4	4.060	4.122	4.184	4.246	4.310	4.375	4.440	4.506	4.573	4.641	4.710	4.779	4.850
5	5.101	5.204	5.309	5.416	5.526	5.637	5.751	5.867	5.985	6.105	6.228	6.353	6.480
6	6.152	6.308	6.468	6.633	6.802	6.975	7.153	7.336	7.523	7.716	7.913	8.115	8.323
7	7.214	7.434	7.662	7.898	8.142	8.394	8.654	8.923	9.200	9.487	9.783	10.089	10.405
8	8.286	8.583	8.892	9.214	9.549	9.897	10.260	10.637	11.028	11.436	11.859	12.300	12.757
9	9.369	9.755	10.159	10.583	11.027	11.491	11.978	12.488	13.021	13.579	14.164	14.776	15.416
10	10.462	10.950	11.464	12.006	12.578	13.181	13.816	14.487	15.193	15.937	16.722	17.549	18.420
11	11.567	12.169	12.808	13.486	14.207	14.972	15.784	16.645	17.560	18.531	19.561	20.655	21.814
12	12.683	13.412	14.192	15.026	15.917	16.870	17.888	18.977	20.141	21.384	22.713	24.133	25.650
13	13.809	14.680	15.618	16.627	17.713	18.882	20.141	21.495	22.953	24.523	26.212	28.029	29.985
14	14.947	15.974	17.086	18.292	19.599	21.051	22.550	24.215	26.019	27.975	30.095	32.393	34.883
15	16.097	17.293	18.599	20.024	21.579	23.276	25.129	27.152	29.361	31.772	34.405	37.280	40.417
16	17.258	18.639	20.157	21.825	23.657	25.673	27.888	30.324	33.003	35.950	39.190	42.753	46.672
17	18.430	20.012	21.762	23.698	25.840	28.213	30.840	33.750	36.974	40.545	44.501	48.884	53.739
18	19.615	21.412	23.414	25.645	28.132	30.906	33.999	37.450	41.301	45.599	50.396	55.750	61.725
19	20.811	22.841	25.117	27.671	30.539	33.760	37.379	41.446	46.018	51.159	56.939	63.440	70.749
20	22.019	24.297	26.870	29.778	33.066	36.786	40.995	45.762	51.160	57.275	64.203	72.052	80.947
24	26.973	30.422	34.426	39.083	44.502	50.816	58.117	66.765	76.790	88.497	102.174	118.155	136.831
25	28.243	32.030	36.459	41.646	47.727	54.865	63.249	73.106	84.701	98.347	114.413	133.334	155.620
30	34.785	40.568	47.575	56.085	66.439	79.058	94.461	113.283	136.308	164.494	199.021	241.333	293.199
40	48.886	60.402	75.401	95.026	120.080	154.762	199.635	259.057	337.882	442.593	581.826	767.091	1,013.70
50	64.463	84.572	112.797	152.667	209.348	290.336	406.529	573.770	815.084	1,163.91	1,668.77	2,400.02	3,459.51
60	81.670	114.052	163.053	237.991	353.584	533.128	813.520	1,253.21	1,944.79	3,034.82	4,755.07	7,471.64	11,761.9

Period, n	14%	15%	16%	17%	18%	19%	20%	24%	28%	32%	36%	40%
1	1.000	1.000	1.000	1.000	1.000	1.000	1.000	1.000	1.000	1.000	1.000	1.000
2	2.140	2.150	2.160	2.170	2.180	2.190	2.200	2.240	2.280	2.320	2.360	2.400
3	3.440	3.473	3.506	3.539	3.572	3.606	3.640	3.778	3.918	4.062	4.210	4.360
4	4.921	4.993	5.066	5.141	5.215	5.291	5.368	5.684	6.016	6.362	6.725	7.104
5	6.610	6.742	6.877	7.014	7.154	7.297	7.442	8.048	8.700	9.398	10.146	10.846
6	8.536	8.754	8.977	9.207	9.442	9.683	9.930	10.980	12.136	13.406	14.799	16.324
7	10.730	11.067	11.414	11.772	12.142	12.523	12.916	14.615	16.534	18.696	21.126	23.853
8	13.233	13.727	14.240	14.773	15.327	15.902	16.499	19.123	22.163	25.678	29.732	34.395
9	16.085	16.786	17.518	18.285	19.086	19.923	20.799	24.712	29.369	34.895	41.435	49.153
10	19.337	20.304	21.321	22.393	23.521	24.709	25.959	31.643	38.592	47.062	57.352	69.814
11	23.044	24.349	25.733	27.200	28.755	30.404	32.150	40.238	50.399	63.122	78.998	98.739
12	27.271	29.002	30.850	32.824	34.931	37.180	39.580	50.985	65.510	84.320	108.437	139.235
13	32.089	34.352	36.786	39.404	42.219	45.244	48.497	64.110	84.853	112.303	148.475	195.929
14	37.581	40.505	43.672	47.103	50.818	54.841	59.196	80.496	109.612	149.240	202.926	275.300
15	43.842	47.580	51.660	56.110	60.965	66.261	72.035	100.815	141.303	197.997	276.979	386.420
16	50.980	55.717	60.925	66.649	72.939	79.850	87.442	126.011	181.868	262.356	377.692	541.988
17	59.118	65.075	71.673	78.979	87.068	96.022	105.931	157.253	233.791	347.310	514.661	759.784
18	68.394	75.836	84.141	93.406	103.740	115.266	128.117	195.994	300.252	459.449	700.939	1,064.70
19	78.969	88.212	98.603	110.285	123.414	138.166	154.740	244.033	385.323	607.472	954.277	1,491.58
20	91.025	102.444	115.380	130.033	146.628	165.418	186.688	303.601	494.213	802.863	1,298.82	2,089.21
24	158.659	184.168	213.978	248.808	289.494	337.010	392.484	723.461	1,322.66	2,443.82	4,450.00	8,033.00
25	181.871	212.793	249.214	292.105	342.603	402.042	471.981	898.092	1,706.80	3,226.84	6,053.00	11,247.2
30	356.787	434.745	530.321	647.439	790.948	966.712	1,181.88	2,640.92	5,873.23	12,940.9	28,172.3	60,501.1
40	1,342.03	1,779.09	2,360.76	3,134.52	4,163.21	5,529.83	7,343.86	22,728.8	69,377.5	207,874	609,890	*
50	4,994.52	7,217.72	10,435.6	15,089.5	21,813.1	31,515.3	45,497.2	195,373	819,103	*	*	*
60	18,535.1	29,220.0	46,057.5	72,555.0	114,190	179,495	281,733	*	*	*	*	*

*These interest factors exceed 1,000,000

● TABLE IV

Present Value of an Annuity Interest Factor (PVIFA) ($1 per period at *i*% per period for *n* periods);

$$\text{PVIFA} = \frac{1 - \frac{1}{(1+i)^n}}{i}; \quad \text{PVAN}_0 = PMT(\text{PVIFA}_{i,n})$$

Period, *n*	1%	2%	3%	4%	5%	6%	7%	8%	9%	10%	11%	12%	13%
1	0.990	0.980	0.971	0.962	0.952	0.943	0.935	0.926	0.917	0.909	0.901	0.893	0.885
2	1.970	1.942	1.913	1.886	1.859	1.833	1.808	1.783	1.759	1.736	1.713	1.690	1.668
3	2.941	2.884	2.829	2.775	2.723	2.673	2.624	2.577	2.531	2.487	2.444	2.402	2.361
4	3.902	3.808	3.717	3.630	3.546	3.465	3.387	3.312	3.240	3.170	3.102	3.037	2.974
5	4.853	4.713	4.580	4.452	4.329	4.212	4.100	3.993	3.890	3.791	3.696	3.605	3.517
6	5.795	5.601	5.417	5.242	5.076	4.917	4.766	4.623	4.486	4.355	4.231	4.111	3.998
7	6.728	6.472	6.230	6.002	5.786	5.582	5.389	5.206	5.033	4.868	4.712	4.564	4.423
8	7.652	7.325	7.020	6.733	6.463	6.210	5.971	5.747	5.535	5.335	5.146	4.968	4.799
9	8.566	8.162	7.786	7.435	7.108	6.802	6.515	6.247	5.995	5.759	5.537	5.328	5.132
10	9.471	8.983	8.530	8.111	7.722	7.360	7.024	6.710	6.418	6.145	5.889	5.650	5.426
11	10.368	9.787	9.253	8.760	8.306	7.887	7.499	7.139	6.805	6.495	6.207	5.938	5.687
12	11.255	10.575	9.954	9.385	8.863	8.384	7.943	7.536	7.161	6.814	6.492	6.194	5.918
13	12.134	11.348	10.635	9.986	9.394	8.853	8.358	7.904	7.487	7.103	6.750	6.424	6.122
14	13.004	12.106	11.296	10.563	9.899	9.295	8.745	8.244	7.786	7.367	6.982	6.628	6.302
15	13.865	12.849	11.938	11.118	10.380	9.712	9.108	8.559	8.061	7.606	7.191	6.811	6.462
16	14.718	13.578	12.561	11.652	10.838	10.106	9.447	8.851	8.312	7.824	7.379	6.974	6.604
17	15.562	14.292	13.166	12.166	11.274	10.477	9.763	9.122	8.544	8.022	7.549	7.120	6.729
18	16.398	14.992	13.754	12.659	11.690	10.828	10.059	9.372	8.756	8.201	7.702	7.250	6.840
19	17.226	15.678	14.324	13.134	12.085	11.158	10.336	9.604	8.950	8.365	7.839	7.366	6.938
20	18.046	16.351	14.877	13.590	12.462	11.470	10.594	9.818	9.128	8.514	7.963	7.469	7.025
24	21.243	18.914	16.936	15.247	13.799	12.550	11.469	10.529	9.707	8.985	8.348	7.784	7.283
25	22.023	19.523	17.413	15.622	14.094	12.783	11.654	10.675	9.823	9.077	8.422	7.843	7.330
30	25.808	22.397	19.600	17.292	15.373	13.765	12.409	11.258	10.274	9.427	8.694	8.055	7.496
40	32.835	27.355	23.115	19.793	17.159	15.046	13.332	11.925	10.757	9.779	8.951	8.244	7.634
50	39.196	31.424	25.730	21.482	18.256	15.762	13.801	12.233	10.962	9.915	9.042	8.304	7.675
60	44.955	34.761	27.676	22.623	18.929	16.161	14.039	12.377	11.048	9.967	9.074	8.324	7.687

Period, *n*	14%	15%	16%	17%	18%	19%	20%	24%	28%	32%	36%	40%
1	0.877	0.870	0.862	0.855	0.847	0.840	0.833	0.806	0.781	0.758	0.735	0.714
2	1.647	1.626	1.605	1.585	1.566	1.547	1.528	1.457	1.392	1.332	1.276	1.224
3	2.322	2.283	2.246	2.210	2.174	2.140	2.106	1.981	1.868	1.766	1.674	1.589
4	2.914	2.855	2.798	2.743	2.690	2.639	2.589	2.404	2.241	2.096	1.966	1.849
5	3.433	3.352	3.274	3.199	3.127	3.058	2.991	2.745	2.532	2.345	2.181	2.035
6	3.889	3.784	3.685	3.589	3.498	3.410	3.326	3.020	2.759	2.534	2.399	2.168
7	4.288	4.160	4.039	3.922	3.812	3.706	3.605	3.242	2.937	2.678	2.455	2.263
8	4.639	4.487	4.344	4.207	4.078	3.954	3.837	3.421	3.076	2.786	2.540	2.331
9	4.946	4.772	4.607	4.451	4.303	4.163	4.031	3.566	3.184	2.868	2.603	2.379
10	5.216	5.019	4.833	4.659	4.494	4.339	4.193	3.682	3.269	2.930	2.650	2.414
11	5.453	5.234	5.029	4.836	4.656	4.486	4.327	3.776	3.335	2.978	2.683	2.438
12	5.660	5.421	5.197	4.988	4.793	4.611	4.439	3.851	3.387	3.013	2.708	2.456
13	5.842	5.583	5.342	5.118	4.910	4.715	4.533	3.912	3.427	3.040	2.727	2.469
14	6.002	5.724	5.468	5.229	5.008	4.802	4.611	3.962	3.459	3.061	2.740	2.478
15	6.142	5.847	5.575	5.324	5.092	4.876	4.675	4.001	3.483	3.076	2.750	2.484
16	6.265	5.954	5.669	5.405	5.162	4.938	4.730	4.033	3.503	3.088	2.758	2.489
17	6.373	6.047	5.749	5.475	5.222	4.990	4.775	4.059	3.518	3.097	2.763	2.492
18	6.467	6.128	5.818	5.534	5.273	5.033	4.812	4.080	3.529	3.104	2.767	2.494
19	6.550	6.198	5.877	5.584	5.316	5.070	4.844	4.097	3.539	3.109	2.770	2.496
20	6.623	6.259	5.929	5.628	5.353	5.101	4.870	4.110	3.546	3.113	2.772	2.497
24	6.835	6.434	6.073	5.746	5.451	5.182	4.937	4.143	3.562	3.121	2.776	2.499
25	6.873	6.464	6.097	5.766	5.467	5.195	4.948	4.147	3.564	3.122	2.776	2.499
30	7.003	6.566	6.177	5.829	5.517	5.235	4.979	4.160	3.569	3.124	2.778	2.500
40	7.105	6.642	6.233	5.871	5.548	5.258	4.997	4.166	3.571	3.125	2.778	2.500
50	7.133	6.661	6.246	5.880	5.554	5.262	4.999	4.167	3.571	3.125	2.778	2.500
60	7.140	6.665	6.249	5.882	5.555	5.263	5.000	4.167	3.571	3.125	2.778	2.500

TABLE V

Normal Distribution (Area of the Normal Distribution That Is to the Right of +*z* or the Left of −*z* Standard Deviations from the Mean)

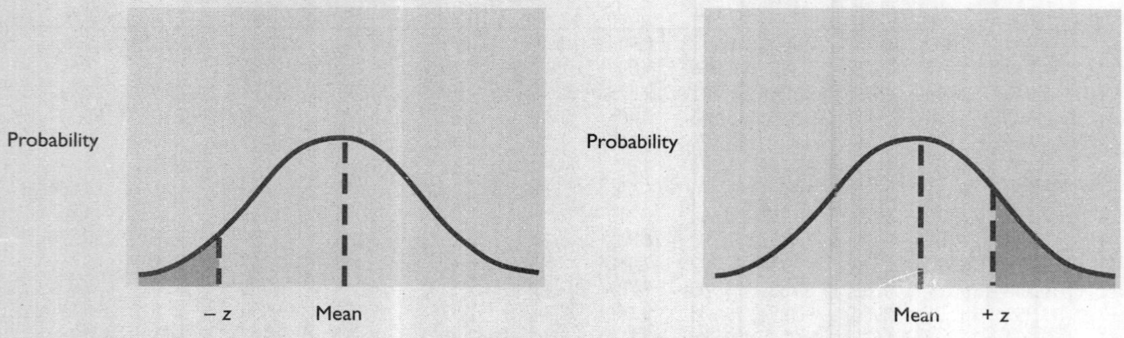

z*	.00	.01	.02	.03	.04	.05	.06	.07	.08	.09
0.0	.5000	.4960	.4920	.4880	.4840	.4801	.4761	.4721	.4681	.4641
.1	.4602	.4562	.4522	.4483	.4443	.4404	.4364	.4325	.4286	.4247
.2	.4207	.4168	.4129	.4090	.4052	.4013	.3974	.3936	.3897	.3859
.3	.3821	.3783	.3745	.3707	.3669	.3632	.3594	.3557	.3520	.3483
.4	.3446	.3409	.3372	.3336	.3300	.3264	.3228	.3192	.3156	.3121
.5	.3085	.3050	.3015	.2981	.2946	.2912	.2877	.2843	.2810	.2776
.6	.2743	.2709	.2676	.2643	.2611	.2578	.2546	.2514	.2483	.2451
.7	.2420	.2389	.2358	.2327	.2296	.2266	.2236	.2206	.2177	.2148
.8	.2119	.2090	.2061	.2033	.2005	.1977	.1949	.1922	.1894	.1867
.9	.1841	.1814	.1788	.1762	.1736	.1711	.1685	.1660	.1635	.1611
1.0	.1587	.1562	.1539	.1515	.1492	.1469	.1446	.1423	.1401	.1379
1.1	.1357	.1335	.1314	.1292	.1271	.1251	.1230	.1210	.1190	.1170
1.2	.1151	.1131	.1112	.1093	.1075	.1056	.1038	.1020	.1003	.0985
1.3	.0968	.0951	.0934	.0918	.0901	.0885	.0869	.0853	.0838	.0823
1.4	.0808	.0793	.0778	.0764	.0749	.0735	.0721	.0708	.0694	.0681
1.5	.0668	.0655	.0643	.0630	.0618	.0606	.0594	.0582	.0571	.0559
1.6	.0548	.0537	.0526	.0516	.0505	.0495	.0485	.0475	.0465	.0455
1.7	.0446	.0436	.0427	.0418	.0409	.0401	.0392	.0384	.0375	.0367
1.8	.0359	.0351	.0344	.0336	.0329	.0322	.0314	.0307	.0301	.0294
1.9	.0287	.0281	.0274	.0268	.0262	.0256	.0250	.0244	.0239	.0233
2.0	.0228	.0222	.0217	.0212	.0207	.0202	.0197	.0192	.0188	.0183
2.1	.0179	.0174	.0170	.0166	.0162	.0158	.0154	.0150	.0146	.0143
2.2	.0139	.0136	.0132	.0129	.0125	.0122	.0119	.0116	.0113	.0110
2.3	.0107	.0104	.0102	.0099	.0096	.0094	.0091	.0089	.0087	.0084
2.4	.0082	.0080	.0078	.0075	.0073	.0071	.0069	.0068	.0066	.0064
2.5	.0062	.0060	.0059	.0057	.0055	.0054	.0052	.0051	.0049	.0048
2.6	.0047	.0045	.0044	.0043	.0041	.0040	.0039	.0038	.0037	.0036
2.7	.0035	.0034	.0033	.0032	.0031	.0030	.0029	.0028	.0027	.0026
2.8	.0026	.0025	.0024	.0023	.0023	.0022	.0021	.0021	.0020	.0019
2.9	.0019	.0018	.0018	.0017	.0016	.0016	.0015	.0015	.0014	.0014
3.0	.0013									
3.05	.0011									
3.10	.0010									
3.25	.0006									
3.50	.00023									
4.00	.00003									
5.00	.0000003									

*Absolute values of z

Glossary

A

ABC inventory classification A method of dividing inventory items into three groups—those with a relatively large dollar value but a small percentage of the total items, those with a small dollar value but a large percentage of the total items, and those items in between.

absolute priority rule A rule used in bankruptcy proceedings that states that the claims of creditors are satisfied before the claims of stockholders.

affirmative loan covenant A portion of a loan agreement that outlines actions a firm's management *agrees to take* as conditions for receiving the loan.

after-tax cash flow (ATCF) Earnings after tax plus noncash charges, such as depreciation and deferred taxes.

agency costs Costs incurred by owners of a firm when the firm is managed by others; includes monitoring costs, bonding costs, and any losses that cannot be eliminated economically by monitoring and bonding.

agency relationships Occur when one or more individuals (principals) hire another individual (agent) to perform a service on their behalf. Agency relationships often lead to agency problems and costs. Two of the most important agency relationships in finance are the relationship between stockholders (owners) and managers and the relationship between owners and creditors.

agent The party who acts on behalf of the principal and has a legal responsibility to act in the best interests of the principal in an agency relationship.

amortization schedule A schedule of periodic payments of interest and principal owed on a debt obligation.

annual financing cost (AFC) The simple, annual interest rate for a short-term credit source.

annual percentage rate (APR) The true annual interest rate paid on a loan. Also called the *effective rate* of a loan.

annuity The payment or receipt of a series of equal cash flows per period for a specified amount of time. In an *ordinary annuity*, payments are made at the end of each period; in an *annuity due*, payments are made at the beginning of each period.

annuity due A series of equal periodic payments or receipts that occur at the beginning of each period.

arbitrage The process of simultaneously buying and selling the same or equivalent securities in different markets to take advantage of temporary price differences.

asset management ratios Financial ratios that indicate how efficiently a firm is using its assets to generate sales.

assignment The process of informally liquidating a business. Assignment occurs outside the jurisdiction of the bankruptcy courts.

asymmetric information The assumption that managers of a company, as insiders, have access to information about expected future earnings and cash flows that is not available to outside investors.

auction rate preferred stock A form of preferred stock in which the dividend yield is adjusted every 49 days through an auction process and investors can exchange their stock for cash.

average collection period The average number of days between the date when a credit sale is made and the date when the customer's payment is received.

B

bad-debt loss ratio The proportion of the total receivables volume that is never collected by a business.

balance sheet A financial statement that lists a firm's assets, liabilities, and stockholders' equity at a point in time.

balloon loan A loan that requires a large final payment greater than each of the periodic (principal and interest) payments.

bankers' acceptance A short-term debt instrument issued by a firm as part of a commercial transaction. Payment is guaranteed by a commercial bank.

bankrupt A situation in which a firm is unable to pay its debts and its assets are turned over to the court for administration.

Bankruptcy Reform Act of 1978 A U.S. bankruptcy act that significantly changed certain aspects of the federal bankruptcy laws.

beta A measure of systematic risk. It indicates the volatility of a security's returns relative to the returns of a broad-based market portfolio of securities.

beta risk (project) The risk contribution of a project to the systematic risk of the firm.

bond A long-term debt instrument that promises to pay the lender a series of periodic interest payments in addition to returning the principal at maturity. Most corporate bonds are offered in $1,000 principal amounts (par value).

bond rating An evaluation of a bond's probability of default. This is performed by an outside rating agency, such as Standard & Poor's or Moody's.

bond refunding The redemption of a callable bond issue and replacement with a lower-interest cost issue.

book value The historic cost of a company's assets.

book value per share The book value per share of common stock is equal to the total book value of the common stockholders' equity, divided by the total number of shares of common stock outstanding.

breakeven analysis An analysis tool that considers the relationship between sales, fixed costs, variable operating costs, and operating income at various output levels.

bullet loan A loan that requires only the periodic payment of interest during the term of the loan, with a final single repayment of principal at maturity.

business risk The variability in a firm's operating earnings (EBIT).

C

call feature A provision that permits an issuer of bonds (and sometimes preferred stock) to retire the obligation prior to its maturity.

call option An option to *buy* an asset at a set price. Also referred to as a *call*.

call premium The difference between a bond's call price and its par value.

call price The price at which a bond may be retired, or called, prior to its maturity.

capital asset pricing model (CAPM) A theory that formally describes the nature of the risk-required rate of return relationship on investments in financial assets (securities) or physical assets.

capital budgeting The process of planning for purchases of assets whose cash flows are expected to continue beyond one year.

capital expenditure The amount of money spent to purchase a long-term asset, such as a piece of equipment. This cash outlay generally is expected to result in a flow of future cash benefits extending beyond one year in time. (Also called *capital investment*.)

capital gains Profits on the sale of a capital asset.

capital gains yield The expected percentage increase in the price of the stock.

capital losses Losses on the sale of a capital asset.

capital markets Financial markets in which long-term securities are bought and sold.

capital rationing The process of limiting the number of capital expenditure projects because of insufficient funds to finance all projects that otherwise meet the firm's criteria for acceptability or because of a lack of sufficient managerial resources to undertake all otherwise acceptable projects.

capital recovery problem An annuity amount necessary to recover a capital investment.

capital structure The amount of permanent short-term debt, long-term debt, preferred stock, and common equity used to finance a firm.

capitalization of cash flow valuation method A method of determining the present value of an asset that is expected to produce a stream of future cash flows. This involves discounting the stream of expected cash flows at an appropriate rate.

carrying costs All costs associated with holding items in inventory for a given period of time.

cash breakeven point The level of output (units) required to cover a firm's fixed cash operating outlays.

cash budget A projection of a company's cash receipts and disbursements over some future period of time.

cash conversion cycle The net time interval between the collection of cash receipts from product sales and the cash payments for the company's various resources. The cash conversion cycle is calculated by subtracting the payables deferral period from the operating cycle.

cash discount A discount offered for early payment of an invoice.

cash flow The actual amount of cash collected and paid out by a firm.

certainty equivalent The amount of cash someone would require with certainty in order to make him or her indifferent between that certain amount and an amount expected to be received with risk at the same point in time.

Chapter 7 of the Bankruptcy Reform Act The liquidation chapter of the Bankruptcy Reform Act. Under Chapter 7, a company's assets are sold off, and the proceeds are distributed to creditors.

Chapter 11 of the Bankruptcy Reform Act The reorganization chapter of the Bankruptcy Reform Act. Under Chapter 11, a company continues to operate while it attempts to work out a reorganization plan.

characteristic line A regression line relating the periodic returns for a specific security to the periodic returns on the market portfolio. The slope of this regression line is an estimate of the *beta* of the security—a measure of its systematic risk.

chattel mortgage A lien on personal property, such as machinery, as security for the repayment of a loan.

clientele effect The concept that investors will tend to be attracted to companies that have dividend policies consistent with the investors' objectives.

coefficient of variation The ratio of the standard deviation to the expected value. It provides a relative measure of risk.

commercial paper Short-term unsecured promissory notes issued by major corporations with good credit ratings.

common-size balance sheet A balance sheet in which a firm's assets and liabilities are expressed as a percentage of total assets, rather than as dollar amounts.

common-size income statement An income statement in which a firm's income and expense items are expressed as a percentage of net sales, rather than as dollar amounts.

common stock Shares in the ownership of a company. Common stock represents a residual form of ownership in that dividends are paid out only after more senior financial obligations are fulfilled, such as interest on debt.

comparable multiple methods A method that uses multiples paid for other merger candidates that are comparable to the company being valued.

comparative analysis An examination of a firm's performance based on one or more financial ratios, which are compared with the financial ratios of competitive firms or with an industry standard.

compensating balance A minimum (absolute or average) balance that a bank requires a customer to keep in its checking account. This balance, which the bank can invest in interest-earning assets, compensates the bank for the services rendered to the customer.

competitive bidding The process of selling a new security offering to the highest-bidding underwriting syndicate.

composition A situation in which a failing business is permitted to discharge its debt obligations by paying less than the full amounts owed to creditors.

compound interest Interest that is paid not only on the principal but also on any interest earned but not withdrawn during earlier periods.

concentration banking The use of decentralized collection centers and local banks to collect customer payments. This speeds up a firm's collections.

conditional sales contract A financing agreement in which the seller of a piece of equipment retains title until all payments have been made.

conglomerate merger A combination of two or more companies in which neither competes directly with the other and no buyer-seller relationship exists.

consolidation A combination in which all of the combining companies are dissolved and a new firm is formed.

contingent claim A security whose payoffs depend on the value of another security.

contingent project A project whose acceptance depends on the adoption of one or more other projects.

contribution margin per unit In *breakeven analysis*, the difference between the selling price per unit and the variable cost per unit.

conversion premium The amount by which the market value of a convertible security exceeds the higher of its conversion value or straight-bond (preferred) value.

conversion price The effective price an investor pays for common stock when the stock is obtained by converting a convertible security.

conversion ratio The number of common shares an investor obtains by converting a convertible security.

conversion (stock) value The value of a convertible security, based on the value of the underlying shares of common stock.

convertible debt A bond that may be exchanged for common stock at the holder's option.

convertible securities Fixed-income securities that may be exchanged for a firm's common stock at the holder's option. The two most common types of convertible securities are *convertible preferred stock* and *convertible debentures.*

corporation A business organization that is created as a "legal person" separate and distinct from the individual or individuals who own the firm's stock. The primary characteristics and advantages of incorporating include limited liability for the firm's owners, permanency, and flexibility with respect to making changes in ownership.

correlation A relative statistical measure of the degree to which two series of numbers, such as the returns from two assets, tend to move or vary together.

cost of capital The equilibrium rate of return demanded by investors in the securities issued by a firm.

coupon rate of interest The interest rate stated on a bond. The coupon rate of interest times the par, or principal, value of a bond determines the periodic dollar interest payment received by the bondholder.

covariance An absolute statistical measure of how closely two variables (such as securities' returns) move together. It measures the degree to which increases (decreases) in the level of one variable tend to be associated with increases (decreases) in the level of another variable over time.

covered interest arbitrage A risk-free transaction in which short-term funds are moved between two currencies to take advantage of interest rate differentials. Exchange rate risk is eliminated through the use of forward contracts.

credit default swap A type of credit insurance contract in which one party pays another party a fee (premium) to protect itself from the risk of default on a debt instrument.

credit period The length of time a credit customer has to pay the account in full.

cumulative (dividends) A typical feature of preferred stock that requires past-due preferred stock dividends to be paid before any common stock dividends can be paid.

cumulative voting A voting procedure by which stockholders may cast multiple votes for a single board of directors candidate. Cumulative voting makes it easier for stockholders with minority views to elect sympathetic board members.

current yield The annual interest payment divided by the current (market) price of a bond.

D

debenture A bond that is not secured by a mortgage on any specific asset but instead by the general credit and earning power of the issuing firm.

debt capacity The amount of debt contained in a firm's optimal capital structure.

declaration date The day on which the directors of a company declare a dividend.

default risk The risk that a borrower will fail to make interest payments, principal payments, or both on a loan.

degree of combined leverage (DCL) The percentage change in a firm's earnings per share (EPS) resulting from a 1 percent change in sales or output. This also is equal to the degree of operating leverage times the degree of financial leverage used by the firm.

degree of financial leverage (DFL) The percentage change in a firm's EPS resulting from a 1 percent change in EBIT.

degree of operating leverage (DOL) The percentage change in a firm's EBIT resulting from a 1 percent change in sales or output.

depository transfer check (DTC) An unsigned non-negotiable check used to transfer funds from a local collection bank to a concentration bank.

depreciation The systematic allocation of the cost of an asset over its expected economic life or some other period of time for financial reporting purposes, tax purposes, or both.

derivative A financial contract that derives its value from some other security or asset, such as stocks, bonds, currencies, commodities, or interest rates. The two broadest categories of derivatives are options and forward-type contracts.

deterministic model A financial planning model that projects single number estimates of a financial variable or variables without specifying their probability of occurrence.

direct lease A lease that is initiated when a firm acquires the use of an asset that it did not previously own.

direct (or private) placement The sale of an entire security offering to one or more institutional investors rather than the general public. This also is termed a *private placement.*

direct quote The home currency price of one unit of a foreign currency.

discount period The length of time a credit customer has to pay the account and still be eligible to take any cash discount offered.

discount rate The rate of interest used in the process of finding present values; also called the required rate of return.

discounted cash flow (DCF) method A method for valuing merger candidates similar to the calculation of the net present value in capital budgeting.

discounted loan A loan in which the bank deducts the interest in advance at the time the loan is made.

discriminant analysis A statistical technique designed to classify observations (firms) into two or more predetermined groups based on certain characteristics (such as financial ratios) of the observations.

diversification The act of investing in a set of financial (securities) or physical assets having different risk-return characteristics.

dividend reinvestment plans Options that allow shareholders to have their cash dividends automatically reinvested in additional shares of the company's stock.

dividend yield The annual dividend payment divided by the price of the stock.

divisional cost of capital A risk-adjusted discount rate for investments being evaluated by a firm's various divisions. It reflects both the differential required returns of equity investors, estimated from the security market line, and a division's differential debt capacity.

draft A financial instrument that is similar to a check except it is not payable on demand. Rather, a draft must be presented to the issuer for approval before a payment is made.

E

earnings The difference between revenues and costs.

EAT The acronym for *earnings after taxes.*

EBIT The acronym for *earnings before interest and taxes* (also called *operating earnings*).

EBIT-EPS indifference point That level of EBIT where the earnings per share of a firm are the same, regardless of which of two alternative capital structures is employed.

economic exposure The extent to which changes in *real* exchange rates lead to a change in the value of a firm's operating cash flows, and hence its value. Also known as *operating exposure.*

economic order quantity The quantity of an inventory item that should be ordered to minimize total inventory costs.

economic value added (EVA®) A measure of operating performance defined as the return on capital minus the cost of capital, times the amount of capital.

effective interest rate The actual rate of interest paid by the borrower or earned by the lender.

efficient capital market A financial market in which new information is quickly reflected in security prices in an unbiased manner.

efficient frontier The set of efficient portfolios.

efficient portfolio A portfolio that, for a given standard deviation, has the highest expected return, or, for a given expected return, has the lowest standard deviation.

EPS The acronym for *earnings per share.*

euro The European single currency that went into circulation in 2002.

Eurobond An international bond issued outside the country in whose currency the bonds are denominated.

Eurocurrency A currency that is deposited in a bank outside of the country of origin.

Eurodollars U.S. dollars deposited in banks outside the United States.

EVA® The acronym for *economic value added.* This measure of operating performance is equal to the difference between operating profits after tax and the cost of capital and indicates a firm's success in creating MVA.

exchange rate The rate at which a currency can be converted into another currency.

exchange ratio The number of shares an acquiring company must give, or *exchange,* for each share of an acquired company in a merger.

ex-dividend date The date on which the right to the most recently declared dividend no longer goes along with the sale of the stock. The ex-dividend date is two business days prior to the *record date.*

exercise price The price at which an option holder can purchase or sell a company's stock. This also is termed the *strike price.*

expected market return The return investors expect to earn on stocks with average risk, i.e., a beta of 1.0.

expected return The benefits (price appreciation and distributions) an individual anticipates receiving from an investment.

expected value A statistical measure of the mean or average value of the possible outcomes. Operationally, it is defined as the weighted average of the possible outcomes with the weights being the probability of occurrence.

ex-rights A stock sells ex-rights when stock purchasers no longer receive the *rights* along with the shares purchased.

extension A situation in which a failing business is permitted to lengthen the amount of time it has to meet its obligations with creditors.

F

factoring The sale of a firm's accounts receivable to a financial institution known as a *factor.*

field warehouse financing agreement A loan agreement in which the inventory being pledged as collateral is segregated from the company's other inventories and stored on its premises under the control of a field warehouse company.

FIFO The acronym for the *first-in, first-out* inventory valuation method. The method assumes that a firm uses the oldest items in the inventory first. Thus, they are *priced out* of the inventory based on the oldest inventory acquisition costs rather than the most recent.

financial analysis The utilization of a group of analytical techniques, including financial ratio analysis, to determine the strengths, weaknesses, and direction of a company's performance.

financial distress costs The costs incurred to avoid bankruptcy plus the direct and indirect costs incurred if a firm files for bankruptcy protection.

financial forecasting The projection and estimation of a firm's future financial statements.

financial lease A *noncancelable* agreement that obligates the lessee to make payments to the lessor for a predetermined period of time. These payments are usually sufficient to amortize the full cost of the asset plus provide the lessor with a reasonable rate of return on the investment in the asset.

financial leverage The extent to which a firm is financed by securities having fixed costs or charges, such as debt and preferred stock.

financial leverage management ratios Financial ratios that measure the degree to which a firm is financing its assets with fixed-charge sources of funds such as debt, preferred stock, or leases.

financial planning models Computerized representations of some aspect of a firm's financial planning process.

financial ratio A statistical yardstick that relates two numbers generally taken from a firm's income statement, balance sheet, or both at a specific point in time.

financial risk The additional variability of a company's earnings per share and the increased probability of insolvency that result from the use of fixed-cost sources of funds, such as debt and preferred stock. In general, the more financial leverage a firm uses, the greater is its financial risk.

financial slack Highly liquid assets (i.e., cash and marketable securities) plus unused debt capacity that allow a firm to take advantage of any attractive investment opportunities.

financial structure The amount of current liabilities, long-term debt, preferred stock, and common equity used to finance a firm.

Fisher effect A relationship indicating that nominal (and risk-free) interest rates are approximately equal to the sum of the real interest rate and the expected inflation rate.

fixed costs Costs that do not vary as the level of a firm's output changes.

float The difference between an account balance as shown on the bank's books and as shown on the firm's books. Float represents the net effect of the delays in the payment of checks the firm writes and the collection of checks the firm receives.

floating lien An inventory loan in which the lender receives a security interest or general claim on all of a company's inventory.

flotation costs The costs of issuing new securities. This includes both underwriting expenses and other issue expenses, such as printing and legal fees.

fluctuating current assets Current assets affected by the seasonal or cyclical nature of the company's sales.

foreign bond An international bond denominated in the currency of the country in which it is issued. The issuer, however, is from another country.

forward contract A contract calling for the delivery of a specified amount of some item at a future point in time at a price set at the present time. Compared to *futures contracts,* forward contracts are not liquid, can be customized with regard to the date or amount, and carry performance risk.

forward rate The rate of exchange between two currencies being bought and sold for delivery at a *future* date.

future value (or terminal value) The value at some future point in time of a present payment (or a series of payments) evaluated at the appropriate interest (growth) rate.

futures contract A contract calling for the delivery of a standardized quantity and quality of some item, such as a foreign currency, crude oil, or government securities, at a future point in time at a price set at the present time.

G

general partnership A business organization where each partner has unlimited liability for all obligations of the business.

generally accepted accounting principles (GAAP) A broad set of accounting rules followed in preparing financial statements.

going-concern value The value of a firm, assuming that the firm's organization and assets remain intact and are used to generate future income and cash flows.

goodwill An intangible asset equal to the premium over fair market value of the acquired assets that is paid for a company in a merger.

H

hedge A transaction in which a position is taken in another market, such as the forward or futures market, to offset the risk associated with a position in the current cash (spot) market.

holding company A corporation that controls the voting power of one or more other companies.

holding period return The change in price from holding an asset (security) plus distributions received from the asset divided by the initial price at which the asset was acquired.

horizontal merger A combination of two or more companies that compete directly with each other.

hurdle rate The minimum acceptable rate of return from an investment project. For projects of average risk, it usually is equal to the firm's cost of capital.

I

income bond A bond that pays interest only if the firm earns sufficient income.

income statement A financial statement that indicates how a firm performed during a period of time.

indenture The contract between the issuing firm and the lenders in a debt obligation.

independent project A project whose acceptance or rejection does not result directly in the elimination of other projects from consideration.

indirect quote The foreign currency price of one unit of the home currency.

informational content The concept that, for a company following a stable dividend policy, changes in dividend payments convey information (i.e., a signal) to investors concerning management's expectations about the future profitability of the company.

insolvency A situation in which either a firm's liabilities exceed its assets or the firm is unable to pay its creditors as required.

interest The return earned by or the amount paid to an individual who forgoes current consumption or alternative investments and "rents" money to a business, bank, the government, some other form of institution, or another individual.

interest rate parity The theory that the percentage differential between the spot and the forward rate for a currency quoted in terms of another currency is equal to the approximate difference in interest rates in the two countries over the same time horizon.

interest rate risk The variation in the market price (and hence in the realized rate of return or yield) of a security that arises from changes in interest rates.

interest rate swap The exchange of floating rate interest payments for fixed rate interest payments, or vice versa.

internal rate of return (IRR) The discount rate that equates the present value of net cash flows from a project with the present value of the net investment. It is the discount rate that gives the project a net present value equal to zero. The IRR is used to evaluate, rank, and select from among various investment projects.

international Fisher effect The theory that the difference in interest rates between two countries should be offset by equal but opposite changes in the future spot exchange rate.

inventory conversion period The length of time required to produce and sell the product.

inventory cycle The time between placement of successive orders of an item.

investment banker An employee of an investment bank who assists client companies with security offerings, mergers, private placements of securities, and long-range financial planning.

investment opportunity curve A graph or listing showing a firm's investment opportunities (projects) ranked from highest to lowest expected rate of return.

J

joint venture A business combination in which two unaffiliated companies contribute financial, physical, and/or personnel assets to a new company formed to engage in a specific economic activity.

junk bond A high-yield debt security issued by a company with a low credit rating.

just-in-time inventory management system An approach to inventory and production management in which required inventory items are supplied exactly as needed by production.

L

lead time The time between when an order is placed for an item and when the item actually is received in inventory.

lease A contract that allows an individual or a firm to make economic use of an asset for a stated period of time without obtaining an ownership interest in it.

leasing A means of obtaining economic use of an asset for a specific period of time without obtaining an ownership interest in the asset.

legally insolvent A situation in which the recorded value of a firm's assets is less than its liabilities.

lessee The user and renter of the property in a lease transaction.

lessor The property owner who collects rental payments from the lessee in a lease transaction.

leveraged buyout A transaction in which the buyer of a company borrows a large portion of the purchase price, using the purchased assets as partial collateral for the loans.

leveraged lease A type of financial lease in which the lessor borrows up to 80 percent of the cost of the leased asset on a nonrecourse basis from a group of lenders. The lessor receives the full tax benefits of ownership. This is also sometimes called a *third-party equity lease* or a tax lease.

LIFO The acronym for the *last-in, first-out* inventory valuation method. The method assumes that a firm uses the most recently acquired items in the inventory first. Thus, they are *priced out* of the inventory based on the most recent inventory acquisition costs rather than the oldest.

LIBOR The London Interbank Offered Rate is the rate of interest at which banks in the Eurocurrency market lend to each other.

limited partnership A business organization in which the liability of the partners is generally limited to their investment.

line of credit An agreement that permits a firm to borrow funds up to a predetermined limit at any time during the life of the agreement.

liquidation value The value of a firm, assuming that it sells all its assets and stops using them to generate future income and cash flows.

liquidity The ability of a firm to meet its cash obligations as they come due.

liquidity ratios Financial ratios that indicate a firm's ability to meet short-term financial obligations.

listed security exchanges Organized secondary security markets that operate at designated places of business. The New York Stock Exchange (NYSE) is an example of a listed security exchange.

loan amortization schedule A schedule of periodic payments of interest and principal owed on a debt obligation.

lockbox A post office box maintained by a bank to speed up the collection of payments from customers.

London Interbank Offered Rate (LIBOR) The interest rate at which banks in the Eurocurrency market lend to each other.

M

MACRS depreciation The Modified Accelerated Cost Recovery System of depreciation, established in 1986.

marginal cost of capital The weighted after-tax cost of the next dollar of capital the firm expects to raise to finance a new investment project.

marginal tax rate The tax rate on the next dollar of taxable income earned by an individual person or firm.

market portfolio The portfolio of securities consisting of all available securities weighted by their respective market values.

market value The price at which a stock trades in the financial marketplace.

market value added (MVA) The market value of debt, preferred equity, and common equity capitalization, less capital.

marketability risk The ability of an investor to buy and sell an asset (security) quickly and without a significant loss of value.

market-based ratios Financial ratios that measure the market's (investors') assessment of the risk and performance of a firm.

matching approach A financing plan in which the maturity structure of a firm's liabilities is made to correspond exactly to the life of its assets.

maturity The length of the life of a debt obligation.

merger A combination of two or more companies into one surviving company. Mergers also are called *acquisitions* or *consolidations.*

misdirected funds Funds that cross an international border unintentionally.

Modified Accelerated Cost Recovery System (MACRS) An accelerated depreciation method used by most firms when computing taxable income.

money markets Financial markets in which short-term securities are bought and sold.

mortgage bond A bond secured by a pledge of a specific asset or group of assets.

multilateral netting A process of international cash management designed to minimize the cost associated with misdirected funds.

multinational corporation A firm with direct investments in more than one country.

multiple internal rates of return Two or more internal rates of return from the same project. This situation sometimes arises when the IRR method is being used for project selection. It occurs only with nonnormal projects or with those whose cash flow patterns contain more than one sign change.

mutually exclusive project A project whose acceptance precludes the acceptance of one or more alternative projects.

MVA The acronym for *market value added.* The difference between the market value of a firm's debt and equity and the capital that has been invested in the firm.

N

negative loan covenant A portion of a loan agreement that outlines actions a firm's management *agrees not to take* during the term of the loan.

negotiated underwriting A process whereby a firm wishing to sell new securities to the public negotiates the terms of the underwriting with the investment banker or bankers.

net (operating) cash flow Cash inflow minus cash outflow. It is measured as the change in net operating earnings after taxes plus the change in depreciation minus the change in net working capital requirements associated with a particular investment project.

net investment The net cash outlay required at the beginning of an investment project.

net present value (NPV) The present value of the stream of net cash flows resulting from a project, discounted at the firm's cost of capital, minus the project's net investment. It is used to evaluate, rank, and select from among various investment projects; the contribution of an investment to shareholder wealth.

net working capital The difference between a firm's current assets and current liabilities. The term *net working capital* is used interchangeably with *working capital.*

nominal interest rate The periodic rate of interest that is stated in a loan agreement or security. Frequently, the *effective interest rate* is greater than the nominal rate because of such factors as the frequency of compounding and the deduction of interest in advance.

normal project A project whose cash flow stream requires an initial outlay of funds followed by a series of positive net cash inflows. This is sometimes called a *conventional project.*

O

operating cycle Includes the three primary activities of purchasing resources, producing the product, and distributing (selling) the product. The operating cycle is calculated by summing the inventory conversion period and the receivables conversion period.

operating lease A *cancelable* lease agreement that provides the lessee with the use of an asset on a period-by-period basis. This sometimes is called a *service* or *maintenance lease,* especially if the lessor provides maintenance services as part of the lease contract.

operating leverage The extent to which a firm uses assets having fixed costs.

opportunity costs The returns (cash flows) that can be earned on funds if they are invested in their next best alternative use.

optimal capital budget The level of capital spending at which a firm's investment opportunity curve just intersects its marginal cost of capital curve.

optimal capital structure The capital structure that minimizes a firm's weighted cost of capital and, therefore, maximizes the value of the firm.

optimization models Financial planning models that determine the values of financial decision variables that maximize (or minimize) some objective function such as profits (or costs).

option A contract (often in the form of a security) that gives its holder the right to buy or sell an asset at a set price during a specified time period.

ordering costs All costs associated with placing and receiving an order.

ordinary annuity A series of equal periodic payments or receipts that occur at the end of each period.

outlays The costs incurred to undertake an investment project.

Over-the-Counter (OTC) Securities Markets A network of security dealers connected by a communications system of telephones and computer terminals that provides price quotations on individual securities.

P

par value (bond) Represents the amount of principal borrowed (usually $1,000) and due at maturity.

par value (common stock) An arbitrary value assigned to common stock by the issuing firm.

par value (preferred stock) An arbitrary value assigned by the issuing firm.

partnership A business organization in which two or more persons form a business with the intention of making a profit. In a *general partnership*, each partner has unlimited liability for the debts of the firm. *Limited partnerships* allow one or more partners to have limited liability.

passive residual policy A theory of dividend policy that suggests that a company should retain its earnings as long as there are investment opportunities available promising a rate of return higher than the required rate of return.

payables deferral period The length of time a firm is able to deter payment on its resource purchases.

payback (PB) period The period of time required for the cumulative cash inflows from a project to equal the initial cash outlay.

pecking order theory A capital structure theory indicating that firms prefer internal financing (retained earnings) to external financing (new security issues) and that, if external financing is required, debt is preferred to new common stock.

percentage of sales forecasting method A method of estimating the additional financing that will be needed to support a given future sales level.

permanent current assets Current assets held to meet the company's long-term minimum needs.

perpetual bond A bond that has no maturity date.

perpetuity A financial instrument that pays an equal cash flow per period into the indefinite future (that is, infinity).

pledging accounts receivable A short-term borrowing arrangement with a financial institution in which a loan is secured by the borrower's accounts receivable.

pooling of interests method A method of accounting for mergers in which the acquired company's assets are recorded on the acquiring company's books at their cost when originally acquired. No goodwill account is created under the pooling method.

portfolio A collection of two or more financial (securities) or physical assets.

post-audit A capital budgeting procedure that consists of comparing *actual* cash flows from a project with *projected* cash flows that were estimated at the time the project was adopted.

preauthorized check (PAC) Similar to an ordinary check except that it does not require the signature of the person (or firm) on whose account it is being drawn. PACs are useful for firms that receive a large volume of payments of a fixed amount each period.

preemptive right A provision contained in some corporate charters that gives common stockholders the right to buy on a pro rata basis any new common shares sold by the firm.

preferred stock A type of equity with a claim on earnings and assets of a firm—in the form of a (normally) fixed periodic dividend payment—that takes precedence over the claims of common stockholders.

present value The value today of a future payment (or a series of future payments) evaluated at the appropriate discount rate.

primary financial markets Financial markets in which *new* securities from an issuing firm are bought and sold for the first time. Investment bankers are active in the primary markets.

prime rate The lowest rate normally charged by banks on loans made to their most creditworthy business customers.

principal An amount of money that has been borrowed or invested.

principal In an agency relationship, the party who employs someone else, the agent, to perform service on behalf of the principal.

private (or direct) placement The sale of an entire security offering to one or more institutional investors.

pro forma financial statements Financial statements that project the results of some *assumed* event, rather than an *actual* event.

probabilistic model A financial planning model that uses probability distributions as inputs and generates a probability distribution for financial variables as output.

profit The difference between revenues and costs.

profitability index (PI) The ratio of the present value of net cash flows over the life of a project to the net investment. It is used to evaluate, rank, and select from among various investment projects. Frequently it is used in conjunction with resource allocation decisions in capital rationing situations.

profitability ratios Financial ratios that measure the total effectiveness of a company's management in generating profits.

promissory note A formal short-term credit obligation that states the amount to be paid and the due date.

prospectus A document that contains information about a company's legal, operational, and financial position. It is prepared for the benefit of prospective investors in a new security issued by the firm.

proxy statements Reports or forms (also called 14A Filings) that publicly traded firms are required to file with the SEC prior to their annual meetings detailing, among other things, matters to be discussed and voted upon.

purchase method A method of accounting for mergers in which the total value paid or exchanged for the acquired firm's assets is recorded on the acquiring firm's books. Any difference between the acquired assets' fair market value and their purchase price is recorded as goodwill.

purchasing syndicate A *group* of investment bankers who agree to underwrite a new security issue in order to spread the risk of underwriting.

put option An option to *sell* an asset at a set price. Also referred to as a *put.*

R

rate of interest The percentage on the principal that the borrower pays the lender per time period as compensation for forgoing other investment or consumption opportunities.

real option Managerial opportunities to make decisions that will impact the expected cash flows of a project, their timing, or the future acceptability of the project.Real options include the option to abandon, the option to defer investment, flexibility options, and growth options.

receivables conversion period The length of time required to collect sales receipts. Receivables conversion period is another name for the average collection period.

record date The date on which a company makes a list from its stock transfer books of those shareholders who are eligible to receive the declared dividend.

reinvestment rate The rate of return at which cash flows from an investment project are assumed to be reinvested from year to year. The reinvestment rate may vary, depending on the investment opportunities available to the firm.

reinvestment rate risk Risk that occurs when a bond issue matures (or is called) and, because of a decline in interest rates, the owner has to reinvest the principal at a lower coupon rate.

relative purchasing power parity The theory that the spot exchange rate between two currencies should change by an amount approximately equal to the difference in expected inflation rates in the two countries.

reorder point The inventory level at which an order should be placed for replenishment of an item.

repurchase agreement An arrangement with a bank or securities dealer in which an investor acquires certain short-term securities subject to a commitment that the securities will be repurchased by the bank or securities dealer on a specified date.

required rate of return The rate used to value a stream of expected cash flows from an asset (also called the *discount rate*). The riskier the expected cash flows from the asset, the higher the required rate of return.

restrictive loan covenant A portion of a loan agreement that limits the scope of certain actions a firm may take during the term of the loan.

reverse stock split A stock split in which the number of outstanding shares is reduced.

revolving credit agreement A binding agreement that commits a bank to make loans to a company up to a predetermined credit limit. To obtain this type of commitment from a bank, a company usually pays a *commitment fee* based on the unused portion of the pledged funds.

right A short-term option issued by a firm that permits an existing stockholder to buy a specified number of shares of common stock at a specified price (the subscription price), which is below the current market price.

rights offering The sale of new shares of common stock by distributing stock purchase rights to a firm's existing shareholders. This also is termed a *privileged subscription.*

rights-on A stock sells rights-on when purchasers receive the rights along with the shares purchased.

risk The possibility that actual future returns will deviate from expected returns; the variability of returns.

risk-adjusted discount rate A discount rate that reflects the risk associated with a particular project. In capital budgeting, a higher risk-adjusted rate is used to discount cash flows for riskier projects, whereas a lower risk-adjusted rate is used to discount cash flows for less risky projects.

risk-free rate of return The return required by an investor in a security having no risk of default; equal to the sum of the real rate of return and an inflation risk premium.

risk premium The difference between the required rate of return on a risky investment and the rate of return on a risk-free asset, such as U.S. Treasury bills. Components include maturity risk, default risk, seniority risk, and marketability risk.

S

S corporation A small business that takes advantage of the corporate form of organization while having its income taxed directly to the stockholders at their individual personal income tax rates.

sale and leaseback A lease that is initiated when a firm sells an asset it owns to another firm and simultaneously leases the asset back for its own use.

scenario analysis A procedure used to evaluate the change in some objective, such as net present value, to simultaneous changes in several variables influencing that objective, such as price, unit sales volume, and operating costs.

seasonal datings Credit terms under which the buyer of seasonal merchandise is encouraged to take delivery well before the peak sales period. Payment on the purchase is deferred until after the peak sales period.

secondary financial markets Financial markets in which *existing* securities are offered for resale. The New York Stock Exchange is a secondary market.

Securities and Exchange Commission (SEC) The government regulatory agency responsible for administering federal securities legislation.

security market line (SML) The relationship between systematic risk and required rates of return for individual securities.

senior debt Debt that has a higher claim on a firm's earnings and/or assets than junior debt.

sensitivity analysis A method of analysis in which a financial planning model is rerun to determine the effect on the output variable(s) (for example, profit) of given changes in the input variable(s) (for example, sales). Sensitivity analysis is sometimes called *what if* analysis.

shareholder wealth Present value of the expected future returns to the owners (that is, shareholders) of the firm. It is measured by the market value of the shareholders' common stock holdings—that is, the price per share times the number of shares outstanding.

short selling Selling a security you do not own (by "borrowing" it from another investor) and then replacing it by buying the security at a later date, hopefully at a lower price.

signal Changes in investment, financing, or dividend policies that convey information to outside investors concerning management's assessment of the expected future returns of the company.

simple interest Interest paid or earned on the principal only.

simulation A financial planning tool that models some event, such as the cash flows from an investment project. A computerized simulation is one technique used to assess the risk associated with a particular project.

sinking fund problem An annuity amount that must be invested each period (year) to produce a future value.

sole proprietorship A business owned by one person. The owner of a sole proprietorship has unlimited liability for debts incurred by the business.

spot rate The rate of exchange between two currencies being bought and sold for *immediate* delivery.

spread The difference between the *bid price*, which is the price a dealer is willing to buy a given security, and the *ask price*, which is the price the dealer is willing to sell a security.

stakeholders The constituent groups in a firm, including stockholders, bondholders, suppliers, customers, employees, community neighbors, and creditors.

standard deviation A statistical measure of the dispersion, or variability, of possible outcomes around the expected value, or mean. Operationally, it is defined as the square root of the weighted average squared deviations of possible outcomes from the expected value. The standard deviation provides an absolute measure of risk.

statement of cash flows A financial statement showing the effects of a firm's operating, investing, and financing activities on its cash balance.

stock dividend A payment of additional shares of common stock to stockholders.

stock split The issuance of a number of new shares in exchange for each old share held by a stockholder.

stockholders' equity The total of a firm's common stock at par, contributed capital in excess of par, and retained earnings accounts from the balance sheet. It sometimes is called the *book value* of the firm, *owners' equity, shareholders' equity,* or *net worth.*

stockout costs The cost of lost sales associated with the inability to fill orders from inventory.

straight-bond value The value a convertible debt security would have if it did not possess the conversion feature. Also referred to as the *investment* value.

subordinated debenture A bond with a claim on the issuing firm's assets that is junior to other forms of debt in the event of a liquidation. The claims of subordinated debenture holders can be met only after all the claims of senior creditors have been met.

swap A contract to exchange cash payments at specified points in time based on the value of an underling asset.

systematic risk That portion of the variability of an individual security's returns that is caused by the factors affecting the market as a whole. This also is called *nondiversifiable risk.*

T

target capital structure The proportions of permanent short-term debt, long-term debt, preferred stock, and common equity that a firm desires to have in its capital structure.

tax deduction An amount subtracted from taxable income. For a corporation with a 35 percent marginal tax rate, a $100 tax deduction reduces taxable income by $100 and reduces taxes owed by $35.

tax shield The amount of tax savings from the deductibility of interest payments on debt or depreciation in computing corporate income taxes.

technical insolvency A situation in which a firm is unable to meet its current obligations as they come due, even though the value of its assets may exceed its liabilities.

tender offer A public announcement by a company or individual indicating that it will pay a price above the current market price for the shares "tendered" of a company it wishes to acquire.

term loan A debt obligation having an initial maturity (i.e., maturity at the time of issue) between 1 and 10 years. Term loans are usually repaid in installments over the life of the loan. This often is referred to as *intermediate-term credit.*

term structure of interest rates The pattern of interest rate yields for debt securities that are similar in all respects except for their length of time to maturity. The term structure of interest rates usually is represented by a graphic plot called a *yield curve.*

terminal warehouse financing agreement A loan agreement in which the inventory being pledged as collateral is stored in a bonded warehouse operated by a public warehousing company.

transaction exposure The potential for a change in the value of a foreign-currency–denominated transaction due to a change in the exchange rate after the transaction is entered into but before it is settled.

translation exposure The change in owners' (accounting) equity because of a change in exchange rates that affects the "converted" value of foreign assets and liabilities.

treasury stock Common stock that has been reacquired by the issuing company.

trend analysis An examination of a firm's performance over time. It is frequently based on one or more financial ratios.

trust receipt A security agreement under which the borrower holds the inventory and proceeds from the sale of the inventory in trust for the lender. This is also known as *floor planning.*

trustee The bondholder's representative in a public debt offering. The trustee is responsible for monitoring the borrower's compliance with the terms of the indenture.

U

underwriting A process whereby a group of investment bankers agrees to purchase a new security issue at a set price and then offers it for sale to investors.

underwriting spread The difference between the selling price to the public of a new security offering and the proceeds received by the offering firm. This also is termed an *underwriting discount.*

unsystematic risk Risk that is unique to a firm. This is also called *diversifiable risk.*

V

variable cost ratio Variable production, administrative, and marketing costs per dollar of sales.

variable costs Costs that vary in close relationship with changes in a firm's output level.

vertical merger A combination of two or more companies that have a buyer-seller relationship with one another.

W

warrant A company-issued long-term option to purchase a specified number of shares of the firm's stock at a particular price during a specified time period.

weighted cost of capital The weighted average of the marginal costs of debt, equity, and preferred stock in proportion to their inclusion in the firm's target capital structure.

wire transfer The process of electronically sending funds from one bank to another through the Federal Reserve System or private bank wire systems.

working capital The difference between a firm's current assets and current liabilities. The term *working capital* is used interchangeably with *net working capital.*

Y

yield-to-maturity The discount rate that equates the present value of all expected interest payments and the repayment of principal from a bond with the present bond price.

Z

zero-balance system A payment system that uses a master disbursing account that services all other disbursing accounts. A zero balance is maintained in all but the master account until payments must be made.

Solutions to Self-Test Problems

Chapter 2

ST1. $$\text{Holding Period Return}(\%) = \frac{\$8.75 - \$11.00 + \$0.10}{\$11.00} \times \$100\%$$

$$= -19.55\%$$

ST2. $$\text{Annual \% Premium} = \left(\frac{\text{Forward} - \text{Spot}}{\text{Spot}}\right)\left(\frac{12}{n}\right)(100\%)$$

$$= \left(\frac{\$1.0739 - \$1.0728}{\$1.0728}\right)\left(\frac{12}{3}\right)(100\%)$$

$$= 0.41\% \text{ (annualized)}$$

This implies that the value of the Swiss franc is expected to rise relative to the value of the dollar over the next 90 days.

ST3. The evidence in Table 2.3 indicates that the value of the euro is expected to increase slightly relative to the dollar. From Table 2.3 it can be seen that the dollar cost of one euro is expected to be \$1.0650 in December 2015 and \$1.0678 in March 2016.

ST4. Indirect quote = 1 ÷ direct quote (given in Table 2.1).
Rand: 1 ÷ \$0.1129 = 8.86 rand/\$
Rupee: 1 ÷ \$0.01845 = 54.20 rupee/\$
Yen: 1 ÷ \$0.010891 = 91.82 yen/\$

Appendix 2A

ST1.

Sales	\$3,000,000
Less: Cost of goods sold	1,800,000
Gross profit margin	\$1,200,000
Less: Operating expenses	800,000
Operating earnings before interest and taxes	\$ 400,000
Less: Interest expense	200,000
Earnings before tax (taxable income)	200,000

Tax calculation:

Total tax = \$22,250 + .39 (\$200,000 − \$100,000)
= \$61,250

The marginal tax rate is 39 percent (34 percent bracket plus 5 percent surcharge). The average tax rate is 30.63 percent (\$61,250 ÷ \$200,000).

Note that there are no tax consequences associated with the retirement of maturing debt or the payment of common and preferred stock dividends. None of those outlays is tax deductible.

ST2.

Sales		$5,000,000
Less: Cost of goods sold		$3,000,000
Gross profit margin		$2,000,000
Less: Operating expenses		$1,000,000
Operating earnings before interest and taxes		$1,000,000
Less: Interest expense		200,000
Earnings before tax and gains from asset sales		$800,000
Plus: Gain on sale of plant and equipment		
Sale price	$1,200,000	
Book value	500,000	700,000
Earnings before tax (taxable income)		$1,500,000

$$\textit{Total tax} = \$113{,}900 + .34\ (\$1{,}500{,}000 - \$335{,}000)$$

$$= \$510{,}000$$

Note that a portion of the gain on the sale of the plant and equipment might have been classified as a capital gain if the sales price had exceeded the original cost of the asset. However, because the corporate capital gain and ordinary tax rates are currently (2016) the same, this distinction is unimportant.

Chapter 3

ST1. a. $\text{Current ratio} = \dfrac{\text{Current assets}}{\text{Current liabilities}}$

$$= \frac{\$52{,}000}{\$25{,}000}$$

$$= 2.08$$

b. $\text{Quick ratio} = \dfrac{\text{Current assets} - \text{Inventories}}{\text{Current liabilities}}$

$$= \frac{\$52{,}000 - \$33{,}000}{\$25{,}000}$$

$$= 0.76$$

ST2. a. $\text{Average collection period} = \dfrac{\text{Accounts receivable}}{\text{Annual credit sales}/365}$

$$= \frac{\$15{,}000}{\$130{,}000/365}$$

$$= 42.1 \text{ days}$$

b. $\text{Inventory turnover} = \dfrac{\text{Cost of sales}}{\text{Average Inventory}}$

$$= \frac{\$103{,}000}{\$33{,}000}$$

$$= 3.12$$

c. $$\text{Fixed asset turnover} = \frac{\text{Sales}}{\text{Net fixed assets}}$$

$$= \frac{\$130{,}000}{\$35{,}000}$$

$$= 3.71$$

d. $$\text{Total asset turnover} = \frac{\text{Sales}}{\text{Total assets}}$$

$$= \frac{\$130{,}000}{\$87{,}000}$$

$$= 1.49$$

ST3. a. $$\text{Debt ratio} = \frac{\text{Total debt}}{\text{Total assets}}$$

$$= \frac{\$47{,}000}{\$87{,}000}$$

$$= 0.54$$

b. $$\text{Debt-to-equity ratio} = \frac{\text{Total debt}}{\text{Total equity}}$$

$$= \frac{\$47{,}000}{\$40{,}000}$$

$$= 1.18$$

c. $$\text{Times interest earned} = \frac{\text{Earnings before interest and taxes (EBIT)}}{\text{Interest charges}}$$

$$= \frac{\$11{,}000}{\$3{,}000}$$

$$= 3.67$$

d. $$\text{Fixed charge coverage} = \frac{\text{EBIT + Lease payments}}{\text{Interest + Lease payments + Preferred dividents before tax + Before-tax sinking fund}}$$

$$= \frac{\$11{,}000 + \$200}{\$3{,}000 + \$200}$$

$$= 3.50$$

ST4. a. $$\text{Gross profit margin} = \frac{\text{Sales} - \text{Cost of sales}}{\text{Sales}}$$

$$= \frac{\$130{,}000 - \$103{,}000}{\$130{,}000}$$

$$= 20.8\%$$

b. $$\text{Net profit margin} = \frac{\text{Earnings after taxes (EAT)}}{\text{Sales}} = \frac{\$5{,}000}{\$130{,}000} = 3.85\%$$

c. $$\text{Return on investment} = \frac{\text{Earnings after taxes (EAT)}}{\text{Total assets}} = \frac{\$5{,}000}{\$87{,}000} = 5.75\%$$

d. $$\text{Return on stockholders' equity} = \frac{\text{Earnings after taxes (EAT)}}{\text{Stockholders' equity}} = \frac{\$5{,}000}{\$40{,}000} = 12.5\%$$

ST5. a. $$\text{Price-to-earnings ratio} = \frac{\text{Market price per share}}{\text{Current earnings per share}} = \frac{\$9.50}{\$5{,}000/5{,}000} = 9.50$$

b. $$\text{Market-to-book ratio} = \frac{\text{Market price per share}}{\text{Book value per share}} = \frac{\$9.50}{\$8.00} = 1.19$$

ST6. $$\text{Return on stockholders' equity} = \text{Net profit margin} \times \text{Total asset turnover} \times \text{Equity multiplier}$$

$$= \frac{\$5{,}000}{\$130{,}000} \times \frac{\$130{,}000}{\$87{,}000} \times \frac{\$87{,}000}{\$40{,}000} = 12.5\%$$

ST7. Return on total assets = 9% = EAT/\$100 million
EAT = \$9 million
EAT = EBT(1 − T)
\$9 million = EBT(1 − T)
EBT = \$15 million
Return on stockholders' equity = EAT/Stockholders' equity
Because the company has no debt, EBT = EBIT
Return on stockholders' equity
= [(EBIT − I)(1 − T)]/Stockholders' equity
0.15 = [(\$15 million − I)(1 − 0.4)]/(\$100 million − Debt)
The interest payments are 10% of the debt amount. Thus,
I = 0.1 (Debt). Substituting for I, the following equation with one unknown (Debt) is obtained:
0.15 = [(\$15 million − 0.1(Debt))(1 − 0.4)]/(\$100 million − Debt)
Debt = \$66.7 million

Chapter 4

ST1. a. Depreciation expense = Increase in accumulated depreciation

= $575 – 500 = $75

b.

Sales	$500
Operating expenses	–125
Depreciation	–75
EBT	$300
Taxes	–120
EAT	$180

c. ATCF = EAT + Depreciation

= $180 + $75

= $255

d. Increase in net fixed assets (NFA):

$100	Increase in gross fixed assets (GFA)
– 75	Increase in accumulated depreciation
$ 25	Increase in net fixed assets

EAT less increase in NFA = ATCF less increase in GFA
$180 – $25 = $255 – $100
$155 = $155

ST2. Rate of sales increase is one-third (33.33%; i.e., from $60 million to $80 million).

Accounts receivable	$ 9 million
Inventories	15 million
Net fixed assets	21 million
Assets that vary with sales	$45 million

Increased funds needed for these asset increases = ⅓ × $45 million = $15 million
Funds provided by accounts payable increase = $4 million
Funds required for cash balance increase = $3 million
Increased retained earnings = $12 million – $2 million (dividend)
= $10 million
Additional financing needed = $3 million (cash) + $15 million (other asset increases)
– $4 million (accounts payable increase)
– $10 million (increased retained earnings)
= $4 million

ST3.

$$\text{Additional financing needed} = \left[\frac{\$10{,}500{,}000}{\$20{,}000{,}000}(\$5{,}000{,}000) - \frac{\$3{,}000{,}000}{\$20{,}000{,}000}(\$5{,}000{,}000)\right]$$

$$-[\$1{,}000{,}000 - \$300{,}000]$$

$$= \$1{,}175{,}000$$

Notes: \$10,500,000 = assets that vary with sales
\$3,000,000 = accounts payable
\$5,000,000 = sales increase
\$20,000,000 = current sales

ST4.

Summit Furniture Company Statement of Cash Flows
For the Year Ended December 31, 2016
Increase (Decrease) in Cash and Cash Equivalents (000)

Cash Flows from Operating Activities:		
Cash received from customers	\$ 142,000	
Cash paid to suppliers and employees	(120,000)	
Interest received	600	
Interest paid (net of amount capitalized)	(2,000)	
Income taxes paid	(6,000)	
Net cash provided (used) by operating activities		\$14,600
Cash Flows from Investing Activities:		
Proceeds from sale of asset	\$1,000	
Capital expenditures	(22,000)	
Net cash provided (used) by investing activities		(\$21,000)
Cash Flows from Financing Activities		
Net borrowings under bank line-of-credit agreement	\$1,000	
Repayments of long-term debt	(2,600)	
Proceeds from issuance of long-term debt	4,000	
Dividends paid	(800)	
Net cash provided (used) by financing activities		\$1,600
Net increase (decrease) in cash and cash equivalents		(\$4,800)
Cash and cash equivalents at beginning of year		5,000
Cash and cash equivalents at end of year		**\$200**

Chapter 5*

ST1. $FV_n = PV_0(1 + i)^n$

a. $FV_5 = \$1{,}000(1.08)^5$
$= \$1{,}000(FVIF_{0.08,5})$
$= \$1{,}000(1.469)$
$= \$1{,}469$

Key	Enter
n	5
i	8
PV	−1,000
PMT	
FV	
	Solution
FV	1,469.33

*Note: Differences between the financial calculator solution and the solution obtained using the present value tables are due to roundoff errors (three decimal places) in the tables.

b. $FV_5 = \$1{,}000(1.02)^{20}$
$= \$1{,}000(FVIF_{0.02,20})$
$= \$1{,}000(1.486)$
$= \$1{,}486$

Key	**Enter**
n	20
i	2
PV	−1,000
PMT	
FV	
	Solution
FV	1,485.95

ST2. $PVAN_0 = PMT(PVIFA_{0.12,10})$
$= \$1{,}000(5.650)$
$= \$5{,}650$

Key	**Enter**
n	10
i	12
PV	
PMT	−1,000
FV	
	Solution
PV	5,650.22

ST3. $FV_n = PV_0(FVIF_{i,n})$
$1.52 = 0.90(FVIF_{i,5})$
$FVIF_{i,5} = 1.689$

Using Table I and reading across the 5-year row, 1.685 is found in the 11 percent column. Thus, the growth rate is approximately 11 percent per year.

Key	**Enter**
n	5
i	
PV	−.90
PMT	
FV	1.52
	Solution
i	11.05

ST4. $PVAN_3 = \$2{,}000(PVIFA_{0.14,5})$
$= \$2{,}000(3.433)$
$= \$6{,}866$

This step calculates the present value of the 5-year *ordinary* annuity at the beginning of year four, i.e., the end of year three. Next, $PVAN_3$ must be discounted to the present:

Key	**Enter**
n	5
i	14
PV	
PMT	−2,000
FV	
	Solution
PV	6,866.16

$$\begin{aligned} PVAN_0 &= PVAN_3(PVIF_{0.14,3}) \\ &= \$6.866(0.675) \\ &= \$4,635 \end{aligned}$$

Key	Enter
n	3
i	14
PV	
PMT	
FV	−6,866.16
	Solution
PV	4,634.46

ST5. $$\begin{aligned} PVAN_0 &= \$50,000(PVIF_{0.10,20}) \\ &= \$50,000(8.514) \\ &= \$425,700 \text{ (amount needed in account on 60th birthday)} \end{aligned}$$

Key	Enter
n	20
i	10
PV	
PMT	−50,000
FV	
	Solution
PV	425,678.19

$$\begin{aligned} FVAN_{25} &= PMT(FVIFA_{0.10,25}) \\ \$425,700 &= PMT(98.347) \\ PMT &= \$4,329 \end{aligned}$$

Key	Enter
n	25
i	10
PV	
PMT	
FV	−425,678.19
	Solution
PMT	4,328.33

ST6. $$\begin{aligned} i_{eff} &= [1 + (i_{nom}/m)]^m - 1 \\ &= [1 + (0.0475/12)]^{12} - 1 \\ &= 1.0485 - 1 \\ &= .0485 \text{ or } 4.85\% \end{aligned}$$

Appendix 5A

ST1. $$\begin{aligned} FV_7 &= \$1,000(e)^{0.10(7)} \\ &= \$2,013.75 \end{aligned}$$

ST2. $$\begin{aligned} PV_0 &= \$5,000(e)^{-0.09(8)} \\ &= \$2,433.76 \end{aligned}$$

ST3. $$\begin{aligned} i_{eff} &= e^{0.12} - 1.0 \\ &= 1.1275 - 1.0 \\ &= 0.1275 \text{ or } 12.75\% \end{aligned}$$

Chapter 6

ST1. $P_0 = \frac{I}{k_d} = \frac{\$80}{0.10} = \$800$

ST2. $P_0 = M(\text{PVIF}_{k_d,n})$

$n = 6;\ M = \$1{,}000;\ P_0 = \$650$

$\$650 = \$1{,}000(\text{PVIF}_{k_d,6})$

$(\text{PVIF}_{k_d,6}) = 0.650$

Using Table II and reading across the 6-year row, 0.650 is found between the 7% (0.666) and 8% (0.630) interest rate columns. Interpolation between these two values gives an approximate yield to maturity (k_d) of

$$k_d = 7\% + \frac{.666 - .650}{.666 - .630}(1\%)$$

$$= 7.44\%$$

Key	Enter
n	6
i	
PV	−650
PMT	0
FV	1,000
	Solution
i	7.44

ST3. $$P_0 = \sum_{t=1}^{n} \frac{I}{(1+k_d)^t} + \frac{M}{(1+k_d)^n}$$

$n = 10; I = .09375(\$1{,}000) = \$93.75$

$M = \$1{,}000; k_d = 0.10$

$P_0 = \$93.75(\text{PVIFA}_{0.10,10}) + \$1{,}000(\text{PVIF}_{0.10,10})$

$= \$93.75(6.145) + \$1{,}000(0.386)$

$= \$962.09(\text{or } \$962)$

Key	Enter
n	10
i	10.0
PV	
PMT	93.75
FV	1,000
	Solution
PV	−961.60

If the investor pays $961.60, the expected yield to maturity is 10 percent. If the investor pays more than $961.60, the expected yield to maturity is less than 10 percent. Therefore, the maximum price the investor should be willing to pay is $961.60.

ST4. $P_0 = \frac{D_p}{k_p} = \frac{\$3.50}{0.06} = \$58.33$

ST5. a. Coupon rate: 3.875 percent
Year of maturity: 2025

b. $1003.82

c. Time Warner is perceived to be riskier than Lockheed Martin.

ST6. a. $108^{26}/_{32}$ percent of $1,000, or $1,088.125

b. $^{-10}/_{32}$ of 1%($1,000) = $−3.125

Chapter 7

ST1. $P_0 = \dfrac{\$3.00}{0.12 - 0.04} = \$37.50$

ST2. Present Value of First 3 Years' Dividends

$D_0 = \$2.00 \quad g_1 = 0.20 \quad k_e = 0.20$

Year	Dividend	PV Interest Factor	Present Value
t	$D_t = \$2.00(1 + 0.20)^t$	$PVIF_{0.20,t} = 1/(1 + 0.20)^t$	$D_t \times PVIF_{0.20,t}$
1	$\$2.00(1 + 0.20)^1 = \$2.400$	0.833	\$2.00
2	$2.00(1 + 0.20)^2 = \$2.880$	0.694	2.00
3	$2.00(1 + 0.20)^3 = \$3.456$	0.579	2.00
PV (First 3 Years' Dividends)			\$6.00

Value of Stock at End of Year 3

$$P_3 = \frac{D_4}{(k_e - g_2)};\ g_2 = 0.06$$

$$D_4 = D_3(1 + g_2) = \$3.456(1 + 0.06) = \$3.663$$

$$P_3 = \frac{\$3.663}{(0.20 - 0.06)} = \$26.164$$

Present Value of P_3

$$PV(P_3) = \frac{P_3}{(1 + k_e)^3} = \frac{\$26.164}{(1 + 0.20)^3}$$

$$= \$26.164(PVIF_{0.20,3}) = \$26.164(0.579) = \$15.15$$

Value of Common Stock

$$P_0 = PV(\text{First 3 Years' Dividends}) + PV(P_3)$$
$$= \$6.00 + \$15.15 = \$21.15$$

ST3. a. No. of shares = No. of shares outstanding × Percentage of shares voting × .50 + 1
With a majority rule voting procedure, each winning director must receive more than 50% (i.e., 50% + 1) of the votes cast.

i. No. of shares = 7,000,000 × .80 × .50 + 1
= 2,800,001

ii. No. of shares = 2,800,001

iii. No. of shares = 2,800,001

b. $\text{No. of shares} = \dfrac{\text{No. of directors desired} \times \text{No. of shares outstanding}}{\text{No. of directors being elected} + 1}$

Since not all of the shares are voted in the election, the No. of shares outstanding is replaced by the No. of shares *voting*, i.e., 7,000,000 × .80 = 5,600,000.

i. $\text{No. of shares} = \dfrac{1 \times 5{,}600{,}000}{7 + 1} + 1$

$= 700{,}001$

ii. $$\text{No. of shares} = \frac{2 \times 5{,}600{,}000}{7+1} + 1$$

$$= 1{,}400{,}001$$

iii. $$\text{No. of shares} = \frac{4 \times 5{,}600{,}000}{7+1} + 1$$

$$= 2{,}800{,}001$$

ST4. a. $115.13
b. −$3.54
c. 1.1%
d. 23
e. 22.23%

ST5. $$\text{Book value per share} = \frac{\text{Total common stockholders' equity}}{\text{No. of shares outstanding}}$$

$$= \frac{\$510{,}000{,}000 - \$50{,}000{,}000}{15{,}000{,}000}$$

$$= \$30.67$$

Chapter 8

ST1. a. $$\hat{r} = \sum_{j=1}^{n} r_j p_j$$

$$= -\$1{,}000(0.20) + \$1{,}500(0.60) + \$2{,}500(0.20)$$

$$= \$1{,}200$$

b. $$\sigma = \sqrt{\sum_{j=1}^{n}(r_j - \hat{r})^2 p_j}$$

$$= [(-\$1{,}000 - \$1{,}200)^2(0.20) + (\$1{,}500 - \$1{,}200)^2(0.60) + (\$2{,}500 - \$1{,}200)^2(0.20)]^{0.50} = \$1{,}166$$

c. $$v = \frac{\sigma}{\hat{r}}$$

$$= \frac{\$1{,}166}{\$1{,}200}$$

$$= 0.97$$

ST2. $$z = \frac{r - \hat{r}}{\sigma}$$

$$= \frac{0 - 15}{12} = -1.25$$

$$p = 0.1056 \text{ (or } 10.56\%)$$

ST3. a. $\hat{r}_p = w_A\hat{r}_A + w_B\hat{r}_B$

$= 0.75(12) + 0.25(20)$

$= 14\%$

b. $\sigma_p = \sqrt{w_A^2\sigma_A^2 + w_B^2\,\sigma_B^2 + 2w_A w_B\,\rho_{AB}\,\sigma_A\,\sigma_B}$

$= [(0.75)^2(6)^2 + (0.25)^2(15)^2 + 2(0.75)(0.25)(.50)(6)(15)]^{0.50}$

$= 7.15\%$

ST4. a. $\beta_p = \sum_{j=1}^{n} w_j\beta_j$

$= 0.25(.95) + 0.25(1.25) + 0.25(1.15) + 0.25(1.05)$

$= 1.10$

ST5. a. $k_j = \hat{r}_f + \beta_j(\hat{r}_m - \hat{r}_f)$

$= 6 + 0.60(15 - 6)$

$= 11.4\%$

b. $k_j = 7 + 0.60(15 - 7)$

$= 11.8\%$

c. $k_j = 6 + 0.60(16 - 6)$

$= 12.0\%$

ST6. a. Maturity risk premium: 7.55% − 6.11% = 1.44%. The maturity risk premium on the Xerox bond will be the same as on the Treasury bonds.

b. Default risk premium: 8.40% − 7.55% = 0.85%

Chapter 9

ST1. Net investment calculation:

Asset cost	$1,200,000
Plus Delivery and installation	100,000
Installed cost	$1,300,000
Minus Proceeds from sale of old asset	150,000
Minus Tax savings on loss from sale of old asset ($50,000 (loss) × 0.4)	20,000
Net investment	$1,130,000

ST2. a. Net investment calculation:

Asset cost	$700,000
Plus Delivery and installation	50,000
Installed cost	$750,000
Minus Proceeds from sale of old asset	275,000
Plus Tax on sale of old asset ($275,000 − $250,000)(0.4)	10,000
Plus Net working capital	40,000
Net investment	$525,000

b. Net cash flow calculation:

$$NCF_{1-4} = [\$100{,}000 - (-\$20{,}000) - (\$150{,}000 - \$50{,}000)](1 - 0.40) + (\$150{,}000 - \$50{,}000) - \$10{,}000$$
$$= \$102{,}000$$

$$NCF_5 = NCF_{1-4} + \text{recovery of accumulated net working capital investment} + \text{after-tax cash flow from sale of new unit}$$
$$= \$102{,}000 + \$90{,}000 + \$70{,}000\,(1 - 0.4)$$
$$= \$234{,}000$$

ST3. Net investment:

Cost of store	$7,000,000
Cost of fixtures	700,000
Installation of fixtures	50,000
Present land value	500,000
Initial working capital	600,000
Net investment	**$8,850,000**

Chapter 10

ST1. $NPV = -(\$20{,}000 + \$5{,}000) + \$7{,}000(PVIFA_{0.11,10}) + \$5{,}000(PVIF_{0.11,10})$
$= \$17{,}983$

The value of the firm, and therefore the shareholders' wealth, is increased by $17,983 as a result of undertaking the project. The project is acceptable because its NPV is positive.

ST2.

$$NPV = \text{PV cash inflows} - \text{Net investment}$$
$$0 = \$75{,}000(PVIFA_{r,8}) - \$360{,}000$$
$$(PVIFA_{r,8}) = 4.80$$
$$r \approx 13 \text{ percent (from Table IV)}$$
$$PI = \frac{\$75{,}000(PVIF_{0.12,8})}{\$360{,}000}$$
$$= 1.035$$

ST3. a. Project G: $\$10{,}000 = \$5{,}000\,(PVIFA_{r,3})$

$PVIFA_{r,3} = 2.0$

$r \approx 23.4$ percent (from Table IV)

Project H: $\$10{,}000 = \$17{,}000(PVIF_{r,3})$

$PVIF_{r,3} = 0.588$

$r \approx 19.3$ percent (from Table II)

b. $NPV_G = -\$10{,}000 + \$5{,}000(PVIFA_{0.12,3})$
$= \$2{,}010$

$NPV_H = -\$10{,}000 + \$17{,}000(PVIF_{0.12,3})$
$= \$2{,}104$

c. Project H should be adopted because it has the higher NPV. It is assumed that the firm's reinvestment opportunities are represented more accurately by the firm's cost of capital than by the unique internal rate of return of either project.

ST4. Net investment (cost of baboon) = \$12,000

Annual depreciation on baboon = \$12,000/20 years = \$600

Net cash flow calculation:

$$\text{NCF}_{1-20} = (\Delta R - \Delta O - \Delta \text{Dep})(1-T) + \Delta \text{Dep}$$
$$= (0 - (\$4{,}000 - \$7{,}000) - 600)(1 - .4) + 600 = \$2{,}060/\text{year}$$
$$\textbf{NPV} = -\$12{,}000 + \$2{,}040(7.963) = \mathbf{\$4{,}245}$$

Yes, buy the baboon, since NPV > 0.

Chapter 11

ST1.
$$z = \frac{\$50{,}000 - \$250{,}000}{\$100{,}000} = -2.0$$

It can be seen from Table V at the back of the book that the probability of a value less than 2.0 standard deviations from the mean is 2.28 percent. Thus, there is a 2.28 percent chance that the actual net present value for the project will be less than \$50,000.

ST2.
a. $k_e = 4\% + 1.0(10\% - 4\%) = 10\%$
b. $k_a^* = 4\% + 1.6(10\% - 4\%) = 13.6\%$
c. NPV @ 10% = −\$9 + \$1.9(6.145) = \$2.68 million (using Table IV interest factors).
d. NPV @ 13.6% = −\$9 + \$1.9(5.299) = \$1.07 million (using calculator accuracy)
The project is acceptable using the required return for average risk projects, and remains acceptable after adjusting for risk.

ST3.
a. NPV calculation:
$$\text{NPV} = -\$75{,}000 + \$30{,}000(0.870) + \$30{,}000(0.756) + \$30{,}000(0.658) + \$20{,}000(0.572) = \$4{,}960$$
b. Certainty equivalent NPV:
$$\text{NPV} = -\$75{,}000 + \$30{,}000(0.90)(0.962) + \$30{,}000(0.80)(0.925) + \$30{,}000(0.65)(0.889) + \$20{,}000(0.5)(0.855) = -\$940.5$$

Chapter 12

ST1. Net proceeds = \$946 − \$11 = \$935

$$\$935 = \$80(\text{PVIFA}_{k_d,10}) + \$1{,}000(\text{PVIF}_{k_d,10})$$

Try $k_d = 9\%$

$$\$935 = \$80(6.418) + \$1{,}000(0.422)$$
$$\$935 \approx \$935.44$$

Therefore, $k_i = 9\%(1 - 0.4) = 5.4\%$

Key	Enter
n	10
i	
PV	−935
PMT	80
FV	1,000
	Solution
i	9.01

ST2. a. $k_e = \frac{D_1}{P_0} + g$

$$= \frac{\$3.50(1 + 0.068)}{\$60} + 0.068$$

$$= 0.13 \text{ or } 13\%$$

b. $k_e' = \frac{\$3.50(1 + 0.068)}{\$60 - \$3} + 0.068$

$$= 0.134 \text{ or } 13.4\%$$

ST3. $k_e = r_f + \beta(r_m - r_f)$

$$= 7.5\% + 1.3(8.6\%)$$

$$= 18.7\%$$

ST4. $k_a = 0.60(k_e) + 0.15(k_p) + 0.25(k_i)$

$$= 0.60(18\%) + 0.15(15\%) + 0.25(9\%)$$

$$= 15.3\%$$

ST5. $k_i = k_d(1 - T)$

$k_i = 0.10(1 - 0.4) = 0.06$ up to \$60 million debt

$k_i = 0.14(1 - 0.4) = 0.084$ above 60 million debt

First increment of debt (\$60 million) will support total financing of \$150 million (\$60 million/0.4 (proportion of debt in capital structure))

$k_e = \frac{\$3.60}{\$60} + 0.06 = 0.12$ for first \$180 million of equity

$k_e' = \frac{\$3.60}{\$56} + 0.06 = 0.1243$ for equity over \$180 million.

First increment:

$\frac{\$60 \text{ million debt}}{0.4} = \$150$ million (including \$90 million retained equity)

$$k_a = 0.6(0.12) + 0.4(0.06) = 0.096 \text{ or } 9.6\%$$

Second increment:

$\frac{\$90 \text{ million retained equity}}{0.6} = \$150$ million (including \$60 million higher cost debt)

$$k_a = 0.6(0.12) + 0.4(0.084) = 0.1056 \simeq 10.6\%$$

Additional funds:

$$k_a = 0.6(0.1243) + 0.4(0.084) = 0.1082 \simeq 10.8\%$$

Break Point	WCC
\$150 million	9.6%
\$300 million	10.6%
Above \$300 million	10.8%

Chapter 13

ST1. **Proportion of Debt**

$\left(\frac{B}{B+E}\right)$	Cost of Debt, k_i	Cost of Equity, k_e	Weighted Cost of Capital, k_a
0.00	—	10.0%	10.00%
0.10	4.0%	10.1	9.49
0.20	4.2	10.3	9.08
0.30	4.4	10.8	8.88
0.40	4.8	11.4	8.76
0.50	5.5	12.5	9.00
0.60	6.6	14.5	9.76
0.70	8.0	18.0	11.00

Note: $k_a = \left(\frac{E}{B+E}\right)k_e + \left(\frac{B}{B+E}\right)k_i$

The optimal capital structure consists of 40 percent debt and 60 percent equity since this minimizes the firm's cost of capital.

ST2. a.

Debt Ratio [B/(B + E)]	Pre-tax Cost of Debt (k_d)	Cost of Equity (k_e)	Weighted Average Cost of Capital
0.00	—	14.0%	14.0%
0.10	7.0%	15.0	13.92
0.20	8.0	16.5	14.16
0.30	10.0%	18.5	14.75
0.40	12.5	21.5	15.9

b. A capital structure of 10% debt and 90% equity minimizes the weighted average cost of capital (13.92%).

ST3. a.

	Leverage Ratio 0%	25%	50%
Total Assets	$25 m	$25 m	$25 m
Debt	0	6.25 m	12.5 m
Equity	25 m	18.75 m	12.5 m
Total Debt + Equity	$25 m	$25 m	$25 m
EBIT	$ 4 m	$ 4 m	$ 4 m
Less: Interest	0	0.625 m	1.875 m
EBT	4 m	3.375 m	2.125 m
Less: Taxes	1.6 m	1.35 m	0.85 m
EAT	$2.4 m	$ 2.025 m	$ 1.275 m
ROE	9.6%	10.8%	10.2%

b.

	Leverage Ratio		
	0%	25%	50%
Total Assets	$25 m	$25 m	$25 m
Debt	0	6.25 m	12.5 m
Equity	25 m	18.75 m	12.5 m
Total Debt + Equity	$25 m	$25 m	$25 m
EBIT	$ 3.2 m	$ 3.2 m	$ 3.2 m
Less: Interest	0	0.625 m	1.875 m
EBT	3.2 m	2.575 m	1.325 m
Less: Taxes	1.28 m	1.03 m	0.53 m
EAT	$ 1.92 m	$ 1.545 m	0.795 m
ROE	7.68%	8.24%	6.36%

c.

	Leverage Ratio		
	0%	25%	50%
Total Assets	$25 m	$25 m	$25 m
Debt	0	6.25 m	12.5 m
Equity	25 m	18.75 m	12.5 m
Total Debt + Equity	$25 m	$25 m	$25 m
EBIT	$ 4.8 m	$ 4.8 m	$ 4.8 m
Less: Interest	0	0.625 m	1.875 m
EBT	4.8 m	4.175 m	2.925 m
Less: Taxes	1.92 m	1.67 m	1.17 m
EAT	$ 2.88 m	$2.505 m	$ 1.755 m
ROE	11.52%	13.36%	14.04%

Chapter 14

ST1. a.

$$\text{DOL} = \frac{\text{Sales} - \text{Variable costs}}{\text{EBIT}}$$

$$= \frac{\$5{,}000{,}000 - \$1{,}000{,}000}{\$2{,}000{,}000}$$

$$= 2.0$$

$$\text{DFL} = \frac{\text{EBIT}}{\text{EBIT} - I - D_p/(1 - T)}$$

$$= \frac{\$2{,}000{,}000}{\$2{,}000{,}000 - \$500{,}000 - \dfrac{\$100{,}000}{(1 - 0.4)}}$$

$$= \frac{\$2{,}000{,}000}{\$1{,}333{,}333}$$

$$= 1.5$$

$$\text{DCL} = \frac{\text{Sales} - \text{Variable Costs}}{\text{EBIT} - I - D_p/(1-T)}$$

$$= \frac{\$5{,}000{,}000 - \$1{,}000{,}000}{\$2{,}000{,}000 - \$500{,}000 - \dfrac{\$1{,}000{,}000}{(1-0.4)}}$$

$$= 3.0$$

Check: $\text{DCL} = \text{DOL} \times \text{DFL}$

$$= 2.0 \times 1.5$$

$$= 3.0$$

b. $\text{Current EPS} = \dfrac{\$800{,}000}{400{,}000 \text{ shares}} = \$2.00$

A sales increase to \$5.5 million represents a 10 percent increase in sales. Hence, EPS should increase by 30 percent (10% × 3.0), to \$2.60.

ST2. $p(\text{EPS} < \$0) = p(\text{EBIT} < \$250{,}000)$

$$z = \frac{\text{EBIT} - \widehat{\text{EBIT}}}{\sigma}$$

$$= \frac{\$250{,}000 - \$1{,}750{,}000}{\$1{,}200{,}000}$$

$$= -1.25$$

$$p = 0.1056 \text{ (or } 10.56\%)$$

ST3. a. $$\frac{(\text{EBIT} - I_d)(1-T) - D_p}{N_d} = \frac{(EBIT - I_e)(1-T) - D_p}{N_e}$$

$$\frac{(\text{EBIT} - \$18)(1-0.40)}{100} = \frac{(\text{EBIT} - \$0)(1-0.40)}{110}$$

$$\text{EBIT} = \$198 \text{ (million)}$$

b. $p(\text{EPS} < \$0) = p(\text{EBIT} < \$18.0)$

$$z = \frac{\text{EBIT} - \widehat{\text{EBIT}}}{\sigma}$$

$$= \frac{\$18.0 - \$250}{\$200}$$

$$= -1.16$$

$$p = 0.1230 \text{ (or } 12.30\%)$$

c. $p(\text{EBIT} > \$198)$

$$z = \frac{\$198 - \$250}{\$200}$$

$$= -0.26$$

$$p = 1 - 0.3974 = 0.6026 \text{ (or } 60.26\%)$$

ST4. a. $CB_0 = \$20$ million; $FCF_R = \$60$ million; $\sigma = \$60$ million

$$CB_R = CB_0 + FCF_R$$
$$= \$20 \text{ million} + \$60 \text{ million}$$
$$= \$80 \text{ million}$$
$$z = \frac{\$0 - CB_R}{\sigma}$$
$$= \frac{\$0 - \$80}{\$60}$$
$$= -1.33$$
$$p = 0.0918 \text{ (or 9.18\%)}$$

b. $CB_R = \$20 \text{ million} + S60 \text{ million} - \$10 \text{ million}$

$$= \$70 \text{ million}$$
$$\sigma = \$60 \text{ million}$$
$$z = \frac{\$0 - \$70}{\$60} = -1.17$$
$$p = 0.1210 \text{ (or 12.10\%)}$$

Appendix 14A

ST1. a. $$Q_i = \frac{F}{P - V} = \frac{\$10{,}000{,}000}{\$4{,}000 - \$2{,}000} = 5{,}000 \text{ units/year}$$

b. $$\text{Target volume} = \frac{F + \$2{,}000{,}000}{P - V}$$
$$= \frac{\$10{,}000{,}000 + \$2{,}000{,}000}{\$4{,}000 - \$2{,}000} = 6{,}000 \text{ units/year}$$

ST2. The probability of having operating losses is the probability of selling 20,000 units or less.

$$z = \frac{\$20{,}000 - \$22{,}000}{\$4{,}000} = -0.5$$

The probability of a $z \leq 0.5$ (i.e., the probability of selling 20,000 units or less) can be determined from Table V as 0.3085, or 30.85%.

Chapter 15

ST1. a. **Post–Stock Dividend Common Stockholders' Equity**

Common stock ($1 par, 120,000 shares)	$ 120,000
Contributed capital in excess of par	2,480,000
Retained earnings	3,400,000
Total common stockholders' equity	$6,000,000

A total of $1,600,000 (20,000 shares × an assumed market price of $80 per share) is transferred from retained earnings to the other stockholders' equity accounts. Of this $1,600,000, $20,000 ($1 par × 20,000 shares) is added to the common stock account and the remaining $1,580,000 is added to the contributed capital in excess of par account.

b. $\text{Post-stock dividend price} = \dfrac{\$80}{1 + 0.20}$

$= \$66.67$

ST2. a.

EBIT	\$1,000,000
Interest	200,000
EBT	\$ 800,000
Taxes	320,000
EAT	\$ 480,000

$$\text{Earnings per share} = \frac{\$480{,}000}{50{,}000 \text{ shares}}$$

$$= \$9.60$$

b. $$\text{Dividends per share} = \frac{\$100{,}000}{50{,}000 \text{ shares}}$$

$$= \$2.00$$

$$\text{Dividend payout ratio} = \frac{\$2.00}{\$9.60}$$
$$= 20.8\%$$

c. $$\text{Dividend yield} = \frac{\text{Dividend per share}}{\text{Price per share}}$$

$$0.02 = \frac{\$2.00}{\text{Price per share}}$$

$$\text{Price per share} = \$100.00$$

d. Equivalent (pre-stock dividend)
dividend per share: $\$2.00 \div 2 = \$1.00$

$$\text{Dividend rate increase} = \frac{\$1.10 - \$1.00}{\$1.00}$$
$$= 0.10 \text{ or } 10\%$$

Chapter 16

ST1. a. $$\text{Inventory conversion period} = \frac{\text{Average inventory}}{\text{Cost of sales}/365}$$

$$= \frac{\$2.120}{\$6{,}946/365}$$

$$= 111.4 \text{ days}$$

b. $$\text{Receivables conversion period} = \frac{\text{Accounts receivable}}{\text{Annual credit sales}/365}$$

$$= \frac{\$2{,}075}{\$11{,}990/365}$$

$$= 63.2 \text{ days}$$

c. Operating cycle = Inventory conversion period + Receivables conversion period

$$= 111.4 + 63.2$$

$$= 174.6 \text{ days}$$

d. $$\text{Payables deferral period} = \frac{\text{Average accounts payable}}{(\text{Cost of sales})/365}$$

$$= \frac{724}{(6{,}946)/365}$$

$$= 38.0 \text{ days}$$

e. Cash conversion cycle = Operating cycle − Payables deferral period

$$= 174.6 - 38.0$$

$$= 136.6 \text{ days}$$

ST2. a.

	Policy A	**Policy B**
Current assets	\$ 90,000,000	\$ 60,000,000
Total assets	190,000,000	160,000,000
Total equity	76,000,000	64,000,000
Total debt	114,000,000	96,000,000
Short-term debt	34,200,000	57,600,000
Long-term debt	79,800,000	38,400,000
EBIT	30,000,000	30,000,000
Interest {STD (10%) / LTD (14%)}	14,592,000	11,136,000
EBT	15,408,000	18,864,000
Taxes	6,163,200	7,545,600
EAT	9,244,800	11,318,400
Rate of return on equity	12.16%	17.69%

b. Policy B is riskier than Policy A since it results in a lower net working capital position (\$2,400,000 versus \$55,800,000) and a lower current ratio (1.04 versus 2.63). (This answer assumes there are no current liabilities other than short-term debt. If there were, the numbers would differ but the relative magnitudes of both calculated measures of risk would be unchanged.).

ST3. a. $$\text{AFC} = \frac{\text{Percentage discount}}{100 - \text{Percentage discount}} \times \frac{365}{\text{Credit period} - \text{Discount period}}$$

$$= \frac{2}{100 - 2} \times \frac{365}{120 - 10}$$

$$= 6.77\%$$

b. $$\text{AFC} = \frac{2}{100 - 2} \times \frac{365}{122 - 30} = 8.10\%$$

ST4.

$$\text{AFC} = \frac{\text{Interest cost}}{\text{Usable funds}} \times \frac{365}{\text{Maturity(days)}}$$

$$\text{Interest cost} = 0.105(\$25{,}000) \times \frac{274}{365}$$
$$= \$1{,}971$$
$$\text{AFC} = \frac{\$1{,}971}{\$25{,}000 - \$1{,}971} \times \frac{365}{274}$$
$$= 11.4\%$$

ST5. a.

$$\text{AFC} = \frac{\text{Interest costs} + \text{Commitment fee}}{\text{Usable funds}} \times \frac{365}{\text{Maturity (days)}}$$

$$\text{Interest cost} = 0.11(\$2{,}000{,}000) = \$220{,}000$$
$$\text{Commitment fee} = 0.005(\$8{,}000{,}000) = \$40{,}000$$
$$\text{Usable funds} = 0.90(\$2{,}000{,}000) = \$1{,}800{,}000$$
$$\text{AFC} = \frac{\$220{,}000 + \$40{,}000}{\$1{,}800{,}000} \times \frac{365}{365}$$
$$= 14.4\%$$

b.

$$\text{Interest cost} = 0.11(\$7{,}000{,}000) = \$770{,}000$$
$$\text{Commitment fee} = 0.005(\$3{,}000{,}000) = \$15{,}000$$
$$\text{Usable funds} = 0.90(\$7{,}000{,}000) = \$6{,}300{,}000$$
$$\text{AFC} = \frac{\$770{,}000 + \$15{,}000}{\$6{,}300{,}000} \times \frac{365}{365}$$
$$= 12.5\%$$

ST6.

$$\text{AFC} = \frac{\text{Interest costs} + \text{Placement fee}}{\text{Usable funds}} \times \frac{365}{\text{Maturity date(days)}}$$

$$\text{Interest costs} = 0.085(\$25{,}000{,}000)\left(\frac{91}{365}\right) = \$529{,}795$$

$$\text{Usable funds} = \$25{,}000{,}000 - \$529{,}795 - \$75{,}000 = \$24{,}395{,}205$$
$$\text{AFC} = \frac{\$529{,}795 + \$75{,}000}{\$24{,}395{,}205} \times \frac{365}{91} = 9.94\%$$

ST7. a.

Average level of receivables	\$4,000,000
Less Factoring commission	
$0.02 \times \$4{,}000{,}000 =$	−80,000
Less Reserve for returns	
$0.10 \times \$4{,}000{,}000 =$	−400,000
Amount available for advance before interest is deducted	\$3,520,000
Less Interest on advance	
$0.12 \times \$3{,}520{,}000 \times \frac{70}{365} =$	−81,008
Amount of funds advanced by factor (Usable funds)	\$3,438,992

b. Interest costs	$ 81,008
Factoring commission	80,000
Total interest and factoring costs	$ 161,008
Less Credit department savings per 70-day period	
$\$3{,}000 \times \frac{70}{30} =$	− 7,000
Less Average bad-debt losses per 70-day period	
$\$9{,}000 \times \frac{70}{30} =$	−21,000
Net financing cost per 70 days	$ 133,008

$$\text{AFC} = \frac{\$133{,}008}{\$3{,}438{,}992} \times \frac{365}{70}$$
$$= 20.2\%$$

Chapter 17

ST1. a. Increase in average cash balance = Average daily sales × Decrease in payment processing time
= ($219,000,000/365) × 2 = $1,200,000

b. Increase in (pretax) earnings = Increase in average cash balance × Interest rate
= $1,200,000 × 0.07 = $84,000

ST2. a. Reduction in collection time = Reduction in mailing time + Reduction in processing and clearing time
= (3.0 − 1.5) + (5.0 − 2.0) = 4.5 days

Average daily collections = Annual credit sales/365
= $292,000,000/365 = $800,000

Amount of funds released = Average daily collections × Reduction in collection time
= $800,000 × 4.5 = $3,600,000

b. Annual (pretax) earnings on released funds = Amount of funds released × Interest rate
= $3,600,000 × 0.10 = $360,000

c. Annual bank processing fee = Fixed cost + Number of payments per year × Variable cost per payment
= $50,000 + (600,000 × $0.20) = $170,000

d. Net (pretax) benefits = Annual (pretax) earnings on released funds + Reduction in firm's payment processing costs − Annual bank processing fee
= $360,000 + $40,000 − $170,000 = $230,000

Chapter 18

ST1. a. Average collection period = 30 + 10 = 40 days

Average daily sales = Annual sales/365
= $54,750,000/365
= $150,000

Investment in receivables = Average daily sales × Average collection period
= $150,000 × 40 = $6,000,000

b. Investment in receivables = {[$54,750,000 × (1− 0.15)]/365} × (30 + 25)
= $7,012,500

ST2. a. Additional sales = \$5,475,000

Marginal profitability of additional sales = Additional sales × Profit contribution ratio
= \$5,475,000 × (1 − 0.75) = \$1,368,750

b. Additional investment in receivables = (Additional annual sales/365) × Average collection period
= (\$5,475,000/365) × 75 = \$1,125,000

Cost of additional investment in receivables = Additional investment in receivables × Required rate of return
= \$1,125,000 × 0.18 = \$202,500

c. Additional bad-debt loss = Additional sales × Bad-debt loss ratio
= \$5,475,000 × 0.05 = \$273,750

d. Cost of additional investment in inventory
= Additional investment in inventory × Required rate of return
= \$800,000 × 0.18 = \$144,000

e. Additional cash discounts = Additional sales × Percent taking discount × Cash discount percent
= \$5,475,000 × 0.10 × 0.02 = \$10,950

f. Net change in pretax profits = Marginal returns − Marginal costs
= \$1,368,750 − (\$202,500 + \$273,750 + \$10,950 + \$144,000)
= \$737,550

ST3. Reduction in receivables balance = Annual sales/365 × Reduction in average collection period
= (\$21,900,000/365) × (55 − 35) = \$1,200,000

Return on reduction in receivables balance = Reduction in receivables balance × Required rate of return
= \$1,200,000 × 0.18 = \$216,000

Cost of discount = Sales × Percent taking discount × Cash discount percent
= \$21,900,000 × 0.50 × 0.02 = \$219,000

Net change in pretax profits = Marginal returns − Marginal costs
= \$216,000 − \$219,000
= −\$3,000

ST4. a. $S = \$72$; D = 360,000 baseballs;

$C = 0.20 \times \$1.25 = \$0.25$/baseball

$$Q^* = \sqrt{\frac{2SD}{C}}$$

$$= \sqrt{\frac{2(\$72)(360{,}000)}{\$0.25}}$$

= 14,400 baseballs (1,200 dozen)

b. $$TC = \frac{D \times S}{Q^*} + \frac{Q^* \times C}{2}$$

$$= \frac{360{,}000 \times \$72}{14{,}400} + \frac{14{,}400 \times \$0.25}{2}$$

= \$3,600

c. $$T^* = \frac{365 \times Q^*}{D}$$

$$= \frac{365 \times 14{,}400}{360{,}000}$$

$$= 14.6 \text{ days}$$

Chapter 19

ST1. NAL = Installed cost ($777,000), *less* Present value of after-tax lease payments ($575,000), *less* Present value of depreciation tax shield ($210,000), *plus* Present value of after-tax operating costs if owned but not if leased ($140,000), *less* Present value of the after-tax salvage value ($42,600)
= $89,400

Based on the numerical analysis, Pepsico should lease. It would be a good idea to test the sensitivity of this conclusion with alternative estimates of the salvage value and the operating cost differential between leasing and owning.

ST2. a.

End of Year	Principal Payment	Interest Payment	Total Payment	Remaining Balance
0	—	—	—	$2,000,000
1	$ 250,000	$160,000	$ 410,000	1,750,000
2	250,000	140,000	390,000	1,500,000
3	250,000	120,000	370,000	1,250,000
4	250,000	100,000	350,000	1,000,000
5	1,000,000	80,000	1,080,000	0

b. Funds available for use:

$\$2{,}000{,}000 - \$50{,}000$ processing fee $= \$1{,}950{,}000$

$$\$1{,}950{,}000 = \$410{,}000(\text{PVIF}_{i,1}) + \$390{,}000(\text{PVIF}_{i,2}) + \$370{,}000(\text{PVIF}_{i,3}) + \$350{,}000(\text{PVIF}_{i,4}) + \$1{,}080{,}000(\text{PVIF}_{i,5})$$

$i = 8.83\%$ (by calculator)

ST3. Calculation of the amount to be amortized:

Initial outlay	$385,000
Less: PV of $31,500 after-tax salvage value at 12% ($\$31{,}500 \times \text{PVIF}_{0.12,5}$) ($\$31{,}500 \times 0.567$)	17,861
Less: PV of annual depreciation tax shelter ($\$77{,}000 \times 0.40 \times \text{PVIFA}_{0.12,5}$) ($\$77{,}000 \times 0.40 \times 3.605$)	111,034
Amount to be amortized	256,105

Calculation of the annual after-tax lease income

Amount to be amortized = PMT ($PVIFA_{0.12,5}$)(1 + 0.12)

\$256,105 = PMT (3.605) (1 + 0.12)

PMT = \$63,430

Calculation of lease payment required from lessee:

$$\text{Lease payment required from lessee} = \frac{\text{Lease payment required by the lessor(after-tax)}}{\text{1 minus lessor's marginal tax rate}}$$

$$= \frac{\$63{,}430}{1 - 0.40}$$

$$= \$105{,}717^{*}$$

Chapter 20

ST1. a. Conversion value = Conversion ratio × Stock price

$$= \left(\frac{\$1{,}000}{\$40}\right)(\$35)$$

$$= \$875$$

b. $$\text{Straight-bond value} = \sum_{t=1}^{n} \frac{\text{Interest}}{(1+k_d)^t} + \frac{\text{Principal}}{(1+k_d)^n}$$

$$= \sum_{t=1}^{20} \frac{\$80}{(1+0.11)^t} + \frac{\$1{,}000}{(1+0.11)^{20}}$$

$$= \$80(PVIFA_{0.11,20}) + \$1000(PVIF_{0.11,20})$$

$$= \$80(7.963) + \$1000(0.124)$$

$$= \$761$$

c. Conversion premium = \$925 − Max{\$875; \$761}

= \$50

d. Conversion value = Conversion ratio × Stock price

$$= \left(\frac{\$1{,}000}{\$40}\right)(\$55)$$

$$= \$1{,}375$$

e. \$1,375. At this price, the bond issue is likely to be called, effectively forcing conversion. Therefore, the debenture cannot be expected to sell at a premium above the conversion value.

ST2. a. Formula value = Max{\$0; (Common stock price − Exercise price) × Number of shares per warrant}

= Max{\$0; (\$32 − \$40)(1)}

= \$0

Premium = \$1.50 − \$0 = \$1.50

*Calculator solution (\$105,720.74) differs slightly from the solution obtained from the present value tables because the tables are rounded to three decimal places.

b. Formula value $= \text{Max}\{\$0; (\$40 - \$40)(1)\}$

$= \$0$

Premium $= \$3.50 - \$0 = \$3.50$

c. Formula value $= \text{Max}\{\$0; (\$48 - \$40)(1)\}$

$= \$8$

Premium $= \$10.00 - \$8.00 = \$2.00$

ST3. a. Rights-on case

$$R = \frac{M_o - S}{N + 1}$$

$$= \frac{\$25 - \$22}{10 + 1}$$

$$= \$0.27$$

Ex-rights case

$$R = \frac{M_e - S}{N}$$

$$= \frac{\$24.73 - \$22}{10}$$

$$= \$0.27$$

b. $0.27

c. $$R = \frac{M_o - S}{N + 1}$$

$$= \frac{\$30 - \$22}{10 + 1}$$

$$= \$0.73$$

Chapter 21

ST1. a. Maximum total revenue 5,000 oz. × $1,750/oz. = $8,750,000
Minimum total revenue 5,000 oz. × $1,450/oz. = $7,250,000

b. Total revenue 5,000 oz. × $1,630/oz. = $8,150,000

c. Total revenue 5,000 oz. × ($1,630 − $4.25)/oz. = $8,128,750

ST2. *Unhedged*
Cost 1,000,000 gal. × $4.00/gal. = $4,000,000
Hedged
Cost 1,000,000 gal. × $3.45/gal. = $3,450,000
Cost is $550,000 higher if it remains unhedged.

Chapter 22

ST1. A U.S. trader could sell U.S. dollars, buy spot Canadian dollars, and invest in Canadian securities to earn 12 percent. Simultaneously, the trader could sell Canadian dollars forward at a 3 percent annual discount. At the end of the forward period, the trader could convert Canadian dollars back to U.S. dollars. The net effect of these transactions is the trader earns 9 percent (12 percent interest less 3 percent depreciation in value) compared with the 8 percent return available in the U.S. market.

ST2. a. Yen price = 140 yen/dollar × $12,000 = 1,680,000 yen.
b. Yen price = 120 yen/dollar × $12,000 = 1,440,000 yen.
A decline in the value of the dollar relative to the yen makes U.S. goods more attractive abroad.

ST3.

$$\frac{S_n}{S_0} = \frac{(1+i_h)^n}{(1+i_f)^n}$$

$$\frac{S_3}{\$0.61/\text{CHF}} = \frac{(1+.04)^3}{(1+.05)^3}$$

$$S_3 = \$0.5928/\text{CHF}$$

The higher Swiss interest rate relative to the U.S. rate implies (using IFE) that the Swiss franc should decline in value relative to the dollar, as this computation verifies.

Chapter 23

ST1. a. Low end of range:
$40 × 1.25 = $50
High end of range:

$$P_{max} = (\text{P/E})_1(EPS_2) = (10)(\$6.00) = \$60$$

b.

$$EPS_c = \frac{EAT_1 + EAT_2 + EAT_{1,2}}{NS_1 + NS_2(ER)} = \frac{\$30\text{ million} + \$12\text{ million} + 0}{6\text{ million} + 2\text{ million}(1.0)} = \$5.25$$

ST2. First, solve for terminal value of cash flows beyond year 4:

$$\text{Terminal value in year 4} = \frac{\$550{,}000(1.05)}{0.14 - 0.05} = \$6{,}416{,}667$$

Next, determine the present value of net cash flows in years 1–4 and the terminal value at the end of year 4:

$$\text{Target firm value} = \frac{\$350{,}000}{(1+0.14)^1} + \frac{\$400{,}000}{(1+0.14)^2} + \frac{\$475{,}000}{(1+0.14)^3} + \frac{\$550{,}000}{(1+0.14)^4} + \frac{\$6{,}416{,}667}{(1+0.14)^4} = \$5{,}060{,}242$$

The most Melissa's Kitchen should pay for Takeshi's Takeout is $5,060,242.

Check Answers to Selected Problems

2

1. a. +0.3%
5. 8.72%
6. a. 15%
10. $14,853
11. a. Total cost = $1,351,728
    Cost per watch = $135.17
12. a. −17.94%

2A

1. $855,100
5. a. $14,100,000
6. $2,640,000
8. a. $33,400,000

3

1. a. $219,178
2. a. 15%
3. $3,945,205
5. a. Firm A: ROE = 30%
   Equity multiplier = 1.5
8. b. Current ratio = 2.2x
13. a. ROE = 28.57%
17. a. 5.0 times
18. c. $16

4

1. $1,150,000
3. b. $500,000 additional financing
4. Cash loans needed at the end of January = $40,000
6. $108 million
8. b. $300,000

5

1. a. $1,191
3. $240,410.40 (Tables); $240,420.73 (Calculator)
5. a. $37,204.70 (Calculator)
6. 13% (Tables); 12.98% (Calculator)
7. a. $584.80 (Tables); $584.55 (Calculator)
9. 20%
11. a. $1,281.58 (Tables); $1,281.88 (Calculator)
14. $13,018.71 (Tables); $13,019.63 (Calculator)
16. a. $29,806 (Tables); $29,810.44 (Calculator)
18. $3,386
19. $51,354 (Tables); $51,357 (Calculator)
20. $690,274 (Tables); $690,295 (Calculator)
22. a. $31,401 (Tables); $31,403 (Calculator)
24. $51,980.44 (Tables); $51,983.14 (Calculator)
25. $94,337 (Tables); $94,335 (Calculator)
26. a. $12,653
29. $21,879 (Tables); $21,872 (Calculator)
30. $5,907.83 (Tables); $5,909.40 (Calculator)
33. $3,890 (Tables); $3,869 (Calculator)
39. $16,333

5A

2. $2,744
4. d. 22.14%
6. $123.13

6

1. b. P_0 = $800
3. a. P_0 = $1,139
4. P_0 = $964
7. a. k_d = 13.65% (Calculator)
10. a. P_0 = $38.89
13. b. YTM = 10.42% (Calculator)
15. a. P_0 = $768
18. $10.97

7

2. a. $88.33
4. $57.36
8. $21.34
9. $16.21
13. a. $40.36
15. a. 300,001
17. $12.10
19. b. $30.97
21. $16.81
23. $20.25

8

1. a. r_x = 15%
   b. σ_x = 11.62%
2. p(Loss) = 2.28%
5. a. i. r_p = 8.2%
      ii. σ_p = 4.87%
6. b. r_p = 13.05%
   c. σ_p = 3.64%
9. b. Rate of return = 9.74%
12. b. i. σ_p = 7.8%
       ii. σ_p = 6.18%
14. 47%
17. a. p(Loss) = 4.75%
22. b. 62.93%
27. 82.89%

9

2. $5,100
4. a. $122,500
8. $402,000
11. $144,730

13. $NCF_1 = \$14,716$
$NCF_2 = \$18,796$
17. $2,780,000
18. $NCF_2 = \$347,960$
19. $148,000

9A

2. year 4 depreciation = $2,304

10

1. NPV = $−3,050
2. a. $158
3. 9.11%
5. $364.53
9. $13,844
10. 8%
13. a. NPV = $19,031
16. $n \approx 19$
18. a. $−250,800
20. b. $NCF_1 = \$2,537,400$
$NCF_3 = \$2,729,400$

10A

1. a. $NPV_A = \$1,888.50$
$NPV_B = \$2,292$
2. Alternative P

11

2. a. 5.48%
6. a. 17%
9. a. $703,600
11. b. $−0.1795 million
13. a. $230,250
15. c. $29,599
19. 19.8%
22. 12.6%
23. 14.2%

12

2. 7.2%
4. b. 13% (Tables); 12.96% (Calculator)
7. a. 13.4%
8. 17.3%
11. First break: $33.33 million
k_a = 13.1% (for first block)
13. First break: $60 million
k_a = 13.19% (for first block)
19. a. $27.65
20. a. 1.4
23. a. $10.10

13

1. $10,000
3. a. $600,000
5. a. i. 45% debt + 55% equity

14

1. a. EPS (Sales = $6 million) = $5.40
d. i. DCL = 2.778
2. b. i. DOL = 1.875
ii. DFL = 1.67
iii. DCL = 3.13
5. a. DOL = 10.67
b. DFL = 1.765
9. 9.18%
12. b. DFL = 1.6
d. EPS = $2.46
14. EPS = $3.36
15. 24.51%
16. 2.28%
18. a. EBIT = $15 million
20. a. EBIT = $2.4 million
21. a. EBIT = $170,000
22. a. EBIT = $133.2 million
25. a. Approximately 26%
26. a. EBIT = $17.5 million
27. a. 2.28%
29. a. 4.01%

14A

1. a. i. 5,000 copies
d. ii. $0
4. $250,000

15

1. b. $0.50
3. 16.7%
4. $1,425,000
7. b. $1.60
14. Friday, August 20

16

1. b. $50,703,000
2. Aggressive: ROE = 14.55%
3. c. 124.1 days
e. 69.35 days (using the equation in footnote 4 or 63.3 days and using Equation 16.5)
4. a. i. Aggressive: ROA = 12.29%
5. a. iii. Aggressive: CA/CL = 1.25
6. a. i. Aggressive: 10.85%
7. c. ii. Interest = $7.79 million
8. a. $889,980
12. a. 46.7 days
13. b. $340,000
14. b. APR = 12.40%
15. a. AFC = 14.9%
19. a. AFC = 8.7%
21. a. AFC = 11.67%
24. AFC = 23.23%
26. c. AFC = 20.4%
29. AFC = 22%
31. a. AFC = 12.89%
33. AFC = 19.66%

17

1. a. $7,500,000
2. b. $177,534
3. d. $−18,424
4. $411,044
5. c. $90,959
7. a. $10,471.50
9. a. $257,849
12. a. $−1,562

18

1. b. 38.5 days
3. $−932
6. c. $−11,363
8. $158,062
10. $17,329
11. $1,163,836
15. $104,700
16. a. 80,000 units
18. a. 17,678; 10,607
20. c. 14.6 days
21. d. 24,658

19

3. a. 4.96% (Calculator)
4. a. $10,624 (Tables); $10,603 (Calculator)
7. Year 1 cash flow = $3.6 million
10. a. PMT = $1,467,567 (Tables); $1,467,633 (Calculator)
14. a. $972,373
16. 11.8% (Calculator) Approx. 12% (Tables)
17. a. Year 1 = $25,082 (Tables); $25,083 (Calculator)
18. a. 13%

20

1. c. $0
2. c. $10
3. a. $1,000
b. $726
4. a. 11.98 shares
6. a. $1.50
b. $3.50
7. c. $0
8. c. $131.25 million
12. c. $1.15
13. a. Formula value = $0
Premium = $1
14. b. $783
16. c. Stock: 33.33%
Warrant: 116.67%

20B

2. $8,486,832
3. $14,812,741 (Tables); $14,813,304 (Calculator)

21

2. a. $26.90
4. a. $202,500

22

1. 9.57% per annum
3. a. $50,000
7. a. $294,000

23

1. b. 19%
2. a. EPS = $4.045
d. EPS = $4.258
3. a. 0.5 shares of Ball for 1 share of Keyes
7. EPS_c = $3.24

Index

Note: Page numbers suffixed by an f, t, or n refer to figures, tables, and notes, respectively.

A

F

G

H

I

Q

R

S